WOODWORKING WISDOM & KNOW-HOW

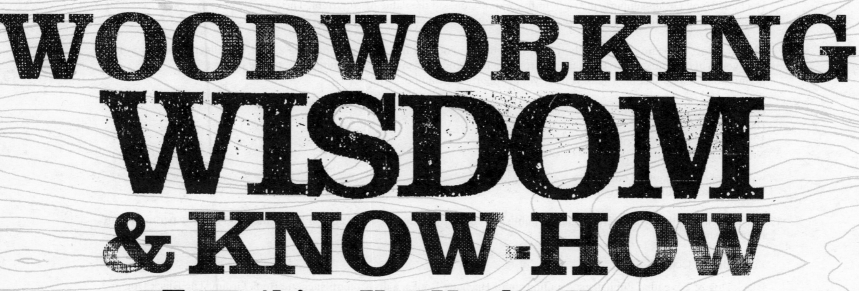

WOODWORKING WISDOM & KNOW-HOW

Everything You Need to Know to Design, Build, and Create

From the Editors of Fine WoodWorking **Compiled by Josh Leventhal**

BLACK DOG
& LEVENTHAL
PUBLISHERS
NEW YORK

Cover design by Ohioboy Design
Cover illustration © Elara Tanguy

Hachette Book Group supports the right to free expression and the value of copyright. The purpose of copyright is to encourage writers and artists to produce the creative works that enrich our culture.

Black Dog & Leventhal Publishers
Hachette Book Group
1290 Avenue of the Americas
New York, NY 10104

www.hachettebookgroup.com
www.blackdogandleventhal.com

The materials in this work were originally published and copyrighted by The Taunton Press, Inc., and used by permission of the publishers.

First Edition: October 2014

Black Dog & Leventhal Publishers is an imprint of Hachette Books, a division of Hachette Book Group. The Black Dog & Leventhal Publishers name and logo are trademarks of Hachette Book Group, Inc.

The publisher is not responsible for websites (or their content) that are not owned by the publisher.

The Hachette Speakers Bureau provides a wide range of authors for speaking events. To find out more, go to www.HachetteSpeakersBureau.com or call (866) 376-6591.

Print book interior design by Ohioboy Design and Liz Trovato

ISBN: 978-1-57912-981-1

Printed in the United States of America

WW

10 9 8 7 6 5 4 3

Contents

Continued ➜

The Wood

TYPES AND SPECIES OF WOOD

Cherry: America's Premier Cabinatewood

by Jon Arno

Of the hundreds of woods I've spent a lifetime studying, none has so captivated me as cherry. Even now, when I bring it into my shop, its pleasant scent, subtly warm appearance, and satiny feel soothe me with a sense of familiarity and comfort. And yet every time I choose it for a project, my confidence is shaken. This species often seems to have a hidden personality—always friendly but never totally forthcoming. There are, of course, tangible and physical reasons behind the mysteries and magic of cherry; at least, I've discovered a few of them.

In many ways, our native North American black cherry (*Prunus serotina*) is a nearly ideal cabinetwood. Its density, texture, stability, durability, working properties, color, and figure are as beckoning to some woodworkers as a cold beer on a hot summer day. And history would seem to second that conclusion, because cherry has figured prom-

inently in American furniture. Museum-quality pieces turned out by skilled 18th-century cabinetmakers are among the finest examples of American craftsmanship of that period. Also, the Shaker craftsmen of the 19th century, who certainly knew a thing or two about practicality and function, chose cherry for much of their best work.

So, how could the beginning woodworker go wrong in selecting cherry? Actually, it's surprisingly easy. In experienced hands, cherry yields results of uncommon beauty, and it deserves its place as one of the world's most prestigious cabinetwoods. But learning the whims and ways of cherry is one of woodworking's great challenges, and cherry bestows its many charms only upon those who toil for the privilege.

Why the Wood Can Vary So Much

You never can count on any two shipments of cherry being quite the same in either color or texture. Nor can you ever completely count on its consistency from board to board within a given shipment. While one board may display the classic flesh-pink color and subtly intricate figure that is most common to this species, another will reveal a noticeably wavy curl in the grain. The next may be peppered with jet-black gum pockets, while still another

will be slightly coarser textured, perhaps even flaunting decidedly greenish or chartreuse highlights. And if you're tempted to blame all of this inconsistency on sloppy handling and sorting at the mill, you'd probably be wrong. In fact, much of the varied lumber in each shipment you receive actually may have come from the same log.

The average cherry tree lives a hectic and stressful life because it is what ecologists and foresters refer to as a nurse tree. It performs the role of being one of the first species to get established when forest lands have been clear-cut or burned. Its roots help to hold the topsoil against erosion, while its foliage provides a sparse canopy for the retention of moisture and the protection of the seedlings of other species. In other words, cherry is a transitional player in the natural process of reestablishing a mature forest because it serves the needs of other species that will overtake it eventually. It helps to jump-start the reforestation process with its ability to disperse very quickly. Because birds eat the fruit and then pass the pit intact through their digestive systems, cherry arrives where it's needed, so to speak, by airmail. Given this symbiotic relationship with birds, cherry can become established on fallow land even

Continued →

though the parent trees may be located many miles away. In fact, so mobile is this species that pockets of it exist along bird-migration routes as far south as Central America. Also, cherry grows rapidly in full sunlight, but it is exceptionally shade intolerant and doesn't grow tall enough to compete for sunlight in the canopy of a forest with other more robust species like maple and oak.

What all this means from the woodworker's perspective is that a typical cherry log represents a microcosm of perpetual change. Because a cherry tree spends its life struggling in an immature forest setting, exposed to constant shifts in the source of light and the ever-increasing competition from other species, it is in a state of constant adjustment. All trees compete for their place in the sun, but cherry virtually never wins. And as the surrounding canopy closes in above them, cherry trees often are weakened to a point where they are susceptible to infestation by insect larvae, triggering their natural defense mechanism to produce more gums. Those gums contain chemicals that affect cherry's pigmentation, its patina-forming properties, and its potential toxicity—all topics of considerable importance to the woodworker.

A Color Like No Other

The chemical compounds produced by cherry, which wood technologists refer to as extractives, are the building blocks of the wood's unique pigmentation. As with all species, once the living tree produces these extractives, they are transported inward through the rays, where they are stored in the inner wood tissue that eventually becomes heartwood. It is the greater concentration of these extractives in the heartwood tissue, and their tendency to form more complex compounds called polymers, that produces the wood's natural heartwood color. With most species, these polymers develop more or less completely while the tree is still alive. They may oxidize and undergo subtle changes once the log has been milled, but the dominant pigmentation of most woods is relatively stable once the heartwood develops.

While cherry's extractives do polymerize to some degree in the living tree and give the wood its initial flesh-pink color, they remain exceptionally reactive, even after the log has been beenmilled. Unlike most other species, the extractives in cherry are photosensitive. They tend to darken, rather than fade, when exposed to light. There are a few other woods with photosensitive extractives—purpleheart, for example—but in most cases, the exposure to light causes a rather quick and complete conversion of their extractives into relatively stable pigments. Cherry is different: While the initial darkening effects of light can be seen almost immediately, continued exposure to light seems to result in an ever-deepening patina over the span of years or even decades. To be sure, strong light eventually will bleach the pigments in cherry, as it will in all woods, but it is a long time coming before it happens to cherry.

The patina that cherry develops is one of the key reasons cherry has such a dedicated following among experienced woodworkers. The beautiful translucence and ever-darkening depth of color can't be faked, and there's no substitute. But getting the most out of cherry isn't an easy task, either when processing it from the log or when using it in the shop. As is the case with walnut, mills often steam cherry to make its color as uniform as possible. The heat generated by steaming darkens the sapwood in both species, but it seems to work more quickly and permanently with walnut because the extractives already present in the sapwood are more immediately and indelibly converted. At least up to the level of its raw, flesh-pink color, steamed cherry has this same initial advantage. However, the benefit is fleeting as its less stable, long-term patina-forming process kicks in.

I'm not certain whether the ultimate long-term color of cherry is more dependent upon differing quantities of extractives present in the sapwood versus the heartwood, but there is no permanent fix that will make cherry sapwood keep pace with the heartwood as the color changes

An Ideal Cabinetwood

PROPERTIES

Cherry is unique among cabinetwoods in that it is the only major timber belonging to the Rose family (Rosaceae). Its darker color, more pronounced figure, and unusual, light-stimulated patina also make it unique among the world's most prestigious timbers.

Density:	Medium
Stability:	Good
Texture:	Fine
Porosity:	Diffuse
Durability:	Good

WHERE IT GROWS

North American black cherry primarily grows in the eastern half of the United States. Cherry trees reproduce with the help of birds that eat the fruit and distribute the seeds during migration.

LEAF PATTERN

Leaves are bright green, lance-shaped with serrated edges, and taper at both ends to a sharp point. Fruit is small (less than $1/2$ in. dia.) and grows in clusters of six to 12 cherries, which become a dark, reddish black as they ripen in the early autumn.

over time. Woodworkers skilled in the art of touch-up staining can do wonders to mask the initial contrast between sapwood and heartwood, and the use of finishes that block ultraviolet light will retard the patina process, but nothing short of perpetual darkness will stop it. For this reason, most experienced cabinetmakers are a little more particular in avoiding cherry sapwood than they might be with other species.

To be sure, there is nothing wrong with using cherry that contains sapwood, if your objective is to achieve a strikingly variegated appearance. But when you intentionally employ this artistic license, it is important to maintain a sense of balance so that the sapwood streaks are both plentiful enough to be an obvious part of the composition and well distributed throughout the piece.

From an artistic perspective, variegated cherry is just one of several legitimate options this species offers. I can think of at least four, or possibly five, subtly distinct cherry cabinetwoods: first, this variegated look, with its sharp contrast between heartwood and sapwood; the equally rustic look offered by the spotted or streaked appearance of gummy stock; the classic, mellow warmth you get when using top-grade, clear heartwood; and the fancier and more complex effect that comes from using a pronounced curly figure.

The fifth incarnation of cherry, and one of my personal favorites, is when the stock contains vivid greenish or chartreuse highlights. This unusual trait typically is seen in conjunction with stock that is a little coarser textured than normal and also is somewhat lighter in weight. It may in part be the product of cherry trees that have experienced spurts of unusually rapid growth, possibly in combination with something in the soil that interacts with one of cherry's extractives to create the greenish highlights. But whatever causes it, this trait is beautiful to my eye. The highlights are fugitive, and stock with this unique

The Quirks of Working with Cherry

No other wood is so demanding in every step of the woodworking process, from start to finish. Each cherry board needs to be chosen carefully at the beginning of the project. The woodworker who buys too little or miscuts a piece is in trouble. While the wood's density and texture give it remarkably good machining and shaping qualities, cutting the joinery demands considerable concentration and care. Cherry's brittleness causes it to chip more easily than most woods, and its natural gums burn almost instantly when exposed to friction from sawblades and router bits. To minimize heat buildup, use exceptionally sharp blades and bits. For the same reason, it is absolutely critical that the stock be passed at a steady rate of feed into shapers, routers, planers, jointers, and even sanders. Just a fraction of a second of stall in the rate of feed, and cherry presents you with virtually indelible and very dark burn marks. To avoid them, I prefer scrapers when working with cherry and use only a fine abrasive (220-grit aluminum-oxide paper) to remove the last vestiges of light scraper marks at the very end of the final prep-for-finish process.

The final finishing process also cannot be taken lightly. While some cherry has flamboyantly curly figure, virtually all cherry has a subtly undulating grain. This sneaky feature of the wood's inconsistent anatomy is often missed by the inexperienced eye. However, the resulting variation it produces in the wood's porosity can cause cherry to accept finishes unevenly. Even clear varnishes or penetrating oils can produce blotches or patches of uneven luster. And then there is the mystery of cherry's light-sensitive patina-forming process: Patience pays a big reward to those who are willing to wait for the wood to darken from its exposure to light.

pigmentation never seems to darken quite as deeply as typical old-growth cherry heartwood. As with any of the other four variations this species yields, it is important to sort the stock carefully and use whatever form you choose exclusively in any given project.

Admittedly, for the small-time avocational woodworker, being extremely picky when it comes to stock selection isn't always an easy thing to do. Most hardwood retailers will allow their customers some reasonable freedom in sorting through their inventories. But in my experience, the best way to buy cherry is in the largest quantity you can afford. Because of the variability of cherry, I cannot overstress the advantage of having an abundance of it on hand in your shop while a project is in progress.

Maple: A Versatile Timber

By Jon Arno

Maple has something to offer every woodworker, from general contractors to turners. Even though maple's inconspicuous figure lacks the striking contrast that gives ring-porous woods, such as oak and ash, their bold character, this diffuse-porous wood is subtly beautiful. Unlike colorful walnut or cherry, light-colored maple has warm brown accents and a translucent, opalescent quality in the way light plays off its surface. And most maple is easy to work and readily takes a finish, and can be used in anything from the finest furniture to packing crates, floors, bowling alleys and pins, cabinets, chairs and eating utensils.

Best of all, maple is exceptionally plentiful and often inexpensive. The latest USDA Forest Service statistics estimate that approximately 42 billion cu. ft. of maple stock (including both hard and soft maple species) is growing on timber lands in the Eastern United States. Most of it is relatively young second growth, but enough of it is of adequate size to produce sawtimber yielding more than 90 billion bd. ft. And this doesn't include stands of bigleaf maple in the Pacific Northwest, maple in unharvestable reserves, or both soft and hard maple available for logging in Canada. Of the commercially important hardwood cabinetmaking timbers native to North America, only the oaks are more plentiful than maple. Sugar maple, Acer saccharum, which is harder than most oaks, is the most common maple cabinetmaking wood; however, softer maples, such as red maple (*A. rubrum*), are also abundant and can be cost-effective substitutes.

There are about 125 species of maple distributed primarily in the Northern Hemisphere. About two-thirds of all these maples are native to China and the bulk of the remainder is spread out from England to Japan. North America claims only 13 native species and just 6 of these represent important commercial sources of timber. Despite the limited number of species, though, the United States and Canada provide the vast majority of the world's total production of maple lumber. Commercially, the lumber is divided into two groups: hard maple and soft maple.

Differences Between Hard and Soft Maple

Hard maple is stronger than soft maple and is better suited to woodwork that takes abuse, such as floors and countertops. Hard maple is cut from two closely related species: sugar maple and the less plentiful black maple, *A. nigrum*. The woods of these two trees, which grow in the Northeastern and Central United States and Southeastern Canada, are virtually indistinguishable in appearance. While black maple tends to be slightly lighter in weight, sugar maple has an average specific gravity of 0.56 (oven dry weight/green volume). Both hard maples are about as heavy as northern red oak and heavier than black walnut and black cherry.

Even though all of the soft maples are substantially lighter in weight than hard maple (and therefore inferior for applications such as flooring), red maple really isn't all that soft. Its average specific gravity is 0.49, which falls midway between that of black cherry 0.47) and that of black walnut (0.51). When it comes to first-rate domestic cabinetwoods, that's pretty good company to be keeping. And red maple is more plentiful and usually much less expensive.

With a little careful selection, cost-conscious woodworkers can come up with some excellent wood among the soft maples. The key is choosing the right species for any given job, and soft maples are diverse enough to span a great many applications. Most of the grain patterns found in hard maple also occur in soft maple, but some of the soft maple species actually possess more interesting color. For example, the heartwood of red maple, which grows throughout most of the Eastern United States, is usually darker than that of sugar maple. It has interesting gray highlights and sometimes dark, chocolate-brown markings.

The softest and lightest soft maple is box elder (*A. negundo*), which is found throughout most of the United States. It's also the finest textured of the maples, making it very pleasant to work with and a favorite among turners. Bigleaf maple, a Western species, and silver maple (*A. saccharinum*), which is plentiful throughout the East, are the remaining two major U.S. timber-producing soft maples. Both of these species are relatively soft and easy to work, and they have the additional advantage of being much more stable than hard maple. In fact, bigleaf has an average volumetric shrinkage of only 11.6%, which is quite comparable to black cherry.

Maple's Many Faces

In most woods, figure is produced by variation in texture between the springwood and summerwood. In maple, however, the figure is produced by bands of warmbrown- or amber-colored fibrous tissue demarcating the annual rings from the wood's overall creamy yellow hue. Like the annual rings, the medullary rays in maple are much darker than the background tissue, and they pepper the tangential surface with short, thin lines, which are similar to the ray flecks in beech. But maple's rays are softer and more subdued, like the weave of shear fabric. Even plain-figured maple, shown in the top, left sample on the facing page, seldom produces absolutely straight grain and the figure on its tangential surface usually curls and contorts like the veins in fine marble.

In some instances, ordinary maple trees may produce extraordinary figures, which are commonly referred to as fiddleback, quilted and bird's-eye maple. Bird's-eye figure ranks among the world's finest and most sought after cabinetwoods. Curly figure (shown in the is sometimes called fiddleback or tiger-stripe maple and is often used for the back of stringed instruments, like violins. Quilted figure, which occurs most often in the Western bigleaf maple, A macropbyllum, is prized for tabletops and inlay. Only a small percentage of maple woods brought to market have these special figures, which are the result of abnormal growth. In some instances, the tree's living, wood-producing layer (the cambium layer, located just inside the bark) develops spots that fail to produce wood tissue at a normal rate. While this process may not affect the entire tree, it generally persists for years, as the spots enlarge and build up layer upon layer of convoluted grain. Depending upon the degree of malformation and how you cut the log, a number of distinct figures may be obtained from a single piece.

Matching and Finishing Maple

Plain-figured maple machines exceptionally well and will hold very sharp details. In fact, the latin name for the maple genus, Acer, means sharp because lances and skewers made from it held a sharp point. Plain maple's even grain allows it to be sawed, chiseled, handplaned or machine planed, or drilled without much chipping or tearout. When it is routed, it has a tendency to develop burn marks that are difficult to sand out, and so you must use a sharp, clean bit and keep your feed speed high. Because of hard maple's density, working it with hand tools requires some muscle, but the results are gratifying. Figured maple, on the other hand, can be very difficult to handplane or scrape cleanly, and it requires using a plane with a surgically sharp blade. Hard maple turns so predictably and yields such defect-free products that it has long been favored for commercial production of round items: kitchen utensils, bowling pins, furniture parts, dowels, spindles, spools and heavy-duty conveyor rollers. And when hard maple is sanded on the lathe, it doesn't gum up sandpaper as cherry does.

Few woods are as easy and as pleasant to finish as maple. It has a moderately high natural luster, and you can quickly smooth its surface with scrapers or fine-grit abrasives. Some soft maples can be more difficult to work to a smooth surface free of fuzzy grain, and they may require more sanding with fine-grit paper than hard maple. A single coat of tung oil on maple tabletops, counters and cutting boards may be sufficient protection against stains from food and drink spills. But bare maple does have adequate porosity to accept stain and allow glue to bond. Also, because of maple's fine texture, you can finish it to a high gloss without using special fillers. Only a coat or two of light-bodied varnish is needed to build up a glassy smooth surface. And since maple is so hard, it supports virtually any finish without a great risk of denting or chipping.

There are no chemicals in maple that threaten its utility. Although there are minute traces of talmin in maple bark, it is absent from the wood. Volatiles in common varnishes, lacquers and glues don't react adversely with maple to destroy their bond or affect drying time. In fact, given its fine texture, maple is excellent for painted projects because its featureless grain won't telegraph through the finish.

Limitations

Given maple's pleasant working characteristics and subtle beauty, there is little mystery as to why it is used in so many diverse applications. But it is not suited to every purpose and indeed has some significant shortcomings. First of all, since hard maple is not very stable compared to most other popular cabinetwoods, woodworkers should prepare for wood movement. Hard maple's average volumetric shrinkage of 14.7% (green to oven dry) is nearly 30% greater than that of black cherry (11.5%) and almost twice as large as that of Honduras mahogany (7.8%). Hard-maple spindles and tenons tend to loosen when exposed to seasonal fluctuations in humidity. Furthermore, hard maple has a rather pronounced tendency to warp because it develops severe stresses when drying. Its high volumetric shrinkage is compounded by a somewhat large difference between its 9.9% tangential shrinkage and its 4.8% radial shrinkage.

Another limitation is that maple has a low resistance to decay. Because maple lacks tannin or other strong chemical defenses often found in more durable woods, it is quickly attacked by fungi. On the positive side, though, the stains caused by fungi can produce a very attractive spalted pattern, which is actually prized for use in cabinetry and in turned decorative bowls. Spalted box elder can be especially nice. It is susceptible to attack by the fungus *Fusarium negundi*, which produces beautiful, coral-colored streaks, rather than the usual brown or blue-black coloration found in most spalted woods. Spalted wood, however, must be thoroughly seasoned as soon as possible after the staining occurs in order to force the fungi into dormancy. Otherwise, the wood will structurally deteriorate as the fungi multiply and literally devour the wood tissue. Unless producing spalted wood is your objective, maple should be dried quickly to remove all surface moisture, before the fungi can get established. Even when properly dried, though, maple is a very poor choice for marine or exterior projects of any kind.

Walnut: The Cabinetwood Par-Excellence

by Jon Arno

In lists of the various properties of cabinetwoods, American black walnut, *Juglans nigra*, stands near the middle in every category. There are dozens, if not hundreds, of woods that are stronger and denser. There are a few woods with better figure and richer color. Some hardwoods are substantially easier to work than walnut. And many fine cabinetwoods are a good deal less expensive.

Yet walnut is so flexibly appropriate for a broad range of uses that, overall, it rivals any other wood in the world. It might, in fact, be the very best cabinetwood of all. What does walnut bring the party that causes it to stand out? To answer this question, we must consider not only its physical properties, but a number of subtle things that appeal to other senses and to our emotions.

Take gunstocks, for example. Of the four woods commonly used, only walnut is rated "excellent" in the physical attributes a gunstock requires. It has been the favored gunstock wood since colonial times, long before laboratory testing could confirm our pioneers' instincts. The substitutes, hard maple, yellow birch, and sycamore may surpass walnut in one or two respects, yet, in the final balance, walnut becomes the standard, the perfect gunstock wood. In weight it is heavy enough to absorb some recoil, yet not so heavy as to be arm-wearying. For its weight, it is outstanding in strength, hardness and shock resistance. It is stable enough not to endanger the precise alignment between metal and wood. It machines beautifully. Walnut's dark color, aesthetics aside, is a particular asset-the runners-up all require staining lest they be conspicuous in the field, and are, therefore, more difficult to touch up if dented or scratched.

Notice how many of these attributes are also desirable for furniture. In the gamut of cabinetwoods, there are only a handful of woods as well endowed. In addition, walnut is neither ringporous like oak or diffuse-porous like maple. It is what most experts call "semi-ring-porous," with a gradual transition between earlywood and latewood. This helps to make for little, if any, chatter in its resistance to the cutting edge, allowing shavings to peel off with a wax-like roll. Walnut has adequate ring-porosity to show a beautiful grain pattern, but is diffuse-porous enough to make the use of fillers optional in most furniture applications—if unfilled the pores will show but not be objectionable.

In walnut, we have a wood that is not too hard, not too soft, not too open-textured, not too plain . . . not too anything (except maybe too expensive). Like Baby Bear's porridge, it's just right.

I suspect that walnut has been so long entwined with human to history that we have developed a genuine emotional attachment it, one that runs deep. Walnut of the English or European variety, *j. regia*, has been with us both in our cabinetmaking and in our diet since ancient times, when our ancestors imported the tree from the Middle East and reestablished it in western Europe, where it had been extinct since the last ice age. In the 1600s, European walnut supplanted oak as the premier furniture wood, until it, in turn, was supplanted by Honduras mahogany. During the American colonial period, when mahogany furniture imported from England was in style, walnut was sometimes stained red by domestic cabinetmakers in an effort to emulate the imports. It could be argued that, in Europe, mahogany is still the standard by which other cabinetwoods are measured. Yet in America this has not been the case for a long time. Today, we take Philippine "mahogany" (lauan and other species of *Shorea*) and stain it dark brown to imitate the walnut that is closer to our hearts.

Strictly speaking, current style is an intangible. Walnut has other intangible features as well. Particularly high on such a list is the pleasant aroma of a piece of walnut as it passes through the planer or the tablesaw. I am abnormally fastidious about keeping my shop clean because I know a clean shop is a safer shop. In fact, I will sometimes stop in the middle of a project to sweep the floor, but I have been known to let walnut shavings lie for days. To me, the scent of walnut ranks with fresh-ground coffee as one of life's great treats. Under certain conditions, however, particularly when a carving block of unseasoned walnut has been set aside to dry slowly, thriving micro-organisms can imbue the wood with a lasting, sourish odor best described as a stink. Even so, it helps clear the sinuses.

I should defer to the medical profession on this topic, but the reason the aroma of walnut evokes such pleasant emotions and a sense of well being may be more than psychological. According to a USDA Forest Products Laboratory publication, walnut contains ellagic acid, a sedative and tranquilizer. They report an incident in which a dog chewed on a black walnut statue and fell into a deep sleep for two days. There are also reports that various tribes of American Indians used to throw crushed walnuts or butternuts into ponds to stupefy fish.

Walnut's chemical potency should come as no surprise to gardeners. One of our native black walnut's most active constituents is a substance called juglone, which is apparently part of the tree's biological defense system. Juglone is toxic to other plants, such as apple trees, and especially to members of the tomato family. It would appear to pose no problem to cabinetmakers, however. It polymerizes into dark pigments in the wood tissue, which, I presume, makes it inert.

One of the walnut tree's few shortcomings is that it produces logs with a relatively large amount of almost pure white sapwood. Slicing it all off would be an appalling waste. Fortunately, by injecting hot steam into the kiln during the drying process, the sapwood can be darkened somewhat. This procedure is certainly beneficial in view of our limited supply of walnut, but it seems to dull the richness of the wood's overall color. To my way of thinking, there is something special about a piece of carefully air-dried walnut with its subtle, almost translucent bluepurple highlights. Unfortunately, like flowers, youth, and so many of this world's beautiful things, the magic of a freshly planed piece of air-dried walnut is a fleeting pleasure. Age and exposure to light will bleach its vivid tones, and over the years the strikingly blue-purple highlights mellow out toward the gold or amber side of the spectrum.

Walnut is a pretty tree with its deep brown, almost black bark and its bright light green compound leaves, but it is a beauty that belongs in the forest where competition for sunlight forces it to produce a tall, unmarred trunk. In this setting it is a capable competitor and will develop diameters in excess of 5 ft. and heights of 100 ft. or more. In the open, like most hardwoods it has a propensity to branch out, forming a dome-like crown which much reduces its value as a timber source.

Although its crop of tasty nuts is an important asset, the tree is not that popular for landscaping. Because walnut leafs late in the spring and loses its leaves early in the fall, its appearance is stark and dead looking for much of the year. There is no particular beauty to its flowering, it is a catkin producer, and a messy tree on a well-manicured lawn. Its nuts attract squirrels that are generally more skillful in collecting the crop than all but the most watchful homeowner, and add injury to insult by planting a few of them in gardens where they are chemically hostile to other plants.

While we woodworkers might unanimously agree that walnut plantings should be sharply increased, the economics of growing hardwood timber on valuable eastern land is, pardon the pun, a tough nut to crack. But contrary to popular opinion, on good sites walnut is not a slow grower. It spurts up rapidly for the first decade or so and then begins to slow down as it enters into nut production. The tree seems to oblige us woodworkers with the reasonably quick accumulation of woody tissue, but then it taunts us in taking its own sweet time mellowing it into the rich brown heartwood we seek.

About the Other Walnuts

My vote for the royal family of cabinetwoods must be *Juglandaceae*. This botanical family includes *Carya*, the hickories (including pecan), and the true bluebloods of the line, the *Juglans*, which are the walnuts and butternut. There are broad differences among the *Juglans* species, but most walnuts overlap so much in color and density that you may have to examine cell structure to tell them apart for certain.

The walnuts and the hickories comprise some 50 or so species worldwide. The hickories are limited to eastern North America and southern China, while the walnuts have a broader range in North America, Central America and northern South America, as well as in Eurasia.

The wood of the old-world tree, *J. regia*, is slightly softer and lighter in color than our black walnut, *J. nigra*. European walnut also shows subtle differences resulting from the climate and soil where it has grown, and for marketing reasons may be called French, Balkan, Italian, etc. but it is all the same species. Very little solid stock escapes Europe, although the veneer called circassian burl is sometimes seen on the market here.

Black walnut is not our only domestic species—there are *J. major*, or Arizona walnut, and *J. microcarpa*, which is called little walnut, Texas walnut or nogal. Occasionally, wood from the several species of walnuts from South and Central America shows up, called either tropical walnut or nogal. These are beautiful woods, a little softer, a little coarser textured and somewhat darker than our black walnut, judging from the few samples I have seen. These species are true walnuts, unlike African walnut (mansonia) and Queensland walnut, which have borrowed the name but not the pedigree.

The several Oriental species of true walnuts, native from northern India to Japan, produce woods that are almost never seen in our market. I haven't worked with Japanese walnut, *J. cordiformis*, but it is reputed to have a warmer, yellowish hue than our native wood.

Butternut, *J. cinerea*, is our other major domestic species of *Juglans*, and one of my personal favorites. While butternut is somewhat coarser in texture, its figure is virtually the same as black walnut. If you have ever wished there was a wood that worked as easily as pine or basswood yet looked like walnut, butternut is as close as you will ever get. With an average specific gravity of only 0.36, it is actually less dense than Ponderosa pine at 0.38 and substantially less dense than black walnut at 0.51. At the extreme ends of the scale, though, the hardest, darkest-colored butternut and the softest walnut can be difficult to tell apart. Yet even then, butternut tends toward gray-tan and gingery tones, while walnut shows more purple.

Butternut has prevalent tension wood and tends to fuzz up a little in sanding. Being soft, it will generally drink an extra coat of varnish before it fills to a polishable surface, and it will not endure as well in daily use—this may be important if you are making a table, but it's almost irrelevant for a mantel clock or a picture frame.

Finally, claro walnut is a term used freely by lumber dealers on the West Coast, usually to describe highly figured walnut harvested from overmature trees in nut plantations. Some of this wood is probably English walnut that was grafted to a native rootstock, a practice that can promote a flame figure low in the stem. Other possibilities are two species native to California, *J. hindsii* and *J. californica*, found respectively in the northern and southern parts of the range. All of these claro walnuts are true *Juglans*, but the name is no guarantee of which species the walnut is, nor that it is particularly showy. I suspect at this point that I'm just splitting hairs. Let me affirm that in the walnut family tree there are some beautiful dark woods but no black sheep. I, for one, will welcome walnut under any name in my shop—none of it is what you could call bad.

Making Walnut-husk Stain

The pigments in all parts of the walnut tree are plentiful and, for better or worse, downright indelible. Anyone who has tried to husk walnuts by hand knows all about the durability of this stain. Even crushing the fresh leaves with bare hands will leave you with a dirty, two-pack-a-day, yellow stain on your fingers that defies a scrub brush. The pigments in the husk of the nuts and the root bark make excellent dye for cloth and, of course, they give the wood its much prized color. In the case of American black walnut, this is the well-known and often strikingly purple-streaked chocolate brown.

Those cabinetmakers with a flair for experimentation can get at this pigment and produce a stain that will transfer some of walnut's beauty to other less-endowed woods. To begin, collect a few pounds of the nuts, preferably those that have fallen to the ground and are beginning to darken and decompose. Husk them and loosely pack a quart jar full of the husks (sans the nuts—eat those). Fill the jar brim-full with non-detergent ammonia, the ordinary sort, not the sudsy kind.

Cap the jar and allow it to stand for a few weeks. The ammonia will leach out the pigment, and this mess can be strained through cheesecloth to produce a jet black liquid that, admittedly, is something of a trial to work with. Wear rubber gloves and apply the stain with a rag in a well-ventilated work space, preferably outdoors. The stain is water based, and two coats are generally necessary because the first coat raises the grain and must be rubbed down with fine sandpaper or steel wool.

It's a foul-smelling, messy process, but it works, and I promise that the results are definitely worth the trouble.

Red, White, and Live Oaks: A Versatile Trio

by Jon Arno

Our senses tell us it is nothing more than a coarse-textured wood with showy rays, and a harsh acidic scent. Yet there's something about oak that causes most of us to think of it in human terms: bold, strong and dependable. There can be little doubt why.

This genus of trees, its fruit and its timber are an inseparable part of the story of humanity since the beginning. Acorns predated grain as a mainstay in the diet of our Stone-Age European ancestors. The pagan Germans worshipped oak, and in England dense groves of the European white oak, *Quercus robur*, served as holy places for Druid rites well before written history began. From ancient times until just before our grandfathers were born, oak served as a strategic military and economic commodity, being the primary naval timber for ships-of-the-line and tall Yankee clippers.

Oak's role in the modern world may be somewhat less romantic, but it has not diminished. Oak remains our most-used hardwood for interior trim, cabinets, flooring, furniture and for many heavy construction applications. The two primary factors that have made oak so enduringly popular are its abundance and its utility. Before exploring these topics, though, let's examine the great diversity of the timbers we lump together botanically as oak.

Oak's Family Tree

Oaks belong to the beech family, Fagaceae. That this family should be referred to as the "beech" family is one of the more irrational snubs in taxonomy. Of the 600 or so species in the family—including the beeches, chestnuts and chinkapins, well over 500 of its most important members belong to the oak genus, *Quercus*.

The oaks are also the most abundant and widespread genus of hardwoods in the Northern Hemisphere. In the United States alone we have a growing stock of 100 billion cubic feet of oak—more than twice our reserves of any other hardwood genus. The natural abundance of the oaks is due to their genetic vigor and their resulting adaptability. Oaks hybridize with very little difficulty. Over millions of years, this natural, genetic experimentation has resulted in a host of species ideally suited to almost any viable environment, from swamps to arid highlands.

In the course of evolution, the genus divided into two botanically distinct groups: white oaks and red oaks, which are sometimes called black oaks. (There's also a third group—the live oaks, which are climatic variants of the white and the red. I'll discuss live oaks later.) The most significant botanical difference between the two is that white oaks mature their acorns within a single season while the red oaks require two seasons. To tell them apart, all you really need to know is that most white oaks have round-lobed leaves, while the lobes on red-oak leaves come to a point.

Other differences—in the cellular anatomy of the woods—are of particular interest to the woodworker. Woods in the white oak group tend to have larger rays and smaller, but more abundant, thin-walled pores. The red oaks have fewer, but larger, thick-walled pores, and the rays tend to be smaller and darker in color. Also, the pores in white oak are almost always clogged with foam-like structures known as tyloses, while the pores in red oak are normally unobstructed. Because these features are responsible for many of the functional properties of these woods, the lumber industry has adopted essentially the same groupings as the botanists, marketing oak lumber as either white or red. Beyond this, however, little or no effort is made to differentiate from species to species. For most construction applications this broad-brush approach is adequate, but for furniture and finer craft work it leaves much to be desired.

Within the oak genus there's an extremely broad range of cabinetwoods. The softest of our domestic oaks, with a specific gravity of 0.52 (see the box for definition of specific gravity and a comparison of some of the more common North American species), is the Southern red species *Quercus falcata*. This species is only about as dense as black walnut (0.51). Some of the live oaks have specific gravities approaching 0.90, making them even denser than rosewood. No other genus of domestic hardwood spans such a broad range. In the United States alone, there are 58 formally classified domestic species and perhaps a third again as many recognized hybrid varieties and naturalized foreign species.

Genetics alone, however, do not account for all of the variation in the oaks sold as cabinetwood. Climate, soil, and even the way the lumber is processed can produce lumber of the same species with strikingly dissimilar characters, both in appearance and working properties.

The most significant factor besides genetic makeup that determines an oak's character is climate. Red oaks and white oaks that grow in our temperate North-American forests are ring-porous woods. At the beginning of each growing season these trees produce a band of large earlywood pores, which accent the annual rings and give the wood a showy, open-grained character. Some live oaks are botanically related to the white oaks and some to the reds. But because live oaks do not experience seasonal interruptions in growth they do not produce the usual bands of large earlywood pores. Instead, they tend to be less figured and much harder woods. As seen on the end grain, the pores in live oak form long radial chains, like the strings of bubbles in a glass of champagne, extending outward from the pith to the bark.

From the woodworker's perspective, categorizing the oaks into these three basic groups—red, white and live—provides a logical and useful framework, although this is really only a starting point. The woods in each group share similar functional properties, but there can be considerable variation from one species to another even within each group. The live oaks make up the hardest and heaviest group; the white oaks are next in terms of weight, strength and durability; and the red oaks are the softest and lightest. Most species of white oak have slower growth rates, producing smaller-diameter pores and a much more compact cellular structure. This gives the wood great strength and a high resistance to splitting. White oak's rays tend to be larger, tying the vascular (vertically oriented) cells together and giving the wood greater resistance to compression.

All oaks contain high concentrations of tannin, which provide at least a modest amount of protection in inhibiting decay. But white oak is substantially more durable than red oak when exposed to the elements because the pores of white oak are clogged with tyloses, which retard the absorption of moisture and help to prevent decay organisms from getting established.

THE OAKS
Some common North American oaks arranged by group

Common and botanical names	Specific gravity	Volumetric shrinkage
WHITE		
Eastern white, Q. alba	0.60	16.3
Bur, Q. macrocarpa	0.58	12.7
Overcup, Q. lyrata	0.57	16.0
Post, Q. stellata	0.60	16.2
Chestnut, Q. prinus	0.57	16.4
Swamp chestnut, Q. michauxii	0.60	16.4
RED		
Northern red, Q. rubra	0.56	13.7
Southern red, Q. falcata	0.52	16.
Cherrybark, Q. falcata, v. pagodifolia	0.61	-
Scarlet, Q. coccinea	0.60	14.7
Willow, Q. phellos	0.56	18.9
Water, Q. nigra	0.56	16.1
Black, Q. velutina	0.56	15.1
Laurel, Q. laurifolia	0.56	19.0
Pin, Q. palustris	0.58	14.5
LIVE		
Live, Q. virginiana	0.80	14.7

Specific gravity is the ratio of the weight of a given piece of wood to the weight of water occupying the same volume. It reflects the relative density of the wood in question. The figures above are based on the wood's green volume and oven-dry weight.

Volumetric shrinkage is expressed as a percentage decrease from original green volume to oven-dry volume. Shrinkage indicates a wood's relative in-use stability.

Continued ➡

END-GRAIN SECTIONS

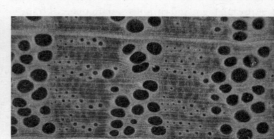

White Oak

White Oak

Red Oak

Red Oak

Live Oak

Live Oak

Size and distribution of rays and pores are the best way to identify the oaks. White oaks have smaller but more abundant pores than the red oaks and larger rays. Live oaks, because they're largely tropical in origin, have the most even distribution of pores of any of the oaks, as well as the greatest density and the least figure.

End-grain sections show one of the biggest differences between the oaks. White oak, which has been used for barrels for centuries and is still considered to be the best wood for aging fine wines, holds liquids because its pores are largely clogged by tyloses. Red oak's pores, on the other hand, are largely unobstructed, and so allow liquids to pass right through. The pores of most live oak are also open, like those of red oak, but much smaller.

Which Oak to Use?

White—Given white oak's many favorable attributes, it is not surprising that many of the cabinetmaking and wood technology texts published in the 19th and early 20th centuries cite white oak as the preferred, or at least most useful, of our oak timbers. White oak's durability and strength made it superior for uses such as bridge beams and railroad ties, and its low permeability to moisture made (and still makes) it ideal for wine barrels and other cooperage applications. In contrast, a red-oak barrel, regardless of how well the staves were fitted, would leak because its contents would simply flow out through the wood's large, unobstructed pores.

For cabinetmaking, white oak also possesses the virtue of being much more flamboyantly figured than red oak, especially when quartersawn. This radially cut white oak is sometimes called silvered oak and was the height of fashion a century ago. Although red oak also can be quartersawn, its rays' darker color and relatively smaller size don't provide the same degree of splashy contrast as does the white.

Today, silvered oak is no longer the rage, and many of the construction and container duties that were once the exclusive domain of white oak are now being performed by metals and synthetics. White oak's clear-cut advantage over red oak has faded.

Eastern white oak is also not as plentiful today as it once was. In the American market a century ago, the term "white oak" was all but synonymous with Eastern white oak (*Quercus alba*). This plentiful species (along with a few virtually indistinguishable hybrids) provided almost all of the commercially processed, higher-grade cabinetwood in the white oak group. Although *Q. alba* still accounts for a large portion of the annual harvest, other species, most notably bur oak (*Q. macrocarpa*), are quite commonly sold as white oak today. Bur oak is a much coarser textured wood with a grayish color and exceedingly large rays. It doesn't turn as well or finish as smoothly as Eastern white oak, but it is not without its virtues. With an average volumetric shrinkage

of 12.7%, green to oven dry, it is more stable than Eastern white oak (at 16.3%), and makes excellent hardwood flooring. However, the two woods are not totally interchangeable and should not be used together where their differing shrinkage properties could cause problems, such as in edge-glued table tops or wide panels. Because of the lumber industry's propensity to comingle these species, buying white oak these days can be tricky. If at all possible, you should inspect any white oak before buying, or at least buy from a supplier who can guarantee that all the lumber you purchase for a project will be of one species.

Red—There's plenty of variety among the red oaks as well, with their average specific gravities spanning an even greater range than the whites. Southern swamp (or cherrybark) red oak (*Q. falcata var. pagodifolia*) is actually slightly heavier than Eastern white oak. Species like cherrybark, that are native to the extreme south where the climate is moist and the growing season is long, grow rapidly and produce proportionately more dense latewood within each annual ring than do northern-grown oaks. Oaks from the temperate North tend to produce softer and more flamboyantly figured woods.

In recent years, southern red oak has developed a somewhat tarnished reputation in the interior trim and cabinetmaking fields for being too streaky and often curly grained. Personally, I prefer this streaked, curly, southern-Appalachian oak for the special character it lends some furniture projects, especially in tabletops and bookmatched panels. But then again, I prefer red oak over white in most applications for rather pragmatic reasons.

Red oak is stocked by more of the high-volume lumberyards where construction contractors buy, so it's generally a little less expensive than white. Red oak is also softer than white, so it's easier to work. This is most noticeable with hand tools and when thickness planing, because white oak's rays have a greater tendency to tear out. Neither red

nor white oak are particularly well suited for turning, but typically gouges stay sharp a lot longer with red oak.

The rays in red oak are less pronounced than in white, so it's not as difficult to match boards. The thing to look for when selecting boards is whether a board is flatsawn or quartersawn. While both grain patterns are attractive, they tend to clash when used together in the same project, so I regard them almost as two different woods.

Finally, because the ray flecks are darker than the background wood in red oak, relatively dark stains can be used without any danger of overemphasizing the rays. With white oak, using a dark stain is not a good idea unless you really want to accentuate the rays. They'll inevitably stand out as very contrasty yellow bands against the surrounding, more porous (therefore darker) wood tissue. If you're going to stain white oak, use a blonde stain.

Live—Live oak has never been a commercially important furniture wood. One reason why is that live oak is absolutely punishing to work with. Historically, live oak has only been used in very specialized applications. Our most plentiful domestic live oak, *Q. virginiana*, was much prized during the 18th and 19th centuries for building warships, because of its superior ability to withstand a broadside. But given the handtools of the time, it was never the oak of choice for finer work and it never became associated with a popular period-style of furniture. This may change, though, in the years ahead. Modern power tools can handle it at least as well as rosewood, bubinga or purpleheart.

Moreover, prospects are high that the live oaks will remain in good supply. In Mexico alone there are well over 100 species of oaks, and the vast majority of them belong to the live oak group. Though they contain fewer species, the forests of Central and extreme northern South America also contain large quantities of live oak, some of which have strikingly unusual ray patterns and vivid color. In fact, they're so different from our domestic species

that often the only clues to their kinship with oak are the wood's tannic scent or the use of Spanish trade names containing the words "roble" or "encino."

By whatever name, these tropical oaks are a world apart from our ring-porous domestic oaks in either the red or white oak groups. With few exceptions they're brutally hard, but they polish extremely well. Although generally considered diffuse-porous woods (because the pores do not congregate in the earlywood), the live oaks are still relatively coarse textured and open grained compared to the familiar domestic species we think of as typical, diffuse-porous woods, such as maple and birch.

The live oaks have much potential as cabinetwoods, but there has not yet been much research or technical data gathered on their working properties. While our domestic live oak (*Q. virginiana*) is relatively stable, some imported species with very high volumetric shrinkage have caused disappointment when brought into our somewhat dryer and more temperate climate … so be forewarned.

Forever in Fashion

In construction, cabinetry and furnituremaking, as well as in a host of other fields, oak has been in style almost since Western history began. As many a surviving royal throne, treasure chest or ancient armoire will attest, it was the preferred wood throughout the middle ages and in the Jacobean period. Even in the 18th and 19th centuries, when mahogany alone would do for elegant pieces, oak was the primary wood for common, utilitarian items such as drysinks, cupboards, tables and chairs.

Tannin, Pro and Con

Chemically speaking, one of the most distinctive features of oak is its high tannin content. Indeed, the scent of most species is so powerful that it will linger in the air for hours after the wood has been milled. Although I very much enjoy the fragrance of many woods and view their aromas as one of the more pleasant aspects of working with wood, I find oak to be downright offensive. And for those of us who are sensitive to oak, exposure to the dust can cause watery eyes, skin rashes and even heartburn.

Even so, the offending agent—tannin—magnifies oak's utility in many ways. Tannin has antiseptic properties, and the highest concentrations of it are in the bark so oak bark has long been used for preserving or "tanning" leather. Tannin also reacts with iron to produce black pigment, and oak-leaf galls were once a major ingredient in the making of ink.

For woodworkers, the interaction between tannin and iron is a mixed blessing. On the one hand, care must be taken in using steel nails or screws in oak, because over time the surrounding wood will develop an ever enlarging black blotch. Yet when oak logs are submerged in a swamp, this same chemical reaction creates bog oak, a unique and beautifully highlighted, silver-black cabinetwood that is much prized in the British Isles.

Tannin, because it's highly acidic, also reacts with ammonia to produce rich brown pigments. Although modern oil-based wood stains are a lot easier to work with, ammonia-fumed oak was once a very popular finish. In this process, trays of highly concentrated (industrial-strength) ammonia are placed in an airtight area along with whatever unfinished oak items are to be fumed. In a matter of hours (or days, depending upon how dark a hue is desired), the raw oak becomes indelibly and deeply pigmented.

In the New World, the Spanish conquest of the Southwest left us the legacy of mission oak. At the turn of the century, massive pedestal tables and rolltop desks in golden oak were popular. At mid-century our soldiers returned home from World War II to raise their families in houses furnished with limed-oak coffee tables and dining-room sets. Oak still dominates the furniture and cabinetmaking scene, although nowadays much of that coarse-grained look is actually veneer or synthetic laminate. And for kitchen cabinets, flooring and interior trim, the use of oak still far exceeds any other hardwood—and probably all other domestic hardwoods combined. Given their history, enduring popularity and the existing stock of oaks, they're likely to remain stalwart favorites for a long time.

Pine: Special Charm from a Common Timber

by Jon Arno

Pine is so relatively inexpensive, readily available and easy to work that it is often dismissed as a wood for beginners to practice on until they're experienced enough to work with more expensive hardwoods. This theory is wrong. Pine is a very respectable cabinet wood with a long tradition in American furniture-making. And although some species of pine are easily worked, others can be fairly difficult to handle and a nightmare to finish.

While there is no such thing as "good" pine or "bad" pine, generally speaking there is a right pine for any given project based on the wood's structural properties or its traditional use. To get the most out of pine, therefore, you must know something about the limitations and applications of the more than 30 native North American species. Fortunately, for practical purposes, these species can be divided into three main groups: white pine, western yellow pine and southern yellow pine.

Although white pine is structurally the weakest and least durable of the three groups, it has the best working characteristics. Eastern and western white pine are virtually interchangeable and are ideal woods a pleasure to work because of it's uniform, fine texture and sweet aroma, but it is inappropriate for period reproductions due to dle large, dark resin canals that produce flecks in the grain pattern.

The southern yellow pine group contains the hardest and heaviest of the pines. These pines have showy figures with high contrast between the soft earlywood and the hard latewood. This group is most frequently used as construction timber, but is authentic for some antebellum furniture as well.

Ponderosa and lodgepole are the dominant species of the western yellow pine group, and are the species most commonly found at lumberyards. These pines have a tamer figure, with more earlywood and thinner bands of latewood than southern yellow pine, and are softer and easier to work. In fact, unfinished western yellow pine looks similar to white pine, but the abrupt transition between earlywood and latewood requires different finishing techniques.

Grades of Pine

With experience, it is not difficult to distinguish the various pines by sight and feel, but normally they are clearly labeled with a grade stamp. Because of the great demand for pine in the construction industry, there is a premium on long, clear and structurally sound boards. Clear white or sugar pine, when you can find it, can cost as much as walnut. This economic reality often forces woodworkers to use the lower grades of wood.

Usually clear stock is not that essential; knots that are tight and structurally sound can add charm and character to some furniture styles. Just make sure the knots are at least 1 in. from the ends of the boards, where they won't interfere with joinery. Avoid knots ringed with a black line, as they will almost surely work loose or fall out.

If you need clear pine for repairing period pieces or reproductions, you can get fairly sizable sections from lower grades of stock. Pines produce branches in whorls 18 in. to 24 in. apart along the main trunk, which results in beautifully figured clear wood between the whorls. My rule of thumb is to buy plenty of the lowest grade of wood that will yield at least 50% usable material for a given project. When I need long, clear pieces, I buy the top grade for just those pieces, provided I can get both grades in the same type of pine. Unless the piece is going to be painted, don't mix pines from the different groups because they don't generally finish the same way, and grain patterns and colors will vary considerably. You should also buy your stock from lumberyards that allow customers to select their own wood. Woodworkers can usually find the right kind of light, soft pine even in a pile that has already been picked over by construction contractors, who tend to prefer the stronger heartwood that is too resinous and bland for furniture. If you only need short, clear pieces, you can use boards with loose or missing knots.

Working with Pine

Pine's scent is one of the most pleasant fragrances in the world, but this benefit only compliments the primary pleasure of working with a wood that machines with so few problems. You do need sharp cutting edges and sawblades to prevent tearout with a soft wood like pine. Pine is also resinous enough to gum up cutting edges, so clean the blades frequently But the resin has lime effect on most glues; glue joints will be stronger than the wood itself. In addition, pine's spongy texture absorbs shock and, while pilot holes are needed for screws, nails can be driven into all but the hardest southern yellow pines without splitting the wood.

Even though pine is a soft wood, you can build furniture for rough, daily use by taking a tip from woodworkers of an earlier era and bulking up the design. Thicker stock makes for rugged components and stronger joinery, which traditionally has included everything from dovetails to butt joints and nails. Because pine has always been a timber of choice for utilitarian pieces, the joinery has tended to be simple, cheap or easy. Mortise-and-tenon and dovetail joints were preferred in colonial days as alternatives to scarce and expensive nails and screws. Pegged joints were frequently used, but as iron and steel became more readily available, square-cut nails and screws proved to be a more convenient choice.

When cutting joints like dovetails or mortises and tenons, you have to compensate for pine's spongy, easily compressed texture by cutting the pieces to fit a little snugger then you would if you were working with hardwoods. Also, minimize test fitting the joints to avoid excessively compressing the wood before final assembly. Tenons should be cut as large as possible and slightly longer than those used width hardwoods. A mortise cut in 3/4-in. stock should be no wider than 1/4 in. using stock a full 1 in. thick or heavier will not only leave more material for the walls of the mortise, it will also allow for a thicker tenon. Cut dovetails with wider pins and at a slightly greater angle than you would for hardwoods—a 1:5 ratio should work well. This angle will reduce the likelihood of failure due to compression of the wood. However, the greater the angle, the greater the chances that the corner of the tail will split, so don't go overboard.

In developing your designs, remember that early American pieces were generally built with stock of various thicknesses rather than with today's standard 3/4-in. stock. It was easier to get odd sizes of stock years ago when the woodworker could order virtually any thickness from the local sawmill. But even today it's worth the extra effort to plane down thicker stock or add edge moldings to achieve a thicker appearance.

Applying Finishes

Perhaps the greatest challenge in working with pine is to select an appropriate finish and apply it properly. As with any other wood, preparation is the key to the quality of the final finish. Because pine is usually predimensioned hard-

Continued →

woods are commonly bought rough—you might think that sanding with 120- or 180-grit paper would be sufficient. These fine abrasives don't cut deep enough, however, to remove the chatter marks left by fast-feed, high-speed commercial planers. The results are blotchy lines across the boards when stain is applied. I have found that belt sanding with 80-grit prior to assembly and then finishing up with progressively finer-grit paper yields dependable results.

For more authentic reproductions, handplane the wood, and then use a scraper to remove any planing marks. Further surface preparation will depend on the type of finish to be applied, and there are many choices. As a common utility wood, pine was often left raw to develop a natural patina, or simply rubbed with linseed oil or beeswax to protect the surface. Other finishes have ranged from shellac to varnishes to paint, each with its own peculiar problems due to the basic nature of pine. Pine's aggravating characteristics include the wood's natural resins, solvents that will dissolve many finishes, and showy figures caused by a large variation in grain density, ranging from as low as 0.28 specific gravity for the soft earlywood to as high as 0.78 for latewood. If pine is not sanded properly, the variation in grain density can result in wavy surfaces and uneven absorption of stains and finishes.

Shellac is one of the primary weapons in combating pine's finishing problems. As a final coat, shellac tends to spot or cloud when exposed to moisture, and has generally been superseded by harder, more durable varnishes. However, shellac is alcohol based and therefore not affected by pine's natural turpenes, so it can be used to seal knots and prevent the turpenes from bleeding into the modern topcoat varnishes. Turpentine- or mineral spirit-base finishes may not harden or dry if they are contaminated by the turpenes. A single coat of 3-lb. cut orange shellac works well as an undercoat; an additional coat serves as a very heavy-bodied sealer that compensates for pine's grain swelling tendency by building to a glassy-smooth surface. Shellac can help control color variations and stain penetration as well when used by itself or in conjunction with other finishes, as will be explained in the following discussion.

Oil and/or beeswax are common finishes on early American pieces. Oil finishes, unprotected by varnish, oxidize, absorb dust and grime, and eventually turn almost black. Beeswax or clear finishes on eastern white pine develop an orange patina known as pumpkin pine. Because time is an essential ingredient in developing this mellow appearance, pumpkin pine is hard to duplicate. A technique I have used to simulate this patina is to first wipe on a tint coat made by dissolving 1/4 oz. of raw sienna oil pigment in a quart of mineral spirits. When this is dry, seal the surface with several coats of orange shellac rubbed out with 0000 steel wool. The shellac further softens the color and creates an authentic, traditional look since the finish was used as early as the late 1600s.

To achieve the dark-look of oxidized oil or to make yellow pine resemble white pine, staining is necessary. Applying stain directly to yellow pine will result in a reversal of the grain contrast as the soft earlywood absorbs most of me stain and very little stain penetrates the hard latewood. To temper this high contrast, apply a wash coat of diluted shellac, one part of 3-lb. cut white shellac to two or three parts alcohol, prior to staining. The shellac penetrates into the earlywood and reduces its porosity, while a light sanding, once the shellac is dry, removes most of the sealer from the latewood. Now stain penetration of the earlywood is reduced, but the latewood will absorb the stain at nearly its original rate, so the color contrast between the two areas will be less obvious. Because stain penetration is decreased, you may have to use a darker stain to achieve the desired results. To reduce yellow pine's natural hue and make it look more like white pine, the stain should be made slightly redder by adding about 1/2 oz. of burnt sienna pigment per quart of stain. A coat of orange shellac applied over the stain, but prior to the final varnish coat, will also give this finish a warmer tint.

Distressed Finishes

Although I prefer a reproduction piece to look as it did when it was new, it is possible to simulate centuries of use by distressing edges, feet and work surfaces by rubbing them with sand or otherwise denting and abrading selected areas. By applying the finish before the piece is distressed, a more natural antique appearance can be duplicated. Once the piece has been abused to taste, apply a final coat of either black paint or dark brown stain and immediately rub it off, but leave some of the pigment on the wounds and in corners. The previously applied finish makes this rub coat, designed to simulate the grime of ages, easy to lighten with rags and turpentine if the contrast first appears too vivid.

While pine is often stained, historic evidence indicates that paint was a more traditional finish. Some of the fancier pieces were painted in several tones, with lighter tints on panels and darker, complimentary colors on frames. Also, pine was often painted to simulate the natural figure of more prestigious woods. A base coat was applied and then mottled, sometimes in conjunction with another tint or pigment, using a dry stiff-bristle brush, rags, feathers, combs or crumpled paper to achieve a grain-like appearance. Although with paint you don't have to worry about what species of pine is used, the knots should still be sealed with shellac to prevent their resins from bleeding.

Generally, early American pigments were somewhat loud, and it is helpful to visit museums to get a sense of the colors that were popular for certain period pieces. Milk paint was the primary vehicle for these pigments and its lack of opacity and tendency to raise the grain gave it a character all its own. While milk paint is still available, a reconstituted, syrupy mix of non-fat dry milk colored with universal pigment or acrylic artist's pigments will achieve comparable results. This homemade variety is not moisture resistant, but it can be protected with a coat or two of varnish. Also, malting your own milk paint allows unlimited choice of colors. Although the colors aren't authentic, flat latex paints can be used. Since they tend to raise the grain on raw wood, they simulate the look of milk paint better than oil-base paint, but a satin varnish topcoat is needed to provide a little luster.

A scrubbed pine or limed look can be achieved by rubbing a thin, almost transparent coat of oil-base white paint on raw wood and sealing it with satin varnish. This finish compliments even the racy figure of yellow pine. The paint tends to soften the grain's contrast, while the wood's natural yellow tones mellow out the paint's stark white pigment to achieve a rich, creamy beige finish.

A very striking appearance can be achieved by layering coats of different color paints and then sanding through to expose the lower layers at points where normal wear would occur. Any combination of two or more colors can be used. Apply two coats of the first color and then a coat of clear varnish between each succeeding coat of different color paint. This allows for a greater margin of error when sanding down to expose a previous layer. A final coat of satin varnish will enhance durability and soften contrast.

Mahogany: Five Varieties of a Fine Furniture Wood

By Matt Kenney

Mahogany is one of the finest furniture woods. Tremendously stable, it has beautiful grain and figure, and ages to a lovely, warm brown. Its diffuse pores give it a consistent density that makes it easy to work and exceptional for carving. It is the wood of choice for classic styles such as Chippendale and Federal. But makers of more modern furniture would be unwise to ignore mahogany's qualities.

Before you head out to the lumberyard to buy mahogany, you should be aware of a few things. First, a great many species are sold as mahogany, and some are no more mahogany than poplar. Cuban is the original mahogany, and Honduras is closely related to it. Khaya, sapele, and sipo, which all grow in Africa, are kin to Cuban and Honduras mahogany, but distant kin. Each is a strong, though not perfect, substitute. Woods like Philippine mahogany and Santos mahogany aren't mahoganies at all. Although they might be similar in color or grain, they don't offer the same overall quality of workability, beauty, and finishing.

Second, mahogany can be quite expensive. Cuban mahogany costs at least $20 per board foot, and Honduras mahogany around $10 per board foot. However, you can buy the three African woods for $6 to $7 per board foot. For a period reproduction where authenticity is critical, there is no substitute for Cuban or Honduras mahogany. But if you're making a contemporary chest of drawers and want stellar figure for the drawer fronts, sapele is the way to go. To help you choose, I've put together a profile for each that covers price, looks, workability, and other key factors. Also, if possible, go to the lumberyard to pick your boards. Grain, figure, color, and density can vary widely within the same species. If buying over the phone or Internet, ask to see pictures before you buy.

Two Options for Purists

Cuban
A rare treasure
Cuban mahogany is the finest of the mahoganies, perhaps even the finest of all furniture woods. Its density, grain, and texture make it perfect for handwork. Working Cuban mahogany is almost like working a cold stick of butter.

It Ain't Easy Being Green

I feel a bit guilty when I buy imported lumber. If possible, I'd like to buy lumber certified by the Forest Stewardship Council, which sets guidelines for the environmentally responsible management of forests. Any species of lumber, including the mahoganies in this article, can be FSC certified.

Lumber is FSC certified only if everyone involved in the chain of custody, from the landowner to the retailer, is individually certified. But finding an FSC-certified retailer isn't easy.

I called more than 20 lumber dealers around the country, and only two were FSC certified. One told me that there wasn't enough demand to justify maintaining an FSC-certified retail store, which requires that certified and non-certified stock be kept separate.

So, buying certified lumber at the retail level isn't easy, but things could be changing. Rick Hearne of Hearne Hardwood in Pennsylvania told me that his company was recently certified, and that he will maintain separate bins for his FSC-certified lumber.

A Wood that Spans the Centuries

Mahogany is usually associated with period furniture, like the secretary by California furniture maker James Betts. However, it's versatile enough to shine in contemporary designs like a curvaceous chair by Don Gray, also of California. Both pieces are made from Honduras mahogany.

It's especially good for carving, because it works so easily and has fine pores that allow it to hold very fine and crisp detail. It also takes an excellent finish.

This is the wood prized by furniture makers during the 18th and early 19th centuries. If you're making a reproduction of a Chippendale, Sheraton, Hepplewhite, or Federal piece and you want it to be as much like the original as possible, then clean out your wallet and spring for Cuban mahogany. It would also be a great choice for any piece that is heavily carved. Otherwise, I'd leave it alone. It's too pricey for a coffee table, and there are better choices for contemporary furniture.

Cuban is expensive because the supply is so limited. It has been commercially extinct since the early 20th century and is no longer exported from any of the Caribbean islands where it grows. Salvaged trees are milled in Florida, and there are several stands growing on the island of Palau (www.bluemoonexoticwood.com).

HONDURAS
Popular substitute, but still pricey
When Cuban mahogany was no longer commercially viable, Honduras mahogany took its place. So unless you're more than a century old, this is probably the wood you know as mahogany. Fortunately, it isn't far behind Cuban mahogany as a furniture wood. It's just as stable, works easily, and carves well. The most notable difference is that its pores are more open, so getting a glossy finish requires filling the grain.

Philip Lowe, a noted period furniture maker who runs the Furniture Institute of Massachusetts, recommends Honduras mahogany to his students for period reproductions. It's also used for Greene and Greene furniture, where the understated grain doesn't clash with the piece's lines. It can be used to great effect in contemporary pieces as well. Unfortunately, Honduras mahogany is becoming ever scarcer. Brazil, which accounted for 75% or more of the world supply, banned its export in 2001. And with limited availability comes higher prices.

Honduras mahogany might go by another name at the lumberyard, because little, if any, actually comes from Honduras now. Its natural range stretches from southern Mexico to Peru, so it might be called Central or South American mahogany, or named for the country where it was logged.

African Alternatives

SIPO
Best value, if you can find it
The demand for sipo, like the demand for khaya and sapele, has risen since the Brazilian ban on mahogany exports. But this wood hasn't caught on as well, and isn't as widely available as a result. It is, however, worth the effort to find it. Don Thompson, president of Thompson Mahogany (an importer of mahogany since 1843), ranks sipo above khaya and sapele as a substitute for Honduras mahogany. And just about everyone I spoke to agreed that sipo is the best of the three African woods.

Sipo is easier to work with hand tools and machines than sapele. The grain pattern is subdued, if not quite as handsome as what you find on Cuban and Honduras mahogany. It would do very well where figure might be a distraction, like the side of a secretary or sideboard. Still, it's possible to come across sipo with the same dramatic ribbon striping as sapele. If you prefer one or the other, you should pick out boards in person or at least see pictures.

Sipo is a better carving wood than khaya, which means that it's a good choice for a period reproduction with carvings, like a Goddard-and-Townsend-style lowboy with shell carvings. Sipo is also consistently close in color to Honduras mahogany, another advantage for period furniture makers.

KHAYA
Price is right, but grain is tough
Long recognized as a good alternative to Cuban and Honduras mahogany, khaya became much more in demand after the Brazilian government banned the export of mahogany in 2001. Khaya is similar to Cuban and Honduras in color and figure, and costs much less. Stock 24 in. wide or wider is still readily available. But khaya is more difficult to work because its grain tends to be interlocking rather than straight. The grain can be fuzzy, too. When it is, it doesn't plane well. And khaya's pores are larger. That means it doesn't take detail as well when carved, and the pores must be filled to get a good finish. But that's in comparison with Cuban and Honduras mahogany. It's definitely better for carving and finishing than a ring-porous wood like oak or ash.

Philip Lowe recommends khaya to his students for period work, but only if Honduras isn't an option. Jamie Cumming, a furniture maker in Boston, was drawn to khaya because of its closeness to Honduras mahogany in color, texture, and grain, and because of its price. It doesn't hurt that he can get slabs thick and wide enough to use as tops for large tables. Khaya is sometimes called African mahogany.

SAPELE
Known for its figure
Long used as a veneer and in architectural millwork, sapele exploded as a furniture wood after Brazil banned the export of mahogany. Khaya was the first choice to meet the demand, but there just wasn't enough of it.

Sapele is deep reddish-brown in color and usually has exceptional figure, ribbon stripes being common. Boards 30 in. wide or wider are available, and 45-in.-wide boards aren't unheard of. There is a cost to pay, however, for sapele's dramatic figure. It's caused by reversing and interlocking grain, so sapele requires much more sanding or scraping to get a surface ready for finishing.

When highly figured, sapele is quite distinct and won't be mistaken for Cuban or Honduras mahogany. So it's usually not a good choice for 18th-century-style furniture. But it would be great for elements of Federal-style pieces, or for drawer fronts and door panels on contemporary furniture. Jamie Cumming likes sapele because he can get wide slabs for tabletops, and he has used dramatically figured sapele veneers to complement the clean, straight lines of his pieces.

Ebony, the Dark Knight of Details

by Garrett Hack

When I saw my first ebony tree in Java more than 30 years ago, I was stunned by its small stature. In a climate where trees grow year-round, this 90-year-old was about 11 in. in diameter. Such stunningly slow growth helps explain ebony's extreme density, why typical boards are so small, and why the wood is so valuable that it's sometimes sold by the pound.

There are more than 450 species of ebony, mostly found in the tropics. All species are endangered, and you should be mindful that what you purchase is certified to have been harvested legally, to ensure its sustainability. A certified board will have a detailed chain of ownership, from its source all the way through the milling process to the sale.

In my woodworking I've used three types of ebony: Gabon (Diospyros crassiflora), Macassar (Diospyros celebica), and Mun (Diospyros mun). Unfortunately, Mun is no longer being exported, at least legally. Each is stunning, very expensive, and hard to find. Veneer is a more economical option.

Gabon Works Small Wonders
Gabon, or African, ebony is mostly available in small sizes, but with its jet-black color, a little goes a long way. This rare beauty is somewhat brittle, but the texture is very consistent, with almost no visible growth rings. It machines well and planes smoothly, but your tools have to be sharp, because the wood can be prone to tearout. Gabon's bold color never fades and the wood is very stable, making it ideal for inlay, beads, pulls, knobs, and edging.

Make Bold Statements with Macassar
Quite unlike its African cousin, Macassar ebony has rich brown and black striping (mostly in quarter-sawn faces). A favorite of the Art Deco designer E.J. Ruhlmann, the wood's grain can vary from widely spaced to so tight it appears almost all black. It's not as brittle as Gabon and can be found in somewhat longer and wider sizes. Surfaces can be hard to plane smooth, but they scrape wonderfully. Macassar's grain patterns make it well-suited to larger surfaces, such as drawer and door fronts, but it's also suitable for cabinet and table feet.

Go Lightly on the Machines
To avoid wasting any of the ebony, I tend to use the bandsaw, handsaws, and handplanes to cut pieces to size, rather than the tablesaw or jointer. I've never sent ebony through a planer for fear of it blowing up, quickly dulling my blades, or both. I will occasionally use the jointer to straighten an irregular edge. I've also turned ebony, with beautiful results, as the material is able to take the finest detail.

Hand-shaping the wood requires sharp tools and some finesse. When planing the long grain, fine tearout is common because of ebony's hardness and interlocking grain. I've had success with both standard and high bevel angles. Just start with a super-sharp blade and expect to resharpen frequently. For best results, set the plane for a fine cut, with a tight throat. I clean up any fine tearout with a scraper.

When working end grain in these brittle woods, chipout is common, so I prefer to use a low-angle plane, taking a light cut with a tight throat and skewing the plane acutely.

To shape the material, I often use scratch stocks and sand occasionally. Though carbide router bits work, I avoid using a router with ebony because it creates more dust (a problem for some) and tends to produce clunky profiles. For other shapes, say for pulls and finials, you can use rasps and files.

THE BLACK DUST MIGRATES, SO SAND BEFORE ASSEMBLY
The dust created while sanding ebony can foul mating surfaces. For the bandings and inlays I make of holly and ebony, bold and bright contrast is my goal. In my experience, sanding to level them after they're glued in turns the holly gray. Planing and scraping cuts the cleanest and preserves the sharp contrast I'm after. With any ebony element, sand before assembly if at all possible.

Though ebony has a reputation for being highly toxic to some people, I have not had issues with it.

IT'S SURPRISINGLY BENDABLE
Despite ebony's toughness, it actually bends well, when both steaming and laminating. To make bent-laminations easier I cut the plies thinner than I normally would, closer to 1/16 in. thick than 1/8 in.

Continued ➜

SCUFF BEFORE GLUING

Both Gabon and Macassar ebonies contain oils that can migrate to the surface and can ruin a glue bond. To avoid problems, I glue parts right after they've been handplaned, and I scuff the freshly planed surfaces with 220-grit paper. I'll even wipe parts with acetone to remove any oil that's built up on the surface.

IT DESERVES A SHINE

When it comes to finishing ebony, I've had great success with shellac and oil/varnish. Being both dark and naturally shiny, ebony shows defects easily, so careful surface prep is a must. Regardless of the finish you choose, build up enough coats to make the prized ebony stand out. Using no finish is an option, too, but be sure to burnish the wood to a high polish with shavings.

Tricks for Working with Ebony

Thin blades save material. To get the most yield from the rough ebony chunks, in this case Macassar, Hack uses a bandsaw. He flattens the slices with handplanes and returns to the saw later to cut parts to size, though sometimes he uses fine handsaws to cut smaller parts.

Plane to thickness. When thicknessing small ebony parts, Hack prefers hand over machine. He often uses a jig to ensure that all parts are uniform. It's simply a piece of plywood with thin runners that the plane rides on. A brad in front works as a stop.

Shape with a scratch stock. Machines can cause wicked tearout on the brittle ebony, so Hack uses scratch stocks to shape the material. Here he shapes a bead applied to a door frame.

Keep the contrast. When bringing an ebony inlay flush to a surface, a sharp handplane or scraper is your best bet. Avoid sanding these elements, because it often embeds the fine black dust into the surrounding surfaces.

High-Quality, Low-Cost Woods

by Matt Kenney

Like most woodworkers, I love beautiful wood. And I want to use the best I can find in the furniture I make. Woods like cherry, walnut, and white oak, however, can cost $6 or $7 per board foot, and much more in some regions. Even in the best of times, that adds up quickly. In these hard times, with everyone's purse strings cinched tighter, it's not easy to drop several hundred dollars on wood.

It's possible to find cherry and walnut for less than retail if you buy green lumber from a small sawmill and dry it yourself, or if you're able to cut your own lumber. But those options are not open to everyone.

That's why I began to look around for some furniture woods that were high in quality but lower in cost. I asked editors and longtime authors, I queried lumber dealers around the country, and I scoured the Internet. I was given plenty of suggestions for low-cost woods, but not all of them panned out.

In the end, I whittled down the list to 12. True, most aren't suitable for high-style period furniture, but they work beautifully for almost everything else. Better yet, all cost less than $5 per board foot, some much less. Mind you, these prices are for rough lumber. You'll pay more if you need it surfaced.

Here's something else I learned. It makes sense to stay local. Being from the South, I've used white ash for furniture and never paid more than $2 per board foot. But I'd never heard of aspen or red alder, which are available out West, and at bargain prices.

So take a look at these low-cost but overlooked furniture woods, find one that grows in your area, and head out to the lumberyard. Don't let the economy keep you from making beautiful furniture.

Available Throughout the United States

BEECH

Once favored for handplanes and other tools, beech is tough, even-grained, attractive, and fairly easy to work. It has the soft, fleshy tones of pear, with very fine, light flecks. Beech isn't known for its stability, so design accordingly.

"If oak is masculine, beech is feminine, and sexy too."
—Garrett Hack, contributing editor

HICKORY

With a warmth and tone similar to raw cherry, hickory is a beautiful furniture wood, even if doesn't darken with age. It's extremely difficult to work with hand tools, but power tools can get the job done. Be wary of cracks: Once one starts, it tends to dive deeper. There are several types of hickory, shagbark being common, but there's little difference among them.

"Hickory often has wonderful, flame-like grain patterns like walnut or butternut. The more I use hickory, the more I like it."
—Peter Turner, frequent contributor

POPLAR

Poplar is often used as a secondary wood in furniture, and most woodworkers are hesitant to let it take center stage. One reason is its green streaking, which some try to hide under a coat of stain. But staining doesn't work well, because poplar is prone to blotching. Instead, finish with oil and let the poplar age gracefully.

"The creamy color of poplar ages to a mellow gold, while the green streaks turn dark brown. Arranged with care, these colors can be used to nice effect."
—Mike Pekovich, FWW art director

RED OAK

Plainsawn red oak, with big cathedrals of grain swathed in stain and encased in polyurethane, is often associated with factory-made furniture that has little personality. But rift- or quartersawn red oak is a different story. The straight grain adds a clean, linear element to furniture, and its subtle ray fleck shimmers. It's often stacked, and priced, with the plainsawn stuff. You'll sometimes find curly boards in the same stack.

"Quartersawn red oak is sleek, handsome, hard wearing, and it works nicely."
—Mario Rodriguez, frequent contributor

SOFT MAPLE

It's hard to believe that soft maple isn't more popular as a primary wood. It has a uniform color and a nice grain pattern that is often indistinguishable from hard maple, and it's much easier to work. Soft maple is great for ebonizing. There's more than one species sold as soft maple, but they're all maples and are essentially the same.

"Often, figured soft maple isn't separated out from the regular boards. So to find it, you only need to dig through the stack."
—Roland Johnson, contributing editor

WHITE ASH

Less dense than oak, white ash is a joy to work with hand tools. It's easy to work with machines and power tools, too. Given its weight, ash is tremendously strong, and it steam-bends very well, even when kiln-dried. So it's a great wood for chairs or any furniture parts, like legs and aprons, that might be curved. And the rich, creamy color of white ash makes it a great wood for fine furniture.

"Quartersawn boards, still available in wide widths, are especially stunning, and cost less than cherry and walnut."
—Matt Kenney, associate editor

Midwest/West

ASPEN

Aspen is creamy white with a faint grain, and is slightly softer than cherry. Once dry, it's remarkably stable. The occasional tree can have as much flash and pop as the best curly maple. Aspen usually works well with hand tools or power tools, glues easily, and takes paint very well.

Behind the Numbers

The best way to identify a wood's hardness, workability, and proclivity to warping and checking, without using subjective terms such as fair, good, hard, or soft, is with numbers. That's why we give the specific gravity and percent shrinkage for each species listed. More information about wood shrinkage can be found by visiting the Forest Products Laboratory Web site at www.fpl.fs.fed.us.

A wood's **specific gravity** speaks to how hard, dense, and heavy it is. The higher a wood's specific gravity, the tougher and stronger it is, basically. These numbers also mean that cherry and walnut are easier to work—by hand or machine—than white oak.

The **percent shrinkage** indicates a wood's stability. There are three numbers to consider: tangential and radial shrinkage, taken on their own, and the ratio of the two. As the ratio of tangential to radial shrinkage gets higher, wood is more prone to warping.

WOOD TYPE	Specific Gravity	Percent Shrinkage		
		Tangential	Radial	T/R ratio
Cherry	0.50	7.1	3.7	1.9
Walnut	0.55 sec.	7.8	5.5	1.4
Oak	0.68.	10.5	5.6	1.8

"Aspen is my favorite alternative to woods like cherry and walnut. It's an ideal secondary wood, but also is beautiful enough for an entire piece of furniture."

—Garrett Hack

RED ELM

The distinctive grain of red elm is a cross between ash and red oak, and when quartersawn it lacks the medullary rays (ray fleck) prominent in oaks. In color, red elm can vary from light tan to reddish brown, with hints of yellow and green. When roughsawn, it might appear a bit sickly, but once milled and given a handplaned surface, it's very attractive.

"Easy to work and dimensionally stable, red elm makes a great furniture wood. It's one of my personal favorites."

—Roland Johnson

RED ALDER

Often referred to as poor-man's cherry, red alder has a grain pattern similar to cherry. It's dimensionally stable, relatively light, and works beautifully. Wide, clear, and long pieces are readily available. It takes a stain or dye well, and with the right color is a good cherry imposter.

"Red alder has a nicer grain pattern than cherry, and its sapwood is less of a headache when it's time to apply a finish."

—Mark Edmundson, frequent contributor

East

EASTERN WHITE PINE

Plentiful, beautiful, and still available as wide planks, eastern white pine is a great furniture wood. It's easy to work, and a sharp handplane will leave a beautiful luster on the surface. Knots and pitch pockets can gum up your tools, but you can cut ruthlessly around them to get beautiful boards. You can do the same with a less-expensive grade, and save money.

"My favorite softwood, because it smells great, is a pleasure to work, and when quartersawn, it's more stable than any other native North American wood."

—Christian Becksvoort, contributing editor

SASSAFRAS

A soft, open-pored wood with distinct grain patterns, sassafras gives off a unique but pleasant aroma when worked. Because of its light brown color, it can be substitutes for chestnut. As a secondary wood, it has a stroner impact than poplar or maple, and it looks great as a primary wood, too.

"Sassafras is a pleasure to work. It's soft, cuts cleanly, and has a tangy aroma."

—Jon Arno, Fine Woodworking's late, great expert on wood

YELLOW BIRCH

Because it's used heavily in kitchen cabinets, yellow birch is available at most lumberyards. Take your time going through the stack and you'll find some beautiful boards. It can be brittle and difficult to work, but patience gets around those problems. Curly yellow birch is also available, and is less expensive than curly maple or flame birch.

"Yellow birch isn't used enough as a primary wood, which is a shame, because it's beautiful."

—Christian Becksvoort

Overlooked Woods of the West Coast

by Anissa Kapsales

Growing up in the East with an interest in furniture making, I was aware of the typical furniture woods—oak, walnut, maple, and my favorite, cherry. Then I learned about a few of the "exotics"—mahogany, teak, ebony, rosewood—and I was excited about the new colors and textures. However, these woods come with big question marks for me: How sustainable are the harvest practices? Should I care about that? Also, I like the idea of using wood grown closer to home, or at least on the same continent. I can't say I've never used exotics, but I always have pangs of environmental guilt.

Just when I had resigned myself to the charming but usual local-wood suspects, I spent a year living and making furniture in northern California. There, I discovered five fantastic local woods: alder, bay laurel, madrone, tanoak, and claro walnut. Of these five, alder is the easiest to find in lumberyards across the country because it is the only one grown as a commercial timber product. The other four come primarily from private landowners and smaller lumber mills. But because of the Internet, these woods are now simple to find and order online, and are becoming increasingly available around the country as solids and veneers.

Without turning to expensive exotics, harvested with questionable methods in faraway lands, you can choose from among these five Western woods and add new colors, hardnesses, and textures to your furniture that you won't find anywhere else.

TANOAK
The oak imposter

Tanoak is not a true oak; in fact, it belongs to the beech family. But it has characteristics similar to oak. For one, the fruit looks like the acorn of the oak tree, but with a woolly or spiny cap rather than the scaly cap of the true acorn. Also, the wood itself somewhat resembles oak. It is exceptionally hard and heavy, though, with finer grain and lighter, more uniform color than the true oaks, ranging from a creamy white to a light tan. The grain can be very straight, with a mix of traditional oak characteristics such as prominent wide rays on quartersawn surfaces.

Tanoak is hard and brittle (more so than the oaks), dulling tools quickly and chipping out easily. The way to manage tanoak is to keep your cutting edges sharp and your patience level high. Taking light passes with a handplane or a router bit and sneaking up on a fit or profile will help eliminate chipout. Tanoak sands well and takes finishes even better.

BAY LAUREL
Color and character abound

The best reason for using bay laurel is its colors, which range from blond to black with many shades of gold, brown, gray, and red in between. There isn't a strong distinction between the heartwood and the sapwood. It's not uncommon to see vivid dark streaks and figure running through the wood. Once, while resawing a board for veneers, I was astounded by the character and pigment that were revealed in each layer. With age, the colors mellow and blend somewhat, taking on golden tones while still maintaining variations.

Bay laurel is heavy, durable, and hard with very fine grain. It tends to have swirly, interlocked grain that tears out. The trick to machining and handplaning bay laurel is sharp blades and light passes. Unfortunately, this wood dulls tools quickly. Depending on the specific piece, a sharp scraper could work well, but sanding is your safest bet. Work methodically through the grits to avoid visible scratches on this fine-grained wood. Bay laurel is finicky, but the results are worth the extra care. The grain and colors pop and shimmer when finish is applied, and it takes finishes very well. Because it is so distinctive, bay laurel is a great choice when building a piece with a subtle design that allows the wood to be the star.

Behind the Numbers

It's important to identify a wood's hardness, workability, and proclivity to warpage and checking. The best way to express these qualities, without using subjective terms such as fair, good, hard, or soft, is (much to my dismay) with numbers. More information about wood shrinkage can be found by visiting www.fpl.fs.fed.us.

A wood's **specific gravity** speaks to how hard, dense, and heavy it is. The specific gravity is a comparison of the weight of the wood with the weight of an equal volume of water. The higher a wood's specific gravity, the more it weighs and the harder and stronger it should be. As examples, black cherry has a specific gravity of 0.47; poplar is 0.40, and red oak has a specific gravity of 0.56. In woodworking this means that poplar is softer and easier to work by hand and with machines than black cherry and oak.

Tangential shrinkage is the amount wood shrinks tangentially (parallel to growth rings and perpendicular to the grain). Black cherry shrinks 7.1% tangentially as it dries, poplar 8.2%, and red oak 8.6%.

Radial shrinkage is the amount wood shrinks radially (perpendicular to growth rings). Black cherry shrinks 3.7% radially as it dries, poplar 4.6%, and red oak 4.0%.

Healing Tree

Tanoak, known as the healing tree, has a long history in Native American culture as well as in the leather industry of northern California. Tanoak is high in tannin, a natural chemical used in the tanning process of leather and a necessary ingredient for fuming and ebonizing wood, making tanoak an ideal candidate for both.

Latin name: *Lithocarpus densiflorus*
aka California chestnut oak, tanbark oak
Specific gravity: 0.58
Percent shrinkage, green to kiln-dried:
Tangential 11.7
Radial 4.9
Tangential/radial ratio 2.38

The **percent shrinkage** indicates how stable a wood will be. There are three numbers to consider: tangential and radial shrinkage, taken on their own, and the ratio of the two.

As the **ratio of the tangential to radial shrinkage** gets higher, wood is more prone to warping. Black cherry's T/R shrinkage is 1.92, poplar's is 1.78, and red oak's is 2.15. As you are deciding where to use woods, consider their T/R shrinkage. A wood with a very high T/R might not make the best door panel or solid tabletop.

MADRONE
Pretty in pink

Madrone wood is gorgeous, ranging from a creamy light pink to a reddish brown. It's extremely hard, fine-grained, and uniform in texture, with interesting fleck patterns.

Although they need a lot of light, madrone trees thrive in dense stands because they will grow—leaning, twisting, and bending—toward the sunlight. This drive to survive creates a complication for woodworkers. Because the tree doesn't always grow straight, the wood can be under tension and warp during drying. This can be controlled by pre-steaming, closely spaced stickering, and slow air drying

Continued ➜

Headache Tree

Bay laurel is related to the Mediterranean laurel (*Laurus nobilis*), source of the aromatic bay leaf you find in the spice section at the grocery store. But the leaf of a California bay laurel is much more potent. Bay laurel is sometimes called the "headache tree" because the smell of the leaves can be so strong that it causes headaches. The wood itself is pleasantly fragrant, especially during milling and working.

Latin name: *Umbellularia californica*
aka myrtle, pepperwood, Oregon myrtle
Specific gravity: 0.51
Percent shrinkage, green to kiln-dried:
Tangential 8.1
Radial 2.8
Tangential/radial ratio 2.89

prior to kiln drying, but unless you have a good relationship with your supplier, it is difficult to know if this has been done. Adding to this, madrone has a higher water content when green (68% to 93%) than most other woods, so of the woods described here, it shrinks and warps the most during drying, decreasing stability. Quartersawing minimizes shrinkage, and using veneers and preemptive design consideration helps, too. All that aside, madrone is a pleasure to work with.

Despite its hardness, madrone machines exceedingly well and doesn't dull tools excessively. It's a very dense wood, so slow down the feed rate while machining. Hand-planing or scraping madrone can be a huge ego boost, as you can produce thin, lacy shavings with almost any cutting angle, leaving a beautiful, polished surface. Sanding is tricky because the fine texture of the wood will show scratches, but if you are set on sanding, work through the grits to P320.

Hardy Evergreen

The madrone is a beautiful evergreen with distinctive red, peeling bark, under which is a smooth green skin. Madrone trees are hardy and drought-tolerant because the root systems can be far reaching and abundant, tapping up to 12 ft. in fractured bedrock and holding soil in place. This makes the madrone tree excellent for controlling erosion. The tree flowers in the spring, and berries form late in the summer, providing food for birds.

Latin name: *Arbutus menziesii*
aka Pacific madrone, strawberry tree
Specific gravity: 0.58
Percent shrinkage, green to kiln-dried:
Tangential 12.4
Radial 5.6
Tangential/radial ratio 2.21

CLARO WALNUT
Walnut at its best

There are good reasons why eastern black walnut (*Juglans nigra*) is such a popular furniture wood. It's a consistently straight-grained, beautifully colored wood that is hard and durable without being excessively heavy. It's easy to work by hand and machine, and it finishes beautifully.

Now take all those fantastic attributes and add more color, interesting swirls, and figure, and you get claro walnut (*Juglans hindsii*). While you're adding, throw some extra cash into the mix. Claro walnut is pricier than black walnut, but it's worth it. The rich colors of this wood

range from medium brown to dark chocolate brown, and it often has purple or reddish striping, gold hues, or whitish marbling. Because of the colors and figure, claro walnut is often used for gun stocks.

It isn't a big surprise that claro walnut is a favorite of many woodworkers, including Sam Maloof and George Nakashima. In fact, Nakashima was known to travel from Pennsylvania to California specifically to look over trees and purchase spectacular slabs of claro walnut.

Claro Confusion

There is a lot of conflicting information about claro walnut, much of it misinformation. To clear up the confusion, I went to forestry expert John Shelley at the University of California, Berkeley. Claro walnut, commercially important as rootstock for English walnut orchards, is a real species of wood, native to northern California. The native species of walnut in California is *Juglans californica*. That seems simple enough, but the claro confusion comes from the distinction between the northern and southern varieties. The northern variety (*Juglans californica var. hindsii* or *Juglans hindsii*) is the highly figured, richly colored wood I'm referring to here. The southern variety (*Juglans californica var. californica*) is more like eastern black walnut.

Latin name: *Juglans hindsii*
aka Hinds black walnut
Specific gravity: 0.51
Percent shrinkage, green to kiln-dried:
Tangential 7.8
Radial 5.5
Tangential/radial ratio 1.41

ALDER
Way better than its reputation

Alder, a member of the birch family, is a beautiful wood that has gotten a bad rap—being dubbed "poor man's cherry." Because it is fast-growing and abundant (therefore inexpensive) and takes stain and other finishes exceptionally well, many cabinetmakers stain alder and pass it off (knowingly or not) as cherry.

Left natural, this fine-grained wood has a warm amber color with reddish tones. There is little or no difference between the heartwood and sapwood, so the color and texture tend to be very uniform and the grain is fairly straight. Select-grade alder is not visually overpowering,

Red Inside

Red alder actually has extremely white bark like the palest of birches, only it doesn't peel as a birch does. Scratching through the outside layer of the bark reveals a rich red, and the wood (nearly white when first cut) turns a reddish amber as it is exposed to air.

Alder also plays an important ecological role; it's known as a nitrogen fixer because its root system hosts a bacterium (*actinomycete Frankia*) that draws nitrogen from the air and enriches the soil, benefiting nearby plants and organisms.

Latin name: *Alnus rubra*
aka western alder, Oregon alder, Pacific coast alder
Specific gravity: 0.37
Percent shrinkage, green to kiln-dried:
Tangential 7.3
Radial 4.4
Tangential/radial ratio 1.65

so it will never distract from the design of a piece. If that sounds mundane, knotty alder is also widely available and can add a different interest to the wood.

Alder is on the softer side of hardwoods (close to mahogany) and tends to decay quickly in the elements, so it is not a good choice for outdoor applications. But it is wonderful for furniture and turnings. It's very stable, machines well, is a pleasure to work by hand, and doesn't dull blades excessively.

The light, warm color doesn't darken quickly as cherry does. It tends to age and color more like maple: warmly and very slowly, not changing much with time.

Best Woods for Outdoor Furniture

by Hank Gilpin

After a long day in the shop, I like to head out to the backyard, sit back in a chair, and have a cold drink. It's relaxing, but I'm only there for a few hours at most. The wood chair beneath me is out in the weather all day, every day. And every minute, the elements are working to tear it down. Outdoor furniture won't last forever, but you can greatly extend its life by using the right wood (and the right joinery).

What makes a wood right for the outdoors? Its ability to resist decay. I've been making outdoor furniture for several decades, and I've used a wide variety of woods to do it. Teak is far and away the best. It resists decay, is very stable, and naturally fades to a beautiful silver-gray. But it also is very expensive, so I don't use it. In fact, I don't use any exotics. There are plenty of domestic species that do great outside and I'll tell you about the five that top my list: white oak, black locust, bald cypress, eastern red cedar, and northern white cedar. Some of these are more difficult to find than others, but you should be able to find at least one of them where you live (and the others you can get from online lumber dealers).

Regardless of which wood you use, here is one bit of advice that applies to them all. Use only the heartwood for outdoor furniture (and anything else you make for the outdoors). Sapwood is too rich in sugars and other tasty treats to survive very long in the wet, wild, and often warm wilderness out the back door. Fungi, the critters most responsible for decay, tear through sapwood, but have a much harder time with heartwood. Wind, rain, and sun also cause decay, but you can mitigate their impact with smart design, like making sure surfaces that face up are sloped and that exposed end grain has plenty of room to breathe and dry.

Also, applying a finish is a Sisyphean task, and it won't preserve the wood forever. The elements catch up with everything. So, skip the finish, let the wood weather to its natural gray, and relax.

White Oak

White oak is widely available, much less expensive than teak and other exotics, and withstands the elements for years. The one knock against white oak is that it can be tough to work. Also, be aware that different parts of the growth rings weather differently. The light-colored early wood (the part of the ring that grows first) is more porous and softer than the darker late wood, so the surface becomes uneven. To minimize that effect, look for lumber with tight annual rings (check the end grain).

Latin name: *Quercus alba*
Availability: throughout U.S.
Specific gravity: 0.68

Percent shrinkage:

Tangential:	10.5
Radial:	5.6
T/R ratio:	1.8

BEHIND THE NUMBERS

A wood's **specific gravity** speaks to how hard, dense, and heavy it is. The higher a wood's specific gravity, the tougher and stronger it is.

The **percent shrinkage** indicates a wood's stability. There are three numbers to consider: tangential and radial shrinkage and the ratio of the two. As the ratio of tangential to radial shrinkage gets higher, wood is more prone to warping.

Black Locust

Of all the domestic woods I know—and I know a lot—black locust resists the ravages of fungi and moisture the best. More durable than white oak, it is the best choice for furniture parts that are in direct contact with the soil. As it never has more than three years' worth of sapwood, there is very little waste. Like white oak, it is tough to work. Although it grows just about everywhere, black locust can be hard to find because it is only just appearing on the fringes of the commercial radar. However, with a bit of leg work (try an online search) you should be able to find it in your area.

Latin name: *Robinia pseudoacacia*
Specific gravity: 0.69

Percent shrinkage:

Tangential:	7.2
Radial:	4.6
T/R ratio:	1.6

Bald Cypress

A light but durable wood, bald cypress is great for furniture that you need to move around often. It works very well with hand tools, and doesn't clog sandpaper as fast as northern white cedar. However, it can be oily, which makes glue-ups tough. Furniture maker Brian Boggs has tested many glues on it and recommends using Oak & Teak Epoxy Glue (glueoakandteak.com), which is specially formulated for oily woods. Bald cypress grows in a fairly large part of the country and isn't difficult to find.

Latin name: *Taxodium distichum*
Specific gravity: 0.46
Percent shrinkage:

Tangential:	6.2
Radial:	3.8
T/R ratio:	1.6

Two Cedars

Red cedar challenges black locust in terms of durability, and is another great choice for any part that is in direct contact with soil. It's not difficult to work, but is often very knotty. However, if you design with foresight you can locate joinery to miss the knots, or use it only for those

---

parts that touch the ground or are buried in it, and use another wood for everything else (it all turns gray in the end). It grows just about everywhere, but to find it in sizes suitable for anything other than fence posts and wood chips for hamster cages, try local sawmills.

Northern white cedar isn't as resistant to decay as red cedar, but still holds it off for many years. It's light and fibrous, but resists splitting very well. It's another perfect wood for furniture that is moved around a lot. Galvanized fasteners will cause staining, so use stainless-steel, brass, or ceramic-coated decking screws instead.

Latin name: *Juniperus virginiana* (Eastern red)
Specific gravity: 0.47
Percent shrinkage:

Tangential:	4.7
Radial:	3.1
T/R ratio:	1.5

Latin name: *Thujus occidentalus* (Northern white)
Specific gravity: 0.31
Percent shrinkage:

Tangential:	4.9
Radial:	2.2
T/R ratio:	2.2

How to Build Furniture That Survives Outside

Building durable outdoor furniture isn't only about picking the right wood. It's just as important to build smart. That's because the parts expand and contract far more than they would indoors.

Start by creating surfaces that naturally shed water, such as angled seats. Keep parts narrow and give them enough space to expand. On a seat, for example, six narrow slats are better than four wider ones. And keep end grain exposed where possible. That allows the wood to dry more easily, making it more difficult for mold and fungi to start growing.

When it comes to joinery, simpler is better. Mortise-and-tenon joints, bridle joints, and lap joints are all good choices. Use a waterproof glue, like Titebond III, to hold the joints together, and reinforce them with a peg or two. Or you can forgo traditional joinery altogether, and use mechanical fasteners such as bolts and screws. Just make sure that you use stainless-steel or brass fasteners. Ceramic decking screws are a good choice, too.

—Matt Kenney is a senior editor.

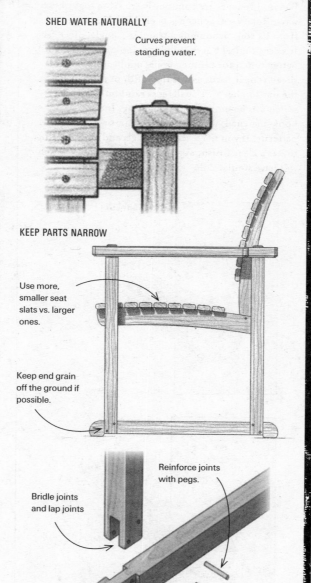

SHED WATER NATURALLY

Curves prevent standing water.

KEEP PARTS NARROW

Use more, smaller seat slats vs. larger ones.

Keep end grain off the ground if possible.

Reinforce joints with pegs.

Bridle joints and lap joints

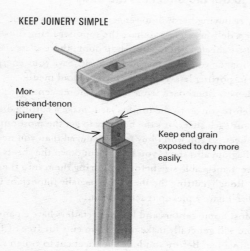

KEEP JOINERY SIMPLE

Mortise-and-tenon joinery

Keep end grain exposed to dry more easily.

Drawings: John Hartman

Plywood for Woodworkers

by Tony O'Malley

In my business making custom built-in cabinetry, I use more plywood and other sheet goods than solid wood. Whether I'm building kitchen cabinets, TV enclosures, window seats, or library shelves, manufactured panels of one type or another make up the lion's share of a project.

The secret to working with sheet goods is to master the balancing act of looks, strength, and cost when buying the material. Buying the best-looking plywood for every piece of a project can be an expensive proposition, particularly when less pricey sheet goods will work just as well, or even better, for painted cabinetry, drawer bottoms, shop furniture, or woodworking jigs.

Sheet goods have a lot of advantages over solid wood for certain projects. When making large or wide surfaces, sheet goods cost less, are stronger and more stable, and resist warping better than solid wood. They're also time-savers, since they needn't be jointed or planed.

There are dozens of varieties out there, but just four types will cover your needs. The first is furniture-grade plywood, which is distinguished by its high-quality face veneers. But you pay a premium for that quality, so this material should be saved for surfaces that will be displayed prominently. Cabinet-grade plywood, which has surface defects like knots, pins, and mineral stains, is cheaper than furniture-grade plywood, and is ideal for painted or hidden surfaces. Then there's multi-ply plywood, usually Baltic birch, which is suitable for drawer boxes, jigs, and other shop tasks. Last is medium-density fiberboard (MDF), a sheet made of fine wood particles compressed and glued together. It makes a remarkably flat and inexpensive material well-suited for jigs, shop furniture, and as a substrate for veneering and counter-top laminate.

Learning the different ways each is used—along with some lumberyard lingo—will help you pick the best panel for your project.

Continued →

Buyers' Guide to Furniture-Grade Plywood

Core considerations

For cabinetry and built-ins, I typically buy three different core types of furniture-grade plywood: veneer, MDF, and a combination of the two. Veneer-core panels are the most common, lightest, and usually the most expensive. They can be fastened easily, but any flaws in their cores can telegraph to the face veneer, showing up after they're finished. MDF-core panels have a smooth, easily finished surface, but are very heavy and don't hold fasteners as well. Combination-core panels are a hybrid. Their inner cores are made of hardwood plies, sandwiched between layers of MDF. They combine the strength and screw-holding properties of a veneer core with the surface perfection of an MDF core.

Making the grade

Grades for face veneers on domestic plywood use a letter-number combination. The better face receives a letter grade (AA, A, B, C, D, E) with "AA" being the best, and the opposite face receives a numerical grade of 1 through 4, with 1 being the best. Furniture-grade plywood is an AA or A grade. I most often use A-1 or A-2 panels, which have excellent-looking face veneer on the front, and a veneer that is very close in appearance on the back. For cabinet-grade plywoods (see below), I usually use a B-1, although home centers often sell "C" grades as cabinet-grade stock.

Furniture-Grade Is Best in Show

Pick furniture-grade plywood for large, conspicuous wood surfaces, and then choose a core suitable for how the panel will be used. For open casework, such as a bookcase or fireplace cabinetry, select veneer-core plywood with an A1 or A2 grade (see "Making the grade," above). Veneer-core is the lightest of the plywoods and holds screws best, making construction much easier. Because it is light, it is less likely to sag when used for shelving or other long spans. Plus, it's easier to reinforce its edge by screwing it to a cabinet case or other support. In most cases, go with 3/4-in. thickness.

On desktops and similar surfaces where flatness is critical, 3/4-in. MDF-core panels are a better choice. They also tend to have better veneers and fewer flaws. In 1/2-in. and 1/4-in. thicknesses, MDF-core is the best choice for cabinet doors or other framed panels, since its ultra-flat surface will look better when finished. Combination-core plywood works well in any of those situations, too. It combines the best of both worlds—the flatness of MDF and the holding power of plywood—and is an excellent all-around choice.

The best bet for purchasing furniture-grade panels is a retail lumberyard. Wholesale plywood dealers will sometimes sell to non-professional builders, usually on a cash-and-carry basis. Choosing between the three cores often depends on availablitiy. As a rule of thumb, opt for the most flattering veneers available on a core that makes sense for the project at hand.

Prices can vary widely depending on the hardwood and core. For a 4-ft. by 8-ft. sheet of 3/4-in. cherry, expect to pay between $115 and $150 for an A-1 grade, with veneer-core being at the costlier end of the spectrum.

- **Surface perfection.** Using a furniture-grade, cherry plywood for this built-in gives a fine furniture look without the warping and instability of solid wood. Plus, it's less expensive and easier to work with.

Cabinet-Grades Work Behind the Scenes

For painted or hidden surfaces, such as the backs and sides of cabinetry or drawer parts, go with cabinet-grade plywood. There's no need to spend extra money on faces that no one sees. Plus, it's widely available at both home centers and lumberyards and costs significantly less than furniture-grade panels.

Cabinet-grade plywood is almost always veneer-core and has rotary-sawn or plain-sliced veneers. For most of my projects, I use B-grade maple with plain-sliced veneers. I also make drawer parts of cabinet-grade plywood, and use solid-wood edging to cover the cores.

Cabinet-grade plywood can be used for jigs and other woodworking accessories and fixtures. It is a bit pricier and less flat than MDF, but it holds screws better.

Home centers sometimes sell cabinet-grade plywood, commonly with red oak, maple, or birch veneers. Depending on the hardwood, a 3/4-in. sheet of cabinet-grade material can vary from $45 to around $80 for a 4-ft. by 8-ft. sheet.

- **Shop furniture.** Cabinet-grade, veneer-core plywood holds screws well and is inexpensive, making it an excellent choice for shop furniture like this planer cart.
- **Cabinets, too.** Use cabinet-grade plywood for painted cabinetry, such as these kitchen cabinets. Buying it prefinished with a clear coat is great for interiors, saving time and adding minimal expense.

Multi-ply Fills Many Roles

Multi-ply plywoods are manufactured from thinner plies than normal veneer-core plywoods. They are pricier, but have cores that are virtually void-free, and surfaces that are flatter than regular veneer-core plywood. They are also the only plywoods attractive enough to be used without edge-banding.

Two Ways to Slice Veneer

Plywood veneers are commonly cut from logs in two ways. Rotary-cut veneer is peeled like a paper towel from its roll, producing a seamless, single-piece face. It's economical but more bland-looking, making it better suited for cabinet-grade applications. Plain-sliced veneer is cut across the width of a log just the way lumber is. Usually it is random-matched, which can be more natural-looking. It also can be book-matched, which produces mirror-image grain patterns. If you need several panels and are planning to use a clear finish, ask for sequential panels, which will have similar color and grain characteristics.

ROTARY-CUT

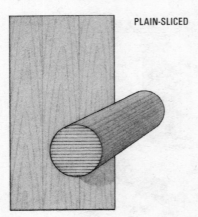

PLAIN-SLICED

Multi-ply is a good choice for drawer parts, and its flatness and screw retention make it the best choice for jigs and shop furniture, too.

Baltic birch is the most common version, but Finnish birch, Russian birch, Appleply, Europly, and similar plywoods are also available. It's rotary-cut, and graded differently than standard plywood. Baltic birch, for instance, has both sides graded—from B, to BB, CP, and C, with "B" being the highest.

It's usually available through lumber dealers only. In 3/4-in. thickness, a 5-ft. by 5-ft. sheet costs about $75 to $90, and a 4-ft. by 8-ft. sheet costs around $110 to $120.

- **Distinctive drawers.** Multi-ply is a good choice for drawer parts, as its void-free edges are attractive as is.

MDF Is a Shop Workhorse

MDF is a versatile, widely available sheet good that will work for a variety of furniture projects and woodshop tasks. Price is the main advantage: A 4-ft. by 8-ft. sheet of 3/4-in.-thick MDF costs less than $40.

MDF's stable, smooth faces make it an excellent material for cabinetry, door panels, and other projects that will have colored lacquers or paints. Plus, the edges can be shaped with a router bit, sanded smooth, and painted. Its ultra-flat surface makes it an excellent material for laminating with veneers or countertop material, or building jigs and workshop templates—particularly if they're curved.

There are a few downsides. At around 90 lb. per sheet, MDF is heavy, although some dealers sell "lightweight" versions that can reduce the weight by up to 30%. It does not hold screws well, although specialty fasteners such as T-nuts or Confirmat screws can help when joining pieces. Cutting MDF produces a lot of fine dust, so dust collection is a good idea. Water is a problem, too: It will cause MDF to swell and lose its structural integrity, so avoid uses where it will get wet, such as countertops or toe-kicks in a kitchen.

- **Top choice for templates.** When building tenoning jigs or other jigs, MDF's flatness and cost make an excellent choice. It's easily shaped, too, making it a go-to material for templates.
- **Flat panels.** For painted, flat-panel doors, MDF will resist warping better than plywood. Glue it into the grooves for added stability.

Handling Plywood

by Gregory Paolini

Plywood, melamine, and other sheet goods are great for cabinets, shelves, racks, and more. These materials are large, flat, and stable, but they're also heavy, awkward to handle, and hard to transport. Being a solo woodworker, I've learned lots of tricks for buying and handling sheet goods safely and efficiently. It all starts at the lumberyard.

How to Get the Sheets to the Shop

If you're buying hardwood-veneer plywood, it's worth paying a delivery charge to have the supplier bring those expensive sheets right to your shop door; there's less risk of having the veneer damaged in transit. Save your energy for transporting less-expensive plywood and medium-density fiberboard from the local home center.

Before you go to the lumberyard, make a cutting diagram for each sheet. It's the best way to get the most out of each sheet, so you won't buy more material than you need. The diagram also shows you how to cut down the sheets to a more manageable size before you bring them into the shop. Rough-cutting the sheets is especially important if you don't have a pickup truck or a van.

Most home centers and lumber retailers have a panel saw and will generally make one or two cuts for free or for a nominal fee. Before you have the sheet cut to rough size, mark the factory edges for later reference if they don't already have a mark from the mill.

If it's not possible to cut down the sheets at the home center, you'll need a truck to carry full sheets home.

The bed on a full-size pickup is wide enough to hold 4x8 sheets flat between the wheel wells; with a short-bed pickup, you'll have to fold down the tailgate. Compact pickups can't fit a 4x8 sheet between the wheel wells, but many have indentations in the bed sides for 2x lumber that will support a load above the wells. If you don't have a way to keep the sheets flat, slide them over the closed tailgate and tip them down so the edge butts against the front of the bed. Don't overload the tailgate. A tie-down near the tailgate secures the load. Use cardboard or a blanket to protect the sheets where they contact the truck. Flag any load that extends past the truck bed.

Handling Sheets at the Shop

If you rough-cut the sheets to size at the home center, getting them into your shop is simple. If not, you have a bit of work to do.

With a larger truck, you can rough-cut the sheets with a circular saw as you slide them out of the truck, using the tailgate as a makeshift sawhorse. Just be sure to leave a factory edge on each piece, marking it if necessary with chalk or pencil. In the shop, you'll use the factory edge to begin cutting the piece to final size.

As an alternative, position sawhorses near the back of the truck, with one or two sheets of rigid building insulation on top of them. Slide a sheet out of the truck, onto the insulation, and then make your cuts. Adjust the saw's depth of cut so it's only slightly deeper than the sheet you're cutting. If you have to carry a full sheet more than a few feet, use a panel-carrying handle that lets you support the weight with one hand and steer with the other. This is the best way to get through a door or around a corner.

How to Make Precise Cuts

To prevent chipout on expensive veneer plywood, especially when crosscutting, I favor a blade with 60 to 80 teeth and a triple chip grind. Sometimes called laminate/melamine blades, they make flawless cuts in plywood and composite materials.

If a dedicated tablesaw blade isn't in the budget, then make a 1/8-in.-deep scoring cut on the bottom followed by a through-cut. Or run masking tape over the cut line on the bottom of the sheet to minimize chipping. Be sure to keep the good side up when you cut.

In my experience, factory edges and corners aren't true enough or clean enough to use in furniture. So I cut them away when I trim pieces to their final size. Begin by ripping pieces 1/8 in. to 1/4 in. oversize, with a factory edge against the rip fence. Rotate the piece end for end, reset the rip fence to the exact size, and rip the piece again. This yields two clean, parallel edges. There won't be much tearout when ripping along the grain lines.

Crosscuts, on the other hand, are prone to tearout, but you can prevent it. Don't use the rip fence to crosscut long pieces. It won't control the workpiece safely, nor will it ensure that your crosscuts are at a perfect 90°. Instead, if you have a large enough crosscut sled, use it. With mine, I can cut pieces up to about 32 in. long and 24 in. wide. Position one of the newly cut edges against the sled's fence and square one end. Flip the piece around and cut it to the desired length.

If the piece is too big for a sled, rough-cut it about 1/2 in. oversize with a circular saw, then square and smooth the edges with a router. To guide the router, I use a simple shopmade panel-cutting jig made to work with a 3/4-in. straight bit. I can align the jig right to the layout line and make a perfect splinter-free cut. Make the first cut so the workpiece is square but still about 1/4 in. oversize, then cut it to exact size when you run the router along the opposite edge.

I can use the same router jig to joint a long panel down its full length. If I forget to mark factory edges, I can use the router jig to cut a fresh jointed edge.

Fine Furniture from Reclaimed Wood

by John Tetreault

To a budding woodworker interested in art and in building things, the old barn boards that my father salvaged from historic buildings in my native western Massachusetts held an allure that's hard to describe. They were damaged by weather, pockmarked by insects, scarred with leftover joinery cuts, and had countless other defects that lent each board a character and feel vastly different from new lumber. His unusual finds inspired me to try building with antique wood, and after the first few pieces, I was hooked.

Now as a woodworker, I look at furniture as usable art—a chance to make something beautiful with your hands that can be used in everyday life—and reclaimed wood is by far the best way I've found to guarantee each piece is one-of-a-kind. I've used it to build more than 50 pieces for myself and clients, and I keep coming back to it. Designing furniture from reclaimed wood forces me to flex my art and design muscles because I have to work with what I have in front of me. It's hard to go back and get matching old boards, so I play it a little loose and let the wood guide the size and look of a piece. Plus, deciding where and how to highlight knots, tool marks, or other aspects of the wood's character is among the most rewarding parts of the process.

And as a frugal Yankee, I take a lot of pleasure in reusing materials to make furniture that hopefully will last several lifetimes more. Using reclaimed wood allows me to work with American chestnut or old-growth pine, beautiful species that are lost to us otherwise. And often, because of the extra labor involved, reclaimed wood is much less expensive than new hardwood from a lumberyard. But you may pay a premium for wide boards or extinct species.

To master using reclaimed wood, you'll have to learn a couple of new tricks. The basic technique is to lightly joint and plane the lumber flat, straight, and square, then go back after glue-up to repair some defects. That leaves most the wood's aged character intact, while simplifying layout and joinery. Once dimensioned, reclaimed wood will easily adapt to designs and plans you like. And it's easy to start using it because, aside from a few tweaks, the approach differs just slightly from what most woodworkers already do.

Another option is to skip milling altogether to show off the as-found, unsurfaced look of the boards. You won't have flat, straight or square boards to work with, but you can get around it by cutting or clamping on straightedges to guide layout and tools where needed. It's a bit more challenging, and won't adapt as easily to plans you already have, but using untouched reclaimed boards guarantees truly one-of-a-kind furniture.

Working with Flat Boards

Let's start with the more straightforward approach: milling the stock and using it the way you would use new wood, with a few modifications to the process.

I tend to use this approach for tables and other surfaces that frequently will be wiped down or spilled on. Light jointing and planing leaves a surface that's easier to clean, won't make containers tippy, and can be finished, so it resists damage from liquids. But to preserve the priceless character of the material, I approach milling carefully, using a few tricks to spare the surface, and fill holes and cracks.

Keep milling minimal—Dimensioning reclaimed wood is a balancing act: Remove too much and you strip away all the patina; remove too little and the boards aren't flat or straight. The key to reaching a happy medium is taking lots of very thin cuts, keeping a close eye on the surface with each pass.

To illustrate my basic approach to working with reclaimed wood, and touch on most of my favorite tips, I built a dovetailed coffee table from four old, chestnut floor boards. As always, when there is finish on the wood, I removed it with my planer. This step often dulls one edge

of the knives. I then flattened (jointed) that side by taking extremely thin cuts with a handplane, although I would have used a jointer if I'd had one wide enough. Last, I used the planer to take equally thin cuts from the opposite side, using a fresh set of knives. I made only enough passes to get the wood flat, or comfortably close to it. I removed bumps, but left small depressions in the middle of boards that still allowed me to safely rip them on the tablesaw. Once I got the boards flat enough, without losing the telltale dark spots, patina, and surface defects common in reclaimed wood, I stopped.

Oversize joinery suits the surface—One way I keep from over-milling the surface of a board is to cut dovetails that stand proud of the corners they join. That way, I don't have to plane the dovetails flush to the surface, and remove more of the patina. For minimalist, simple designs, the oversize, handcut detail can really complement the overall look.

In my coffee table, I joined the top and shelf to the sides with oversize dovetails. I also used them to join the top to the sides of my bookcase, although I needed to use a couple of extra tricks there. The procedure is just like normal dovetailing, except that I add an extra 1/4 in. when I'm scribing the shoulder lines. I also generously chamfer the tails and pins, not only to prevent them from being damaged, but also to add to the rustic-yet-refined look.

Cracks, defects, and finishing touches—Before glue-up, I fill and repair holes, bumps, knots, and other defects, paying special attention to the top or any other surface where flatness is critical. For areas that aren't wiped down regularly, like a drawer front or the sides of a cabinet or coffee table, I leave the smaller holes and cracks. Defects highlight reclaimed wood's character, and leaving them in some areas adds to the look without affecting the design.

Next, I surface the boards with a handplane or sand up to P220-grit with a random-orbit sander. Satin polyurethane brings out the beauty of the wood without looking too glossy. I brushed on two coats, sanded with P400-grit, and wiped on a third.

Where to Find It

Over the last decade, growing environmental awareness has made reclaimed wood much easier to find, both locally and online. With a little creativity and vision, you can give this beautiful material another life.

Craigslist.com, eBay.com, and other websites can connect you with people selling salvaged lumber. There are also dealers who specialize in reclaimed lumber, and particularly rare or nearly extinct species like chestnut. I find most of my antique wood through word of mouth. I keep my eyes peeled for old barns and buildings, and have even helped homeowners clean up sites in exchange for wood. I've also used wood salvaged from house fires, just like the wood used in my coffee table. Owners are happy to see the material reused rather than going into a landfill. You can use anything from moldings and trim to structural beams and timbers.

A word of caution: Watch out for bugs. They are notorious for hiding in reclaimed materials. I avoid pieces that look infested, or at least cut out the sections that do. For this reason, I prefer to store reclaimed wood outside, covered, before bringing it into the shop. The damp pieces will still dry up, but it lets me keep an eye out for holes, sawdust, or other telltale signs of bugs.

Continued ➔

GET IT CLEAN BEFORE DIMENSIONING

Spare your planer by removing hidden hazards like old nails, hardware, dirt, and gravel. Then use a dedicated set of planer knives to take off the finish, if any.

Inspect closely. A metal detector can help spot nails or other metal hidden in the wood (above). To protect the surface from dents, leverage pullers against a piece of scrap (above right). Then use a wire brush and a vacuum to remove dirt and gravel that could damage a cutterhead (right).

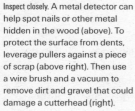

Plane first. To get rid of the old finish, Tetreault ran all of the boards through his planer first (above). That dulls the knives, so you might need to change them (left), but this method is still faster and cheaper than chemical strippers.

MATCH THE JOINERY TO THE MATERIAL

Big, bold dovetails that stand proud of the surface fit nicely with the reclaimed material, and add to the handmade look.

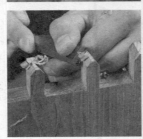

Pencil the intersections. Dry-fit the piece to mark the overhang (above) and then chamfer down to the lines on the tails with a chisel or block plane (above right). Mark and chamfer each pin individually (right), cutting the longer sides first. Chisel in from both sides to avoid tearout.

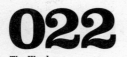

DECORATIVE DEFECTS

Here are some attractive ways to fill gaps and cracks.

Plug holes with scrap. Chisel random-shaped pegs from offcuts and glue them into nail holes or worm holes (left). Then trim them flush (below).

Use a contrasting crack-filler. Darkened epoxy looks more natural than sawdust or clear epoxy once it's finished. Just mix quick-set epoxy with a few drops of India ink, then apply it quickly in any cracks (above). Let the mixture gel for a few minutes, and then scrape off the excess with a razor blade.

Skip the stain. Low-luster finishes like satin polyurethane bring out the natural look of reclaimed wood.

The Next Level: Learn to Join Lumber that Hasn't Been Flattened

Weathered boards plucked from the side of an old house or barn are not hard to find, and they scream "rustic" like no other wood. But they won't keep that look if you joint or plane them. It's impossible to re-create that naturally acquired character with a finish, so when I want to highlight it, I just use the boards as I found them. Of course, that means having to join workpieces that are warped, deformed, or even roughsawn. But if you start with just one straight surface, preferably where no one sees it, you can add a variety of clamps, jigs, or fences to make square or parallel cuts. Here's how I do it.

JOINT HIDDEN FACES

For cabinets like this bookcase, I start by jointing a perfectly straight edge along the back of the case. The back edge will be unseen, since it's against the wall, but it will let you line up a T-square jig or edge guide to rout grooves or dadoes.

I also joint the bottoms and edges of the shelves and the backsides of the rails so that I can lay them out squarely and glue their edges so they fit tightly. Like the back edge, those jointed faces aren't visible when the case goes together.

RABBETS SIMPLIFY JOINERY

I use rabbets in a couple of different ways to build a piece. In the bookcase, I made a glue-tight fit where shelves slot into dadoes by rabbeting across the top ends of both shelves. I scribed the rabbets with a marking gauge and cut them with a handplane. I clamped a fence to the shelf to guide the cut straight.

TIP

Simpler pieces spotlight the unique character of reclaimed wood, and are also easier to adapt to your lumber and any surprises it gives you along the way.

I also use rabbets to line up and mark dovetails in unsurfaced wood. By planing shallow rabbets across the inside faces of the pin boards and tail boards, I can butt the boards together squarely, and mark the pins from the tails. When the joint goes together, the rabbets stay hidden and are never seen.

JOINT ONLY WHERE NEEDED
Inconspicuous jointing lets you line up square cuts afterward.

Hide it in the back. A jointed edge along the back of a case (left) can help line up a jig for routing dadoes and grooves. Paired with a tablesaw sled, the jointed edge also allows you to safely and squarely cut workpieces to length (above).

Flat bottoms make joinery easier. Since the bottoms of shelves aren't seen, joint them to help cut even rabbets.

MARK THROUGH-MORTISES INSIDE OUT

Drill the corners. Mark the mortises on the inside, then drill tiny holes to transfer the marks for the corners to the outside (above). Scribe a line between the pilot holes and chop the mortises from the outside in (right). Then mark the tenon from the mortise (below).

CLAMP THINGS STRAIGHT
Wide boards often cup or warp, which causes problems when cutting joinery. I get around this by clamping the board between thick pieces of scrap, which pulls the board straight enough to join easily.

TWO TRICKS FOR MORTISING
Cutting mortises in reclaimed wood can be tricky, because you don't want to mar or tear out the wood surface when marking and cutting the joint. Plus, the surface you're marking is not likely to be flat or straight, which means you could end up with crooked joinery. There are two easy ways to get around that problem.

For a blind mortise (one that isn't seen from the outside), I cut the tenons before the mortises. It's a backward approach from traditional joinery, where mortises are usually cut first. Once I cut the tenons on a piece, I put it in position against its mating pieces and simply trace around the tenons to mark the mortises.

For through-mortises, which will be seen from the outside, it's easier to mark the mortise first, but you should do so in a way that your layout marks get covered up. Usually, that means marking from the inside out.

In the bookcase, for instance, I marked the through-mortises for the shelves on the inside of the dadoes. Then I drilled pilot holes through the corners of the mortise, and used them to mark and chop out the mortise from the other side. Then I marked the tenons directly from the mortises, like normal.

SKIP THE FINISH
I don't use any kind of finish when I've built a piece with an original patina. Oil tends to darken it too much and mute the color, and wax fills the nooks and crannies. I figure that the wood has been building its finish naturally for years, and nothing I can do would beat it

STRAIGHTEN DOVETAILS IN WOBBLY WOOD

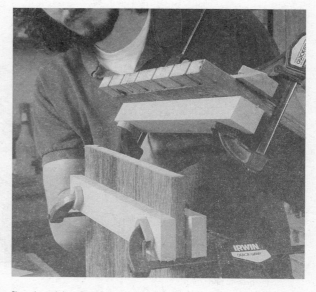

Clamp the workpieces flat. Cut a shallow rabbet on the inside faces and once again squeeze the boards between thick pieces of scrap to help line them up evenly for marking the pins.

JIGS FOR RABBETS AND DADOES

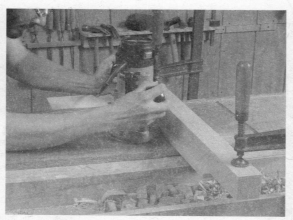

A T-square for dadoes. Square the jig from the back edge and then use a thick caul to clamp the whole board flat.

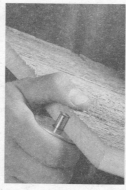

Rabbet the shelves to fit. The jointed bottoms of the shelves create a reference face for scribing perfectly even rabbets (left). Tetreault rabbets the shelf using a thick piece of wood to guide a rabbeting block plane (right).

SHOPPING FOR LUMBER

Lumberyard Basics

by Steve Scott

Buying wood at a lumberyard is like ordering dinner in a French restaurant. For the unprepared, the choices are confusing, the menu offers scant help, and the waiter speaks a foreign language. Asking for what you want can be an intimidating and frustrating experience. On the other hand, the offerings in a French restaurant are richer and more varied than the average fast-food joint. Master a few key phrases, and you can eat like a king.

For the woodworker who usually buys stock from the home center, the lumberyard or hardwood retailer offers a similar step up in quality and variety. It gives you the chance to buy roughsawn stock and mill it to dimension yourself, freeing you creatively from the standard thicknesses of pre-surfaced material. Study the dialect of the lumberyard and you'll soon be making sense of the wide variety available there, choosing wisely and dealing confidently with the host (the person driving the forklift).

What follows is a kind of English-to-lumberyard phrase book. Study it and take it with you on your next trip to buy wood.

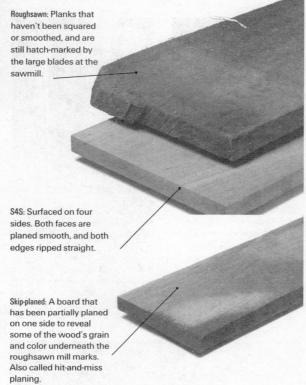

Roughsawn: Planks that haven't been squared or smoothed, and are still hatch-marked by the large blades at the sawmill.

S4S: Surfaced on four sides. Both faces are planed smooth, and both edges ripped straight.

Skip-planed: A board that has been partially planed on one side to reveal some of the wood's grain and color underneath the roughsawn mill marks. Also called hit-and-miss planing.

How It's Measured

WHEN AN INCH ISN'T AN INCH

Lumberyards measure a roughsawn board's thickness in $1/4$-in. increments, so 4/4 (four-quarter) stock is 1 in. thick, 8/4 stock is 2 in. thick, and so on. If your project calls for finished pieces 1 in. thick, you'll want to buy 5/4 roughsawn stock to allow for losses as you mill them smooth. When you buy boards that have already been surfaced, the stated thickness will match the board's original roughsawn thickness. The actual thickness will typically be

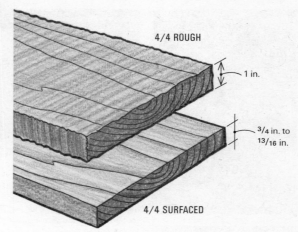

4/4 ROUGH

1 in.

3/4 in. to 13/16 in.

4/4 SURFACED

One Board, Many Woods

A single log contains different types of wood, with very different properties and appearance, depending on how it is cut.

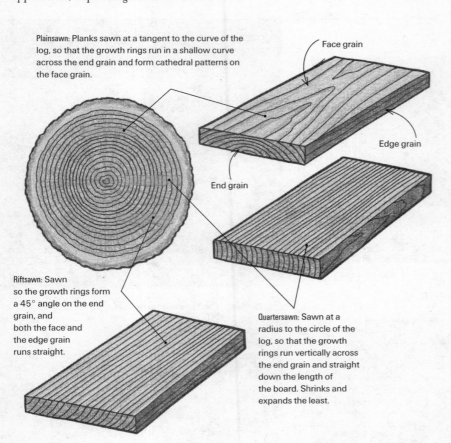

Plainsawn: Planks sawn at a tangent to the curve of the log, so that the growth rings run in a shallow curve across the end grain and form cathedral patterns on the face grain.

Face grain

Edge grain

End grain

Riftsawn: Sawn so the growth rings form a 45° angle on the end grain, and both the face and the edge grain runs straight.

Quartersawn: Sawn at a radius to the circle of the log, so that the growth rings run vertically across the end grain and straight down the length of the board. Shrinks and expands the least.

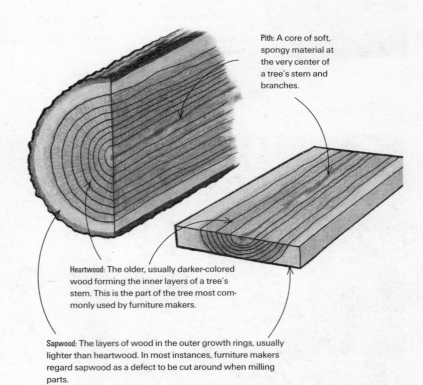

Pith: A core of soft, spongy material at the very center of a tree's stem and branches.

Heartwood: The older, usually darker-colored wood forming the inner layers of a tree's stem. This is the part of the tree most commonly used by furniture makers.

Sapwood: The layers of wood in the outer growth rings, usually lighter than heartwood. In most instances, furniture makers regard sapwood as a defect to be cut around when milling parts.

Early and late wood: A tree's annual growth takes place in two distinct stages that leave their mark on the wood the tree produces. The early season growth of an individual growth ring is called early wood, and typically is made by cells that are larger and less dense than the late wood. The visible difference between the two is more pronounced in some species than in others.

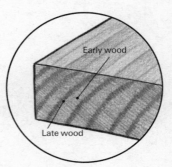

Early wood

Late wood

When a Foot Isn't a Foot

Lumberyard operators say one of the biggest challenges new customers face is in understanding the board foot—the basic unit of measurement for roughsawn stock. The board foot (144 cubic in.) is confusing because it measures a board's volume, not its length. This means that a piece of stock 1 ft. long can contain more than 1 board foot of material. A good visual way to understand 1 board foot is to picture a board 1 in. thick by 12 in. wide and 12 in long. Add an inch to the board's thickness, and you now have 2 board feet. To calculate a plank's board footage, multiply its thickness by its length and width (all in inches) and divide the result by 144.

In contrast, surfaced lumber is typically sold by the linear foot, a simple measurement of a board's length. The price per foot will vary according to the board's width and thickness.

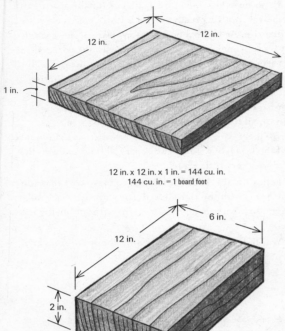

12 in. x 12 in. x 1 in. = 144 cu. in.
144 cu. in. = 1 board foot

12 in. x 6 in. x 2 in. = 144 cu. in.
144 cu. in. = 1 board foot

What to Look Out for

One of the best ways to ensure flat, square stock is to leave bad boards at the lumberyard. But a little perspective is important because, nature being what it is, every board is imperfect in some way. So, when you're sorting through the stacks, bear in mind that many defects can be milled away or cut around. For example, a badly bowed long board can be cut into smaller lengths to make the problem manageable.

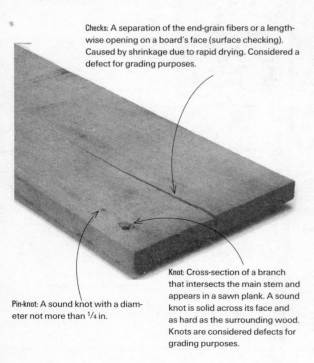

Checks: A separation of the end-grain fibers or a lengthwise opening on a board's face (surface checking). Caused by shrinkage due to rapid drying. Considered a defect for grading purposes.

Pin-knot: A sound knot with a diameter not more than 1/4 in.

Knot: Cross-section of a branch that intersects the main stem and appears in a sawn plank. A sound knot is solid across its face and as hard as the surrounding wood. Knots are considered defects for grading purposes.

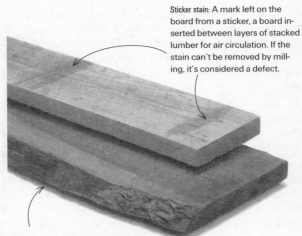

Sticker stain: A mark left on the board from a sticker, a board inserted between layers of stacked lumber for air circulation. If the stain can't be removed by milling, it's considered a defect.

Wane: Bark or the lack of wood at a board's edge caused by the round edge of the log. A defect, for grading purposes.

Hardwood Lumber Grades

Established by the National Hardwood Lumber Association, these grades are based on the percentage of clear wood, or wood that is free from certain defects like checks, knots, pitch pockets, and sticker stain. The upper grades yield clear pieces that are longer and wider than those from the lower grades. Naturally, they also cost more. It's not crucial to memorize all the rules, but it helps to know which grades yield larger clear boards versus smaller ones. Knowing the lumber grades can help you figure out which pile to sort through, whether you need smaller stock for, say, a wall-hung cabinet, or larger, clear boards for a dining table.

FAS: At least 6 in. wide and 8 ft. long

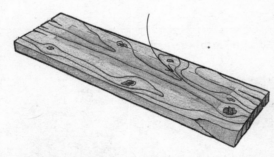

FAS (First and Second): Boards must be at least 6 in. wide and 8 ft. long, and each must yield clear pieces totalling 83% of the board's face. The clear pieces must be at least 3 in. wide by 7 ft. or 4 in. wide by 5 ft. Both faces of the board must meet these requirements to be graded FAS.

F1F (FAS One Face): A step down from FAS, in which the board's better face must meet all the FAS requirements and the opposite face must meet the standards for No. 1 common.

Selects: Essentially the same as F1F except that the minimum overall board size is reduced to 4 in. wide and 6 ft. long.

No. 1 Common: Sometimes called cabinet grade. Boards must be at least 3 in. wide and 4 ft. long, with clear pieces totalling between 66% and 83% of the board's face. The clear boards must be at least 3 in. wide by 3 ft. long or 4 in. wide by 2 ft. long. Both faces must meet these requirements to be graded No. 1 Common.

No. 2A Common: Sometimes called economy grade. Overall size requirements are the same as for No. 1 Common, but the clear cuttings need only total 50% of the original face. If either face of a board is graded as No. 2A, then the board's grade is 2A, regardless of the opposite face.

Every Warp Has a Name

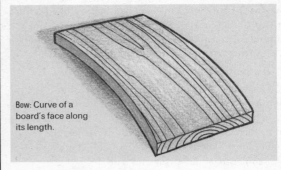

Bow: Curve of a board's face along its length.

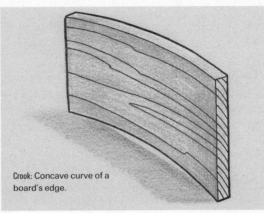

Crook: Concave curve of a board's edge.

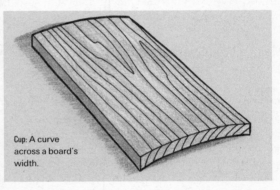

Cup: A curve across a board's width.

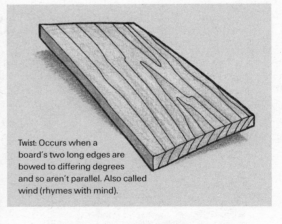

Twist: Occurs when a board's two long edges are bowed to differing degrees and so aren't parallel. Also called wind (rhymes with mind).

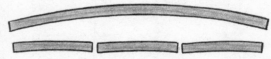

LESS WASTE FROM WARPED STOCK
Cutting a board into shorter or narrower pieces reduces the severity of warp, meaning less stock must be removed to flatten each piece.

Continued ➔

by Asa Christiana

Imagine for a moment that you had the run of a furniture factory: all the tools you needed at your disposal and a bottomless stack of roughsawn cherry, maple, and walnut to pick from.

It's a nice daydream, isn't it? Not exactly.

On a rushed assembly line, the worker doesn't get to choose boards individually or map out furniture parts for the best appearance of the grain. You, on the other hand, have a huge advantage: the time to choose just the right lumber—just like the time you'll spend making sure every joint comes together strong and true.

Choosing lumber is a process, maybe the most important one of all. Here's how to do it so you come home with the right boards to make your project come alive.

Start with a Drawing

If you are not working from a detailed, dimensioned drawing like one of the exploded illustrations in *FWW*, take the time to make one. It will help clarify your ideas about how the piece will go together and how it will look—the joinery you will use, the lumber species and thicknesses you need, the correct grain patterns for each part, and so forth.

Done thoroughly, the drawing is the most direct way to fully document your project, to literally have a clear picture of every part that goes into it. And you'll need that knowledge when you head to the lumberyard.

Make a Woodworker's Shopping List

Every new woodworker eventually hears about the advantages of buying lumber from a "cutlist," an organized inventory of all the wood needed to complete a project.

Recently, though, I decided I like the term "parts list," much better than "cutlist." Where a cutlist might encourage you to think in simple terms of sizes and saw cuts, a "parts list" tells you to think of the components as distinct parts, each having a different role in the finished piece and in many cases coming from different types of boards, even though they might be the same species. Regardless of what you decide to call your list, compile it this way: Spread the drawing out in front of you and refer to it as you make a list on a separate sheet. Write down the name of every part in the project—one to a line. On each line, note how many of that piece the project requires ("4 legs," for instance), and the part's finished thickness, width, and length, including joinery.

If you buy your lumber from a lumberyard that sells roughsawn stock, be sure to also list the thickness of the rough stock you want for each part. To get a 3/4-in. finished thickness, for example, you'll want 4/4 roughsawn boards. For good measure, add roughly 1/2 in. to the width and an inch or two to the length of each piece.

Make note, too, of instances where you'll want to take parts from the same board for good grain and color match. And, just to be safe, you might also want to mark down types of grain: flatsawn, riftsawn, quartersawn.

Because you'll almost never find boards that fit your needs exactly, you're likely to wind up with a bit more stock than you strictly need. That's fine. You'll want the extra for test cuts or repairs. In fact, if you think you may have cut it too close, throw in one nice extra board to be sure.

A Smart Buyer Makes A Smart List

The most basic parts list includes the type and number of each part, along with dimensions. Make your list more helpful by including notes about the type of grain you want in each part and the rough thickness.

How to Pull Diamonds from the Rough

All of this work leads to the lumberyard, where you will find those beautiful finished parts in the piles of rough lumber.

Remember: The decisions you make here are ones that you will live with for years to come. So take your parts list, and take your time. Start by spending a few minutes to make friends with your lumber guy. Explain that you are a furniture maker and need some extra time to pick through the piles.

For the two walnut end tables I made recently for our free video series, *Getting Started in Woodworking*, I needed a couple of 4/4 flatsawn boards for the tabletops, each with a very nice grain pattern, so I could cut it into three pieces, match the grain at the edges, and turn it into a beautiful panel.

I also needed some more 4/4 stock for the aprons and the shelves, nothing really special but still clear and close to final size. As I added boards to my take-home stack, I kept track by making a check mark next to the corresponding parts on my list. Then I headed over to the 8/4 walnut for the legs. Here I didn't want flatsawn grain anymore; I wanted riftsawn stock. That's where the growth rings are diagonal on the end grain, so you get relatively straight grain on all four faces of the leg. I found a nice clear, narrow piece with very straight grain, one that I could take all of the legs from, going two across all the way down the board with very little waste.

Following this process, it's easy to make sure that you come home with the right boards for your project, and that you bring home enough material without buying too much.

You'll drive home worrying only about potholes and sharp curves, instead of your project.

At the Lumberyard

Step one—bring the list. Attach it to a clipboard (left) or leave it in the tablet so it's easier to make notes as you work. Also bring a tape measure, a block plane, and a lumber crayon (and a friend?). Lumberyards stack boards of each species by thickness, so it makes sense to choose all of your 4/4 boards at the same time, for instance. Sort by eye at first, looking for the grain and width you want. Use the tape measure to gauge the amount of clear stock between defects.

Mark out parts. Once you're home, it's easy to get mixed up about which boards you intended for which part. To keep things straight, it can help to mark the parts directly on the stock with a lumber crayon before you leave the lumberyard.

One Table from Three Boards

For this table, Christiana used a single board for each of the three major components, greatly enhancing the consistency of color and grain in each finished piece.

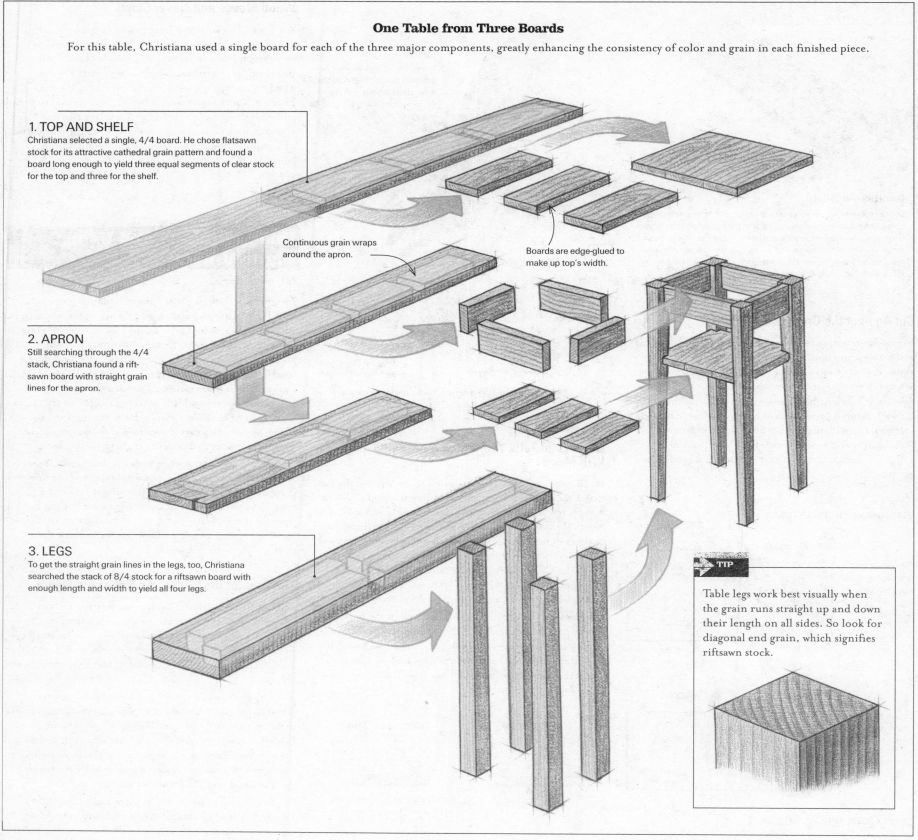

1. TOP AND SHELF
Christiana selected a single, 4/4 board. He chose flatsawn stock for its attractive cathedral grain pattern and found a board long enough to yield three equal segments of clear stock for the top and three for the shelf.

Continuous grain wraps around the apron.

Boards are edge-glued to make up top's width.

2. APRON
Still searching through the 4/4 stack, Christiana found a rift-sawn board with straight grain lines for the apron.

3. LEGS
To get the straight grain lines in the legs, too, Christiana searched the stack of 8/4 stock for a riftsawn board with enough length and width to yield all four legs.

TIP

Table legs work best visually when the grain runs straight up and down their length on all sides. So look for diagonal end grain, which signifies riftsawn stock.

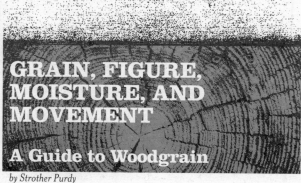

GRAIN, FIGURE, MOISTURE, AND MOVEMENT

A Guide to Woodgrain

by Strother Purdy

As one of our contributing editors is fond of saying, a board's grain is a bit like a cat's fur. If you brush the cat's fur in the wrong direction, you tend to make the cat hiss. Brush it in the right direction, and the cat purrs. Working wood with the grain will yield smooth boards. Cutting it against the grain will give you endless grief. Grain, however, is a bit harder to read than fur. But being able to read wood grain is an important part of working the material successfully. Grain can tell you quite a bit about a board. It can tell you where a board's strengths and weaknesses are and the direction the wood will move most. Grain patterns will also recommend the best ways to cut a particular board.

Grain Patterns Describe the Structure of Wood

Lines of grain delineate the annual growth rings of the tree and, therefore, its structure. Depending on how a board has been milled, you will see flat grain, quarter grain or end grain on a board's face. Usually, though, lumber isn't cut with end grain on the face. The grain's orientation not only makes the lumber look different but also makes it behave differently (see the drawing at right).

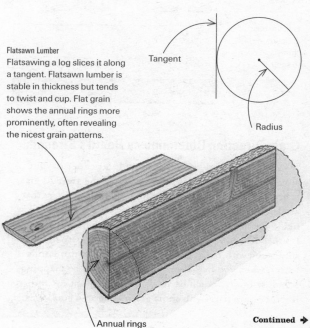

Flatsawn Lumber
Flatsawing a log slices it along a tangent. Flatsawn lumber is stable in thickness but tends to twist and cup. Flat grain shows the annual rings more prominently, often revealing the nicest grain patterns.

Tangent

Radius

Annual rings

Continued ➔

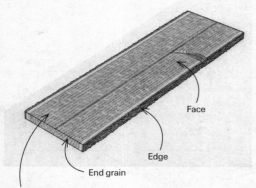

QUARTERSAWN LUMBER

Quartersawing a log slices it along its radius. The term quartersawn comes from a sawing technique that cuts the logs into quarters, then into boards. It's more expensive and less common, but it's twice as stable in width than flatsawn and doesn't warp much. Quarter grain has a subtle figure but reveals beautiful ray patterns in oak—a feature taken advantage of by Arts-and-Crafts designers.

Cut Against the Grain at Your Peril

In woodworking, as in life, it never pays to go against the grain unless you must. If you don't cut a board with the grain, the blade will tear out bits of wood to remind you. When the grain is straight, you are in luck. Frequently, though, it's impossible to avoid cutting against the grain. Strongly figured woods such as bird's-eye maple have grain that goes in every direction at once. In this situation, making light cuts with very sharp tools helps. And if you still get tearout, remember that scrapers and sanders can get rid of it.

IDEAL BOARD WITH STRAIGHT GRAIN

Cut against the grain and the wood will tear out.

Cut with the grain for a smooth edge.

COMMON BOARD WITH WAYWARD GRAIN

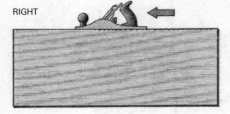

Pick the best direction, cut lightly and plan to sand.

Grain Direction Determines a Board's Strength

If you've tried, you know that wood is far easier to split along the grain than it is to break across the grain. This is because wood is made up of tough cellulose fibers that are about 100 times longer than they are wide. They're held together by a glue-like substance called lignin, which is much less strong than the fibers themselves. When you split wood with the grain, you're breaking lignin bonds (easy); when you break across the grain, you're snapping cellulose fibers (much harder). Though tempting, designing furniture parts with short grain is never a good idea.

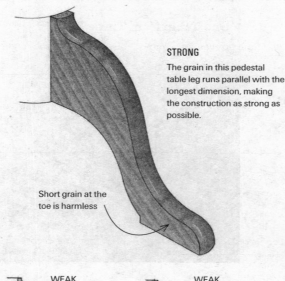

STRONG
The grain in this pedestal table leg runs parallel with the longest dimension, making the construction as strong as possible.

Short grain at the toe is harmless

WEAK   WEAK

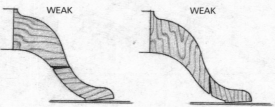

Weight of table will split the short grain in the ankles of these feet.

Grain Even Tells You Where Your Wood Will Move

Wood's wayward ways are not more evident than in the way that it moves. Even after you mill a board straight, flat and square, it will grow and shrink, bend, twist and cup. Wood moves for two reasons: internal stresses in its structure and changes in moisture content because of changes in relative humidity (you can ignore this only if you live in sunny Southern California where the relative humidity never changes). Helpfully, a board's grain will tell you how much and in which directions a given board will move.

Flatsawn lumber will tend to cup toward the bark, flattening out its annual rings. Quartersawn lumber doesn't warp as much, but it can shrink unevenly in thickness, less toward the pith (the center of the tree) and more toward the bark. These reasons and others make it unwise to join boards with different grain.

WHEN YOU BUILD   **THREE YEARS LATER**

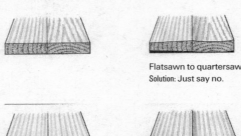

Flatsawn to quartersawn
Solution: Just say no.

Pith to bark
Solution: Say "bark to bark and pith to pith" 10 times fast.

Repeating or alternating flatsawn orientation
Solution: It's your choice, but repeating seems more predictable.

Wood Moves and Never Stops

When wood absorbs and loses moisture from the surrounding air, it moves. Because the relative humidity can vary sharply between seasons and even between rooms (think of the proverbial damp basement and dry attic), wood expands in the summer and shrinks in the winter. Expect a North American hardwood (such as oak) to shrink and swell about 1/4 in. across 12 in. of flat grain and 1/8 in. across 12 in. of quartersawn grain between highs and lows of humidity. Finishes will reduce movement, but won't eliminate it.

Understanding and Using Figured Wood

by Thomas R. Schrunk

Imagine woodworking without any figured woods: no bird's-eye maple, no crotch mahogany, no walnut burl, no curly cherry—just foot after board foot of straight-grained, uniform wood. Sure, life would be easier: Straight-grained wood dries predictably, works easily, and can be used to make solid-wood furniture. On the other hand, burl or crotch wood can crack or warp on drying; solid pieces may be impossible to work with; and just try planing that board of bird's-eye maple. But like moths to the flame, woodworkers are drawn to highly figured wood by its unique beauty and even the challenges it presents.

We all know figure when we see it, but how is it defined scientifically? What causes one maple tree to have uniform grain and its neighbor to have the wildest fiddleback pattern? Not all the causes of exotic figure are known, but I'll describe some theories, give a glossary of the many names for wood figure, and offer a few tips for working these difficult but beautiful woods.

The Greater the Stress, the Better the Figure

"Figure" is a deviation from normal straight-cell orientation. This deviation can be quite organized, as in fiddleback or blister, or it can be random, as in bird's eye or burl. While the individual cells are too small to see, we read the figure by a change in luster, and sometimes in cell color.

The causes of figure are much debated, but stress seems to be a factor, whether it comes from climate, insect or fungus attack, or physical damage. Bigleaf maple trees that lean tend to produce both blister and quilt figure; the northern range of the sugar maple produces far more bird's eye than warmer regions; burl is likely started by a dormant bud that divides and subdivides profusely.

Some types of figure begin more easily than others. Development of a corrugated or washboard pattern is common in large trees. It is normally found in the radial or quartersawn plane and produces the pattern known as fiddleback. When this undulant growth occurs on the tangential or flatsawn plane, the result is a trunk that looks like a corrugated drainage pipe. This curly figure, frequently found in birch, gives luster of varying beauty, but the variation in vessel openings can result in a blotchy look when stained.

While figure may begin development in young trees, it tends to become more intense as the tree grows. This is probably due to increased crowding of newly divided cells in the cambium (the thin layer between the bark and the wood). The cells enlarge first by elongation. If there isn't room to squeeze between adjacent cells, their only option is to bulge outward. Some species (maple, sapele) tend to exhibit more figure than others, which may be due to cell shape and thickness, as well as the vigor of the cell-division process.

Because of figured wood's scarcity and value, it is often easiest to find by mail order. But first you must understand the terminology. Fiddleback, curly, tiger, pommele, blister—the variety of names is almost as broad as the types

Figure Found in Normal Growth

CROCH WOOD

The juncture between two major limbs produces this distinctive figure. As each branch adds its annual cylinder of growth, the cylinders impinge on each other in the crotch, creating chaotic growth patterns. However, too sharp an angle entraps the bark and compromises the appearance and workability (old-time lumber men said that for optimal figure a person must be able to sit in the crotch like a saddle). Crotch wood is available as both veneer and solid wood.

RAY FLECK

Also known as flake, this figure is not actually a deviation from normal growth, but is the result of cutting wood on the radial plane to expose the medullary rays that run horizontally from the center to the outer edge. Normally too small to be noticed, in some species the rays are so pronounced they become a visual feature. Quartersawn white oak is the most well-known example. Sycamore also has abundant rays, but lacewood (left) is the exotic champion.

SPALTING

The distinctive dark brown and black lines of spalted wood are unlike any other figure type. Representing the boundaries of different colonies of fungi, spalting shows up best in light-colored woods such as maple and birch. Because this is a decay process, spalted wood may be compromised in strength, and for this reason is rarely available as veneer. But when the decay is stopped soon enough, the solid wood is quite usable.

STUMP OR BUTT

As the base of a tree transitions from typical vertical wood cells to root cells, it widens and abruptly branches in all directions, causing pressure ridges and convoluted growth. Angel Step is a stump-wood figure type that looks like lustrous stairs, and is found most frequently in walnut, ash, and maple. Because of its location, stump wood comes in limited sizes. This is not a problem for gun stocks, where stump figure and luster are much prized.

of figure, and in truth the labels given are inexact. I hope the brief guide to wood figure in this article will encourage you to go out and try some of these exotics in your next project.

How to Work Figured Wood

Part of the higher price you pay for figured wood is the greater difficulty working with it. However, there are tricks worth learning.

Planing bird's eye, either by hand or machine, often pulls out the eyes. A better method is to sand the wood, if necessary renting the use of a wide-belt sander at a commercial furniture shop.

When thicknessing any curly wood with a power planer, you can reduce tearout by wetting the surface and waiting a few minutes. This causes the fibers to swell, raising the short fibers so that they can be cut cleanly.

Another way to get clean cuts is to angle the board through the planer so that the knives will shear shavings on the bias rather than make chopping cuts along the grain.

The narrow bands of grain running in opposite directions in ribbon-stripe boards make hand-planing problematic, but closing down the mouth of the plane reduces tearout. Alternatively, use a scraper plane or a cabinet scraper to tame this wild grain.

Figure Caused By Abnormal Growth

Although not all the reasons are known, stress and disease seem to play a role in creating the best figure in trees.

BIRD'S EYE

This unique figure is caused by a series of depressions in the cambium as new wood is added each year. Though it occurs in many species, bird's eye is best known in sugar maple. The eyes radiate out from the center, so plainsawn lumber gives the roundest eyes, and wide boards may display oval eyes at the edges.

BLISTER/QUILT

This figure consists of a series of forms, often varying in size, that visually resemble three-dimensional domes. Found most frequently in bigleaf maple, blister is usually round or oval. If the ovals are elongated, the figure may be referred to as cigar, while a rectangular shape is called quilted. If this type of wood is book-matched (left), one side will look concave, and the matching side will look convex.

BURL

The most difficult and beautiful of veneers, burl is the wood of kings and sultans. Starting from dormant buds, burls may be individual (and quite large) wartlike growths on trees, normally toward the bottom. Or there may be a number of smaller burls among normal straight-wood growth, a type known as cluster burl.

Burl occurs in many woods but is harvested commercially in relatively few, among them ash, maple, myrtle, and redwood. Most walnut burl comes from California orchards, where English walnut stems (for nut production) are grafted to black walnut or California walnut rootstock. The irritation caused at the graft line frequently causes large (up to 6 ft. dia.) and highly prized

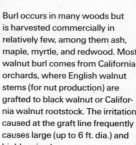

Because of the great complexity of grain direction, burl is difficult to use as lumber, though careful drying may give marvelous blanks for turning. Burl is rotary-cut as veneer.

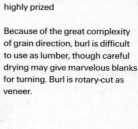

CURLY/TIGER/FIDDLEBACK

Curly is a generic term that refers to undulant or wavy growth patterns. These range from modest irregular waves (left) to full-blown fiddleback (third from top). The latter is named for its use in stringed musical instruments from the mid-16th century onward. A favorite of woodworkers, this intense figure consists of regularly spaced light and dark bands that look like hills and valleys. Where curly might be measured in rows per foot, fiddleback is measured in rows per inch. It occurs in many types of maple, and I've seen especially stunning examples from redwood, makore, and anigre.

The term tiger was once used to describe vigorously curly figure (left) in soft maple. It has been extended to include figure in soft and hard maple that is better than curly but not quite fiddleback.

MOTTLED/BEE'S WING

Found in tropical woods, mottle is ribbon-striped wood with the addition of tangential curly figure. The mottling may be fine and tight, as in razor mottle, or large and regular, as in this block mottle bubinga (left). An inconsistent pattern is called broken mottle.

A very tight mottle that looks like an insect's wing under a magnifying glass is known as bee's wing. The most sought-after, expensive examples come from Ceylonese satinwood, but bee's wing also occurs in andiroba, eucalyptus (below right), mahogany, and narra.

Continued ➜

POMMELE/PLUM PUDDING

One of the most distinctive figure types, pommele has the appearance of rain on the surface of water. The many rounded forms, often of surprising density, produce a luxurious figure. Pommele finds frequent use in high-end furniture and yachts, and comes from the largest of tropical trees including bubinga, sapele, and makore.

Mahogany occasionally develops a distinctive variant of pommele known as plum pudding. Popular in Chippendale period pieces, the plum-size rounded shapes sometimes feature color variations in the plums.

RIBBON-STRIPE

While we think of trees as growing straight, almost all trees grow with a slight twist, normally counterclockwise. Many tropical trees develop a significant twist for several years and then reverse to grow in the opposite direction. After many direction changes over the years, the entire trunk has interlocking grain, which when quartersawn reveals a ribbon-stripe light-dark pattern caused by light refracting from the differently angled cells. The closer the cut is to true radial, the tighter the spacing. Stripes as tight as ¼ in. apart are described as pencil stripe.

Water and Wood

R. Bruce Hoadley

What is the relative humidity in your workshop? Or in your garage where you are "seasoning" those carving blocks? Or in the spare room where you store your precious cabinet woods? Or for that matter, in any other room in your house or shop?

If you're not sure, you may be having problems such as warp, checking, unsuccessful glue joint, or even stain and mold. For just as these problems are closely related to moisture content, so is moisture content a direct response to relative humidity. Water is always present in wood so an understanding of the interrelationships between water and wood is fundamental to fine woodworking. In this article we'll take a look at water or moisture content in wood and its relationship to relative humidity, and also its most important consequence to the woodworker-shrinkage and swelling.

Remember that wood is a cellulosic material consisting of countless cells, each having an outer cell wall surrounding an interior cell cavity. A good analogy for now is the familiar synthetic sponge commonly used in the kitchen or for washing the car. A sopping wet sponge, just pulled from a pail of water, is analogous to wood in a living tree to the extent that the cell walls are fully saturated and swollen and cell cavities are partially to completely filled with water. If we squeeze the sopping wet sponge, liquid water pours forth. Similarly, the water in wood cell cavities, called free water, can likewise be squeezed out if we place a block of freshly cut pine sapwood in a vise and squeeze it: or we may see water spurt out of green lumber when hit with a hammer. In a tree, the sap is mostly water and for the purposes of wood physics, can be considered simply as water, the dissolved nutrients and minerals being ignored.

Now imagine thoroughly wringing out a wet sponge until no further liquid water is evident. The sponge remains full size, fully flexible and damp to the touch. In wood, the comparable condition is called the fiber

Average Moisture Content (Percent) of Green Wood		
	HEARTWOOD	SAPWOOD
Ash, white	46	44
Beech	55	72
Birch, yellow	74	72
Maple, sugar	65	72
Oak, northern red	80	69
Oak, white	64	78
Walnut, black	90	73
Douglas fir	37	115
Pine, white	62	148
Pine, sugar	98	219
Pine, red	32	134
Redwood	86	210
Spruce, eastern	41	172

saturation point (fsp), wherein, although the cell cavities are emptied of water, the cell walls are fully saturated and therefore fully swollen and in their weakest condition. The water remaining in the cell walls is called bound water. Just as a sponge would have to be left to dry-and shrink and harden-so will the bound water slowly leave a piece of wood if placed in a relatively dry atmosphere. How much bound water is lost (in either the sponge or the board), and therefore how much shrinkage takes place, will depend on the relative humidity of the atmosphere.

A dry sponge can be partially swollen by placing it in a damp location, or quickly saturated and fully swollen by plunging it into a bucket of water. Likewise a piece of dry wood will regain moisture and swell in response to high relative humidity and can indeed be resaturated to its fully swollen condition. Some people erroneously believe that kiln drying is permanent, but lumber so dried will readsorb moisture. There is a certain amount of despair in the sight of rain falling on a pile of lumber stamped "certified kiln dried"!

It is standard practice to refer to water in wood as a certain percent moisture content. The weight of the water is expressed as a percent of the oven dry wood (determined by placing wood in an oven at 212-221 °F until all water is driven off and a constant weight is reached). Thus if a plank weighed 115 pounds originally, but reached a dry weight of 100 pounds in an oven this would indicate 15 pounds of water had been present and the original moisture content would have been 15 ÷ 100 or 15%.

The fiber saturation point averages around 30% moisture content (higher in some species, lower in others). Living trees always have moisture content in excess of this level, although the moisture content (MC) may vary widely. Hardwoods commonly have original moisture contents ranging from 50 to 100%. In softwoods there is usually a noticeable difference between sapwood and heartwood; heartwood moisture content being just over the fiber saturation point whereas the sapwood commonly exceeds 100% moisture content-that is, the sapwood may be more than half water by weight.

When wood dries, all the free water is eventually lost as well as some of the bound water, depending on the relative humidity. When the bound water moisture content is in balance with the atmospheric relative humidity, the wood is said to be at its equilibrium moisture content (emc).

When lumber is left out-of-doors in well-stickered piles, protected from soaking rain and direct sun, it eventually becomes "air-dry." In central New England, the relative humidity (RH) averages around 77%, so air dry lumber will have a moisture content of 13 to 14%.

In heated buildings, in coldest winter weather, the relative humidity may drop quite low. The actual moisture content of thin pieces of wood or unprotected wood surfaces may be as low as 2 to 3%, only to return to 10 to 12% in muggy August weather. Therefore, for indoor uses, average moisture content should be attained to begin with. A moisture content of 6 to 8% is usually recommended

for furniture manufacture in most northern and central regions of the United States. In the more humid southern and coastal regions the appropriate average equilibrium moisture content might be somewhat higher; in the arid southwest, somewhat lower. The only way commercially to get lumber this dry (that is, below air dry) is to dry it in a kiln; hence" kiln dried" lumber suggests this sufficient degree of drying. The drying can also be accomplished by simply leaving wood exposed indoors until it assumes the proper emc-remembering, of course, that it fluctuates as indoor relative humidity does.

Certain common terms which have been associated with drying are unfortunately misleading. "Curing" lumber suggests the involvement of some chemical reaction as in the setting of resin, or the curing of hides or meat. To some persons, the term "seasoning" suggests the addition of an appropriate chemical or some special aging process to others; it probably originated in connection with certain seasons of the year when natural drying was optimum for efficiency and quality of drying. But in reality, the drying of lumber is basically a water removal operation that must be regulated to control the shrinkage stresses that occur.

The claim that lumber is kiln dried can probably assure only that the lumber has been in and out of a kiln; it does not assure that the lumber has been dried properly (to avoid stresses), that is has been dried to the desired moisture content, or that subsequent moisture regain has not taken place. On the other hand, lumber which has been kiln dried properly is unsurpassed for woodworking.

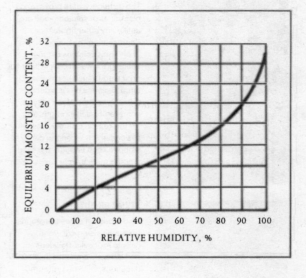

The curve above shows the approximate relationship between relative humidity and equilibrium moisture content for most woods. Below, the curves show the seasonal indoor variation of moisture content in wood. A is unfinished thin veneers or wood surfaces, B is furniture of kiln-dried lumber and well coated with finish, and C is furniture of air-dried lumber and well coated with finish.

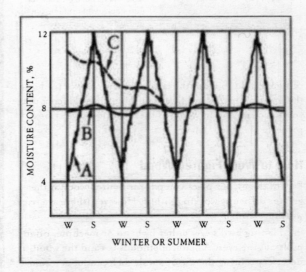

The woodworker's success in dealing with moisture problems depends on being able to measure or monitor either the moisture in the wood directly, or the relative humidity of the atmosphere, or both. Direct measurement of moisture content is traditionally done by placing a sample of known initial weight into an oven (212-221 °F) until constant weight is reached (usually about 24 hours for I-inch cross-sectional wafer). Reweighing to obtain oven-dry weight enables determination of moisture loss and calculation of moisture content (moisture loss ÷ oven-dry weight). By so determining the moisture content of wafers taken from the ends of a sample board, the board moisture content can be closely approximated. Simply monitoring the sample board weight in the future will then indicate changes in moisture content.

An interesting application of this idea is to suspend a wood sample of known (or approximated) moisture content from one end of a rod, horizontally suspended on a string at its balance point. As the wood looses or gains moisture, the inclination of the rod will give a constant picture of changing moisture content. Such an improvisation can be calibrated (by adding known weights) to make a "moisture meter". Of course, there are also commercially made moisture meters, which are surprisingly accurate and simple to operate and will take the guesswork out of measuring moisture content. Measuring and controlling relative humidity in the shop can be equally important. Simple and inexpensive wet and dry bulb hygrometers give accurate readings. Common sense will indicate where humidifiers or dehumidifiers (or some improvised means) are necessary to control humidity. One summer I suspected the humidity in my cellar workshop was high. I distributed 1/8-inch thick spruce wafers around and after several days determined their moisture content by the oven-dry technique. To my horror it was up to 21%! I immediately installed a dehumidifier and within a few weeks the emc was lowered to about 9%.

For the woodworker, then it is important either to obtain lumber of proper dryness or to be able to dry it properly (a subject we must leave to the next issue. Further, once having dried wood to the proper moisture content and built something out of it, some consideration must be given to future moisture exchange with the atmosphere. To some extent, design should allow for lumber movement, but usually the principal measure should be that of sealing the finished piece to prevent exchange of moisture and avoid the highs and lows of seasonal humidity fluctuation by holding close to the original average. Somehow the notion has prevailed that "wood has to breathe." Unfortunately, the term "breathe" suggests something positive or even necessary for the well being of the wood, but in reality, depriving wood of its tendency to adsorb and desorb moisture in response to humidity fluctuation is the best course of action.

Finishing materials vary widely in their ability to seal off wood surfaces and prevent moisture exchange with the atmosphere. Among the least effective is linseed oil. So-called penetrating oil finishes vary from low to moderate in moisture excluding capability depending on resin content and, as with linseed oil, give improved results when many coats are applied. Shellac is also relatively permeable to moisture. Lacquers are even better, but modern varnishes, such as the urea alkyd or urethane types, offer the best clear-finish protection against moisture adsorption. For end sealing lumber during drying or storage, aluminum paint or paraffin provide the ultimate in moisture barriers, as do commercial end sealing compounds.

Moisture extremes-either too high or too low-sometimes give rise to problems in chemical bonding of adhesives and finishes or high moisture (above 20%) may invite mold, stain or decay. But clearly the most common trouble-maker is the dimensional change-shrinkage and swelling-which accompanies moisture variation over the range below fiber saturation point.

As we begin to unravel the subject of shrinkage, three considerations should be taken into stride: when (over what moisture content range), where (in what direction relative to cell structure) and how much (quantitively in terms of actual dimensions). In the first consideration, as with a sponge, wood shrinks (or swells) as bound water escapes (or is picked up) in seeking its balance with the atmosphere. So only moisture change below fiber saturation point (about 30% MC) results in dimensional change, which is directly proportional to the amount of moisture lost. In considering where and how much, we must leave our sponge analogy, because a sponge has similar structure and properties in all directions; wood on the other hand, has oriented structure related to the "grain direction" (predominant longitudinal cells) and to the growth rings. Longitudinal shrinkage (i.e., along the grain) is drastically different from shrinkage across the grain; shrinkage across the grain in turn is variable from the radial direction (perpendicular to growth rings) to tangential (parallel to growth rings).

Shrinkage in wood is commonly expressed as a percentage loss in dimension due to loss of bound water, that is, in drying from the fiber saturation point to the oven dry condition. Parallel to the grain, shrinkage is only about 1/10 of one percent, and in most cases can be neglected. However, in juvenile wood (near the pith) or in reaction wood (in limbs and leaning stems) longitudinal shrinkage may be up to ten times the normal amount, and variable-resulting in extreme warp.

The greatest concern is transverse (across-the grain) shrinkage, which averages about 4% radially and 8% tangentially. However, there is considerable variation among species, ranging from 2% to about 12%.

These values indicate the degree to which some species are apparently "more stable" than others. However, the greatest cause of trouble arises from the difference between radial and tangential shrinkage. As a result, cylinders of wood may become oval, squares may become diamond shaped, and flat sawn boards cup. This shrinkage difference also accounts for wood containing the pith cracking open, as anyone who has tried to dry cross-sectional discs of wood well knows. For it is impossible for wood to shrink more around the growth rings than across them without the development of stress. We also realize why edge-grain (quarter sawn) boards remain flat and shrink less across the width and are therefore preferable for many uses such as flooring.

Shrinkage in wood tissue results when water molecules leave the microstructure of the cell walls and the cellulosic structure is drawn more closely together. As sapwood transforms into heartwood, molecules of extractives (which usually give heartwood its darker color) may occupy this space and thus reduce total shrinkage. For this reason, woods with high extractive content may tend to be more stable (e. g. redwood, mahogany). At the same time, in a particular piece of wood there may be a troublesome-difference between shrinkage of heartwood and sapwood, resulting in noticeable difference in shrinkage or even checking of sapwood.

The woodworker has several options and approaches, which can be applied singly or in combination, for dealing with the instability of wood. First, the wood can be preshrunk, i.e., properly dried to optimum moisture content. And secondly, the subsequent dimensional response to the atmosphere can be reduced or virtually eliminated by proper finishing. Third, sensible design can allow for dimensional change to occur without consequence; the classic example being the traditional feather-edge paneling allowed to move freely within each frame. Fourth, shrinkage and swelling can be overpowered or restrained, as the veneers making up a plywood sheet mutually do, or as the battens on a cabinet door will do.

Fifth, chemical treatments may stabilize wood, although this approach is probably least convenient. Controlling moisture content-and therefore dimensional change-involves an awareness of relative humidity and also the dimensional properties of wood. Understanding and mastering wood/moisture relationships should be looked upon as an integral part of woodworking expertise.

CALCULATING WOOD SHRINKAGE OR SWELLING

The approximate dimensional change expected in a piece of wood can be estimated by application of the following formula:

$$\Delta D = D_0 \times S \times \Delta MC \div fsp$$

where
ΔD = Change in dimension
D_0 = Original dimension
S = Shrinkage percentage (from tables)
ΔMC = Change in moisture content
fsp = Average value for fiber saturation point, approximately 30%

Example: How much will a 14-inch wide, unfinished colonial door panel attempt to "move" (shrink and swell) if made from flat-sawed Eastern white pine?

Solution: Original dimension (width), D_0 is 14 inches.
S (from tables) is 6.0% = 6/100 = 0.06
Assuming the humidity may fluctuate such that moisture content will vary from 4% in winter to 12% in summer, then ΔMC = 8%.

$$\Delta D = (14 \text{ inches})(0.06)(8\% \div 30\%) = 0.224 \text{ inches}$$

The door panel will thus attempt to change width by nearly a quarter-inch during seasonal humidity changes. Loose framing to allow the panel to move, or finishing with a moisture-impervious finish are therefore recommended.

The formula clearly suggests ways of reducing the consequences of shrinkage and swelling. For example, reducing the dimensions (D_0) of the members: Narrow flooring will surely develop smaller cracks between boards than wide flooring. Choosing a species with a small shrinkage percent (S) can obviously help; e.g. catalpa is obviously more stable than hickory. Reducing the moisture variation is best accomplished by starting with wood of the correct moisture content and giving the completed item a coat of moisture-impervious finish.

Continued →

Drying Wood

by R. Bruce Hoadley

It is ironic that our environment has us surrounded by trees—yet wood seems so inaccessible and expensive for the woodworker. Actually, abundant tree material is available to those who seek it out from such sources as storm damage cleanup, construction site clearance, firewood cuttings and even direct purchase from local loggers. With chain saws, wedges, band saws and a measure of ingenuity, chunks and flitches for carving or even lumber can be worked out. Also, it is usually possible to buy green lumber, either hardwood or softwood, at an attractive price from small local sawmills.

But what to do next? Many an eager woodworker has produced a supply of wood to the green board stage, but has been unable to dry it to usable moisture levels without serious "degrade" or even total loss. Certainly, the most consistent and efficient procedure would be to have the material kiln dried. Unfortunately, however, kilns may simply not be available. The cost of custom drying may be prohibitive, or the quantity of material too meager to justify kiln operation. But by understanding some of the basic principles of drying requirements and techniques, the woodworker can dry small quantities of wood quite successfully.

The so-called "seasoning" of wood is basically a water-removal process. Wood in the living tree has its cell walls water saturated and fully swollen with "bound" water and has additional "free" water in the cell cavities. The target in drying is to get the wood moisture content down to the equilibrium level of dryness consistent with the atmosphere in which the finished product will be used. In the Northeast, for example, a moisture content of about seven percent is appropriate for interior cabinetwork and furniture; in the more humid Southern states, it would be higher; in the arid Southwest, lower. Since removal of bound water is accompanied by shrinkage of the wood, the object is to have the wood do its shrinking before, rather than after, the woodworking.

Wood dries first at the outside surface, creating a moisture imbalance. This moisture gradient of wetter interior and drier surface zone is necessary to cause moisture in the interior to migrate to the surface for eventual evaporation. On the other hand, if a piece of wood is dried too quickly, causing a "steep" moisture gradient (i. e., extreme range between interior and surface moisture content), excessive surface shrinkage will precede internal shrinkage; the resulting stress may cause surface checking or internal defects (collapse or later honeycomb). Gradual drying with a moderate moisture gradient allows moisture from the interior to migrate outward, replacing moisture as it evaporates from the surface, thus maintaining gradual and more uniform shrinkage. Shrinkage in wood per se is a natural and normal part of drying which should be expected and accommodated; uneven shrinkage due to uncontrolled drying, however, is the culprit which we must deal with. On the other hand, drying cannot be too slow or unnecessarily delayed, lest fungi causing decay, stain, or mold have a chance to develop. In other words, the key to drying is manipulating conditions of humidity, temperature and air circulation to attain a compromise drying rate fast enough to prevent fungal development, but slow enough to prevent severe uneven shrinkage.

The practice of drying includes (1) proper cutting and preparation of the pieces, (2) appropriate stacking and location to allow regulated drying (and in lumber, restraint of warp), and (3) systematic monitoring of the drying progress. Let's review the application of these basic concepts to typical situations of drying small quantities of wood. We will consider the drying of short log segments or short thick stock, commonly used for wood carvings or stout turnings, as well as regular lumber or boards. We will also assume that fairly small quantities such as several log chunks or up to a few hundred board feet are involved-as occurs when one suddenly falls heir to a storm-damaged tree or purchases enough lumber for a single piece of furniture.

First let's look at proper preparation of the material. Selection of pieces should favor those with normal structure and straight grain. If possible, avoid pieces with large obvious defects. Lumber from trees with special grain will invariably twist upon drying. Irregularities such as crotch grain or burls are esthetically interesting but chancy to dry, since their cell structure usually has unpredictable shrinkage. Knots are troublesome if they are large enough to involve grain distortion. Logs with sweep or from leaning trees having an eccentric cross-sectional shape probably contain reaction wood and will almost surely develop warp and stress due to abnormal shrinkage.

Whether preparing lumber or carving blocks, remember that normal shrinkage is about double tangentially as radially. My initial rule in splitting carving chunks from logs is to avoid pieces containing the pith. A half log or less which does not contain the pith can dry with a normal distortion of its cross-sectional shape (like slightly closing an oriental fan).

Another advantage of not boxing in the pith is being able to see if any overgrown knots are present which may not have been apparent from the bark side. Every knot-causing branch developed from the pith, so it is important to examine pieces from the pith side to discover hidden branch stubs, especially if they have decay. Additionally , the pith area is often abnormal juvenile wood that might best be eliminated.

In sawing lumber, cup will be minimized by favoring quartersawed boards, which have no tendency to cup, or flatsawed boards taken furthest from the pith. Boards sawed through the center of the log, containing the pith or passing very close to it, will usually cup severely (or split open if restrained) along the center and might as well be ripped into two narrower boards before drying.

End drying is about 1 2 times as fast as drying through sidegrain surfaces. Consequently, the regions near the ends of pieces drop below the fiber saturation point first. As the ends begin to shrink while the rest of the piece is still fully swollen, end checking usually results. In boards that are relatively long compared to their thickness, most moisture will leave slowly via the side surfaces; the influence of the end-checking problem is confined to a zone near each end of the board (about 6 inches from the ends of 1-in. boards). With relatively thick material, e. g., an 8 x 8-in. chunk 20 in. long, the end checking under uncontrolled drying can extend inward so far from each end that it riddles the entire piece.

To prevent the rapid end drying which will ruin carving chunks and the ends of lumber, the end-grain surface should be coated. Any relatively impervious material (such as paraffin, aluminum paint or urethane varnish) in ample thickness will do nicely. End coating can be applied to relatively wet surfaces by giving a primer coat of latex material first. It is important to end coat as soon as possible after sawing, before even the tiniest checks can begin to develop. Once a check develops, the cell structure failure will always be there even if it later appears to have closed. Also, when normal drying stress develops, a small check can provide the stress concentration point for further failures which otherwise might not have even begun in check-free wood. The purpose of end coating is to force all moisture loss to take place from lateral surfaces.

In some species, radial drying may be significantly faster than tangential drying. Therefore, if the bark on larger carving blocks is tight (as with winter-cut wood), it may best be left on to slow the radial drying. If the bark has been removed from a heavy slab, it should be watched carefully during the early drying stages for signs of surface checking. Another reason for prompt end coating is to prevent ever present airborne fungal spores from inoculating the surface. If the bark is loose, it should be removed; otherwise the layer of separation will become a fungal culture chamber with undesirable results.

Don't forget to mark a number and date on each piece. It is amazing how easily your memory can fail once you have several batches of wood in process. Next, consideration must be given to the correct piling and location of the material so proper drying will result. Piling must ensure maximum air circulation around virtually every surface of the material . Some means of elevating the bottom of the stacks should be provided and some sort of sticker strips are usually recommended to separate adjacent pieces. With irregular carving blocks, merely piling them loosely may suffice, as long as flat surfaces do not lie against one another. No attempt should be made to restrain distortion of large chunks. With lumber, however, carefully designed systematic piling is best.

The usual piling method is to arrange boards in regular layers or courses separated by narrow strips or stickers. This permits the free movement of air around the lumber, uniformity of exposure of the surfaces, and restraint to minimize warp. The stickers should be dry and free of fungi and at least as long as the intended width of the pile. In planning the pile, stickers should be placed at the very ends of each course and at least every 18 inches along the length of the boards, since loose ends hanging out of the pile lack restraint and dry too rapidly (resulting in excessive warp) . It is best to have lumber uniform in length, but if random lengths are unavoidable, they should be arranged in a pile as long as the longest boards; within each course, stagger the position of alternate boards so their alternate ends are lined up with the end of the pile. This " boxed pile" system prevents excessive drying of overhanging ends. To prevent excessive drying degrade to the top and bottom courses or layers, extra outer courses of low-grade lumber or even plywood might be added to the pile. Stickers should be lined up in straight vertical rows. To ensure uniform restraint in a course, lumber and stickers should be as uniform in thickness as possible.

In large piles, the majority of the boards are restrained by the weight of others above. In small piles, extra weight (old lumber, bricks, cinder blocks, etc.) should be placed atop the pile. An alternate method of applying restraint is to assemble rectangular frames to surround the pile. The pile can be wedged against the frames and the wedges tapped further in to maintain restraint as the pile shrinks. Obviously the weighting or wedging should not be so extreme as to prevent shrinkage of the boards across their width.

In a commercial dry kiln, the operator can manipulate air circulation, temperature and humidity to dry the lumber gradually. He begins with a moderately low temperature and high relative humidity until the lumber (based on monitored samples) drops to a certain moisture content, say , near the fiber saturation point. He then establishes a slightly higher temperature and drier condition which he holds until the next lower prescribed moisture content is reached. Then he again establishes another warmer, drier level and so on until the lumber is dried. The so-called "kiln schedule" is a sequence of successively drier conditions which are regulated according to the moisture content of the lumber.

In home drying of wood, we must therefore try to choose locations or regulate conditions to allow only moderate drying at first, followed by more drastic conditions once the lumber has reached a lower moisture level. One logical starting place is out-of-doors. Except for especially arid regions, the relative humidity is usually moderately high. For example, in the New England area the humidity averages around 7 5 to 80 percent, which would give an equilibrium moisture content of 12 to 14 percent. Piles of blocks or stacks of lumber should be kept well up off the ground to avoid dampness, and should be protected from direct rainfall and sun rays as well. Any unheated building which has good ventilation, such as a shed lacking doors and windows, is ideal. Most garages serve well and even unheated basements are suitable if plenty of air space around the pile is provided. In air drying out-of-doors, some rather obvious seasonal variations will be encountered. In many Eastern areas, slightly lower humidity and more prevalent winds favor drying in spring months. In winter, if temperatures drop to near or below freezing, drying may be brought to a standstill. You must therefore interpret conditions for each particular area. If wood is intended for finished items that will be used indoors, outdoor air drying will not attain a low enough equilibrium moisture content. The material must be moved indoors to a heated location before it is worked.

Surface checking should be closely watched. Minor shallow surface checking that will later dress out can be ignored. However, deeper checks should be considered unacceptable. The worst type are those which open up but later reclose. Often they go unnoticed during subsequent machining operations only to reveal themselves when staining and finishing of a completed piece is attempted. If any serious

end checks develop, don't pretend they don't exist, or will ever get better or go away. For example, if a large carving block develops a serious check, this indicates fairly intensive stress; it is probably best to split the piece in half along the check, thus helping to relieve the stresses, and be satisfied with smaller pieces.

If wood must be located indoors from the very start, drying may be too rapid. Any signs of surface checks in the material suggest that some retardation may be necessary. This can be accomplished by covering the entire pile with a polyethylene film. Moisture from the lumber will soon elevate the humidity and retard the drying. However, this arrangement must be closely watched, since air circulation will likewise be stopped. Moisture condensation on the inside of the plastic covering or any mold on the wood surfaces may mean the pile has been turned into a fungi culture chamber and signals the need for speeding up the drying again. Common sense and intuition will suggest how often to check the wood and how to modify the storage location to speed up or slow down the drying. The seasonal humidity fluctuation commonly encountered in heated buildings must also be allowed for in determining the equilibrium moisture level.

Drying progress can be monitored by weight. Weights should be taken often enough to be able to plot a fairly coherent graphical record of weight against time. Weighing should be accurate to within one or two percent of the total weight of the piece. A large chunk in the 100-pound range can be weighed on a bathroom scale. Pieces in the 10 to 25-pound category can be weighed with a food or infant scale. Small stacks of boards can be monitored by simply weighing the entire pile if this is convenient. In larger piles, sample boards can be pulled and weighed periodically. Electrical moisture meters are perhaps the simplest means of keeping track of the drying progress in boards.

The last stage of drying should be done in an environment similar to the one in which the finished item will be used. The weight of the pieces will eventually level out and reach a near constant equilibrium with only faint gains and losses of weight in response to seasonal humidity fluctuations.

When material comes into equilibrium weight with the desired environment, it's ready. Don't pay attention to overly generalized rules like "one year of drying for every inch of thickness." Such rules have no way of accounting for the tremendous variation in species' characteristics or in atmospheric conditions. Basswood or pine decoy blanks four inches thick dry easily in less than a year, whereas a four-inch thick slab of rosewood may take much longer to dry without defects. In general, the lower density woods are easier to dry than higher density woods. Since the average cell wall thickness is less, moisture movement is greater and this results in faster drying. In addition, the weaker cell structure is better able to deform in response to drying stresses, rather than resisting and checking. After some experience is gained for a particular species and thickness dried in a certain location, a fairly reliable estimate can be made as to the necessary drying time. Here, the initial date you marked on the piece will serve you well.

Whether drying log sections or boards, remember that the drying must be somewhat regulated; usually at the beginning, indoor drying proceeds too quickly and needs slowing down.

In drying your own lumber or carving wood, one common problem is hesitation. You can't wait! If you do, fungi or checks will get ahead of you. Try to think out all the details before you get your wood supply; don't wait until you get it home to decide how you are going to end coat or where you are going to stack it.

But perhaps the greatest pitfall is greed. Most woodworkers never feel they have enough material put aside and tend to overstock if the opportunity presents itself. With green wood, this can be disastrous. Don't try to handle too much. Don't even start if you can't follow through. More material is ruined by neglect than by lack of know-how.

Finally, in drying wood, nobody has ever proved that it doesn't pay to cross your fingers.

Understanding Wood Movement

by Christian Becksvoort

For centuries, granite has been quarried along the Maine coast. Way back in the woods behind my shop, on a granite outcropping, sit a few leftover slabs 10 in. thick by 2 ft. wide by 12 ft. long. The granite faces show a series of 1/2-in. holes drilled 12 in. to 18 in. apart. The old-timers would have driven dried wood into these holes, then walked down the row pouring water onto the wood. Eventually, the granite slabs would split apart. When wood cells absorb water, they swell and expand, and not even granite can stop it. So forget about pins, glue, screws, or fancy joinery; wood will move and break apart your work if you don't follow the rules.

The exact amount of wood movement depends on any combination of several factors, including the environment (the degree to which humidity fluctuates) and how the lumber has been sawn (see below).

The amount of movement also varies among wood species, particularly among the hardwoods. For example, beech, hickory, oak, and hard maple move substantially more than cherry, walnut, and butternut.

Last, the type of finish you apply to a piece affects wood movement. Because light skin finishes such as wax and oil allow greater moisture absorption, wood that has been coated with either of them moves more than wood that has been finished with deeper-penetrating sealants such as urethane and lacquer.

As a professional woodworker, I can't afford to cut corners when it comes to wood movement. So I devote my energy to building furniture right the first time—whether it's a chest, a case, a bed, or a table.

How Wood Moves

Grain Orientation Determines the Amount of Movement

You can predict how lumber will behave by looking at the growth rings. Flatsawn boards revealing long ring sections that are parallel to the pith of the log will move the greatest amount.

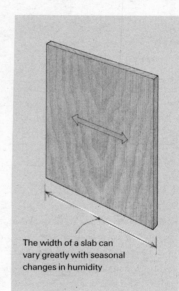

Flatsawn board

Quartersawn board

Pith

FLATSAWN BOARD
Most seasonal movement in a board is along the rings. With annual rings nearly parallel to the surface, flatsawn boards exhibit more seasonal movement and are prone to cupping.

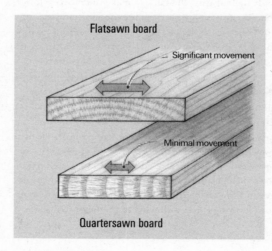

Flatsawn board

Significant movement

Minimal movement

Quartersawn board

QUARTERSAWN BOARD
A quartersawn board has annual rings running perpendicular to the surface, so the board will experience far less seasonal movement and will be less likely to cup.

FRAME-AND-PANEL CONSTRUCTION ISOLATES MOVEMENT
Your approach to controlling wood movement will depend a lot on whether the piece is made using slab or frame-and-panel construction.

Slab construction is typical in chests, tabletops, and headboards and consists of single, wide boards or narrow boards glued up edge to edge. With solid-wood slabs, you have to worry about cross-grain movement, which can be significant with large widths.

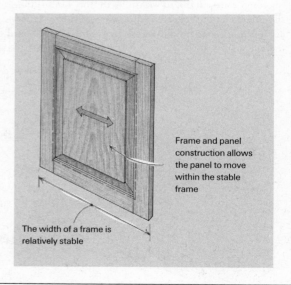

Frame-and-panel construction, on the other hand, minimizes the effects of wood movement by isolating large areas (the panel) and restricting movement to relatively small areas (the frame). The panel is set into grooves of the appropriate depth, but it is not glued in place. Instead, this "floating" panel is free to expand and contract within the frame.

The width of a slab can vary greatly with seasonal changes in humidity

Frame and panel construction allows the panel to move within the stable frame

The width of a frame is relatively stable

Continued ➡

Blanket Chests

SLAB CONSTRUCTION ALLOWS ENTIRE PIECE TO MOVE

A blanket chest, in which the grain runs in a band around the entire box, is an example of slab construction. The depth and width of the chest remain constant, because the wood does not move lengthwise. But the wood does change in height in response to changes in humidity. The blanket chest gets slightly taller in summer and shorter in winter. Because movement in the top is from front to back, the hasps of the lock don't always fit. The solution is to use quartersawn wood for the top, file the hasp parts to increase clearance, and use a good sealing finish.

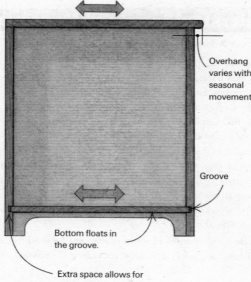

Overhang varies with seasonal movement.

Groove

Bottom floats in the groove.

Extra space allows for expansion

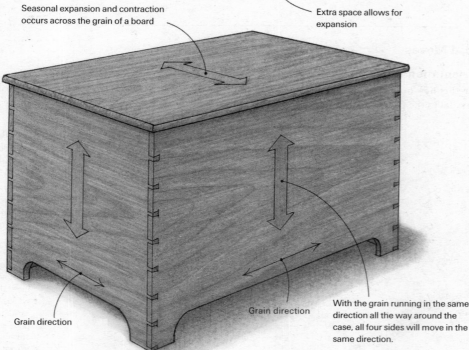

Seasonal expansion and contraction occurs across the grain of a board

Grain direction

Grain direction

With the grain running in the same direction all the way around the case, all four sides will move in the same direction.

Tables

BREADBOARD CONSTRUCTION KEEPS TABLETOPS FLAT

Breadboard ends are added to tabletops to help prevent the top from warping or cupping. But they must be attached so as to allow the top to expand and contract.

The preferred method for making breadboards is a single tongue with cutouts. For a stronger joint, parts of the tongue are cut out to within 1/4 in. to 1/2 in. of the shoulder, and the corresponding areas of the mortise are left in place to hold the weak faces of the breadboard together.

The trickiest part of construction is pinning and gluing the breadboard ends. I like to plane a slight (1/16-in.) concave bow into the breadboard to keep the ends tight against the table. I make the mortise longer than the tongue, center the breadboard, and clamp both ends onto the table. I drill a 3/8-in.-dia. hole in the center and then one (for narrow tabletops) or two holes (for wider ones) on either side of center.

I remove the breadboard end and scribe a line along the edge of the holes closest to the end. Next, I elongate all but the center holes with a 3/8-in. rat-tail file. The farther from center, the longer the oval. For very dry wood (6% moisture content or less), elongate away from the center to allow the top to expand. For wet wood (12% moisture content or more), elongate toward the center to allow for shrinkage. Do not file beyond the scribe lines; doing so will relieve the pressure holding the breadboard to the table shoulder.

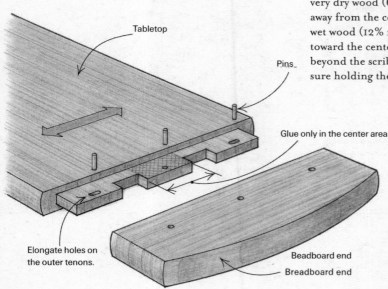

Tabletop

Pins

Glue only in the center area.

Elongate holes on the outer tenons.

Beadboard end

Breadboard end

Mortise-and-Tenons That Breathe

You may have have surmised that cross-grain gluing is a no-no. That is correct up to a point. Wood has a small amount of give to it, and aliphatic resin (yellow) glue is slightly elastic. So you can feel relatively safe making cross-grain joints, such as mortise-and-tenons, as long as the tenons aren't too wide. With cherry, for example, I limit cross-grain joints to a width of 5 in. As a precaution, I glue only the top half of the joint. Theoretically, the top of the rail will stay flush, and the bottom will move ever so slightly. That also should work for hardwoods that are less well-behaved than cherry.

Narrow Apron can be glued and pinned

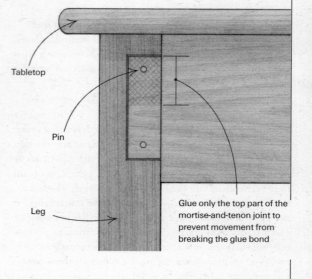

Tabletop

Pin

Leg

Glue only the top part of the mortise-and-tenon joint to prevent movement from breaking the glue bond

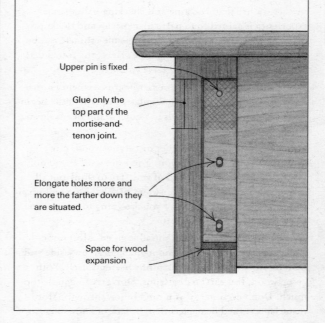

Upper pin is fixed

Glue only the top part of the mortise-and-tenon joint.

Elongate holes more and more the farther down they are situated.

Space for wood expansion

Slab Headboards Need Extralong Mortises

A slab headboard that's 12 in. to 14 in. wide may move up to 1/4 in., which means the mortise into which it fits needs to be that much wider. If the headboard is to be pinned and glued in the middle (fixed), leave an 1/8-in. space at the top and bottom of the mortise. But the headboards on some beds, such as pencil-posts, sit loosely in the mortises on the posts. The unit is held together by bolts in the rails. Extratall headboards (as in old Victorian styles or sleigh beds) require extradeep grooves or large shoulders and mortises.

ATTACHING A LOOSE HEADBOARD

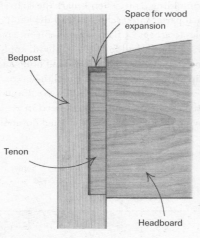
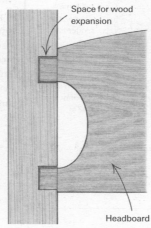

Bedpost

Space for wood expansion

Tenon

Headboard

Space for wood expansion

Headboard

ATTACHING A FIXED HEADBOARD

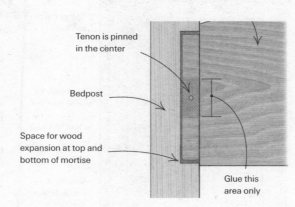

Headboard

Tenon is pinned in the center

Bedpost

Space for wood expansion at top and bottom of mortise

Glue this area only

Tabletops Need Room to Move

No matter how I go about attaching a top to its base, I anchor it firmly in the middle, ensuring that both halves are free to move equally. As a matter of course, I orient the grain in the long direction to minimize the amount of movement.

A good way to attach tops is to make 1/4-in. grooves, or a series of 1/4-in. slots, 1/2 in. below the inside top of the rail. I then install shopmade wood buttons, which grip the grooves and screw to the underside of the top. The buttons at the ends of the tabletop can go to the full depth of the groove, while the buttons along the

sides must be placed according to the wood's moisture content and the time of year. (Fit them tighter in summer, looser in winter.)

For a table with rails substantially thicker than 3/4 in., I countersink 1/2-in.-dia. holes from the bottom of the rails. Then I drill 1/4-in. holes all the way through. I use a rat-tail file to elongate holes away from the center. Holes in the center of the end rails stay as they are. Because the wood movement is side to side, the ovals in the long rails run across the thickness of the rail. That's why I don't recommend this method for thin rails.

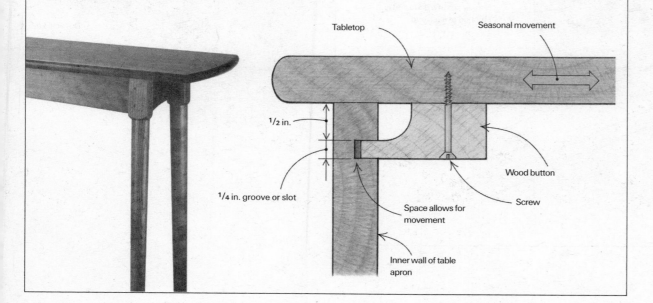

Tabletop

Seasonal movement

1/2 in.

1/4 in. groove or slot

Space allows for movement

Inner wall of table apron

Wood button

Screw

Case Pieces

A FRAME-AND-PANEL BACK ACCOMMODATES MOVEMENT

Building high-end furniture and having a preference for solid wood, I make my backs as frame-and-panel units, set into rabbets and glued into place. This method creates a totally sealed back, which allows for movement yet provides racking resistance.

The success of this method depends on the width and grain orientation of the outside frame members. Because the frame is glued into the rabbets, any excess wood movement will break out the lips of the side and top rabbets. I have determined that by using quartersawn cherry no wider than 1 3/4 in. for the sides and top of the frame members, there is enough give in the wood to accommodate any potential movement. Less well-behaved woods require correspondingly narrower stock. In any event, the stock must be quartersawn.

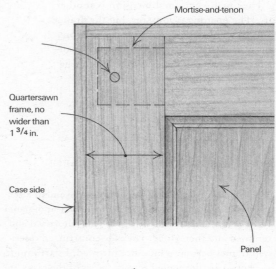

Mortise-and-tenon

Quartersawn frame, no wider than 1 3/4 in.

Case side

Panel

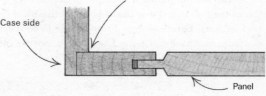

Case side

Panel

Continued ➜

FITTING DOORS AND DRAWERS

The issue of wood movement in doors and drawers must be taken into account. Because they will change in width over the course of a year, I install slab doors only in narrower case openings using quartersawn wood and then stabilize the door with battens.

Frame-and-panel doors are much less of a headache. For quartersawn cherry, I aim for a gap at the lock side of the door that is between the thickness of a nickel (5/64 in.) and a dime (3/64 in.). The hinge-side gap is constant year-round; the top gap is a dime fit; and the bottom gap is a nickel fit.

Fitting drawers is bit more involved. Again, I prefer to use quartersawn stock to minimize wood movement. I start by making drawers the same size as the opening, side to side. When assembled, I trim them to fit, with a 1/64-in. (minimum) to 1/16-in. (maximum) total side clearance.

The top-to-bottom dimension is another story. The opening is constant, but the drawer front changes in height. I also make my front about 1/32 in. narrower than the sides by planing that amount off the bottom (after cutting the grooves for the drawer bottom).

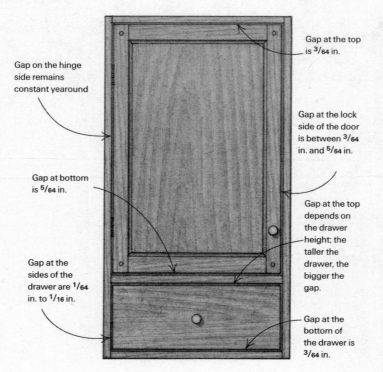

Gap on the hinge side remains constant yearround

Gap at the top is 3/64 in.

Gap at the lock side of the door is between 3/64 in. and 5/64 in.

Gap at bottom is 5/64 in.

Gap at the sides of the drawer are 1/64 in. to 1/16 in.

Gap at the top depends on the drawer height; the taller the drawer, the bigger the gap.

Gap at the bottom of the drawer is 3/64 in.

SIDE MOLDINGS THAT HOLD

Most antiques that I've looked at have the side molding glued (and/or screwed) at the miter and nailed the rest of the way back. As the case side moves over the years, the nail holes widen and the nails lose their grip. The long-lasting solution is to use dovetailed keys and slots. I cut my molding and miter the corners to fit. The side molding receives a dovetail slot that runs its full length, in the meatiest portion of the molding, not necessarily its center.

To locate the dovetail keys, I hold the molding in position, then make knife marks on the case side at the top and bottom of the slot, at both the forward miter and at the back. I connect these tick marks, then cut a dovetail key the length of the cabinet side. Ideally, you want it to be 0.003 in. to 0.005 in. thinner than the depth of the slot to draw the molding tight. Then I mark the strip into five or six equal parts. Into each segment I drill and countersink two holes to accept #4 flathead screws, 1 in. apart. Between these holes, I drill for a 20-ga. brad, apply a drop of glue around the underside of the brad hole, and position the strip between scribe lines. I nail the brads, then sink the screws. Once the long length of the dovetail key has been installed, I chisel out a 3/8-in. section at each pencil mark, leaving five or six perfectly aligned dovetail keys.

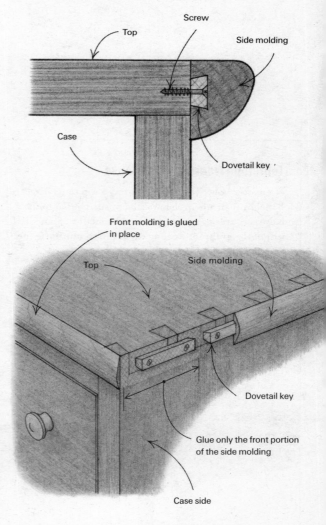

Screw

Top

Side molding

Case

Dovetail key

Front molding is glued in place

Top

Side molding

Dovetail key

Glue only the front portion of the side molding

Case side

WEB FRAMES PROVIDE UNDETECTABLE MOVEMENT

Web frames provide lightweight, low-movement alternatives to solid drawer dividers. For frame-and-panel cases, web frames are merely four slats—mortised and tenoned and then glued. For slab-constructed cases, web frames become a bit more involved. I start with four slats. Two are dovetailed into the sides of the case; one slat in the front, and one in the back (flush with the back rabbet). Before gluing, I rout a dado to connect the front and back dovetails. Then I cut a mortise into each end of both dovetailed slats. I measure the length of the drawer runners and add the depth of the two mortises, minus 1/16 in. for dry wood, or minus 3/8 in. for damp wood. I glue the front slat into the dovetailed slots and then cut the tenons on the front-to-back runners. The front tenon is glued into the mortise, and the runner is forced into the connecting dado. The back slat is then glued into its dovetail slot, but the back mortise-and-tenon is not glued.

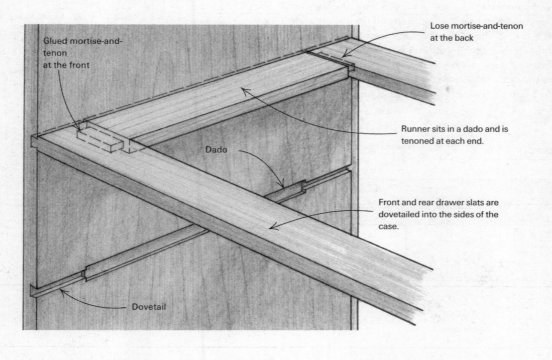

Glued mortise-and-tenon at the front

Lose mortise-and-tenon at the back

Dado

Runner sits in a dado and is tenoned at each end.

Front and rear drawer slats are dovetailed into the sides of the case.

Dovetail

The Workshop

HAND TOOLS

Essential Tools for Furniture Makers

by Michael Pekovich

I started out as a power-tool guy, but I've learned that even if you have every conceivable machine, you still need hand tools to produce your best work.

So now I use machines for the heavy lifting of milling and dimensioning lumber, and for joints that are never seen, like rabbets, dadoes, mortises, and tenons. I save my hand tools for where they really make a difference: layout, cutting dovetails and fitting joints, and surface prep. As a result, I don't need every hand tool ever made. In fact, there are only about a dozen essential ones. You probably already have some of them, and the rest you can pick up over time. And it's well worth the effort, because using them will help you to make better furniture, period.

In addition to these tools, you'll also need a sturdy workbench, but you don't need to spend a fortune on a massive bench or spend months making one.

Tools for Layout

Accurate layout is an essential part of making fine furniture, and it's just as important for power-tool work as it is for handwork. That's because regardless of the tools you're using, you need precisely located and square joints. If you're just starting out in woodworking, these should be the first hand tools you buy.

MARKING GAUGE

Marking gauges excel at cutting a line parallel to the edge of a board, which is vital for laying out accurate tenons, mortises, and the baseline for dovetails. A cut line is better than a pencil line because it provides a precise location and line for starting a chisel or handsaw. Gauges with a knife or cutting wheel cut cleaner lines than pin gauges, but wheel gauges are easier to find. I recommend one like the Veritas standard wheel gauge for your first.

Continued →

COMBINATION SQUARE

A combination square is indispensable for penciling or knifing a line at 45° and 90°. It's important to get a good one, like those made by Starrett, because it will be accurate out of the box and it will stay that way. The 12-in. model is a workhorse, long enough to mark wide boards or across multiple pieces at once. It's a good one to get first, but I've found a second, 6-in. version is just as handy. Because of its small size, it fits better in your hand and is easier to use when laying out joints in tight places and across end grain.

MARKING KNIFE

You also need a sharp marking knife. I've owned and used many different types, but the one I reach for time and again is a chip-carving knife. I like the blade's double bevel, which lets me mark on either side of the blade. And the bevels extend the entire height of the blade (the cross-section is triangular) so I can rest the blade against the side of the workpiece and strike a line exactly adjacent to it. The blade also is long, thin, and stiff, so it fits in tight places without flexing.

BEVEL GAUGE

Because it has a pivoting blade that can be locked into any angle, a bevel gauge is useful for transferring angles from plans to workpieces and setting tablesaw blade angles. However, you'll probably use it first to lay out dovetails, a task it is perfect for. When buying a bevel gauge, look for two things: First, the blade should lock down tightly, so it doesn't move accidentally. Second, the nut used to lock it down shouldn't get in the way of using the gauge (a frequent problem with the wing nut used on some gauges).

The Big 12

- Coping saw
- Smoothing plane
- Combination square
- Bevel gauge
- Marking knife
- Dovetail saw
- Card scraper
- Marking gauge
- Spokeshave
- Shoulder plane
- Block plane
- Chisel set

Tools for Joinery

Dovetails are the hallmark of craftsmanship, and the effort to cut them by hand is well worth it. However, even if you use power tools to cut all of your joinery, hand tools are still the best way to fine-tune the fit. For hand-cut dovetails and tight-fitting tenons, I recommend a dovetail saw, a coping saw, a set of chisels, and a shoulder plane.

DOVETAIL SAW

You have two options for a dovetail saw: a Western backsaw or a Japanese pullsaw (dozuki). Japanese saws are a good place to start, because even the inexpensive ones are very sharp straight from the box. However, after 25 years of making furniture and using both types of saw, I can tell you that the pistol grip of Western backsaws positions your hand and arm for straighter cuts, so you will get more consistent and accurate results than from a dozuki. But don't feel bad about buying the dozuki first. You'll find plenty of uses for it, like cutting small parts and flush-trimming pegs.

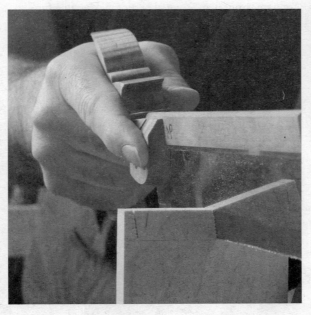

CHISELS

Start with at least four: $\frac{1}{4}$ in., $\frac{3}{8}$ in., $\frac{1}{2}$ in. and $\frac{3}{4}$ in. The six-chisel Irwin Blue Chip set is a great value, with a $\frac{5}{8}$-in. and a 1-in. chisel in addition to the other four. Steer away from chisels sized in millimeters; the first set I bought was metric and that was a mistake. Although their widths approximated their U.S. equivalents, they were far enough off to prove frustrating when squaring up mortises or cleaning out grooves made with fractional bits. After you have the basic set, add a wide chisel (1 $\frac{1}{2}$ in. to 2 in.) for paring and chamfering in tight spots.

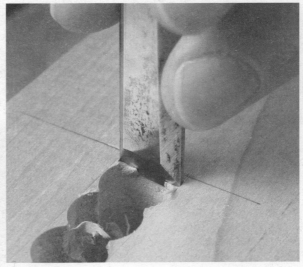

COPING SAW

There is no need to be precious about getting rid of the waste between pins and tails, so I use a coping saw to do it before paring to the baseline with a chisel. You will save a huge amount of time compared to chopping away all of the waste with a chisel. In addition to cutting fast, coping saws also turn on a dime—perfect for maneuvering between pins or tails—and the cheap, replaceable blades mean you can always have a sharp one ready.

SHOULDER PLANE

Regardless of how you cut joinery, you should have a shoulder plane, because nothing is better for fine-tuning joints for a perfect fit. What makes this plane unique is that the blade extends the full width of the sole, so you can plane right into a corner. If you try to plane a tenon cheek with a block plane, you'll end up with a tapered tenon. Shoulder planes come in a range of widths from 1/2 in. to 1 1/4 in. wide, but I find a wider plane is more versatile, handling broad tenon cheeks as well as narrow shoulders. It also has a ton of mass, which helps it stay flat on its sole and move with force when making cross-grain cuts.

CARD SCRAPER

On woods with tricky grain, like tiger maple, or when you've got a small bit of tearout on an otherwise clean board, there's no tool like a card scraper. Unlike a handplane, a scraper has no risk of tearout. Even when I handplane a surface, I'll often follow up with a card scraper to remove any imperfections.

SPOKESHAVE

The spokeshave is probably the most overlooked tool in the shop. This odd-looking tool is actually a short-soled handplane with handles on the side, rather than in front of and behind the blade. Nothing is faster at smoothing bandsawn curves. The tool is available with a flat or curved sole, but I recommend the flat sole, as it works well even on concave surfaces.

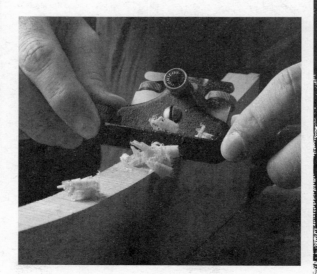

SMOOTHING PLANE

At last we come to that most iconic hand tool, the bench plane. I fared well for many years using only sanders to smooth surfaces, though today I couldn't imagine being without a plane. You can go from machine marks to a glass-smooth surface in just a few swipes. It's that rare instance in woodworking where the most enjoyable path is also the most efficient, and the results are superior to sanding. The size to start with is a No. 4. If you mill all your lumber with machines, you don't really need the flattening ability of a longer plane. The easiest path to making shavings is to buy a good-quality new plane—Lie-Nielsen and Veritas are proven products. An old plane, like a venerable Stanley Bailey, offers good quality at an initial savings, but requires some tune-up work and probably a new replacement blade. Regardless of the plane you buy, it has to be razor sharp. Even the most expensive plane is nothing but a paperweight if it's dull.

Tools for Shaping and Smoothing

A good finish starts with good surface preparation, and hand tools are the fastest way to remove machine marks and tearout. The flat surfaces and crisp chamfers that handplanes create are impossible to replicate with a sander. A smoother and a block plane are the two planes to have. Add a card scraper to work really difficult grain, and a spokeshave for cleaning up curved surfaces.

BLOCK PLANE

For chamfering edges, leveling joints, and smoothing end grain, the block plane is indispensable. It also is perfect for paring the end grain on dovetails. Block planes are available in standard and low-angle models. I recommend a low-angle plane with an adjustable throat. This allows you to take a fine cut with a small mouth, which helps to prevent tearout.

Essential Handsaws

by Matt Kenney

I regularly use four handsaws in my shop, not because I'm a hand-tool nut but because a handsaw is often the smartest, most efficient choice for the job at hand. Take the job of crosscutting or mitering delicate moldings and miter keys. You could do those tasks at the tablesaw or miter saw, but you'd need to devise a jig to hold the workpiece during the cut, and there's no guarantee that the spinning blade won't chew up the workpiece. It's much quicker, safer, and cleaner to make the cut with a backsaw.

Handsaws are great for getting into tight spaces, too. A coping saw is the perfect tool to cut out the waste between dovetails. The thin blade can fit into even the tightest pin socket and make a turn along the baseline, removing the waste in seconds. Chopping out waste with a chisel takes much longer, and routing it out is possible only when there's enough clearance between the tails to fit the bit.

And then there are jobs that a power tool simply couldn't (or shouldn't) do, like cutting pegs flush. The only power-tool option is a router, and you have to make an auxiliary base to raise the router and then dial in the bit's cut depth so that it doesn't ruin the surface. Not to mention that pegs are often used on narrow parts, like legs, where the router can tip and ruin the part.

Continued ➔

There are lots of handsaws out there, but I think the four you need most are a dovetail saw, a backsaw set up for crosscuts, a dozuki, and a coping saw. I'll show you some tips on getting the best from each one.

1. Dovetail Saw

I bought my dovetail saw to make hand-cut dovetails, but over the years I've found that it's good for other tasks, too, such as notching a shelf or drawer divider to fit in a stopped dado cut in a case side. For a smooth cut, I'd recommend a saw with about 19 teeth per inch (tpi), sharpened for a ripcut. Western-style saws cut on the push stroke and come with two different handle styles—pistol grip or straight. I prefer a pistol-grip handle, which makes it easier to push the saw and control the cut.

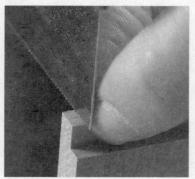

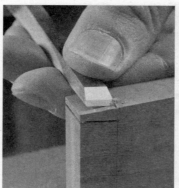

Cut a clean shoulder. A crosscut backsaw is perfect for getting rid of the waste in the half sockets on the edges of a tail board. For the best results, chisel an angled groove along the scribed baseline (left) and use the vertical wall of the groove to get the saw started. The groove helps to start the saw in a straight cut, so that it naturally cuts down along the baseline, leaving no waste that needs paring.

Sandpaper prevents scratches. Where the spine trick won't work, fold a small piece of sandpaper (abrasive side in) and put it under the blade to prevent the teeth from marring the wood.

Easy way to start the cut. After cutting a line with a knife or marking gauge, put the nail of your forefinger and thumb into it, place the saw's teeth against the nails, and push lightly.

A sawhook is great for small parts. The saw cuts on the push stroke, which helps keep the part against the fence while you cut. A large fence with two kerfs in it—one at 90° (top) and the other at 45° (bottom)—improves the accuracy of your cuts and prevents tearout. Locate the kerfs so that the fence will support a workpiece on either side of each one.

4. Coping Saw

With its thin blade and tall frame, the coping saw is adept at cutting curves. It was used in the past to cope molding to get perfect miters. But I use it when cutting dovetails. I was taught to chop out all of the waste with a chisel—a tedious job. When I tried sawing out the waste with a coping saw, it was a watershed moment for me and I'll never go back. You don't need a super-expensive frame, but don't go with a hardware store cheapy, either. I spent about $20 on mine and it's easy to tighten and adjust the blade. The handle is comfortable, too. As for blades, get ones with a fine cut. They cut slower, which means the saw is less likely to jump the kerf at the end of the cut and damage the tail or pin.

2. Crosscut Saw

When you're making furniture, there are always small parts—like moldings, pulls, drawer stops, and pegs—that need to be cut to length. Instead of using a tablesaw, which could destroy those delicate parts in a flash, I use a Western-style carcass backsaw. A crosscut saw with about 12 to 14 tpi and a blade that's a bit taller and longer than on a dovetail saw can easily make clean, accurate cuts in parts up to 1 in. thick and 3 in. to 4 in. wide. To increase accuracy, I use the saw with a sawhook, which is simply a flat board with a square fence (and a cleat that goes in your vise). The hook is great because it gives you a way to hold the workpiece still during the cut (both you and the saw press it against the fence) and helps to keep the saw cutting straight and square.

3. Dozuki

A dozuki saw has a thin, flexible blade, with fine teeth and a straight handle, which makes it well-suited to flush-cutting pegs. The flexible tip helps it get close to the base of a pin, and the straight handle is easier to hold and control with the saw on its side than a pistol grip would be. Get a crosscut dozuki with about 20 tpi. So why not just use a flush-cut saw? Their teeth have no set, so they clog and don't cut as well. Dozukis don't have those problems. The thin blade can kink, so get a saw with a replaceable blade.

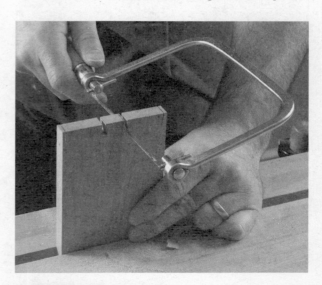

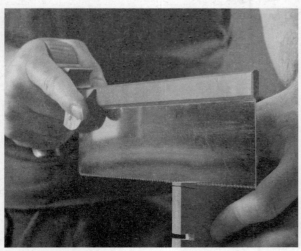

Ride the spine. As you saw, press down on the spine to keep the teeth away from the surface. Use a chisel or block plane to flush the edging.

The teeth face the handle. This means the saw cuts on the pull stroke, which puts the thin, narrow blade under tension so it won't buckle.

One More Worth Having Around

If you've ever found yourself at the lumberyard with several boards that are too long for the bed of your truck, you'll appreciate having a panel saw. Carrying around a circular saw and hoping to find an outlet is more hassle than it's worth. But leaving a panel saw (8 to 12 tpi) in the truck is no problem. Lay the boards in the bed with the gate down, and cut them to fit. I even use a panel saw in the shop to cut a board to rough length when it's too big for my chopsaw.

Mastering the Backsaw

by Chris Gochnour

There's no doubt that power tools like the tablesaw and router are efficient and put perfect joinery within the reach of even the newest woodworker. But that doesn't mean you don't need a backsaw. With a bit of practice a backsaw can become an extension of your arm, allowing you to make very accurate cuts quickly.

At that point, you'll find that there are times when a backsaw is actually a better option than a tablesaw or router, such as when you're building one piece of furniture rather than several identical pieces at once. For a one-off table, you can cut tenons on the aprons with a backsaw as quickly as you can with a tablesaw, because you don't spend any time setting up the blade's height, positioning a stop on your miter gauge, or dialing in the settings on your tenoning jig.

A backsaw makes even better sense for difficult joinery like angled tenons, where a tablesaw and routing jigs would require too many fussy setups. And there are parts, like bed rails, that are just too big to tenon on a tablesaw. Also, don't forget that for many woodworkers, making furniture is as much about the journey as it is about the destination, and hand tools connect them to the act of creating a piece of furniture in a way that is more fulfilling than using power tools. Making furniture (and not just the furniture itself) becomes part of the reward.

In any case, to get to the point where you can use a backsaw with efficiency and accuracy, you need to learn proper technique and then practice it. I'll demonstrate how to cut straight, which is the most important skill, and I'll show you some exercises to help you ingrain the correct mechanics in your body. I'll also give you some tips on sawing the two most common joints: dovetails and tenons.

One note before we get started. Although Japanese saws are wonderful tools, I prefer Western backsaws for joinery. I find their pistol grip and D-shape handles are more comfortable and make it easier to control the saw. Also, in my experience, Western saws are less prone to drift and deflect in use, because their blades are thicker and stiffer than those on Japanese saws, which are designed to be pulled rather than pushed.

Good Posture Is the Key to Cutting Straight

Sawing well is an activity for your entire body, from your feet and legs to your arms and hands. So, before you pick up a saw, take time to learn how to position your body. Your legs should be spread, one foot in front of the other, with knees slightly bent. Your torso should be turned, too, so that your arm can move forward and back in a straight line. If you have to swing your arm around your body, you cannot saw straight.

The distance between you and the workpiece is also critical. If you're too far away or too close, your arm will curve and your cuts will, too.

When you pick up the saw, hold it gently. And don't put any downward pressure on the saw as it cuts. A sharp saw—which yours should be—needs no more than its own weight to get the job done.

In addition to having the right body mechanics, you also need a bench that's rigid, so it doesn't flex or deflect under use. And it should be heavy or bolted down, so it doesn't skip over the floor. It needs a vise and a saw hook for holding parts. And don't forget to have good lighting around the bench so you can see what you're doing.

▶ SET UP

Start with Proper Posture

To saw straight lines, the tool must move back and forth in a straight path, like a piston. If you align your body with the saw, that straight cut happens naturally.

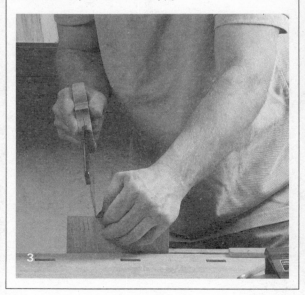

Hang on loosely. Grip the handle lightly with three fingers, your index finger pointing forward and your thumb wrapped around the back of the handle (1). For righties, the left foot goes out front (2). For lefties, it's the opposite. And your legs should be slightly bent. Finally, think of the saw as an extension of your hand, with a straight line running along the spine and through your hand, wrist, forearm, elbow, and shoulder, so they all work in harmony (3).

Your First Saw Should Be for Ripcuts

The best reason to get a backsaw is to cut dovetails and tenons by hand. Both involve a lot more cutting along the grain (ripcuts) than across it (crosscuts). So, when you get your first saw, choose one that's sharpened for ripcuts. The secret to a great-cutting saw is a great sharpening job. That means a saw from the home center won't cut it. Instead, get one from one of the best saw manufacturers, who do this well. I've had good experiences with saws from Lie-Nielsen, Veritas, Bad Axe, Gramercy, Adria, and Wenzloff & Sons.

Ripsaws come in a variety of sizes. Don't get the dovetail size—they are too small for large dovetails in casework. Instead, get a carcase saw, which can handle tenons and case dovetails, as well as dovetails for drawers and smaller items like boxes. Your first backsaw should be around 11 in. to 12 in. long, have 14 ppi (points per inch), and 2 in. to 2-1/4 in. of cutting depth beneath the spine. Don't worry about the crosscuts you'll have to make—a ripsaw works just fine for them. I've been using backsaws for decades and I don't own a crosscut saw. I've never had a problem with tearout or rough cuts. However, if you are willing to spend a bit more, there's a new type of saw that handles both rip- and crosscuts extremely well. The teeth have an old-school shape (called a "hybrid cut") that lets them cut across the grain just as well as along it. Both Gramercy and Bad Axe make this type of saw.

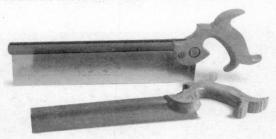

▶ BASIC TECHNIQUE

Learn to Cut Straight

The point of learning to saw is to cut joinery, but before you jump into dovetails or tenons, learn to cut a line straight and square to a board's face. That's the essential skill you'll need.

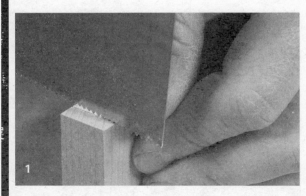

Start on the far edge. Align the cut with your thumb (1). Without putting any weight on the saw, gently push it forward. It's easier to get just a few teeth started straight at the back edge than to get a straight start across the board's entire thickness. Lower the back of the saw as you cut deeper (2). After reaching the front edge, bring the saw horizontal (3) and cut down to depth.

Continued ➡

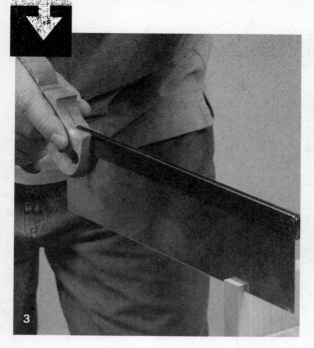

Hold Steady

It's difficult to saw fluidly and straight in a chattering board, a common event with cast-iron front vises, which only clamp a board on one edge. To eliminate vibration, clamp the board's other edge to the bench.

Break Down Tenons, Too

Shoulder and cheek cuts are straight but big, and there's a strategy for handling each one. Shoulder cuts are first. The cheeks follow.

PRACTICE THE TWO BASIC CUTS

It takes crosscuts and ripcuts to make a tenon. Practice them separately.

Here's the drill for shoulders. Use a saw hook and your off hand to keep the board still. To get used to cutting down to a horizontal line, mark the depth on both edges.

Long cuts for cheeks. It's important that the depth of your test cuts replicate what you'll do for tenons, so they should be 1-1/2 in. to 2 in. deep.

HOW TO CUT CLEAN SHOULDERS

Shoulder cuts are tricky because aprons and rails can be several inches wide. It's hard to track a straight cut across that distance.

Make a track. After cutting your layout lines with a knife or marking gauge, use a chisel to create a V-groove along the shoulder line. You'll get a clean shoulder that will keep the saw cutting straight down.

Shoulder tracks the saw. Set the teeth in the V-groove, against the shoulder. Lower the blade until it rests in the groove across the board's entire width before you begin to cut.

Let the saw do the work. There is no need to put any downward pressure on the saw. Its own weight is enough. The teeth will cut without any resistance or catching.

Conquer Dovetails One Cut at a Time

Repetition of good technique is the key to good joinery because it creates muscle memory. Don't worry about complete joints at first. Instead, spend time practicing the individual cuts that make up a tail and pin.

TAILS

Practice should simulate the real thing. Lay out both sides of the tail on the same board. For the cuts right of center, always cut to the right (waste side) of the layout line as you would on real dovetails. On the left side, do the opposite.

Stay to the left of the line.   Cut to the right of the line.

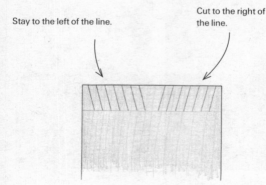

PINS

Same goes for pins. Lay out both angles on the same board and cut to the right of the line on the right half and the left of the line on the left half. Line up your body with the angled cuts.

Stay to the left of the line.   Cut on the right side of the line.

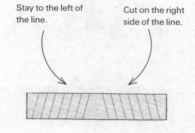

4 Steps to Great Cheeks

This method lets you cut along just one layout line at a time, with each new cut guided by the previous one.

1. Across the end grain. Make a shallow kerf, starting at the far corner. You'll use it as a guide to keep the saw straight as you continue.

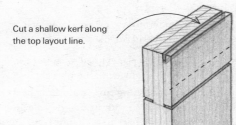

Cut a shallow kerf along the top layout line.

2. Work down the near edge. Angle the saw up and cut down the layout line closest to you.

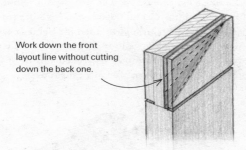

Work down the front layout line without cutting down the back one.

3. Cut down the other edge. Turn the board around in the vise and make another angled cut.

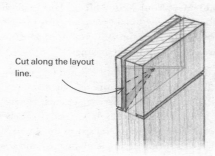

Cut along the layout line.

4. Level out and finish the job. All that's left now is a triangle of waste, but you have three straight kerfs to guide the saw as you cut down the middle.

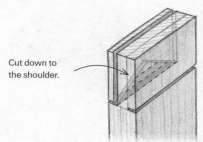

Cut down to the shoulder.

Essential Handplanes

by Garrett Hack

Every shop—even one that relies heavily on power tools— needs handplanes.

For some tasks, such as smoothing a surface or fitting a joint perfectly, handplanes fine-tune work that was begun on a machine. In other instances, they handle jobs that machines can't do as quickly or nimbly. Handplanes are quiet, safe, and clean. They encourage working at a slower pace that is less prone to mistakes. And did I mention enjoyment? The swish of a plane across a surface and the smell of fresh shavings are reason enough to pick up a handplane.

To reap these rewards, though, you first have to spend some effort in learning to handle the tools and, most importantly, in learning to keep them sharp.

The planes on this list are tools that I use day after day. Most do a variety of things very well; a few are the best tools for specialized tasks. I've listed them in rough order of importance.

1. Bench Plane

Best at: Flattening and smoothing surfaces
Model shown: Old Stanley Bedrock No. 604 fitted with a thick replacement blade
Available new: Contemporary versions by Lie-Nielsen, Veritas, Clifton, and others feature unbreakable castings and thick alloy blades (good for chatter-free cutting).

If you have just one plane in your shop, make sure it's a No. 4 bench plane. I use mine all the time to flatten and smooth surfaces or to joint and trim edges in ways that power tools and sandpaper can't.

If you're fitting a drawer front, for instance, the plane lets you dial it in carefully, one 0.001-in.-thick shaving at a time. In contrast, a single mistake on the tablesaw can render the workpiece useless. You'll also find that, with practice, you can use a No. 4 to smooth a fairly large drawer face with a few passes in less than a minute. Unlike a sander, the plane leaves a smooth surface that has deep clarity and is flat right to the edges.

The No. 4 also is great for cutting bevels in a profiled edge and does a respectable job smoothing end grain, like that on the edge of a tabletop. It even works well for shaping convex curves such as a bowed drawer front.

The key to the No. 4's versatility lies in its middle-of-the-road size. It takes a two-handed grip that delivers enough power to flatten and smooth large parts, yet it's small enough to use in tight places or for more delicate work. The blade can be adjusted to take a coarse shaving, or a very fine one that leaves a beautifully smooth surface.

You can tackle both tasks with a single No. 4 plane by opening the throat wide for the rough work, then narrowing the opening for the smoothing passes. For some No. 4s with a "Bedrock" frog, this adjustment takes 15 seconds; with others, the blade must be removed in order to adjust the frog forward and tighten the mouth.

Continued ➜

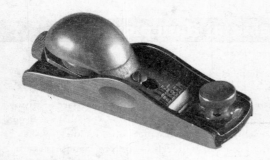

2. Adjustable Block Plane

Best at: Shaping curves and chamfers, smoothing small surfaces, trimming dovetails, and cutting end grain

Model shown: Lie-Nielsen No. 60½

Also available new: Veritas makes a nice version of this low-angle, adjustable-throat plane. Stanley continues to make the classic 60½.

This plane, patterned after the Stanley No. 60½ is another tool to keep within easy reach. Like the No. 4, it can be adjusted for rough or fine work, and it does a multitude of things well.

I like this plane for the precise trimming of small surfaces, such as where stile and rail meet on a frame. In similar fashion, I keep the No. 60½ handy when sizing small parts because it can take fine shavings from edges too narrow for For these reasons, the 60½ is perfect for the very exact business of sizing inlays and trimming them flush after glue-up, where the grain might be going in many directions. For the smoothest cutting in these situations, you need a plane with a throat that can be adjusted to the thickness of a piece of thin paper.

The block plane is also the best tool for trimming dovetail pins flush after glue-up. Because the plane cuts at a low angle, much like a paring chisel, it is ideal for cutting end grain smoothly.

This plane is also great for shaping wood, giving you great flexibility when cutting tapered chamfers or rounded edges. In contrast to a router setup, the block plane lets you refine or alter a profile easily as you go.

3. Jointer

Best at: Jointing edges of any length, flattening large surfaces

Model shown: Old Stanley Bedrock No. 607

Available new: Clifton, Stanley, and Lie-Nielsen all make a No. 7.

I rely on the mechanical jointer in my shop every day, but I wouldn't be without my jointer plane. The No. 7 is ideal for jointing edges on boards that are too long, heavy, or awkward to handle on the jointer. I often use it to clean up machine-jointed edges, especially those that will be glued. This is because jointer knives that are slightly dull or improperly set can create a scalloped surface that leaves gaps in the glueline. And that could mean a glueline that shows or a joint that fails.

The No. 7 perfectly trues the edge and cuts a clean glue surface. I also can use the plane to make an edge slightly concave along its length for a sprung joint.

This plane and its beefier sibling, the No. 8, also are hefty and long enough to make quick work of flattening large surfaces or cutting a set of tapered legs dead straight. The long sole bridges valleys that a No. 4 would follow, making the jointer plane a better choice for flattening.

The accuracy of a jointer plane depends on a sole that is flat from end to end. These planes cost more to make and thus are considerably more expensive than a No. 4. Otherwise, look for the same basic characteristics: comfortable handles, a thick blade, and easy throat adjustment.

4. Shoulder Plane

Best at: Truing up tenon shoulders and trimming tenon cheeks

Model shown: Stanley No. 93

Also available new: Veritas makes a nice midsize shoulder

I like to say that a perfectly fitted mortise-and-tenon joint looks like it grew together. Even with precise tablesaw tenoning jigs and hollow-chisel mortisers, though, it's hard to get this sort of fit straight from the machines.

So many things can prevent a joint from fitting perfectly. A tablesaw blade, even with stabilizers, can wobble and cut a shoulder that's not perfectly straight. Or you could wobble when cutting the cheeks (even using a jig). You might have a joint ever so slightly out of square in either plane, in which case one shoulder hits before the other or the bottom hits before the top. The longer the shoulder (breadboard ends being the extreme), the more likely or more obvious the problems.

The shoulder plane fixes these slight imperfections, leaving you with a perfectly fitting joint. It can take a fine shaving precisely where you need it, whether on a shoulder or cheek. For slightly angled joints, a shoulder plane is safer than trying to use jigs, where it is very easy to get something backward and cut at the wrong angle.

I regularly use my Stanley No. 93 for adjusting rabbets cut by machine, such as on the meeting rails of two cabinet doors or when fitting a rabbeted panel. It also works respectably across the grain in other situations, such as sizing the bottom of a wide dado.

5. Smoothing Plane

Best at: Cutting a smooth, highly polished surface that is ready for a finish

Model shown: Lie-Nielsen No. 4½

Also available new: Clifton, Lie-Nielsen, and Stanley make a Bailey pattern No. 4½. Ray Iles makes an infill smoother reproduction. Vintage Norris or Spiers infill smoothers can be found. Sauer and Steiner make infill planes superior to many originals.

Woodworkers smooth lots of surfaces. A smoothing plane is amazingly efficient at this, cutting flat surfaces so polished they shine with deep clarity. A No. 4 is an OK smoother, but it is a little light for really difficult grain. It's more efficient to have a plane dedicated to smoothing. It should have some mass, a super-fine throat, and a solidly supported, thick blade. That No. 4 is still very useful as a pre-smoother, flattening a surface and doing the bulk of the work. That way, the smoothing plane need cut just a few gossamer shavings and stays at peak sharpness longer.

A good smoother may be the most expensive plane on this list, but it's worth it. Among the best designs are heavy British planes such as those made by Norris and Spiers, with steel bodies infilled with dense rosewood, and very thick blades. A number of contemporary versions are available, some better than the originals. The heavy body and wide blade of the No. 4½ make it a very good smoother, especially with a 50° cutting angle (frog). Length is not important for a smoother, but some like the mass of a No. 7, No. 6, or No. 5½ for this work.

6. Spokeshave

Best at: Shaping, smoothing, and refining curves

Model shown: Old Stanley No. 52

Available new: Contemporary versions by Veritas, Lie-Nielsen, Woodjoy, and others

For the most part, all of the planes listed so far work well to make wood flat, smooth, and square. But what about curves?

For shaping or smoothing curves, nothing beats a spokeshave. The spokeshave, with its narrow sole and winglike handles, doesn't look like a handplane, but it works like one. It holds a relatively wide iron at a fixed angle and depth. It registers the cut against a sole, and it takes a shaving. The spokeshave's long handles and narrow sole are ideal for steering around curves and working into tight places. They help maintain a consistent angle easily when cutting chamfers where a block plane won't reach, such as along a concave curve. The narrow sole allows the tool to work both inside and outside curves. Soles come in a variety of shapes, including rounded for tighter curves. The spokeshave is a great tool for shaping the profile on the edge of a curved tabletop or an arched apron, or for smoothing the bandsawn profile of a cabriole leg.

7. A Second Block Plane

Best at: Roughing out curves, wide bevels, or simple molding profiles.

Model shown: Lie-Nielsen No. 102

Available new: Your second block plane could be another No. 60½, adjusted to take rougher cuts. Lie-Nielsen's No. 102 fits a large palm well, and its open throat is suited to aggressive work and big shavings.

If you already have a No. 60½ tuned for precise work, you'll find you can work more quickly if you set up a second block plane to make coarser cuts. Having twin block planes ensures that each is tuned precisely the way I want it for the work and spares me the hassle and variation of adjusting a single plane back and forth.

I use this second plane to rough out a wide chamfer or bevel, or to shape a bullnose profile for a cabinet molding. The plane offers good control despite making aggressive cuts. I also use my second block plane, set for a light cut, to remove freshly dried glue from a panel, a far safer bet than risking tearout by scraping it off.

8. Small Router Plane

Best at: Cutting and cleaning up small grooves, cleaning up hinge mortises

Model shown: Old Stanley No. 271

Available new: Lie-Nielsen makes a small router plane based on this design. It offers a ¼-in. blade as well as pointed- and square-tipped ³/₃₂-in. blades for inlay work.

When working on just a few parts, I often find that to set up a machine to do 100% of a task takes far more time (what with test cuts and jigs) than to do 95% of the job quickly and the rest by hand. A stopped groove for a box bottom is a good example. I can set up a tablesaw with a dado blade in a minute, but it leaves curved ends to be cleaned out. A small router plane is just the tool, with its right-angled blade projecting below the sole and working as a paring chisel. The blade can be locked to cut consistently at any depth. For a long time this was a shopmade tool, with a simple wooden body and a bent chisel blade.

The No. 271 router plane, the pint-sized sibling to the No. 71 router plane, is one of those planes that can make your life a lot easier. It can work in a groove or dado as narrow as ¼ in. wide, and it can work along a curve as easily as a flat surface. For leveling the bottom of an inlay recess, a router plane is far easier to use than a chisel, and less apt to damage the walls. It's also useful for installing drawer locks that mortise into the back of the face, and for cutting hinge mortises at a consistent depth. The No. 271 is worth having for cleaning up stopped dadoes and sliding dovetails alone.

Handplaning 101

by Chris Gochnur

The smoothing plane is one of my best friends in the shop, and I reach for it frequently. A sharp smoothing plane meticulously shaves the surface of a board, creating a glass-smooth sheen that highlights the wood's figure while leaving a dead-flat surface in its wake. For most furniture parts, a handplaned surface is good enough for finishing. But not everyone has success with the handplane. Many who buy a smoothing plane have so much trouble getting good results that they set the tool on a shelf, where it becomes a dusty spectator to the real action in the shop.

Problems occur for three main reasons: The blade is not sharp, the tool is out of tune, or it's not being used properly. This article focuses on the third factor, showing how to set up and adjust a traditional bevel-down plane, and how to use it for optimal performance. For space reasons, we will assume a handplane is in good working order with a blade that is razor-sharp.

Install the Chipbreaker and Blade

The first task is to understand the parts of the plane and to make sure they are assembled correctly. Mounted on top of the blade, the chipbreaker deflects shavings up and out of the plane. The first step in setting up the plane is to secure the chipbreaker to the blade. Put the assembly on the frog (the angled bed that connects the plane body to the iron) and secure it with the lever cap. Set the tension on the lever cap just enough to hold the blade assembly in place while allowing for blade adjustments.

Open the Mouth

As the plane cuts, shavings pass through an opening in the sole called the mouth. How wide you open the mouth depends on how thick you want the shavings. Heavier cuts need a larger opening, while lighter cuts need a smaller one.

To adjust the mouth opening, advance the blade until it barely projects through the plane's mouth. Then move the frog forward or backward until you get the desired mouth opening. The bedrock-style frog offered by Stanley, Lie-Nielsen, and Clifton makes these adjustments convenient. Simply loosen the two side screws at the rear of the frog, then use the central adjusting screw to move the frog to open or close the mouth. Once set, tighten the side screws to lock the frog in position. The Bailey pattern planes require the blade to be removed to access the frog screws, making the adjustments a little less convenient.

Adjust the Blade

With the mouth opening set, it's time to adjust the blade laterally and to fine-tune the depth of cut. First adjust the blade laterally so that the shaving is coming through the mouth in the center. Now set the depth of cut by advancing the blade. Aim for a shaving about 0.001 in. to 0.002 in. thick that's near full width and tapers to nothing at its edges. A cut is too heavy if it causes excessive strain on the user, causes the plane to jump and chatter, or leaves unsightly plane tracks on the surface.

If the cut is too heavy, lighten it by rotating the adjustment knob counterclockwise. After raising the blade in this manner, remove the backlash, or slop, from the plane's adjusting mechanism. Rotating the knob clockwise until it is snug does it. Eliminating backlash prevents the cut from changing as you plane.

Anyone Can Plane Like a Pro

If you've struggled with your plane, it may surprise you to know that a handplane naturally wants to make surfaces flat and smooth. But to get there, you need to pay attention to your grip, stance, and planing motion—all at the same time.

Secure the board to the bench—Be sure the grain is oriented in the direction you wish to plane. The best way to hold the board is with the benchdogs on a cabinetmaker's bench. Do this by opening the tail vise, placing the board between the dogs, and closing the vise to clamp the board. Do not overtighten the vise because this will bow the board upward. Complete the clamping process by tapping each dog slightly downward with a hammer. This draws the board firmly against the bench. Alternatively, a

planing stop, which is basically a wood strip that is secured across the width of your bench, will do the trick.

Power through the cut—Once the board is secured, grasp the plane by the tote (the rear handle) and the knob. Use a three-fingered grasp on the tote with the index finger pointing forward. Hold the knob in a way that feels comfortable. Some use a fingertip grasp, while others hold it in the palm of their hand.

I also recommend skewing (angling) the plane throughout the cut. Skewing lowers the blade's cutting angle, reducing resistance and helping to eliminate chatter, which is especially useful on unruly grain. A skewed plane is also the most natural and comfortable way to hold the tool. Because your stance is in a slightly forward position, it's awkward to align your hands one in front of the other. It is far more natural to have them spread apart, side to side.

Use your entire body to drive the plane. At the beginning of the cut, concentrate pressure on the knob to counter the natural tendency of your hands to rock the plane as it meets the board. Then transfer pressure to both the knob and tote evenly. As you exit the cut, put more pressure on the tote and ease up on the knob.

On the return stroke, it's OK to maintain contact with the board, but tilt the plane slightly on edge so as not to add needless wear to the cutting edge.

Continue planing end to end, working from the near edge to the far edge with consistent, overlapping passes. (It is a lot like mowing the lawn, but far more enjoyable.) Repeat the pattern until all the mill marks and snipe are eliminated, leaving a surface ready for finishing.

Install the Blade Properly

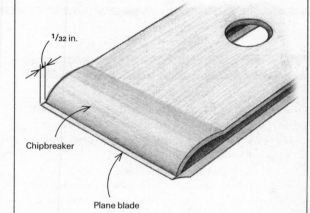

1/32 in.

Chipbreaker

Plane blade

Secure the chipbreaker. Keep its leading edge slightly inset from the front of the blade, and parallel to it (above).

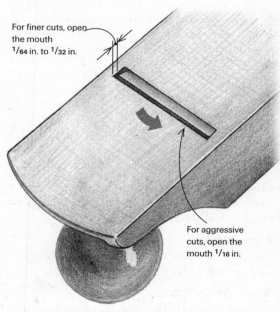

For finer cuts, open the mouth 1/64 in. to 1/32 in.

For aggressive cuts, open the mouth 1/16 in.

Set the mouth opening. Small screws allow you to adjust the mouth opening to accommodate heavy or light cuts (above).

Dial in the Depth of Cut

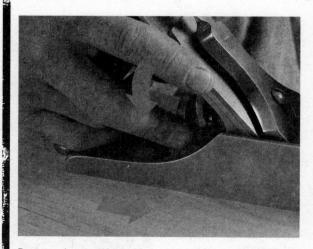

Retract and rotate. With the blade retracted fully, move the plane across a flat board, slowly advancing the blade with the depth-of-cut knob. Stop when the blade contacts the board.

Watch the shaving. Make a short pass, looking at where the shaving is coming up through the mouth. More than likely, the shaving is leaning to the left or right.

Continued ➡

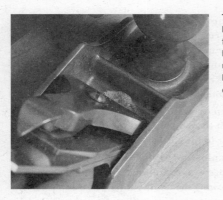

Move it to the center. Swing the lateral lever to bring the shaving closer to the center. If the shaving comes out on the left, move the adjuster to the left. Do the opposite if the shaving is on the right.

That's more like it. You're finished with lateral adjustments once you have the shaving centered.

LATERAL ADJUSTMENT

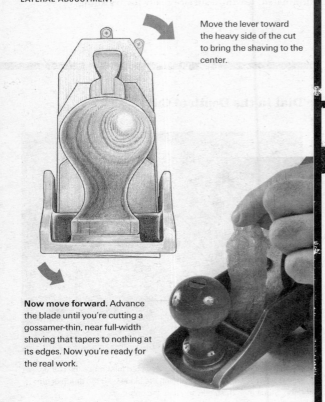

Move the lever toward the heavy side of the cut to bring the shaving to the center.

Now move forward. Advance the blade until you're cutting a gossamer-thin, near full-width shaving that tapers to nothing at its edges. Now you're ready for the real work.

Use Your Whole Body to Push the Plane

Power up. For stability and power, stand with your legs comfortably spread apart and your feet facing forward. Lean slightly forward, and put firm, downward pressure on the knob as you begin the cut.

Full contact. Once the plane's sole is completely on the board, apply pressure equally to both the tote and knob. Skewing the plane will reduce resistance and help eliminate chatter. Be sure to maintain your wide stance and use your body to drive the tool forward.

Exit strategy. As you exit the board, ease up on the knob and focus pressure more on the tote. Continue working across the board using consistent, overlapping passes.

Simple Solutions to Common Problems

A smoothing plane is not a complex tool, so it's pretty easy to diagnose and cure the most common ills. By the way, none of these solutions will work if the blade isn't sharp.

CHATTER

Problem: When your plane stutters or skips through a cut, it's called chatter. The problem often leaves a rippled surface, but you usually can feel it happening as you plane.

Solution: Take a lighter cut; put more pressure on the knob as you power into the cut; increase the angle of skew; resharpen the blade.

PLANE NOT CUTTING

Problem: Sometimes a plane stops cutting, even after successful passes.

Solution: Check for a clogged mouth; advance the blade to take a heavier cut; inspect the chipbreaker for poor contact with the blade; resharpen the blade.

TEAROUT

Problem: Tearout is one of the most common problems associated with planing. Instead of shaving the wood cleanly, the iron pulls up the wood fibers, leaving a fuzzy, rough surface.

Solution: Take a lighter cut; change planing direction; plane straight on (don't skew the plane); resharpen the blade.

TRACKS

Problem: A plane is supposed to leave a smooth, flat surface in its wake. But a plane that's not set up right can make tracks, or ridges, in the surface.

Solution: Readjust the blade laterally; take a lighter cut; when resharpening the blade, push down on the corners to relieve them slightly, creating a cambered edge.

Mastering the Card Scraper

by Matthew Teague

Of all the tools in my shop, my favorite is the basic card scraper. It's nothing more than a thin piece of steel that costs a few dollars, but it greatly reduces my least favorite part of woodworking: sanding.

The scraper cleans up tool and milling marks, levels glue-ups, and smooths surfaces. It removes material as efficiently as sandpaper but doesn't leave scratches in its wake. A scraper is easier to control than a handplane and can surface tricky grain where even a well-tuned plane does more harm than good.

Tuning a card scraper is relatively easy using only a mill file, sandpaper, and a screwdriver. Using a card scraper takes practice, but only a little. In a very short time, you'll be able to cut continuous shavings akin to those you get with a handplane.

Uses

Remove Mill Marks

A scraper is ideal for cleaning up light tearout and marks from jointers, planers, and handplanes.

Clean Glue

Dried squeeze-out comes off easily. Avoid an aggressive cut, which can dish the glueline.

Trim Edging

The cut is adjustable enough to trim solid edging flush and avoid damaging the plywood veneer.

Work Tricky Grain

The scraper works lightly, taking clean shavings despite treacherous changes in grain direction on a walnut-burl board.

Tune-Up Starts with a Mill File

New scrapers need a tune-up, and you'll have to repeat it from time to time, but the good news is that the process only takes three or four minutes.

First, file the long edges flat and square to the faces of the scraper. You can clamp the scraper in a vise and work the edge freehand with a standard mill file, or lay the file flat on the bench and work the scraper across it. Take full-length strokes until you feel and hear the file cut continuously.

Next, flatten the scraper's faces. Use a flat sharpening stone or 180-grit wet-or-dry sandpaper attached to a flat surface. Don't work the entire face, just the leading ½ in. or so. Use all eight fingers to apply even pressure, and work until you see a smooth surface with fresh steel exposed all the way to the edge. Then move to 320-grit paper to achieve a cleaner surface. If I'm trying to achieve a very fine, finish cut, I sometimes move on to 400 or even 600 grit.

These filing and flattening steps build up a "wire edge" of thin and brittle waste material that must be removed. To do this, hold the face of the scraper at 90° to the stone or sandpaper and work the edge using light pressure. It's easier to maintain the 90° angle if you skew the scraper. After a few strokes, the wire edge should fall off. If not, give the faces of the scraper a few passes across the sandpaper.

Draw and Turn the Burr

To create a tough burr for cutting wood, you need a burnisher—a rod of highly polished steel that is harder than the soft steel in the scraper. I've owned several commercially made burnishers over the years and they all worked fine. My favorite now is an old screwdriver.

Creating a burr begins with the scraper flat on the edge of the bench. Hold the burnisher flat against the face while pushing it away from you for several strokes along the length of the edge. Concentrate downward pressure on the cutting

Tune-Up

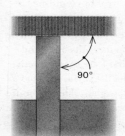

FILING AND HONING
Before you can form consistent burrs at the edges, it is crucial that the edge and sides are smooth and meet at 90°.

Sharpening starts with a file. Secure the scraper in a vise and use a mill file to remove hardened steel and square the edge. Be sure to keep the file at a 90° angle to the faces of the scraper.

Next hone the faces. Work the scraper back and forth on a sharpening stone or sandpaper set on a flat surface. Use eight fingers to apply even pressure. A mirror finish isn't crucial, but a smoother surface ½ yields a more uniform burr.

Remove the wire edge. A few light strokes on edge should accomplish this. Skewing the scraper to the direction of cut helps keep it square to the sanding surface. This also hones the edge, removing any rough file marks.

RAISING A BURR
Burnishing each edge forces the metal into a hook shape, creating a cutting burr.

1. Draw the burr. Apply firm downward pressure with the burnishing rod at the scraper's edge. Take several strokes, always pushing away from you. Skew the burnisher to help force material past the edge of the scraper.

2. Turn the burr. Use a piece of scrap as a reference to set the scraper's edge at a consistent height. Then ride the burnisher's handle along the bench to maintain a consistent angle, and make several firm pushing strokes away from you.

Drawing the burnishing rod over the flat face at a very slight angle extends the corner of the edge out into a ridge.

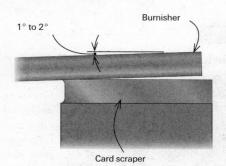

1° to 2°   Burnisher

Card scraper

Use the burnisher at an angle of 1° to 15° to flatten this ridge and create a hook-shaped cutting burr. A steeper angle yields a more aggressive cut.

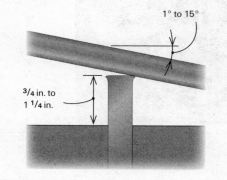

1° to 15°

¾ in. to 1 ¼ in.

edge to draw out the burr. Some woodworkers like to angle the burnisher down on the edge, but this angle should be very slight, only a degree or so. Work until you feel a slight burr when you carefully touch the edge with your fingertip. Draw the burr along each of the scraper's four long edges.

Now clamp the scraper upright in a bench vise with the edge to be burnished parallel to the benchtop. You can turn the burr with the burnisher held freehand or, to ensure a consistent angle, let the handle of the burnisher ride on the benchtop during each stroke. Following this second approach means that adjusting the scraper's height in the vise will alter the burnishing angle and, as a result, the cutting angle of the finished burr. The steeper the angle, the more aggressive the cut, but any angle between 1° and 15° works well.

Turning the burr should take only two or three passes. Once you feel a turned burr along the entire edge, test the cut. If you're making only dust, burnish some more. Once you're making shavings with both sides, you're ready to start scraping.

Two Ways to Take a Shaving

A scraper can either be pushed or pulled. I usually push the scraper to make aggressive, slightly concave cuts when removing tearout or smoothing tricky grain. For finer cuts, I pull the scraper to flatten any dished areas and leave a surface ready for finishing.

To push the scraper, hold it with your fingers on the short edges and your thumbs together in the middle of the back, about ½ in. or so above the cutting edge. Use your thumbs to create a slight bow along the bottom edge. The deeper the bow, the more aggressive the cut. Conventional wisdom says to start by holding the scraper vertically and angling it forward until you feel the burr bite into the wood. It works, but in my experience, it's easier for beginners to start with the scraper held at about 60° and, while pushing, slowly increase the angle until the burr begins to cut the wood. Then push forward in one smooth motion to get continuous, paper-thin shavings.

To pull the scraper, place your fingers on the far side and your thumbs on the face closest to you. Unlike when pushing, your thumbs should be positioned higher on the face of the scraper and your fingers lower. A pulled scraper is held with the edge bowed only enough to prevent the corners from digging into the wood. Some woodworkers avoid this problem by rounding the corners with a file or grinder.

A Scraped Surface That's Finish Ready

In my shop, a card scraper touches virtually every surface of a project, and is almost always the last tool to do so before the finish goes on. If I'm working easily planed, straight-grained stock, I typically clean up jointer and planer marks on larger surfaces with a handplane, then use the scraper to remove plane tracks and clean up tearout. To ensure a uniform appearance under a finish, I give all the surfaces at least a light scraping. In general, I scrape the entire surface using a push stroke, then flatten the slightly dished area using a pull stroke.

For stock with trickier grain, such as bird's-eye or burl, I skip handplaning altogether. A scraper is much easier to control than a handplane, and there is almost no chance of tearout.

In any case, if the milling marks are especially heavy, I usually start by power sanding to 120 grit. I prefer the way a scraped surface looks under a finish, so at this point I thoroughly brush or vacuum away the sanding dust and scrape until the entire surface is uniform.

Restore the Edge

A dull scraper takes more effort to push and a steeper cutting angle. It also creates dust instead of wide shavings.

Fortunately, it's possible to restore the burr several times simply by reburnishing the face and then the edge in the same way you initially turned the burr. After four to six burnishings, the metal becomes brittle and you need a new surface. Return the scraper to the vise and start over with a

file, removing any nicks along the edge that you've created by scraping. Then burnish the faces and edges to draw and turn new burrs.

Because each tune-up removes so little steel, I still use the first scraper I bought a dozen years ago. Sandpaper, however, usually wears out in minutes.

Making Shavings

TIP

An inexpensive heat shield. A flat refrigerator magnet helps protect your thumbs from the heat generated in use.

Two thumbs down. Grasp the scraper with your fingers wrapped around each side and your thumbs together on the back, near the bottom edge. Push forward with your thumbs, applying enough pressure to create a slight bow. The more pronounced the bow, the more aggressive the cut.

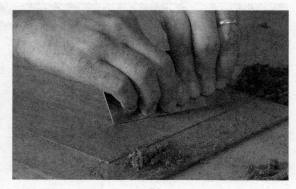

Use caution near edges. Avoid letting the scraper dig into the workpiece edges and leave them ragged. Here, Teague bows the scraper enough to concentrate cutting pressure in the center of the workpiece.

Pulling leaves a flatter surface. Align your fingertips behind the cutting edge to apply uniform pressure.

Continued ➜

Cabinet Scrapers and Scraper Planes

by Chris Gochnour

When bench planes begin to tear out tricky grain or balk at tough woods, many woodworkers reach for a card scraper. But that isn't always the best choice. Often, especially on large, flat surfaces, the job can be done easier, faster, and better by using one of the card scraper's bigger, lesser-known brothers: the cabinet scraper and the scraper plane.

I use all three scrapers in my shop, because each one has its place. Once you understand what they can do for you, what they cost, and how to use them, you can decide for yourself whether to add one or more to your tool cabinet.

Basic Card Scraper Is Best on Smaller Surfaces

Because it's held in both hands with finger pressure slightly flexing the steel, a card scraper lets you make light to moderate cuts depending on how it is held and engaged with the wood surface. The scraper can be pushed or pulled. To make cutting easier, I sometimes create a shearing cut by holding the scraper about 30° to the direction of travel.

As useful as a card scraper is, though, it has significant limitations. It is not an aggressive tool, so it won't remove a lot of material quickly. It cuts with a lot of resistance and, consequently, the cutting edge dulls fairly rapidly. Mainly, though, the card scraper is uncomfortable to hold because your hands are always in contact with sharp corners. Then, too, it creates a lot of friction as it cuts, so the steel can get hot to the touch within minutes. And because it lacks a flat sole to maintain a consistent cutting depth, you have to work carefully to avoid creating shallow dips and valleys.

So, I use a card scraper mostly to smooth smaller surfaces, typically under 18 in. sq. By the time my fingers are hot and my hands are tiring, the work is done.

Cabinet Scraper Is Better for Everything Else

Compared to the card scraper, the cabinet scraper is considerably more comfortable to use, even over extended time periods. The handles provide a place for the hands, and because fingers never touch the blade, heat is a nonissue. Plus, a cabinet scraper is more likely to maintain a flat, even surface because its sole helps regulate and control the depth of cut. The sole also makes it easy to start and finish cuts on the edges of panels. And a thumbscrew at the center of the scraper keeps the blade flexed for you.

Versatile and easy to use—The cabinet scraper excels at removing mill marks from board edges. Its sole provides the control needed to ensure that a board edge stays true as it is worked.

I typically use a cabinet scraper when the surface gets into the 18-in.-sq. to 36-in.-sq. range, such as a tabletop or panel. You can use one on even larger surfaces with good results, though that is where I turn to the scraper plane, which I'll cover shortly.

In use, I normally push the tool, but it cuts just as well when pulled. Like a card scraper, a cabinet scraper generally cuts better when skewed to about 30°.

Two ways to sharpen the blade—You have two options when it comes to sharpening a cabinet scraper. You can sharpen it as you would a card scraper, with its edges filed at a right angle to its face and a small burr, or hook, burnished onto each of its cutting edges. I find that cabinet scrapers work very well with this configuration. They are easy to sharpen, and, like on a card scraper, you get two working burrs along each edge.

To sharpen a blade to 90°, I start by securing it in a vise. Then, I use an 8-in. bastard file to create a flat, straight edge. As I push the file, I try to keep it at a right angle to the face surfaces of the blade. Three or four strokes usually are enough to get the job done. Then, with the blade still in the vise, I use a fine-grit, flat slipstone to smooth each side of the scraper at the filed edge. Once the edge is prepared, I'm ready to use a burnisher to form the cutting burr.

The second approach is to sharpen the scraper edge with a 45° bevel. This method produces a more aggressive cutting edge, useful if you want to remove material faster. For example, if a thickness planer produced some fairly heavy tearout, I'd use the 45° edge to speed up the process of thinning the stock until the tearout disappeared.

Setting up a cabinet scraper—Place the freshly sharpened blade into the body of the scraper. To establish the blade extension, place one or two pieces of paper on a flat surface. Then, to elevate the sole ever so slightly, place the front of the sole on the paper. Press the blade down against the flat surface while tightening the thumbscrews to secure the blade. This step sets the blade extension to match the thickness of the paper, typically about 0.004 in. per sheet.

Next, turn the scraper over and sight down the bottom of the sole. The cutting edge of the blade should be parallel to the sole. If it isn't, lightly tap the side of the blade with a hammer until it is. Finally, turn the thumbscrews that flex the blade until the blade has a very slight (about 0.002 in. to 0.003 in.) crown. The scraper is now ready to go to work.

Scraper Plane: Best Choice for Large Surfaces

All the scraper planes on the market are patterned after the Stanley No. 112, a tool that was developed in 1874. Like the original 112, the new scraper planes have a pivoting lever-cap and thumbscrew that clamp the blade to the frog. The frog is adjustable from zero to 25°, making it easy to dial in the cutting angle of the plane. This adjustment is critical, as the scraper's cutting angle needs to work in harmony with the angle of the burr on the scraper's edge. The pivoting frog also regulates the depth of cut.

Use it like a handplane—Handle the tool just as you would a bench plane. I find that a light touch, with a smooth, steady stroke, produces the best results. Just as with a bench plane, start the cut with pressure on the front knob. As the cut proceeds, equalize the pressure on the knob and the rear handle. Then, upon completing the pass, shift your weight to the rear handle.

Choosing a scraper plane—Of the scraper planes on the market, the one made by Veritas (www.leevalley.com) is the only one with an adjustment screw that lets you flex the 0.055-in.-thick blade to produce a slight camber, a feature that makes it less likely that you'll dig into the wood and also gives a very smooth cutting action. On the other models, I keep dig-ins under control by rounding the corners of the blade to about a 1/16-in. radius.

Sharpening a scraper plane—The 45° bevel can be created with a file, but I get the best results by "grinding" the edge with sandpaper. First I use spray adhesive to mount 120-grit sandpaper to a flat surface such as a chunk of granite or a piece of plate glass. Then I mount the blade in a Veritas Mark II honing guide (the only guide I've found that can hold a thin, wide scraper blade without causing distortion). With the guide set to create a 45° bevel, I roll it back and forth until the bevel is formed. With the blade still in the jig, I hone the beveled edge on a 1,000-grit waterstone. Then I use a 6,000-grit stone to polish the edge. After honing the edge, I form the cutting burr using a burnisher.

Setup is easy—When setting up a scraper plane, the first thing to do is tilt the adjustable frog 15° forward. Then set the plane on a flat benchtop and insert the blade into the plane with its bevel facing toward the back. With the blade resting on the benchtop, clamp the blade in place by tensioning the thumbscrew. Next, to extend the blade slightly from the sole, move the frog forward slightly. This is done by backing the rear locking nut a quarter-turn off the post and tightening the front nut up against the post.

Test the cut on a flat piece of wood and make depth adjustments accordingly. If the blade isn't parallel to the sole, you will feel the plane turning sideways as it cuts. If this occurs, make lateral adjustments by tapping the side of the blade with a hammer.

A scraper plane works best when set for a light cut. That said, it should produce a nice, wide shaving, not dust. If your scraper is not cutting shavings, adjust the frog angle so that it is working in harmony with the burr you have created on the blade's edge.

To find the best angle, remove the blade from the plane and make a pass or two while holding it like a card scraper. Find the angle at which the blade best engages the stock, then adjust the scraper frog to that angle, reinstall the blade, advance it slightly, and take another test cut. After using the scraper plane for a while, the blade will dull and the cut will be lighter and less efficient. Tilt the frog forward a degree or so to reengage the blade.

Wood with uneven grain is an inevitable part of woodworking. Short of sanding forever, the next best option is to use a tool from the scraper family. You'll end up with a smoother board, in less time, with less dust. That's a rare win-win situation.

When to Plane and When to Scrape

Whenever I'm working to smooth a relatively straight-grained wood, my tool of choice is a handplane. In my opinion, there's no better way to prepare a wood surface for a finish. But wood is not always straight-grained. Sometimes grain is wavy, curly, bird's eye, or has some other form of general nonconformity. I often use such wood for panels and tabletops, as it's a sure way to add a dramatic look to a furniture piece. As you might expect, wild grain—with wood fibers going up, down, and sideways at all angles—can be difficult to smooth. No matter how well the blade is sharpened, or how light a cut you make, a handplane tends to tear grain that runs helter-skelter. That's when I skip the plane and use a scraper.

Contrary to the names, card scrapers, cabinet scrapers, and scraper blades don't scrape—they cut. Sharpened and properly tuned, they can produce a pile of shavings. A couple of factors enable them to smooth wood without tearing the wood fiber. First, scrapers meet the wood at a steep cutting angle. That means it's almost impossible for the steel to get under the wood and lift and pry the fibers. Second, as a scraper cuts, the wood chip breaks immediately. That way, a long chip can't peel back, only to ultimately break and create a noticeable tear.

Cabinet Scraper

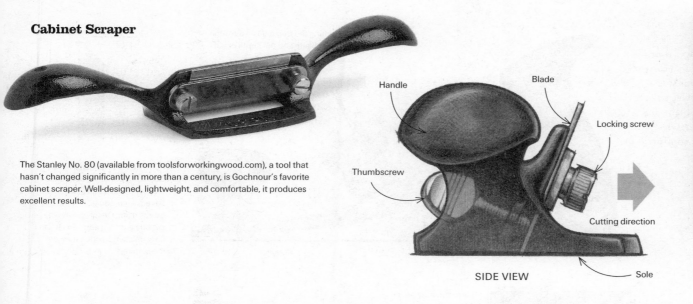

The Stanley No. 80 (available from toolsforworkingwood.com), a tool that hasn't changed significantly in more than a century, is Gochnour's favorite cabinet scraper. Well-designed, lightweight, and comfortable, it produces excellent results.

Handle

Blade

Thumbscrew

Locking screw

Cutting direction

Sole

SIDE VIEW

Create shavings, not sawdust. Properly sharpened and tuned, a cabinet scraper produces long, thin shavings, much like a plane. A typical stroke ranges from 12 in. to 24 in.

CREATING THE CUTTING BURR

A cabinet-scraper blade can be honed to either 90° or 45°. Of the two options, a 90° angle produces a smoother finish. Plus, you get two cutting burrs along one edge of the blade. See previous page to find out how to sharpen a blade to 45°.

90°

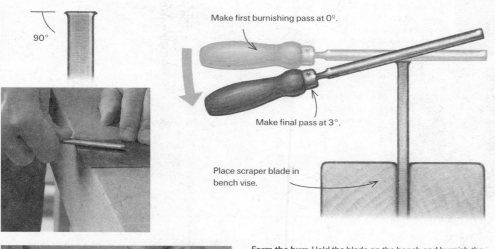

Make first burnishing pass at 0°.

Make final pass at 3°.

Place scraper blade in bench vise.

Form the burr. Hold the blade on the bench and burnish the face, keeping the burnisher flat against the blade (1). Clamp the blade in a vise and create the burr, starting the burnisher at 0° to the edge. Tilt the burnisher 3° and make a few more passes (2).

TIPS FOR SETUP AND USE

Set the cutting depth. A sheet of paper and a flat surface are all you need to set the depth of cut.

Set the blade flex. Tighten the thumbscrew to flex the blade about 0.002 in. to 0.003 in.

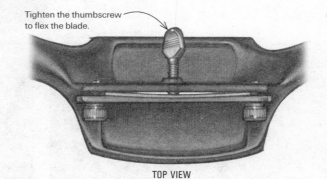

Tighten the thumbscrew to flex the blade.

TOP VIEW

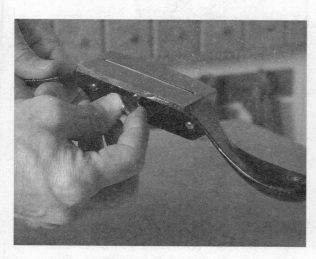

Start flat. The scraper cuts with less effort when at about 30° to the direction of travel. To start a cut at an edge, add pressure to the forward handle so that extra force is applied to the front of the sole. As the sole slides onto the stock, shift the hand pressure so that both handles end up with downward force.

Finish flat. As the sole of the cabinet scraper begins to extend over the end of the board, reduce pressure on the forward handle while maintaining pressure on the trailing handle. Finish the cut with full pressure on the back handle.

Keep the edges flat. When scraping close to the edge of a board, allow the sole to overhang only slightly, keeping most of it on the board. That way the cabinet scraper can't tip and give the surface an unwanted taper.

Continued →

Scraper Plane

The scraper plane has some advantages over a cabinet scraper. First, it's secured to a cast-iron, plane-like body with a generous sole that helps ensure that the board surface stays flat and true. Also, the angle of the blade and the depth of cut can be adjusted precisely. The handle and knob provide extra comfort and control.

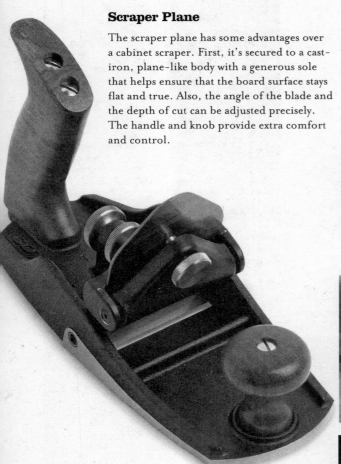

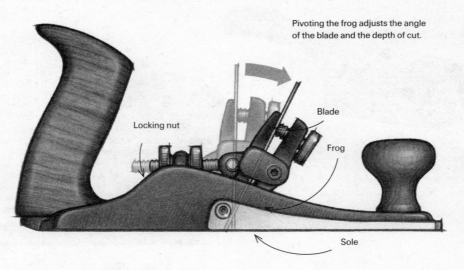

Pivoting the frog adjusts the angle of the blade and the depth of cut.

Locking nut

Blade

Frog

Sole

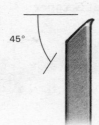

45°

FORMING THE BURR

Gochnour prefers to sharpen the scraper-plane blade at a 45° angle because it produces a more aggressive cut. On the downside, you get one working edge and it can't be burnished as often between sharpenings.

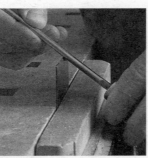

Form the burr on a 45° angle. Make the first pass along the bevel using a burnisher held at 45° (left). Then make a series of passes flattening the angle by about 5°, with the last pass at 15°. A board with a 15° line provides guidance for the final pass (bottom).

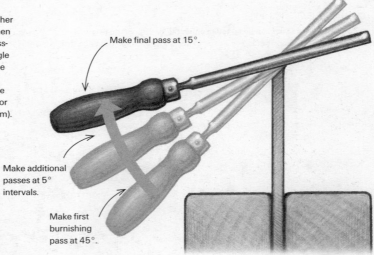

Make final pass at 15°.

Make additional passes at 5° intervals.

Make first burnishing pass at 45°.

TIPS FOR SETUP AND USE

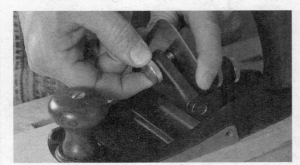

Load and lock. With the frog of the scraper plane set to a 15° angle, and with the plane on a flat surface, slip the blade (bevel facing back) into the plane until the burred edge bottoms out on the flat surface. Then turn the locking nut to secure the blade.

Set the depth of cut. To set the depth of cut, pivot the frog forward 15°. When the blade begins to dull, pivot the frog farther forward to improve the cutting action.

Skew the plane for easier cuts. Like a cabinet scraper, a scraper plane cuts more easily when angled about 30° to the direction of travel.

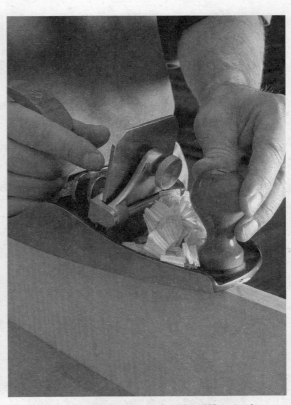

Scraper plane has the edge when doing edges. When an edge requires scraping, the scraper plane has the best balance and control, so you're less likely to tip the scraper and create an out-of-square edge.

The machine area of my shop is stocked with Western woodworking machines. But over at my workbench, all the hand tools are Japanese. Just as it's hard to beat hefty Western machines, I think Japanese hand tools clearly outperform their Western counterparts. When it comes to chisels, the Japanese variety takes a sharper, more durable edge than Western chisels; these tools simply work better and for a longer period of time.

What Makes Them So Good?

Japanese chisels, like other Japanese edge tools, are laminated, and this is the key. A thin layer of very hard and finely tuned high-carbon steel—the cutting edge—is forge-welded to a thicker piece of iron or low-carbon steel that forms the body of the blade. The thick layer of softer metal provides mass and shock dampening and prevents the hard, brittle steel from fracturing.

When you buy a new Japanese chisel, there's some setup to do before you can put it to work—flattening the back, creating the cutting bevel, and setting the hoop. Here I'll explain the anatomy of Japanese bench chisels, walk you through the various types, and give you guidelines and specific suggestions for which chisels to buy. Good-quality Japanese chisels are still made one at a time by individual blacksmiths in small shops, and I like the idea that while buying the best tool I can find I'm also helping keep an age-old craft alive.

Using a Japanese Chisel

Using Japanese chisels doesn't present anything like the radical shift users experience when going from Western to Japanese planes and saws. Japanese bench chisels are generally shorter than Western chisels and have a different feel and balance, but you'll work with them in the same ways.

One slight difference in use is due to the hollows on the back of the blade. When you are paring with a Japanese chisel and the back is registered against a flat surface, you have to adapt to the fact that you don't have the full width to ride on as you would with a Western chisel. Also note that Japanese chisels should never be used with a prying motion, as this action risks breaking the edge.

Sharpening the laminated blade may actually be easier than what you're used to. Because the thin steel cutting edge needs to be fully supported, the bevel of a Japanese chisel shouldn't be hollow-ground or given a microbevel—the whole bevel stays flat and the whole thing is honed at each sharpening. But since the backing iron is soft, sharpening the bevel on stones is quick. And dispensing with the grinder simplifies the sharpening process.

If you use a mallet with your chisels, you might consider getting a Japanese hammer to use with these chisels. The hoop at the end of a Japanese bench chisel keeps the wood from splitting when it's struck with a metal chisel hammer. These hammers are lighter, smaller, and easier to control than large wooden mallets, and deliver a more accurate blow.

Choosing a Chisel

Although there's no real learning curve in using a Japanese chisel, it will have a subtly different heft and feel in use than a Western one. If you are new to these chisels, consider buying one in a size that you use often and working with it for a while to see how you like it. If you prefer it, I still wouldn't advise buying a full set unless cost is no object. You get almost no discount for buying a set of 10 and you pay a hefty premium for the larger sizes. Instead, I'd buy five or so in the sizes you use most. For me, that would be: 3mm (1/8 in.), 6mm (1/4 in.), 9mm (3/8 in.), 12mm (1/2 in.), and something wide like 24mm (1 in.) or 36mm (1-1/2 in.). Japanese chisels are usually sized metrically, and are slightly narrower than their imperial equiv-

Basic Features

Nearly all Japanese-style chisels share a common anatomy, give or take the hoop, which is not found on dedicated paring chisels. But there are interesting variations in the blades, some significant and some not.

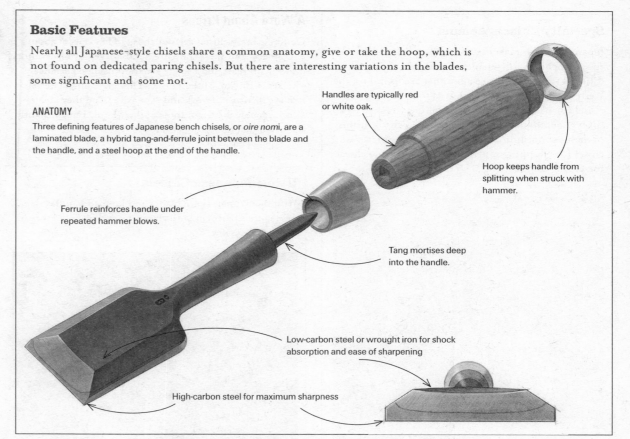

ANATOMY

Three defining features of Japanese bench chisels, or *oire nomi*, are a laminated blade, a hybrid tang-and-ferrule joint between the blade and the handle, and a steel hoop at the end of the handle.

Handles are typically red or white oak.

Hoop keeps handle from splitting when struck with hammer.

Ferrule reinforces handle under repeated hammer blows.

Tang mortises deep into the handle.

Low-carbon steel or wrought iron for shock absorption and ease of sharpening

High-carbon steel for maximum sharpness

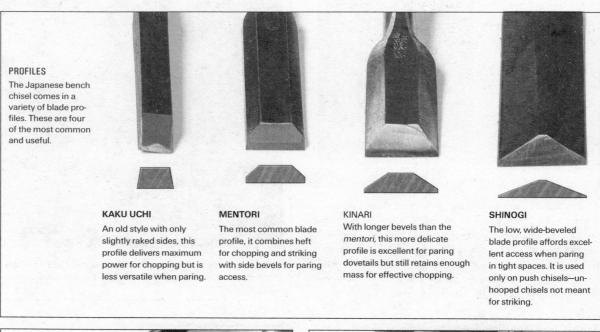

PROFILES

The Japanese bench chisel comes in a variety of blade profiles. These are four of the most common and useful.

KAKU UCHI
An old style with only slightly raked sides, this profile delivers maximum power for chopping but is less versatile when paring.

MENTORI
The most common blade profile, it combines heft for chopping and striking with side bevels for paring access.

KINARI
With longer bevels than the *mentori*, this more delicate profile is excellent for paring dovetails but still retains enough mass for effective chopping.

SHINOGI
The low, wide-beveled blade profile affords excellent access when paring in tight spaces. It is used only on push chisels—unhooped chisels not meant for striking.

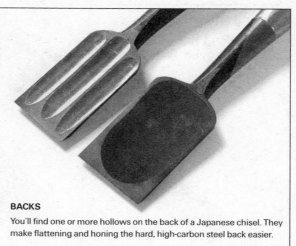

BACKS
You'll find one or more hollows on the back of a Japanese chisel. They make flattening and honing the hard, high-carbon steel back easier.

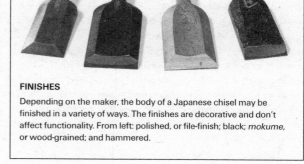

FINISHES
Depending on the maker, the body of a Japanese chisel may be finished in a variety of ways. The finishes are decorative and don't affect functionality. From left: polished, or file-finish; black; *mokume*, or wood-grained; and hammered.

alents. The smaller widths—1/8 in. to 1/2 in.—are good for the relatively small dovetails I use on drawers. The 1/4-in. and 1/2-in. chisels are also good for squaring mortises cut by machine. And having one or two wider chisels is nice for larger dovetails and larger mortises. All these chisels would work well for the various paring tasks that come up while making furniture.

Depending on need, you could fill out the set over time. Or use the money not spent on a complete set of bench chisels to buy some specialty chisels. Because hand-tool use is still a living part of the woodworking culture in Japan and because much of the woodworking there is highly specialized, there is a wide variety of chisel types.

Continued ➔

Specialty Chisels Abound

Japanese chisel-makers still produce a wide array of specialty chisels for Japanese craftsmen plying traditional trades. Here are a few that are useful on the Western workbench. From left: a long *shinogi* push chisel for paring; a *hiramachi* chisel for access to tight spaces; a cran\-neck chisel for cleaning the bottoms of dadoes and sliding dovetails; a heavy mortise chisel for chopping mortises; and a very wide chisel for paring or chopping.

Fishtail chisel is worth reeling in. With its flared blade, the *bachi nomi* is superb for getting at otherwise inaccessible corners while paring.

You could get a wide *shinogi*-style push chisel, which is great for general-purpose paring (and not meant to be struck); a cran\-neck chisel with a short foot for cleaning the bottoms of dadoes; a heavy mortising chisel for hand-chopping large mortises; or a fishtail-shaped chisel, or *bachi nomi*, for working in tight spaces like the hard-to-clean rear corners of half-blind dovetails.

Steels and Handles

The cutting edge of Japanese chisels is usually made from either "white steel," which is a very pure high-carbon steel, or "blue steel," which is white steel to which tungsten and chromium have been added to make the steel tougher. The names white and blue steel have nothing to do with the color of the metals—they refer to the paper that the steel comes wrapped in from the mill. There are different grades of both white and blue steel. White is said to take a sharper edge, blue to hold it longer in use. In my experience, either kind can make an outstanding chisel. One of my favorite chisels is made with #1 white steel. It's easy to sharpen, holds a great edge, and is fairly durable. But I also have chisels made with blue steel that perform similarly. To me, the skill of the blacksmith is more important than the choice of steel.

Japanese chisel handles are often made from red or white oak, but boxwood, gumi, ebony, and rosewood handles are also fairly common. All except the ebony and rosewood are strong, tough, and resilient enough to make excellent handles. I find rosewood and ebony too brittle for chisels that will receive hammer blows, but they are fine for push chisels, which are meant only for paring.

A Word About Prices

Good Japanese chisels are not cheap. They start at about $70 apiece. But these tools are hand-forged by blacksmiths drawing on years and usually generations of experience who are at the top of their craft. They are using materials that are difficult to work and expensive. And they are creating arguably the finest tools of their kind. I'm constantly surprised that they don't cost more.

That said, in Japan there is definitely a level of "tools as art," and there are collectors around the world who buy them. It is not necessary—and it may be counterproductive—to go to that level to find a wonderful tool. For me, the most beautiful tools are those that perform their jobs the best.

Using Japanese Chisels

With their super-sharp blades and hooped handles, Japanese chisels perform both chopping and paring tasks with ease and accuracy.

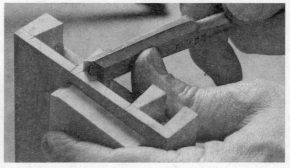

Precision paring. Japanese bench chisels are superb for paring, but shouldn't be used with a prying action, which could chip the very hard cutting edge.

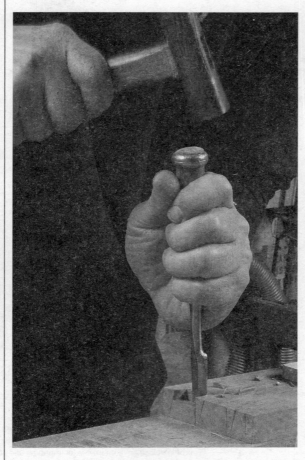

Specialty tools in action. The *shinogi* push chisel (above) excels at paring wide recesses like hinge mortises; the ultra heavy duty *tataki* (right) excels at hand-chopping large mortises.

Chopping. Its hooped handle lets the Japanese chisel take a pounding. A steel striking hammer, or *dai dogyu*, delivers a sharp, accurate blow.

Buying Guide

Japanese chisels fall into three general categories according to cost.

LOW END ($20–$40)

In this range, the maker's name will not be known—possibly because the tools are mass-produced. The handle may be dyed to mask inferior wood, and poorly fitted to the ferrule. Blades may be stamped from sheet material and painted. Cutting steel may be soft and abrade away quickly. Hollows may be ill-formed. Blades won't get as sharp as better brands and will lose their edge more quickly.

MID RANGE ($60–$300)

Although made one at a time in small shops and typically attributed to a particular blacksmith, these chisels offer the best value to furniture makers. Made with high-quality white or blue steel tempered to Rockwell c65 or higher, they should take a razor-sharp edge and hold it. Care in the making will be evident in the even shape of the hollow, a clean lamination line, a graceful transition from the neck to the body, and the fit of the handle to the ferrule.

HIGH END ($500 AND UP)

Some Japanese tools are treated as art, and with collectors in the picture, prices can get stratospheric. The provenance of a chisel—whether the blacksmith is a national figure—and features like folded-steel blades, exotic handles, and rustic, hammered surface treatments can increase the value of a chisel, but they don't improve its performance.

Hammers and Mallets

by Mario Rodriguez

Fine woodworking is usually characterized by the careful cutting and fitting of joints that then slide together with only hand pressure. However, sometimes a little coercion is the most efficient response to a stubborn joint. In my shop I employ a variety of hammers and mallets to help me in a multitude of tasks: interior demolition and disassembly of existing work, dry-fitting of carcases, built-in installations and adjustment of tools such as the blades on molding planes. My favorite hammers and mallets are laid out here, along with explanations of what I use them for.

12-oz. curved-claw hammer

For light assembly, this hammer's compact size reduces the chance of causing inadvertent damage. The red-oak handle feels good, but I have had to tighten it with oak shims a couple of times. The curved claw gives good leverage for pulling out nails without destroying the work.

16-oz. straight-claw hammer

This hammer is great for heavy work in the shop: assembling large-scale dovetails, driving lag bolts before wrenching them and setting the pronged drive center for a lathe into a blank. The head and handle are one piece, making this hammer a favorite among the pros because of its indestructible nature. At 21 years, this is my oldest hammer.

20-oz. straight-claw hammer

I use this heavy bruiser for construction and installation. The weight and length of this hammer are sufficient to drive an 8d common nail in two blows. The straight claw is useful for chipping stuff out of corners as well as for prying things apart. I prefer a fiberglass handle for a tight and permanent fit with the head; the rubber sheath gives a nonslip grip.

Japanese hammer

This hammer is useful for setting the irons in Japanese planes, and for woodworking in tight corners. The head is of cast steel with a handle fitted through the eye and held tightly with wedges.

12-oz. ball-pein hammer

A small-scale, machine-shop staple comes in handy in my woodshop. There is always some bit of metal needing to be coaxed into place or straightened out. This hammer also does more mundane duty, such as tamping down paint-can lids.

Cross-pein hammers

Also known as a Warrington hammer, this style is considered a versatile shop hammer, as evidenced by the wide range of sizes it comes in. I use the 3 1/2-oz. hammer for delicate tasks such as nailing brads in picture frames, while the 12-oz. size does universal duty. The tapered pein— the end of the head opposite the main striking head— can be used for starting small nails with less chance of hitting your fingers.

6-oz. tack hammer

When I picked up this hammer almost 20 years ago at a five-and-dime store, I replaced the original, flimsy lauan handle with a hickory one. Now I love the feel of this tool. It is perfect for restoration work such as setting small, solid-wood patches and inlays. I also use it for setting wedges into joints and for adjusting blades and cutters on my antique planes.

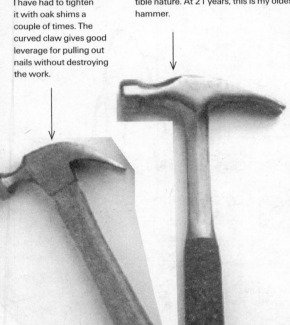

2-lb. mason's lump hammer

I use this brute for light demolition work such as removing interior trim and woodwork. It also provides just the right force for assembling the undercarriage of my Windsor chairs. I replaced the original handle with one made of hickory.

Deadblow hammer

This rubber mallet features a hollow head filled with lead shot that delivers a solid blow without damaging the work. It doesn't have much visual or tactile appeal, but it's good for assembling large carcases.

Brass-headed mallet

This mallet definitely punches above its weight. I use this compact tool mostly for carving because its ergonomic shape reduces fatigue. An added bonus of its small size is that it takes up less space in a tool bag.

Laminated mallet

The head on this mallet comprises 1/16-in.-thick layers of laminated beech, making it stronger, heavier and less prone to splitting than a solid-wood mallet. The face of this mallet is designed to strike the work at a more efficient angle than a square-headed mallet would.

Lignum vitae carver's mallet

I use this when cutting mortises and carving. Unlike the square mallet, the round shape of this tool allows me to pick it up without having to orient its face to the work. I bought this mallet for $2 because of its crooked handle, but I wouldn't part with it for $20.

Sharpening Planes and Chisels

by Deneb Puchalski

For many woodworkers, sharpening plane irons and chisels is an intimidating and frustrating task. I've traveled the country teaching and demonstrating sharpening and hand-tool techniques for Lie-Nielsen Toolworks for the past nine years, and I've met plenty of woodworkers who struggle to get a consistently sharp edge on their tools and are convinced that sharpening is beyond their reach.

Sharpening doesn't have to be difficult and mysterious. The method I'll show you combines ideas I've picked up over 25 years of working with hand tools. I've demonstrated it countless times.

The heart of this approach is a collection of simple tools: a $15 side-clamping honing guide, a supply of sandpaper in several grits, 1,000- and 8,000-grit waterstones (or a combination stone if you like), a thin metal ruler, and a shopmade stop board that will help you quickly and reliably set the correct honing angle every time. With these tools, you can handle the most common sharpening tasks— honing, grinding, and repairs—for every kind of blade.

Using this method, you'll get a truly sharp edge, allowing your tools to cut more cleanly and efficiently with less effort.

Start with a Time-Saver: The Ruler Trick

Many woodworkers buy a high-end handplane with the idea that their woodworking will get better. It's true that a better tool makes for a less frustrating experience. But

Continued ➜

although you may think a new plane is ready to go right out of the box, think again. Even a new tool should be sharpened before you put it to wood.

A brand new, high-quality plane iron should have a flat back. If it doesn't, or if you're working with an older iron, flattening is a must. Fortunately, this should take no more than 5 or 10 minutes using the sandpaper technique shown on p. 46. Your goal is not a high polish but simply a flat back with no heavy milling marks running to the cutting edge. This is because, once I have the back flat, I use David Charlesworth's ruler trick to create a subtle bevel on the blade's back. The ruler trick puts the honed surface at the cutting edge where it belongs and eliminates the tedium of polishing the entire back.

Here's how it works: Place a thin metal ruler (0.020 in. thick or less) on one side of the 8,000-grit stone. Now place the back of the blade on the ruler and lower the blade's tip onto the stone. Work it up and down until you can see an even mirror polish about 1/32 in. wide, from corner to corner, at the edge of the blade. Now you're ready to hone the bevel.

The typical bevel-down smoothing plane blade comes with a primary bevel of about 25°. There's no need to hone the entire primary bevel to get a sharp edge, though. It's more efficient to create a small, steeper secondary bevel right at the cutting edge. For the most common primary bevel of 25°, a secondary bevel of 30° works well.

I use steeper angles with scraper planes, as well as bevel-up tools for working in hard, highly figured woods. The harder the wood, the higher the angle.

How to Find and Hold the Right Angle

To hone the secondary bevel, I use a honing guide. Some woodworkers call this cheating. As someone who learned long ago to sharpen freehand, I say it's not. A honing guide holds the blade at a consistent angle as you work the edge and move from stone to stone. The secondary bevel remains flat, and each successive grit reaches all the way to the tip of the edge.

I use a simple, side-clamping honing guide. To set the angle consistently, I constructed a stop board (see drawing, right), which consists of a plywood base and several stops to set the blade a certain distance from the front of the guide. The shorter the distance, the steeper the honing angle. My board has stops for five common angles: 25°, 30°, 35°, 40°, and 45°. I also use a 1/8-in. shim to increase an angle at any of the stops. With a long projection like 25° to 30°, 1/8 in. represents roughly a 2° increase in angle. With a short projection like 45°, the same 1/8 in. represents about 5°.

Honing Takes Less Than a Minute

Set the blade to the correct angle and tighten the guide so the blade won't shift. Begin with the 1,000-grit stone, working back and forth and applying even pressure. After four or five passes, you should be able to see and feel a burr or "wire edge" on the back of the blade. This burr indicates that you have removed the dulled edge and it's time to change stones.

Before sharpening on the 8,000-grit stone, wipe off the roller wheel of the honing guide so that you don't transfer grit from stone to stone. To ease off some of the burr, take one pass on the blade's back, drawing the blade toward you. Now work the bevel side, taking another four or five passes. When you see a clean and brightly polished parallel line right at the blade's tip, you are done. However, if you applied uneven pressure on the blade, the polish line will be wider at one corner than the other. This can be corrected easily on the 8,000-grit stone by placing extra pressure on the narrower side with just a few more strokes. As a final step, remove the blade from the honing guide and touch up the back using the ruler trick to fully remove any burr that is still present.

An All-In-One Honing Station

A board with multiple reference stops is a great way to set honing angles reliably. This compact jig also supports your sharpening stones. The measurements shown give approximate angles for most side-clamping honing guides. For best results, set your own stop distances as shown below.

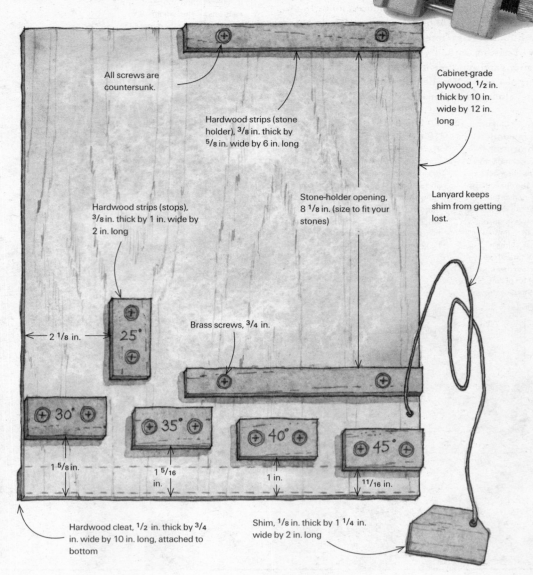

All screws are countersunk.

Cabinet-grade plywood, 1/2 in. thick by 10 in. wide by 12 in. long

Hardwood strips (stone holder), 3/8 in. thick by 5/8 in. wide by 6 in. long

Hardwood strips (stops), 3/8 in. thick by 1 in. wide by 2 in. long

Stone-holder opening, 8 1/8 in. (size to fit your stones)

Lanyard keeps shim from getting lost.

2 1/8 in.

25°

Brass screws, 3/4 in.

30°

35°

40°

45°

1 5/8 in.

1 5/16 in.

1 in.

11/16 in.

Hardwood cleat, 1/2 in. thick by 3/4 in. wide by 10 in. long, attached to bottom

Shim, 1/8 in. thick by 1 1/4 in. wide by 2 in. long

SET YOUR OWN ANGLES

To locate a stop at the correct distance for a given angle, place an iron in the honing guide and use a protractor to set the angle. Then, butt the guide against the board and place the stop against the iron's edge. Use brass screws to secure the stop parallel to the edge.

Grinding Without a Grinder

With repeated honings, the secondary bevel will grow wider. When it becomes too large, and you're spending 20 to 30 passes honing on the 8,000-grit stone, you need to re-establish the primary bevel. A lot of woodworkers use a grinder for this, but I've found that working by hand on sandpaper is just as fast, won't burn the tip and soften the steel, and gives me more control. You need a flat, hard substrate to attach the sandpaper to. I use granite, but plate glass works too.

Re-establishing the primary bevel—Use the stop board to set the blade in the guide to the correct primary bevel. Attach three or four grits of 3-in.-wide adhesive-backed paper to the substrate. Take 10 to 15 passes on each grit, switching from a coarse (P80 to P180 grit) to a medium (P220), to a fine grit (P400). Switching grits often avoids working too long in the same scratch pattern. It also helps prevent unintentionally crowning the blade, which makes honing difficult. Continue cycling through the grits until you achieve a consistent and straight bevel at the desired angle. Do not work the edge down to a point. Stop just short of creating a burr. You are done when you can see a very thin, flat line on the tip of the blade, about 0.01 in. or 0.02 in. thick. A jeweler's loupe can help you see this line. If you are having trouble, you can work down until you feel a very slight burr. With the primary bevel re-established, rework the secondary bevel, starting with the ruler trick.

A New Blade Only Needs Honing

Hone just the tip of the back

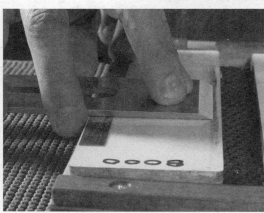

Tiny ruler is a huge time saver. Lifting the iron's back off the stone lets you polish only a thin band at the cutting edge, instead of the entire back. The work is done with just 10 to 20 passes on an 8,000-grit stone.

Why I Like Waterstones

You can use this technique with any abrasive. I like waterstones, 1,000 and 8,000 grit, specifically the new Shapton glass-backed stones. These stones cut aggressively but have a ceramic binder holding the stone together, so they only need to be spritzed with water. Don't soak them as you would a regular waterstone; they will soften and can be ruined. You may also want a 4,000-grit stone for occasionally lapping the back of a plane iron or chisel. Keep your stones flat for consistent results. This is easily done by lapping frequently with a coarse wet-or-dry paper (150 to 220 grit) on a flat reference plate, granite or glass, or a coarse diamond lapping plate (45 to 55 micron).

Also, be sure to wipe off the roller of your honing guide before switching stones, to avoid transferring grit from one to another.

Keep your stones flat. Lap your sharpening stones often with a diamond plate or coarse wet/dry sandpaper on a flat surface. Do this often and it will be less work each time.

Same Goes For The Bevel

Honing on the 1,000-grit stone removes a narrow band of metal near the cutting edge. A few passes on the 8,000-grit stone creates the highly polished surface needed for a sharp edge.

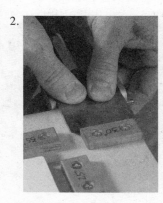

1.

2.

This should take only a minute. Use the 30° stop on the board to set the iron in the honing guide (1). Four or five passes on the 1,000-grit stone should be enough to raise a burr on the iron's back (2). Take a handful of passes on the 8,000-grit stone to create a highly polished narrow band at the tip (3). Finally, repeat the ruler trick to remove any remaining burr on the back (4).

3.

4.
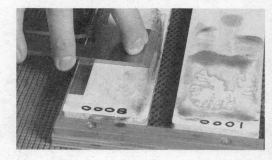

Test the edge. Replace the iron and set it for a light cut. See-through shavings should be the result.

Same Method for Chisels, With a Few Tweaks

Like new plane blades, chisels aren't ready to go right out of the box. The good news is that this sharpening method works for chisels, too. The bad news is that the ruler trick won't work. You need to flatten (on sandpaper) and polish (on stones) the entire back because it serves as a reference for paring and other fine work.

Once the back is flat, mount the chisel in the honing guide. Its lower position in the guide creates a honing angle that is about 5° shallower than the marked angles on your board. So your 30° stop becomes 25° and so on.

Because I can control the angle and am not removing much material, I work the entire face of the primary bevel on the 1,000-grit stone, then hone a secondary bevel a few degrees steeper on the 8,000-grit stone. Use the 1/8-in. shim to increase the angle. I avoid sandpaper grinding unless I get a heavy nick in the edge.

Fix the nicks first. There's no point in honing this edge until the nicks have been removed. Puchalski uses a block of wood to hold the chisel perpendicular to the sandpaper as he grinds the edge back to remove the nicks. Then he regrinds the primary bevel with the chisel in a honing guide. The same method works for plane blades.

Fitting the chisel in the honing guide. The chisel rides in the lower set of jaws. The lower jaws also hold narrow plane blades.

The angles are different. Chisels ride lower in the honing guide and project farther out of it. To compensate, choose a stop that is 5° steeper than your desired angle.

Continued ➜

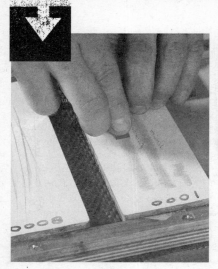

Honing in two steps. Puchalski works the entire face of the bevel on the 1,000-grit stone, then hones a secondary bevel a few degrees steeper on the 8,000-grit stone.

IMPORTANT NOTE!
Avoid the ruler trick with chisels. Once you're done honing, take a couple of passes on the back to remove the burr. Keep the back flat on the stone.

Keeping Tools Sharp
by Roland Johnson

One of the most time-consuming tasks in a woodworking shop is sharpening, whether that means grinding and honing chisels, running to the store for a new cutter, or sending planer blades out to be sharpened. Although it's a chore that can't be avoided, it can be delayed. A variety of hazards will dull cutting edges prematurely. Steering clear of them will let you work more and sharpen less.

Among the worst of these is dirt. Cleaning debris off rough lumber before machining can help maintain a sharp edge on jointer and planer knives and sawblades. Removing pitch and sawdust to prevent buildup helps prevent cutters from dulling too soon. It's also important to protect your tools from collisions with other metal or hard surfaces that can mar a sharp edge.

Clean Lumber Before Milling

Roughsawn lumber holds lots of dust and debris, which can act like sandpaper on cutting tools. A light brushing will not always get it out of the surface pores. The best way to clean the surface is to use compressed air and a wire brush. A quick blast will remove the bulk of dirt and debris, and a good brushing will dislodge the remaining grit. It's best to clean lumber outdoors so as not to spread dust on nearby material, tools, or workbenches. Although it cleans a bit more slowly than compressed air, a good shop vacuum can be used indoors because it will not spread dust around the shop. Used lumber poses different hazards. I use a metal detector to find embedded nails or screws that can dull or damage tool edges and remove them before proceeding with the cut.

Hand-scraping or chemical removal will take care of old paint, which will dull a cutting edge quickly and leave a residue on tools. But the wood has to be pretty valuable to go through all that hassle. The best bet is to avoid painted lumber altogether.

Scrub and Lubricate Cutters

Toothed cutting blades on bandsaws, tablesaws, and chopsaws rely on clearance immediately alongside the sawteeth to help eliminate drag, and on gullets behind the cutter to remove the freshly cut wood fibers. If the teeth have pitch baked on their sides or if the gullets have crud built up on their edges, the blade will heat up and dull quickly. I clean my tablesaw blade frequently with a blade cleaner such as OxiSolv Blade & Bit Cleaner or CMT Formula 2050 Blade and Bit Cleaner. I am careful to keep the gullets clean on my bandsaw blade, especially when resawing—a brass brush can clear blocked bandsaw gullets quickly without dulling the edges. In addition, a regular waxing or dry lubricant coating on the blade will minimize buildup and reduce friction in the cut. I find that paraffin wax or DriCote works well. Before applying DriCote, clean the blade with a solvent because this product needs to adhere to bare metal.

Drill bits, especially twist bits, suffer when chips build up in the flutes and can't be extracted from the bore hole. This is an especially big problem with bits used in hollow-chisel mortisers. The friction from the compacted chips can create enough heat to turn the metal of the chisel and the bit blue, effectively ruining the temper, or hardness, in both. Once steel loses its hardness, the cutting edge won't stay sharp for long. To improve the ability of bits to eject chips, I coat bits with DriCote.

Specialized lubricants can significantly enhance the operation of tools that rely on metal tables to support work being sawn, edged, or molded. Products such as Empire's TopSaver will keep a steel or cast-iron top slick, resulting in less effort needed to push material past a blade or cutter. Constant feed rates, essential to producing a consistent knife-mark pattern on molded edges, are easier to maintain when the table's friction is low.

REMOVE PITCH AND SAWDUST

Clean bandsaw gullets. With the machine turned off, rotate the upper wheel by hand as you pass a brass brush over the blade.

Use a blade-and-bit cleaner on tablesaw blades. Spray it on the buildup and let it sit before scrubbing with a brass brush.

LUBRICATION SLOWS DULLING, RUST

Apply a dry lubricant on chisel mortisers. The lubricant helps prevent buildup and keeps bits from dulling prematurely.

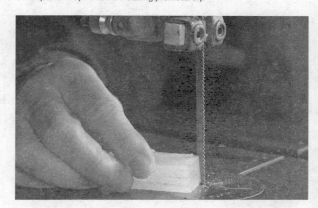

Wax bandsaw blades to reduce friction. With the blade running, hold a piece of paraffin wax on the table and against the blade.

Protect Sharp Tool Edges from Hard Knocks

I have an ongoing debate with a friend about the proper way to set a sharp handplane on a benchtop. I always set mine on the sole with the blade resting on a fairly clean wooden benchtop surface. I reason that there is less chance of damaging the blade, or myself, when the blade is covered. Resting the plane on its side exposes the blade, increasing the chances that I'll get a flesh wound or my plane will be damaged by another metallic tool.

Chisels laid on a benchtop should always point away from the woodworker, the project, and the other tools on the bench. Be careful to avoid clutter on a workbench; it is too easy to bump sharp cutting edges against metal.

Debris in tool trays, and the trays themselves, can nick and dull cutting edges. Keep trays clean and organized. Put a divider between each tool in a toolbox and if the toolbox is metal, line the interior with wood or heavy card stock.

Provide a safe haven for all cutting edges. I have a rack for my chisels; dowels on the wall for my files, rasps, and planes; trays for my router and drill bits that keep the sharp sides up and separated from one another; individual shelves for my tablesaw blades; and a separate dowel for hanging each of my bandsaw blades.

Touch Up That Edge Before It's Gone

It is faster and easier to hone a slightly dull tool than to regrind a really dull tool. As soon as the performance drops in any cutting device, it is time to give it a touchup. Sometimes honing is as simple as running the flat face of a bit over the edge of a diamond stone to restore full performance.

Steel cutters such as plane blades and chisels also should be honed frequently during use and ground only occasionally. Carvers are seldom far from their honing system, whether it is a leather strop and diamond paste or a buffing system.

The same goes for scrapers. The burr that does the cutting on a scraper is relatively fragile and can start to lose its sharpness within a few strokes. But a quick once-over with a burnishing tool will restore the edge.

There's nothing like seeing fine shavings roll off the cutting edge of a tool. Protecting those edges and touching them up often will extend your working time between full sharpenings.

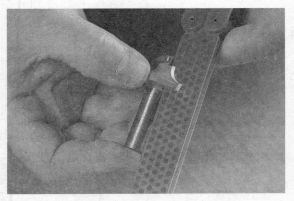

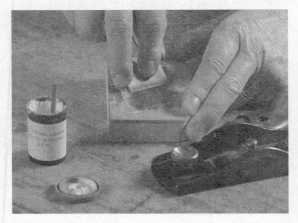

Sharpen router bits with a small diamond stone. Run the flat face of a bit over the stone, using the same number of strokes for each edge.

Hone plane irons regularly. Diamond paste on a piece of leather quickly renews an edge.

POWER TOOLS

Ripping and Crosscutting on the Tablesaw

by Marc Adams

Ripping and Crosscutting

Most woodworkers, including me, will answer yes to the following two questions, while looking sheepishly at their penny loafers. Did you ignore the "Using Your Saw" section in the owner's manual when you got your first tablesaw? Have you experienced kickback?

I have had workpieces kick back a few times in my life. Fortunately, I wasn't hurt. For others, though, that instant on the tablesaw has been tragic and life-altering.

With hundreds of students passing through my school each year, I've developed firm guidelines for safe tablesaw use, regardless of skill level. My first rule is to keep all 13 saws properly set up and maintained. But this article focuses on the second part of the equation: a knowledgeable operator. If you understand how the saw works and know the best practices for its use, the chance for a bad accident can be virtually eliminated. Machines don't think, but you can.

Kickback Is The Main Danger

Kickback accounts for the majority of tablesaw accidents. Unfortunately, I encounter many woodworkers who don't understand the cause of kickback, or the cure.

Here's how it happens. The teeth at the front of the blade do the cutting, and they move downward, helping to

Three Core Principles

Staying safe begins with these three core concepts. No. 2 is specific to the tablesaw, but the others are critical on any piece of machinery.

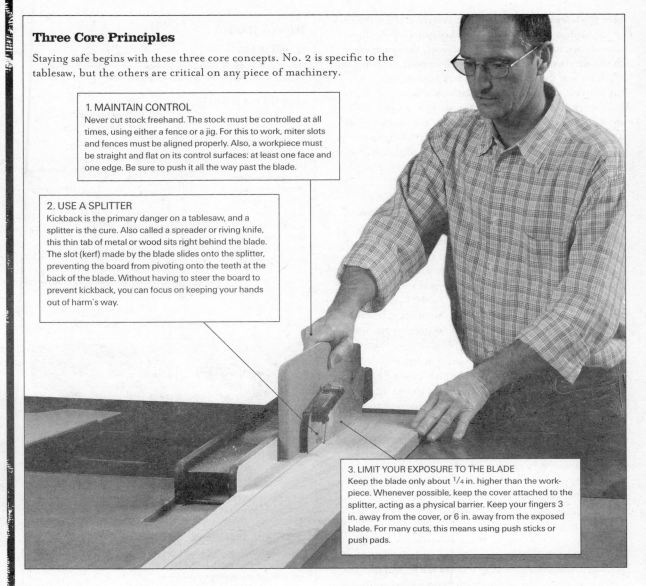

1. MAINTAIN CONTROL
Never cut stock freehand. The stock must be controlled at all times, using either a fence or a jig. For this to work, miter slots and fences must be aligned properly. Also, a workpiece must be straight and flat on its control surfaces: at least one face and one edge. Be sure to push it all the way past the blade.

2. USE A SPLITTER
Kickback is the primary danger on a tablesaw, and a splitter is the cure. Also called a spreader or riving knife, this thin tab of metal or wood sits right behind the blade. The slot (kerf) made by the blade slides onto the splitter, preventing the board from pivoting onto the teeth at the back of the blade. Without having to steer the board to prevent kickback, you can focus on keeping your hands out of harm's way.

3. LIMIT YOUR EXPOSURE TO THE BLADE
Keep the blade only about $1/4$ in. higher than the workpiece. Whenever possible, keep the cover attached to the splitter, acting as a physical barrier. Keep your fingers 3 in. away from the cover, or 6 in. away from the exposed blade. For many cuts, this means using push sticks or push pads.

Today's Saws Have Better Guards

A few years back, Underwriters Laboratories mandated that all saws sold in the United States have much-improved, European-style safety systems, and all North American manufacturers complied.

Better blade covers and splitters. Today's blade covers are narrower, allowing a push stick to pass by more easily. And the riving knife, an improved version of the splitter, moves up and down with the blade, hugging it closely to prevent kickback.

Low-profififile option. For very thin rips (above left) and non-through-cuts (above right), the blade cover comes off easily, and you can either adjust the riving knife downward or replace it quickly with a low-profile version.

Older Saw? You Have Options

Older splitter systems are inconvenient, and often discarded. But no worries—there are two good ways to replace them.

Buy a better splitter. Available online as an "Anti-Kickback Snap-In Spreader" for about $150, the Biesemeyer aftermarket splitter was designed for Delta saws but works in many others. You install its holder in the throat of your saw, and then the splitter pops in and out quickly.

Or make a stub splitter. This little tab of wood goes into the saw slot (above left) on a shopmade throat plate and can be cut short so it works for non-through-cuts too (above right). You'll need to lengthen the saw slot to accommodate it. If it binds in the sawkerf, just sand or plane the sides a bit. Be sure the grain runs vertically for strength.

Continued ➡

keep the board safely on the table. But the teeth at the back of the blade are not your friend; they spin in your direction at over 100 mph. During a safe cut, the slot made by the blade brushes past the back teeth without incident. But if the back of the board pivots as you push it, or one of the halves is pinched into the blade somehow, only one of those back teeth needs to grab the workpiece to set kickback in motion. And it happens in milliseconds, as the lifting action converts almost instantly to horizontal force aimed right at you. The projectile can hurt you, obviously, but it can also pull your hand into the blade. The good news is that kickback is easy to prevent.

Use a splitter whenever possible—Also called a spreader or riving knife, a splitter keeps a board from making contact with the teeth at the back of the blade. Problem solved? Not exactly. The splitter has to be there to do its job, and until recently, most splitters were downright inconvenient and were therefore discarded. North American saws that are more than a few years old will have a crude splitter that extends high above the blade and too far behind it. The main problem is that these splitters have to come off the saw for all non-through-cuts, such as grooves. The big blade covers are just as inconvenient.

This outdated safety equipment is difficult to detach and reinstall, so most of these splitter/blade cover assemblies find a permanent home in a shop cabinet. If you have one of these saws, you still owe it to yourself to use a splitter.

A riving knife is a blessing—Fortunately, a few years ago Underwriters Laboratories (UL) proposed that all new tablesaws have a riving knife, a more versatile type of splitter borrowed from European tablesaws, and all of the North American tablesaw manufacturers complied.

If you can afford to buy a new saw, you'll find safety much more convenient. The riving knife can stay on for almost every type of cut, and the new blade covers are narrower and come off the saw more easily when they get in the way. Unfortunately, today's riving knives still include "anti-kickback fingers," which are basically useless and often in the way, so I remove them.

One gray area is getting your riving knife or splitter to fit through a shopmade throat plate. On my saw, I just extend the blade slot (using my scrollsaw) to allow the low-profile riving knife to fit through. But the taller knife won't work because it is longer, and I'd have to make the slot so long it would weaken the insert plate. So I use my zero-clearance throat plate for crosscutting only, where tearout is the biggest problem and where I need to use my low-profile knife anyway to fit through the fence on my miter gauge and crosscut sled. For ripping, I use the standard throat plate. That lets me use the full-height riving knife and blade cover.

A Few More Tips

Even if a board is already jointed straight and flat, it might not stay that way as internal tensions are released during a cut. If a board jams during the cut, use one hand to turn off the saw, wait for the blade to stop, and finish the cut on the bandsaw. Also, be aware that a short board is more likely to pivot onto the back of the blade. If you are not sure about a workpiece, rip it on the bandsaw. And on some smaller, portable saws, the rip fence won't stay parallel to the blade when you move it, which can cause binding, so you'll need to check it each time.

One no-no when crosscutting is using the rip fence as a stop. This traps the offcut, and the friction against the fence can cause it to pivot and bind, causing kickback. For the rest of my safety rules, see the photos and illustrations throughout this article.

Follow these basic safety guidelines and you'll turn the most dangerous machine in the shop into a trusted friend. In Part 2, I'll show you how to get even more value from this versatile tool, demonstrating a variety of fast, accurate joinery cuts.

Ripcut Basics

SET UP FOR SAFETY

When ripping boards, you need the fence to be parallel to the blade, and you need a few shopmade push sticks on hand.

ALIGN THE SAW IN TWO STEPS

How you adjust the table is different on different saws, but you need the miter slots to be parallel to the blade for safe crosscutting. Then you adjust the rip fence parallel with the slots and you're set for ripping, too.

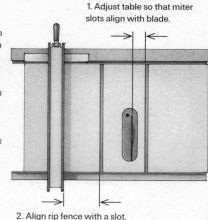

1. Adjust table so that miter slots align with blade.

2. Align rip fence with a slot.

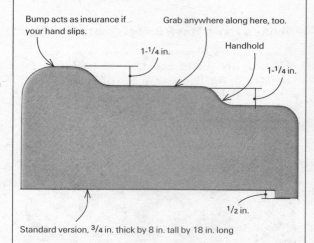

Rip fence is easy to correct. Use the adjustment screws to align the fence with a miter slot, and it should stay parallel in any position.

SMART PUSH STICK DESIGN

Adams's push sticks hook over the back of a board, of course, but also extend over the top of it for full control. He makes them in MDF in a number of sizes and thicknesses.

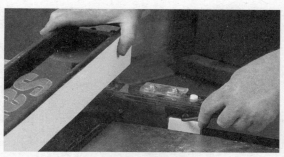

Bump acts as insurance if your hand slips.

Grab anywhere along here, too.

1-1/4 in.

Handhold

1-1/4 in.

1/2 in.

Standard version, 3/4 in. thick by 8 in. tall by 18 in. long

Crosscut Basics

SET UP FOR SAFETY

Make a zero-clearance throat insert. Crosscuts produce the most tearout at the bottom edge, and a zero-clearance insert will prevent it. It will also keep small offcuts from diving into the throat of the saw.

Safe Ripping Is a 3-Step Process

GOOD BODY POSITION

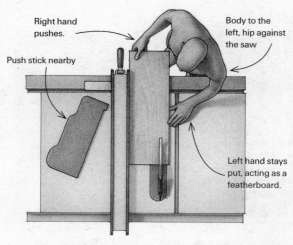

Right hand pushes.

Body to the left, hip against the saw

Push stick nearby

Left hand stays put, acting as a featherboard.

1.

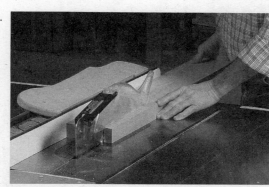

Start the cut with your hands (1), as a push stick could tip the back of the board down and the front up. When your back hand is within 6 in. of the blade, stop pushing for a moment and grab the push stick (2), keeping the board stable with your left. Finish the cut (3) with the push stick, moving your left hand safely out of the way and pushing the stock all the way past the blade. Note how the outfeed table supports the board, so you don't have to.

2.

3.

HOW TO HANDLE PLYWOOD

Safe and accurate. Focus on the area where the panel rides the rip fence, but remain aware of your hands, too, keeping them clear of the blade. Again, outfeed support is critical.

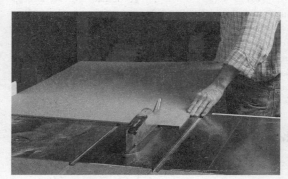

Simple job. Trace your stock insert plate onto a piece of MDF (above) of the right thickness to fit your saw, and then bandsaw it close, using a sander to work up to the line. On most saws, a 10-in.-dia. blade won't go low enough to let you insert the blank plate, so make a ripcut along the bottom to create clearance (above right). Then install the blank insert, place the rip fence on top of it, and bring the spinning blade up through it (right). Last, extend the slot with a jigsaw (below) or scrollsaw to accommodate your splitter or riving knife. You might also need to use tape or screws underneath to shim the plate level with the table.

MAKE A MITER-GAUGE FENCE

A standard miter gauge needs some help. A long fence will improve control and accuracy, tame tearout on the back edge, and push the offcut safely past the blade.

Smart, safe design. Screw a long piece of MDF to your miter gauge, cut a slot through it, and then attach a wood block (as shown) on the back edge where the blade emerges.

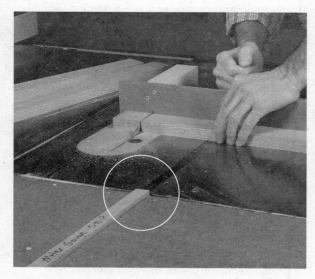

Stick trick. The slots in your outfeed table, designed to accommodate miter gauges and sled runners, are the perfect spot for a simple stick that limits their travel, making sure the blade doesn't pass through the safety block (or box) at the back of the fence.

ACCURATE CROSSCUTTING

Zero clearance is your friend. After cutting one end of the stock square, mark the length at the other end, and use the slot in your miter-gauge fence to set up the final cut.

Set the stop. The long MDF auxiliary fence lets you set up a stop at the far end for cutting a series of workpieces to the same length.

Perfect support. With a big, stable bed, and two runners in the miter slots, a crosscut sled cuts big workpieces with unmatched accuracy. Again, you can clamp stops to the fence. For longer workpieces, clamp a hook-type stop above the workpiece (see above).

CROSSCUT SLED IS BEST

For the most accurate crosscuts of all, even on large panels, nothing beats a crosscut sled.

Cutting Joinery on the Tablesaw

by Marc Adams

In my previous article, I demonstrated how to get better ripcuts and crosscuts—and stay safe in the process. But the tablesaw can do more than make rectangles. If you add a dado set and a few shopmade jigs and fixtures, it can become your favorite machine for cutting flawless joinery, too. The tablesaw offers an unmatched combination of accuracy, repeatability, speed, control, and endless jig potential.

To produce joint-quality cuts, both across the grain and with it, you'll need two types of blades. You can stick with your normal combination blade, but make sure you keep the teeth clean of pitch buildup. A clean blade will always cut better. For wider notches in wood, whether rabbets, dadoes, grooves, tenons, or lap joints, I use an 8-in. stack dado set. Quality is very important here. You need a set that cuts clean edges and flat bottoms.

A dado set's inside and outside blades have angled teeth designed to eliminate tearout at the edges of the cut. A variety of chipper blades go between, allowing $1/4$-in.- to $7/8$-in.-wide dadoes. Thin shims go in to fine-tune the width, if necessary. Be aware that dado sets take big cuts and can cause underpowered saws to bog down, and that the shorter arbors on some portable saws won't allow the full stack to be used.

Add a Few Key Jigs and Fixtures

You can cut most of the common joints on the tablesaw with just four simple jigs and fixtures: a zero-clearance throat plate, a miter-gauge extension fence, a crosscut sled, and a sacrificial fence for rabbeting. I showed how to make the first three in my earlier article, and I'll cover the last one here.

The cool thing about learning the fundamental joints, like dadoes and rabbets, is that the same techniques work for many others, such as laps, tongues, and bridle joints. In fact, the design of a tablesaw invites a host of joints and jigs. This article is just the beginning. Soon you'll be calling this versatile machine "the variety saw," like I do.

Two Kinds of Blades Do It All

DADO

For many joinery cuts, you'll need a good dado set. Get the best stack-type dado set you can afford. It should cut slots with clean edges and flat bottoms.

Continued ➡

COMBO

A basic combination blade is fine for miters and grooves. For the cleanest cuts, buy a good one and keep its teeth free of pitch.

The Simple Groove

Grooves are the easiest joint to cut. Since they are aligned with the grain, you can use the rip fence to guide the workpiece. I normally use my combo blade, adjusting the fence and taking multiple passes for a wider groove. If the bottom needs to be dead flat, you can also use your dado set.

The advantage of the single blade is that it lets you use a riving knife to prevent kickback. If your saw doesn't have one, you can use a shopmade stub splitter.

In any case, always use a push stick or push pads to maintain good control while keeping your fingers safe (you can't see the blade until it exits the board). Pay special attention to keeping the workpiece flat at the point of contact.

Ride the fence. Adams makes grooves with a single blade, making multiple cuts for wider grooves. A long push stick gives better downward pressure and control.

Use a push pad for short pieces. On these shorter drawer sides, a push pad, lined with rubber and/or sandpaper, gives better control.

Clean Dadoes

A dado is a groove cut across the grain and is usually sized precisely for a second piece to fit into. Since dadoes are crosscuts, tearout can be a problem without a zero-clearance surface below the cut. If the back edge will show, you'll need zero clearance there, too. You can use a variety of fences to make a dado cut safely, but it depends on the size of the workpiece and location of the dado. On wide workpieces with the dado close to the end of the piece, you can run the stock against the rip fence.

But the crosscut sled is my favorite tool for dadoing, because it carries pieces with excellent control and great accuracy. That control is especially important because you can't use a splitter or riving knife in conjunction with a dado set on most saws. A crosscut sled also accepts all types of stops.

NEAR AN EDGE, RIDE THE FENCE

Tame tearout. You'll need a fresh throat plate to prevent tearout. Adams showed how to make these in his earlier article. Insert a blank one, position the rip fence to hold it down without getting in the way of the blade, and then bring the dado set up through it.

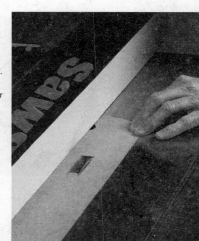

Push pad stars again. A push pad works better than a push stick to keep a big panel down on the table and tight to the rip fence.

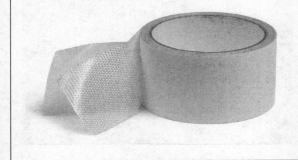

> **TIP**
>
> ### Carpet Tape Grips Better
>
> To add holding power to jigs, Adams uses double-sided carpet tape with mesh inside. It is thicker and far stronger than the thin plasticky type.

Accurate Rabbets

To cut rabbets, you should bury the dado set in a sacrificial rip fence. This makes it easy to adjust the width of the rabbet: You simply nudge the fence a bit instead of fine-tuning the width of the dado stack.

But a sacrificial fence can be hard to clamp to the short sides of a standard rip fence without the clamps getting in the way. My solution is to build a simple MDF box that fits snugly over the fence, and then tape the sacrificial piece to that. The box allows the sacrificial fence to be removed and replaced easily, on either side, so it works with the fence on either side of the blade. And a single piece of MDF can be positioned four different ways to extend its use.

IN THE MIDDLE, USE A SLED

Refresh your crosscut sled. To prevent tearout on a sled, tape down a piece of 1/4-in.-thick MDF (above). Do the same on the fence (below), and then cut a zero-clearance slot through both.

Why the sled is best. A crosscut sled controls workpieces of almost any size, and is a must for the middle dadoes on these long bookcase sides. A hook-style stop offers a long reach and is easy to attach.

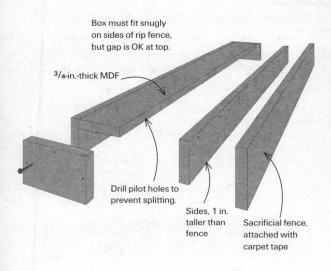

Box must fit snugly on sides of rip fence, but gap is OK at top.

¾-in.-thick MDF

Drill pilot holes to prevent splitting.

Sides, 1 in. taller than fence

Sacrificial fence, attached with carpet tape

Fast, accurate rabbets. Whether the rabbets are along the edge (above) or end of a workpiece (right), you can run the workpiece against the fence. But you'll need a zero-clearance throat plate to prevent tearout when working across the grain. Push pads do a good job controlling the workpiece, but you'll need to support narrow workpieces with the miter gauge.

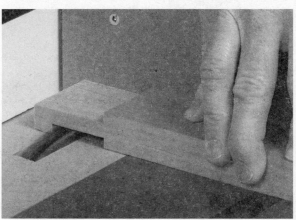

Quick Tenons

One way to cut tenons on the tablesaw is to first make shoulder cuts with the pieces lying flat, and then make the cheek cuts using a tenoning fixture. But my favorite method is to cut them with a dado set, which is faster and easier and works on larger workpieces. Long pieces are a problem on a tenoning jig, because they have to stand straight up in the air. With a dado set, the workpiece lies flat on the table, where it is easier to control.

You can control the work with a miter gauge and use the rip fence as the stop. You'll need a zero-clearance throat plate to prevent tearout at the shoulders. I stack my dado set to about ¾ in. wide, and I always start with the stock against the rip fence for the first cut and then nibble away the rest. Do not lift the stock when you finish a cut; just keep a tight grip as you pull it back.

Start with the two opposite cheeks, testing the fit in one of your mortises as you dial in the setup. Then change the blade height to trim the tenons to width. You'll notice that the outside blades leave fine lines on the surface, but these will not affect joint strength. Some woodworkers leave the tenon a bit fat and finish the job with a shoulder or rabbeting plane. Using a test mortise, I am able to get a good fit right off the tablesaw.

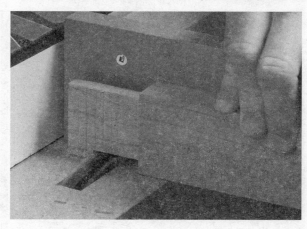

Tenons in minutes. Set the rip fence to position the first cut at the shoulder (top), and make a series of nibbling cuts (center) to finish the job. To cut the top and bottom of the tenon, change the height of the blades if necessary and just flip the workpiece on edge (bottom).

How to get a snug fit. Cut the sides 1 in. taller than the rip fence, and long enough to allow clearance for the lever at the end. Clamp the sides in place to measure for the top plate and attach it as shown. Drill pilot holes to prevent splitting. Keep the clamps on as you screw on the end caps.

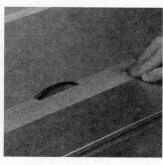

Add the fence and bury the blades. Use thick carpet tape to attach a tall MDF fence (above), then move the fence over the top of the dado set and bring the spinning blades up into it (left), only as high as needed.

TIP

Get Square First

To get even tenon shoulders, you need a perfectly square miter gauge. You can place a square or drafting triangle against the blade to check, but inconsistencies in the fence or blade

can throw it off. Instead, do this simple test. It works for squaring up fences and blades for all sorts of joinery tasks. Rip parallel edges on a long piece of scrap, and mark one side for reference. Make a crosscut (above) and then flip one of the pieces. Set both against a straight surface like the rip fence (below). A gap means you need to adjust the miter gauge and try again.

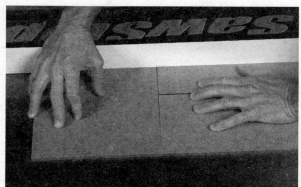

Tight Miters on a Crosscut Sled

The most common type of miter is the flat type used to join frame pieces. They often surround a plywood panel to make a door or a tabletop, and standard moldings are cut this way, too.

The challenge with flat miters is the wide cut, which makes it hard to end up with a 90° corner and no gaps. If you rely on your miter gauge, you will struggle with accuracy and repeatability. That's why I cut them on my crosscut sled using a simple 45° fence. You use the sled to make the fence, too, and the whole process is easy.

In this case, with flat stock and zero-clearance below the blade, you could keep the fence in one position for all of the miter cuts, simply flipping the pieces to miter the second side. But if the front of the stock is molded or you are getting chipout on the bottom edge, you'll want to flip the fence to the other side of the blade when cutting the second end of each piece, in order to keep the same side up.

Aside from accuracy, what I love about this setup is how easy it is to attach a stop: You just tape it down.

Continued ➜

MAKE AN ACCURATE FENCE

Start with a perfectly square piece of MDF and use your crosscut sled to turn it into an accurate 45° fence.

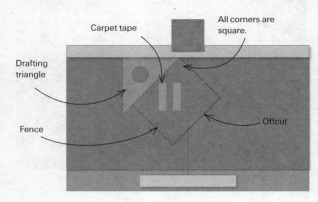

Carpet tape
All corners are square.
Drafting triangle
Fence
Offcut

HOW IT'S USED

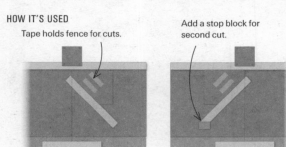

Tape holds fence for cuts.
Add a stop block for second cut.

Easy to make. Use a 45° drafting triangle to position the MDF fence on the sled. Use carpet tape to hold it down, but keep the triangle in place as you cut, to be sure the workpiece doesn't shift.

Miter one end of each workpiece. Put the fence on the left or right, pressing it down very firmly on the carpet tape, and then use it to miter one end of each workpiece. Hold the workpiece firmly to be sure it doesn't drift.

Switch sides. Flip the fence over to set it up on the other side. This time you'll need a stop to set the final length of each piece, but that's as simple as taping a block to the sled. The miters should come out perfect.

Bandsaw Tips and Fundamentals

by Michael Fortune

In my first year of design school in the early 1970s, I remember the shop manager telling me that the bandsaw was the most useful piece of equipment in a woodshop. This struck me as a dubious statement, given that we were standing in a workshop filled with state-of-the-art European woodworking equipment. But time and again he proved it.

After I graduated in 1974, my first purchase was a 15-in. General bandsaw. However, I soon realized I could achieve the accuracy and versatility I had experienced at school only if I set up the saw the way my shop manager did.

Once I figured out the keys to success, I came to rely on that bandsaw. With a single blade, I routinely cut smooth tenon cheeks, fine inlay stringing, and perfect veneers that use the entire height capacity of my machine.

I also do all of my ripping on that 15-in. bandsaw. The task is safer and requires less horsepower than the tablesaw, and the narrow kerf consumes less wood. New employees and students are surprised at first by my preference for ripping on the bandsaw, but they are converted quickly.

Although I have three excellent industrial tablesaws in my shop, they are used almost exclusively for dadoing, squaring panels, and cutting shoulders on joints.

There are three key elements to getting the most from your bandsaw: blade type, blade alignment, and moderate tension. My approach contradicts some of the common advice for setting up bandsaws. It does not require high blade tension, special equipment, exotic blades, high horsepower, or continual fence adjustments to accommodate blade drift.

Start with a Coarse Blade

During teaching assignments, I run into many woodworkers experiencing difficulties with their bandsaws. They complain about severely cupped kerfs, poor tracking, and saws that seem underpowered, so their bandsaws are relegated to cutting curves in thin stock.

The number-one culprit behind all of these difficulties is a bandsaw blade that has too many teeth, with small gullets in between. Sawdust generated in the kerf must be removed efficiently. A tremendous amount of heat is created by the friction from the sawdust that is jam-packed in each small gullet right at the point where the wood fibers are being cut. The intense heat can cause the blade to lose

 TIP 1

A Single Blade Can Handle Most Tasks

A 1/2-in.-wide, 3-tpi blade—properly set up—will handle general ripcuts, resawing, and even cutting curves in thin stock, not to mention cutting precise tenons.

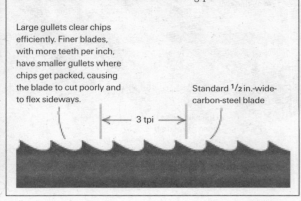

Large gullets clear chips efficiently. Finer blades, with more teeth per inch, have smaller gullets where chips get packed, causing the blade to cut poorly and to flex sideways.

Standard 1/2 in.-wide-carbon-steel blade

3 tpi

its temper and dull prematurely. The heat and pressure buildup also can cause the blade to flex sideways and backward, creating a dished cut. A typical reaction here is to tighten the tension on the blade. But overtensioning the blade creates a whole new set of problems (see Tip 2).

My bandsaw does everything, every day: cutting joints, resawing wide laminates in exotic woods, making curved patterns in 1/16-in.-thick stock. It is not practical to change the blade and the guide blocks for each situation, nor is it necessary, in fact.

With rare exception, a standard carbon-steel 1/2-in.-wide, 3-tpi, skip-tooth blade installed on my bandsaw performs all of the above tasks.

Blades are inexpensive, so keep a sharp one loaded— The blades I use are made by Starrett but are welded and distributed by BC Saw and Tool in Canada. By delightful coincidence, these blades are relatively inexpensive. It helps that I buy them in groups of 10, which earns me a 25% discount.

Unfortunately, not all blade distributors weld bandsaw blades properly. A poorly welded, misaligned sawblade will not give you the smooth and effortless results you are after.

Simply using a 3-tpi blade, with its larger gullets, will eliminate many problems. Even 4 tpi is too fine a tooth pattern for general woodworking and resawing. If you want a fine cut, use a coarse blade, even on thin stock. In my experience, the old rule of thumb about having two teeth engaged in the stock at all times is bogus. The reason I use a 1/2-in.-wide blade is that it is stiff enough to resaw but flexible enough to follow a curve down to a 2 1/2-in. radius. A cautionary note: Cutting particleboard is extremely hard on carbon-steel bandsaw blades and can reduce their life by 75%.

High horsepower is another myth—For most 14-in. bandsaws with a 1/2-in.-wide, 3-tpi blade, a 1/3-hp motor is fine. The same saw with a riser block in the column could use a 1/2-hp motor for big resawing tasks, but anything larger is overkill. If the motor is bogging down, you are either forcing the cut or using a dull blade.

Don't Overtension the Blade

It is important that the tires on the bandsaw remain in excellent shape. Grooves in the rubber tire on either the upper or the lower wheel will make it impossible to keep the blade on the centerline, in line with the rip fence. And the most common cause of grooves in the tires is overtensioned blades. Very high tension even can flex the saw frame out of alignment.

I slightly undertension my 1/2-in.-wide blade. Because of its excellent ability to clear sawdust, the blade is not inclined to flex, wander, or heat up. For the 1/2-in.-wide blade I adjust the tension scale to the 3/8-in. setting. If no scale is present on the machine, I tighten the adjustment knob (with the machine off and unplugged) until the blade deflects about 1/4 in. to the side without making my fingertips go white.

High Blade Tension Is Not Necessary

High tension eventually will groove the tires, pulling the blade out of alignment (for more on blade alignment, see Tip 3). High tension even can flex the machine's frame out of alignment.

Use less than the recommended tension. For a 1/2-in.-wide blade, turn the tension gauge (above) to the setting for a 3/8-in.-wide blade. The first step in overhauling a bandsaw is to check the tires for grooves (left). If necessary, replace them.

A side benefit of lower blade tension is that I seldom have to release the tension on the saw, as is commonly recommended to prolong blade life.

Align the Blade to Eliminate Drift

When I bought my bandsaw in 1974, I set the fence parallel to the miter-gauge slot in the table, and I haven't had to adjust it since. The reason is that I use the tracking adjustment on the upper bandsaw wheel to align the blade. A nightmare of fence adjustments ensues if each new blade is allowed to track differently.

Simply by keeping the centerline of the blade (regardless of width) in line with the centerline of the upper wheel, I am able to keep the blade aligned correctly at the blade guides.

The relationship between tracking the blade on the centerline of the upper wheel and having the fence aligned parallel to the miter slot should produce a kerf with equal space on either side of the blade.

Much has been made in books and articles of the alignment of the two wheels to each other. In my shop and in my travels to schools around North America, I have never found this to be a problem. Tracking the blade properly on the upper wheel has always been enough, except in the case of a severely damaged bandsaw.

Now square the table and align the fence—The table is now aligned with the cutting direction, but it also should be adjusted so that it is square with the vertical line of the blade.

Last, the fence should be aligned parallel to the blade and square to the table. I use a 3 1/2-in.-high birch plywood rip fence screwed onto the mtal fence. I have shimmed the plywood with masking tape to get it perpendicular to the table. Taller plywood fences can be screwed to the existing plywood fence, but I use these only when I am resawing to the maximum capacity of my bandsaw, about 6 1/2 in.

Use Metal Guide Blocks, Set Close

Again, simple is the way to go. When setting up my bandsaw in 1974, I took out the metal guide blocks and squared their working faces against the side of the wheel on my bench grinder, being careful to check the blocks for square. I have not had to replace them or resquare them since.

The sequence for setting the guide blocks is as follows. Unplug the saw, pull the guides well back, tension the blade, and then spin it a few times backward and forward by hand. Now turn on the saw and adjust the tracking of the blade to center it on the upper wheel.

Next, turn off the saw again, and bring the guide assembly forward so that the front of the blocks aligns with the back of the blade's gullets. Then adjust each guide block to within the thickness of cigarette paper, or 0.001 in., of the blade. The Allen screw might pull the blocks in or out when they are tightened, so this process could require one or two attempts. With practice, you will be able to adjust the guides by eye, looking for the smallest crack of light between the blade and the guide blocks.

Last, bring the thrust bearing in the rear to within 1/32 in. of the blade. This bearing is the only part that requires replacing, when it becomes stiff or scarred. But it is a standard part and can be bought in most automotive- or bearing-supply houses.

With the guide blocks set this close, and with the back of the gullets just aligned with the front of the blocks, there is no room for the blade to twist or for the teeth to hit the metal guide blocks.

You Can Eliminate Blade Drift by Adjusting the Tracking

Advice on blade alignment usually centers on the rip fence instead of the blade. You can eliminate blade drift by adjusting the position of the blade on the upper wheel.

ADGUST THE ALIGNMENT OF THE BLADE, NOT THE FENCE
First, align the rip fence parallel with the miter-gauge slot and leave it there. Then eliminate blade drift by centering the blade on the upper wheel. The upper wheel has a slight crown on it. Therefore, if the blade is close to the front of the upper wheel, it will be angled on the wheels, causing the saw to cut to the right. If the blade is close to the back of the wheel, the reverse will be true.

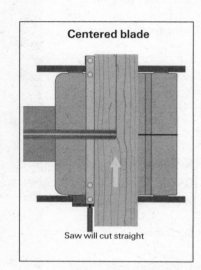

Centered blade

Saw will cut straight

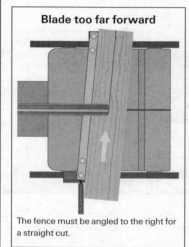

Blade too far forward

The fence must be angled to the right for a straight cut.

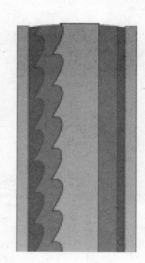

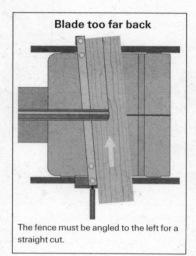

Blade too far back

The fence must be angled to the left for a straight cut.

ALIGN THE FENCE JUST ONCE

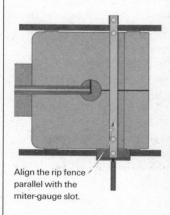

Align the rip fence parallel with the miter-gauge slot.

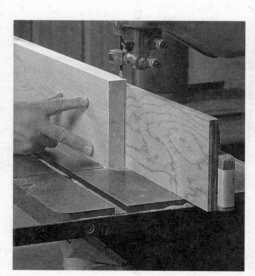

Now push gently and let the blade do the work. Pushing too hard will make the blade flex sideways, which will cause it both to overheat and to drift off line. With the blade, fence, and guides properly aligned and adjusted, the back of the blade should be centered in its kerf (inset).

Continued →

If I thought there was some advantage to replacing the guides or the blocks, then I would, but I find the original system gives me excellent results. With the blade and fence aligned properly, the metal guide blocks are not rubbing constantly against one side of the blade or the other and creating friction heat.

The lower guides are set in the same way as the upper ones, though I often leave them backed slightly away from the blade, unless I am resawing particularly difficult wood. I have worked in several shops in Europe, and none of the bandsaws I used there had lower bearing assemblies.

Feed Stock with Mild Pressure

With the saw properly set up, it is necessary to place only two of your fingers against the workpiece: You should be able to use one finger to push the stock and the other to hold it against the rip fence. If you have to use the butt of your hand to push the stock, something is wrong—either the blade is dull or it is no longer tracking on the center-line of the upper wheel and is misaligned with the fence, causing the wood to bind.

Use mild but consistent feed pressure, allowing the blade to do the work. The sawdust must have a chance to be cleared from the kerf. For safety, once your pushing fingers are within 6 in. of the blade, use a push stick.

 TIP 4

Replacement Guides Aren't Necessary

A set of metal guide blocks will keep your blades on track for many years. The key is to set them very close to the blade and just behind the gullets.

Closer than you might think. Many people use a dollar bill for setting the blocks, which keeps them 0.003 in. away from each side. Cigarette paper (or a feeler gauge) will set each block closer to 0.001 in. away, resulting in smoother, more precise cuts.

Other important guide settings. The guide assembly should be adjusted so that the metal blocks remain just behind the blade's gullets. Then the thrust bearing is set 1/32 in. behind the blade, as shown, so it contacts the blade only during use.

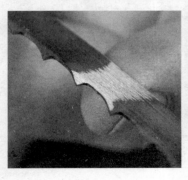

The blade weld must be smooth. A good sawblade company will weld blades precisely and grind the welded area flat. After setting the guides, turn the wheel by hand to be sure the weld passes through the guides smoothly.

 TIP 5

Add Dust Collection to Keep Your Saw Running Well

Sawdust extraction is very important. Wood dust will get compressed onto the lower wheel by the revolving blade. The resulting bumps will cause the blade to vibrate and wander off center.

Many saws provide for some dust extraction directly below the cutting area, but that isn't enough. Attach a second dust pickup at the lower left corner, where the air current generated by the lower wheel makes dust accumulate.

Also, attach a wooden brush with stiff natural bristles to the frame of the saw so that it continually cleans off the lower wheel. The lower dust port will catch the debris.

Collect dust at two points. Many bandsaws have dust collection below the cutting area, but Fortune also recommends installing a vacuum port at the bottom left of the lower wheel. If dust and pitch build up on the tires, the blade will not track properly. Install a brush (left) to remove dust from the lower wheel.

Miter Saw Basics

by Marc Adams

Because miter saws were not around when many of us took a high school shop class (remember the radial-arm saw?), the majority of us were never taught how to use them. The hosts of those television DIY shows are no help.

Although relatively lightweight and portable, the "chopsaw" deserves as much respect as any machine in the shop. It certainly carries as much potential danger. On the other hand, it is capable of more than you might know.

With a few tips and upgrades, you'll be able to do almost all of your crosscutting and mitering on the miter saw, like I do, getting furniture-quality cuts in half the time it takes to drag out your crosscut sled. Of course, the miter saw is also the quickest way to rough-cut lumber to size, and I have tips for that, too.

My tips and techniques are based on the type of saw that I favor, the simple chopsaw (see "Basic chopsaw is better for woodworking"), but many will work for sliding miter saws, too.

A Few Key Upgrades

The first step is to replace the blade that came with your saw. It will struggle through big hardwood lumber, and it won't have enough teeth for the finest cuts. You don't have to buy the most expensive one, but do get a good blade designed for a miter saw.

Basic Chopsaw Is Better for Woodworking

Designed for carpenters and contractors of all stripes, miter saws come in a bewildering variety of configurations. One advantage of running a woodworking school is that I get to purchase lots of tools and learn which features are truly worthwhile. For woodworkers, I've found that the simple chopsaw is the best bet and the most accurate. You don't need to pay extra for a big sliding model if you have a tablesaw and crosscut sled for wider stock.

But the cost savings don't end there. You also can skip the double-bevel feature, since you'll get better cuts when pivoting the head rather than tilting it. And I'm not a fan of laser guides. They don't work in every blade position, and they need regular adjustment.

On the other hand, I would go for the full 12-in. blade over the 10-in. size, and I'd make sure the saw has an automatic brake (most do) that stops the blade when the trigger is released. You'll see why shortly. Another feature I find handy is a miter range of 50° or more.

With any crosscutting tool, you have to deal with tearout. One of the best ways to enhance your miter saw is to add a zero-clearance throat plate and a sacrificial fence. These simple upgrades do three great things: They eliminate chipout at the bottom and back edges of the cut; they show you exactly where the blade will cut, at any angle, making it easy to line up a mark accurately; and they make the saw safer, preventing small offcuts from getting trapped against the blade and kicking back at you.

To tame tearout along the bottom edge, some woodworkers cover the base of the saw with a full layer of plywood, but I prefer to replace the throat plate. That way, you don't lose thickness capacity. Also, the saw always comes down in the same slot, even when pivoted for miter cuts, so you don't have to replace that shopmade plate unless you change blades or make a bevel cut with the head tilted.

I've made these inserts successfully for at least five different brands of saw. Just trace the standard plastic insert on a piece of 1/4-in.-thick MDF. Then bandsaw and sand the edges to fit. If necessary, you can plane the insert to bring it flush with the surface. To install it, you can use thick (exterior grade) carpet tape, or redrill the screw holes and use those.

To prevent tearout along the back edge of the board, you can't easily make a sacrificial insert in the metal fence. So I use a full layer of plywood there, which does steal some width capacity. I recommend 1/2-in.-thick MDF or plywood cut roughly 6 ft. long and just wide (tall) enough to fit under the motor or handle in its lowest position. The extra length comes in handy for attaching stops. Again I use carpet tape to hold the fence in place, making it easy to change. You'll need to replace it when you change cutting angles.

Using stops for repeat cuts is one of the best moves you can make on a miter saw. You can place them on either side of the saw, but for shorter cuts, the stop might need to go on the opposite side from the motor to avoid bumping it.

The Right Technique Makes All the Difference

All miter saws have a degree of slop in the arbor, which allows blade runout. That's why proper technique is so critical to getting accurate cuts.

I don't actually like the term "chopsaw" because it reminds me of words like "hack" and "slash." Forcing the blade will make it deflect and wobble. Also, a blade with more teeth needs more time to get through the wood. On the other hand, if you go too slowly, you'll get a burnt or burnished cut. So let the blade cut at its own pace— not yours. Go by feel. The same blade will cut differently in soft and hard wood, through larger and smaller workpieces.

If yours is a sliding model, pull it all the way toward you before lowering it and pushing it through the cut. Again, go by feel.

The second important rule is to let the blade come to a stop before raising it back up through the cut. The cutting action tends to stabilize the blade, but it can wobble again when the cut is done. Also, you tend to raise the blade faster than you cut with it. That's why you will hear that "twangggg" sound when you bring a spinning blade back up through the cut, and will see deep sawmarks.

If the brake is working well, you'll only have to wait a couple of seconds for the blade to stop, but the quality of the cut will be considerably better. So force yourself to develop this habit.

Miters vs. bevels—Because of the way the guard works, I do not like using a miter saw's bevel function, in other words, tilting the head. There is just too much blade exposure, and it ruins the zero-clearance insert. It also puts the weight of the motor on the side of its pivot point, causing it to flex sideways as you pull it downward, compromising the cut.

The good news is that you can stand a narrow board up against the fence, turning a wobbly bevel cut into an accurate miter cut. There is also a great trick for avoiding compound-angled (bevel and miter) cuts on crown molding, turning those into simple miters, too.

Coax extra width out of your saw—There are a number of ways to get more width capacity from your saw. This is most often a problem when cutting rough lumber to approximate length, and usually on a chopsaw. Sliding miter saws are not my favorite, but they do have significantly more cutting capacity.

First let's cover an important safety tip. When cutting bowed, twisted, or cupped boards, always make sure the stock is touching the fence and base in the cutting area. Otherwise it will dive down or backward as you finish the cut, pinching and binding dangerously against the blade.

The first tip is that if your cut leaves ½ in. or less to be nicked off at the end, you often can simply lift the front edge of the board a bit to finish the cut. The other trick for rough lumber is to make as wide a cut as possible and then let the blade stop, flip the board over, realign the blade with the kerf or mark, and finish the job.

For accurate, furniture-quality cuts, I have another handy tip. Just put some scrapwood underneath to raise up your stock to the bigger part of the blade. You can add an inch or more to the width of the cut this way on a 12-in.-dia. blade.

A Few More Safety Tips

In 2010, the University of Cincinnati did a study at our school on woodshop noise levels. The miter saw produced more decibels than any other tool in the shop. So always wear ear muffs or plugs, and of course, protect your eyes at all times.

Never cross your arms. Most people do this when cutting miters, choosing to use their normal trigger hand no matter which way the miter is pointing. Miter-saw triggers will work with either hand, and for miter cuts you want to stand opposite where the saw is pointing. That might mean putting the board on the opposite side you are used to, and switching hands. This will give you better visibility and help you hold the stock more tightly so it isn't pulled sideways by the blade. Another time you might want to switch hands is to hold onto the piece that is trapped against a stop.

I have a 3-in. rule on all power tools, making sure my hands always stay out of this danger zone. So for smaller pieces, I use a special stop and hold-down to keep the stock safely in place against the fence and table. These are easy to make.

So make a few upgrades to your saw, let it come to a stop after each cut, and follow a few simple rules. Then you'll really see what a miter saw can do.

Set Up for Success: Zero Clearance Is Essential

This is a crosscutting tool, so without sacrificial surfaces below and behind the cut, you'll get tearout.

Replace the plate. Remove the stock throat plate and trace around it (left) onto ¼-in.-thick MDF. Saw and sand it to fit, and then screw it into place (above), or attach it with carpet tape. You might have to plane the MDF to make it flush with the base.

Cut the slot. Make a cut through the plate and fence, and say good-bye to tearout. The zero-clearance slots also show exactly where the blade will cut, making it easy to line up a mark precisely.

Add a fence. A 6-ft.-long piece of ½-in. MDF or plywood makes a good sacrificial fence. Attach it with carpet tape.

SIMPLE BUT EFFECTIVE STOP

This basic stop block hangs on the fence. The cleat keeps it square to the blade, with a slight gap between it and the table so dust doesn't interfere.

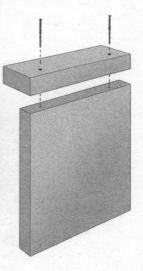

Using a stop safely. Always hold the workpiece on the stop side. That part is trapped against the blade, and should be controlled at all times.

Advantages of Table-Mounting

If you can dedicate some counter space to your saw, there are a number of advantages.

Better work support. Bolt down the saw and build long boxes to extend the fences and support long boards and stops.

Continued ➜

SIMPLE SUPPORTS, SNAZZIER STOPS

Adams bolts his saw in place, and also screws down these work supports, so their fences line up with the center insert. Shim the saw to bring it level.

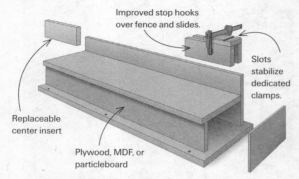

Improved stop hooks over fence and slides.

Slots stabilize dedicated clamps.

Replaceable center insert

Plywood, MDF, or particleboard

Replaceable insert. You don't have to replace the whole fence every time you make a miter cut and ruin the zero-clearance slot. You just replace the center insert, which is held in place with carpet tape.

Get Furniture-Quality Cuts

You can get smooth, accurate cuts of all kinds with this lightweight machine. Proper technique is the key.

THREE STEPS TO CLEAN CUTS
Power up. Let the blade get to full speed before lowering it.

1.

2.

Let it cut. It takes time to get 100 teeth through a big piece of wood, so let the blade cut at its own pace.

3.
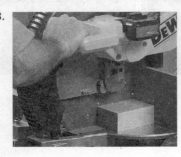

Now wait. This is the most important part. Let the blade come to a full stop before lifting it or moving the stock. This is where an automatic brake speeds things up.

Perfect Miters

NO

Stay away from the blade. Pivoting the saw toward your body (left) is less safe and makes it hard to reach in and hold the stock steady. Change hands and stand on the other side (below) to give yourself more room.

YES

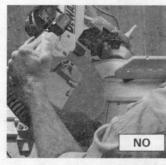
NO

Turn tricky bevels into happy miters. A miter-saw motor is less stable when tilted on its side (left), affecting the quality of the cut on this base molding. Also, too much of the blade is exposed. By standing the molding up (below), you turn a bevel cut into a safer, more accurate miter.

YES

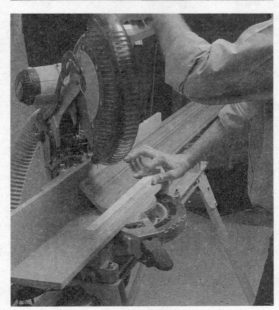

Convert compound angles, too. Laid flat on the saw, this crown molding would require a combination miter and bevel cut. Add a sacrificial base to the saw with a cleat that stands the molding up in its installed position. Then you can make a simple 45° miter cut for perfect joints.

Going Bigger and Smaller

Get More Width in a Pinch
When chopping up boards into rough lengths, the saw's width capacity often falls short. These tricks add capacity.

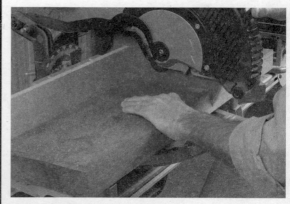

Lift it. If you have only a sliver of wood left (above), you can safely lift the near edge into the spinning blade (left) to finish the cut.

Flip it. To almost double your cutting capacity, make a full cut on one side (above), and then flip the board to finish the job (left).

A trick for fine cuts, too. To add an inch or more to a cut without compromising the quality, raise the board on a sacrificial piece in order to use a wider portion of the blade.

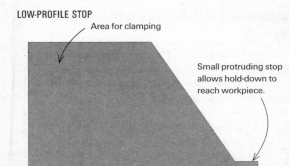

Area for clamping

Small protruding stop allows hold-down to reach workpiece.

LONG HOLD-DOWN

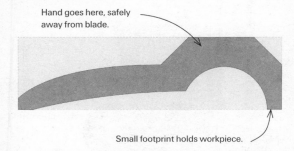

Hand goes here, safely away from blade.

Small footprint holds workpiece.

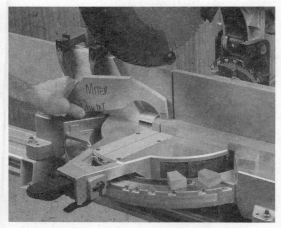

Cut precise pieces. A low-profile stop and special hold-down let Adams safely control small, precise parts for segmented turnings, for example.

Trim veneers cleanly. Veneers (and plastics) will shatter on the miter saw, but if you hold them down with a sacrificial board (above), you can get a perfect cut on a whole stack (bottom).

Three Essential Routers

by Jeff Miller

Doing a quick inventory of my shop recently, I discovered that over the years I have accumulated nine routers. Nine! How did that happen? Does the average woodworker really need that many routers?

The short answer, happily, is no. Still, the argument for having more than one router is powerful. You can leave one in your router table and have another for handheld work. Second, adding a router with particular strengths can make certain tasks much more convenient, whether you're cutting edge profiles with large, heavy bits or routing shallow hinge mortises on narrow stock.

There are many router types available, but which ones do you really need? I'll suggest two approaches. Either one will tackle a wide range of work, but the first is kinder to your wallet.

For Good Value, Start With a Combo Kit

A combination router kit (we reviewed them in "Router Combo Kits," *FWW* #173), is a very cost-effective way of setting up your shop for both table and handheld routing. The kit comes with one router motor and two bases—one fixed, one plunge. This lets you mount the fixed base in a table and keep the other for topside use.

I recommend putting the fixed base in the table, mainly because the plunge base is so much more versatile for topside use. Second, when the router is mounted in the table, it's often easier to adjust bit height with the fixed base than it is with the plunge. This makes for an economical choice—you can find a good combination kit for around $200, saving $50 to $100 or more compared with the purchase of two individual routers of a similar size and power.

To the combo kit, add a trim router. Although its limited horsepower confines it to lighter-duty tasks, it is much easier to control than a larger router. It is also limited to working with 1/4-in.-shank bits, but its lower torque and one-handed size are perfect for hinge mortising, inlay, and small edge profiles like chamfers and roundovers. It's great for any task that doesn't call for large bits, deep cuts, or lots of horsepower.

With this package of routers, you can tackle almost everything.

Stepping Up

The combination kit is a great value, but it does force a few compromises. For one, switching one motor between table and topside is much less convenient than having two individual routers. Second, in most combination kits, the motor is limited to 2 hp or 2¼ hp. If you cut deep mortises with your router or work with large shaping or panel-raising bits, you should consider investing in more horsepower. A heavy-duty plunge router like those reviewed in *FWW* #214 ("Heavy-Duty Plunge Routers") will typically come with better features than the plunge base in a combo kit. You'll get height adjustment that is easier and more accurate, a smoother plunge mechanism, and a handle-mounted power switch. Also, the 3¼ hp motor will provide smooth, effortless action on the heaviest cuts.

As another step up from the combination-kit approach, I'd recommend getting a router built to be installed in a table. Routers of this type—all of which come with a through-the-table lift—were reviewed in *FWW* #189 ("Routers for Router Tables"). This lets your router table become a dedicated shop tool with excellent controls, like a tablesaw, instead of something you have to fuss with for 15 minutes just so you can spend 30 seconds cutting an edge.

Again, add a trim router to this combination and you're set to tackle the full range of routing tasks.

1. ONE IN A ROUTER TABLE
Whenever possible, you should do your routing on a table. Moving the workpiece against a solid fence and table is simply more accurate than moving the router.

2. ONE THAT CAN PLUNGE
There are lots of tasks that can't be done on a router table, such as most stopped cuts, and cuts in the middle of large surfaces. For those jobs you'll need a handheld router, and a powerful plunge router will handle them all.

3. AND ONE IN THE HAND
While you can live without a small "trim" router, the truth is that many routing tasks are light ones, and this compact tool acts like an extension of your arm.

Kill Two Birds with One Combo Kit

A combination kit will handle both table and topside routing and costs much less than two separate routers. So you'll have plenty of money left over for a good-quality trim router. Also called laminate trimmers, these small, simple, one-handed routers are easy to set up and even easier to use.

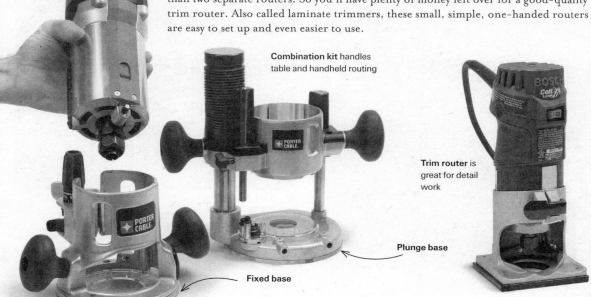

Combination kit handles table and handheld routing

Trim router is great for detail work

Plunge base

Fixed base

...ed ➡

ONE THAT CAN PLUNGE

The plunge base is best for handheld routing. The motor switches quickly between the two bases for topside use (above). The plunge function lets you lower the bit safely into the work while the tool is running. This allows you to make stopped cuts like the dadoes at right, and do them in several passes.

ONE IN THE TABLE

The fixed base lives in the table. Attach the base to the router-table insert (left). Look for a combination kit that offers through-the-table height adjustment (center). The table's flat surface and square fence simplify dozens of tasks, like routing precisely along a narrow edge (right).

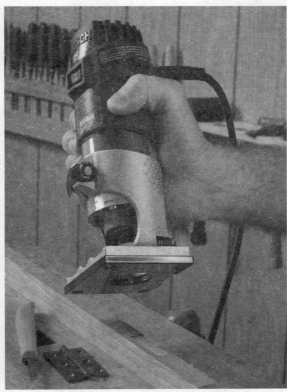

AND ONE IN THE HAND

Hinge mortises and much more. The easily balanced trim router is perfect for this application, which requires delicate control and good visibility. You'll also love it for flush-trimming face frames, inlay work, and when you need to chamfer or round over all the edges on a project.

Stand-alone Routers are a Heavy-duty Upgrade

A router combo kit will cover your table- and heldheld routing needs, but not as well as two separate routers will. A router designed for table use makes above-the-table bit changes and height adjustments easier, and also collects dust efficiently. A dedicated plunge router offers better height and plunge adjustments. And both offer bigger motors for smoother cuts.

Large router designed for router tables

Trim router for detail work

Large plunge router for handheld routing

One job to do. A dedicated table router stays put, ready for action at a moment's notice.

ONE IN THE TABLE
Easy adjustments. This Triton router (TRC001) was a favorite in past reviews of table-mounted routers. It includes an automatic spindle lock that makes above-the-table bit changes a breeze.

Bigger bits. In addition to more convenient features, a heavy-duty table router easily removes a lot of stock safely in one pass, as with this panel-raising bit.

ONE THAT CAN PLUNGE
Serious power. These maple bed posts require a mortise 1/2 in. wide and 1 1/4 in. deep. Tasks like this call for serious routing power, and extra heft helps too.

Still Not Satisfied? There's Always Room for More

Even with three versatile routers in your shop, there are some situations when it can be nice to have another router or two dedicated to specific tasks. Many woodworkers, especially pros, settle into patterns of work, and do certain jobs over and over.

A fixed-base router makes a great fourth router because it's less expensive and very simple to operate. The assembly typically has a low center of gravity and handles easily. The motor also slides into the base in a way that makes depth adjustment simple.

In my case, I often cut edge profiles with larger bits. So I keep a fixed-base router set up with an extrawide base that has a handle to help prevent tipping. I don't use it for anything else.

Or suppose that you regularly cut dovetails with a jig or cut sliding dovetails with an edge guide. You might want to have a router set up with a straight bit to clear the waste and another one set up with the dovetail bit to cut the socket.

A router for every router bit? Now that's excessive.

Ten Essential Router Bits

by Gary Rogowski

You've bought a new router, unpacked it, and even found the switch on it. But that's only half the battle. Woodworkers new to the router will encounter a bewildering array of bits that do all sorts of work. Which ones do you buy first?

High-quality router bits are not cheap, and making the wrong choices can hurt your wallet and limit your woodworking. So I've come up with a basic set of bits that will do a lot of things well, from cutting joinery to shaping profiles to pattern-routing. You can get the entire kit for around $260—well worth the money when you consider all the jobs you can complete with it.

Most of the bits in this group are carbide-tipped, which makes them more durable than high-speed steel bits but less expensive than solid carbide bits. Also, most have 1/2-in. shanks, which are less prone to breaking than bits with 1/4-in. shanks. I don't claim that these bits will be the only ones you'll ever need, but they will create a rock-solid, versatile foundation for routing that can be expanded as your woodworking repertoire expands.

Operating: Handheld vs. Table Mounted

For safety, Rogowski does most of his routing on a table, because it provides a stable worksurface. He uses a handheld router when a workpiece is too unwieldy to handle on a table or when the task simply is more suited to handheld routing, such as chopping mortises or running dadoes across a case side. When using a handheld router, work left to right. When routing on a table, work right to left.

A Basic Bit Kit

- 1/4-in. straight bit
- 1/2-in. straight bit
- 3/8-in. spiral-fluted straight bit
- Rabbeting bit with four bearings
- 1/2-in. dovetail bit
- 1/4-in. roundover bit
- 3/8-in.-radius cove bit
- 45° chamfer bit
- Three-wing slot cutter
- 1/2-in. flush-trimming bit

GROOVES AND DADOES

A groove is cut along the long grain of a board, while a dado is cut across the grain. A sharp straight bit makes quick work of both tasks and gives you grooves and dadoes of uniform size.

Generally, grooves are easier to cut on a router table, but it's possible to cut them with a handheld router. Use a plunge router for stopped grooves. For accuracy, you'll need to employ the router's edge guide or secure a straightedge to the workpiece to guide the router.

Dadoes often are cut in multiples and on longer, wider stock for case goods, so it makes sense to cut them with a handheld router. For speed and accuracy, it's a good idea to use a right-angle jig that clamps to the workbench and across the stock. Fed properly, the router base will be pushed by the cutting action against the fence of the jig,

ensuring a straight cut.

Make the jig out of 3/4-in.-thick plywood: Screw a fence to the base (both about 4 in. wide) at a precise 90° angle. Place the router base against the fence, then rout a dado in the base of the jig. Use that dado to align the jig with layout lines on the workpiece.

Grooves are best cut on the router table. For smooth cuts with little burning, take light passes, gradually raising the bit to full height.

Right-angle jig ensures straight dadoes. Align the dado in the jig with the layout lines on the workpiece, then clamp the jig in place.

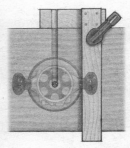

Work on this side of the fence. Then the bit's rotation will pull the router base against the jig's fence, ensuring an accurate cut.

EDGE TRIMMING

You can use straight bits to make edge cuts just like a jointer. I often use this technique on workpieces such as tabletops that are too unwieldy to clean up on a jointer.

To ensure a straight cut, make a jig a bit longer than the longest edge you need to rout. The jig should have a base of 1/4-in.-thick medium-density fiberboard (MDF) and a 3/4-in.-thick fence (see drawing, right). Start by using the router to trim the edge of the base. Then just place that edge on the line you want to cut. Be sure the cutting edge of the bit is long enough to reach past the bottom of the workpiece.

Router as jointer. With the help of a jig, you can clean up rough-sawn edges on large workpieces such as tabletops. Work from left to right.

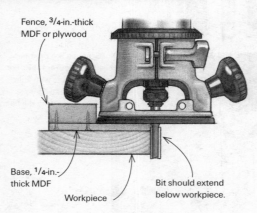

Fence, 3/4-in.-thick MDF or plywood

Base, 1/4-in.-thick MDF

Workpiece

Bit should extend below workpiece.

Use a Spiral Bit for Mortising

It's tough to find carbide-tipped spiral bits these days, so I chose a solid carbide bit for the kit. It's an expensive piece of tooling, but if you plan to cut mortises with a router, this is the bit to have. The flutes spiral around the bit, similar to the way a drill bit is cut, so it pulls chips up and out of the mortise. And with spiral flutes, there are always two cutting edges in the work, making for a smooth, shearing cut.

Mortises in a flash. Mounted in a plunge router, a spiral bit cuts a mortise easily. Use a router fence for accuracy. To prevent the router base from wobbling on narrow stock, support it with an extra piece of stock.

 TIP

Don't toss your loose bits in a drawer. If they roll around and bump into each other, the cutting edges could get chipped. Instead, hold bits in their original packaging, or drill a wood scrap to make a simple holder for the set.

Rabbeting Bit

As the name implies, a bearing-guided rabbeting bit excels at cutting rabbets of varying sizes. Although a straight bit can do the job, the bearing-guided bit ensures uniformity, an advantage if you're cutting a number of identical rabbets.

A rabbeting bit with a set of different-diameter bearings allows you to change the width of the rabbet simply by switching out the bearings. Rabbets typically are not much deeper than 1/2 in., so the set I recommend adjusts to cut rabbets from 5/16 in. to 1/2 in. wide. You can use the bit in a router table or in a handheld router.

One advantage of a bearing-guided rabbeting bit is that you can cut rabbets in frames after they have been glued together, which ensures perfect alignment. The bearing controls the rabbet's width, so there's no need for a fence to guide the cut. Move the router clockwise around the inside of the frame (see drawing, below).

PROFILING THE EDGES OF A FRAME

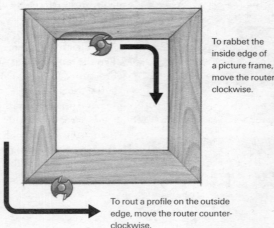

To rabbet the inside edge of a picture frame, move the router clockwise.

To rout a profile on the outside edge, move the router counterclockwise.

Three-Wing Slot Cutter, 1/4-in. Thick

A slot cutter makes grooves to a specific, consistent depth and width, with a cleaner cutting action than a straight bit. It is used mainly for cutting grooves for a frame-and-panel assembly, but it also can be used to rabbet the edges of panels and to carve decorative grooves in panels or pilasters. Each of these jobs is best done on a router table.

I chose a bit with three wings that cuts a 1/4-in. kerf. Three wings provide more balance than two. The smaller kerf allows you to cut grooves for 1/4-in.-thick panels as well as larger ones with a series of passes. You can change the depth of cut by changing the bearing.

 TIP

Buy quality bits from reputable sources. Generally, a cheap bit won't last as long as its pricier cousin because it's not as well made. You could end up spending twice as much to replace a bit that dulls prematurely, breaks, or chips.

1/2-in. Dovetail Bit

Dovetail bits are designed to make dovetails for drawers or carcases as well as sliding dovetails. Most dovetail bits have angles ranging from 7° to 14°. I prefer the 10° angle, which works well for both hard and soft woods.

Both parts of a sliding dovetail joint can be cut on a router table. Dovetail bits are made to cut full depth. So before you cut a sliding dovetail slot, run a 1/2-in. straight bit through first to clean out most of the waste. Follow with the dovetail bit. This will extend the life of the bit and leave a cleaner cut.

Cut the slot first, with the stock held flat on the table and a backer board behind it to keep the workpiece square to the fence and prevent blowout. With the bit height unchanged, reset the fence to cut the dovetail on the end of the mating piece. Make test cuts in a scrap piece the same thickness as the stock.

Sliding dovetail: solid and sturdy. Make the slot first, holding the board flat on the table (above). Leave the height of the bit as-is, and adjust the fence to cut the mating dovetail with the stock held vertically against the fence (right). Again, use a backer board to prevent tearout and to keep the workpiece aligned.

45° Chamfer Bit

The chamfer bit is used to bevel the edge of a workpiece. The 45° model I've included in this kit (1 1/4 in. dia.) is the most common. It's faster than a block plane for creating uniform chamfers on legs, aprons, and tabletops. You also can use it to achieve great visual effects (see photo, bottom right). The bearing on the bottom of the bit allows you to make cuts without a fence. To increase the depth of the chamfer, raise the bit.

Thick and thin. You can make a beefy top look thinner by chamfering the bottom edge (bottom), and a thin top look thicker by chamfering the top edge.

Eased edges. A 45° chamfer bit can soften the edges of legs, aprons, and tabletops.

1/4-in. Roundover Bit

A bearing-guided roundover bit eases sharp corners and softens the look of a piece. The 1/4-in. bit is a good moderate size to start your collection, because it will cut roundovers with or without a step (fillet) and can be used to create 1/2-in.-thick loose tenon stock as well as molding profiles (see drawings, below).

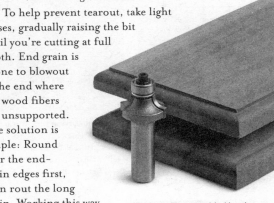

To help prevent tearout, take light passes, gradually raising the bit until you're cutting at full depth. End grain is prone to blowout at the end where the wood fibers are unsupported. The solution is simple: Round over the end-grain edges first, then rout the long grain. Working this way removes any blowout that occurs on the end grain.

Two profiles, one bit. Use the roundover bit to create a soft edge (bottom) or a rounded edge with a step, or fillet, along the top of the profile.

3/8-in.-Radius Cove Bit

Some router bits are designed simply to make decorative cuts. One example is the cove bit, which creates a simple concave edge. I use this bit often to create a hidden pull in a drawer front. Because the cove bit is designed to make profile cuts, this choice is simply a matter of taste (I like the shape). You might choose a different profile, depending on the work you do. The bonus of having both a cove and a roundover bit in your kit is that you can use the bits in tandem to create a complex profile (see photo and drawings, right), or a drop-leaf table edge if both bits are the same radius.

Hidden pull. You can use a cove bit to carve a drawer pull on the back lower edge of a drawer front.

1/2-in. Flush-Trimming Bit

With a bearing-guided flush-trimming bit, 1/2 in. dia. is pretty standard, but you could choose a different diameter if you'd like. I recommend getting a 1 1/2-in.-long bit, though, because the extra length comes in handy when working with thick stock.

The flush-trimming bit is indispensable for trimming face frames flush to carcases, and for trimming edge-banding flush.

With the flush-trimming bit, you also can duplicate pieces easily on a router table (called pattern, or template, routing). The bearing rides either against the original piece or against a pattern or template secured in a jig with hold-down clamps (see drawing, below). Before mounting the workpiece in the jig, cut away most of the waste on the bandsaw. Be careful not to rout uphill (against the grain), which could cause severe tearout. When you reach the point where the grain changes direction, reverse the workpiece in the jig.

Trim face frames flush to case. The bearing on a flush-trimming bit is the same diameter as the cutter, allowing you to bring a frame flush to a carcase using a handheld router.

Create identical parts on the router table. Cut away most of the waste on the bandsaw first, then place the workpiece in a jig with the template on top (see drawing). The bearing will ride against the template, making an exact copy of the original. Cut with the grain, and reverse the workpiece in the jig (if possible) when the grain changes direction.

PATTERN-ROUTING JIG

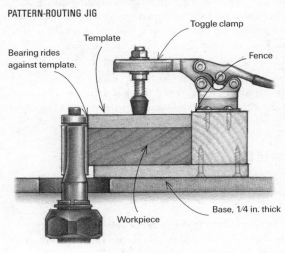

- Toggle clamp
- Template
- Bearing rides against template.
- Fence
- Workpiece
- Base, 1/4 in. thick

Roundover and Cove Bits Create a Classic Profile

You can combine roundover and cove bits to create an ogee profile with a fillet. Make the first pass with the cove bit, then finish with the roundover cutting full depth.

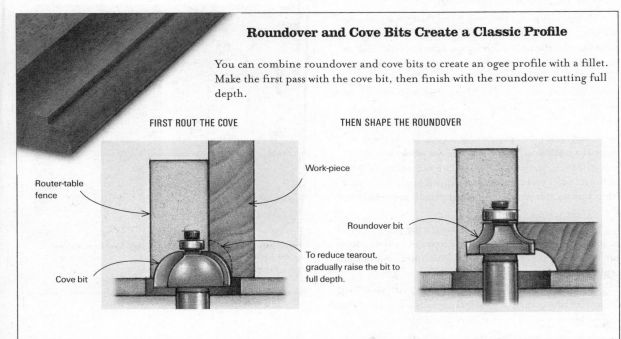

FIRST ROUT THE COVE
- Router-table fence
- Cove bit

THEN SHAPE THE ROUNDOVER
- Work-piece
- Roundover bit
- To reduce tearout, gradually raise the bit to full depth.

Drill Press Fundamentals

by Asa Christiana

There's no disputing the usefulness of a handheld drill. It's perfect in situations when you need to bring the tool to the work. It can drill pilot holes and drive screws at the bench or inside cabinets.

But that flexibility comes at a cost. A handheld drill is prone to tearout and lacks the power to drive larger bits. And even with careful layout, drilling in exactly the right place at the right angle can be hit-or-miss.

To do your best work, you need a drill press.

The drill press is all about control. It lets you precisely determine the placement and angle of the hole as well as its depth. It also provides power and leverage to drive the bit easily, even in hard stock, and it lets you raise and lower the bit repeatedly without altering the shape of the hole.

The table supports the workpiece nicely, and makes it easy to place a backer board below the hole, which prevents ugly blowout on the bottom side. You'll end up with perfect holes, plus counterbores and countersinks that are precise and chatter-free.

The drill press is a useful machine, but not an especially expensive one. It's designed for metalworking, so even the less-expensive models have plenty of power and stability for woodwork. And they are hard to damage, so it is easy to find a good used one. I bought a big, strong benchtop model out of the local classifieds for $100.

You won't want to throw out your cordless drill, but once you have a drill press in your shop, you'll appreciate the power, accuracy, and control of a real drilling machine.

First Things First

The first thing to do with a new drill press is to fit it with an auxiliary table. That's because the typical drill-press table is too small to support big workpieces. The stock table also has a big hole in the center for bit clearance. That big opening allows far too much tearout on the bottom of the workpiece.

To eliminate that problem, and to give yourself plenty of room to work, you can install one of the snazzy auxiliary tables available in woodworking catalogs. These typically feature accessories like zero-clearance plates in the middle, and handy fences that lock down quickly and accurately. Or just make your own table. It can be as simple as a piece of MDF, with the occasional fence clamped on for repetitive work. Two other accessories you'll love are a clip-on light (the top of a drill press tends to cast a shadow on the work area), and a foot-activated switch.

Continued →

Setting Up

1. ADJUST THE TABLE HEIGHT

You can raise or lower the table to accommodate any drilling task. Set the height so you'll have enough room for the bit to clear the work, but not so much travel that it makes drilling inconvenient.

2. SET THE DRILLING DEPTH

A stop on the drill-press column (below and right) lets you make repeated cuts at the same depth. Mark the desired depth on the side of the stock, plunge the bit to that point, then adjust and lock the depth stop. Plunge the bit once more to be sure it stops at the right spot.

3. ADD A FENCE FOR ALIGNMENT

Once you've established the distance between the bit and the edge of the workpiece, you can lock down the fence and drill dozens of holes in a row.

Know the Controls

The three adjustments you'll make most often are speed, table height, and plunge depth. Each of these takes less than a minute.

You can buy a variable-speed model for on-the-fly speed changes—and spend a lot more money—but I think the old-fashioned pulley-style machines offer plenty of speed settings for woodworking tasks.

On pulley-driven drill presses, you'll find a speed guide somewhere near the top of the machine, often inside the pulley cover. The recommended speed varies with the size of the bit. To quote FWW contributing editor Roland Johnson, "Basically, you should not run any bit faster than 3,000 rpm, and you should slow the speed considerably for bigger bits. For example, a 1-in.-dia. bit should run at 300 rpm to 500 rpm in hardwood."

After setting the speed, put the bit in the chuck and tighten it. Unlike modern handheld drills with keyless chucks, most drill presses still use a keyed chuck that must be tightened manually to hold the bit in place. Be sure the bit isn't bottomed out in the chuck, or hung up between two of the three jaws. The chuck is self-centering, meaning that all three jaws move in unison when the key is turned. This means it is not necessary to tighten each jaw individually. Always remove the chuck key right away! You don't want any surprises when you hit the "on" switch. Also, find a way to keep track of the chuck key. Mine hangs on a chain, but I've also seen lots of ideas for chuck-key holders, using magnets, pen caps, etc.

Now, with the bit in place and the workpiece on the table, you'll know where to set the table's height. For deep holes, you want the tip of the bit just above the workpiece so you can take advantage of the drill press's full plunge depth.

Finally, if you are not drilling all the way through the workpiece, you'll need to set the depth stop. This is easy, too: Mark the desired depth on the side of the stock, plunge the bit down to that point, spin the depth stop down until it is snug, and lock it there. Plunge the bit once to be sure it stops at precisely the right spot, and you are set.

Location, Location

Another great thing about a drill press is that you can put a fence on it. This means that once you've dialed in the distance between the bit and the edge of the workpiece, you can lock down the fence and drill dozens of holes in a row. Add a stop block to the fence, and you've locked in the hole location in both directions.

I still recommend laying out the holes carefully (or at least the first one in a series) using a crisscross mark, and sighting carefully along both axes as you bring the tip of the bit down. When it looks perfect, turn on the machine, and touch the tip down lightly to double-check the position. Fine-tune the fence or the stop if necessary.

Even if I have only one hole to drill, I still use the fence in most cases. If nothing else, it keeps the stock from spinning when the going gets tough. By the way, the lower the fence the better; tall fences sometimes get in the way of the crank handles.

How to Drill Clean Holes

Even with all this heavy-duty drilling hardware at your fingertips, getting the best results calls for some attention to the details.

To avoid burning the stock, be sure to use a sharp, high-quality bit. Also, don't set the bit speed too fast or lower the bit into the work too slowly.

Clogged chips are the only other thing that will cause burning. The solution is simple: As you feel the bit start to hesitate in the hole, withdraw it momentarily to allow the flutes to clear themselves. But here's the trick: Don't bring the bit all the way out of the hole. If you do, it will sometimes tear the rim. Just bring it up high enough to let the packed chips fly free.

Tearout is more of a problem on the bottom of the workpiece, but again prevention is painless: Make sure there is a fresh wood surface under the workpiece at the exit point. Some auxiliary tables have removable panels in the middle, and these can be flipped around to find a fresh surface. Or you can loosen the drill-press table and shift it sideways.

A simpler approach is just to keep a big piece of MDF or plywood on the table, shifting it around to find a fresh surface. When it becomes riddled with holes, you can just replace it.

There are lots more things you can do with your drill press, like tilting the table or making ramp-like jigs to drill angled holes, but I'll leave it to you to discover those.

Bits Matter, Too

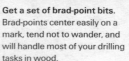

Get a set of brad-point bits. Brad-points center easily on a mark, tend not to wander, and will handle most of your drilling tasks in wood.

And a set of twist bits. You'll need them to drill metal and plastic. They also stay centered well when drilling a small hole below a larger one.

Cleaner countersinks. The drill press makes it easy to bore even countersinks of precise depth. The single-edge type with a diagonal hole through the tip makes chatter-free cuts.

Fun with Forstners. With the drill press's control over location and depth, it's an ideal setup for mortising with a Forstner bit, which can drill partial or overlapping holes (left) without wandering. The drill press also handles large Forstner bits, making it easy to drill holes as large as 2 1/8 in. diameter. The hole's flat bottom makes it ideal for applications like this hardware mortise (right).

How to use a plug cutter. Use a thick board so the cutter doesn't go through (left). Then use the bandsaw (right) to free the plugs. A piece of tape keeps the plugs on the table.

OTHER TOOLS AND ACCESSORIES

Essential Measuring and Marking Tools

by Chris Gochnour

Careful layout is important to every woodworking project. Measure or mark a part inaccurately and it almost certainly will cause problems along the way.

That point was driven home recently as I taught a woodworking class where students used mostly hand tools to build a Hepplewhite writing desk. As the class progressed, the correlation between effective layout and successful woodworking was clear. Students who carefully laid out their projects with crisp, concise markings built their desks quickly and efficiently, with fewer setbacks. Students who laid out their projects with faint and irregular markings had to work at a slower, less productive pace. Not surprisingly, the latter group took longer to complete their desks, and the quality level was not up to that of the other students.

All that led me to consider my favorite measuring and marking tools, the ones I keep within easy reach and use nearly every day. These 11 tools are as important to my work as any hand or powered cutting tool. A well-equipped workshop, I feel, should include one of each

12-in. Combination Square

The 12-in. combination square is an 8-in-1 tool that I find indispensable. Its versatility comes from the unique shape of its head and an adjustable blade that's incrementally marked as a rule.

A 12-in. combination square can be used as a long- or short-bladed try square, as well as a miter square. The adjustable rule enables it to serve as a depth gauge to verify the depth of a mortise, dado, or hole. It also can be set up as a height gauge to check tablesaw-blade or router-bit height. Used with a pencil, it can scribe lines parallel to board edges, much like a marking gauge.

A glass level vial, set in its head, verifies that things are plumb and level. As a final benefit, the blade can be removed altogether and used as a precision rule or straightedge.

Inexpensive, discount-store varieties are usually not well marked or machined. To get the most from a combination square, it's best to purchase one from a reputable maker of precision engineer's tools.

Framing Square

Another square I find useful, particularly for large-scale work, is the framing square. Although generally viewed as a carpenter's tool, it is extremely useful in the woodshop. Made from one piece of aluminum or steel, roughly 1/8 in. thick, with one arm incrementally marked to 16 in. and the other to 24 in., it serves as a jumbo try square for larger work.

Among other tasks, I use mine to lay out cut lines on panels or wide lumber, to define joinery across wide case pieces, to test the corners of panels to verify accuracy, and to check case assemblies for squareness during glue-ups.

Although framing squares are not expensive and generally are not viewed as precision tools, I've used the same one for 20 years and have never had to true it up. I treat it with care, and like an old friend, it has never let me down.

4-in. Engineer's Square

A 4-in. engineer's square is great for setting up or checking machinery blades, fences, or tables for accuracy. It also helps in verifying that stock is square and true. I use it for layout tasks where pencil or knife marks are scribed on board edges or narrow faces, as in door, chair, or frame construction. It also can be used to verify the squareness of smaller assemblies, such as doors, drawers, cases, and the like.

Made of precision-milled steel, engineer's squares are dead accurate. And they stay that way indefinitely, given proper care. They are relatively inexpensive, and the little extra spent on a reputable brand will pay for itself in the long run.

12-ft. Tape Measure

I use a steel tape for many of my day-to-day measuring tasks. Tapes range in length from 8 ft. to 25 ft.; the blade widths run from 1/2 in. to 1 in. I like a 12-ft. tape. It's long enough for most furniture-making needs, but not so heavy as to weigh down my pocket or belt.

I prefer a 3/4-in.-wide blade, simply because it is more rigid than the 1/2-in. That's useful when the blade must extend unsupported in order to make a measurement. The blade markings should be clear and easy to read.

I use a tape for most inside and outside measuring tasks. The hook on the tape end is designed to move in or out its exact thickness, enabling the tape to read inside and outside measurements accurately. If the hook is bent, the measurement will be inaccurate. Periodically check the hook against an accurate rule, and correct as needed.

If real precision is required, I like to bypass the tape's hook and line up the tape on the 10-in. mark, take the reading, and then subtract 10 in.

6-in. Steel Rule

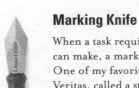

A 6-in. steel rule is handy for setting the fences on tablesaws, routers, marking gauges, or plow planes. I also use it to set up blade or bit heights and to check stock thickness. It's great for laying out the full range of joinery, from mortise-and-tenon and dovetail joints to dowels and biscuits.

Look for a rule with markings etched into the steel, as they generally are easier to read. The markings should run from end to end so that you can measure from an inside corner. A rule that also has marks parallel to one end (not shown) is a plus, as it makes some height adjustments easier.

Marking Knife

When a task requires a finer line than a pencil can make, a marking knife is my tool of choice. One of my favorites is a version made by Veritas, called a striking knife. It has a slender blade that tapers to an acute point, which is easy to slip between tight spaces and reach into tight corners. The blade is flat on one face but has two bevels on the other, making it suitable for both left- and right-handed marking. The flat face also allows it to fit right up to an edge. The blade is housed in a comfortable rosewood handle that is easy to grasp and enhances precision and control. The sides of the handle are flattened so that it won't roll off the workbench.

Pencils

I use a variety of pencils, each suited to a particular task, such as marking boards for rough dimensions, basic joinery layout, designating waste areas, and shop math. For general shop use, I prefer a No. 2 pencil, sharpened to a point with a conventional sharpener. For jobs such as dovetailing, where a finer, more precise line is needed, I use a No. 3 pencil because it has harder lead. I shape the point with a block plane and sandpaper to create a fine, knifelike edge.

Colored pencils also are useful. For dark-colored woods like walnut and wenge, the mark from a white-lead pencil is easier to see. I use other colors on all wood types to define and designate cabinet or chair parts.

Fractional Dial Caliper

Dial calipers generally are viewed as machinists' tools, but they are great in the woodshop. They are capable of inside, outside, and depth measurements. A thumbscrew locks the jaws for measurement transfer. I find dial

calipers helpful for verifying stock thickness, checking joinery size and spacing, and measuring turned parts. Unless you enjoy reading conversion charts, I would recommend the type with a dial incrementally marked in both fractions and decimals.

Marking Gauge

A combination-type marking gauge offers the user two options. One side of the gauge has a single pin, the other has a pair of pins. It is important to sharpen all the pins to a keen edge that will produce a knifelike cut.

The single pin is used to scribe lines parallel to a board edge. It's used across the grain for such tasks as scribing a baseline for dovetails or a tenon shoulder. Working with the grain, the single pin on a combination gauge can define a rabbet cut, or scribe a reference line to work to while preparing stock with hand tools.

The side with two pins can serve as a mortise gauge, allowing you to scribe simultaneously two lines parallel to a board's edge.

Scratch Awl

Traditionally, an awl was used for scribing lines with the grain or on end grain where knife marks are more difficult to see. I like to use an awl to mark the center of drill-hole locations. The impression left by this pointed tool helps to center the bit and ensure precise drilling whether you use a twist, brad-point, or auger bit. It also can be used to locate or start a center for lathe work.

Awls come in all shapes and sizes. The bottom line is to get one with a comfortable handle. I like it to have a few flat spots to keep it from rolling off the bench and a tapered, cylindrical shaft that terminates in a sharp conical point. Plain or fancy, take your pick.

Precision Work with Pencil and Paper

by Hendrik Varju

You don't need to be high-tech to achieve high precision. Whether you need to move your tablesaw fence a few thousandths of an inch or craft a perfectly fitted mortise-and-tenon joint, you can see and control nearly invisible differences by using two of the most common and ancient tools around—a pencil and paper. The next time you want to dial in a higher level of accuracy, don't reach for your credit card to buy the latest alignment gadget. Instead, pull a few business cards from your wallet and a pencil from your tool belt.

Pencil Strokes Highlight Your Progress

Whether sharpening, planing, or routing, sometimes the amount that needs to be removed is so little it's hard to see with the naked eye. Drawing pencil lines on the workpiece or the tool can make your progress easily visible.

GET A WATERSTONE TRULY FLAT

A waterstone needs to be perfectly flat to work well, but it is hard to tell when this has been achieved. To track your progress, draw light pencil strokes on the face of the stone before flattening it. The marks will disappear first on the high points, so keep rubbing until all pencil strokes are gone.

AVOID TAPERING TOO FAR

A jointer or handplane is used to refine tablesawn tapers on a leg, with each pass extending the taper farther up the leg. But stray into the designated flat area, and you'll see a gap when the apron is attached to the leg. A few pencil strokes near the start of the taper highlight when to stop planing.

FIT A MORTISE AND TENON

When fitting a tenon to its mortise, it can be difficult to assess where the tenon is too thick. Pencil strokes on the tenon cheeks will rub off where the fit is too tight, showing where to pare the tenon for a proper fit.

SEE WHERE YOU'RE PLANING

If you're flattening a glued-up panel, start by finding all of the high areas using a straightedge and marking them with pencil strokes. This way you can concentrate on the areas that need the most wood removed. You'll also be able to track any places you missed. Use a different pattern of pencil strokes in the lowest spots as a warning to avoid planing these areas.

SET A ROUTER'S DEPTH PRECISELY

When bringing trim or a plug level with its surroundings, you need to set a straight bit to cut exactly level with the surface. Mark a piece of plywood with some heavy pencil strokes, then gradually lower the bit until the pencil marks get lighter but are just visible. While this might sound difficult to attain, a good microadjust system on your router will easily allow you to dial in just a couple of thousandths of an inch at a time. If you go too deep, back off, draw some more lines, and try again.

Paper Shims

I constantly need to adjust a setup, fence, or workpiece by a few thousandths of an inch to achieve perfect accuracy. Paper is a great way to make precise adjustments. A non-embossed business card is typically 0.011 in. to 0.012 in. thick, standard 24-lb. printer paper is 0.005 in., and phone-directory paper 0.002 in. to 0.003 in.

Clamping Tips and Tricks

by Roman Rabiej

A common saying among woodworkers is, "You can never have too many clamps." Turns out, it might be more accurate to say that you can never apply too much force. Most woodworkers have only the vaguest idea of how much clamping force to apply when gluing boards. Even those perfectionists who rely on dial calipers and feeler gauges when cutting and planing wood often judge clamping pressure simply by the amount of glue that squeezes out. The results are occasional joint failures and embarrassing gaps between boards on the ends of tabletops.

During my career in wood technology I've done scientific studies of glue joints using different types of glue, different clamping pressures, different species of wood, and even different grain orientations.

Rather than blind you with science and make your next glue-up even more nerve-wracking, I'll assume you're using yellow (polyvinyl acetate—PVA) glue and I'll try to answer the following questions: What is the optimum force when clamping soft and hard woods? How many clamps should you use and how should you arrange them? And last, how can you test a sample joint to see if you are getting good results?

Use this information to approach your next glue-up with newfound confidence, and the only thing under pressure will be the wood.

Why Correct Clamping Pressure Matters

Optimum clamping pressure creates strong glueline joints in several ways. First, it overcomes the viscous resistance of the glue and forces it into a thin, continuous film in contact with the wood, which is necessary for a strong joint. Second, as the glue releases moisture, causing the wood to swell, clamping overcomes this pressure and prevents the joint from opening up. Third, it overcomes minor surface imperfections between mating surfaces. And fourth, clamping holds parts in position until the glue cures.

Keys to Success

1. Match the clamping pressure to the wood

2. Make sure you have enough clamps

3. Distribute the pressure effectively

Too little pressure will fail to achieve any of these benefits. Conversely, extreme pressure can produce weaker joints, although as I'll explain later, this is unlikely with common woodworking clamps. Because modern glues are stronger than the wood fibers, a good glue joint should break in the wood, a process known as wood failure, rather than along the glueline. So rather confusingly, the higher the percentage of wood failure, the better the joint. The wood-failure percentage starts to diminish as clamping pressure is increased beyond a certain point, because excessive pressure begins to starve the joint of glue and also to compress the wood and reduce its ability to absorb the glue.

The Chart Simplifies the Science

The chart below shows the recommended glueline pressure for selected furniture woods. The optimal pressure is roughly twice as high. This peak pressure is the point just before the glueline is starved or the wood fibers are crushed. For most hardwoods, however, normal woodworking clamps can't get close to these levels of force. But joints clamped at the recommended levels will be quite strong enough, with the glueline being stronger than the wood itself. You'll achieve a glueline thickness well under the recommended maximum, which is about 0.004 in. To give a point of reference, the cover of this magazine is 0.005 in. thick.

The next step is to find out how much pressure you are applying with each type of clamp.

Different Woods Require Different Clamping Pressure

Both the wood species and the grain orientation affect the clamping pressure required for a strong glue joint.

In general, dense and tight-grained woods require the application of greater force. On hardwoods, glue joints between radial or quartersawn faces require half the pressure of tangential or flatsawn face joints. This is because on hardwoods, the quartersawn face has half the compression strength of the flatsawn face, so the fibers are more easily crushed. On softwoods, the reverse is true, with the quartersawn-face gluelines requiring twice the pressure of the flatsawn-face gluelines.

WOOD ORIENTATION
When determining whether a joint is flatsawn or quartersawn, con-

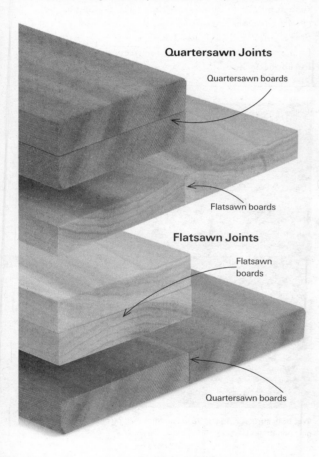

Quartersawn Joints
Quartersawn boards
Flatsawn boards

Flatsawn Joints
Flatsawn boards
Quartersawn boards

РЕΨОММЕΝΔЕΔ ΨΛΑΜΠΙΝΓ ΠΡΕΣΣΩΡΕ Σποθνδσ περ σϑθαρε ινψηΠ		
WOOD TYPE	QUARTERSAWN GLUE FACE	FLATSAWN GLUE FACE
SUGAR MAPLE	600	1,200
RED OAK	450	900
BLACK WALNUT	300	600
BLACK CHERRY	250	500
PONDEROSA PINE	300	150

Not All Clamps Are Created Equal

The force applied by each type of clamp varies greatly depending on the strength of the operator. We conducted a test using four different staff members; two Fine Woodworking editors, our female copy editor, and a brawny Fine Homebuilding editor. The numbers below are the average of the FWW editors. The copy editor in our test consistently applied about 60% of the average clamp pressure, while the hand strength of the FHB editor was about 40% higher.

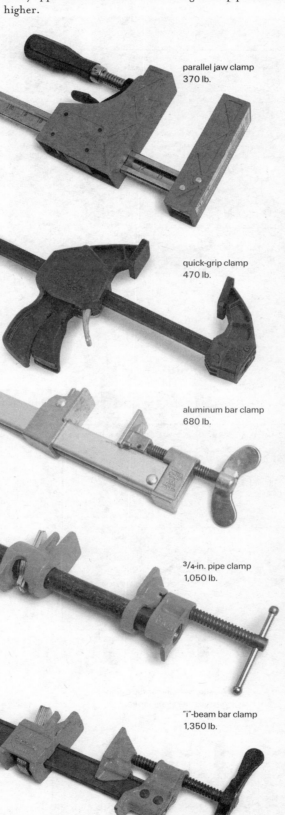

parallel jaw clamp
370 lb.

quick-grip clamp
470 lb.

aluminum bar clamp
680 lb.

3/4-in. pipe clamp
1,050 lb.

"i"-beam bar clamp
1,350 lb.

Calculating Clamp Requirements

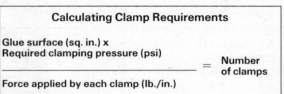

$$\frac{\text{Glue surface (sq. in.)} \times \text{Required clamping pressure (psi)}}{\text{Force applied by each clamp (lb./in.)}} = \text{Number of clamps}$$

EXAMPLE 1

Less pressure for pine. These two pine boards have a glue surface area of 16 1/2 sq. in. Because the glue faces are nearly flatsawn (left), the recommended pressure is 150 psi, requiring a total force of 2,475 lb. This can easily be met by using three 3/4-in. pipe clamps.

EXAMPLE 2

More pressure on maple. The effective glueline area is the same as for the pine (even though there are three boards to glue instead of two). The glue faces are quartersawn (left), so the recommended pressure is 600 psi. This total force of 9,900 lb. requires nine pipe clamps.

Continued ➡

We Tested the Common Bar Clamps

In his book, Understanding Wood (The Taunton Press, 2000), R. Bruce Hoadley illustrated that the amount of force applied by different types of woodworking clamp varies widely. He also found that the force of an individual clamp can differ by a factor of two depending on the strength of the operator.

To compare traditional bar and pipe clamps with newer designs and to see how the force they apply varies by user, Fine Woodworking rigged up a jig linked to a set of bathroom scales. The magazine's female copy editor represented one end of the strength scale, a brawny former builder at Fine Homebuilding represented the other, and

a couple of Fine Woodworking editors fell in betwee. Generally, clamps with T-handles exert more pressure than those with round handles.

The first step when gluing boards is calculating the square inches of glue surface. For example, if you are gluing two boards 3/4 in. thick and 36 in. long, a single glue surface equals 27 sq. in. Even if you are edge-gluing several boards, you still need to measure only one glue surface because the clamping pressure is transmitted across the width of the boards. If you are edge-gluing flatsawn red oak boards and wish to apply about 450 lb. psi, then 27 multiplied by 450 equals a force of 12,150 lb. that must be applied. Using the average of the editors' clamping forces, this could be supplied by around nine heavy-duty

bar clamps, a dozen 3/4-in. pipe clamps, or 26 quick-grip clamps. Obviously it would be hard to fit 26 clamps along a 36-in. board, so add some more powerful clamps if you have them. It's fine to mix and match types of clamp.

Just as important as the overall force is how it is distributed. You want even pressure along the whole glueline. This can be done in two ways. The force applied by a clamp radiates outward at 45° on either side, so you'll need to space the clamps so that the force from them just overlaps along the glueline.

When edge-gluing wide boards, such as for a tabletop, you can employ powerful clamps spaced widely, alternating the clamps above and below the workpiece to prevent the boards from bowing. If the glueline is close to

Put the Pressure Where You Need It

The force from a clamp spreads out in a 45° cone from each head. For the cones to overlap and the glueline to receive even pressure, the clamps need to be spaced correctly. The 45° angle makes the cones of pressure easy to measure. The force will radiate sideways in both directions the same distance as the clamp is from the glueline. So, in the example below, the 6-in.-wide board creates 12-in.-wide cones of pressure at the joint.

Cauls spread the force. When clamping a narrow strip, the clamps have to be close together in order to have the pressure cones overlap (at right in photo). A solution is to employ a wide caul that spreads out the force before it meets the glueline (below).

CLAMPING WIDE BOARDS

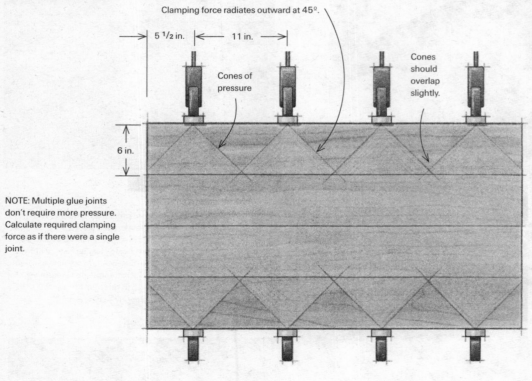

Clamping force radiates outward at 45°.

5 1/2 in. | 11 in.

Cones of pressure

Cones should overlap slightly.

6 in.

NOTE: Multiple glue joints don't require more pressure. Calculate required clamping force as if there were a single joint.

CLAMPING THIN EDGING

Where the glueline is close to the clamp head, place the clamps very close together or use a wide caul. Otherwise, some parts of the glueline will not receive sufficient pressure.

Unpressured area between cones

A wide caul spreads the clamping pressure along the entire length.

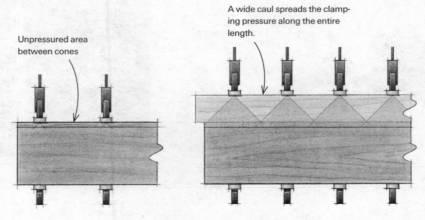

Tips on Gluing

It is important to get even, continuous glue coverage on the surfaces to be bonded, so apply yellow glue to both surfaces when you can. This provides instant wetting of both surfaces without relying on pressure and surface flatness to transfer the glue from one surface to the other. You will, however, have to work fast as the open time for yellow glue can be around five minutes at a temperature of 70° F (21° C) and relative air humidity of 50%.

How long should the joint be subjected to clamp pressure? The time varies from species to species, with woods that have an even density across the growth rings, such as maple, requiring less time. But in general, the glueline reaches around 80% of its ultimate strength after 60 minutes of clamping. After this, joints can be released from the clamps, but the full glue strength won't develop for about 24 hours.

Wet both surfaces. To ensure the uniform wetting of the wood that aids glue penetration, apply glue to both surfaces.

HOW STRONG IS YOUR GLUELINE?

Even if you have used the correct pressure, it is still reassuring to make sure that you are achieving well-glued joints. A simple test is to place a sharp chisel exactly on the glueline, and strike it with a mallet. A weak joint will split in the glueline, either because the glue was too thick or the glue didn't penetrate the wood correctly. The percentage of wood failure will be very low or nonexistent. A good joint will split mostly in the wood adjacent to the glueline.

Glue failure. A poor joint fails along the glueline.

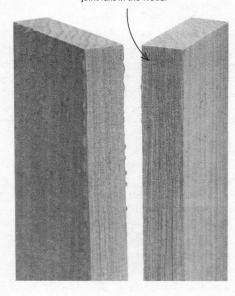

Wood failure. A good joint fails in the wood.

the face of the clamp, such as when applying solid-wood edging to plywood, to avoid having a clamp placed every inch or two, you can use wide cauls that will spread the clamp pressure as well as protect the edge of the workpiece from the clamps.

Glue-Up Gear and Accessories

by Michael Fortune

As I say in "Great Glue-Ups, Guaranteed", glue is a slippery film. And as you'll see in that article, I use a few types of clamps and a wide variety of cauls to put pressure right where I want it and to keep parts in place. That article covers a variety of specific situations; this one covers the glue-up gear I keep on hand. The beauty of these basic cauls and supplies is that they will handle the vast majority of work you will encounter.

I use common types of clamps. Instead of spending your money on a pricey parallel-jaw models, buy more of the low-tech kind. Then spend your time making cauls. I use a bunch of custom cauls in my work, made from whatever hardwood I can spare, but I keep a variety of common sizes in buckets.

When clamping pieces that are prefinished or will be hard to sand or repair later, I use small pads under the clamp heads. If the jaws don't have pads already, I tape pieces of wood to the workpiece. You don't want to be wrestling with little wood pads as you try to position the clamps perfectly and tighten them. I keep a pile of these pads on hand, made from basswood and poplar—softer than the furniture woods I use but strong enough to stand up to the pressure. As for glue, some people pour it into little dishes before spreading it, but I almost always apply it right out of the bottle, and I use my finger, wiping it clean on one of the world's crustiest aprons.

How Clamps and Cauls Team Up

DIRECT
Pressure needs to be centered on a joint, so Fortune prefers clamps that focus their force. Cauls add insurance.

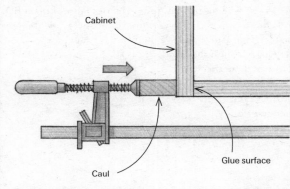

SPREAD
Just as pressure needs to be centered in one direction, it often needs to be spread in the other. Cauls handle that, too.

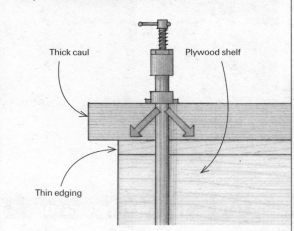

CONSTRAIN
Even if the pressure is centered, pieces can shift. Cauls keep them perfectly in line.

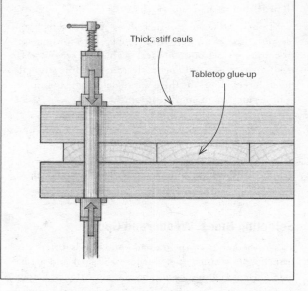

Clamps

Fortune keeps a wide variety of clamps on hand, and none are high-tech. His favorites are Jorgensen F-style bar clamps, because you can align the deep clamp heads precisely on almost any joint. When F-clamps fall short, he turns to Jorgensen pipe clamps. He finds parallel-jaw clamps to be heavy and imprecise.

PIPE CLAMPS

There is no better and more affordable way to reach long distances than with pipe clamps, in both the 3/4-in. and 1/2-in. sizes. The larger ones are stronger; the smaller, more nimble. He sometimes uses plastic jaw protectors (available online) on these.

F-STYLE CLAMPS

Fortune has Jorgensen F-style bar clamps in many sizes and lengths, and most have little plastic jaw protectors.

EDGE CLAMPS

Although he could get by without them, Fortune really likes these specialty clamps.

Targeted pressure. With edge clamps, you don't need to reach long clamps across a panel. You still need a caul, though.

Accessories

You can keep it simple with the glue, too. Simple PVA (yellow) glues are super-strong, and the best spreader is your finger, though Fortune also uses cheap brushes and sticks.

GLUE

Fortune almost always uses Titebond III, which has 20 to 25 minutes of working time. It leaves a tan glueline, so for the whitest woods he uses Titebond I, which sets up a bit faster.

Continued ➡

SPREADERS

To get glue into crannies like mortises and dovetails, Fortune uses popsicle sticks, trimmed square, and cheap brushes, which he takes a moment to fine-tune.

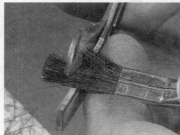

Brush trick. As is, cheap flux brushes are too floppy and tend to drop bristles into the glue. So hammer the ferrule to tighten up the bristles, and trim off some of the length.

Cauls

Fortune keeps a few types of hardwood cauls in buckets, always ready to go. He prefers to use packing tape to prevent glue from sticking, but for two-sided cauls with one edge curved and one straight, he waxes both faces, as clamps would tear up the tape. A marker line, straight or curvy, shows which face goes against the glue-up.

How to Make a Curved Caul

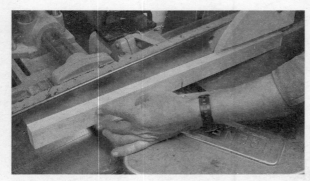

Simple setup. Mark the midpoint of the caul, and set up a stop block on the jointer so that point will drop right at the leading edge of the outfeed table. Set the jointer for a 1/32-in.-deep cut.

Drop and go. Put the caul against the stop block with a push stick hooked on that end, and lower the caul onto the cutterhead. Then push it forward. Do the same to the other end to create a gentle camber.

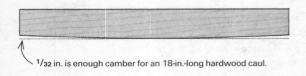

↖ 1/32 in. is enough camber for an 18-in.-long hardwood caul.

LONG AND STRONG

In one bucket, Fortune keeps long cauls for larger glue-ups. These are roughly 7/8 in. thick by 1-3/4 in. wide by 18 in. long. Several are slightly cambered so when clamps are applied at the ends, pressure is exerted in the middle.

SHORT AND FLAT

In the other bucket, he keeps 20 short cauls, each roughly 7/8 in. by 1-1/2 in. by 6 in. long. He uses most of them flat side down, where they have more surface area and are more stable. That said, half have their packing tape wrapped around the edge. He uses them that way for the added stiffness and better visibility.

TIP

KEEP GLUE FROM STICKING
Tape or wax. The tape lasts indefinitely, but the paste wax needs to be refreshed from time to time.

Best Glues for Woodworking

by Mark Schofield

Unless they confine their woodworking to knockdown furniture, all woodworkers rely on glue. As a result, there are dozens of types of glue and masses of competing brands all proclaiming their superiority.

To help make sense of it all, Fine Woodworking ran a test with three main objectives. The first was to compare six common types of woodworking glue; the second was to see if the type of wood might affect the bonding strength of the different glues; the third was to determine how tolerant the glues are to poorly cut joints.

The results were revealing. Some older glues performed superbly, while a newer glue was less than impressive. The wood type does make a difference, but don't believe the stories that say all dense tropical woods are hard to glue. And, while glue starvation seems to be a myth, so does the gap-filling ability of certain glues.

Selecting Glues, Woods, and Gaps

To see whether an open-grained wood bonds differently from a tight-grained one, we chose white oak and hard maple. Dense tropical woods have a reputation as being difficult to glue. We intended to use teak, but the lumberyard owner suggested ipé, as he had heard many complaints about glue failure with this wood.

We chose a traditional interior polyvinyl acetate (PVA) yellow glue represented by Elmer's carpenter's glue; a newer PVA glue with a Type I waterproof rating in the form of Titebond III; two types of hide glue, a room-temperature version by Old Brown Glue and traditional granules that must be mixed with water and heated; a two-part, slow-set epoxy from System Three; and Gorilla Glue's polyurethane.

If a joint is sloppy, will the glue fill the gaps? Conversely, if the joint is so tight it has to be hammered home, will it be starved of glue? Does a perfectly fitting joint produce the strongest glue bond? To answer these questions, we tested bridle joints with three types of fit: tight, snug, and loose.

Bridle Joints: First Make 'Em, then Break 'Em

We settled on a bridle joint, also known as an open mortise-and-tenon joint, because it has no mechanical strength and instead relies entirely on the glue bond. It also was easy to adjust the width of the tenon to change the fit of the joint to test each glue's gap-filling ability.

Precise milling—To lessen the impact of a rogue result, John White, Fine Woodworking's shop manager, made three samples of each joint for a total of 162 samples. To keep wood variables to a minimum, he cut the joints from a single, straight-grained board of each species.

The joints were cut using a Freud box-joint blade set in the 1/4-in.-wide configuration, as these blades give a very clean cut with a flat bottom. White cut all the tight joints first, spacing them so that they needed a light tap to bring them together. Using a dial indicator to adjust the tenoning jig, he cut the snug-fitting joints so that they required only hand pressure to bring them together and would represent a perfect fit to most woodworkers. Last, he cut the loose joints with a 1/64-in. gap, split evenly on each side of the tenon. We chose this spacing because there was no wood contact on the tenon, but the joint was still tight enough that most woodworkers would take a chance and hope that glue would fill the gap.

Applying the glue—Each glue was prepared and applied according to the manufacturer's instructions. We used ample glue because squeeze-out was not a consideration.

The final step was to make a 45° cut at the end of each arm to prepare the joints for the joint-breaking machine. To give the glues time to develop maximum strength, we allowed the joints to rest for three weeks.

Off to the lab—We shipped the joints to the Department of Materials Science and Engineering at Case Western Reserve University in Cleveland, Ohio. Under the direction of associate professor David Matthiesen, the samples were placed in an Instron testing machine. The force it took to break each joint was recorded on a computer, and then the values for the three joints were averaged and a standard deviation calculated.

The Types We Tested

We picked six brands to represent the spectrum of common woodworking glues, including two types of PVA glue, a polyurethane glue, an epoxy, and two types of hide glue.

PVA glue

Making the Joints

All 162 joints for the test were cut on a tablesaw using a tenoning jig. To maintain even spacing on either side of the tenon in the loose joints, White machined each joint carefully and clamped both pieces to a piece of dead-flat glass while the glue dried.

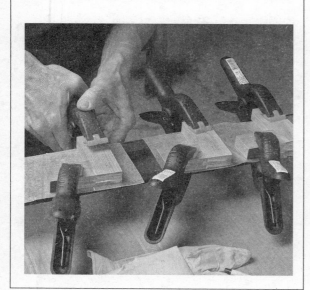

Which Glue Is the Strongest?

The chart shows the glues ranked by the average force it took to break their joints. To give a guide to each glue's relative performance, its average joint strength is shown as a percentage of that of the strongest glue. We rated Type I PVA as the best overall, with interior yellow glue (PVA) as the best value.

GLUE	JOINT FIT	MAPLE	OAK	IPÉ	AVG. JOINT STRENGTH (LB.)	JOINT STRENGTH AS % OF TYPE I PVA GLUE	COMMENTS
Type I PVA glue (waterproof)	Tight	1842	1843	2554	2024	100%	This proved to be a good all-around glue with no weakness in any of the woods or joint fits. Combined with its ease of use and moderate cost, this glue wins the best overall label.
	Snug	1700	1822	2733			
	Loose	1593	1603	2525			
Slow-set epoxy	Tight	1690	1908	2425	1994	99%	The betting before the test was that this glue would be the strongest. It came in a close second, but given its high cost and longer preparation time, this was disappointing. In particular, it didn't prove to be the clear choice for gap-filling.
	Snug	1680	1832	2712			
	Loose	1635	1557	2503			
PVA glue	Tight	1737	1769	2696	1924	95%	Many woodworkers will be relieved to see that their first-choice glue performed so well. Amazingly, it produced the strongest bonds on tight and snug ipé joints. This glue is the best value.
	Snug	1543	1684	2842			
	Loose	1474	1537	2036			
Liquid hide glue	Tight	1468	1850	1716	1595	79%	Not as strong as epoxy or the PVAs, this glue still gave a very credible performance. It performed particularly well on oak, but was relatively less strong on ipé.
	Snug	1516	1699	1779			
	Loose	1436	1521	1374			
Hot hide glue	Tight	1488	1847	1769	1531	76%	Proponents of hide glue have never claimed that it is as strong as PVA, but instead promote its reversibility and compatibility with stains and finish. From this test, it appears that hot hide glue is only a little weaker than yellow glue and is stronger on oak.
	Snug	1412	1765	1459			
	Loose	1485	1618	936			
Polyurethane	Tight	1414	1491	1875	1164	58%	The surprise of the test was this glue's poor showing. The snug joints were poor, and the loose joints were unacceptable. Polyurethane may be a tough finish, but it isn't a tough glue.
	Snug	1336	1055	1455			
	Loose	564	571	716			

THE WEAKEST LINK

The joints failed in three different ways: With the strongest glues, particularly in maple and oak, the failure was usually 100% in the wood. With the weakest glues, particularly in the strongest wood, ipé, the failure was 100% along the glueline, with the wood fibers remaining intact. But the majority of the joints showed some combination of both types of failure.

Glue failure

Wood failure

Combination

Type I PVA glue	Polyurethane glue	Slow-set epoxy	Hot hide glue granules	Liquid hide glue

Breaking the Joints

Under pressure. Under the direction of David Matthiesen (left), Chris Tuma placed each joint in the machine at Case Western and applied force gradually.

Continued ➜

Breaking point. Eventually, the force became great enough for the joint to break within the wood or, as in this case, along the glueline.

Monitoring the test. The computer displays the force applied and the amount the joint was compressed. The line's peak marks the point where the joint failed.

Use Screws Like a Pro

by Robert J. Settich

Some purists will tell you there's no place for screws in woodworking. If they mean that screws can't replace a snug mortise-and-tenon or a seamless dovetail joint … OK. But the fact is, screws do the job—and do it well—in many woodworking applications. The trick is to select the right screw for the job, and to understand how to get the most holding power from it.

The Basics

Most crucial to a screw's holding power is its resistance to being pulled out. The more thread surface in contact with the wood, the more resistance. So, to muscle up holding power, use a longer or thicker screw, one with a deeper thread pattern, or any combination of those properties.

A thicker root (around which the threads are wound) also beefs up a screw's torsional strength, or resistance to twisting forces that can snap it, usually after its head hits the wood. To avoid this, choose the right screw, drill the right-size pilot hole, and don't overdrive. Set the power driver's clutch to a lower setting or make the last few turns by hand. Overdriving also spins the screw after it reaches full depth, reducing the wood fibers to a fluff and leaving the screw with no holding power.

Pilot holes—In woodworking, always drill pilot holes. Without them, screws simply push the wood fibers aside. This is OK in carpentry, but with the harder woods and often thinner pieces used in making furniture, it's a recipe for splitting. The general rule is to drill a pilot hole in the target piece that's the size of the screw's root. This is easy when using a rolled-thread screw, in which the root diameter is consistent throughout the length of the screw, tapering only at the tip. For a cut-thread screw, in which the root diameter gradually tapers toward the tip, optimal drilling requires a tapered drill bit.

Clearance holes—Another critical element in a successful screw joint is the head of the screw. No matter how great a screw's holding power, the joint won't hold tight if the pieces being fastened are "jacked," or not drawn tightly together. That's where clearance holes come in. These are drilled through the top board (or piece to be fastened), allowing the head of the screw to pull that piece fast against the target board. To achieve this in most cases, the clearance hole should be as wide as the outer diameter of the screw's widest threads.

Dialing in a precise screw fit—Here's an easy way to confirm the pilot-hole and clearance-hole sizes for a batch of screws. This works for all screws and woods, but you need dial calipers ($16 for a 6-in. version from Grizzly; www.grizzly.com; product No. G9256) and a full set of drill bits, graduated by 64ths of an inch.

What We Learned About Glue

The first lesson is that most (but not all) of these joints are incredibly strong. As Matthiesen joked, "You could park a car on these joints!" Given that the majority of the joints showed either complete or partial wood failure (with the exception of hide-glued ipé and all three woods glued with polyurethane), we concluded that most woodworkers can rely on their glue. That said, there are significant variations between the different glues, between the three woods, and according to the fit of the joint. Many of the results directly contradict conventional wisdom.

ORDINARY YELLOW GLUE IS AS STRONG AS THE EXPENSIVE STUFF

If you are confident in your joint-making ability, then stick with good old-fashioned interior yellow glue. It was only a little weaker than Type I PVA on tight and snug maple and oak joints, and it was stronger on ipé. If your joint-making skills still need a little help, go with the more expensive Type I PVA.

LIQUID HIDE GLUE IS AS GOOD AS HOT HIDE GLUE

Based on the average strength of all the joints, liquid hide glue beat out hot hide glue. However, if you look at specific joints and woods, hot hide glue was strongest in five of the nine categories. I had expected liquid hide glue to be weaker due to the addition of urea to keep it workable at room temperature, but in this test the two glue types were about equal. Where hot hide glue was comparatively weakest was on snug and loose ipé joints.

OPEN-PORED WOOD PRODUCES STRONGER JOINTS

In only two of 18 categories did maple produce a stronger joint than oak. Hide glues in particular seem to get a better bond on open-pored woods. This may explain why period furniture makers have great success using hide glue on mahogany, another relatively open-pored wood.

EPOXY ISN'T NECESSARY ON A DENSE TROPICAL WOOD

The strongest joint in the whole test was yellow glue on ipé—a real surprise. Indeed, both yellow glue and Type I PVA were stronger than epoxy in tight and snug ipé joints. On loose ipé joints, epoxy showed no great advantage, so I would stick with either interior PVA or Type I PVA on this tropical wood. At all costs, don't hope that polyurethane will fill a loose ipé joint—it won't.

TIGHTNESS DIDN'T STARVE THESE JOINTS

With oak, all six glues created stronger bonds on tight joints than on snug ones, and the same was true with five out of six glues on maple. If oak and maple are representative of domestic woods, you don't need to worry about a tight fit causing glue starvation. Of course, these "tight" joints are far less tight than a clamped joint. On ipé, and perhaps other dense tropical woods, leaving a little extra room for the glue seems like a good idea. That said, both PVA glues and epoxy create incredibly strong joints whether the joints are tight or snug.

POLYURETHANE GLUE FAILS IN LOOSE JOINTS

With the exception of hot hide glue on maple, all glues were slightly weaker on loose joints compared to tight and snug ones. All but polyurethane, however, were strong enough. If you want the best adhesive for a sloppy joint, use epoxy for maple, hot hide on oak, and Type I PVA on ipé. Polyurethane gluelines failed on loose joints in all three woods.

Anatomy of a Screw Joint

Drill with the right bits, in the right sequence, and the screw will bring the boards tightly together.

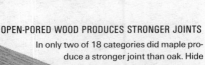

Head pulls top board to target board.

Threads not engaged in top board

Screw length, 3x thickness of top board

Threads engaged in target board only

Countersink is equal to or greater than head diameter.

Head diameter

Thread diameter

Clearance hole equals thread diameter.

Root diameter

Pilot hole equals root diameter.

First, measure the root diameter of the screw by reaching into the space between threads. This is the diameter of the pilot hole. For very soft woods like pine, go down one bit size; for very hard woods like maple, go up a size. Next, measure the outside of the threads. This is the diameter of the clearance hole. And if you need a counterbore (see next section), use a bit that matches the screw's head diameter—or the diameter of the plug that will cover the screw head.

Countersinking and counterboring—Beginners sometimes use the terms "countersinking" and "counterboring" interchangeably, but they are distinctly different processes. Countersinking chamfers the rim of a hole so that a flathead screw seats flush to, or slightly below, the surface of the wood.

My favorite countersink bits are the single-cutter design (created by drilling a hole through the bit) because the cone point positively engages the hole and the cutter slices the wood instead of grinding it. Countersinks usually have an 82° angle to match the underside of flathead screws.

Another countersink is attached to a drill bit. For woodworking, this bit should be sized to make the clearance hole. These combination tools are often sold in sets to accommodate a wide range of screw gauges. The countersinks also match various plug sizes, so if the bit is driven deeper into the wood, the countersink also makes a counterbore for plugging.

A counterbore is a hole with parallel sides, stopped partway through the top board. Sometimes you'll make one simply to extend the reach of a screw, but it's more commonly used to create a home for a plug to conceal the screw head.

The drilling sequence—In furniture making, where accuracy is essential, the order in which you drill your holes can be critical. If you're not careful, you can get into a situation in which a subsequent bit can't pick up the center of an earlier hole.

To attach two pieces of wood with a countersunk screw, clamp the pieces together first. Next, drill the pilot hole through the top board and into the bottom board. Then, using a twist bit (which, because of its tapered tip, centers itself over the pilot hole), drill the clearance hole in the top board.

To create a plugged screw joint, clamp the boards together and drill the counterbore in the top board. Make the counterbore about 1/16 in. deeper than the penetration of the plug. Drill the pilot hole next, driving the bit through the center dimple left by the first bit. Then make the clearance hole with a twist bit.

Screws in Solid Wood

Now the question becomes which screws—and what fastening techniques—work best in which situations. Let's begin with the most common application in making furniture: fastening solid wood to solid wood. Here are a few general rules:

1. Drive the screw through the thinner piece of wood into the thicker one.

2. Avoid "jacked" joints by making sure the threads aren't engaging the top board, and also by clamping parts together tightly before driving screws. Otherwise, the screw entering the target board can raise a tiny eruption of wood that can permanently separate the two pieces of wood.

3. Another cure for jacked joints is to countersink the pilot hole on the bottom of the board you're fastening. This creates a clearance zone for the raised wood fibers.

4. If you must drive a screw into end grain, a cross-dowel in the target board will boost strength.

Slotted holes allow movement—Solid wood's seasonal expansion and contraction is a concern that arises most often when fastening the tops of tables or cases. One common solution is to drill slotted screw holes in the cleats used to attach them. The slots allow the top to expand and contract across its grain while being held flat by the screws.

Slotted holes work similarly for screws attaching solid-wood drawer bottoms.

Another common solid-wood screw application involves breadboard ends for table and casework tops. Screws in slotted holes hold the breadboard to the tongue but permit the top to freely change in width. (A screw-slot router bit is the perfect tool for most slotting applications. Lee Valley offers styles for either flathead or roundhead screws.)

Sizing the Pilot and Clearance Holes

A caliper zeroes in on the screw's root and outside-thread diameters. You'll need both measurements in order to choose the proper bits for the drilling sequence.

A Clearance Hole Prevents Jacking

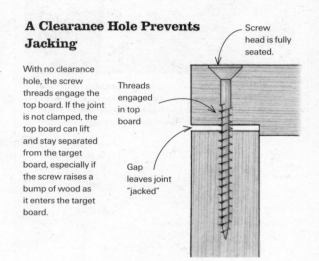

With no clearance hole, the screw threads engage the top board. If the joint is not clamped, the top board can lift and stay separated from the target board, especially if the screw raises a bump of wood as it enters the target board.

Screw head is fully seated.

Threads engaged in top board

Gap leaves joint "jacked"

Counterboring

COUNTERBORE

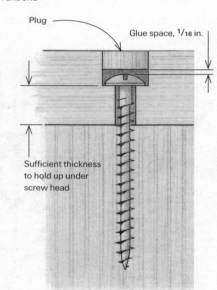

Plug

Glue space, 1/16 in.

Sufficient thickness to hold up under screw head

Combo Bits

Using an appropriate-size combo bit saves steps, letting you make the clearance hole and countersink in one drilling (left). Before or after this step, use a smaller bit to drill the pilot hole (below).

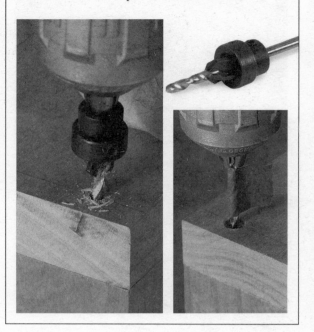

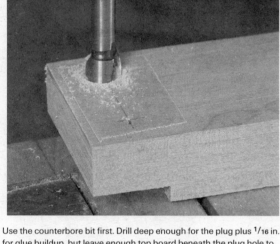

Use the counterbore bit first. Drill deep enough for the plug plus 1/16 in. for glue buildup, but leave enough top board beneath the plug hole to support the screw head. Using a Forstner bit and masking tape helps ensure a straight-walled plug hole with a round, sharp rim.

Two twist bits are next. Drill the narrow pilot hole through both pieces, and then use the larger bit to widen the hole in the top board for clearance (left)). Bring the joint home with screws, and tap in the glued-up plugs (right).

Joining Plywood and MDF

Building cabinets, jigs, and other items with sheet goods such as plywood and medium-density fiberboard (MDF) poses other fastening challenges. Though wood movement is not a major concern, these materials are especially prone to end- and edge-splitting. This can leave the screws that fasten them with very little holding power.

Continued ➔

Slotted Holes

CROSS-GRAIN FASTENING

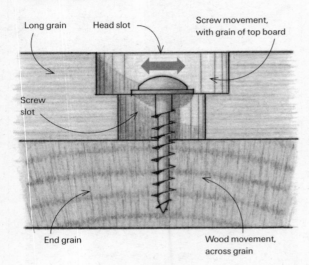

- Long grain
- Head slot
- Screw movement, with grain of top board
- Screw slot
- End grain
- Wood movement, across grain

FLAT BOTTOM BITS

bottom slot not only accommodates any screw at-bottomed head, but it also allows you to add a further ensuring freedom of movement over the surface.

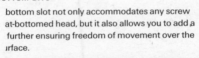

Rout the slot. With a screw-slot bit in his router, Settich plunges it into a bracket for a solid-wood cabinet top (top). The resulting slot (left) leaves ample room for the top to expand and contract.

TAPERED BITS

The tapered-bottom screw-slot bit matches the design of the flathead screw, as with this mounting slot for a solid-wood drawer bottom.

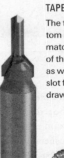

End Grain

Use a dowel for grip. Screwing into end grain, as when applying a breadboard end, is risky because the threads don't grip the wood fibers well. Solve this problem by inserting a dowel near (but not too close to) the edge of the target board and screwing into the dowel.

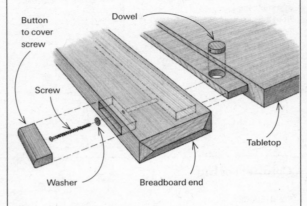

- Button to cover screw
- Dowel
- Screw
- Tabletop
- Washer
- Breadboard end

Sheet Goods

PLYWOOD

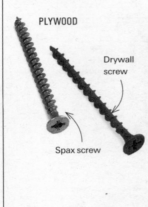

- Drywall screw
- Spax screw

Use deep, sharp threads in plywood. Most screws won't hold well in the cross-layered fibers of plywood. The solution: Use deep-threaded fasteners such as Spax screws and Type-W drywall screws, especially when fastening into an edge such as a plywood cabinet shelf (above)).

MDF

- Confirmat bit
- Confirmat screw

Special screws for MDF. Getting a good grip in medium-density fiberboard requires a shallow-threaded fastener with a substantial root diameter such as the Confirmat screw. A special bit allows you to drill the matching pilot hole, clearance hole, and countersink.

Plywood—You can achieve decent strength screwing into the face of a plywood panel because you're working into face-grain wood fibers. But screwing into a plywood end or edge offers no more than thin layers of edge and side grain, and it takes more thread surface to get a good bite. With conventional screw designs, this means moving to a larger gauge—for example, a #10 screw instead of a #8. But edge-driving a thicker screw also increases the risk of splitting the plywood by separating its layers. So your best bet is to use a fastener that has a deeper thread circling a slimmer shank. That includes Spax screws and Type W drywall screws.

Medium-density fiberboard—Unlike plywood, MDF lacks the structural advantages of continuous wood fibers. As a result, it's even more prone to splitting and causing spinout. The best solution is to use a low thread design, as seen in the Confirmat screw.

Fastening Hardware

You rarely have to deal with seasonal movement or edge-grain liabilities when fastening hardware to wood. Yet this job is not as easy as it seems. Many hardware items, such as hinges, have countersunk holes and include mounting screws. While convenient, this does not ensure that the screws will fit properly or hold well. So, begin by test-fitting each screw into its countersink to be sure that the head is flush with the surface of the leaf. If the head stands proud, and it's the only type of screw available, modify the hinge with a countersink bit, preferably chucked into a drill press.

Start with the right bit. A special self-centering drill bit takes the frustration and guesswork out of drilling precisely positioned pilot holes for hardware. Many such bits (including the most common brand, the Vix bit) enable you to replace the twist drill component of the assembly to extend the life of the tool.

Then, go with the right fastener. Use the screws that come with the hinge, or substitute special hinge screws. When you drive screws, the threads typically raise a tiny

Hardware

HINGE BIT

Hinges require extra precision. Drill pilot holes with a self-centering hinge bit. It's best to have two or three different sizes of these bits, to match the most common hinge-screw sizes.

SWITCHEROO

Steel first, brass later. Brass screws are soft and often wind up with scratched or stripped heads when driven into hardwood. To avoid that, drive a steel screw into the pilot hole first, then replace it with its brass twin.

curl of wood that can become trapped under the head of an ordinary screw and prevent it from fully seating. The undercut head of the hinge screw provides room for the curl, so you can drive the head flush.

If the hinges are brass, the hinge screws should be brass, too. But brass screws are soft, and their heads are easily marred by a struggling screwdriver tip. Avoid problems by first driving an identical steel screw into the pilot hole. This will cut the threads into the wood, reducing the strain on the brass. If you still meet resistance, enlarge the diameter of the pilot hole.

Robert J. Settich is a writer, photographer, and woodworker in Gladstone, Mo. He is the author of Taunton's Complete Illustrated Guide to Choosing and Installing Hardware (The Taunton Press, 2003).

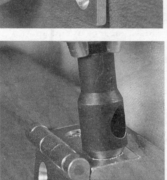

AVOID WRONG-HEADEDNESS
If the tapers of a screw head and hinge hole don't match (top), the screw might seat proud and prevent the hinge from closing fully. If you don't have the right screw on hand, reshape the hinge hole with a countersink (center). With the hole re-shaped, you can re-seat the screw at its proper depth (bottom).

Jigs 101

by Gary Rogowski

A good workshop jig will hold your work accurately and safely so you can make consistent, repeatable cuts quickly. Take the template-routing jig I use at the router table. It protects my fingers and allows me to reproduce a shape over and over. It also speeds up the shaping process. So in one jig I get safety, accuracy, and speed.

The purpose of any jig is to make life in the shop easier. Whether building a simple one-use jig for the job at hand or a more complex jig to last a lifetime, choose materials wisely and take your time.

I design jigs to be easy to use, with stable materials that are flat and straight; I won't grab just any piece of scrap and waste time trying to make it flat and square. I stick to plywood or medium-density fiberboard (MDF), with an occasional piece of hardwood where I need a high degree of accuracy or durability. I use glue or simple fasteners so that the jigs are quick to build yet hold up in use. And I ease edges to make them friendly to the touch.

Sacrificial plywood. This jig for cutting key slots in miter joints is made from scraps of ³/₄-in. plywood.

Thin MDF. Two layers of ¹/₄-in. MDF create a handy jig for cutting butterfly keys. A pencil eraser holds down the work.

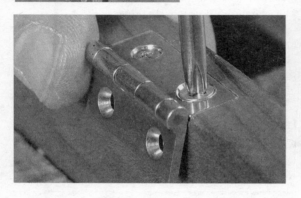

Hardwood for durability. Hardwood components, like these runners on a crosscut sled, can withstand repeated movement and rubbing. Note that the fence is also hardwood, milled perfectly straight and square.

Low-cost option. Particleboard is an inexpensive material for building up thick bending jigs.

The Right Materials

The purpose of the jig will determine what materials you should use. Mostly I use ³/₄-in.-thick MDF or veneer-core plywood.

When I need an absolutely square fence on a jig, I'll use a piece of straight-grained hardwood milled flat and square. When I need to glue up layer after layer, such as when I make a thick bending jig, I'll use particleboard. It's inexpensive and works just fine. If you need material with no voids or gaps in its edges, then use a material like Bal-

tic-birch plywood. (In the western United States, a product known as ApplePly is also widely used for jig making.) I've used Masonite for router templates, but I generally prefer MDF because it's easier to see pencil lines on the lighter surface. For jigs that get screwed or nailed together on edge, I use solid wood or plywood and drill pilot holes to avoid splitting the material.

Material that's ³/₄ in. thick allows enough room for countersinking large screw heads or bolt heads. It also reduces the chance of splitting if I have to screw into the edge of a piece. There are times when using thinner stock helps me hold a jig easier or maneuver it faster. When I cut butterfly keys on the bandsaw, for example, I hold the small workpieces steady in a simple jig made from two layers of ¹/₄-in. MDF. It's nice to have a thinner profile on the jig to hold a thin wedge piece.

The Right Fasteners

Some jigs need to be assembled with glue to remain accurate through years of regular use. Just be sure that the surfaces you're gluing are clean and clamp them together for about half an hour. The trouble with glue is that it acts as a wonderful lubricant for 10 seconds or so, then locks your pieces into the wrong position. Or so I've heard.

To combat that creep, use brads or pin nails to lock pieces in place. Spread the glue, align the pieces, shoot several nails in place, then put on the clamps. If you don't have a nailer, clamp the pieces of the jig at the edges so they won't slip when you clamp the faces together. Or, dry-clamp the pieces, predrill screw holes, then glue and screw the jig together.

For jigs that don't require the permanence of glue, use drywall screws or round-head wood screws. Obviously, you shouldn't put any screw where it will get in the way of a blade or bit. For example, my tenoning jig fits over the tablesaw fence, but I made very sure that the screws holding it together are above any blade-height setting. And, obviously, don't use a round-head screw where it might prevent part of the jig from sitting flat, pivoting, or sliding smoothly.

Some jigs slip out of adjustment over time, and you can't always tighten screws enough to bring the jig back into line. On my crosscut jig, for instance, I bolted the fence to the sled. That leaves a little wiggle room for adjustment, and makes it easy to crank down hard on the bolts, both when building the sled and when it needs to be realigned.

The Right Hold-Downs

Many jigs are designed to work with some type of clamp to hold the jig down on the bench or on a workpiece, to hold a stop block on the jig itself, or to hold a workpiece in place. There are several types of clamp you can use. But always make sure there's no way in the world that the clamp can be nicked by a blade or cutter. And if the clamps will double as handles, be sure you position them where they keep your hands out of harm's way.

Standard C-clamps or F-style bar clamps work great, especially for holding a jig in place. They're easy to adjust and provide plenty of clamping pressure. When I need only a little holding power—to secure a stop block, for example—I'll use spring clamps. For the ultimate in low-tech clamping solutions, use opposing wedges to clamp your work in place.

For holding workpieces in place, as on a tenoning jig or template-routing jig, DeStaCo-style toggle clamps are the ticket. Screw these in place or mount them in T-tracks screwed into slots routed into the jig base for clamping pressure exactly where you need it. There are several types of toggle clamps available, so pick the one that best suits your needs.

Tips for More Comfortable Woodworking

by Art Liebeskind

I have been woodworking for more than three decades, since I was a comparative stripling of 42 years. Now I'm an old oak, and when I work in my shop for any length of time, muscles shriek and nerves buzz. My body tells me that certain tasks have grown more difficult.

If you want to work wood for decades to come, you'll need to find ways that are gentler on sinew and bone. Fortunately, the market these days is brimming with ergonomically friendly tools and accessories. This article highlights some of my favorites—tools that have helped keep woodworking fun and relatively pain-free.

Don't wait until you're old and sore to take advantage of these innovations. Make woodworking easier right now by eliminating many of the small, sometimes hidden, struggles in the workshop. You'll find sources for the tools on p. 83.

Get a Better Grip

Some woodworking tasks are just plain hard on your hands. I'm thinking especially of turning, as in driving screws; twisting, as in tightening clamps; and holding during assembly or while gripping a plane. Common aches and pains can magnify these difficulties, turning a simple task like driving a nail or planing a surface into an endurance test.

Recently I've been asking my wife to open beverage bottle caps. My wrist strength is not what it was and I am not even embarrassed. What did humble me, however, was the pliers marks on several of my parallel-jaw clamps. I just could not crank them tight enough by hand alone. Then I began using foam-rubber grips that slip over the clamp handles. The grips let me tighten the jaws without pain or mechanical leverage. Some clamp makers now offer bigger, "grippier" handles.

Chisels also can be difficult to handle, especially those with slender, rounded grips. If you find a square or octagonal handle on a good chisel, buy it. If not, refit your chisels with larger handles that are well shaped for your grip.

For a better grip in all kinds of applications, some woodworkers like to use cotton gloves with a latex coating on the palms.

Saw on the Pull Stroke

The Japanese-type pullsaw was an exciting discovery for me even when I had lots of strength. The saw rewards a gentle grip and action with a cut that's smoother and more precise than a Western backsaw. The saws are relatively inexpensive, and there are a variety of blade types. The flexible blade with zero set is great alternative for cutting plugs and pegs flush to a surface, reducing time spent planing or sanding.

Sharpen by Machine

Sharpening chisels and plane irons using a stone or sandpaper can be an exercise in suffering. The strokes are tiring and the grip—even with a honing guide—can be painful. This pain becomes a reason to postpone sharpening, which in turn causes more pain and danger from using dull tools. A dry-abrasive horizontal sharpener, which I purchased a year or so ago, rescued me from all of that. Its slow speed and controlled angles let me sharpen and hone a chisel or a plane blade in less than three minutes.

Scrape with Less Effort

A sharp card scraper removes wood smoothly and quickly with great control. But I came late to hand-scraping and frankly too late to comfortably hold and flex a scraper by hand enough to get good shavings. The Lee Valley card-scraper holder makes it simple and painless to scrape a wood surface. Another real arm-saver is the heavy scraping plane, versions of which are made by Lie-Nielsen and Lee Valley. Properly sharpened and tuned, it saves hours of hand- or random-orbit sanding.

Power Tools Can Prevent Pain

Cordless power drivers are a godsend to the woodworker with arthritis in the hands and wrists. Their use as a drill is obvious, but their real gift is allowing you to drive screws without pain. With current advances in batteries and ergonomics, a lightweight 12-volt model can handle almost any drilling task.

Even more powerful are the cordless impact drivers that effortlessly "melt" large screws into hardwood. I recently used one to install a new deck surface, a job in which driving the screws by hand would have been impossible.

A small but powerful trim router that can be held with one hand is much easier to use than a full-size router in roundover or hinge-setting operations, for example. The Bosch Colt router has become a mainstay in my shop for profiling the edges of already assembled cases and drawers. It is not only quite powerful, but it's also ergonomically designed for one-handed use. Fitted with a flush-trimming bit, it saves much hand-scraping and planing when trimming edge-banding on plywood.

Make the Work Easier on Your Eyes

As we grow older, many of us need corrective lenses to read a ruler or see a layout line. There are other tools that can help you see what you're doing.

Safety goggles or safety glasses with a magnifying insert act as tiny bifocals that allow you to read the fractional increments on a ruler or place a drill hole accurately. At the same time, of course, they protect your eyes from flying particles.

Look for measuring tapes with large, clear, and distinctive markings. Electronic digital calipers have a large, liquid-crystal readout that is much easier to read than a vernier gauge or a $1/64$-in. increment on a ruler.

Use a desk lamp that is equipped not only with an articulated light but also with a magnifying lens for easy close-up work. These lamps, as well as the magnifying safety glasses, are useful for inspecting the progress made while sharpening edge tools.

Save Your Back

I won't belabor back braces and proper lifting procedures to avoid damaging your back. Let's focus on the stuff that is just too heavy to lift, even if you once could bench-press 250 lb. A good friend, partner, or strong spouse is the best tool ever invented to save your back. Get one and treat him or her well. Remember, this helper plays a dual role: He or she can also be blamed for any errors in judgment.

A small scissor-lift hydraulic table (prices start at $220) can lift equipment or cabinet assemblies from 5 in. off the floor to bench or machine-table height. It's also great for loading or unloading a pickup truck. This device makes a superb assembly table: It can position the work at proper height to minimize stretching and awkward reaches.

An anti-fatigue floor mat is great. Your feet and back will be even more grateful if you keep a padded stool near the bench. Many tasks, such as chopping dovetail waste or wiping finish on small parts, lend themselves well to working from a seated position. Look for a stool that's adjustable so you can set it at your optimum working height.

Try an Upright Shop Vac

For the last several years, the shop cleanup routine involved tedious broom action and a loud call to my beloved spouse to come hold the dust pan. A canister-type shop vacuum can reduce that nuisance, particularly if it has a long enough wand to allow an upright stance. Better still for me was a "Shop Sweep" from Shop-Vac. This machine is kind of a super upright vacuum with a huge bag. It sweeps up chips, nails, coins, and small careless children—all without my bending down. My wife has not been called to help with cleanup since we bought the Shop Sweep. (Some of you will not consider this progress, but your significant other will.)

WORKSHOP PLANS AND LAYOUTS

Floorplans for Workshops of All Sizes

by Asa Christiana

Since workspaces vary so widely—from cavernous lofts in industrial buildings to the corners of basements and garages, down to hallways and closets (I've seen it!)—it's hard to make definitive statements about shop layout. Except one: It matters, a lot.

Just like having a workspace that is too hot, too cold, or too dark, a disorganized floor plan means woodworking won't be as much fun. With too much fussing between every task, your frustration level will mount. Ever wonder why you are hesitating to head out to the shop? If it's not plain laziness, it might be one of the culprits listed above.

I can't help with chronic lassitude, but I can give some advice on shop layout, with help from a few of my friends. To fathom the feng shui of an efficient shop, I reached out to a number of FWW authors with well-organized workspaces, and settled on three that reflect the most common situations.

I discovered a number of common themes. For one, while shop spaces range widely, most of us end up with a similar set of equipment. Most also need some storage space for lumber, power tools, and other supplies; a router-table solution; and at least one other waist-high work surface, aside from the workbench.

Another common theme is that each of these woodworkers took the time to think about how he works and what he uses most often. In all cases the tablesaw and workbench were placed first, since they are used the most and require the most elbow room. But after that, these guys came up with a variety of smart layout solutions. Also, space needs vary for hobbyists vs. professionals. That's because time is money for the latter. The rest of us can live with a bit of shuffling to make things work.

One last note: If you choose to work with hand tools only, many of these rules don't apply. Even if you make exceptions for a jointer and bandsaw to speed things up, you'll be able to work comfortably in much less space, with only a workbench and tool cabinet to accommodate.

Large

Working pro needs extra space, but layout still matters
Christian Becksvoort, professional furniture maker
New Gloucester, Maine

Outbuilding, 24x40 Chris Becksvoort built his shop in the early 1980s out of lumber from the local sawmill. He did most of the framing and installed the floor, which is 1-$1/2$-in.-thick hemlock. A few friends helped with the main support beam down the center of the shop, and the roof shingles. An electrician did the 120/240 wiring. This year Becksvoort updated the roof to standing-seam metal, and reports that "snow slides off in a hurry."

The center of the shop is obstructed by a support post and a set of stairs, which lead up to his lumber loft and can be folded upward if necessary. But Becksvoort has never had to do that. Instead, he parked three machines around the stairs, and tucks scrap bins and other items below.

Becksvoort keeps his big Lie-Nielsen workbench out in the open, and most of his work happens on or around it. Nearby is a long counter with storage for routers and bits, sanders, clamps, fasteners, a Bose audio system, and the phone ("It's a dial phone with a really loud bell I can hear when machinery is running"). Above the countertop and close at hand for benchwork is his big wall-mounted tool cabinet (see FWW #153).

The other dedicated workstation that juts into the shop is Becksvoort's 7-ft. glue-up table with slotted rails for bar clamps. Most everything else in this shop is along the walls, leaving plenty of assembly and work space in the middle, critical for a working pro. Like many woodworkers, Becksvoort realized that his tablesaw doesn't need any

extra room on the extension end, so he parks that against a wall, leaving plenty of room for infeed and outfeed on both sides. His lathe sits in front of an east-facing window, which offers wonderful light for morning turning sessions.

A Corner For Glue-Ups.

Becksvoort's solid-cherry Shaker furniture usually starts with glued-up panels, so a dedicated clamping table is a worthwhile investment in floor space. He assembles doors there, too.

No Space Goes to Waste.

Longer scraps find a home in bins along the attic stairs, with bins for smaller scraps tucked under the staircase. The ceiling beam holds clamps and sawblades.

Little Island at the Support Post.

Becksvoort turned an obstruction into an asset by attaching power outlets to it, and clustering his bandsaw, jointer, and sander nearby. Related accessories hang on the post, too.

Medium

A small garage can pack a punch
Michael Pekovich,
hobbyist/part-time pro
Middlebury, Conn.
Garage, 20x20

FWW art director and frequent contributor Mike Pekovich also makes furniture professionally, at least part-time, in his vintage two-car garage. The 20x20 building was small to begin with, but after insulating the cinder-block walls, the usable space was reduced to a cozy 18x18. "I knew that I had to make every inch count," Pekovich says. "That meant I had to give up on the idea of storing lots of lumber in my shop. A lumber shed is in the plans, but for now, I buy stock as projects come along, and when scraps build up too much, they go into the woodstove. Finally, anything that is only used on occasion goes up to the attic and out of my way."

Pekovich has never been a fan of mobile machines, and not just because he doesn't want to have to stop working to rearrange them. "The rolling bases I've used are too wobbly, and once the shop gets cluttered up, it's difficult to move things at all." His solution is a central machinery island, an idea favored by many woodworkers. He says the "doughnut of space" around the island serves as infeed and outfeed for the machines, and offers easy access to everything else in the shop.

But the heart and soul of the shop is the hand-tool area, Pekovich says. He is not the first to center his workbench under a window, both for the visibility and the view. And a wall-hung tool cabinet is another common touch. But his tablesaw's outfeed table, which has a solid maple top and cast-iron front vise, is innovative. "I use it both as a workbench and assembly table, and it's the smartest move I made in my shop." Also near the bench is a 15-drawer cabinet that holds a variety of fasteners and power tools, with the top serving as a sharpening station.

Storage, storage, storage.

Hand tools are stored in a wall cabinet near the workbench. A 15-drawer cabinet, which houses hardware, router bits, and power tools, also serves as a sharpening station. Most of the wall space is taken up by hanging cabinets, shelves, and plywood backboards for hanging up jigs.

Machine central.

The tablesaw, jointer, and planer are clustered in the center of the shop where a dust collector can easily pick up the chips. A shopmade stand raises the planer to allow infeed and outfeed clearance over the jointer bed in front and tablesaw outfeed table behind.

Long boards, no problem.

Pekovich's chopsaw and bandsaw are centered on separate walls, allowing for maximum infeed and outfeed clearance. For additional support at the chopsaw, Pekovich slips a board rest under the lathe bed.

Hand tools within easy reach. One corner of Becksvoort's shop is dedicated to benchwork. His custom-height bench is located near his wall-mounted tool cabinet. And counter-height cabinets along the wall provide ample storage for handheld power tools.

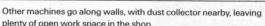
Other machines go along walls, with dust collector nearby, leaving plenty of open work space in the shop.

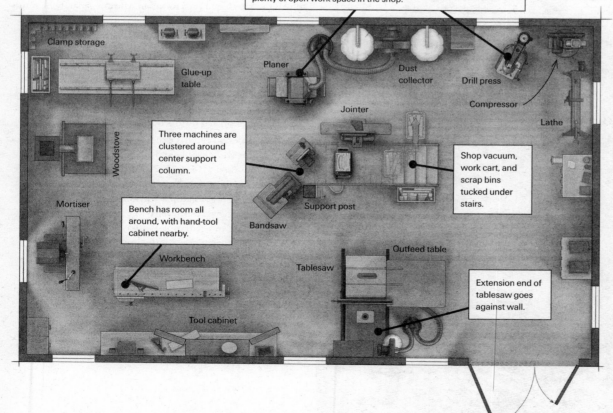

Clamp storage

Glue-up table

Planer

Dust collector

Drill press

Compressor

Jointer

Lathe

Woodstove

Three machines are clustered around center support column.

Shop vacuum, work cart, and scrap bins tucked under stairs.

Mortiser

Bench has room all around, with hand-tool cabinet nearby.

Bandsaw

Support post

Workbench

Outfeed table

Tablesaw

Extension end of tablesaw goes against wall.

Tool cabinet

Double-duty outfeed table. Pekovich built his tablesaw outfeed table with a sturdy trestle base and solid maple top. Outfitted with a cast-iron vise, the table serves as a second workbench and an assembly table. On large projects, even the tablesaw top lends a helping hand.

Small

In the smallest spaces, plan vertically and horizontally
Rob Porcaro, hobbyist/part-time pro
Medfield, Mass.
Spare room, 11x17

Rob Porcaro is "quite proud of his little workshop," which is in a spare room of his house. That gives him the benefit of hardwood floors, climate control, and a very short commute. Acoustic paneling on the doors keeps the family happy.

To make the space work for the usual mix of hand and power tools, Porcaro has engineered almost every inch, both horizontally and vertically, the latter by closely matching infeed and outfeed surfaces, letting him place tools much closer together, and building a number of smart racks for clamps, lumber, and parts in progress. He has enjoyed fine-tuning the space and has covered the process extensively in his blogs at RPWoodwork.com/blog.

Porcaro began his layout like most people do, by locating the workbench. His first thought was to put it under the windows, but he decided to place it along the opposite wall for a number of reasons particular to his space. For one, he anticipated that the baseboard heater element under the windows would get packed with chips from the bench. Also, he wouldn't have as much wall space for placing his tool cabinet nearby. And last, his electrical outlets were on the window side. So it made more sense to park his machines there.

Porcaro took a calculated risk with his tablesaw, cutting down the rip-fence rails to the maximum capacity he tends to use, just over 24 in. That allowed him to create more room around the other side of the saw for infeed, outfeed, and crosscuts. He says he has rarely had to move the saw. A small cyclone dust collector is tucked in near the wall between the saw's rails. One 4-in.-dia. dust hose reaches all the machines, with a simple press-fit connection. No blast gates needed. This is where having a small shop is a good thing, Porcaro points out.

He is able to keep his bandsaw in place most of the time, but his router table and 12-in. jointer/planer must be moved to work. He stores an additional thickness planer (with a Shelix cutterhead) on top of a secondary tool chest. When needed, it goes atop a Workmate stand which normally hangs on a wall. Similarly, he "muscles" a benchtop drill press and an oscillating sander onto the Workmate from their storage places on the long shelf.

To make his cozy workshop work, Porcaro keeps only what he needs: "It's like the salary cap on a pro sports team—every tool has to perform with value."

FLEXIBLE LIGHTING.

A desk lamp attaches to the left side of the workbench (above) for the sharpening station, and to the right for the small fold-down drafting table.

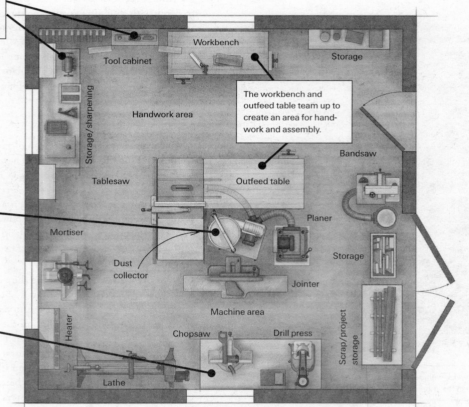

Wall cabinet keeps hand tools near bench, and sharpening station is also close by.

Tool cabinet

Workbench

Storage

Handwork area

Storage/sharpening

The workbench and outfeed table team up to create an area for handwork and assembly.

Bandsaw

Tablesaw

Outfeed table

Central machinery island makes dust collection easier and creates a circle of space all around.

Mortiser

Planer

Dust collector

Storage

Jointer

Additional tools go against the wall to complete the machine zone.

Machine area

Heater

Chopsaw

Drill press

Scrap/project storage

Lathe

Smart tool choices. Porcaro stores his hand tools in a large floor-standing cabinet. Even so, space is limited and he says that any new tool must be an upgrade for an existing one.

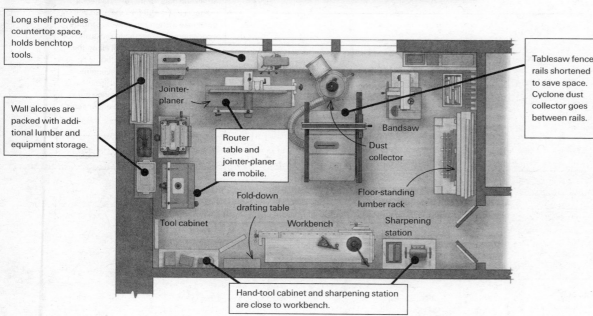

Long shelf provides countertop space, holds benchtop tools.

Wall alcoves are packed with additional lumber and equipment storage.

Jointer-planer

Router table and jointer-planer are mobile.

Fold-down drafting table

Tool cabinet

Workbench

Bandsaw

Dust collector

Floor-standing lumber rack

Sharpening station

Tablesaw fence rails shortened to save space. Cyclone dust collector goes between rails.

Hand-tool cabinet and sharpening station are close to workbench.

DUST COLLECTION IS SIMPLE BUT EFFECTIVE.

A portable cyclone with a single hose and slip fitting can service the tablesaw, bandsaw, and jointer/planer without being moved.

CHOPPED SAW.

Porcaro cut down the rip fence rails on his tablesaw to save floor space. The resulting 24-in. capacity is more than enough for the type of work he does. Instead of a dedicated outfeed table, he breaks out a tilt-top support stand only when needed for long rips.

JOINTER/PLANER PACKS A LOT OF MILLING INTO A SMALL FOOTPRINT.

The 12-in. machine can handle heavy milling tasks but rolls neatly out of the way. Porcaro makes sure to tackle all of the milling tasks on a project at one time, and doesn't see the mobile machine as an inconvenience. "It forces me to really think through a project before I begin, which has increased the efficiency in my work."

Tips for Basement Workshops

by Thomas McKenna

In medieval times, miscreants and criminals were tossed into the bowels of a dungeon for their offenses. Below ground, these dungeons were dark, dank, foreboding places, characterized for centuries as hideous homes for torture or cramped imprisonment.

It may be a stretch to compare a basement shop to a dungeon, but they do have similarities. Like a dungeon, a basement is a hole in the ground and attracts all manner of moisture, with issues such as mildew, rust, even small floods. Basements aren't flooded with natural sunlight, either; single incandescent fixtures are the norm, usually scattered where you don't need them. On top of that, basements are where household items go to die, so space is tight.

Still, for lack of an alternative, many woodworkers set up shop in the basement and have to deal with any or all of these medieval horrors. To help them out, we asked our extensive and experienced online audience for tips on making a basement workshop drier, brighter, and more space-efficient. We also asked folks how they prevent noise and dust from infiltrating the living areas above.

The response was overwhelming, and we got plenty of nifty solutions to common problems. We used those ideas to create a virtual basement shop that is as comfortable to work in as it is unobtrusive to the rest of the household.

How to Keep Moisture at Bay

Basement walls are concrete, a porous material that allows moisture penetration if you don't take measures to stop that migration. It's well worth the effort, though. Here in the Northeast, for instance, many basements are moist, and folks who have basements are familiar with the term "musty." In summer, there's an odor in the basement that's impossible to miss but hard to pinpoint. In winter, the cold, moist air can chill even your fingernails. And the moisture does not just create an uncomfortable working environment. It also will rust your tools and increase the moisture content of lumber to undesirable levels.

If you get standing water regularly, you may have issues that need to be addressed by a professional waterproofing contractor before placing expensive tools and materials in harm's way. But if you simply have a damp space, there are many ways to fight the fog.

Look outside—If you're battling moisture, the cause may be rooted outside the house. Check that the house gutters are not clogged and that the downspouts are directed away from the foundation. Where possible, try to grade the property so that it slopes away from the house. This may be easier said than done.

Continued →

Get a dehumidifier—One of the first things we heard from our online responders was to add a dehumidifier. You can get one at any home center. Depending on the size, the cost will run from about $150 to $250. When you install the dehumidifier, make a habit of emptying it regularly, especially during the humid summer months.

Seal walls and floor—You can reduce moisture by sealing the walls and floor with a moisture-blocking paint, such as Drylok or Damplock. These thick coatings have the added benefit of giving the area a bright face-lift that reflects light.

Guard against rust—Finally, you can fight rust directly by placing desiccants in tool drawers or coating surfaces lightly with paste wax.

Fight Dust and Noise Migration

Dust is a known carcinogen, so it's important to prevent as much of it as possible from floating around. If you work in a basement, the dust also becomes a nuisance upstairs, as it will migrate into living areas. So get a dust collector and an air cleaner to help keep the particles at bay. You'll also appreciate the fact that there will be less to sweep up.

Along with dust, a woodworker's passion for building things comes with another inhospitable by-product: noise. When you're working below the living area of your home, you must be mindful of others above. Our online survey uncovered some nuggets that help reduce the noise that can invade living areas.

You can launch a systematic, all-out offensive against sound, as Mark Corke did for us in 2004. In that article, he showed how to frame and insulate the basement walls and ceiling to eliminate sound migration into the upper living areas. But there are smaller steps you can take to help turn down the volume.

Separate drywall from framing—One way to reduce sound transmission is to isolate the drywall from the framing. You can install resilient metal channel (www.truesoundcontrol.com) in the ceiling, as Corke did, but a cheaper alternative is stapling polystyrene sill sealer (available at home centers) to studs and ceiling joists to create a cushion between the wood and the drywall. Insulation between framing also will help reduce sound transmission; the higher the R-value, the better the insulation will dampen sound.

Put a lid on your compressor and shop vacuum—Although you can't put a muffler on your tools, you can reduce the output of two of the more annoying accessories in the shop: the compressor and the shop vacuum. By housing each of these in a soundproof chamber made of plywood and acoustic padding, you drop the noise level of each machine. Just make sure the box has enough holes or vents for airflow.

Get a better door—One of the unique aspects of a basement shop is that there's often a door leading directly to the living areas of the home. Choosing the right door, or modifying your existing one, can help reduce the amount of noise and dust that enters the home. For advice in that area, I turned to veteran Fine Homebuilding editor Chuck Miller, who's also a talented woodworker.

High-frequency noises generated by routers and shop vacuums get in through cracks, Miller says, while low-

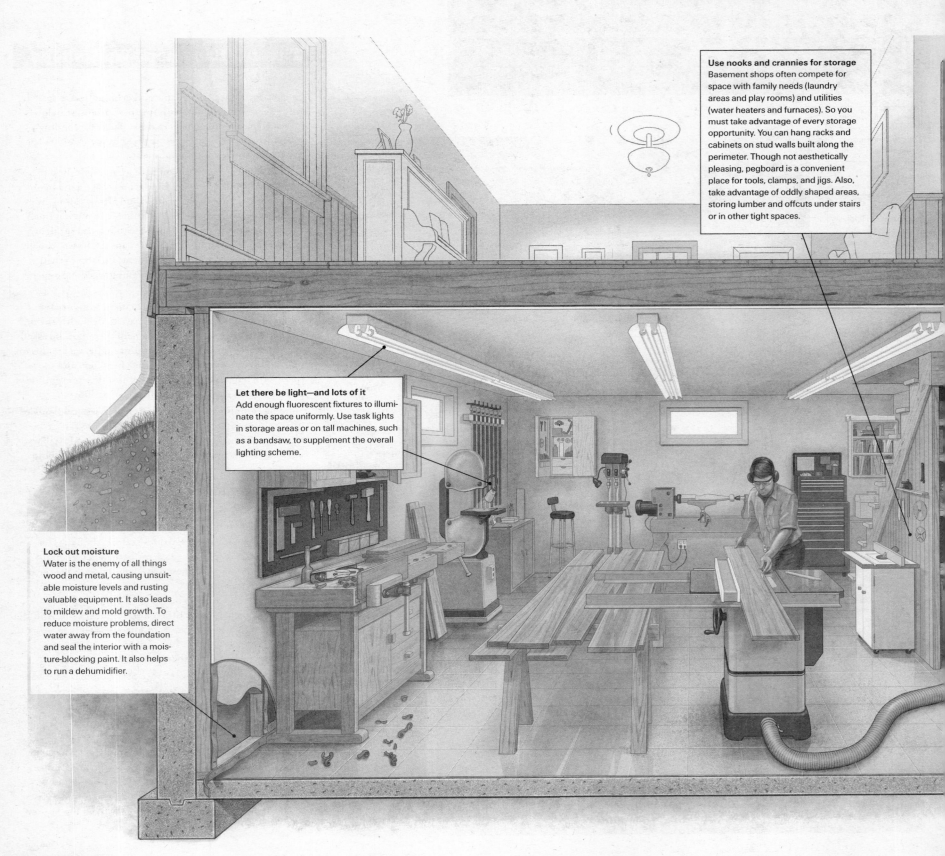

Use nooks and crannies for storage
Basement shops often compete for space with family needs (laundry areas and play rooms) and utilities (water heaters and furnaces). So you must take advantage of every storage opportunity. You can hang racks and cabinets on stud walls built along the perimeter. Though not aesthetically pleasing, pegboard is a convenient place for tools, clamps, and jigs. Also, take advantage of oddly shaped areas, storing lumber and offcuts under stairs or in other tight spaces.

Let there be light—and lots of it
Add enough fluorescent fixtures to illuminate the space uniformly. Use task lights in storage areas or on tall machines, such as a bandsaw, to supplement the overall lighting scheme.

Lock out moisture
Water is the enemy of all things wood and metal, causing unsuitable moisture levels and rusting valuable equipment. It also leads to mildew and mold growth. To reduce moisture problems, direct water away from the foundation and seal the interior with a moisture-blocking paint. It also helps to run a dehumidifier.

frequency sounds, such as those generated by a deadblow mallet on a workpiece, migrate through mass. Miller recommends treating the basement door as though it were an exterior entry, where you want to stop air infiltration.

Your first choice is install a heavy, prehung exterior door, with all the attendant weatherstripping in place. The weatherstripping will cut down on the high-frequency sound, and the mass of the door itself will muffle the low-frequency noise. If you don't want to add a new door, retrofit the basement door with weatherstripping along the door stops, and add a vinyl sweep to the door bottom.

Pump Up the Lighting, and Make the Most of Space

By their nature, basements don't get natural light, so you need a boost here. Typically, basement lighting schemes are not well-thought-out by builders. You often get a small handful of single bulbs scattered here and there. But you can change the lighting scheme to create a more inviting, comfortable work area.

The goal is to create uniform lighting from corner to corner, and fluorescent fixtures are the most economical way to do it. If you have existing incandescent fixtures, replace them with banks of fluorescent lights to illuminate as much of the space as possible. If you don't have existing fixtures and wiring, it's worth the investment to hire an electrician to run the wiring and install the fixtures.

To help with light reflectivity, paint the walls white and coat the concrete floor with epoxy paint. Another option is to lay down light-colored vinyl tile. Treating the floor not only helps with light reflection, but it also fights moisture and makes it easier to sweep up any debris.

If you need to, add task lighting at your bench or at machines that cast shadows on their own tables, such as a floor-standing drill press or a bandsaw. It's also beneficial to illuminate storage areas.

As with most woodworking shops, a basement can get filled with equipment quickly. But basement spaces can be small to start with, and often store stuff for everyone in the family, so storage for your lumber, tools, and accessories becomes even more of a challenge.

Many readers suggested using narrow or oddly shaped areas, such as the space under stairs, to store lumber and scraps. Those with larger basements built separate storage rooms around their furnaces and water heaters. This solution not only creates a neat storage option, but it also isolates the utilities from wood dust. Some folks simply store most of their wood outside or in the garage, bringing in stock as they need it.

Some readers built wood stud walls over the concrete surfaces, making it easy to hang cabinets, lumber racks, or other storage systems. The bottom line: Use spaces smartly, and you'll stay well organized and avoid mixing your lumber scraps with the laundry.

Working in a Basement Is Not So Bad

A basement may not be the ideal place to set up shop, but for many folks it's the best option.

Instead of toiling in a dungeon, you can create a clean, well-lighted place. In the end, you'll be more comfortable and so will your housemates—a win-win for everyone.

Do not disturb the household
Let's face it, building furniture is a noisy hobby, and when you're engaging your passion below the rest of your family, the muffled roar can be annoying. We got some great tips from readers on how they manage sound transmission, ranging from isolating framing from drywall, to beefing up the basement door, to muffling shop vacuums and compressors, to simply not working after hours.

Don't choke on dust
There's not a lot of airflow in a basement, so airborne dust will just hang in the air or migrate to living areas above. To control and capture it, use a dust collector and install an air cleaner. To prevent dust from tracking upstairs on the bottom of your shoes, place a doormat at the bottom of the stairs or use a pair of shop shoes.

Design Tips for Stand-Alone Shops

by Matt Kenny

It's possible to build furniture just about anywhere—I've done it in an attic and on a narrow balcony—but it's more enjoyable and easier in a shop dedicated to woodworking. You don't have to pack up your tools and projects at the end of the day or work around a lawn mower, bicycles, or cars.

The good news is that it's not as difficult as you might think to have a dedicated shop. The three shops featured here are great examples of how it can be done on a variety of budgets. And all of them are detached from the house, which minimizes the amount of dust and noise that make it into the living space.

Convert a Garage

When looking for a new house, Anatole Burkin found one for sale that had two garages: one attached to the house for the cars, and a detached garage, which he knew would make a great shop. He jokes that he was sold on the house before he even took a look inside.

By using an existing structure for his shop, Burkin avoided the cost of constructing a new building. The only structural changes he made were to remove one of the overhead doors and replace it with an entry door and window. He also insulated the roof, hung a ceiling, and laid prefabricated wood tiles on the floor. All these changes help keep the shop warmer in the winter. At 440 sq. ft., Burkin's shop is cozy, but by paying close attention to workflow he was able to arrange all of his tools and workstations to make it feel bigger.

ROLLING RACKS ARE VERSATILE.

To make the most of the shop's wall space, Burkin used inline-skate wheels to create four rolling tool racks. They allow him to use the space in front of the windows without permanently blocking them.

MOBILE TOOLS ARE THERE WHEN HE NEEDS THEM.

When he doesn't, he pushes them against the wall to open up floor space.

No cars allowed. A single overhead door is the only hint that Burkin's shop was once a two-car garage. He kept it because it's great for bringing materials into the shop and furniture out.

Continued ➔

TABLESAW TAKES CENTER STAGE.

Paolini uses his tablesaw all the time, so it needs a central location and lots of space. He keeps just about everything on rolling carts so he can quickly clear out the area around it for cutting large pieces and assembling big cabinets.

TALL WORK IS NO PROBLEM.

Paolini used scissor trusses on the back half of his shop. The extra height they provide lets him assemble very tall pieces.

SHEET GOODS GO ON A ROLLING RACK.

Offcuts are stored in bins to keep them organized and easy to find. Full sheets are stacked together, making it easier to sort through them and pull one out.

CLAMP CART ROLLS, TOO.

Paolini saves time by always having clamps close at hand, rather than walking back and forth to a wall-hung rack.

COMPLETE SHOP IN A SMALL SPACE.
Although this shop is less than 500 sq. ft., Burkin laid out work areas in a smart way so it holds every tool a furniture maker needs.

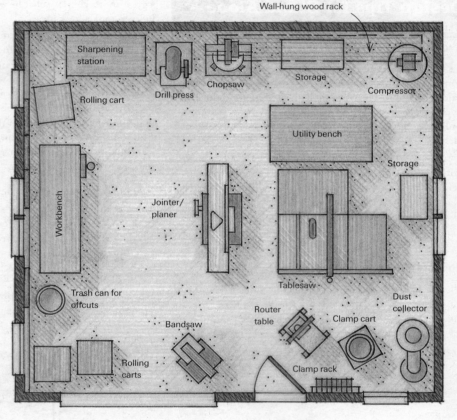

Wall-hung wood rack

Sharpening station
Rolling cart
Drill press
Chopsaw
Storage
Compressor
Utility bench
Storage
Workbench
Jointer/planer
Tablesaw
Dust collector
Trash can for offcuts
Router table
Clamp cart
Bandsaw
Clamp rack
Rolling carts

A place in the sun. Paolini placed his bench alongside two south-facing windows, which let in light year round. Living in the South, he can open the overhead doors most of the year to let in an extra flood of light.

Build a Garage Shop with Retail in Mind

Greg Paolini wasn't a full-time professional woodworker when he built his shop, but he knew that one day he would be. He needed a shop that would be big enough to run a business from, but didn't want to be burdened with a limited-use building if he ever outgrew it. That's why Paolini built an oversize two-car garage tailored to fit the needs of a professional furniture maker.

New construction is always expensive, but Paolini cut down on the expense by building a garage 24 ft. wide by 32 ft. deep, with studs 16 in. on center, which meant he didn't need to cut down any sheathing, insulation, or wall covering. He used attic trusses in the front for overhead storage and scissor trusses on the back half to get 11-ft. ceilings, space he needs to assemble large cabinets. But if Paolini ever moves his shop or sells the whole property, he would only need to remove his tools, and the garage would be ready for cars, bikes, and a lawn mower.

Easy conversion back to a garage. Paolini knows that as his business grows, he might outgrow his home shop or sell the whole property. The oversize garage he built will easily house cars when it no longer houses his business.

VERSATILE GARAGE SHOP

Spacious and filled with carts and tools on mobile bases, this shop can be reconfigured quickly to meet the changing needs of a professional cabinet maker.

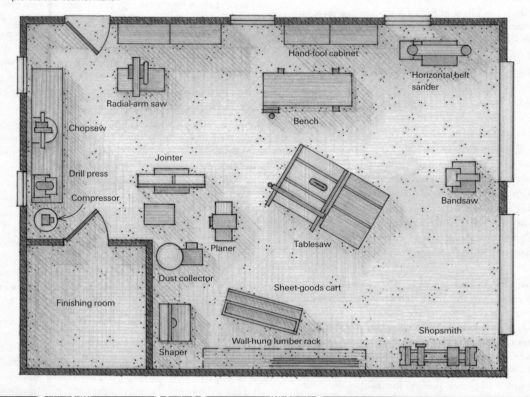

Hand-tool cabinet
Horizontal belt sander
Radial-arm saw
Bench
Chopsaw
Jointer
Drill press
Compressor
Bandsaw
Planer
Tablesaw
Dust collector
Sheet-goods cart
Finishing room
Shopsmith
Shaper
Wall-hung lumber rack

Take the lathe for a spin. Waters likes to make chairs, which need turned parts. A treadle lathe allows him to stay true to his love for traditional, human-powered tools.

Or Make No Compromises

Sunny Waters lives in the Pennsylvania countryside. His home is an accurate reproduction of a classic three-level home, down to the interior plank doors with wooden latches and leather pulls. That's the perfect setting for his woodworking, as he makes period chairs using traditional techniques and doesn't use any power tools.

When Waters set out to design his shop, he was less concerned about the budget than he was that the shop not conflict with the historical accuracy of his home, the idyllic countryside, and the pre-industrial bent of his woodworking. That's why his shop appears to be a two-horse barn, why its bones are a timber frame raised by local Amish craftsmen, and why he built the interior of the shop over three years, using hand tools whenever possible. But that doesn't mean he completely shunned the modern world. The walls, floors, and ceiling are insulated, and although the primary means of heat is a woodstove, Waters installed a propane heater for really cold mornings. And he took advantage of full-extension drawer slides in a clever way to make his tools easy to store and easy to reach.

A FEW MODERN CONVENIENCES FIT IN FINE.

The Noden Adjust-a-Bench isn't out of place in Waters's hand-tool shop, and its versatility allows Waters to carve without bending over.

BEAUTY AND WARMTH.

A woodstove is the primary source of heat in winter. It looks perfect set against a wall made from local stones.

TURN DRAWERS ON END.

Vertical panels, mounted on full-extension slides, pack Waters's large collection of hand tools into a small space, and the setup makes it easy to reach them.

Timber frame creates dream shop. To complement the pre-industrial charm of his home, Waters designed his timber-frame shop to look like a horse barn. The inside is beautiful, too.

HAND-TOOL HAVEN

An emphasis on hand tools and man-powered machines led to this un-cluttered but well-outfitted shop.

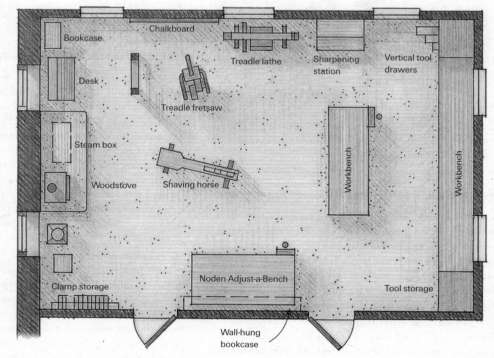

Bookcase
Chalkboard
Treadle lathe
Sharpening station
Vertical tool drawers
Desk
Treadle fretsaw
Steam box
Workbench
Workbench
Woodstove
Shaving horse
Clamp storage
Noden Adjust-a-Bench
Tool storage
Wall-hung bookcase

Continued ➜

Tips for a Comfortable Garage Workshop

by Michael Pekovich

I set up shop in the two-car garage of my Connecticut house when I started at Fine Woodworking 13 years ago. Coming from California, I wondered why so many folks in this area chose to work in their cramped basements rather than their spacious garages.

But when November came around, I understood. The propane heater I had installed was no match for the uninsulated roof and walls, cold concrete floor, and leaky garage doors. After emptying a 60-gal. propane tank in less than a month, my shop quickly became a three-season workplace and its floor space was increasingly devoted to bikes, camping gear, and chicken feed.

With access to the Fine Woodworking shop at work, I asked myself if I even needed a home shop, but after sharing the shop for years and watching rust develop on my woodworking machines at home, I finally decided I really needed my own heated workspace. This meant insulating the floors, walls, and ceiling, hanging and finishing drywall, and installing new doors. I also bought a manufactured shed to house all of the non-woodworking items that had been slowly encroaching on my workspace.

I'm a woodworker, not a carpenter, so a lot of the tasks on this project were new to me. Fortunately, with the folks at Fine Homebuilding just down the hall, I had access to decades of collective building knowledge. Admittedly, some of the building solutions I came up with might not be realistic on a typical building site where speed and efficiency dictate how to accomplish every task, but they made sense to me as a woodworker on a very tight budget. I hope they make sense to you, too.

4 Steps to a Warmer Shop

1. Install new doors

2. Add a wood floor

3. Finish the ceiling

4. Insulate the walls

Two Garage Doors—Two Different Approaches

It was easy to see I was losing many of my heating dollars through the gaps in the garage doors. Weatherstripping and insulation kits are available for doors in good repair, but my old rotting doors had to go. The question was how to replace them. I thought about a set of steel insulated doors, but I didn't like the idea of hoisting open a roll-up door in the middle of winter and letting the cold air rush in.

Instead, I decided to replace one of the overhead doors with a normal walk-out door. This would provide easy entry and create a few extra feet of much-needed wall space. I did this by framing in a pair of narrow panels that would flank an inexpensive, prehung steel entry door.

Each panel consists of a 2x4 frame faced with CDX plywood (rated for exterior use). The frame is filled with rigid insulation and covered with drywall on the interior face. To dress up the exterior, I glued and nailed pine boards to the plywood for a frame-and-panel look. Windows with square corbels below the sill added an Arts and Crafts element that would complement my home's bungalow style.

For the second bay, I needed a different approach. Even though I never intend to park a car in the space, I still wanted to leave a door wide enough to drive through in case we ever decide to sell the house. I also like the idea of having a large opening for machinery and lumber, and letting in sunshine on nice days.

Instead of a roll-up door, I opted for a pair of swing-out carriage doors. I thought the carriage doors would be easier to weather-seal and would offer more insulation. Eliminating the garage door's overhead tracks would also give me additional headroom and provide greater flexibility with the lighting layout. After getting a quote of $4,000 for professionally made doors, I decided I could make my own.

Carriage doors anyone can build—I wanted the doors to be lightweight, well insulated, and really rigid to resist sagging over time. True frame-and-panel construction didn't seem to be a good way to accomplish any of those tasks. Instead, I chose a torsion-box design consisting of a solid-wood frame with plywood on each face, similar to the way a hollow-core door is made. This would create a very rigid structure with plenty of room for insulation.

I started with a 1 1/2-in.-thick poplar frame joined with stub tenons. Long tenons aren't necessary; in fact, biscuits would work fine, because all the strength comes from the plywood skins. I used a dado blade to cut a 1/2-in.-wide by 1-in.-deep groove in the frame parts. I also used the dado blade to cut stub tenons on the ends of the parts to fit the groove. The frame was glued and screwed through the tenons.

I filled the cavity with rigid insulation and glued and nailed plywood to each face. This created a very rigid torsion box that should resist sagging for many years. The outer face is 1/2-in. plywood while the inside face is 1/4-in. plywood to help keep the weight down. I added windows and framed the outside face with 3/4-in.-thick lumber for a frame-and-panel look similar to the other bay. The final result is 48-in.-wide door that weighs less than a typical solid-oak entry door, and at $300, is far cheaper than a custom-built door. The guys at Fine Homebuilding were impressed.

I mounted the doors with long strap hinges that are plenty strong and look great. They were also very easy to install. First, I attached the hinges to the doors with lag screws. Then I set the doors in place using shims to locate them properly. With consistent gaps all around, I bolted the hinges to the door frame.

A Wood Floor Is Warm and Easy on the Feet

For the floor, I took a cue from an article on shop flooring by Scott Gibson. I glued and nailed pressure-treated 2x4s to the concrete floor, placing rigid insulation in between. The insulation I used was the same thickness as the 2x4s, so I spaced the sleepers 24 in. on center. Normally a spacing of 16 in. would be necessary to prevent the floor from sagging under the weight of heavy machines, but since the rigid insulation has good compressive strength, 24 in. is fine. Before screwing the 3/4-in T&G (tongue-and-groove) plywood in place, I stapled 6-mil plastic over the insulation to act as a vapor barrier, just as Gibson recommended.

I moved as much as possible out of the shop by filling an 8-ft. by 12-ft. portable storage container (pods.com) that was dropped off in my driveway before construction started. Unfortunately, some machinery didn't fit, so I had to install the floor in two parts, moving the equipment from one side to the other. Installation would have been easier in an empty shop, but I was able to get the entire floor done in a day. The new floor is warmer, easier to sweep, and much kinder to my feet and joints.

Enclose the Ceiling for a Brighter, Warmer Shop

The ceiling posed a challenge. I like the looks and reflected light provided by an enclosed ceiling, but the bottom of my ceiling joists were now only 7 1/2 ft. off my new plywood floor. The space felt more cramped and claustrophobic. My first thought was to spray insulation on the underside of the roof and leave the ceiling joists open. The insulation contractor said I'd still need to cover the insulation with plywood or drywall if the joists were left open, so I decided to look into raising the joists and enclosing the ceiling.

I spoke to the local building department about my situation and an engineer in the department concluded I could raise the ceiling joists 2 ft. without creating structural problems. I had always thought of building inspectors as something best avoided on small home-improvement jobs, but on this project, they were a big help.

Again, I'm a woodworker, not a carpenter, so the idea of raising ceiling joists was a little scary. Fortunately, the actual process wasn't that bad. I was able to reuse the existing joists by cutting them one at a time and nailing them in their new location (some local codes don't allow the reuse of materials, so check first). One smart thing I did was to rent a cordless Paslode framing nailer from my local home center.

The final ceiling is a lofty 9 ft. While the floor plan didn't grow, the shop now has a more spacious feel and by adding some 1/2-in OSB (oriented strand board) on top of the ceiling joists, I have some much-needed storage above the ceiling. To access that space, I installed a fold-down attic ladder and wired a light in the attic. For insulation, I decided to spray the underside of the roof with open-cell foam insulation. Since my rafters are only 6 in. deep, I only was able to achieve an R20. But since foam practically eliminates air movement, which experts say is the real nemesis in heat loss, it should perform very well.

When it came time to reinstall the lights, I decided on an upgrade. I replaced my three old 8-ft. two-bulb fixtures with nine 4-ft. four-bulb fixtures, effectively tripling the amount of light in the shop. With the addition of the white ceiling and walls, my shop now glows like a beacon.

Basement Approach to Wall Insulation

The walls of a typical frame-construction garage are easy to insulate. But the walls of my shop are concrete block, so I used an insulation method more suited to a basement shop, but with a modern twist. Rather than frame out the concrete wall in the typical fashion with studs on edge and the insulation in between, I took a different approach.

On the advice of Rob Wotzak, an expert on green construction at Fine Homebuilding, I started by covering the masonry wall with a continuous layer of rigid insulation, wedging it between a top and bottom plate that I nailed to the block wall. Over that, I attached the studs flat against the insulation, nailing them to the plates. From there, I installed a second layer of insulation between the studs and finished with drywall. Installing the studs on edge would have created a thermal bridge from the block wall to the drywall, reducing the insulating properties of the wall. The continuous layer of insulation between the block wall and studs acts as a thermal break and should result in lower heating bills. The finished wall is only 3 1/2 in. thick but boasts an R-value over 20.

A True Transformation

What started as a long-overdue insulation job ended up as completely transformed workspace. In replacing the doors, I wasn't looking to beautify my home, but the result is a quaint backyard shop that's bright and inviting.

It's not just the shop that has had a makeover. I've also picked up a few new skills. I've done some serious framing and remodeling. I've acquired new drywall skills and an appreciation for those people who do it well. Basic wiring is no longer a mystery to me. But, as much as I've enjoyed the new challenges, I'm happy to put my tool belt aside and get back to woodworking.

The Big Picture

With its drafty doors and concrete floor, Pekovich's uninsulated shop was limited to warm-weather woodworking. Even in the summer, the low ceiling, dark walls, and minimal lighting made the space feel cramped and dreary. By adding insulation, improving the lighting, and replacing the garage doors with shopmade carriage doors, he transformed the space into a comfortable, year-round workspace.

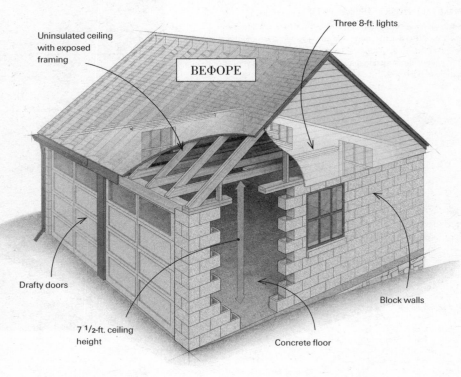

BEΦOPE

Three 8-ft. lights

Uninsulated ceiling with exposed framing

Block walls

Concrete floor

7 1/2-ft. ceiling height

Drafty doors

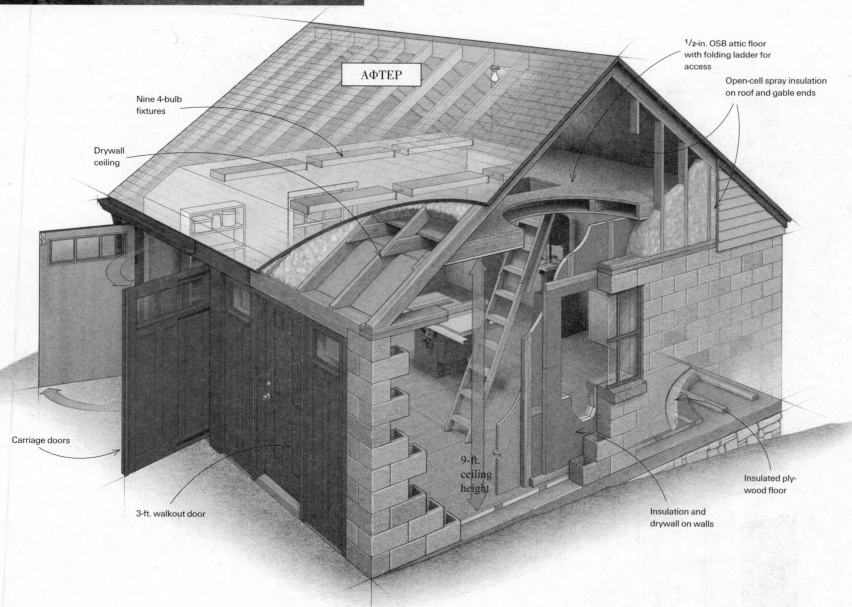

AΦTEP

1/2-in. OSB attic floor with folding ladder for access

Open-cell spray insulation on roof and gable ends

Nine 4-bulb fixtures

Drywall ceiling

Carriage doors

3-ft. walkout door

9-ft. ceiling height

Insulation and drywall on walls

Insulated plywood floor

Continued →

Two Options for Drafty Garage Doors

MAKE LIGHTWEIGHT CARRIAGE DOORS

Filled with rigid insulation and covered with a frame-and-panel treatment, Pekovich's shopmade carriage doors are an attractive and energy-efficient upgrade over conventional overhead garage doors. Torsion-box construction makes them lightweight yet very strong—and simple to build.

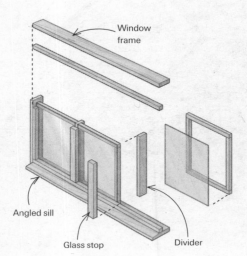

Window frame

Angled sill

Glass stop

Divider

1 1/2-in.-thick poplar frame

1 1/2-in. rigid insulation

3/4-in. pine

1/2-in. CDX plywood

Groove, 1/2 in. wide by 1 in. deep

1/4-in. plywood

1-in.-thick stub tenons

FRAME IN A WALKOUT DOOR

Compared to a garage door, a 3-ft. (prehung) steel entry door makes it easy to come and go and its smaller opening reduces heat loss. Side panels flanking the walkout door were used to shrink the garage's original 8-ft. opening. They also provide additional light and boost curb appeal.

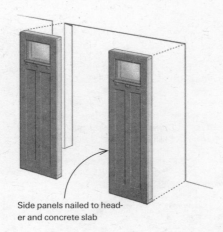

Side panels nailed to header and concrete slab

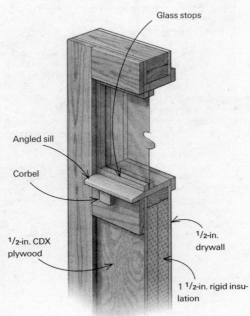

Glass stops

Angled sill

Corbel

1/2-in. CDX plywood

1/2-in. drywall

1 1/2-in. rigid insulation

3 strap hinges lag-bolted to door and post

3x3 post lag-bolted to framing

Water-shedding pressure-treated threshold

Stop

Raised plywood floor

2x6 pressure-treated bottom plate

Shims

Concrete

Poplar frame, plywood skin. A groove in the center of the 1 ¹/₂-in. thick poplar stock receives stub tenons formed on the ends of the rails with a dado set (left). Although most of the strength comes from the plywood skins, stub tenons help keep everything square during the large glue-up (right). Once the glue dries, the interior compartments are filled with 1 ¹/₂-in.-thick rigid insulation.

Pine dresses up the plywood. Pekovich applied flat pine pieces to create a frame-and-panel effect and an Arts and Crafts look.

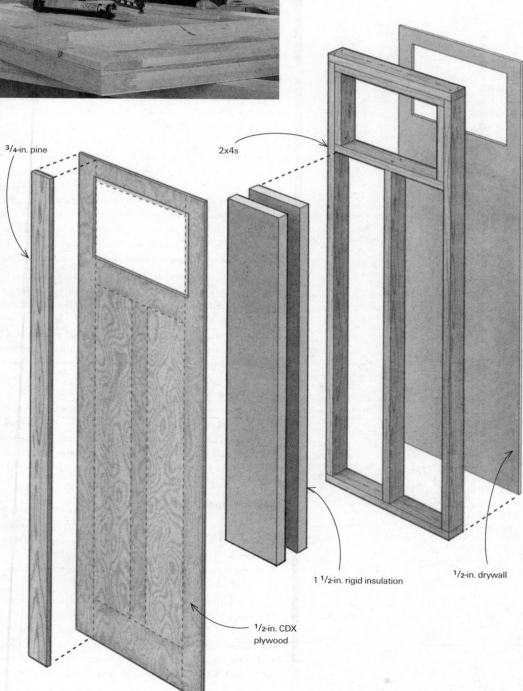

³/₄-in. pine

2x4s

1 ¹/₂-in. rigid insulation

¹/₂-in. drywall

¹/₂-in. CDX plywood

Plywood Floor Adds Warmth and Comfort

A plywood floor installed over rigid insulation is easier on the knees and helps dampen noise and vibration from shop machines. Three coats of polyurethane protect the plywood from spills and wet shoes and make sweeping easier.

Simple process. Working from one wall toward the opposite wall is an easy way to ensure the 2-ft. by 8-ft. foam panels and 2x4 pressure-treated sleepers fit tightly together. After applying a generous bead of construction adhesive (bottom), Pekovich uses fasteners from a powder-actuated tool to keep the sleeper in position while the glue sets (below). Then the whole floor is covered with a layer of 6-mil polyethylene and ³/₄-in. tongue-and-groove underlayment-grade plywood (top).

Continued →

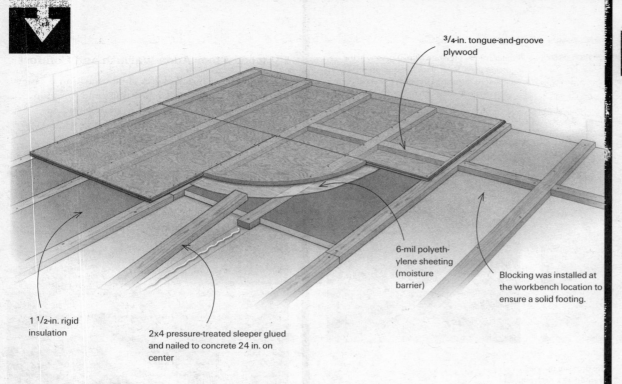

¾-in. tongue-and-groove plywood

6-mil polyethylene sheeting (moisture barrier)

Blocking was installed at the workbench location to ensure a solid footing.

1 ½-in. rigid insulation

2x4 pressure-treated sleeper glued and nailed to concrete 24 in. on center

How to Insulate Concrete Walls

To get the maximum insulation value, the first layer of insulation spans the wall without interruption and a second layer is fit between studs. Finally a layer of 1/2-in. drywall painted white was placed on top, creating a bright and inviting workspace.

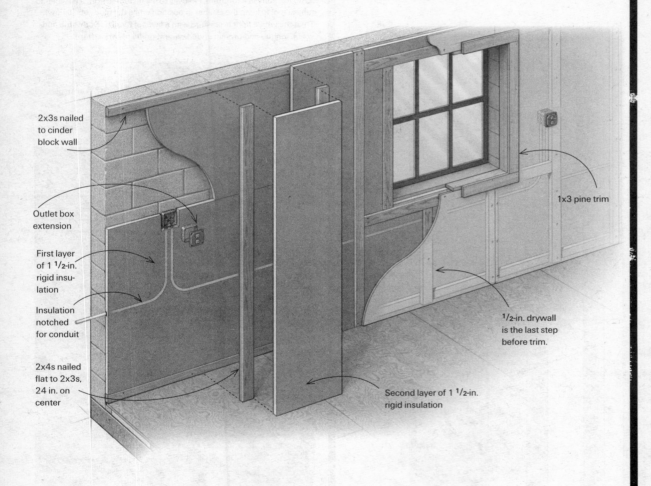

2x3s nailed to cinder block wall

Outlet box extension

First layer of 1 ½-in. rigid insulation

Insulation notched for conduit

2x4s nailed flat to 2x3s, 24 in. on center

Second layer of 1 ½-in. rigid insulation

1x3 pine trim

1/2-in. drywall is the last step before trim.

Garage Workshop from the Ground Up

by Matthew Teague

When I left the staff of Fine Woodworking and headed south a few years ago, my wife and I bought a '50s ranch just east of downtown Nashville. I set up shop in the flat-roofed, one-car garage out back while we figured out if I could make a living building furniture and writing about the craft. Two years later, both careers were going well. The workshop, however, was growing smaller every day.

I didn't need an industrial shop for a big crew, but I did want a well-equipped workshop for a single pro, with plenty of bench space, versatile storage, adequate lighting, dust collection, and enough uncramped space to allow for tools and efficient workflow—the same requirements a serious hobbyist might have. I moved into my new shop recently, and the lessons I learned should be valuable to anyone thinking about building a small, detached shop for woodworking. Many of these tips also will work for updating an existing garage.

An Architect Is a Good Value

If you're building a shop and you're concerned about either its look or resale value, hiring an architect is worth the relatively small outlay of money (ours charged $560). In my case, he devised construction alternatives to raise the ceiling without raising the roof; he helped convince me—against the contractor's suggestion—to keep the bumped-out roof over the entry door; and he was available for last-minute phone calls to help solve the inevitable snafus that pop up during construction. Also, at least in my county, having full renderings of the building plan helped us skate past an otherwise overbearing inspection department. In short, if I had to do it again, I'd probably ask more of the architect instead of less.

For resale reasons, we designed the building to serve as a two-car garage, though we'll never park a car in it ourselves. And even if codes had allowed for a larger shop, I'd have stayed near the 700-sq.-ft. limit (we ended up at 698). Even on paper, anything larger looked like a monstrosity alongside our humble home.

The architect helped to ensure that the design complements our brick ranch house: He drew in a low-slung (4/12 pitch) hip roof like the one on the house and then, to prevent the building from looking like a box with a cap, he set the front door in a small bump-out under a cantilevered roof. Though the house is brick, we opted for Hardiplank siding on the shop and saved about $5,000.

While the architect worried mostly about the exterior of the shop, I spent countless hours sketching the interior. I wanted plenty of natural light inside, a comfortable office space, and, for waterstones and general cleanup, the luxury of running water. I settled on a half-bath (a toilet and a mop sink), with room for later expansion, combined with a small office for books and a computer—together the two rooms take up only 96 sq. ft. of space, but they save countless trips to the house.

With the office and bath in the back corner of the shop, I was left with a generous 600 sq. ft. of L-shaped shop space. Once we had a working drawing, I made scaled cutouts of all my tools and set them in place. Before we broke ground, I needed to know that everything would fit.

Shop Around for a Builder

Construction bids from general contractors were at least $50,000. We then called a contractor who builds garages exclusively. His bid came in at just over half that of the cheapest general contractor. I checked out some of his work, called his references, and signed on.

The builder would be responsible for pouring the foundation, framing, roofing, and installing the windows and doors. I opted to subcontract the plumbing, electrical, insulation, drywall, and exterior painting myself. Being a nice guy, the builder even helped me negotiate lower prices with a few of the subs. In retrospect, I don't think

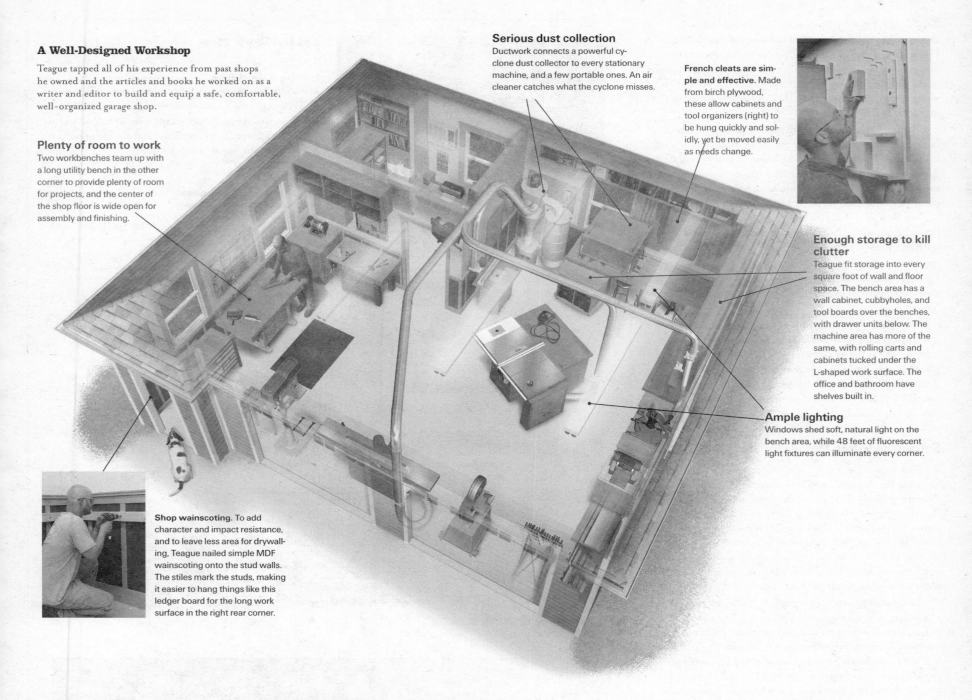

A Well-Designed Workshop

Teague tapped all of his experience from past shops he owned and the articles and books he worked on as a writer and editor to build and equip a safe, comfortable, well-organized garage shop.

Plenty of room to work
Two workbenches team up with a long utility bench in the other corner to provide plenty of room for projects, and the center of the shop floor is wide open for assembly and finishing.

Serious dust collection
Ductwork connects a powerful cyclone dust collector to every stationary machine, and a few portable ones. An air cleaner catches what the cyclone misses.

French cleats are simple and effective. Made from birch plywood, these allow cabinets and tool organizers (right) to be hung quickly and solidly, yet be moved easily as needs change.

Enough storage to kill clutter
Teague fit storage into every square foot of wall and floor space. The bench area has a wall cabinet, cubbyholes, and tool boards over the benches, with drawer units below. The machine area has more of the same, with rolling carts and cabinets tucked under the L-shaped work surface. The office and bathroom have shelves built in.

Ample lighting
Windows shed soft, natural light on the bench area, while 48 feet of fluorescent light fixtures can illuminate every corner.

Shop wainscoting. To add character and impact resistance, and to leave less area for drywalling, Teague nailed simple MDF wainscoting onto the stud walls. The stiles mark the studs, making it easier to hang things like this ledger board for the long work surface in the right rear corner.

I saved much money by subbing out work myself. When a contractor calls a sub he deals with every day, he gets a better price than you do when you ask them to squeeze a single job into a busy schedule.

What to DIY

As for what to do on my own, like many of you I had to weigh what I was willing to do against how much money I could make working the same number of hours. In most cases, it was cheaper to hire out. Case in point: I was willing to buy rolls of insulation and install it myself. But at the behest of my builder I checked with a local insulation crew. They installed better insulation than I had planned to buy—and for about $350 less than I would have paid for materials alone. They showed up a day after I called them and were gone in an hour and a half. Better yet, I didn't itch at all.

As for enlisting the help of friends, on large construction jobs, you realize pretty soon that you'll need a crew of buddies for almost every task at hand. And since you can call on them only so often, you have to pick your battles. Consider this, too: If you can't get to a task immediately, it puts off all the subcontractors in line behind you (you can't drywall until you install insulation, etc.). Even with all I subbed out, there were plenty of construction concerns to keep me busy.

In cases where the work was relaxing or really mattered to me, I did it myself. I built the cabinetry and storage units and did all of the trim work. I also installed the dust collector and ducting.

A Great Option for Heating and Cooling

I've worked in shops that aren't climate-controlled, and neither 20°F nor 100°F is very inspiring. Installing central heating and air seemed like a no-brainer. However, for a fraction of the price, a number of HVAC guys told me, an electric 15,000-Btu packaged terminal air conditioner (PTAC) would work as well. PTACs essentially are small heat pumps and are common in hotel rooms.

The framers left an opening for the unit, and the electrician ran an extra 220v outlet on a dedicated circuit. All I had to do was set the unit in the wall and plug it in. I spent an extra $50 to add a thermostat—a good decision. After paying the bills through a harsh winter and a Nashville summer, the PTAC seems just as efficient as the central heat-pump system we put in the house.

Electrical: More Is More

My builder led me to an electrician who called back promptly, showed up when he said he would, and actually seemed to like what he does for a living. To boot, his prices were reasonable. He re-routed a 100-amp panel from the old shop and installed both 220v and 110v outlets everywhere I might want to place a tool; adding an outlet during construction costs only a few extra bucks but doing so later is both pricey and a hassle. For convenience, we located all of the outlets 42 in. off the floor—above bench height. He also supplied and installed six 8-ft. strips of fluorescent lighting.

Walls Made for Woodworking

Once the shell of the building was up, I did the bulk of the interior work, beginning with the extrahigh walls. If I went with drywall from floor to ceiling, I worried that I'd punch countless holes in the walls as I moved boards around the shop. So I designed and installed medium-density fiberboard (MDF) wainscoting around the lower 40 in. of the walls—to just above bench height. I milled all of the trim pieces for windows, doors, and wainscoting from a few sheets of MDF, at a fraction of what off-the-shelf molding would have cost. I centered each wainscoting stile on a stud—when I hang cabinets on the wall, I don't need a stud finder.

Once the drywall contractors were done (I'm no fan of that job), I painted the top of the walls a light tan color; it masks dust and it's less bland than stark white. I painted the wainscoting panels red, but left the MDF trim natural with just a shellac finish.

As much as I'd prefer wood floors—they're much easier on your back and dropped tools—I had to draw the line somewhere. I sealed the concrete floor with a durable epoxy paint. In front of my workbenches and tablesaw I rolled out anti-fatigue floor mats.

Work Flow: From Machines to Benches

In any efficient shop, work flow determines the tool layout. In my shop, raw lumber comes in the garage door and goes straight onto the lumber racks. With only slight tweaks, I used the lumber-rack design outlined by Andy

Continued ➡

Beasley in FWW #181. Boards slide easily off the racks and onto the chopsaw, where I cut them to rough length. I then stack them on a mobile cart near the jointer, the planer, and the tablesaw. By the time I'm toting workpieces to the workbench, router table, or one of the work areas along the back and side walls, they're already milled to a manageable size.

Big tools first—To accommodate long boards, I set the tablesaw at an angle in the center of the shop, and behind it I put my old outfeed table that doubles as a storage unit. The tablesaw is also outfitted with a router table on the left extension wing. Having two router tables comes in handy when I'm using paired router bits. My main router table is located along the short wall opposite the office. It's built to the height of the tablesaw, and rolls out to provide extra outfeed support.

I left both garage doors operable but realized that I'd only need access to one. A new 12-in. jointer (a shop-warming gift to myself) sits against the garage door I seldom use.

The bench area is an oasis—I didn't get into wood-working because I like heavy, loud machines. What I enjoy most is time at the workbench with hand tools. For that, I placed my two real workbenches in the smaller section of the shop. When I walk in the door, seeing the two walls of benches and hand tools makes me feel like I'm walking into a woodshop instead of a factory.

Storage and More Storage

Whenever possible, I try to design storage into my work-stations. My chopsaw stand is outfitted with shallow metal drawers available from Lee Valley (www.leevalley.com) that slide on grooves cut directly into cabinet sides. The outfeed table for the tablesaw holds my handheld power tools, and the auxiliary table sits on a cabinet for tablesaw accessories. All of the wall-storage units—including cabinets and tool boards—are hung on French cleats, making it easy to move or rearrange them later.

Long workbench accommodates roll-out carts—One of the best moves I made was to build a long work surface that starts at the chopsaw station, turns the corner at the back wall, and extends to the dust collector. The surface is simply two thicknesses of plywood glued and screwed together, and it's supported by 3/4-in.-thick plywood panels instead of cabinet bases. Underneath I keep a low, rolling assembly table, as well as storage cabinets of various designs. I also keep my pancake-style compressor there, on its own rolling base.

At Last, Real Dust Collection

Because the shop shares space with my office, I wanted to keep dust to an absolute minimum. I could have gotten away with a few smaller mobile units for dust collection, but not only do they take up more space, they also have to be wrangled around the shop constantly. After consulting numerous experts and manufacturers, I went with a 3-hp, 2-stage cyclone collector from Oneida (www.oneida-air.com). I provided them with a drawing of the shop's floor plan, and they gave me a parts list and a drawing of the ductwork layout.

For the ductwork itself, I spent about twice the price of traditional materials in favor of quick-release ducting from Nordfab (www.nordfab.com). This ducting snaps together without tools and goes up in a fraction of the time it takes to rivet and route traditional ductwork. Better still, it can be disassembled and rearranged easily should my tooling or layout change.

Even with a great dust-collection system, a little bit of dust is inevitable. To help manage airborne dust, I hung an air cleaner over the tablesaw. The cost was minimal, but it makes a noticeable difference.

Let the Work Flow

The office/bathroom shortens one end of the shop, creating distinct areas for machine and bench work. Materials flow in the garage door, onto the lumber rack; through the nearby milling machines; onto the bandsaw, drill press, and router table; and then into the bench area for joinery, assembly, and finishing before heading out the way they came in.

Comfort and self-sufficiency. An office for computer, stereo, and books, along with a small bathroom, keeps Teague on task all day long.

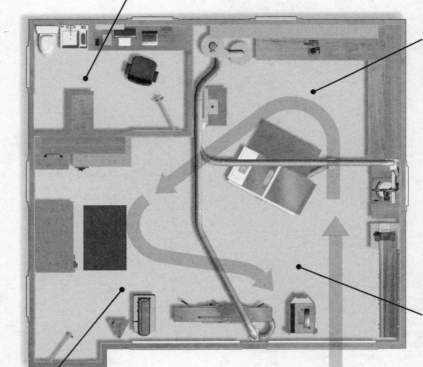

Power central. The larger portion of the shop consolidates the machines and dust-collection ducting, with plenty of lumber storage and all-purpose benchtop space around the outside.

Materials and milling. With the lumber rack built next to the garage door (left), Teague can move materials easily into the shop. The jointer and tablesaw are nearby (below) for milling, and a planer cart and lumber cart roll between them to complete an efficient array.

Hand-tool oasis. The smaller corner of the shop houses two real workbenches with storage for hand tools and hardware, and plenty of natural light.

Now that the shop is done and I've spent a few months building furniture there, I don't miss the few corners I cut, but I do appreciate all the extras I insisted on. The floor paint, wainscoting, half-bath, top-flight dust collection, and smart storage solutions all work together to create a comfortable and inspiring workspace. When I walk through the door each morning, I know I'm set up to build almost anything that pops into my mind. It's become my home a few feet away from home.

Rolling Carts Do Double Duty

Storage and work space. Teague prefers an open-based bench with room for rolling carts below (above). One unit has simple drawers (left) that bring the tools to the job, with a hinged top that can flip onto another storage cart (below) to create a larger surface for assembly or finishing.

Rolling, Rotating Planer Cart

Planers require a lot of infeed and outfeed space, so I've always stored my benchtop planer on a cart under the right wing of my tablesaw, pulling it out when I needed it. But that meant either lifting the heavy planer onto a benchtop or working crouched over. In this shop I've found a better way.

A pivoting-top tool station is not a new idea, but this one works especially well and is easy to build. The planer is bolted to a top that spins on a 1/2-in. steel rod.

For support at the chopsaw, I simply screwed a length of hard maple to the other side of the top. A more versatile option would be to install an adjustable roller on the side of the cabinet. Then I could use the other side of the top for another tool, such as a disk/belt sander combination.

The secret is to start by building the top, and then size the cabinet parts to fit it. The top is two 3/4-in.-thick pieces of birch plywood glued onto an inner hardwood frame, creating a torsion box of sorts. The frame is the exact thickness of the steel rod, and its two halves are positioned snugly against the rod so it is supported on four sides. The pivot mechanism is deceptively simple: The top is edged with maple, and the rod passes through that edging, ending in two support strips that sit atop the cabinet sides. Before attaching the side edging to the top, drill a 1/2-in. hole through its center points. Then glue on the edging with the rod in place. Now slide two washers onto each end of the steel rod, and epoxy the rod into the outer support strips.

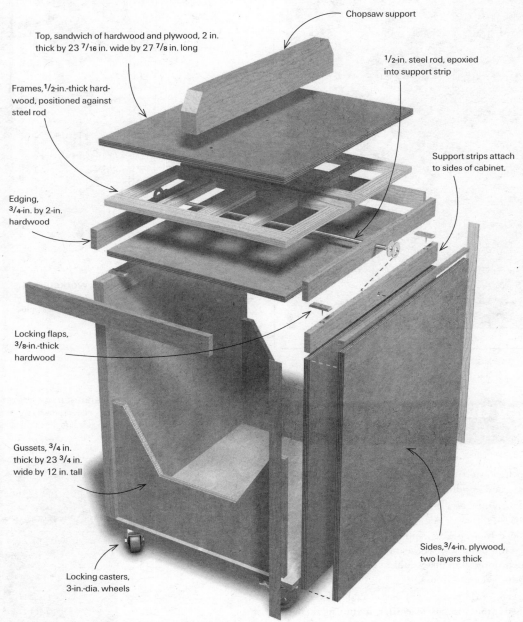

Chopsaw support

Top, sandwich of hardwood and plywood, 2 in. thick by 23 7/16 in. wide by 27 7/8 in. long

1/2-in. steel rod, epoxied into support strip

Frames, 1/2-in.-thick hardwood, positioned against steel rod

Support strips attach to sides of cabinet.

Edging, 3/4-in. by 2-in. hardwood

Locking flaps, 3/8-in.-thick hardwood

Gussets, 3/4 in. thick by 23 3/4 in. wide by 12 in. tall

Sides, 3/4-in. plywood, two layers thick

Locking casters, 3-in.-dia. wheels

NOTE: The cabinet is 27 7/8 in. deep by 26 3/4 in. wide by 27 7/8 in. tall, not including casters. The overall height, 32 1/8 in., positions the planer bed at tablesaw height.

Continued →

It's a snap. Teague spent a lot more to get Nordfab ducting, which goes together in a toolless snap and can be dismantled and rearranged just as easily. Oneida, the cyclone manufacturer, eased the process further by producing a ductwork diagram and parts list, based on a drawing of the floor plan.

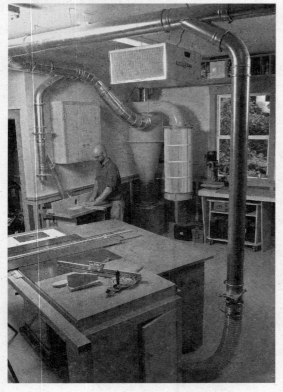

Making the Most of a Small Space

by Stelios L. A. Stavrinides

At the very least, starting a woodworking shop requires two things: good woodworking tools and adequate space. Where I live, on the Mediterranean island of Cyprus, both are in short supply.

But I love woodworking, and I didn't want to let these problems stand in my way. So, using SketchUp, I designed a fully functioning shop that would fit into a 5-ft. by 5-ft. storage room when not in use.

To make it work, I converted the portable power tools I already had into stationary machines, mounting them on a compact, rolling bench. This bench houses five major tools: tablesaw, router table, jigsaw, drill press, and disk sander. And it leaves plenty of space in my store room for lumber and other tools.

Of course, the shop has limits. I don't have a jointer or a planer, so I have to start with stock that is already jointed flat and milled to thickness. Also, the tools must be rolled out into the covered parking area of my apartment complex for use. It's not good for cold weather, but fortunately, we have very little of that here.

Apart from those drawbacks, my little shop can do a lot of woodworking. Here's a look at how it works.

How to Fit a Whole Hobby Into a 5x5 Closet

Stavrinides packs all of his woodworking tools and supplies into this storage room in the parking area of his apartment building. The room measures approximately 5 ft. square and 8 ft. high—a little more than twice the volume inside Volkswagen's modern Beetle.

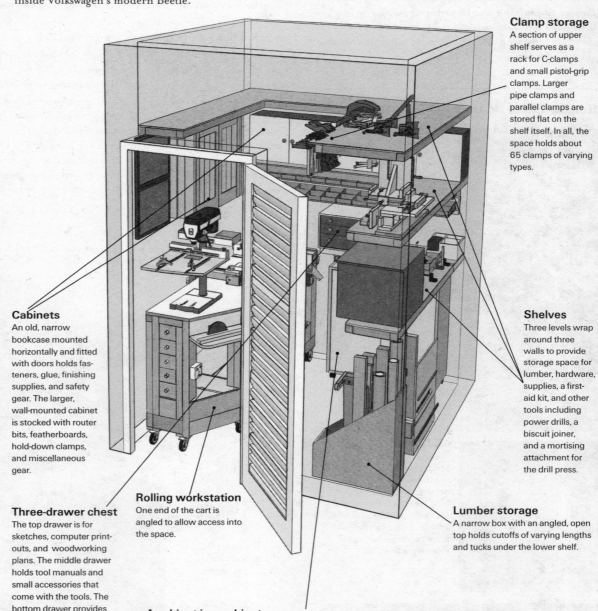

Clamp storage
A section of upper shelf serves as a rack for C-clamps and small pistol-grip clamps. Larger pipe clamps and parallel clamps are stored flat on the shelf itself. In all, the space holds about 65 clamps of varying types.

Cabinets
An old, narrow bookcase mounted horizontally and fitted with doors holds fasteners, glue, finishing supplies, and safety gear. The larger, wall-mounted cabinet is stocked with router bits, featherboards, hold-down clamps, and miscellaneous gear.

Three-drawer chest
The top drawer is for sketches, computer print-outs, and woodworking plans. The middle drawer holds tool manuals and small accessories that come with the tools. The bottom drawer provides storage for sandpaper of all types—sheets, circular pads, and rolls.

Rolling workstation
One end of the cart is angled to allow access into the space.

Shelves
Three levels wrap around three walls to provide storage space for lumber, hardware, supplies, a first-aid kit, and other tools including power drills, a biscuit joiner, and a mortising attachment for the drill press.

Lumber storage
A narrow box with an angled, open top holds cutoffs of varying lengths and tucks under the lower shelf.

A cabinet in a cabinet
Interior doors provide space to hang more tools inside this rolling storage piece, which measures 32 in. square by 13 in. deep. To get the most out of the space, Stavrinides planned the tool layout on paper first.

Rolling Workstation:
The Big Idea Inside the Small Shop

Stavrinides designed this power-tool bench on wheels to serve multiple functions and fit inside his storage space. The bench, 20 in. wide by 59 in. long, is built on a frame of 2x4 and 2x2 lumber, with a plywood skin and a 3/4-in. MDF top surfaced with plastic laminate for durability. In addition to the power tools, the bench also features a vise, five small drawers for accessories, and eight electrical sockets.

What's under the hood?
A table-mounted array of portable power tools serve as standard shop machines. Shown here are the jigsaw, circular saw, and router.

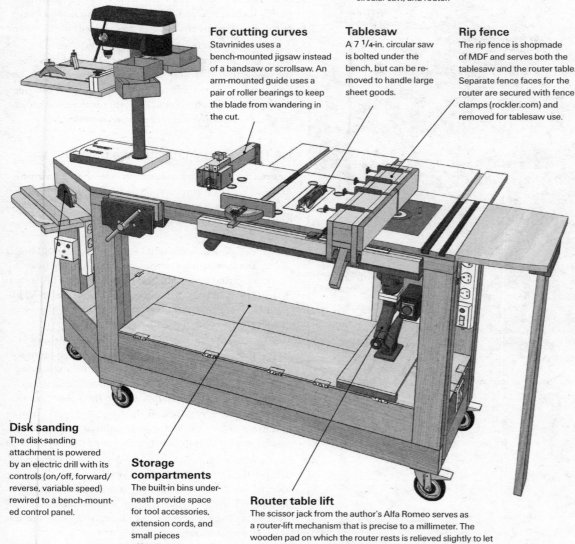

For cutting curves
Stavrinides uses a bench-mounted jigsaw instead of a bandsaw or scrollsaw. An arm-mounted guide uses a pair of roller bearings to keep the blade from wandering in the cut.

Tablesaw
A 7 1/4-in. circular saw is bolted under the bench, but can be removed to handle large sheet goods.

Rip fence
The rip fence is shopmade of MDF and serves both the tablesaw and the router table. Separate fence faces for the router are secured with fence clamps (rockler.com) and removed for tablesaw use.

Disk sanding
The disk-sanding attachment is powered by an electric drill with its controls (on/off, forward/reverse, variable speed) rewired to a bench-mounted control panel.

Storage compartments
The built-in bins underneath provide space for tool accessories, extension cords, and small pieces of lumber.

Router table lift
The scissor jack from the author's Alfa Romeo serves as a router-lift mechanism that is precise to a millimeter. The wooden pad on which the router rests is relieved slightly to let air circulate over the motor vents.

Low-Cost Shop Floor

by Scott Gibson

Many a shop is a converted two-car garage built on a concrete slab. I'll say this much for concrete: It's easy to sweep clean. It's also unforgiving. By mid-afternoon, feet hurt. By evening, a dull ache creeps up the back. Tools can be damaged if they're dropped on concrete. And in cold climates, concrete can be a heat sink.

One solution is to install a wood floor directly over the concrete. A wood surface is easier on your feet as well as any tools that roll off the bench. There are other advantages. Electric cable can be routed beneath the floor to power equipment located away from walls. Stationary tools, workbenches and other fixtures can be screwed down easily. If there is enough headroom, a wood floor can be raised enough to locate dust-collection ducts below. And the cost of material for covering a concrete floor with wood is minimal—about $1.60 per square foot.

However, if a wood floor is going to drop the ceiling height to less than 8 ft., I'd think twice about adding one. But a floor consisting of 2x4 sleepers and 3/4-in.-thick plywood is only 2 1/4 in. thick.

Lay Out the Sleepers First

Because the sleepers will be in direct contact with concrete (for a permanent floor), they should be pressure-treated material rated for ground contact. Concrete can absorb water like a sponge, and untreated wood not only decays, but it also invites carpenter ants and termites.

Don't forget to wear eye and lung protection when cutting pressure-treated wood and to wear gloves when handling it (splinters are nasty). Even though damp concrete won't degrade pressure-treated material for a very long time, really serious water problems should be cured before the new floor goes down. In a basement shop, that may mean cutting a trench at the perimeter of the room and installing a subsurface drain system and sump pump. Better to do that now.

Sleepers are laid flat, not on edge, over the concrete. They should be spaced 16 in. on center so that the long edges of the plywood always fall on solid wood. An easy way to get the layout right is to snap chalklines on the concrete to mark the edge of each 2x4. Snap the first line 14 3/4 in. from the wall, then add 16 in. to each successive line. Sleepers will span minor gaps and voids in the concrete,

but serious dips should be filled before installing the floor. Be sure to use a cold chisel to knock off any obstructions that would prevent the sleepers from lying flat.

Once all of the sleepers have been cut to size, place them on or near the layout lines. Then, starting at one end of the room, pick up a sleeper and lay a fat bead of construction adhesive on the floor where the center of the sleeper will fall. Press the sleeper into place. Adhesive alone should hold down the 2x4s, but I recommend using powder-actuated nails, which will ensure that the wood is secure. Powder-actuated nails are inexpensive, and you can find them at a local hardware store. Don't, however, skip the adhesive and rely on powder-actuated fasteners alone. Over time, the floor can wiggle loose. Because the adhesive starts to dry quickly, glue down one sleeper at a time. Remember to leave a 1/2-in. gap between the walls and perimeter sleepers. In a cold climate, a layer of rigid-foam insulation cut to fit snugly between the 2x4s helps keep out the chill.

Follow with Plastic Sheeting and Plywood

Once the 2x4s have been anchored to the floor, they should be covered with a layer of 6-mil polyethylene sheeting. The sheeting prevents moisture from migrating up through the floor and protects the plywood from damp air. Overlap any seams by 6 in. and tape them with housewrap tape. If the floor is not to be permanent, omit the adhesive and fasteners and allow the sleepers to float on the concrete. Lay the polyethylene directly over the concrete first, then lay the sleepers on top of the polyethylene (see the bottom drawing on p. 61).

Plywood is next. My first choice would be 3/4-in.-thick tongue-and-groove, exterior-grade plywood, but you also can use oriented-strand board (OSB), which is less expensive. Arrange the sheets so that the seams are staggered. That is, start in one corner with a half sheet. On the next course, start with a full sheet. That way, the seams will be staggered 4 ft. apart. The plywood can be nailed to the sleepers, but screws allow you to remove and replace damaged plywood sheets easily. Fasten the plywood every 16 in. with either steel wood screws or drywall screws.

Although plywood is more dimensionally stable than

Concrete: The Floor of Hard Knocks

Industrial ergonomists—specialists who look for ways to make the workplace more user-friendly—would rather see you work on almost any surface other than plain concrete.

"Concrete floors are a very hard, very dense material. As a result, if you have to stand on them for any length of time, most likely you're going to experience some level of discomfort," said Rob Nerhood, director of consultative services for the NC Ergonomics Resource Center in Raleigh, N.C.

Dan MacLeod, a consultant in ergonomics in Milford, Pa., said standing on hard surfaces can result in a variety of ailments, including fatigue, stress on the spinal column and heel spurs. "The latter is more or less a type of tendinitis of the heel," he said, "the symptoms for which are sore heels, particularly in the morning when you first get out of bed."

Adding a floor of 2x4 sleepers and plywood over a concrete slab does provide some relief. But consider also using antifatigue mats. Nerhood said the goal is to provide a material that can be compressed, even slightly, as a buffer between a worker's feet and a hard floor.

Don't overlook your work shoes, either. Insoles can wear out long before the outside of a shoe shows much wear and tear. "If you can't improve the floor," Nerhood said, "improving where your body interacts with the floor at the feet is one of the good steps you can take." No pun intended.

Continued →

solid wood, it's not a good idea to run the edge of the sheets right up to the wall. Leave a gap of 1/2 in. all the way around to give the plywood a little breathing room. You can cover the gap with a piece of baseboard or shoe molding.

Finishing the floor is a matter of personal preference. A coat or two of paint or clear finish will help protect the plywood from the inevitable coffee or paint spill. But for a shop, that may be more trouble than it's worth. Your feet, knees, ankles and back—as well as your edge tools—will be just as happy with an unfinished floor.

Plywood Floor Over Concrete Slab

For permanent floor, attach 2x4s to the concrete slab using construction adhesive and powder-actuated nails

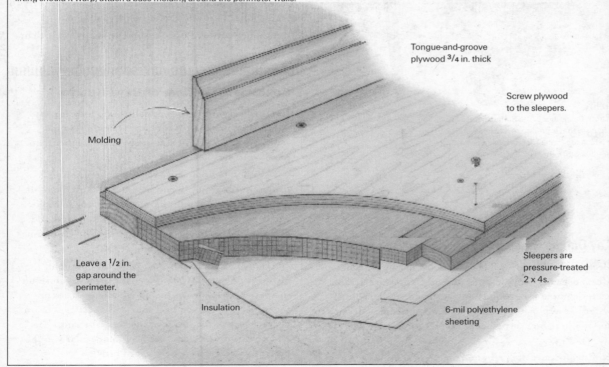

Tongue-and-groove plywood 3/4 in. thick

Screw plywood to the sleepers,

Leave a 1/2 in. gap around the perimeter.

6-mil polyethelene sheeting

Sleepers are pressure-treated 2x4s located 16 in. on center.

Sleepers are driven into the floor with powder-actuated nails.

Rigid-foam insulation

Construction adhesive

TEMPORARY FLOOR

For a removeable floor, leave out the adhesive and fasteners, and place the polyethylene sheeting directly on the concrete. To keep the floor from lifting should it warp, attach a base molding around the perimeter walls.

Tongue-and-groove plywood 3/4 in. thick

Screw plywood to the sleepers.

Molding

Leave a 1/2 in. gap around the perimeter.

Sleepers are pressure-treated 2 x 4s.

Insulation

6-mil polyethylene sheeting

Wiring Your Workshop

by Clifford A. Popejoy

The electrical wiring, outlets, and lighting in your shop should be as specialized as your tools. It's hard to turn out high-quality work—or to work safely—in a poorly illuminated shop. It is equally frustrating and potentially dangerous if your tools keep tripping breakers on underpowered circuits or if your floor is a tangle of extension cords. To upgrade your workspace to meet the special needs of woodworking, you should know how to identify your needs and then communicate them to an electrician

with the skills to turn your plan into reality. If you put these ideas to use, your woodworking will be safer and more satisfying.

Shop Features Dictate the Wiring Layout

Installing the wiring for a woodshop is done most easily during construction or remodeling with the walls open, but it can be done anytime. If the walls are closed in, either have the wiring run in surface-mounted conduit or hire an "old work" electrician who can run wires in existing walls and make a minimum of holes to be patched later.

To feed the shop circuits, the best approach is to install an electrical subpanel (breaker box) specifically for the shop. In a well-designed system a breaker will rarely trip, but if it does, it helps to have the panel nearby. There's a wide range of subpanels available, and your choice will depend on how much power and how many circuits you need.

At any given time, most one-person shops will be running one major stationary tool, a dust collector, an air filtration system, and lights. In this case, 60 amps at 240/120v likely will provide enough power. If there's heating or air conditioning running as well, a 100-amp subpanel probably will be adequate. I suggest a panel with room for 16 or 20 circuit breakers. These are starting points. Because each shop is different, you should calculate the number of circuits and power needs of your own.

There are two interdependent aspects to wiring a shop. One is circuit design—how the various things that use power (called "loads") are arranged and grouped, and how they are connected to their electricity source through wiring and circuit breakers. The other is the choice and location of light fixtures, receptacles, and switches.

Let There Be Light (On Its Own Circuit)

Depending on the size of the shop, you should have one or more 120v, 15-amp circuits dedicated to lighting. That way if you are ripping a board and your tablesaw trips a breaker, you won't be plunged into darkness and into a dangerous situation.

To compute how many lighting circuits you will need, add up the total wattage of the lights and provide one 15-amp lighting circuit for every 1,500 watts. This is based on loading each circuit to about 80% of its capacity. This cushion, though not required in noncommercial applications, is still a good idea.

For example, to provide lighting for a single-car garage-size shop (240 sq. ft.) with 96-in., high-output (HO) fluorescent lights, you would need four separate 2-lamp fixtures. Each 8-ft. lamp requires 110 watts, so you would need a total of 880 watts to light this shop. Consider installing some task lighting (say a track fixture with three, 65-watt floodlamps or equivalent fluorescent floods) as well. I'd put this lighting on one 15-amp circuit.

Consider setting up the lighting so that the general lighting fixtures are wired to two or more separate switches, with the task lights switched separately from the general lighting. This way, if your machine and bench areas are separate, you can save energy by illuminating only the area in which you're working.

Outlets: The More the Better

It's a fact that a shop can never have too many clamps, and it's equally true that it can't have too many receptacles. Receptacles should go on 20-amp circuits. There's no limit set by the National Electrical Code (NEC) for the number of outlets that can go on a circuit in a residential application. For a shop, it makes sense to identify the loads you expect to operate at the same time and group the receptacles onto circuits so that each circuit can comfortably support the expected demand. A 120v, 20-amp circuit can provide 2,400 watts, although it's a good idea to keep the load to 80% or less, or about 1,900 watts. To figure out how many circuits are needed, look at the power needed as shown on the tool nameplate (some nameplates will specify watts, and some amps). If the tool specs give amps only, convert from amps to watts for a 120v tool by multiplying amps times 120. For instance, if you have a small air compressor that draws 13 amps (1,560 watts), put in a receptacle supplied by its own 20-amp circuit, called a "dedicated" circuit. For outlets that won't be supplying a specific tool, as in an area like an assembly bench where you will be using various small power tools, I suggest three or four outlets on a 20-amp circuit.

The NEC requires ground fault circuit interrupter (GFCI) protection for any 15-amp or 20-amp branch circuits supplying a garage or other work area at grade level. You can meet this requirement by using a GFCI circuit breaker or by having a GFCI receptacle first in line and wired to protect the downstream receptacles.

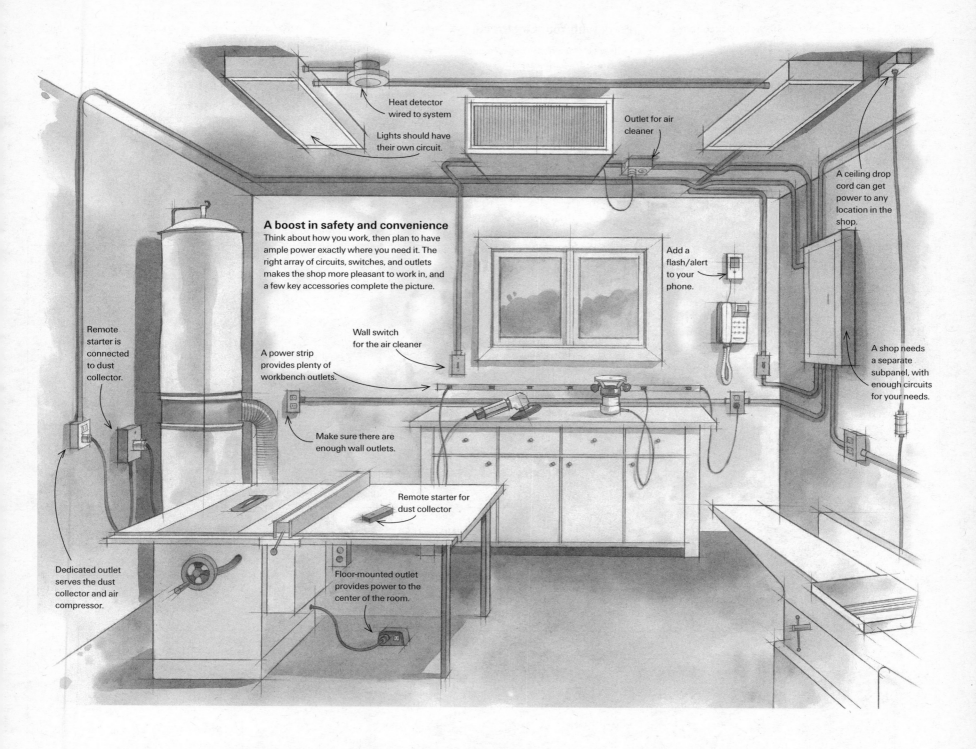

A boost in safety and convenience
Think about how you work, then plan to have ample power exactly where you need it. The right array of circuits, switches, and outlets makes the shop more pleasant to work in, and a few key accessories complete the picture.

Heat detector wired to system

Lights should have their own circuit.

Outlet for air cleaner

A ceiling drop cord can get power to any location in the shop.

Add a flash/alert to your phone.

A shop needs a separate subpanel, with enough circuits for your needs.

Remote starter is connected to dust collector.

A power strip provides plenty of workbench outlets.

Wall switch for the air cleaner

Make sure there are enough wall outlets.

Remote starter for dust collector

Dedicated outlet serves the dust collector and air compressor.

Floor-mounted outlet provides power to the center of the room.

For general-use outlets, like the ones used for routers, hand sanders, and corded drills, it is a good idea to set up circuits based on the area served. For example, you might set up a separate circuit for each wall. Or you may want a couple of 20-amp circuits to serve your workbench, where you might have three or four outlets on each circuit. A neat trick is to run two circuits along the wall and feed alternating receptacles from the two different circuits. Don't use a shared neutral circuit for this; you have to GFCI-protect the outlets, and keeping the two circuits completely separate makes this easier.

A product called Plugmold (www.wiremold.com) is useful for providing workbench power. It is a steel channel with outlets spaced at intervals. Plugmold stands about 1¼ in. wide and above the surface and is available in various receptacle spacings (12 in. is best for shop use). Plugmold is much sturdier than a typical cord-connected "power strip" and is the right way to pack a lot of outlets along a wall.

It's a good idea to place wall outlets 50 in. above the floor (to the bottom of the box). That way if you lean sheet goods against the wall, they won't cover the outlets. And the outlets will be well above any benchtop or other worksurface. Another nice setup is to set aside a shelf area for cordless-tool chargers, and put a 3-plus-ft. strip of Plugmold with 6-in. receptacle spacing on the wall behind the shelf. Put this on a separate 20-amp circuit, so you can leave it powered up while turning the other receptacle circuits off at the breakers for safety when you're not in the shop.

Get Plenty of Juice to Stationary Tools

The big guns—stationary tablesaw, jointer, planer, dust collector—draw so much power that they each require their own circuit. (Without it, running two simultaneously will trip a breaker.) If the motor can be set up to run on 240v, have an electrician do it. It will probably require taking the motor out of the machine. There's no power efficiency advantage to running a machine at 240v vs. 120v in a single-phase system, but the higher voltage means lower amperage, and as a result, you can use smaller-gauge power-supply wiring. That translates into less expense to run the wire and to hook it up.

To figure out what size circuits you will need, check the amp rating on each tool's data plate or in its product manual. Keep in mind that the circuit breaker at the subpanel is designed to protect the building's wiring from an overcurrent condition—it does not, however, ensure that the machine's motor won't overload. If the motor does not have an internal circuit breaker for overload protection (the tool manual will indicate this), a fused disconnect may be required. Ask the electrician to install it. The fuses in the disconnect box will protect the motor windings from overheating.

Some tools are an island—Getting power to a machine in the middle of the floor can be a challenge. You don't want a cord running along the floor that you might trip over. If there's a basement or crawlspace below, I would run cable or conduit below the floor and use a monument-style housing to hold the receptacle at the base of the machine. A flush-mounted floor outlet is a poor choice for a shop. It will fill with debris and could be shorted out by a stray nail or staple.

If you plan to move shop machines around and you want to keep the floor clear, use a hanging (pendant) outlet about 6 ft. to 7 ft. above the floor. To prevent accidental unplugging, a locking cord cap on the receptacle end of the pendant outlet is a good idea. This will require you to put a compatible locking plug on the machine cord, or make an adapter.

Custom Touches Add Safety, Convenience

Even though they are full of flammable materials, most woodshops have no smoke alarms. That is because airborne sawdust can set off the photo-ionization or photoelectric sensors typically used in smoke alarms to detect smoke. The solution is to install a heat-detecting fire alarm that can activate the smoke alarms in the house. Firex (www.icca.invensys.com/firex) has a complete line of smoke alarms that includes compatible heat-detector units.

It's nice to have a phone in the shop, but how do you hear it ring while planing boards and wearing hearing protectors? You can add a flashing visual alert.

Continued →

Another convenience is to have your dust collector start automatically when you switch on a machine it serves. It's possible to build a current sensor/relay setup, but there are commercially available ones. Ecogate (www.ecogate.com) sells a system that not only turns on the dust collector when it senses that a tool has started, but also opens and closes the adjacent blast gate. Alternatively, you could install a relay and receiver on the dust collector's cord that switches on and off with a remote-control transmitter that can sit in a convenient spot or hang on your key ring (like a car-door remote).

Work with Your Electrician

Unless you're a qualified electrician or are willing to take the time to become familiar with the techniques of the trade, the many requirements of the NEC, and any local codes pertinent to shop wiring, you should find a licensed electrician or electrical contractor to wire your shop. Look for one who does both residential and commercial work; a strictly residential electrician might not be familiar with some of the products and design elements suggested here.

When working with an electrician, it's more productive to explain the objective or goal than to try to dictate a precise method or approach. Sit down with the electrician before work begins, and lay out your requirements clearly. If your plan and goals are not clear at the outset, be prepared to pay for changes.

Finally, don't expect to find an electrician who will "just do the hookups" after you've pulled the wires, etc. Few licensed electricians will take the risk of putting the finishing touches on work they didn't do themselves.

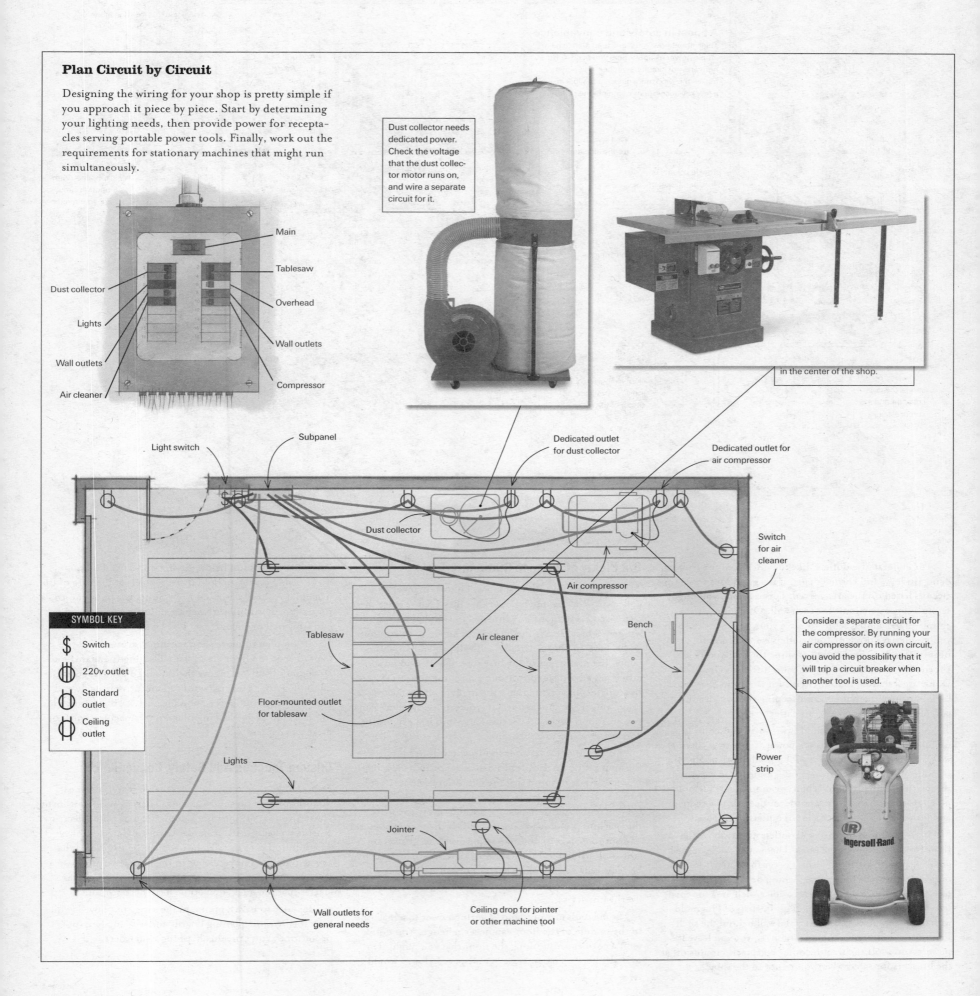

Plan Circuit by Circuit

Designing the wiring for your shop is pretty simple if you approach it piece by piece. Start by determining your lighting needs, then provide power for receptacles serving portable power tools. Finally, work out the requirements for stationary machines that might run simultaneously.

Dust collector needs dedicated power. Check the voltage that the dust collector motor runs on, and wire a separate circuit for it.

Main

Tablesaw

Overhead

Wall outlets

Compressor

Dust collector

Lights

Wall outlets

Air cleaner

in the center of the shop.

Light switch

Subpanel

Dedicated outlet for dust collector

Dedicated outlet for air compressor

Dust collector

Switch for air cleaner

Air compressor

Bench

Consider a separate circuit for the compressor. By running your air compressor on its own circuit, you avoid the possibility that it will trip a circuit breaker when another tool is used.

SYMBOL KEY

$ Switch

220v outlet

Standard outlet

Ceiling outlet

Tablesaw

Air cleaner

Floor-mounted outlet for tablesaw

Power strip

Lights

Jointer

Wall outlets for general needs

Ceiling drop for jointer or other machine tool

Ingersoll Rand

Improve Your Workshop Lighting

by Nancy McCoy and Peter Judge

Have you ever had to squint to see a scribe line or line up a pencil mark? Maybe a recent finish looked great in the shop, but once you brought it into the house you found sanding scratches. Your problem might be inadequate shop lighting. Light fixtures are seldom at the top of tool and equipment wish lists, so most home shops are illuminated with a collection of mismatched, outdated fixtures, with little thought given to their overall placement and how they're switched.

As a result, improving your shop lighting will likely mean starting over with new wiring and fixtures. Many woodworkers will think they can handle this job, but it's probably better to hire an electrician who'll let you do some of the work yourself.

An electrician looking at the job can confirm that your electrical panel isn't overtaxed and that there are no other pressing electrical problems. Then you can save some money by mounting the fixtures and running the conduit yourself. Later, the electrician can check your work, run the wires, and make the connections inside the panel. Some electricians are fine with this type of arrangement. Others will want to do everything themselves, so make sure you work out the division of labor in advance.

We used Fine Woodworking associate editor Matt Kenney's shop to demonstrate the techniques discussed in this article. Like most woodworkers, Matt thought his shop lighting was just fine. But when the upgrade was finished, he was amazed: "I don't have to get my eyes right up to the work to see what I'm doing anymore. More light just makes everything easier." The lighting upgrade also allowed Matt to start using the entire shop instead of the single well-lit area near his bench. Matt and local electrician Steve Foss worked together on the installation, with Matt installing the fixtures and Steve doing the wiring.

Two Types of Lighting

Any discussion of artificial light starts with the distinction between ambient and task lighting—you'll want both types for a well-lit shop. Ambient lighting describes general lighting for common cutting and shaping tasks. Task lighting describes a higher level of illumination focused right on the work. However, it's important to remember that once you have an even blanket of bright light, task lighting is reserved for filling in the dark areas.

Don't skimp—It might be tempting to save money on lighting by arranging the ambient overhead lights so that they're strategically placed over benches and machines. But we recommend against this approach because the lights will be in the wrong locations if you ever decide to change your shop setup.

And you never know quite where you'll need light: Will it be on the floor when cutting up a sheet of plywood, or in the corner when picking through the scrap pile? With an even blanket of ambient light, you'll be able to work anywhere. You can save the task lighting for when you really need it, like finishing and joinery.

The Illuminating Engineering Society of North America (IES) recommends between 20 and 50 foot-candles for woodworking. One foot-candle is the amount of light produced by an ordinary candle measured from 1 ft. away. We suggest 75 foot-candles because you'll need more light as you age, and the cost difference is negligible. Even if your eyes are fine now, you'll need the additional light soon enough.

Light-colored surfaces boost light—Another consideration is how much of the light produced by your fixtures is reflected by the ceiling and walls. A clean, white surface may reflect as much as 85% of the light that initially hits it, while a dark, rough surface can reflect as little as 10% or 15%. If your shop is cluttered and dusty or has exposed insulation, you'll need to boost lighting levels by another 30% to 50%, compared to shops with clean white walls and ceilings.

Flourescents Are the Foundation

Light every corner of a workshop—you never know where you might need a clear view. Overhead fluorescents arranged on a grid are the most cost-effective way to create a blanket of bright light.

SHOP READY FIXTURES

Buzz-free and efficient. Modern fluorescents are the obvious choice for shop lighting. They have electronic ballasts that don't hum or flicker, and they're energy-efficient and affordable. The SB 432 from Lithonia (www.lithonia.com) has a wraparound lens that keeps out dust and spreads the light.

Lower-cost option. Strip (no lens) fluorescents are sold in 2-, 4-, and 8-ft. lengths. If you choose 8-footers, make sure to get them with pairs of 4-ft. bulbs instead of 8-ft. bulbs, which are harder to find and transport.

THE RIGHT BULBS

Modern fluorescents save energy. The fluorescent fixtures shown in this article take 4-ft. T8 bulbs, which sell for between $3 and $4 each.

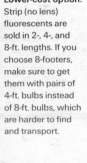

True colors. A bulb's color temperature can make a big difference in the appearance of wood species and finishes. Ideally, you should select bulbs rated 3000 K, so the shop lighting matches your home lighting. Color temperature is found on packaging and sometimes right on the bulb.

Cherry under incandescent light

Cherry under 3000 K fluorescent

Cherry under 7500 K flourescent

Hang your own fixtures. Fluorescent fixtures are surprisingly light, so toggle bolts let you put them wherever you want on a drywall ceiling (left). You also can fasten the lights directly to framing members with screws. Another task you can do yourself is to install the straight conduit between fixtures (above). Before tightening the toggles or screws completely, use the wiggle room to squeeze in the pipe. Always be sure to ream the conduit ends, as any sharp edges will damage the wires' insulation.

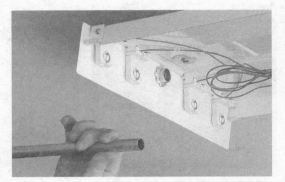

Leave the wiring to a pro. With the fixtures placed, you can bring back the electrician to install the rest of the conduit, run the wire, and make the necessary connections. This will likely take a day or less.

A Functional Lighting Layout Is Simple

Once you've made a decision on the level of lighting you want in your workshop, laying it out is as easy as 1-2-3.

1. Choose your fixture—The most common shop fixture is an open "strip" fluorescent (see photo, above). These work pretty well, but without a cover they experience more "dirt depreciation," which is the drop in light output caused by dust on the bulbs and housing. It's easy enough to clean off the fixtures once in a while with compressed air, but it's even easier to select fixtures with an acrylic lens. Not only does the lens keep out much of the dust and spread the light, but it also provides a bit of safety when you're swinging around long boards.

Our favorite fixture for a home workshop is Model SB 432 from Lithonia (see above). They have a lens, and their electronic ballast means they won't hum loudly and they'll work in cold temperatures. This fixture used to cost about 25% more than strip fluorescents, but we found them at Amazon.com for $55, which is the same as or less than some strip lights.

2. Select the bulbs—One of the complaints we often hear about fluorescent bulbs is that the light is bluish and unnatural. This used to be true, but fluorescent bulbs are now available in a wide variety of "color temperatures." Measured in kelvins (K), color temperatures of fluorescent lights commonly range from 2000 K (warm red) to 7500 K (cool blue).

Continued →

Task Lighting

With most of the light provided by overhead fluorescents, task lighting is about filling the gaps.

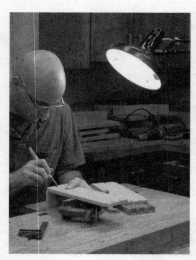

Desk lights shine bright. When the shadow from your own body makes it tough to see, an inexpensive swing-arm desk lamp can fill in the dark areas.

Attach a mounting block to your bench. Many desk lights have a post that can fit into a block screwed to your bench for easy installation and removal.

Tall machines cast a shadow. Bandsaws and drill presses, with their large cabinets and motor housings, often block overhead lighting, but the fix is easy: a magnetic-base task light aimed right at the work.

Raking light reveals surface flaws. Inexpensive stand-mounted halogen worklights are a great way to provide low-angle light for surface prep and finishing (above). The raking light can highlight machine marks that are invisible under overhead light (right).

Why is a bulb's color temperature important? Ideally, the lighting in the shop should be the same as the lighting inside your home, so your projects look the same in both environments. Most likely you have warm incandescent lighting in your home, so you should select warm fluorescent bulbs with a 3000 K color temperature. This will help your finished projects look the way you intended, and the cost difference compared to standard bulbs is negligible.

3. Plan your layout—Most electricians and lighting showrooms can provide a lighting layout for a garage shop easily, but if you want to do the layout yourself, we suggest using Visual Basic, a free program found on the Lithonia Web site (www.lithonia.com). Start the program by entering the shop dimensions and ceiling height, then specify a lighting level (75 foot-candles in our case). The program then gives you several options on the reflectivity of your walls. You can then select a light fixture from a pull-down menu, choose the type of ceiling and lens cover, and the software will tell you how many fixtures you need and how to arrange them.

Using the SB 432 fixture and assuming a 22-ft. by 24-ft. two-car-garage shop with 8-ft. ceilings as an example, the program says we need nine fixtures, arranged in three columns of three fixtures each.

Zoning saves money and energy—Rather than having all your lights controlled by a single switch, it's a good idea to divide the space into work zones. For example, you could put the finishing table in one zone, the bench or assembly table in another, and the machine area in a third. For the cost of a little extra cable and a few switches, the energy savings is well worth it.

Another nice feature is an occupancy sensor that turns on a single light whenever you walk into the shop, especially when your hands are filled with tools or materials. Because an occupancy sensor will turn off the lights when it doesn't detect movement, it can occasionally leave you in the dark.

Task Lighting

Overhead fluorescents are good for general ambient light, but for finishing and bench work you'll need additional task lighting. Swing-arm lamps like those found on drafting tables are great for aiming light directly where you need it. Twin-head halogen work lights are great for finishing because they can provide raking light that makes it easier to see runs and other problems.

Having a well-lit shop is a lot like having a well-heated one. The shop becomes a more welcoming place, a playground for your creativity.

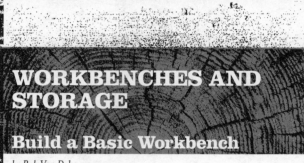

WORKBENCHES AND STORAGE

Build a Basic Workbench

by Bob Van Dyke

A workbench with an end vise and front vise is easily the most important tool in your shop, one that you use on every project. If you don't already have one, or if yours is old and rickety, it's time to upgrade.

You could just buy a bench—there are some good ones out there—but you could easily spend $1,000 and not improve on the bench I'll show you how to build in this article for around $300.

This bench is everything a good workbench should be: It is heavy and strong, so it won't skate or wobble. It has a flat surface big enough to support a medium case side or tabletop. And it's capable of holding your work securely, with an end vise that can be used with benchdogs to hold work flat or like a front vise to clamp work upright. Best of all, you can make this bench in a weekend, to your own dimensions, and you don't need a ton of tools.

If you're wondering whether a bench like this can really do the job, I have more than 25 of these benches in my school and they are still going strong after 11 years and 3,500 students.

Simple Joinery and Fasteners Make a Sturdy Base

I like to make the base from ash, maple, poplar, or oak. The base consists of two end assemblies, each built from a pair of crosspieces dadoed into the legs. These end assemblies are connected by two long stretchers bolted in place on each side. The top long stretchers are rabbeted into the tops of the legs.

All of this joinery is best cut on the tablesaw with a dado set but it's also possible, if more tedious, to do the work with a standard blade and a miter gauge. Either way, a single fence setting and a spacer block is used to cut each corresponding joint exactly the same width and in exactly the same place on each leg. If you leave the crosspieces and stretchers a bit wide, you can edge-plane them in the thickness planer for a precise fit in the dadoes and rabbets.

With the joinery cut, begin construction of the base with the two end assemblies. Before starting, break all the edges with a chamfer or roundover. Check for square during glue-up by measuring diagonally across the assembly in each direction. Adjust at the corners if needed until the measurements match.

The rest of the assembly consists of connecting the two ends by attaching the long stretchers. Set the base upside down on a level work surface and clamp the stretchers in place while drilling the bolt holes. With the base assembled, you can turn it over and use it to build the top.

Easy Dadoes on the Tablesaw

You don't need a dado set to cut the joints on this bench. Here's how to do it with your standard blade and miter gauge.

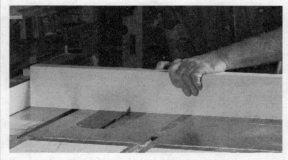

First the fence gets set. The rip fence will be your stop. Lay out one of the legs and set the fence so the blade lines up with one end of the dado.

Then the fence stays put. Use a spacer block (left) to reposition the leg for cutting the dado's opposite end. Cut each wall cleanly, supporting the leg with the miter gauge, and then make passes to remove the material between them (right).

The Top: A Triple-Decker Sandwich

Cutting 4x8 sheets of medium-density fiberboard (MDF) and particleboard by yourself is no picnic. Buy one sheet of each and have your supplier rough them down so each piece is 1 in. bigger than final size in each direction. You can use the particleboard offcuts to piece together the top's middle layer. If you plan your cuts carefully, the middle layer will consist of two pieces with only one seam.

Before assembly, use a tablesaw or a router and straightedge to cut the top layer accurately to final size. Cut the other layers about 1/4 in. to 3/8 in. bigger than this layer.

Start the glue-up with the top layer facedown on the base. Roll yellow glue onto the surface, then place the pieces of the middle layer on the waiting piece. Make sure the middle layer extends beyond the top on all sides, then screw them together. Make sure you don't drive any screws where you plan to drill dog holes. Afterward, use a router and a flush-trimming bit to bring the middle layer flush with the top. Finish the glue-up by repeating the entire process to attach the bottom layer.

Cut the stock for the solid-wood edging no more than 1/8 in. wider than the thickness of the top, with each piece about 1 in. longer than its finished length. When gluing the edging to the sides, use thick clamping cauls to distribute the pressure evenly. After gluing the edging in place (long sides first) and trimming the ends, use a router to flush-trim the protruding edging to the core—top and bottom. Then switch bits and round over all the edges. Now is also a good time to sand the benchtop.

A Single Vise Does Double Duty

This bench has one vise, which acts a both a front vise and an end vise. You can use it to hold your work vertically for any sawing or chiseling task or you can use it in conjunc-

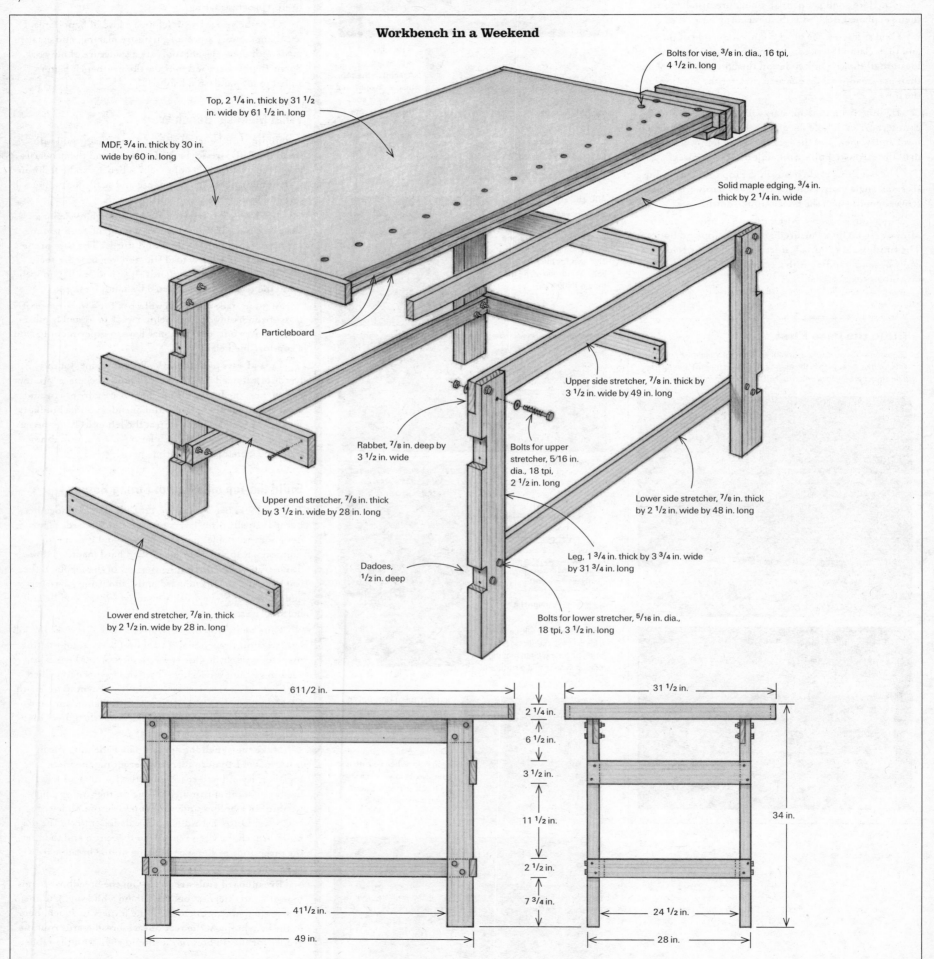

Workbench in a Weekend

Bolts for vise, 3/8 in. dia., 16 tpi, 4 1/2 in. long

Top, 2 1/4 in. thick by 31 1/2 in. wide by 61 1/2 in. long

MDF, 3/4 in. thick by 30 in. wide by 60 in. long

Solid maple edging, 3/4 in. thick by 2 1/4 in. wide

Particleboard

Upper side stretcher, 7/8 in. thick by 3 1/2 in. wide by 49 in. long

Rabbet, 7/8 in. deep by 3 1/2 in. wide

Bolts for upper stretcher, 5/16 in. dia., 18 tpi, 2 1/2 in. long

Lower side stretcher, 7/8 in. thick by 2 1/2 in. wide by 48 in. long

Upper end stretcher, 7/8 in. thick by 3 1/2 in. wide by 28 in. long

Dadoes, 1/2 in. deep

Leg, 1 3/4 in. thick by 3 3/4 in. wide by 31 3/4 in. long

Lower end stretcher, 7/8 in. thick by 2 1/2 in. wide by 28 in. long

Bolts for lower stretcher, 5/16 in. dia., 18 tpi, 3 1/2 in. long

61 1/2 in.

31 1/2 in.

2 1/4 in.

6 1/2 in.

3 1/2 in.

11 1/2 in.

2 1/2 in.

7 3/4 in.

34 in.

41 1/2 in.

49 in.

24 1/2 in.

28 in.

Continued ➔

tion with benchdogs to easily hold a board flat on the benchtop.

Before installing the vise, I use an inexpensive 3/4-in. spade bit to drill a row of holes in the top for the benchdogs. I start the row 5 in. from the vise end of the bench and space them about 4 in. apart, but the spacing can vary according to your needs. What is important is that the holes line up with the dog in the vise.

To mount the vise, first make a spacer to fit between the vise and the bottom of the benchtop. It should be slightly longer and wider than the vise's footprint, and thick enough to drop the cast-iron jaws about 1/2 in. below the top. Hardwood jaw pads go on before installation, then get planed flush with the benchtop.

Glue and screw the block to the underside of the bench and then clamp the vise in its final position. Mark the location of the vise bolt holes on the bottom of the bench, then use an adjustable square to transfer the locations to the top.

Drilling from the top, start with a Forstner bit to counterbore each hole deep enough to fully recess the bolt head and washer. Use the center dimple left by the bit to drill the through-holes, and bolt the vise in place.

The last thing to do is attach the top to the base. I use six small angle irons available from any hardware store and screw them in (turn the bench upside down).

For a tough, water-resistant finish, I use four coats of Minwax High Gloss Polyurethane on the top and bottom. The finish is exceptionally durable, and can be renewed easily by scuff-sanding with 220-grit sandpaper and brushing on a new coat.

Build the Base First

Glue and screw the end assemblies. Drill pilot holes and countersink for the screws while the assembly is dry-fit (below). Clamp the side stretchers in place when drilling their bolt holes (bottom).

The Top Goes Together in Layers

**TRIM, THEN TRIM AGAIN
Assemble the top.** Start with one layer cut to exact size, then use a router and flush-trimming bit to trim the adjacent layers.

ADD THE EDGING

Biscuits align it. Van Dyke uses a shim to offset the biscuit joiner when cutting the slots in the top's edge. This ensures the edging will stand proud of the top for trimming flush.

Overhanging base

Straight bit

Trim the edging with a router. This simple base allows a straight cutting bit to trim the edging flush with the surface of the top.

OUTFIT WITH DOG HOLES AND A VISE

Install the vise. Sighting along an upright square (left) helps in drilling a straight dog hole. When you attach the vise (below), add a spacer block to keep the jaws even with the tabletop.

A Workbench 30 Years in the Making

by Garrett Hack

When I built my first bench well over 30 years ago, I had limited furniture-making experience, so I adapted the design from some benches I had used in various classes. That first bench has been a solid friend in the shop for many years. But as my experience level increased, I kept a mental list of improvements I'd make if I were to build a new one. I recently said as much in a lecture at Colonial Williamsburg, and Fine Woodworking decided to pay me to stop procrastinating.

Over the years, I've developed a love of hand tools. I use them in every aspect of furniture making, and details made with these elegant tools are a signature of my work. So my first priority was to make the new bench better suited to my hand-tool habits.

What Makes a Bench Work

In building this bench, I wanted a tool that would withstand the daily stresses heaped upon it, and the materials and design reflect that approach. A bench can be fashioned with humble materials (any dense and stable hardwood will do) and basic joinery and work very well.

Add beef—The benchtop is big enough to clamp a large case piece in almost any arrangement, with room for many tools, and it's thick and sturdy. The base of the bench can hold a heavy load (the top weighs more than 200 lb.), but more importantly, it's rigid enough to withstand the racking forces created by handplaning.

At 35 in. tall, my bench will work for a wide range of tasks, from handwork to machine work to assembly jobs. But I'm over 6 ft. tall. You may have to experiment to find a comfortable height.

Lots of ways to hold work—Because I do a lot of handwork, I need surefire ways to hold workpieces. In my experience, the best tools for the job are a front vise and a tail vise, used in tandem with benchdogs and a holdfast. Finally, I added a sliding stop at the left end. It can be set high or low and is useful for planing panels, thin drawer bottoms, tabletops, or multiple parts.

Build the Top on a Pair of Strong Horses

The top looks like a bunch of 12/4 planks glued together, but it's actually three layers of 1-in.-thick boards. This design is very stable so it will stay flat, and it's an economical way to use materials. I used hard maple, yellow birch, and beech, dedicating the best of the maple to the top layer and the breadboard ends, and using narrower and somewhat lower-quality material for the middle and bottom layers.

Glue up the top one section at a time. To make the job less stressful, I recommend Unibond 800, a slow-setting urea-formaldehyde glue (www.vacupress.com) typically used in vacuum veneering. Once you have the top glued together, use a circular saw to trim the benchtop to length. Clean up the edges with a scraper and a handplane, and flatten the top. When the top is flat, rout the rabbet for the till bottom on the back lower edge.

Make the benchdog apron—The benchdog apron is laminated from two pieces. After gluing the pieces together, lay out and cut the mortise for the front vise hardware in the apron; depending on the vise, you may need to cut a hollow under the top to accommodate the hardware. Once that's done, use a dado set to cut the dog holes. Attach the vise's rear jaw to the apron and then set the piece aside as you start working on the breadboard ends.

Breadboard ends are next—Cut the breadboard ends to width and thickness but leave them a bit long. Cut them to size after you lay out and cut the joinery to attach them to the benchtop. At the rear of each breadboard, rout the groove for the till bottom; it should align with the rabbet

in the benchtop. Then drill holes for the lag screws that will help anchor the breadboards to the top. Finally, lay out and cut the dovetails.

Use a router and fence to cut the tenon cheeks on the ends of the top. Then lay out and cut the long tenons that will go deep into the breadboards. Clean up the inside corners with a chisel, and fine-tune the fit using handplanes.

Once the breadboards have been fitted, drill the pilot holes for the lag screws. To give the screws extra purchase (so they don't just go into weak end grain), I mortised hardwood dowels from under the benchtop, in line with the pilot holes.

Attach the breadboards, apron, and till—Start by gluing the apron to its breadboard end. Then apply glue to the apron and front edge of the benchtop. Screw on the breadboard end, and clamp the apron in place, working from the corner out. Don't worry about exactly where the apron ends; you'll be notching out that end of the bench-top for the tail vise. Finally, install the other breadboard end.

After the glue cures on the breadboard ends and the benchdog apron, install the till parts and 1x blocking underneath, which increases stiffness and gives better clamp purchase.

Assemble the base—Once the top has been glued together, build the trestles and make the stretchers of the base. Before gluing and wedging the top of the trestles, notch both ends to go around the benchdog apron in front and the till in back.

Base Is Rock Solid

To withstand the rigors of handplaning, the base is made from thick hardwood stock and held together with sturdy joinery.

Peg the short rails. The trestles are assembled with beefy mortise-and-tenons. The rails are reinforced with hardwood pegs.

Wedge the shoes. The mortise-and-tenons in the top and bottom of the trestles are wedged.

Big stretchers. Threaded rod gives a secure connection between the stretchers and trestles.

Add the Tail Vise

Building a smooth-working tail vise can take nearly as long as building the benchtop or base. The work is worthwhile because a tail vise is unmatched at holding work flat on the benchtop between dogs. Have the hardware in hand before you start and make a full-scale drawing of the whole assembly to make layout easier. Use a circular saw and hand tools to cut a notch in the benchtop for the vise, and tune the vertical surfaces square with the top. Rout the groove for the top plate a bit oversize to provide a little clearance and leave room for adjustment, if needed. Now attach the vertical mounting plate to the bench (with only two screws so you can adjust it later if need be), aligned with the top-plate slot and perfectly parallel with the benchtop.

The core is key—The core of the vise accommodates the screw and nut, and is laminated from two pieces. Before gluing them together, hollow out the interior of one piece with a core-box bit and router. The other piece has a rectangular section removed with a saw. Glue these two pieces together and let them dry.

Now make the dog-hole plank and dovetail it to the end cap. Cut two mortises in the end cap and mating tenons on the end of the core, for alignment and added strength. Also, cut the shallow mortise into the end cap and a tenon on the end of the top cover. Cut a shallow rabbet in the top edge for the top guide plate.

Attach the top and bottom guide plates to the core and slide it onto the plate on the bench. Test the action—there should be little wiggle when you lift the front edge, and

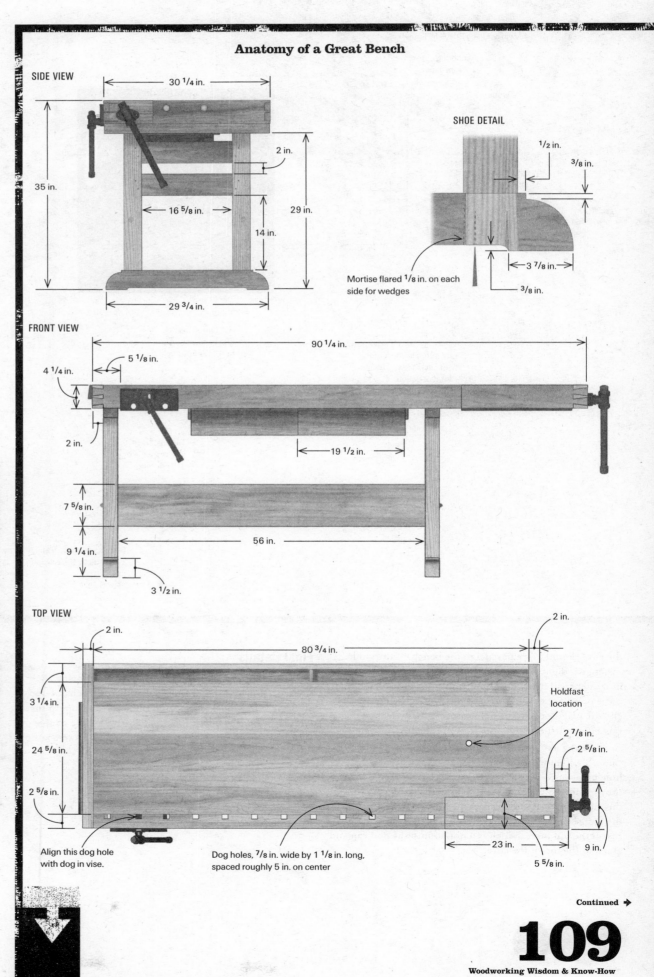

Anatomy of a Great Bench

SIDE VIEW

30 1/4 in.

35 in.

2 in.

16 5/8 in.

29 in.

14 in.

29 3/4 in.

SHOE DETAIL

1/2 in.

3/8 in.

3 7/8 in.

3/8 in.

Mortise flared 1/8 in. on each side for wedges

FRONT VIEW

5 1/8 in.

4 1/4 in.

90 1/4 in.

2 in.

19 1/2 in.

7 5/8 in.

56 in.

9 1/4 in.

3 1/2 in.

TOP VIEW

2 in.

80 3/4 in.

2 in.

3 1/4 in.

Holdfast location

24 5/8 in.

2 7/8 in.

2 5/8 in.

2 5/8 in.

Align this dog hole with dog in vise.

Dog holes, 7/8 in. wide by 1 1/8 in. long, spaced roughly 5 in. on center

23 in.

9 in.

5 5/8 in.

Continued ➡

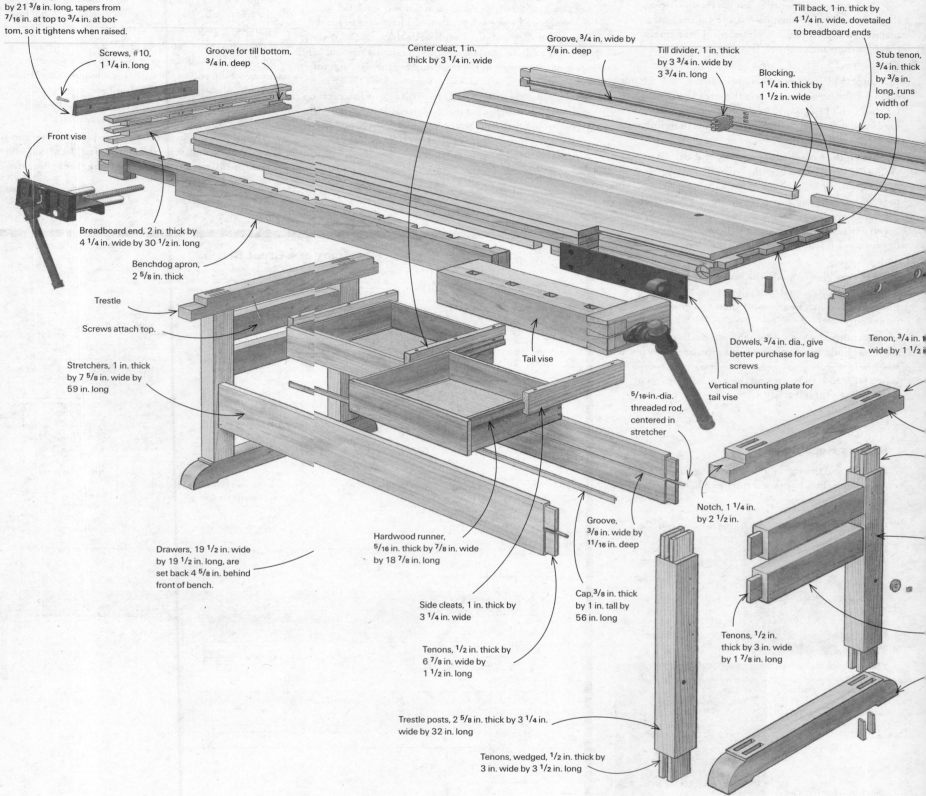

Slide-up hardwood stop for handplaning, 2 1/2 in. wide by 21 3/8 in. long, tapers from 7/16 in. at top to 3/4 in. at bottom, so it tightens when raised.

Screws, #10, 1 1/4 in. long

Groove for till bottom, 3/4 in. deep

Center cleat, 1 in. thick by 3 1/4 in. wide

Groove, 3/4 in. wide by 3/8 in. deep

Till divider, 1 in. thick by 3 3/4 in. wide by 3 3/4 in. long

Till back, 1 in. thick by 4 1/4 in. wide, dovetailed to breadboard ends

Blocking, 1 1/4 in. thick by 1 1/2 in. wide

Stub tenon, 3/4 in. thick by 3/8 in. long, runs width of top.

Front vise

Breadboard end, 2 in. thick by 4 1/4 in. wide by 30 1/2 in. long

Benchdog apron, 2 5/8 in. thick

Trestle

Screws attach top.

Stretchers, 1 in. thick by 7 5/8 in. wide by 59 in. long

Tail vise

Dowels, 3/4 in. dia., give better purchase for lag screws

Tenon, 3/4 in. wide by 1 1/2

Vertical mounting plate for tail vise

5/16-in.-dia. threaded rod, centered in stretcher

Notch, 1 1/4 in. by 2 1/2 in.

Drawers, 19 1/2 in. wide by 19 1/2 in. long, are set back 4 5/8 in. behind front of bench.

Hardwood runner, 5/16 in. thick by 7/8 in. wide by 18 7/8 in. long

Groove, 3/8 in. wide by 11/16 in. deep

Tenons, 1/2 in. thick by 3 in. wide by 1 7/8 in. long

Side cleats, 1 in. thick by 3 1/4 in. wide

Cap, 3/8 in. thick by 1 in. tall by 56 in. long

Tenons, 1/2 in. thick by 6 7/8 in. wide by 1 1/2 in. long

Trestle posts, 2 5/8 in. thick by 3 1/4 in. wide by 32 in. long

Tenons, wedged, 1/2 in. thick by 3 in. wide by 3 1/2 in. long

the core should move parallel to the bench. If the guide plates grip the steel plate on the bench too tightly, the core movement will be stiff. Shim the bottom guide plate with a piece of veneer or a business card. If you have lots of wiggle, the plates need to be tighter together, so deepen the rabbet for the top guide into the core slightly and retest.

Add the dog plank and top—When the core moves smoothly, remove it from the bench. Now glue the dog-hole plank and end cap together and to the core. Mount the assembly to the benchtop, adding the last screws to the mounting plate. Thread in the lead screw and fasten the flange to the end cap and test the vise action. Finally, install the top piece, which is tenoned into the end cap and glued to the top of the core.

Final Details

Now finish the surface prep on the benchtop. Bring all surfaces flush and smooth using handplanes. I chamfered all edges with a block plane. Add the slide-up stop on the end of the bench, install the drawers, and make a couple of handles for your vises. Last, finish the top with two coats of boiled linseed oil.

Till bottom, 3/4 in. thick by 3 3/8 in. wide by 82 1/4 in. long

Breadboard end, 2 in. thick by 4 1/4 in. wide by 24 7/8 in. long

Elongate holes for cross-grain movement.

Lag screw, 5/16 in. dia. by 4 1/2 in. long

Notch, 1 1/4 in. by 7/8 in.

Trestle top, 2 5/8 in. thick by 3 in. wide by 30 1/4 in. long

Tenons, wedged, 1/2 in. thick by 3 in. wide by 3 in. long

Pegs, 1/4 in. square at ends

Intermediate rails, 2 in. thick by 4 in. wide by 20 3/8 in. long

Trestle shoe, 2 5/8 in. thick by 3 1/2 in. wide by 29 3/4 in. long

Tackle Top in Sections

Assemble the benchtop in sections on a pair of sturdy sawhorses. Offset the pieces in each section to create a strong tongue-and-groove interlock and guarantee alignment.

TONGUE-AND-GROOVE TRICK

First section kicks it off. Glue the first three boards together, then let the assembly dry. Clean up squeeze-out so it won't interfere with the following section.

Three boards at a time. After the glue dries from each previous section, add the next three boards, applying glue to all mating surfaces. Clamp across the faces and edges. Repeat until the whole slab of the top is assembled. You'll need lots of clamps. Use cauls to keep the assembly flat.

SECTION THROUGH TOP

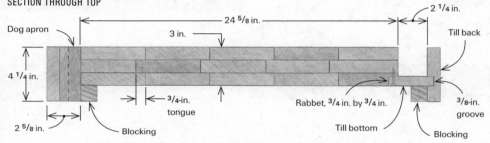

Dog apron — 24 5/8 in. — 2 1/4 in.

3 in. — Till back

4 1/4 in.

3/4-in. tongue — Rabbet, 3/4 in. by 3/4 in. — 3/8-in. groove

2 5/8 in. — Blocking — Till bottom — Blocking

BREADBOARDS KEEP IT FLAT

How to handle big breadboards. After mortising the breadboard pieces, cut the tongue and tenons on the top. Use a router and fence to make the cheek cuts and a handsaw to remove the waste between the long tenons. Clean out the corners with chisels.

Tail Vise Is Worthwhile Challenge

Hack begins by notching out the front right corner of the benchtop. The vise design uses readily available steel hardware for the mechanical parts ($80; Woodcraft #144807), housed in a shopmade wooden sliding jaw.

CHECK THE ACTION OF THE HARDWARE

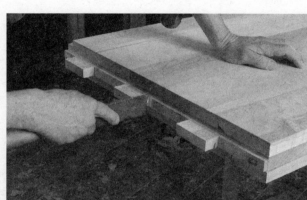

Make way for the top plate. Use a three-wing slot cutter to rout a groove parallel to the benchtop to house the top plate. The vertical board tacked in the corner acts as a spacer to prevent the bit from cutting too far.

Attach the vertical plate. Clamp the bottom plate in place. Align the top of the vertical plate with the groove, drill pilot holes, and drive in the top screws. Now attach the top and bottom plates and try the sliding action.

Continued →

The Apron Frames the Top

To allow for wood movement, the breadboard ends are tenoned to the top, with lag screws cinching the parts. Use slow-setting urea-formaldehyde glue everywhere else to buy time for fine-tuning.

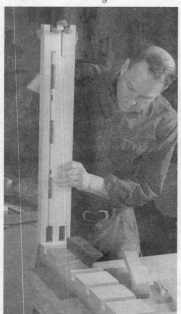

Start at the front left corner. Connect the breadboard to the apron (left). Then apply glue to the breadboard tenons and to the interior face of the apron. Go lightly to avoid squeeze-out into the dog holes. Clamp the breadboard in place to help support the long dog apron (upper right), then drive in the lags. The right-hand corner of the top (reversed in lower-right photo) will be notched for the tail vise, so there's no need to make the dog apron the full length of the bench.

The till goes on last. Screw the till bottom into its rabbet under the top. Glue the divider in the till back, then glue the assembly to the breadboard ends and the top.

CROSS-SECTION

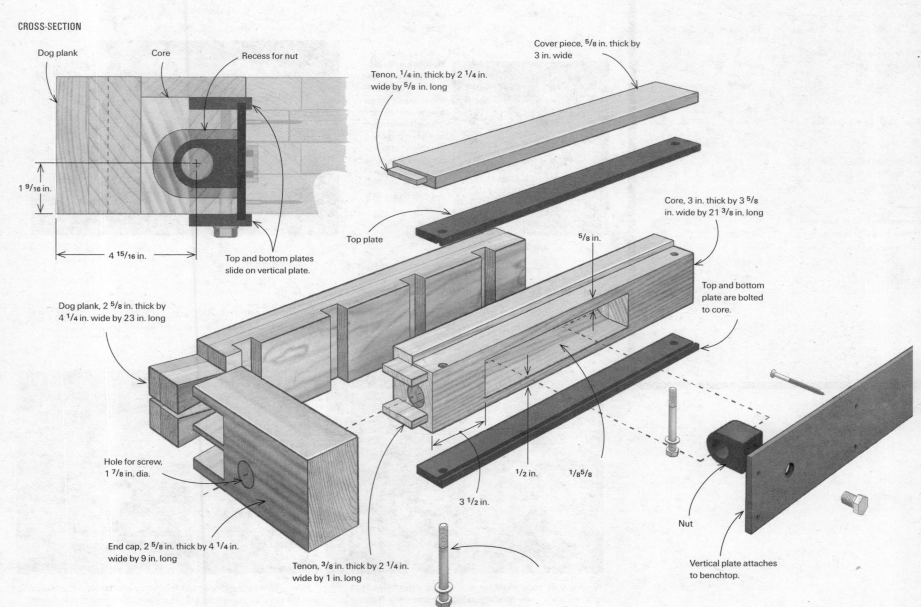

Dog plank

Core

Recess for nut

$1\ 9/16$ in.

$4\ 15/16$ in.

Top and bottom plates slide on vertical plate.

Tenon, $1/4$ in. thick by $2\ 1/4$ in. wide by $5/8$ in. long

Cover piece, $5/8$ in. thick by 3 in. wide

Top plate

Core, 3 in. thick by $3\ 5/8$ in. wide by $21\ 3/8$ in. long

$5/8$ in.

Top and bottom plate are bolted to core.

Dog plank, $2\ 5/8$ in. thick by $4\ 1/4$ in. wide by 23 in. long

Hole for screw, $1\ 7/8$ in. dia.

$1/2$ in.

$1/8$ $5/8$

$3\ 1/2$ in.

Nut

End cap, $2\ 5/8$ in. thick by $4\ 1/4$ in. wide by 9 in. long

Tenon, $3/8$ in. thick by $2\ 1/4$ in. wide by 1 in. long

Vertical plate attaches to benchtop.

Assemble the Wood Parts

FINAL ASSEMBLY

Mount the wood jaw to the hardware. Be sure to clean up the wood parts to remove any glue squeeze-out that could interfere with the assembly (above). Thread the bolts through the core, and then screw each plate to the core. Glue the top cover to the core and to the end cap (below).

The Wired Workbench

by John White

In a modern shop, a lot of work gets done with power tools such as routers, biscuit joiners, and random-orbit sanders. But most of us use them on benches designed around handplaning, which means everything from the height to the mass to the vises and benchdogs is geared toward hand-tool use. So the editors at Fine Woodworking decided to build a bench designed for power tools. They posted a blog on FineWoodworking.com, asking readers what they thought a "wired workbench" should be. A lot of great suggestions came in, and being a veteran of the FWW shop and an inveterate inventor, I was given the task of distilling readers' ideas into a user-friendly whole.

Power tools need electricity to run and they make dust by the fistful. So most people agreed that the first thing this bench needed was a built-in source of electricity and dust collection. I kept things simple by attaching a commercially available automated vacuum outlet, the iVAC switch box, that turns on the dust collection when you power up the tool. And I made room in the base for both a shop vacuum and an Oneida Dust Deputy, a miniature cyclone that has proven its value trapping the fine dust (and all of the chips) before it gets to the vacuum and clogs the filter.

This wired workbench also is taller (38 in. total) than traditional benches, moving the tool and the workpiece up to a height where you have better vision and control. It's wider, too, but not as long. I got rid of the traditional front and tail vises, opting for a simple but effective clamping

Collect the Dust, Forget the Fuss

Imagine locking down your workpieces quickly, and using your portable power tools without any dust or distractions.

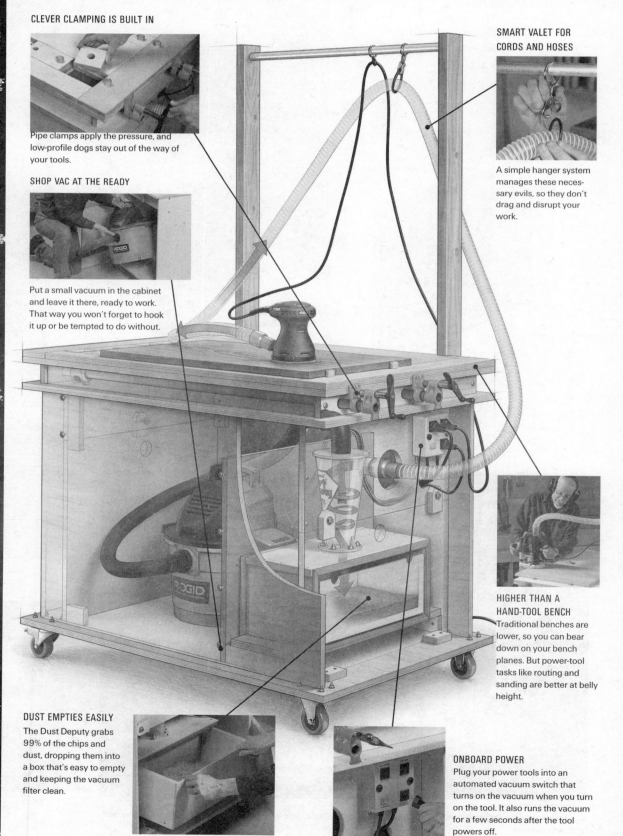

CLEVER CLAMPING IS BUILT IN

Pipe clamps apply the pressure, and low-profile dogs stay out of the way of your tools.

SHOP VAC AT THE READY

Put a small vacuum in the cabinet and leave it there, ready to work. That way you won't forget to hook it up or be tempted to do without.

SMART VALET FOR CORDS AND HOSES

A simple hanger system manages these necessary evils, so they don't drag and disrupt your work.

HIGHER THAN A HAND-TOOL BENCH

Traditional benches are lower, so you can bear down on your bench planes. But power-tool tasks like routing and sanding are better at belly height.

DUST EMPTIES EASILY

The Dust Deputy grabs 99% of the chips and dust, dropping them into a box that's easy to empty and keeping the vacuum filter clean.

ONBOARD POWER

Plug your power tools into an automated vacuum switch that turns on the vacuum when you turn on the tool. It also runs the vacuum for a few seconds after the tool powers off.

Continued →

system made from two pipe clamps. The benchdogs have soft heads that hold workpieces firmly, but won't dent or mar them. And there are locking casters underneath to make the bench mobile.

Finally, the wired workbench is much easier to make than a big, heavy traditional bench. Because it won't take the forces a hand-tool bench does, the entire bench is

made from plywood. And there is no complicated joinery, just butt joints held together by screws. Where they show, I've used stainless-steel deck screws and finish washers for a clean, modern look.

If you already have a heavy hand-tool workbench, this one will make a great, mobile, secondary workstation. And if you rely mostly on power tools, this might be the only bench you need.

The Base Is a Dust Collector

It's not too difficult to cut accurate parts from plywood. I'll skip over that process now and just explain how the parts go together.

I put the vacuum and the mini-cyclone in the base for two reasons: First, enclosing the vacuum muffles it. Second, it makes the bench a self-contained unit. There's

Build the Base First

Rather than fill the interior with drawers, we designed it to hide and muffle a shop vacuum and hold a dust separator. Construction is simple and solid: 3/4-in. plywood and drywall screws.

Sources of Supply

Dust-Deputy Miniature Cyclone

Oneida-air.com, No. AXD001004, (90° elbow, No. AHA000004)

Ivac Switch ivacswitch.com

Cleat, 2 in. wide by 25 1/2 in. long

End apron, 6 in. wide by 27 in. long

Door latch, 2 in. wide by 3 in. long

Front and back, 28 in. wide by 44 in. long

End apron, 12 in. wide by 27 in. long

Hole for dust-collection hose, 4 1/2 in. dia.

Side cleats, 2 in. wide, also serve as door stops.

Hole for power cord, 2 in. dia.

Door, 22 in. wide by 27 in. long

Door stop, 2 in. wide by 3 in. long

3-in. locking swivel caster

Finger hole, 2 in. dia.

Door, 16 in. wide by 27 in. long

Door stops, 2 in. wide by 3 in. long

Foot, 2 in. wide by 10 3/8 in. long

3-in. fixed caster

Interior divider, 22 in. wide by 27 in. long

Ventilation hole, 2 1/4 in. dia.

Bottom, 32 in. wide by 47 1/2 in. long

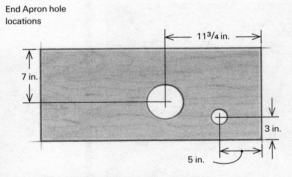

End Apron hole locations

11 3/4 in.

7 in.

3 in.

5 in.

Get a third hand for assembly. White used a simple plywood corner block to hold parts still and square to one another while he drove in screws.

Add aprons for stiffness. Screw through the face into the cleats. On the cyclone end, pre-drill holes for the vacuum hose and power cords with a circle cutter.

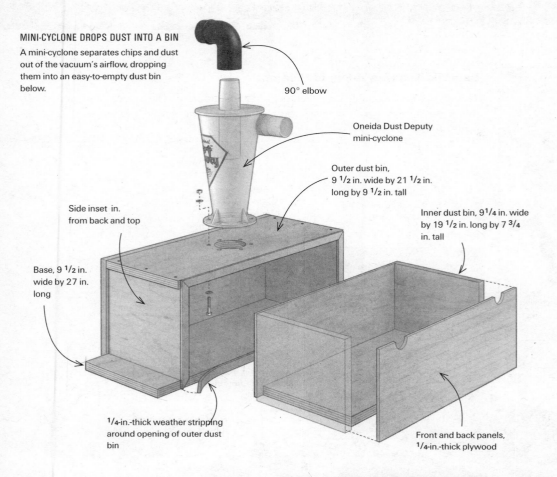

MINI-CYCLONE DROPS DUST INTO A BIN
A mini-cyclone separates chips and dust out of the vacuum's airflow, dropping them into an easy-to-empty dust bin below.

90° elbow

Oneida Dust Deputy mini-cyclone

Outer dust bin, 9 1/2 in. wide by 21 1/2 in. long by 9 1/2 in. tall

Side inset in. from back and top

Inner dust bin, 9 1/4 in. wide by 19 1/2 in. long by 7 3/4 in. tall

Base, 9 1/2 in. wide by 27 in. long

1/4-in.-thick weather stripping around opening of outer dust bin

Front and back panels, 1/4-in.-thick plywood

FINE-TUNE THE AIR SEAL
A door on the cabinet presses tightly against weather stripping on the dust bin, so the inner bin can be loose. Stops at the bottom and latches at the top of the door create even pressure.

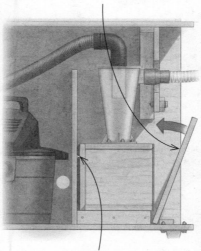

Use drywall screws on the back of the dust bin to push it back and forth to fine-tune how much the weather stripping is compressed by the door.

Weather stripping makes an airtight seal. Miter the corners with a chisel after you apply the stripping, and glue the corners together with cyanoacrylate glue.

Put the Deputy on the case. To create an airtight seal, apply a bead of acrylic caulk to the mini-cyclone's flange before putting it on the bin.

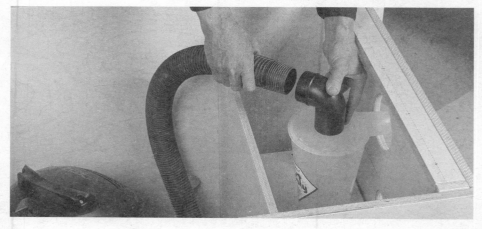

Connect the vacuum to the mini-cyclone. A 90° elbow makes the tight turn under the bench's top without restricting airflow like a crimped hose would.

no vacuum trailing behind it like a baby elephant behind its mother.

Start assembling the base with the bottom panel, predrilling holes for the casters. Then attach the front panel to the bottom. Screw the interior divider to the base and then to the front panel. Next, attach the back panel to the base and divider, but before you do, drill the ventilation hole (the power cord for the iVac switch also passes through this hole).

An apron runs across the top of the door opening at both ends of the base. Each apron is screwed to plywood cleats. The top cleat attaches the top assembly. The side cleats serve as door stops. After assembling the aprons and cleats, screw them between the front and back panels.

Then turn over the base and bolt the casters to it. Flip the cabinet back over and install the doors. Attach the lower door stops to the sides of the cabinet and to the bottom panel. Then screw the pivoting door "locks" to the apron.

Collect the dust in an airtight box—The Dust Deputy is a plastic cyclone typically attached to the lid of a 5-gallon bucket, which collects the chips and dust when they fall out of the cyclone. But such an assembly is too tall to fit inside the base cabinet, so I came up with another way to collect the debris. Of course, that meant overcoming a big challenge, because for the cyclone to work properly, the box needs to be airtight. Fortunately, I found an easy way to do that, because—and this is the cool part—you don't need any special tools or materials to make it.

The cyclone sits on top of a box, and inside the box is a removable drawer that catches the dust and chips. When it is full, you just open the box, pull out the drawer, dump it in a trash can, and put it back in.

The butt joints in the box are tight enough to prevent airflow and the door can be used to create a tight seal around the opening. Just apply foam gasket—the kind used for weather stripping on entry doors—around the opening for the door, mitering the corners and gluing them together using cyanoacrylate glue. When the door closes against the gasket, it creates an airtight seal.

To fine-tune how much the door compresses the gasket, I drove two drywall screws into the back of the outer dust bin. Adjusting the screws in and out moves the box farther from and closer to the door and compresses the gasket less or more.

Finally, to complete the airtight box, apply a bead of acrylic caulk around the opening for the cyclone before bolting it in place.

The Top Is a Vise

The cool thing about this top is that, like my new-fangled workbench, it has a clamping system built into it. All you need are two 3/4-in. pipe clamps—this bench is designed for Jorgensen No. 50 Pony clamps—some 3/4-in.-dia. dowel, and 3/4-in.-internal-dia. vinyl tubing. The dowel is cut into short lengths to make benchdogs and the tubing slides over the dogs to keep them from marring or denting your work, something you don't want to have happen when you're sanding a door just before applying a finish.

Here's how it works. A block of plywood with a dog hole drilled in it is pushed against the sliding jaw of the pipe clamp. The other jaw is fixed to the apron. You can move the sliding jaw wherever you need it, and the dog hole moves along with it.

The top is made from layers of plywood strips, but it is plenty rigid for power-tool work (and some hand-tool work like light planing). Screw the top and middle layers together. Mark the locations of the stationary benchdogs, partially disassemble the parts, and drill the holes.

Now that the basic structure of the top has been assembled, make and attach the riser layer. The two end risers need holes for the pipes to pass through. Drill them at the drill press.

Next, make and install the sliding benchdog blocks.

Continued ➜

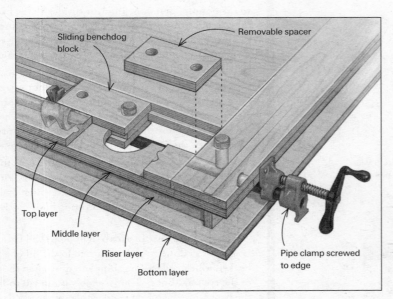

Sliding benchdog block

Removable spacer

Top layer

Middle layer

Riser layer

Bottom layer

Pipe clamp screwed to edge

Layered Top Has Room for Clamps

This plywood top assembly has a clamping system built into it. The layered construction makes it easy to create tongued channels for the sliding benchdog blocks and a cavity for the pipe clamps.

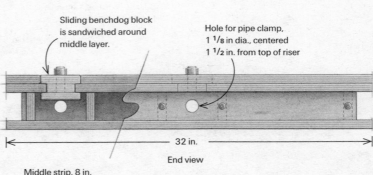

Sliding benchdog block is sandwiched around middle layer.

Hole for pipe clamp, $1\frac{1}{8}$ in. dia., centered $1\frac{1}{2}$ in. from top of riser

32 in.

End view

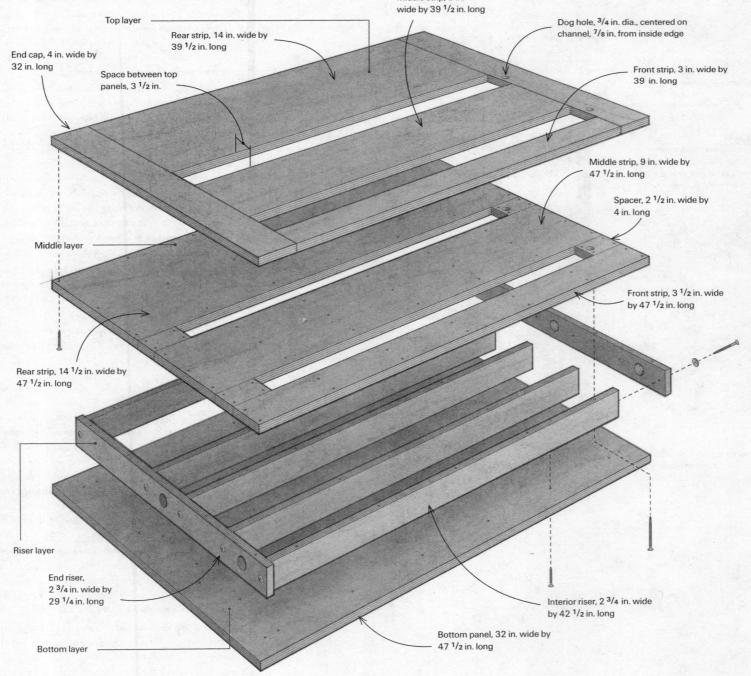

Top layer

Middle strip, 8 in. wide by $39\frac{1}{2}$ in. long

Rear strip, 14 in. wide by $39\frac{1}{2}$ in. long

Dog hole, $\frac{3}{4}$ in. dia., centered on channel, $\frac{7}{8}$ in. from inside edge

End cap, 4 in. wide by 32 in. long

Space between top panels, $3\frac{1}{2}$ in.

Front strip, 3 in. wide by 39 in. long

Middle strip, 9 in. wide by $47\frac{1}{2}$ in. long

Middle layer

Spacer, $2\frac{1}{2}$ in. wide by 4 in. long

Front strip, $3\frac{1}{2}$ in. wide by $47\frac{1}{2}$ in. long

Rear strip, $14\frac{1}{2}$ in. wide by $47\frac{1}{2}$ in. long

Riser layer

End riser, $2\frac{3}{4}$ in. wide by $29\frac{1}{4}$ in. long

Interior riser, $2\frac{3}{4}$ in. wide by $42\frac{1}{2}$ in. long

Bottom panel, 32 in. wide by $47\frac{1}{2}$ in. long

Bottom layer

BUILD THE TOP TWO LAYERS FIRST

Connect the top and middle layers. Pre-drill and countersink for the screws and use an offcut from the plywood to keep the edges aligned as you drive the screws.

Use spacers to locate slots for clamps. Make sure they're dimensioned and placed accurately, because they determine where you drill holes for the stationary benchdogs.

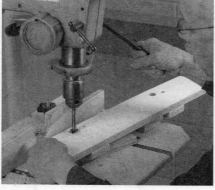

Drill for the stationary benchdogs. Leave the spacers attached and drill through both pieces at once. Use scraps to support the far end of the assembly.

ADD THE RISER FRAME AND SLIDING DOGS

Long screws. Screw down through the frame pieces and into the top.

Make the sliding benchdog blocks. After drilling dog holes through the assembled blocks, take off the bottom layer and put the blocks in place. Three stacked pieces of blue tape, added after the dog holes are drilled, create enough play for the block to slide easily (use a knife to cut openings in the tape).

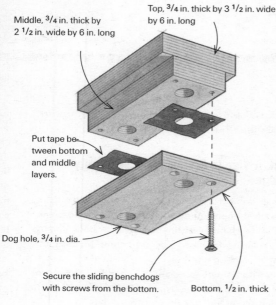

Middle, 3/4 in. thick by 2 1/2 in. wide by 6 in. long

Top, 3/4 in. thick by 3 1/2 in. wide by 6 in. long

Put tape between bottom and middle layers.

Dog hole, 3/4 in. dia.

Secure the sliding benchdogs with screws from the bottom.

Bottom, 1/2 in. thick

Assemble the layers and drill a hole for the benchdog. Take off the bottom layer, add some tape to make the groove a bit wider than the tongue on the top, and install the blocks. Now attach the bottom panel to the risers. Then set the entire assembly onto the base and attach it by screwing through the cleats and into the bottom panel.

Make filler blocks for the slots. Then make some benchdogs from a length of dowel and slip some vinyl tubing over one end. Finally, install the pipe clamps.

Install the Low-Cost Clamping System

Whether you're sanding or routing, the workpiece needs to be held still. White's ingenious "vise" is nothing more than 3/4-in. pipe clamps and a clever system of sliding blocks and dogs, but it gets the job done and applies pressure close to the bench's surface—without sticking up and getting in the way.

Install the pipe clamps. Put the bare end in and through the adjustable clamp head. Tighten it completely, and mark it where it's flush with the top's edge. Take it out, cut it to length, and put it back. Screw the fixed head to the bench through pre-drilled holes (right), so you can open and close it without holding the head.

Continued ➤

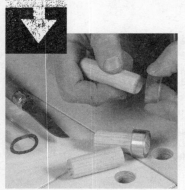

Low-tech benchdogs. A sharp knife is all you need to cut the plastic tubing that fits over the dowels (left) so they won't mar or dent workpieces. Use filler blocks to cover the slot (right). You need several of different lengths for complete coverage no matter where the benchdog block and clamp head are.

Tame Hoses and Cords From Above

Nothing is more annoying than a cord or hose that continually catches and drags as you try to control a tool. White solved that problem with an overhead rack for both.

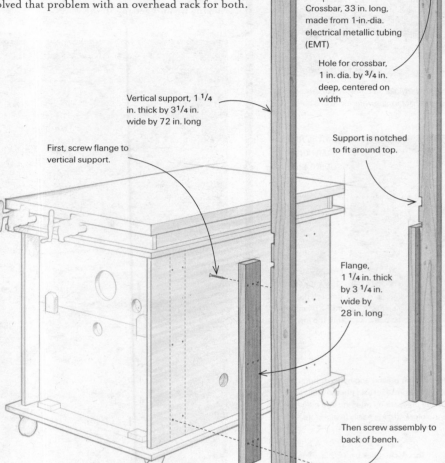

Crossbar, 33 in. long, made from 1-in.-dia. electrical metallic tubing (EMT)

Hole for crossbar, 1 in. dia. by 3/4 in. deep, centered on width

Vertical support, 1 1/4 in. thick by 3 1/4 in. wide by 72 in. long

Support is notched to fit around top.

First, screw flange to vertical support.

Flange, 1 1/4 in. thick by 3 1/4 in. wide by 28 in. long

Then screw assembly to back of bench.

Elegantly simple. White used a key ring and O-ring bought at a local hardware store to suspend the hose. Another one holds the cord. They slide easily over the electrical tubing used for the crossbar.

A User's Guide to Vises

by Garrett Hack

A good bench vise is nearly as useful as a shop apprentice. On my bench I have a front vise and a large tail vise—I call them my right- and left-hand men. It's hard to imagine woodworking without them; they hold my work firmly so that I can concentrate fully on powering and controlling the tool I'm using.

In general, you'll find vises at two locations on a woodworker's bench: one on the long side of the bench, typically at the left-hand corner for right-handed woodworkers, and another on the short side at the opposite end.

The first, known variously as a side vise or front vise, matches the mental picture that most people have of a vise, with a movable jaw capturing work between it and the edge of the bench.

The second, called an end vise or tail vise, can clamp work like a front vise, but is more often used to hold boards flat on the bench, pinched between a pin or dog in the vise and another in one of the many holes along the benchtop. Together, these two vises can meet all of a woodworker's basic needs when it comes to holding work firmly and within reach.

Up Front: A Vise to Clamp Work Vertically or On Edge

A front vise, typically found on the bench's left-front corner, is ideal when you need to clamp a board to plane an edge, hold a chair leg while shaping it, or hold a board upright for sawing dovetails. The most common design is quite simple: a jaw of wood, or cast iron lined with wood, that moves with a single screw and a T-handle. The rest of the vise is mortised into the front edge of the bench. Mine opens about 10 in. and has about 4 in. of depth.

Many of the front vises on the market are fairly easy to fit to a benchtop. Look for one that has a large screw with well-cut Acme threads. These are the same square threads found on good clamps; they can smoothly deliver lots of force over a long life.

To hold long boards, wide panels, or doors securely on edge in a front vise, you need the added support of the deep front apron of the bench. Properly installed, the fixed half of the vise should be mortised into the bench so that the movable jaw clamps against the apron. This creates a great deal of stability, making it possible to clamp most boards on edge with no other support. For very long boards, just put one end in the front vise and rest the other on a short board clamped in the tail or end vise, much like a board jack on traditional benches. You can clamp a large tabletop vertically against the front edge of a bench, one end held in the front vise and the other held by a bar clamp across the bench.

A problem can arise, though, when clamping on just one side of the vise, such as when holding just the end of a much larger piece, clamping pieces vertically for laying out or sawing dovetails, or holding tapered or oddly shaped pieces. When one side of the jaw is applying all the pressure—or trying to—it is very hard on the screw and any alignment rods, and can even distort them. One solution is to slip a block as thick as the workpiece into the other side of the jaw (use a wedge for odd shapes). This keeps the jaws parallel so you can apply all the pressure you need. Some bench manufacturers equip their front vises with a threaded stop that does the same job.

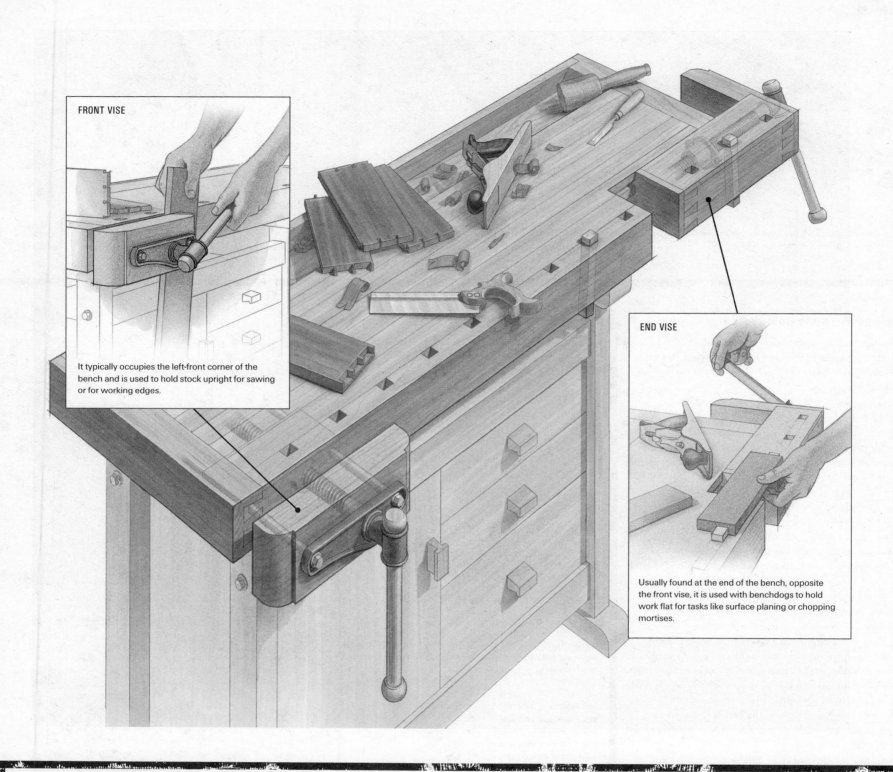

FRONT VISE

It typically occupies the left-front corner of the bench and is used to hold stock upright for sawing or for working edges.

END VISE

Usually found at the end of the bench, opposite the front vise, it is used with benchdogs to hold work flat for tasks like surface planing or chopping mortises.

Types of Front Vise

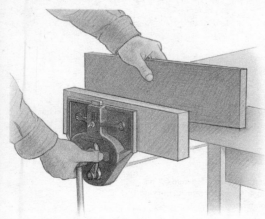

CAST IRON

The most popular front vise is cast iron. A steel rod or two keep the jaw aligned. Some also have a quick-action release for faster jaw adjustments.

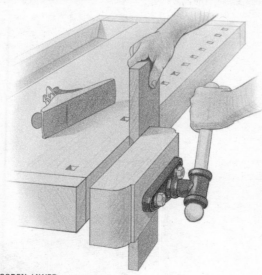

WOODEN-JAWED

A wooden-jawed vise operates like its cast-iron cousin. The movable jaw is typically made from the same material as the bench. Some models offer quick-release.

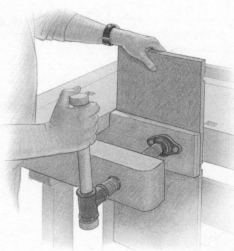

ARM VISE

An arm vise works well on wide boards. There are no screws or rods in the way. But the right-angled arm limits clamping force, which reduces the ability to clamp long boards horizontally.

Continued →

Build it yourself. Many companies sell the hardware for these vises. Look for a large screw with square-cut threads.

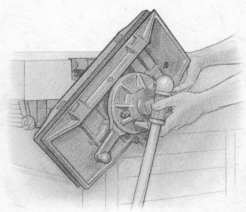

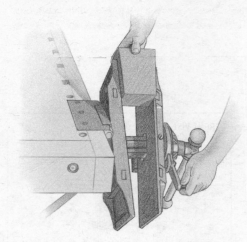

PATTERNMAKER'S VISE

A patternmaker's vise can hold oddly shaped work at any angle. The vise body can pivot up and over the bench until the jaws are parallel to the benchtop. The jaws also can rotate 360° and angle toward one another for holding tapered work.

At the End: A Vise to Hold Work Flat

At the other end of the bench, you typically will find one of two distinct types of vises, known as end vises or tail vises. Their main purpose is to hold work flat on the surface of the bench.

A traditional tail vise, with one row of dog holes along the front edge of the bench and several more in the movable jaw, allows you to hold work flat over nearly the entire length of the bench. This is ideal for holding long boards to smooth a face, bead one edge, or hold a leg while chopping a mortise. You can also clamp across the grain to bevel a panel end or shape the skirt of a chest side. Be careful to apply only modest pressure to hold the work, or you will bow it up.

The tail vise is also great for holding long or odd pieces at any angle—there are no screws in the way and the hefty construction tends to prevent racking on odd shapes. Also, it can hold a workpiece at right angles to the bench edge, ideal for planing an end-grain edge, shooting a miter on a molding, or paring a tenon shoulder.

One drawback with this vise is that the large movable jaw can sag. A misaligned jaw makes it difficult to hold work flat on the benchtop. Avoid chopping or pounding over the movable jaw; it isn't as solid as the benchtop itself. Support the work as much as possible over the bench, with the least amount of jaw open. I keep small, square blocks handy to shim my work toward the bench or protect it from the dogs. I shouldn't have to say this, but never sit on your tail vise.

Another type of end vise—The other popular type of end vise looks and works like a front vise, except that the movable jaw is mounted to, and set parallel with, the end of the bench. If I had to outfit a bench with just one vise, it would be this type (see drawing, right). My small traveling bench has an old front vise mounted on one end in line with a row of dog holes.

Some end vises of this type have a jaw that spans the entire width of the bench. Equipped with a dog on each end of the jaw, and paired with a double row of dog holes down the front and back of the bench, this is a great system for holding wide parts flat on the benchtop. Several ready-made benches are built this way. Lee Valley also sells the necessary hardware for making the vise yourself.

Types of End Vise

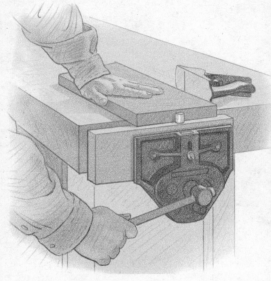

CAST IRON

Same vise, different location. The cast-iron front vise also works well as an end vise—a smart solution if you have room or money for only one vise.

FULL WIDTH

A modern variation spans the width of the bench. With two rows of dog holes, the wide jaw of this vise is ideal for holding wider panels.

TAIL VISE

The traditional end vise. The movable jaw is a thick section of the bench's front edge, about 18 in. long. Dog holes hold work flat on the surface. The jaws also can hold work at an angle.

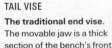

TWIN-SCREW

A twin-screw model can clamp wide stock vertically. A chain connects the two screws to prevent racking.

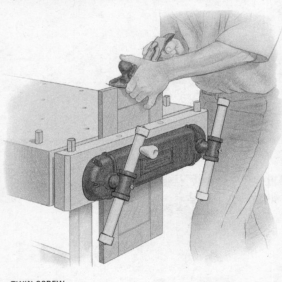

The guts. Tail-vise hardware comes with instructions for making the wood components.

Bench-Vise Tips

by Steve Latta

The bench vise is one of woodworking's most necessary and fundamental tools, vital for holding work while you saw, chop, pare, plane, scrape, and perform any number of other tasks on your projects.

Despite the vise being used so often, it is commonly misused. In my class or at workshops, I routinely see beginning students clamping stock the wrong way in the vise, sawing or paring in the wrong direction, and risking injury when the work slips and the tool jumps.

You can avoid mishaps like that by adopting a few basic techniques to hold your work securely and prevent it from slipping. And with a few simple shopmade fixtures, you can use your vise to tackle an even wider variety of tasks safely.

Many Ways to Use the Vise Alone

I typically use my bench vise in one of three ways: by itself, with benchdogs, or with other clamping fixtures. Let's look at all three.

On its own, the vise is great for holding smaller workpieces during sawing, chisel work, edge-planing, or other tasks. But for best results—and safety—it's important to orient the work properly in the vise.

For vertical work, consider your task and orient the workpiece so that you'll be working across the jaws and not in line with them. You want the back jaw to brace against the thrust of the saw or chisel. Also, to reduce the likelihood of slipping and racking the vise, position the stock between the vise screw and a guide bar, as low in the jaw as possible. The farther up from the jaws the operation gets, the greater the potential for losing control.

For horizontal work, you may need support under the workpiece if the task calls mainly for downward force. So I keep a piece of 3/4-in. stock handy that is as long as my vise and comes to about 1/8 in. below the top of the jaws when resting on the guide bars. Resting a workpiece on top of this board provides additional support and enhances safety.

For edge-planing short pieces, simply clamp them in the vise. For longer pieces, I add a support block with a piece of sandpaper glued to both faces. The sandpaper bites into both jaw and workpiece, keeping it from slipping when I get to the ends of the board.

A Vise and Dogs Hold Work on the Bench

For surface planing and some other tasks, the workpiece needs to be held flat on the benchtop. You can do this using the sliding stop on top of the vise and a row of dog-holes bored into the bench surface.

Many vises come with a metal stop that slides up out of the front jaw. If yours doesn't have one, you can create one by boring a hole in the front auxiliary jaw to fit a commercially available or shopmade dog. For best support underneath the work, don't open the vise wide to accommodate the workpiece. Instead, use the most distant doghole you can, and keep the vise opening narrow. This puts the bulk of the stock over the bench surface, making planing easier and more stable.

Also, make sure the dog is below the board's surface. Nicking a steel or brass dog can damage a plane iron.

Add a Few Simple Helpers

There are several accessories and attachments that work well with a vise. The simplest is just a cutoff scrap that matches the thickness of the workpiece. Inserting this scrap in the opposite end of the vise helps prevent the vise from racking (pivoting and losing its grip) when work is clamped on the other side of the vise. Taking this further to prevent racking with any thickness of stock, I made an angled block that slides in a dovetail key cut along the length of the vise. Also in the very simple category, just about any bench hook or shooting board that typically braces against the edge of

the bench can be made more stable by clamping it into the vise—a practice I recommend.

Other accessories help with larger stock or specialized tasks. For instance, when edge-planing longer stock or working the end grain of wider boards, you need a way to hold the free end of the workpiece. I do this with a clamping block made from two pieces of scrap joined at a right angle. This block gives me a surface against which I can clamp the work, and a plate that lets me secure the block to the workbench. A different fixture helps when dovetailing the top of a table leg. To hold the work and support the router, I use an L-shaped block that clamps securely in the vise. The fixture anchors the leg, letting me remove much of the socket with a router and do final cleanup with a chisel.

Work in the Right Direction

Brace the work from behind. Applying force in line with the jaws can make the workpiece slip (left). Instead, orient the stock so that you're sawing perpendicular to the jaws (below).

Even wide stock can slip. It's natural to place the broadest faces against the jaws (left), but clamping on the edges still provides enough pressure to hold the work securely (below). Now the piece is braced against the force of the cut and won't slip.

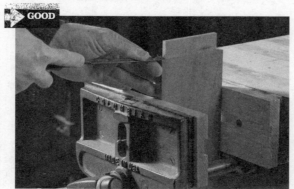

Work at the Right Height

Too tall. It's tempting to place the stock high in the vise so you can work without stooping. But this lets the workpiece flex (left), making the task more difficult and the results less accurate. For the best support, keep the stock low in the vise (below left) or brace it with a backing block of thick scrap stock (below right).

This is dangerous. With no support underneath, the workpiece and chisel can slip under downward pressure (left). Place a support block in the vise underneath the work (below).

A safe setup. Resting on the vise's bars, Latta's support block is about 5/8 in. lower than the vise jaws. With the block in place, the workpiece doesn't slip.

Continued ➡

Tips for Flat Surfaces

How a drawer fits in a vise. Clamp the drawer front lightly in the vise to avoid racking, and use a short piece of stock as a bridge between the benchtop and the top of the vise. This bridge braces the drawer side against downward pressure.

Secure longer stock for surface planing. Butt the workpiece against a thin batten laid across the benchtop. Hold the batten in the vise with an attached cleat, and brace it with a benchdog. This simple setup gives all the support you need, and lets you change out boards quickly.

Use Clamping Blocks for Long and Tall Stock

LONG

Fixture helps hold wide or long boards. The block is as thick as the vise's rear jaw. Leave the crosspiece long to accommodate a clamp.

Just add clamps. To hold the free end of a long board for edge-planing, secure the crosspiece to the bench and the workpiece to the block. The setup also works for wide boards.

LONG

A fixture for legs. Latta uses a panel with an L-shaped bracket to support long work vertically (left). The fixture's top provides a bearing surface for the router when cutting dovetail mortises in the top of a table leg (right). The bottom of the L provides an index for clamping into the vise.

Two Cures for Racking

When a workpiece is placed near the end of the jaws, all front jaws rack (deflect) to some degree, compromising the grip. Here are two great solutions.

USE AN OFFCUT

Match its thickness to your workpiece to prevent the front jaw from pivoting. A spring clamp keeps the scrap from falling before the vise is closed.

A DOVETAIL WEDGE

Latta's anti-racking wedge won't fall out because it slides on a dovetailed key routed into the inner jaw. Slide the wedge farther in to accommodate thicker stock.

Durable Yet Simple Sawhorses

by Anissa Kapsales

A few years ago, after moving into a small apartment, I needed a desk—and fast. I had a big slab of planed, live-edge walnut that would make a perfect top—but what to put it on? Then I spied the two sawhorses I made while studying at the College of the Redwoods, in the furniture-making program founded by James Krenov. Turns out, the horses balanced the mass of the slab perfectly. And their spare, elegant, and well-proportioned design actually made for a nice-looking desk that got tons of compliments from woodworkers and non-woodworkers alike.

But don't let the good looks fool you. These are real workhorses, designed to be versatile and durable—holding up that desk is probably the lightest duty my horses have seen yet. And with straightforward mortise-and-tenon joinery, the horses also are easy to build. The basic design was developed by Krenov, but students add their own flair, as I have to the feet and joinery. I encourage you to do the same.

Why These Are Better

Every woodworker needs a stout pair of sawhorses. They're great for rough-milling lumber and assembling projects—and can even be used as a sturdy base for a temporary worktable. But these horses are different from the standard types, made of 2x4s with splayed legs. Those clunky designs can be hard to use and don't store very easily.

These horses are light and have a small footprint. They are easy to move and the long feet give the horses a wide stance that resists tipping. The upright design lets you position them close together for small glue-ups or veneer pressing jobs. Traditional sawhorses with splayed legs won't cozy up as easily. This nesting ability is also great for stowing the horses when you're done with them.

Despite their sleek profile, these horses can support hundreds of pounds. I often pile a big stack of lumber on top of them for storage or milling. I attribute this strength to the solid mortise-and-tenon joinery and an overall design that carries stresses downward instead of out so the joints aren't pushed apart.

The stretchers not only add strength and stability, but they also are functional. The lower stretcher can hold clamps and lumber. The top stretcher is notched into the uprights and screwed in place without glue. It's easy to remove and replace when it gets worn. This top stretcher also can act as a caul during a glue-up.

Building a Pair Is a Half-Day's Work

The beauty of these horses is their simplicity, and the materials and construction reflect that. They will get knocked around and loaded heavily, so choose materials accordingly. Avoid softer woods like poplar or pine. Hardwoods will last longer, but these are just workhorses, so consider your wallet, too. Ash, red oak, and hickory are low-cost options.

Mortises and tenons first—After milling the lumber, mark the upright mortises in the bases and cut them using a plunge router and edge guide with a spiral upcutting bit. Cut the through-mortises in the uprights for the lower stretcher the same way, but use a backer board underneath to prevent any blowout on the other side and to protect the surface you are routing on. This joint is wedged, so I flare the mortises slightly, top and bottom, with a rounded file to accommodate the wedges.

Now cut the tenons on the bottom of the uprights and the ends of the lower stretcher. Cut the shoulders on the tablesaw using a stop on the crosscut sled, and cut the cheeks with an over-the-fence tenoning jig, also on the tablesaw. Then chisel and file the tenons round to match the mortises.

Fitting the top, shaping the bottom—The notched top stretcher sits in corresponding notches in the uprights and gets screwed in place through the uprights, making it easy to replace when it gets worn. The distance between the inside shoulders of the notches should match the length of the lower stretcher from shoulder to shoulder.

Cut the notches in the upper stretcher using a crosscut sled on the tablesaw. Because there are only four narrow notches, I don't bother with a dado blade; instead, I make a series of cuts between stops. I do the same for the uprights, using a tall fence on the sled. I hit the two outside edges of the notch first and move the fence incrementally to waste away the middle area.

Elegantly Simple

Made popular by legendary teacher James Krenov, this horse is made from just six pieces of stock, simply joined. Choose an inexpensive but durable hardwood such as ash, hickory, or red oak.

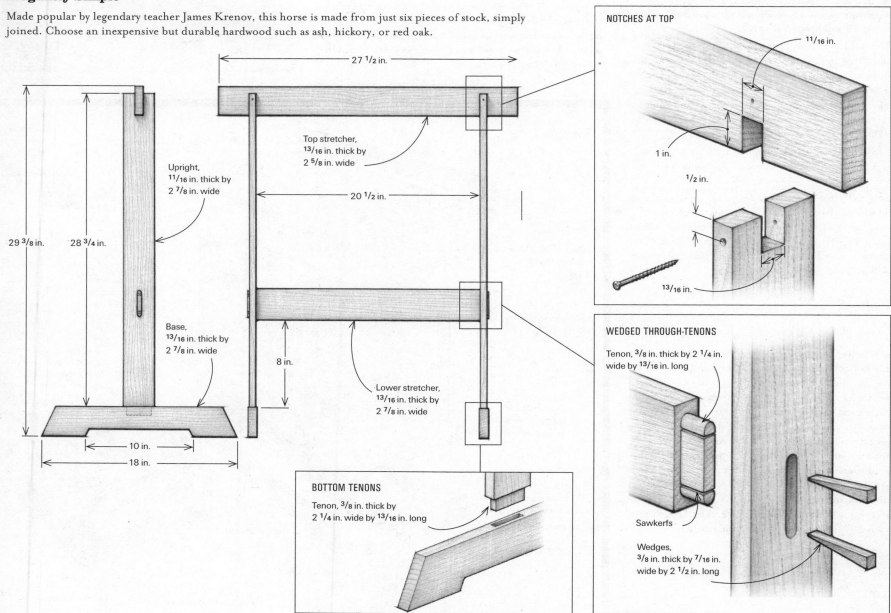

27 1/2 in.

Top stretcher, 13/16 in. thick by 2 5/8 in. wide

Upright, 11/16 in. thick by 2 7/8 in. wide

20 1/2 in.

29 3/8 in.   28 3/4 in.

Base, 13/16 in. thick by 2 7/8 in. wide

8 in.

Lower stretcher, 13/16 in. thick by 2 7/8 in. wide

10 in.

18 in.

NOTCHES AT TOP

11/16 in.

1 in.

1/2 in.

13/16 in.

BOTTOM TENONS

Tenon, 3/8 in. thick by 2 1/4 in. wide by 13/16 in. long

WEDGED THROUGH-TENONS

Tenon, 3/8 in. thick by 2 1/4 in. wide by 13/16 in. long

Sawkerfs

Wedges, 3/8 in. thick by 7/16 in. wide by 2 1/2 in. long

The shaped base pieces are the design element that changes most from maker to maker, ranging from curves to angles or straight lumber. My bases have just an angled cut (done on the miter saw) on each end and a shallow cutout with the same angle on the bottom (cut freehand on the bandsaw and cleaned up with a scraper). Whatever the shape, this cutout on the bottom is important because it creates four feet instead of just two long planks that sit on the floor. Without the center area cut out, the horses are likely to wobble.

Final details—Before glue-up, use a file or block plane to break the sharp edges, and use a handsaw to cut kerfs in the tenons that will hold the wedges. Drill and counterbore the top of the upright for the screw that will secure the top stretcher. Now dry-fit the assembly. Mark and trim the through-tenons on the lower stretcher so they protrude about ⅛ in.

Glue-up is easy—Glue the uprights into the bases. Once they are dry, glue the lower stretcher into the two uprights. When this assembly is in clamps, glue and tap the wedges (I used cherry) into place before the glue sets up in the mortise. After the glue dries, trim and file the wedge flush on the end of the tenon. Screw the top stretcher in place, and you're ready to put the horses to work.

How to Make a Wedged Through-Tenon

ADD SOME FLARE

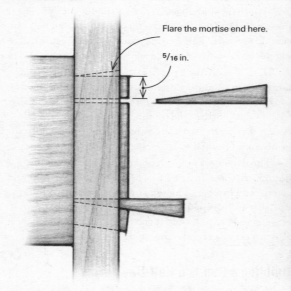

Flare the mortise end here.

5/16 in.

Room to spread. These through-tenons are wedged for strength and a decorative touch. Flare the mortise ends with a rounded file so the tenons can spread as you drive the wedges home.

Simple materials, simple joinery. With the exception of the MDF top, White built the cabinets entirely from Baltic-birch plywood. Basic butt joints, held with plenty of countersunk, coarse-thread drywall screws, make a sturdy box.

Two ways to meet the floor. For the fixed cabinets, White mounted the boxes on skids milled from kiln-dried 4x4s, with a ½-in. lag screw at each corner for leveling. The scrap is there to set the initial height. The rolling cabinets ride on heavy-duty casters (fixed in back, swivel in front).

Workshop Storage Ideas

by John White

By the time you're into woodworking seriously enough to set up your own shop, several things may have already happened, or will happen soon.

You will search catalogs, yard sales, and the Internet for tools large and small that you need, think you need, or just plain want—and you will buy them. You will bring home great-looking lumber because it is beautiful, even though you have no immediate plans for it. And someone, possibly a friend, will tell you that "you can never have too many clamps," and you will believe that person.

Each of these things will happen repeatedly, and your space, no matter how voluminous, will soon be a cluttered mess.

This collection of my favorite storage ideas from shops I've set up, and from Fine Woodworking's readers, will help you keep clutter at bay. To show you how the cabinets, racks, and holders all work together, we built them all into the garage of Fine Homebuilding's Project House, where they will get good use.

Cabinets

BUILD TO FIT

I especially like base cabinets in the shop because they provide horizontal work surfaces along with plenty of storage. For the Project House shop, I made a set of fixed and rolling cabinets (two each) that occupy most of a long wall. The fixed units create 20 square feet of countertop in addition to nearly 50 cubic feet of storage in the spaces underneath. The top rank of shallow drawers works well for smaller items, while the deeper drawers underneath can hold routers, belt sanders, biscuit joiners, and other large tools. One open cabinet provides space for a shop vacuum, and an opening in the MDF top makes it easy to connect to any tool you roll into place. A backsplash prevents anything from falling behind the cabinet.

I build shop furniture like this from ¾-in. Baltic- or Russian-birch multi-ply. You probably won't find this at your local home center, but it's worth seeking out at a plywood or lumber dealer because it is rigid, stable, and without voids. The cabinets are sized to be cut efficiently from standard 4x8 sheets. The boxes can be assembled easily with coarse-thread drywall screws. Be sure to drill pilot and clearance holes for each screw or you'll split the plywood and lose strength.

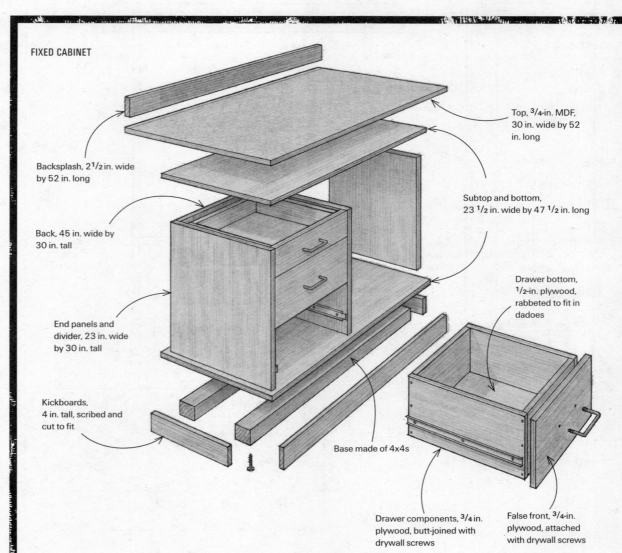

FIXED CABINET

Backsplash, 2½ in. wide by 52 in. long

Back, 45 in. wide by 30 in. tall

End panels and divider, 23 in. wide by 30 in. tall

Kickboards, 4 in. tall, scribed and cut to fit

Top, ¾-in. MDF, 30 in. wide by 52 in. long

Subtop and bottom, 23½ in. wide by 47½ in. long

Drawer bottom, ½-in. plywood, rabbeted to fit in dadoes

Base made of 4x4s

Drawer components, ¾-in. plywood, butt-joined with drywall screws

False front, ¾-in. plywood, attached with drywall screws

Topping it off.

To the plywood subtop, White screwed a layer of ¾-in. MDF for a replaceable, low-friction surface. He had to create a large overhang in back to accommodate a protruding foundation wall, but you might not have to.

White used a measured length of plywood to locate each pair of drawer slides at the correct height. This ensured that the drawer hung level, and in the right place.

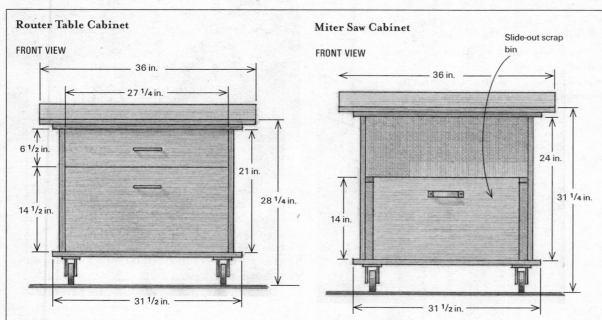

Router Table Cabinet

FRONT VIEW

36 in. / 27 ¼ in. / 6 ½ in. / 21 in. / 14 ½ in. / 28 ¼ in. / 31 ½ in.

Miter Saw Cabinet

FRONT VIEW

Slide-out scrap bin

36 in. / 24 in. / 31 ¼ in. / 14 in. / 31 ½ in.

INSTALLATION

Whenever possible, I like to position base cabinets on a long stretch of unbroken wall. This makes an ideal location for a chopsaw station, offering plenty of room to orient long stock for cutting, with the countertops working as long support wings.

I leave space between the fixed cabinets to accommodate a rolling tool stand. I built two of those: a low one to hold the compound-miter saw and a second to carry a benchtop router table. A benchtop planer would be another great candidate for a rolling cart. The rolling cabinets swap in and out of a central "parking space" when I'm ready to use them, and hook up in seconds to the shop vacuum that lives just next door.

There's no need to anchor the fixed cabinets to the wall; they aren't going anywhere. Once they're in position, adjust the lag-screw feet to make sure they are level and in the same plane. Then roll the chopsaw into place and adjust the saw's height so that its bed is level with the countertops. To do this, I measured the distance between the bed and countertops and then bolted the saw to a pair of riser blocks milled to that thickness.

Level the tops

Just the turn of a wrench. After moving the fixed cabinets into place, White used a long level to span the gap between them and adjusted the lag-screw feet to make sure the tops were level and coplanar.

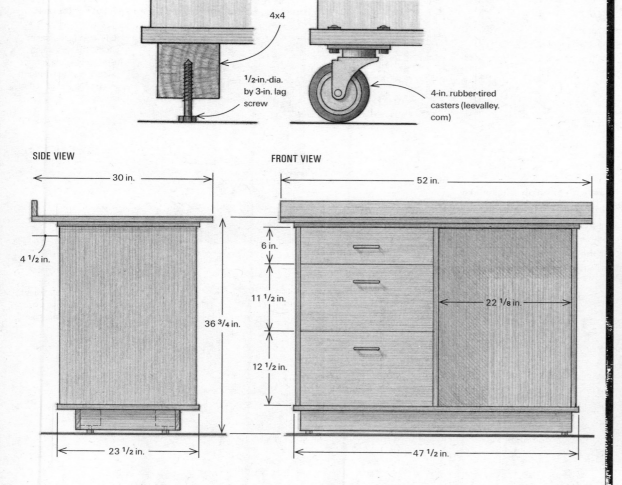

TWO FEET OPTIONS

Fixed cabinet base   Rolling cabinet base

4x4

½-in.-dia. by 3-in. lag screw

4-in. rubber-tired casters (leevalley.com)

SIDE VIEW

30 in. / 4 ½ in. / 36 ¾ in. / 23 ½ in.

FRONT VIEW

52 in. / 6 in. / 11 ½ in. / 22 ⅛ in. / 12 ½ in. / 47 ½ in.

Continued ➜

Align the saw

Smart riser blocks. White deliberately built the chopsaw stand low, so the tool's height could be dialed in precisely to match the cabinet height. To do this, he measured from the saw's bed to the countertop height (below), then mounted the saw on blocks milled to the corresponding thickness.

Change Out Tools In Minutes

Built-in dust collection. An open cabinet bay holds a shop vacuum. The hose threads through a hole in the cabinet's top for connection to the miter saw and router table, as well as any power tools used on the countertop. A sliding bin underneath the saw collects cutoffs.

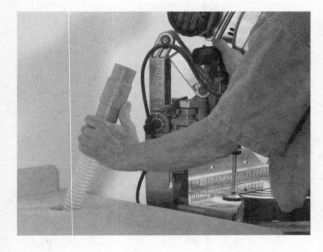

Ready to rout. The router-table cabinet is sized to put the tool's work surface at a comfortable working height. After rolling either cart into place, White secures it with two simple screen-door hooks (right).

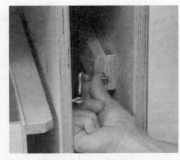

Storage

WALL STORAGE

Cabinets are great for stowing tools and supplies that don't see action every day. Tools used all the time should be closer at hand.

This is especially true near the bench, where I keep chisels, saws, and layout tools in open racks on the wall. This makes them easy to find, retrieve, and stow. The same system works terrifically for clamps. A lot of woodworkers stow their clamps on a cart that rolls out of the way when not in use. For a smaller shop, it makes more sense to use open wall space.

A fast and flexible way to create this storage is by covering the studs or wallboard with sheets of T-III plywood (grooved siding with a roughsawn face). I like T-III because, like any plywood, its strength means you can install tool racks anywhere, without searching for a wall stud. But I like the roughsawn look of T-III, and its surface disguises abandoned screw holes.

The plywood surface makes it easy to attach an assortment of shelves and custom holders for a wide variety of tools and clamps. And the arrangement is easy to reconfigure as your tools and needs change.

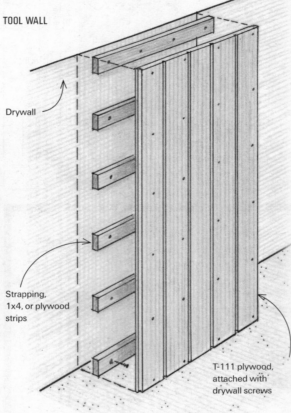

TOOL WALL

Drywall

Strapping,
1x4, or plywood
strips

T-111 plywood,
attached with
drywall screws

Start with a Sturdy Backboard.

White used T-III plywood, an inexpensive exterior sheathing product, as a base for mounting tools and clamps. Battens screwed to the wall provide more attachment points for the siding and eliminate the worry of aligning seams with stud locations.

Tools

Custom holders. Near the bench, White mounted an array of holders for hand tools of all kinds. For chisels, he routed dadoes of differing widths in a long board, and then added strips on the front side to keep the chisels in place. The tool walls make it easy to find, retrieve, and stow the items you need most often.

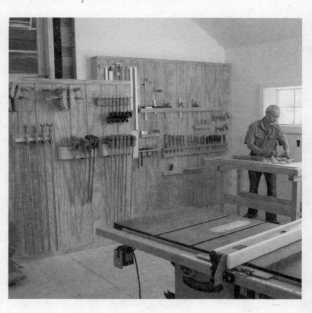

SHEET GOODS

Because they are heavy and hard to handle, the most efficient place to store sheet goods is near the entrance where you bring them into the shop. In this shop, I placed the plywood rack right next to the twin carriage doors. And, because the tablesaw is only a couple of steps away, there won't be any trouble maneuvering through the shop with a cumbersome 4x8 sheet.

The smart vertical design was suggested by reader Karen McBride. The rack holds the sheets between the wall and a support arm that can mount to a wall (as shown) or a ceiling joist. The support arm stops the travel of the sheet tops; this lets the user flip the sheets forward to view and retrieve a sheet from anywhere in the pile. The bottom ends of the sheets rest on a slightly raised platform covered with melamine particleboard with a UHMW plastic strip on the open end for easy sliding in and out of the rack.

Safe storage for sheet goods. The restraining bars lift out of the way for loading. A lipped platform secures the sheets at the bottom.

Take your pick. The restraining bars let you leaf through the stack to find a sheet and remove it easily without removing others.

LUMBER

Lastly, some folks say that a shop is only as good as its lumber stash. But how good is that, really, if the stash is disorganized? The solution is to get your lumber up on a good sturdy rack. It's not much more expensive to buy one than build one, so we bought one. I put the rack along the shop's back wall, with long stock below the window and shorter boards higher up, between the back door and the back window.

Rock-solid rack. A heavy-gauge steel rack, mounted to the wall studs with lag screws, can hold several hundred pounds of lumber. These brackets and standards are sold individually at leevalley.com.

Wall Cabinet for Hand Tools

by Michael Pekovich

When I stop to think about it, I probably spend as much time in my shop with power tools as I do with hand tools. But when the dust and noise from milling parts finally settles and I head to my bench, that's when the fun begins—when I feel like I'm really woodworking. And that's why my cobbled-together hand-tool cabinet was always the heart of my shop. Over the years, though, as my tool collection grew, I finally had to admit that I had outgrown my old friend and it was time to build a new one.

Space is limited in my shop, so I needed a way to pack more storage into the new cabinet without taking up more wall space than the old one. I solved the problem in two ways. First, I made the case deeper, giving me more room for handplane storage in the lower portion and enough depth for swing-out panels above. Also, I built the doors as shallow boxes instead of flat panels, an idea I borrowed from contributing editor Chris Becksvoort. These deeper doors combine shelf space for smaller planes and swing-out panels for extra space to hang tools. After some careful design and layout, I now have all my hand tools in one easy-to-reach place—and the cabinet looks great, too.

Tools Drive the Design

Designing a tool cabinet can be a challenge. It's not just the number of tools. You have to figure out ways to store tools of varied sizes and shapes. Even a bigger cabinet would not have room for every tool I own, so I took a hard look at my collection to determine which tools I use regularly, which ones I use only occasionally, and which ones simply gather dust. I wanted to make sure that the tools I use most are always within easy reach; that the tools I use once in a while, like carving gouges, are stored in less accessible parts of the cabinet; and that the dust gatherers

find a home somewhere else. By the way, I also built in a little extra space for new tools I have my eye on. To help with the design, I made a full-sized mock-up out of plywood scraps. This gave me a better idea of the space I had and how to use it to its fullest. To customize the cabinet for your tools, I'd recommend you do the same.

Exposed Joinery Is Beautiful and Strong

I'm not big on dressing up most shop cabinets, but I think a tool cabinet deserves some extra attention. For me, that means a solid-wood case with dovetails at the corners, and frame-and-panel doors mounted with mortised butt hinges. Still, I made good use of Baltic-birch plywood in the back and door panels as well as in the interior of the case. It provides a solid surface for mounting tool holders and its thin, void-free plies mean that the exposed edges look nice. You could certainly build the whole cabinet from plywood or go to the other extreme by adding veneer or marquetry. It's a great place to show some flair and dress up your shop, or you can keep it simple.

I cut the dovetails on the tablesaw. Then I cut the pins with a handsaw, hogging out the waste between pins with a router and paring to the line with chisels.

To give the case more rigidity, I joined the fixed shelf to the sides with through-tenons. Normally I start by cutting the mortises, but in this case it was easier to transfer the tenon layout to the mortises rather than vice-versa.

First I cut the tenon shoulders using the tablesaw. I formed the cheeks by cutting a shallow rabbet, with the blade buried in a sacrificial fence. The rabbet has three benefits. First, it provides a consistent shoulder line to pare to when removing waste between the tenons. Second, it obscures any gap at the mortise. And finally, I can give a shelf a final handplaning without affecting the thickness of the tenons.

For the mortises, I started by marking the shelf location on the back edges of the sides and then carried those lines across the faces. Next, I stood the shelf on each case side to mark the mortises on the inside and outside faces. I roughed out the mortises on the drill press and squared them up with a chisel.

Once the joinery was completed, I dry-fitted the case, making sure the assembly was square. I also lightly chamfered the ends of the dovetails and through-tenons with a block plane because I planned to leave them proud instead of trimming them flush after glue-up. After gluing up the case, I made and installed the plywood back panel. I cut it and the lower French cleat from the same piece, beveling their mating edges at 45°. The bevel cut is hidden by the fixed shelf and centered in its thickness. Then I assembled the doors and the door boxes.

Inside, Planes Get Priority

With the case complete, it was time to work on the storage components. I started at the heart of the cabinet with the plane till and the gallery, designed to hold my collection of handplanes. The till not only displays the larger planes nicely but it also makes them easily accessible because it tilts back at 30°. Triangular cleats screwed to the case sides support the till.

The planes are separated by a series of dividers screwed to the till. I used the actual planes and a 1/4-in.-wide spacer strip to locate the dividers.

At the bottom of the cabinet I created a gallery that also includes a couple of drawers, useful for everything from drill bits to tape measures. The whole section slides in and out as a unit and is screwed to the base of the cabinet at the back.

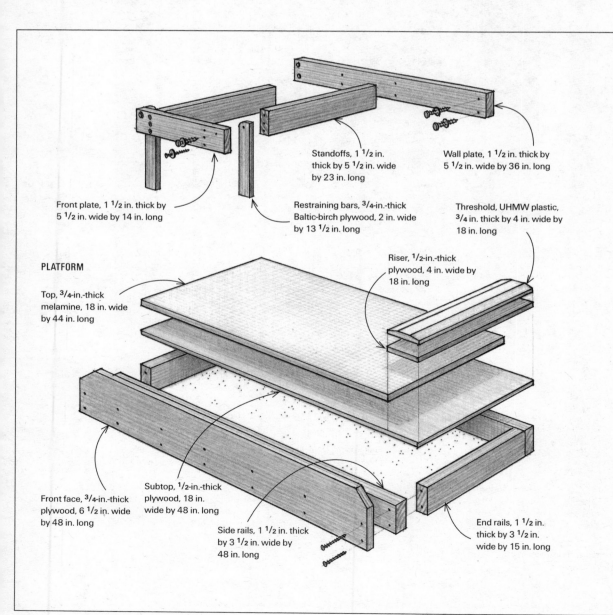

Standoffs, 1 1/2 in. thick by 5 1/2 in. wide by 23 in. long

Wall plate, 1 1/2 in. thick by 5 1/2 in. wide by 36 in. long

Front plate, 1 1/2 in. thick by 5 1/2 in. wide by 14 in. long

Restraining bars, 3/4-in.-thick Baltic-birch plywood, 2 in. wide by 13 1/2 in. long

Threshold, UHMW plastic, 3/4 in. thick by 4 in. wide by 18 in. long

Riser, 1/2-in.-thick plywood, 4 in. wide by 18 in. long

PLATFORM

Top, 3/4-in.-thick melamine, 18 in. wide by 44 in. long

Subtop, 1/2-in.-thick plywood, 18 in. wide by 48 in. long

Front face, 3/4-in.-thick plywood, 6 1/2 in. wide by 48 in. long

Side rails, 1 1/2 in. thick by 3 1/2 in. wide by 48 in. long

End rails, 1 1/2 in. thick by 3 1/2 in. wide by 15 in. long

Continued →

The gallery is narrower at the top than at the bottom, and the dividers are curved. This allows easier access to the handplanes. The 1/4-in.-thick plywood dividers slide into dadoes in the 1/2-in.-thick top and bottom. I added horizontal dividers to two of the partitions to double-up block plane storage, gluing in stops to keep the smaller planes from sliding in too far.

Doors within doors double the storage area—At the top of the cabinet, just above the plane till, I added cleats to the cabinet sides. These not only support a small shelf but also act as a place to attach a pair of swing-out plywood panels made from 1/2-in.-thick Baltic-birch plywood. I relieved the bottoms of each panel so they wouldn't block access to the planes below. I also added swing-out panels to the inside of each cabinet door. The panels give me another strong surface to attach tool holders, helping the cabinet pack in even more storage in a shallow space.

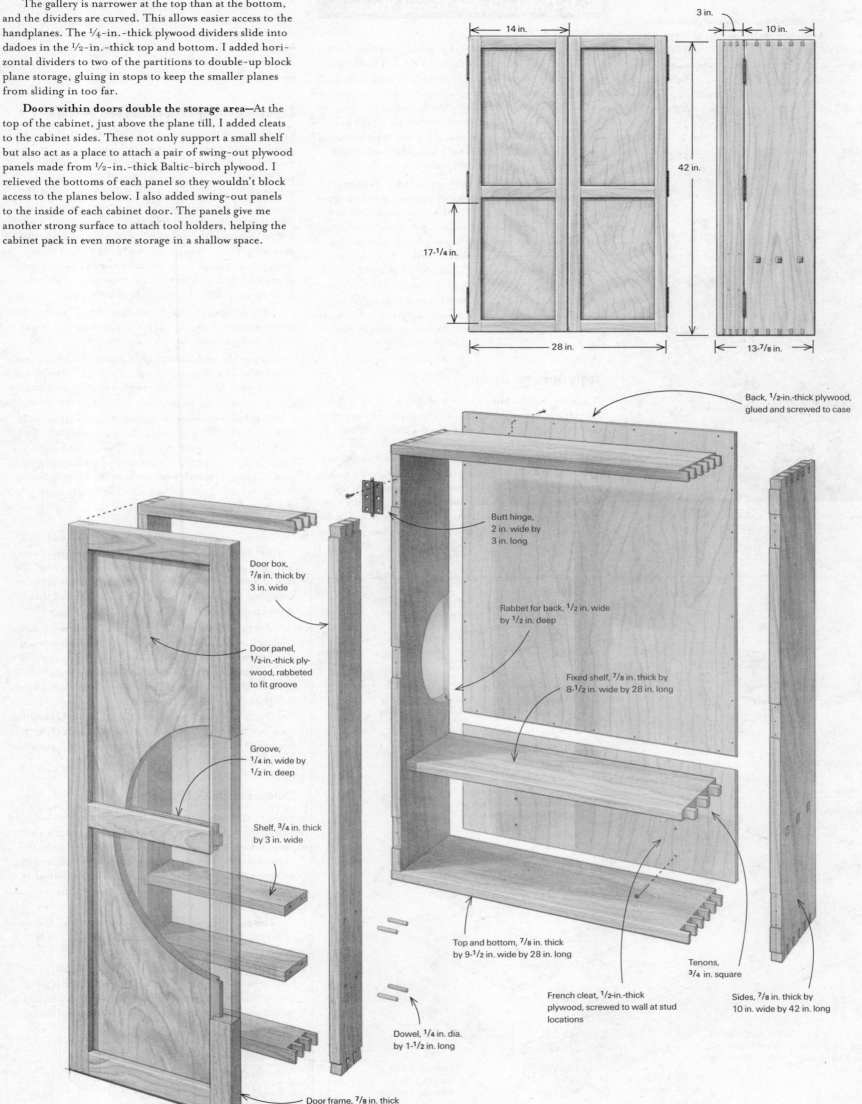

14 in.

3 in.

10 in.

42 in.

17-1/4 in.

28 in.

13-7/8 in.

Back, 1/2-in.-thick plywood, glued and screwed to case

Butt hinge, 2 in. wide by 3 in. long

Door box, 7/8 in. thick by 3 in. wide

Rabbet for back, 1/2 in. wide by 1/2 in. deep

Door panel, 1/2-in.-thick plywood, rabbeted to fit groove

Fixed shelf, 7/8 in. thick by 8-1/2 in. wide by 28 in. long

Groove, 1/4 in. wide by 1/2 in. deep

Shelf, 3/4 in. thick by 3 in. wide

Top and bottom, 7/8 in. thick by 9-1/2 in. wide by 28 in. long

Tenons, 3/4 in. square

French cleat, 1/2 in.-thick plywood, screwed to wall at stud locations

Sides, 7/8 in. thick by 10 in. wide by 42 in. long

Dowel, 1/4 in. dia. by 1-1/2 in. long

Door frame, 7/8 in. thick by 1-3/4 in. wide

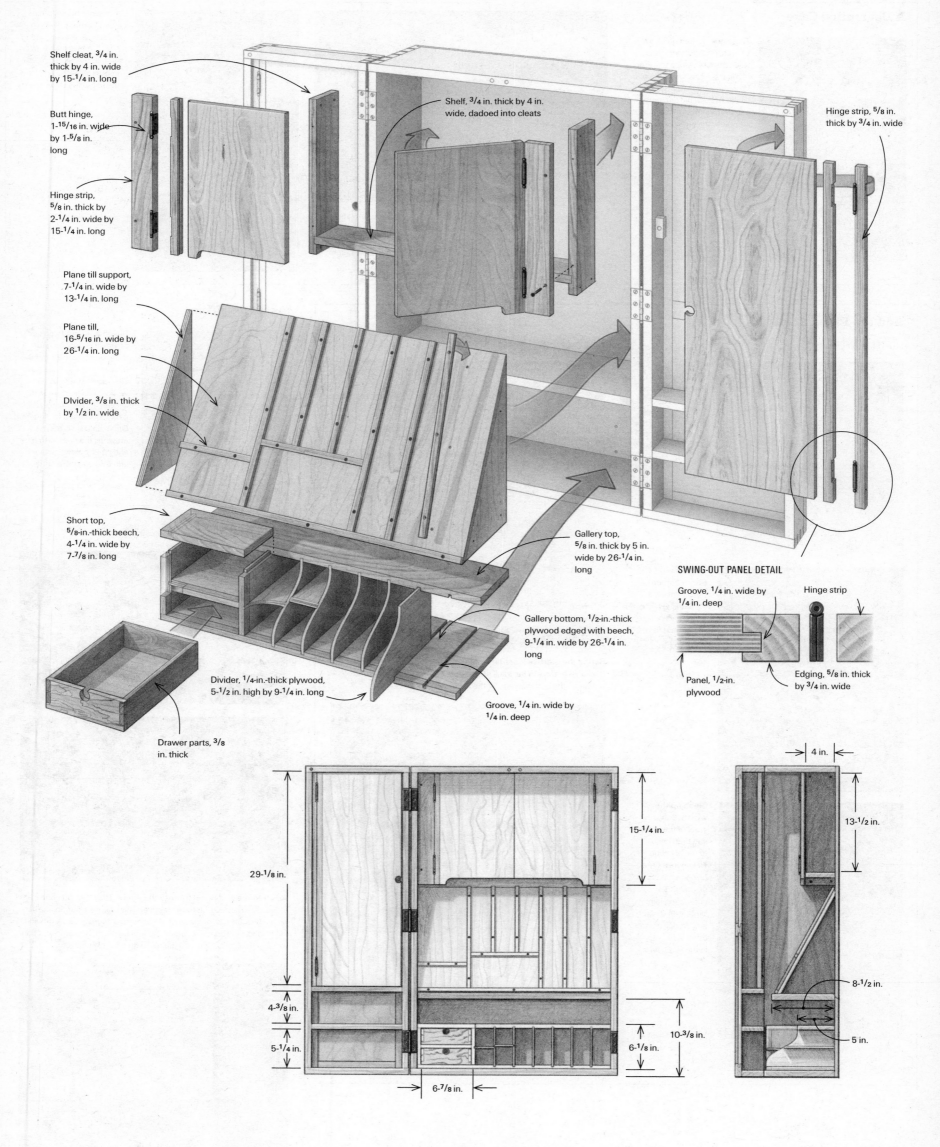

Shelf cleat, 3/4 in. thick by 4 in. wide by 15-1/4 in. long

Butt hinge, 1-15/16 in. wide by 1-5/8 in. long

Hinge strip, 5/8 in. thick by 2-1/4 in. wide by 15-1/4 in. long

Plane till support, 7-1/4 in. wide by 13-1/4 in. long

Plane till, 16-5/16 in. wide by 26-1/4 in. long

Divider, 3/8 in. thick by 1/2 in. wide

Short top, 5/8-in.-thick beech, 4-1/4 in. wide by 7-7/8 in. long

Drawer parts, 3/8 in. thick

Divider, 1/4-in.-thick plywood, 5-1/2 in. high by 9-1/4 in. long

Shelf, 3/4 in. thick by 4 in. wide, dadoed into cleats

Hinge strip, 5/8 in. thick by 3/4 in. wide

Gallery top, 5/8 in. thick by 5 in. wide by 26-1/4 in. long

Gallery bottom, 1/2-in.-thick plywood edged with beech, 9-1/4 in. wide by 26-1/4 in. long

Groove, 1/4 in. wide by 1/4 in. deep

SWING-OUT PANEL DETAIL

Groove, 1/4 in. wide by 1/4 in. deep

Hinge strip

Panel, 1/2-in. plywood

Edging, 5/8 in. thick by 3/4 in. wide

29-1/8 in.

15-1/4 in.

4-3/8 in.

5-1/4 in.

6-7/8 in.

6-1/8 in.

10-3/8 in.

4 in.

13-1/2 in.

8-1/2 in.

5 in.

A Dovetailed Case

Tablesaw makes quick work of tails. Pekovich attaches a sled with a tall fence to a pair of miter gauges to cut the tails. With the blade tilted, he makes a pass at each pin location and then rotates the board to complete the pin socket.

The pins are next. Start by scribing the pins from the tails board (above). After sawing to the scribe lines with a backsaw, remove the waste in between the pins with a router equipped with a spiral straight bit. Pekovich uses a simple box (right) to bring the workpiece to a comfortable height for routing.

A custom blade leaves clean corners. The top of each tooth is ground to 7-$\frac{1}{2}$°. When the blade is tilted to the same angle, it creates a flat-top cut, leaving just a sliver of waste in the middle.

Add the Fixed Shelf

CUT TENONS FORST

Cut the shoulders. Use a marking gauge to scribe shoulder lines on the shelf and then mark the tenon locations with a pencil. Set the blade height to the scribe line to form the tenons.

Cheeks next. Bury a portion of the sawblade in a sacrificial fence to cut the shallow rabbet that forms the cheeks.

Clean up the waste. Bandsaw most of the waste and then chisel to the baseline. To ensure a tight fit, chop halfway down, undercutting the joint slightly, then flip and work from the other side in the same way.

THEN CHOP THE MORTISES

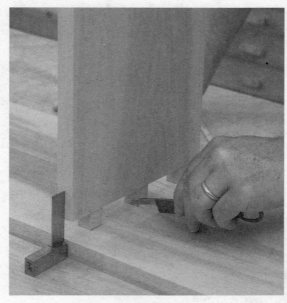

Scribe the mortise locations. Stand the shelf in place, using a square to align it flush with the back edge. Knife around each tenon and repeat on the opposite face of the case side.

Drill and chop. Remove most of the waste on the drill press. Then use a chisel to chop out the rest, working back to the scribe lines gradually. Chop halfway down, undercutting slightly, then flip to complete the cut.

Assembly Tips

Big glue-up made easier. To provide clearance for the proud dovetails and the through-tenons, Pekovich elevates one side using wood strips (left). Then he assembles the main carcase, checking it for square. Once the case is dry, he attaches the back with glue and nails (below). Screws add a little extra security.

Add a frame-and-panel front to the doors. The plywood panels are glued into a stub-tenon frame (above). This creates a handsome yet rigid assembly that helps keep the door from sagging while providing a solid, flat surface for attaching tool holders. The frame-and-panels attach to the door boxes (below) with a simple glue joint.

Neat tricks for customized tool storage—The final step of the construction was to create a safe, secure home for each tool in the cabinet. Some solutions, like chisel racks, fit a variety of tools. Others, such as holders for marking gauges and saws, are customized for each tool. Finding the right solution for each tool is half the fun.

My chisels hang on a holder with concentric-sized holes that accommodate a variety of handle diameters. I have several spokeshaves of various shapes and sizes, but a pair of racks with upward-angled arms handles all of them. Squares can be secured with a simple slotted block of wood. Handsaws require a custom-fit holder. I started by making a block to fit the opening in the handle, then screwed on a pivoting tab to hold the saw in place. Rare-earth magnets set into blocks help keep long tools from swinging. For the finish, I kept it simple. I just wiped on a few coats of shellac to give the case a little protection and make it easier to clean.

To hang the cabinet, start by attaching the French cleat to the wall with 3-in. screws at the stud locations. Rest the cabinet on the cleat and screw through the back of the case into the studs.

Customize the Interior

PLANE TILL AND GALLERY

Build the dividers around your tools. The plane till is simply a plywood panel screwed to triangular cleats mounted to the case sides. It's easier to add the plane dividers before installation. Set each plane in place and slide a 1/4-in.-thick shim against it to create some wiggle room. Screw down the dividers without glue to make future alterations easier.

Clean dadoes for the gallery dividers. Cut the dadoes for the dividers with a dado blade and a crosscut sled. A fresh plywood base taped to the sled eliminates tearout.

Six dividers, one cut. Tape the dividers into a single stack and cut all the profiles at once. A symmetrical curve creates offcuts with the same profile.

Make It Your Own

The interior is divided into three basic zones that can be customized to fit anyone's tool collection. The vertical surfaces are great for saws, spokeshaves, chisels, screwdrivers, and layout tools. The angled till keeps handplanes within easy reach. The shelves at the bottom can be outfitted with dividers for even more plane storage or filled with drawers for screws, hardware, router bits, and small tools.

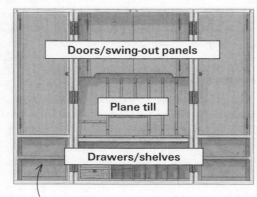

Doors/swing-out panels

Plane till

Drawers/shelves

Leave out the shelves in the doors and extend the swing-out panels for even more vertical storage space.

Glue up the gallery and slide it in as a unit. The left side of the gallery is outfitted with a pair of drawers for odds and ends. The shelves are for block planes.

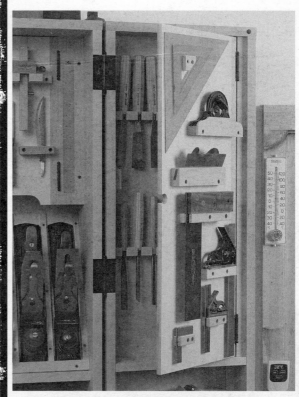

Add the door shelves. Use spacer blocks to locate each shelf while you drill and pin them in place. You can change the location of the shelves later by drilling out the pins.

A swing out panel increases storage. The 1/2-in. plywood panel is edged with a thicker hardwood strip on one side to allow for hinge mortises. The panel is attached to a cleat that is mounted to the drawer box.

Continued ➜

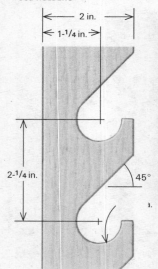

2 in.

1-1/4 in.

2-1/4 in.

45°

Simple spokeshave rack. A pair of uprights hold the shaves securely. Start by drilling holes, then finish the profile at the bandsaw.

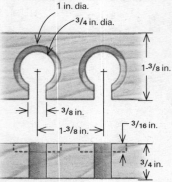

1 in. dia.

3/4 in. dia.

1-3/8 in.

3/8 in.

1-3/8 in.

3/16 in.

3/4 in.

Versatile holder for chisels and gouges. The stepped holes fit handles large and small. After drilling, cut the access slots on the tablesaw.

Simple Rack for Handplanes

by Chris Gochnour

Let's face it. Handplanes are expensive, costing as much as or more than a benchtop power tool. To keep these investments safe, many woodworkers tuck their planes inside drawers or cabinets. Though the tools are safe and sound, it's a nuisance to keep opening a door or drawer to access the planes while they're working. For convenience, many folks end up keeping their most-used planes on top of the bench.

That method is not so convenient, however, because the planes can get in the way, and they're just inches from getting knocked to the floor accidentally. My plane rack solves all of those problems.

Though simple in design, the rack has a unique way of holding the planes. The knobs are suspended from loops made from bootlaces, and the soles rest on an angled panel. The system is strong and stable, and the bootlace hangers allow me to grab and store planes with ease.

This rack holds what I consider to be a full set of handplanes—a jointer, fore, jack, two smoothers (Nos. 4 and 4 1/2), three block planes—with room below for some specialty planes, such as a shoulder plane. But the rack can be modified to fit more or fewer planes, or planes of different sizes.

Joinery Is Straightforward

The case is assembled with simple dadoes and rabbeted dadoes. After cutting these joints, you can take on the trickiest part of the assembly: cutting the grooves for the angled back panel. Start by making the grooves in the

Bootlaces Are the Secret

Planes rest on the angled back panel and are held in place with sturdy bootlace loops. The rack hangs on a hidden french cleat, screwed into studs.

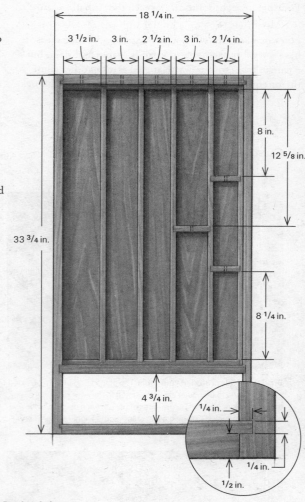

18 1/4 in.

3 1/2 in.   3 in.   2 1/2 in.   3 in.   2 1/4 in.

8 in.

12 5/8 in.

33 3/4 in.

8 1/4 in.

4 3/4 in.

1/4 in.

1/4 in.

1/4 in.

1/2 in.

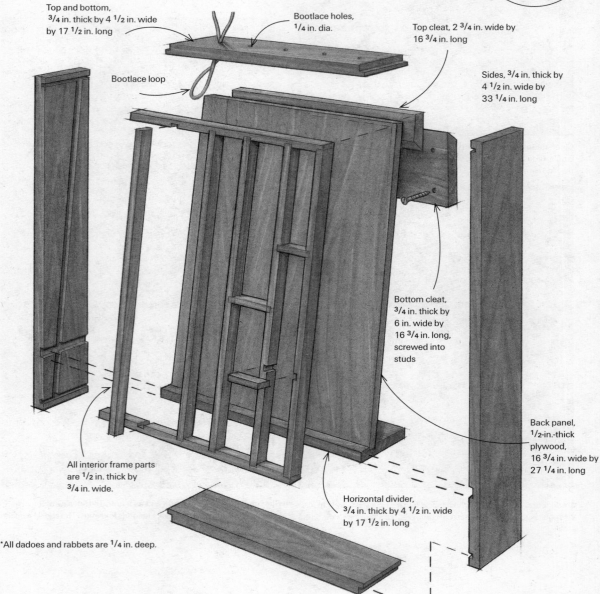

Top and bottom, 3/4 in. thick by 4 1/2 in. wide by 17 1/2 in. long

Bootlace holes, 1/4 in. dia.

Bootlace loop

Top cleat, 2 3/4 in. wide by 16 3/4 in. long

Sides, 3/4 in. thick by 4 1/2 in. wide by 33 1/4 in. long

Bottom cleat, 3/4 in. thick by 6 in. wide by 16 3/4 in. long, screwed into studs

Back panel, 1/2-in.-thick plywood, 16 3/4 in. wide by 27 1/4 in. long

All interior frame parts are 1/2 in. thick by 3/4 in. wide.

Horizontal divider, 3/4 in. thick by 4 1/2 in. wide by 17 1/2 in. long

*All dadoes and rabbets are 1/4 in. deep.

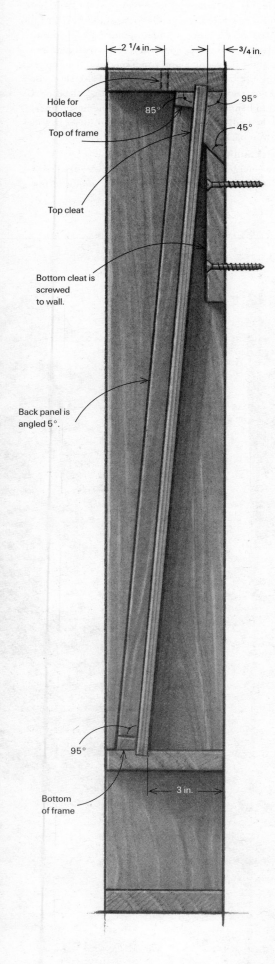

2 1/4 in. ← → ← 3/4 in.

Hole for bootlace

85°   95°

Top of frame

45°

Top cleat

Bottom cleat is screwed to wall.

Back panel is angled 5°.

95°

Bottom of frame

3 in.

underside of the top and in the top of the horizontal divider. These through-grooves are cut on the tablesaw using a dado set tilted to the panel angle (5°). Then, dry-assemble the case. Place a spacer, the same thickness as the back panel and about 1 in. wide by 3 in. long, into the grooves in the top and divider. Knife around the spacer to locate the grooves in the sides.

Clamp the sides together and to the benchtop and clamp a long plywood fence to one side, aligned with the groove marks. Rout the groove using a plunge router and a 1/2-in.-dia. pattern bit. Rout the groove in the other side piece in the same way. With all the grooves made, cut and fit the plywood back panel and glue up the case. Then make and fit the french cleat. Note how it is angled to sit flat against the back panel.

Cut and Fit the Interior Frame

Start by making the top and bottom pieces of the frame. Cut them to length, then bevel one edge 5° so that the inward facing edge is at a right angle to the back panel. That means you bevel the top edge of the top piece and the bottom edge of the bottom piece.

Angled Cuts Made Easy

Cut the top and bottom grooves for the back panel with a tilted dado blade. Then use a plunge router and angled fence to make the grooves in the sides.

Tilt a dado. Cut the grooves in the top and the horizontal divider at 5°.

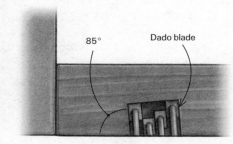

85°   Dado blade

Layout blocks ensure that all the grooves meet. With the case dry-assembled, use offcuts from the back-panel stock to lay out the side grooves. Place these blocks in the top and bottom grooves and scribe around them with a knife.

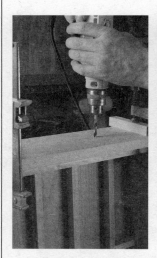

Rout the sloping side grooves. Clamp a fence aligned with the scribe marks, and use a plunge router and 1/2-in. pattern bit.

Next, cut the dadoes for the vertical frame pieces in the top and bottom of the frame. Fit the vertical pieces, then cut the dadoes in them for the short horizontal frame pieces. After cutting and fitting the shorter pieces, drill 1/4-in.-dia. holes in them for the lower bootlace hooks. Now glue the interior frame into the case. These tight-fitting parts require only spring clamps to hold them while the glue cures. After the interior frame has been installed, drill holes through the top of the case for the top bootlace hooks. Clamp a backer board to the opposite side to prevent tearout.

Assembly's a Cinch

Gluing up the case won't be hard. Assemble the carcase first. Once that's done, make the french cleat, then cut and assemble the interior frame.

Build the box first. The plywood back panel is glued into its grooves, making the cabinet rigid.

Glue in the interior frame. Install the top and bottom frame pieces first, then attach the vertical pieces. You can glue them to the back panel without clamps, but the joinery must be tight. Drill the bootlace holes in the short horizontal pieces before gluing them in.

Holes for the hooks. Once the case is glued up, drill holes through the top piece for the bootlace hooks. Clamp a backer board underneath to prevent tearout.

Custom hooks. Make a loop using a square knot (top) and thread it through its hole (above). Experiment to get the right-length loop for each plane.

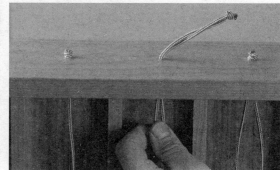

Continued →

Finish the Rack and Tie Up Loose Ends

I finished the rack with three coats of Watco Danish Oil, which brings out the beauty of the wood, protects it from grime, and touches up easily if needed. Once the finish is dry, make the bootlace hooks. It will take some tries to get the right-length loop for each compartment. Don't get frustrated. As long as you can hook the knob of the plane through the loop and the plane sits in its compartment, you're good to go. Singe the ends of the loops to prevent fraying.

It won't take long to get the hang of this rack. Soon you'll be removing and replacing the planes with just one hand.

WORKSHOP SAFETY

Essential Workshop First-Aid Kit

by Patrick Sullivan

Woodworkers spend a lifetime handling razor-sharp tools, power equipment with exposed blades, and boards that harbor splinters and fasteners. In this environment, there's always the risk of an injury.

Usually woodworkers cut their fingers, and occasionally the palms of their hands. Although the hand often will recover from minor injuries even if it receives no care at all, recovery is faster with less scarring and less risk of infection if it's treated properly. For more serious cuts and eye injuries, however, what you do first can have an impact on the rest of your life.

As a woodworker and physician, I understand the types of injuries that are common in the shop, and I know how they should be treated. Forget the first-aid kits offered in drug stores. Forget much of the misguided advice found in popular manuals. The woodworking environment is unique, and I'll tell you about some specialized equipment and supplies that work well there. I'll also show you a few tricks on treating wounds—from stopping bleeding to cleaning to bandaging—based on proven medical principles. In the end, you'll learn how to treat injuries in a way that gets you back to work as soon as possible.

Patrick Sullivan is an internal medicine specialist with extensive emergency room experience. Now retired from his medical practice, he has more time for woodworking.

Build a Custom Kit

A first-aid kit for woodworkers looks very different from the kits sold in drugstores. It contains materials for closing cuts, flexible coverings for wounds, tools for removing splinters, and eye wash. Many of these products are available from multiple manufacturers.

How to Handle Most Cuts

1. Soap and Water

The enemy of healing is infection. The germs that live on lumber and tools generally do not cause disease; essentially, all the risk is from bacteria you already carry on your skin. A wound allows those skin germs to reach the more vulnerable tissue beneath the skin. The problem gets worse if there is dirt, sawdust, debris, or dead tissue in the wound.

The most effective treatment for all wounds is immediate washing with soap and clean water. (You can skip this if you need to go to the emergency room, because they will clean it there). Washing drastically reduces the number of germs, and takes away dirt and debris in which bacteria can hide and multiply.

I have seen several Internet pictures and videos that show first-aid techniques in which they advocate wiping the wound clean with a damp paper towel or gauze pad. This is the most ineffective way to wash a wound.

The surest way to clean a wound is to hold the cut under running water for several minutes and lather thoroughly. If soap is not available, plain water will do a credible job. Wash every wound, whether you can see contamination or not. Waterless hand cleaners and antiseptic solutions may be better than nothing, but they are not a proven substitute for washing. If you can wash effectively, you do not need these products.

Doctors and first-aid manuals in the past have routinely recommended the use of an antibiotic ointment, but recent surgical research proves that clean wounds need no antibiotic if they are washed well and closed promptly. Moreover, the ointment preparation discourages the formation of a scab, which is the most effective wound closure available. Skip any antibiotic ointment unless dirt and debris were driven into the wound and cannot be washed out.

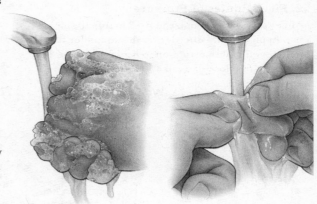

LATHER UP

Wash both hands vigorously enough to generate lots of lather under a strong stream of warm running water for several minutes. While washing, hold the cut open and flush the wound for at least a minute. Ignore any bleeding this may cause. Dry both hands on a clean paper towel.

Do You Need a Doctor?

VULNERABLE AREAS OF THE HAND

Areas highlighted in green contain very few vulnerable structures, such as tendons. Unless the wound obviously penetrates into a bone or joint, cuts here typically can be treated easily at home.

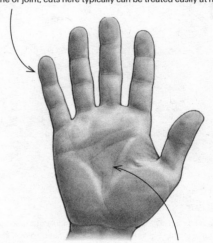

Areas in red, however, contain tendons. Deep cuts in these areas are likely to have damaged the tendons or tendon sheaths and should be examined by a doctor.

IF THE CUT WON'T CLOSE, GET IT STITCHED

Cuts that do not slice all the way through don't require stitches because the lower layer of skin keeps the wound reasonably closed.

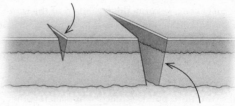

The cut on the right penetrates all the way through the skin, revealing the fat beneath. A deep cut like this that's under 1 in. long usually can be treated at home; if it's longer than 2 in., the wound needs to be stitched. In between 1 in. and 2 in., the decision to get stitched depends on the location of the wound (see below).

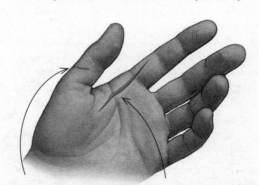

The cut on the thumb can be treated at home. It is short, and although deep, tends to close itself. Normal hand movements will not apply stress to the wound.

The cut on the palm and index finger begs for stitches. It is long and deep and in a location where every hand activity will stretch the wound apart.

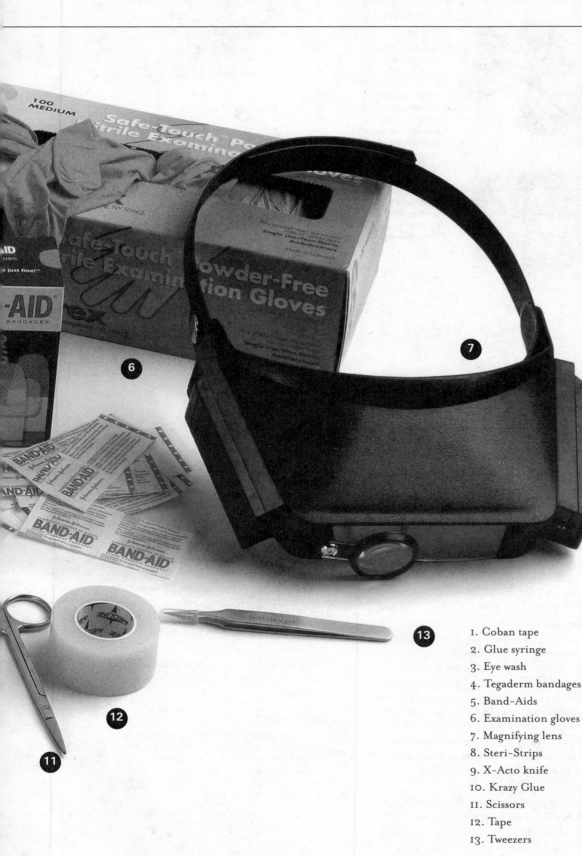

1. Coban tape
2. Glue syringe
3. Eye wash
4. Tegaderm bandages
5. Band-Aids
6. Examination gloves
7. Magnifying lens
8. Steri-Strips
9. X-Acto knife
10. Krazy Glue
11. Scissors
12. Tape
13. Tweezers

Continued ➜

2. Five Minutes of Pressure

After washing the wound, you need to stop the bleeding. Apply pressure directly over the wound for five minutes without interruption to help form a clot. If you peek, the clock starts all over again.

Right   **Wrong**

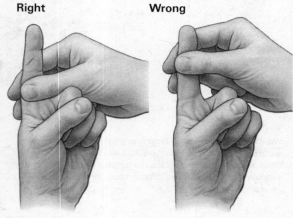

BE DIRECT
Don't be afraid to touch the cut. Apply pressure directly over the wound (right), not below it (left).

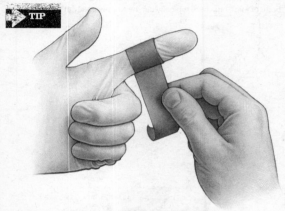

WHEN YOU CAN'T STOP WORKING, USE A GLOVE
If you get a minor cut, say, while you're in the middle of a glue-up, you don't have to stop working. Put on an examination glove, and wrap masking tape snugly around the finger directly over the cut. The glove keeps blood off the woodwork, and pressure from the tape will usually stop the bleeding in 5 to 10 minutes. After removing the tape and glove, wash your hands thoroughly, and close and dress the wound.

3. Close the Wound Before Bandaging

When you get cut, keeping the two edges of the wound firmly closed will help it heal rapidly. Cuts from sharp tools penetrate cleanly, which makes them easier to close and faster to heal. Wounds with frayed or crushed edges (such as those made by a spinning tool) take a bit longer to heal. In either case, you want to wash and close the wound to pull the sliced skin back together.

Standard adhesive bandages cover the wound but don't securely close it. As soon as you start using your hands, skin movement will reopen the cut. Hospitals often use a specialized tape product called Steri-Strips, which you can buy without a prescription in most drugstores or online.

It is also possible to glue wounds closed with ordinary cyanoacrylate glue. Both methods work better if you have a helper to either hold the wound closed or to apply the Steri-Strips or glue.

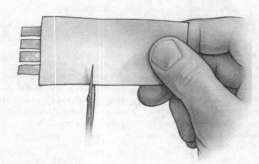

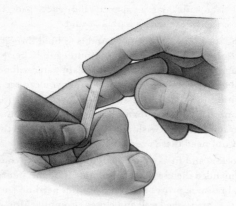

ADHESIVE-BACKED STERI-STRIPS KEEP CUTS CLOSED
Dry the skin around the wound, then cut the strips to length. Remove the paper backing, and apply. Adhere the strip to one side of the cut, push the wound edges together so they just meet, and stick the strip down on the other side.

Wrong

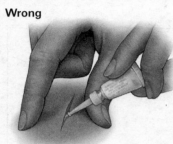

Right

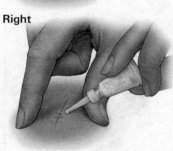

A DIFFERENT KIND OF GLUE-UP
Cyanoacrylate glue works for closing a wound. But the job is not like butting two boards together. Do not apply glue inside the wound. Instead, push the skin edges together and spread a thin layer of glue across the top of the skin, interrupting the glue at short intervals to preserve flexibility. Don't use the activator spray that comes with some glues.

4. Smarter Bandages

If you go to an emergency room with a hand injury, you'll come home with a huge, fluffy bandage that will attract a lot of sympathy but render you unable to work. Emergency rooms use gauze as the main element of bandaging. Gauze is light as air, extremely flexible, and breathes like it wasn't there at all. However, you cannot work wood while wearing gauze.

Woodworkers need bandages that are flexible, thin, and tough. It is also convenient to have bandages that shed water, sawdust, and glue, and yet breathe so the skin stays dry. Here are two bandages that you can use after you've closed the wound or after you've come home from the ER.

The first option is to cover the area with a Tegaderm dressing. Tegaderm is a transparent medical dressing (made by 3M) that's flexible, tough, and stretchy. It is great for hand wounds because it can be conformed to a number of shapes and is so smooth that it won't catch on any sharp edges, like an adhesive bandage can. This product is available with and without a non-stick, absorbent pad in the center. Many wounds will seep a small amount of serum in the first few hours after bandaging, and the absorbent pads are useful then. Later, they may be unnecessary.

This might be all you need. If you have to handle rough lumber, or do work that applies a lot of friction or abrasion to your hands, consider wearing leather or fabric gloves to protect the dressing.

Injuries that involve the palm or the webs between the fingers are very hard to bandage. For these areas, cover the closed wound with Tegaderm,

and then wrap Coban around the hand as necessary. Coban is a very stretchy bandage that sticks to itself, but not to anything else. It is excellent for bandages involving the palm or wrist, because it stretches greatly, but always remains snug.

BETTER THAN A BAND-AID
After closing the wound with a Steri-Strip, apply a Tegaderm bandage. Put on the bandage and then peel off the paper frame. If you need to cut the bandage to a smaller size, do it while all the backing paper is still in place. The bandage is thin and flexible, allowing nearly full knuckle movement.

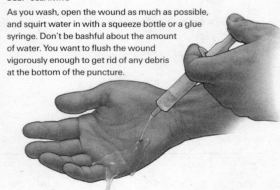

WHEN YOU NEED MORE HOLDING POWER, USE COBAN TAPE
It's hard to keep a bandage in place on the palm of your hand, so wrap the dressing with Coban tape (1 in. wide usually is sufficient). First take a couple of wraps around the wrist. This serves to anchor the whole bandage. Then continue with several wraps around the palm. End the Coban on the back of the hand or wrist, where it will receive the least rubbing.

Punctures

Wash Away Debris

Punctures from clean, sharp tools like narrow chisels, scratch awls, and marking knives should pose very little hazard and require very little treatment (unless they penetrate into joints or cut tendons). The wounds tend to close themselves. Wash thoroughly and apply a small bandage until bleeding stops.

If you have a puncture wound caused by a dull tool, you have an increased chance of infection (see drawing, below). First wash the area thoroughly. As you wash, flush out the wound with water using a squeeze bottle or glue syringe. Apply Tegaderm with an absorbent pad. If the wound becomes more puffy and painful over a period of several days, have it seen by a doctor.

Puncture wounds carry a very small risk of tetanus. You were immunized against tetanus in childhood, but your immunity needs a booster every 10 years. Keep this up to date.

DEEP CLEANING
As you wash, open the wound as much as possible, and squirt water in with a squeeze bottle or a glue syringe. Don't be bashful about the amount of water. You want to flush the wound vigorously enough to get rid of any debris at the bottom of the puncture.

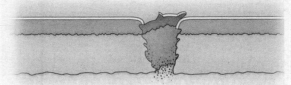

DULL TOOLS CAUSE MORE HARM
Punctures from dull tools like screwdrivers leave more crushed and damaged cells, and the dull edge often pushes the skin, dirt, and debris back into the wound, creating more chance for surface skin bacteria to be lodged in underlying tissue. These wounds really need to be flushed out.

Splinters

Pull or Slice Them Out

Everyone who works with wood has had splinters in their skin, and virtually everyone has struggled to remove them. If you have trouble seeing the splinter, use magnifying glasses, whether it's a pair of inexpensive reading glasses or visor-type magnifiers that you can wear over eyeglasses. These magnifiers may come in handy for other shop uses, too, like working with small parts or chiseling to a line in tight spaces between dovetails.

Usually you can pull out the splinter with a pair of tweezers. However, if a splinter has tunneled a long distance under your skin, you'll have to gently slice the skin to reach it using a No. 11 blade in either a disposable scalpel or an X-Acto knife. After slicing, pull out the splinter with tweezers.

Be sure to wash your hands and the blade thoroughly before you probe around in the skin. Sterility is not necessary, but cleanliness is very important. Usually no dressing is needed; but if you had to dig so deeply that the wound bleeds significantly, then dress this as you would a cut.

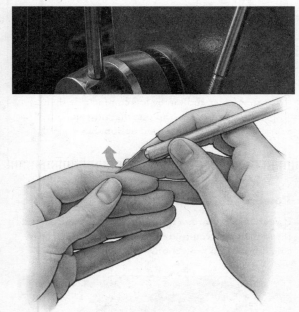

STUBBORN SPLINTERS NEED TO BE SLICED OUT
To reach long slivers that tunnel through the skin, use an X-Acto knife with a No. 11 blade. First wash your hand and the blade. Insert the back of the blade along the top of the splinter, and gently slice open the skin with the tip of the blade. Slice along the splinter's length to expose it as much as possible, then pull it out with tweezers.

Eyes

Rinse Carefully or See a Doctor

When you cut wood, especially with a router or tablesaw, sawdust (and sometimes other material) will fly. If some of that small debris ends up in your eye, your natural tears will usually wash it away. If the debris digs in and resists being washed away by tears, the best answer is to retract the eyelid away from the eyeball, and flush the eye with an eye-wash solution.

Get someone to help you. Lie on your back—it is hard to flood the eye with solution while you are upright. Have your helper put on your magnifiers and look in your eye for the debris. Regardless of whether they see the offending particle or not, have them squirt the solution under both lids. Use towels or tissues to sop up the excess, and use plenty of liquid. If that does not work, do it again. If repeated irrigation of the eye does not dislodge the particle, seek professional help. Never use tweezers or hard instruments in the area of the eye.

If there is so much spasm of the eyelids that you cannot open the eye enough to see what is going on, that suggests a more serious eye injury, and you should get immediate professional help.

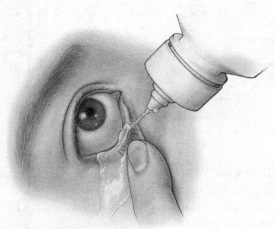

RINSE AND REPEAT
The safest and easiest way to remove foreign particles in the eye is to rinse them away with a spray of eye wash. Lift the eyelid and spray vigorously. If necessary, repeat several times.

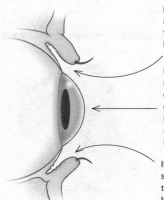

If particles embed themselves in this area, it is safe to try to wash them out at home.

If particles embed themselves in the clear layer over the iris and pupil (the cornea), have the eye examined by a doctor. Even tiny scratches in the cornea can lead to vision impairment.

If particles embed themselves in this area, it is safe to try to wash them out at home.

Dust Protection

by Jeff Miller

Wood dust is a woodworker's constant companion and a constant threat. It doesn't take much airborne dust to exceed the exposure limits recommended by the National Institute for Occupational Safety and Health. In fact, you'll quickly blow past them when machining or sanding wood. Dust collectors and air cleaners help control wood dust, but even when optimized for your shop they don't catch it all. The smallest and most dangerous particles escape them.

Exposure to those minute particles can cause nasal and sinus-cavity irritation, allergies, lung congestion, chronic cough, and cancer. That's why it's important to wear a dust mask or a powered respirator whenever you're producing dust, or working in the shop afterward.

You're more likely to wear a dust mask or respirator if it's comfortable and fits well. You might need to look beyond your local hardware store, but great choices are out there. In fact, there are so many options you might feel overwhelmed. But that won't happen if you know how dust masks and respirators work, how to tell if one fits you well, and which features make one more comfortable.

I recently tested a large selection of masks and respirators, and had the editors at *Fine Woodworking* do the same. I'll tell you what we liked about them and what we didn't. That will help you know where to begin your search for a good-fitting and effective dust mask or respirator.

After all of our testing, it's clear that there are a few key features that make for a great mask or respirator. You should put them at the top of your list before you shop.

Comfort and Fit Matter Most

An exhaust valve is an indispensable feature on a dust mask. In fact, we recommend you steer clear of any dust mask that doesn't have one. Exhaust valves clear the warm air you exhale, prevent safety glasses from fogging, and help keep your face cooler.

You also should look for a mask that is made from face-friendly material. The interior of the 3M 8511, for example, is soft and fleece-like. An adjustable nosepiece is important, because it allows the mask to form a tighter seal against your face and allows you to customize the mask to the shape of your nose.

Adjustable straps are a big plus, because they make for a tighter fit. Testers liked the adjustability of the straps on

Continued ➜

the Willson Saf-T-Fit Plus, and applauded the versatility of the Moldex Handy Strap, which allows you to hang the mask comfortably around your neck.

Some features don't reveal themselves until you have a mask on. You don't want a mask that interferes with your vision or safety glasses, prevents you from speaking audibly, or interferes with hearing protection.

Because they have nearly all of these features, two masks really stood out from the rest: the 3M 8511 and the Willson Saf-T-Fit.

Respirators are harder to peg than dust masks, but there are a few key features to look for. The weight and balance of the helmet, for example, are important. If a respirator doesn't sit well on your head, you'll take it off very quickly. And the face shield shouldn't distort or interfere with your vision. You also should be able to wear some kind of hearing protection with the respirator on.

Of the respirators we tested, the Trend Airshield and Airshield Pro distinguished themselves for comfort, clarity of vision, and overall user-friendliness.

Keep the Clean Air Flowing

Dust masks don't last forever. Replace yours when it becomes difficult to breathe through, when the mask no longer seals properly, or when it is damaged.

If you use a respirator, make sure to check its airflow regularly. When it doesn't move enough clean air, it's time to replace the batteries, the filter, or both.

Dust Masks

Get a Vent
Our testers clearly favored vented masks because they are more comfortable. They allow hot air to easily escape through the front of the mask, so your face stays cooler and your glasses won't fog.

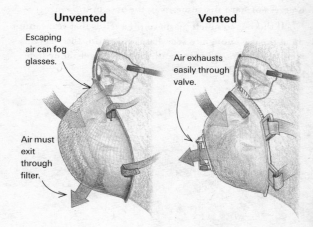

Unvented

Escaping air can fog glasses.

Air must exit through filter.

Vented

Air exhausts easily through valve.

Filters for Wood Dust

For protection from wood dust, look for a mask rated N95, N99, or N100. The ratings don't apply to powered respirators, but all the respirators tested clean the air as well as an N95 mask.

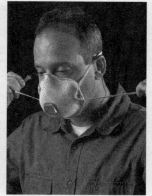

A place to hang your mask. The Moldex Handy Strap makes hanging a mask around your neck a snap (above), a big plus when you need to take it off momentarily to speak, get a drink, or make an adjustment. The strap makes putting the mask on easier, too (above right).

A better fit for more noses. Masks with adjustable nosepieces work for more people because they can be tailored to the individual's nose. The nosepieces help prevent fogging by giving a better seal around the nose.

Which One Is Right for You?

For most people, a high-quality dust mask works great. A powered respirator is a better choice if you need protection from flying chips, or if you have facial hair, which keeps a dust mask from working properly. Most respirators have integrated, safety-rated face shields.

Reusable Masks: a Good Alternative for Some

Disposable masks and those with replaceable filters clean air in the same way. The difference shows up when it's time to replace the filter. With a reusable mask, you replace just the filter section, and keep the "frame" that holds it. Although they cost more up front, their filters last longer and are less expensive. They are heavier and can be less comfortable than disposables, but if you find one that fits you well, a reusable mask could be a good option.

Powered Respirators

If you've got a beard, a respirator is the way to go. And if you turn, you can find one with a safety-rated face shield for added protection.

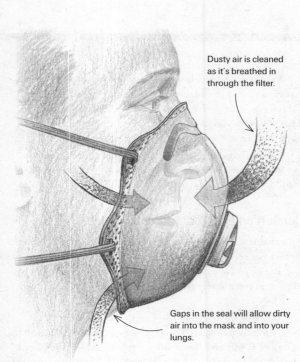

Dusty air is cleaned as it's breathed in through the filter.

Gaps in the seal will allow dirty air into the mask and into your lungs.

DUST MASKS REQUIRE A TIGHT FIT
A dust mask should seal tightly against your face. That keeps bad air from seeping in.

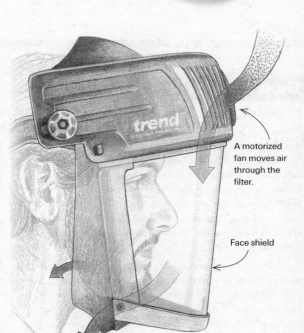

A motorized fan moves air through the filter.

Face shield

Clean air exits through the loose-fitting shroud.

POWERED RESPIRATORS USE POSITIVE PRESSURE
Respirators use a fan to pull dirty air through a filter. The clean air flows down over the face, preventing bad air from flowing into the mask.

Protection from the big stuff, too. Many respirators have an integrated safety-rated face shield, which makes them great for turners.

A Revolution in Dust Collection

by Asa Christiana

In 2002, wood dust went from being a nuisance to an official health risk. That's when the U.S. government put it on their list of "known carcinogens," linking it to a variety of nose, throat, and lung cancers. But it has taken our corner of the woodworking industry a while to catch up with reality.

The best way to manage dust is to collect it at the source, and one of the industry's first important realizations was that the dust ports were sadly lacking on most woodworking tools, and nonexistent on others. That was pretty easy to fix, and the improvements have been steady and significant. So before you spend money on ceiling-hung air filters or expensive respirators, go to the source of the problem. Connect your dust collector and shop vacuum to every possible power tool. If you are buying new tools, look for manufacturers that make dust collection convenient and effective. For your existing tools, take a day in the shop to improve the ports. Fine Woodworking has done lots of articles on this topic.

The Filtration Story

Fifteen or twenty years ago, if you collected dust at all, you probably did it with a single-stage collector and a 30-micron polyester bag. Those porous bags act like fine-dust delivery systems, blasting out a cloud of the most dangerous stuff at head height. The irony is that people who didn't bother with dust collection at all, leaving big piles of sawdust under their tablesaws, were probably safer!

The trouble with wood dust is that the most dangerous particles, the very fine ones, are the hardest to collect. Under 10 microns in size, they hang longest in the air, penetrate deepest into the lungs, and are the hardest for the body to eject.

So the tool companies knew they had to get serious about filtration. Felt bags were an early response, borrowed from industry. But the finer the felt, the taller the bag needed to be in order to have enough surface area for good airflow. There's room for that in a factory but not a small shop. Enter the pleated filter, which packs hundreds of square feet of surface area into a small canister. You see these now on the latest cyclones, single-stage dust collectors, and shop vacuums, and they certainly are a major upgrade from the filters of the past. But for everything but the cyclones, there is a problem: The filters can only get so fine before they start clogging and killing airflow.

Why the cyclone is still best—Filters work best on two-stage collectors (like cyclones). A two-stage system catches most of the dust before it can get to the filter. That means the filter can be much finer.

On single-stage dust collectors (and most shop vacs), most of the fine dust reaches the filter, so the very finest pleated filters will quickly pack with dust and start killing suction. At least five manufacturers of single-stage dust collectors told me the same thing: that they had to stop at 2-micron pleated filters when outfitting those machines. On the other hand, cyclone collectors can have state-of-the-art filters that capture particles as small as 0.3 microns. (For the bottom line on filter ratings, see "The truth about filtration," on p. 140.)

So my first piece of advice is to buy a cyclone dust collector if you can. While the first cyclones for small shops were big, expensive, stationary machines, requiring long hose or rigid-duct runs to reach all four corners of a shop, almost every cyclone manufacturer now makes compact, roll-around models, and many are under $1,000.

Separators for the Rest of Us

I would love to trade up for a cyclone collector, but I recently exhausted my marital capital on a bigger bandsaw and a planer/jointer with a segmented cutterhead. So I have the same setup you probably have: a single-stage collector and a shop vacuum.

I've done my best to upgrade them. I put a "2-micron" cartridge filter on my dust collector and replaced the standard filter on my vac with a HEPA model (the finest filtration available). But the HEPA filter came with a cost: I have to bang it against my trash can regularly to unclog it and restore the vacuum's suction. That's not only a pain, but it also fills my head with the same fine dust I'm trying to avoid. And I've known for some time that the 2-micron filter on my collector was not up to snuff.

The light went on for me when I recently reviewed Oneida's new Dust Deputy. It is a small plastic cyclone separator for shop vacuums, and I was astounded at how clean it kept my HEPA filter, and how much more powerful the airflow was as a result.

Why Two Stages Are Better Than One

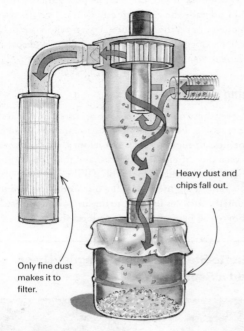

THE CYCLONE IS KING

A cyclone has two stages. Dust is drawn first into the cyclone itself. All but the very finest particles fly to the outside of the cone and spiral down into a collecting bucket, leaving mostly clean air to be drawn up through the center of the funnel cloud and into the filter stage.

Heavy dust and chips fall out.

Only fine dust makes it to filter.

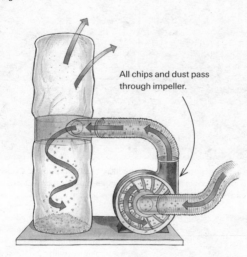

All chips and dust pass through impeller.

MOST COLLECTORS AND VACS ARE SINGLE-STAGE

Single-stage dust collectors (and most shop vacuums) draw air and chips directly into the collection area, where they clog filters, choking airflow and reducing suction.

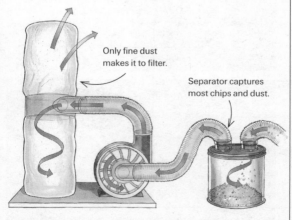

Only fine dust makes it to filter.

Separator captures most chips and dust.

ADD A SEPARATOR TO CREATE A TWO-STAGE SYSTEM

A dust separator turns a single-stage collector (or vac) into a two-stage system, grabbing the vast majority of the dust before it reaches the filter, keeping it clean and effective.

Small Cyclones, Tiny Cyclones

One of the breakthroughs in dust collection involves downsizing. There is no doubt that the cyclone is the best way to collect dust. New portable models (below left) are a more affordable option for small shops, while even smaller versions work wonders as dust separators for shop vacuums (below right) and single-stage dust collectors.

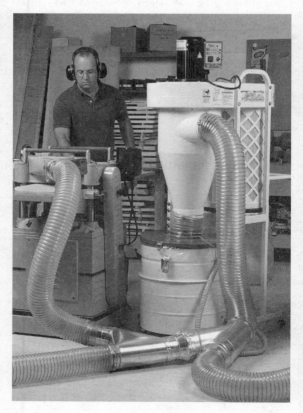

Continued ➜

Dust separators are nothing new, and they are made for both shop vacuums and single-stage dust collectors. The common type is not much more than an inlet and outlet that attach to the top of a barrel. Dust reaches the barrel first, where the larger particles spin around and settle out before the air passes out of the barrel and into the dust collector itself. Oneida's little cyclone is just a new type of separator.

My experience with the Dust Deputy got me thinking: Could I upgrade the cartridge filter on my single-stage dust collector and then install a separator to keep that filter from clogging constantly? Or do I have to spring for a cyclone to be truly safe?

Testing, Testing

To answer these questions and more, I started researching this article. I spoke with product managers from eight companies; brought in the best cyclones, single-stagers, shop vacuums, aftermarket filters, and dust separators for testing; and enlisted the help of *FWW* shop manager Bill Peck, a retired engineer. He dug our pitot tube and digital manometer (devices for measuring airflow) out of storage, and borrowed bags of dust from a local shop.

Single-Stagers: Clean Frequently or Add a Separator

Use a dust separator to keep the filter clean. This Veritas Cyclone Lid is an affordable upgrade for any single-stage dust collector. Separators are also easier to empty than bags are.

Or clean the filter yourself—frequently. Spinning the internal flappers or blowing with compressed air will return the airflow to normal, but you must do it after each woodworking session.

No surprise: Cyclones rule—First, Peck measured the initial airflow on every dust collector and vacuum to get a baseline for each with a clean filter. Then he turned them on, and sucked up enough dust to fill each one to capacity, measuring flow the whole time. That told us that the experts are right about cyclones: They work better than any other type of collector. While the airflow/suction on the other dust collectors and vacs dipped up to 40 percent as their filters clogged, the filters on the cyclones stayed clean and the airflow barely wavered.

How to test single-stagers?—After seeing what a dust separator did for my shop vacuum, allowing it to have a much finer filter without clogging, I couldn't wait to try out the separators made for single-stage dust collectors. That's when we hit a roadblock: No one makes an after-market filter for single-stage collectors that's any better than the standard-issue models.

So we couldn't upgrade the filters on the single-stage collectors, but we could do two things that would get us very close to a definitive answer. First, we could test the effect of a dust separator on a single-stage collector with its standard pleated filter in place. If the separators worked well for those, they should help even finer filters too. Second, we could do the full test on our army of shop vacuums, since there are dust separators *and* upgraded filters available for all of those.

Separators work wonders on single-stage collectors—We started by testing a number of typical single-stage collectors, trying them without a separator in place, and the results were sobering: Airflow dropped by an average of 40 percent after filling the bags just once. One has to assume that number would be even higher with finer filters. Then we picked a typical performer, the Jet DC1100CK, and tried it with various dust separators. With the best separators, the airflow hardly budged! By the way, Jet makes a "Vortex" version of its single-stage collectors, and the one we tested recently kept its filter clean without the need for a separator.

We also tested the effectiveness of those internal flappers that manufacturers have included on their cartridge filters. They worked great, too. A few spins of the handles this way and that unpacked the pleats and brought the airflow back to normal. Blowing compressed air through the pleats also worked very well, and won't abrade the filter media the way flappers might. We also found that a full bag drives the dust swirl higher, clogging the filter more quickly, so we recommend emptying the bag when it is half full or so.

Separators are a must-have for shop vacuums—The next test was tougher. We put both standard and HEPA filters onto a number of shop vacuums, sucked up gallons of dust, and measured the flow. Sure enough, the HEPA filters clogged more rapidly than standard models, just as I experienced in my own shop. Then we attached the separators, and they did their magic once again, keeping the filters clean and flowing free.

By the way, our tests showed that adding a separator does steal a small amount of initial airflow, but that loss is vastly outweighed by their advantage once you start pouring dust into the system.

The Bottom Line for Safe Woodworking

If you want to be safe from fine wood dust and have a cleaner shop in general, you should focus on two things: Bringing the proper amount of suction to the source, and putting the finest filtration you can buy at the other end.

Choose the right power plant—Your primary source of suction for woodworking machinery should be a dust collector, not a shop vacuum. That's because you need as much as 700 cfm of airflow at the end of the hose for larger machines. But it is possible to overbuild your system. Too much air pressure is actually a bad thing, since it can force dust right through a fine filter. So unless you are installing a full-shop system, with a stationary collector and permanent duct runs to every corner, a 2-hp dust collector (either cyclone or single-stage) with a 12-in. impeller is probably right for a basement or garage shop.

With anything smaller, and even for 2-hp collectors, I recommend keeping the biggest machines as close as possible to each other to keep hose runs shorter (long runs add friction and slow airflow).

Check your filters—If you can afford it, get one of the new compact cyclones, with a filter that has been rated by a reputable third party. We found three manufacturers with certified, state-of-the-art filters—Grizzly, Oneida, and Penn State. And filters from those companies can be purchased as accessories and retrofit onto an existing cyclone. But other manufacturers are upgrading all the time, so check websites for current stats and testing info.

If a single-stage collector is a better fit for your budget, or if you already own one, consider the upgraded filters coming from Grizzly and Oneida. Most collectors have similar dimensions and designs, so there should be an aftermarket filter that will fit yours. After upgrading, consider adding a dust separator to keep the filter clean and the airflow powerful.

Of course, no matter what type of collector you get, you'll need a shop vacuum that can go where its big brother can't. Put a HEPA filter on yours, or buy a new one with HEPA standard. And unless your vac has some kind of self-cleaning feature (a few have built-in filter shakers), add a dust separator to keep that HEPA filter from clogging and killing airflow. By the way, while doing all this testing, we ended up testing the best new vacuums.

The Truth About Filtration

There is a lot of mystery and misinformation surrounding filtration specs, so I took a closer look. Manufacturers tend to give vague ratings like "2 micron." If a filter rating doesn't tell you what percentage of what size particles it can capture, the manufacturer probably doesn't know exactly. Although the science of filter ratings is new to our corner of the woodworking industry, there are plenty of independent companies in Europe and the United States that can test and rate filter media at very low cost, and a few manufacturers have taken advantage of that.

Ratings are standardized. The widely accepted standard in the United States comes from the American Society of Heating, Refrigerating, and Air-Conditioning Engineers (ASHRAE), and is expressed as a minimum efficiency reporting value (MERV), or as HEPA (high-efficiency particulate air), a rating that exceeds the MERV scale. True HEPA filters capture 99.97% of 0.3-micron particles, which is as small as wood dust gets. For shop-vacuum filters, buy a certified HEPA filter, not "HEPA-type" or anything vague-sounding. For all other dust collectors, look for a filter that is third-party-rated to capture more than 85% of the 0.3-micron to 1.0-micron particles (MERV 15 or higher).

Working with and Shaping Wood

DEVELOPING AND ORGANIZING PROJECTS

7 Habits of Highly Effective Woodworkers

By Matt Kenney

Making furniture isn't easy, especially if you do it in your spare time. When it comes to complicated tasks like dovetailing a carcase or sanding a big piece, it's challenging to get consistent results when working in short bursts.

I've long thought that if I could make wiser use of my limited shop time, I'd make fewer mistakes, get more done, and build better furniture. To that end, I recently asked our contributing editors for suggestions, tapping their combined decades of experience. Surprisingly, none of them focused on technical skills; I guess these just come naturally over time. Instead, their advice dealt with things like project planning, tool maintenance, and basic milling operations. And there was a surprising amount of agreement among them.

In all, their tips boiled down to a set of good bedrock habits that will enhance anyone's work and enjoyment in the shop. With apologies to Dr. Stephen R. Covey (author of *The 7 Habits of Highly Effective People*), here they are.

1. Plan Your Work

Begin each project by drafting an overall plan. This plan should start with a detailed drawing and cutlist, but just about everyone agreed it pays to think through the whole project in advance and map out a logical step-by-step sequence for every facet, from milling and shaping parts to joinery, glue-up, sanding, and finishing.

Planning ahead yields a number of benefits. It helps ensure that you won't forget any crucial steps. It also breaks up the project into a series of tasks, each of which can be made small enough to treat as a goal for an individual shop session.

As you develop your plan, you'll learn to spot natural breaks in the action that afford their own very real woodworking advantages. For instance, if you conclude a shop session with a final sanding of your project, you'll be ready to apply finish when the next session starts—after the sanding dust has completely settled. You'll also find that short shop sessions are ideal for applying a single coat of finish that can dry during the interval between them.

2. Warm Up and Take Your Time

Gary Rogowski points out that great woodworkers work quickly, but they never rush. Hurrying leads to mental mistakes like chamfering the wrong edge of a stretcher or cutting an apron too short. Make a conscious effort to slow down and work carefully. You'll make fewer big mistakes and avoid major backtracking, like remaking parts or even a whole assembly. As a result, you'll finish your work more quickly.

A routine hand-tool exercise like Rogowski's 5-minute dovetail is a great way to begin a shop session because it helps ease you into a focused, deliberate pace.

3. Prepare for Mistakes

Careful planning can help you avoid many mistakes, but we're human, so something will go wrong eventually. Accept your fallibility. Mistakes are far less likely to ruin your fun if you're ready for them.

One way to prepare, Steve Latta suggests, is to mill extra parts—five legs instead of four, for example. That way, if you cut a mortise in the wrong place, you can grab a spare and keep going. It's also wise, as Chris Becksvoort points out, to mill stock for test cuts and test joints

Continued →

while milling the workpieces, cutting to exactly the same dimensions. A test piece that is even a few thousandths off will cause inaccurate setups. Lastly, avoid working while frustrated. Frustration has caused me to drill holes in the wrong place, cut tenons too narrow, and accept iffy results just so I could move on. It's better to stop, walk out of the shop, and stay away until your head clears. Ten minutes or ten days—it's worth the wait.

4. Keep Tools Where They Belong

Organize your shop in a way that keeps tools close to where they will be used most often. And make a point of returning them to their places when you are done. We've all had work come to a screeching halt while we searched a jumbled and dusty shop for a tool that "was just here!"

A good shop apron is like a shop assistant. It can keep handy the tools you use most often: a square, a ruler, a marking knife, a pencil, a sliding bevel, and your safety glasses. If these tools are always at hand, you won't waste time hunting for them or making do with a substitute.

5. Tap the Power of Hand Tools

The block plane is a great introduction to the utility of hand tools, according to power-tool lover Roland Johnson. Unlike a fussy router setup, it takes just a few quick passes to flush-trim a plug or the tails and pins of a dovetail joint. Leveling an apron with the top of a leg is also quicker and cleaner with a block plane than any power tool. And it's far quicker to break a sharp edge with a block plane than with a router. Hand tools are also great for smoothing convex curves and rough-shaping wood.

6. Document Your Progress

Sometimes, I leave the shop and don't get back until a week or more has passed. The lapse of time can make it hard to remember details. Suppose, after measuring a cabinet opening at the end of a previous shop session, I decided to widen the stiles for the door I'm about to build. Or did I? With no reminder, I might go merrily on my way at the start of the next session, milling the pieces to the width shown on the drawing, and end up having to remake them.

To avoid such gaffes, take detailed notes about what you are doing and thinking before you leave the shop. A quick note—"widen stiles 1/4 in."—will put you right on track when you return. In addition, a note or two made on your original drawings will help you keep track of modifications to the design should you decide to build the piece again.

7. Sharpen and Tune Tools Regularly

Sharpening tools isn't fun. Neither is checking the accuracy and setup of your machinery. But it's really an investment in the quality of your work and the quality of your experience in the shop. Nothing slows you down more than dull or out-of-tune tools, Rogowski says. Plan a shop session specifically to sharpen and maintain your machines. Perhaps the best time to do this is between projects, so you won't be interrupting other work. In this way, you'll have come full circle and be ready again for step one, which is planning your next project.

More Tips: Avoiding Shortcuts

by Asa Christiana

We're all busier these days, feeling the pressure for quick results in every area of life, even in the last place we woodworkers should tolerate it—the shop.

So we take shortcuts—at least, I do. I trick myself into believing I can skip vital steps that prevent mistakes but slow me down. I ignore the quiet voice in my head that tells me I am gambling.

Temptation arises at every stage of a project, from choosing what to build to buying lumber and milling it, from cutting joints to assembly and finishing. And a mistake at any stage can show in the final product.

On the other hand, if you go the extra mile, you'll appreciate the gorgeous surfaces, tight joints, and flawless finish for years to come. I've never regretted taking my time on a piece.

The Payoff

If you are a hobbyist like me, don't put yourself on a deadline. Leave those for your day job. Take a breath, clear your mind, and let that quiet voice guide you. It will warn you about every shortcut, and you'll be surprised at what you can accomplish.

Spend Time on Design

When I was starting out, I couldn't wait to begin cutting and building, so I designed pieces without much forethought. As a result, my work wound up with proportions, moldings, and other elements that I didn't like. I keep my first bookcase well hidden in a basement playroom.

If you're creating a design from scratch or even from a photograph, you'll need to iron out the details before you buy lumber. The best approach is to make scale models and mock-ups—a tall order for a beginner.

So build your first projects from trusted sources, such as books like this one. After the bookcase, I built a cradle from a plan in a book. That one came out great, and sits proudly in my daughter's bedroom.

Don't Skimp on Wood

We all get sticker shock at the lumberyard, but it's not worth the savings to buy subpar wood, or just enough to cover your cutlist. The ugly trade-off comes when you are forced to accept defects in the finished piece, or make the long drive to get more wood later.

You won't regret buying 10% or 20% extra. You can cut around defects, reject a board that warps severely or looks worse than you thought it would, or replace one if you make mistakes (you will).

Before you open your wallet, though, take care at the lumberyard to find the right board for each part. Look for matching color and great grain where it counts most. Then use a lumber crayon to mark each board for the parts it will yield.

Also, if you buy your wood already surfaced, take extra care to make sure that each board is straight, flat, and smooth before putting it in the take-home pile.

Milling Is the Most Important Step

You need patience and attention to detail when cutting pieces to rough length and width, then jointing and planing them to achieve flat, parallel faces and square corners. These tasks are crucial, but dull, and it's too easy to treat them like a speed bump on the road to building your project.

You might decide, for instance, to skip the step of milling your stock slightly oversize and letting it acclimate (and move) for a few days before bringing it to final dimension.

You might choose not to bother marking which faces you've already milled, and end up with lumber that is not straight or square.

Attention to these details will make you much happier when the work is done. It's also worth remembering to mill extra pieces as replacements or test parts.

Pause for a Sharpening Session

If I don't sharpen my hand tools at the beginning of a project, I tend to avoid it when I'm in the thick of things later. So I try to make do with dull tools, swearing when they dive too deep or tear at the wood. I end up with torn-up surfaces and joints that don't fit well.

I've learned to commit to a sharpening session early on. At a minimum, I hit my block plane, smoothing plane, and scraper. If there are any mortises and tenons, I also sharpen my shoulder plane and chisels.

If you don't know how to sharpen blades well, stop now, read a few articles, buy the gear you need, and learn to use it. I recommend a high-quality honing guide and waterstones, getting the final polish on an 8,000-grit stone. Once you use a truly sharp tool, you'll know what all those hand-tool nuts have been crowing about.

Check the bits and blades on your power tools, too. They should be free of gunk and sharp to the touch.

Joinery Requires Some Prep, Too

Cutting joinery is another place where I sometimes have tempted fate. In a rush and overconfident, I sometimes try to make the first cut on my actual workpieces. And about 50% of the time, I am sorry I did. That's where extra lumber can come in handy. Mill an extra part here and there to dial in your setups for perfect results.

Another trap I sometimes fall into is trying to work around the fact that I don't have the right tool or jig for the job. For example, I used to struggle to cut tenons with my sloppy shopmade tablesaw jig until I finally made a second one—carefully.

Sometimes you need a certain tool for best results. I use spiral upcutting bits for mortising. Until I got serious and bought a few of these pricey bits in different sizes, I struggled with straight bits that wouldn't clear chips, stopping every five seconds to blow them out.

Pause Before Gluing Up, Or Else

Once all the joinery is cut, I can't wait to get the whole thing glued up so I can show my wife what I've been doing in the shop for weeks.

At that point, two huge temptations arise: avoiding a bunch of sanding and scraping, and not doing a dry-fit to test the clamping setup. Skip either, and you'll be sorry.

Some beginners try to skip surface prep—either in part or entirely—leaving behind jointer, planer, and tablesaw marks that become painfully obvious once a finish is applied.

Once the surfaces are prepped, don't rush into a glue-up. Stop to do a real dry-fit, and you won't have any surprises once the glue is spread and the clock is ticking. You don't want to be caught scrambling around the shop for a missing clamp or caul, or be forced to pull apart a whole assembly that doesn't fit right.

Don't Run Out of Gas at the Finish

By now the surface should be mostly prepped, with just a bit of touch-up to do after the clamps come off and the squeeze-out is scraped away, but you still need to apply a nice finish. Once again, you'll be tempted to dive right in, slapping finish on the real piece. Don't.

Stop, take a breath, and make a test panel. A test panel is simply a piece or two of extra project wood, used to test the finish. Even if you are using a finish you've already mastered, you shouldn't skip this step, because each board can respond differently to a finish. You should try out most or all of any process, coat by coat, on some scrap. If you are unsure of your surface-prep method, try that out too.

Build in the Right Order

By Philip C. Lowe

Drawings are important in any furniture project, but they don't tell you where to start building.

The choice is an important one. Building in the right order helps ensure that parts fit properly, and it gives you the flexibility to work around the small variations that are bound to occur. Choose poorly and the project can get a lot more complicated.

This approach goes hand in hand with another important idea, which is to avoid precutting all of your parts to final dimension. Instead, leave them slightly oversize. That way, you can cut them to fit the piece perfectly as it comes together.

So how do you choose where to start? The clearest general rule is to build the case first. Doing so lets you start with a single assembly that will control the dimensions of just about every other part in the project. Even in pieces that aren't case pieces, this underlying idea still applies: Look for the assembly with the most control over other parts, and start there.

Practice this and you'll find that for any piece of furniture, there's a sequence that will make the task simpler.

Here are four basic furniture types, with time-tested advice on what to build first, next, and last. If you understand these, you should be able to handle almost everything else.

Cabinet with Face Frame and Door

This small wall cabinet is a good example of a piece with a sol-id-wood face frame. The rest of the piece is solid wood, too, but it could just as easily be plywood or have more complex joinery.

STEP 1 BUILD THE BOX

As with any case piece, the basic box comes first. You need to see the exact size of the case before you can measure for the shelf and size the face frame. Don't forget to cut the shelf dadoes and rabbet the case parts for the back, if need be, before gluing up the case.

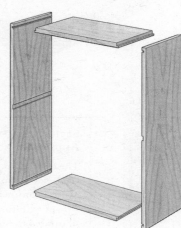

STEP 2 ADD THE SHELF AND SIZE THE FACE FRAME

With the case glued up, measure the inside width just below the top and add the dado depths for a perfect-fitting shelf. Build the face frame slightly over-size—$\frac{1}{32}$ in. on each side—so it can be planed flush. The frame should be attached before any other work is done, as it will define the opening for the door and could even pull the case slightly out of square when it is attached.

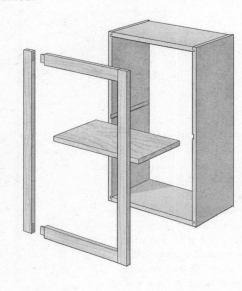

STEP 3 FIT THE DOOR

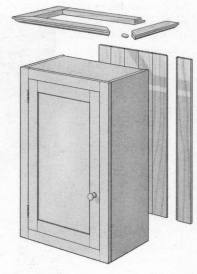

Size the door to fit the opening in the face frame. Dry-fit the door frame and measure from groove bottom to groove bottom to size the panel. Then glue up the door. Fit the door by planing the top, bottom, and one edge to fit with the correct clear-ance. Now install the hinges and mark the door's overlap. Remove the door, cut and plane it to size, and re-install.

STEP 4 ADD THE BACK AND THE TOP

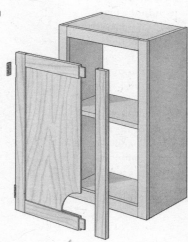

The back and the top go on last. Leaving the back off until the end makes it easier to fit the door because you can see the gaps when the door is backlit. Rip and crosscut the boards or back panel to size, cut the rabbets for shiplaps if called for, and install the back. An exception to this approach would be a larger piece, where it's a good idea to install the back after the face frame but before the door, to add rigidity. Finally, fit and attach the top moldings.

Table with Drawer

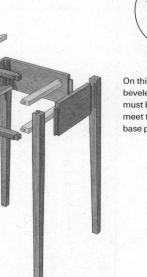

This project has legs and aprons joined with mortises and tenons, but the same basic rules apply.

STEP 1 BUILD THE BASE

Start with the base because it controls the size of the draw-er opening and the top. Mill the legs and aprons to finished dimension and mark out for the mor-tise-and-tenon joinery. Mortise and taper the legs, then tenon the aprons and the lower front rail. Dove-tail the top rail and (with the base dry-fitted) mark out its sockets in the front legs. Cut the sockets, then glue up the front and back assemblies separately before joining them with the side aprons. The drawer kickers and runners go in last.

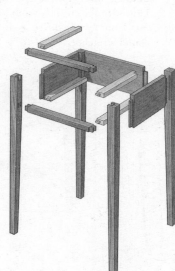

STEP 2 SIZE THE TOP

First, check the finished dimensions of the base. After gluing up and flattening the panel for the top, cut it to size and shape the edge. Then, go ahead and fasten it to the base. If any bow exists in the top front rail, attaching the top will change the shape of the drawer opening. That's why this needs to be done before fitting the drawer.

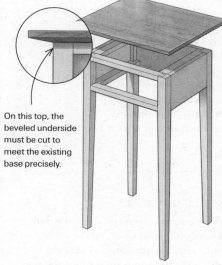

On this top, the beveled underside must be cut to meet the existing base precisely.

STEP 3 FIT THE DRAWER

The drawer comes last for the best fit. Plane the edges and ends of the drawer front and sides to fit the opening before cutting the joinery.

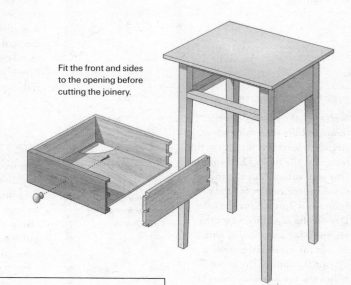

Fit the front and sides to the opening before cutting the joinery.

Building From Plans

Avoid the temptation to mill all your pieces to the dimensions specified in the cutlist before you start the project. On a case piece, for example, the box you build will vary slightly from your plan. It may be a little larger or smaller; it may even be slightly out of square. When that happens, you'll have to make adjustments to the parts and pieces that follow. Leaving them slightly oversize gives you the flexibility to do this.

Continued ➡

You'll often hear woodworkers say that it's much easier to build a drawer to fit an opening than it is to build an opening to fit a drawer. This is even more true when multiple drawers are involved.

STEP 1 BUILD THE CASE

The case is first, because its final size and shape will determine the dimensions of just about every other component in the piece, and you can tailor the rest of the components for a precise fit. In this piece, the case is solid wood, with dovetail joinery. But the concept would be the same for post-and-panel construction.

STEP 2 ADD THE DIVIDERS

After gluing up the basic box, install the horizontal drawer dividers, along with the interior components, all of which define the opening for each drawer. The runners are tenoned into the dividers with a relieved shoulder to accommodate wood movement, and held fast with a single screw at the back.

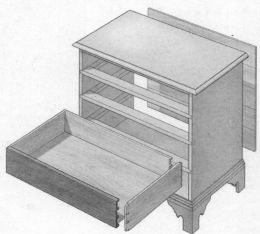

STEP 3 ATTACH THE TOP, BASE, AND MOLDINGS

Wait until the case is assembled so you can measure its bottom for the base. This lets you fit the base accurately and accommodate any imperfections, like corners that might not be precisely 90°. This will affect the fit of the base molding as well. Install the top and attach the base before fitting the drawers. As with a table, if there's any bow in the top stretchers, or twist in the base frame, attaching the base will alter the shape of the drawer openings.

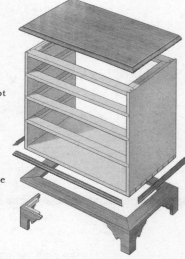

STEP 4 FIT THE DRAWERS AND ADD THE BACK

Again, fit the drawer front and sides before cutting the joinery. Install the back last: Without the back in the way, it will be easier to see what you're doing when fitting drawers and installing stop blocks.

> ### Styles Vary, But the Approach Is the Same
>
> The concept of building in a particular order and fitting parts as you go isn't confined to one particular style of furniture making. The logic illustrated in these game plans can be applied to any piece, whether it's a Queen Anne lowboy, a Shaker chest of drawers, or a contemporary chest on stand.

With compound angles in all directions, chairs strike fear in the hearts of many woodworkers. But if you realize that the back is the foundation and start there, you'll find you can use the fit-as-you-go principle to divide and conquer almost any chair.

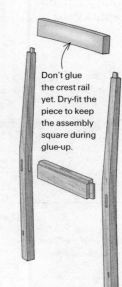

STEP 1 THE BACK ASSEMBLY

Start with the posts: Shape them, cut the seat-rail and stretcher mortises, and form the tenons at the tops. Then size the rear seat rail and cut its tenons as well as the rabbet for the seat frame and mortise for the splat. Dry-fit the assembly, mark the crest rail for an exact fit, and lay out the crest-rail mortises against the tops of the posts. To help keep the assembly straight and parallel while you glue it up, dry-fit the crest rail during the process.

Don't glue the crest rail yet. Dry-fit the piece to keep the assembly square during glue-up.

STEP 2 THE SPLAT

Together, the back assembly and the crest rail create the opening for the back splat. Install the splat now because you don't want other parts in the way when clamping it. Mortise the bottom of the crest rail for the splat. Then, fit the splat's bottom tenon into its mortise and, with the crest rail removed, use a straightedge across the tops of the posts to mark out for the top tenon. When the joinery is fitted, glue the splat and crest rail in place.

STEP 3 THE FRONT LEG ASSEMBLY

The front leg assembly—legs and front seat rail—establishes the width of the chair at the front. Building this assembly separately in advance also simplifies the final glue-up. Otherwise, the clamp needed for the front rail would interfere with the side-rail clamps.

STEP 4 SIDE RAILS FIRST AND STRETCHERS LAST

Wait until the back and front assemblies are complete before laying out the tenons on the side rails and stretchers. If the two assemblies vary from your original drawing, the angles for the joinery will change, and you'll need to adjust them. With the joinery for the side rails done, the front and back assembly can be dry-clamped together to mark out the joinery for the side stretchers. Last, with the entire assembly dry-fit, mark out for the dovetails on the center stretcher.

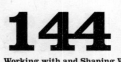

Step-By-Step Process to Developing Your Own Designs

by Michael Fortune

For many furniture makers—even those with advanced technical skills—design is the most daunting aspect of the craft. Learning to design can seem intimidating, even mysterious. But there's no magic involved. Anyone with the desire and a little perseverance can be creative. In fact, the overall concept for a piece of furniture can be discovered and its details beautifully resolved by walking through a series of simple steps. When strung together, these steps form a dependable design process. The more you use it, the more intuitive it becomes.

Whether I'm designing a chest, a chair, a bed, or a bench, I follow the same steps. I always generate multiple options to choose from—the more the better. To keep the ideas flowing fast, I focus only on the visual aspect of the pieces at this point and figure out how to build them later. This approach has the great benefit of forcing me to explore new woodworking techniques, which makes the work more fun and adds arrows to my quiver for future designs. Along the way, I discard nothing, so with each project I add to my idea bank, building up a repository of sketches, models, photos, and techniques that I'll draw from for the rest of my life.

Here are the seven basic steps:

1. Identify and analyze—I start my design process by identifying what I want to make—a chair, a cabinet, a built-in bench—and analyzing the hard constraints on the piece: what functions it will serve, what space is available, and the requirements of weight, stability, and traffic around it.

2. Set the goal—I clarify what I want from the piece aesthetically and technically. Do I want a completely new design, or something to match an existing style? Do I want to learn new techniques? Work with specific materials? Is the priority function or appearance? Or are the two equal?

3. Generate ideas—This is the fun part—and it's the heart of the matter. The key is to generate as many ideas as possible, either on paper or in model form. The tools can include transparent paper and a soft pencil for doodling and drawing, and whatever else works for making quick models: wire, foam, MDF, softwood, Popsicle sticks, and straws.

4. Select—Withhold judgment on your ideas for a couple of days. Then give them a careful review and pick one. The trick here is to make a decision and proceed. Remember that you can make any of the other ideas at a later date. If you procrastinate, you don't learn anything.

5. Build—Make a full-size mock-up if you need one, but make it quickly and cheaply. You're looking to refine the proportions of the piece, not work out all the details. Then make a full-size drawing to determine the details of joinery. Proceed to construction of the real piece.

6. Document—While you're building the piece, take photos and make sketches and notes to document the process. Add them to a file with all your design sketches for the piece, along with photographs of the models and mock-ups.

7. Evaluate—When you've built the piece, always review the steps you took and look for ways to make the process more enjoyable and productive. Next time you design, revisit the files for successful pieces to see how their designs developed.

Fine-Tune Your Designs with Scale Model Mock-Ups

By Gary Rogowski

Woodworkers, as we all know, love to roar into a weekend project. They can then spend weeks or months on it, as we also know, only to find out one sad day that the finished piece doesn't look quite right. It may in fact be a bit homely or ungainly. But didn't those plans look promising? Didn't that drawing seem right? You can avoid this dilemma with a simple and rewarding exercise: Build a scale model first. This is the advice I give my students; those who latch on to this technique never again build without it.

Don't get me wrong: Drawings and plans, whether full- or partial-scale, are very useful. But adding a three-dimensional model made with ordinary shop tools and available materials will help you learn more. The model will show you form, help you fix proportions, balance, and symmetry, even help you think about the best way to build a piece. In the end, you can save a load of time and money building the right design instead of one that may never feel quite right.

Start By Drawing Ideas in a Sketchbook

Building a model will help you visualize and refine a new design, but it's best to launch the project on paper first. How do you get from an idea you saw once in a magazine or at someone's house to the point where you can build a model? I find it easiest to begin by sketching or doodling, without censoring my ideas. I do this in a notebook that I keep for future reference. You never know how the germ of one idea may give life to a totally new design later on.

This process usually yields several ideas that appeal to me for my current project. At this point, I establish basic outside dimensions and draw a box that represents the proportions of the piece. With this visual key, I now can sketch to general proportions so I don't end up with a great-looking cabinet design in my notebook and a squashed-looking shoebox in reality.

Materials Are Inexpensive

Cardboard

Commonly available and inexpensive, it's best for full-scale or half-scale models, and great for modeling full-size tabletops. Cardboard cuts easily with a bandsaw, a tablesaw, or a knife and straightedge, holds with yellow glue or hot-melt glue, and is sturdy enough for simple tenon joints. Details can be drawn or painted on the surface.

Foamcore

Sold at art-supply houses in 1/8-in., 3/16-in., and 1/2-in. thicknesses, its higher price makes it a better choice for small-scale models or full-size mock-ups of small pieces. Any saw or sharp knife will cut it. Use pins, glue, or even packing tape to hold it together. Advantages are its stiffness, light weight, and white color, which forces you to concentrate on the shape of the piece. Its surfaces can be painted, inked, stenciled, you name it.

Wood

Material can come from the shop scrap barrel, typically 1/8-in. or 1/4-in. resawing offcuts or other scraps. Working in small scale makes parts easier to handle and the design easier to see. Wood scraps can be cut with saws and joined with a variety of glues.

I narrow down my notebook sketches to three ideas and work up more detailed ideas on drawing paper. Then I let these ideas percolate for awhile. Finally I boil down the best elements in each to a single design and do a final sketch.

Once a design is sketched and I like its elements, I make my elevation and plan drawings to scale. Afterward, if I'm confident about the elements of the piece, I can do full-scale drawings. But if I still have questions about the form or proportions, I might want another level of information. That's when I make a model.

See It Before You Build It

Models can help you work out design ideas for all types of pieces. They don't require much time or material to build, but they can save a lot of both in the construction of your furniture.

- Softwoods are easy to shape and carve.
- Experiment with design details.
- Photocopied contents can fill out an interior.
- Models can be as detailed as the final piece.
- Components can simply be drawn in place.

From Sketchbook to Model

First, decide on scale. Are your questions about the design primarily about the rightness of its basic proportions? Do you need to transport the model and show it to clients? A small-scale model will probably answer. Or do you need to live with the piece for a while, to see how it casts shadows and fits into its intended space? If so, full-scale is probably your best bet.

When I built library tables for the Oregon State Archives project, I made a 1/8-scale model for several reasons. One was to impress the selection jury with my design, giving them something tangible to see and discuss. I built the model in cherry, the same as the tables would be, but I sketched in the inlay details with a pen. The other advantage? It forced me to walk through the stages of building the piece and led me to resolve key questions about construction. Which parts would I put together first? What steps had to be completed before moving to the next phase? Would this design hold up over time, or did I need to modify the structure?

For my Greene and Greene table, I worked full-scale with cardboard. I made up hollow table legs that were 1 1/2 in. thick by 2 1/2 in. wide by slicing up parts on the saw and hot-gluing them into elongated boxes. Having a leg that doesn't collapse when you walk by is great. I cut apron pieces to length and made up a top with drawn-in bread-board ends. I made simple mortise-and-tenon joints and used corner blocks on the inside corners for strength. Now here was something to walk around and examine.

Working Small

Small-scale models are easy to build and transport, and they take up little space. They also can be made from the same stock as the full-scale piece. Nothing beats a wooden model for selling a furniture design to a client or spouse.

First, mill the stock to whatever thickness you need. Cut lengths using a tablesaw crosscut sled or chopsaw. Be cautious in cutting these smaller parts. Sometimes a pencil eraser end is a better and safer grip than your fingertip for holding things in place. Simple joints can be made on this scale, but most pieces are just butt-jointed together and glued. Strengthen where needed with gussets and corner blocks.

Continued ➡

Working Big

When you want to see how a piece will take up space and work with other furniture around it, build a full-scale model. Cardboard works best for full-scale or half-scale models. In just a few hours, Rogowski can create models as large as 2 ft. by 7 ft. with moving parts to help clients see how something might fit or look. Draw in door stiles and rails, or stack one layer of cardboard on another to create depth and texture. Use a sheet of single-wall cardboard and glue on an edge to give it thickness. Spray-paint the cardboard if you want to look at another color besides tan. Use white if you simply want to concentrate on the form of the piece.

At this point in the process, you can congratulate yourself for building the model, but then let it rest for a couple of days. Let it sit in a corner of your shop or in the place where the finished piece will finally live. Then come back to it and see how it feels. Your gut will tell you a lot about whether you got it right. If it's not right, then you'll need to start figuring out where to cut and where to add. I tell my students that planning at this stage may feel like it's slowing you down, but in the end it can save you time as you build with confidence, knowing you have a design that works, fits the space, and looks great.

Tools for Designing and Drawing Curves

By Michael Fortune

I use all manner of curves to spring my furniture to life. Once I've nailed down the design, I like to create full-size drawings of any curved parts. These make it easier to transfer the pattern to a template or to the workpiece. Having accurate drawings of curved parts also makes it easier to visualize joinery details and ultimately to cut those parts.

I'll show you how to draw both regular and irregular curves (see drawing, below), and then how to transfer those drawings to your work. My methods are simple and effective, and the tools involved won't cost an arm and a leg.

Two Types of Curves

A regular curve is a section of a circle. Irregular, or fair, curves appear more lively than a regular curve. The latter type can be symmetrical or asymmetrical.

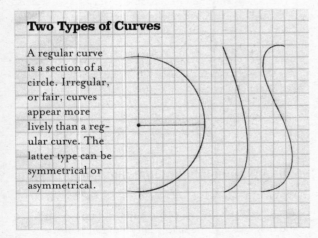

Use a Compass for Regular Curves

When drawing a circle or a section of a circle, it's hard to beat a compass for simplicity and accuracy. There are different types, and your choice will be based on the size of the arc you need.

Small radii, usually up to 6 in., are best drawn with a divider-style compass. The most basic compass uses a standard pencil as one leg of the divider. These are available at office-supply stores and woodworking stores for as little as $3.

A mechanical compass is a more refined tool. Costing about $10 to $20 at office-supply stores, it uses a special pencil lead in a holder that's sharpened along the outside at a 30° angle. To maintain that point, you can use a fine-grit sanding block or a sharpening stone. Choose a hard lead (2H), which will hold its point longer than soft lead and will render a finer line.

Beam compasses, or trammels, are used to draw radii from 1 in. to many feet. A beam compass has two separate heads that are mounted on a beam, usually wood. One head has the radius point and the other holds the lead or scribe that draws the arc. Again, use a hard lead and sharpen it in the same manner as the lead in a mechanical compass.

You can buy more robust beam compasses (available from www.toolsforworkingwood.com or www.generaltools.com) that can be attached to thicker, sturdier beam stock, allowing you to draw large arcs with radii from 5 ft. to 10 ft. These are ideal for working with curved dining tables or other large pieces.

Regular Curves

To draw a regular curve, you need a tool that will render a perfect arc, or section of a circle. Your choice will depend on whether you are drawing a small, medium, or large curve.

- **Small.** A divider-style compass or mechanical compass is ideal for radii 6 in. or smaller.
- **Medium.** A beam compass is a two-part drawing tool that attaches to a strip of wood. It can render curves from 1 in. to several feet in diameter.
- **Supersize.** Heavy-duty beam compasses are attached to thicker stock to draw ultralarge-diameter arcs.

Use French Curves and Bows For Irregular Shapes

Small irregular curves, such as those found on the feet of cabinets or on door handles, can be drawn using french curves. They are made of plastic and are often sold at art-supply stores in sets of three (the largest is 12 in. long) for about $10.

For larger irregular shapes, I have come to rely on easily adjusted drawing bows. The bow has a stick that's bent under stress and held in that shape with a string or strap. This versatile tool works for both symmetrical and asymmetrical curves. Drawing bows do not generate a consistent radius; instead, the curve is always straighter at the ends than in the middle.

I've been making my own wooden bows for years. But these bows tend to develop a kink or two and a twist along the length over time. Drawing bows made with carbon-fiber-impregnated plastic are much more consistent and reliable than the shopmade wood versions. Lee Valley (www.leevalley.com) sells two versions: asymmetrical and symmetrical. The stick of the asymmetrical bow is tapered in thickness to generate the asymmetry.

Irregular Curves

Irregular curves appear more natural to the eye, and it takes some specialized tools to draw them.

- **Small.** Use french curves to render small details such as door handles or knobs.
- **Large.** Drawing bows, both symmetrical (yellow) and asymmetrical (green), are bent into shape by tensioning and locking the strap.
- **Parallel.** To add thickness to a curved part such as a drawer front, you need to draw two lines that are evenly spaced apart. Simple metal washers or shop-made MDF versions work well.

Whale of a Hold-Down

Heavy helping hands. It's tough to hold the bow and trace a line at the same time. If you don't have a helper, use spline weights, often called whales by boat-builders, to keep the bow still as you scribe the curve.

These weighted hold-downs are easy to make, but if you prefer, you can buy them online from boat-building supply stores (search for "spline weights").

Re-Creating Shapes on the Workpiece

Once you have the drawings done on paper, you need to get them to the workpiece. I like to draw my pieces full size, so transferring is fairly easy to do.

One way is to attach the drawing directly to the workpiece using spray adhesive. Then simply cut out the pattern following the drawing. This technique is great for making templates, but unless you make a copy of the drawing, you lose it.

Another way is to lay a sheet of carbon paper on the project and tape the drawing in place on top. Then it's a simple matter of retracing the lines. A variation of this involves scribbling with a soft pencil lead (HB, 2B) on the back of the drawing and retracing the pattern on the workpiece.

My favorite method of transferring irregular curves from a full-size drawing is using the drawing bow. I reconstruct the important straight lines (as reference lines) on the project or template. Then I stretch the drawing bow to the appropriate shape, use a pencil to mark the tangent, or end, points of the curve on the bow, and move it to the workpiece, aligning the end-point with the straight lines on the project.

Once you have the pattern in place on your workpiece, you can move to the bandsaw and start cutting the curves.

From Paper to Project

To transfer full-size drawings to a blank, you can stick the pattern right on the piece, trace the shape over carbon paper, or reproduce the shape using a drawing bow.

Attach the pattern to the workpiece using spray adhesive.

This method works especially well when making templates from MDF or hardboard, but avoid using it on the actual workpiece. The glue makes the surface gummy and may cause problems with finishes. Use double-sided tape instead.

Retrace using carbon paper.

Tape the carbon paper and pattern to the workpiece and simply trace along the lines firmly. When you lift off the paper, the pattern is perfectly reproduced.

Don't have carbon paper?

Try this. Use a soft lead pencil to shade over the lines of the drawing on the back. Then tape the pattern to the workpiece and retrace.

Re-create the curve using a bow.

First find the curve's end points (where the curve meets a straight reference line) on the pattern and transfer those to the bow (top). Next, re-create the reference line on the workpiece (or use a straight edge of the piece), align the marks on the bow with the reference line, and trace the shape.

Keep Track of Parts with the Triangle Marking System

By Michael Pekovich

They say that good joinery starts with good layout. I'd add that good joinery and good layout require clear orientation marks. If you've ever spent half a day dovetailing a drawer only to cut the last set of pins in the wrong direction, you know how important it is to mark your parts clearly and refer to the marks often.

As your projects become more ambitious, and doors and drawers multiply, so do the opportunities for mix-ups. Without a system for quickly identifying and orienting all those otherwise indistinguishable parts, you're inviting mistakes.

To avoid the pain and suffering of miscut joinery, I use the carpenter's triangle, a deceptively simple mark that magically unravels the DNA of every part I'm working with, and heads off mistakes before they happen.

Unlike more complicated marking systems that use matching numbers, letters, or hieroglyphics, the simple triangle gives you all the information you need for every part—which face and edge go out and up, and which joints go where. Whether you're doing a simple tabletop glue-up or making a complicated case piece with lots of parts, using the triangle is the easiest, most intuitive way to keep track of all of them.

How Triangles Help

Every part gets marked with a partial or complete triangle on its face or top edge, with points facing forward or up. For a frame-and-panel door, for example, you'd start by ganging up the stiles. Mark one triangle, pointing up, across the front face of both pieces. Then gang up the rails and mark them with another triangle that points up. Finally, mark the panel. Each part now has a mark to identify its placement on the door, its front face, and its vertical orientation.

Instead of their faces, drawers get triangles across their top edges, pointing forward. Draw one across the tops of the sides, then another across the tops of the front and back. Treat case assemblies and table aprons the same way, with triangles on the front and top edges.

Table legs get a different approach. If you mark one triangle across the top of all four, the front two legs will get just a slash each, making it easy to confuse them. Instead, mark the tops in pairs, using right triangles to distinguish the left legs from the right. This way, you have enough information to taper the legs and cut the joinery with confidence. Right triangles also come in handy anytime you have two of the same elements in a piece, like drawers or doors. If you have more than two, number them in the most straightforward, systematic way possible.

For Quality Joinery, Eyes on Your Marks

A few seconds spent marking triangles really pays off when you lay out and cut your joinery.

No matter how patient you are setting up your machines and dimensioning stock, no two pieces of wood will ever be identical. The dimensions of any piece can vary slightly over time. By referencing off your triangles you can make sure that at least one face (usually the front) of each assembly ends up flat and flush.

Here's how it works. To get all the joints of a frame-and-panel door flush on the front face, orient the show faces of the rails and stiles against the rip fence when you cut the panel groove, and orient those same faces against the fence of the mortiser when you cut the mortises. This ensures that the distance from the show face to the panel groove and from the show face to the mortise are the same. Any variations in the thickness of the parts will be apparent on the back of the door, not the front. The same goes for cutting tenons. Make the front-facing cheek cuts first, at that same distance from the face of the rail. Then, if you need to make any adjustments for fit, make them on the back-facing cheek.

Power of the Pyramid

Drawing one triangle across multiple parts tells you how each one should be oriented for joinery and glue-up.

A simple case piece. Even if the piece has just one door and drawer, using consistent, unambiguous orientation marks will help you build it faster, with fewer mistakes.

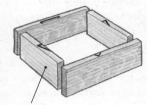

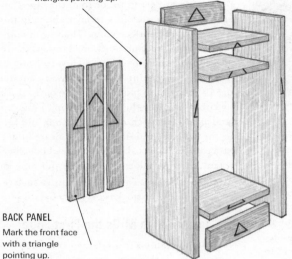

CASE PARTS
Sides and shelves get marks on the front edges with the triangles pointing up.

BACK PANEL
Mark the front face with a triangle pointing up.

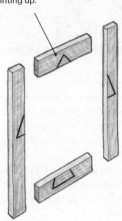

DRAWER
Draw a triangle across the top edges of the sides, and one across the back and front, both pointing forward.

DOOR
Draw one triangle across the rails and one across the stiles, both pointing up.

ORIENTING TABLE PARTS

One approach tackles any table. Whether it's this simple side table or a dining table that seats 12, the same intuitive system applies to tops, aprons, and legs.

RIGHT TRIANGLES MAKE SENSE OF MULTIPLES

For doubled doors and drawers, or table legs, a single triangle isn't enough. If using one triangle would create confusion, a pair of right triangles helps distinguish left- from right-handed parts.

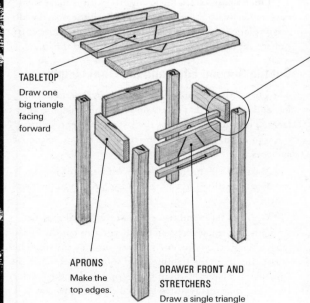

TABLETOP
Draw one big triangle facing forward

APRONS
Make the top edges.

DRAWER FRONT AND STRETCHERS
Draw a single triangle before they're ripped.

MARK LEGS IN PAIRS

Avoid confusion by marking the left and right legs with one right triangle on each pair.

Using one triangle would leave just a single mark on the two front legs, making it easy to confuse them with each other.

MULTIPLE DOORS, DRAWERS

A more complex case piece. A second door and drawer mean more potential for mix-ups. Right triangles clear up the confusion.

Continued ➜

As you move from machine to machine, it can be easy to flip-flop a piece without realizing it. But keep an eye on the triangles, and they'll let you know if you're about to cut a part the wrong way.

When hand-cutting joinery—for example, dovetailing a drawer—triangles help you keep faces and edges straight. This is especially helpful when you're scribing the pins on the drawer front and back.

It's important to locate and orient your parts correctly during glue-ups, too. So before you plane or sand off the triangles, be sure to re-mark them on the joinery where they'll be out of the way.

MILLING AND SHAPING WOOD

Essential Milling Machines

By Tom Begnal

Imagine trying to build a skyscraper from bent or twisted beams. It would be an overwhelming challenge, if not downright impossible. Woodworkers face the same dilemma when they try to work with boards that have more curves than straight lines. It's a common problem, because almost
all boards we bring home from the lumberyard or home center have at least some measure of warp. And once they acclimate to the humidity level in your shop, they tend to warp even more.

So before you begin any project, some preliminary work is in order. That work, called milling, is done with the jointer, planer, and tablesaw. When you're done, the six surfaces of each board—two faces, two edges, and two ends—should be flat and straight, with all the corners perfectly square.

Select Flat, Square Stock and Cut It Longer and Wider Than You Need

To make the milling process as easy as possible, begin thinking about flat, straight, and square stock when you're selecting the wood, no matter if it has been planed already or is still rough-sawn. Avoid badly warped stock. You'll have to remove far too much material from a board with a big bend or a substantial twist to get it flat, straight, and square.

And even if the boards look good, buy them somewhat thicker, wider, and longer than the final dimensions you need. That way, when you do mill away some extra material to remove whatever warp is there, you'll have enough stock remaining to provide the right-sized board.

As a general rule, I start by cutting each board to a manageable length and width. I cut the board about an inch longer than its approximate final length. Then I use a bandsaw to rip the boards to their approximate final width. The bandsaw is safer than the tablesaw when cutting warped stock. Depending on the width, I allow an extra 1/4 in. to 1/2 in. of stock during this initial cut. Keep in mind, though, that the maximum width is limited by the size of your jointer. If you need to end up with a 10-in.-wide board and you have a 6-in. jointer, you'll want to rip two pieces of stock to about 5-1/2 in. wide and edge-glue them after they've been milled.

First Flatten One Face on the Jointer

The next step is to flatten one face of each board. The jointer gets that job. For safety, always use push blocks when planing a face surface.

I generally take light cuts, no more than 1/32 in. If I have a lot of material to remove, I might increase the next couple of cuts by an additional 1/64 in., but rarely do I remove more than a fat 1/32 in. with a single pass. A cut that's too heavy requires you to exert more pushing force on the board and is likely to produce tearout or splintering.

To plane the face, place the board on the infeed table with one edge against the fence. Using a push block in each hand, feed the board into the knives. Once the knives start cutting, I use the push block in my left hand to apply downward pressure to the lead end of the board, pressing it against the outfeed table while pushing it forward.

As soon as I get 12 in. or so of the board on the outfeed table, the push-block in my right hand joins the one in my left at the outfeed table. Then, with both hands in line on the board, and positioned toward the front of the outfeed table (but not over the knives), I push the boards forward. At this point, all the downward and forward pressure from the push block is over the outfeed table, just past the knives. To keep the board moving, I pick up my lead hand and place it behind the other one and keep repeating the process until the board has cleared the knives. Use extra care as the board exits the infeed table because, for an instant, the guard doesn't cover the spinning knives.

Keep making passes until the entire surface is planed. At that point, your stock is perfectly flat on one face.

The Jointer Also Mills the First Edge

Now, use the jointer to straighten and smooth one edge of the board, making it square to the face you just planed. The planed face goes against the fence. If the edge has a front-to-back bend (called crook), be sure to place the concave edge against the jointer table. This ensures that the board won't rock because two points are always in contact with the table.

For safety's sake, I never push with my fingers over the blade area. Continue making passes until the board is planed along its entire length.

A Planer Makes Parallel Faces

Now it's time to work on the remaining face. It should be flat and straight, parallel to the opposite face. Your first instinct might be to use the jointer again. After all, it excels at making boards flat and straight. But unless you are very lucky, the jointer won't make the second face parallel to the first. Only a thickness planer can do that.

Once again, check the grain direction. I make light cuts, typically no more than 1/32 in. Feed the board with the unplaned surface faceup. Make passes until the entire surface is planed and reduced to the desired thickness.

Cut the Second Edge and the Final Length

The board now has both faces flat, straight, and parallel, and one edge that's flat, smooth, and square to the faces. The tablesaw handles the last assignment, cutting the second edge parallel to the first and square to the face surfaces.

Make the ripcut first. If you want a smoother edge, cut the board a little wide and then edge-joint it to the final width.

With two faces and two edges of the board now flat, straight, and square to each other, you can cut the board to length. First, trim one end to make sure it's square. Then, measuring from the trimmed and squared end, mark the final length. Now, crosscut the second end at the marked line. The board is ready to be used on your project.

FLATTEN A FACE ON THE JOINTER

The milling process starts on the jointer. To minimize tearout or splintering, take a reading of the grain direction by looking at the edge of the board. If it tends to run more in one direction than another, feed it into the planer with that grain direction in mind.

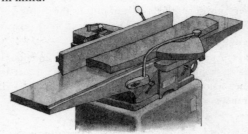

SQUARE ONE EDGE TO THE JOINTER

After making sure the fence is square to the jointer table, place the planed face of the board against the fence and joint one edge.

PLANE THE SECOND FACE PARALLEL TO THE FIRST

With the previously flattened face against the bed of the thickness planer, feed the board through the machine to plane the other face.

RIP TO WIDTH ON THE TABLESAW

Place the planed edge against the tablesaw fence, then rip the board to final width. The tablesaw is the machine of choice here because it cuts an edge parallel to the opposite edge.

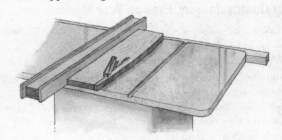

CUT TO LENGTH

Use the tablesaw and miter gauge to cut one end square. Measure from the trimmed end of the board, then cut it to final length on the tablesaw.

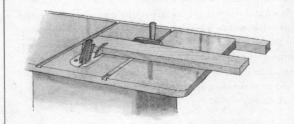

How the Jointer Flattens Lumber

The infeed and outfeed table surfaces are flat and parallel to each other. All the cutterhead knives are flush with the top of the outfeed table. The infeed table is set slightly below the outfeed table. As the board travels from the infeed table to the higher outfeed table, the knives shave an amount equal to the difference in table height.

With the bowed, cupped, or crooked surface facedown, the board rests steady on two points. The flattened area gets wider with each pass over the cutterhead until the entire surface is flat.

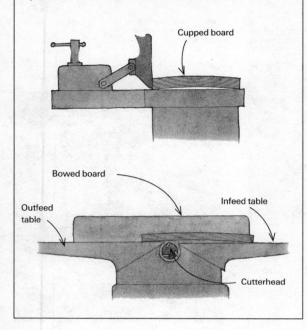

Cupped board

Bowed board

Outfeed table

Infeed table

Cutterhead

Milling Lumber with a Bandsaw and Jigsaw

By Michael Fortune

The switch from using surfaced lumber to milling your own boards from rough stock is a watershed for most woodworkers. It saves you money, unchains you from the standard thicknesses available in surfaced lumber, and gives you greater control over the accuracy of your work and the look of your boards.

But this business of taming roughsawn stock can be a challenge. The wood is rarely flat to start with, and it often releases inner stresses when cut that can pinch or bind a sawblade, resulting in a violent kickback.

I eliminate these dangers by using a bandsaw instead of a tablesaw for initial ripping and by using a jigsaw instead of a chopsaw for crosscutting rough stock to length. Both of these saws employ narrow blades that make them less susceptible to binding.

Besides being safer, the process I follow is simple and straightforward. Make sure your machines are set up properly and check the stock with an accurate square as you progress through these steps. Your goal, of course, is boards that are completely flat, straight, and square.

Start with the Jigsaw and the Bandsaw

Rough lumber that is twisted or cupped won't sit flat on a chopsaw. As the cut is made, the stock can drop into the blade, pinching and binding. For this reason, I use a jigsaw with the stock set across three or (better still) four sawhorses. A jigsaw with an oscillating cutting action and a very coarse blade will cut through the hardest wood up to 2 in. thick.

Always cut off the rough ends of the boards, which may be checked (cracked) and embedded with grit, staples, and other debris that could nick your jointer and planer knives. Now use the jigsaw to cut the rough stock into pieces that are 1 in. or 2 in. over the finished length.

The next step—cutting pieces to rough width—is the point at which many woodworkers use the tablesaw. Here's why I head for the bandsaw instead: Wood can release inner tension when sawn down its length, springing apart after being cut. On the tablesaw, the wood may bow away from the fence and into the blade, or the kerf can close up on the blade, with either one potentially resulting in a violent kickback. On a bandsaw, the short fence is less likely to push bowed stock into the blade, and the blade's downward cutting action isn't aimed at the operator.

Use the bandsaw to cut the pieces to rough width, about 1/8 in. oversize. Run one straight edge of the stock along the bandsaw's fence to get a straight cut. Depending on the straightness of each piece, you may need to pass an edge over the jointer first to get this straight reference edge.

Sometimes, if I can't joint the edge because it is too wavy, still has bark on it, or has a big knot, I'll mark a pencil or chalk line and trim the entire edge freehand on the bandsaw. Most importantly, this technique allows you to lay out the first edge so the board will have straight grain.

A surer way of cutting a straight line is to attach a straightedge (a piece of plywood or long stock with a jointed edge) with a couple of finishing nails in the overlength portion of the stock. The jointed edge will ride the fence and guide the stock through a straight cut. Don't sink the nails flush; you'll pull them out when you are done.

At the Jointer, Flatten a Face and Square an Edge

After the stock has been ripped to rough length and width, and after it has rested overnight, the next step is to joint one face flat. A thickness planer cannot do this job—it can only mill one side of a board parallel with the other. Inspect the stock for grain orientation and pass it over the jointer (cup side down) in the appropriate direction.

Sometimes the grain direction won't be obvious, so use several light passes rather than one heavy cut. If particularly bad tearout occurs in one area, then you still have the option to flip it end for end to reorient the grain and try again. Bear in mind that you will be removing material from the other face later with the planer. Try to balance out how much wood is removed from each face. This will help prevent an unbalanced release of tension, which would cause twist or cup.

Next, if I haven't done so already, I'll joint one edge, using the freshly jointed face as a reference surface against the fence of my jointer. Then it's back to the bandsaw.

Bring the Stock to Finished Width and Thickness

Because I usually bring the piece to finished width on a benchtop planer, I find it helpful to rip again on the bandsaw—this time to about 1/16 in. over finished width. This lets me take the lightest possible passes, saving wear and tear on the planer knives and ensuring the best performance. Sometimes there is so little waste material left after jointing that this step isn't necessary. But most often I'll return to the bandsaw, even if it means the blade is not fully embedded in the cut. With a properly set up saw and an unhurried feed rate, the blade does not wander.

Next, if the stock is much thicker than the finished thickness, I'll "resaw" it (bandsaw the stock on edge) a little over thickness, about a heavy 1/16 in. If you resaw away a large amount, or to yield two or more boards from thick stock, be sure to let the pieces sit for a day or so and then re-mill as needed to alleviate any twist or cup.

Once the piece is close to final thickness, mill the unjointed face in the planer to make it parallel with the opposite surface and to bring the piece to final thickness. Again, light passes are best. Roughsawn lumber can vary in thickness; you don't want your planer to bog down if the wood increases in thickness down the length (if you've re-sawn the stock, this shouldn't be an issue). Also, a heavy cut will yield a rough surface and promote snipe at the ends.

Next, clean up the bandsawn edge and bring the piece to final width by standing the piece on its jointed edge and passing it through the planer. I use the 1-to-5 rule here. If the stock is 1 in. thick, I can plane a board up to 5 in. wide. If it is 1/2 in. thick, then the maximum width is 2 1/2 in., and so on. Always use the center portion of the planer for this. Because the infeed rollers are mounted on either end and held in place with springs, they will tilt the wood slightly if it is put too close to either end.

If the dimensions exceed the 1-to-5 rule, then I trim to final width on the tablesaw. Because so little waste material is left, this cut is often exposed on the waste side, cutting away just 1/16 in. or so. I actually prefer this because it avoids creating narrow strips of waste that can fall into the throat plate and cause problems.

The last step is to cut the ends. If the pieces are too long to handle with a tablesaw's crosscut sled, cut them on the chopsaw.

1. Cut to Rough Length with a Jigsaw

Chopsaws can bind.
Because roughsawn stock isn't flat, it won't always sit still under the circular cutting action of a chopsaw. It may fall into and bind the blade during the cut.

With a jigsaw, the vertical cutting action doesn't push the stock around. The narrower blade is also much less likely to be pinched.

Cupped, bowed, or twisted boards can cause the blade to bind.

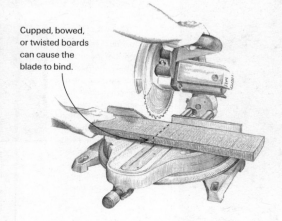

Crosscut to rough length. Position the sawhorses so that stock on both sides of each cut is fully supported.

Continued ➜

2. Layout: Snap a Line or Add a Guide

A straight rip follows a straight line.
A carpenter's chalk line produces a bright, straight line on stock that's too long for marking with a straight-edge (left). A surer path to a straight rip is to attach a piece of edge-jointed stock, nailing into the waste area of the rough board (below left). The jig's jointed edge rides the bandsaw fence and guides the stock in a straight path through the blade.

Straightening the grain.
On the bandsaw, it's easy to "correct" grain that runs out of parallel to the edge of roughsawn stock. Just make your first cut follow the grain.

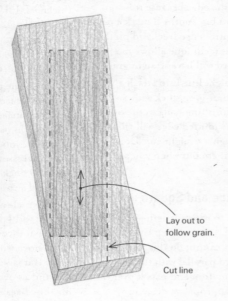

Lay out to follow grain.

Cut line

3. Cut a Straight Edge on the Bandsaw

Tablesaws can kick back.
On the tablesaw, tensions in the wood may cause a long rip to close up again behind the blade, pinching it and creating a kickback hazard. Because the bandsaw's blade is much narrower from front to back, it is much less likely to be pinched in the same way.

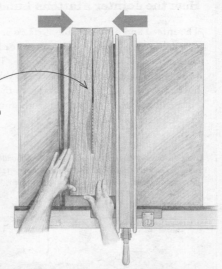

Binding can cause kickback on a tablesaw.

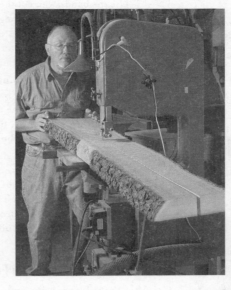

Rip without resistance.
Fortune sets up his bandsaw with a coarse, 3-tpi, skip-tooth blade, tracked on the centerline of the upper wheel. This makes it easy to cut thick stock. Boards without a straight reference edge can be ripped free-hand (left). Or use a straight-line jig (right) to guide the stock through the blade.

4. Rip to Rough Width

Stay at the bandsaw.
With one relatively straight edge established, you can rip your stock to rough width, about 1/8 in. over final width to accommodate any uneven-ness in your straight edge and for the release of any tension in the wood. Let the stock rest over-night before milling to final dimension. To provide adequate support to long or heavy stock, Fortune mounts an outfeed roller on an adjustable stand modified to mount directly to the saw's housing (below). This provides a sturdy outfeed that stays level and doesn't tip.

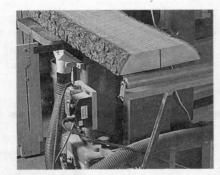

5. Joint a Face and Square an Edge

Joint a face.
Joint with the cupped side down. Take light passes until the face is flat.

Board

Feed direction

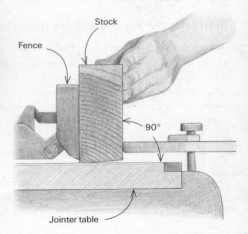

Cutter direction

Cutterhead

Joint an edge.
Register the freshly jointed face against the fence (left) and again take light passes until the edge is flat. If the fence is set at 90° to the jointer table, the two jointed surfaces should now be square to one another.

Grain matters.
To reduce tearout, consider the rotation of the cutterhead and the direction of the grain when de-ciding which way to feed a board. Fortune marks his jointer near the cutterhead for easy reference. The diagonal lines represent proper grain orientation.

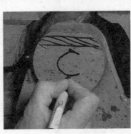

Stock

Fence

90°

Jointer table

6. Saw and Plane to Thickness

Bandsaw first?

If you still have a fair amount of material to remove, a thin bandsaw cut lets you approach final thickness quickly and avoid repeated passes in the planer.

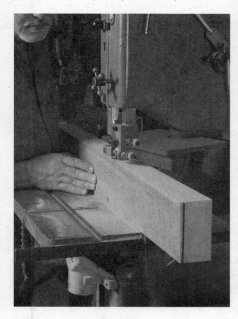

Plane to final thickness.
Take passes of no more than 1/16 in. The planed surface will now be parallel to the previously jointed face.

Taking a heavy resaw cut.
It's also possible to resaw to yield two or more boards from one piece of stock.

REJOINT IF YOU RESAW

If you resaw away a lot of material, the tensions released in the wood might cause twist or cupping. In that case, rejoint the boards.

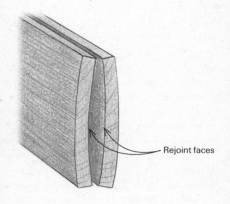

Rejoint faces

7. Trim to Final Width

Plane narrower stock on edge.
This is a safe method of trimming to width as long as the stock is no more than five times as wide as its thickness (left). Trim wider stock on the tablesaw (below).

8. Cut to Final Length

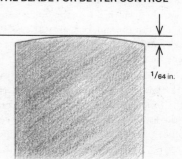

Cut one end square, then cut the other to length.
Fortune makes his final crosscuts on the chopsaw (left). If the stock is too wide (above), he uses a crosscut sled on his tablesaw.

Hone Your Handplane Skills

By Philip C. Lowe

You often don't learn the value of stock that is flat, straight, and square until you've made furniture from material that isn't.

You find out soon enough. A cupped drawer side fights back when you try dovetailing it to the front. A twisted apron can set a table's legs askew.

That's why the first task my students must complete is to mill by hand a piece of hardwood stock flat, straight, and square. This assignment trains the eye to recognize properly milled stock, and it builds basic skills in layout and handplaning.

Start by Tuning Your Plane Iron

Start with a No. 5 jack plane or a No. 4 smoothing plane. If the edge of the plane iron is perfectly straight, the corners of the iron will score the work as you plane. You can avoid this by sharpening the iron with a very slight convex edge. This "crown" is especially useful when planing edges.

I get a convex edge by bringing the iron across a grinding wheel at a slight arc. You also can use a coarse stone and apply greater downward pressure at the corners of the iron. For a smoothing plane, aim for a difference of about 1/64 in. between the crown's peak and the edges of the iron. For a jack plane, aim for 1/32 in.

Flatten the First Face

Start with a piece of stock roughly 1 in. thick, 8 in. wide, and 10 in. long. Lay a straightedge across one of the broad surfaces from end to end, edge to edge, and diagonally across the corners. Note the high and low spots. Begin taking strokes to bring the high spots in line with the lowest point on the surface. If the board is slightly twisted, with one or two high corners, take diagonal passes from high corner to high corner, working enough of the surface to bring the high areas down to the low spots.

A board that is slightly cupped across its width can be worked with the convex face either up or down. With the

Continued ➔

CROWN THE BLADE FOR BETTER CONTROL

1/64 in.

The Curve is Very Slight
Grinding a slight curve into the cutting edge of a plane iron prevents the corners from scoring the wood's surface. It also allows better control when squaring edges.

convex side down, make straight cuts along both edges to lower the high corners, or make strokes across the board from edge to edge with the plane in a skewed position, working your way down the length to remove the high corners. Use the same technique if the board is tapered, removing thickness at one end. If the board is cupped and the convex side is up, plane straight down the middle until you have flattened the high center.

Check your progress frequently with the straight-edge. When the board is nearly flat, finish with a series of straight smoothing cuts along the board's length and in the same direction as the grain. For the first pass, align the center of the blade—the peak of its crown—with the left- or right-hand edge of the board. The cut will be deepest at the board's edge. Overlap each stroke by about half the blade's width. This will put the blade's crown into the shallowest part of the previous cut, minimizing surface undulations. Check your work again. You'll know the surface is flat when no light can be seen under the straightedge in any direction. Mark the flattened surface for use as a reference face in laying out subsequent cuts.

Next, Straighten and Square an Edge

The next step is to plane one long edge straight and flat so that it is square to the reference surface you just flattened. Beginners often want to correct an angled edge by tilting the plane's body to compensate. This would be required if the iron were ground and honed straight. With a crowned iron, it's unnecessary. Instead, set the sole in full contact with the edge, aligned so the blade's crown cuts on the high side of the angle. As you make cuts to remove the angle, shift the plane with each cut until the blade is centered on the edge, bringing the high side down and into square.

To remove a convex surface on an edge, simply make short strokes in the center of the edge and lengthen each consecutive cut until the edge is straight. For an edge that is twisted or high at opposite corners, move the plane laterally from one edge to the other, starting with the plane off to one side as though you were addressing an out-of-square edge. As the cut progresses, the plane will shift so that it is making a cut with the crown in the center, at the square point of the twist, and then gradually will shift to have the opposite side of the crown cutting to remove the opposite angle of the twist.

Use a straightedge to check that the edge is straight and flat. Use a square, with the head registered against the reference face, to check that the edge is square. Once the edge is straight and square, mark it, too, as a reference edge. You'll use it to check that the ends are square and that the opposite edge is parallel.

Next, use the edge-planing techniques to plane the ends of the board so that each is square to both reference surface and edge. With the iron adjusted to make a finer cut, use deliberate strokes, working in from both edges and stopping short of the corners to avoid chipping out.

Make the Opposite Edge and Surface Parallel

Set the head of the square against the reference edge and use the square's blade to scribe a reference line indicating the board's finished width. Plane the opposite edge to this width, checking with the square against the reference face for squareness, and using the head of the square and the blade to check for parallel.

Finally, plane the remaining surface to bring the stock to finished thickness. Use a cutting gauge to scribe a line indicating the final thickness. Working off the reference face, scribe the line all the way around the piece of stock. This line will be parallel to the original reference face.

Work to bring the high spots in line with the low point on the surface. As you approach the scribe line, you'll begin to create a feather edge just above it that falls away as you reach final thickness. This feather edge provides good visual evidence that you are getting the surface flat and parallel. If the feathering develops evenly on all four edges, you're on the right track.

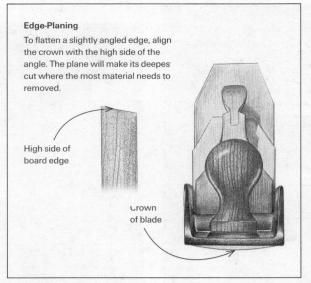

Edge-Planing
To flatten a slightly angled edge, align the crown with the high side of the angle. The plane will make its deepest cut where the most material needs to removed.

High side of board edge

Crown of blade

If you've reached the scribe line and still don't have a parallel surface, strike another line and keep going. Don't get discouraged. By the time some of my students have completed this exercise, their original 1-in.-thick workpiece is no more than ½ in. or ⅝ in. thick.

Hand-planing to Smooth Wood and Fit Parts

By Chris Gochnour

There's no denying my love of hand tools and the romantic notions I have about building furniture by hand. To my ear, the swoosh of a sharp plane gliding along the face of a board is music worthy of an iTunes track, or at least a ringtone.

But I don't turn a deaf ear to the need for woodworking machinery. When I'm building furniture on commission, time is money, and easy listening must give way to the heavy-metal roar of machinery. Fortunately, my hand tools, planes in particular, don't sit backstage for long.

In my shop, machines tackle the rough work, with handplanes following to eliminate evidence of machine work. But planes are more than cleanup tools. No matter what piece of furniture you are building, whether a case or a table, a chair or a box, handplanes can step in to polish a surface with a sheen unmatched by machine or paper. And these tools excel at fine-tuning and trimming components, allowing you to creep up on the fit of parts in almost microscopic increments. Most of the time, I go straight from planing to finishing, but if I am dealing with tricky cross-grain situations, such as breadboard ends or some obstinate figured wood, I reach for a scraper or sandpaper to eliminate tearout.

The two bench planes I use most often are the jack and the smoother. Here I'll show you where and how to incorporate these planes into your furniture making, not only for basic stock preparation but also for refining glued-up assemblies such as doors and drawers. Let's start with the basics.

Make Mill Marks Disappear

Even a well-tuned machine will leave its fingerprints on a board. But have no fear: The smoothing plane is usually all you need to remove the machine marks, leaving a glassy surface ready for finishing.

Lube the sole. Waxing the bottom of the plane with paraffin makes it easier to push. Reapply when resistance increases.

Just like mowing the lawn. The face of a board fresh from the jointer or planer can be polished with a smoothing plane, working with the grain. Skewing makes it easier to push the plane through the stroke. For heavy snipe or milling marks, start with the jack plane.

How to keep an edge square. Before planing the edge, make pencil marks across it every few inches (left). Then use your fingertips to hold the plane square to the face of the board (right). Plane so that the marks disappear evenly across the edge.

Smoother and Jack Work as a Team

The workhorse planes in my shop are the jack (No. 5) and the smoother (No. 4). If I'm simply removing light machine marks from a board, I typically can get by with the smoother alone. But I often team up the jack and smoother to surface a single board or a whole assembly quickly and efficiently. The jack, set with a mouth opening of ¹⁄₁₆ in. to ⅛ in., is used for stock removal. Its length allows the tool to span any dips in a board, creating a surface that's true and flat; a smaller plane will tend to ride the dips like waves, making them more pronounced. I follow the jack with the smoothing plane. With a fine mouth opening of ¹⁄₆₄ in. to ¹⁄₃₂ in., the smoother leaves a polished surface after just a few passes.

Pick Up Where Machines Leave Off

The most basic task of a handplane is to remove the ripples and ridges left by machines on the faces, edges, and ends of parts. So let's begin by planing the edges. Although some woodworkers use a block plane on an edge, I prefer the heft and control that bench planes offer. Whether you choose a jack or a smoother depends on the amount of work that's needed. If the machine work is not high-quality, start with a jack to remove heavy mill marks and finish with the smoother; otherwise, you can clean up marks with the smoother.

First, secure the board in a front vise, with the edge about 2 in. to 3 in. above the bench, and make pencil lines across the edge every 4 in. or 5 in. Grasp the tote (rear handle) of the plane in one hand and the front of the plane's side rail with the other. Holding the tool this way will help your fingertips keep the plane level as you work the edge of the board.

As you plane, watch the pencil lines you made earlier. If the lines are removed along one side only, adjust the pressure on the tool to make a more uniform cut. Work until all pencil and mill marks are gone.

Once you've mastered the fundamental skills of planing, you can use those skills to refine furniture parts, giving them a fit and finish that no machine can achieve. Let's begin with a glued-up panel.

Level and Smooth Glued-Up Panels

A glued-up panel, whether for a door or a tabletop, usually has high spots where the boards didn't align perfectly. A wide-belt sander will produce a flat surface, but these machines cost thousands of dollars yet still leave a lot of hand-sanding to be done. The most precise way to level and clean up those surfaces is with handplanes.

Secure the panel to the bench between benchdogs in the tail vise and benchtop. Mark surfaces with a pencil to show high and low spots. Make passes diagonally across the surface with the jack plane to bring everything into alignment. Work corner to corner, using overlapping passes.

Next, plane with the grain from end to end, starting at one edge and working to the other using overlapping passes. Repeat the process until all remnants of the diagonal passes are eliminated.

Complete the surface preparation with a smoothing plane, working with the grain. After finishing the top and bottom, clean up the end grain and edges.

End grain is tough—End grain is prone to tearout and chatter, and it's murder on a plane iron. But you need to clean it up if the edges are to be exposed, as they often are on a tabletop. The smoothing plane, set for a very light cut (a mouth opening of about 1/64 in. to 1/32 in.), deftly handles the challenge.

Be sure to skew the plane throughout the cut. This not only makes the work easier but also produces a high-quality surface. Prevent chipout at the end of the cut by clamping a backer block to the far end. If needed, lubricate the end grain with paint thinner, which makes the ends slick and supple, reducing chatter and extending blade life. Use the sawmarks on the board end as a reference, planing until the marks just disappear.

The last step is to plane the edges. A smoother may be enough here, but if there's any damage from clamping, I'd recommend starting with a jack to handle the heavy planing.

Tame Panel Glue-Ups

A glued-up panel often has surfaces that are not flush and edges that are marred from glue and clamps. The jack and smoother team up to remedy these flaws with precision.

PREP THE PARTS
Use the jack and smoother to prep long boards for glue-up. When gluing up boards for a large panel, a tabletop for instance, Gochnour refines the machine edge with planes. To ensure that the edges are straight, he first takes a few passes with a jack plane; then he finishes with a swipe or two with the smoother.

PLANE THE FACE OF THE PANEL
Work diagonally first. Secure the glued-up panel between benchdogs in the tail vise and benchtop. To bring the boards into alignment, plane diagonally using a jack plane.

Work from corner to corner and back again.

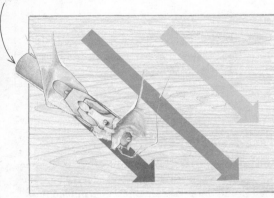

Now plane with the grain. Once the boards are flush to one another, use the jack plane (left), going with the grain until marks from the diagonal passes are gone. Finish with the smoother. If the grain reverses direction from one board to the next and wants to tear out, stay between the gluelines and work on one board at a time.

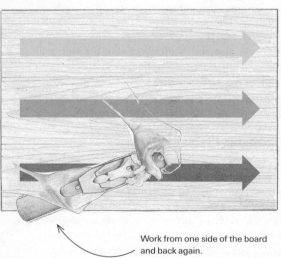

Work from one side of the board and back again.

Fix Ill-Fitting Door Parts

Glued-up door frames (and face frames) often have problems with misalignment of parts, such as a rail that's proud of a stile, and often have blemishes and scars from glue squeeze-out and clamps. Handplanes are the cure-all for these issues.

With the door secured to the benchtop, visually identify any high spots. If the rail or stile is high on one end and low on the other, use a tapering approach. Take the first couple of passes with a jack plane in the vicinity of the high spots. Gradually extend the length of each successive stroke toward the flush end until both ends are flush with the mating parts. If the rail or stile is offset equally on both ends, simply plane uniformly with the jack plane until everything is flush.

Finally, take a few final passes with a smoothing plane, starting with the rails. Be sure to skew the plane to reduce the chances of tearout across the grain of the stile. If you get a few catches, don't worry—you'll clean up the stiles in the next step. Also, lift the plane on the return strokes so that its heel doesn't accidentally bruise the stile. When the rails are smooth and blemish-free, plane the stiles.

Once you have the surface of the door planed smooth and even, use handplanes to dial in the reveal, or gap, around the door.

Continued ➔

Tackle the End Grain

Use the smoothing plane here. Set for a gossamer-thin cut, the smoothing plane deftly navigates end grain. To prevent chatter, lubricate the end grain with paint thinner (above) and skew the plane (below). To prevent tearout as the plane exits the cut, clamp a backer block to the far end of the panel.

Fine-Tune Frames

LEVEL RAILS AND STILES

During glue-ups, the rails and stiles of a door or other frame can become misaligned along their faces. Use the jack plane to level the surfaces and remove any squeeze-out and clamp marks. Save the smoother for the final passes.

Work uphill with the jack plane. If a rail is proud of the stile on one end and flush on the other, plane toward the high end. Begin the cut in the middle and gradually increase the length of the stroke until the members are flush.

Clean up marks from the jack using the smoother. Start with the rails. Skew the plane throughout the stroke (left) and increase the angle as you approach and cross the stile (right). Finish with the stiles.

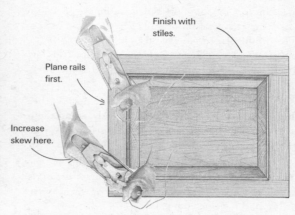

Finish with stiles.

Plane rails first.

Increase skew here.

Skew to smooth. Increasing the skew of the plane as you near the stile decreases the cutting angle and reduces the chances of tearout across the grain.

Level Face-Frame Parts

Frequently, a woodworker applies a solid-wood face frame to a plywood case to conceal the plywood edges. The frame often is left proud of the case and must be trimmed flush later without damaging the veneer. The safest tool for the job is a handplane.

Start by making a series of pencil marks every 3 in. to 4 in. across the face frame edge and onto the veneered surface to serve as reference lines to gauge your progress. Use the jack plane to begin working the solid wood flush. Watch the pencil lines and use your fingertips to feel the surfaces for misalignment to determine where and how much material must be removed. Skew the plane so that its heel references on the veneered panel, and work with care until you have planed to within 1/64 in. of the veneer.

Now switch to the smoothing plane and work until the pencil marks on the veneer just begin to disappear. Stop at this point and, if necessary, blend things in with a scraper or a sanding block.

Trim Dovetails Perfectly Flush

The easiest way to get perfectly flush joints in a dovetailed drawer is to leave the tails proud and then take a few skilled swipes with a handplane to trim them flush after assembly. The ideal tool for the job is the smoothing plane, set for a very light cut. Before planing, it's a good idea to protect the fragile edges of the dovetails by chamfering the corners.

Plane parallel to the row of dovetails (across the drawer) until the surfaces are just flush. Skewing the plane (with the toe facing into the drawer) makes end grain easier to handle and gives the tool sure footing on the workpiece. Finish by planing from the end of the drawer toward the center.

The top and bottom rims often need a touch—When you glue up a drawer, edges don't always align perfectly; typically one edge is proud. On a small drawer, you can use a smoothing plane to level the parts, but a large drawer (or case) requires the longer jack plane, which will help keep the edges straight.

Plane uphill (toward the high end) near the high spot and gradually extend the length of the stroke until the parts are flush. Finish by going around the rim with the smoother.

Fit Doors

Ideally, you want an even reveal, or gap, around a door. It's easiest to make the door fit snug and then take incremental cuts with a handplane to achieve that uniform reveal.

Mark tight spots. Mount the door and wedge it closed with shims. Highlight tight areas with a pencil.

Jack and smoother again. Use the jack plane for the heavy work, removing the marked areas in steps. After the jack's work is done, a full stroke with the smoother is the final touch.

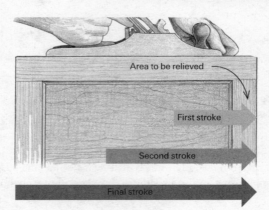

Area to be relieved

First stroke

Second stroke

Final stroke

Tapered cuts remove high spots. Sometimes you have to taper the edge of a door for a consistent reveal. The first stroke starts close to the spot that needs to be taken down. Gradually increase the stroke with each pass.

Trim Face Frames

A handplane takes controlled, even cuts to bring a face frame flush to the side of a plywood case, with no chance of the damage that can be inflicted in a flash by a router or power sander.

Pencil marks guide the way. Make a series of marks across the edge of the frame and onto the case side (above). To avoid biting through the plywood's thin veneer, plane just until the pencil marks disappear on the case side (left). Unless the frame is proud by more than 1/16 in., the smoother is the best tool for the job.

Clean Up Dovetails

For perfect dovetails on a drawer or case, leave the pins and tails proud, and handplane them flush after the glue dries. Use a smoothing plane set for a feather cut.

No-tearout zone. Chamfer the corners of through-dovetails before planing.

Simple way to support a drawer for planing. Clamp two long boards so that they overhang one side of the bench. Slide the drawer over the boards and then prop a short length of hardwood between the boards to wedge them against the inside of the drawer.

Skew for best results. When planing pins or tails flush, skew the plane to lessen the chances of tearing out the cross-grain surfaces that lie below the end grain.

Finish with the grain. Once the joint is flush, plane from each corner to the center to even things out.

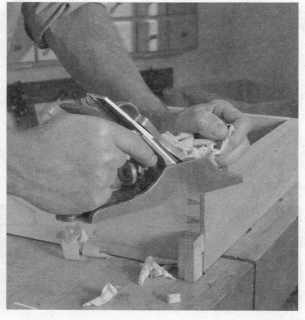

Trim the rim, too. Plane high spots first (see top of p. 51), then take a final pass around the edge with a smoother. Skew the plane throughout, but increase the angle as you turn the corner.

Board Too Wide for Your Jointer? Flatten It by Hand

With the proliferation of jointers and planers in most shops, the skill of flattening a board by hand has become a lost art. After all, it's hard to argue against the efficiency and speed of these machines. But what if your board is too wide for your jointer? Well, you can flatten one face with a jack plane and then send it through a power planer to do the rest.

First, work diagonally, taking heavy cuts. Once the high spots have been leveled, reset the jack plane for a lighter cut and go with the grain. You don't have to touch every inch with the jack plane; just create a good reference surface for the next step. You can tell if the wood is flat by using winding sticks and a straightedge, or you can lay the planed face on top of a reliably flat surface, such as a tablesaw top, and see if it rocks.

When you have the surface flattened, send the board through the planer with its handplaned face down.

Wedges won't wobble. Secure the board between dogs and add wedges to prevent it from rocking as you plane.

Coarse work. With the jack plane set for a heavy cut, plane diagonally across the board from corner to corner. Shavings will pile up quickly.

Status report. Use winding sticks and a straightedge (shown) to find the remaining high spots.

Go with the grain. After taking down the high spots, use a jack plane to even out the surfaces. Skew the plane as needed.

Ripping on the Tablesaw

By Paul Anthony

The tablesaw is a wonderful tool for cutting parts to size, and ripping is its most common task. "Ripping" means sawing wood parallel to its grain—usually when cutting boards to narrower widths. You can do the job with a bandsaw or a portable circular saw, but a tablesaw is much more efficient. It is powerful, and the rip fence allows you to cut identical multiples. The large surface also makes handling stock of all sizes much easier.

This article will tell you how to safely and accurately use the tablesaw to rip solid lumber as well as sheet stock. To do the work safely, you need to follow the proper

steps and use the right accessories, including—most importantly—a splitter. A riving knife is a more sophisticated splitter, and works even better.

Prep the Saw

Most tablesaw accidents result from violent kickback during ripping, but a properly aligned splitter will prevent kickback by keeping the workpiece from contacting the rising rear teeth of the blade and being thrown back at you. Also, when possible, use a blade guard to prevent hand-to-blade contact and keep sawdust out of your face.

Safety and quality of cut also depend greatly on a straight fence that's set parallel to the blade. Even a premium fence goes out of alignment after a while, so make

sure to check it for parallel occasionally by measuring from the blade to the locked fence at both the front and the rear of the blade. Some woodworkers cock the outfeed end of the fence away from the blade by $1/32$ in. or so, which is fine.

Finally, an outfeed table is an absolute necessity, even when ripping short pieces. Without one, your work just falls to the floor, possibly damaging edges and corners. Outfeed support is critical when ripping long stock, which may otherwise start to tip off the saw table before the cut is complete, forcing you to bear down on the trailing end of the board right at the spinning blade.

You might also want to set up infeed support, especially for long, heavy boards or sheet goods.

Continued ➜

Prep the Stock

To rip safely, the edge that contacts the rip fence must be straight, and the face that bears against the table should be flat. That way, the board doesn't pinch against the blade or rock as you're feeding it.

So the first step is to create a straight edge. If the edge is already reasonably straight, the quickest approach is to run it across the jointer. If the edge is severely crooked or is a waney, "live" edge, you'll need to saw it.

You can trim the edge straight on the tablesaw by temporarily tacking a straightedge guide board to the workpiece and running that edge against the fence. Alternatively, strike a cut line on the board and saw to it using a bandsaw, which poses no danger of kickback. After bandsawing, joint the edge straight.

Ideally, your stock should be jointed and planed to final thickness before ripping. In the process, you create the flat face for safe feeding. But this isn't always possible. For example, a board that's too wide for your jointer may have to be ripped into narrower widths first.

Let It Rip

With one edge of the board jointed straight (and a push stick at hand) you're ready to make the cut. The exact way you handle the workpiece will depend on the material itself, how long, thick, or heavy it is, and how wide a rip you're making.

Turn on the saw first, then lay the board on the table against the fence with the leading end a couple of inches from the blade. Use your left hand to press the board downward and against the fence at the same time. With your right hand on the trailing end, push the board steadily forward into the spinning blade. When the trailing end of the board is completely on the table, pick up the push stick with your right hand and use it to continue feeding

the stock. As the cut nears completion, remove your left hand from the board for safety's sake, continuing forward with the push stick until the right hand is past the splitter.

Get Some Support

The key to ripping large sheets of MDF or plywood is proper support. Best is a large outfeed table that extends at least 50 in. beyond the splitter. You might also want infeed support for heavier panels.

For easiest handling, begin with the cut closest to the center. Lock the rip fence in position. Instead of hoisting the panel onto the saw and infeed support at the same time, place the panel on the saw (with blade lowered and splitter removed), then drag it onto the infeed support.

With the blade raised and the splitter reinstalled, turn on the saw and stand at the left rear corner of the panel. Keep your eyes glued to the fence, push the panel forward with your right hand, and apply enough sideways pressure with your left to keep the panel against the fence. Push until the saw table is carrying the full weight of the sheet. Let

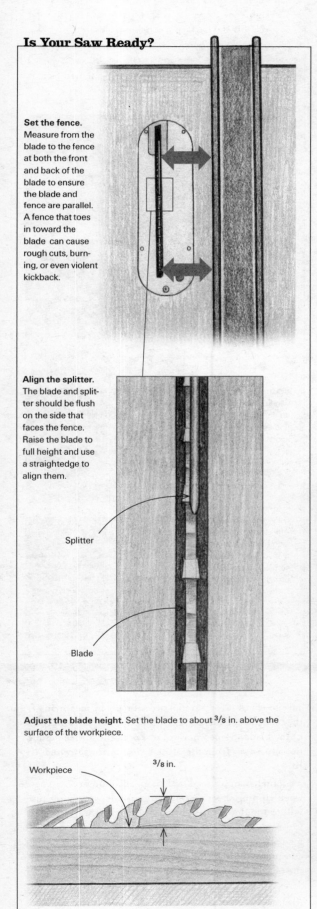

Is Your Saw Ready?

Set the fence. Measure from the blade to the fence at both the front and back of the blade to ensure the blade and fence are parallel. A fence that toes in toward the blade can cause rough cuts, burning, or even violent kickback.

Align the splitter. The blade and splitter should be flush on the side that faces the fence. Raise the blade to full height and use a straightedge to align them.

Splitter

Blade

Adjust the blade height. Set the blade to about 3/8 in. above the surface of the workpiece.

Workpiece

3/8 in.

Crooked Edge Spells Danger

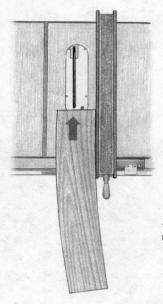  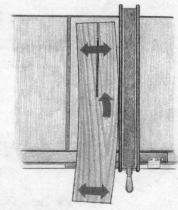

...ng a concave edge against the fence can cause the ...to push against the blade, inviting kickback.

A convex edge is no better; it allows a board to rock, also making kickback more likely.

TWO GOOD SOLUTIONS

 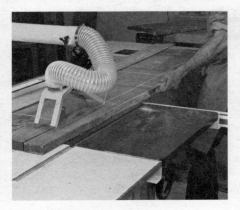

Mild curve? Joint it. With relatively straight stock, a pass or two over the jointer should yield an edge straight enough to run against the table-saw fence.

Serious curve? Saw it. Tack a straightedge guide board to the workpiece (above left). The guide runs against the fence so the saw can make a straight cut (below left). Anthony keeps several lengths of 1/4-in. plywood on hand for this. He puts the nails into a waste area of the board.

A Dance with 3 Steps

Take a balanced stance. Stand slightly to the left of the workpiece, facing the fence with your legs roughly parallel to the blade. The idea is to remain solidly grounded and well balanced throughout the cutting process.

SHOPMADE PUSH STICK

A shoe-style push stick like this offers the best control. The long sole holds the workpiece down and also helps you keep it against the fence to prevent kickback. The heel hooks over the end for feed force.

Hanger hole

3/16 in.

Sole, approx. 8 in.

Heel, 2 in. min.

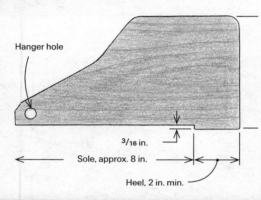

Start the cut. Push the stock with your right hand on the board's trailing end. Use your left hand to press the board downward and against the fence at the same time. If the leading edge isn't on the table, the blade can slap it down ferociously.

Reach for the push stick. When the board's trailing end is on the table, pick up the push stick and use it to continue feeding the stock. Feed the stock as quickly as you can to prevent burning. There's no reason to go slow unless the saw is bogging down.

Follow through with one hand. As the cut nears completion, take your left hand off the board. Keep pushing with the stick until the right-hand piece is past the splitter. Throughout the cut, be sure to keep the board against the fence.

---

the panel sit for a moment, move around to its rear edge, and place your hands so that each one is centered between the blade and the panel edge. Maintain your focus on the fence. Push straight forward until the cut is complete.

How to Rip Sheet Goods

WHAT NOT TO DO
If a panel is wider than it is long, don't try to run it against the rip fence. It is too easy to rotate the panel, sending it dangerously onto the back of the blade. Use some other method for a cut like this.

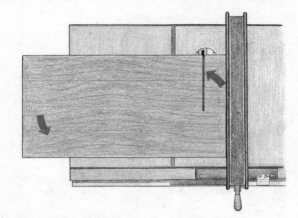

Lift the sheet onto the table. It's easiest to place a large panel on the saw first (with the blade lowered and the splitter removed), and then drag it onto the infeed support, in this case a router table that's the same height as the saw table.

Stand at the rear corner. Position yourself at the left rear of the panel, with your right hand on the trailing edge and your left as far forward as is comfortably possible. Keep a wide, balanced stance.

Focus your attention on the fence. Push the panel straight forward with your right hand, and apply enough sideways pressure with your left hand to keep the panel against the fence.

Finish the cut at the rear. Once the saw table is carrying the full weight of the sheet, move around to the rear and place your hands so that each is centered between the blade and the panel edge.

Resawing on the Bandsaw

By Lonnie Bird

Resawing thick stock on the bandsaw to create thinner lumber or veneer offers a variety of benefits to woodworkers. It not only allows you to move beyond the standard lumber dimensions available at lumberyards and home centers, but it also opens all sorts of design options. For instance, you can slice a board in half to create bookmatched panels; you can slice extrathin stock for dividers and delicate boxes; and you can cut your own veneers to get the most from a prized plank of figured wood.

Yet, with all the benefits resawing offers, few machine techniques seem as difficult to master. Because the blade is embedded along the width of the wood, resawing places a lot of demands on both the bandsaw and the blade. If the saw isn't powerful enough or the blade isn't sharp enough, the blade can buckle and bow, the motor can bog down and stall, or the blade can wander out of the cut and spoil the workpiece. But with the right setup, you'll overcome these obstacles and achieve uniform, flat cuts every time.

Probably no factor affects your success as much as blade selection. I find a coarse, narrow blade with a positive rake angle (the angle at the front of the tooth) works best. For most resawing, I'd use a hook-tooth blade with 2 tpi to 3 tpi, 3/8 in. to 1/2 in. wide and 0.025 in. thick. This coarse blade effectively pulls sawdust out of the kerf, allowing the blade to run cooler and thus cut faster. The positive rake angle pulls the wood forward, making it easy to feed with a light touch. The only downside of such a coarse blade is that the cut will be somewhat rough and prone to vibration, so it may not be suitable for resawing thin veneers, which are spoiled easily. If you plan to resaw veneers from thicker stock, you may want to use a variable-tooth, hook-type blade. The teeth on this blade are the same shape but vary in size, which results in less vibration.

Ready the Bandsaw for Resawing

Not only does resawing require the proper blade, but for consistent results and smooth cuts, it's also critical to adjust the bandsaw. These adjustments must be made in the proper sequence. First mount, track, and tension the blade; then square the table to the blade and adjust the guides. Finally, if the fence on the machine is too short to support wide stock, build an auxiliary fence. Because resawing generates a lot of dust, use dust collection at the source as well as an ambient air cleaner.

Start with the Right Blade and Tension

USE A COARSE, NARROW BLADE
A narrow (3/8 in. to 1/2 in. wide), coarse (3-tpi), hook-tooth blade will clear sawdust out of the kerf easily, and a positive rake angle will make it easy to feed a board through with a light touch.

3 tpi

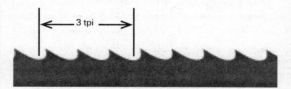

Two ways to check blade tension. A simple method is to set the tension one mark higher on the tension scale of your bandsaw (for instance, set it to the 1/2-in. mark for a 3/8-in.-wide blade). You also can check the tension by pressing your finger against the side of the blade (right); if it deflects more than 1/4 in., crank up the tension.

Increased blade tension produces flatter cuts—Resawing places a greater burden on a bandsaw blade because of the increased forces and the heat generated during the process. As the stock is fed into the blade, it places the front of the blade in compression and the back in tension. The combination of these opposing forces can cause the blade to buckle and spoil the workpiece. The best way to avoid this scenario and ensure smooth cuts of uniform thickness is to place the blade under lots of tension (15,000 psi is a good target) and employ a steady feed rate; don't force the stock.

The most accurate method for measuring tension is with a tension gauge, but this device costs around $300.

Continued ➝

Adjust the Table and Guides

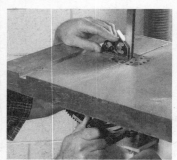

Make sure the blade is perpendicular to the table. Place a square against the side of the blade, and adjust the table until the sawblade is flush against the blade of the square.

Adjust the guides. Guides should be 0.002 in. to 0.003 in. from the blade and should not touch the teeth. You have the right spacing if you can just slide a slip of paper between the guides and the blade (left). The same goes for the thrust bearing (right), which shouldn't spin until you begin to feed stock into the blade.

If you don't want to shell out that kind of cash, you'll have to rely on your saw's built-in tension scale. Unfortunately, most of these scales tend to provide a low reading, so I came up with a low-tech solution. Simply adjust the blade tension to the next mark on the scale; for instance, if you are using a 3/8-in.-wide blade, adjust the tension for a 1/2-in.-wide blade. To reduce strain on the saw, I reduce the tension when I'm finished resawing.

Setting up the table and guides—With the blade tension set, make sure that the table is square to the blade. Next, position the guide blocks and thrust bearing about 0.002 in. to 0.003 in. from the blade (about the thickness of a piece of paper). Be sure that the guide blocks do not contact the teeth. Then, adjust the upper guides so that they're no more than 1/8 in. above the workpiece.

Tall fence adds support and can be adjusted for drift—If you're sawing just a few drawer parts from inexpensive stock, you can use the fence that came with your bandsaw. But for precise, uniform cuts, it's better to build a taller auxiliary fence.

ADD A TALL FENCE TO SUPPORT WIDE STOCK

A tall auxiliary fence made from 3/4-in.-thick plywood or medium-density fiberboard (MDF) helps support wide stock for resawing, ensuring cuts that are true (parallel) and smooth.

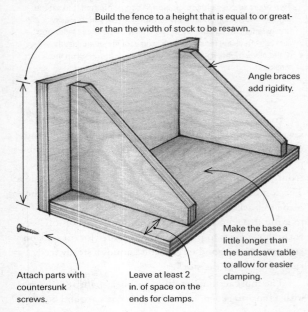

Build the fence to a height that is equal to or greater than the width of stock to be resawn.

Angle braces add rigidity.

Make the base a little longer than the bandsaw table to allow for easier clamping.

Attach parts with countersunk screws.

Leave at least 2 in. of space on the ends for clamps.

Before resawing, it's important to determine and adjust for blade drift, the tendency of the thin blade to begin cutting out of parallel with the fence. One way to reduce drift is to track the blade so that it's in the exact center of the tire, which can be difficult to do with the flat tires on many European bandsaws. I find it easier to adjust the fence for drift (see photos, right).

Adjust for blade drift when installing the fence. Raise the guides and cut along a scribed line freehand (right). Stop midway through the cut, hold the test piece in place, and clamp the auxiliary fence against it (below). This ensures that the blade won't wander during the cut.

Listen to the Machine as you Cut

The process of resawing is straightforward. It starts with stock that is flat and square so that you have a flat surface to register against the fence.

As you resaw down the thickness of a board, you typically eliminate the tension in the wood that was keeping it square and flat. With that tension unleashed, the natural side effect is that the resawn stock can tend to twist, cup, or bow. Resawing parts a bit oversize allows you to straighten and flatten them later. For thicker stock, such as that used for drawer fronts or sides, I cut boards about 1/16 in. to 1/8 in. thicker than I need (factoring in the sawkerf). I cut veneer sheets only about 1/32 in. thicker than necessary, just enough to allow for easy removal of sawmarks.

As you cut, listen for the sounds of overfeeding. If you push the saw too hard, the motor may bog down, or the blade may twist or bow and ruin the cut. At about 6 in. from the end of the cut, replace your pushing hand with a push stick for safety. If you're resawing a long board, pull the last length of the workpiece through.

When resawing veneer, run the workpiece lightly over the jointer after each cut, removing only about 1/64 in. of material. This gives you one flat face to glue to the substrate, allowing you to smooth the rough outer face easily without fear of spoiling the veneer. Then place the jointed face against the bandsaw fence, and continue cutting. If you plan to book-match the resawn boards, stack them in the order that you cut them so that it will be easier to find good matches.

Tips for Better Resawing

SLICING THICK, LONG STOCK

SLICING THIN VENEER

Keep the workpiece flat against the fence. To ensure a true (parallel) cut, use one hand to push the board and the other to hold it flat against the fence throughout the cut.

Pull long stock through at the end of the cut. Before the board starts to fall off the table on the back side, walk around to the other side of the saw and pull the board through. Support the board with one hand while using the other to hold it flat against the fence. This method also keeps your hands away from the blade.

For consistent results, hold the flat face of the workpiece against the fence. As you near the end of the cut, push the stock through with a push stick to keep your fingers clear of the blade.

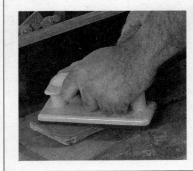

Joint after each cut. Run the just-cut face of the workpiece lightly over the jointer (removing about 1/64 in. of material) before slicing the next sheet.

158

Avoiding Tearout

By Asa Christiana

Wood is an amazing material, widely available in all sorts of colors, with beautiful grain patterns. It cuts easily with small machines and tools—products that are accessible to the home craftsman—and its strength-to-weight ratio rivals high-tech materials. But it is organic, and therefore comes with some strings attached.

One is movement, and there is no stopping it. The other is tearout. A budding hobbyist soon encounters splintered edges and pockmarked surfaces, damage that grows more obvious when finish is applied. It happens with almost every tool in the shop. The good news is that it can be stopped, in most cases easily.

Tearout happens when wood is cut and its plant fibers aren't held firmly in place. There are two main types: One happens when wood is cut across its grain, and the other when the surface is planed. I'll start with crosscutting, which is the easiest to handle.

Crosscut with No Worries

Ripping happens along the grain, and generally causes little to no tearout. The few long fibers involved simply shear away from each other. But crosscutting applies pressure across every fiber in a board. That's fine through most of the cut, but near the bottom or back edge, the last few fibers have nothing behind them and would much rather splinter away than be sliced through. On most tools, there is nothing there to stop them.

Manufacturers build those tools to make both square and angled cuts, so the opening in the table or fence needs to be extra large to allow the blade to be tilted. Carpenters don't mind, because tearout doesn't matter on framing, and they usually can hide the bottom side of a trim- or

deck board. But furniture makers can't always hide a splintered edge, and they quickly learn to close up that big gap with a "zero-clearance" plate, usually just a piece of plywood tacked or clamped onto the tool.

The principle is always the same: The blank plate is attached, and the sawblade is used to cut a kerf through it. Then, when wood is crosscut on top or in front of that plate, the lower or back edge is supported completely on both sides of the blade. Granted, that plate will need to come off or be replaced for angled cuts, but most cuts are at 90°.

Saws are simple—On tablesaws, you should replace the throat plate (the one with the big slot) with a blank plywood one for all square cuts. But you can use a zero-clearance plate on the miter gauge fence, too, to support the back edge of the cut. This is nothing more than some plywood or MDF (medium-density fiberboard) screwed to the existing fence.

The same goes for any crosscut sled you build for the saw: You can tape or tack sacrificial surfaces onto the base and the fence. Don't use thick pieces on the base; you'll steal too much of the blade's height capacity. Later, when the zero-clearance slots on these plates get beat up by angled cuts or different-size blades, you just attach new ones. On miter- and chopsaws, you can eliminate tearout on both square and 45° cuts by attaching similar plates to the bed and fence. The principle even holds true for handheld power tools. A shopmade straightedge jig for a circular saw uses the same zero-clearance idea to eliminate tearout on at least one side of the cut, where it matters most.

Same deal for drill presses and router tables—Although these don't exactly crosscut wood, they cut across the fibers in a similar way. And you use the exact same treatment.

Most drill presses have a big hole in the cast-iron table to accommodate the largest drill bits. Without a backer board under your workpiece, you'll get terrible blowout on the bottom side of the hole you are drilling. A simple piece of plywood or MDF prevents this. Just move it around to get a solid surface under each new hole.

On router tables, the force of the spinning bit is horizontal, so you will sometimes need a zero-clearance plate on the fence, but almost never in the table. There are a number of ways to do it: Make the whole fence sacrificial and replaceable, attach a thin blank plate to the fence, or design a fence with replaceable inserts.

Surface Tearout is Trickier

Jointers, planers, and handplanes all can create nasty tearout in wood surfaces, especially when they hit grain that changes directions. But the power tools require a different approach than the hand tools.

I don't believe there is a way to use the zero-clearance principle on the jointer and planer (it's difficult to get support close to the spinning cutterhead), but there are other ways to reduce tearout. Cut with the grain as much as possible. If you are getting tearout, try reversing direction. Also, try replacing dull knives with sharp ones. Sometimes it also helps to dampen the surface with water before sending the board through. Handplanes, on the other hand, do benefit from the zero-clearance principle, or, more accurately, the tight-clearance principle.

The force of the blade tends to pry fibers upward, while the plane's sole holds them down. A tighter blade opening puts the sole closer to the front of the blade and prevents the fibers from lifting during the cut. For the final, critical passes on a board, resharpen the blade, set it for a fine cut, and adjust the mouth to a very tight opening.

Depending on the plane, you either adjust the frog forward or adjust the toe of the sole backward to close the mouth. And on planes with a chipbreaker, it helps to place it as close as possible to the tip of the blade, so it applies additional downward pressure on the chip as it curls it, fighting its tendency to tear upward.

Last, when tearout is unavoidable, use scrapers and/or sandpaper to work past it and produce a flawless surface.

Two Main Types

TEAROUT FROM CROSSCUTTING

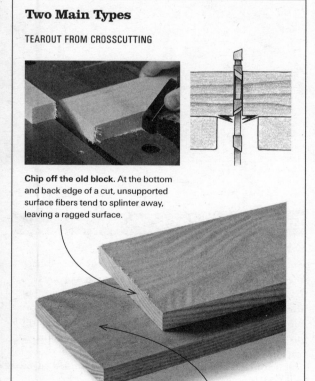

Chip off the old block. At the bottom and back edge of a cut, unsupported surface fibers tend to splinter away, leaving a ragged surface.

TEAROUT FROM PLANING

Scarred surface. Jointers, planers, and handplanes can lift surface fibers and break them instead of cutting them cleanly, leaving pockmarks in the surface.

Zero Clearance for Tablesaws

Replace your tablesaw insert. A zero-clearance throat plate helps control tearout by supporting the fibers on the bottom of a workpiece.

Add support to your miter gauge, too. A hardwood or MDF fence screwed to the front of the miter gauge will prevent the wood from splintering at the rear of the cut.

CROSSCUT SLEDS

Also works on sleds. Clamp a piece of ³/₄-in. MDF to the fence and tack down a sheet of ¹/₄-in. plywood. Then cut a new slot to match the crosscut or dado you plan to make.

Zero Clearance for Other Tools

MITER SAW

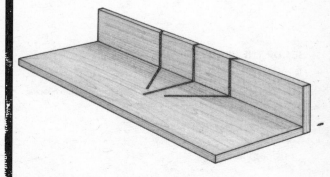

Cut cleanly on the chopsaw. This L-shaped auxiliary table supports the bottom and rear of the stock when cutting small parts.

Continued ➔

CIRCULAR SAW

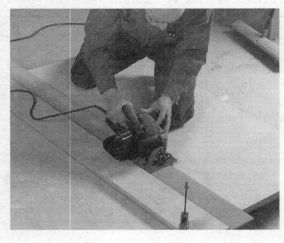

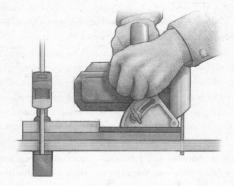

Get straight, square edges without splinters. A shopmade cutting guide keeps a handheld circular saw on a straight line. The MDF base helps support the fibers on the top surface, where the blade exits the cut.

ROUTER

Bury the bit in a sacrificial fence. A clean cut is crucial for delicate joinery like these sliding dovetails. Attach an extra board to the fence, then pivot the assembly into the spinning bit.

Torn fibers vs. a clean cut. The zero-clearance fence supported the wood adjacent to the cut on the lower piece, preventing tearout.

Handplanes

The goal. A properly set up handplane with a sharp iron should produce thin, fluffy shavings like these and a glassy surface with no tearout.

HOW TEAROUT HAPPENS

If the mouth is set too wide, there is nothing to hold down the wood fibers, allowing cracks to travel forward, deep into the surface.

When the plane's mouth is tightly set, the sole holds down the wood fibers in front of the cut. The iron shears them off cleanly.

SET UP THE PLANE FOR A CLEAN CUT

Move the frog (blade carriage) forward to create a tight mouth opening. For fine cuts, open the mouth $1/64$ in. to $1/32$ in.

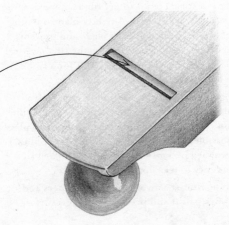

Strategies for Surface Tearout

Pay attention to grain direction. On the jointer, the edge grain should run downhill toward the rear of the board. On the planer, the downslope should point to the front of the workpiece.

JOINTER

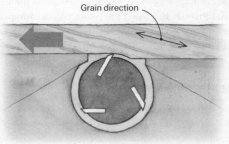

Grain direction

PLANER

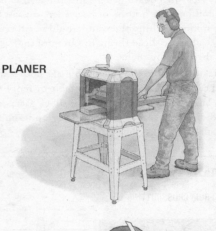

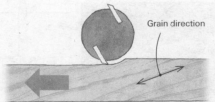

Grain direction

Breaking Edges

By Garrett Hack

Some tasks in woodworking are so basic and crucial that they apply to virtually every piece of wood in a project. Basic milling and surface preparation come to mind, but for me, breaking edges is just as vital. I use sandpaper or a block plane to relieve every edge of just about every part of my furniture. It's quick work, but it needs to be done systematically. Do too little, and your furniture won't look or feel finished. Overdo it, and your heavily rounded edges will look like unskilled factory work.

Not all furniture should get the same edge treatment, however. Contemporary furniture, for example, usually wants crisp edges, which work fine if relieved adequately. Arts and Crafts goes to the other extreme with rectangular parts broken with sensible—sometimes bold—chamfers.

The process calls for two skills that take a little practice but aren't at all hard to master: the cleanly planed chamfer and the lightly sanded roundover.

Chamfers Create a Strong Visual Impression

I like the visual effect of chamfers so much that I typically cut a light chamfer into all the visible edges of a piece. I do this with a block plane rather than a router because this is

light work; to effectively break an edge, a chamfer doesn't need to be more than about 1/32 in. wide. The block plane is also easy to maneuver one-handed, works well in tight quarters, and leaves an attractive flat and polished cut.

Set up the plane for a light cut, with a narrow throat opening. A well-tuned plane will often chamfer an edge flawlessly, regardless of grain direction, but if you're getting resistance or small tearouts, turn around.

Align the plane's body lengthwise with the corner you're chamfering. Tilt the body with the blade centered on the workpiece edge. Keep a standard grip on the plane but, if possible, ride a knuckle or the tip of your thumb on the stock to help maintain a consistent chamfer angle. Skewing the plane, on the other hand, lets you cut cleaner chamfers in end grain and work deeper into inside corners.

Break most edges before assembly—On almost any project, you can simplify the task of breaking edges by doing some of the work before assembly. On a table, for example, all the edges can be worked beforehand. This includes the legs and the bottom edges of the aprons, inside and out. The tabletop edges can be done before or after assembly, but you'll find them easier to work as long as you can run around all four edges at once. Even with an underbeveled edge, you'll need to break the edges on this bevel with sandpaper or a light chamfer.

A frame-and-panel door is another good example. I chamfer the inside edges of the stiles and rails before putting the frame together. These edges are harder to reach once the panel is in place. To avoid creating a gap at the end of the rails, be sure to stop well short of the joinery when chamfering the inside edges of the stiles. After glue-up, use a paring chisel and a rabbet plane to carry these chamfers into the corners. Now chamfer the outer edges.

Work carefully on the top and bottom areas where the long grain of the rails joins the cross grain of the stiles. Giving the plane a healthy skew as you come onto the cross grain should leave a polished facet there. Finally, give the inside of the closing stile an extra pass or two, to ease this area of potential wear.

Rounded Edges are Quick and Comfortable

The simplest way to break an edge is to round over the corner with fine sandpaper (P220-grit, then P320). This technique is quick and effective. And it's perfect for preserving wood's wonderful tactile quality, softening sharp, sometimes fragile corners and making them easier to handle for builder and user alike.

I tend to use the roundover technique primarily on less-visible parts like drawer sides (guides and runners, too) and the inside edges of table aprons. Out of sight as they are, these areas still get handled and require protection from wear and tear.

Sanding freehand can make it challenging to get a consistent shape on all of your edges, especially when working into corners. You'll improve your results by supporting the sandpaper with some type of backing that gives a little and lets you control the shape you're creating. Woodworking suppliers sell foam or cork sanding blocks, but I find it simple and effective to attach sandpaper to a narrow scrap of 1/4-in.-thick softwood or a scrap of leather.

The sandpaper also makes it simple to control the size of the roundover you're creating. If a few passes aren't enough, keep going. Stop when the edge feels comfortable and fits your design.

Again, some of this work is easier done before the piece comes together. On a drawer, for example, I lightly round the inside edges of the drawer sides and both top edges of the back before assembly. I do the rest after the drawer is together, using a file or chisel to hit the corners on the back of the drawer front. I use a block plane to chamfer the visible front edges of the drawer front.

How to Cut Clean Chamfers
Even the lightest flat chamfer will catch light and give life to an edge.

For long chamfers, guide the plane with both hands. Align the plane's body roughly lengthwise with the corner you're chamfering. Ride a knuckle on the stock to help steady the plane at a consistent angle.

A block with a V-shaped notch helps support square work at a convenient angle for breaking edges.

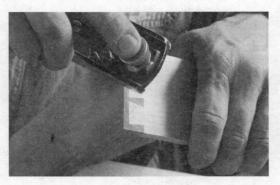

Get the right angle on end grain. Skewing the iron to the plane's line of travel lowers the cutting angle and pushes the fibers downward, creating a cleaner chamfer at the end of a piece.

Before or After Assembly?

Most edges are easiest to access and work before assembly, but some must wait. Also, be sure to complete surface preparation before breaking edges, as sanding and smoothing can erode the chamfers you've created.

Advance work. The bottom edges of a table apron are easily chamfered before glue-up (far left), as are the table's legs. Assemble the leg and apron after cutting the chamfers. Cutting these chamfers after assembly would be next to impossible because the adjoining parts obstruct the work (left).

DOORS ARE TRICKIER
The easiest way to chamfer the edges on a door frame is to treat the inside edges before assembly. But you'll need to finish off the inside corners after the frame is glued up. The outside edges must wait until the door is assembled, trimmed, and sanded.

Mark the stiles. With the frame dry-fitted, mark the stile at the point where the mating rail will meet it.

Don't go too far. If the chamfer on the stile goes beyond your reference line, it will create a gap in the joint with the rail.

The rails are easier. Because the rails die into the adjoining stiles, the chamfers can continue to the end of the workpiece.

Finish after assembly. Use a chisel to carry the chamfer into the corner on the inside of the stile.

Roundovers are Friendly to the Hand

Some woodworkers prefer light roundovers throughout their projects. Sandpaper is quick and effective, but it needs some kind of backer for consistent results.

Out of sight but not out of hand. Hack uses a gentle roundover on parts like drawer sides that will be handled but not often seen (left). He supports the paper with thick leather. Use a common mill file to get into tight corners (above), skewing it as you push it along the edge.

HEAVIER ROUNDOVERS

A heavier roundover is great for edges that are prone to damage, such as tabletops or the top edges of drawer sides. Another example is the bottom inside edge of table aprons, where you'll grip when moving the table.

Start with a block plane. When you want edges more rounded than you can achieve quickly with sandpaper alone, start with a block plane (above left) and use sandpaper to turn the facets into a roundover.

Perfect Tapers on the Tablesaw

By Steve Latta

It's no secret why woodworkers taper the legs of tables and chairs: It improves the appearance of the entire piece. Tapering breaks up that boxy square look, lightens the visual weight, and helps direct the eye toward the center.

Tapered legs are found across the range of furniture styles. The majority have tapers on two adjacent faces that begin just below the apron or rail, keeping the joinery square. But you can also find tapers that extend to the top of the leg, and tapers on all four sides. What they all demand is a way to cut them accurately and safely.

While you can cut tapers on the bandsaw or the jointer, tablesaw cuts are cleaner and more accurate. However, the standard commercial tapering jig (two aluminum sections hinged on the end) has always scared me—strike that—terrified me. Because the workpiece isn't clamped to the jig, your fingers have to come dangerously close to the blade.

Tapered legs on fine furniture. You need a jig that can make dead-accurate tapers on two, three, or four sides.

Why I Favor Foolproof

At the college where I work, many of my students are new to woodworking, so any jig has to be simple and safe to use. The jig we use to taper legs ticks both these boxes. It falls under the broader category of what I call carriage jigs, in that the work is carried on some sort of sled. Because one edge of the sled lines up with the path of the blade, setting the location of the workpiece is very easy, and with a built-in clamp to secure the workpiece, your hands remain well clear of the blade.

Instead of the sled being guided by the miter slot, as in most cases, I have it hooked to the fence. If the sled only rides in the miter slot, it wants to dip and come out of the slot before and after the cut. Some people try to use one knee to support the sled while doing an odd little one-legged dance in front of the spinning saw. Not with this sled. It is tied to the fence with an interlocking strip that keeps it flat on the table at all times.

What's more, one edge of the jig is near-zero-clearance, so it tells you where the blade will cut. That means you can simply align the layout marks on a leg with the edge of the jig, and cut with confidence.

Construction is Straightforward

To make the jig, start with a piece of hardwood, roughly 7/8 in. thick by 2 in. wide by 38 in. long, rip off a 3/8-in.-wide strip, and cut it to 33 in. long. This strip will ride

A Smarter Sled

The sled is guided simply and safely by an L-shaped guide that clamps to the rip fence, and a little hardwood strip that is nailed to the sled.

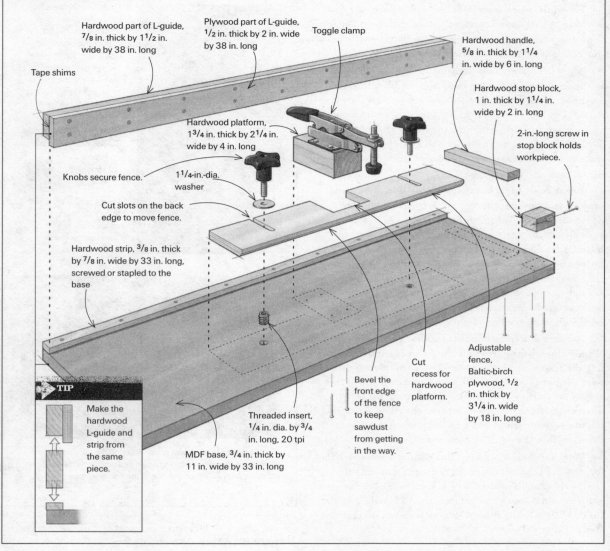

Hardwood part of L-guide, 7/8 in. thick by 1 1/2 in. wide by 38 in. long

Plywood part of L-guide, 1/2 in. thick by 2 in. wide by 38 in. long

Toggle clamp

Hardwood handle, 5/8 in. thick by 1 1/4 in. wide by 6 in. long

Tape shims

Hardwood stop block, 1 in. thick by 1 1/4 in. wide by 2 in. long

Hardwood platform, 1 3/4 in. thick by 2 1/4 in. wide by 4 in. long

2-in.-long screw in stop block holds workpiece.

Knobs secure fence.

1 1/4-in.-dia. washer

Cut slots on the back edge to move fence.

Hardwood strip, 3/8 in. thick by 7/8 in. wide by 33 in. long, screwed or stapled to the base

Bevel the front edge of the fence to keep sawdust from getting in the way.

Cut recess for hardwood platform.

Adjustable fence, Baltic-birch plywood, 1/2 in. thick by 3 1/4 in. wide by 18 in. long

Threaded insert, 1/4 in. dia. by 3/4 in. long, 20 tpi

MDF base, 3/4 in. thick by 11 in. wide by 33 in. long

TIP Make the hardwood L-guide and strip from the same piece.

against the rip fence, so you want it just proud of the edge of the sled. To achieve this, place a piece of masking tape along the edge of the sled, place the strip and the sled base against the rip fence, and then glue and either screw or staple the strip to the sled. Peel off the tape, and you're all set.

The two long sides of the sled must be parallel, so with the sled riding against the rip fence, trim the opposite side. But before you do that, attach the stop block, so it gets trimmed flush, too. Afterward, attach the sled's adjustable fence, push handle, and toggle clamp.

An L-guide locks the jig parallel to the fence yet allows it to glide smoothly with no slop. To make the guide, glue and nail or staple a 2-in.-wide by 38-in.-long strip of 1/2-in.-thick plywood to the remaining piece of hardwood that you ripped earlier. Place the side of the base with the maple strip adjacent to the saw's fence and clamp the guide to the fence. Check to see if the sled slides back and forth. If it is too tight, simply add a strip or two of blue painter's tape to the hardwood side of the guide before re-clamping it and testing the movement again.

Two-Sided Tapers are the Most Common

On traditional furniture across a range of styles, there is a basic rule for which faces of a leg to taper: If it falls under the aprons, it gets tapered. A tapered leg lends a piece the lightness and grace mentioned earlier, plus gives it a stable-looking stance without making it look splay-legged. On a typical four-legged table with a rectangular top, or even variations such as a bow or serpentine front, the two inside faces of the legs are tapered. To show how the jig works, I'll cut one of these legs.

First, cut any joinery on the leg. It is much easier while the blank has straight sides. Layout, or more accurately the lack of it, is another advantage to this jig. A line marking the start of the taper and another on the bottom of the foot are all you need. The taper usually starts where the bottom of the apron or rail intersects the leg. I use a combination square to set the lines on the top, being careful to mark only the sides to be cut. Too many lines leads to mistakes! If the taper has a finished dimension of, say 5/8 in. at the bottom, I cut a piece of stock that thick, line up the blanks, and mark the bottoms with one swipe of the pencil. I rotate each leg 90° and make a second mark. Finally, I use a wax crayon to highlight the faces to be tapered.

When using the sled, the thin end of the tapered leg should always be closest to the operator. This way not only are you cutting "downhill" with the grain, but the action of the blade helps push the blank onto the sled. You also want to rotate the leg clockwise after the first cut, so the leg is resting flat on a non-tapered face during the second cut (see photos, left).

MAKE THE FIRST CUT

Adjust the jig and cut the first taper.

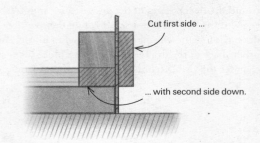

Cut first side ...

... with second side down.

ROTATE FOR NEXT CUT

There is no need to adjust any setting; just reposition the leg while the blade is spinning and clamp it down.

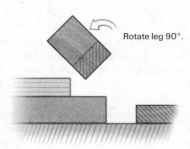

Rotate leg 90°.

CUT THE SECOND TAPER

With the first taper facing up, make the second tapering cut.

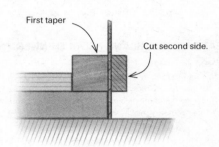

First taper

Cut second side.

To position the leg in the sled, align the mark on the bottom of the foot with the edge of the sled and push the foot into the tip of the screw protruding from the stop block. Now align the start of the taper with the edge of the sled and set the adjustable fence against the leg. Finally, deploy the toggle clamp. Leave a little extra material to handplane and sand by setting the saw fence so that the side of the sled is about 1/32 in. from the blade. Make the cut, using the handle to push the sled so that your fingers come nowhere near the blade. Pull the jig back to the front of the saw, loosen the clamp, rotate the leg 90° clockwise, and secure it again. Cut the second taper. When cleaning up the saw marks, don't remove any wood above the taper because this will leave a gap between the leg and the apron. To sneak up on the line, I mark the area below the line with a crayon, and then plane up the marked area, stopping just before the line. A final light sanding completes the job.

Clean Up the Cuts Carefully

Precise planing. To avoid extending the taper too far, mark the surface of the leg a few inches below the layout mark with a wax crayon. This makes it easier to measure your progress and to stop before you reach the line.

Two-Sided Tapers in Minutes

You need to set up the sled only once to cut tapers on two adjacent sides, but lay out each leg to keep track of your cuts.

Align the foot. Line up the layout mark with the edge of the sled and stop block, and push the leg gently against the screw in the block.

Align the top. You need only a small tick mark at the start of the taper. Line it up with the edge of the sled, then slide the adjustable fence against the back of the leg blank.

Adjust the rip fence. You want the edge of the sled to be about 1/32 in. away from the blade. In this way the taper is cut slightly proud to leave room for handplaning and sanding.

Three or Four-Sided Tapers Are No Problem

On a round or oval period table with corresponding shaped aprons, the legs can be tapered on three or four faces. Further, on contemporary furniture, it is common to find legs tapered on four sides, often extending all the way to the top, or even inverted with the wider part at the base of the leg. Never fear, this jig can handle all of these tapers and then some.

For example, with four-sided tapers, cut the first two adjacent sides as above. To cut the last two sides, first adjust the sled's fence to take into account the tapered side of the leg that will now be against it. After cutting the third taper, you may need to place an offcut under the blank to support it during the fourth cut.

Four-sided Tapers? Just One Extra Step

Set up for tapers three and four. After cutting the second taper, rotate the piece clockwise and align the marks with the sled as before (left). This time, because the opposite side of the leg has already been tapered, you'll need to move the adjustable fence (right).

Cut tapers three and four. There is no need to adjust the fence after the third cut, but you might need to adjust the toggle clamp or place a shim under it to maintain pressure on the thinner leg.

8 Tips for Flawless Mouldings

By Steve Latta

A crisp molding lends the same touch of elegance to a well-made cabinet that a silk tie bestows on a sharp-dressed man. But in order for their magic to work, neckties and moldings both must be treated with care. A molding with torn-out grain or fuzzy edges will spoil the effect—like a soup stain in the middle of your chest.

I don't have to fuss with a necktie very often, but my students and I do run plenty of molding. I've adopted several techniques for making sure the results fit well and look their best. Creating molding safely and cleanly requires careful attention in three areas: cutting profiles, cleaning them up, and, finally, ripping the individual molding strips. The suggestions here touch on all of these areas.

1. Use a Sacrificial Fence to Tame Tearout

To eliminate tearout, I like to bury the bit in a wooden fence, creating a zero-clearance cavity that lets the fence serve as a chipbreaker. There are two types of this fence that I make most often; both start with a good scrap of wide 2x stock with a jointed face and edge.

The first is a very simple fence that I make by using the bit itself to cut the zero-clearance cavity. Clamp one end, bury the bit a little deeper than you need, then bring the fence back to the appropriate setting and clamp the free end. If you are raising the bit into the fence, go only as high as necessary. Creating a cavity taller than your final bit height reduces the chipbreaking effectiveness.

For complex bits or those that can't cut their way into the fence, such as bearing-guided bits, I drill the fence opening with a Forstner bit. This also makes it easier for me to joint the infeed side if I need an offset fence. I also cut a channel in the back of the fence for chip removal.

To prevent chipout in heavily figured stock, I re-orient this fence so that the bit is literally buried in the infeed side. To do this safely, clamp a straight backer board behind the fence. Loosen the clamps that hold the fence and, with the router running, slide the infeed side of the fence into the bit. The movement is very controlled because the rotation of the bit pushes the fence against the backer board. After setting the fence, reclamp and continue running the molding.

Another advantage of any sacrificial wooden fence: I can quickly screw guards or hold-downs in place.

Of course, a good table and router are also important. Reinforce an MDF top with angle iron or C-channel, if need be, to prevent sag. As for routers, I recommend a fixed-base model with at least a 1 1/2-hp motor.

A SIMPLE FENCE FOR SIMPLE BITS

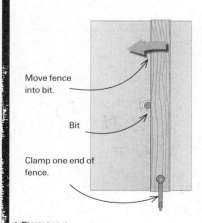

Move fence into bit.

Bit

Clamp one end of fence.

A bit with no bearing or post on top can cut its own deep, zero-clearance cavity. Start with a jointed piece of 2x stock.

Continued ➜

Bury the bit. Clamp one end of a wooden fence to the router table and, from the other end, carefully pivot the fence into the rotating bit. Then clamp it down.

A FENCE FOR COMPLEX PROFILES

Drilling the opening is easier for tall, complex profiles. To create zero clearance, bury the bit on the infeed side.

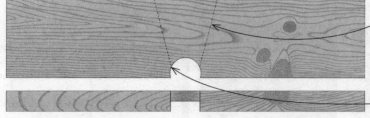

Cut away a shallow dust chute on the underside.

Drill a bit-clearance hole.

1. Clamp a backer board to the table.

2. Move fence into bit along the fixed board and clamp it in place.

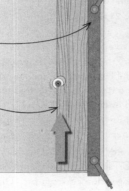

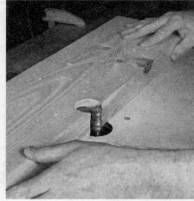

Push the fence into the bit. The infeed edge of the bit is buried, so the workpiece fibers are fully supported where the bit exits the cut.

2. Use the Tablesaw to Hog Off Waste

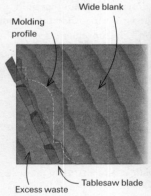

Wide blank

Molding profile

Excess waste

Tablesaw blade

Saw away the waste. Doing so saves wear on router, bits—and ears.

After drawing the profile on the end of a piece, I use the tablesaw to cut away as much waste material as I can, making sure the blade is tilting away from the fence. Roughing away this extra stock allows lighter passes with the router.

3. Cut Molding on a Wide Blank

Choose a piece of stock that is wide enough to run a profile on each edge while leaving a few inches in the middle. A bigger workpiece means less vibration and better results. It also lets you run the molding much more safely, keeping your hands well clear of the spinning bit while controlling the stock. It's also much easier to clean up moldings while they are part of a wider piece that can be clamped easily while the profile is scraped or sanded.

Pay close attention to the feed rate. Too fast leads to chipping; too slow can cause burns. Wax the table and fence to keep resistance to a minimum.

After the molding is done, rip it away on the tablesaw (Tip 8).

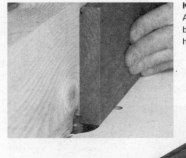

Keep fififingers safe. A wide workpiece can be fed into the cut with hands well clear of the bit.

4. Glue Up Your Own Stock to Produce a Wide Molding

When you want to cut a wide molding in figured wood like bird's-eye maple, you might not find stock thick enough. My solution is to make my own.

I do this by ripping a thinner board into strips a little wider than the thickness I want. Stand these strips on edge and laminate them face-to-face to create a glued-up board with enough thickness for the desired moldings. Glue up the blank with a piece of scrap stock as a backer board. This lets you cut multiple molding strips in the reoriented face grain while keeping your hands safely away from the bit.

Assemble the blank so that each glue joint falls in a tablesaw kerf when the moldings are ripped. You'll need to account for the kerf width, the amount of stock removed in cutting the profile, and the thickness of the finished molding.

CREATE A THICK BLANK FROM THINNER STOCK

Rip 1 1/2-in. strips from 4/4 stock, flip the strips on edge, and glue them together, face-to-face. Use a scrap of jointed pine as a backer board in the center of the glue-up. After the glue is dry, surface the stock to the necessary thickness.

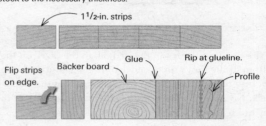

1 1/2-in. strips

Flip strips on edge.

Backer board

Glue

Rip at glueline.

Profile

Cut from a wide board. This keeps your hands safe and, because a wide board is more stable, ensures that the work doesn't chatter as you cut.

5. Reduce Chipout by Cutting in the Right Sequence

Sometimes a simple profile requires multiple passes of the same bit. The simple cove shown above is a case in point. Because I don't have a specific bit that cuts the proportions I need, I run this molding with multiple passes using a core-box bit.

In this situation, I find that I can reduce chipout dramatically by making the first pass with the bit set at the point farthest from the fence. I then raise the bit and move the fence toward the workpiece with each successive pass. In this way, the chipout created by each pass is removed by the subsequent passes. For the final run, I make sure the bit is buried in the fence, reducing the likelihood of any chipout.

This technique also helps when cutting complex profiles using a combination of different bits. This is sometimes necessary because many complex-profile bits don't quite fit specific design requirements. By combining cutters, you can match older moldings or create original designs.

The delicate crown molding at right—for a small chest—is made by combining three cutters: an oversize beading bit from Eagle America (www.eagleamerica. com), a core-box bit, and a straight bit.

Start by cutting a sample section of the profile to use as a setup piece. Creating this piece also brings to light any unforeseen problems in the process. If you create the molding often, hang the sample on the wall for future use.

6. Use an Offset Fence When Molding an Entire Edge

Profiling an entire edge is very much like jointing the edge of a board: all of the original surface is removed to create the profile. With a standard setup, this means the profiled workpiece won't ride against the outfeed fence. For proper support, the outfeed fence should be set flush with the cutter while the infeed fence steps in about 1/32 in. Make passes on a scrap piece to dial in the offset.

Although this might sound a little complicated, it's actually quite simple to set up. Take a jointed piece of 2x stock and drill an opening for the bit. Set the jointer to a 1/32 in. depth of cut and joint the edge of the fence just to the cutout. Lift it off the table and … shazam! You have an offset fence.

THE PROBLEM: NO OUTFEED SUPPORT

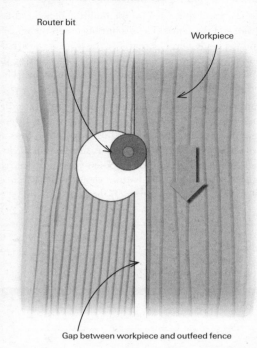

Router bit

Workpiece

Gap between workpiece and outfeed fence

No fence support. When the bit removes the entire bearing surface, a standard fence can't support the outfeed side.

THE SOLUTION: MAKE AN OFFSET FENCE

An offset fence in one easy step. Simply joint the infeed edge, stopping at the bit cutout.

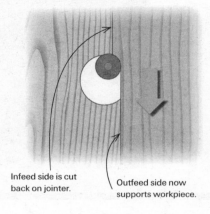

Infeed side is cut back on jointer.

Outfeed side now supports workpiece.

SINGLE-BIT PROFILE

Multiple runs with a core-box bit yield a custom cove. Each cut removes tearout from the previous pass.

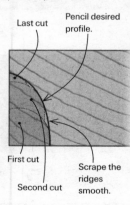

Last cut

Pencil desired profile.

First cut

Second cut

Scrape the ridges smooth.

Cover your tracks. When using multiple passes to cut different sections of the same profile, sequence the cuts so that each pass removes any tearout left by the previous cut.

MULTIPLE-BIT PROFILE

Sequence the profiles to remove tearout, starting at the bottom and inside on the molding.

1. START ON THE INSIDE

Drawn-in profile

Waste cut on tablesaw

Quarter-round bit

Tearout

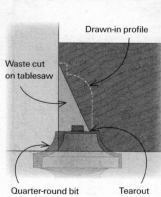

Start with the lower quarter-round. Running this bit first will cause some tearout at its top edge. This line of tearout will be removed when the core-box bit establishes the cove.

2. THEN WORK IN THE MIDDLE

Tearout

Core-box bit

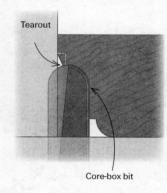

Run the cove in multiple passes. Raise the bit a little each time. Any chipout along the outside edge will be removed when the fillet is cut.

3. FINISH AT THE OUTERMOST PORTION OF THE MOLDING

Straight bit cuts fillet.

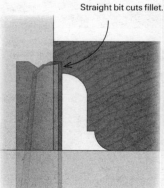

Finish with the fillet. Use a straight bit buried in a fresh fence to prevent tearout.

---

7. Clean Up Before Ripping

Moldings generally need some cleanup, especially if the profile was generated by a combination of bits. Still, if the milling was executed properly, that cleanup should require minimal effort.

A variety of tools come into play for taking off tearout, tool marks, chatter, or burn marks. The list includes scrapers, a shoulder plane, files, and various sanding blocks.

Scrape first, using scrapers fashioned to a variety of profiles to fit the need. Shape cutoffs from card scrapers into an assortment of beads and rounds. For moldings like bracket feet, grind a scraper close to the profile. Don't go for an exact match because you'll need to attack from various angles.

Detail files work well for small radii and leave marks small enough to be removed quickly with sandpaper. Sanding, however, should always be kept to the essential minimum. I tell my students that after just a few minutes of sanding, the only thing they are really sanding away is their grade.

I tend to use aluminum-oxide paper ranging in grit from P150 to P220. Most times, I use a sanding block or a piece of dowel stock for an appropriate curve. Contour sanding grips are available, but these seem like one more thing I don't really need to accomplish a basic task.

This should be light duty. With proper cutting technique, moldings should need only minimal cleanup. Latta grinds custom shapes in card scraper stock.

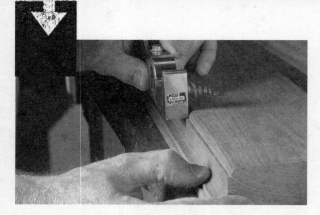

Use a shoulder plane for flats and fillets. The Stanley No. 92 works great at getting into corners.

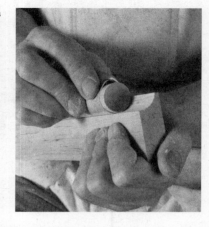

Sand sparingly. Dowels of different diameters work well for coves and other hollows. Be careful to avoid rolling the dowel over any hard edges. Doing so takes away essential detail.

8. Rip Between the Blade and Fence for Consistency

When cutting molding from a blank, standard safety practice calls for setting the tablesaw fence so that the ripped molding falls to the outside of the blade. The fence is then reset and the process repeated for the molding on the other edge. But repeatedly resetting the fence can lead to variations in the thickness of the different pieces. This problem can make it harder to install the molding properly.

To avoid this, I rip off the molding between the blade and the fence. The distance between the fence and the blade never changes, so the thicknesses are far more consistent. And because you're not resetting the fence after each cut, the work also goes more quickly.

But this method demands extra precautions. Use a splitter to prevent the molding from curling into the back of the blade and causing kickback. Stub splitters stay out of the way but get the job done. Push sticks and hold-downs are also important. A small bandsaw cut in the end of the molding stock lets you hook a narrow push stick into it. A hold-down clamped to the fence keeps the stock from lifting off the table.

Rip to a consistent width. When ripping thin strips like this, a notch in the end of the stock provides a secure grip for a narrow push stick.

How to Fix Flaws and Mistakes

By Mark Schofield

It's an old chestnut, but it's true: The difference between a professional and an amateur is that the pro knows how to cover up his mistakes. We all make mistakes, so it is almost certain that the hole you find yourself in has been previously occupied—and that a former occupant found a successful way out. To compile a woodworker's survival guide, I talked to FWW's top authors to get their greatest tips on fixing mistakes. I've divided the problems into defects and flaws in the wood, miscut joinery, and undersize parts, but there are some tips that apply to every mistake and every project.

Will Neptune told me about a student in the musical instrument department at North Bennet Street School who had almost completed a violin. He was applying a French polish when his pad stuck to the surface, leaving a blemish in the otherwise flawless finish. In a rage, the student smashed the violin to pieces.

Too bad he didn't take Garrett Hack's advice and sleep on the problem. More often than not inspiration will strike, either in the early hours or the next morning when you are no longer angry at yourself. In the case of the violin, rubbing the spot with an alcohol-dampened pad would have removed the error in minutes!

Michael Fortune said his universal tip is to hang onto every piece of scrap until a project has left the workshop. It's much easier to get a good grain and color match for a patch if you still have part of the board left over.

Defect or Damage? Don't Lose Hope

Nobody's perfect, not even nature. So as well as self-inflicted damage, someday you'll face a beautiful board marred by a loose knot or a large wormhole. Learn ways to overcome both.

Smart scoop, invisible patch

When Chip Ogg drilled through the top of a 48-in.-dia. tabletop, he knew his boss, Charles Shackleton, wouldn't be happy. So he did some fast thinking. Using nothing but a carving gouge, he created a repair that was so good, he challenged his fellow cabinetmakers to find it.

Scoop around the hole. Take a deep carving gouge that is slightly wider than the damage, in this case #8/10mm, and carve out a shallow depression around the hole. Practice on some scrap first.

Glue and clamp. After dry-fitting the patch (it should fit evenly and be slightly proud), glue it and clamp it in place with plenty of pressure. Waxed paper prevents the caul from sticking to any squeeze-out.

Replace a loose knot

A loose knot doesn't add character; it detracts from the wood's beauty. Instead of scrapping a nice board or cutting it in two, Steve Latta shows how to save it with a clever plug that looks like an area of nice figure.

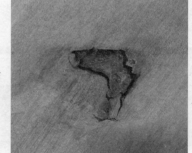

Trace the knot. Draw the outline of the loose knot on a piece of clear plastic, such as a three-ring file divider.

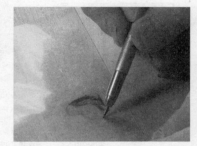

Find your patch. Use the transparent pattern to find a nice, tight knot of similar size on a piece of scrap and resaw it to about 3/16 in. thick. Draw a similar outline and cut it out on a scrollsaw.

Draw around it. Place the patch so that it covers the whole knot and draw around it with a very sharp pencil.

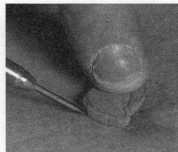

Make a recess. Use a small plunge router or a rotary tool in a plunge base to excavate to a depth of about 1/8 in. After that, work up to the layout lines with a small chisel or gouge.

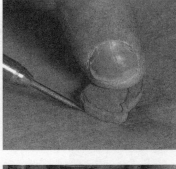

Magic Moulding Repair

Sometimes tearout just happens, particularly on curly wood. If it occurs while profiling the edge of a tabletop, you may not be able to simply trim that edge and re-rout, as that will affect the overhang. Instead, Steve Latta shows how to add a strip and conceal the joint in the profile.

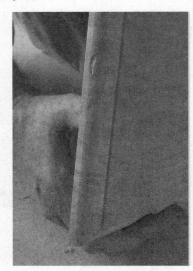

Tabletop · Fillet · Damaged edge

Cut away the damage. Saw in line with the fillet (step) of the profile to leave the center of the tabletop untouched.

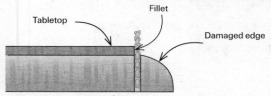

Glue on a closely matched strip.

Glue on a strip. Find a piece of scrap that closely matches the rest of the top in color and figure and glue it on.

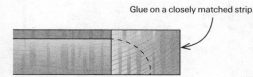

Roughly 3/32 in.

Make a test cut. After trimming the strip to leave the tabletop approximately 3/32 in. wider than the desired final width, re-rout the profile.

Dial in the location. Measure how far the fillet of the profile is from the glueline of the repair. Set the tablesaw to rip off this exact amount, leaving a flat edge (as shown).

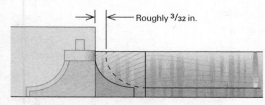

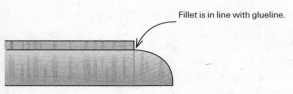

Fillet is in line with glueline.

Last pass. Make one final pass on the router table to bring the fillet of the molding in line with the joint for a nearly invisible repair.

Hide a misguided mortise

The secret to many repairs is to avoid straight lines. They aren't found in nature and they will attract the eye. Michael Fortune shows that even a large patch will blend right in if it is curved.

Cut around the patch. Glue a piece of tracing paper over the damaged area, then glue the patch to the paper over the hole. When the glue is dry, mark around the patch with a knife. Then break off the patch at the paper line.

Check the fit. Adjust the size and shape of the patch using sandpaper until it fits seamlessly.

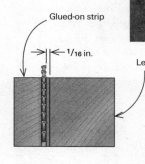

Where's the repair? The curved shape of the patch helps it blend into the background.

Glued-on strip

1/16 in.

Leg

Rip trick. Now just rip away the waste, leaving 1/16 in. glued to the damaged face. Trim the strip to match the leg's taper, then break its edges to conceal the seam.

Remove a groove

It's a common mistake to cut a groove for the drawer bottom on the wrong side of a drawer side. Instead of cutting all those dovetails again, Latta shows how to quickly replace the miscut section only.

Cut a half-dovetail at each end. This goes quickly compared to dovetailing a brand-new side completely.

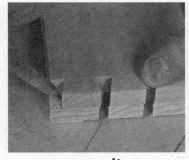

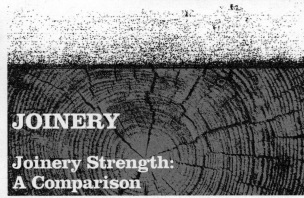

JOINERY

Joinery Strength: A Comparison

By Douglas Moore and Thomas McKenna

We Applied Racking Force

Our test used diagonal compression to simulate racking force, the most common cause of failure in frame joints. The samples were placed in a servo-hydraulic materials testing machine—essentially a hydraulic ram hooked up to a computer to record force and movement.

WHAT IS RACKING FORCE?

One example is gravity pulling down on the free side of a door, making the frame rack, or deform into a parallelogram, and creating diagonal stresses across the four joints. In other cases, just one or two joints are affected.

When it comes to making furniture, woodworkers typically base their joinery preferences on aesthetics, efficiency, and available tools.

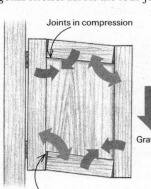

Joints in compression · Gravity · Joints in tension

The post-to-seat-rail joints take a beating when your well-fed uncle leans back at Thanksgiving.

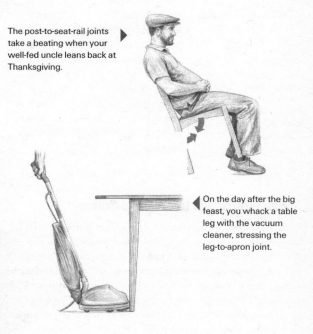

On the day after the big feast, you whack a table leg with the vacuum cleaner, stressing the leg-to-apron joint.

Continued ➜

However, joint strength also is a primary concern; after all, we want our furniture to last generations, without embarrassing joint failures. But how do you know which joint is strongest?

In an attempt to provide some insight, Fine Woodworking teamed up with a group of research engineers at a lab in Providence, R.I., to break ... er ... test a bunch of common woodworking joints.

This sounds straightforward on the surface, but many joints have specific applications within woodworking. So, to simplify things and facilitate comparisons, we focused on a single application that appears in a variety of furniture forms and offers many joinery options: the frame joint. Unlike a standing type of joint such as a dovetail or box joint, which is most often used to attach case or box sides, the frame joint is a flat connection typically used to construct face frames, doors, and other frame-and-panel assemblies. Table and chair joints would also fall roughly into this category. We made five sets each of 18 different types of joints using cherry, a species used often by furniture makers. All of the samples were ¾ in. thick by 2½ in. wide by 8 in. long, and all were cut by machine to close tolerances. We did break out hand tools to clean up shoulders and to chamfer the tips of tenons slightly so they would slide more easily into their mortises.

All of the joints were glued with Titebond III waterproof Type-I polyvinyl acetate (PVA) adhesive, the peak performer in our recent test. Per the manufacturer's instructions, we clamped the joints for at least an hour, and let them cure for five days before shipping them to the lab.

The joints were tested to failure in compression using a servohydraulic materials testing machine—essentially a powerful hydraulic ram mounted in a rigid load frame. The test was designed to simulate a racking load, the most common cause of failure in frame joints. As the joints were tested, we recorded actuator displacement and resultant force using a computerized digital data acquisition system. Then we analyzed the data to generate numbers for the average peak strength (the force at which the joint failed) for each type of joint. We also inspected the joints to determine how they'd failed.

Surprising Results

The hallowed mortise-and-tenon joint was not the strongest, even after we fattened the tenon to ⅜ in. thick. Instead, the bridle and half-lap joints, with their broad glue surfaces, withstood the most racking force. The miter was another surprise performer. Bear in mind, though, that none of these joints went through the decades of expansion and contraction that a furniture joint must endure. For other caveats, check the boxes at right. For more on each joint's performance, turn the page.

HALF LAP	1,603 lb.
bridle	1,560 lb.
splined miter	1,498 lb.
⅜-in. Mortise & Tenon	1,444 lb.
⅜-in. Floating M&T	1,396 lb.
MITER	1,374 lb.
⅜-in. Wedged M&T	1,210 lb.
⅜-in. pinned M&T	1,162 lb.
⁵⁄₁₆-in. M&T	988 lb.
BEADLOCK	836 lb.
Dowelmax	759 lb.
¼-in. M&T	717 lb.
Pocket Screw	698 lb.
Domino	597 lb.
Biscuit	545 lb.
Butt	473 lb.
COPE & STICK	313 lb.
Stub tenon	200 lb.

Some Surprises at the Top and Bottom

Before the test, we surveyed the Fine Woodworking staff and our online audience at FineWoodworking.com to find out which joint they'd predict to be strongest. Among editors, the pinned mortise and tenon was picked to finish first (it was a close race). Folks who took our online poll predicted the regular mortise and tenon would be king. It turns out, however, that the half-lap joint proved strongest in our test, with the stub tenon bringing up the rear.

Top two have lots of glue—Although we were surprised to find the half-lap and bridle at the top of the heap, in retrospect it was predictable: Both joints have large long-grain glue areas and are clamped across both faces. The only way they can fail is if one or both of the "legs" fracture across the grain.

Thicker tenons are stronger—Most of our survey respondents predicted the trusted mortise and tenon would be strongest, so it's no surprise that two ⅜-in. versions were at the top of the list. What's significant is the margin by which they outperformed their lankier ¼-in. and ⁵⁄₁₆-in. cousins. We noticed that reinforcing the joint with a pin or with wedges did not help the pieces resist racking forces; in fact, pins and wedges made the joint slightly weaker.

The lowly miter steps up—The miter has always been considered one of the weak links in the joinery world, so we were shocked to see two versions nestled near the top. The fact that the splined version did well was surprising given the reinforcement and increased long-grain glue surface provided by the spline. However, our testing configuration may have stacked the deck for both miter joints, loading the tip of the glueline in tension while compressing the fibers of each leg across the grain.

Even so, as well as the basic miter performed, it's hard to recommend it as a top-notch furniture-making joint without adding a key or spline of some kind. It has no inherent mechanical interlock, so all its strength comes from its glueline. And, as the parts expand and contract, the glueline will be stressed repeatedly and intensely, eventually opening at the outside corner. With a deep key at the outside corner, however, this joint might prove to be very strong over the long haul.

Store-bought systems prove their mettle—We tested several store-bought joinery systems (pocket screws, biscuits, Beadlock, Dowelmax, and Domino) and each put up respectable numbers. We like the fact that they all go together quickly.

Bottom of the heap—The two weakest joints were the cope-and-stick and stub tenon, coming in behind the basic butt joint. These joints are widely used to make production cabinet doors, and they are strong enough for this application, especially when reinforced with a glued-in plywood panel.

Broad Glue Surface Adds Muscle to Bridle and Half-Lap

These two heavy hitters ranked one and two in our test, with an average peak load of 1,581 lb., enough to support a full-grown cow. The two joints are similar in their geometry: Both have large glue surfaces and are clamped across their faces, which strengthens the glue bond. When stresses were applied, the joints failed only because the wood sheared across its fibers. Even though the half-lap and bridle joints have great strength, they are exposed joints, and may not look right on every project.

HALF-LAP
Peak load: 1,603 lb.
Rank: 1 of 18

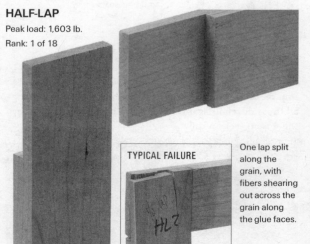

TYPICAL FAILURE

One lap split along the grain, with fibers shearing out across the grain along the glue faces.

BRIDLE
Peak load: 1,560 lb.
Rank: 2 of 18

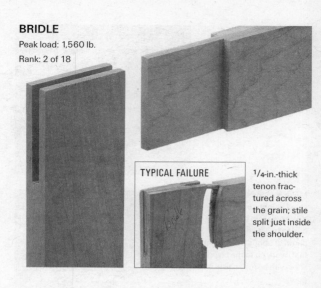

TYPICAL FAILURE

¼-in.-thick tenon fractured across the grain; stile split just inside the shoulder.

Thick Spline Adds Backbone to the Miter

Though the miter was surprisingly strong, structural limitations make it hard to recommend the unreinforced miter for furniture-making tasks. When assembled, the joint is angled at the typical 45°. However, as wood expands and contracts over time, the 45° geometry will change (see drawing, below), causing joint failure at the outside corner. The spline creates long-grain glue surface, which helps explain the splined miter's No. 3 position overall.

MITER
Peak load: 1,374 l
Rank: 6 of 18

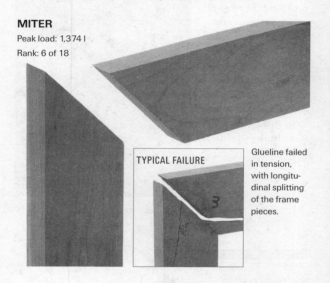

TYPICAL FAILURE

Glueline failed in tension, with longitudinal splitting of the frame pieces.

ANGLE CHANGES AS WOOD MOVES

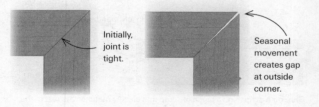

Initially, joint is tight.

Seasonal movement creates gap at outside corner.

SPLINED MITER
Peak load: 1,498 lb.
Rank: 3 of 18

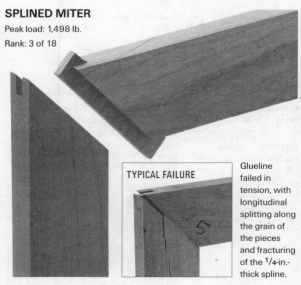

TYPICAL FAILURE

Glueline failed in tension, with longitudinal splitting along the grain of the pieces and fracturing of the ¼-in.-thick spline.

A Thicker Tenon Makes a Stronger Joint

The 3/8-in. mortise and tenon did well in the test, but the performance of thinner versions was surprisingly average. The results prove that making tenons thicker increases strength: The 3/8-in. tenon was almost twice as strong as the traditional 1/4-in. tenon. Adding pins or wedges slightly compromised joint strength; however, they do provide insurance against glueline fatigue in decades to come. A floating tenon acted just like a traditional mortise and tenon in our testing.

-IN. MORTISE AND TENON

Peak load: 1,444 lb.
Rank: 4 of 18

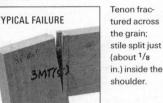

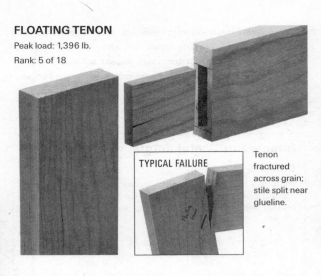

TYPICAL FAILURE — Tenon fractured across the grain; stile split just (about 1/8 in.) inside the shoulder.

SIZE MATTERS

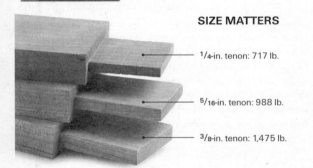

1/4-in. tenon: 717 lb.
5/16-in. tenon: 988 lb.
3/8-in. tenon: 1,475 lb.

WEDGED MORTISE AND TENON

Peak load: 1,210 lb.
Rank: 7 of 18

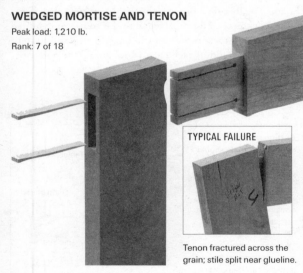

TYPICAL FAILURE — Tenon fractured across the grain; stile split near glueline.

PINNED MORTISE AND TENON

Peak load: 1,162 lb.
Rank: 8 of 18

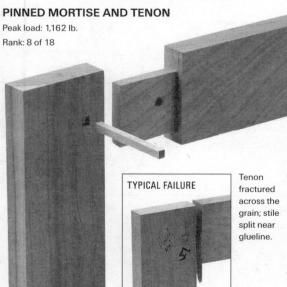

TYPICAL FAILURE — Tenon fractured across the grain; stile split near glueline.

FLOATING TENON

Peak load: 1,396 lb.
Rank: 5 of 18

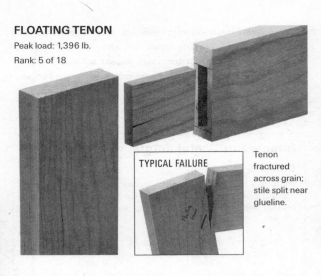

TYPICAL FAILURE — Tenon fractured across grain; stile split near glueline.

Store-Bought Tenons are a Bit Weaker Than Shopmade

Biscuits, dowels, and premade tenons are all floating tenons of a sort. In general, however, they don't reach as far into the stile as shopmade tenons, allowing the stile to split along the grain without fracturing the tenon. Though we used the manufacturer's dowels and tenons (and followed their directions), we recommend that you choose or make longer ones. Still, these fast and efficient systems made strong joints. When time is money, one of these speedy systems makes a lot of sense.

BEADLOCK

Peak load: 836 lb.
Rank: 10 of 18

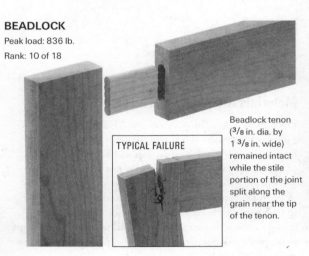

TYPICAL FAILURE — Beadlock tenon (3/8 in. dia. by 1 3/8 in. wide) remained intact while the stile portion of the joint split along the grain near the tip of the tenon.

DOWELMAX SYSTEM

Peak load: 759 lb.
Rank: 11 of 18

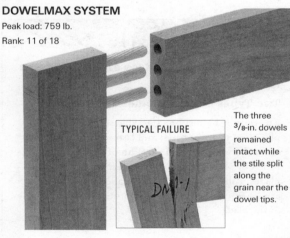

TYPICAL FAILURE — The three 3/8-in. dowels remained intact while the stile split along the grain near the dowel tips.

DOMINO BY FESTOOL

Peak load: 597 lb.
Rank: 14 of 18

TYPICAL FAILURE — Tenon (size 10x50) remained intact while the stile split along the grain near the tenon tip.

BISCUIT

Peak load: 545 lb.
Rank: 15 of 18

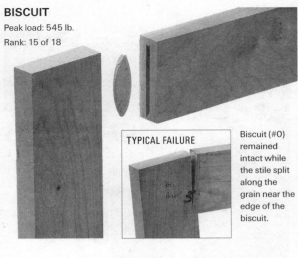

TYPICAL FAILURE — Biscuit (#0) remained intact while the stile split along the grain near the edge of the biscuit.

Glue in a Panel to Strengthen Stub Tenons

Most folks expected the butt or miter joint to bring up the rear. But it was the stub tenon and cope-and-stick joints that sank to the bottom of the pile. Even copious amounts of glue did little to help. Both are too weak to be used as-is in large doors. For real strength, stub tenons and cope-and-stick joints need a glued-in plywood panel for reinforcement.

STUB TENON

Peak load: 200 lb.
Rank: 18 of 18

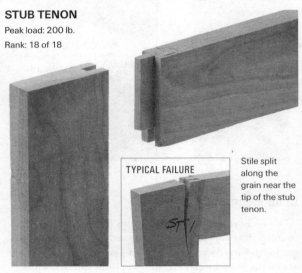

TYPICAL FAILURE — Stile split along the grain near the tip of the stub tenon.

COPE-AND-STICK

Peak load: 313 lb.
Rank: 17 of 18

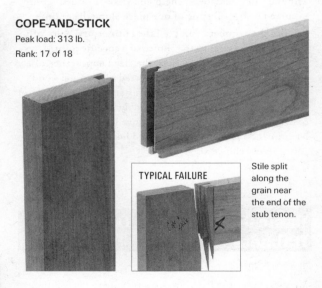

TYPICAL FAILURE — Stile split along the grain near the end of the stub tenon.

Pocket Screws Beef Up The Butt Joint

We included the butt joint in the test to serve as a baseline against the others, but it didn't perform badly. Even so, the butt joint isn't suitable for furniture because the small glue surface depends on end grain, making it very susceptible to seasonal stresses. Pocket screws increased the load capacity enough to make this joint a good option for situations where the interior of the frame is hidden.

Continued ➜

BUTT

TYPICAL FAILURE

Stile split along the glueline, tearing out fibers from the stile.

POCKET SCREWS

TYPICAL FAILURE

Stile split along the grain at the ends of the screws.

Conclusions

When we looked closely at how joints tended to fail, we found a clear correlation with our test results. The stronger joints forced their component pieces to fail by fracture across the grain or right at the glue joint (miter), while with the intermediate-strength and weakest joints, failure occurred by the splitting of one piece along the grain.

But the numbers don't tell the entire story. A lot of considerations go into the choice of a specific joint: How it will look (exposed joinery vs. the clean appearance of a hidden joint); how it will be affected by seasonal wood movement (is there mechanical resistance to keep the joint together over time?); ease of assembly (fast sometimes is best); and how it will be used (picture frame vs. apron-to-leg joint). So take all those issues to heart when making your joinery choice.

Basic Joinery with Dadoes and Rabbets

By Mario Rodriguez

My students always find it more satisfying to perfect their joinery by creating a piece of furniture rather than by adding to the kindling in the scrap bin. The dado and the rabbet are fundamental woodworking joints found in all kinds of furniture, from bookcases to highboys. Building this organizer, which either can be hung on a wall or stood on a table, allows you to practice these joints while creating a useful piece of furniture.

This piece features dadoes that run the width of the sides to support the shelves, and stopped dadoes in the upper shelf and the underside of the top to receive the partitions. Rabbets in the cabinet include those at the top of each side piece and partition as well as in the drawer

construction. Both joints provide accurate alignment of the parts, load-bearing capability, and increased glue surface. They can be cut accurately on the tablesaw, with or without a dado set, and with a router using various fences and jigs.

Simple But Useful Joints

DADOES

The dado, a square, flat-bottomed recess cut across the grain of one board to receive the end of another, can run the full width of the board or stop short of one or both edges.

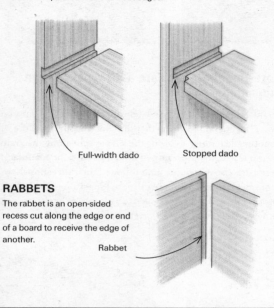

Full-width dado   Stopped dado

RABBETS

The rabbet is an open-sided recess cut along the edge or end of a board to receive the edge of another.

Rabbet

Materials Are Cheap and Easy to Find

I chose red oak as the primary wood for this project and pine for the drawer boxes and the back slats. If you can find 11-in.-wide oak boards, you will be spared the step of gluing up panels, but glue-up is not a big procedure for a project this size. The oak for the partitions needs to be thicknessed to 1/2 in., and most of the pine needs to be 3/8 in. thick; this is best done with a planer rather trying to resaw thicker stock. You will need about 18 ft. of 8-in.-wide oak boards, and 7 ft. of pine, which includes an extra 20% to be on the safe side.

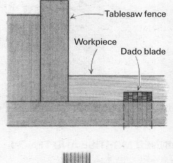

Cut Full-Length Dadoes and Rabbets on the Tablesaw

Two Types of Dado Blades are Available

The outside cutters of a stackable set of blades are placed on the arbor first and last, with chipper blades between them. The width of the cut is fine-tuned by placing metal or paper shims between the blades. Adjustable blades, also called wobble blades, can be adjusted to width by rotating a dial on the side of the blade.

Dadoes and Rabbets Can Be Cut on the Tablesaw

Most of the dadoes and rabbets for this project can be cut on the tablesaw using a set of dado blades. There are two types of dado blades: stackable blades, which consist of two outside blades to cut the sides of the joint and multiple chipper blades to remove the waste in the middle, and adjustable blades, also known as wobble blades. I prefer the stackable dado set because it makes a cleaner cut. Install a throat insert made for a dado set. Mount the two outside blades and sufficient chippers to make a cut just under 3/4 in. wide. Using a piece of surplus oak as a gauge to make test cuts, fine-tune the width by adding or removing shims between the blades until you achieve a snug fit.

Each side piece gets a pair of dadoes for the shelves, and the top and bottom shelves each receives one narrow dado for the drawer divider. Dadoes shallower than 1/4 in. deep can be cut in one pass, but feed the workpiece slowly to achieve a clean cut and avoid straining the motor. Use the rip fence to guide the location of each dado, making the same cut on both side pieces before adjusting the fence for the next dado. Apply firm downward pressure on the workpiece to ensure that the depth of each dado is consistent throughout its length.

Even though the cut for the rabbets on the top of each side piece is 3/8 in. square, there is no need to reset the width of the dado set. Instead, clamp a piece of 3/4-in.-thick plywood or medium-density fiberboard (MDF) to the rip fence, locate the fence for the cut, and gradually raise the blade so that it eats into this sacrificial fence.

The final cuts with the dado blade are 1/8-in.-deep by 3/16-in.-wide rabbets on both sides of each end of the three partitions, and 3/16-in.-deep by 1/4-in.-wide rabbets on overlapping sides of the pine back slats. Known as a shiplap joint, this allows the boards to move seasonally without creating a gap between them.

Stopped Dadoes Are Best Cut with a Router

On this project the partitions are secured in stopped dadoes in the upper shelf and the top.

The stopped dadoes must be cut in identical positions on the top shelf and the underside of the top piece. To achieve this I use a rub collar (also called a template guide) in conjunction with a template. The collar has a tubelike piece of metal that surrounds the router bit and guides it by means of a template placed on the workpiece. When laying out the job and making the router template, the difference between the outer diameter of the rub collar (in this case 9/16 in.) and the router bit (1/4 in.) must be taken into account. Blocks of wood glued to the underside of the template act as stops to ensure accurate placement on both of the pieces to be cut.

I also use the router to cut 3/8-in.-square stopped dadoes on the sides for the back slats and on the underside of the top for the sides. Because these cuts are near the edges of the workpiece, a fence attached to the router and guided by these edges works well. You will need to stop the router just before the end of each cut and square up the end with a chisel.

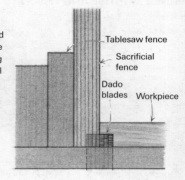

Cutting a dado. The depth of the dado should equal about a third of the wood's thickness. Apply constant pressure both against the fence and downward to ensure that the cut is consistent in depth across the piece. With narrow workpieces, use a miter gauge for guidance and support.

Tablesaw fence
Workpiece
Dado blade

Cutting a rabbet. After cutting the dadoes for the shelves, flip the board and cut the rabbet on the top of each side, creating a narrow tongue that will enter the top. To avoid damage to the rip fence, clamp on a sacrificial plywood fence.

Tablesaw fence
Sacrificial fence
Dado blades
Workpiece

Small Storage Case Assembles Easily

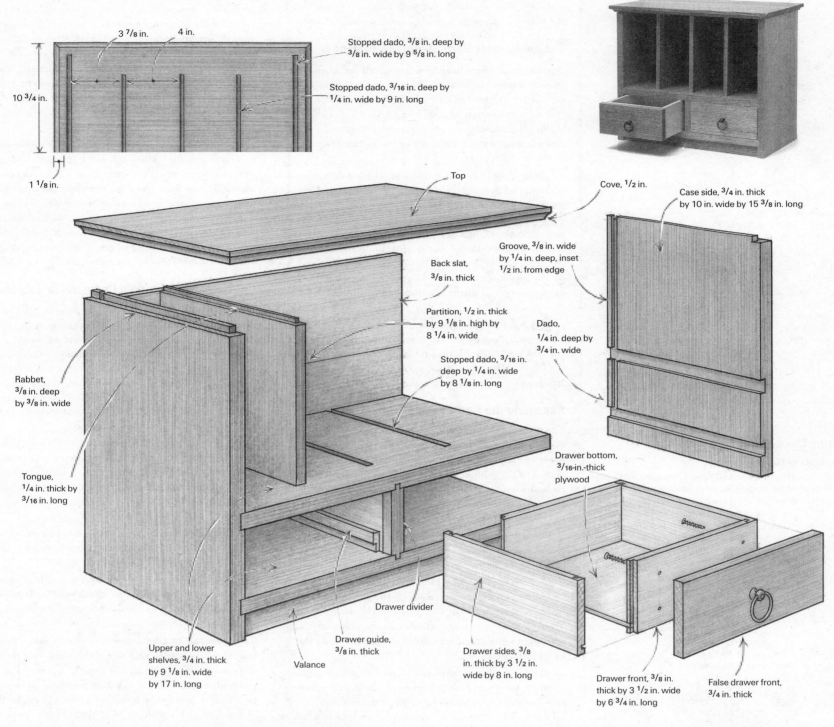

3 7/8 in.   4 in.

Stopped dado, 3/8 in. deep by 3/8 in. wide by 9 5/8 in. long

Stopped dado, 3/16 in. deep by 1/4 in. wide by 9 in. long

10 3/4 in.

1 1/8 in.

Top

Cove, 1/2 in.

Case side, 3/4 in. thick by 10 in. wide by 15 3/8 in. long

Back slat, 3/8 in. thick

Groove, 3/8 in. wide by 1/4 in. deep, inset 1/2 in. from edge

Partition, 1/2 in. thick by 9 1/8 in. high by 8 1/4 in. wide

Dado, 1/4 in. deep by 3/4 in. wide

Stopped dado, 3/16 in. deep by 1/4 in. wide by 8 1/8 in. long

Rabbet, 3/8 in. deep by 3/8 in. wide

Drawer bottom, 3/16-in.-thick plywood

Tongue, 1/4 in. thick by 3/16 in. long

Upper and lower shelves, 3/4 in. thick by 9 1/8 in. wide by 17 in. long

Valance

Drawer divider

Drawer guide, 3/8 in. thick

Drawer sides, 3/8 in. thick by 3 1/2 in. wide by 8 in. long

Drawer front, 3/8 in. thick by 3 1/2 in. wide by 6 3/4 in. long

False drawer front, 3/4 in. thick

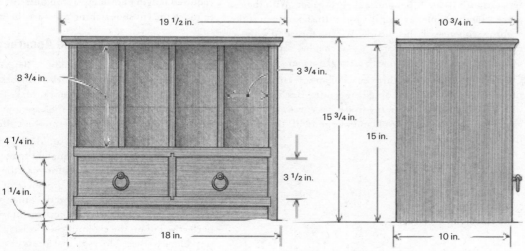

19 1/2 in.

10 3/4 in.

8 3/4 in.

3 3/4 in.

15 3/4 in.

15 in.

4 1/4 in.

3 1/2 in.

1 1/4 in.

18 in.

10 in.

Red oak is the primary wood for this project because it is handsome, hard wearing, and not difficult to work. Pine was used for the drawer boxes and the back slats. Both woods are readily available at home centers at a moderate price. Look for oak boards that are quartersawn (growth rings perpendicular to the face of the board) for a sleek, high-quality appearance. Most home-center lumber is milled to 3/4-in. thickness, so the board's grain should be easy to see.

Continued →

A Quick Drawer Joint Made with Dadoes and Rabbets

The front, back, and sides of the drawer boxes are connected by dado and rabbet joints cut on the tablesaw. The false fronts are mounted with screws after the drawers have been assembled.

Drawer-box front

Rabbet, 1/4 in. by 3/16 in.

Dado, 1/8 in. wide by 3/16 in. deep

Drawer side

False drawer front

Groove for drawer bottom, 3/16 in. by 3/16 in.

The template guides the router. A rub collar (or template guide) screwed to the router base runs against the template, guiding the router bit.

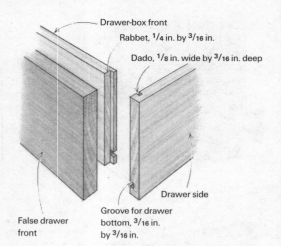

Routing Dadoes

Use a Template for Matching Dadoes

The partitions are secured in stopped dadoes in the upper shelf and the underside of the top. Because the cuts must be in matching positions, use a rub collar (also called a template guide) in conjunction with a template. Make the template out of a piece of plywood and cut guide slots and access holes for the router bit and rub collar.

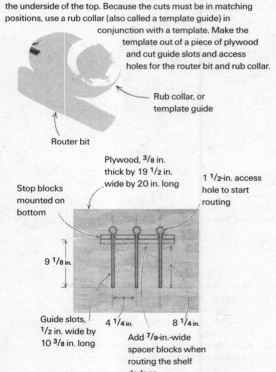

Rub collar, or template guide

Router bit

Plywood, 3/8 in. thick by 19 1/2 in. wide by 20 in. long

1 1/2-in. access hole to start routing

Stop blocks mounted on bottom

9 1/8 in.

Guide slots, 1/2 in. wide by 10 3/8 in. long

4 1/4 in.

8 1/4 in.

Add 7/8-in.-wide spacer blocks when routing the shelf dadoes.

While you have the router out, now's a good time to profile the edge of the top. Although the piece shown here has a cove on the underside of the front and sides of the top piece, you may prefer the look of a chamfer. Regardless, use a bearing-guided bit running along the edge of the workpiece. For a clean cut with minimal tearout or burning, make the cut in two stages with the second cut at the final depth removing only a small amount of wood.

Cut the Drawer Parts Using the Tablesaw

Because the drawers have false fronts and are fitted with guides, it is safe to make up the drawer boxes before the carcase is assembled. The front, back, and sides of the boxes are connected by dado and rabbet joints cut on the tablesaw: First cut two dadoes on each side piece; the distance from the end is determined by the thickness of the front and back pieces.

Because the next cut is made with only a thin section of wood in contact with the tablesaw, install a zero-clearance insert around the sawblade to prevent the workpiece from getting wedged between the table and the blade. In two cuts you can make rabbets on the ends of the drawer back and sides to create a tongue that connects with the dadoes on the drawer sides. Before assembling the boxes, cut grooves on the inside of the front and sides, and cut away the back of the drawers so that the bottom can be slid in.

The drawer partition simply is a 3/4-in.-thick piece of pine that is joined to the two shelves with 1/4-in. dadoes. These can be cut on the tablesaw with two passes over a conventional blade. To avoid having end grain exposed on the front of the cabinet, use a tongue-and-groove joint to attach a thin facing piece of oak.

Assemble the Carcase and Fit the Drawers

You will find that the assembly of this project will be much easier to do on a pair of sawhorses, because the gap between the horses allows more room for clamping. Glue the shelves to the cabinet sides and slide in the drawer divider from the front. When these joints are dry, slide in the back slats, glue in the three partitions, and then glue on the top. Screw the center of each back slat to the sides.

Before fitting the drawers, mill some rabbeted drawer guides from pine and set them in place with glue. The rabbet along the bottom and the fact that they are 1 1/2 in. short allow them to be trimmed in place with a block plane.

Once you have achieved a snug fit for each drawer box, mark its location on the back of each false drawer front. Transfer the location of the holes on the drawer box and drill pilot holes in the false front to avoid splitting the wood with the screws.

The last pieces to add are a valance that is set just in from the sides and glued to the lower shelf, and a two-part French cleat if you are going to hang the organizer on a wall. Before assembly you should sand the interior sections with 100-, 150-, and 220-grit paper. With the piece assembled, plane all of the joints flush and repeat the sanding sequence on the outside. Wiping the wood with denatured alcohol will reveal any glue that has squeezed out. Sand these areas again with 220-grit paper.

Finish the wood with three coats of an oil-varnish mixture, such as Waterlox, sanding between the first two coats with 220-grit paper. When the finish has cured, rub the cabinet with 0000 steel wool, and wax and buff the wood for a smooth, satin finish.

Master the Miter Joint

By Gary Rogowski

The attraction of a miter joint is easy to see. It is an elegant and straightforward method for joining parts that meet at an angle without showing any end grain. Whether you are building the frame for a veneered panel (tabletops, case goods), applying wrap-around molding or constructing a simple picture frame, a miter joint will serve your needs. But as the saying goes, the devil is in the details. The very visibility of the miter joint means that errors in machining or assembly are hard to conceal. However, with a little patience and lots of practice cutting and assembling miters, you too can master the joint.

Generally used for right-angle corners between two boards of equal thickness and width, miters are made with matching cuts. These cuts are at 45° so no end grain shows. But the miter joint isn't reliable solely as a glue joint for most constructions. Where any real tenacity is required, strengthening with biscuits, splines or keys is always the prudent choice. In short, to get perfect miters requires perfectly mating joints, a slip-proof gluing system and at least one form of strengthening.

Cut Miter Joints with a Chopsaw or Tablesaw

No matter what type of saw you cut miters with, use a sharp, clean blade. Generally the more teeth to a blade, the smoother the cut, but no blade will cut well if it's dull or covered with pitch. Every cut is made in two directions: at 45° across the width of a board and at 90° across its face. For a miter to close up well, both angles need to be cut exactly. Make rough adjustments using a plastic 45° drafting triangle, then take several practice cuts, checking the results with a combination square.

A chopsaw works great at cutting miters. Just make sure the fence is flat and straight. If necessary, add an auxiliary fence and shim it to make it square to the table. Frame parts can lie flat on the chopsaw table. Angle the blade 45° to the fence to make the cuts. Clamp stops onto the auxiliary fence to index matching cuts.

When cutting miters on a tablesaw, you'll get the best results using a jig that holds your work to move it past the blade.

The miter gauge is, of course, the standard jig used for cutting miters. Be sure to check your settings for the angle of cut. Attach an auxiliary fence to the miter gauge to support the workpiece near the blade.

When cutting frame miters, angle the gauge down and away from the blade. This way, if the workpiece slips, it will slide away from the blade, not into it. A piece of sandpaper glued to the fence will help prevent slipping. Make certain that your gauge is cutting a true 45° angle, then cut one end of each matching part. Measure and mark off the required length and clamp a stop onto the auxiliary fence to index the cut so matching parts are the same length.

Picture-Frame Jig Ensures Accuracy

A picture-frame jig has four parts: a flat base, two runners, a fence and clamping blocks. The base can be made of any flat 1/2-in.-thick sheet stock. Make the runners, which attach to the bottom of the base, out of quartersawn hardwood, so seasonal movement won't affect their fit.

The fence of the jig is 3/4-in.-thick plywood. Cut the corner of the fence at a right angle, then screw it to the base. It won't matter if it's mounted a little off a true 45° angle as long as you always cut one piece of the miter joint on the left side of the fence and the other on the right side. The cuts will always be complementary and mate perfectly. Put on the clamping blocks last. You can clamp a stop block to these blocks to make cuts of uniform length.

Miter-Gauge Tune-Up

Although the miter gauge is the standard jig for cutting miters, the basic model can be improved with several simple modifications.

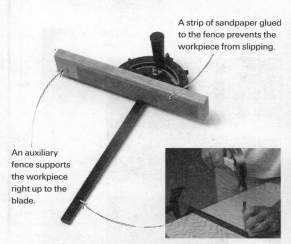

A strip of sandpaper glued to the fence prevents the workpiece from slipping.

An auxiliary fence supports the workpiece right up to the blade.

A tighter fit. If your miter gauge has some side-to-side slop in the miter slot, punch the edge of the gauge bar with a center punch. This spreads out the metal to tighten the fit.

MAKE A TEST CUT AND CHECK FOR SQUARE

To set the miter gauge at exactly 45°, first align a drafting triangle against the miter slot in the tablesaw (top). Make a cut in a piece of scrapwood (lower left). Flip over the cut-off piece and hold both pieces tightly against a square (lower right). Adjust the miter gauge until there is no gap, and you are set to cut perfect miters.

Picture Frame Jig

Cut adjoining parts on opposite sides of the jig to guarantee a 90° joint.

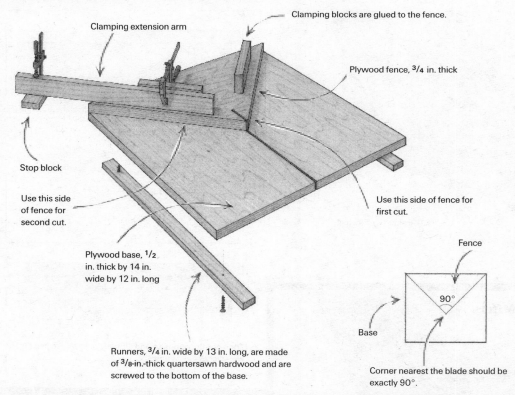

Clamping extension arm

Clamping blocks are glued to the fence.

Plywood fence, 3/4 in. thick

Stop block

Use this side of fence for second cut.

Plywood base, 1/2 in. thick by 14 in. wide by 12 in. long

Runners, 3/4 in. wide by 13 in. long, are made of 3/8-in.-thick quartersawn hardwood and are screwed to the bottom of the base.

Use this side of fence for first cut.

Fence

90°

Base

Corner nearest the blade should be exactly 90°.

The first cut is made on the left-hand side of the jig. If the work slips, it will do so away from the blade.

Uniform length. Mark the length on the workpiece and on the right-hand fence. Clamp a stop block against the mitered end.

Make the second cut on the right-hand side of the jig. With the stop block in place, you are assured of consistent cuts.

Fine-Tune the Fit Before Glue-Up

After cutting the miters, do yourself a favor and take some time to prepare them for gluing. First check your cuts to see how well your saw performed. There are several ways to remedy a cut that is less than smooth. Trim the miter with a low-angle block plane, tuned up with a freshly sharpened blade. Put the workpiece in a vise and take a few light passes off each mating face, but don't change the angle. Check your results with a combination square.

A disc sander outfitted with a miter-gauge jig can also be used to fine-tune miters. This jig rides in the slot in the sander table and has a plate on it cut at 90° but positioned 45° to the sanding disc. Work on both sides of this fence to ensure that mating pieces get complementary cuts, but always work on the left side of the moving disc. In this way your work will always get pushed down into the supporting table. Take only light passes, and try to move the work past the disc so you don't burn the wood or load up the disc in one spot. Before starting, double-check that the sander's table is exactly 90° to the disc.

A third method of trimming is to use a shooting board. A stop angled 45° on both sides is screwed to the base. When used with a square-sided plane, this jig will trim the miter at 45° across its width and at 90° to its face.

Even Clamping Pressure Is Critical

Wood is made up like a bundle of straws. Crosscut or miter the end of a board, and you expose the ends of those straws, which suck up glue and starve a joint, weakening it. The faces of a miter joint should be sized by precoating them with a light wash of glue to fill the pores. Scrape off any excess glue before it dries. Despite the normal warning not to apply glue to an already glued surface, in this case sizing will strengthen the glue joint.

Dry-fit and clamp everything before the final glue-up, and you'll thank yourself later for your calm demeanor and slow heart rate. Mind you, I am a yellow-glue devotee, so all of this advice comes from using quick-setting glue, not some expansive, messy polymer.

Band clamps fit around a box or a picture frame to apply even pressure to the miter joints. Practice locating and tightening the band clamp in place right over the joint. Use several clamps for wider glue-ups, and stagger the clamp heads so they're not in each other's way.

You can put clamping corners over the joint to help spread the pressure. Some band clamps come with self-adjusting corners suitable for any angle; you can also buy aftermarket versions. Again, practice with these systems before gluing.

When gluing up miters with splines or keys that would interfere with a band clamp, I use shopmade clamping blocks clamped right onto the frame side. These blocks have a notch cut right into them where you can place another clamp to apply pressure directly across the joint. If your clamping blocks slip too much, glue a piece of sandpaper to them on the side that rests against the workpiece.

How to Strengthen Miters

Reinforce miter joints by using splines or biscuits, which are inserted before the joint is glued up, or keys, which are added after glue-up. Which method you use is determined by several factors, the most important being aesthetic considerations. Do you want to conceal the strengthening for a seamless look, as with a gilded picture frame, or do you prefer to emphasize it, as with face-frame keys? The second factor is the difficulty and length of time involved.

Splined miters in frames—Through spline cuts are made along the length of the miter. They're most easily made on the tablesaw. Use a spline-cutting jig to support the workpiece at a 45° angle to the blade. Make this jig out of a straight piece of 3/4-in.-thick plywood and a support piece glued and screwed on at a 45° angle. Make certain that your fasteners are higher than the tablesaw blade at its highest setting.

Continued ➔

With your frame piece in the jig, set the fence so that the sawkerf is centered in the thickness of the stock. If it's not, the faces of your frame members will not be flush. One way to prevent this is by having a miter jig with two fences on it for each side of the miter. The jig is rotated 90° to cut the spline in the adjoining workpiece.

Set the blade height for a 1/4-in.- to 3/8-in.-deep cut, but no deeper. Because the grain direction of a spline in a solid-wood frame has to run in the same direction as the frame members, too deep a spline cut makes for a wide and fragile spline. Hold or clamp the work firmly in the jig. Place your hands carefully out of harm's way and make a pass. Use a flat-grind blade to put a flat bottom on the cut.

Mill up the spline material out of a contrasting wood to set off the joint. Using a tenoning jig, hold the board vertically and run it past the blade to trim your spline to thickness. Then cut the spline to length. If your spline doesn't quite fit, use a block plane to trim it to thickness. Be careful not to snap the short grain of the spline as you plane. You're looking for a snug fit, not one that's overly tight.

Fit one side of the spline and check to see that it will let the joint close up nicely. Trim its end grain with a block plane, if needed. Size the end grain of the miter, then put glue in one of the spline cuts with a thin piece of wood. Set the spline in place all the way down to the bottom of the groove. Then put glue on the rest of the joint and clamp it up. If the fit is a bit loose, clamp across the face of the joint as well. You can also pin this spline in place with dowels for extra strength and an additional design detail.

Biscuit splines—You can also strengthen a miter with a biscuit joint. Mark the frame members across their faces with a pencil at the center of the joint or closer toward the inside corner of the joint so that the cut won't show at the corners. Center the joiner in the thickness of the stock. Support or clamp the frame members securely, and hold the joiner tight to the miter as you cut.

Keys Can Reinforce Miter Joints

Mitered frames may also be reinforced after glue-up using exposed keys. These keys are inserted into mitered corners from the outside after cutting the appropriately sized slots. Slots may be cut on a tablesaw or on a router table.

Cutting straight keys on the tablesaw—A keyed miter jig works great for holding a glued-up frame in place while you pass it through the sawblade (see the photos and drawings on this page). Set the blade height for the full depth of cut, and use a flat-grind blade if you have one. Cut each corner, holding the same face of the frame to the jig.

Mill up key stock wider than the depth of the key cut. Trim the stock to thickness on the tablesaw. You should use a thin push stick to help you move the work safely past the blade. Use a handplane to trim the key exactly to thickness, then cut it longer than necessary.

Fit keys in their cuts so that they're snug and only require a light tap to position them. Make sure when gluing that they fit all the way down in the key cut at both its sides. Once the keys are dry, clean them up on the bandsaw. Sight along the edge of your frame as you make the cut so you don't cut into the piece. Then handplane away from the corner in each direction to trim the key flush. If you plane toward the corner, you will tear out the tip of the key.

Cutting face-keyed miters—Face-keyed miters for frames probably originated when someone made a straight key cut in the wrong spot. It was a pretty mistake. Make these cuts using the keyed miter jig on the tablesaw. Place the cut just on the outside edge of each corner on both faces of the frame. Make up key stock as before, but this time just make it conveniently thick. When gluing, make sure the keys fit down to the bottom of the cut on both sides of the joint. Put clamps across the keys to hold them in place. The final step is to plane the keys flush with the face of the frame, being careful of the contrasting grain directions.

Splined Miters

Splines are cut prior to the joint being glued. They strengthen the joint by providing a face-grain glue surface.

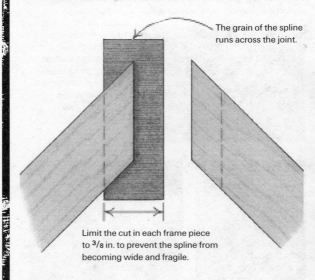

The grain of the spline runs across the joint.

Limit the cut in each frame piece to 3/8 in. to prevent the spline from becoming wide and fragile.

SPLINE-CUTTING JIG
This jig has two 45° fences, which allow miters to be cut on both ends of the workpiece while keeping the same face registered against the jig. All parts are made of 3/4-in.-thick plywood.

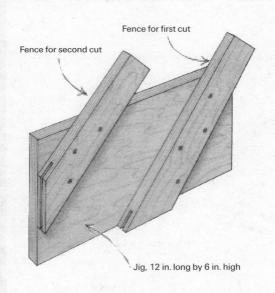

Fence for first cut

Fence for second cut

Jig, 12 in. long by 6 in. high

Keyed Miters

FACE KEY   STRAIGHT KEY

Keys are added after the joint has been glued. Both face keys and straight keys add to the glue area of the joint.

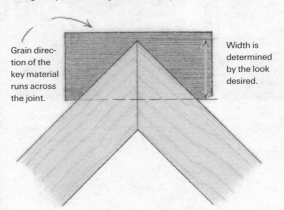

Grain direction of the key material runs across the joint.

Width is determined by the look desired.

Cutting the spline. Use a tenoning jig to trim the spline to thickness.

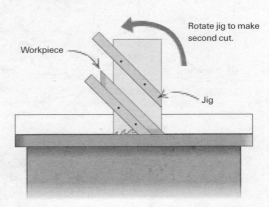
No band clamps here. Because the spline extends beyond the outside corner, it is necessary to use block clamps.

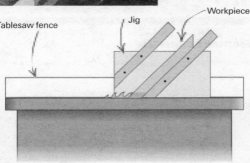

Tablesaw fence   Jig   Workpiece

Cut one end. Hold the workpiece firmly in place and register the jig against the tablesaw fence.

Rotate jig to make second cut.

Workpiece

Jig

Then cut the opposite end. Rotate the jig and register the workpiece against the other fence.

KEY-CUTTING JIG
Use this jig to cut straight keys as well as face keys in mitered frames.

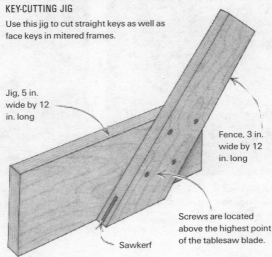

Jig, 5 in. wide by 12 in. long

Fence, 3 in. wide by 12 in. long

Screws are located above the highest point of the tablesaw blade.

Sawkerf

One jig cuts two keys. Simply by adjusting the fence of the tablesaw, the key-cutting jig can cut either straight keys in the center of the frame or face keys on the front of the frame.

Quick Mortises with a Drill and Chisels

By Christian Becksvoort

Many woodworkers cut mortises by drilling away much of the waste with a drill press, then cleaning up what remains using a bench chisel. The technique is popular because it doesn't require a special machine or jig. It's a challenge, though, mainly because the chiseling process is slow and easily goes awry.

I've been building furniture full time for more than 30 years, and I still use drilling and chiseling to make many of my mortises. But I've managed to refine the process to just a few surefire steps.

The tools are simple. After removing most of the waste using the drill press, I use a mortising chisel to square an end and lever away—in one shot—most of the waste. A bench chisel quickly cleans up what's left.

This method delivers clean, accurate mortises, and quickly. Including the drill-press work, I can finish a 3/8-in.-thick by 1½-in.-wide by 1½-in.-deep mortise in about 4 to 5 minutes. By the way, if you don't have a drill press, use a doweling jig and handheld drill to remove the waste accurately.

Mortise Chisel Is the Star

A bench chisel is ideal for a lot of applications, but it's not the best choice to clean up the waste after drilling a mortise.

When driving a bench chisel with a mallet to square the end of the mortise, the chisel tends to twist. That's because the blade is relatively thin and the edges are beveled, so there is little side support. Typically, you'll need to start and stop the cut several times to keep it on track. And chances are it won't be as clean a cut as you'd like.

It's also challenging to keep a bench chisel square when cleaning up the sides. So the mortise may not end up straight and smooth. Plus, compared to my method, it's slow.

The solution is a mortise chisel. They come in two basic types: One has a blade with a rectangular cross-section (parallel sides), and the other has a blade with a trapezoidal cross-section (tapered sides). You want the rectangular one. A rectangular mortising chisel won't twist easily as you bang it with a mallet to square the end of the mortise. And because the corners of the chisel meet at sharp right angles, you get a shearing cut when you lever it forward. That means much of the sidewall waste can be removed in one quick motion.

In addition, while bench chisels are normally sharpened to 25°, most mortising chisels are sharpened to 30°. That means the sharpened edge is less likely to fracture when levered.

Last, mortising chisels are thicker and longer than bench chisels. That adds stiffness and leverage, making them better suited to the forceful levering action.

It takes just four steps to cut any mortise. But first, make sure your chisels are sharp.

Keep in mind that this technique requires that the mortise and the mortising chisel are the same width. That means if you want a 3/8-in.-wide mortise, you need a 3/8-in.-wide mortising chisel. I find that three different chisel widths—1/4 in., 3/8 in., and 1/2 in.—cover almost any mortise I need.

Layout is Critical

Begin by carefully laying out and marking the length and width of the mortise. Use a sharp pencil to mark the ends. Then use a marking gauge to cut the two scribe lines for the sides. Now, with a square and a marking knife, cut scribe lines at the mortise ends. The cut lines are important: When you slip the sharpened edge of the chisel into them, they align it perfectly for the start of the cut.

Drill Out the Waste

Now you're ready to start removing waste wood to create the mortise. You could remove all the waste with the mortise chisel, but it's a lot faster to remove most of it by drilling a series of holes. Plus, drilling makes it easier to maintain a consistent depth along the length of the mortise.

I put the drill press to work here. Either a brad-point or Forstner bit works fine. Both of these bits let you drill overlapping holes to remove the maximum waste from the mortise. Just be sure that the bit diameter is the same as the mortise width, and position the fence carefully so that all the holes are bored dead-center into the mortise.

Start by drilling the first hole at one end of the mortise, and then do the same at the other end. After that, drill as many non-overlapping holes as possible. Then cut overlapping holes as needed to remove most of the remaining waste.

Plunge and Lever

With most of the waste drilled out, mark the depth of the mortise on the chisel blade. Place the tip of the cutting edge into the scribe line on one end with the bevel facing away from the end. Make sure the chisel is plumb. Also, with thin stock, it's a good idea to clamp the sides of the stock at the mortise so it won't split.

Now, use the mallet to pound the chisel to the full depth. Keep the chisel plumb as you go (see tip).

Once you reach the full depth, lever the chisel forward, toward the opposite end of the mortise. This is where the rectangular chisel pays big dividends. Because the chisel sides are parallel, their leading edges slice away—in one quick motion—a good portion of the waste at one end. Repeat the cut-and-lever technique on the opposite end. If the wood is hard, use both hands and lean into the chisel a bit.

Just a Bit of Cleanup Left

You now have only a small triangular section of waste in the middle of the mortise. Since this is mainly a paring operation, use a normal, bevel-edged bench chisel. Simply start at the top of the waste triangle and carefully pare down to the bottom. Use the mortise chisel to clean up what remains.

TIP

Keep the mortise at least 3/4 in. away from the end of the workpiece. Otherwise the end-grain at the end of the mortise could blow out when you drive in the chisel.

STEP 1 **Scribe Lines Show the Way**

Scribe the sides. After marking the location with a pencil, use a marking gauge to scribe each side of the mortise, stopping at the pencil lines.

Scribe the ends. To complete the layout, use a knife to scribe a cut line at each end of the mortise.

Mark the depth. With an ink marker and a square, mark the mortise depth on the blade of the chisel.

Drive the chisel. Place the tip of the chisel into the cut line on one end of the mortise (bevel facing away from the end), then use a mallet to drive it to the full mortise depth.

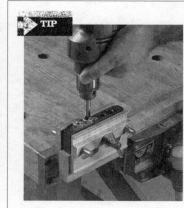

TIP

No drill press? Use a doweling jig. It's nearly as fast and just as accurate as a drill press.

STEP 2 Drill the Waste

SETUP

Drill press does the grunt work. Use a bit that matches the mortise width. Clamp a fence to the table to ensure that the bit drills into the center of the piece.

Dial it in. After drilling a single hole in the test piece, use a dial caliper to make sure the hole is centered.

DRILLING SEQUENCE

Drill the end holes and 'tweeners. With the stock against the fence, drill a hole at each end of the mortise. In between, drill as many non-overlapping holes as possible (left), leaving 1/8 in. between holes. Then drill overlapping holes, anchoring the center spur in the material between each hole to help keep the bit from drifting.

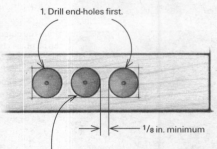

1. Drill end-holes first.

← 1/8 in. minimum

2. Drill non-overlapping holes second.

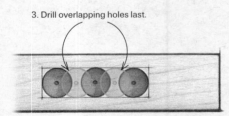

3. Drill overlapping holes last.

STEP 3 The Mortise Chisel Trick

Lever the chisel. Lever the chisel toward the opposite end of the mortise. As you do, the square corners of the mortise chisel shave a good part of the waste stock. Repeat from the other end. The levering trick removes all but a small triangle of waste (see drawing, below).

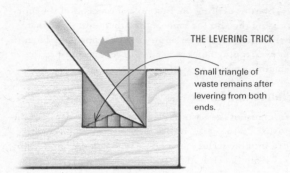

THE LEVERING TRICK

Small triangle of waste remains after levering from both ends.

STEP 4 Finish with a Bench Chisel

Clean out the last of the waste. A bench chisel removes the remaining triangle. Elapsed chiseling time for both the mortise and bench chisels: one to two minutes.

TIP

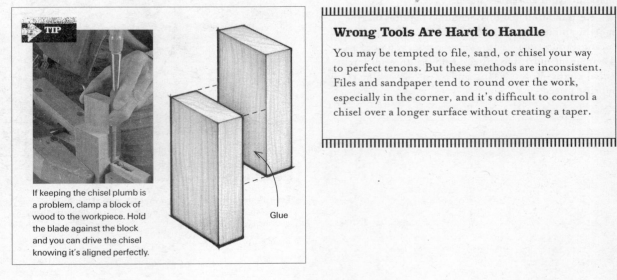

If keeping the chisel plumb is a problem, clamp a block of wood to the workpiece. Hold the blade against the block and you can drive the chisel knowing it's aligned perfectly.

Glue

Fitting Tenons with Hand-planes

By Chris Gochnour

A lot of woodworkers choose to cut tenons with a tablesaw, thinking it will be fast and dead-on, only to get frustrated when their "precise" setup results in ill-fitting cheeks or misaligned shoulders. Truth is, it's hard to cut perfect-fitting tenons using just machinery, whether a tablesaw, a router, or a bandsaw. A better approach is to cut the tenon close and dial in the fit using hand tools. But is there one that's best for the job?

To find the answer, I compared shoulder planes, rabbet block planes, fillister planes, and bullnose planes to see which one is best for trimming tenon shoulders and cheeks. All are essentially planes designed to cut into corners, leaving crisp, square edges and removing material methodically in a way that power tools cannot.

What to Look for in a Tenon Trimmer

For a plane to be effective at trimming tenon cheeks and shoulders, it must have some basic characteristics. First, it must be adept at cross-grain and end-grain cuts, so it should have a low cutting angle. Precision manufacturing also is critical, and the way the blade aligns with the body is important for peak performance. The blade should silhouette the body accurately, projecting slightly (about 0.002 in.—the thickness of a sheet of paper) beyond each side and parallel with the sole to achieve the desired amount of cut. If the blade projects excessively from the side of the plane, it will dig into and mark the joint's side. If it doesn't project enough, the plane is pushed away from the corner and produces a sloping or wandering cut.

The sole of the plane should be flat and the plane sides should be perfectly square to the sole. The blade should hold up to the rigors of end-grain planing. As with any handplane, the depth and lateral adjustments should be easy and should hold. Finally, since these planes may be used in multiple positions, the body should be comfortable to grip with one or two hands.

The Right Planes for the Job

I used all of the planes on tablesawn tenons to fine-tune the shoulders and cheeks, a job that involves tricky end-grain and cross-grain work. The stock was cherry, and the tenons were 1/4 in. thick by 4 in. wide by 1-1/4 in. long. I judged the planes based on the test, as well as on their fit and finish and ergonomics.

After all the testing, bullnose and fillister planes fell out of contention while shoulder and block rabbet planes rose to the fore. With their low cutting angle, both of these planes handle end-grain and cross-grain cuts. And they're made for use with one or two hands, so you can hold them in a number of positions to handle any trimming job.

I'd recommend buying a shoulder plane first, and adding a rabbet block plane later (see "Which Ones to Buy, and in What Order, next page).

Wrong Tools Are Hard to Handle

You may be tempted to file, sand, or chisel your way to perfect tenons. But these methods are inconsistent. Files and sandpaper tend to round over the work, especially in the corner, and it's difficult to control a chisel over a longer surface without creating a taper.

Trim a Tenon for a Perfect Fit

The key to achieving a piston fit is working methodically. Cut the tenon on the tablesaw (or other machine), and then carefully trim the shoulders and cheeks with a shoulder plane and rabbet block plane.

TIP

HOW TO DIAL IN MACHINE CUTS
To reduce the amount of hand-trimming you need to do, cut the tenon close enough that a corner just fits into the mortise. Subsequent handwork will be quick.

SHOULDERS

Lower the step. One of the most common problems with a tablesawn tenon is a step (right), or uneven shoulder that leaves a visible gap in the joint. To fix it, take a light pass with the shoulder plane (below), toward the step, starting near the middle. Take progressively longer strokes until the step is almost gone.

Then level the shoulder. Once the step is almost gone, go back in the other direction. One advantage of the shoulder plane is that you can pull it easily toward you. One or two passes should do the trick.

CHEEKS

A wide berth. To trim long tenons with a shoulder plane (below left) requires overlapping passes, which could taper the tenon if you're not careful. The wider rabbet block plane (below right) is more efficient and helps ensure a flat surface.

Fillister and Bullnose Planes Don't Make the Cut

Bullnose and fillister planes are not designed to trim tenon cheeks and shoulders. The bullnose plane has too short of a nose and does not register properly to start a cut. The fillister is really a joint-making tool, made for cutting rabbets and raised panels. It's not designed to be used on its side for trimming shoulders, and it's too long to use with one hand, a necessary trait for trimming tenons with the workpiece supported on a bench hook.

Which Ones to Buy, and in What Order

With its tall body, a shoulder plane is ideal for trimming tenon shoulders, offering great control while keeping your hands away from the work. It also can be used to trim tenon cheeks. Buy the biggest one you can (see recommendations, opposite page), which can handle any size shoulder and any tenon cheek.

The problem with a shoulder plane, even a large one, is that it's not the most efficient tool for cheeks, requiring multiple overlapping passes to tackle long tenons, which could result in a tapered tenon if you're not careful. That job is best handled by a rabbet block plane, which has a wider blade (see recommendations, above). Though it can be used on a shoulder, its short body is a bit harder to hold on its side.

Out of both, the first one I'd recommend is the large shoulder plane, because it can do both shoulders and tenons pretty easily. Ideally, though, if you can afford it, add a rabbet block plane for cheeks. With both tools you'll be set up to trim tenons perfectly every time, quickly and efficiently.

Through Mortise-and-Tenon Joinery

By Jim Richey

It's hard to hide mistakes in through mortise-and-tenon joints. Both the tenon and the mortise are there for anyone to see. I found it tough to get crisp, chip-free mortises that were uniform and had clean, square corners. Then, not too long ago, I came across a drawing of a simple bench made from 1 x 12 stock, like the one shown in the photo below. I wanted to build several of them, but the joint that held the bench together was a wedged through mortise and tenon. The bench was an incentive. I worked on my technique and experimented with prototypes until I could cut this joint quickly and accurately.

In a through mortise and tenon, the tenon goes all the way through its mating piece and shows on the other side. Wedges are often added to spread the end of the tenon and lock the joint together. It's a strong, attractive joint.

I can cut the mortises by hand, but when I'm faced with making a lot of them, I like to use a machine. In my shop, that means using either the drill press or the router. I prefer using the drill press because it's quiet and setup is fast and accurate. I can easily see the cut in progress.

When I'm boring holes for a through mortise, I try to minimize tearout where the bit exits the stock. If possible,

I'll select the side where tearout will be the least noticeable; then I'll lay out and cut the mortise from the opposite side. If tearout is unacceptable on either side, then I'll use a router and a jig. For this bench, though, I decided I could live with some minor tearout on the back side because this area is fairly well-hidden.

Cut the Mortises First

The usual approach is to build from the "inside out." That is, cut the tenons first, and then use the tenons as a template to mark the mortise locations. The problem is that you drill the mortises from the back, which virtually guarantees some tearout on the face of the piece, no matter how careful you are. I prefer the "outside-in" approach-cut the mortises first by drilling from the face side, and then mark the tenon locations from the mortises.

To do it this way, I set up my drill press with a Forstner bit and a fence to register the workpiece (see step 1 of the drawings below). Forstner bits are best for this operation because they make such clean cuts. Just remember that the bit diameter should be equal to or slightly smaller than the tenon thickness. You can always enlarge a mortise that's too narrow.

To minimize tearout, I set the drill-press depth stop so that the bit just goes through the workpiece or leaves a paper-thin layer of material on the bottom of the mortise. It's best to back up the workpiece with a clean piece of scrap.

I drill the first hole at one end of the mortise. Then I nibble away the remaining waste by sliding the work face down on the fence and drilling successive holes every 1/4 in. or so until I reach the other end. Toward the bottom of each hole, I slow down and use light pressure on the drill-press arm.

Shopmade Saw Cleans out Corners

After roughing out the mortise on the drill press, I trim up those little waves on the sides and any remaining waste on the bottom of the mortise with a sharp chisel. This can be done by eye, but you'll get better results if you clamp a straight piece of 3/4-in.-thick scrap across the workpiece to serve as a guide (see step 2). You can use the guide to square up the corners by working toward the corner from one direction and then swinging the guide 90° and working in from the other. If you use a chisel to square up the corners, be sure to work in from both sides of the workpiece, or you'll tear out some really nasty chipping on the back side.

The way I square up the corners is to saw them out with a small, stiff saw (see step 3). I made my saw by filing teeth into the back of a carbon-steel paring knife. But you could also modify a wallboard saw by hammering the teeth flat, filling the sides of the blade to remove all set and the filing the teeth straight across like a rip saw.

I lay the saw against the wooden guide clamped to the workpiece and saw to the corner of the mortise. I use the saw as a rough me to square out the corners (there will be minor tearout on the back side).

Lay out and Cut the Tenons

I mark the tenon directly from the mortise using a small knife or pencil sharpened to a chisel point. Because the tenon thickness is the full stock thickness, only the width must be marked (see step 4). I use a square to extend this line down the face of the stock (see step 5) and a marking gauge to scribe the tenon length. The tenon should extend completely through the mortised stock with an extra 1/32 in. or so. This will be trimmed flush later, after the wedges have been glued in place. I bandsaw the tenons using the cutting sequence shown in step 6. If all goes well, the tenons will fit snugly into the mortises on the first try. This never happens for me, though, so some fitting is usually required. Filing either the mortise or the tenon usually will take care of a too tight fit. If you have some gaps, don't worry. Small shims cut from the same stock will hide them.

Continued ➔

CUTTING THROUGH MORTISES

Step 1: Back up workpiece with clean scrap; use a Forstner bit to remove most of the waste. Set depth stop so bit just cuts through stock.

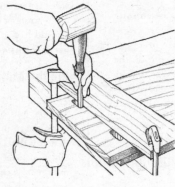

Step 2: Guide chisel with a straight piece of scrap, and pare remaining waste from walls of the mortise.

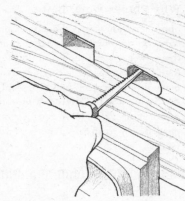

Step 3: A shopmade saw used like a rough file squares the corners. Carefully work the saw into the corner.

MAKING THE TENONS

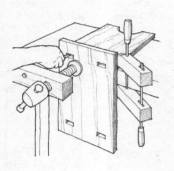

Step 4: Transfer mortise location to tenon stock. Use a knife or sharp pencil to mark out the tenon width.

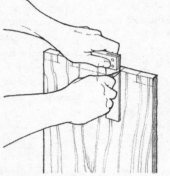

Step 5: Extend tenon layout lines down the face of the stock with a square.

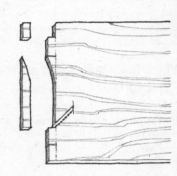

Step 6: Mark the length of the tenons with a marking gauge or knife, and then cut to the line on a bandsaw.

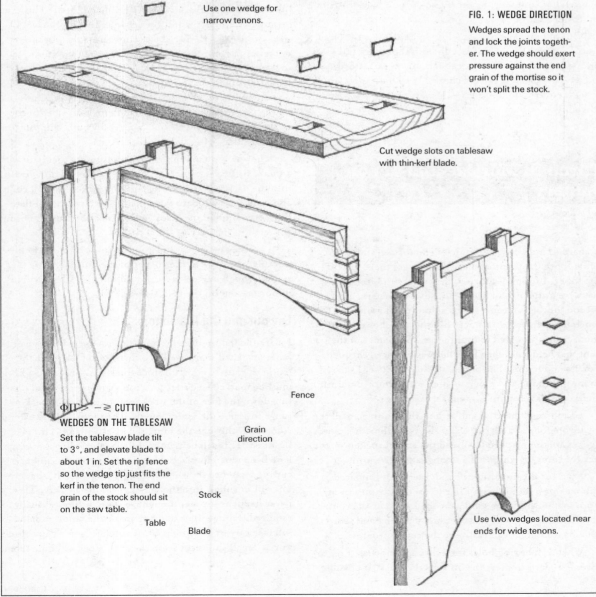

Use one wedge for narrow tenons.

Cut wedge slots on tablesaw with thin-kerf blade.

CUTTING WEDGES ON THE TABLESAW

Set the tablesaw blade tilt to 3°, and elevate blade to about 1 in. Set the rip fence so the wedge tip just fits the kerf in the tenon. The end grain of the stock should sit on the saw table.

Fence

Grain direction

Stock

Table

Blade

Use two wedges located near ends for wide tenons.

FIG. 1: WEDGE DIRECTION
Wedges spread the tenon and lock the joints together. The wedge should exert pressure against the end grain of the mortise so it won't split the stock.

Cutting Wedges and Assembly

After fitting the mortises and tenons, I cut the wedge slots in the tenons. A thin-kerf cutoff blade in a tablesaw will produce a clean slot that's about the right width. Depending on the size of the tenon and its direction in the mating stock, I use one or two wedges to spread the tenon and create a tight joint.

Wedges should always exert pressure against the end grain of the mortise to keep the workpiece from splitting. I locate the slots as shown in figure I below.

I saw the wedge material by ripping the stock, on edge, on the tablesaw, as shown in figure 2 at left. I angle the blade at 30, and adjust the fence until the point o f the wedge will just fit into the kerfs I've sawed into the tenons. I cut the wedge material to length, and now I'm ready to assemble the joint. After clamping everything together, I drive the wedges home with a bit of glue on the leading edge.

Mortise-and-Tenon Joints for Curved Work

By Jeff Miller

My first saw was a bandsaw, so from the very beginning of my woodworking career, I found myself working with curves. If you've only been a straight-shooter until now, you'll find that curves not only open up a world of design possibilities, but they also offer plenty of chances to expand your repertoire of woodworking skills: from laying out eye-pleasing shapes to cutting and smoothing those shapes, or even bending them (with steam or by lamination).

What stops most people, however, is the prospect of cutting and fitting joinery on these curved parts. I'll show you three techniques that I've used over the years with great success. There's nothing exotic or difficult about them, and once you see them in action, you'll soon be adding graceful curves to your own work.

1. Create a subtle flat as an easier landing spot

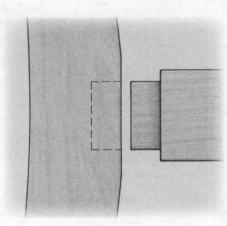

2. Make the flat stand out for a curved transition

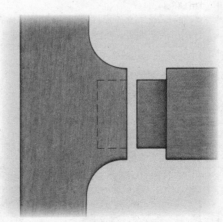

3. For inside curves, scribe the tenon shoulders

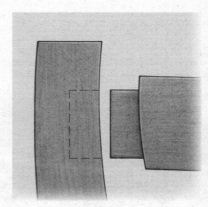

Creating a Flat Spot on the Curve

The simplest way to join two pieces when one of them is curved is by leaving or creating a flat area on the curved work where the mortise is to be cut.

If you are cutting the curved piece out of square stock, it's easiest to locate and cut the mortise while the workpiece is still square. Then you can leave the area around the joint flat when cutting the curve. The tenon on the mating rail can then be cut and fitted just as for any other mortise-and-tenon joint. When creating the flat, be sure to extend it 1/8 in. or so beyond the rail both above and below the joint to accommodate any expansion across the width of the rail. When the piece is glued up, you can sand lightly to ease the transition from flat to curve, leaving about 1/16 in. flat.

Things get more challenging if you're cutting several identical parts from square stock. If you want to minimize waste, you'll need to "nest" the layout of the parts and cut them all out before doing anything else. This means you'll then have to create the flat—and cut the mortise—in an already curved part. To do this, I make a simple jig that holds the work while I create the flat spot and then cut the mortise.

Clamp the curved piece into the jig so that the area to be flattened projects above the jig's fence. Now you can create the flat spot, using a handplane to remove the projecting material and bring the part flush with the top of the fence. To use the jig with a router, screw on a top plate to support the router. Use a spiral upcut bit or a straight bit, set to cut flush with the top of the jig's fence. The first cut should be a clockwise pass around the area to be flattened; this is a climb cut to avoid tearout.

To mortise with the same setup, equip a plunge router with a fence that will ride along the back of the jig. Adjust the fence to locate the mortise on the thickness of the workpiece. Rout between the layout lines in shallow passes (perhaps 1/32 in. of added depth per pass) until you reach the desired depth.

Create a Flat That Stands Proud

Some designs call for seamless curves that flow from one part to the next, regardless of whether the parts themselves are curved.

In these cases, don't shape the curve, or much of it anyway, on the end of the tenoned piece. The outer tips of the curved ends will consist of very fragile short-grained stock. Instead, leave a raised area on the mortised part, and form the transitional curves there. Just rough them in, and then refine the transitions after gluing the joint together. A well-known example of this technique can be seen on the leg-to-rocker joints of a Sam Maloof rocking chair.

By the way, another excellent solution to this problem is the gunstock joint used by Kevin Kauffunger in his hall table.

OPTION ONE: FOR SHALLOW, OUTSIDE CURVES, CREATE A FLAT

This works best with shallow curves so the flat spot won't stand out. It's good for joining straight rails to curved posts on a chair or bed, or straight aprons to curved legs on a table.

...OR ROUT A FLAT ON NESTED PARTS

"Nesting" curved parts saves material. However, it also makes it impossible to leave a precise flat when sawing each part. So Miller uses a simple jig to shape the flat afterward.

LEAVE A FLAT SECTION IF YOU CAN...

The easiest flat. Leave a section of the stock's square edge intact when cutting the workpiece to shape. Mark the flat's boundaries on the pattern and let that section hang over the stock's edge when tracing the layout.

Saw the piece to shape. But before bringing the work to the bandsaw, go ahead and cut the mortise—a task that's much easier while the stock is still square.

Simple Jig Can Flatten and Mortise

The assembly is based on a piece of thick, wide stock screwed to a vertical plywood fence so the mating edges are flush.

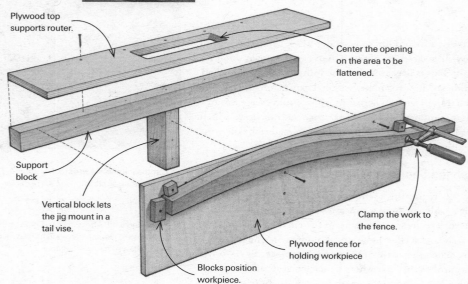

Plywood top supports router.

Center the opening on the area to be flattened.

Support block

Vertical block lets the jig mount in a tail vise.

Clamp the work to the fence.

Plywood fence for holding workpiece

Blocks position workpiece.

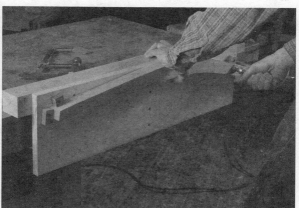

Left: Hold the jig in a bench vise. The workpiece clamps to the jig's fence. Three hardwood stops locate the workpiece so that the section to be milled protrudes above the fence.

Right: Add a top plate to support the router. Use 3/4-in. plywood and make the plate opening larger than the desired flat by 1 1/2 in. in each direction.

Continued →

1. ROUT THE FLAT

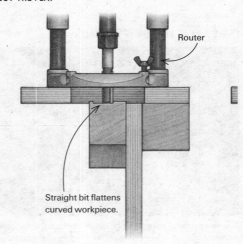

Router

Straight bit flattens
curved workpiece.

2. ROUT THE MORTISE

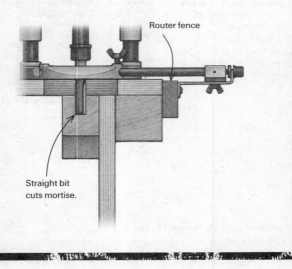

Router fence

Straight bit
cuts mortise.

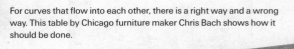

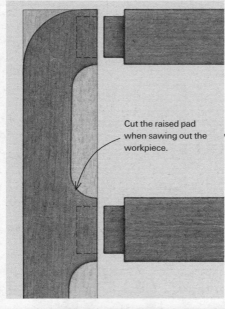

Cut the raised pad
when sawing out the
workpiece.

For curves that flow into each other, there is a right way and a wrong way. This table by Chicago furniture maker Chris Bach shows how it should be done.

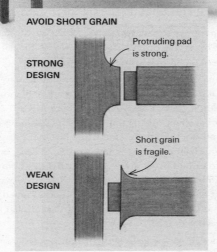

AVOID SHORT GRAIN

Protruding pad
is strong.

STRONG
DESIGN

Short grain
is fragile.

WEAK
DESIGN

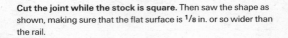

Cut the joint while the stock is square. Then saw the shape as shown, making sure that the flat surface is 1/8 in. or so wider than the rail.

Finish by hand. After the joint is glued, remove the excess material and create a smooth transition using a round or half-round wood rasp, followed by a card scraper.

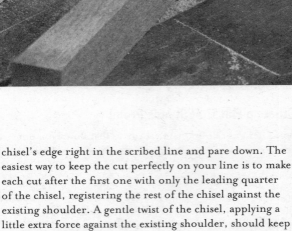

Here's a final point to consider when using this type of joinery: It makes a lot of sense to use quartersawn wood for the rail. This is because, after the joint has been smoothed to seamlessly flow together, seasonal expansion and contraction of the rail across its width could create minor misalignment between the parts. Quartersawn stock, which moves less across its width than flatsawn material, will minimize this problem.

Match the Shoulders to the Curve

When you're joining a tenoned part like a chair's crest rail or a table apron to a concave section of curve, it won't work to create a flat spot on the curve. The simplest approach is to scribe the tenon shoulders on one piece to exactly match the curve of the adjoining piece. By the way, this is another instance where a quartersawn rail is a good idea. Excessive wood movement can cause gaps to appear in a scribed joint, because expansion or contraction will actually change the curvature of the shoulder.

The task of cutting the mortise and tenon is roughly the same as before. You can use the jig again to cut the mortise, although you may need to use a curved offcut as a brace between the jig and the workpiece to help hold the work squarely when clamping.

The real trick in this technique lies in shaping the tenon shoulders to tightly hug the curve of the mating part and create a gap-free joint. This process will be simpler if, when cutting the tenon, you angle the tenon shoulder so that it generally follows the direction of the curve to which you'll be scribing. You can do this with a tablesaw tenoning jig, clamping the workpiece in the jig against a precut wedge. Cut the tenon to normal length to fit in the mortise.

Start the scribing process by inserting the tenon fully into the mortise. Next, use a marking knife to ride along the curved workpiece and scribe a line into the shoulder of the mating part. It's ideal if the scribed line is made with a single-bevel knife so that the straight side of the cut is toward the shoulder—this will leave a very crisp edge to pare toward. Facing the knife that way often will create the offset you need to transfer the full curve to the shoulder, while ultimately shortening the tenoned part as little as possible. But you can use a shim of some kind (an automotive feeler gauge or a small scrap of wood) to increase the scribing offset for deeper curves.

The paring requires a very sharp chisel with a flat back. Nibble a little bit away at a time, until you are just one or two paring cuts away from the scribe line. Now put the chisel's edge right in the scribed line and pare down. The easiest way to keep the cut perfectly on your line is to make each cut after the first one with only the leading quarter of the chisel, registering the rest of the chisel against the existing shoulder. A gentle twist of the chisel, applying a little extra force against the existing shoulder, should keep you from inadvertently crossing the line. It also helps to undercut the shoulder a little. Just be careful not to do that at the corners, where undercutting from one side will leave unsightly gaps on the adjacent face.

As you trim back the shoulders, you might also need to trim the tenon length back so the final depth is about 1/32 in. less than the depth of the mortise. This leaves room for excess glue.

This technique creates tight joints between two pieces when one of them is a concave curve.

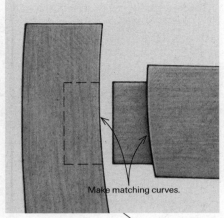

Make matching curves.

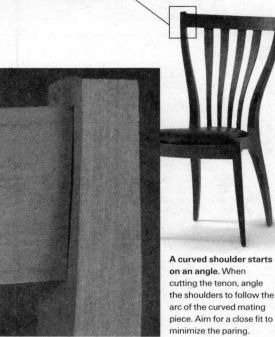

A curved shoulder starts on an angle. When cutting the tenon, angle the shoulders to follow the arc of the curved mating piece. Aim for a close fit to minimize the paring.

Mark the shoulder. An automotive feeler gauge hugs the curve when transferring the layout to the shoulder. Use a wood scrap for a wider gap.

Pare to the scribe line. Nibble away most of the waste, then seat the chisel in the scribe line and pare straight down. Use overlapping cuts, advancing only a quarter of the blade with each new stroke.

Bring the joint home. You may need to shorten the tenon slightly to allow the shoulder to seat completely. With the shoulder pared carefully, the joint should come together with no gaps.

Pegging Mortise-and-Tenon Joints

By Matthew Teague

I seldom cut mortises and tenons—whether in doors, leg-to-apron joints, or on breadboard ends—without pegging the joints. Driving a wood peg through a mortise and tenon not only strengthens the joint, but it also adds a decorative element that I've come to depend on in most of my designs. Because I lean toward joinery that is honest and exposed, using pegs makes the construction process transparent. If you see pegs, you can bet that they're more than ornamental, and you can tell at a glance how the piece is held together.

Reinforcing a joint in this manner involves driving a hardwood peg through the mortise and tenon (though I've seen the same technique used on other types of joinery, including box joints and dovetails). Structurally, the peg strengthens the mechanical connection between mortise and tenon—often to the extent that glue isn't necessary. Aesthetically, the peg can add a subtle or bold detail to your work.

Most of the time, I drive pegs into a mortise-and-tenon joint that has already been assembled. But with proper planning, pegs also can be integral to the assembly process, exerting their own clamping pressure. This method, called drawbored pegging, calls for some drilling and layout work before assembly Both methods make for bombproof joints, and the techniques are relatively simple.

Let the Furniture Dictate the Peg Form

Pegs can be designed to suit most furniture styles. For starters, you can make them round, square, flush, or even proud and faceted. Then there is the species of wood. Because the end grain of the pegs is exposed and will darken

Layout and Design

LOCATE PEGS SMARTLY

Wood pegs create tenacious mortise-and-tenon joints that will never pull apart. For maximum strength, be sure there's sufficient tenon stock above and below the peg as well as toward the front of the tenon. Leaving too little wood in these areas could result in a split when the joint is stressed.

IN FRAME JOINERY

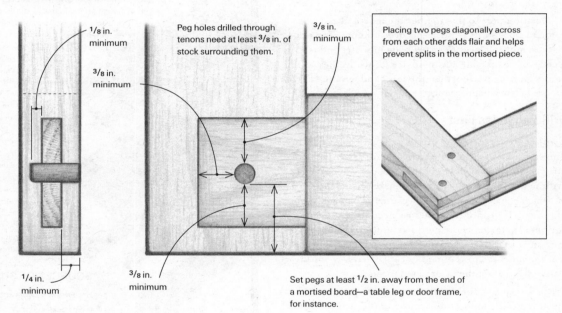

1/8 in. minimum

3/8 in. minimum

1/4 in. minimum

Peg holes drilled through tenons need at least 3/8 in. of stock surrounding them.

3/8 in. minimum

3/8 in. minimum

Placing two pegs diagonally across from each other adds flair and helps prevent splits in the mortised piece.

Set pegs at least 1/2 in. away from the end of a mortised board—a table leg or door frame, for instance.

IN APRON-TO-LEG JOINERY

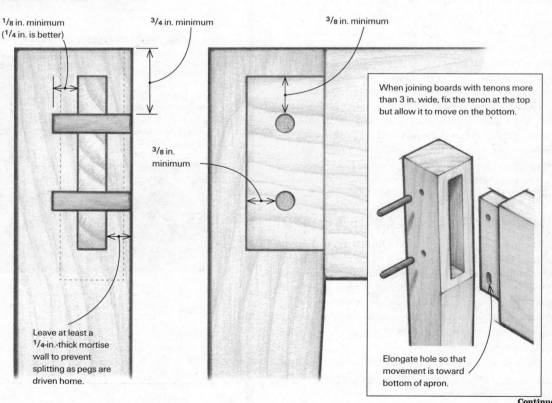

1/8 in. minimum (1/4 in. is better)

3/4 in. minimum

3/8 in. minimum

3/8 in. minimum

When joining boards with tenons more than 3 in. wide, fix the tenon at the top but allow it to move on the bottom.

Leave at least a 1/4-in.-thick mortise wall to prevent splitting as pegs are driven home.

Elongate hole so that movement is toward bottom of apron.

Continued →

with an applied finish, they will offer contrast in some form. For a more subtle appearance, cut the pegs from the same primary wood you're using on the project. To pump up the contrast, choose pegs of a darker or lighter species. I often use walnut to add a darker accent to cherry designs. Ebony is dense and strong, and the near-black color offsets mahogany or walnut well. On occasion, especially if I want a more contemporary look, I'll use pegs of a lighter color: holly pegs in a mahogany door, for instance.

Regardless of your design, choose a dense and strong hardwood peg that is as strong as, or stronger than, the material you are pegging. On a few occasions, I have pegged joints with a softer wood, but in these cases the pegs are simply a design element—not a means of strengthening the joinery.

Maximize Strength Without Sacrificing Appearance

There's more to pegging a joint than the appearance. It's also important to get as strong a mechanical connection as possible. A few factors come into play here: the size, placement, and number of the pegs.

Without calling in the engineers, you can determine the size of the peg by considering the joint you're re-inforcing and the desired effect. In general, I use pegs between 3/16 in. and 3/8 in. dia. That said, even smaller decorative pegs of 1/8 in. dia. would not be out of place on a delicate box, and 1/2-in. pegs might work better on a beefy trestle base.

Position pegs so that neither the mortised nor the tenoned stock splits as the peg is driven home. You also may use multiple pegs to secure wide mortises and tenons, such as those on table apron-to-leg joints. In these cases, double pegs help strengthen the joint and lend the design a more balanced appearance.

Drill Peg Holes First

Whether you're installing round or square pegs, start by choosing a bit that closely matches the peg size. Just make sure the bit isn't much larger than the peg stock. If you're drilling into softer stock, you can make the hole about 1/32 in. smaller than the peg stock because the primary wood will offer a little give. But you may need to whittle the bottom two-thirds of the peg to get it to fit the hole. Shoot for a snug fit, but not so tight that the peg could split either the mortised or tenoned stock. Different woods react differently, so test the fit on scrap pieces.

Before gluing the mortise-and-tenon joint, transfer the mortise/tenon location around to the face of the stock and then mark out the center point of the peg locations. If you are pegging an exposed mortise and tenon, such as a bridle joint, you can mark the locations after glue-up.

Simply drill at the center points all the way through the tenon and about 1/8 in. to 1/4 in. beyond. On thinner stock, common on door frames, 1/4 in. is not always possible. In these cases, simply drill about a third or half of the way into the opposite wall of the mortise—just make sure the back wall of the door stock isn't thinner than about 1/8 in. Use a piece of tape attached to the bit to control the depth, and keep the drill perpendicular to the workpiece. On smaller workpieces, using a drill press guarantees perpendicular holes. If your design calls for square pegs, you'll need to square up the top third of the hole using a chisel.

Metal Hammer Will Sing as You Tap in Pegs

Both round and square pegs need a little prep work before you drive them home. After cutting the pegs to length—they should be about 3/8 in. longer than the depth of the hole—ease the edges on the bottom of the pegs using sandpaper, a chisel, or a small knife. Doing so allows you to drive the peg into the hole without splitting or damaging any parts, and gives excess glue a place to go when you drive the pegs home.

Once both hole and peg are prepped, place a small drop of glue in the hole and apply a thin layer to the lower third of the peg. To drive the peg home, use a small metal fin-

Pegged-Joint Basics

Driving wood pegs into mortise-and-tenon joints adds strength and visual appeal to furniture. Typically, the joint is glued up before pegs are installed, but you don't have to wait for the glue to dry before adding pegs. You might want to leave the clamps on, though.

Mark out the peg locations. Draw the outline of the tenon on the mortised stock. Locate the pegs' center points, then define them with an awl so that the drill bit won't wander.

Drill peg holes. Attach a tape "flag" to the drill bit, and stop drilling when the flag knocks the chips away. Drill perpendicular to the workpiece to avoid tearout.

BUY PEGS OR MAKE YOUR OWN

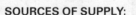

You can buy dowel stock for pegs, but you'll have more design options if you make your own from hardwood scraps in your shop or from purchased pen blanks, which come in a variety of exotic species (see Sources, below). Start with a 3/4-in.-sq. blank. Set the tablesaw fence and the blade height based on the size of the pegs you're cutting. If you're making 3/16-in. pegs, set the fence to 3/16 in. but leave the blade height just shy of 3/16 in. Using a push stick at the end of each cut, rip along each corner of the blank, adjusting the blade height until only a sliver holds each corner together (top photos, right). Eventually, you'll be able to peel away the strips. To make round pegs, place the square strip in a V-grooved trough and plane away equal amounts of stock at the corners.

Square pegs on the tablesaw. Set the fence to match the peg width and set the blade height to just under that measurement. Use a push stick at the end of each cut, and raise the blade until only a sliver of material holds the peg stock to the blank. Then peel away the strips.

Make 'em round if you want. With the blank set in a V-grooved trough, use a block plane to remove the corners, rotating the blank as you go.

SOURCES OF SUPPLY:

Hardwood dowels and pen blanks

www.rockler.com
www.woodworker.com
www.woodcraft.com

TRIMMING PEGS FLUSH

Drive pegs home. The pegs will go in easier if you chamfer the bottom edges (inset). Use a metal hammer to drive in the pegs. Stop when the hammer tone deepens; it means the peg has bottomed out.

1. (Right) Use a handsaw to trim the peg almost flush. Place a shim under the saw to protect the workpiece.

2. (Left) Dampen the peg with water, then mash it a few times with a hammer, causing the head to mushroom slightly. The water softens the fibers and mashing helps spread the peg to fill any gaps.

3. (Right) Pare the peg flush using a chisel. Rest the chisel flat on the work-surface. Slowly work your way around the outside of the peg and toward the middle to avoid tearout as you finish the cut.

ishing hammer. Its light weight won't stress the stock you're pounding, and the tone of the metal hammer will deepen as the peg bottoms out in the hole. Once the peg bottoms out, stop hammering or you'll risk cracking the stock.

Trim Pegs Flush or Leave Them Proud

You can trim pegs flush (see p. 41), but leaving them proud of the surface they're driven into is a good way to accentuate the joinery even more. I often leave small pegs about 1/16 in. proud of the surface, larger ones a little more. After installation, the exposed end of the peg can be softened with sandpaper, chamfered with a chisel or plane, or, my favorite, faceted.

The first few times I tried to use faceted pegs, I made it a lot more difficult than necessary. Brian Boggs, a chairmaker in Kentucky, taught me a better way. Simply drive the peg into place as usual, then wait for the glue to dry. To cut the pegs to a consistent size, use a shim whose thickness matches the desired projection of the peg, and register the saw against it as you trim the pegs to length.

To cut the facets, use a chisel that's wider than the peg, and hold it bevel-side down against the surface adjacent to the peg. Working in from one side at a time, use the bevel as a lever to angle the blade upward as you cut toward the center. To prevent denting or scarring the surface you're bearing against, place a thin shim between the chisel's bevel and the surface of the wood. You'll have the best luck if you cut each facet in a single sweep of the chisel—every time you stop to realign the chisel, you're left with a small ridge on the peg's pyramid top that will have to be cleaned up. Before working on a project, practice the technique on a scrap peg and joint.

Pegged Breadboard Ends Never Loosen

Pegging the breadboard ends of a tabletop is a great way to reinforce that joint. But you must allow for wood movement by elongating the outermost peg holes.

BREADBOARD ENDS NEED ROOM TO MOVE

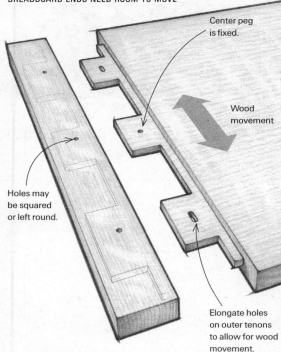

Center peg is fixed.

Wood movement

Holes may be squared or left round.

Elongate holes on outer tenons to allow for wood movement.

Clamp and drill, then widen the outermost tenon holes. With the breadboard ends clamped to the tabletop, drill the holes for the pegs at their marked locations. Again, flag the bit to gauge the drilling depth (left). Remove the breadboard end, use the drill to elongate the holes in the outer tenon, then clean up the holes with a chisel (right).

Drive the pegs. Glue the breadboard ends to the tabletop, being sure the holes in the breadboards align with the holes in the tenons. Clamp them in place, and tap the pegs home.

Drawbored Pegs Pull Joints Tight

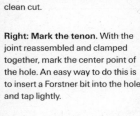

By drilling the tenon peg holes slightly toward the shoulder, the mortised joint will be drawn tight as the peg is driven in.

OFFSET PEG HOLES ARE THE KEY TO A TIGHT FIT

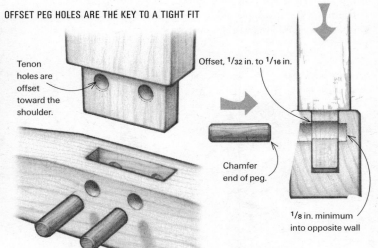

Tenon holes are offset toward the shoulder.

Offset, 1/32 in. to 1/16 in.

Chamfer end of peg.

1/8 in. minimum into opposite wall

Left: Drill the mortised piece. Go through one side and partway into the other. Use a Forstner bit for a clean cut.

Right: Mark the tenon. With the joint reassembled and clamped together, mark the center point of the hole. An easy way to do this is to insert a Forstner bit into the hole and tap lightly.

Scribe the offset. Use a combination square and a knife to offset the hole 1/32 in. to 1/16 in., depending on the hardness of the materials.

Mark offset 1/32 in. toward shoulder.

Center point of peg hole

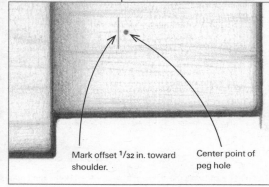

Drill through the tenon. Align the tip of the Forstner bit so that it engages the offset line. If you need to drill multiple holes, using a fence helps ensure consistency.

Continued →

Laying out Dovetails

By Chris Gochnour

Striking a perfect blend of form and function, dovetail joints add great interest and detail while enhancing the structural integrity of a case, box, or drawer.

Cutting dovetails can become second nature after plenty of practice with saw and chisel. Dovetail layout, on the other hand, is where I see students get frustrated. Here are the key steps in laying out a basic through-dovetail joint, with tips on creating an attractive joint that is sturdy enough to last generations.

How to Balance Aesthetics and Strength

Several factors go into the design of a dovetail joint. These include the size and spacing of the tails and pins, and the slope of the tails (see drawings, below).

Most dovetail joints begin and end with a half-pin on the outside, with the rest of the space subdivided into multiple pins and tails. This creates plenty of long-grain glue surfaces as well as mechanical strength to tie the elements together.

A common practice is to span the joint with pins and tails of equal proportions. Although it's structurally very sound and typical of machine-cut dovetails, this joint has little design appeal. A better method is to span the joint with tails that are larger than the pins (see right drawing, below). This is a common practice with hand-cut dovetails and also can be done on the bandsaw or tablesaw, as well as with the better machine-dovetail systems.

Anatomy of a Strong Joint

Dovetails provide not only mechanical strength as the pins and tails interlock, but also plenty of long-grain-to-long-grain glue surfaces for a long-lasting joint.

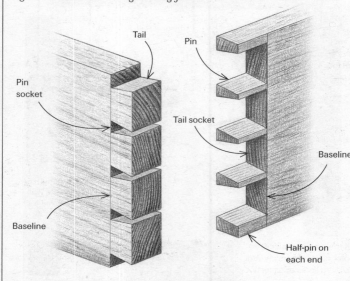

Tail

Pin

Pin socket

Tail socket

Baseline

Baseline

Half-pin on each end

PIN AND TAIL DIMENSIONS

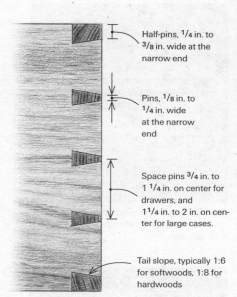

Half-pins, $\frac{1}{4}$ in. to $\frac{3}{8}$ in. wide at the narrow end

Pins, $\frac{1}{8}$ in. to $\frac{1}{4}$ in. wide at the narrow end

Space pins $\frac{3}{4}$ in. to $1\frac{1}{4}$ in. on center for drawers, and $1\frac{1}{4}$ in. to 2 in. on center for large cases.

Tail slope, typically 1:6 for softwoods, 1:8 for hardwoods

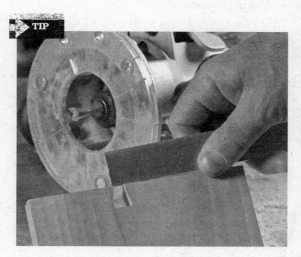

Sizing pins for router-cut dovetails. If you plan to cut dovetails with a router, the minimum pin width will be dictated by the diameter at the base of the bit.

Set the Tail Spacing

Gochnour lays out and cuts the tails first. His method uses the narrowest dimension of the pins, and simple math, to divide the tail board evenly.

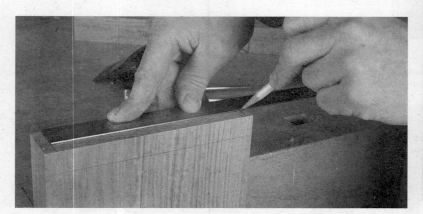

Divide this distance by the number of tails.

Pin width

Distance between half-pins

1. Mark the pin width. Stack both tail boards in the vise. After laying out half-pins, mark the pin width on one end.

2. Measure from the half-pin mark on one end to the pin-width mark on the other. Divide that distance by the number of tails; adjust the dividers to this dimension.

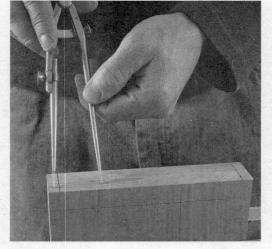

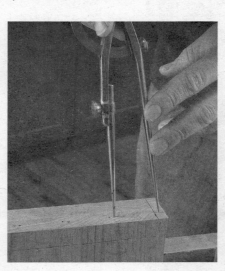

3. Mark the left edges of the tails. Place one point of the dividers on the right half-pin line and walk the dividers across the end grain.

4. Mark the right edges of the tails. Repeat the process beginning from the left half-pin line.

I recommend sizing the half-pins on the outer edges from 1/4 in. to 3/8 in. at their narrow end. Interior pins range from 1/8 in. to 1/4 in. wide and can be spaced anywhere from 3/4 in. to 2 in. on center, depending on the application.

Last, it's important to choose an appropriate slope, or angle, for the tails. That slope is what draws the pin board up tight during assembly. More slope pulls the joint together efficiently; too little slope may require clamps or other aids to pull the joint together, much like a box or finger joint requires clamping pressure in two directions. Partly a matter of preference, the traditional ratio is 1:6 for softwoods and 1:8 for hardwoods; the reason being that the fibers of softwoods can compress more easily and therefore require a bit more angle to ensure that the pins are drawn tight to the tail board.

Keep the Layout Process Simple

When laying out dovetails, use as few steps as possible. Begin by marking out the orientation of the pin and tail boards: inside and outside faces, top and bottom, front and back. Remember that tail boards generally make up the sides of drawers and cases, and the fronts and backs of chests; pin boards are usually the fronts and backs of drawers, tops and bottoms of cases, and ends of chests.

Scribe baselines—With the orientation of the tail board and the pin board established, scribe the baselines on both using a marking gauge. Set the gauge to the exact thickness of the pin board and scribe the tail board on both faces and edges. Setting the gauge to the pin board's exact thickness means there are no proud pins to interfere with clamping and leaves little to trim flush after glue-up. After scribing the tail board, scribe the inside and outside faces of the pin board in the same way.

Determine tail spacing—Though some woodworkers will argue that it's best to lay out and cut the pins first, I prefer to work the tails first for a few reasons. First, I can lay out and cut more than one tail board at a time. Second, I find it easier to align, hold, and transfer the tails to the pin board because the pin board can be held securely in a vise and the tail board can lay horizontally, easily registering on the pin-board ends. Last, any adjustments or fine-tuning during assembly will be done to the pins, and it is much easier to trim and fit the open, right-angled pins than the tight, angular confines of the tails.

Clamp both tail boards in a shoulder vise so that they are 2 in. to 3 in. above the benchtop and square to it. Measure and mark the half-pins across the ends of the boards and perpendicular to the faces. Now divide the tails based on the number that you want and the pin sizes between them.

For example, say you want four tails with 3/16-in.-wide pins and two 3/8-in. half-pins. Lay out the half-pins 3/8 in. from both edges, then make a mark on the end of the tail board 3/16 in. past the half-pin mark on the right side (this distance is based on the width of the full pins). Then measure from that mark to the half-pin mark on the left side. Say that distance equals 6 1/2 in. Because you want four tails, divide the 6 1/2 in. by 4, which equals 1 5/8 in. Now adjust a set of dividers with the points 1 5/8 in. apart.

Lay one point of the divider on the right half-pin and walk it across the board end until you pass the half-pin on the left. If your math has been done correctly, the divider should be 3/16 in. past this mark. Now put one of the divider points on the left half-pin mark and walk back across the board end to the right.

Mark out the tails—The divider technique will leave a series of impressions spaced appropriately, in this case 3/16 in. apart. Place a sharp pencil in each impression, slide a square up to the pencil, and square a line across the ends of the boards.

Next, set a bevel gauge to the appropriate slope and mark the face of the tail board. A dovetail saddle marker can be handy here because it allows you to draw the two lines across the top and down the face quickly and without misalignment. Dovetail saddle markers generally come with one of two slope ratios, 1:6 or 1:8, and are available from a number of sources, such as www.leevalley.com.

Have Fun with Dovetail Layout

Mastering the basics of dovetailing opens the doors to many design options, allowing you to increase the strength of the joint as needed or add visual pop. Each of these designs works with the layout process described in this article.

ADD PINS AND TAILS
This joint has enough pins to ensure that the joint is sound, but not so many that the joint is laborious to execute. The 1:6 slope of the tails ensures that the pin board is drawn up tight during assembly.

INCREASE THE SLOPE OF THE TAILS
This joint has a unique visual appeal and a great ability to draw the pins up tight. It also leaves a lot of short grain on the tails, creating a potential weak spot.

ADD PINS AT THE ENDS
The outer edges of a joint are the most susceptible to failure. Fortifying the edge with an extra pin is a great way to strengthen this potentially weak corner. It looks good, too.

ALTERNATE TAIL WIDTHS
The sky is the limit in what can be done to capitalize on both the form and the functional aspects that the dovetail joint affords the craftsman.

Mark the Pin Board

Use the tail board to mark out the pins. Line up the baseline of the tail board with the inside edge of the pin board. Now use a marking knife to transfer the tail locations clearly to the pin board.

Mark the Tail Board

Mark the widths of the tails on the end. Set the pencil point into the depressions from the points of the dividers, slide a square up to the pencil point, and draw lines across.

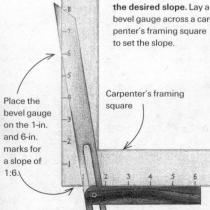

Set a bevel gauge to the desired slope. Lay a bevel gauge across a carpenter's framing square to set the slope.

Place the bevel gauge on the 1-in. and 6-in. marks for a slope of 1:6.

Carpenter's framing square

Mark the tails on the face. Use the bevel gauge to draw in the tails on the face of the board.

TIP

Saddle markers speed the process. A dovetail saddle marker allows you to draw the lines on the end and face of a board in one step and with one tool. These jigs come with preset slopes, or you can make one based on your preference.

Continued →

Now you're ready to cut the tails and remove the waste. The end-grain cuts must be absolutely perpendicular to each face of the board. Otherwise, during the next step the information transferred from inside the boards will not match the outside, causing problems.

Transfer layout to the pin board—With the tails laid out, cut, and pared, secure the pin board in the shoulder vise, with its outside facing you and its end 2½ in. to 3 in. above the benchtop.

Place the tail board with the outside face up on the end of the pin board. Use a spacer to keep the tail board level. Line up the baseline of the tail board with the inside edge of the pin board. If the tail's baseline overlaps the pin board's inner edge, the tails will be too tight. If the baseline is proud of the pin board's inner face, the pins will be too small, resulting in a loose joint.

Holding the tail board securely—use clamps if needed—knife in the tails clearly on the pin board. Extend the marks perpendicularly down the pin board's face to the baseline. Now you are ready to cut the pins and complete the joint.

Dovetails on the Tablesaw

By Gregory paolini

It takes an awful lot of practice to cut dovetails by hand and to do it well. Your sawcuts should be straight, at a consistent angle, and square to the board's face. And you can't cut into the baseline. Later, when you're paring and attempting to make up for bad sawcuts, you can make things much worse.

There are ways to cut dovetails that bypass those challenges. With a router and jig, you'll get straight and square tails and pins that have consistent angles. Unfortunately, they won't look as nice as hand-cut dovetails. It's difficult to reproduce the wide tails and narrow pins that make the hand-cut version so appealing.

However, there is one power tool in your shop that excels at cutting straight and square, and can easily maintain the same angled cut for both tails and pins: the tablesaw. What's more, because tablesaw blades are no more than 1/8 in. thick, you can reproduce hand-cut dovetail spacing, too.

Of course, because both the tails and the pins are cut at the tablesaw, you're limited to through-dovetails. That's great for case joints and the back joints on a drawer, but what about the half-blind dovetails we all use to join the drawer front to the sides? No problem. I have a trick that turns a through-dovetail into a half-blind, with added benefits you can't get the traditional way. But let's start with the basics.

Use a Rip Blade and Auxiliary Fence

To cut dovetails this way, you need only your stock miter gauge and a blade. I use a rip blade because these are ripcuts and because it has a flat-top grind, which leaves a flat shoulder when I cut the pins, with no paring needed. However, any standard blade will leave a bit of material between tails, so you'll still have some paring to do. If you're going to cut dovetails this way all the time, get a blade with the teeth ground to match the dovetails' slope. Any saw-sharpening service can do it. Use it for the tails and you won't have any paring to do in the corners, either.

You also need two L-shaped fences for the miter gauge—one for the tails and one for the pins. They should be at least twice as long as the drawer sides are wide, so the sides always have support as you move them to cut the pins and tails. After the fence is attached to the gauge and a kerf is cut into it, it's easy to align layout lines with the kerf so the blade cuts exactly where you want it to.

Bevel Gauge Guides the Way

To take advantage of the tablesaw's accuracy, you need to set it up precisely. Using a bevel gauge is the secret.

Mark the tails, setting the gauge at your favorite dovetail angle (left). Paolini likes 10°. Then use the same bevel-gauge setting to angle the blade (above) to cut the tails.

With the blade at 90°, angle the miter gauge for the pins. Don't change the setting on the bevel gauge, and the pins are sure to match the tails.

Angle the Blade to Cut the Tails

The tablesaw locks in the cutting angle and a stop block allows you to make eight cuts from a single layout line. So all you need to do is lay out the tails at one end of one board.

Scribe the baselines, then lay out the tails. Scribe all the boards (top), wrapping the marks around the edges on the tail boards. You can space the dovetails any way you want (bottom), but they should be symmetrical around the centerline.

Angle the blade. Make sure the bevel gauge's setting hasn't changed and that it's flat against the blade's plate, coming up in a gullet between teeth.

GET ACCURATE WITH AN AUXILIARY FENCE AND STOP BLOCK

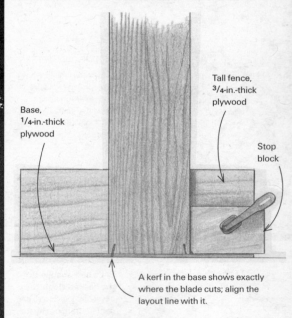

Tall fence, ³/4-in.-thick plywood

Stop block

Base, ¼-in.-thick plywood

A kerf in the base shows exactly where the blade cuts; align the layout line with it.

Four cuts from a single setup. Flip the board to make two mirror-image cuts, then rotate it end for end to make the same two cuts on the opposite end. When you've done the same with the second tail board, you've made eight cuts without moving the stop block.

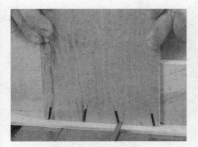

The mirror effect. As you work across the board, moving the board (and stop block) to a new layout line and making all four cuts each time, you naturally begin to cut the second side of every tail.

Nibble the ends. A few eyeballed cuts knock off most of the waste at the ends.

Clean out the waste. After defining all of the tails at the tablesaw, cleanup goes quickly. Work to your scribe lines.

Angle the Miter Gauge for the Pins

Move the blade back to 90°. One side of every pin is cut with the miter gauge angled in one direction. Angle it in the other direction to cut the second side.

CUT THE FIRST SIDE OF THE PINS

Transfer the tails to the end grain. Do this on all your boards. Paolini uses a 0.5mm mechanical pencil because of its very fine line.

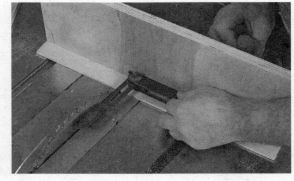

Wrap the line onto the face grain. You can't see the end grain when the board is standing on the auxiliary fence, so you'll need these lines to align the board for cutting.

Adjust the miter gauge. Use the bevel gauge, still set to the angle used for the tails. Paolini attaches a new auxiliary fence so that the kerf for this cut doesn't overlap the one used for the tails.

MAKE ALL THE CUTS YOU CAN

You can't flip the board this time to make a mirror-image cut on the same end, but you can invert it. Keep the same face out.

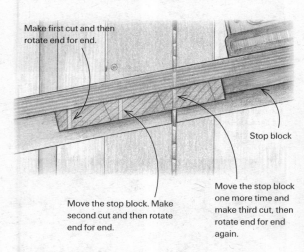

Make first cut and then rotate end for end.

Stop block

Move the stop block. Make second cut and then rotate end for end.

Move the stop block one more time and make third cut, then rotate end for end again.

Don't cut into the pencil line. If you do, the pin will be too narrow and you'll have gaps in the joint. Take advantage of the zero-clearance kerf, aligning the board so that the pencil line is right next to the kerf, but not in it.

Cut the Second Side of the Pins

Reset the miter gauge. There's no way around it to cut the second side of the pins. Be sure the bevel gauge is still locked into its original setting.

OPPOSITE ANGLE FOR SIDE TWO

This is just like cutting the first side of the pins, except the board goes through the blade at a different angle.

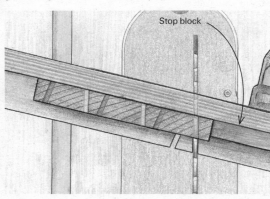

Stop block

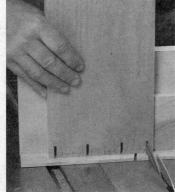

Nibble the waste by eye. Most of the waste can be cut out with the fence at the second setting, but you'll need to move it back to the first setting to get all of the waste.

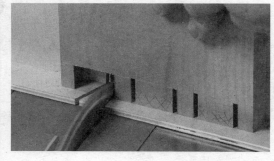

Payoff is perfect joints. After cleaning up the baseline of the pin board with a file, the joint should come together square, without gaps, and without much persuasion.

Use the Same Technique to Make Half-Blind Dovetails

You can use through-dovetails in lots of places, but typically not drawer fronts. There, you want half-blind dovetails. But you can still use this dovetailing method by gluing a thin board (1/8 in. to 1/4 in. thick) to the front of the drawer box after it's glued together. That allows you to use through-dovetails for all of the joints, but still get the half-blind look. As a bonus, you get more mileage from your best lumber, which you can resaw to get book- and slip-matched fronts.

1. Cut through-dovetails using the tablesaw technique.

2. Glue thin board to front for the half-blind look.

Cut the fronts. Resawing from a thicker board lets you spread a beautiful board over several drawers.

Brads lock it in place. Cut them off short and they'll stick into the front and prevent it from creeping under clamping pressure.

Don't skimp on clamps. Paolini uses a caul made from melamine-covered particleboard to protect the front and help spread the pressure over the entire surface (for a tight glueline around all four sides).

Just rout it flush. Routing is faster than a handplane and makes it easier to keep the edge square to the face. Do the ends before the long edges, and use a pin in your router table to help you enter the cut safely.

Miter Your Dovetails

By Josh Metcalf

Among my favorite things about making this small dresser mirror is the joinery—two different combinations of dovetails and miters that are strong, look great, and allow me to cut molded profiles on the edges and faces of the piece.

On the case, the lap of the half-blind dovetails enables me to cut a continuous ovolo edge detail around the top. The miter at the front of the joint also lets me cut a molded profile on the front of the case.

I wanted the same molding details on the edge and face of the mirror frame, and I wanted its joinery to visually echo the dovetails on the case. The joint I use—a dovetailed through-tenon with a miter in front and a half-lap in back—is challenging but fun to execute, and the results speak for themselves.

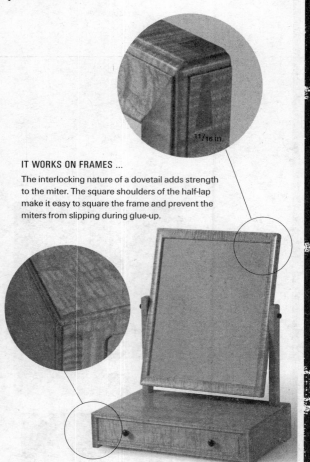

IT WORKS ON FRAMES ...

The interlocking nature of a dovetail adds strength to the miter. The square shoulders of the half-lap make it easy to square the frame and prevent the miters from slipping during glue-up.

... AND CASES

Like the frame version, the mitered front on the half-blind dovetailed case sides lets Metcalf cut a continuous decorative profile on the case front and along the edges.

The Frame Version

This joint can be used in a variety of applications, such as mitered cabinet doors or picture frames. It works especially well for small frames that are too thin for a standard mortise and tenon. The joint has great mechanical strength and it clamps easily across the face to ensure the best bond. However, it's not an easy joint to cut. Visualizing it can be confusing, and the sawing and fitting must be accurate. Also, the dovetail layout is a little out of the ordinary. The dimensions of the joinery make it very awkward to transfer the layout from one workpiece to another, so Metcalf lays out the tail and socket separately using the same gauge settings for each. Still, with careful layout and saw work, the result is strong and pretty.

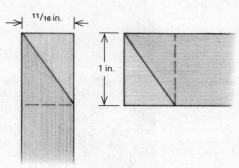

LAYOUT IS CRITICAL

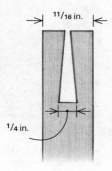

Start with the miter. Use a marking gauge to scribe the width of each piece onto both edges of its mate. Then use a bevel gauge to lay out the angles on the front faces.

Cut the dovetailed tenon. The front cheek is cut at an angle (left) with the saw stopping just before the outside corner of the miter. The rear cheek is cut to the baseline. Clamp the stock horizontally to cut away the waste (right). Cut on the waste side of the line and pare with a chisel.

Mark out the socket. Use the bevel gauge to mark the angled socket cheeks on the edge of the piece. For the pin, the straight lines are on the edge and the angles go on the end grain.

Bevel gauge alternative. For easier layout on narrow stock, Metcalf made an adjustable jig by fitting Plexiglas into a kerf in a hardwood block and adding screws. A cleat on the end helps locate the jig.

A single, long socket. A pair of angled cuts establishes the socket walls. Carefully saw to the waste sides of your marks (left), and then use a bandsaw or coping saw to hog out the majority of the socket (right). The remaining waste can then be cleared with a coping saw and chisel.

Add a Miter to Half-Blind Dovetails

The dovetails for the case are, for the most part, ordinary half-blinds. However, the mitered front complicates the layout and joinery slightly. To begin with, you'll need to dimension the top piece so that it is the full length of the case, to allow for the miter at the front. And before laying out for the tails, you'll need to remove a narrow band of stock so that the tails will come up short of the end of the case.

On this case, the top and sides were also of different thicknesses. This meant the miter wasn't 45°, requiring different bevel-gauge settings to create the mating angles.

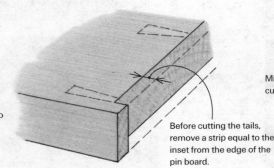

Before cutting the tails, remove a strip equal to the inset from the edge of the pin board.

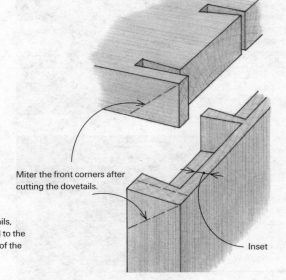

Miter the front corners after cutting the dovetails.

Inset

1. CUT THE TAILS

Trim the tail board. With a router and fence, remove the extra material (left). Use a chisel to square up the tab (right), which will form one half of the mitered front. Its rear face also captures the half-pin behind the miter.

Mark and cut the tails. Scribe a line for the tail length using a gauge setting picked up from the pin board. You can scribe the underside of the top all the way across, but scribe the show face only between your angled pencil lines. To pare the waste from the narrow sockets (left), Metcalf uses a chisel that he ground to 1/16 in. wide.

2. CUT THE PINS

Transfer the layout and cut the pins. Scribe the socket shoulders with a knife (left), then flip the piece in the vise and mark the vertical portion of the pins with a pencil. After sawing to the lines and hogging away the waste with a router, Metcalf does a careful final cleanup with a chisel (below).

3. MITER THE CORNER LAST

Mark out the miter for the top. Adjust the sliding bevel to the angle between the top's outside corner and the scribe line for the tails on the underside. Trim the miter. After sawing tight to the line with a fine saw, the paring required should be minimal.

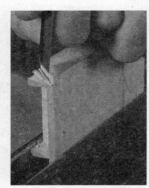

Check the fit. If all is well, you should now be able to tap the top and sides together, and you should have a tight-fitting miter at the front.

Biscuit-Joint Basics

By Tom Begnal

It will never match the beauty of a dovetail or the strength of a mortise-and-tenon, but for speed, accuracy, and ease of use, it's hard to beat the biscuit joint.

Biscuit joints can be used on all wood products: solid wood, plywood, medium-density fiberboard (MDF), and particleboard. For this reason, they are great for cabinetry, which typically involves a mix of solid wood and sheet goods. Biscuits are a great way to join a plywood carcase and attach an assembled face frame. They also help keep things aligned when gluing solid-wood edging to plywood or assembling solid boards into a wide panel.

Biscuit Joiner Cuts the Slots

A dedicated tool and an oddly shaped tenon combine to create a biscuit joint. At the heart of the process is a power tool called a biscuit joiner or a plate joiner. To make a joint, use the tool to cut a shallow slot in each of the mating parts. Then, after adding glue to each slot, insert a thin, football-shaped biscuit into one slot. A little more than half the biscuit's width goes into the slot; the other half sticks out. To complete the joint, just slip the mating slot onto the "tenon" and clamp the parts together.

The biscuit joiner has just four main parts: a motor, a blade that cuts the slot, an adjustable fence that aligns some types of cut, and a base that houses the blade and also can align cuts.

The 4-in.-dia. blade looks like a miniature tablesaw blade. Unlike a tablesaw blade, however, the biscuit-joiner blade cuts horizontally. The kerf it creates, commonly called the slot, measures about 1/8 in., just wide enough to accept standard-thickness biscuits.

Thanks to a spring-loaded sliding "way" that connects the base and motor, you can butt the front of the base against a workpiece, start the motor, and push it forward. The spinning blade emerges from the front of the tool to cut a shallow arc-shaped slot in the workpiece. Release the forward pressure, and the springs push the motor back to retract the spinning blade safely into the base.

Expanding Biscuits Fill the Slots

The second element in this joint is the biscuit. Made from beechwood or white birch that has been thoroughly dried, biscuits are compressed by machine to a standard thickness. For maximum all-around strength, the biscuits are cut so the grain runs diagonally.

When a biscuit comes into contact with moisture, it swells. So when you insert a biscuit into a glue-lined slot, the biscuit expands, creating a snug fit and a tight joint. It is important to use only water-based glues such as common yellow PVA glue. Biscuits won't work with epoxy, cyanoacrylate ("super") glue, or polyurethane glues.

Reference Off the Fence

Using the fence to locate the cut lets you adjust the position of the biscuit slot to any point between 3/16 in. and 1 in. from the reference surface.

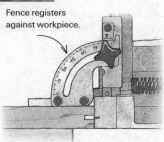

Layout is simple. Just align the workpieces, then draw a line across the mating faces to mark the centerline of the biscuit.

Center the cutter on the stock's thickness. With the fence flat on the workpiece, adjust its height to locate the cut. To make the cut, simply align the joiner with the single layout mark, start the tool, and push the joiner's body forward.

Fence registers against workpiece.

Continued ➜

Biscuits come in three standard sizes, No. 0, No. 10, and No. 20. The biscuit joiner has preset depth stops that match these sizes.

Use the Fence or the Base to Locate the Slot

When using a biscuit joiner, you have two ways—the fence or the base—to register the slot in the workpiece. Each has advantages.

For extra flexibility, the adjustable fence lets you position the slot anywhere between 3/16 in. and 1 in. from the fence (if the biscuit is any closer than 3/16 in. to the surface of the workpiece, its swelling could create a bulge on the surface). Also, you can set the fence to cut slots in angled joints.

However, if all you want to do is center a slot on 3/4-in.-thick stock, it's easier to register off the base. This is because the center of the kerf is located 3/8 in. from the bottom of the base. To create a slot in 3/8-in.-thick stock, place the base and the stock on the same flat surface and make the cut. It's OK if the slot isn't exactly centered; just remember not to flip the parts when it comes time to glue them.

Cut and Assemble a Simple Biscuit Joint

With a biscuit joiner in hand, it takes just four steps to join a pair of 3/4-in.-thick boards end to edge. This joint is useful for making light-duty door frames, especially when the panel is plywood or MDF. That's because plywood and MDF don't expand and contract with changes in humidity, so they can be glued in place to add strength to the frame.

Step 1: Align and mark—Align the boards as you want to see them joined, and use a single line to mark the biscuit centerline on the top face of both parts.

Step 2: Determine the biscuit size—Based on the width of the board, choose the largest biscuit that it can accept. For the 3-in.-wide stock shown, No. 20 biscuits are a good choice.

ANGLE THE FENCE FOR MITERS

Setting the fence to 45° allows the joiner to cut a slot in the end of a mitered workpiece. Align the joiner for a cut toward the inside of the miter, so there is plenty of material in which to sink the slot.

A Variety of Uses

Biscuit joinery is useful in a wide range of applications, from aligning edge-glued boards to securing shelves to assembling and attaching frames, miters, and more.

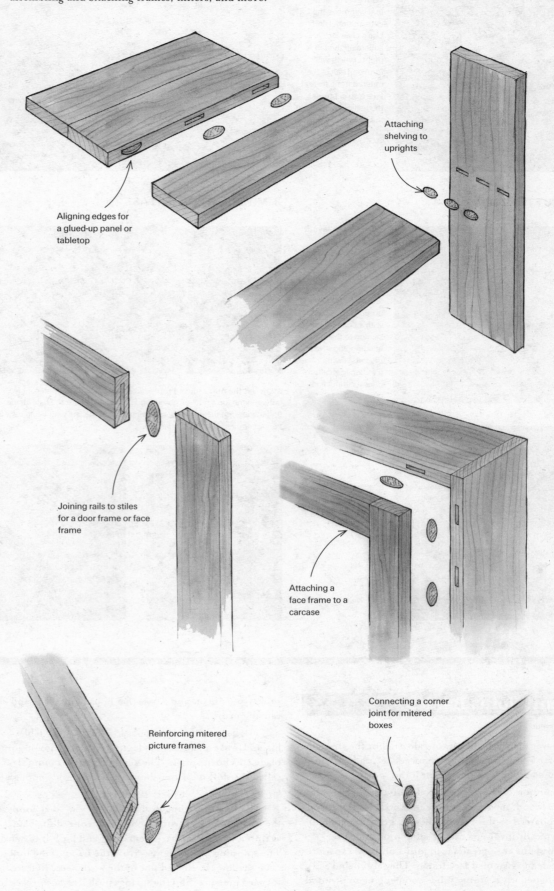

Aligning edges for a glued-up panel or tabletop

Attaching shelving to uprights

Joining rails to stiles for a door frame or face frame

Attaching a face frame to a carcase

Reinforcing mitered picture frames

Connecting a corner joint for mitered boxes

Step 3: Cut the slots—Clamp one of the workpieces in place (never hold the workpiece by hand). Set the depth-adjustment knob for the No. 20 biscuit. Align the center-registration mark on the biscuit joiner with the biscuit-centerline mark made in step one. Start the motor and, with one hand on the top handle and one hand on the motor housing, push the motor toward the stock. Continue cutting until you reach the stop, and then allow the spring action to return the motor to the starting point. Repeat the process to cut a slot in the second piece.

Step 4: Apply glue—Use a small brush (I use a throwaway soldering brush) to apply a generous coat of glue to each slot. Be sure to coat the sides of the slots—that's where a lot of the glue strength comes from. Add glue to the biscuit and insert it into one of the slots, then attach the other piece and clamp them together. Don't answer the phone after the biscuit has been inserted into the first slot. By the time you come back, it will already have swelled enough that you won't be able to insert it in the second part of the joint. The only thing you can do then is let the glue dry, saw away the protruding part of the biscuit, and recut the slot.

Reference Off the Base

Registering a cut from the joiner's base always puts the biscuit slot 3/8 in. from the reference surface, or centered on 3/4-in. stock. This can make for quick biscuiting, as when attaching a fixed shelf to an upright.

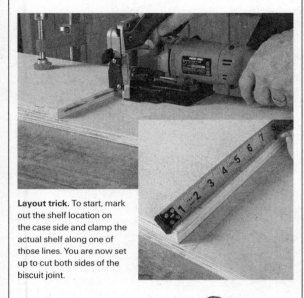

Layout trick. To start, mark out the shelf location on the case side and clamp the actual shelf along one of those lines. You are now set up to cut both sides of the biscuit joint.

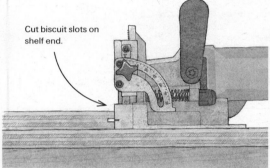

Cut biscuit slots on shelf end.

Just butt and cut. With the joiner base on the side piece, cut the biscuit slots in the end of the shelf (above). Reposition the joiner so the base butts against the end of the shelf, and cut the mating slots in the side piece (below).

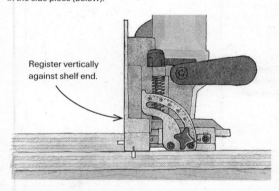

Register vertically against shelf end.

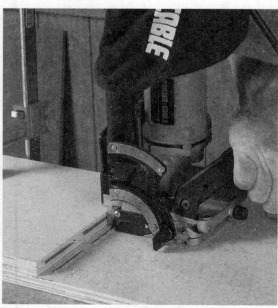

Strong, Simple Joints with Dowels

By Asa Christiana

In all of woodworking, no joint is as undervalued or underused as the one held together by the lowly dowel. Why? The answer lies in a mountain of broken chairs and cabinets. Decades of bad factory-made furniture have given the sturdy little peg a rickety reputation. But savvy pros know better. Dowel joints offer a simple, strong way to make fine furniture, and they often succeed where other joints can't.

Dowels are easy to use in part because they are cylindrical, meaning you can quickly create accurate holes for them using a handheld drill. As to strength, our recent joint test showed that properly executed dowel joints are strong enough for all but the most demanding applications. This strength means you only have to make simple butt joints before drilling holes. And the best news, especially for beginning woodworkers, is that all you need is that drill, a couple of good drill bits, and an inexpensive jig. Here are my favorite ways to use dowels.

Align Glued-Up Panels Perfectly

Woodworkers often edge-glue several boards into a panel for a wide part like a door or tabletop. Dowels work well to keep the boards aligned so their surfaces stay flush.

To mark out for the joinery, draw tick marks across the joints, about 6 in. or 8 in. apart. Use these marks to align the doweling jig for drilling. This joint's strength comes from the long, edge-grain glue surface, so the dowels don't need to be numerous or large. I usually use 3/8-in.-dia. dowels, unless the panel is less than 5/8 in. thick.

Be sure to drill 1/16 in. or so deeper than needed to hold excess glue when the joint goes together. Also, when gluing any dowel joints, don't put glue on the dowel itself; the hole will scrape it off and create a mess. Instead, put glue in each hole and spread it with a small brush or stick.

Build Sturdy Tables, Doors, and Cabinets

Almost any joint that calls for a mortise-and-tenon—table bases, door frames, face frames—is a candidate for dowel joinery.

Because this joint relies exclusively on the dowels for strength, you need longer dowels—and more of them. A good rule for dowel size here is one-half the thickness of the workpiece, with 3/4 in. or more extending into each hole. A 3/8-in.-dia., 2-in.-long dowel works great in most situations. To ensure that the holes in the mating pieces line up accurately, start with the jig referenced along a common edge. In this case, use the top edge of the rail and the top of the leg, which will be flush when the pieces are assembled. Also, don't apply glue to the mating surfaces. The end grain won't add much strength and you'll get excess squeeze-out, which is best avoided.

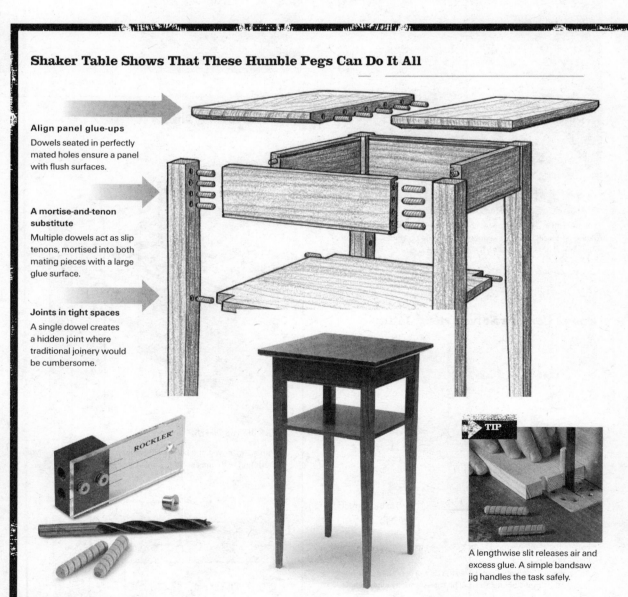

Shaker Table Shows That These Humble Pegs Can Do It All

Align panel glue-ups
Dowels seated in perfectly mated holes ensure a panel with flush surfaces.

A mortise-and-tenon substitute
Multiple dowels act as slip tenons, mortised into both mating pieces with a large glue surface.

Joints in tight spaces
A single dowel creates a hidden joint where traditional joinery would be cumbersome.

ROCKLER

TIP

A lengthwise slit releases air and excess glue. A simple bandsaw jig handles the task safely.

SECRETS OF SUCCESS

A good dowel joint depends on a snug fit between dowel and hole. Hardware-store dowels won't do, but good, cheap dowels are available from online woodworking suppliers.

To drill accurate holes, use a brad-point bit. Its center spur prevents the bit from wandering and enlarging the hole. To keep mating holes aligned and ensure that the holes are square to the surface, you'll need a doweling jig. The $14 model from Rockler works with dowels of 3/8-in. diameter, a good all-purpose size.

For places where the jig can't go, a set of dowel centers is a smart accessory. These metal plugs fit a hole precisely and transfer its location to the mating piece.

Continued ➔

Hide a Joint Where There's No Room to Hide

Furniture makers often draft an overall design for a piece first and sort out the joinery afterward. This allows creative freedom but can lead to situations where traditional joinery won't work.

One example is the lower shelf on this table. Rest it on stretchers or cleats and it will look clunky. Traditional joinery would be difficult to execute or visually distracting. Dowels offer a clean solution. You can use the jig to drill the dowel holes in the table legs, but the jig won't work on the small notched corners of the shelf. Instead, dry-fit the legs to the aprons, and clamp a support block to each leg so that its top is level with the shelf bottom. Then insert a dowel center into each hole and rest the shelf on the blocks. A light mallet tap on the outside of each leg will press the dowel center's point into the shelf edge, marking for the mating hole. Now drill the dowel hole in the shelf edge. Again, place glue only in the dowel holes.

The strength in a panel glue-up comes from the large long-grain mating surfaces. Be sure to apply glue on these surfaces as well as in the dowel holes, spreading it evenly inside and out.

Dowel Centers Solve Tricky Joints

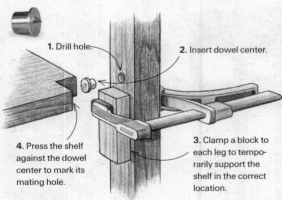

1. Drill hole.

2. Insert dowel center.

4. Press the shelf against the dowel center to mark its mating hole.

3. Clamp a block to each leg to temporarily support the shelf in the correct location.

- Locate the shelf. A support block clamped to the leg holds the shelf in place.
- Tap once. A light mallet tap drives the dowel center into the shelf edge. The dimple locates the drill bit for a perfectly aligned hole.
- Drill the shelf edge. Eyeball the drill and the edge of the shelf to make sure the hole is straight and square.

Glue Up Perfect Panels

Set the depth. Insert the drill bit into the doweling jig until the point protrudes to the desired depth. To create a simple depth stop, wrap a piece of painter's tape into a "flag" around the bit where it enters the top of the jig.

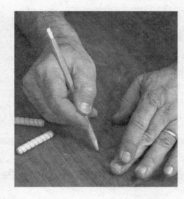

Layout is simple. Make a series of pencil marks squarely across each joint to locate the mating holes.

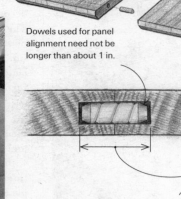

Dowels used for panel alignment need not be longer than about 1 in.

In this joint, the depth of each hole should be half of the dowel's length, plus 1/16 in. or so at each end to accommodate excess glue.

Drill the holes. Registration marks on the doweling jig align with your pencil marks to locate the jig. When the depth-stop flag begins sweeping chips from the work surface, you've reached the correct depth.

Build Strong Joints

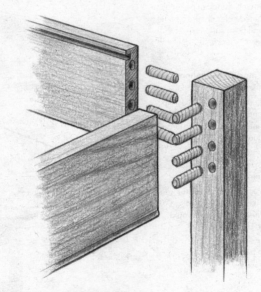

HOLE DEPTHS DIFFER

With a 2-in. dowel, the holes in the leg must be shallower to avoid interfering with one another.

OFFSET JOINERY

The apron's outside face is set in from the leg by 1/8 in. As a result, the holes in the leg must move over by 1/8 in. to accommodate the difference. Modify the jig to accomplish this.

TRICK FOR ACCURATE SPACING

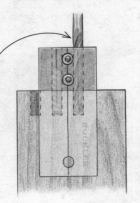

Start with the jig flush to the edge of the workpiece.

Drilling the first two holes. Secure the apron in a vise and clamp the jig so its edge is flush with the top of the apron.

Move the jig and secure it with a spare dowel.

Move the jig over. To continue the line of holes beyond the jig's reach, use a dowel to hold the jig in the last hole you drilled.

With the jig secured, drill the next hole in line.

Drill and repeat. With the jig secured, drill the next hole. Repeat as needed for a line of evenly spaced holes.

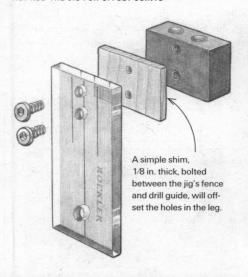

A simple shim, 1/8 in. thick, bolted between the jig's fence and drill guide, will off-set the holes in the leg.

Drill like usual. Drill the leg holes with the jig shimmed out by 1/8 in. (left). When the joint comes together, the apron will have an attractive reveal (above).

TIP

The leg-to-apron joint derives no real strength from glue on the mating surfaces, so apply glue to the dowel holes only.

The Rule Joint Done Right

By Michael Zuba

Most commonly found on drop-leaf tables, the rule joint allows the outside leaves to be lifted to create a large, useful surface, or folded down to save space. The beauty of this molded joint is that it looks attractive whether open or closed, and it keeps the hinges hidden.

You need to understand the mechanics of this joint in order to lay it out and cut it accurately, and project articles rarely go into enough detail. A rule joint consists of a board with a bead (typically the fixed top of a table) and a board with a cove, or cope (typically the movable leaf). When the joint is closed, the two boards meet tightly and on an even plane. As the leaf is lowered, the cove rolls evenly around the bead. Two or more hinges support the leaf. The secret is to place the center of the hinge barrel in line with the center of the bead.

Although you can create this joint with matching molding planes or shaper knives, the method I'll explain uses two widely available router bits. And construction is easy when divided into three main steps: Cut the bead, cut the matching cove, and finally, install the hinges.

Dial In the Setup on a Sample Board

It is vital to the smooth operation of the rule joint that the boards remain flat and true, so rough-mill the boards a little oversize and allow them to rest in your shop for a week or so to make sure they are stable and don't cup or twist. Then mill them to final thickness, in this case 3/4

in. I always mill a sample board to the same thickness as the tabletop and use it for layout and test cuts all the way through the process to ensure the rule joint fits properly. This makes me confident that everything will work when I start cutting my valuable tabletop.

The rule joint revolves around the barrel of the hinge, so start laying out the joint by setting a marking gauge to the distance from the flat side of a drop-leaf hinge to the center of its barrel. The grain of the tabletop and the drop leaf runs parallel to the rule joint, so the layout is done on the end grain. Scribe a line along the end grain of the sample board, registering off the bottom edge of the board. Make sure you lay out the end of the board that will contact the router bit first on the router table.

I used a 3/8-in. radius half-round or bullnose bit to cut the bead, so I set a compass to this distance. Put one point of the compass on the scribe line and the other where this line reaches the edge of the board. Now draw an arc of about 180° whose apex just touches the edge of the board. Use a knife and a square to mark a line perpendicular to the scribed line at the location of the compass point away from the edge of the board. You now have established the location of the hinge and the profile of the bead.

I use a full half-round bit rather than a quarter-round beading bit because the half-round bit will cut a return past the centerline. If this is not cut, the bottom edge will bind as the leaf drops and the cope of the drop leaf will not roll evenly. You'll also need a 3/4-in. diameter core-box or round-nose bit, which should nest perfectly with the half-round bit. I used Freud bits 18-122 and 82-116, available

at www.woodworker.com.

With the half-round bit mounted in a router table, use the sample board to set the correct height of the bit and then gradually move the fence back to sneak up on the exact line of the bead. Once set, clamp a hold-down board to the fence, and make the cut to both sides of the fixed part of the tabletop. With a sharp bit, you can do this easily in one pass. Depending on the thickness of the board, you may be left with a thin strip of wood attached to the fillet (the vertical surface above the bead). Cut this away on the tablesaw and clean up the edge with sandpaper wrapped around a block, using a light touch. With the bead side complete, the next step is to cut the matching coves on the leaves.

Sample Board Strikes Again

To get the approximate location of the cove, I butt the beaded board against the uncut side of the sample board and trace the bead onto the end of the board.

Remove the bulk of the waste with a 1/4-in.-wide dado blade on the tablesaw, staying away from the traced line. This will prevent the core-box bit from having to make too large of a cut in a single pass. Set up the router table with the 3/4-in.-dia. core-box bit. Use your sample board to make a trial cut just below the outline you drew. Now check the fit of cove to bead, and raise the height of the bit accordingly. The cut should produce a cove that perfectly matches the bead when the boards are mated on a flat surface.

When set up, I take a secondary fence and align it parallel to the primary fence with the sample board as a spacer. This fence acts like a featherboard to keep the leaf tight to the fence, ensuring a smooth, consistent cut. With the beads and coves cut, you can move on to the hinges.

A Rule Joint Hinges on the Hardware

Locating and installing the hinges is the most critical part of the process. The first step is to determine the number of hinges. For smaller pieces such as a Pembroke table, I use two hinges. For large tables such as a William and Mary gate-leg or a dining-room table, I would use up to four.

Set a marking gauge to the width from the edge of the bead to the vertical line you drew during layout. Now take the actual tabletop, and scribe a line along the underside of the bead to mark the centerline of the hinges.

Clamp the top and a leaf together, face down. Now place the hinge upside down with the barrel in line with the scribe mark. Using a knife, outline the location of the hinge across both boards. Set up a router with a 1/4-in. straight bit and adjust the depth of cut to the thickness of the hinge leaf. Separate the boards and rout away the waste,

Anatomy of the Joint

Fixed tabletop

Drop leaf

Barrel

Long side of hinge attaches to leaf.

When exposed, the joint shows a thumbnail profile.

HOW IT WORKS
The joint revolves around the barrel of a special drop-leaf hinge. When the leaf is raised, it should be flush with the tabletop. When lowered, there should be no gap between the parts.

Table leaf swings down to save space.

A PAIR OF ROUTER BITS MAKES THE JOB EASY

Bead

Cove

A 3/8-in. radius half-round or bullnose bit cuts the bead.

A 3/4-in. core-box bit cuts the cove.

For the two halves of the rule joint to meet without a gap, it is critical that the radii of these two router bits match exactly.

Continued →

Lay Out the Bead

1. LOCATE THE CENTER OF THE HINGE

Because the joint revolves around the center of the hinge's barrel, you need to mark this location. Set a marking gauge to the distance from the flat side of the hinge to the center of the barrel, and scratch a line on the end of the sample board that will enter the router bit first.

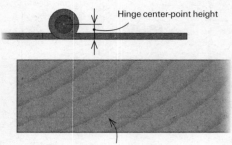

Hinge center-point height

Mark line at hinge center-point height.

2. MARK THE ARC OF THE HALF-ROUND ROUTER BIT

Set a compass to equal the radius of the half-round bit you'll be using, in this case 3⁄8 in. Place one point on the edge of the board and the other on the center-point line created in step one. Draw an arc of about 180°.

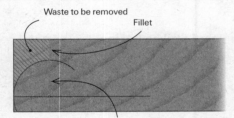

Mark the arc.

3⁄8-in. radius

3. COMPLETE THE LAYOUT

Drop a line at right-angles to the center point. This gives the location of the fillet, or straight section above the bead. The shaded area is removed on the router table to leave the beaded half.

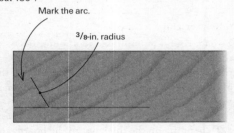

Waste to be removed

Fillet

Mark a vertical line at the center point.

staying away from the knifed line. Then clean up the walls with a chisel.

To make room for the hinge barrel, I use a #8 carving gouge to create a round-bottomed trench. You also could use chisels to create a straight-sided recess.

Set the hinge in the mortise to check that no part of the hinge projects above the bottom surface of either board.

Fasten the hinge with appropriate screws and swing the leaf to check the fit. You may have to sand the surfaces very lightly, but that should be the limit to your fine-tuning.

Although this joint takes patience, you'll see the reward on your next table, whether the leaves are open or closed.

Rout the Bead

Fine-tune the setup. Using the layout on the end of the sample board, set the half-round bit to the correct height. Make the first pass with the fence slightly forward, and then ease it back until the bead is cut perfectly.

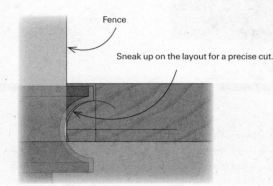

Fence

Sneak up on the layout for a precise cut.

Bead the tabletop. Now that the router has been set up using the sample board, clamp a hold-down board to the fence of the router table and cut the bead on both sides of the fixed tabletop (above). Because only a small amount of wood is being removed, you can cut each bead in one pass. If a thin strip of wood is left attached to the top of the fillet (above), cut it off on the tablesaw and carefully sand it flush.

Cut the Matching Cove

Transfer the layout. Butt the tabletop to a fresh edge of the sample board with the fillet in line with that uncut edge. Transfer the outline of the bead.

Saw away the waste. Use dado blades to cut away the bulk of the waste in what will become the cove.

Set up to cut the bead. Align the sample board with the round-nose bit, but make the first cut with the bit slightly too low.

Check the fit. After the first cut, the bead and cove should nest perfectly, but the coved sample board should still sit a little higher than the beaded board. Sneak up on the cut until the two boards are level.

Cove the drop leaves. Once the sample board is right, clamp a second fence to the router table so that the wide leaves won't wobble as they pass the router bit.

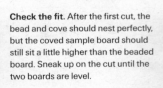

Install the Hinges

THE RIGHT HINGE FOR A RULE JOINT

A regular hinge with its barrel in the middle won't work for this type of joint. Instead you need a drop-leaf hinge with sides of different lengths. The short side is attached to the beaded board, while the longer side is attached to the drop leaf so that the underside swings under the beaded board.

SOURCES OF SUPPLY:

Drop-Leaf Hinges
www.horton-brasses.com
www.londonderry-brasses.com

FLATTEN THE HINGE IF NECESSARY

How to check it. The drop-leaf hinge should sit flat with the barrel facing up (top). If the leaves rise up as they approach the barrel, the hinge may not work properly.

Gentle persuasion. Hold one leaf tightly in a vise and use a block of wood and a hammer to gently straighten the leaf.

LAY OUT THE POSITION

Inset the hinge. Set a marking gauge to the distance from the edge of the bead to the vertical line below the fillet (1). This marks the center of the hinge barrel. Scratch a line where the hinges will be centered (2). Then clamp the drop leaf to the tabletop, and locate the hinge upside down straddling the joint, with the barrel centered on the scribed line (3). Mark the outline deeply with a knife.

CUT THE MORTISE

Set the router depth. Set the depth of a straight bit to match the thickness of a hinge's leaf. Clean up the recess after routing away the bulk of the waste. Use a chisel to square up the sides of the hinge recess (right).

ATTACH THE HINGE

One last cut, and it drops in. Use a carving gouge or a chisel to cut a trench for the barrel of the hinge (above). Use full-threaded screws to attach the hinge to the tabletop and the drop leaf (above right). Check that the two surfaces of the rule joint remain parallel throughout the movement with no binding or unsightly gaps (right). A bit of sanding smooths out the action.

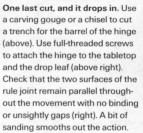

A Guide to Gluing and Stamping

By Gary Rogowski

No movie chase scene could provide as many heart-pounding thrills as gluing up a project in the woodshop. After weeks of effort and preparation, all of your careful work comes down to 15 minutes of heart-palpitating frenzy. Few other things in life can compare to this, except perhaps getting to the airport late for your flight.

Just as there are strategies for milling lumber and cutting joinery, there are strategies for gluing that increase your chances of success. Organizing your tools beforehand, planning for contingencies, gluing up in stages, applying glue intelligently, and practicing assembly techniques will help you to avoid most of the stress of glue-ups. Notice that I did not say all of it. Most of these important factors come under the heading "preparation."

Preparation is the Key to Success

The assembly of your project may be the most important job you face during its construction. Before you squeeze out any glue, check that your assembly tools are at the ready. This will save you precious time during glue-up. It also may send you to the store to get the right tools for the job.

A lamentable truth is that you will never have enough clamps. Get over it; it's true. Choose clamps appropriate for each job, and buy as many heavy-duty ones as you can afford. Before using clamps, unscrew them as much as possible so you have plenty of adjustment available, and arrange them so that the head and tail stops are at the proper distance.

Different clamps have different jaw depths. Put clamps on your project to check that you'll get pressure where you need it. Make sure any caul or clamp pad you use is free of dried-up glue. Nothing dents wood as well as that hard old stuff.

This may seem simple, but number the parts clearly so there is no confusion when you are under the gun. There is no worse feeling than finishing your clamping only to discover that tenon A is in mortise C. Use big, bold letters or numbers. You won't have time in the midst of your gluing frenzy to look for neat little script.

In every case, do a dry run to make sure everything is in order beforehand. Check the parts to see that they are not twisted or bowed by the clamping pressure. Adjust the pressure to keep frames flat while still pulling them tight at the joints. This may mean changing the position of the clamp heads.

Just Enough Glue, Just Where You Need It

The age-old question asked by most new woodworkers is: How much glue should I use? The age-old answer is: Just enough. Unfortunately, experience is the best teacher. I used enough glue on my first large bookcase to glue three of them together. More glue is not usually better, and the cleanup can be time-consuming and difficult, especially if you are following with a finish (such as oil) that highlights glue residue.

A little bit of squeeze-out is what you're shooting for in most situations. Let the glue dry until it's reached a plastic state. Then it can be lifted from the surface of the wood with a sharp chisel or scraper. Do not wet a rag and smear the glue around unless you're painting the piece or you have no other choice. If the glue does dry completely, you'll have to get it off. Dried glue is hard, so in this case use your second-best chisel, one that you don't mind resharpening often.

The best glue joint is long grain to long grain, so don't worry about gluing end-grain surfaces unless that's all you've got to work with.

There are a variety of gluing situations, but I've drawn up a few of the more common scenarios that you'll run into. Advice on these specific glue-ups can be applied to many variations.

Continued ➡

Essential Clamps and Supplies

Like everything else in woodworking, successful assembly depends a lot on having the right gear. This includes the right type and number of clamps, the right clamp pads and cauls, the right mallet, and the right gluing accessories.

GLUE

Which type of adhesive to use depends on several factors: strength, open time, clamp time, and appearance. For 90% of my projects, yellow glue has proven to be great. However, it has a short open time so you must be prepared to work quickly once you wipe it on.

LIGHT-DUTY CLAMPS

For simple assemblies, spring clamps will suffice. For slightly larger glue joints, small, sliding-arm bar clamps will work. Have an array of these from 6 in. to 18 in. in length..

BAND CLAMPS

Use band clamps for glue-ups of everything from chairs to mitered picture frames.

C-clamps put a lot of pressure in a small area, and work for both light- and heavy-duty clamping. Be sure to use clamping pads, as C-clamps can mar the work surface.

DEADBLOW MALLET

Persuasion comes in many forms. Rather than using a framing hammer and a block of wood to protect the work surface, use a deadblow mallet. They pack a wallop without leaving marks.

HAND SCREWS

Wooden hand screws won't mar the workpiece, but practice closing them before the glue-up. They can provide light to moderate pressure over a wide area.

HEAVY-DUTY CLAMPS

For bigger jobs like pulling together frames, carcases, or panels, you'll need heavy-duty bar or pipe clamps of sufficient size and length. Use a threaded pipe coupler and pipe that is threaded at both ends to make two shorter bar clamps into a long one.

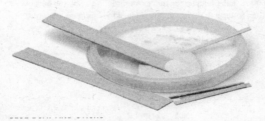

To make the glue accessible, use a glue boat of some sort—a plastic lid, a folded-up piece of cardboard. To avoid getting glue on your fingers, spread it with wood sticks.

CAULS

Clamps often need help to do their jobs properly. Clamping cauls vary from thin, protective pads to curved and angled pieces that redirect or distribute clamping pressure. Use cauls made of melamine or cover the cauls with tape so glue won't stick to them. Thin, flat strips of wood will protect your project, while thicker cauls will spread clamp pressure. Save your bandsawn offcuts to act as shaped cauls.

Dovetailed Cases: Keep Glue on the Outside

Carcase dovetails usually need some clamping help to come together. I like to leave the long grain of the case just slightly proud of the end grain so I can put a flat caul right over the joint. If you leave the pins and tails proud, you'll have to use notched cauls for clamping. I also find it easier to plane the long grain flush than to work on the end grain of protruding pins and tails.

Dovetails can be a messy glue-up. Use melamine cauls or cover the cauls with tape so they won't become glued to the case. Put glue on all of the long-grain surfaces but only lightly touch the outer half of the end-grain surfaces with glue. Gluing the end grain doesn't help and causes a lot of squeeze-out inside the case.

Plywood Cases: Curved Cauls Spread Pressure

Everyone builds plywood boxes eventually. In some cases, you can use simple butt joints and biscuits to join the pieces. If the cabinet is going to be painted or if the sides won't be exposed, you can use screws or nails to hold the biscuited assembly together while the glue dries.

However, for maximum strength and clean looks, you probably will opt for rabbet and dado joints, and you'll need clamps for the glue-up. In that case, you'll have to plan the assembly more carefully.

For deep cases, use convex curved cauls, which will extend pressure to the center of interior panels. Curved cauls also can distribute pressure along a long edge, bailing you out if you don't have enough bar clamps. You can curve a caul with a few passes of your handplane or belt sander.

Put glue in the rabbet and dado joints, with just a touch along the end grain of the horizontals. Excess glue will squeeze out into tight corners, causing problems later. After clamping, check the diagonals and make any necessary adjustments.

Use Glue Size to Avoid Starved Miters

Large, mitered solid-wood carcases will test your band-clamp supply. If you don't have enough, glue angled cauls directly onto the case and use small clamps to put pressure exactly where you need it. Attach the cauls with hot-melt glue, double-stick tape, or even a thin bead of yellow glue. If you use yellow glue, make sure the caul is a wood that's softer than your project stock. After the glue has cured, you can take a chisel and knock off the bulk of the cauls. Clean up any wood sticking to the carcase with a handplane or belt sander.

Miters soak up a lot of glue, so apply a preliminary coat of glue—called size—to close up all of the porous end grain.

I use band clamps to close up mitered picture-frame-type joints, but there are other good methods. One strategy I've used is to make thick cauls with V-cut notches in them at each end. Clamp these cauls to the two mating pieces, with the notches positioned over the glue joint. Then clamp across the notches.

Blind Mortise-and-Tenons: Put More Glue in the Mortise

Different mortise-and-tenons require different gluing strategies. The two basic types involve through-tenons, which we'll deal with shortly, and blind tenons. A blind tenon ends inside the mortised piece. A good example is a standard table base.

Put glue in the mortises all the way to the bottom, with a little bit extra near the mouth. Then just kiss the tenon cheeks with glue right before pushing the joint together. Do not put any glue on the end-grain tenon shoulders or mortise ends because those surfaces won't do much holding, and you're just asking for more squeeze-out.

Make sure the rail, when assembled, is a bit higher than the ends of the legs. This way, the joinery will be easy to clean up using a handplane. Otherwise, you'll have to remove end-grain wood from the tops of the legs. Check that the legs don't twist when you apply clamping pressure.

Case Work

DOVETAILED CASES: APPLY GLUE SPARINGLY

Avoid squeeze-out inside the case. Apply glue to the cheeks of the pins and tails, but put only a dab on the outside edges of the end grain. Drive the joint home with a deadblow mallet, which won't mar the workpieces. Wipe away the squeeze-out before clamping.

Use melamine cauls and check the diagonals. On dovetails, Rogowski keeps the long grain proud, which allows him to use flat cauls. Later, he planes the sides flush with the pins and tails. If the diagonals don't match, use a long clamp to draw the assembly square.

PLYWOOD CASES: CURVED CAULS REACH ACROSS LONG SHELVES

Clamp at the ends.
Convex caul
Shelf
Curve applies pressure in the middle, where clamps cannot reach.

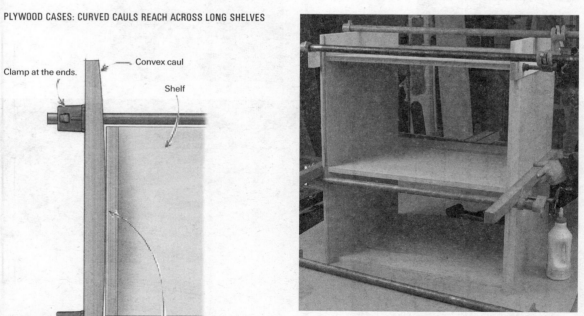

Glue large cases in stages. Here the case is upside down, and the top panel is only dry-fit in its rabbet, while the other panels are glued. To apply pressure along the entire edge of the middle shelf, Rogowski uses a convex caul.

Miter Joints

BAND CLAMPS HANDLE MOST PICTURE FRAMES

Size miters to avoid starved joints. Size is a preliminary coat of glue that seals the end grain. Scrape away any excess and wait a few minutes before applying glue again.

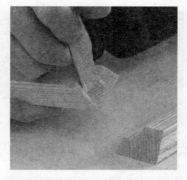

A band clamp makes tight miters. This one, from Jorgensen, is ratcheted tight with a small wrench.

BAR CLAMPS ARE A BETTER CHOICE FOR MITERED CASES

Use these with angled cauls to ensure that miters close completely and accurately. Cauls can be glued, taped, or clamped to workpieces.

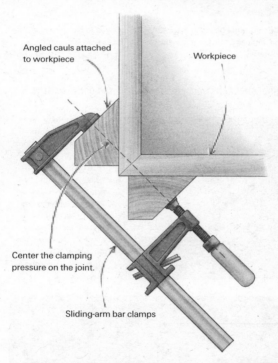

Angled cauls attached to workpiece
Workpiece
Center the clamping pressure on the joint.
Sliding-arm bar clamps

Attach cauls onto large mitered cases. Angled cauls direct clamping pressure through the joints. If you glue on the cauls, make them out of a softer wood so they are easy to remove.

Continued ➔

Mortise-and-Tenons

BLIND TENONS ARE STRAIGHTFORWARD

The mortises get the glue. Handle the pieces carefully so the glue doesn't drip out. To minimize squeeze-out, the tenon cheeks get just a touch of glue, and the shoulders get none.

Glue up table bases in stages. This allows you to check and adjust the flatness and squareness of subassemblies before the final assembly.

THROUGH-TENONS SQUEEZE GLUE WHERE YOU DON'T WANT IT

Seal the end grain of through-tenons with shellac. The ends always wind up with glue on them, which soaks quickly into the grain, where it can interfere with the final finish. Use clamps to pull the tenon evenly and safely through the mortise. Wipe away the squeeze-out as soon as possible.

Sliding Dovetails

A QUICK AND EASY METHOD FOR DRAWERS

To begin assembly, clamp the drawer face to the bench. Apply a good amount of glue to the female part of the joint but just a touch of glue to the male part.

The drawer back also is dovetailed. Use two clamps to push the workpiece evenly downward. Note the small slip of wood used to align the slots for the drawer bottom.

Use pipe clamps to drive the dovetail home. Have another one ready to finish where the first clamp leaves off. With steady, focused pressure, the joint won't bind. The small dovetailed strip taped to the drawer side protects it as it is driven fully home.

Edge Joints

STRAIGHT PIPE CLAMPS MAKE FOR FLAT PANELS

Run a bead of glue and spread it. Rogowski props the middle board against the bench to apply glue to both edges. Rubbing the edges together creates a good glue bond.

Let glue stiffen before removing it. Wait 15 or 20 minutes, and the gelled glue will peel off easily with a sharp paint scraper.

Be sure the boards are seated on the pipes. Use C-clamps and pads to align any wayward edges. Cover black pipe at the glue joints with tape or clamp pads, so that it doesn't stain the wood.

Through-Mortises and -Tenons: Seal the End Grain

Through-tenons squeeze their way through a glued mortise like a car through a car wash. They come out completely wet with glue. Almost inevitably, your carefully crafted tenon end will develop blotches where the glue soaked in and prevented the finish from penetrating.

Plan ahead by prefinishing the tenon end and any other part of the tenon that will show. Apply several coats of thinned shellac to seal it completely, being careful to keep the finish off the gluing surfaces. Later, you can follow with any other finish. Wet down the entire tenon with glue, but put less in the mortise.

Sliding Dovetails: Use Steady Clamping Pressure

This joint makes for quick drawers (among many other uses), often with metal drawer slides placed in the extra space along the sides. But sliding dovetails can be a challenge to glue. I'm lying—they're much worse than that. If they fit properly, there's no way to get them home without applying steady, perfectly centered pressure. A clamp is better for this than a mallet, which can force the parts in crookedly, causing them to bind.

Pipe clamps offer a long screw length, which is important for keeping the joint moving steadily over a longer distance. Have two pipe clamps ready to go.

Spread glue into the female part of the joint, with just a touch on the male part, and start driving the joint home with a pipe clamp. Do not take any time to scratch your nose; the joint will swell up and be tough to get moving again. When one clamp runs out of thread, grab another and keep that drawer side moving until it's in place. Breathe.

Panels: Check for flatness

Edge laminations should come out flat. But they will not if your assembly table is not flat, if your clamps are not straight, or if your wood isn't true. Check those things first. Have pipe clamps ready to go. To avoid staining the lumber, put tape on black pipe clamps where they contact the glue joints or use galvanized pipe.

Make sure all of the boards are numbered or the joints marked so you know how the pile of lumber goes back together.

Keep a deadblow mallet close by as you apply pressure to persuade the faces to line up. If they won't, a C-clamp on the ends will pull the faces into line. The right amount of clamp pressure for panel glue-ups is the maximum force you can apply comfortably with your off hand (I'm right-handed, so everything is left-hand tight). Make sure the boards are sitting flat on the clamps. Bang them down if they're not.

If you are helping a friend glue up a project, you will marvel at how calm you remain while he or she is going nuts. And the reverse is also always true. So, to keep your blood pressure low, plan ahead.

Fast Fixes for Joinery Mistakes

In the article "How to Fix Flaws and Mistakes," we asked the magazine's most frequent contributors for their favorite methods for concealing flaws in the wood, whether self-inflicted mistakes or courtesy of Mother Nature. Their clever tricks for getting out of a problem without having to go back and start over struck a chord with our readers.

That article focused on cosmetic fixes for surface flaws, but we saved a whole other family of invaluable remedies, for mistakes made while cutting joinery. While these mistakes may or may not affect the look of a piece, they most certainly have an impact on its strength, and can force you to scrap a valuable workpiece. Once again, the pros have a bunch of tricks up their sleeves.

Solutions For Gappy Dovetails

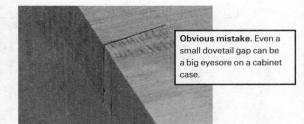

Obvious mistake. Even a small dovetail gap can be a big eyesore on a cabinet case.

Insert the shim. Chop the bottom of the strip at an angle so it will fit the widened gap, then glue it in place. Be sure to orient the end grain of the strip in line with that of the tail board.

ANGLED SHIM FOR THROUGH-DOVETAILS

A common mistake when hand-cutting through-dovetails is to cut on the wrong side of the scribe line, which leaves a small but noticeable gap between the pin and tail when the piece is glued up. A surefire solution is to fill the gap with a thin shim that's the same wood species as the project. Widen the gap first, glue in the shim, then trim it flush.

Widen the gap. A slight gap can be hard to fill. To make it easier, widen it slightly with a dovetail saw, angling the saw and cutting to the baselines of both the pins and tails.

Trim it flush. After the glue dries, use a wide chisel to slice the shim flush.

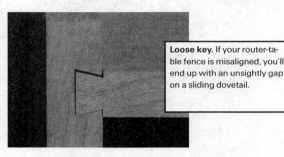

Loose key. If your router-table fence is misaligned, you'll end up with an unsightly gap on a sliding dovetail.

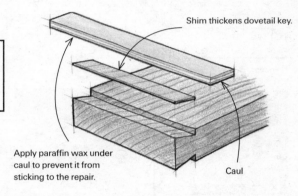

Shim thickens dovetail key.

Apply paraffin wax under caul to prevent it from sticking to the repair.

Caul

WIDE SHIM FOR A LOOSE SLIDING DOVETAIL

This fix came to me while I was working on a wall shelf made with sliding dovetails. As always, I'd set up the router-table cuts using test pieces and verified the fit. But after I finished routing the dovetail keys, I discovered that I was off by a little more than 1/16 in. Yikes! Turns out that I'd not tightened down my fence sufficiently, and it shifted slightly as I made the cuts. Fortunately, I came up with a fix that was pretty quick and easy. I filled the gap with a piece of thick veneer, and glued along the face of the key. Be sure to run the grain in the same direction. Then I re-routed the joint to get a tight fit.

Tight joint. After re-routing the shimmed key, it fits perfectly.

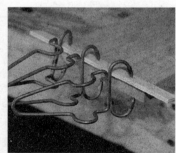

Spring into action. Glue a piece of veneer or a thicker shim to the face of the dovetail key. Brown uses spring clamps and a thin caul to ensure a good glue bond across the width.

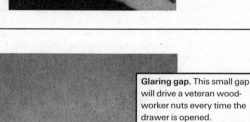

Glaring gap. This small gap will drive a veteran woodworker nuts every time the drawer is opened.

TAPERED SHIM FOR HALF-BLINDS

Here's a simple way to fix a gap in a half-blind dovetail. Use end-grain shims that closely match the color and grain pattern of the pin. This fix is slightly different from the through-dovetail fix above, which uses a triangular, flat shim. Because there's no way to widen the gap cleanly, and it's trapped by the edge of the drawer front, I taper the shim to create a wedge that is easier to put in. I tap it into the gap with a hammer, then trim it flush.

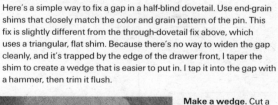

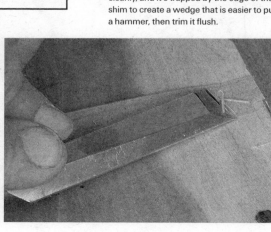

Make a wedge. Cut a shim slightly wider and thicker than the gap. Then taper the sides and ends using a chisel and block plane.

Continued ➜

When Miters Don't Meet

RELIEVE THE BACK, NOT THE CORNERS

When trimming the miters on moldings, it's easy to take off too much from one end, leaving a small gap. Instead of cutting a new piece of molding, you can fix the pieces you have. Simply take a very light jointer pass off the back face of the molding (a handplane will work too). This has the effect of lengthening the distance between the miters, giving you one more chance to close the gap.

Open corner. It's easy to trim too much off a miter, creating a gap.

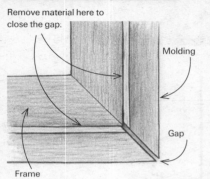

Remove material here to close the gap:

Molding

Gap

Frame

Joint the back. Run the back of the molding over the jointer, taking a shallow cut. Be sure to use push blocks. If the molding is too small for a safe jointer pass, use a handplane.

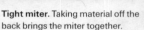

Tight miter. Taking material off the back brings the miter together.

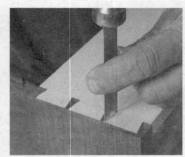

Drive it home. Put glue on the tip of the shim and tap it in place (left). Saw off the excess and trim the patch flush (below).

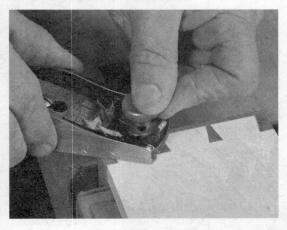

Rx for Tenon Troubles

Shim splint. Add a strip of veneer to thicken a loose tenon. Cut the veneer so that it overhangs the tenon just a hair on each side.

FATTEN UP A THIN TENON

It's easy to trim too much from a tenon, creating a loose fit in its mortise. There is an easy fix, which I learned from Phil Lowe. You just glue veneer to the tenon cheek and try again. First partially assemble the joint and look for a gap to see which face of the tenon is undercut (shimming the wrong face can mess up the alignment of the parts). Now resaw a strip of veneer just a bit thicker than the gap. Glue it on, using a small caul to get even pressure and a tight glueline, and then trim the tenon again to creep up on a perfect fit.

A little off the top. Trim the edges of the veneer flush, and then plane the fattened tenon until it fits.

Hanging tight. A perfect fit is one where the joint stays together when you hold it in mid-air.

Bad shoulder. Get an offset tenon wrong and the problem is obvious. But even this can be fixed without starting from scratch.

REPLACE A TENON COMPLETELY

It's all too common to orient an offset tenon backwards on a rail, creating a big step on the finished frame. But it's not a fatal error. You can simply slice off the miscut tenon, cut a big stopped groove in the rail, and slide in a slip tenon. This fix works for bad tenons of all kinds. Here's how to do it.

Install a dado set on the tablesaw equal to the tenon thickness. Set the height for the width of the tenon and use the rip fence to locate the dado set in the rail thickness. Be sure you have the location right this time! Feed the rail in far enough to cut a reasonable-size pocket—stop the cut just after you reach the apex of the blade. Turn off the saw and wait for the blade to stop. Use the same species of wood to make a slip tenon that fits snug in the curved pocket. Cut the tenon to length and glue it into the rail. When the glue dries, clean up the bottom edge and fit the new tenon to its mortise.

Remove the tenon altogether. Cut off the tenon at the shoulder.

Clear a path for a new one. Use a dado set to plow a groove where the tenon should have been. Stop the cut when the blade is at the apex of the curve, turn off the saw, and hold the piece until the blade stops.

Bad corner. When fitting a long through-tenon, it's easy to chip out a corner or just over-trim it, ruining the look.

Make a cap. Mill a slip tenon for a snug fit in the outside of the mortise. Then cut off a piece long enough to meet the end of the real tenon.

Top it off. Glue in the cap over the tenon for a seamless repair.

Curved piece fits right in. Mill a slip tenon for a snug fit in the groove, with one end curved to match the arc of the blade. You can use the blade to trace the arc.

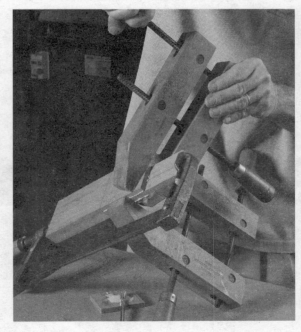

Slippery glue-up. When gluing in the tenon, you need to clamp it in three directions: One clamp pushes the tenon in, one keeps it from pivoting out, and one goes across the face to ensure a good bond with the cheeks.

BENDING

The Basics of Steam-Bending

By Lon Schleining

Steam-bending is fast, strong and authentic. You'll never see a glueline nor have a piece break because of short-grain weakness. Steam-bending does not require green wood. Nor does it require a vast array of tools. What it does require, though, is lots of heat, a box to capture steam and a sturdy bending form.

Once you realize that each of the components works in conjunction with the others, the setup for bending is straightforward. There is almost no limit to the parts you can make by steam-bending—chair parts, table legs, curved drawer parts—except your imagination. I usually start with a drawing of the finished part, then design a form to bend it, allowing for a bit of springback (how much the part relaxes after it's been bent). The size of the bending blank determines the size of the steambox you'll need to use. The larger the box, the larger the steam generator it takes to heat it, so the box should be only as large as necessary for the parts you plan to bend.

The easiest way to understand the basics of bending is to see it done, so for this article I'll demonstrate by bending the back slat for a chair. The slat is made of ¹/₂-in.-thick material, and the radius is not very tight, which makes this is a good bend to warm up on.

The bending techniques illustrated here will work for simple bends of a slight radius as well as for more complex bends using compression straps. Whatever bending you

design into your projects, what you learn here should lay the groundwork for success. As you gain experience, your confidence in bending will build, and your designs will grow bolder.

The Best Wood for Steam-Bending

Many experts claim that you must use green or air-dried lumber for steam-bending, but in the Los Angeles area where I live, air-dried stock is not a convenient option. I've had no choice but to bend kiln-dried material, and the results have been quite successful.

Kiln-dried wood is not only easily available, even if you live in the city, but it's also dimensionally stable, dry and ready to be milled as soon as bending is complete and the piece has had time to cool.

Any wood will bend somewhat, but long-grained woods such as hickory, ash and oak bend easiest. Dense woods, such as cherry, hard maple and most exotics, are certainly more challenging. Ideally, wood for steam-bending should have straight grain, which enables you to bend without stressing the areas already weakened by grain direction. I suggest starting with oak, because it is much easier to bend than most other species.

Predicting Springback is Not an Exact Science

If at all possible, use a full-sized drawing of the part to help design the bending form. Be sure to take into account that the shape will relax, or spring back, somewhat after it's been bent. Build some overbend into the form so that the part will relax to the shape you want.

Numerous factors affect springback, such as the radius, the thickness of the part, degree of bend, how quickly the part is bent, how long it was steamed, how long it stayed

on the form to cool, the type of wood and its moisture content. The bad news is that if you're going to bend just a couple of parts, you'll have a difficult time predicting the amount of springback.

The rule of thumb is to allow for more—rather than less—springback than you expect. While a piece that has been overbent can be straightened out easily, it is nearly impossible to add more bend after your initial effort.

Build the Steambox

I typically use ³/₄-in. exterior plywood for the box itself. It's inexpensive and is fairly stable, even when it's steaming hot. Inside, dowels are used for racks, which allow the steam to circulate around all four sides of the blanks so that the heat will penetrate evenly.

Build the box only large enough for the number and sizes of parts you'll be bending at one time. I usually build a new box for every project.

The box should not be tightly sealed. Drill ¹/₄-in. holes in several areas to provide access for a thermometer and to allow the steam to circulate. Use a common meat thermometer to measure the temperature in several places to make sure it's uniform. Resist the use of metal in steamboxes. Hot steam, hot wood and wet steel react in such a way as to turn the wood black.

Plastic pipe is a tempting material to use as a steambox. It works okay, but as it heats, it also softens. Unless its entire length is supported in a wooden V-trough, it will sag in the middle. It also lets heat easily escape, so you might need to insulate it. As with a wooden box, use dowels for racks to hold the pieces away from the sides and bottom of the pipe and to allow air to circulate.

Find a Source of Steam

The boiler's size must be proportionate to the size of the steambox. The larger the box, the larger the boiler because more steam is required to keep the box as hot as it needs to be: at least 200°F. No matter how big the heat source is, the steambox will never get any hotter than 212°F as long as there is a pressure release in the box, creating the perfect temperature control.

If the steambox doesn't reach 200°F within 20 minutes or so, chances are your boiler is too small for the size box you're trying to heat. Often it's a matter of simply using two kettles instead of one to get the box up to temperature.

Electric heating is probably safer than devices that have an open flame, but as long as you are careful, any sort of heat source works fine.

The electric kettle available from Lee Valley Tools puts out a lot of heat for its small size. It is possible to rent or buy a wallpaper steamer. But an electric deep fryer is cheap (look for one in a thrift store) and puts out a great deal more heat than an electric cooking pot or wallpaper steamer. A two-burner propane steamer will heat a very large steambox but must be used outside only. Whatever sort of boiler you use, there must be a convenient way to add water. Even the small kettle goes through 2 qt. of water an hour.

Off the shelf. This kettle, available from Lee Valley Tools, comes with an extralong spout to accommodate a steambox.

From the kitchen. The author's electric deep fryer, on longtime loan from his mother, is outfitted with a frame to hold a steambox.

Off the wall. A wallpaper steamer can be bought or rented and provides a reliable source of steam.

For the outdoors. This shopmade propane burner will put out an exceptional amount of steam, but because of its open flame, it should be used only outdoors.

Keep water in the pot. When using this small electric kettle, the author adds water often, ensuring that there's plenty of steam to keep the temperature inside the box above 200°F.

Take note of the the time. Once the blanks are inside the steambox, monitor the temperature and note the time it reaches 200°F.

Continued →

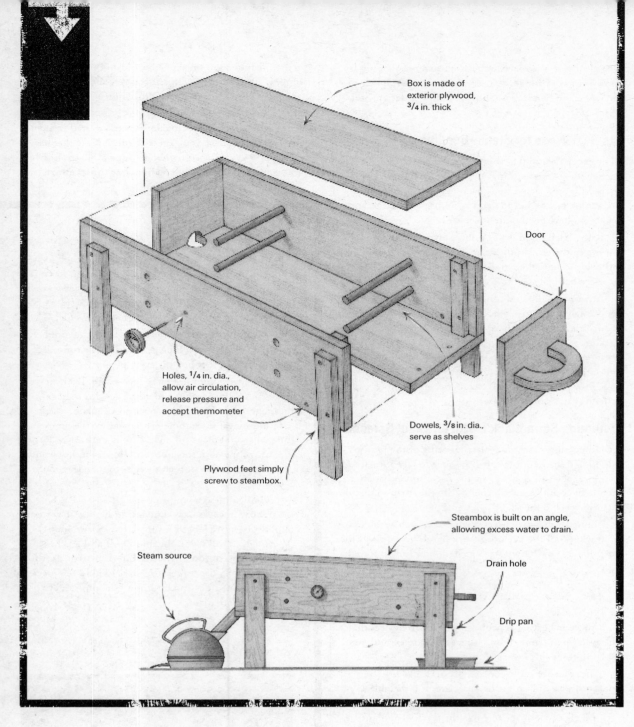

Box is made of exterior plywood, ³/₄ in. thick

Door

Holes, ¹/₄ in. dia., allow air circulation, release pressure and accept thermometer

Dowels, ³/₈ in. dia., serve as shelves

Plywood feet simply screw to steambox.

Steambox is built on an angle, allowing excess water to drain.

Steam source

Drain hole

Drip pan

Make a Sturdy Bending Form

The form serves as a mold for the shape of the part being bent. I usually draw the part full sized so that I can plan the form accordingly. The drawing shows both finished and rough sizes for the part and serves as a map for building the form. This is the time to build in overbend to allow for springback.

Use layers of plywood shaped like your drawing to build the form. Any flaw in the curvature here will telegraph into the final product, so shape carefully. Clamp pockets or a wedge system provide a means to clamp quickly. Speed is important because of the limited time the part will stay hot enough to bend.

Add a cleat of some kind so that the form can be held securely to a bench. Build the form stronger than you think it needs to be. It must absorb the stress of bending.

To accommodate springback, bending forms must be built to a tighter radius than the finished piece.

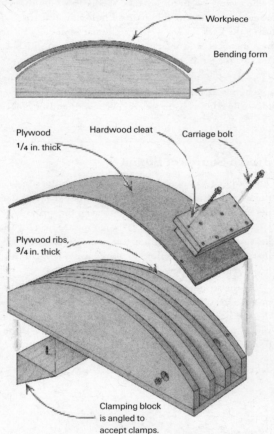

Workpiece

Bending form

Plywood ¹/₄ in. thick

Hardwood cleat

Carriage bolt

Plywood ribs, ³/₄ in. thick

Clamping block is angled to accept clamps.

It's quite easy to straighten out the piece a little if it's bent too far. A wet rag placed on the concave part of the bend will straighten it out some. Heating the part with a hair dryer will accelerate the process. Do not try to bend the part just a little more once it's cooled—it will break almost every time.

Make a Practice Run Before Bending a Piece

Begin by cutting several practice blanks out of oak. To determine grain runout, hold up the blanks so that light reflects along the surface of the edge that will be curved. The straighter the grain, the better. Oddly, it seems to make little difference how the end grain is oriented: whether vertically, flat or diagonally.

I usually load the blanks into the box while it's cool so that I don't have to work around the steam any more than necessary. Once the pieces are in place, close the lid, plug in the boiler and wait for the temperature in the box to rise above 200°F. Check the temperature with a thermometer in several spots to make sure it's uniform. Note the time when the box reaches the correct temperature.

Because the heat must penetrate to the core of the material, monitor the temperature throughout steaming; add water as needed. Remember, it's heat, not moisture, that allows the piece to bend. Wood should be steamed for one hour per inch of thickness. For a ¹/₂-in.-thick chair back, leave the piece in the steam for a half-hour—or just a bit longer. If wood stays in the steamer too long, it begins to get dry and brittle and becomes harder to work.

When the blank comes out of the box, it will be very hot. When I work around steam, I wear gloves that cover my forearms. Once the piece is out of the steambox, it cools rapidly, so bending must be done immediately. It's important to work both quickly and deliberately—quickly to begin bending, deliberately to get the right shape. Don't force it. Give stock time to get used to the idea that its surfaces are changing length. After a few tries, you'll begin to develop a feel for the material and become a better judge of how quickly or how slowly you need to go.

Use clamps or wedges to hold the part on the form while it cools. You want to be sure that the piece has had time to dry completely before you remove it from the form. Whenever possible, let the piece cool for 24 hours.

When the part comes off the form, it will spring back a bit. If the curve is correct, congratulations. If it's bent too much, use a hair dryer and a wet cloth. If it's not bent far enough, start from scratch and make a new bending form with more curvature in it. Once the kinks have been worked out, make a series of cooling forms, which will enable you to bend a number of pieces in assembly line fashion.

Bending wood is not the answer to every woodworking application, but in certain situations, it's the only viable option. With careful setup, it's also a simple task. And no matter how many times I do it, I'm amazed when a blank comes out of a steambox so pliable that I can bend it into a knot.

Bend and Twist with Free-Form Steam Bending

By Michael Fortune

If you can create a shape with a strip of paper without tearing or folding it, in theory you can bend wood to that same shape. However, because wood compresses much better than it stretches, conventional steam-bending requires the use of a compression strap, and it can be difficult to create a compression strap for unusual shapes.

Master Class

The method I'll describe uses a compression strap to pre-bend the wood, but does away with it when bending the desired shape, allowing you to bend wood through two planes at once and even twist it, adding a new dimension to your woodworking. For example, the table leg on the next page sweeps outward at the bottom along a 45° axis.

Bend the Wood Twice to Make It Pliable

The first step is to make a traditional bending form with a radius tighter than the desired final shape. This will allow the wood fibers to be compressed and the lignin bonds loosened in the areas that you will later bend free-form.

The blanks to be bent should be approximately ⅛ in. larger in thickness and width and about 4 in. longer than the final length. In this way, any torn wood fibers can be removed when the wood is shaped to the desired dimensions.

Steam the blank for an hour per inch of thickness, then take it from the steambox, secure it in the strap assembly, and bend it around the form. Almost immediately, straighten out the blank (holding one end in a vise if needed), roll it over face-for-face in the strap assembly, and bend it around the form again. Remove the blank from the strap and straighten it again. Now that the entire bent section has had the lignin loosened, the blank can be bent free-form without a compression strap.

Although the wood cools fairly slowly, complete all the steps as quickly as possible and get the blank clamped onto its final form. If it takes more than five or 10 minutes, the blank can be reheated in the steambox. This should take only five or 10 more minutes because the inside of the blank has remained hot.

Bend the softened wood into free-form designs

When you bend the wood a third time, without the compression strap, you'll be able to create shapes beyond the scope of traditional steam-bending.

Bend a leg that is strong and elegant—A leg that sweeps out near the bottom along a 45° axis usually must be cut from a large blank. This invariably leaves short grain, making the foot weak and unattractive. Steam-bending would make more sense as it consumes less wood and allows the grain to follow the shape of the leg, maintaining its strength and improving the look.

However, using a compression strap is impractical because there is only a corner of the blank for the strap to bear on. By double-bending the leg as described, you can then bend it along the edge without a compression strap. The first step is to build a V-shaped form made from two sections shaped with a large chamfer bit. You'll also need to cut some clamping blocks with V notches. Clamp the double-bent blank into the form and leave it to dry. The drying time depends on the size of the blank and the temperature and humidity in the workshop. A 1½-in.-sq.

A Look Inside Steam Bent Wood

Wood fibers are held together by a natural adhesive called lignin. The lignin bond can be loosened temporarily by heating the wood to between 190°F and 230°F, usually with steam. The heated wood can then be bent and will retain its new shape when cool.

The key concept here is that wood will only stretch about 2% of its length before the fibers begin to fail. But it will compress to a phenomenal degree before it fails—I routinely bend 1½-in.-thick hardwoods to as little as a 1-in. radius.

The traditional solution is to use a compression strap. This has two drawbacks: First, complicated shapes are impractical for a metal strap. Second, there is no compression on the outside face next to the strap, so there is more chance of the shape springing back. However, if the wood is rolled 180° and immediately bent again, then the lignin bond is loosened throughout the blank. The wood can now be bent and twisted at will without a strap and with almost no springback.

Wood That Steam-Bends Well

When wood is kiln dried, the lignin is set permanently in place, so try to steam-bend only air-dried wood with a moisture content of around 15%. This is usually available from smaller sawmills and lumberyards. Among the best woods for steam-bending are ash, red and white oak, walnut, hickory, and elm. Slightly more difficult are cherry, maple, and birch. Woods that do not steam-bend include softer hardwoods like basswood and poplar, curly domestic hardwoods, all softwoods, and most exotic woods including mahogany and teak.

THE AUTHOR'S METHOD STARTS WITH A COMPRESSION STRAP

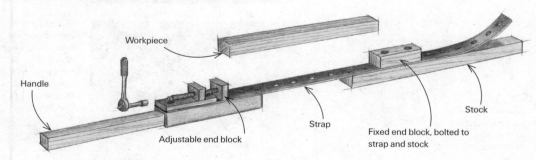

Workpiece · Handle · Adjustable end block · Strap · Fixed end block, bolted to strap and stock · Stock

Pre-bend with a compression strap

After steaming, place the blank in a compression strap and bend it around a form. Then quickly remove the wood, roll it 180°, and bend it in the opposite direction.

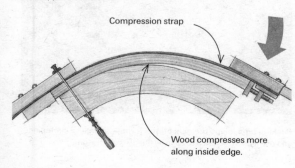

Compression strap · Wood compresses more along inside edge.

Then bend to desired shape

Now that all of the fibers are loosened, the blank can be easily shaped.

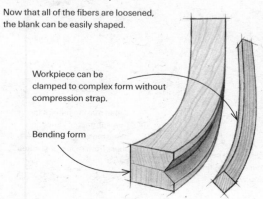

Workpiece can be clamped to complex form without compression strap. · Bending form

1. STEAM THE WOOD

In the box. Let the blank steam for an hour per inch of thickness. Use gloves when removing the hot wood.

1. DOUBLE BEND THE WOOD TO LOOSEN THE FIBERS

Bend, straighten, and bend again. Place the blank in the compression strap, tighten the end clamp, and then bend it around the form (left). Remove the blank from the strap, place it loosely in a vise, and lever it until it is almost straight (lower left). Flip the blank so that the face that was against the strap is now against the form, and bend it again. In this way the lignin that bonds the wood fibers is loosened across the width of the blank (below).

3. BEND THE WOOD AROUND THE FORM...

Create an angled form. To make the bending form that holds the blank on its edge, use a 45° chamfer bit in a router table to shape the two halves of the form (left). There is no need to use a compression strap on the double-bent blank, but you do need "V"-shaped clamp blocks (right).

...OR GIVE IT A TWIST

Twist the wood and preserve the new shape. With one end of the blank clamped in a vise, twist the wood 180° using a long board as a handle. To let the wood dry in its new shape without springing back, clamp the turning handle to a fixed object.

Continued ➜

piece of ash will take about a week to dry down to 7% to 8% humidity if there is a modest airflow across the wood.

A new twist on steam-bending—With conventional steam-bending, getting wood to twist is difficult and the results often are disappointing. You'd be lucky to achieve 90° of twist before the fibers separate, and then the shape will untwist even after the wood is dry because the lignin bond was not completely broken. Wood that has been double-bent can be twisted to around 180° before the wood fibers fail.

Square or rectangular cross sections work best for twisting. Before you start, cut a hole that matches the end of the blank in the middle of a piece of wood 3 ft. to 4 ft. long and at least 3 in. wider than the blank. This will serve as a handle. Double-bend the blank around a form with about a 20-in. radius. Reheat it and then clamp one end of the hot blank in a heavy-duty vise and insert the other into the handle, applying a clamp on either side.

Twist the blank slowly. There will be some springback, so I recommend overtwisting by about 10° to 15°. When you've achieved the desired twist, clamp the handle to a stationary object and allow the blank to dry.

Variations on the twist include tapering the wood before it is twisted to cause the twist to "speed up" as the wood narrows. You also can rabbet the corners and inset a contrasting wood (use epoxy to withstand the temperature and moisture).

Curved Panels Made Easy

By Michael C. Fortune

Furniture with curved panels stands out from the crowd. But common approaches to making them are imperfect. When made from solid wood, either by shaping thick planks or coopering thin staves, curved panels aren't very stable. You can make a more stable panel by laminating several thin plies between a pair of forms, because the plies are arranged at right angles to one another. However, making the perfectly mated forms is tedious, and distributing pressure evenly across them is not easy.

The answer is a vacuum-bag system. With a vacuum press, you get the stability of a laminated panel but need only one form, and the press applies pressure evenly across the entire panel.

Most of my work is curved, and I've refined my techniques for making the form and panel. My methods are not difficult, and they allow you to pursue exciting design possibilities. I won't cover the basics of buying and setting up a vacuum-bag system.

First Trick: Make Multiple Parts from One Core

To simplify the door and drawer panels for this bedside table, Fortune laminated a large core in the vacuum press and then cut out the smaller pieces. Note that the grain on the core runs horizontally because the show veneer hasn't been applied.

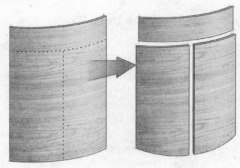

Trick 2: Use the Bag to Make the Form

Curved panels require a ribbed bending form, designed to hold its shape under the extreme pressure of the vacuum press. Glue up the entire form at once in the bag to create even pressure and a uniform surface, which is necessary to get a strong bond between the panel plies.

Beveled strips keep ribs aligned on the base. If not held in place on both sides, the ribs will slide out of alignment in the vacuum bag.

Pattern jig creates matching ribs. Fortune cuts his pattern oversize, then adds a fence and some toggle clamps to make routing the ribs quick, safe, and accurate.

Outer ribs come first. Glued and clamped manually, these prevent the other ribs and spacer blocks from sliding toward the ends of the form.

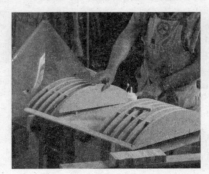

Add the inner ribs. The ribs are 2 in. apart. Spacer blocks hold them perpendicular to the base.

In the bag. The press applies uniform pressure from all directions, so there won't be any bumps in the form. Leave it in the bag overnight.

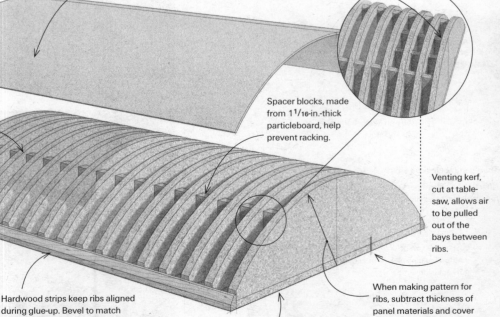

Cover sheet, 5/16-in.-thick bendable plywood

First three bays at each end get four spacer blocks to offset increased pressure. All other bays get two spacer blocks.

Ribs, 1 1/16-in.-thick particleboard, spaced 2 in. apart.

Spacer blocks, made from 1 1/16-in.-thick particleboard, help prevent racking.

Venting kerf, cut at tablesaw, allows air to be pulled out of the bays between ribs.

Anatomy of a bending form
Ribs, spacer blocks, and a cover sheet make the form strong enough to withstand the vacuum's pressure.

Hardwood strips keep ribs aligned during glue-up. Bevel to match curve on ribs. Keep flush with or just below end of rib.

Base, 1/2-in.-thick particleboard, cut 2 in. larger than the finished panel in length and width

When making pattern for ribs, subtract thickness of panel materials and cover sheet from radius of finished panel.

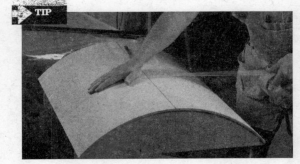

Packing tape keeps the glue off the form. Also, mark a centerline and use it as a reference to align all the plies on the form.

Simple Materials Work for Most Panels

Except for the edge-banding, a laminated curved panel is made up of glue, a core, and show veneer.

Titebond Cold Press for Veneer glue is great for laminating because it remains workable long enough to lay up the panel and get it in the bag. It's also non-toxic, inexpensive, and flexible enough to accommodate the movement of the plies. However, when the show veneers are arranged decoratively, as with parquetry, the pieces are taped together and the grain can run in various directions. In these situations, I use Unibond 800 because its alcohol base greatly reduces the risk of the individual pieces rolling up or moving about.

Bendable plywood (also known as wiggle wood) is usually my first choice for the structural plies. It is extremely flexible: Pieces 3/16 in. thick can be bent to a radius as tight as 10 in.; 5/16-in.-thick pieces bend to a 14-in. radius. This material has three plies: a very thin inner ply sandwiched between two thicker plies. The grain on the outer plies runs in the same direction, which is why bendable plywood is so flexible. But you don't want a floppy panel, so you add structural plies of veneer, laminated at a right angle to the grain direction on the outer plies of the bendable plywood, to lock it in the desired curve and make the panel stable. If the grain on the veneer and bendable plywood ran in the same direction, the panel would look like a potato chip.

However, if the curved panel will be supporting any significant weight, like a chair seat would, use lauan rather than bendable plywood. Lauan isn't as light or flexible, but it is stronger.

Bending Form Needs to Be Strong

I use my bending forms to laminate and square the panel core, and to apply show veneer to the outside curve of the panel. Vacuum presses apply tremendous pressure from every direction. To prevent the bending form from collapsing, I make it by gluing a series of ribs, reinforced with spacer blocks, to a flat base, and then covering the ribs with a sheet of bendable plywood. I use 1/2-in.-thick particleboard for the base and 11/16-in.-thick particleboard for the ribs and spacers. To get a panel that is smooth and symmetrical, all of the ribs must be identical, so make a pattern of the curve and then rout the ribs flush to it. Glue a strip of hardwood, beveled to match the curve of the ribs, to either side of the form's base. Then, glue in a rib at each end of the base.

Before gluing on the remaining ribs, use the tablesaw to cut a kerf through the base along its length and to one side of the center. This kerf allows air to be pulled out of the form's interior by the vacuum press, ensuring that the ribs and cover sheet receive uniform pressure. Use the vacuum press itself to glue in the remaining ribs, the spacers, and the cover sheet. The press applies even pressure from every direction, producing a smooth and uniform curve—impossible to achieve if you use clamps to glue the ribs in place.

Let the form sit in the bag overnight. When you take it out, draw a centerline down the cover sheet, and then apply clear packing tape over the entire surface to prevent glue from sticking to the form.

Laminate the Core and Apply the Edging

I laminate curved panels in three steps. First, I make the panel's core. Then I band the core's edges with solid hardwood. I apply the show veneers last.

To make a 3/4-in.-thick panel core, you'll need two pieces of 5/16-in.-thick bendable plywood and three pieces of veneer. One piece of veneer is glued between the bendable plywood, the other two to the outside faces. Cut the bendable plywood and veneer about 1 in. oversize in length and width. Mark a centerline on the ends. Spread the glue on the plywood. If you spread glue on the veneer, it will roll up like a tube. After spreading the glue and stacking the plies, top off everything with a 1/8-in.-thick hardboard cover sheet, 1/4 in. larger all around than the panel core plies. The cover sheet should have a centerline marked on its face and two ends.

Trick 3: Cross-Grain Sandwich Makes a Rigid Core

Three pieces of veneer run across the grain of the bendable plywood, locking it into the desired curve and stabilizing the core. You'll add the face veneers later.

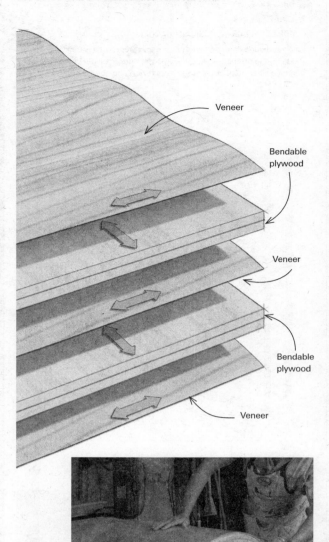

Veneer

Bendable plywood

Veneer

Bendable plywood

Veneer

Place everything on the form, aligning all the centerlines. Use packing tape to hold the core and cover sheet to the form. Seal everything inside the bag and turn on the vacuum press. As the bag is pulled tight around the form, make sure it doesn't get caught under the panel core. Titebond Cold Press for Veneer glue needs just a few hours in the bag. Unibond 800 should be left in overnight.

After you take the form and panel core out of the bag, let them sit for an hour or two to let any remaining moisture from the glue dissipate. Then square up the panel core. I square the curved ends with a router and the straight edges at the tablesaw.

After the core is square, glue on the edge-banding. I glue on the piece that will be least visible first and the one that will be most visible last, which minimizes the amount of visible end grain. Keep the edging no more than 3/8 in. thick. If it's any thicker, there will be differences in wood movement between the solid-wood banding and the laminated panel, and the glueline between the two will be noticeable.

Apply Show Veneers One at a Time

The show veneers must be applied in two steps. The outside curve can be done using the form, but the inside curve might not match the form perfectly. Any gaps between the inside curve and the form will leave bubbles between the panel core and show veneer. Fortunately, the core is strong enough to hold its shape under the pressure. So you can just flip the panel, concave side up, and the bag will mold the veneer to it. Each show veneer needs about 45 minutes in the bag. After the veneers have been glued in place, chamfer the edges of the panel to hide the glueline between the show veneers and the banding.

Spread glue on the plywood only. Moisture in the glue would curl the veneer if applied directly to it. Fortune uses a notched spreader to get a thin, even coat.

Thin caul spreads pressure. A 1/8-in.-thick piece of hardboard keeps the top veneer flat. Cut it oversize to hold plies tight to one another at the edges of the panel.

Keep panel core on centerline. Fortune aligns the bendable plywood, veneer, and cover sheet on the form's centerline, holding them in place with packing tape, to ensure that the panel has a symmetrical curve.

WHERE TO FIND BENDABLE PLYWOOD

Bendable plywood, also known as wiggle wood, flexply, and wacky wood, can be found at local plywood and lumber dealers. If it's not in stock, the dealer should be able to order it for you.

Trick 4: Use the Same Form to Trim the Ends

Bonus: The bending form becomes a router jig for trimming the curved ends of the core.

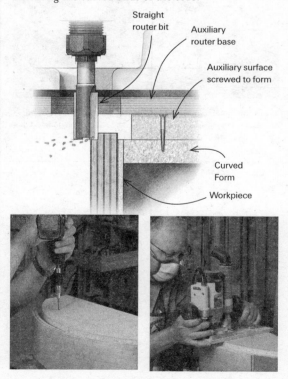

Straight router bit

Auxiliary router base

Auxiliary surface screwed to form

Curved Form

Workpiece

Attach an auxiliary surface to the form. Running the router on it allows you to move the panel up past the edge of the form, which in turn keeps the spinning bit from damaging it. To avoid tearout, work around the outside of the panel rather than trimming the full width in one pass. A long auxiliary base helps Fortune balance the router.

Continued ➡

Trick 5: Digital Gauge Dials in the Edges

Use a digital angle gauge to ensure the tablesaw cuts are square to the panel's faces.

1. Square edges at the tablesaw. Fortune uses a Wixey angle gauge to set the edges flat on a crosscut sled (right). The pencil line marks the finished edge of the panel. Support the underside with a block of wood, clamp the panel in place, and make the cut. The edge will be square to the face of the panel.

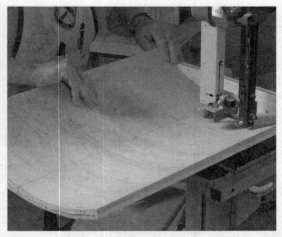

2. Cut out the drawer front. The safest way to separate the drawer front is at the bandsaw. A steady hand, well-set-up bandsaw, and sharp blade will give a clean and straight edge.

3. Cut the panel to make doors. Fortune again used a Wixey angle gauge, this time straddling the centerline, to adjust the panel so that the cut is square to the faces of the panel.

Trick 6: Band Edges Before Gluing On Face Veneer

TIP

HIDE END GRAIN WITH SMART BANDING

Mitered edge-banding hides its own end grain, but it is tricky to apply. Use butt joints instead, starting with the bottom piece. Unless you go in for a close inspection, the end grain won't be noticeable.

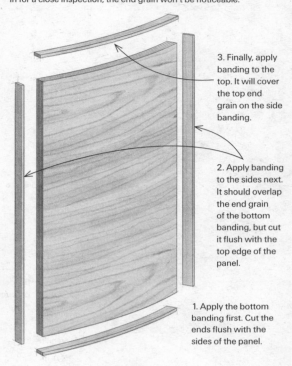

3. Finally, apply banding to the top. It will cover the top end grain on the side banding.

2. Apply banding to the sides next. It should overlap the end grain of the bottom banding, but cut it flush with the top edge of the panel.

1. Apply the bottom banding first. Cut the ends flush with the sides of the panel.

BANDING THE ENDS

Cut out curved banding. In most cases that's all you need, but if the banding will be highly visible, like on the top of a drawer, you can laminate it from thin plies (and rip it into thin strips), so the grain follows the curve. Glue banding on the bottom first, using a caul to apply even pressure across its full width and length. Rout the banding flush. To prevent tearout, start in the middle and work down the curve.

Trick 7: Face Veneers Go On One at a Time

Veneer for the outside of the curve can be done with the form, but for the inside, do away with the form and press the veneer directly to the panel.

USE THE FORM TO GLUE THE OUTSIDE VENEER

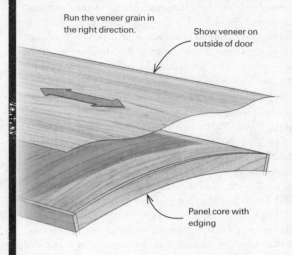

Run the veneer grain in the right direction.

Show veneer on outside of door

Panel core with edging

NO FORM NEEDED ON INSIDE VENEER

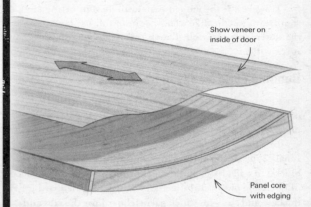

Show veneer on inside of door

Panel core with edging

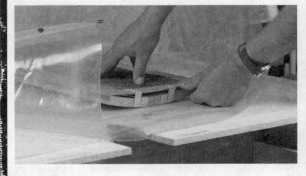

No form needed. The panel is strong enough to hold its shape while the veneer is pressed into the curve. Tape a cover sheet over the veneer.

BANDING THE EDGES

Tape instead of clamps. Because the panel is curved, clamping across it can be tricky. Instead, place a caul over the banding and use tape to apply pressure.

Fence in the panel. The process is much the same as it was for the panel core, but this time nail small fences on each side of the door panel to hold it in place, and use a 1/8-in.-thick hardboard cover sheet.

Trim the veneer. Use a utility knife or razor blade to cut away any overhanging veneer. Cut with the grain, and keep the blade angled slightly away from the panel.

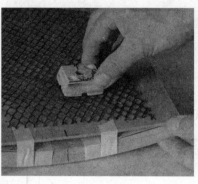

Create suction without a platen. A piece of gutter guard helps air to escape the bag, and a small block connects to the air hose. The grooves in the bottom of the block provide channels that allow the air to escape. After attaching the press's hose, turn it on. The bag will pull tight around all of the panel's surfaces.

Tapered Laminations Made Easy

By Michael C. Fortune

Incorporating tapered, curved laminations in your furniture opens up an incredible range of designs. However, tapering the component after it has been laminated has two disadvantages. If too many gluelines are broken, then the part will begin to straighten. Also, the severed gluelines are likely to show as a series of ugly lines.

A better way is to taper the individual plies, so that when they are glued together, both the inside and outside curves are continuous wood with no disfiguring gluelines. I have a jig that makes creating tapered plies a snap. It works not only to cut the tapered plies on the bandsaw, but also to clean them up on the planer.

Determine the Dimensions of the Plies

After creating a full-scale drawing of the piece, the first step is to figure out the number and thickness of the plies. This is a balancing act: The bond between thick, curved plies with only a few gluelines might weaken, letting the part slowly straighten, a process known as "cold creep." Conversely, too many plies introduces too much glue, increasing the risk that the piece will contract or warp as it dries. As a guide, a 1-in.-thick laminated part bent around a 12-in. radius should comprise about 10 plies. You should be able to bend the plies around the form by hand; if not, make them thinner and add more.

When calculating the number of plies, start at the thin end of the finished part, maintaining a minimum thickness of 1/16 in. at the tapered end of each ply. Any thinner and they may not survive being passed through the planer. Then divide the thick end by the number of plies to get the maximum thickness of each ply. I recommend making the plies 1/4 in. wider than the finished part, and 1 in. longer (measured along the outside of the lamination) at both ends, to allow for cleanup and final sizing.

Make the Bandsaw/Planer Taper Jig

The dimensions of the jig can be changed to suit the project. I've used these jigs for making tapered parts from 1 ft. to 14 ft. long. Make the jig 2 in. longer at each end than the length of the plies. This 2-in. space accommodates end stops on the jig and any planer snipe. Make the jig wide enough to accommodate your plies, but be aware that the width of the jig is limited by the resaw capacity of your bandsaw. The jig is made up of three pieces: two solid-wood parallel runners (3/4 in. thick is best) and an inclined solid-wood or plywood bed that provides the taper. The three pieces should be jointed and planed as straight as possible. Two inches from each end of the runners, carefully measure down from the top edge and mark the thin dimension of the ply on one end and the thick dimension on the other. Draw a line connecting the two points. Align the top surface of the bed with this line and clamp the parts together without glue. Drive in two or more small finishing nails on each side so that they penetrate the bed by 1/8 in. Leave the nail heads proud so they can be pulled out later.

Taper the Plies for a Clean Look

By tapering the individual plies before they are glued into a lamination, the tapered outer surfaces remain solid with no visible gluelines (left). If you taper the piece after it has been laminated, you will cut through the gluelines, spoiling the appearance and potentially weakening the piece (right).

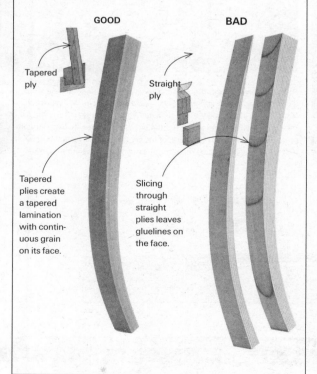

GOOD

Tapered ply

BAD

Straight ply

Tapered plies create a tapered lamination with continuous grain on its face.

Slicing through straight plies leaves gluelines on the face.

Separate the parts, apply glue, and reassemble them, aligning the nails in the holes to stop the parts from sliding as clamps are applied. Remove the nails when the glue is dry.

Position the end stops so the blank just slips in and out between them. If more than one blank is involved, all must be cut to the same length. To keep sawdust from accumulating and affecting the fit, the stops are rabbeted on the inside with space on either side next to the runners.

Set Up the Bandsaw and Make Tapers

Make sure your bandsaw is tuned up and ready for resawing. Set the fence so that the blade is 1/32 in. to the right of the jig and cutting parallel to the fence. If both runners don't contact the fence, attach a taller auxiliary fence. Bring a guide platform with a small cutout around the blade up to the jig and attach it to the bandsaw table. This can be done with double-sided tape, or with screws set into a block of wood clamped to the edge of the table. The platform helps to support the blank while it is carried past the blade. For this reason, the thickness of the platform should match that of the jig's runners. The guide platform should extend beyond the front and back of the blade by a little over half the length of the blank. When cutting long plies, the ends of the platform can rest on adjustable stands.

The tapered plies are cut from a blank of solid wood. It is a good idea to draw a triangle on the top surface of the blank to keep the laminates in order.

The blank must be flipped end-for-end each time a tapered ply is cut away. If not, the thick end of each ply comes from the same end of the blank, and the blank becomes increasingly tapered. You will quickly run out of wood on one end of the blank, and each successive ply will have more and more weak cross-grain. The blank should be wide enough to provide enough plies for at least two packets of laminations.

Place the blank in the jig (triangle pointing up) and run it through the bandsaw. The thick stop should be toward you so the blank is less inclined to slip off. After each pass, lightly joint the bandsawn face of the blank, then flip it end-for-end so the triangle is pointing down, reinsert it in the jig, and cut another taper. Pile the tapered plies in these two groups according to the triangle marks as they come off the bandsaw.

Shim the Plies and Run Them Through the Planer

The bandsaw leaves surfaces too rough for making tight glue joints, so you'll need to plane these surfaces smooth. Glue a piece of veneer or thick card to the face of the thicker end stop on the jig. When inserted, the plies should bow up about 1/8 in. at the center point. The infeed roller on the planer will press the bow flat, which in turn will jam the ply against the end stops, greatly reducing or eliminating shredding. The 1/32-in. gap you set between the jig and the bandsaw blade will provide enough material to plane before you get down to the tops of the jig's runners.

Install a ply in the jig, bandsawn face up. The thick end of the ply usually enters the planer first so that the grain slopes away from the rotating planer knives, reducing tearout. The exception is plies with crooked grain, so examine the grain first.

Run the sled through the planer, carefully lowering the cutterhead until it begins cutting the taper. One pass might do it, but be cautious about taking off too much material at once. Also, be certain that the plies retain their desired thickness.

A Better Form for Bending

For all my laminating and steam-bending, I use a one-piece "male" bending form (the plies are bent over the form rather than into a concave form) made from particleboard or medium-density fiberboard. The shape is bandsawn and the inside curve runs parallel to the outside so the clamps won't slip off. Attach battens long enough to guide the unclamped plies as they are brought around the form.

Continued →

Make the Tapered Plies

BANDSAW AND PLANER TAPERING JIG

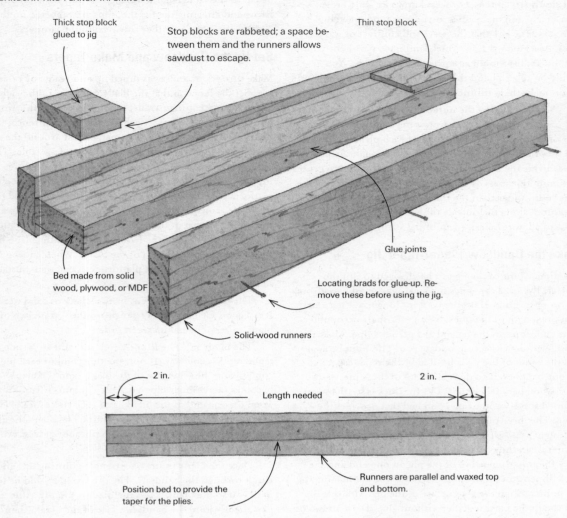

Thick stop block glued to jig

Stop blocks are rabbeted; a space between them and the runners allows sawdust to escape.

Thin stop block

Glue joints

Bed made from solid wood, plywood, or MDF

Locating brads for glue-up. Remove these before using the jig.

Solid-wood runners

2 in.

Length needed

2 in.

Position bed to provide the taper for the plies.

Runners are parallel and waxed top and bottom.

BANDSAWING

Stop blocks secure the blank. On either end of the jig, glue and clamp a stop block. You should just be able to slip a piece of paper in between the blank and each stop block.

To keep sets in order, mark a triangle on the stock before bandsawing.

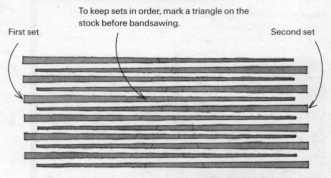

First set

Second set

Two sets of plies. After cutting each tapered ply, joint the face, flip the blank end over end, and cut the next one. Note the simple guide platform that keeps the workpiece level.

PLANING

Run each ply through the planer. Glue a piece of veneer to one stop block (left), causing the ply to bow upward about 1/8 in. When pushed down by the infeed roller of the planer, this bow greatly reduces the risk of the ply being picked up and shredded by the planer knives. With straight-grained wood, feed the thick end of the ply into the planer first (above) so that the knives are cutting downhill and not against the grain.

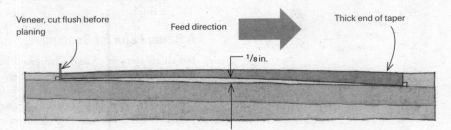

Veneer, cut flush before planing

Feed direction

Thick end of taper

1/8 in.

One board, two sets of plies. After planing the plies, use the triangle drawn on the original blank to stack the two groups in their correct sequence for grain-matched laminations.

The form's surface should be smooth and true. You can either remove the bandsaw marks with a stationary disk or belt sander, or surface the face with a 1/8-in.-thick layer of Masonite, taking into account the extra thickness when designing the form. Cover the surface with packing tape, and apply paste wax to all the other parts of the form to resist glue adhesion.

Before you apply glue, do a dry run

Pressure radiates from a clamp's pad at about a 45° angle. To achieve uniform pressure but avoid having clamps placed almost next to each other, you need to position the clamp pads farther away from the workpiece so that the cones of pressure overlap. I use at least a 1-in.-thick stack of padding strips made from 1/8-in.-thick plywood, and apply packing tape to the face of the strip in contact with the plies.

For most woods I use urea/formaldehyde glue. Its rigidity and lack of cold creep make it ideal for laminations. I always do a dry-clamping run and time it to ensure I am within the adhesive's open time of about 30 minutes, depending on temperature. I use a metal mastic spreader with 1/32-in. curved notches stamped along the edge (Hyde Co., part No. 19120; www.hydetools.com). The notches deposit the perfect amount of glue (for veneer work, too), and the spreader is easy to clean with a damp cloth.

Tape the ends of the plies down to a piece of cardboard on a bench, paying attention to the triangle mark sequence. Leave aside the top piece, which isn't glued. Pour the glue onto the plies and spread it with the notched spreader. Draw the glue down the length of the plies to avoid forcing it between them.

On oily tropical woods I use an epoxy, applying the glue to both sides of each laminate. After gluing one face using the above procedure, I take the strips off the cardboard one at a time and glue the second side with a 2-in.-wide piece of spreader.

Gather the plies and the packing strips together and move the entire assembly to the form. Starting at one end, clamp the lamination to the batten, then clamp it to the form, and then repeat these steps until you reach the far end, alternating clamps front and back of the form. Let the lamination dry overnight.

Remove the dried glue from one face with a paint scraper, run that face across the jointer, and then finish the cleanup as shown in the photos above. You are now ready to use my mortising jig to do the joinery on these curved parts.

Cleanup

Clean up the squeeze-out. Use a paint scraper to remove the hard glue that has squeezed out from between the plies.

Joint one edge. Run the edge that was scraped across the jointer.

Saw safely to width. Using a bandsaw to rip the lamination to width is safer than using a tablesaw and risking kickback.

Plane to thickness. Run the lamination through the planer to remove the bandsaw marks and bring the lamination to final thickness. Trim the ends on a miter saw using a jig, or on the tablesaw using a sled.

Glue-Up

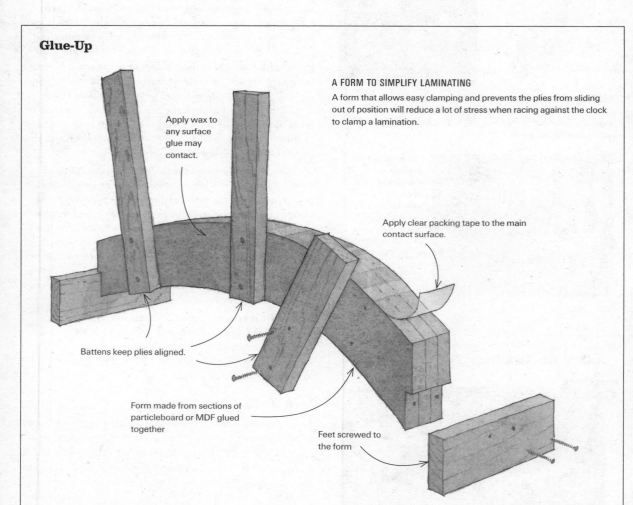

Apply wax to any surface glue may contact.

Apply clear packing tape to the main contact surface.

Battens keep plies aligned.

Form made from sections of particleboard or MDF glued together

Feet screwed to the form

A FORM TO SIMPLIFY LAMINATING
A form that allows easy clamping and prevents the plies from sliding out of position will reduce a lot of stress when racing against the clock to clamp a lamination.

Apply the glue. With a limited open time, it is important to apply the glue quickly. Tape the plies to a piece of cardboard and use a metal spreader with a serrated edge to apply an even coat of glue.

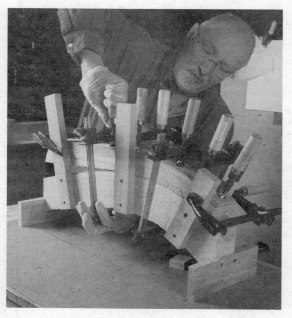

Clamp from one end. Place the plies and the packing strips on the form, and keep them parallel by clamping them to a batten (left). Then begin clamping them to the body of the form, working from one end to the other (above).

TURNING WOOD AND MAKING CURVES

The Basics of Turning Furniture Parts

by Peter Galbert

I had almost no idea how to use a lathe when I built my first Windsor chair 13 years ago, even though I'd built plenty of furniture by then. So I set about teaching myself to turn by digging through books and magazines for more information. As a woodworker new to turning, I discovered pretty quickly there's a lot they don't tell you.

There is a learning curve in jumping from curious furniture maker to competent turner. I'll show you how to get through it quickly as you turn a basic cylinder, the starting point for any spindle, and then add some tapers and tenons. Along the way, I'll share the tips I wish I'd known when I started turning, particularly things like how to hold the tool and move your body for clean cuts. Master the basics here, and in a future article, I'll take you through adding swells, beads, and coves to fully flesh out an endless array of crisply turned parts for fine furniture.

Luckily, getting started isn't expensive. Furniture makers turn mostly spindles (workpieces secured at both ends on a lathe), which doesn't require an especially powerful machine, although a longer one is better. And you can cut almost any shape with a 3/4-in. roughing gouge, 1/8-in. diamond parting tool, a 3/8-in. detail gouge, and a 3/4-in. oval skew chisel. Buy those four tools instead of a whole "kit" and you'll save a pretty penny. You can spend that savings on a few essential accessories I'll recommend later.

Start From Square One

Whether you're making table legs or drawer pulls, every turned piece starts as a blank. Begin with a square one at least 1/8 in. wider than the widest diameter of the finished spindle. That should leave room for roughing and shaping.

It's important to get the blank centered properly on the lathe because if it's off on one end, you'll remove a lot of extra material to get an even cylinder. So draw corner-to-corner lines on both ends, punch the two intersections with an awl, and use the indent to line up the lathe's drive center and tail center.

If you're using a traditional spur center, remove it from the lathe and hammer it into the end of the blank before mounting the whole piece back in the lathe. Use the spur marks to line up the workpiece. If you don't have a center yet, I recommend you buy a steb center instead. A steb center has a circle of teeth with a spring loaded-pin in the middle, and acts like clutch if a spinning piece catches a gouge. It's a more forgiving design, especially for beginners, and it's easier to mount because it stays in the lathe. Just line up the pin by eye. It's a spring, so you can always loosen the tail and move it if need be. With either type of center, tighten the tailstock enough that the piece won't spin freely by hand. Don't over-tighten or you can damage the lathe's bearings.

Now set the tool rest about 1/8 in. from the widest part of the blank, about even with the center. Rotate the blank by hand to make sure it will clear the tool rest as it spins. Keep the rest in the same relative position as you rough out the blank and the diameter shrinks.

Basic Roughing Technique

A perfect cylinder actually starts as a series of gentle, overlapping tapers that eventually get evened out. That initial taper ensures you're always cutting downhill later on when you smooth the surface. Downhill cuts mean you won't run the risk of catching the gouge on an exposed bit of end grain, which can pop out a wood chunk and or send the tool skittering. For both initial tapering and subsequent straightening, use the roughing gouge.

The basic strategy is simple. A right-handed turner would start cutting at the headstock end, always working

Mount the Blank

Find the center by drawing corner-to-corner lines on both ends, and then use the marks to line up the workpiece on the lathe's centers.

Punch the intersection. The indentation left by an awl helps locate the drive and tail centers.

TRY A STEB CENTER DRIVE

1/2-in. "stebcentre"

A steb center acts like a clutch, so a workpiece won't keep spinning if it grabs a tool's edge. The design minimizes tearout, so it's great for beginners and veterans alike. Plus, the small diameter is better for turning small or thin pieces.

Line it up. The awl and spur marks will register the piece when you seat it between the drive and tail centers. Line everything up and then tighten the tailstock to secure the blank.

Adjust the Tool Rest

> **TIP**

GIVE IT A TUNE-UP

Remove dings and divots. Tools will glide more easily over a smooth, straight tool rest, so file it smooth and polish it with diamond plates or sharpening stones. Then coat it with wax.

Keep it close. Move the tool rest about 3/8 in. away from the workpiece, and keep it at about the height of the centerline.

---

from right to left to break the edges and rough out the subtle taper. Start the first pass about 3 in. from the headstock and cut back toward the headstock. Start each subsequent pass about that same distance farther away. Once you reach the end of the tool rest, or the spindle, keep cutting lightly along the full length of the section until the edges have all broken and the piece has begun to turn round. Then slide the tool rest down the lathe's bed and repeat the process until the whole spindle tapers roughly from end to end. There may be bumps, particularly where you've moved the tool rest, but don't worry, you'll smooth them away afterward.

At this stage of bringing the piece from square to round, there are couple of important points to keep in mind.

First, move with your legs. Your body position and stance are difference-makers when it comes to clean cuts. New turners make the mistake of moving the gouge by pushing their arms or rotating their waist. Those movements make the tool travel in an arc, and leave the turner constantly trying to compensate to cut evenly. Instead, keep your arms and upper body fixed in the same position and generate side-to-side movement from your legs and hips, pivoting your weight from one foot to the other. This keeps the gouge straight throughout the cut. This is easier to do if you align your body so that it feels comfortable at the end of the cut, rather than the beginning. Face the lathe in front of where your cut will end. Then pivot your weight to your right foot to start the cut. As you move through the cut, pivot your weight back to your left foot.

Also, never stab the gouge straight into a workpiece or it will scrape the wood instead of cutting it. Scraping leaves a poor surface and creates lots of dust and the potential for serious tearout. Instead, ride the bevel up high on the spinning piece without cutting, and slowly draw it back, lifting the bottom of the handle to drop the edge and engage the workpiece. Exit the cut the same way, by riding the bevel back up. Always skew the gouge, too. That way, the bevel rides on the just-cut surface, which will support the cutting edge ahead of it as you move. This, too, makes for cleaner, safer cuts.

Lastly, throughout the whole motion, don't hold the gouge too tightly. A heavy grip limits the range of movement and makes it hard to feel the feedback from a spinning workpiece. Grip it like a bird, just tight enough to keep it from flying away.

Even the Cylinder

Finish straightening the taper and evening out the cylinder by taking a series of straight passes with the gouge. Start at the tailstock end and drop the bevel in so that you're taking a very light cut. This time, run the gouge straight along the tapered piece. The cutting edge will take increasingly thinner shavings until at some point the gouge's edge will naturally come out of the cut as it moves along. Keep cutting with thin, straight passes to even out the taper, trim any high spots, and leave a uniform shape. Check the diameter of the cylinder with a caliper to make sure it's thin enough. If not, keep taking long, thin passes to remove material evenly and to leave a smooth surface for cutting shapes.

Tapers and Cigars

I'll cover more complicated turnings in Part 2, but we can turn your uniform cylinder into two elegant furniture parts right now, complete with precise tenons on the ends. The easiest shape is a simple taper. Create it by sizing the beginning and end of the taper with the parting tool, checking with a caliper set to the desired dimension.

Don't stab the parting tool straight into the workpiece. Enter a cut with the bevel riding on the round, and draw the tool back slowly to engage the tip. Exit the cut the same way. It helps to wiggle the parting tool side-to-side just a bit to widen the kerf while cutting. It also makes it easier to check your progress with a caliper as the work spins.

For measuring diameter, I prefer my Galbert Caliper because it won't catch the kerf's edges and reads dimensions directly without any setup.

Use a roughing gouge to remove the waste between the

two parting-tool cuts, but don't cut down to the very bottom of the kerf. Leave just a little bit of material that you can remove during final smoothing with a skew chisel, which I'll cover in Part 2.

For a basic cigar shape, like those on turned Shaker legs or Windsor-chair stretchers, cut slightly rounded tapers on both ends of the cylinder the exact same way.

You can use the same technique to form accurate tenons. Just size the shoulder and ends and then gouge out the waste. Check that the diameter is even along the tenon using an open-ended wrench. Its wider surface makes it easier to see high and low spots.

Tapers and Tenons

¹/₈-in. diamond parting tool

Now you are ready for the next stage of turning: Using a parting tool to set distances and depths, and then using those cuts as references.

USING A PARTING TOOL

Point the tool straight at the blank with the bevel riding it. Draw the edge back and down to enter the cut.

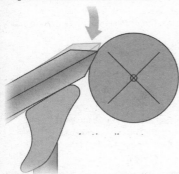

As the diameter shrinks, you'll need to keep the edge moving down and toward the center.

Roughing Out a Cylinder

The wide bevel and deep flute make this tool easy to control while hogging out material from a blank.

2 KEYS TO SUCCESS

Drop the tool into the cut. Let the bevel ride high on the blank before entering the cut. Draw the gouge back slowly and angle it down to drop the cutting edge into the workpiece.

TURN A CYLINDER IN 2 STEPS

Start with a taper. Start at the headstock and cut a slight taper a few inches from the end. Repeat the cut, starting a bit farther away each time. Keep working with overlapping passes to create a rough taper along the blank. Keep working toward the headstock to bring the taper closer to a straight cylinder before moving the tool rest to the next section. When you are done, the whole blank will have a slight taper.

Make straight cuts, starting at the fat end, to create a smooth, even cylinder.

MAINTAIN A SKEW CUT

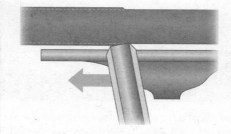

Move with legs and hips. Galbert starts a cut with his arms, waist, and torso locked in position, and his weight on his right foot (left). This ensures even cuts because he can hold the gouge in the same position, and move by shifting his weight to his other foot (right).

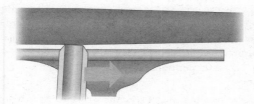

Skewing the gouge stabilizes the bevel against the already-cut section, leaving a cleaner surface and an easier-to-control tool.

TAPERS ARE EASY

Set your landmarks. Galbert starts taper cuts by first sizing the diameters at the beginning and end. Set a caliper for the desired diameter, and slide it into the parting-tool cut.

Other landmarks. This turning will get tapered at both ends, with a flattish section between. Shallow parting-tool marks define the thick ends of the taper.

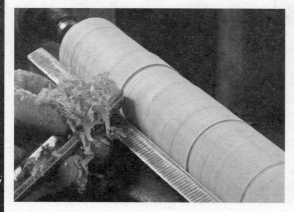

Start cutting at the end. Make a series of ever-widening passes to work down to your narrowest diameter without going deeper than your high point at the fat end of the taper. The taper will be a bit rough, but Galbert will smooth it with a skew chisel in Part 2.

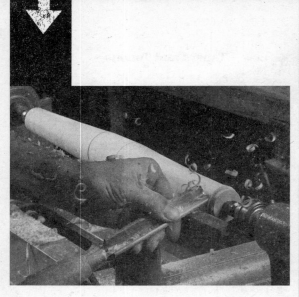

Switch directions on double tapers. To do the other taper, work toward the tailstock, moving left to right. Remember to skew the gouge into the cut.

TURNING A TENON

Size the shoulder and ends first. Cut tenons like tapers, but with the same diameter at both ends. The parting tool works better if used slightly away from the end, suported on both sides of the cut

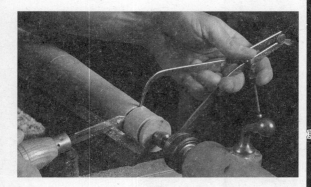

Scoop out the middle. Remove the waste at the end, and then take straight, even cuts with a roughing gouge (below). The thick jaws of a wrench (right) make it easy to find high spots, whether the piece is spinning or not.

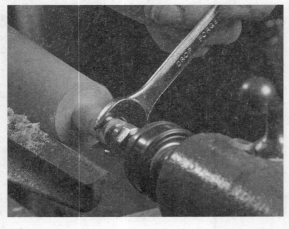

Create Smooth Surfaces and Intricate Designs with Turning

by Peter Galbert

One thing furniture makers don't realize when they approach turning is that the smooth surfaces, sharp notches, and lovely beads and coves they covet all take a bit of practice. The great thing about a practice session is that you don't have to fret over making something precious.

The basic drills in this article will teach you the subtleties involved in planing a surface smooth, plus cutting the precise notches, beads, and coves seen in traditional furniture parts. Master these cuts in practice and real furniture spindles will be a breeze.

I'll demonstrate some techniques that the usual sources neglect to explain, such as how to adjust your footwork and grip to put the tools and your body in the most comfortable position.

You won't need as many tools as you think. Furniture work requires only four tools, a roughing gouge and parting tool, plus an oval skew chisel and spindle gouge that have been specially reground and honed. For the skill-building exercises in this article, you'll need blanks 12 in. to 18 in. long that have been roughed down to 2-1/4-in.-dia. cylinders, as you learned to do efficiently in Part 1.

A Step-By-Step Tutorial

After learning to make perfect cylinders and tapers, Galbert's students learn more intricate cuts by running through a series of short exercises on scrap or firewood. By cutting the key shapes over and over, they develop confidence and muscle memory. It also is easier to see and fix errors in technique when you make the same mistake a few times in a row.

Planing with the Skew Chisel

Although planing all of the flat surfaces with an oval skew chisel is typically the last step I take in turning a spindle, it's one of the first skills I teach novices because it's simple to learn and develops a feel for the tool. The key is learning to balance the bevel of the tool on the spinning workpiece and rotate/angle the edge as needed to take whisper-thin, even shavings and leave behind a glass-smooth surface. Turners try to minimize sanding, which blunts sharp details.

You'll need to learn to plane in both directions, but there is a more natural direction for lefties (going left to right) and righties (vice versa) to start with when getting a feel for the technique.

Hold the oval skew chisel like a roughing gouge, with one hand bracing the bottom of the handle against your hip. Press the barrel of the chisel against the tool rest with the thumb of your other hand. Keep the edge of the tool at about 45° to the axis of the workpiece with the toe pointed up. That position keeps the bevel bearing on the workpiece, stabilizing the cut.

Engage the blade either by rotating the tool down a bit so the curved edge begins to shave, or by swinging the handle up in an arc. In either case, the point of contact with the spindle should stay in the middle of the edge, as high on the workpiece as is comfortable. Staying high on the round limits the depth of cut. With a little practice, you'll find that the skew will cut from any number of positions once you find the right balance between the angle of presentation and the rotation of the tool. Use the same side-to-side movement with your hips and legs that you use with a roughing gouge. This ensures that the edge will move along the spindle in a relatively constant position, making it much easier to cut straight.

To avoid catches, always keep the skew moving forward in a constant, fluid motion, and don't try to cut too deep. Most problems with the skew come from moving backward to get a missed spot. Be content to simply shave away high spots at first. Subsequent passes will even out the surface. The shavings will become more uniform and continuous once the spindle is straight and smooth. To finish a skew cut, rotate or push the edge back up again so that the edge no longer contacts the round. Don't pull the tool away from the blank or lower the cutting edge; that will deepen the cut and could catch the edge.

Now try it in the other direction, this time planing away from your body. First use the rouging gouge to rough up your nice surface, and then switch to the skew for planing. It's a little trickier this way for new turners, who often block the handle as they position themselves. Rotate your body close to the lathe. This will let you angle the edge properly, and give you plenty of room to enter and exit cuts cleanly.

Exercise 1: Learn to Smooth a Cylinder

The goal is to plane a roughed-down cylinder until it's glass-smooth and even. Practice moving in both directions, and smooth a number of spindles.

Balancing act. Galbert braces the handle against his hip and uses thumb-pressure on the barrel to keep the tool in a consistent position (above left). The trick with a planing cut is to ride the bevel of the tool while keeping the cutting action at the center of the edge (left). Avoid cutting with the toe or heel, which can cause catches. The other key is to always be moving

THE OVAL SKEW CHISEL HANDLES BOTH TASKS

The oval-shaped barrel is especially important for planing cuts, making it easier to pivot subtly on the tool rest and find that perfect angle of attack.

Exercise 2: Cut a Row of V-Notches

The V-notch is the easiest shape to learn, but the trick is to cut one consistently and confidently in three clean strokes.

Start with a relief cut. Use a chopping motion with the toe of the skew chisel to cut straight into the workpiece (above left). Then cut the side walls. Angle the chisel and follow its outer bevel down into the notch.

V-Notches Open the Door to Other Shapes

For new turners, V-notches are a gateway because they serve both as decorative elements and as preliminary cuts for other shapes. Also, the V-notch is the easiest shape to learn—it takes just three short cuts with the toe of a skew chisel. To practice that, make a series of notches about 1 in. apart along one of your practice cylinders. Make a notch and move quickly to the next without recutting or cleaning up the last. The goal is to repeat the gestures until you develop a feel for them, moving seamlessly from one side of the V to the other. After a few blanks, you'll be able to do this handily.

After making the relief cut in the center, rotate the chisel slightly to cut each sidewall. The outer bevel is the one that matters. Line it up with the cut you want to make, and then raise the handle of the tool to slice off a nice, clean ring of wood. If the chisel skitters one way or the other, rotate it in the other direction a bit more and try again. Just as with a planing cut, the skew must constantly travel forward to cut a V-notch without catching. You'll need to sidestep a little and get your torso out of the way before making the cut that is closest to your body.

Skew Can Cut Beads, Too

To cut beads, start with your series of V-notches and use the same tool you've been getting comfortable with, the skew chisel. To develop consistency, practice cutting a row of half-beads along a cylinder that has a V-notch about every inch, and then come back and cut the other half-bead.

To enter the cut, lower the skew until the edge is about to contact the workpiece, then roll the heel of the skew toward the V-notch and lift the handle. Stay in contact as you roll around the bead by moving the handle sideways.

Here's a secret seldom told to new turners: The technique is much easier if you hold the tool so it's most comfortable at the end of the cut. In this case, it's important to keep the skew cutting high on the round, which is easier if you start with your hands in a slightly unnatural position. Hold the chisel with its toe pointing straight up. Then rotate it back to the starting position without changing your grip. Now you'll always be moving toward a more comfortable grip as you rotate the tool, and your motion will be much smoother.

By the way, I leave a nearly imperceptible flat on the center of my beads, so I have a good starting point for both sides of the cut. I finish it off afterward.

Cutting Beads with a Gouge

When cutting a bead with a spindle gouge, new turners often find the cutting motion tough to master, because it involves rotating the tool while simultaneously lifting the handle and swinging it sideways along the tool rest. Again, if you do the drill, you'll build the skill.

Start by cutting the left side of each bead, working down the entire row. The handle will swing away from you, which is easier. The process is the same for cutting right-side beads, but it requires you to step a little farther to the left to get your body out of the way as you swing the handle of the tool toward you.

Back to that turner's secret again, where you start off a little awkward and move toward comfortable. For a right-side bead, this means you should grip the gouge so the flute faces all the way to the right before putting it in position to start the cut.

Cutting Coves with a Gouge

To cut coves, the concave shapes found in all types of spindles, you'll use the spindle gouge in a maneuver that looks similar to cutting a bead in reverse. As with beads, the choreography is tough to get used to at first. You'll practice cutting two sides from the same position, and the entire spindle will be less likely to vibrate and chatter if it's thinned out in only one place at a time. Lay out the ends of the coves by penciling a line every inch and then get the cove started by using a parting tool to size the diameter between the marks down to 1 in.

Making a cove cut is like scooping wood out of the spindle, working toward the middle in ever-widening scoops until you reach the pencil line. Finish each cut before you encounter any end grain that's exposed on the other side of the cove, which will cause a catch. Work back and forth, making passes on the right and left until the cove is done before moving on to the next one. As before, it helps to grip the gouge so that your hands are in a comfortable position at the end of the cut. Your body needs to be out of the way, too.

Bring It All Together

After practicing the basic shapes, you're ready for a more complicated shape. I have students bring them together into a series of alternating beads and coves, each shape beginning and ending at a crisp shoulder line. Here, the goal is to create consistent shapes and move fluidly from one to the other without cutting into the shoulder. For a workpiece, rough down one of the practice pieces from earlier. I tell students to aim for about a 2-in.-dia. cylinder, but being exact doesn't matter, as long the diameter is consistent and thick enough to leave the bottom cove at least ³⁄₄ in. thick. Any thinner and the spindle could flex, causing chatter as you cut.

Locate the shoulder lines by making a pencil line every inch, down the entire workpiece. But once again, you will work one section at a time to avoid excessive vibration. That section will consist of a half-bead, then a shoulder cut, a full cove, a shoulder cut, and then a half-bead.

Start each section by cutting a pair of shoulder lines down to 1¹⁄₄ in. dia. Then remove most of the waste between them with the spindle gouge, stopping just before you reach the depth of the shoulders. The slightly proud surface gives a reference point to begin the cove cuts. Cut the beads last, smoothing them with the skew chisel if needed. If your gouge is sharp, they probably won't need it. And remember, it's just practice.

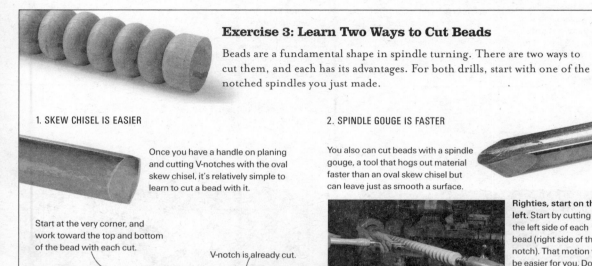

Exercise 3: Learn Two Ways to Cut Beads

Beads are a fundamental shape in spindle turning. There are two ways to cut them, and each has its advantages. For both drills, start with one of the notched spindles you just made.

1. SKEW CHISEL IS EASIER

Once you have a handle on planing and cutting V-notches with the oval skew chisel, it's relatively simple to learn to cut a bead with it.

Start at the very corner, and work toward the top and bottom of the bead with each cut.

V-notch is already cut.

Lead with the heel. Begin by taking a small cut on the corner of the V-notch, rotating the heel of the chisel to peel a thin shaving all the way down to the bottom. Remove a bit of wood with each pass.

Pivot from the thumb. Use the tool rest as a fulcrum when slicing through the wood. The motion looks and feels like a planing cut in which you ride the bevel. You'll need to move the handle away from the center of the bead to do so.

Vertical limit. With each pass, you'll start closer to the center of the bead, and finish with the tool more and more vertical until it's close to 90°.

2. SPINDLE GOUGE IS FASTER

You also can cut beads with a spindle gouge, a tool that hogs out material faster than an oval skew chisel but can leave just as smooth a surface.

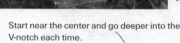

Righties, start on the left. Start by cutting the left side of each bead (right side of the notch). That motion will be easier for you. Do a whole row.

Start near the center and go deeper into the V-notch each time.

Now the right. To cut a bead with a spindle gouge, enter the cut near the center and simultaneously roll the tool and ride the bevel down the side of the bead.

Tricky motion. To keep the cutting edge engaged, you'll need to roll the tool sideways while both lifting the handle and moving it sideways.

Finish on the side. The gouge will end up tipped all the way onto its side on your final pass.

Continued ➡

Exercise 4: Cut a Row of Coves

Unlike beads, you can practice coves on a straight cylinder and it's best to cut them one at a time.

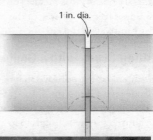

Start with a pencil and a parting tool. Mark pencil lines every 1 in. and make notches between them to roughly 1 in. dia. To use the parting tool, start by riding the bevel and then raise the handle to lower the tip.

1 in. dia.

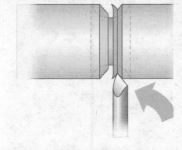

A few small cuts in the middle. Holding the gouge on its side, take shallow cuts on each side of the parting-tool cut. Enter the cut by rolling the gouge back toward level while pushing it forward in a scooping motion. Keep the bevel of the gouge bearing on the wood as you roll and push.

Work toward the pencil lines. Scoop out the sides of the cove, working from side to side to widen and deepen the shape. Continue feeding the cutter forward to raise it out of the cut.

Map out the spindle and excavate. Use two parting-tool cuts to define the shoulders, and the spindle gouge to remove most of the waste in between.

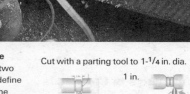

Cut with a parting tool to 1-1/4 in. dia.

1 in.

Remove most of the middle.

Define the center. Use a parting-tool cut to define the depth of the cove at roughly 3/4 in. dia.

Parting tool defines cove depth.

Exercise 5: Put It All Together

Use another one of your practice cylinders. The goal is crisp transitions between each element.

Beads first. Stick with the gouge, shooting for a clean, sharp transition to the flat shoulder.

Gouge defines the beads.

Now the cove. To avoid excessive vibration, hollow out this section last. If the beads are rough, plane them a bit with the skew chisel.

Smooth and refine the bead if needed with a skew chisel.

Form the cove with the gouge.

Faceplate Turning

by Jimmy Clewes

When it comes to turning, most furniture makers, not surprisingly, confine themselves to making furniture components. Regardless of the style, whether Shaker legs or period finials, almost all parts are turned between centers with the grain running parallel to the lathe's bed, a process known as spindle turning. However, there is another dimension to turning—faceplate turning—where the blank is attached just to the headstock end with the grain perpendicular to the bed.

Faceplate turning allows you to explore a whole new world of artistic woodworking, creating beautiful objects from start to finish in a few hours. Yet the tools and techniques are not that different from the ones you spindle

turners are already familiar with. I'll demonstrate the steps involved by turning a platter, but a bowl is turned in the same way.

Freed from the conventional restrictions of furniture making, you'll find that turning stand-alone artistic pieces allows you to use a far wider range of wood. You only need an interesting chunk of a log, not a clear, 8-ft. section cut into boards and dried for a year. And in faceplate turning, the contrast between sapwood and heartwood is often prized, and irregularities like bark inclusions and burls are put on full display. However, you still want to avoid wood with cracks and checks in it, because the blank can fly apart. Although you can turn green wood, in this case I used kiln-dried curly maple.

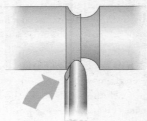

The Basic Sequence

The sequence for most faceplate turning is as follows: First, draw a circle on the wood using a compass. This not only gives you a line to follow on the bandsaw but also marks the center of the blank. After sawing away the waste, mount the blank with the outside or underside of the platter facing the tailstock. The simplest and most secure way to attach it to the lathe is using a faceplate, hence the name for this type of turning. Most lathes come with at least a small faceplate, but aftermarket plates in all sizes are inexpensive and easy to find. Next, shape the base or foot so that it can be attached to a four-jaw chuck, and turn, sand, and finish the rest of the outside. Remove the workpiece from the faceplate and mount the base in the four-jaw chuck. Now you can turn and finish the inside and top of the platter.

Completely Finish the Outside First

The first thing to consider when turning the base of your platter is how you want the jaws of the chuck to grip the workpiece. They can either apply pressure outward against a recess or inward against a spigot. I prefer a recess because I think you get a better grip. The diameter of the recess will determine the size of the foot, and so it should be in proportion to the rest of the piece. About a third of the total radius is a good rule of thumb. If you are turning a recess with a foot, as I am, never make the outside of the foot the same depth as the recess (see drawing, next page). If you do, you will end up with a potentially weak ring of wood on the base of the platter, which may break out when hollowing the inside.

The recess must be cut as accurately as possible so that the jaws of the chuck sit perfectly. It only needs to be deep enough to enclose the serrated ends of the jaw (see photo, below). I use a 1/8-in. parting tool to define the rim of the recess and a 3/8-in. bowl gouge to remove waste from the center. Feel free to use other tools you are comfortable with. Finish-sand the recess.

Profile the outside of the piece—With the recess and foot complete, it's time to shape the rest of the outside. Simple shapes please me most and my favorite is the softened ogee, which is attractive to the eye.

Don't turn at an excessively slow speed. Once the blank is balanced, higher speeds lessen the resistance of the cut and produce a better finish from the tool. To shape the outside of the platter, work from the center to the edge going with the grain. I remove the bulk of the waste material with a 3/8-in. long-grind bowl gouge (see "Simple Set of Tools").

When you have shaped the outside of the platter, there will almost certainly be some tearout on the end grain. There are a couple of steps to take care of this. Make a finishing cut with a 1/4-in. bowl gouge, also cutting from the center to the outside and removing only a little wood—up to 3/32 in. The more even your movements, the smoother the finish, but the odd ripple can be removed by the next step.

Shear-scraping, which is really shear cutting, leaves a surface that needs very little sanding. When preparing the scraper, try sharpening the tool upside down. This produces a longer, more even burr, as the grinding wheel draws the steel away from the tool edge. By the way, when the burr is worn away on one part of the cutting edge, a slight adjustment in tool angle will give you a fresh burr to work with.

Take your time sanding—The outside of the platter should be ready for sanding. I start with P180-grit paper and work through P240, P320, P400, and then CAMI 600, 800, 1,000, and 1,200 wet-or-dry paper, used dry.

The first sanding is the most important—any tool marks or disturbed grain should be sanded out to leave an even surface. If you can see any light lines in the piece, they are probably areas where the grain has been disturbed and they show up because dust has entered the disturbed grain. These lines must be sanded out before you go to the next grit.

Simple Set of Tools

You only need four tools to create beautiful faceplate turnings—two bowl gouges, a parting tool, and a scraper—but the way you grind them is key.

TIP GRIND A LONG BEVEL ON A BOWL GOUGE
Most bowl gouges come with a short bevel. To make it more versatile, Clewes grinds a long bevel that extends farther back. He uses Oneway's Wolverine sharpening system, set up as follows.

3/8-IN. BOWL GOUGE WITH LONG BEVEL GRIND

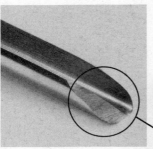

This gouge removes the bulk of waste material. The long wings can be used for light, cleanup cuts inside the rim, around the foot, and on the outside.

Place the gouge in the Vari-grind jig with its adjustable arm in the second stop from the bottom. Place the jig against the back of the V-arm support and extend the tip of the gouge until the base of the bevel is level with the front of the V.

Set the base of the jig in the V-arm and swing the jig back and forth until the wings are fully shaped.

1/4-IN. BOWL GOUGE

The standard short-grind bevel makes a light cut that removes tearout left by the 3/8-in. gouge.

PARTING TOOL

This tool starts cuts in flat surfaces, leaving a trench that a bowl gouge can engage.

ROUND-NOSE SCRAPER

The tool is ground bevel-side up to create a fine cutting burr.

I usually power-sand using small hook-and-loop-backed sanding disks attached to a corded drill. This speeds things up dramatically and gives better control and more even pressure. If you see the disk detaching itself from the pad, you are probably spending too much time sanding with too fine a grit and creating too much heat. You will be better off dropping back to a coarser grit.

When satisfied with the initial sanding, go through the grits, removing the sanding marks made by the previous abrasive. By the end, the wood should be polished enough to see your fingers reflected in it before you apply any finish.

Seal and then apply a finish—I finish my platters with Watco Danish Oil, my favorite finishing product. It is extremely durable, with just the right amount of body, and it allows you to re-oil items later to rejuvenate them, providing you didn't apply a topcoat of paste wax.

However, don't apply the Danish oil to bare wood. On figured wood in particular, you would have to saturate the wood before you'd get an even sheen. Instead, seal the surface with either dewaxed shellac or an oil-based sanding sealer. Once dry, smooth the surface with Liberon's 0000 steel wool. Use a fine-weave, lint-free cloth such as an old T-shirt to apply the Danish oil in a circular motion with the piece stationary on the lathe. If you see any white dots, they are pores filled with dust; apply more oil to these areas until they disappear.

Remove any excess oil using a clean cloth with the lathe turning slowly. Let the oil dry for about a half-hour before buffing to a satin sheen with a clean cloth. Second and third coats are optional based on the sheen you desire.

Remount the Piece and Turn the Inside

Now to the inside of the platter. Remove the faceplate from the unfinished side of the platter and screw the four-jaw chuck to the lathe. When mounting the piece in the chuck, make sure you put pressure right in the center of the workpiece. This will ensure that it is sitting squarely before the chuck jaws are tightened. Tighten until there is just a little resistance on the jaws, enough to hold the workpiece securely but not enough to dent the recess.

The first task is to flatten the face of the workpiece and bring it to the desired thickness. When laying out the inside of the platter, bear in mind that the width of the rim looks good if it is about one-third of the radius. Make a cut with a parting tool to define the rim edge. This will also serve as a shoulder for the bevel of your bowl gouge when you start hollowing the center.

Finish the rim first, leaving the bulk of the wood in the middle for support. I also divide the rim roughly into thirds with the outer third sloping toward the outer rim while the inner section slopes toward the inner rim but terminates in a kind of very small ski jump. This gives your fingers something to register against when you handle the platter. You also will be cutting downhill with the grain. I shear-scrape if necessary as I cut the wood, ready for sanding.

To remove waste from the inside of the platter, I again use the long-grind bowl gouge and the 1/4-in. bowl gouge for the finishing cuts, working from the outside to the middle, as this is the way the grain is running. I erase any ripple marks by shear-scraping. Make sure the inside profile of the platter is a nice continuous curve with no hump or depression in the middle, a common oversight. To detect any discrepancies on the inside profile curve, simply use the tips of your fingers and run them back and forth over the surface; it's surprising how sensitive they are and how fine a flaw they can detect. When satisfied that everything is in order, sand, seal, and finish the inside in the same way as you did the outside.

Continued ➤

1. Mount the Workpiece on the Lathe and Turn the Foot

Screw on the faceplate and then attach the faceplate to the lathe. Start by turning the outside of the blank round and the face flat. Then turn a recess that will accommodate the four-jaw chuck, used when shaping the inside of the platter.

Attach the faceplate. Screw the faceplate to what will become the top or inside of the platter.

Measure the chuck. When gripping a recess, four-jaw chucks have the most contact with the wood when the jaws are nearly closed. Set your calipers to that diameter.

Lay out the recess. Use the calipers to mark the diameter of the recess on the spinning workpiece. Mark the outside of the foot, too, and then use a parting tool to cut the shoulder.

Complete the recess. Use the long-grind 3/8-in. bowl gouge to remove the rest of the waste from the recess.

Grip with the tip. There is no need to create a recess that matches the full depth of the chuck's jaws. Only the serrated tips need to grab the wood.

2. Rough Out and Refine the Bottom

Use a series of tools to quickly shape the overall profile, and then produce a smooth surface with no tearout.

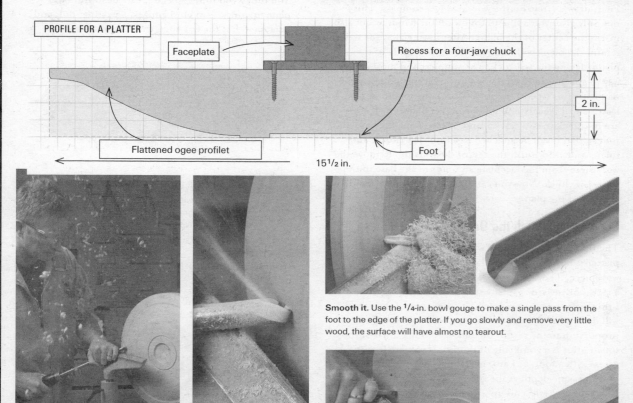

PROFILE FOR A PLATTER

Faceplate

Recess for a four-jaw chuck

2 in.

Flattened ogee profilet

Foot

15 1/2 in.

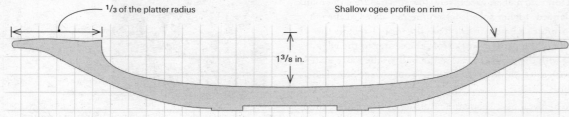

Smooth it. Use the 1/4-in. bowl gouge to make a single pass from the foot to the edge of the platter. If you go slowly and remove very little wood, the surface will have almost no tearout.

Rough it. When shaping the outside of the workpiece, cut from the center toward the edge, going with the wood fibers. Use the 3/8-in. bowl gouge. The side bevels, or wings, on the gouge can be used to make light, shaving cuts to clean up the surface.

Scrape it. Use the burr on a round-nose scraper to clean up the surface prior to sanding.

4. Turn the Inside Last

When turning the inside, reverse the process and work from the edge to the center.

PROFILE FOR A PLATTER

1/3 of the platter radius

Shallow ogee profile on rim

1 3/8 in.

Work toward the center. Turn the rim using the same tools as the bottom of the platter, then hollow out the center. Weight in the center keeps the blank more stable.

Rule of thirds. The rim should be about a third the radius of the platter. Use a parting tool to define the inside edge, and then divide the rim itself into thirds to help determine its profile.

The reward for good sanding. The oil-based finish will highlight any tearout or scratches, so don't skimp on surface preparation.

Flip and regrab. With the outside finished, remove the faceplate and use the recess you turned in the base to mount the platter on the chuck.

Smooth Curves with Hand Tools

By Jeff Miller

When I started building furniture, my designs were simple, squarish Shaker and Mission-style pieces. But as my skills grew, I began drawing curves inspired by the human body, nature, or architecture. Curves became crucial to my work, making it more expressive, more appealing to eye and hand.

Whether you bandsaw curves or template-rout them, they'll need smoothing afterward. Many woodworkers struggle with this and resort to sanding—dusty, tedious work that doesn't yield fair curves or crisp surfaces. I'll show you a better way to smooth both convex and concave curves using a handful of basic tools: handplane, spokeshave, rasp, and scraper. You'll get smooth curves without kinks, flat spots, or bumps—surfaces that invite hands to run along the edges of your work.

Bear in mind that these tools are for flat (so to speak) edges, as opposed to sculpting freeform, rounded shapes.

Handplanes Can Handle Some Curves

For gentle-to-moderate convex curves (or very gentle concave ones), I start with a sharp handplane set up for a light cut. A plane chatters less and smooths more efficiently than lighter tools.

With a bench plane, I use a standard grip on the handle and tote. I also hold a block plane with two hands. On convex curves, very little of the sole rides the surface, so control the

tool by balancing downward pressure, fore and aft, to keep the edge in the cut. Two things help: First, power the stroke with your lower body, not your arms. Second, roll the plane forward as you move, as if you're pushing it around a large wheel. On concave curves, skew the tool to shorten its sole. With any curve, if you can't follow the curve with a plane, it's time to switch tools.

Essential Kit for Curves

You can smooth curves quickly with just a bench or block plane, a spokeshave, a rasp, and a scraper. Miller keeps them all handy, and starts with the largest tool that can handle the curve. Mass equals momentum.

BLOCK OR BENCH PLANE

The popular No. 4 smoother works well; a smaller bench plane perhaps a little better (Miller often uses a No. 2). Most versatile is a high-quality block plane. Miller says it doesn't need an adjustable throat opening or a low angle. Just sharpen the blade and set it for a light cut.

SPOKESHAVE

The shave's short sole lets it smooth hollows that a longer tool would bridge over. A flat-soled shave works well on steep convex curves and moderate concave ones. A convex sole reaches into tighter concave curves, but is harder to control.

RASPS

The rasp fits where edge tools won't. Miller uses a fine-grain Auriou (their No. 13) but has a coarser rasp (a 9 or 10) for heavier stock removal. There are even coarser models, but they are for 3-D shaping and rounding.

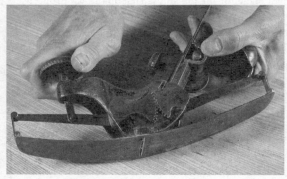

SCRAPER/SANDING BLOCK

Use a card scraper or sanding block on tearout-prone areas where grain changes direction, or for smoothing spots that have already been worked by the other tools. Set up the scraper with a light to moderate burr.

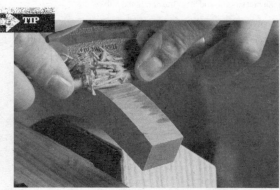

COMPASS PLANE IS A CURVE SPECIALIST

If you do curved work often, consider getting a compass plane. Its flexible sole adjusts to a range of curves. A few companies make new models, but an old Stanley 113 is fairly easy to find and is still the best.

Convex Curves

PLANES FOR LARGE CURVES

Miller likes to start with the largest plane that can navigate the curve. A heavier tool will chatter less and leave a smoother surface, but its longer sole requires more finesse to control.

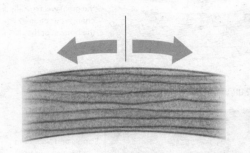

PLANE WITH THE GRAIN

Hold a block plane with a forefinger on the front knob and the opposite hand wrapped around the front to apply downward pressure as you move forward.

SPOKESHAVE FOR TIGHTER CURVES

A spokeshave handles steep curves more nimbly than a handplane. Control the shave with your thumbs on the back edge of the blade or the shave's body. Your index fingers regulate downward force on the front of the tool.

TIP

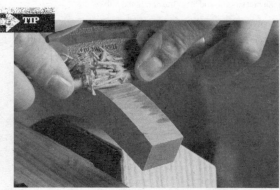

WATCH THE LINE

To avoid beveling the edge, use the bandsaw marks to track your progress. Try to remove them evenly as you go. Once they're gone, switch to a square as a final check.

---

3. Finish Before Flipping

Take this opportunity to completely prep and finish the bottom of the platter. You'll use the same finishing sequence on the top.

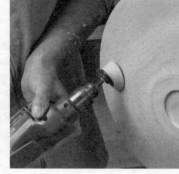

Power sanding. Although you can use sheets of sandpaper or random-orbit sander disks, the fastest and most effective way is to use hook-and-loop disks and a foam backer pad attached to a drill while the workpiece spins at a moderate speed.

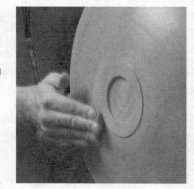

Seal and steel. After sanding, seal the surface with shellac or sanding sealer. When dry, smooth the surface with good quality 0000 steel wool.

A flawless finish. Because you sealed the wood first, the subsequent oil-based finish leaves an even sheen.

Continued ➡

Concave Curves

START WITH A SPOKESHAVE

With its minimal sole, a spokeshave can settle into concave curves that are too deep for a handplane to fathom.

WORK DOWNHILL

On a concave edge, the grain will typically change direction at the bottom of the valley.

SCRAPE OR SAND THE TRANSITIONS

After working the surface with edge tools and a sanding block, use a card scraper to remove any tool marks and refine the surface, especially in tearout-prone transition areas.

Most curved edges can be smoothed with a sanding block shaped to fit the workpiece. It's great for tight curves or where grain direction changes. Start with P150 grit.

VERY TIGHT CURVES? USE A RASP

Two hands. Angle the rasp slightly, push forward (rasps do not cut on the pull stroke), and lift at the end of the stroke.

Remove the rasp marks. The surface left by a relatively fine-grain, higher quality rasp is easily cleaned up with a scraper.

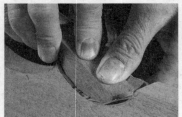

Sand for consistency. After smoothing with edge tools, you may want to give the entire edge a light sanding with P220-grit to achieve a consistent surface.

Shaves Work Curves, Inside and Out

Spokeshaves are made to smooth curves, both convex and concave. The short sole makes it easier to follow a curve, especially when the radius is tight or changing.

Hold the tool with your thumbs pushing on or near the blade and your fingertips at the front. This lets you vary the angle of attack to follow the curve as you push with your lower body. The shave has very little mass to dampen vibration, so work slowly to avoid chatter. A sharp blade is crucial.

Skewing the tool lengthens the sole on the surface, reducing chatter, bridging high spots, and making it easier to start a cut. Be careful not to bevel the surface sideways, though. Check it periodically with a square.

To avoid tearout where the grain changes direction at the bottom of a concave curve, try rolling the tool back so that the edge stops cutting as you approach the bottom. Finish those transition areas with a scraper or sanding block to remove any tearout.

Keep a Rasp Ready

On some curves, the radius is too tight, the curve dies into a corner, or the surface just can't be reached with an edge tool. A rasp's half-round face is ideal for tight inside curves and its cutting action lets you approach the work from any angle. Hold it by the wooden handle (a must) with the other hand guiding lightly at the tip. A well-sawn curve needs only a light touch with a fine rasp, but the surface will be rougher than one left by a plane or spokeshave. Follow with a scraper or sanding block.

Flawless Curves on the Bandsaw

By Michael Fortune

I have exhibited my work for many years and have noticed that people respond to curves. They'll stop, look, and then run their hands along the curved edges of a piece. Square furniture rarely invites this personal interaction.

I use all manner of curves in my work, from irregular, free-form curves to regular curves with exact radii. All of them must be free of irregularities that could catch the light unevenly or be easily detected when you pass your hand along the edge. The fastest way to cut curves is on the bandsaw. The bandsaw is a crude machine, however, and the results can be rough, with major smoothing and sanding required. I will show you how to cut curves on the bandsaw so smooth and close to the line that they require very little cleanup afterward.

The first step to cutting attractive curves, whether true arcs with a single radius or irregular, flowing curves, is knowing how to draw them.

Start with the blade and guides

A 14-in. bandsaw is a good size for cutting curved furniture parts. The key to great performance is picking the right blade for the job and setting up the saw properly.

Pick the right blade—It might seem counterintuitive, but a coarse blade (3 tpi to 4 tpi, skip tooth) will make very clean cuts. A finer blade, with too many teeth and small gullets in between, will clog with sawdust pretty quickly, causing it to overheat and dull prematurely. The blade will also tend to dodge left or right as it works to avoid the compressed sawdust, resulting in a wobbly cut line.

Be sure to match the blade width to the radius you are cutting. In general, tighter curves require narrower blades. Finally, be sure the blade is sharp and clean. A dull blade will always seek the path of least resistance, and it is rarely in the direction you want to cut. You can tell a blade is getting dull when it takes extra pressure to cut the stock. A dull blade also runs hotter, and the end of the kerf will be dark where the teeth were in contact with the wood. You may also notice that the sawdust appears slightly toasted.

Set the tension and guides—Once you have the proper blade in hand, it's critical that you set the tension and guides to ensure good results.

With the guides pulled away from the blade, adjust the tension and track the blade so that it's centered on the upper wheel. I do not overtension bandsaw blades. In fact, I lean toward undertensioning them. For example, my 1/2-in. blades will be tensioned only to the 3/8-in. mark on the blade tension scale. The lower tension works because the coarse blades I use cut flawlessly and are easy to steer along a pencil line. The lower tension also saves wear and tear on the bandsaw tires and doesn't overstress the frame of the bandsaw. Overtensioning a narrow blade, such as the 1/8-in., 3/16-in., and 1/4-in. sizes, risks having the blade create a groove in the tires. Once that happens, any blade will become almost impossible to track.

Next, adjust the guides and the thrust bearing to ensure sufficient blade support for the curved cuts. Finally, check that the table is square to the blade, lower the upper guide to within 1/2 in. of the workpiece—enough to block your fingers from passing under—and you're ready to cut.

Cutting Close to the Line Means Less Cleanup Later

An essential woodworking skill is being able to cut to a curved line on the bandsaw. I see a lot of students and beginning woodworkers struggle with this task. I'll show you the secrets to making smooth cuts within 1/32 in. of any cut line, without the need for fancy jigs.

Let the blade do its job—When cutting, don't push too hard. Feed the workpiece slowly and steadily. With a sharp blade, the work should practically feed itself. Trying to make the blade cut too fast will create a rough surface and a wandering cut.

It's also helpful to have good task lighting focused on the cutting area so the pencil line is clearly visible. As you cut, always be aware of where your hands and fingers are. It's easy to lose track of them as you navigate the curves.

Plan the sequence of any curved cut so that it is not necessary to back out along the curved kerf. Backing out can be problematic, especially if the kerf has closed up, and you risk inadvertently pulling the blade off the bandsaw wheels.

A really twisted trick—The most common problem encountered when cutting a freehand curve is that the cut is wavy and not always precisely parallel with the line you want to follow. The set on the blade's teeth (the distance the teeth project from the sides of the blade) allows the wood to move from side to side until it encounters the flat sides of the blade.

I found a way to overcome this problem by slightly twisting the wood during the cut so that one side of the kerf remains in contact with the back edge of the blade. In essence, the back of the blade serves as a steady rest, eliminating the side-to-side wobble and allowing you to control the cut with precision. The technique certainly takes some practice (you may want to try it with a wider blade at first), but you'll be shocked at the results.

Offer support where needed—If you're cutting a large piece, the small table of the bandsaw may not provide enough support. Also, the workpiece or the offcut will tilt slightly and snag on the edge of the bandsaw table as it is swung around. To avoid this problem and make the cut safer, use either an outfeed support or a large auxiliary table that's clamped to the bandsaw table, or both.

When bandsawing thin stock, tearout is often a problem. To prevent tearout on the bottom of a thin workpiece, back up the cut using a thin sheet of hardboard taped to the bandsaw table. With this method you can make splinter-free cuts in stock as thin as 1/16 in. By the way, the rough blade still works in thin stock.

Tricks for compound curves—There are cases where it is not possible to have the wood always in contact with the bandsaw table. Cutting a compound curve can require that the part be lifted off the table at various points. This is not safe, because the cutting action can slam the wood onto the table, drawing your fingers in or pinching them underneath. One common method of supporting the workpiece

is to tape the offcuts to the blank after each side is cut. This is a typical procedure for making cabriole legs, but it works for any leg that is shaped on multiple sides.

Another method is to use a block under the concave area of a workpiece, a technique especially useful when you're cutting a curved apron or drawer front. Be sure to orient the workpiece with the show face on top.

Simple Methods to Remove Sawmarks

Any cuts made on the bandsaw, no matter how skillfully done, will need to be cleaned up to remove the sawmarks. Curves can be smoothed using hand tools or sandpaper. Whatever your approach, the goal is to create a flawless surface that's easy on the eyes and fingers.

When working with solid wood, I always look first at using a compass plane or spokeshave to smooth or fair a curve.

I use custom sanding blocks made to match the curve. I often make these blocks from the offcuts or trace the pattern onto a separate blank. The closer the sanding block is to the shape you're after, the better you will be able to smooth the curve. If the workpiece is convex, the sanding block is concave; a concave workpiece gets a convex sanding block. Serpentine curves or curves made from variable radii may require several sanding blocks.

I also fair curves using a belt sander fitted with a curved wooden block mounted to the sander's platen. I mount my sander to a custom table so that I have more control over the workpiece and I keep the platens for future jobs.

Remember, once a surface has been sanded, by hand or by machine, grit will invariably be left behind. Any hand-tool work or routing should be done first; otherwise, the embedded grit will destroy your cutting edges.

Success Starts with Setup

A coarse blade for a smooth cut. For all bandsaw cuts, including curves, a coarse blade like this 1/2-in., 3-tpi model will run cool and track a line more effectively than a fine blade. The finer blade will run hotter and will clog with sawdust quickly, making it wander.

Tighter curves require narrower blades. For example, a 1/2-in.-wide blade won't make it around a 1-in. radius.

BLADE SIZE	MIN. RADIUS
1/8 in., 14 tpi	1/8 in.
3/16 in., 4 tpi	3/8 in.
1/4 in., 4 tpi	5/8 in.
3/8 in., 3 tpi	1 1/4 in.
1/2 in., 3 tpi	2 1/2 in.
3/4 in., 3 tpi	5 in.

Bring the Guides Close to the Blade

To keep the blade from twisting excessively during a curved cut, it's critical that you keep the guides and thrust bearing close to the blade.

Paper-thin gap. Space the guides about 0.001 in. (about the thickness of tracing or cigarette paper) from the sides of the blade. Also, the front of the guides should align with the back of the blade's gullets.

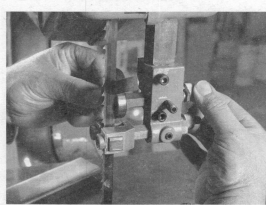

Square the table to the blade. The sides of the blade should sit flush against the blade of the square.

Adjust the thrust bearing. Move the bearing within 1/32 in. of the rear of the blade. Fortune uses a thin rule as a gauge.

Smooth Cuts Guaranteed

A LITTLE TWIST MAKES ALL THE DIFFERENCE

Use the back of the blade to steady the cut. A bandsaw blade typically leaves a bumpy surface in its wake. But by lightly twisting the workpiece so that the back of the blade rides along one side of the kerf, you can make a smooth cut and control the blade's path with marksman-like precision. What side of the kerf you press on will depend on the direction of the curve.

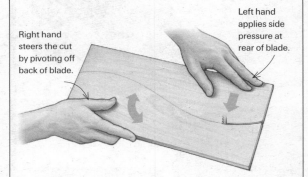

Right hand steers the cut by pivoting off back of blade.

Left hand applies side pressure at rear of blade.

USE RELIEF CUTS TO CHEAT

How to bandsaw a radius tighter than a blade will allow. First remove the bulk of the waste. Next, make the relief cuts perpendicular to the cut line. The number of relief cuts you make depends on the severity of the curve. Now you'll be able to remove the rest of the waste along the line, steadying the workpiece against the back of the blade.

Continued ➤

Customize Your Bandsaw Table

A simple auxiliary table can help support large work-pieces and can prevent tearout on thin stock.

MAKE A BIGGER WORK SURFACE

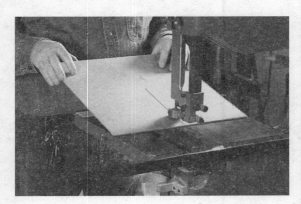

Got MDF? By clamping a larger table to the bandsaw table, you can support a workpiece and its offcuts throughout the cut.

USE A ZERO-CLEARANCE TABLE FOR THIN STOCK

No tearout allowed. A piece of 1/8-in.-thick hardboard supports the workpiece and reduces tearout as the blade exits the cut. Use double-sided tape to attach it to the table.

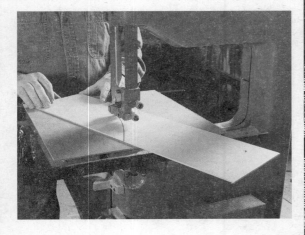

Straight Cuts in Curved Work

CONCAVE SHOW FACE

CONVEX SHOW FACE

Bandsaw cuts are rougher on the bottom side. So, when ripping a curved panel, such as a table apron or drawer front, be sure the show side is face up. If the concave side is the show face, cut it against a fence (left). If the show side is the convex face, support the cut with a block screwed to a fence (right). Locate screws where the blade won't hit them.

Compound Curves, Step by Step

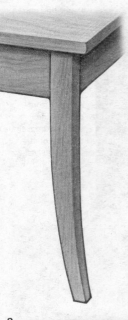

Cutting a curve, such as that on a leg, can be tricky and dangerous because the cutting action can slam the workpiece onto the table, drawing your fingers in or pinching them underneath. Taping offcuts to the blank is a tried-and-true method of working safely.

1.

2.

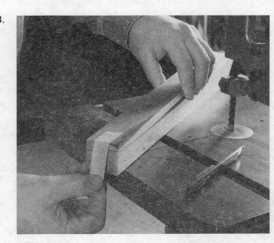

3.

4.

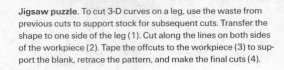

Jigsaw puzzle. To cut 3-D curves on a leg, use the waste from previous cuts to support stock for subsequent cuts. Transfer the shape to one side of the leg (1). Cut along the lines on both sides of the workpiece (2). Tape the offcuts to the workpiece (3) to support the blank, retrace the pattern, and make the final cuts (4).

Flawless Smoothing

Here are four great options for polishing off your carefully cut curves.

PLANE OR SHAVE

Follow the grain when planing. On a curved piece, the grain changes direction. So if you use a compass plane or spokeshave to refine the shape, pay attention to the grain to avoid tearout.

Convex curve
Work from the middl the ends.

Concave curve
Start at the ends an middle.

SANDING BLOCKS

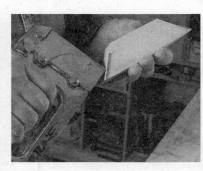

Make curved sanding blocks that match the profile. Staple sandpaper to the bottom of the block. For a concave block, it's better to use spray adhesive. If you have problems with the paper tearing, reinforce the back of the sheet with duct tape.

PRECISE BELT-SANDING

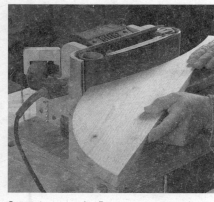

Soup up your sander. Fortune mounts curved wooden blocks on the metal platen of his belt sander. He mounts the sander in a shopmade table to add even more precision.

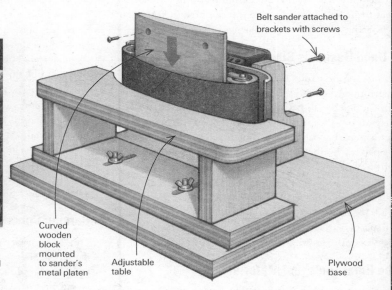

Belt sander attached to brackets with screws

Curved wooden block mounted to sander's metal platen

Adjustable table

Plywood base

CARVING

Beautiful Carving Starts with a Keen Edge

by Dan Faia

It is not the artistic side of carving that keeps some woodworkers from trying it, but the mechanics of how to sharpen the multitude of carving tools. This article will teach you how to sharpen a curved gouge, one of carving's most basic and useful tools. Gouges of various widths and curvature (sweep) are used throughout the carving process: the initial roughing out, the "setting in" of the carving's primary outlines, and the final details and finished surfaces. Some of the techniques you'll learn also apply to other types of carving tools. On FineWoodworking.com, I'll show how I sharpen two others.

Gather Your Equipment

Master Class

To sharpen a gouge or any other carving tool, you need sharpening stones (one coarse stone, like an India stone, and one fine Arkansas). I use oilstones because they wear more slowly than other types of stones. If you plan to carve a lot, get a separate set of stones for your carving tools. Otherwise, you'll spend too much time keeping the stones flat for your straight-edge tools.

You'll also need a fine, profiled slipstone, a leather strop, and a bench grinder with a tool rest. A slow-speed grinder is best, but a high-speed one with a white or pink wheel is fine, too.

Start By Jointing the Edge

The first thing to do with a new gouge is to joint the edge. Jointing flattens and trues the edge and creates a narrow, flat surface on the tip. This flat serves as a visual reference to aim for when grinding the bevel, helping you to keep the edge consistent. Jointing is also important in repairing a damaged edge or if you need to grind the edge again to re-establish the bevel angle. I joint the edge on a fine India stone. Using a two-handed grip, hold the edge perpendicular to the stone and take six to 10 strokes, drawing the tool toward you. Your goal is a flat that's no wider than $1/64$ in. or so.

The next step is to grind the bevel. First, consider whether to bevel both sides of the edge or only one. Some carvers bevel both sides, but I find it easier to maintain the tool with a bevel only on the outside of the flute. Then consider the angle of the bevel itself. In general, a shallower bevel cuts more easily while a steeper bevel creates a longer-lasting edge. I like a 30° bevel because it gives you a durable edge that cuts effectively in all but the hardest woods. The steepness of the bevel also means that the tool's handle sits high enough when I'm cutting that my knuckles can ride underneath without bumping the work.

Setting the tool rest is easy. Most new tools come with the bevel set between 24° and 26°, and with a little experience you'll be able to use this angle as a reference to set the tool rest by eye. You also can set the angle using a protractor or angle gauge. The diameter of the wheel is not critical (because all of the hollow will be honed away). There's also no need to dress the wheel with a special shape—a flat grinding edge is what you want. To grind the bevel, hold the gouge flat to the tool rest and lightly touch the edge to the wheel. Steadily rotate the handle to ensure even grinding, and move the tool from side to side, using the whole width of the stone. Check your progress often. You'll know you're done when the jointed surface on the edge is almost gone.

Grinding a Smooth Bevel

Joint the edge flat. Faia rests his forearms on the benchtop to help keep the tool perpendicular to the stone. The goal is a flat that's no more than 1/64 in. or so wide.

Grind with a light touch. Steadily rotate the handle to work the entire edge. Also slide the tool from side to side to use the wheel's whole width. When you're done, the jointed surface should be almost gone.

Continued →

Honing Refines the Edge

I start honing on the India stone. Orient the stone with its long side facing you. Start in the middle of the stone, with the middle of the flute facing down. As you move the tool toward the side, rotate the handle so that the stroke ends with the trailing wing in contact with the abrasive. The next step is to bring the tool all the way back across the stone, rotating as you go, so the opposite wing is touching when you reach the other end. But first, I back up just a little and work the same wing once more. This helps ensure even wear between the wings and the bottom of the flute.

Work until you raise a burr on the inside of the flute.

Get the Hang of Honing

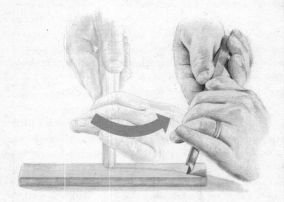

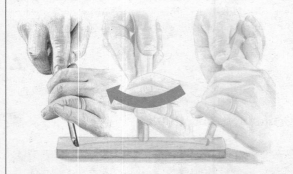

1. **Center to side.** Place the stone on the bench so its long axis crosses your body. Tilt the handle upward until the blade is seated on its bevel.
2. **Start in the center of the stone.** Rest the tool on the bottom of the blade's curve.
3. **Work the gouge from side to side.** Rotate the tool as you go. End each stroke as the tool's corner touches the stone.
4. **Move to the finer stone.** Continue honing in the same pattern, switching to the Arkansas stone to polish the bevel.
5. **Push back the burr.** Use a slipstone, working the edge with short strokes along the tool's long axis. Return to the Arkansas stone and repeat the process until the burr is gone and the bevel fully polished.

Stropping Is the Secret

1. **Pull and roll.** Faia starts with the edge on one corner and pulls the tool toward him, rotating it onto the opposite corner as he goes.
2. **Put a curl in it.** Faia simply folds the strop over to work the inside of the gouge.
3. **Do your carving tools cut like this?** A series of clean cross-grain cuts with clearly defined ridges and no tearout indicates a sharp gouge.

Then use the translucent white Arkansas slipstone to push the burr back, holding the slipstone dead flat against the inside of the flute. Move on to the finer stone, repeating the process to polish out the scratches from the India stone. Using the stones, chase the burr from bevel to flute until the hollow is flattened, the bevel is polished, and you can no longer feel the burr. Finish by lightly stropping the bevel and flute to polish away any rough spots and create a highly sharpened edge. I charge the suede side of a piece of leather with honing compound (I like Herb's Yellowstone), and hold the strop flat on the bench with my hand as I work the tool across it.

•

Surface Carving
by Michael Cullen

Surface carving adds depth and richness to any piece. But what intrigues and excites me most is repetitive patterns and texture, and the dynamic quality they bring to furniture. Walk past a piece with carving, and light dances on and off the carved surface, creating highlights and shadows that are in motion from every vantage point. Although this may sound dramatic, the effect tends to be subtle: It intrigues and suggests, inviting the eye to further inspect and enjoy the piece.

What draws me to this particular style of carving, as opposed to more traditional period designs, is the informality of both the execution and the product. Surface carving is simultaneously irregular and regular. Inconsistency is apparent in the individual cuts and yet the overall pattern is predictable and consistent. I'll take you through my process, from design to finishing. I'll cover a clear finish in this article, and you can turn to Finish Line, to learn how I enhance the carvings with milk paint.

A Good Design is Simple but Not Perfect

My inspiration comes from observing everything in the environment: an old fence, the bark on a tree, even the pattern in a box of nails. Beyond inspiration is whether the pattern will translate well to surface carving. Simple patterns are best because the repetition is easily discerned. If a pattern is overly complex or "muddy," the eye becomes confused.

Another aspect of a successful pattern is a combination of irregularity and regularity. Inspect a pine cone, and you'll see that the shapes of the individual segments and the spaces between them are unique, yet the whole pattern appears uniform, with both flow and life.

The Right Tools and Materials

Good carving woods are those that render crisp lines, don't tear out, and hold together under the force of the gouge. Avoid open-grain woods such as oak and ash since that characteristic can compete with the pattern.

Whether you intend to paint or add clear finish to a carving plays a role in wood selection: Woods best suited for clear finish have even color and little grain. Pear, maple, mahogany, and many of the exotic woods are excellent candidates.

If you'll be adding milk paint to the carving, mahogany and walnut are at the top of the list. Both carve well in all directions and the grain is almost nonexistent. I choose hard woods such as maple or some of the exotics when the pattern has fine details or tightly curved cuts that push the strength of the material to the limit. On soft woods, such as cedars and some of the pines, carving is almost effortless but the tools need to be razor-sharp or the results will be poor. Basswood is a bit soft for furniture, so best confined to smaller items.

You can encounter strange grain in even the best carving woods, so always do a carving sample before committing to a large canvas of wood that may turn out to be extremely difficult and frustrating to carve.

Get Started with a Basic Pattern

Before you begin carving, handplane or sand the surface to remove all machine marks. Sanding afterward dulls a carving's crisp lines. Make sure you remove all the sanding particles with a vacuum or compressed air to avoid dulling the tools.

Clean Cuts Need Sharp Tools

- **Sharpen both edges.** Cullen uses an Arkansas slip stone to refine both the inside and outside of a gouge.
- **Honing secret.** Cullen has a great trick for final honing. Use the gouge to cut its own groove in MDF, put honing or buffing compound in the groove, and then pull the gouge through it backward.

My most basic pattern is the ripple because it reminds me of the small patterns water leaves on the beach. Although I use all sorts of gouge sizes to create variations on this theme, the most common is a #8/13mm gouge. The 8 refers to the sweep or curve of the tool, and the 13 to the width across the front edge in millimeters.

Subsequent cuts are made parallel to the first, paying particular attention to the proximity of the past cut and to creating a complementary depth. After half a dozen grooves, the pattern will begin to appear; the slight variations between cuts will impart a rhythm to the whole.

It's easier with a mallet—There are two reasons for driving the gouge with a mallet: greater ease when cutting through dense woods, and more control in all woods. In denser material, the mallet becomes important because it gives absolute control over how fast or slow the gouge cuts.

However, while heavy hits with the mallet create long cuts, they leave evidence of where the stroke begins and ends. It is better to make quick, light taps that drive the gouge more delicately and with more continuity through the material. The cut should appear as if the gouge simply swept though the wood unimpeded.

It's faster by hand—When carving without a mallet, the hand gripping the tool in the forward position (straddling the handle and the steel) plays the part of the brake, while the hand at the back is the driving force. It requires practice and a high level of coordination between both hands to avoid disaster. Once you're comfortable with a mallet you can try switching to hand power, but begin with narrow tools and shallow cuts.

Carving Concentric Circles

One of my favorite patterns is Spring Rain, a pattern I developed after watching raindrops on puddles outside my workshop window. Years ago, I spent a great deal of time laying out the concentric circles with a compass. As I learned to love the slight irregularities found in nature, I abandoned the compass for free-drawn circles, which brought immediate spontaneity and life to the pattern.

I carve this pattern using a V-gouge (#12/6mm). Carving circles takes practice and is best done with the aid of a mallet. The tool should move almost effortlessly through the wood, creating a V-groove of uniform depth and width. Gently walk around the piece while tapping and guiding the gouge to create one seamless circle. Slight variations between the freshly cut circles are desirable, but avoid obvious straight sections or wild cuts off course because these create a disquieting effect in the overall pattern. Avoid going back to fix a cut that may appear slightly off or not deep enough. It's better to leave the minor imperfection than to risk increasing the problem.

A variation on this pattern is one I call the Thousand Suns. After completing the Spring Rain pattern, use a #8/7mm gouge and a mallet to dish the surface between the V-grooves. This is a challenging cut, loaded with risk, so practice before attempting the final piece. Controlling the gouge as the grain changes direction around the circle is crucial. More than likely you'll need to make the cut from several directions to avoid tearout.

Get the Basics Down

Power and precision. When carving, your feet should be spaced wide apart for stability and your entire upper body should be applying power to the gouge. Place a hand close to the tip of the gouge and rest an arm on the workpiece to direct and control the gouge.

The right angle. Each gouge has a correct angle that will produce a long curling chip, leaving a groove that is consistent in depth and width. Holding the handle too low will cause the tool to rise out of the workpiece, while holding the handle too high makes the gouge go deep until eventually the tips cause tearout on the surface. Give the tool only small taps with the mallet.

By hand alone. In the less dense hardwoods, you can dispense with a mallet and apply power just by hand. This tends to produce a cleaner cut and is quicker, but it also requires more control. To avoid blowout, cut the last part of the groove from the far side (left).

Texture Adds Subtle Support

If pattern is the lead actor in surface design, texture typically plays a supporting role, adding details that set off the carving.

The pattern called Fields combines a straight version of the Thousand Suns with some texturing. After laying out the pattern and cutting the V-groove and furrowed sections, I texture the uncarved sections using a small gouge (#9/3mm). Don't use a mallet—you need a light touch and careful cuts to create an overall uniform texture. The trick to making clean cuts is to roll the gouge as it cuts through the fibers. When the texturing is complete, note how it recedes in comparison to the adjacent patterns.

Selecting a Finish: Color or Clear?

Unpainted carvings can be both stunning and understated, imparting a subtle beauty and elegance that is unmatched. I seal the wood with Danish oil or preferably a thin coat of shellac. Finishes that build quickly tend to pool in the grooves, leaving unsightly shiny spots. You also want to avoid sanding because it can easily eliminate details in the carving. Typically, after sealing, I apply a light coat of wax with 0000 steel wool to burnish the surface and even out the luster.

Intricate Leaf Pattern Works Well On Smaller Surfaces

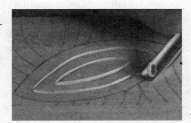

Work from the center. With a #12/6mm or similar V-parting tool, begin carving the "leaves" that overlay the others and work from each center toward the outside.

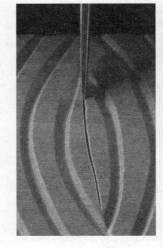

Central groove adds texture. Use a double-beveled knife to create a stop cut down the middle of the leaf (left). Then use a #9/3mm gouge to make relief cuts (above) creating a V-shaped, textured groove.

Combine texture and patterns

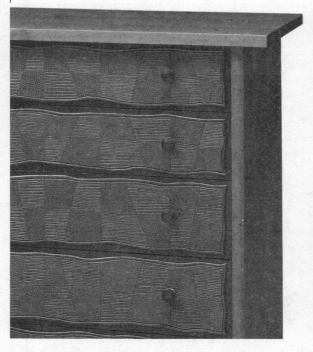

Extra texture. In Cullen's Fields pattern, cutting lines of small hollows adds interesting texture to the surface.

Concentric Circles Look Best on Large Surfaces

Top to bottom. As with all overlapping patterns, start by cutting the top elements first (in this case, the small "raindrops" that fell most recently) and then the larger background ones.

Sun spots. A variation on Cullen's "Spring Rain" (left) is "Thousand Suns," (above) where he cuts a shallow furrow between the grooves using a #9/5mm gouge.

Continued ➡

Applied Carving

by Will Neptune

Woodworkers often react to applied carving as "cheating," a somewhat grudging admission of its effectiveness. It is a traditional but still very useful technique. Sure, every applied carving could be done "in the solid," with the carving outlined by vertical stop cuts, and then the background lowered with numerous relief cuts or perhaps with a router. But achieving the smooth background normally needed for furniture can be very time-consuming.

With applied carving, the outline of the carving is cut with a coping saw or scrollsaw. You then temporarily attach the blank to a backing board, carve it, and glue it to the workpiece.

If the carving is particularly large and complex or narrow and fragile, you take a different path: After sawing out the blank you apply it to the workpiece and carve it in place. I'll explain the first approach and show you when to use the alternative one. With a little practice, soon you'll be accused of cheating, too.

Wood Selection is Critical

Grain that is straight and not pronounced generally gives better results than figured wood. In addition, the appliqué should match the background. A carving with clashing color or grain patterns will look stuck on.

One way to get a good match is to resaw a thick piece, using one piece for the background and the other as the carving blank. Remember to mark the parts and keep track of the match when you saw and carve. The other way to get a good appearance is to slip-match. The carving blank comes from an adjacent section of the same board as the background and slides on top so that the growth rings nest when you look at the end grain. This works best if the board has mild grain and a similar look along its length. Before I cut the carving blank to the pattern, I lay it on the background piece to see where it best matches the growth-ring pattern on the end grain.

In Most Cases Carve First, and then Apply

Carving a blank before you attach it to the workpiece is the preferred method: Carving on a waste block reduces the risk of damaging the background, and mistakes can be discarded.

Transfer the pattern to the blank—You have several choices for transferring the pattern to the carving blank. Stencils are worthwhile if the pattern is one you'll use often. I cut these from thick oak tag or matboard. You can leave small connecting tabs to secure thin, flexible areas. Soaking the edge with cyanoacrylate glue makes the stencil hold up better. With identical parts, the sawing can be done in a stack to save time and parts can be flipped over to make lefts and rights. It's also easy to mount multiples in a row and carve them as a group.

For one-off carvings, you can photocopy a design and stick it down with low-tack spray adhesive. This method is great for dark woods where it is hard to see a pencil line. You will need to clean off the back of the carving with solvent before you try to glue it down.

For mirror-image carvings, I photocopy a drawing onto tracing paper from both sides to make matching patterns.

In all cases, put the pattern on what will be the underside of the carving. In this way, any tearout from sawing out the pattern will be on the top edges where it will most likely be carved away, instead of on the bottom where it would leave gaps against the background.

Saw out the pattern carefully—A jigsaw, a scrollsaw, or a coping saw with a bird's-mouth support are all good ways to cut out the parts. The more accurately you saw, the less cleaning up you'll need to do. There is always a tendency to saw a little wide of the line but this makes everything rather heavy.

Use files to clean up the edges. Don't sand or you risk carving into residual grit, blunting your tools. I usually hold the part in a hand screw clamped vertically in my vise, which makes it easy to see what I'm doing and quickly reposition the part. File away from the bottom to avoid chipping. Try to work right up to the lines while keeping the edges square.

Carve the Blank on a Backer Board

I mount the carving blank on plywood using double-stick tape. Scraps of 1/2-in.-thick Baltic-birch or marine meranti are excellent backers and very strong. Lightweight, thin carpet tape is good. Most of the carving force is downward, so you don't need a killer grip. I trim away the excess so it won't collect chips while I carve.

From this point, the carving is the same as if you were working in the solid with the ground established. Start by establishing the main contours, then sketch in as much information as needed to guide the detail work. If necessary, you can clean up the surfaces with fine files and/or sandpaper.

When you're done, a thin putty knife and some solvent make it easy to dismount the blank. Fanning the carving with a heat gun will also help to loosen the tape's grip.

Clever Tricks for Gluing and Clamping

Attaching the carving securely and completely is very important. If you use too much glue, cleanup will be almost impossible without damaging the background. Too little glue or uneven clamping pressure and you risk parts lifting later on.

The first step is to prepare the background as you would before finishing. Be sure all mill marks and tearout are cleaned up. Position the carving dry and mark the location with tape or light pencil marks.

One of the problems when clamping small pieces is that if they slide while you're clamping them down, you may not notice with cauls and clamps in the way. I have a couple of ways to overcome this: If the carving is fairly sturdy, without narrow branching parts, I tap two or three fine brads into the background board and nip them off to leave short nibs. Then I press the carving into place, making dimples that hold it there.

If the carving is more fragile or flexible, I trap it with thin tabs of wood taped around its edges. These strips can be shaped as necessary to control every part of the carving.

The trick for gluing is to "ink" the back of the carving with an even coat of glue. You should do tests to learn how heavy a coat is needed. Too light a coat and the background will absorb it and starve the joint. Too much and you get messy squeeze-out.

A Variety of Clamping Techniques

Clamping pressure is as important as using the right amount of glue. The goal is to get small dots of squeeze-out along all of the edges, without any areas having a continuous bead.

Simple shapes can be clamped with cork or Homasote pads. On complex carving, one easy way to get even pressure is to use a vacuum bag without a caul. If there are pointy areas, cover the carving with soft leather to protect the bag.

Whatever clamping method you choose, remove the clamps when the glue is dry but not fully cured, so it is easy to remove the squeeze-out. I use a Popsicle stick sharpened like a skew chisel. Don't try to wash off extra glue with water and a brush. This risks washing out glue from under the carving and weakening its bond, or getting glue in the background wood, which will show up under a finish.

Attaching the Carving

The challenge is to securely apply a delicate carving in an exact location with the minimum of squeeze-out.

Stop the squirm or corral the carving. If your carving is thick enough, you can push it onto small brads clipped close to the surface (above). This will stop the carving from moving around when clamping pressure is applied. Another way is to attach thin wood tabs with double-sided tape in a few key spots (left).

Molded caul. To apply uniform pressure to complex carvings, make a custom caul. Place a piece of plastic food wrap over the carving, then build up a layer of non-hardening modeling clay (left). Remove the plastic and clay carefully (right) and refrigerate for at least 30 minutes to harden.

The "inking" trick. Roll glue onto an impervious surface and then lower the carving straight down onto the glue. This way, you get an even application of glue on the bottom of the carving and none on the sides. Use the point of a knife to lift up the edge of the carving before removing it.

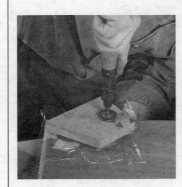

Even pressure for a good bond. Place the carving on the workpiece in the marked location and apply the cold, stiff, molded caul followed by a plywood caul. Then apply the clamps. The clay will stay stiff long enough for the glue to set.

Apply, then Carve

Complex or delicate carvings may need to be carved in place. It is more time-consuming, but still easier than working in the solid. As before, the blank is temporarily mounted on plywood.

ALTERNATE METHOD

Add a backer and plane to thickness. Roll PVA or hide glue on the plywood and the carving blank, and then clamp them with a layer of coarse brown shopping-bag paper in between. The paper holds moisture, so these joints dry slowly. Once dry, you can thin the blank in a planer if necessary.

MAKE A SANDWICH

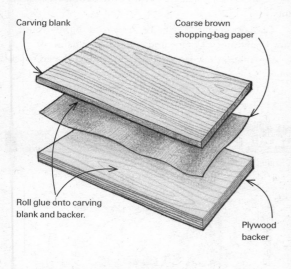

Carving blank

Coarse brown shopping-bag paper

Roll glue onto carving blank and backer.

Plywood backer

Saw out the pattern. Spray-mount the pattern to the blank and then cut it out on the bandsaw. The plywood keeps the carving blank intact.

Locate the carving. On delicate carvings, tabs of wood attached to the workpiece work better than snipped brads, which might split the workpiece.

Plywood acts as clamping caul. The plywood now distributes the clamping pressure. Once the glue is cured, split the paper joint with a wide chisel to remove the plywood, as shown.

Start carving. The carving is done as before but you have to work next to the finished background. The risk is no greater than when carving from the solid and you've avoided the labor of removing all the background waste.

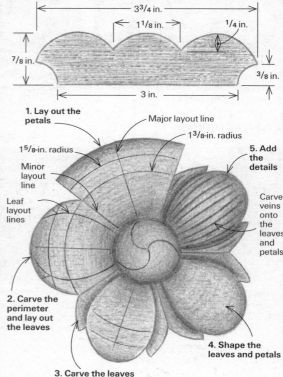

3³/₄ in.

1¹/₈ in.

¹/₄ in.

⁷/₈ in.

3 in.

³/₈ in.

1. Lay out the petals

Major layout line

1⁵/₈-in. radius

1³/₈-in. radius

Minor layout line

Leaf layout lines

5. Add the details

Carve veins onto the leaves and petals.

2. Carve the perimeter and lay out the leaves

4. Shape the leaves and petals

3. Carve the leaves

Carve a Rosette

by Tony Kubalak

To many furniture makers, carving is intimidating and frightening. A great way to overcome these fears is to carve an applied rosette: It requires only a small amount of wood; it's independent of the piece it eventually will reside on; and it has a small number of elements that are repeated multiple times. Rosettes come in many variations, and although small in size, they significantly refine a high chest or a clock case.

Master Class

When I became interested in building period furniture, I didn't think that I'd be able to tackle the carving. I assumed that you had to be an artist and I didn't consider myself one. I've since learned that carving is as much science as art, a process taken in logical, repeatable steps. That said, carving is a skill that you can continue to hone for a lifetime.

Turn a Blank on the Lathe and Lay Out the Design

Start with a blank that's approximately ⁷/₈ in. thick by 3⁷/₈ in. square. After cutting out a rough circle on the bandsaw, screw the blank to a screw chuck that already has a ¹/₂-in.-thick disk of wood attached to it. You need to include this other piece of wood because you will undercut the back of

the rosette and you don't want the turning tool hitting the chuck. Use a gouge or a scraper to turn the profile shown in the top drawing above. This rosette is one element repeated five times, so divide the disk into five equal sections.

You'll need a backer board to hold the rosette for carving. Lay out this board with lines radiating out from a center point at the desired spacing and extending about 3 in. beyond the blank. In this case there are five major divisions, so draw a major line every 72° marking the midpoint of the petals, with minor lines dividing the petals halfway between the major ones. Drill a hole through the center of the backer board and screw on the blank, penetrating the blank by no more than ¹/₂ in. Place a pencil dot at the center of the blank, and by eye, extend the backer-board lines onto the blank. Draw two circles and lay out the petals.

Carve the Outside Profile First

You carve this rosette working your way in from the perimeter. First, carve along the arcs that define the petals. Don't do this in one cut, but use a V-tool to cut away small increments beginning at the perimeter. Then round over the edges using a #7-20mm gouge. The exact gouge is not critical, but avoid one that's too narrow; a #7 sweep gives the petals a pleasing curve.

The next step is to refine each large petal into a

smaller petal with a leaf on each side. Draw an arc ¹/₈ in. on both sides of a minor line out to where the adjacent major line meets the perimeter. Then draw a short curve from where this new arc crosses the outer circle out to the perimeter of the leaf (see drawing, above). Carve to the lines using the same V-tool and rounding technique as the petals but using a #7-6mm gouge for the short sections and the #7-20mm for the longer sections.

Refine the Petals and Leaves

There are a couple of things to keep in mind while carving the petals and leaves. First, the leaves are lower than the petals; second, the pairs of leaves are divided by a ridge. To define the petals, start by making perpendicular or stop cuts along each petal's perimeter with a #3-20mm gouge. From the leaf side of this cut, make a shallow angled cut known as a relief cut that terminates at the stop cut to remove a small wedge of wood. Repeat these two cuts until the depth matches the base of the central dome where they meet, and is slightly deeper at the perimeter. Work on the adjacent sides of two petals at a time, so that the angle into the stop cut does not get too steep. Repeat until all the petals are established.

From each centerline, round over the petals down

Continued →

to the cuts you just made using a shallow gouge, say a #3-20mm. Use a small file to smooth the facets into a continuous surface.

The ridge line between each pair of leaves begins at the base of the central dome, divides at the inner circle, and terminates at the outer circle. The ridge should be lower than the high point on the petal, but higher than the rest of the leaves. It is this variation in depth that gives life to the carving. Use a shallow gouge, say a #3-12mm, to define the ridge.

Now that the face of the perimeter is defined, you can give the rosette a crisper, more delicate look by extending the undercut area by about 3/8 in. toward the center using a shallow gouge. Strive for a nice crisp "V" between the leaf pairs around the perimeter and crisp, thin tips for the leaves.

Work on the Central Dome

The rosette's dome is carved to look like the central reproductive parts of a flower: the stamen and the stigma. I'm no botanist, so I'll just refer to the parts as leaves. With a

pencil, sketch in three lines that curve out from the center and divide the dome into roughly equal thirds. Use a #7-10mm gouge to make a stop cut along each of the three curved lines, and with the same gouge make an angled relief cut. Repeat this process until the channel is about 1/8 in. deep.

You now need to round the tip of each leaf at the center of the dome. With a #7-6mm gouge near the center, connect one of the stop-cut edges with the adjacent edge formed by the angled cut. With the same gouge, step back from this line toward the center a bit and angle into it. This angle will be rather steep because there is not much room left without impacting another leaf. When completed there should be three well-defined leaves.

Use a relatively flat and narrow gouge, say a #3-8mm, to round each leaf from the high edge down to the bottom of the stop cut. Blend this cut smoothly into the outer baseline defined by the perimeter of the dome. The more refined the carving becomes, the more delicate the cuts, so a lighter hand will yield better results. Now create a small leaflet from each leaf, using a #7-4mm gouge to make a perpendicular cut followed by a relatively steep angle cut. Deepen this a bit and gently feather the line so that it disappears near the base of the dome.

Delicate Details Complete the Rosette

What remains is to add some detail lines. Use a #11-0.5mm veiner to add shallow veins to the petals, the leaves, and the dome leaves. Take care to avoid tearout on cross-grain cuts.

Looking at your finished rosette, you'll understand how something that appeared complex and daunting became manageable with a few types of cut repeated several times.

1. LAY OUT THE TURNED BLANK

Lay out a backer board. After turning the blank, lay out the 10 divisions on a plywood square. Score the lines with a knife and then darken them with a pencil.

Lay out the blank. Attach the blank to the backer board. Extend the lines onto the blank and use a compass to draw two circles.

Draw the petals. Starting where a line crosses the inner circle, draw two arcs out to where the next line meets the perimeter.

2. CARVE THE PERIMETER

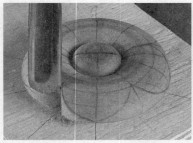

Define the petals. Use a V-tool to cut into the perimeter and then a #7 sweep gouge (shown) to profile the edge of the petals.

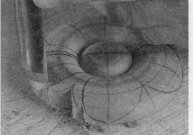

Finish the perimeter. Draw a pair of arcs either side of every other line to lay out the leaves. Then cut notches in each edge of the petals to define the tips of the leaves.

3. CARVE THE LEAVES

Relieve the petals. Make vertical "stop" cuts and then angled "relief" cuts (shown) to create V-shaped channels around the petals.

4. SHAPE THE LEAVES AND PETALS

Round over and smooth the petals. Use an inverted gouge to round over the sides of the petals and bring them down to the adjacent groove. Use a fine file to smooth the facets into a continuous surface.

Undercut the back. To give the edges of the rosette a crisper, lighter look, carve away some wood near the edge of the back and deepen the V between the leaves. Lay out a rough circle to guide your cuts.

5. ADD THE DETAILS

Work on the dome. Draw three lines that curve outward from the center of the dome, and then create grooves with stop cuts and relief cuts. Each third of the dome is further divided into two sections with another outward sweeping curve.

Add the details. With a small veining tool, add narrow channels to the petals, leaves, and central dome to represent the veins in the flower.

Carve a Decorative Fan

by Philip C. Lowe

Cabriole legs may give a Queen Anne lowboy its signature grace, but the fan is its visual centerpiece.

The fan, which decorates the bottom center drawer of the lowboy, was a popular element in Queen Anne furniture. It is a fairly simple relief carving that requires a handful of gouges and chisels.

Master Class

I begin with the drawer front cut to size and its edge detail shaped. To lay out the fan, draw a baseline 1 1/4 in. from the bottom of the drawer front. From the center point of this line, draw a perpendicular line. Where these lines intersect, place the compass point and draw a half-circle the radius of the fan, a second one 1/4 in. smaller, and a third circle with a 3/4-in. radius.

Next, divide the semicircle into 12 equal pie-slice segments. You can use a protractor to mark the 15° segments, or you can use 45° and 30°-60°-90° drafting triangles anchored to a straightedge held parallel to the baseline. Make certain the scribe marks extend inside the smallest circle and beyond the largest one.

Twelve Easy Pieces

Geometrically, the fan is essentially a pair of nested semicircles with the larger one carved into a dozen identical slices. Each slice is 15° wide.

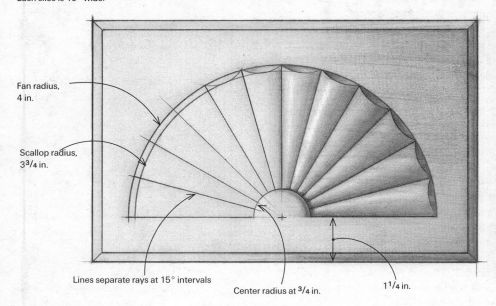

Fan radius, 4 in.

Scallop radius, 3³/₄ in.

Lines separate rays at 15° intervals

Center radius at ³/₄ in.

1¹/₄ in.

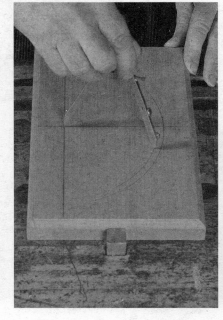

Draw the arcs and rays. Use a compass to mark the perimeter of the fan, the inner boundary of the scalloped edges, and the hub (left). Use 45° and 30°-60°-90° triangles in combination to lay out the rays (below).

Broad Strokes Set the Background

To begin carving, match a carving gouge to the radius of the inner hub. Use a mallet to drive overlapping vertical cuts about ¹/₄ in. deep. Also deepen the baseline on either side of the hub, using a straight chisel for cuts that are shallow at the outer arc but ¹/₄ in. deep at the hub.

The fan's illusion of depth comes in part from the fact that the rays are recessed at the fan's hub and flush with the surface near the outer radius, so they project forward as they radiate outward. To achieve this, use a wide, flat gouge (I like a #3 or #5 sweep, 20 mm wide) to make a series of cuts from the outer area of the fan to the hub. These cuts should deepen to about ¹/₄ in. deep at the inner circle. This series of cuts removes most of the layout lines. But because you drew them long, you can re-establish them before moving on to define the individual rays.

Define and Shape the Rays

Begin this task by using a V-tool to cut a sharp trench along the segment lines that separate each ray. Next, use a back-bent gouge to round over the tops of the rays into the trenches you just cut. When making these cuts, particularly on the center rays, you'll be working at an angle across end grain that you exposed previously with the V-tool. To prevent tearout, cut in a direction that ensures that the fibers are supported from behind. This means working in opposite directions on opposing sides of each V-groove—toward the center on the top of each ray, away from the center on the bottom. You'll likely need a second pass to refine the shapes further and make the rays stand out in appropriate relief.

A Trick for Cutting Scallops

I cut the scalloped shapes around the fan's outer edge with two gouges: a specially ground #2 sweep, 25 mm wide, for the vertical outside wall of each scallop and a #5 sweep, also 25 mm wide, for the inside. Start with the outside cuts. Tap the gouge in vertically to about ¹/₈ in. deep. Next use the #5 to make angled paring cuts that meet the first cut at its bottom.

To make these cuts intersect cleanly, I grind a shallow convex curve onto the end of the #2, so the bottom of its cut matches the radius of the #5. In this way, the second cut neatly severs the chip and creates a semicircular bottom. With the scallops done, the carving is nearly finished.

Use the back-bent gouge to round over the edge of the inner hub to a quarter-round profile. Once this is done, continue defining and refining the lines and shapes as needed, using your eye as a guide. The tool marks can be reduced by scraping and sanding to the desired texture.

Establish the Outline

Begin the carving by establishing its boundaries. Scribed and chiseled lines help limit the travel of gouges and other tools.

The first cutting tool is a gauge. Scribe the baseline on either side of the hub with a marking gauge. This creates a channel in which to register further cuts.

Define the hub. Use a gouge whose sweep matches the fan's inner radius. Vertical cuts about ¹/₄ in. deep create a stopping point for gouges when carving toward the center of the work.

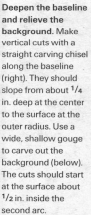

Deepen the baseline and relieve the background. Make vertical cuts with a straight carving chisel along the baseline (right). They should slope from about ¹/₄ in. deep at the center to the surface at the outer radius. Use a wide, shallow gouge to carve out the background (below). The cuts should start at the surface about ¹/₂ in. inside the second arc.

Continued ➡

Shape the Rays

Lowe uses a variety of gouges and chisels to separate the rays so that they stand out against the background.

Pick up your pencil again. You erased some layout lines with the shallow gouge. You'll need them for the next step.

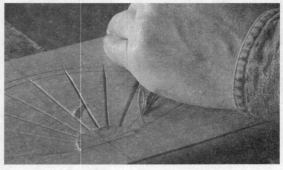

Separate the rays. Follow those newly redrawn lines with a V-shaped parting tool to furrow between the individual fan blades.

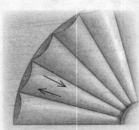

Shaping comes next. A back-bent gouge is ideal for rounding the beveled edges left by the parting tool. Blend the curves across the top of each ray. Avoid tearout by cutting in the right direction.

Work toward the center on the upper edge of the ray and away from the center on the lower edge.

Cut the Scallops

The rays are decorated with scalloped tips, throwing them into further relief and creating greater visual interest.

The last course is scallops. Lowe uses a #2 gouge with a convex tip to establish the outer walls (left). Next, he pares from the center out with a #5 gouge to finish the cut cleanly (below).

VENEER, MARQUETRY, AND INLAY

An Introduction to Veneering

by Thomas R. Schrunk

Veneering has an image problem: Woodworkers see it as difficult; non-woodworkers consider it inferior to "solid wood." Both perceptions are untrue. As with many woodworking procedures, the steps of veneering are easy to master and, with practice, you can produce beautiful results. Veneering opens up a world of exotic and beautiful woods such as burls and crotches, many of which would be difficult and prohibitively expensive to use as thicker lumber.

As an introductory project, we'll veneer a plywood panel that can be inserted in a frame to form the door to a cupboard or bedside cabinet, or the lid for a box. The frame means there is no need to veneer the panel edges. And because it is not solid wood, the panel can be glued into its groove, strengthening the assembly. This is especially helpful with router-made cope-and-stick joinery, which has limited strength on its own.

Select and Prepare the Veneer

Start with a core of 3/16-in.-thick birch plywood an inch wider and longer than the final size. After it is veneered and cut to size, it will fit into a 1/4-in.-wide groove.

If you don't have a local supplier, try mail-order and online veneer sources. For this project, I selected some attractive cathedral-grain cherry for the outside, or face, of the panel, and quartersawn cherry veneer for the back side. You must veneer both sides to prevent the plywood from warping. The back veneer need not be the same species, but the grain direction should be the same as the face veneer.

Book-matching shows off figure—You could use a single piece to veneer the panel, but a more interesting way to present some veneers is to take sequential leaves

---

||||||||||||||||||||||||||||||||||||||||||||

Wavy Veneers are Easy to Flatten

The unique figure of burls and crotches puts them among the most sought-after veneers, but a drawback is that they often arrive wrinkled and curled. Before you can use them, you must flatten them.

Large Pieces are Dampened and Clamped

If the veneer is highly contorted and brittle, lightly spray the front and back with a flattening solution. I use three parts water, two parts white glue, one part glycerin (available at drug stores), and one part denatured alcohol. This solution keeps the veneer flatter for longer than water alone, but it fills the pores, which will color differently from the wood if a stain is applied (so use water if you plan to stain the wood). After wetting the surface, place the veneer between paper towels and clamp between 3/4-in.-thick particleboard or MDF cauls. Change the towels after 10 minutes, after 30 minutes, then every few hours until the veneer is dry.

Small Pieces Can Be Ironed

A household iron can be used to flatten small pieces and works well on burls. Place the veneer on a nonporous surface such as melamine. Beginning at one end, move the iron slowly up the veneer, covering the heated veneer with another piece of melamine to prevent water vapor from escaping. The lignin in the wood plasticizes at around 180° and the layers of melamine keep it flat as it cools.

With both methods, keep the veneer clamped until use.

||||||||||||||||||||||||||||||||||||||||||||

Choose and Orient the Veneer

A perfect match. When orienting veneer for a book-matched panel, overlap the two sheets (above) until you find the best place to make the joint. Identifying marks on the wood (right) are a great help in achieving perfect vertical alignment.

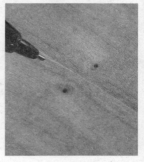

from the same log, and flip one piece over like the page of a book to form a mirror image, a process known as book-matching.

Compare the two pieces of veneer to find the location of the best match, and then lightly mark the cut line with a No. 2 pencil on the first piece. When cutting veneer, a self-healing mat used for fabric works well, but you also can cut on a piece of medium-density fiberboard (MDF). For most veneer I use a utility knife with a fixed blade (it is less wobbly than a retractable-blade knife) and I change blades frequently. I hold down the veneer with a 2-in.-wide aluminum rule with P80-grit sandpaper stuck to the back to prevent slipping. Make a light scoring cut, then four or five cuts of moderately increasing pressure until the cut is complete. Lay the freshly cut piece over the second piece of veneer, mark the exact matching line, and cut it, too.

The next step is to sand the mating edges of the pieces. Place one piece on the workbench with the cut edge hanging over the bench by about 1/8 in. Place a metal straightedge on top of the veneer, even with the edge of the workbench. Sand the cut edge with a sanding block, gently moving it with even, horizontal strokes. I use a square section of dead-flat aluminum with P180-grit sandpaper stuck to one side, but you could use two bits of plywood glued into a T. Stop when you see sawdust all along the cut. Repeat with the mating half.

Sanding the cut has a second benefit: On many book-matches, the joint shows up as a dark line called the "glueline." It is the result of liquid finish getting into open pores. When the cut is sanded, however, the pores tend to become plugged with fine dust that the finish has trouble penetrating. With practice, the glueline will be almost invisible.

Tape the matching veneers together—The side of the veneer that will be visible is referred to as the show face, while the back side is the glue face. To lock in a symmetrical alignment, place the veneers together, show face up, and join them with pieces of blue tape. Flip the veneer over and put 3-in. to 4-in.-long strips of blue tape across the joint spaced every 3 in. to 5 in., pulling and stretching the tape so that it acts like a clamp. Then place an additional piece all along the joint and press it down firmly. Now turn the veneer over to the show face again and remove the blue tape used for alignment. The veneer tape you are about to apply is thin enough not to imprint the veneer when it is in the press. Its adhesive is moisture ac-

tivated. You can use a wetted sponge or you can simply lick the tape, but practice first on a piece of scrap veneer. Too little or too much moisture and the tape won't stick. Put veneer tape all along the joint. When the tape is dry (about 5 minutes) you can place the core on top of the veneer and cut the veneer to size with a utility knife. Finally, remove the blue tape from the back side.

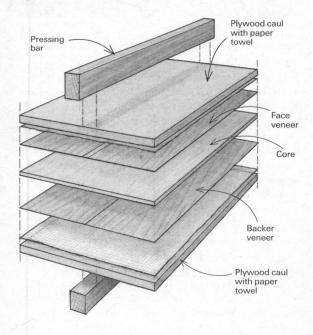

Pressing bar

Plywood caul with paper towel

Face veneer

Core

Backer veneer

Plywood caul with paper towel

Create an Invisible Seam

1. Cut veneer carefully
2. Sand the cut edges
3. Tape both sides with blue tape
4. Retape the show face with veneer tape
5. Trim veneer to size and remove the blue tape

Veneer Both Sides of the Panel at the Same Time

Because the veneer will begin to curl as soon as the glue makes it wet, you should have the clamping method prearranged to allow you to work quickly. If you're new to veneering, I'll assume that you don't have a vacuum pressing bag, but for panels like these, C-clamps, pressing bars, and plywood work just as well. I begin by placing a couple of 4-in.- to 5-in.-tall support blocks on the bench to support the workpiece and allow clamps and bars to pass underneath. On this I place a caul of 3/4-in.-thick plywood or particleboard and a single layer of paper towels, both cut to the same size as the panel. These towels will absorb moisture as the glue evaporates and will prevent the

cauls from bonding to any glue squeeze-out. If the towels stick to the panel, any residue can be sanded away later.

There are a number of specialty veneer glues available, but I use standard yellow glue for most work. It's important to coat the entire surface evenly. I pour the glue onto the core, never the veneer, and spread it with a short-nap roller, 3 in. to 4 in. wide. This type of roller should apply the proper amount of glue, leaving the surface lightly wetted and evenly glistening. Starting out, one usually applies a bit too much glue; try a practice piece first.

Glue one side of the core and place it onto the backer veneer, then apply glue to the front of the core. Set it on the lower caul and paper towel, and place the face veneer over it, glue face down. Add the paper towel and the upper caul, and you're ready to press. You may want to put blue tape over the edge of the veneer near the corners to prevent "squirm" or slippage of the veneer as it is clamped.

I use clamps spaced every 3 in. to 4 in. around the perimeter, which exert good pressure in a 4-in.-dia. to 5-in.-dia. circle. If the workpiece is wider than about 9 in., you should add one or more pairs of pressing bars to apply pressure where the clamps can't. The bars are 2-in. to 3-in.-wide boards with convex profile of around 1/8 in. per foot on the contact edge. Leave the veneer clamped for at least six hours, preferably overnight.

Cut the Panel to Size, then Sand It

With the veneer dry, the next step is to cut the panel to the frame. To minimize tearout, I cut the panel show-face up with blue tape applied to the back along the lines to be cut.

Some like to remove the veneer tape with a scraper or to lightly moisten it and peel it off. I prefer to begin sanding with P120-grit paper on a random-orbit sander until the tape is sanded away, and then move up the grits until I get to P220. Be sure to sand the back panel in the same way; you will finish it identically so that you'll have an equal moisture barrier on both sides to prevent warping. Use caution near the edges to avoid sanding through the thin veneers. Wet the surface with mineral spirits to see that no veneer tape or adhesive is left, then glue the panel into the frame and apply a clear finish.

Glue and Trim Panel

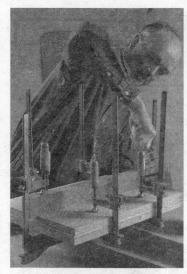

Clamping press. Schrunk spaces clamps around the perimeter of the panel, and then uses a pair of pressing bars to add pressure at the center where the clamps can't reach.

Strong and beautiful. Because it is not solid wood, the veneered panel can be glued into the frame to strengthen the assembly.

by David Welter

The main reason for using veneer is the same now as in Tutankhamun's time: Veneering makes it much easier to cover a large area with very attractive or rare wood. Used with man-made sheet goods as a substrate, veneer also minimizes the construction difficulties posed by solid wood, which moves with moisture changes. These days, there are veneer options that weren't available when the pharaohs reigned, commercially cut veneers as well as shop-sawn. However, I only work with veneers I resaw myself at the bandsaw. And that's what we teach at College of the Redwoods, in the cabinetmaking program founded by James Krenov.

Commercial veneers are available in thicknesses from 1/32 in. to 1/60 in., but the slightest misuse of furniture with these thin veneers can cause damage that requires a repair with the same vulnerable material. And it is rare that you'll be able to perfectly match commercial veneers to the solid wood you'll need for the other parts of a furniture project.

In stark contrast, shop-sawn veneer, described by Krenov as "real," with a finished thickness of 1/16 in. to 3/32 in., can better withstand everyday use. And if the veneer is damaged, it is thick enough to sand or even plane, restoring the surface. Also, you can cut veneer from the same boards you use for solid wood, providing harmony throughout a project. Furniture made this way stands out from the arranged marriages of commercial veneer and solid wood. And because shop-sawn veneer is thicker, it's easier to work with and doesn't bubble as much as commercial veneer during pressing.

Successfully sawing and using your own veneers isn't difficult. The keys are careful bandsaw setup, thoughtful layout, and a few edge-banding tips.

Choose the Right Blade

No method of ripping or resawing is better than a bandsaw. And a few minutes of careful setup will yield great resawing results without great risk.

The first thing to consider is the blade. A resaw blade needs deep gullets that can eject all of the sawdust that these tall cuts generate. I suggest a 3 tpi (teeth per inch) blade at least 1/2 in. wide. For dedicated resawing in widths greater than 6 in., a 11/2 tpi, 1-in.-wide blade reduces the effort needed to feed the stock and has more room to clear waste from the kerf.

Even if you have the blade set up just right, you might have to negotiate for drift, the tendency for the stock to wander away from the fence or for the blade to cut a wavy line. The solution is easy: Just angle the fence to match the blade's natural cutting angle.

Get Ready to Cut

In most cases, the veneered panels will need edge-banding of some kind, and you want that to blend in seamlessly. So before you cut your first sheet of veneer, you need to cut the edge-banding from your board.

Estimate that you'll be cutting five veneers from 1 in. of stock. Most likely, you will be able get at least six veneers, but the pessimist is rarely disappointed. Plan to cut the veneers slightly under 1/8 in. thick. If you are cutting a width greater than 8 in., favor a slightly heavier cut, but no thicker than 1/8 in.

Now you are ready to resaw. Start by surfacing one face of the board and then squaring an edge to it. After each cut, lightly joint the sawn surface. Each leaf then will have a jointed face and a sawn face. If the veneers will be thicknessed by machine, having one clean surface will give you a head start.

In your first outing, plan to cut veneers about 4 in. longer than the finished dimension. The extra length allows room for bobbles at the ends when cutting and for snipe at the planer. Additionally, it provides latitude for

Continued ➜

aligning grain. Also, give yourself ½ in. of extra width to accommodate jointing the edges before gluing the veneer leaves into a panel and squaring up the panels.

Remember, there's nothing like the security of having at least a couple more leaves of veneer than you need for a project. The extra leaves will allow more options for the arrangement of the grain pattern and serve as a backup in the event of a mishap.

Arranging Leaves

After you have cut a stack of veneers, you have an opportunity to play with the grain pattern to create a pleasing effect. The leaves can be arranged in a number of ways: book-matched, slip-matched, end-for-end, or a combination.

Of course these are only starting points. When book-matching, notice the way that light reflects from the veneer surfaces. A phenomenon known as chatoyance often occurs. One leaf may seem brighter than another. The effect may be most apparent on vertical surfaces. The resulting impression of striping can either be unsettling or used to good effect.

Smart Setup for Smooth Resawing

Center the blade. The upper wheel is crowned, and the blade needs to run on the center of it to cut straight. While spinning the upper wheel by hand, gradually turn the tilt adjustment screw. A small tweak may be all that is necessary. Spin the wheel a few turns to see that the blade has settled in the right position.

Adjust the guides. Back the guides and thrust bearings away from the blade on both the top and bottom guide assemblies, and then set them as close as possible to the blade without touching it. You should just barely be able to see light between the guides and the blade.

Match the fence to the drift. To find out if your blade wants to drift one way or the other as it cuts, draw a straight line on a scrap piece, parallel to its edge, and move the rip fence out of the way. Now try to cut along the line. The angle you need to hold the board at is the angle of drift. Hold the scrap at that angle and turn off the saw. If the saw's fence allows adjustment, set its angle parallel to the scrap. Otherwise, use that angle to set up a shopmade fence.

Join the Veneers Like Solid Wood

When you are ready to glue the veneer leaves together to create a bigger panel, you must first joint the edges. Using the jointer isn't a good option because it will leave tiny scallops in the finished joint. But a handplane does a great job, as long as you sandwich the veneer between boards.

Some woodworkers use painter's masking tape to pull the leaves together. Because it is a bit of a pain to remove the tape and it obscures the fit of the joint, I prefer a clamping method that uses small wedges to apply pressure. If you go with tape, do it on both sides, use more strips

Resawing, Step by Step

Remove edge-banding first. Slice off solid banding now, and you'll be sure it will blend seamlessly into the veneered surfaces later. Mark the edges and ends of the board so you know which side the banding came from, and the order in which the veneers were cut.

Start at the jointer. Joint one face and one edge of the board. These will be your reference points against the table and fence. After each bandsaw cut, rejoint the same face of the board to maintain a solid reference and give you a jump on smoothing the veneer. Stack the veneers in order.

A few tips from a pro. If you are cutting through the entire board, the last ⅜ in. can be tricky to handle. This problem can be solved by taping a ¾-in. backer board to the back face of the board (above). A steady feed yields the best cuts (right), so find a position from which you can feed the cut with little or no shifting. Use additional support such as rollers if the stock is long. Keep the stock in contact with the fence with the right hand, and use your left to feed the workpiece at a constant rate no faster than the blade will allow.

How to Plane Veneer Safely

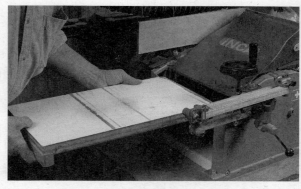

Make an auxiliary bed for your planer. If your resawing skills are good, the unjointed face of the veneer may not need to be machine surfaced. But if you need to smooth it further, use a thickness planer with sharp blades and a simple melamine auxiliary bed to support the thin pieces.

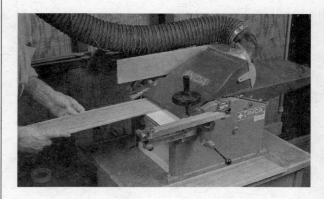

than you would clamps, and pay extra attention to keeping the veneer surfaces flush with each other.

After the leaves have been joined and the glue is dry, trim the veneer sheets to size. If you are applying an edge-banding after you veneer, you'll want to make the sheets the same size as the substrate, or slightly smaller. The exposed substrate edge makes it easier to trim the panel to finished dimensions. If the sheets are to be applied to a substrate with captured banding, remember to include the banding dimension when you size the veneer sheet. After the veneers are glued to the substrate, you can trim them down to the banding.

On the jointer, joint one long edge of the sheet straight, then use a tablesaw sled to crosscut the piece to length before ripping it to width. A quick word about the substrate: You are taking pains to create an item of quality, so glue the veneers to a good, void-free substrate. Use multi-ply birch or maple plywood. Fiberboard products may be flat, but they do not hold fasteners well and will swell if they get wet, to say nothing of the off-gassing and noxious dust. So I don't use products like MDF.

The shrinkage of glue exerts significant force on the substrate. To minimize the risk of cupping, be sure to veneer both sides of the substrate at once, and orient the plywood substrate so that its outer veneer is perpendicular to the direction of the veneer you are applying.

Edge-Band Before or After?

Unless your veneered panel is trapped in a frame-and-panel door and the edges won't be seen, you'll need to apply an edge-banding that covers the substrate, either before or after you veneer. This banding can be made wide enough to take on a shape, or at least to allow the edges to be softened. If you followed my advice and cut the banding from a board before it was sawn for veneers, your edging matches the faces of your panel, and the color or grain pattern continues from the top across the edge. This shows care and attention.

Captured bandings, about ¼ in. thick, are glued to the substrate before the veneer is applied. They are most often used where the appearance of after-the-fact framing would be undesirable; for instance, if you want a pattern to flow uninterrupted from a door to a drawer above. Here, an applied edge-banding would be a visual distur-

bance and look like a production job on shop plywood.

Applied edge-banding is glued to the substrate after the veneers are in place and is rarely more than ½ in. wide. The thickness of an applied banding provides you with the opportunity to shape a profile on a tabletop or cabinet top.

Also, the two types of banding can be used on a single panel, such as a door. A panel can look like a solid board if the top and bottom are captured and the sides are applied. Applying banding at the sides of the door also allows for the shaping of overlapping rabbets where two doors meet.

Two Edging Options

In general, use captured banding for end-grain edges and applied banding for long-grain edges.

1. CAPTURE EDGE-BANDING BEFORE VENEERING

Tape does the trick. Because the veneer will cover this glue joint, tape is plenty strong for clamping. The edging should be proud of the substrate on each side and a little longer. Glue two opposite sides at a time, trim the banding to length, and then band the other two sides. Last, using a handplane, flush all the banding to the level of the substrate.

Veneer both sides at once. This will balance out the tension as the glue dries, and prevent cupping. You can use a different wood on each side, but the woods should be of a similar nature, such as quartersawn with quartersawn.

Pressing issues. Welter manages smaller work with hand clamps and cauls to distribute pressure. Larger panels go in a vacuum bag. For both, Welter goes through a dry run first, and uses blue tape to keep the veneers aligned.

2. OR APPLY EDGE-BANDING AFTER VENEERING

Applied edge requires more pressure. The banding should be slightly wider than the panel is thick. Blue tape helps with alignment but isn't enough. Cauls and clamps must be used to keep this visible joint tight.

Plane banding flush after the glue dries. To keep the plane from tilting and overcutting near the edges, concentrate your pressure over the substrate. Welter uses one plane set for a thicker cut initially, and then switches to another plane to take thin cuts and flush the banding to the panel.

How to Veneer a Sunburst Table Top

by Mark Arnold

Veneer can replicate solid lumber, but if you use it only for that purpose, you are missing out on some dazzling design opportunities. One of the most spectacular of these is to arrange consecutive sheets around a center point. Known as a sunburst, this pattern is ideal for circular tabletops. It creates interesting concentric patterns, and the tapered shape of each segment draws the eye from the perimeter toward the center.

If you try this with solid stock it will fail, either from radial splitting caused by shrinkage or from cupping caused by expansion. I'll show you how to work with veneer to create a beautiful sunburst tabletop, from laying out the pattern to cutting and installing the segments. I'll also show how to install a simple border that frames the sunburst.

Crotch veneers create stunning effects and are the traditional choice for sunbursts, but plain sliced veneers also yield interesting results. Cross-grain figure works, such as curly and fiddleback, but bird's-eye and burl tend to understate the sunburst effect. For this tabletop, I chose a blistered cherry veneer with an African satinwood border.

Choose an Even Number of Segments

An accurate layout is critical to success. The first step is to decide upon the number of segments in the sunburst pattern. This may be dictated by the size of the veneer sheets you have. The key to good results is to assemble the pattern in small sections first and then join those sections. In this 12-piece sunburst, the total number of segments is divisible by four, so I'll assemble the pattern in quarters first. An eight- or 16-piece design can be created using the same basic layout.

Sunbursts with an even number of segments not divisible by four must be assembled in halves, each with an odd number of segments. Whatever method you choose, for best grain and color match, you'll need a stack of veneer sheets that were sequentially sliced.

Make sure the veneer is wide enough—Before you lay out the pattern on the substrate, make sure the veneer will fit the pattern. Divide the circumference of the sunburst you want to create by the desired number of segments to find out how wide each sheet must be. In this case, the top has a diameter (D) of 30 in. The formula for the circumference (C) of a circle is C=πD, so the circumference of the table is slightly more than 94 in. (30 × 3.14 = 94.2). Each segment of a 12-piece sunburst will therefore need to be 7.864 in. wide, or about 7⅞ in.

Lay Out the Pattern and Cut the Veneer

Sketch the sunburst pattern on the substrate to use as a template. I use ¾-in.-thick Baltic-birch plywood, but MDF or stable, quartersawn solid wood is also acceptable. Cut the substrate to an exact square, slightly larger than the intended final diameter of the tabletop. Draw out the sunburst pattern as shown in the drawings on p. 73.

Use sequentially cut veneer—Number the veneer sheets in the order they were sliced from the log. Then number the segments on the template as shown on p. 73. In this way, no adjacent pieces of veneer will be more than two sheets from one another as sliced from the flitch. No stack of veneers is identical from the first piece to the last, so if you simply lay them out clockwise, the first and last sheets would likely be noticeably mismatched along their seam. To help make accurate cuts, use a ¾-in. MDF template cut to the shape of a segment, but a little longer. Double up the MDF to create a fence on one edge (see photos 1 and 2, p. 74). Align the veneer sheets in the same direction. Locate the four pieces that border the Y-axis (Nos. 5, 6, 7, and 8) at the bottom of the stack.

The best way to cut a stack of veneers is with a veneer saw. Because the saw cuts on the pull stroke, start with the stack upside down and cut the left-hand side first to reduce the likelihood of losing a segment tip on the second cut. After the first cut, remove sheets No. 5, 6, 7, and 8, leaving them oversize for now. Align the cut edge of the remaining eight sheets with the far edge of the angled template, and make the second cut to create the 30° segments.

Assemble the Sunburst One Quarter at a Time

Continued ➤

Lay Out the Sunburst

HOW TO DRAW A 12-PIECE PATTERN

Begin with a perfectly square piece of plywood or MDF. Draw lines from opposite corners, then use a trammel to draw a circle slightly larger than the desired circumference (1). Without adjusting the trammel, place the point where one of the diagonals, or axes, meets the circumference, sweep the pencil in an arc, and mark where it crosses the circumference on either side (2). Repeat this on the three other axis points, and then connect each pencil mark with the one diagonally opposite to divide the circle into 12 equal segments (3).

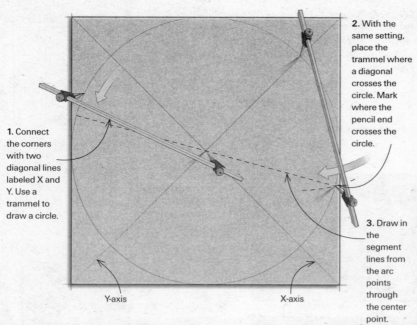

1. Connect the corners with two diagonal lines labeled X and Y. Use a trammel to draw a circle.

2. With the same setting, place the trammel where a diagonal crosses the circle. Mark where the pencil end crosses the circle.

3. Draw in the segment lines from the arc points through the center point.

Y-axis   X-axis

1.

2.

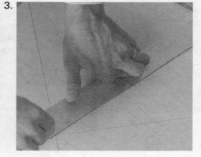

3.

PREPARE THE VENEER

Make sure that the veneer is flat and dry. Treat it with a veneer-flattening solution such as Rockler's Veneer Glycerin and keep it clamped flat until you are ready to use it. To determine where to cut the veneer, use two mirrors taped along one edge and opened, with the aid of a slice of wood, to 30° (360° divided by 12 segments). Placed over a sheet of veneer, the mirrors give you a preview of the finished sunburst. Find a pleasing pattern, and then faintly trace the outline onto the first sheet. Number the sheets in their correct order in a location that will not be trimmed off later.

Keep the sheets sequence. Number the sheets of veneer in the order they were cut from the log.

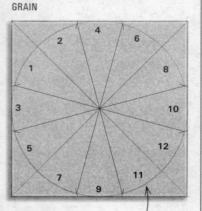

HOW TO MINIMIZE THE DIFFERENCE IN GRAIN

Grain and figure change progressively from sheet to sheet. For the best match throughout the sunburst, arrange each numbered segment as shown. In this way, adjacent slices of veneer are never more than two away from each other in the sequence.

Lay the cut segments on the back of the substrate and, using the numbered pie chart as a guide, assemble them into quarters as shown on p. 74. Begin with a larger piece that overlaps the Y-axis, such as segment 5. Flip over segment 3 so that it forms a mirror image, or book-match, with segment 5. Pull the two segments together with masking tape, making sure the tips align perfectly. This is more critical than a having adjacent halves be perfectly symmetrical. Now connect segment 1, faceup, to segment 3. Repeat the process starting with segment 7 facedown; book-match it to segment 9 faceup, and then add segment 11 facedown. Repeat for the two other quarters.

Once all four quarters are taped up, join the two pairs across the X-axis (segments 1 to 2 and 11 to 12) to create two halves. Next, fold one half over onto the other and align the seams of the two X-axes. Verify that all the segment tips meet at one point, then lay a straightedge across the diameter, perpendicular to the X-axis and aligned to the point where all segment tips meet.

Trim the waste from all four segments at once, open up the two halves, and attach them with masking tape. Then flip over the sunburst and apply veneer tape to all the seams on the show face. For adhesion, you need to moisten the veneer tape, but don't use too much water or you'll distort the cut seam. Instead, pull the tape across a damp sponge, then apply it. Allow the veneer tape to dry, then remove all the masking tape from the opposite face. The sunburst is now ready to be glued to the substrate.

I use Better Bond (www.veneersupplies.com), a polyvinyl acetate (PVA) adhesive formulated to reduce the risk of glue bleeding through the veneer, and apply it with a paint roller. Veneering only one side of the substrate could cause warping, so stabilize it with a backing veneer. Apply adhesive to the underside of the substrate and position the backing veneer perpendicular to the face grain of the plywood. Then flip the panel onto a 3/4-in.-thick MDF caul covered with a sheet of plastic, apply adhesive to the top of the substrate, and center the sunburst face on it, taped side up. Cover the veneer with a sheet of plastic and another MDF caul, and press the stack in a vacuum bag or veneer press for six hours.

A Border Made from Contrasting Veneer

A border is a classic way to frame the sunburst veneer. It can either be a simple circle of consistent width, as shown here, or a more ambitious pattern.

When the glue has cured, remove the panel from the clamps or vacuum bag, dampen the tape, and peel it away. Much of the remaining work is done referencing off the center of the sunburst. First, use a trammel (with the metal point in a plastic tip to protect the veneer) to draw the circumference of the table on the veneer, and cut just outside the line using a bandsaw. Next, make a pivot block with a hole in it that matches the diameter of the metal rod or drill bit you intend to use. Align the hole with the center point of the tabletop and attach the block to the top with double-sided tape. Set up a router on a trammel whose pivot point is connected by a metal rod or drill bit to the pivot block. Use a 3/4-in.-dia. mortising bit and set the depth of cut to the thickness of the border veneer. Subtract 2 in. from the intended radius of the finished top, and cut a shallow rabbet from that point to the edge of the top. Go clockwise on all passes to minimize tearout, and keep a firm grasp on the router for this climb cut.

Cut the border veneer into pieces 3 in. wide by a little over 2 in. long, with the grain running perpendicular to the width. Cut enough pieces to go around the tabletop. Mount the trammel point in the center of the pivot block and use the pencil to mark the arc of the sunburst on the stack of border veneer. Use the bandsaw to cut the stack along that mark. Place a piece of scrapwood under the stack to create a zero-clearance surface.

A sharp plane iron is the easiest way to cut the joint between the radial seams of the border, but you can also use a veneer saw. After joining three or four sections together with veneer tape, lay them adjacent to the sunburst (stringing will fill any slight gap) and place masking tape on the substrate at both ends of the border. This will make it much easier to remove glue squeeze-out before adding adjacent sections. Use masking tape to attach the border to the sunburst veneer to prevent it from moving. Apply glue and then clamp the border using a suitably shaped caul. Work around the top in this fashion.

Once all the border has been applied, use the trammel-mounted router to cut the top to final size. This can be done with a straight-cutting bit in 1/4-in. increments, or after the first pass you can go to the router table and trim away the waste using a bearing-guided, flush-trimming bit.

Now wrap the table edge with vertical pieces of the edge-banding veneer. Again, do short sections at a time, place a piece of masking tape at the end to facilitate removing squeeze-out, and use thin strips of wood or bending plywood as cauls. An edge-banding clamp with its steel strapping works best, but you could also employ a nylon strap clamp.

You could use a router to cut the groove for the stringing between the sunburst veneer and the border, but I use a scratch stock indexed to the center point. You could also run it against the table edge. Glue in the stringing and scrape it flush.

To give the vulnerable veneered edge of the tabletop some added protection, I add a thin strip of solid stock. I cut a 1/8-in.-square rabbet in the top corner using the router and trammel and glue in a piece of hard maple. Scrape the edging flush, sand the whole surface, and apply a clear gloss finish to bring out the wood's figure.

Assmble the Sunburst

TAPE THE VENEER SEGMENTS INTO QUARTERS, THEN HALVES

When cutting the sunburst segments to size, the four pieces that adjoin one of the axes are deliberately left oversize. Beginning with these pieces, tape together the three segments in each quarter, flipping and book-matching each alternate piece.

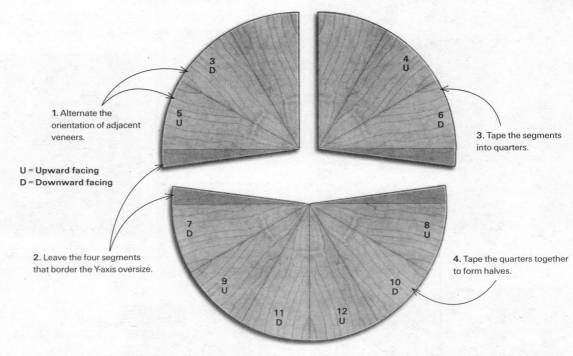

1. Alternate the orientation of adjacent veneers.

U = Upward facing
D = Downward facing

2. Leave the four segments that border the Y-axis oversize.

3. Tape the segments into quarters.

4. Tape the quarters together to form halves.

First cut. Use a veneer saw guided by a straight-edged fence to make the left-hand cut on all 12 sheets of veneer.

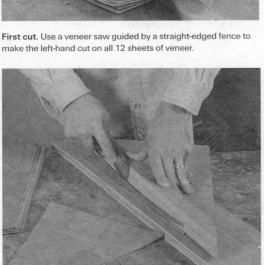

Second cut. Remove the four sheets that border the Y-axis, leaving them oversize for now. Flip the remaining sheets and align them with the left-hand side of the template. Then make the left-hand cut on the segments.

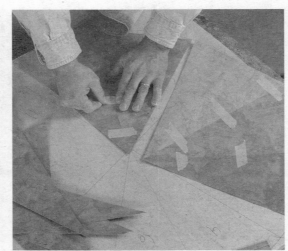

Quarter by quarter. Beginning with an oversize segment, use masking tape to assemble each quarter, flipping and book-matching alternate segments.

Two halves completed. Join adjacent quarters to form two halves that extend about 190º.

THEN TAPE THE TWO HALVES TOGETHER

Finally, align the points of the two halves and their center seams, cut away the surplus from the four oversize segments (shaded), and tape the sunburst together.

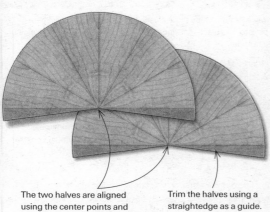

The two halves are aligned using the center points and seams of the segments.

Trim the halves using a straightedge as a guide.

Complete the sunburst. Use masking tape to join the halves into the finished sunburst.

Apply veneer tape. Flip over the sunburst and apply strips of veneer tape to the seams on the show face. Draw the tape over a damp sponge to avoid over-wetting it. When the veneer tape is dry, remove the masking tape from the glue face of the sunburst.

Glue and Trim

Veneer both sides. To avoid the risk of the substrate warping, glue a backing veneer to the underside and press both sides at once.

Bandsaw the top. After the glue dries, use a trammel to redraw the circumference of the table and then bandsaw just outside the line.

Trim the Edge and Band It

CUT THE CIRCUMFERENCE IN TWO STEPS

1. Use a straight bit and a trammel-mounted router to make an initial 1/4-in.-deep cut.

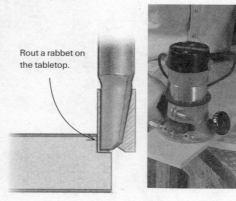

Rout a rabbet on the tabletop.

2. Complete the cut on the router table with a bearing-guided, flush-trimming bit.

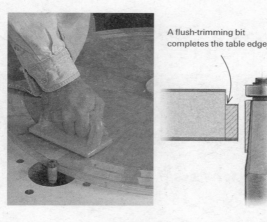

A flush-trimming bit completes the table edge.

Add the edging. Use narrow strips of edge-banding veneer to cover the edge of the tabletop.

Circle clamp. Apply the edging in short sections and use a band or strap clamp. The large triangular section keeps the clamp jaws off the wood. Note that the section being clamped is along the far edge of the table.

Add the Border

HOW TO ROUT A SHALLOW RECESS

Attach the pivot point. A pivot point is attached with double-faced tape directly over the center of the sunburst. Shine a flashlight through the hole to align it over the center point.

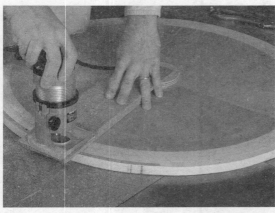

Rabbet for the border. Make a simple trammel to hold the router, attach it to the pivot point, and use a mortising bit to cut a shallow 2-in.-wide rabbet for the border.

CUT AND GLUE THE BORDER VENEER

Prepare the sections. Use a trammel to scribe the sunburst curve onto a stack of border veneer.

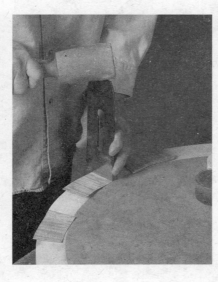

A clean cut. A plane iron creates a tight seam when joining the sections.

Three at a time. Tape three pieces of veneer together, lay them on the substrate, and place masking tape at both ends to help remove glue squeeze-out.

Clamp with a curved caul. After applying glue to the substrate, tape the border to the sunburst to prevent it from moving when clamping pressure is applied.

Add Stringing and a Solid Corner

SCRATCH STOCK CREATES A GROOVE FOR STRINGING

A scratch stock is just a piece of old hacksaw or bandsaw blade with the teeth ground away and a profile filed onto the end. It is held in a simple hardwood block and makes a surprisingly clean cut.

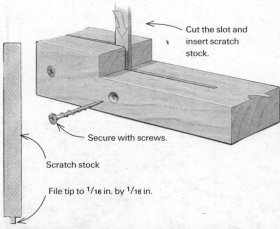

Cut the slot and insert scratch stock.

Secure with screws.

Scratch stock

File tip to 1/16 in. by 1/16 in.

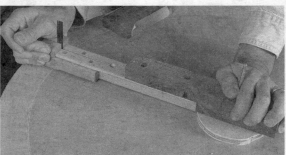

Another trammel. Attach the scratch stock to the pivot point and cut a groove between the sunburst and the border to receive the stringing.

Insert the stringing. Use a syringe to insert glue into the groove, and then add the holly stringing. When the glue has dried, bring the stringing flush with a scraper.

The fifinal cut. Use the trammel-mounted router one last time to cut a 1/8-in.-square rabbet on the top corner of the tabletop.

Rout a 1/8-in. rabbet on the top edge.

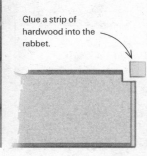

Added protection. A strip of hard maple protects the vulnerable veneered edge.

Glue a strip of hardwood into the rabbet.

Applied Fretwork with Veneer

by Timothy Coleman

I am fascinated with patterns. I see them everywhere—in nature, on fabrics, on buildings, on playing cards—and I am always looking for ways to use them in my furniture to create surfaces that have depth and texture. One way I achieve this is to use my scrollsaw to cut fretwork-like patterns in veneer and apply them to table aprons. This technique produces a surprising amount of depth and shadow using a minimal amount of thickness. I also use a contrasting wood underneath, adding even more interest and flair.

Master Class

The materials and tools involved are few and simple. I begin with veneer resawn to 1/16 in. thick on the bandsaw (you also could lay up sheets of commercial veneer to get the right thickness). I use a handheld fretsaw or a scrollsaw to cut the patterns, and follow with a knife, small files, and sanding sticks to clean up after cutting. Pressing the underlayer of veneer and the fretwork pattern onto the apron involves MDF cauls and hand clamps. This is low-tech woodworking at its finest.

Where the Contrast Comes From

For the best effect, you want the surface under the pattern veneer to be a contrasting wood. I typically use two layers of veneer (an underlayer and the pattern) to create the contrast. However, you can eliminate the underlayer of veneer and apply the pattern directly to the apron if the apron wood is a contrasting color.

For stability, you should orient the grain of the veneer(s) with the grain of the apron. Using a thick apron (1 in.) will eliminate the need for a backer veneer, which is usually applied to prevent a veneered panel from warping. If the apron you're using is 3/4 in. thick or under, it couldn't hurt to add the backer. One other note: I cut all the joinery in the apron before applying the pattern.

LOW-TECH METHOD, HIGH-IMPACT RESULT

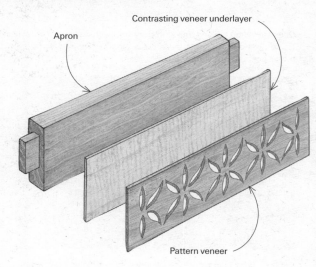

Apron

Contrasting veneer underlayer

Pattern veneer

Thick Veneer Works Best

For this technique, the pattern veneer should be 1/16 in. thick to emphasize the layered effect and create a strong shadow. The thick veneer is also easier to cut with the scrollsaw.

You also could glue together multiple layers of thin veneer to create thicker material. Some woodworkers would recommend orienting the plies cross-grain for stability. But I keep the grain running in the same direction and have had success. When glued and pressed between pieces of 3/4-in.-thick MDF, the assembly comes out quite flat. Cut the veneer slightly wider and longer than the exposed face of the apron. You'll trim it flush after it's applied to the apron.

Lay Out the Pattern

For some people, patterns are not always easy to see, but you just need to look around; they are everywhere. Wonderful patterns can be manmade, such as those seen

in fabrics or in architecture, or natural, like leaves or plants. If you need inspiration, check out The Grammar of Ornament by Owen Jones (The Ivy Press Limited, 2001; available at Amazon.com). If you're doing this for the first time, I would suggest a simple pattern that does not have any delicate or thin elements that could break easily.

If you are using a repetitive pattern—one that will appear more than once on a piece, which often happens on table aprons—draw it on card stock, cut it out with an X-Acto knife, and use the card as a stencil on the veneer. Sometimes I make a scrollsawn sample of the pattern as practice, and this can serve the same purpose as the paper cutout. If the pattern is not repetitive, I draw it directly on the veneer, or use graphite paper to transfer it from my sketchbook to the veneer.

The Right Blade Ensures Clean Cuts

I have used a fretsaw and a homemade scrollsaw to cut patterns, but an electric scrollsaw is fast and easy.

The key to a good cut is using the right blade. When cutting individual patterns, I use a fine, 28-tpi skip-tooth blade; for stacked cuts, I use a coarser 20-tpi blade. The skip-tooth arrangement helps clear the chips from the thicker workpiece.

I aim to saw the pattern right on the line, but any deviations can be cleaned up afterward using a carving knife and fine files.

Use Care When Gluing the Pattern to the Substrate

Take a deep breath and approach this step carefully. I use Titebond II as the adhesive or Titebond Extend for a bit longer open time. Before applying the underlayer of veneer, sand the apron surface smooth.

I use a vacuum veneer press for much of my veneer work, but clamps and cauls work fine for a small surface. Apply a uniform coat of glue on the underlayer veneer,

Continued ➜

Make the Fretwork

RESAW THICK VENEER

Veneers should be just over 1/16 in. thick. Resaw both the underlayer and pattern veneers (left). Clean up the material with a cabinet scraper and sandpaper, holding each piece in place with double-stick tape (below). thick.

CUT AWAY THE WASTE

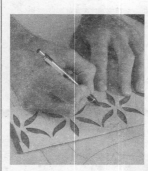

Use a stencil. Cut the pattern into card stock and trace it on the veneer. Make the veneer (and the pattern) oversize to allow the veneer to be trimmed after it's applied to the apron.

Make the cutouts. Drill holes through the cutout areas to make way for the scrollsaw blade. Cut slowly and carefully on the line. To create a repetitive pattern on multiple pieces, tape the layers of veneer together, and cut them all at once.

CLEAN UP

Fine cuts need fine tools. Clean up the sawcuts in each pattern using a knife and needle files. Coleman likes to bevel the edges of the cutouts with the knife and do the final smoothing with fine needle files.

place it on the apron, and put the sandwich between two 3/4-in.-thick MDF cauls. After the glue dries, lightly sand the underlayer, then glue the pattern veneer to the apron. Apply glue sparingly, then lay the pattern veneer carefully onto the apron, using blue tape to keep it in place. Put the sandwich between the cauls and clamp it up.

Assemble the Veneers

CONTRASTING LAYER FIRST

Glue and clamp the underlayer to the apron. Apply an even layer of glue to the underlayer veneer and the apron. Use MDF cauls and lots of clamps to apply even pressure across the surface. Wrapping the top caul in newspaper prevents the caul from sticking to the veneer.

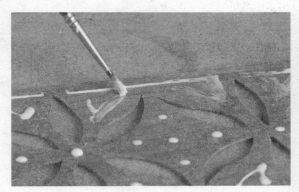

Don't be sloppy here. Because it will be hard to clean up squeeze-out on the interior of the pattern, apply glue so the squeeze-out occurs on the outside. Place little dabs on interior elements of the pattern, and finish with a heavier coat around the perimeter. Use a small paintbrush to spread the glue (above).

Tape and clamp. Put the pattern veneer on the apron and tape it in place so it won't move when it's clamped up (left). Use cauls to protect the pattern and plenty of clamps to spread pressure evenly across the surface (right).

NOW GLUE ON THE PATTERN

Once the assembly comes out of the clamps, trim the veneer layers flush to the apron, and refine the surface with a light scraping and sanding with P220- and P320-grit paper.

When applying a finish, put on light coats to prevent pooling inside the cutouts. To reach tight spots, use a fine, narrow brush.

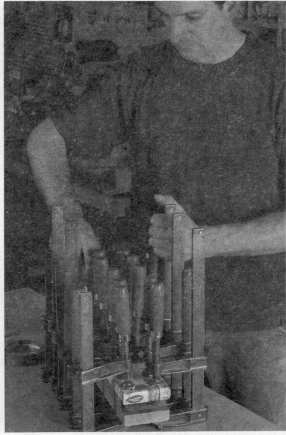

Trim Everything Flush

Scrape the top and bottom. Coleman uses a cabinet scraper to bring the veneer edges flush with the apron edges (left), and a sharp chisel to trim the ends of the veneer (below).

Marquetry, the Italian Way

By Paul Schurch

I didn't know much about marquetry when I got my first big table job in California in 1989. I decided to inlay the solid maple top with wood and stone designs by shaping the inlay, routing out the background, gluing the inlay into the recess, and sanding it flush. I got the job done, but I knew there had to be an easier way.

This spurred me to head back to Europe, where I had done my original woodworking training. There I found work in an Italian shop, producing marquetry for the furniture trades, and learned the efficient techniques of knife-cutting, packet-cutting, and contour-cutting that I still use and teach today.

The three techniques are complementary, and allow me to produce any design I can come up with. They require little investment in tooling, are easier and faster than other methods, and deliver better results.

By the way, to add depth and realism to these pictures, I also use sand-shading, a classic scorching technique for adding shadows. If you haven't tried marquetry, you will be surprised at how simple, practical, and fun it can be. To demonstrate, I'll create a panel of three flowers, with leaves and a curving stem.

You will need a basic scrollsaw that can hold a 2/0 blade, and for larger projects, you'll need a vacuum bag to glue the veneers onto a core. I also recommend thin tongs, for handling the pieces, and a 23-gauge pin nailer, though hand-nailing the packet also works.

Why Packet-Cutting?

Packet-cutting is simply stacking various veneers on top of each other and scrollsawing the pattern simultaneously in both the background and the picture veneers. You then select the right pieces and reassemble them like a puzzle. The kerf is not an issue, since the 0.008-in. gaps created by the blade are so thin that the gluing and finishing process fills them. I also use the sawkerf lines as a design element, as in leaf veins or other accent lines in the design.

The beauty of packet-cutting is that when you wander slightly off the line, the background and the design will still fit. Also, a single packet can yield multiple versions of the same design.

Start with a Drawing

Every marquetry design (called a "cartoon") starts with a line drawing, which acts as a template for cutting out and assembling the pieces. There are many ways to obtain a usable drawing for marquetry. You can trace over photographs in books, using either vellum tracing paper and a 0.5mm mechanical pencil with HB lead, or transparent film and a fine-tipped permanent marker. You can then enlarge, reduce, or reverse the drawing or certain elements of the drawing with a photocopy machine to achieve the proper elements for your project. By the way, a drawing can also be photocopied onto transparent film, which can be used to trace a mirror image for symmetrical designs.

You can also make your own sketch, refining it by placing tracing paper over each new version until you are happy with the picture and all the lines are crisp and clean. My go-to tools are my 0.5mm pencil, an electric eraser (used with an erasing shield), and a photocopy machine. I also use other common drafting tools—from compasses, rulers, and templates I have made in 1/8-in.-thick

MDF, to drafting arms and thin wooden sticks to bend a curve just right.

I find that creating a marquetry cartoon is easier after the furniture has been designed, in order to get the form and proportions just right.

For a workable cartoon, you should make all the pieces in the design or background bigger than 1/4 in. square, or they will be too small to handle while cutting or sand-shading. I always try to simplify the drawing so that the background is connected together as much as possible, and avoiding narrow background sections between the images. I find that the most challenging designs to scrollsaw are straight lines, thin parallel cuts (stems, border work), lettering, and facial features: All of those show mistakes clearly, so beginners should avoid them.

Labeling Is Critical

It's very important to number all of the pieces to help you identify, sort, and assemble the marquetry pattern after it is in a hundred pieces, many of them similar.

You'll also need to add little rows of dots where you plan to sand-shade the pieces, as well as lines to indicate grain direction. After the final drawing is done, I make three photocopies, one for choosing veneers (sometimes I paint it first) to get the colors right, one to be glued onto the packet as a cutting template, and one as an assembly guide.

How to Make the Packet

To build the packet, start with two sheets of grayboard 3/4 in. larger than the final panel size. Also known as thin cardboard, base mat board, or notebook backer, grayboard is about 0.035 in. thick, and can be obtained from an art-supply store in sheets up to 3 ft. by 4 ft. It allows for clean

Design: You Don't Have to Be an Artist

If your design is simple or you can draw well, you can create the design from scratch. But there is an easy way to build a complex design without drawing.

- **Building blocks.** Find line drawings in books, and enlarge or reduce them with a photocopier to make them the right size. Then trace them onto paper or clear film to get clean versions.

- **Arrange to create.** Photocopy those traced drawings and arrange them under tracing paper to create a complete design, drawing in the missing elements.

- **Clean it up and label it.** To make your final, clean drawing, place another sheet of tracing paper over the top. Put clear film between the sheets so the pencil marks don't transfer from below. Last, mark and label your drawing as shown below.

MANAGE THE MADNESS
In order to choose veneers for your packet and keep track of the pieces afterward, you need to label each element carefully.

Number each piece.

Two parallel lines show grain direction.

Decide which edge should be in shadow (sand-shaded), and put a row of dots there.

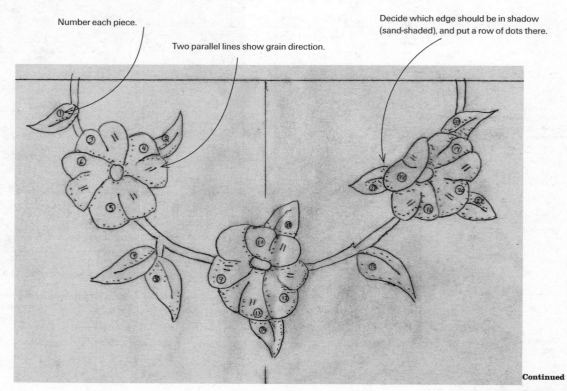

Continued →

nailing, prevents scrollsaw tearout, and helps the thin 2/0 blade to stay vertical while cutting. Glue a copy of the drawing onto one layer of grayboard with a spray adhesive like 3M 77. Then tape the two sheets of grayboard together along one side—hinged like a book.

Now select all the veneers you'll need for your design. The first piece in the packet is the background, the same size as the oversize grayboard. It can be a radial match, bookmatch, or just a single sheet of veneer. After that, if you are not using full sheets, each piece of veneer should be prepared at least 1 in. larger than the image it corresponds to in your drawing.

Apply 25-gram veneer tape (also known as gum tape) to the whole "show face" (the side that you will see once glue-up is done) of each layer of veneer to reinforce it, and rub the tape aggressively with a brass-bristle brush to improve its grip. Then immediately place the pieces under a sheet of MDF or plywood to keep them flat while they dry for 20 to 30 minutes.

After that, you can start building the packet. Using a few pieces of blue tape, secure the background veneer to the bottom layer of grayboard. Then open and close the sandwich rapidly to make sure you are positioning each piece of veneer directly under its drawn outline, and secure each one with a few more pieces of blue tape away from any areas to be cut, if possible. Select veneer pieces and orient the grain for maximum effect. Make sure the gum-taped side of all pieces is facing up.

Nails Lock Everything in Place

Close and nail the packet together with 3/4-in.-long, 23-gauge pins. These thin nails have a sharp point on one end, which separates the fibers rather than crushing them. Still, lighter background woods can show pinholes after glue-up, so you'll need to fill those holes after the design is assembled (before glue-up). Just apply a spot of white glue, burnish the hole closed with the tip of a chisel, and

hand-sand with 100-grit paper, filling the hole with dust and wet glue.

Here are some other important tips: Nail the packet together on a piece of rigid foam so the nails don't stick into your bench. And nail only into the background areas, close to the designs. Hopefully, each piece of background will be secured by at least two nails to keep it from shifting during sawing. I put a 1/2-in.-thick spacer under the body of my nailer, which leaves each pin protruding 1/4 in. on either side of the packet.

Now, bend down (or "clinch") the nails. Don't bend them over a cut line, and be sure to bend both sides in the same direction. If you form an S-shape, you will shift the veneer alignment.

Scrollsaw Success

While cutting the packet on a scrollsaw, remove each stacked element of the design as it is cut free, placing them to one side as you go. To get the pieces out, I use a pencil or dental pick to hold down the stack of pieces I just cut, as I lift the packet. And then I reach under the

packet with a pair of thin tongs or tweezers to pull out the little stack.

Your best bet is to start cutting out pieces from the middle of the design, and work your way out toward the edges. This way, the pin nails holding the packet together will support the veneers throughout the cutting process. I make the starter hole for the scrollsaw blade in the center of the packet, by drilling with a sharpened 18-gauge wire nail or dental pick. The spinning point eases the fibers aside, so they will knit back together later. No drills (or faceted nail points), since they remove wood fibers.

It is wise to save all the pieces until the project is glued up, since you may need an alternate piece to replace a damaged or lost one. After cutting, sort and select each piece including its numbered grayboard drawing on a tray for sand-shading. After shading, you can pull the pin nails out of the packet to release the background, and the pattern can be assembled. To remove the pins cleanly, place the packet on the rigid foam again, and gently lever the pins straight out with some wire nippers, without cutting them. The pin will unbend on the bottom and pull out.

Saw from the Inside Out

Start from the inside elements so the outer elements remain attached to the overall packet for support.

Starter hole. Schürch cuts the head off an 18-gauge nail and chucks it in a drill to create a starter hole for the scrollsaw. The nail parts the wood fibers, which can be re-knit later.

One stack at a time. After sawing an element free, press down on it with a pencil, lift the packet, and then reach under it to remove the small stack of pieces.

Stay organized. Under each part of the drawing is a small stack of veneer parts. Keep each stack together, with its labeled piece on top. Use a big tray and another copy of the drawing to keep track of the pieces.

Pick out your parts. Now take apart each stack, find the piece with the right color and grain direction, and place it on a copy of the full drawing. Since there is veneer tape on the show face, you'll be looking at the glue face for reference. Bring along the labeled cardboard pieces, too.

SAND-SHADING IS NEXT

Build the Packet

To saw out all the pieces in one shot, you need to bind together all of the veneers in a stack, with the drawing on top.

SMART SANDWICH

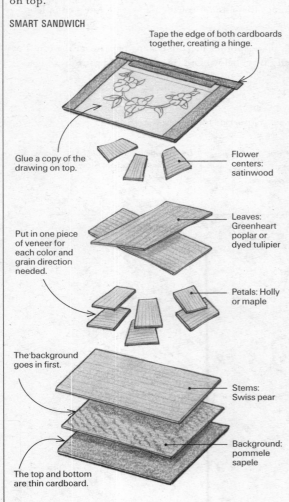

Tape the edge of both cardboards together, creating a hinge.

Glue a copy of the drawing on top.

Flower centers: satinwood

Put in one piece of veneer for each color and grain direction needed.

Leaves: Greenheart poplar or dyed tulipier

Petals: Holly or maple

The background goes in first.

Stems: Swiss pear

Background: pommele sapele

The top and bottom are thin cardboard.

Putting It Together: Tape and Tape Again

When all the veneer parts are ready for assembly, place the background on a flat surface, gum-taped show face down. For this flower design, the stems act as bridge pieces, joining the two background sections together. Use a few pieces of blue tape to secure them.

Now flip the pattern over (show face up) and put wide blue tape over the gum tape on all assembly areas. Then flip the pattern over (show face down again), with the sticky side of the blue tape showing through the voids. The large blue tape will hold it all together, and allow you to stick all the small pieces in place. This is the fun part, watching the picture come together.

Spread the leaf veins apart to snug the leaf perimeter tight to the background, which also opens up and accents the vein lines. Place the outer petals of each flower snugly against the background first and then work your way in toward the center, distributing the gaps evenly. The adhesive on the blue tape will let you shift the pieces sideways. And if you need to move a piece, it's easy to pry it up with the tongs and reset it.

After the basic assembly, most kerf gaps will not need filling, since glue-up and finishing will do this. To fill gaps larger than 1/32 in., you have a few options. You can stipple the veneer by stabbing it along the grain direction with a chisel, opening up the wood fibers. Then add a spot of white glue to fill the gap. You also can insert veneer slivers where needed, and dab white glue into the repair areas (or other fragile spots). Lightly sand the glue spots with 100-grit paper to ensure they will adhere properly to the substrate. By the way, like assembly, repair is always done on the glue surface.

The tape dance isn't over. Cover the glue face with blue tape, flip the skin over, remove all the blue tape from the show face, and replace it with slimy gum tape. Once again, brush down the tape and place the assembled pattern under a platen to dry. Last, remove the blue tape from the glue surface.

Now you can trim the edges, and add stringing or borders if needed. Make both the finished pattern and the substrate 1/2 in. oversize (1/4 in. all around) in case the veneer shifts during glue-up. I use the substrate as a template for trimming the veneer to size. Cut a balancing veneer for the back of the panel, do a final check for overlaps in the marquetry, and glue it up. Afterward, scuff the veneer tape with 100-grit paper, wet it for a minute or two, and it will come off with a sharp putty knife. The glue fills most of the gaps in the marquetry, but if any depressions are left after I've finish-sanded the panel and sealed it with a couple of padded-on layers of shellac, I fill them with Famowood or Dap (both walnut color), sand with 220-grit, and seal again with shellac before applying oil or lacquer.

That's it. Lots of steps, but none difficult. You've learned marquetry; the only limit now is your imagination.

Assembly Is the Fun Part

The process is quick and easy, and it feels great to watch your veneer picture come together.

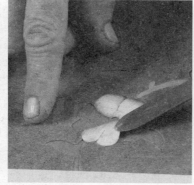

First pull the pins. Use a small nail nipper, gripping the pins in the tool's throat to avoid cutting them. They will straighten as they pull free.

Build bridges. Schürch uses small stem pieces to connect the two halves of the background, working on the glue face.

Tape is the foundation. Working on the show face, now cover all the spaces with blue tape.

Paint your picture. Flip the pattern over to the glue face, and start placing pieces (left). Schürch places his thin tongs into the sawn leaf veins (right) to spread the piece and even out the gaps. The blue-tape adhesive allows the pieces to be shifted easily.

Check the gaps. Place the completed pattern in front of a strong light to check for uniform gaps. Shift pieces around if necessary.

Got a Chunk Missing? Repairs Are Easy

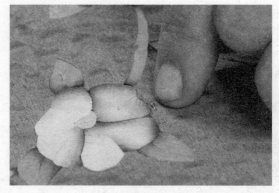

Oops. Sometimes a tiny piece chips away and goes missing.

Stippling means spreading. Use a sharp chisel to spread the nearby wood fibers along their grain lines, filling the gap.

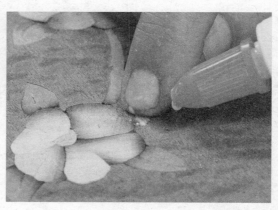

Glue and sand. Apply a dot of glue to the stippled area, rub it in, let it dry, and sand it lightly with 100-grit paper to pack the gap with dust and glue, and to scuff the glue off the veneer surface.

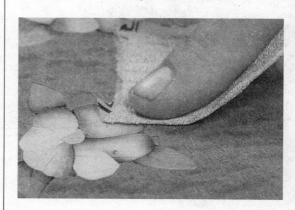

Continued ➔

Dance of the Tape

Most veneering projects involve a back-and-forth between blue tape and gum tape, in order to move all the veneer tape to the show face while keeping the pattern in perfect alignment.

Tape the glue face. Use blue tape on the back side to lock in the pattern and placement. Burnish the tape with a brass-bristle brush for a good hold.

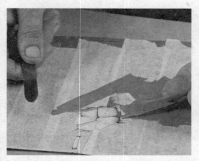

Clean off the show face. Remove all the blue tape from the show face. Keep the tape low as you pull, to avoid pulling up fibers or a whole piece. Hold pieces down if necessary. Some loose gum tape will come off.

Tape the show face. Now gum tape goes on the show face to hold everything together through the glue-up process.

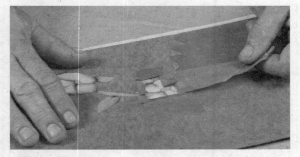

One last layer to remove, then let it dry. Don't forget the blue tape you put on the glue face (above)! Put the veneer under a layer of MDF to keep it flat while it dries.

Sand-Shading Marquetry and Inlay

by Paul Schurch

Without shading, marquetry can be flat and lifeless. With it, you get a 3-D effect that brings pictures to life, whether they are the folds in a linen cloth, the petals of a rose, or the shadows and lines of a face. It brings the same depth to many types of inlay in solid wood, too.

The good news is that shading is easy to do, using a low-tech, traditional method called sand-shading, in which a piece of veneer is scorched along one edge in a pan of heated sand to create a permanent, realistic shadow that goes smoothly from dark to light.

The process starts when you are making the initial drawing of the pattern or image. Pencil a series of small dots on the drawing along the edge to be shaded.

To decide which edges to shade, imagine a light source from the top right or left of an image, projecting down onto the design and creating shadows. Objects that appear to be underneath, or behind, should be shaded accordingly. There is one exception to that rule: When an image has the same type of wood side by side, as in two adjoining flower petals, I shade only one edge or the other, never both, because that would create a dark, unattractive furrow in the picture. But even if I don't shade an edge, I heat each piece a little, so its overall hue doesn't stand out.

How to Shade Safely

After cutting out all the parts, keep each stack of pieces together, including their corresponding "cartoon" drawing piece, then pull the right-color piece out of each stack, and place it and the cartoon onto a tray next to the sand-shading pan. The dots on the cartoon are your guide through the sand-shading process, and assembly, too. I also like to have a full copy of the drawing nearby as a reference.

You'll need 100-grit, clean washed silica sand, the crushed kind used for sand blasting or children's sandboxes, not beach sand, which has debris and salt in it. Put an inch of sand in a large, noncoated metal frying pan and heat it over a natural-gas kitchen, propane, or butane-gas flame. An electric hotplate may not get hot enough, though an electric stove might.

Let the sand heat up for about 15 minutes over a medium flame, and then use tweezers or thin tongs to pick up and insert the edge of a light-colored veneer test piece into the sand to see what happens. If the heat is right, the piece will be shaded with a dark-to-light gradated line in 5 to 10 seconds. If the sand is too hot, the wood edge will char and the piece may crumble. If the sand is not hot enough, the shading will take 20 seconds or more, and the whole piece will darken as it shrinks and curls. Note that some of the shading effect will be removed during final finish sanding, so exaggerate the shading a little bit.

Dark or dyed woods will take more heat to shade, and every wood species shades slightly differently, requiring you to change the depth you plunge some pieces into the sand (the deeper, the hotter).

By the way, if you've taken my advice and reinforced your veneer pieces with veneer tape prior to scrollsawing, don't worry: The heat will penetrate through the paper and work just fine.

You'll find there is a sweet spot of heat in the pan, and long pieces can be shaded by moving them through that spot in stages. Also, the inside of a leaf can be shaded along one edge of a vein by bending or breaking the leaf in the middle of the vein cut, using the veneer tape as a hinge. You can then insert the whole leaf at an angle to shade both a middle edge and an outer edge at the same time.

Pieces Need to Be Rehydrated

Shading the veneer pieces will curl and shrink them slightly, making them brittle. So you need to re-introduce some moisture to make the wood swell back to its original size and become pliable again.

To do this, brush off any sand stuck on the piece and dab its bare face with a moist sponge or wet finger. When the wood starts visibly expanding and becomes pliable again, I place the piece and its cartoon between small 4-in. by 4-in. plywood or MDF cauls to keep them flat and absorb the excess moisture as they dry, which will take 10 to 20 minutes. The cauls stack nicely.

By the way, too much hydration will loosen the veneer tape, over-expand the piece, and create too tight a fit. You definitely don't want pieces to overlap in your marquetry pattern. So you might have to reheat pieces a bit to dry and shrink them, or you'll have to pound the pieces with the butt end of a chisel during assembly to get them to fit. On the other hand, small gaps will fill with glue during the pressing process. As I always say, "Better gaps than laps in marquetry."

New Spin on Fan Inlays

by Garrett Hack

Most furniture makers aspire to have their work stand out, to be original in some way. That's what inspired me to start using various forms of inlay in my work, from traditional cuff bandings to original Morse-code signatures in black-and-white stringing. They've all added uniqueness—and lots of fun—to my furniture.

One of my favorites is the quarter-circle fan, made from ebony and holly rays. These fans appear frequently on 18th-century Federal furniture, where makers used them to brighten the façade of a piece with contrasting flourishes in the corners of drawers and doors, to adorn and connect the corners of a tabletop, or to decorate the back splat of a chair. I've used fans in these traditional ways, but I like to push the envelope, inlaying fans in surprising places, like backsplashes and table aprons. I've also altered the design and construction a bit. Traditionally, fan inlays were created with veneers of contrasting colors (whether shaded, dyed, or of a different species) cut and inset into a shallow mortise one ray at a time. The outer radii of these traditional fans often were scalloped.

My modern approach to making and installing fans is efficient and ensures uniformity. I use thicker stock, with rays cut and assembled in bunches, and fans then sliced off the bundle and glued into a router-cut recess. Each fan has a smooth outer radius. For fun and flair, I add a small ebony dot at the tip. Wood movement is rarely a concern with these small fans, but their orientation should always be face grain—never weak end grain.

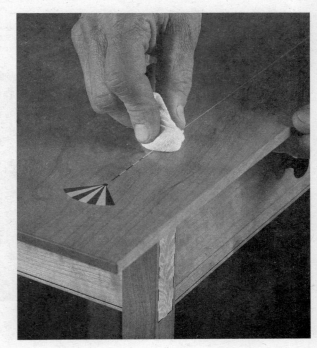

How to Make a Fan Sandwich

When it comes to fans, I like the extreme contrast of white holly and black ebony, because both colors will contrast with most woods. Generally, the most appealing and balanced fan has an odd number of rays, beginning and ending with the dark ebony in lighter-colored woods or with the white holly in darker woods.

Making a fan sandwich sounds simple, but it takes considerable effort to assemble the small wedges accurately. Any slight mismatch of the rays is very noticeable.

Cut rays on the tablesaw—The fans shown here are delicately sized, so you don't need a lot of material. Start by crosscutting 1-in.-thick blanks of ebony and holly about 1⅛ in. long. Blanks that are 4 in. to 6 in. wide should

yield plenty of ray stock for four or more fans, with room to toss any damaged pieces.

Glue each blank to a scrap block the same thickness and length, and about 4 in. or so long (see drawing, facing page). The scrap block will keep your fingers a safe distance from the blade as you cut the rays and will allow you to use as much of the valuable holly and ebony stock as possible.

Stringing Ties Fans Together

Historically, fans were inlaid into corners of doors, drawers, and tabletops and often were connected with stringing. But your fans don't have to be stuck in the corner. They can take a more prominent role in the design.

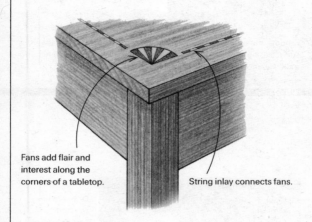

Fans add flair and interest along the corners of a tabletop.

String inlay connects fans.

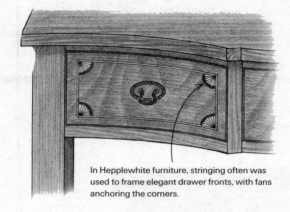

In Hepplewhite furniture, stringing often was used to frame elegant drawer fronts, with fans anchoring the corners.

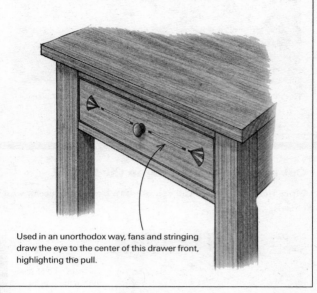

Used in an unorthodox way, fans and stringing draw the eye to the center of this drawer front, highlighting the pull.

Recipe for Fan Sandwiches

Traditionally, fan inlays were made from veneers and inlaid into a shallow mortise one ray at a time. Hack's method is efficient and ensures uniformity. He cuts all the rays at the same time, glues them up into a sandwich, then saws off slices.

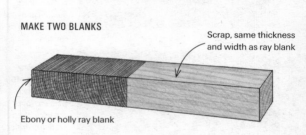

MAKE TWO BLANKS

Scrap, same thickness and width as ray blank

Ebony or holly ray blank

Get the most out of valuable wood. For a better hold on the ebony and holly stock, glue each to a piece of scrap, using a backer to align the pieces.

Slice the rays. Use a thin-kerf blade to reduce waste and a zero-clearance insert to prevent rays from falling into the saw cabinet or getting jammed in the insert slot. For a seven-ray 90° fan, set the miter gauge to just under 6½° and make test cuts in scrap to dial in the setting. Rotate the blank after each cut.

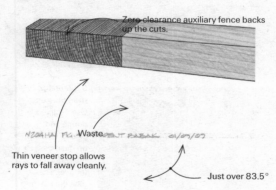

1. FIRST PASS GETS THE ANGLE RIGHT

Zero-clearance auxiliary fence backs up the cuts.

Waste

Thin veneer stop allows rays to fall away cleanly.

Just over 83.5°

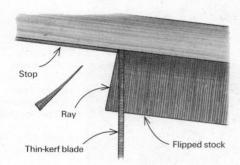

2. ROTATE THE BLANK AFTER EACH CUT

Stop

Ray

Thin-kerf blade

Flipped stock

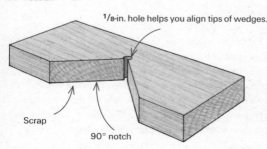

RAY HOLDER

⅛-in. hole helps you align tips of wedges.

Scrap

90° notch

Continued ➜

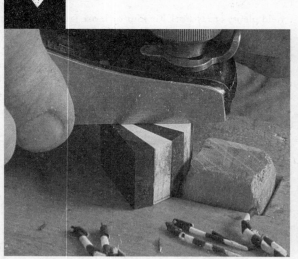

Get rid of the crust. Clean up the sandwich faces using a block plane.

Thin slices, please. Use a dovetail saw to cut the ¹/₈-in.-thick slices. An L-shaped block, tacked to a scrap clamped in a vise, acts as a bench hook to hold the small pieces.

Smooth the outside and make a home for the dot. Fair the curved surface using a file (left) or sandpaper, then use a ¹/₈-in.-dia. file to form a shallow recess in the point of the fan (right).

Cut the Recess and Plug in the Fan

Once the fan is made, you can use it to lay out its recess, which is cut with a router and cleaned up with gouges and chisels.

1. Dot mortise serves two purposes. Lay out the centerline of the fan through its point, and drill a hole for the inlaid dot at the tip of the fan. The hole also becomes a reference point for the rest of the fan layout.

4. Rout a recess. Highlight the scribed lines with a colored pencil, then rout the recess freehand, staying within the lines. Use a ³/₁₆-in.-dia. straight bit with the depth slightly less than the fan thickness.

Dots are easy to make. Chuck a narrow blank of ebony into a drill and use a file to shape the blank into a ¹/₈-in.-dia. rod (left). Slice off a ¹/₈-in.-thick section and glue it into the tip of the fan.

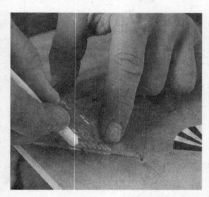

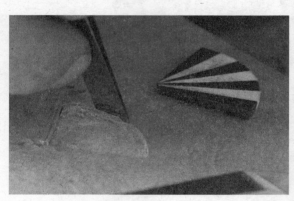

2. Radiate lines outward. Align a drafting triangle with the centerline and the dot hole, and scribe lines to frame the straight edges of the fan.

Plane everything smooth. Use a block plane to level the inlay, then work the entire surface with a smoothing plane and/or scraper.

3. Knife around the fan. Hold the fan firmly. Make the first pass very light, and then bear down a bit more during subsequent passes.

5. Clean up, then glue up. Use a curved gouge and chisels to clean up the recess to the scribed lines (above). Then glue the fan in place (left), using a small scrap block as a caul.

I slice the wedges on the tablesaw. The miter-gauge angle depends on the number of rays you want to cut and on the angle of the fan sides. This fan is 90° and has seven rays, so angle the miter gauge to just under 6 ½°. As you flip the blank, you effectively double the angle, creating wedges just under 13°. For rays of uniform size, tape a thin stop to the auxiliary fence.

Now make a bunch of test pieces to check the overall 90° fan and the stop settings, using stock that's the same dimension as the inlay material. It's critical that the rays end with a knife edge. Any thickness here and the tips will be hard to line up to a single point when gluing. Once the saw is set up correctly, cut the rays, flipping the blank after each pass.

Assemble and slice the fans—The fans are hard to glue up, so I use a notched board to stabilize the rays. Work quickly and carefully, positioning the rays so they come to an even point. Clamping is difficult, but rubbing the rays as you assemble them helps with adhesion so that you usually can just hold the assembly in place with your fingertips for a few minutes.

After letting the assembly cure, clean up the faces of the fan sandwich with a block plane and then use a handsaw to slice off ¹/₈-in.-thick sections. Fair the outer radius with a file or sandpaper.

Now make the shallow recess for the dot at the point of the fan using an ¹/₈-in.-dia. round file. Once that's done, you're ready for installation.

Use the Fan as a Template for its Recess

One advantage of making the fans as complete slices is that you can use them as templates during layout.

Regardless of how the fan will be oriented, you need to draw a centerline through its axis, or point. Drill a 1/8-in.-dia. hole at the point of the fan for the dot inlay. I've tried drilling the hole for the dot after the fan is installed, but it's difficult to drill the small hole into the ends of the rays and background wood without the bit wandering or the wood tearing out. Drilling the hole first also allows you to fit the fan so that it's centered exactly on the dot.

Now draw two lines that meet at the hole at 90°. Hold the fan between those lines and knife around its perimeter. Then rough out the recess with a router.

Clean up to the knifed lines with gouges and chisels and then glue in the fan (I use yellow glue). Now make the dot and glue it in place.

Finishing Tips

Sanding inlays can cause problems, with ebony dust fouling the bright white holly, so my first choice is to plane inlaid surfaces, first with a block plane to bring them flush, then with a smoothing plane to refine the entire surface. If I have any problems with tearout, I resort to a card scraper.

When it comes to finishing, penetrating oil-based topcoats such as varnish, oil-varnish mixes, and straight oils can discolor the white holly as you build up the finish, dulling the contrast you've worked so hard to create. So if you plan to use a penetrating finish, seal the fans first with a thin washcoat of dewaxed shellac. Zinsser Bullseye SealCoat will work.

Better Way to Add Stringing and Banding

by Craig Thibodeau

Whether your tastes run traditional or contemporary, learning to do a veneered tabletop opens up all sorts of design possibilities. For one, you now have access to scores of new wood species and grain patterns, all widely available and affordable. Secondly, you can cut and arrange the veneers into beautiful patterns not possible with solid wood. That's just the beginning. My focus here is bandings and borders. Veneer makes those easier, too.

Master Class

The traditional way to make bandings is to start with a bricklike lamination and slice off layers. Then you inlay them, excavating a channel in solid wood, with issues when you go across the grain. But since my tabletops are fully veneered on a stable substrate using a big vacuum bag, adding beautiful bandings and borders is as easy as cutting out pieces of veneer and taping them to a center field of veneer. After laying up the panel, I add solid-wood edging to protect the veneer and complete the look. Last, I rout a groove along the glueline and inlay the final piece of stringing the traditional way, hiding the glueline and any inconsistencies there. It is a foolproof system.

I also sometimes veneer all the way to the edge of the table, by simply making the bandings wider. I often use crossbanding this way, banding the side of the tabletop with the same veneer for a waterfall effect.

Stringing and banding separate the center field from the edges of the tabletop, and add a dash of both complementary and contrasting color. While you can buy banding in varied patterns, it's just as easy to create your own using small pieces of figured veneer that are too nice to throw away.

A Few Shopmade Helpers

To make all of the bandings in this article, you'll need a freshly sharpened veneer saw (see FineWoodworking.com/extras to learn how I sharpen my saw) and a few simple shopmade devices. First, make a 2- or 3-in.-wide straightedge from MDF to joint edges. Then you'll need a banding-cutting board with a fixed stop that sticks up about 1/4 in. to 1/2 in. The board works in conjunction with a simple cutting guide that matches the width of your desired banding. Both the cutting guide and straightedge need 60- to 120-grit sandpaper stuck to the bottom to stop them from slipping. You'll also need veneer tape. I recommend "water gum" tape from schurchwoodwork.com.

Let's start by making 1/2-in.-wide straight banding of curly sycamore. Cutting any curly veneer along the grain creates interesting stripes across the width. We'll need a 1/2-in.-wide cutting guide.

For bandings, I stack (and tape) two pieces of veneer and cut them at the same time for greater efficiency. But I don't try to cut bandings any longer than 24 in.; it is hard to cut them straight. If I need longer pieces, I join them with a simple scarf cut that hides the seam.

Adding the Stringing and Banding Is Easy

After you have cut and assembled the veneer for the center of the tabletop, usually some sort of bookmatch, be sure all edges are straight, square, and clean.

The inner line of stringing and the shopmade banding go on now, simply stuck down on tape, overlapped at the corners, and mitered with a single cut. For this first line, I tend to use commercial stringing (from originalmarquetry.co.uk). It comes in many widths and colors, and is relatively inexpensive. In this case it is roughly 1/16 in. wide (sold as 1.5 mm), and the same thickness as the commercial veneers I use. The best colors for these thin outlines are black and white. The black is usually dyed, not true ebony. For pure white, holly is best, though maple makes a great off-white stand-in.

Cutting Bandings

INLAY: MAKE IT OR BUY IT
Thibodeau buys his stringing, which is the same thickness as veneer. But he makes his own banding pieces.

Start with a straight edge. After taping a couple of pieces of veneer in a stack, use a veneer saw and an MDF straightedge, with sandpaper stuck to the bottom, to cut one edge straight. Start with a light pass, and then bear down a bit more as you go.

Simple jig. Make a cutting board as shown, plus a hardwood cutting guide the width of your desired bandings. Hold the guide and the veneer firmly against the stop on the cutting board. Cut enough banding to go around your panel, plus a few extra pieces.

Installation Is Easy

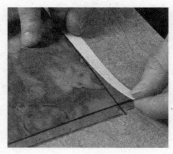
Stick it down. With a strip of overhanging blue tape on the show face, you flip the sheet over and simply stick on the stringing and banding, pulling it tight against the central field, and overlapping it at the corners.

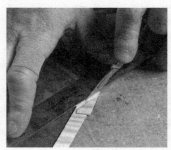
Scarf the banding. Stringing can have butt joints, but where the 2-ft.-long bandings come up short, use an angled cut to hide the joint. Just overlap the pieces, line up the grain, and use a scalpel and steel ruler to cut through both.

Another angle at the corners. Use a similar technique to make perfect miter joints at the corners, cutting both stringing and banding at once. Line up the straightedge carefully with the corners of the overlap.

Tape across the joints. Pull blue tape across the miter joints, and across the all the edges. Stretch and pull the tape as you apply it.

Always burnish. After running long pieces down the joints, burnish down all the tape with a brass-bristled brush for a strong bond.

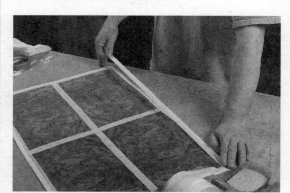
Veneer tape next. Remove the blue tape from the show face, and replace it with 3/4-in. veneer tape. Then throw the sheet under a piece of MDF to stay flat. When it's dry, flip the sheet and remove the blue tape on the glue face.

Continued ➡

Last Piece Goes in After Glue-Up

I use a vacuum press for my veneering, which is wonderfully effective and convenient. The sandwich includes evacuation mesh on top, MDF cauls top and bottom, thin plastic sheeting to keep glue off the cauls, the front and back veneers, and of course, the MDF substrate. Yellow glue works fine.

When the panel is out of the bag, trim the edges right to the edges of the border, and add the wood edging. Now the final piece of stringing goes in, covering the glueline and any gaps.

You can use more commercial stringing here, but installation is much easier if the stringing is a bit thicker and easier to handle. I cut these strips from a solid piece of Gabon ebony, making them a fat 1/16 in. wide by about 1/8 in. tall. Now that I have a drum sander, I just bandsaw my shopmade stringing and sand it to size. But before I had one, I did it as shown in the photos. After routing the tiny 1/16-in.-wide groove and installing the stringing (I use bit No. 5152, stewmac.com), wait 24 hours for the glue to dry, and then sand the entire tabletop smooth. Apply a finish and watch the full beauty emerge.

Sheet Becomes a Panel

In the bag. After laying up the panel (left), you'll need to trim it. To get a first reference edge straight and flush with your banding, you can shim the panel on a crosscut sled (above). Then line up a framing square with that edge, using it to set up a straightedge and router on an adjacent edge. The tablesaw can take over from there.

Different Deal for the Last Piece of Stringing

It is next to impossible to install the last piece of stringing beforehand and then trim the panel precisely flush to it, so Thibodeau installs it after attaching the solid-wood edging to the tabletop, routing a groove right over the glue joint.

Pre-fit the pieces. Mark these at the corner joints (above), using a sanding block or disk sander to make the tiny miters. Thibodeau uses a kids' glue bottle with a narrow tip to inject the glue into the groove, presses in the stringing, and then seats it fully using a small hammer and a wood block (below).

Rout carefully. After the solid edging is sanded flush, rout a 1/16-in.-wide groove that straddles the glue joint. Attach a fence and set the depth at 1/8 in., pivot the router down into the cut, and go slowly so you don't break the tiny bit.

Shopmade stringing this time. To make slightly taller stringing, which is easier to inlay, Thibodeau rips a strip of ebony on the tablesaw, sizing it to fit the groove, and then rips that strip to height on the bandsaw as shown.

Square the corners by hand. Be careful not to rout too far, then finish up the corners with a narrow chisel and scalpel.

Need to fine-tune it? Make a little planing jig like this one, with a low stop, and add pieces of double-stick tape to keep the stringing from bowing as you plane it.

Veneer is the secret. If the central panel is veneered, you can just add the inlay pieces to the edges of the sheet before laying up the panel, with no wood-movement worries.

Crossbanding Isn't Much Harder

Thibodeau likes Macassar ebony for crossbanding, as its striped pattern is eye-catching and hides the seams between the short pieces.

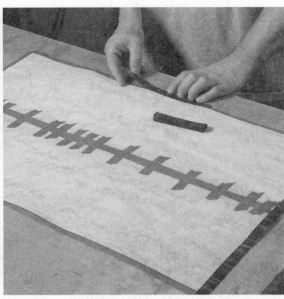

Three good edges. This time you need to cut the two long edges of the stack parallel before trimming one end square. These crosscuts want to tear out at the near end, so make a small reverse cut there before each pass.

Back to the cutting board. Starting at the square end, cut as many strips as you need. As before, make a series of light passes for each cut, with a short reverse cut before each pass.

Installation starts at the center. Install a line of stringing first, as before. Then mark the center points of each edge, and start adding the crossbanding there, working toward the corners and flipping each opposite piece as you go for a balanced look.

Checkered Banding Catches the Eye

Any very dark and light colors work well for this type of banding, in this case maple and wenge.

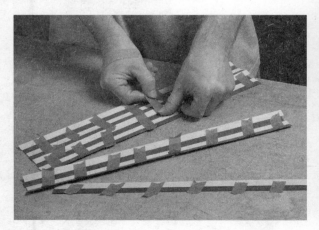

Start with strips. Cut six strips of each color, and join them in pairs first by pulling blue tape across the seams. Then assemble the pairs into a full sheet, before putting a strip of tape along every seam.

Crosscut your bandings. After squaring one end of the sheet, use the banding jig again. Cut tape-side-up, and make more than enough strips for the job.

Start at the corners this time. Overlap dark squares at the corners, then simply remove one of them. To get the rest of the banding to fit, trim a bit off a square or two near the center. No one will notice.

Continued ➡

Fixes for Common Veneering Problems

By Stuart Lipp

No matter how careful you are when working with veneer, you'll need to make the occasional repair. Veneers get chipped, scratched, dented, or blistered, and to be good at veneering, you also must be good at veneer repair. Not to worry. Just ask yourself the philosophical question: If you execute an invisible repair, did the damage ever really occur?

While my focus is on the construction process, the methods described here also can be applied to restoration, and some even work on solid wood. Keep in mind that existing glue and finish (topics I won't address here) are big factors in restoration work. Also, when building a piece, it's important to catch repairs early in the process; otherwise, construction could get in the way, such as with solid-wood edging or a frame around a panel.

Having an arsenal of remedies will get you through even the toughest of repairs, and experience will help you match the appropriate repair to the damage. I work with thin commercial veneers, but the same techniques apply to thicker, shopmade veneer.

Small Repairs Require a Judgment Call

The first thing to do with damaged veneer is judge whether a repair is necessary. Don't jump into a full-blown repair if you don't have to. A small chip or dent on the edge of a piece often disappears when you break the edges, or you can be a little heavy-handed on that spot to ensure that it does. And there is nothing wrong with using putty once in a while to fill a tiny chip, crack, or split. It requires skill to color the putty with water-soluble aniline dye powders to match the wood perfectly. This fix should be used rarely and when the damage is very small, but it can save you from cutting into the veneer when it isn't necessary.

Sometimes, to make a good repair you must first make the damage worse. A chip, loose edge, or split can be too small to repair successfully. If you try, you'll most likely fail, causing a bigger mess. The only option is to "cut back," or extend the damage into the surrounding veneer because it provides the ideal situation for a successful repair because it provides enough space on the substrate to get good adhesion and allows you to control the shape of the patch.

Choose the Right Glue

When choosing glue for a repair, try to match the veneer color as closely as you can. This way, if glue bleeds through the pores it will be less visible. For example, use white glue on maple, a tight-grained wood that is not usually stained. However, rosewood is a dark wood with open pores; white glue would bleed through and ruin it during finishing. Choose something dark instead, like urea formaldehyde glue. Also, any water-based glue can be colored with water-soluble aniline dye powders to match the wood.

Your goal should always be to minimize the visibility of the repair. You don't want to accentuate it with gluelines or glue in the pores. Keep everything as clean as possible, since even the dirt from your fingers can work into white glue and leave a dirty black line.

Slice Blisters to Work In Glue

Blisters are small pockets where the veneer wasn't glued properly to the substrate. A veneer blister is contained; it doesn't have an opening that you can see or reach. The best way to check the size of a blister is to tap all around it with your fingernail. You've located it when you hear a high popping sound. I pencil around the perimeter of the blister so I know where to work.

Once you've located the edges of the blister, the next step is to cut thin slits in it. The number of slits you need will depend on the size of the blister (as a benchmark, I usually cut one slit down the center of a 1-in.-wide blister). Make the slit the same length as the blister to provide complete access for glue.

I use an Exacto knife, a small art spatula, and a bottle of glue that has a tiny opening. Once you are finished gluing, get good pressure on the blister as fast as you can. Whether you use clamps or weights, remember to use a hard caul so the blister glues down smooth and flat.

Fill In Dents

Dented veneer can be tough to repair. Because commercial veneer is thin, scraping and sanding aren't viable options. Filling it with putty is, but the color usually doesn't match, and unless you are very good at touch-ups it will stick out. Fill the dent with glue and spread some about $\frac{1}{16}$ in. beyond the perimeter of the dent. Lay a new piece of veneer over the glue-filled dent, put a rubber pad (available from www.mcmaster.com, or use a piece of old inner tube) and a caul over that, and apply pressure with a clamp. You want a fair amount of pressure to force the veneer into the dent, but not so much that you make a larger dent. Once everything is dry, it's easy to clean up the squeeze-out with a chisel and sandpaper.

Break Veneer to Match a Splinter Pattern

Splinters are chipouts that occur at the end grain of veneer. If you are lucky, the splinters will be connected but just folded up. In that case, just apply some glue to the bottoms of the splinters and clamp them back in place.

But if the splinters are lost and you can't find them after scouring your shop floor, take a matching piece of veneer and break it across its long grain to replicate the missing splinters. This may take a few breaks. To glue a splinter into place, slide it into the void so that it not only glues down to the substrate but also edge-glues to the veneer. When sliding the splinter into the void, use a bit of pressure so that it really smashes into the surrounding veneer, almost to the point of sliding under it. This will eliminate the glueline. Clamp with a nonstick caul to put pressure on the repair.

Cut a Tombstone Over the Damage

Another great repair trick I use is the "tombstone fix." I like this technique because it is quick, controlled, and very effective when the damage is relatively small, on the top of a workpiece, and close to the end. A light-duty router and a straight bit are two great tools to use when repairing veneer this way. The bearing on the router bit gives you complete control over what you remove, and the depth of the cut is easy to set to the veneer thickness.

Set up a $\frac{3}{4}$-in.-thick plywood fence running in the direction of the grain; most of it should sit on the workpiece, with just 1 in. hanging off the end. Clamp it in place, so that a $\frac{1}{2}$-in. straight router bit, with a top guide bearing, will run over the damage as the router base runs along the fence. Set the bit depth to the veneer's thickness and cut away the damaged area. Next, find a piece of veneer that matches the grain and color and cut it to $\frac{1}{2}$ in. wide. Check to make sure it fits well; slightly too wide is good because you can smash it in when gluing. Cut the end of the veneer piece into a half-round to match the cutout. If you have a sharp $\frac{1}{2}$-in. gouge (carving or turning), this will be easy. Test the fit of the piece. To glue, push the piece down and in to the cutout so that the seam disappears.

Make a Curved Template to Cut Veneer

What if damage occurs along one of the long-grain edges: for example, a chip or a cross-grain scratch? The dilemma is how to begin and finish the repair. Angular lines will show, especially on a repair like this where they would run across the grain.

In this situation, the best repair looks something like a section of a circle—tapering in from the edge, hitting its apex right at the damage (make sure you just clear it), and then tapering back to the edge. The patch size will depend on the position and size of the damage. You should also try to match it with the grain.

The first step is to cut out the shape you want from a piece of $\frac{3}{4}$-in. plywood and sand it smooth. Clamp the plywood template in place and cut out the damage. Now cut a piece of mating veneer to match and fill that void. Glue the piece in, and clamp it down with a hard block. This will give you a seamless repair.

Cut Away an Entire Strip

When damage is extensive and is not close to an end or an edge, you may have to replace a strip of veneer that spans the length of the piece. Again, you'll need a router and a straight bit. My method allows you to match the cutout section precisely.

First cut a piece of plywood to a width that covers the damage and a length that overhangs the workpiece by an inch on each side. This piece represents the strip that you will rout out and the patch. Once you have it exactly where you want it, clamp it in place from each end.

Cut two more pieces of plywood, about 4 in. wide and as long as the first piece. Clamp one to each side of the center strip, keeping the clamps back far enough so that they don't interfere with the router. With a hammer, tap in these outer pieces so they tightly butt up next to the middle strip, and then tighten the clamps. Next, unclamp the inner strip and gently tap it out. That leaves you with a gap that will allow you to cut a perfectly straight and parallel strip out of the veneer. When you are finished routing, remove the clamps and plywood from the panel.

Selecting a new strip of veneer to glue into place is easy if you have the next sequential piece in the flitch. If not, choose something as close to the original as you can. Lay the center template over the veneer and clamp it. Cut the veneer by going around the plywood with a single-bevel knife, banking the flat side of the knife against the plywood. This creates a mating piece to glue into the routed area. Lay the piece into place, sliding it where it looks best and taping down one side. Once glue is applied, quickly flip the veneer down. Make sure the loose edge is in place and tape it down. Clamp a 2-in.-wide, nonstick hard caul over this repair, making sure that the caul covers the two seams.

Finishing and Refinishing

FINISHING TOOLS AND FUNDAMENTALS

Why Finish Wood?

by Mark Schofield

Finishing experts tell you how to apply a finish but they never explain *why* you should finish wood. Why not leave a piece in its just-planed state showing the wood's natural beauty? Is it really necessary to go to all that trouble coating your piece with some combination of oil, resin, or plastic?

In fact, there are many important reasons for applying a finish—some aesthetic and some practical. A finish can reduce seasonal movement and the resulting stresses on joinery. It also makes a surface more impact-resistant and protects wood from everyday use, whether the piece is a rarely handled picture frame, a kitchen table, or an outside chair. Also, the right combination of dyes, stains, and clear finishes can turn humdrum wood into an eye-catching piece.

And finally, there *are* some occasions when no finish really is a valid option.

Some Finishes Slow Wood Movement

When it comes to protecting a piece of furniture from the damage that can be caused by wood movement, applying a finish is no substitute for careful construction.

Still, certain finishes will reduce wood's tendency to absorb and release moisture. This in turn will slow seasonal expansion and contraction, reducing stresses that can eventually damage joinery and helping to minimize problems like door panels that rattle in winter or drawers that stick in summer.

Some finishes are better at this than others. No clear finish can match paint at controlling moisture, even over a couple of weeks. Pure oil finishes in particular are ineffective. Spar varnish gives some protection, but the standouts among clear finishes are shellac and polyurethane.

If you do apply an effective moisture-excluding finish, be sure to treat all surfaces equally. Otherwise, each side of the surface will absorb and release moisture at a different rate, causing the boards to cup.

Finished Wood Stays Cleaner

No piece stays looking like the day it was made. The surface gets a slightly rough feeling, sunlight oxidizes the surface cells, and hands leave oil and dirt. A clear finish can give wood varying degrees of protection against environmental damage as well as everyday wear and tear.

The need for protection varies by the intended location and use of the piece. If you want the look of natural wood, a rarely handled piece such as a picture frame or an ornamental turning probably only needs a single coat of finish followed by a coat of wax. That's enough to allow dust to be wiped off and not into the grain.

Tabletops likely to come into contact with food and drink need a finish that can protect the wood. Unfinished, scrubbed-pine tables were fine for the nobles who employed scullery maids, but if you're cleaning up after yourself, you'll find that traces of red wine and ketchup are removed far more easily from a durable film finish such as varnish or polyurethane.

Continued →

No Finish is Waterproof

If you live where there are wide humidity swings between winter and summer, you should weigh moisture control more heavily in choosing a finish. Use this chart to compare the moisture-repelling properties of common finishes. Each finish was applied in three coats on samples of clear Ponderosa pine. The test pieces—along with unfinished control samples—were then kept in a controlled environment of 80°F and 90% humidity to simulate real-world humidity changes. Afterward, each was weighed and compared against its unfinished control piece to gauge relative water gain.

PERCENTAGE OF MOISTURE REPELLED

Finish	1 day	7 days	14 days
Paste wax	17	0	0
Linseed oil	18	2	0
Tung oil	52	6	2
Nitrocellulose lacquer	79	37	19
Spar varnish	87	53	30
Shellac	91	64	42
Oil-based polyurethane	90	64	44
Oil-based paint	97	86	80

Penetrating finishes offer less protection, but minor damage can be repaired more easily by sanding and then wiping on another coat of finish. This easily repairable finish is suitable for surfaces that won't be subject to frequent damage by liquids. The "easily" is relative when compared to repairing a film finish: It is still quite a lot of work to sand out the damage and apply new finish to the damaged area and possibly the whole immediate surface, so you don't want to do this once a month to a kitchen table. Almost any other piece, including the tops of occasional tables (especially in an adults-only house), will be fine with a penetrating finish.

Enhance Wood's Beauty

Yes, beauty is in the eye of the beholder, but even those who hate finishing must have had that moment of pleasure when the first coat of finish lights up the wood. The impact is greatest with highly figured wood—burls, crotches, blister, and ribbon stripe. Finish increases the light/dark contrast and exaggerates the shimmer, or chatoyance.

Applying a finish also increases the contrast between light and dark woods, whether it is walnut drawer pulls, wenge trim, or the mahogany background to holly stringing.

Don't confine yourself to clear coats: Dyes can really put the tiger in tiger maple, while bright dyes help blister and quilt-figured maple to jump out.

Finishing Outdoor Furniture

Whether to finish an outside piece is rather like deciding whether to dye your hair. You can either accept going gray, or you can apply dye/finish on a regular basis. In both cases, make the choice and then stick with it; neither gray roots nor an outdoor piece with peeling finish are attractive.

A finished outdoor piece is much easier to keep clean and dry. After a day of rain, you can wipe it with a cloth or a towel and you have a surface ready for those white trousers or dresses. An unfinished piece will stay damp for hours or even days after a good soaking and will grow lichen, moss, etc.

Outdoor finishes not only need to withstand the elements but also must allow for far more wood movement

than interior finishes. The answer is to use a durable yet flexible finish. Apply many layers of a marine varnish, particularly on end grain. Immediately repair any damage before water can get under the finish, and when the surface loses its shine, apply another coat. If you wait until the finish has begun to crack and peel, the only solution is to go back to bare wood and begin again.

For those determined not to apply a finish, a durable outdoor wood such as teak, white oak, or cedar will give you years of good service before weathering starts to weaken it. You can also avoid finishing some dense, oily tropical hardwoods such as cocobolo or rosewood. Sand them to a high grit and then buff them (on a buffing wheel for small objects) and they'll retain a medium luster.

Outdoors: To finish or not?

Two ways to survive the great outdoors. To finish his outdoor furniture, Sean Clarke applies multiple layers of epoxy sealer and marine varnish. Or you could take Hank Gilpin's approach and apply no finish at all.

The Fundamentals of Surface Prep and Finish Types

by Mark Schofield

One reason many woodworkers find finishing difficult may be because the language is so confusing. If your finish is bleeding, does it need time to cure? If it is blushing, should you be distressed (or perhaps you should be fuming)? Do you call the mob if you need a finish rubbed out?

What follows is a guide to the language of finishing that will explain some of the more common but cryptic words and phrases. We'll start by covering surface preparation and the range of finishes available. Then we'll discuss different methods of applying and polishing a finish.

Surface Prep: The Foundation of Finishing

Surface preparation is the process of using handplanes, scrapers, and sandpaper (powered by machine or hand) to remove surface blemishes left by machines. A handplane and card scraper is the fastest method; sandpaper is typically the last step. Almost all sandpaper now uses the European FEPA scale (a metric system for measuring the coarseness of the abrasive granules), denoted by a P before the number. The older CAMI scale is now mostly confined to grits higher than 600 in wet-or-dry paper used for sanding finishes.

Most random-orbit sanding disks (and some rolls of abrasive) come with a **hook-and-loop** backing (aka Velcro) that can be pricey but lets you remove and reuse the disks. **Sanding swirls** and **pigtails** are visible scratches caused by pressing down too hard on a random-orbit sander. The sander's weight alone is enough to let the disk do its job and yet spin randomly, leaving an evenly distributed scratch pattern.

For a penetrating oil finish, you should sand up to P220-grit on most hardwoods, but on cherry or other woods that tend to absorb oil unevenly, I would go to P320- or even P400-grit to burnish the surface. For a thicker film finish, you can stop at P180-grit, but make sure the surface is flat and smooth. Check your progress with a spotlight or desk light just above the surface of the wood, shining across it. This is known as a **raking light**.

Finish sanding using a **sanding block**. This can be either solid cork, or wood faced with 1/8-in.-thick cork or rubber sheet (a cork floor tile works well). If you are applying a water-based dye or a waterborne clear finish to the bare wood, wet the wood with a damp cloth to **raise the grain**, causing the surface fibers to swell. Let the surface dry, and then hand-sand. This prevents the dye or clear finish from raising the grain and leaving a rough surface.

While you are hand-sanding, you'll want to **break the edges** of the piece. This involves very slightly rounding or chamfering the sharp corners. This makes the edge feel better to the touch, helps resist dents, and is more forgiving under a film finish. Breaking the edge lets the finish flow around the corner, giving the whole surface an even coat.

When you've finished sanding, remove the dust with a vacuum cleaner, blow out any remaining dust in the wood's pores with compressed air, and then wipe the surface with a cloth dampened with denatured alcohol or with a **tack cloth**. This is a cheesecloth impregnated with a kind of sticky varnish to pick up any fine dust remaining on the surface. Unfold the cloth, then lightly bundle it and wipe the surface, applying minimal pressure. Pressing down hard can leave sticky residue on the surface that may interfere with waterborne finishes.

Oil-Based Finishes

Oil and oil-based clear finishes are the finishes that most people use, but their complexity and range of variations also make them the most complicated to understand.

The simplest are **pure oil finishes,** which contain no resins or solvents. These are applied thinly and rubbed into the wood, eventually revealing any luster or **chatoyance** deep in the wood. Over time, pure oil finishes start to look dull but are easily cleaned and renewed.

The most common pure oil finish is **boiled linseed oil,** which is derived from the seeds of the flax plant. It is not actually boiled but has chemicals known as **metallic driers** added to speed up the absorption of oxygen, which is how an oil finish cures. **Raw linseed oil** contains no driers, will take far longer to dry, and will not cure as hard as boiled linseed oil.

Like boiled linseed oil, **pure tung oil** is another **drying oil,** meaning that it will dry to a hard finish and will not remain greasy or sticky.

The range of **oil-based finishes** is immense, but they all share three components. The first is a **binder,** also known as a resin, which when dry forms a film attached to the wood's surface. Binders in oil-based finishes include **acrylic, phenolic, alkyd,** and **urethane.** The second component is a **carrier** to help the binder flow out. The most common are linseed, tung, and soybean oils. Finally, you need a **thinner** (a solvent) to achieve a workable viscosity. Commercial finishes use mostly **mineral spirits,** but shopmade oil-based finishes can be made with some **naphtha** for faster drying, or **turpentine** for slower drying (and a nicer smell).

Varying the ratio of these three components creates different finishes. You'll sometimes hear a finish described as **short oil** or **long oil** as if it were a commodities trader. A short-oil finish will have a higher percentage of binder and will form highly protective indoor finishes such as varnish or polyurethane. Thinned with solvent, it becomes a **wiping varnish,** meaning it can be applied with a clean cotton cloth. A long-oil varnish, also known as **spar varnish,** has more oil to give it a more elastic consistency that can cope with the increased wood movement outdoors. A higher-quality spar varnish is a **marine-grade varnish,** which should contain **ultra-violet absorbers** or **inhibitors** to slow damage to the finish from sunlight. A diluted long-oil finish is known as **Danish oil.** It is poured on the surface and allowed to penetrate the wood, and then the surplus is wiped off.

Gel varnish, gel polyurethane, or simply **gel finish** are all oil-based finishes with a thickening agent. This makes them much less messy to wipe on and off.

The Many Types of Shellac

Derived from the protective casing of a type of insect larvae in southern Asia, this ancient finish has been refined into various grades and sold in flake or granule form. Among the least refined is **seedlac,** a reddish-orange granule mostly used in matching antique finishes.

Buttonlac comes in small coin-sized disks. Like

seedlac, it contains about 5% wax, giving it a cloudy appearance. This makes it good for an antique look but less durable than grades of shellac that have been dewaxed. **Dewaxed** grades of shellac come in flakes and are described by their color, from a dark **garnet** through **ruby, orange,** and **lemon** to a very pale **blond.**

Shellac is an evaporative finish, where one coat melts into the prior one. Its viscosity is measured by its **cut.** When you dissolve 3 lb. of dry shellac in 1 gal. of **denatured alcohol** (ethanol with some methanol added to make it non-drinkable), you get a 3-lb. cut. To thin this to a more easily brushed 2-lb. cut, add one part alcohol to two parts liquid shellac by volume.

Solvent-Based Lacquer

Lacquer is another evaporative finish. **Lacquer thinner** is made from several solvents blended in different combinations. Faster-evaporating thinner is used when spraying lacquer, but slower blends allow you to brush this finish.

The most commonly sprayed lacquer outside commercial operations is **nitrocellulose lacquer,** made from cotton cellulose, nitric acid, and other acids. It dries fast and offers great clarity and depth, but its high solvent content is highly air polluting. It also has a strong yellow color, which increases as the finish ages. For a non-yellowing lacquer, go with **CAB-acrylic lacquer,** which is made with clear acrylic resin.

Waterborne Finishes

Often incorrectly called water-based finishes (a true water-based finish would dissolve in water), **waterborne finishes** consist of acrylic and polyurethane resins mixed with glycol ether solvent and water. As the water evaporates, the solvent makes the resins sticky so that they come together in a continuous film, the definition of a **coalescing finish.**

Waterborne finishes have names like lacquer, polyurethane, and varnish, but are nothing like their solvent-based namesakes. Instead they all have a white, milky appearance in the can, they dry almost colorless, and they clean up with water.

The Fundamentals of Application and Polishing

by Mark Scholfield

Often there are bewildering terms that woodworkers and finishers use to describe the task of preparing a surface for finishing, and for the finishes they use. As it happens, there are more linguistic land mines when describing how to apply a finish and how to give the surface a final polish. Understanding these terms will make you a better finisher, helping you understand your problems—and the solutions given by experts, too.

The Right Rag for a Wipe-On Finish

Wiping on a finish is a relatively simple process, but it's not without pitfalls. I wish I had a dollar for every finishing article I've read that suggests using a lint-free cotton cloth. Many cotton items from socks to underwear contain **lint**—residual flecks of fiber that gradually come loose and disappear after multiple washings. That's why an old, much-washed T-shirt makes a great application tool.

To check a cloth for lint, use it to dry a wine glass or clean a mirror with glass cleaner. Any lint will show up on the glass and will mar your project if you use a linty cloth to apply a finish.

Aside from lint marring a wiped-on finish, you may also encounter a problem known as **bleeding.** This occurs with oil finishes on open-pored woods such as oak when excess oil oozes from the pores long after you've wiped the

surface dry. If you don't repeatedly wipe the surface, these droplets will dry into small, shiny dots that you'll have to sand off.

One important wipe-on finishing technique is known as **French polishing,** in which a **rubber** (a pad made from several layers of cotton cloth) is used to apply the multiple thin layers of shellac that make up this classic finish.

Brush Up Your Language Skills

All brushes have **filaments**—the individual strands, natural or synthetic, that make up the body of the brush. Only a few, though, have **bristles,** a type of natural filament made from animal fiber. These are typically made from hog bristle, also known as China bristle because that is where the material comes from. Other fibers used in **natural-filament** brushes include ox hair and badger hair. All work well for oil-based finishes, shellac, or lacquer. The natural resilience of the fibers allows them to hold a lot of finish and distribute it evenly. Avoid using natural-filament brushes for waterborne finishes, however, because the filaments will absorb water and lose their resilience.

To apply waterborne finishes, use a brush with man-made filaments or **synthetic bristles**. These are mostly made from nylon or polyester. A particularly fine-strand filament is called **Taklon**; these types of brushes are great for applying a thin topcoat that leaves almost no brush marks. Synthetic-bristle brushes can also be used for other finishes and many consider them almost as good as top-of-the-line natural-filament brushes.

Natural or synthetic, look for filaments that are split and frayed at the ends. A brush with this characteristic, known as **flagging,** leaves fewer brush marks. For the same reason, look for a **chisel-ended** brush, where the filaments form a V at the end rather than being flat.

The metal that encloses the base of the filaments is known as the **ferrule.** On any brush you intend to keep, the ferrule should be made of brass or stainless steel to avoid rust that eventually can contaminate the finish.

Learn What to Say Before You Spray

Spraying may leave a great finish, but learning all the terms makes it hard to get started. There are three areas you need to know about. The first is the source of compressed air for the spray gun, either a **turbine** (a self-contained unit with a built-in blower) or an air compressor. Both systems are defined as **HVLP** (high volume, low pressure). They use low air pressure to **atomize** the finish (turn it into tiny particles), so more of the finish stays on the workpiece instead of bouncing off and ending up as **overspray.**

The last group of spraying terms has to do with the quality of the finish. Spraying is meant to speed up the finishing process, so you are aiming for an **off-the-gun** finish, one that needs no further work. Before you reach that nirvana, you will probably experience some problems. One of the most common is known as **orange peel,** a bumpy surface caused by too heavy a film or poor atomization of the finish. To fix it, you can cut back the supply of fluid and either increase the air pressure to the spray gun or reduce the viscosity of the finish.

Another problem when spraying fast-drying finishes such as lacquer or shellac on very humid days is **blushing.** This happens when water vapor gets trapped in the film of finish and creates a whitish haze. The solution is to add a blend of solvents known as a retarder to the finish to lengthen the drying time. A less-common problem is **fisheye,** small craters often caused by silicone contamination from old furniture polish or shop lubricants on the wood's surface.

Finishing the Finish

Unless you are an expert sprayer, with any kind of built-up film finish you will probably need to work on the last coat after it has fully cured. There may well be small bits of dust known as **nibs** stuck in the finish; the surface may be marred by brush marks or perhaps small sags and runs on

vertical surfaces. Or, you may not want a glossy appearance. The solution to all these problems is to rub out the finish using a variety of methods and fine abrasives.

The shine on the surface is referred to as **sheen,** and is a measure of the amount of light it reflects. A **high-gloss** sheen, sometimes called a **piano finish**, requires careful leveling and polishing of the topcoat. A less formal **low-luster** finish is easier to achieve.

Any high-gloss finish must be perfectly flat, so the first step is to level it by **wet-sanding** with wet-or-dry sandpaper lubricated with water and a tiny amount of dish soap. With some finishes, you'll want to lightly "**scuff sand**" between coats to level the surface. If you sand through the topcoat of a finish like varnish where each coat doesn't melt into the previous one, you will create a **witness line.** The only way to cover up this ragged edge of finish is to apply another coat or two and start leveling again.

Final polishing of a high-gloss finish used to be done with **pumice,** a finely ground lava, lubricated with mineral oil, followed by **rottenstone,** a kind of limestone. These days it is much easier to use polishing compounds and liquids formulated for polishing car bodies.

For a lower-sheen satin finish, rub the surface with 0000 (pronounced "4 ought") **steel wool** or a 4,000-grit **Abralon** pad. This foam-backed abrasive disk works well on flat and curved surfaces. After that you can apply some furniture polish or paste wax and rub or buff it out with a lint-free cloth, which gets us back to where we started.

The Shelf Life of Finishes

by Jeff Jewitt

Few things are more annoying than opening a quart of varnish you bought last year, only to find the remaining two-thirds has solidified into a gel. It's an expensive reminder that tools may last a lifetime, but finishes don't.

All finishes have a shelf life, which is the amount of time that a product remains usable. I'll show you how to maximize the shelf life of finishing materials, and more importantly, how to tell when they've gone to the dark side.

Buy It Fresh and Date It

I'm as cheap as anybody, but when it comes to finishes, "buy more, save more" isn't a good strategy. Try to anticipate how much finish you'll use over the next year and don't buy more than that. Some manufacturers publish shelf-life figures and date products clearly, but many don't.

▶ TIP   **Always Date Your Finish**

On the container, write the date that you dissolved the shellac, or mixed your own wiping varnish. After six months, test the finish before use, even if it looks fine. Also, label brand-new finish with the purchase date, or the date provided by the manufacturer.

Continued ➔

Never buy cans with rusty lids, the ones you often see "on sale"—the condition of the can indicates poor storage or old age. Try to buy finishes like you buy milk: Look for a manufacturing date. If you don't understand the dating code, ask a clerk for help. If there is no date, write the date of purchase on the can. Label all your finishes, including those you've mixed yourself.

Store finish in a cool place, between 55°F and 70°F. Chemical reactions accelerate as the temperature rises, and almost all processes that cause finish to go bad involve chemical reactions. A cool basement is better than a hot garage. Most finishes are OK if stored below 55°, with the exception of waterborne. If you work in a cold shop, store your waterborne finishes in the house, and never let them freeze. Bring all finishes up to 55° to 70° before you use them. Also, keep the lid tight. If necessary, transfer the product to a container with a tighter lid.

Keep Oxygen Out of Oil-Based Finishes

Any finish based on a drying oil will harden when exposed to oxygen. These include tung and linseed oils, so-called Danish oils, and oil-based varnishes and polyurethanes. If you're not careful when storing these products, oxygen will cause them to harden prematurely.

When a can is full, there's no room for oxygen. But as you use the finish, you create "head space" as the can fills with air. Exposed to oxygen, the finish will gradually skin over, or the whole liquid may start to gel.

Kept in tightly sealed containers with minimal head space, raw or boiled linseed oil and tung oil can last five or more years. It might thicken with age, but if it isn't cloudy and gummy, it should be usable. Danish oil-type products are mostly oil and solvent. They may thicken, but are usable as long as they are clear and liquid.

On the other hand, when air gets into cans of oil-based varnish and polyurethane, one of two things will happen. In some products, a skin will form. If you can break the skin and get at the liquid, it's generally usable. But, in tung-oil-based varnishes like Waterlox, air can gel the entire contents, rendering them unusable.

To minimize exposure to oxygen, transfer finish to smaller containers as you use it (I use glass Mason and baby food jars). Or, use a product like Bloxygen, which replaces the air with a heavier gas. To test the finish, pour it through a medium mesh strainer (the cone-shaped type available at hardware and paint stores). If it strains, it's good.

Even Flakes Have a Shelf Life

When you dissolve dry shellac flakes in alcohol, the shelf-life clock starts ticking faster. This is due to esterification, a gradual chemical reaction between alcohols and organic acids (shellac is made up of organic acids). The reaction produces chemicals called esters, which are softer and tackier than the normally hard shellac resin. They are also more prone to water-spotting.

Less-refined shellac grades like button, seedlac, and waxy grades will esterify at a much slower rate and may last over a year once dissolved. Dewaxed, bleached grades such as super blond should be used within six months to a year, depending on the "cut," or the ratio of flakes to alcohol. That goes for all mixed shellac: the more alcohol, the shorter the shelf life.

To test whether dissolved shellac is still viable, pour a drop onto an impermeable surface such as glass or laminate. If it's good, it will dry enough to be tack-free (your finger won't stick to it) within an hour.

Dry flakes also have a shelf life. Bleached and dewaxed flakes are the most prone to going bad, while unrefined waxy grades can last for years. In general, try to use flakes within a year after purchase.

There are a couple of myths about prolonging the shelf life of shellac. Some folks say that old shellac can be forced to dissolve by grinding it. Not true. Bad shellac is bad regardless of the size of the flakes.

The second myth is that vacuum-sealing shellac flakes makes them last longer. In fact, dry shellac reacts with itself over time, slowly becoming insoluble in alcohol. Heat accelerates the reaction, but oxygen has no effect. Probably, this myth persists because most folks vacuum-seal flakes and then refrigerate them, which will prolong their shelf life.

Keeping Oxygen Out

Oil-based finishes start to harden when exposed to oxygen, so keep them in an airtight container. To maintain a good seal, remove any dried finish from the lid and rim, and wipe down the rim after each use.

CLEAN THE RIM

Dig it out. To create a good seal with the lid, dig out any dried finish that has collected in the rim.

KEEP THE LID TIGHT

Clean it. If the inside of a lid has become encrusted with finish and won't fully screw on, soak it in lacquer thinner and then scrub it with steel wool.

The self-draining trick. Use a nail to punch four or five holes in the rim of a standard container. When finish gets into the rim, it will drip back into the can.

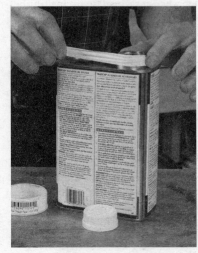

Non-stick finish. Wrap a screw top with Teflon plumber's tape. Finish won't stick to it, you'll get a much better seal, and the lid will screw on and off more easily.

Waterborne Finishes Have Different Problems

It's hard to generalize shelf life and storage needs for waterborne finishes because there are so many types. In general, I try to use them within a year, two at the most. Keep cans tightly sealed in a cool, dry place, and don't let them freeze. Bad waterborne finish has a cheesy, curdled consistency, or it separates like oil and water, even after shaking. The additives in waterborne finishes can deactivate over time, causing them to "fisheye" or become foamy after they're applied. If a product is more than a year old, run it through a mesh filter and test it on a sample board before you use it. (If in doubt, throw it out.)

Head space doesn't cause problems with most waterborne finishes, but dried finish around the lid seal does. Again, transfer unused finish to a smaller container (glass or plastic) with a tight-fitting lid.

Oil-Based Basics

Oil-based finishes can last indefinitely, but only if you keep oxygen away.

Test

Good under the skin. If the finish only has a thin skin on it, the liquid underneath should still be usable. Pour it through a strainer into a new container.

Too far gone. If the finish has started to gel, or if you create lots of small flakes trying to break through the skin, it is probably not worth using.

Prevent

Fill to the brim. Fill a smaller jar with finish from a partially used can. This will prolong the life of the leftover finish by minimizing its contact with oxygen.

Or replace the air. After using some of the contents, spray inert gas into the container to replace the air and prevent the remaining finish from hardening.

■ MYTH

Storing Upside Down Prolongs Shelf Life

Storing a half-empty can upside down does nothing to displace the air and will not prolong the life of the contents.

Long Live Lacquer

One of the few products with a long shelf life is plain old solvent-based furniture lacquer, also known as nitrocellulose lacquer. Because there are no reactive components in the resin, it should store for many years if you keep it close to the 55°F to 70°F range.

Oxygen has no effect on lacquer. It may thicken if the solvent evaporates, but just add lacquer thinner and keep the lid tight. I've seen lacquers yellow in the can over time, but this generally doesn't affect appearance.

Stains and Dyes Last Long

Pigment stains are forgiving when it comes to shelf life and storage. They should store just fine for years. (Oil-based gel stains are an exception; treat them like other oil-based finishes.) One caution: Don't let waterborne stains freeze, or they'll become "cheesy" or curdled.

Concentrated liquid or powdered dyes have a virtually infinite shelf life. Try to use mixed dyes within a year, but as long as you store them in a metal-free container to avoid rust, they can last much longer. Always test older pigments and dyes on a scrap, to confirm the color hasn't changed.

PRODUCT	SHELF LIFE BEFORE OPENING	SHELF LIFE AFTER OPENING	BRAND NAMES	COMMENTS	UNUSABLE WHEN
Linseed oil (boiled and raw)	Indefinite	Indefinite	Kleen Strip, Crown, Sunnyside	Can be thinned with mineral spirits if necessary.	Will not strain, is thick and jelly-like
Tung oil	Indefinite	Indefinite	Hopes, Master Blend, Rockler, Woodcraft	Can be thinned with mineral spirits if necessary.	Will not strain, is thick and jelly-like
Danish oil, oil and varnish blends	Indefinite	Indefinite if properly stored	Watco, Deft, General Finishes	Pour into smaller containers or use Bloxygen.	Hardened or jelly-like
Tung-oil-based varnish	Indefinite	Indefinite in ideal conditions; typically 3-4 years	Waterlox and some spar varnishes	Shortest shelf life once opened. Pour into smaller containers or use Bloxygen.	Jelly-like consistency
Alkyd varnishes	Indefinite	Indefinite if properly stored	Pratt & Lambert, 38 Clear Varnish, Old Masters Super Varnish	Forms skin after prolonged oxygen exposure, but liquid underneath is generally usable.	Hardened or jelly-like
Oil-based polyurethane	Indefinite	Indefinite if properly stored	Minwax, Deft, Varathane, Cabot, Behlen	Forms skin after prolonged oxygen exposure, but liquid underneath is generally usable.	Hardened or jelly-like

PRODUCT	SHELF LIFE BEFORE OPENING	SHELF LIFE AFTER OPENING	BRAND NAMES	COMMENTS	UNUSABLE WHEN
Shellac flakes, waxy Includes seedlac and buttonlac, waxy orange and lemon	5 or more years in cool, dry conditions	(After mixing) 1-2 years in cool, dry conditions	Woodcraft and various online retailers	When mixed, thinner cuts have shorter shelf life Refrigerate unused flakes	Mixed with alcohol, a jelly forms.
Shellac flakes, dewaxed Includes super blond, blond, pale, etc.	1-2 years in cool, dry conditions	(After mixing) 6-12 months in cool, dry conditions	Woodcraft and various online retailers	When mixed, thinner cuts have shorte shelf life. Refrigerate unused flakes.	Mixed with alcohol, a jelly forms
Shellac, premixed	3 years	3 years if properly stored	Zinsser Bulls-eye, Sealcoat	Zinsser dates all its products. Buy the freshest date.	Won't dry quickly or stays tacky

SHELLAC
Shellac has a shelf life both as flakes and when dissolved. Old shellac will take longer to dry and won't create a durable finish.

TEST
Flakes won't dissolve. If flakes don't dissolve, they're no good.
Liquid won't harden. To test the viability of old shellac, pour a small puddle onto an impermeable surface. If it's tacky after an hour, dispose of it.

PREVENT
Keep it cool. Refrigerating shellac flakes slows their deterioration.

MYTH

Vacuum Packing or Grinding Extends Shelf Life

Vacuum sealing a bag of flakes doesn't extend its shelf life. The chemical breakdown isn't affected by oxygen. Turning old shellac flakes into powder may make them dissolve in alcohol, but they will still produce an inferior finish.

WATERBORNE
Use waterborne finishes within a year or two of purchase and store them at between 55° and 70°F. If they freeze, throw them out.

PRODUCT	SHELF LIFE BEFORE OPENING	SHELF LIFE AFTER OPENING	BRAND NAMES	COMMENTS	UNUSABLE WHEN
Waterborne finishes	1–2 years	1–2 years if properly stored	General Finishes, Varathane, Behlen, Target, Minwax, Deft	Don't use waterborne finishes older than 2 years.	Discolored, lumpy, or rubbery when strained; test with strainer

LACQUER
Furniture lacquer is among the longest-lasting clear finishes. It can stay usable for many years when stored correctly.

PRODUCT	SHELF LIFE BEFORE OPENING	SHELF LIFE AFTER OPENING	BRAND NAMES	COMMENTS	UNUSABLE WHEN
Nitrocellulose lacquer	Indefinite	Indefinite	Deft Clear Wood Finish, Minwax, Deft	Store in original container with tight seal	Severely discolored, cloudy, or rubbery sediment

DYES AND STAINS
Concentrated dyes, whether liquid or powder, and pigment stains can last for decades in their pre-mixed form.

PRODUCT	SHELF LIFE BEFORE OPENING	SHELF LIFE AFTER OPENING	BRAND NAMES	COMMENTS	UNUSABLE WHEN
Oil-based pigment wiping stains	Indefinite	Indefinite if stored in an airtight container	Minwax, General Finishes	If skin develops, product underneath should be usable	Hardened
Dye powders and concentrates unmixed	Indefinite	Indefinite	JE Moser, Lockwood, Homestead, Arti	Can last 20 years or more	Doesn't dissolve in solvent
Dyes, premixed with water or solvents	Indefinite	Indefinite	Behlen Solar-Lux, General Finishes	Never store dyes in metal containers. Use plastic or glass.	Severe color change from original; doesn't dissolve in solvent

Continued ➡

The Best Brushes

by Mark Schofield

Many woodworkers use only one finishing tool—a cloth. That is a shame, because applying a finish with a brush has many advantages: You build up a protective finish much faster; you can use waterborne finishes, which are very hard to wipe; and you waste far less finish than with a spray gun and don't need a special spray booth.

One obstacle to getting started, though, are the hundreds of brushes for sale in hardware stores, home centers, and online. They come in all sizes and shapes, at every point on the price scale, and with different types of bristles (some with no bristles at all). You want to apply a perfect finish to your just-completed project, but should you spend $50 on a brush or will a $10 one work just as well?

A brush is simply a tool for spreading finish on a surface. But like all tools, there are specialist versions for different products and situations, and to a great extent price does determine quality. I'll explain what to look for in a quality brush, why you will get better results using one, and how to keep your brushes working well for many years. I'll also tell you what brushes work best with different types of finish, and suggest a selection that won't break the budget. You'll be surprised at how easy brushing can be when you have the right brush.

Buy Quality, Not Quantity

A starter pack of brushes is usually a false economy. The quality will be so-so and you'll probably use only one size regularly. Spend the same amount on one quality brush from a company that specializes in making them. Good choices include Elder & Jenks, Purdy, and Wooster.

Your First Brush

Start with a 2-in. brush. This is small enough to learn on but large enough to finish most surfaces up to small tabletops. Because most brushes are designed to apply paint, they are stiffer than is ideal for applying most clear finishes. Look for a brush that feels relatively flexible and has filaments around $\frac{1}{2}$ in. longer than the brush is wide. Shorter filaments don't have enough flexibility. Buy a natural-bristle brush for solvent-based finish, or a synthetic-filament brush for water-based finish.

SQUARE END

ANGLED SASH

A GOOD PLACE TO START
A 2-in.-wide flat brush with a square end will let you develop your brushing skills.

OVAL

TWO OTHER SHAPES TO CONSIDER
An angled-sash brush is designed to handle areas of different widths as well as corners and tight spots. Get a size between $1\frac{1}{2}$ in. and $2\frac{1}{2}$ in. Once you're comfortable brushing and you're ready to tackle a large surface, buy a round or oval brush. Their extra capacity means fewer trips to reload the brush.

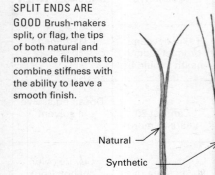

TWO WAYS TO CREATE A CHISEL PROFILE
Brushes work better with a pointed end, but there is a good way and a bad way to form it.

1. Trimming the ends removes the flagging from the edges.

Flat bottom

POOR QUALITY

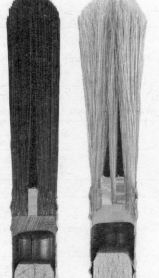

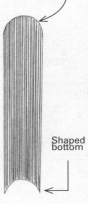

2. Shaping the bundle leaves the flagging intact.

Shaped bottom

OD QUALITY

SPLIT ENDS ARE GOOD Brush-makers split, or flag, the tips of both natural and manmade filaments to combine stiffness with the ability to leave a smooth finish.

Natural

Synthetic

SYNTHETIC FILAMENTS FOR WATER-BASED FINISHES
When hair and bristle hit water, they swell and go limp. This makes them unsuitable for water-based finishes.

When latex paints were introduced, brush manufacturers had to create suitable brushes, and now the majority of brushes in stores are designed for latex paint. They have synthetic filaments: nylon, polyester, or a blend of the two. Brand names include Chinex and Tynex, both nylon, and Orel, made from polyester. Polyester is the stiffer of the two filaments and is probably better just for paint, but even most nylon brushes are too coarse to be able to lay down an even coat of clear finish. Instead, focus on the thinness of the filaments.

Match the Brush to the Finish

Despite some manufacturer's claims, brushes with synthetic filaments can't match a natural-filament brush when applying a solvent-based finish. Most woodworkers refer to a brush's bristles rather than its filaments, but that is rather like calling all cheese cheddar. Bristle refers only to hog bristle, also known as China bristle because that is where nearly all of it comes from.

The other natural filament you're likely to find in brushes is European ox hair, which comes from these animals' ears. Slightly less stiff than hog bristle, it is also softer and much more expensive. You can buy ox hair/bristle blend brushes such as Elder & Jenks' Capital Ox, or you can buy a pure ox-hair brush from Tools for Working Wood. Once you get the feel for brushing a finish, either type of brush is well worth buying if you are using solvent-based varnish.

Your grandfather may have sworn by his badger-hair brush and some catalogs offer "badger-style" brushes. However, genuine badger hair costs around $400 per pound, so it is likely that the brush is really hog bristle with a black streak painted on the bristles to resemble badger hair. Read the fine print closely.

Natural Hair or Bristles for Solvent-Based Finishes

A GOOD START

Your first brush should be made from hog (China) bristle. The black or beige color of the bristle makes no difference, and you can get a fine 2-in. brush for under $15.

TOP OF THE LINE

The Cadillac of solvent brushes is made from pure ox hair. Very fine and soft, it will lay down a coat of varnish with almost no brush marks but costs at least $40 for a 2-in. brush.

NICE COMPROMISE

An ox hair/bristle blend works very well. It can't quite match the surface left by pure ox hair, but this won't matter if you are rubbing out the finish. Expect to pay $20 to $25 for a 2-in. brush.

TAKLON IS THE EXCEPTION TO THE RULE

One synthetic filament, Taklon, works for both solvent- and water-based finishes. The filaments are extremely fine and leave virtually no brush marks, but their flexibility makes them suitable only for thinned finishes and they can't deliver as much finish per stroke. A good way to get a really smooth final coat for fast-drying finishes like lacquer or shellac is to thin them by at least 50% and use a Taklon brush to lay down a coat almost devoid of brush marks. You can expect to pay around $30 for a Taklon brush.

Perfectly smooth final coat. Taklon does an incredible job laying down a thin, smooth coat of solvent-based finish.

ALL-PURPOSE? NOT REALLY

Most synthetic-filament brushes are designed to apply latex paint and are too stiff and coarse to be ideal for clear finishes.

LOOK FOR FINE FILAMENTS

Two good choices are Purdy's Syntox brushes and Wooster's Alpha line.

PURDEY SYNTOX

WOOSTER ALPHA

Continued ➡

Water-based finishes also dry fast but can't be thinned as much as shellac and lacquer. To get around this problem, you can buy slightly stiffer Taklon brushes made especially for these finishes. Some Taklon brushes have a glue size applied that keeps the bristles stiff for packaging and transport. Before first use, submerge them in warm water or alcohol to remove the size.

Thicker version for water-based finishes. The double row of filaments can handle thicker water-based finishes.

Brushing the last coat. Taklon brushes are ideal for the last, thinned coat of finish. But there is a specially made Taklon brush (right) for water-based finishes that can't be thinned as much.

Protect Your Investment

A 75¢ foam brush is disposable, a $40 ox-hair brush is not. Take time to clean a good brush thoroughly each time you are done with it, and you'll be rewarded with many years of flawless service.

CLEANING STARTS BEFORE YOU BEGIN

So you're anxious to see how your new brush works. Before you dip it in the finish, though, there are a couple of steps to take. First, even the best brush may have one or two loose filaments (cheap brushes will have many), so rather than pick hairs out of a wet finish, bend the filaments back and forth with your hand a few times, pulling gently on them. Hold the tip up to the light and remove any filaments protruding above the rest. Now dip the brush into a solvent that matches the finish you'll be using and then squeeze out the solvent onto a paper towel. This coats the filaments with solvent and makes cleaning the brush much easier when you've finished using it.

In use, don't overload the brush with finish. If you are brushing vertical surfaces, periodically squeeze out as much finish as possible back into the can. These steps will prevent finish pooling around the base of the filaments and flowing all over the ferrule or running down the handle.

SHELLAC, LACQUER, AND WATER-BASED FINISHES CLEAN UP EASILY

Shellac and lacquer: let it dry. A brush used for lacquer and shellac don't need to be cleaned thoroughly. Give it a swish in lacquer thinner or denatured alcohol, shake it out, and let it dry hard. When you need it again, just stand it in solvent. It will be soft and ready to use within 30 minutes.

Use soap and water for water-soluble finishes. Use hot water and dish soap to remove water-based finishes from brushes. Lather, rinse, and repeat two or three times.

OIL-BASED FINISHES ARE HARDEST TO CLEAN

Let's start with the good news: You don't need to clean the brush if you plan to use it again within 24 hours. Instead, suspend the brush in mineral spirits that have previously been used for cleaning a brush. Keep the tips of the filaments off the bottom of the container so they don't get bent or contaminated with residue.

When you're done with the brush, rinse it a couple of times in used mineral spirits, then pure mineral spirits, removing the bulk of the solvent on newspaper each time. Now rinse the brush in hot soapy water several times before giving it a final cleaning using either citrus cleaner or household ammonia. If you can't smell any mineral spirits on the filaments, the brush is clean and can be wrapped in paper and put away.

Dip a toe in. Only submerge about a third of the filaments in finish. If you go deeper, it is harder to apply an even coat. Also, finish will tend to pool in the bottom of the brush and then run down the ferrule when brushing vertical surfaces.

Let it soak between coats. If they are going to be reused within 24 hours, brushes containing an oil-based finish can be suspended in mineral spirits. Use a kebab skewer through the handle to avoid bending the bristles.

TIP

Reuse Your Mineral Spirits

Don't toss it. After you have cleaned a brush, pour the contaminated mineral spirits into a sealable container.

Clearly better. After a few weeks, the residue will sink to the bottom of the container and you can pour off clean mineral spirits for reuse.

Spray-Finishing Basics

by Jeff Jewitt

It's a pity that so few woodworkers have taken the plunge and begun spray finishing. Lack of information is the main reason, and manufacturers bear much of the blame. Makers of professional spray systems assume you're already familiar with spraying, while the manuals for entry-level equipment give only basic details, and instructions on cans of finish tell you to consult your spray-gun manual.

To remedy this dearth of useful information, I'll describe the main types of spray guns and show you how to match the gun to the finish. By spraying various pieces of furniture, I can demonstrate the different spray strokes that will work best on each kind of surface.

Match the Finish to the Gun

A spray gun mixes pressurized air and liquid finish in a process known as atomization. For proper atomization, it is critical to adjust the gun to the thickness, or viscosity, of the finish you want to spray.

MEASURE THE VISCOSITY OF THE FINISH

A viscosity measuring cup is small with a precisely machined hole in the bottom. Most turbine-driven spray guns come with this type of cup, but owners of conversion guns can purchase one for around $10.

Viscosity is affected by temperature, so before you try to measure it, make sure the finish is at 70°F. Begin by submerging the cup in the finish, and then take it out. Start timing when the top rim of the cup breaks the surface of the finish. Raise the cup 6 in. over the can, and when the first break appears in the fluid stream, stop the clock. The number of seconds passed is the measure of the finish's viscosity.

SELECT THE APPROPRIATE NEEDLE/NOZZLE

Once you know the viscosity of the finish, the next step is to choose the matching-size needle/nozzle and sometimes air cap. Keep in mind that the different styles of gun (gravity, suction, or pressure feed) use different-size needle/nozzles for the same finish. Always use the smallest needle/nozzle that you can, as the smaller-diameter ones generally atomize finishes best. Try thinning the product before you select a larger needle/nozzle.

Some cheaper guns may come with only one size needle/nozzle, and in extreme cases the manual may not even specify what size needle/nozzle that is. In this case, you'll have to thin the finish until you achieve good atomization. Manufacturers of water-based finishes typically recommend thinning with no more than 5% to 10% of distilled water. Beyond that, you will have to use a viscosity reducer dedicated to that finish. Add the water or reducer in increments of 1 oz. per quart of finish until it sprays properly.

For the best finish "off-the-gun," it is a good idea to strain all finishes as you pour them into the gun. A fine- or medium-mesh cone filter works well to strain impurities from water-based clear finishes; a medium-mesh filter works for paint.

Create a Good Spray Pattern

Once you've matched the finish to the gun, make final adjustments at the gun. Also, select a respirator with cartridges suitable for the type of finish you will be spraying.

SETTING UP A CONVERSION GUN

High-volume low-pressure (HVLP) spray guns have a maximum inlet pressure of 20 to 50 psi; the exact figure is either stamped on the gun's body or given in the instructions. Conversion, or compressor-driven, HVLP spray guns are designed to reduce this inlet pressure to 10 psi at the nozzle, enough to atomize most finishes. With the trigger of the gun slightly depressed to release air but not finish, set the compressor's regulator to slightly above this maximum inlet pressure. This allows for the hose-pressure drop, which is caused by friction as the air passes through the hose. To avoid this calculation, install a miniregulator at the gun to set the pressure.

Turn the fan-width and fluid-delivery valves clockwise so that they're closed. If your gun has a cheater valve (a built-in air regulator), make sure it's open. While the trigger is fully depressed, open the fluid-delivery valve a few turns, which regulates the amount of fluid going through the nozzle. Set it low for delicate spraying of edges and small areas, or open it up for spraying large surfaces. Spray a piece of scrapwood or some corrugated cardboard. Ideally, you want a fine and uniform pattern of droplets across the width of the spray. If you have coarse, large droplets, either the finish is too thin or the needle/nozzle is too large. The reverse is true if the gun sputters or spits. If the finish looks good, keep turning down the air pressure in 5-psi increments until you start to see the finish form a dimpled surface resembling an orange peel. Then raise the air back up 5 psi. Note this as the proper air pressure for the finish you're using. Operating the gun at the lowest pressure possible saves material by reducing bounce-back and overspray.

The fan-width control valve on the gun regulates the spray pattern. As you open the valve, the spray pattern becomes elongated). When you open the valve, you also may have to turn up the air pressure going into the gun, so it's a good idea to keep an eye on your regulator.

SETTING UP A TURBINE-DRIVEN GUN

Fully open the cheater valve on the gun. The correct air/liquid balance is established the same way as on a conversion gun. However, on most turbine guns, the position of the air cap determines the shape and orientation of the spray pattern. When the air cap's horns are in the horizontal position, the spray pattern is wide and oriented vertically. When you rotate the air cap 90°, the spray pattern is horizontal. The intermediate position makes the spray pattern tight and round.

Mastering the Art of Spraying

Before spraying any piece of furniture, dismantle large items as much as you can. Remove backs from carcase pieces and remove drawer bottoms, if possible. If you have a complicated project that includes a lot of slats, consider finishing them before final assembly.

HOW MUCH FINISH TO APPLY

Novice sprayers often get carried away with the ease of laying down a finish, and so they apply too much at once.

You should aim for each coat to be about two thousandths of an inch thick, or in spraying terms, two mils. A mil gauge is a piece of metal with teeth in mil increments. To use the gauge, spray some finish onto an impermeable surface such as laminate or glass. Drag the gauge through the wet finish, keeping it 90° to the surface and pressed down. Withdraw the gauge and note the first tooth that isn't coated with finish, as well as the one next to it that is coated. Your depth of finish will be an intermediate thickness between these marks. If you have trouble seeing clear finishes on the gauge, sprinkle talc on the wet teeth and blow it off. The talc will stick to the wet teeth.

THE BASIC SPRAY STROKE

Lay a flat board or a piece of cardboard on a pair of sawhorses to practice on. Hold the gun perpendicular to the surface, about 6 in. to 8 in. away and about 3 in. off the bottom left-hand corner. Depress the trigger until finish comes out, and move the gun across the board until you get 2 in. to 3 in. past the far edge. Do not arc your pass; rather, lock your forearm so that the gun moves across the board at a constant height and in a straight line. As you make another pass, overlap the first by 50% to 75%. Move the gun fast enough to avoid puddles of finish, but not so fast that the surface feels rough when it has dried.

I start with the surface closest to me and work toward the exhaust fan in my spray booth to reduce overspray landing on the wet finish and leaving it rough. Practice this basic stroke until it becomes second nature, because it is fundamental to all spraying.

Continued ➔

VISCOSITY CHART

Generic finish viscosity	Viscosity time	Appropriate needle/nozzle sizes		
		Gravity feed	Suction feed	Pressure feed
Thin	10–15 sec. [b]	1.1 mm	1.3–1.4 mm	0.7 mm
	15–23 sec.	1.2–.3 mm	1.5 mm	0.8–1.0 mm
	23–35 sec.	1.5 mm	1.7 mm	1.1 mm
Medium	35–40 sec.	1.5–1.7 mm	1.9 mm	1.1–1.2 mm
	40–45 sec.	1.7 mm	N/A	1.2–1.3 mm
	45–55 sec.	1.9 mm	2.2 mm	1.3–1.5 mm
Think	55+ sec.	2.2 mm	N/R	1.5–1.7 mm

[a] Measured in a Ford No. 4 viscosity cup with finish at 70°F
[b] Water = 10 seconds
[c] To convert millimeters to inches, multiply the millimeter figure by 0.03937

HOSE-PRESSURE DROP

Inside diameter of hose	Pressure at compressor	Pressure drop		
		15-ft. hose	25-ft. hose	50-ft. hose
5/16 in.	40 psi	1.5 psi	2.5 psi	4 psi
	60 psi	3 psi	4 psi	6 psi
3/8 in.	40 psi	1 psi	2 psi	3.5 psi
	60 psi	2 psi	3 psi	5 psi

Pressure drop is the amount of air loss from the compressor regulator to the gun's air inlet. For pressures below 40 psi, the pressure drops in the hose are negligible.

FLAT SURFACES

The basic spray technique for flat surfaces is called a crosshatch. Begin with the underside of the piece: At a 90° angle to the grain, start your first pass at the edge closest to you and spray a series of overlapping strokes. Then rotate the top 90° (it helps to have it on a turntable) and spray with the grain.

Choosing a gun

Newcomers to spraying should use a high-volume, low-pressure (HVLP) spray system for the efficient way it converts liquid to droplets (atomization) and transfers those droplets to the object being sprayed.

TURBINE-DRIVEN HVLP

The first HVLP guns were powered by converted vacuum-cleaner motors, which evolved into two-, three-, and four-stage fans known as turbines. These HVLP systems offer a number of advantages to novice sprayers: They're normally sold as a packaged set, including the turbine, an air hose, a gun, and multiple needle/nozzle sizes for different finish viscosities, and generally come with good directions. Systems range in price from $300 to $1,000. You can get a good system for around $600.

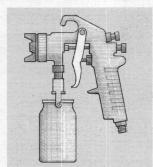

COMPRESSOR-DRIVEN HVLP

If you already have an air compressor, you may want to consider buying a gun that will use the air from this source (see below). Known as conversion guns, they convert the high-pressure air from the compressor to a high volume of low-pressure air at the spray tip. Prices range from $100 to $500, with good-quality guns available for less than $300.

SUCTION FEED
Air expelled through the front of the gun creates a venturi effect, pulling the finish into the gun. Although it's fine for medium- and low-viscosity finishes, this conversion spray gun can't pull up thick finish with enough speed to spray efficiently.

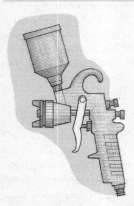

GRAVITY FEED
With the finish container mounted above the gun, this system lets gravity push the material down into the gun. Not only can you spray thicker materials more efficiently, but the gun also is easy and quick to clean. However, it is harder to get the gun into tight spaces.

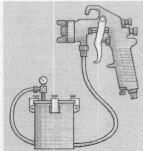

PRESSURE FEED
You can pressurize either a cup attached to the gun or a remote pot that delivers the finish to the gun through a hose (below). The latter system makes the gun smaller and more maneuverable, but there are more parts to buy and clean.

Holding the still-dry edges, turn over the panel and place it back on the nail board. Spray the edges with the gun parallel to the surface, then bring the gun up to 45° to the top and spray the edges again to get extra finish on them. Finally, repeat the cross-hatching on the top side.

If you get a drip, and you won't be damaging a delicate toner or glaze underneath, wipe the drip immediately with your finger and lightly respray the area.

Inside cabinets—Spraying inside a cabinet is a lot easier if you remove the back. If you cannot remove the back, you'll get a face full of overspray unless you turn the air pressure way down, which may result in a poorly atomized finish. Start on the underside of the top and then the two sides, leaving the bottom last so that overspray doesn't settle there and create a rough finish. For each panel, spray all four edges first before doing the center. Rotate the piece so that you always spray toward the back of the booth; this way, the fan will draw the overspray away from the piece. Blow away the cloud of finish left inside by depressing the trigger of the gun slightly so that air but no finish comes through.

VERTICALS

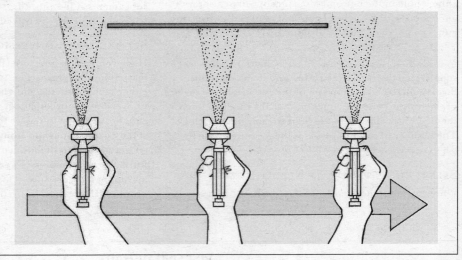

Spraying Flat Surfaces

THE BASIC SPRAY STROKE
Hold the spray gun at the same distance from the workpiece for the entire pass over the surface. Start spraying off the edge of the workpiece and proceed over the surface. Stop spraying off the other edge.

Start at the bottom and lay down a continuous layer of finish until you reach the top. Overlap each pass 50%—as though you were spraying a flat surface—but don't cross-hatch, because the extra finish will cause runs. For face frames, adjust the fan width to match the width of the frame members, if possible.

COMPLICATED PIECES

To spray a stool or a chair, work from the less-visible parts to the most visible. With the piece upside down, spray the underside and inside areas. Though less visible, they still have to be finished. Turn over the stool and rest it on four screws driven into the feet to prevent the finish from pooling around the bottom of the legs.

Now spray the sides of the legs and the slats, working quickly to apply light coats. Finally, finish the outside surfaces that are most visible. As with vertical surfaces, the trick is to keep the coats of finish thin and to avoid sags and runs.

Anatomy of a Spray Gun

The components of most spray guns are the same as this typical HVLP conversion gun.

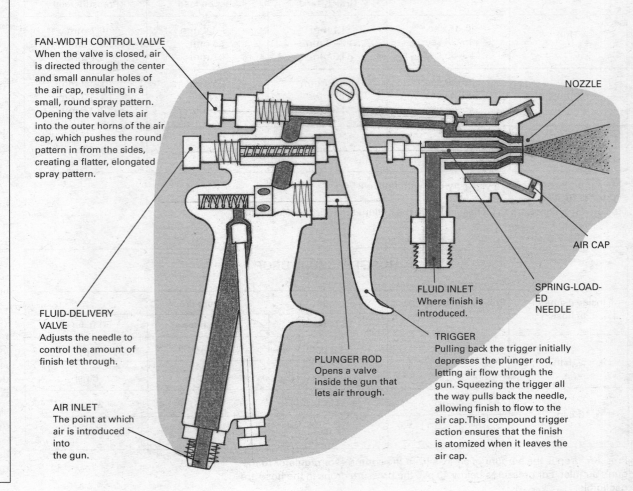

FAN-WIDTH CONTROL VALVE
When the valve is closed, air is directed through the center and small annular holes of the air cap, resulting in a small, round spray pattern. Opening the valve lets air into the outer horns of the air cap, which pushes the round pattern in from the sides, creating a flatter, elongated spray pattern.

NOZZLE

AIR CAP

SPRING-LOADED NEEDLE

FLUID INLET
Where finish is introduced.

TRIGGER
Pulling back the trigger initially depresses the plunger rod, letting air flow through the gun. Squeezing the trigger all the way pulls back the needle, allowing finish to flow to the air cap. This compound trigger action ensures that the finish is atomized when it leaves the air cap.

PLUNGER ROD
Opens a valve inside the gun that lets air through.

FLUID-DELIVERY VALVE
Adjusts the needle to control the amount of finish let through.

AIR INLET
The point at which air is introduced into the gun.

Finish a Panel in Four Steps

To achieve a good finish on a flat panel, you need even coverage on all surfaces. The use of a nail board and turntable allows you to finish the top surface while the bottom is still wet and to direct the spray (and the overspray) toward an extractor fan.

1. **Spray the edges.** With the gun parallel to the panel's surface, make one pass on all four edges **Dealing with runs.** If you spot an area with too much finish, quickly wipe away the surplus and apply another light coat.

2. **Recoat the edges.** With the gun now at a 45° angle to the panel, give the edges a second coat of finish.

3. **Spray across the grain.** Maintaining the gun at an even height over the surface, spray overlapping strokes across the grain.

4. **Then spray with the grain.** Turn the workpiece 90° and spray with the grain in the second half of a crosshatch pattern.

Dial in the Spray Pattern

The type of gun will determine the method of adjustment for the shape and orientation of the spray pattern.

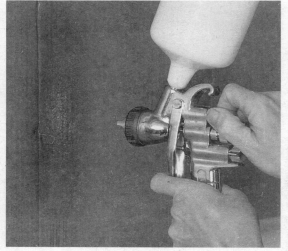

Conversion guns require two adjustments. A valve at the back changes the pattern from circular to elongated. Twisting the air cap changes the orientation of the spray pattern.

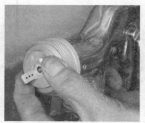

Turbine guns are adjusted at the front. To adjust the pattern from circular to horizontal to vertical, just turn the air cap.

Rather than alter the way you hold the gun, adjust the spray pattern to suit the object being sprayed. For vertical surfaces, a horizontal pattern gives optimum coverage; when spraying flat panels in the crosshatch pattern, adjust the gun to get a vertical pattern. A tight circular pattern reduces overspray when finishing narrow parts, such as slats and legs.

HORIZONTAL

VERTICAL

CIRCULAR

Spraying Furniture

Case Pieces

Get down, and get under your cabinet. Spray the underside of the shelves first. Then complete the inside of a cabinet by spraying the sides followed by the tops of the shelves. In this way, the most noticeable surface is sprayed last and won't be affected by overspray.

Avoid runs on vertical surfaces. Apply overlapping strokes from bottom to top, but do not apply a crosshatch spray across the grain, as too much finish likely will sag or run on a vertical surface.

Slats and Spindles

With the stool upside down, spray the underside of the rails and the inside surfaces that are least visible. Flip the stool (below) and spray the visible areas, keeping the spray gun the same distance from the workpiece.

Raised Panels

The procedure is identical to that of a tabletop, with the addition of a first pass with the gun angled around the inside edge of the frame.

Grids

Treat grids and frames for glass-panel doors as a flat, continuous surface, and apply a crosshatch spray pattern.

PREPARING AND SANDING WOOD

Handplanes vs. Sanding

One of the happiest moments in any woodworking project comes when you begin applying a finish. It's then that you see the wood's final appearance deepening in color and character before your eyes. But the results won't be satisfying if you haven't prepared the wood's surfaces for the finish, which tends to highlight flaws instead of disguising them. The surfaces must be smooth, flat, and free of milling marks, scratches, tearout, and other imperfections that can detract from the beauty of your work.

Preparing the surfaces usually means using one of two time-honored cutting technologies: sandpaper or handplanes. Which is best? To explore the question, we recently set up a friendly competition in our shop. Each contestant was given the parts for a Shaker table with tapered legs. Milled to final dimension and with the joinery already fitted, the parts were ready to be sanded or planed in preparation for a finish. We broadcast the event live on FineWoodworking.com and invited local woodworkers to our shop to watch and judge the results.

Art director Michael Pekovich demonstrated handplanes and scrapers. Editor Asa Christiana used a random-orbit sander and hand-sanding. Afterward, each contestant applied a coat of Waterlox, a wiping varnish, as a way to check the results.

We put each contestant on the clock to see who crossed the finish line first. But we were even more interested in knowing whose finish looked best at the end.

As it happened, Mike and his handplanes appeared to prevail on both counts. He finished his prep with a half-hour to spare, and the audience judged his finish to be superior. In truth, if you follow either method carefully and thoroughly, you'll get great results.

No Sharpening Required: Sanding Is a Sure and Simple Way to Get Flawless Surfaces

By Asa Christiana

When I started out as a woodworker, I didn't know much about sharpening and therefore couldn't get my hand tools to work well. So I used sandpaper to prepare surfaces for finishing. Sandpaper has a short learning curve, and I picked up most of the tips I needed from a great Taunton Press video on finishing by Frank Klausz.

Truth be told, I've since switched to handplanes for a lot of my surface prep. A few passes with my sharp No. 4, and I usually have a dead-flat surface ready for finish. But the handplane doesn't work with every type of wood and figure, so I still break out my random-orbit sander and trusty sanding blocks quite often.

I don't mean to say that sandpaper works better than handplanes and scrapers. But sandpaper is a great equalizer: It works on every wood and in nearly every situation, while handplanes must be perfectly tuned and razor sharp to work at all. With sandpaper and a few tips, anyone can create flawless surfaces.

My sense is that sanding is slower than planing and scraping, even when you factor in sharpening time for the hand tools.

Continued ➔

Handplanes Flatten and Smooth Quickly with No Dust

By Michael Pekovich

I did a lot of sanding in the 15 years between my first run-in with a dull, rusty handplane and my eye-opening test drive with a truly sharp one. Unfortunately, that's not an uncommon experience. A sharp handplane can work wonders, going from machine marks to a glass-smooth surface in minutes. A dull plane can do a lot of damage, both to your lumber and your psyche.

The good news is that it's easier than ever to start working with your first handplane. Years ago, your choices were to buy an inferior new plane that needed a lot of tune-up work or an old high-quality plane that also needed a lot of tune-up work. Today the market offers many excellent new planes that require little more than a five-minute sharpening before the shavings start to fly.

I still keep a scraper and fine sandpaper on hand to fix the occasional tearout, but my smoothing plane has eliminated the dusty hours of sanding that used to accompany every project. In addition to saving time and leaving a smooth surface, the handplane excels at creating dead-flat surfaces and crisp chamfers, hallmarks of fine woodworking that are impossible to achieve with sandpaper alone.

Finish by Hand-Sanding

Shopmade paper cutter. This cutting jig uses an old hacksaw blade to trim sandpaper sheets squarely to fit on padded sanding blocks. The blocks hold the paper flat, ensuring that it will leave a flat surface.

Finish by hand. Begin hand-sanding with the last grit you used on the random-orbit sander, usually P220. Work the sanding block in the direction of the grain to remove the last swirl marks from the sander.

How to keep edges flat. Hold the workpiece in a vise, with the narrow edge horizontal. Use the sanding pad like a block plane, running your fingertips along the workpiece to keep the block flat and the edge square.

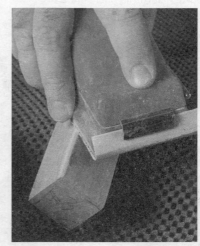

Sand block breaks edges, too. Easing the sharp edges makes them friendlier to fingers and more resistant to damage. Turn the block 45° for a few passes with P150-grit paper to create a light bevel.

SANDING IS STILL A SAFE FALLBACK

Sandpaper can handle the toughest grain without a hitch. But it takes longer. Some suggest using a belt sander for speed, but the random-orbit sander is easier to control.

Also, sanding is easier for beginners. Just work the surface evenly, move patiently through the grits, and use a block for hand-sanding.

Power Sanding: Deal with Dust and Don't Skip a Grit

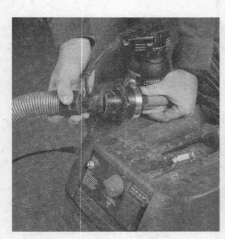

Better than a dust mask. Connect a shop vacuum to the sander's dust port to keep dust out of the air and avoid clogged sanding pads. Better vacuums switch on with the sander when the tool is plugged into an onboard power outlet.

Gang up parts. Start with a coarse grit, P80 or P100, to remove burns and mill marks. Avoid rounded edges on narrow stock by ganging two narrow pieces together. Note, this only works if the surfaces are level.

Change disks frequently. Don't be shy about using more than one disk of the same grit before moving to a finer abrasive. A worn or clogged disk will slow down the work.

Scrape away the glue first. Start work by using a sharp paint scraper to remove any glue.

Sand evenly. It is critical to work the surface evenly and systematically to guarantee it will end up flat. It's easy to linger in one area and create a hollow, which you may not notice until finish is applied.

Work in stages. Use each successive grit to remove the scratches left by the last one, until the abrasive is so fine (P220 or more) that the human eye can't see the scratches under a finish.

When to stop. The final grit depends on the type of finish: P220 for shellac or polyurethane, or as high as P600 for an oil finish, especially on blotch-prone woods like cherry.

Handplaning: Start Sharp and Use Simple Stops

Get sharp first. Using waterstones and a honing guide, polish a narrow band at the blade's beveled tip. Remove burrs with your finest stone.

Easier than benchdogs. A simple planing stop clamped across the benchtop is all you need to secure the work, and it lets you quickly flip the piece or change to another.

Don't bother with hidden surfaces. To save time and wear on the blade, plane only the outside face and bottom edge of each apron. Afterward, chamfer the bottom edges with a block plane.

Holding narrow work. A simple L-shaped jig mount in a vise can hold the narrow legs securely during planing.

Mark the top end of the taper. Planing too much on the tapered area can cause the intersection with the flat area to move. To avoid this, draw a few pencil lines just below the intersection as a guide.

A piece of scrap keeps the workpiece level. To plane the outside faces, insert the taper's matching cutoff underneath to support the leg along its length.

Large Surfaces Get Extra Care

Treatment for tearout. Use a card scraper to remove any tearout.

Plane in two stages. First, level any high spots until the surface is flat on both sides. After re-sharpening the iron, set the plane for a light cut and take a series of smoothing passes over the entire surface of the show side only.

Sandpaper. Because the scraped areas have a different scratch pattern than the planed areas, it's good to blend them by following any scraping with P320 through P600-grit sandpaper over the entire surface.

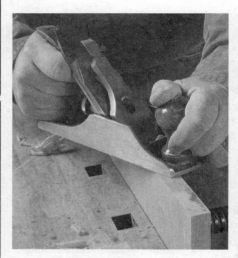

How to tackle end grain. Start by lightly lubricating the plane's sole with paste wax. To avoid chipout at the far edge, take a few short passes from that end first. Then rotate the piece and work normally, stopping short of the far edge.

Dead flat and smooth. Careful surface preparation pays off, especially on your project's broadest, most visible surfaces.

YES, PLANES ARE FASTER, BUT DON'T RUSH

With perfectly straight-grained lumber, planing is a breeze, but in the real world, that's rarely the case. Quarter-sawn grain on legs can be especially tricky and prone to tearout. Spend extra time scraping those parts.

During the contest, I used just one bench plane to show that you don't need to buy a lot of handplanes to get started. But I wound up doing a lot of adjusting for heavy and light cuts. Normally, I'd have set up a No. 5 jack plane for flattening parts quickly and a No. 4 for final smoothing. That would have saved some time and effort.

Continued →

Proper Sanding Techniques

by Teri Masachi

Just about every woodworker has a random-orbit sander. They're cheap to buy, they can handle any job, and you don't need to serve an apprenticeship to use one effectively. But you do need to understand how the tool works. Most people don't. Perhaps they saw one being used on TV, a friend gave them a one-minute lesson, or more likely they simply slapped a disk on their new sander and hit the wood.

The result is too many pieces that show the telltale evidence of poor sanding. These include failure to remove planer and jointer marks or scratches from coarse sandpaper, and surfaces that are smooth but not flat, with depressions and rounded-over edges.

I'll tell you how to handle the sander correctly, what grits to start and end with, and how to check your progress. It's worth learning how to sand correctly, as sanding is the most critical part of the finishing process. A well-sanded piece is already half finished!

A Light Touch and a Slow Hand

One of the biggest sanding debates is about whether to land the sander on the surface running at full speed, to place it on the wood and then turn it on, or to try a compromise, touching down while the motor is still picking up speed. In truth, do whatever feels best (this can vary by model); it really doesn't matter. What is more important is how you sand once you begin.

A key factor is how fast you move the sander over the workpiece. Some people work in a frenzy, moving the sander rapidly back and forth as if they were using a sanding block. Others spend too long sanding the same spot. The correct speed is 8 to 10 seconds per foot. The frenzied among you will find slowing down like coming off the highway and going 25 miles an hour, but skittering the tool around doesn't help: You can't possibly move faster than the sander's vibration. On the other hand, slowing down allows you to keep better track of your sanding pattern and to be sure you are covering the surface evenly.

Random-orbit sanders need to float on the surface with light pressure to produce an optimum orbital pattern. Don't push down on the sander in the belief that it will cut faster. You'll just cause the tool to bog down, load up the paper with dust, and leave swirl marks on the wood. Bearing down also will create excessive heat, which can warp the sander's pad. If the sandpaper is constantly wearing out only around the perimeter, the pad has been distorted by heat buildup around the edge and you need to replace it.

Other Secrets of Success

When sanding a wider surface, overlap each pass by between a third and a half to ensure even coverage. As for the edge of the workpiece, it's fine to overhang it slightly, but keep at least two-thirds of the pad on the surface to avoid the risk of tipping the sander and rounding over the edge. If you are working on narrow surfaces such as legs or the edges of boards that individually can't meet the two-thirds rule, consider clamping identical pieces together and sanding them collectively. The wider surface provides a more stable platform for the sander.

One thing you should never try to do with a sander is to break or bevel an edge. The action is not designed to work on a narrow edge and you'll end up with an irregular surface. Break edges using a sanding block or bevel them with a block plane or a router bit.

There is no doubt that random-orbit sanders create enormous amounts of dust. Effective dust pickup from the sander will not only keep the air clear but also keeps dust from packing the spaces between the abrasive particles and killing sanding efficiency. Hooking up a vacuum to the sander speeds stock removal and will extend the life of the disk.

Choose Your Weapon

5-IN. SANDER IS NIMBLE
Almost everyone owns a 5-in.-dia. random-orbit sander. They aren't expensive, and they can handle almost any task from sanding chair legs and frame-and-panel assemblies to smoothing big tabletops.

6-IN. SANDER COVERS MORE GROUND
The extra inch gives you nearly 45% more sanding surface, which not only covers large, flat surfaces faster but also does a better job of flattening them.

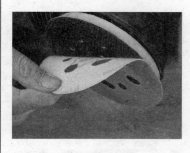

The 5-in. sander is the one most woodworkers should buy first. It's versatile and a must for narrow surfaces such as chair legs, but there are some good reasons a 6-in. machine should be second on your list. Years ago, pressure-sensitive adhesive (PSA) disks were cheaper than hook-and-loop (H&L) ones, but if you were sanding a small piece you often had to discard a PSA disk before it was used up, whereas H&L disks can be reused. Now the cost has nearly evened out and most sanders come with a H&L pad. Yours should, too.

Don't spend extra on a sander with speed control: I have never understood why anyone would sand at lower speeds and not keep the sander at its maximum setting. The only exception is wet sanding or polishing, which you shouldn't do with an electric sander anyway because of the risk of a shock.

AIR POWER FOR HARD-CORE SANDERS
The majority of professional finishers and large cabinet shops use air-powered sanders for several reasons: They are more compact, lighter, and less top-heavy than their electric counterparts. They have fewer moving parts, last longer, and can be repaired rather than being generally disposable. However, these sanders are air hogs and at 90 psi, they need 20 plus cubic feet of air per minute, which translates into a 50- or 60-gal. compressor, compressed air lines, and in-line air filters and driers. That is the real expense of these machines, which makes them hard to justify for a hobbyist.

Even with a vacuum attached, it is still necessary to sweep, vacuum, or blow off the surface before switching sandpaper to the next higher grit. Otherwise, leftover abrasive from the previous grit can create occasional deeper scratches even after you've switched to a finer disk.

Guide to the Grits, from Start to Finish

The first grit is unique: Its job is to remove surface defects. How coarse that grit should be depends on the severity of those defects: For large changes in height such as planer snipe or uneven edge-glued boards, you should start with 80 or 100 grit (it would be quicker, though, to remove the bulk of the high areas with either a handplane or a belt sander with a 100-grit belt). If the surface is essentially level but there is some tearout, you can start with 120 grit. If you have a smooth, flat surface left by either a well-tuned planer or handplane, you can start with 150 grit.

Stick with this first grit until *all* of the defects have been removed, and if it is taking too long, switch to a rougher grit. The purpose of subsequent higher grits is only to refine the scratch pattern of the previous grit, not to remove defects. If you switch to a higher grit when *most* of the defects are removed, you may never get rid of them. Most likely you will go through several disks of this initial grit, so don't be tempted to extend their life. Most disks lose their cutting action dramatically after 15 to 40 minutes for coarse 80- to 120-grit disks and half that time for finer 180- to 220-grit disks. After that, it is time to toss them. Continuing to use these disks can cause the dreaded swirl or "pigtail" marks from sandpaper that is clogged. Secondly, don't think that if you start with 100 grit and use it long enough, it becomes 120 or 150 grit. It just creates 100-grit scratches, more and more slowly.

The Right Rate

Slow and steady. Advance the sander at a rate of about 8 to 10 seconds per foot, rather than rushing the sander all over the place. This lets the sander do the work and lets you keep track of your pattern, so you sand uniformly.

Sand Before You Assemble

Sand first, glue later. It is much easier to sand components before you glue them together.

To see if you've removed all the defects, vacuum the dust, wipe on some denatured alcohol or mineral spirits, and check the surface with a raking light.

The two-line trick—The subsequent grits go much quicker. Draw a light pencil squiggle across the surface and sand the entire surface until it is gone. Draw a second line and sand it off. Now switch to the next-higher grit; it's as simple as that. As you move to higher grits—120, 150, 180, 220—the appearance of the surface will improve as coarse scratches are replaced by finer ones.

The industry standard for what should be the final grit is 220 for softwoods and 180 for hardwoods. This standard applies when using any film-building finish such as shellac, lacquer, and water- or oil-based polyurethane or varnish. But if the surface is going to get a French polish or a thin-finish such as a penetrating oil, then it is a good idea to continue up to 400 grit. If you can't find 320- or 400-grit disks locally, you can mail-order them or, if you have a small project, you can apply these grits by hand using sheets of sandpaper and a sanding block.

In any case, always do the final sanding by hand. Use the last grit that you used on the machine, wrap it around a cork-faced block or any firm sanding block, and sand with the grain in long, straight strokes. This will remove any sneaky swirl marks or other flaws and will soften the edges and refine delicate details. Check the surface again as before. You'll spot any flaws before you apply a clear coat or stain, and you can finish your project confident in its final appearance.

If you've never experienced a well-sanded project, you'll be surprised at how nicely the finish goes on.

TIP · If You Must Sand After Assembly

If you glued parts together before sanding them, it can be difficult to sand corners without damaging adjacent parts. A large dry-wall-taping knife lets you work into the corner safely.

No Tipping Please

Not an angle grinder. Don't try to concentrate the sanding power in a small area by tipping the sander. You'll create hollows in the surface. You also risk overheating the rim of the pad and causing it to expand. A sign this has happened is if the disk wears only toward the outside.

Manage the Dust and Grit

Attach a vacuum. As well as keeping your lungs cleaner, attaching a vacuum lets sanders cut faster and extends the disk's lifespan. Clean between grits. Remove any dust left on the workpiece before switching to a higher grit. It reduces the risk of coarse abrasive contaminating the finer disk, and it keeps the shop cleaner.

It All Comes Together on Tabletops

The tops of cabinets, chests, and tables are the most visible surfaces and therefore require the most careful sanding.

Level first. The first stage is leveling the surface. The grit you choose depends on how much material you need to remove. Letting up to a third of the sander's pad overhang the edge of a work surface helps ensure uniform sanding. But go beyond a third and you risk tipping the sander and rounding the edge.

Check the surface. Looking across the surface into a raking light (above) helps reveal any imperfections. This pigtail squiggle (left) was probably caused by a piece of debris that the sander picked up when it was set down on the bench.

Then smooth. After you've removed surface imperfections with a coarse grit, the role of subsequent finer grits is to refine the scratch pattern. Here's a great way to know when to switch grits. Draw a light pencil line across the surface and sand the whole surface until the line is gone. Repeat and then move on to the next-grit disk.

Hand-sand last. Once you've completed the final grit with the sander, use a sanding block with the same size grit, sanding with the grain. This removes any swirls left by the sander. Finally, use 180- or 220-grit paper and a sanding block to break the edges. Don't attempt this with a sander.

How to Handle a Frame-and-Panel

Right and wrong sanding both before and after glue-up can make or break your frame-and-panel assemblies.

PANEL

Flat surfaces first. It is fine to use a power sander on the raised portion of the panel and its back.

Hand-sand the profile. Don't use the sander, even on a flat, bevel-edged profile. Instead, hand-sand up to the same final grit as used on the sander. Go to 320 or 400 grit on the end-grain sections, so they don't absorb too much finish and end up darker than their surroundings.

FRAME

Gang up parts. To sand the narrow sides of the frame, clamp them in pairs to provide a wider surface for the sander to ride on.

Sand the face after glue-up. After the frame is glued up, you need to level the joints. You may want to reduce major high spots with a handplane, but a random-orbit sander is ideal as it won't leave any cross-grain marks on adjacent parts.

Continued ➜

Test Your Finish on Sample Boards

by Teri Masachi

Spend weeks making a beautiful piece of furniture, and the last thing you want is the finish to be a nasty surprise: a look that magnifies your poor sanding; one that display's the wood's blotchiness; or a stain that's simply the wrong color. That's why you should always test the finish on a sample board rather than on the project. By making all of the potential mistakes on the scrap instead of the project, life can still go on without the huge task of reworking a finishing nightmare. The only disaster is the test piece!

How to Make a Sample Board

For the best results, use a cutoff from each of the woods used to make the project. This includes plywood, veneered panels, and solid lumber. Use a piece that's big enough to give you a good read: at least 7 in. square for each step of the finishing process.

It's important to prepare the sample board's surface exactly as you will the actual workpiece. Sand or scrape it too

A Clear Finish

Even a clear finish needs testing. The sample board below shows how a straight shellac finish will look with one, two, three, four, and five coats.

TEST AN OIL FINISH FOR BLOTCHING

Try different methods. The Danish oil-finished sample board (above) shows how blotches can be overcome in either of two ways: by presanding to a higher grit (right), or by applying a washcoat before the stain (below.)

SANDED TO P150 GRIT

SHELLAC WASHCOAT

SANDED TO P400 GRIT

---

much or not enough, and you'll get a misread on the stain and the sheen. There's a light-year's difference between a stained finish on pine at P150-grit and at P400-grit.

Testing just a clear coat—The basic sample board shows what the wood will look like with just a clear finish. Apply one coat to the whole board. Let it dry, mark off one-fifth of the board at one end, and apply a second coat to the rest of the board. Repeat the process until the last section receives a fifth coat.

This "step sample" is a graphic way to show how many coats must be applied. On certain woods, even a clear coat can blotch, especially if it is oil-based. The sample alerts the finisher to change course by pre-conditioning, sanding to a higher grit, or changing the coating material altogether.

Adding a stain—One up from the basic sample board is one showing a stain first and then a clear coat. But continue with the clear coats up to the desired sheen, as this will give a complete indication of what the stain will be like with the finished or "wet" look.

A Slightly More Sophisticated Sample

When the finishing plan calls for multicolor layering, it becomes imperative to use a step sample.

Like the example showing five coats of shellac on each step is isolated on the board. On the walnut sample below, lemon-yellow dye is applied to the whole board but left uncoated in the first section. A seal coat of shellac is applied as the second step. The third panel shows the application of a glaze, and so on.

This process is necessary to visually document the raw appearance for historical reference. It's important to make notes on every detail of the process including the date; it's vital information when working with cherry and other woods that age dramatically in a short period of time.

Years from now, you'll be able to go to the sample board and make sure that any new or repair work is progressing to match the original piece perfectly.

In short, the test sample helps you achieve two key goals of finishing: predictability and repeatability. The sample predicts the wisdom (or folly) of the finishing plan, and it allows you to repeat or duplicate the chosen plan in the future.

With a test sample, finishing your project can turn a nightmare into a dream.

Sand Between Coats for a Flawless Finish

by Jeff Jewitt

Whether you spray, brush, or wipe, one of the keys to a great finish is learning to sand between coats. When I began finishing in the 1970s, there weren't many choices when it came to sanding a finish: Steel wool shed tiny hairs that got embedded in the finish; regular sandpaper (if you could find it above 240 grit) clogged quickly when sanding shellac or lacquer; and if you wanted to flatten defects between coats of finish, you used wet-or-dry paper, which was messy and made it hard to gauge your progress.

Today, not only are there much better choices among consumer-oriented abrasives, but the Internet also has given everyone access to industrial abrasives. I'll narrow down what to use with film-forming finishes like lacquer, varnish, and shellac (in-the-wood 100% oil finishes and thin applications of oil/varnish mixes typically don't require sanding). I'll describe new products to use for dry-sanding between coats, and I'll cover the better use of wet-or-dry paper for sanding the final coat in preparation for the rubbing-out process.

Fine Grits and a Light Touch

Going from sanding bare wood to sanding a finish involves a change of gears. Instead of power-sanding using grits mostly P220 or coarser, you typically hand-sand using grits P320 and finer.

The first coat of finish, whether a purpose-made sealer or just a thinned coat of the final finish, generally leaves a rough surface with raised grain embedded in the finish. At this stage you aren't flattening the surface, just smoothing it, so there is no need to use a sanding block. Using P320-grit stearated paper, you can make a pad by folding a quarter sheet into thirds. This pad works best if you have to get into corners and other tight areas. Otherwise, you can just grip a quarter-sheet of paper by wrapping one corner around your pinkie and pinching the other corner between your thumb and index finger. An alternative is pressure-sensitive adhesive (PSA) paper in the same grit (P320) that comes in 2¾-in.-wide rolls. You can tear off only what you need and temporarily stick it to your fingers.

Making a Multicolor Sample

A step sample can document a complex coloring process. Start by prepping the sample board and then apply each layer of finish.

From prep to finish. Start by scraping, planing, or sanding the sample board as you will the actual workpiece (left). Then mark the lines separating each step in the coloring process (center). Then apply the finish, coat by coat, until the desired color and gloss are achieved (right). A piece of blue tape offers a way to isolate a section.

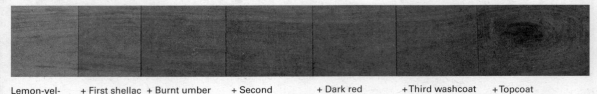

| Lemon-yellow dye stain | + First shellac washcoat | + Burnt umber glaze | + Second washcoat | + Dark red mahogany glaze | +Third washcoat | + Topcoat |

Myth-Buster: New Paper Works with Water-Based Finishes, Too

I've always assumed that stearated sandpaper caused adhesion problems with waterborne finishes. However, after finding little hard evidence, I decided to test several consumer and industrial sandpapers with a variety of waterborne finishes.

I applied one coat of each finish to a separate sample board. When it was dry, I divided the board into sections and sanded this coat smooth with a variety of P320-grit stearated sandpapers. After I removed the sanding residue, I applied another coat of finish and after 72 hours, evaluated the surface for flow-out and adhesion.

I found no compatibility issues with any of the sandpapers and waterborne finishes. If you use a premium stearated paper, you'll have no problems as long as you remove the residue after sanding.

Stearated Sandpaper: No More Clogging

The biggest advance in sanding between coats of finish has been the increasing availability and improving quality of stearated sandpaper. A waxy-feeling powder, zinc or calcium stearate (or a mixture), is incorporated into either aluminum-oxide or silicon-carbide sandpaper. The stearate prevents the dry finish residue from sticking and forming clumps, or corns, or clogging the spaces between the abrasive particles.

Dry-sanding between finish coats is better than wet-sanding because it allows you to see what you're doing much more clearly. If a surface is wet with lubricant, you could be sanding right through the sealer or finish because the lubricant creates an illusion of finish on the wood.

Another option, which costs a bit more, is hook-and-loop pads that allow you to hand-sand using disks designed for random-orbit sanders. If the sandpaper starts to load up with debris or corns, I swipe the grit side of the paper against a piece of thick carpet (Berber is best). You also can swipe it on a gray abrasive pad.

It's important to remove the residue after each sanding, or it will cause problems with the next coat of finish. If your finish is oil-based, solvent lacquer, or shellac, dampen a clean cotton or microfiber cloth with naphtha or mineral spirits and wipe away the debris. I prefer naphtha because it evaporates faster and leaves a little less oily residue. For waterborne finishes, I make a mixture of 5% denatured alcohol in tap water (roughly 1 oz. denatured alcohol to 16 oz. water). It's OK to follow the solvent wipe with a tack cloth, but most tack rags can leave a residue that will interfere with the adhesion of waterborne finishes. One waterborne-friendly tack cloth is 3M's item No. 03192.

Higher grits for subsequent coats—After you have smoothed the sealer coat and applied the first real coat of finish, you should generally use P400- or P600-grit paper to sand; otherwise, you might see tiny sanding scratches in finishes that don't melt into each other, such as oil-based products and most waterborne ones.

You can use a power sander on large, flat surfaces, once you have built up enough finish thickness (at least four to six coats). Use caution when sanding, staying away from the edges and using P400-grit paper or higher. For better visibility, I always do this with dust extraction. The better papers out there have holes punched to match the ports on the sanding pad, or are made up of a mesh like Mirka Abranet. An industrial product called Clean-Sand by 3M is disk paper with a spiral progression of small holes for dust extraction.

Special products for moldings, carvings, and turnings—Although you can use sheet sandpaper with shopmade or commercial profiled sanding blocks on gentle profiles, this won't work on sharp curves and other extreme profiles. For these areas, use ultra-flexible sanding sponges or a synthetic steel-wool substitute. Neither of these products has stearates because the face is more open and clogging isn't an issue. After use, most of them can be cleaned with soapy water and re-used. I like ultrathin synthetic steel wool, which more easily conforms to profiles and turnings. Choices include Mirka's Mirlon Total and 3M's Multi-Flex, both of which are available in a convenient roll, but look for 3M's SandBlaster flexible pads, which last a bit longer and are easier to find at most home centers and hardware stores.

On thin, flat areas like the inside edge of a picture frame or door, hold the pad with your thumb on top and the rest of your fingers underneath. This keeps it level. Or just use a small piece of the PSA paper mentioned earlier.

Wet-or-dry paper still the best for final flattening

Unlike stearated sandpaper, wet-or-dry sandpaper can be either FEPA (P) or CAMI graded. Make sure you know what you're using, because a P600 is equivalent to just under a CAMI 400. All FEPA-graded sandpaper should have a P before the grit number; if there is no P, assume it's CAMI grade unless otherwise specified. One feature of wet-or-dry paper is that you can get it in grits up to 2,000 and sometimes higher. If you have any trouble finding it, try an automotive parts supplier.

Wet-or-dry sandpaper is a very sharp and fast-cutting abrasive and works best for removing final defects and flattening the finish prior to rubbing out (where you polish the flattened surface to the desired sheen). You can use mineral spirits, a light mineral oil called paraffin or rubbing oil, or soapy water as a lubricant. Of the three, soapy water is the least messy, though it seems not to cut as fast or as well as the other two. I add a capful of Dawn dishwashing liquid for every pint (16 oz.) of tap water, and then apply the mixture using a plant mister.

Start with a quarter-sheet of P600-grit paper wrapped around a cork, or a cork-faced, block. Spray some lubricant on the surface and begin sanding with the grain if possible. On a top, I typically rub the outside 3 in. first so I can focus on keeping the block flat and not tipping it off an edge (that happens naturally with my arm motion if I'm taking a long sweep from one end to the other). Once I've gone around a few times, I come back and do the center. Wipe away the slurry and examine the surface. You're done when the surface looks about 80% to 90% dull. Don't try to make the entire surface perfectly dull, because you'll probably sand through the finish.

After using the wet-or-dry sandpaper, you can follow up with paste wax applied with 0000 steel wool for a satin finish. An alternative to steel wool is a very fine abrasive foam pad such as Mirka's Abralon. The 1,000, 2,000 and 4,000 grits can be used for sheens ranging from dull to satin. You don't need compounds or polishes with these products.

> **TIP**
>
> ### Remove the Dust
>
> It is very important to remove all the sanding residue before applying the next coat of finish. For solvent-based finishes, dampen a cloth with naphtha or mineral spirits. The former dries faster (but is harder to spell).

How to Handle Flat Surfaces

2 WAYS TO HOLD PAPER

Fold into thirds for tight spots. Fold a quarter sheet of sandpaper into thirds. All the paper can still be used but there is no grit-on-grit contact.

1.

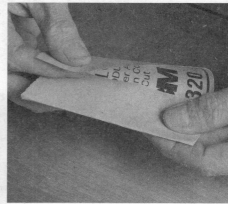

Sand inside corners. Folding the sheet into thirds allows you to work your way into tight spots.

2.

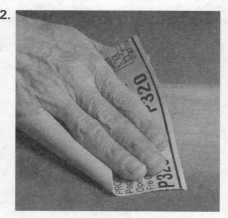

Hand sander. For sanding flat surfaces, just wrap a corner of the sheet around your little finger and grip the opposite corner between your index finger and thumb.

Continued ➡

1.

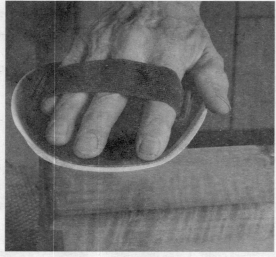

Handy pad. You can hand-sand using disks designed for random-orbit sanders by attaching them to a Velcro-backed pad.

 TIP

Keep Sandpaper Clean

Unlike power sanders with onboard dust extraction, hand–sanding can clog the paper quickly. A quick wipe on a carpet remnant gets it clean again.

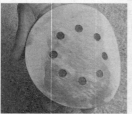 

2.

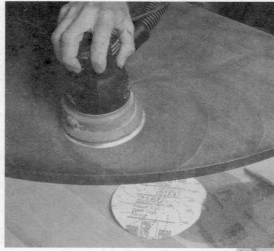

Power-sanding comes later. Once you have applied five or six coats of finish, you can safely use a random-orbit sander equipped with P400-grit disks.

New disks, better dust extraction. Through-the-pad dust extraction has been one of the great innovations in wood finishing. The latest disks work even better and fit all sander models regardless of their hole configuration. Mirka's Abranet is an abrasive-coated mesh (top right), while 3M's Clean-Sand disks have spirals of small holes (right).

New Tools for Curves and Carvings

Foam mesh. 3M's Sandblaster is a drawer-liner type of foam mesh coated with abrasive. It can be folded over to reach into tight corners or wrapped around curves.

Abrasive pads. These pads come in a variety of grits and are thin enough to get into carvings.

Sticky paper. Adhesive-backed sandpaper is useful for sanding narrow surfaces. Simply stick it to a finger.

Sanding sponges. Less flexible than the other products, sanding sponges are good for gentle curves and can be washed out when finished.

Switch to Wet Sanding on the Final Coat

Flat surfaces. Wet-or-dry sandpaper is the best way to smooth the surface prior to rubbing out the finish. Use soapy water as a lubricant and wipe away the slurry to check your progress.

Tight curves. Use 0000 steel wool lubricated with soapy water to remove the gloss on curved surfaces.

Finish up with wax. Apply some paste wax with Liberon's 0000 steel wool and then buff the surface with a cotton cloth for a smooth, satin finish.

Finish While You Build

by Charles Neil

For most woodworkers, finishing is a chore to be put off as long as possible. So they wait until after a piece is assembled to figure it out. Instead, finishing should be one of the first things on your agenda; if it isn't, you will work yourself into a corner—literally.

At age 13, I ran across a guy who painted cars. I really enjoyed watching him work, and later learned to do painting and finishing myself. I worked for years in that industry, and along the way I learned a lesson that has become invaluable in my woodworking: Look at each piece as a collection of parts. Just as a vehicle breaks down into the hood, the trunk lid, the doors, etc., a piece of furniture can be broken down into components.

A step-back cupboard, for example, consists of the doors, the face frame, the shelves, the crown molding, and other distinct parts. Not only is it much easier to sand and pre-finish these parts before they are assembled, but I also have a number of ways to modify the design of the components slightly to simplify finishing.

Think Finish Before You Cut and Glue

Few woodworkers are handy enough with dyes to be able to harmonize boards of different colors. Therefore, spend some time at the lumberyard sorting through the boards for matching color and grain.

Once you get the wood home and begin to lay out the parts on the boards, it often pays to alter the dimensions of your piece slightly. Unless you're building an exact replica, the design usually has a little flexibility. Say you have two beautifully matched boards that are ideal for the tabletop but are 1/4 in. narrower than your planned width. It is much better to compromise on the design and use the best matching boards for the premier surface. No amount of skilled wood coloring will make up for an ill-matched top.

Pre-finish the interiors and anticipate squeeze-out—After finding the best match between the boards and the individual parts of the project but before you do any assembly, think about the finish. For example, on a step-back cupboard, if you assemble the top case and glue in the shelves, sanding or scraping and finishing will be very difficult where the parts meet at 90°. Instead, finish the entire interior of both upper and lower cases now. You may have some touch-up to do later, but finishing these panels while you can lay them flat is much easier than wrestling with the whole case. You also will get much better results.

Mask off areas that will be glued. On shelves that are finished on both sides, screw on end caps sized to cover the entire area on the shelf ends that will fit into the dado in the cabinet sides. In this way, you can turn over the shelves without marring the finish, both sides can dry at once, and the area to receive glue remains unfinished. I find that 1/8-in.-deep dadoes give ample shear strength, are easier and cleaner to cut, and leave plenty of material in the shelf sides for adding the screws and plugs.

After applying the finish, remove the masking tape from the glue surfaces and dry-fit everything. Now apply masking tape to the areas adjacent to glue surfaces. When you glue the cabinet together, any squeeze-out will collect on the tape and be easy to remove. The alternative is trying to remove squeeze-out in hard-to-reach areas that are already finished.

Make and install the face frames—Here again, some pre-finishing and masking tape can spare you a lot of agony. Apply finish to the inside edges of the face frame. Before gluing the face frame to the carcase, place tape on the adjacent surface of the carcase to protect it from squeeze-out. Don't worry about the exterior, because those surfaces will remain accessible and you'll be scraping or sanding them after the piece is assembled. No matter how particular you are, you may still get some glue on the wood. Don't try to wipe it off with a damp cloth; instead, let the glue set until it's semi-firm like chewing gum, then use a chisel or scraper to peel it off the surface. Now clean the wood with acetone; it removes the glue better than water and works with PVA, polyurethane, epoxy, and hide glues.

Pre-Finish Interiors

You dado the sides of the case before assembly, so why not finish them too? A few minutes spent prepping the components for finish saves hours trying to finish the assembled interior.

Sand before you assemble. Scrape or sand boards while they can be laid flat. Once a piece is glued together, it is much harder to reach into corners either by hand or with a machine.

Mask off glue surfaces. Clear finish or paint will interfere with glue's ability to bond wood, so use masking tape to seal off surfaces that will be glued.

Temporary handles. Screw blocks of scrapwood to each end of the shelves. You'll be able to handle the shelves cleanly while finishing them, the glue surfaces are protected, and both sides can dry at once.

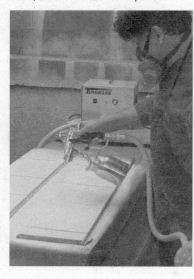

Finish the inside. Whether you use a brush or spray gun, it is much easier to finish the interior of the upper cabinet before the cabinet is assembled.

Continued ➔

Protect from Squeeze-Out

You don't want to scrape dried glue off the pre-finished interior, so position some blue masking tape to catch any glue that squeezes out.

INTERIOR SHELVES

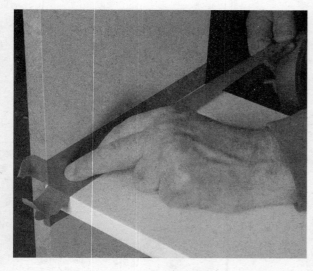

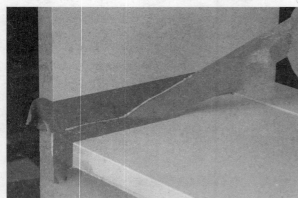

Tape and peel. When you dry-assemble the piece, place masking tape adjacent to glue surfaces (above). Disassemble and apply the glue (below). When the parts are glued up, any squeeze-out goes onto the tape and is easily peeled away (bottom).

A Novel Way to Hide Screw Holes

Neil reinforces shelf-to-side panel joints with screws, but matching filler to the finished wood is problematic. Sink trim-head screws 1/4 in. below the surface. Tap in a square peg with diagonals slightly greater than the hole's diameter. Once dry, saw and sand the peg flush, apply a finish, and it will resemble an antique square peg.

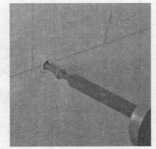

Drive the screws. As well as the hole for the shaft, drill 1/4-in.-dia. holes to receive the head.

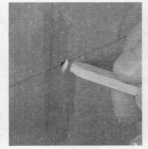

Square peg, round hole. Taper the tip of a square peg and then glue and tap it into the screw hole.

Meant to show. When finish is applied, the square pegs stand out.

Face Frames

Pre-finish adjacent parts. The face frame will be next to the already painted shelves, so pre-finish the edge before attaching it.

Tape the cabinet edges. Apply tape to the interior cabinet adjacent to the face frame (above) to make removing excess glue much easier (below).

TIP

If you get surplus glue on the wood while the glue is curing, remove any residue with acetone.

A Neat Trick for Attaching Moldings

With the two carcases glued up, it's time to focus on the smaller parts, starting with the base and crown moldings. Any time you have a cross-grain application, such as where moldings contact the sides of the cabinet, two issues come into play. First, the expansion and contraction issue prevents gluing on the pieces all the way across—an inch or two at the front is as far as you dare go. Second, there is risk of cross-grain sanding scratches.

However, there's a nice, simple trick that solves both problems at once. For the base molding, rather than using a narrow strip of wood that must be nailed to the cabinet with the subsequent nail holes to fill, make the molding a couple of inches wider and then notch it to fit under the lower case. This allows the base to be screwed to the underside of the cabinet using slotted holes in the sides of the molding that allow for movement. The horizontal top section of crown molding is attached to the top in the same way using slotted screw holes. The base and the crown can now be prepped and finished independently of the rest of the cabinet. The sides of the cabinet can be worked unobstructed, removing the risk of cross-grain scratches.

I have a novel way to reinforce the relatively weak miter joint at the front corners of the molding. After the miter is glued and dried, take as large a Forstner bit as will fit into the notched section of the molding and drill halfway through. Now bandsaw a piece of wood slightly smaller than the diameter and depth of the hole. Glue the circle into the hole with the grain running perpendicular to the miter joint.

Pre-Assemble Moldings

Instead of nailing on pieces of molding at the last minute, make them into a robust separate unit, pre-finish them, and attach them to the cabinet with hidden screws.

Notched molding. The base molding fits under the cabinet instead of being nailed to the front and sides. This means it can be pre-assembled and screwed on.

Drill a hole. Use a Forstner bit just smaller than the corner area to drill a little more than halfway through the wood. Keep the point just to one side of the joint to avoid splitting it.

Shopmade circle. On a piece of wood slightly thinner than the depth of the hole in the miter joint, just start to drill a hole with the same bit and then cut out the circle on the bandsaw.

A stiffer joint. Glue the circle into the hole with its grain perpendicular to the line of the joint.

Divide and conquer. It is much easier to prep and finish the molding and the case sides before joining them.

Prep and Finish a Frame and Panel Before Assembly

Solid-wood panels are designed to move within the frame. While this is a neat solution to the problem of wood movement from a woodworker's perspective, it presents a number of problems to a finisher. When the frame and panel are finished after glue-up, an unfinished area that sits in the grooves becomes exposed if the panel contracts later. On the other hand, if finish "glues" the panel into the frame, either the panel will split as it tries to contract, or it will break the frame as it tries to expand.

Second, it is nearly impossible to scrape or sand the sides or back of a raised panel and the inner edges of the frame after the frame has been glued together. It is much easier to prep these areas while they are still individual parts.

On a raised panel, the end-grain beveled area will absorb more finish and appear darker than the rest of the panel. To avoid this, it is necessary to sand this area with much finer sandpaper or use some other form of absorption control. You can either finish just the profiled part of the panel or, if you prefer, the entire surface. With the components done, check to see if any finish needs touching up before assembling the cabinet. Screw on the moldings and feet, nail or screw on the pre-finished backs, and attach the doors. By taking the time and making the effort to plan ahead, you'll be rewarded with a finish worthy of your masterpiece and a lot less hassle.

Frame-and-Panel Tips

It is almost impossible to finish an assembled frame-and-panel neatly. Plan ahead!

Finer grits for end grain. To prevent the end grain on a raised panel from absorbing too much finish and turning dark, sand it successively with P320-, P400-, and P600-grit paper.

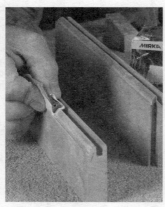

Don't forget the frame. Sand the inside edges of the frame parts before the panel is inserted and the frame is glued together.

Finish the parts. Apply finish to the panel (above) and the inside edges of the frame (left) before glue-up.

Protect the finish. After the frame has been glued together, you probably will need to flush-sand the joints. To avoid damage from the sander, tape off the nearby sections of panel.

Home stretch. By finishing individual parts separately and controlling glue squeeze-out, You can achieve a flawless finish.

Seal First for a Better Finish

by Peter Gedrys

One aspect of finishing that causes great confusion is sealers and their use. Part of the problem stems from thinking that sealers are to clear coats what primer is to paint and that all bare wood should be sealed first. In fact, the first coat of any finish acts as a sealer.

But using the first coat as a sealer isn't always the best choice—if that were the case, this would be a very short article! Clear finishes vary greatly in how effective they are as sealers, and there are many times when you should go with something else. However, a product sold as a "sanding sealer" may or may not be the solution. Now that I've got you confused, let's delve into the world of sealers. I'll make the choice for your next project easy, and your final finish will be better than ever.

Shellac is the Wonder-Product

There are many types of sealer, but if you could use only one it would be dewaxed shellac, either from a can (left) or flakes. It is readily available, cheap, has no strong fumes, goes on easily, and sands well. It is compatible with any finish and wood. Use it on all interior projects except those that will be subject to substantial heat or humidity.

When to Seal Bare Wood

The first coat of any finish on any wood penetrates the fibers and leaves the surface feeling rough and uneven after it dries. This coat needs to be sanded smooth, to provide a good foundation for subsequent coats to build on.

Varnish doesn't sand well, so seal first—Not all types of finish sand easily, especially when applied to bare wood. Varnish tends to gum up the sandpaper and takes a long time to dry. You can overcome these problems by sealing with a coat of dewaxed shellac.

However, I never use shellac with exterior varnishes. Because of shellac's brittle nature, temperature fluctuations can weaken its bond to the substrate and cause the finish to fail. In this case you have a couple of options. You can thin the varnish by 50% with mineral spirits and apply it to the bare wood. It takes longer to dry and is harder to sand than shellac, but you get a durable exterior finish. A more expensive option is a marine-grade sealer that is stearate-free, such as Interlux's Interprime Wood Sealer (jamestowndistributors.com), suitable for interior or exterior work. (For more on stearates, see "Why to Avoid Some Sealers," p. 269.)

For oil-based finishes, seal to avoid blotching—With oil or oil-and-varnish finishes, the problem is not poor sanding, but rather excessive or uneven penetration. Porous woods such as butternut seem to drink this type of finish and never create an even sheen. Others such as pine and cherry can end up blotchy. And on almost all woods, the end grain turns darker than the other surfaces. Thinning the first coat only makes these problems worse. Again, shellac comes to the rescue. Instead of sealing, the aim is to let absorbent areas of the wood soak up the wash-coat while the rest of the surface is minimally changed. To do this, apply only a thin, 1-lb. cut of dewaxed shellac and when dry, lightly sand it with 220-grit paper. You will see slightly less shimmer from figured woods but the overall tone will be more even.

Sealers minimize raised grain—Some waterborne finishes are quite alkaline, which promotes grain raising when they are applied to bare wood. Manufacturers sell neutral-pH sealers, labeled sanding sealers, but you sacrifice some durability, so the better choice is once again shellac. As well as providing a smooth base for the waterborne finish, shellac can enhance and warm the overall tone of a finish, particularly if you use darker grades such

Continued ➜

as dewaxed garnet. This is beneficial with waterborne finishes, which can have a cold and somewhat lifeless appearance.

Use vinyl sealer in hot or moist areas—Vinyl-based sealer may be considered the modern shellac. It dries quickly, forms an excellent barrier, and bonds so well that vinyl resin is the base for many adhesives. Like shellac, it will also lock in contaminants and seal oily woods. Use it for interior projects only. However, it has far better heat and moisture resistance than shellac, so it is a good sealer for kitchens and bathrooms. Although sold to be used under solvent lacquers or two-part coatings to which it is chemically related, it can be used under any type of finish.

The downside is that vinyl sealer is formulated to be sprayed, and is not the friendliest stuff. But you can pad it on after thinning it (with lacquer thinner), and protect yourself with gloves, a respirator, and good ventilation. If applying it by hand, it works best on small projects because it dries rapidly. It doesn't sand as well as shellac, so some sealers include stearates, but better ones use a modified nitrocellulose resin to help with sanding. Examples include Sherwin-Williams' High Solid Vinyl Sealer No. T67F5 and M.L. Campbell's C100 25. Both come in a minimum size of 1 gal., but Behlen's Vinyl Sealer comes in quarts (woodcraft.com).

Seal in the oils in problem woods—The oils in some tropical woods such as rosewood and cocobolo can prevent oil-based finishes from curing, leaving them sticky. The same is true of the chemicals in aromatic red cedar and the resin in pine. In all cases, applying a coat of dewaxed shellac to the bare wood isolates the oil-based finish and allows it to cure normally.

Finally, if you are refinishing an old piece of furniture, surface contamination, particularly silicone oil from

What Can a Sealer do for You?

A sealer can save you time and money, help you avoid disasters, and result in a better-looking finish.

SAVE TIME AND FINISH ON POROUS WOODS

After three coats of wipe-on poly, the side of this butternut board sealed with a 2-lb. cut of dewaxed shellac has good build and an even sheen. The unsealed side absorbed the poly unevenly.

UNSEALED   SEALED

CONTROL BLOTCHING

UNSEALED   SEALED

Many cherry boards will absorb an oil-based finish unevenly, leaving a blotchy appearance. A 1-lb. cut of dewaxed shellac limits absorption in the more porous areas for an even look.

SMOOTH SANDING

The advantage to applying a 2-lb. cut of shellac rather than a thin coat of varnish as a sealer coat is that shellac powders when sanded (left) but varnish gums up the sandpaper (right).

TAME OILY WOODS

The oils in some tropical woods can delay or even prevent an oil-based finish from curing, leaving it sticky. The right side of the board was sealed with shellac, which prevents this problem.

ADD WARMTH

Waterborne finishes can leave some woods, such as cherry, looking gray. The right-hand side of the sample was sealed with dewaxed garnet shellac for a warmer look.

SEAL BETWEEN OIL AND WATER

Applying a waterborne topcoat over an oil-based pigment stain is asking for trouble. Dewaxed shellac seals in the stain and gives a good base for the topcoat.

PROTECT DYE

After the board was colored with a water-based dye, the near side was sealed with dewaxed shellac. When a waterborne topcoat was brushed on, it removed some of the dye on the far side, but not in the sealed area.

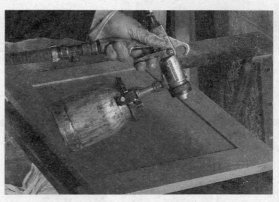

furniture polish, can cause fisheye, where contamination repels the finish and leaves little craters. Again, an initial coat of shellac is the answer.

Sealers Between Finishes

When doing a multi-step finish, product compatibility is a big issue. We all know that oil and water don't mix, so it is good practice to apply shellac or a vinyl sealer between an oil-based stain, grain filler or glaze, and a waterborne clear coat. Otherwise you run the risk of poor adhesion.

Sometimes two similar products must be kept apart to avoid a fatal attraction. A water-based dye can bleed into a waterborne topcoat and leave a muddy, blurry appearance. A thin coat of sealer will lock in the dye or stain and allow you to topcoat with ease. If you plan to use an alcohol-based non-grain-raising dye, brushing shellac as a topcoat can be problematic because the alcohol in the shellac will reactivate the dye. Overcome this by spraying a very thin first coat of shellac. Trust me: Making the right choices will save headaches down the road. Guess how I know that!

Why to Avoid Some Sealers

Ingredients
Copolymer resin.....
Petroleum distillates...
Stoddard solvent......
Vinyl toluene............
VM&P naphtha.......
Zinc stearate........

Usually, in woodworking, your best choice is a tool or product specifically designed for the job. That's not the case with many products sold as "sanding sealers," whether waterborne or oil-based. The latter consist of a vinyl-alkyd resin that seals, a fast-drying solvent such as toluene that allows you to recoat in under an hour, and zinc stearates or metallic soaps to make sanding easier. These last components are the sealers' Achilles heel. They make the sealer soft and tend to produce a weak bond with the substrate and subsequent coatings.

Closely examine the description of the can's contents: Like the example shown above, if you see either stearates or soaps mentioned, then go with another type of sealer.

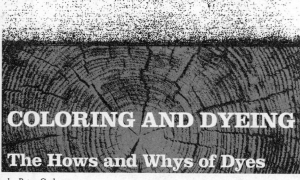

COLORING AND DYEING
The Hows and Whys of Dyes

by Peter Gedrys

Dyes are an indispensable tool for a professional finisher: I use them to give mahogany that rich brown found on antiques, to enhance figured maple, and to brightly color a contemporary piece. However, many woodworkers have a deep fear of coloring wood. I'm reminded of Groucho Marx's witticism: "Die, my dear? Why that's the last thing I'll do!"

In part, this comes from confusion between dyes and pigment stains. Unlike stains, dyes never look muddy or hide the natural beauty of wood. With that in mind, let's take a closer look at what dyes are, where they come from, and how to use them.

What Is a Dye and How Is It Made?

For centuries, dyes were obtained from natural products such as roots, berries, insects, and nut husks. Then in the mid-nineteenth century, William Henry Perkin discovered how to make a synthetic purple dye from aniline, an organic compound derived from coal tar. This was a giant step forward: There was now an inexpensive method to mass-produce dyes. Today, most dyes are derived from crude oil but the term aniline is still widely used.

Many woodworkers think that dyes, like stains, are simply finely ground pigments, but this is not true.

Although you can buy dyes already dissolved, powders offer the widest range of colors and are the most inexpensive option. You also have full control over the color strength by adding powder or diluting the solution.

The three main dye groups associated with woodworking are acid, basic, and solvent dyes. The water-soluble dyes are, for the most part, the acid group, and the alcohol dyes are the basic group. The solvent dyes are soluble in a variety of oil solvents from mineral spirits and naphtha (aliphatics), to xylene and toluene (aromatics), to acetone and lacquer thinners (ketones).

So much for chemistry. Which dye is right for your project?

The Sum of its Parts

Dyes are usually a blend of three colors. This can be seen clearly with a water dye. Drop a pinch in water, watch the colors separate, and get a lesson in basic color theory. A reddish-brown dye may contain yellow, orange, and blue. Since orange and blue are complementary colors (opposite each other on the color wheel), they offset each other. In other words, if the dye has more orange than blue, it will be a warmer red brown. Add more blue and the color shifts to a deeper, less reddish brown.

Water-Soluble Dyes Work for Most Needs

Water-soluble dyes dissolve easily in warm water, have no odor whether dry or dissolved, and resist fading. They are best applied to new wood and are suitable on any species, but particularly dense-grained species such as maple, cherry, or poplar.

Water-soluble dyes are also easy to apply by hand. On large areas, you want to flood the surface; on smaller areas, folded paper towels or a small brush work well. On very large areas, spraying is an option, and because the dye is water based, there is no need for an explosion-proof spray booth.

Don't be fooled by the dead look that dyes have when they dry. They come back to life when a clear finish is applied.

The problem of water-soluble dyes raising the grain is overblown. Some boards swell more than others (use a test sample), and for these, dampen the surface prior to final sanding. On all others, any raised-grain fuzziness disappears when you sand the first coat of clear finish. But what you don't want to do is sand the dye coat, as you will sand through the color in spots.

When preparing your test board, you may find that surface tension prevents these dyes from adding color to the pores of woods like mahogany, oak, and walnut. To ease the surface tension, add a scant drop of dishwashing detergent to the dissolved dye. Don't add too much or you'll get a sudsy dye.

Alcohol-Soluble Dyes Dry Fast

The biggest difference between water-soluble dyes and alcohol-soluble ones is that alcohol-soluble dyes dry much faster, generally in less than 15 minutes even when applied

Dyes and Stains Are Two Different Products

A dye is generally an organic compound that is soluble in water, alcohol, or oil. This creates a color in solution that penetrates the wood. Conversely, a pigment remains in suspension and requires a binder to help affix it to the surface. Think of dyes as sugar and pigment as sand. Drop them into warm water and the sugar will dissolve; the sand will collect at the bottom. This is also what makes dyes transparent and stains cloudy.

Dyes Pop the Figure

On close-grained woods like maple, dyes add uniform color while magnifying any figure that is present. Stains muddy the figure.

Stains Pop the Grain

On open-grained woods, the pigment particles lodge in the pores, highlighting the grain structure. Dyes give a more uniform color.

Plenty of Dye Yields an Even Color

Flood the surface. Don't skimp when applying the dye. You get better penetration if you wet the surface thoroughly.

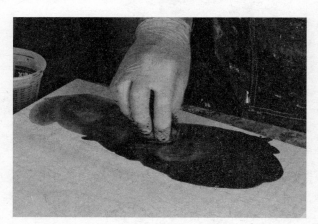

Uniform color. After a minute, the boundary will disappear and when the surplus dye is wiped away, the surface will have an even color.

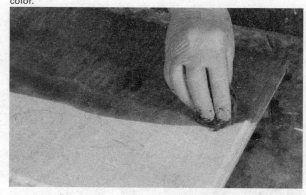

Uneven application? If you pause on a large surface, you can apply more dye as long as the surface is wet. At first the boundary will be obvious because the earlier dye had longer to penetrate.

Continued ➡

by hand. They are considered non-grain raising, which eliminates any need to raise the grain prior to dyeing and makes them excellent for quick touchups. Furniture finishers and restorers often have a plastic box with 18 compartments for a wide variety of alcohol-soluble dye powders. Mixing the dyes with a little shellac quickly rectifies finishing flaws such as sanding through color on edges.

On the other hand, while small areas can easily be dyed by hand with a quick-drying solvent like alcohol, it takes careful planning to avoid unsightly streaks when doing a large area. In these cases, spraying is more effective.

Dissolve the powder in denatured alcohol and stir the mixture occasionally for at least an hour. Once the powder is dissolved, you can use the dye to tint finishes such as shellac and lacquer (when tinting lacquer, use a 3:1 mix of methanol and acetone).

Preparing a Dye

Heat helps. Dyes dissolve best in liquid that is around 160°F. If you are heating anything but water, make sure you do it in a hot water bath and not directly over a heat source.

Why I Don't Use Chemical Dyes

I have deliberately not covered chemical dyes, though a few woodworkers still swear by them. Some, like the vinegar-and-steel-wool concoction, are relatively benign (it you let the hydrogen escape while it brews) but you can get the same color with dye powders with much less hassle. Avoid other chemical dyes at all costs. Potassium dichromate, used to darken cherry and mahogany, contains a heavy metallic salt, hexavalent chromium, which is very dangerous to humans and the environment

Alcohol Dyes Dry Fast

Great for touchups. Alcohol-soluble dyes mixed with some dewaxed shellac are a great way to cover up mistakes such as over-sanded edges.

Oil-Based Dyes Are Best for Tinting Clear

Sneak preview. To see what tinting an oil-based finish will look like, put some finish on a white plate, sprinkle on some dye powder, and rub it around.

Strain the solution. Dissolve the oil-soluble dye in mineral spirits or lacquer thinner, then add it to the clear oil-based finish via a fine paint strainer.

All dyes will fade to some degree, but alcohol powders are not as lightfast as water ones. The most fade-resistant dyes are metal-acid complex types. In a sophisticated piece of chemical engineering, a metal such as chromium, copper, or cobalt is liquefied and attached to a molecule of dye in a 1:1 or 1:2 ratio. This creates a much stronger molecular bond and improves lightfastness. TransTints concentrated dye and Solar-Lux NGR dye contain this metal-complex dye, as do some of Lockwood's water-soluble powders.

Oil-Soluble Dyes Are Best for Tinting

These are probably the dye powders you will use least, but they still have some niche uses. They are useful to add a hint of color in oil-based finishes. By tinting a clear finish, you create a toner that can slightly adjust a wood's color. This is also an easy way to shift a very amber-colored varnish to a more neutral brown. Oil-soluble dyes will dissolve in an aliphatic such as mineral spirits or turpentine, but are best dissolved in lacquer thinner, which mixes well with oil-based finishes. Add the dissolved dye in small increments and don't exceed 5% of the finish by volume, or you run the risk of a streaky surface. Less is more here.

Tips with Dyes

There are a few simple safety precautions for working with dyes. Always wear gloves, and when handling dye powders wear a dust mask—you only get one pair of lungs.

When mixing a dye, it is best to work by weight vs. volume, but if you lack a sensitive scale, 1 oz. of dye as measured in a plastic medicine dispenser is just under 1 oz. in weight. As you gain experience, you'll get a feel for how much powder is needed to create your colors. The standard concentration is 1 oz. of powder per quart of liquid. However, I normally make a stock solution at twice that strength. If I want to dilute the color, I'll pour some of this stock into a measured amount of clear solvent and test the result. Keep records of the ratios and you can re-create any color.

Dye powders dissolve best in solvents warmed to about 160°F. You can directly heat water (distilled is best), but if you warm up flammable solvent always use a hot-water bath as opposed to open flame or microwave. Failure to do so could ruin your day.

Dissolved water-based dyes are susceptible to bacteria, which can form a mold on the surface. However, I keep my dyes in glass or plastic containers out of sunlight and they last a year without problem. Alcohol or oil dyes are not as easily affected by bacteria, but can come out of solution over time and may require stirring and filtering.

If you've never used dyes, you'll be happily surprised at their versatility, brilliance, and clarity. Even though chemists have advanced their quality, some things stay the same. One example is Lockwood's walnut crystals, whose base color comes from a peat found in Germany. Once washed and filtered, it produces a lovely brown we associate with walnut.

Welcome to the wonderful world of dyes.

Success for Dyeing

by Jeff Jewitt

Most woodworkers have read about the benefits of using water-based dye stains to color wood. They are available in a range of colors, from bright primaries to muted wood tones, and their transparency lets the wood's personality shine, popping the figure in woods like curly or bird's-eye maple.

But using dyes for the first time can be a frustrating experience. Newcomers often end up with streaky surfaces or uneven colors, perhaps because they apply the dyes the same way they wipe on pigment stains purchased from the local home center. With a pigment stain, you wipe on a heavy layer in a fairly random manner, wait a few minutes to let it soak in, and then wipe off the surplus. But dyes soak in almost instantly, so the application must be quick and precise to avoid lap marks and streaking.

Here, I'll explain how to use a water-soluble dye stain, giving you the keys to achieving reliable results the first time and every time.

Prepare the Wood, Tools, and Dye

Dyes don't emphasize sanding errors as much as pigment stains do, but you still want a well-sanded surface, so sand up to P180 or P220 grit. The last sanding should be done shortly before applying the dye to lessen the chance of getting dirt or hand grease on the wood, which might interfere with the dye. Remove the sanding debris with a vacuum or compressed air.

Preemptive raising of the grain is advisable only with woods that really "puff" when water hits them, such as red or white oak. Woods that don't react to water as severely, such as maple and cherry, can be smoothed easily after the dyeing process. If you do raise the grain, wipe down the wood liberally with distilled water, let it dry, and then sand with the last grit of sandpaper you used.

You can apply water-based dyes with a spray gun or by hand. A spray gun will really speed up the process, but it isn't mandatory. If you do spray, protect your lungs: A standard organic vapor respirator rated for paints will suffice. When applying the dye by hand, I use cotton cloths, which I buy in 5-lb. boxes. These cloths are somewhat water-repellent straight out of the box, so to increase absorption, I soak each one in hot water and then wring out the excess before using it to apply the dye. Be sure to wear gloves.

It's impossible to keep dye from running over to an adjacent surface, so I always dye all sides at the same time. A nail board made with drywall screws works well because you can dye the underside of an object first, then place it on the nail board and dye the other sides without marring the underside of the project.

Water-soluble dyes are sold as powders or liquid concentrates. I'll focus on the powders, as they are more economical and come in a wider range of colors.

As an example, I want to give a maple side table an amber antique look. A starting ratio is typically 1 oz. dye to 2 quarts water, but don't mix up all the dye at once. Instead, use the same ratio but prepare just a little more liquid dye than you expect to use. For a small table, a pint should be plenty. That way you'll have plenty of dye powder left over to make the liquid darker if necessary. There are a couple of ways to measure small amounts of powder if you don't have a scale. If the dye comes in a transparent container, you can mark the quarter measurements on the outside. Or, pour the powder onto a sheet of paper; divide the heap into two equal halves, and then divide one half in half again to obtain roughly 1/4 oz.

Tap water contains trace iron compounds that react with tannins in woods like cherry or oak and will produce gray spots that might be noticeable under light colors, yellows in particular. Therefore, use distilled water for light dye colors (tap water is fine for darker ones). The water should be about 140°F, or roughly the temperature of hot tap water. Stir in the dye and let the contents cool to room temperature. It's not a bad idea to run the cooled mixture

through a fine paint strainer or, in a pinch, a coffee filter to remove any small lumps of dye powder.

Test this mixture on a scrap of wood from your project to see if it's the color you're after. The color of the wet dye will be very close to how it will look after a clear topcoat has been applied. Once you have the color you want, finish another scrap board, end grain and all. Use this sample board to see if the dye colored unevenly. If you notice dark splotches or excessively dark end grain, you should use a stain controller on your project before dyeing it.

Preparation is the Key

SEAL PROBLEM AREAS

End grain is a usual suspect. Once you have the right color, test it on another sample board to see if the wood absorbs the color evenly.

In this case (above), the end grain has absorbed too much dye and become darker than the surrounding wood. On areas your sample boards indicated would absorb too much dye, apply a coat of a water-based stain controller. This will limit the wood's absorption capacity.

GIVE IT A LIFT

To avoid liquid pooling under the bottoms of the legs and creating dark areas when you apply the dye, drive a drywall screw into the end of each leg.

Dye Quickly, or You'll Live to Regret it

Because it's easier to work on flat boards than inside corners, dismantle your project as much as possible before applying the dye. The next step is to apply a stain controller to areas the sample board told you are likely to absorb too much color.

The most common problem newcomers have with dyes is streaking or lap marks. This is caused by not keeping a wet edge when applying the dye, and consequently applying an overlap of dye to an area that already has started to dry. There are a couple of ways to lessen this problem. First, apply dyes in temperatures between 50°F and 75° F. In addition, avoid strong cross-ventilation such as open windows. There's no smell from water-based dyes and the fumes aren't considered hazardous unless you spray the dye.

Dunk a pre-wetted and wrung-out cotton cloth into the dye solution and let it soak for about 10 to 15 seconds. Take it out and squeeze out the excess. Then apply the dye as quickly and evenly as you can. When staining a tabletop, always start at an edge, never the middle, and go with the grain. Cover the back side, edges, and top, moving as fast and as efficiently as possible. If necessary, dunk the rag in the dye again to recharge it, or you can keep another rag sitting in the mix, ready to go.

Once the top has been covered completely, remove any excess dye with clean paper towels. On larger areas, such as a dining table, you can use the same application methods, but you may want to have one helper to keep recharging the cloths with dye and another to handle the paper towels.

On complicated surfaces such as a table base, a plant mister allows you to apply the dye with one hand and then blot up the excess with a clean cloth in the other. Work from the bottom up, and if you get a drip on any area, apply more dye immediately to that area or it will show up as a dark spot later. If you have even a portable compressor, a spray gun works great.

On drawers, I like to stain only the outside and top edge of the drawer front, which takes a bit of care. I soak a small piece of rag in the dye, wring it out as much as possible, and then carefully apply the dye. The end grain of the dovetails will darken after the topcoat is applied, so I don't bother trying to stain them. If you choose to dye the end grain (for example, if the rest of the piece is being dyed a dark or vibrant color), use a small artist's brush.

Be very careful when dyeing work veneered with standard interior PVA glue (yellow or white). Water-based dyes really soak into the wood and can release the glue's bond, resulting in a bubble under the veneer. If you veneer your own work, use a two-part glue like Unibond 800 or a waterproof glue like Titebond III.

Use a Clear Finish of Your Choice

When the dye has dried, the wood may take on a dry, matte, or mottled appearance that's very different from what it looked like as you were applying the dye. This is normal; the color will take on depth and luster as you apply a clear topcoat.

If the surface feels rough, don't resort to sandpaper; instead, lightly smooth it with a gray abrasive pad, going with the grain. The pad's cushioned surface is less likely to cut through the stain. Most of the time I don't bother; I just apply a couple of coats of clear finish and then sand the surface with P320-grit paper.

One note of caution: Brushing on a water-based clear coat over a dried water-soluble dye will lift some of the color. To prevent this, apply a sealer coat of dewaxed shellac or an oil-based sealer first. If you're planning to use an oil- or solvent-based finish, you don't have to worry; the dye won't lift with these products.

Two Ways to Apply Dye

WIPE FLAT SURFACES

Work fast to avoid streaking on large surfaces. Start at the edges and go with the grain, using a large cloth (above). Jewitt dyes only the face and the top edge of a drawer front (left). He doesn't dye the ends because the end grain will darken under a clear coat.

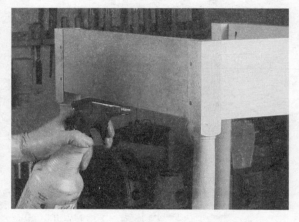

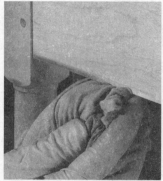

SPRAY COMPLEX SURFACES

You can use a plant mister to apply dye to complex or small shapes or to vertical surfaces such as legs (above). Wear a respirator even with this type of spraying. Use a cloth or paper towel to remove surplus dye (left) before it can dry.

When Things Go Wrong

If you make a mistake, the die is not cast. If you miss a small spot on a large surface, it is best to dye the whole area again. Likewise if the color is too weak, apply the dye again.

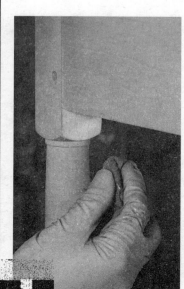

BARE SPOTS

If you overlook an isolated area, wait until the dye dries and then touch up the bare spot.

Continued ➜

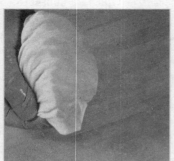

STREAKS

While the wood is still wet, rub the darker areas with a clean, damp cloth to remove some of the dye.

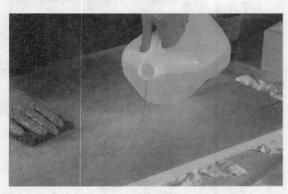

TOO MUCH COLOR

If an area needs a drastic reduction in color, pour a little distilled water on the surface and scrub the wood with a gray abrasive pad.

Fantastic Finishes with Dyes and Gel Stains

by Peter Gedrys

Gel stains have grown in popularity in recent years. Their viscosity and wipe-on/wipe-off application method make them easy to master, and compared with penetrating oil stains, they cause far less blotching on certain woods. However, using them on bare wood is often not the best method. Because of the pigment in gel stains, multiple coats tend to obscure the wood grain. And they come in a limited range of colors.

A better way to use them is in conjunction with dyes. You can apply gel directly over a dye to emphasize the grain and pore structure, or you can seal the dyed surface first and then apply the gel stain. Known as glazing, this is one of the most versatile and forgiving steps in the finisher's arsenal because it's so easy to change or even remove the glaze before it dries. I'll demonstrate on three popular woods—white oak, pine, and mahogany—and give finishing recipes for each.

Mission Oak

Transform pale white oak into the rich, deep brown reminiscent of fumed oak without using hazardous concentrated ammonia.

THE RECIPE

- Lockwood #871 English Brown Oak water-soluble dye
- General Finishes Brown Mahogany gel stain
- Oil-based varnish

White oak is one of my favorite woods because it takes colors and finishes in a very predictable fashion. On this table, I'll show you how to create a deep, rich brown reminiscent of fumed oak, the signature finish of so many Arts and Crafts pieces.

The process starts with a water-based dye, which is used to lighten up or subdue the base or background color of the wood. Water-based dyes are economical and come in a huge range of colors. My choice for this table was Lockwood's English Brown Oak, a cool, deep brown. Dissolve ½ oz. of powder in 8 oz. of warm distilled water, let it cool, and then filter it.

After sanding the table to P180 grit, blow the dust out of the pores, wipe the surface clean with a dry cloth, and apply the dye with a small pad. Use a brush to help dab the dye into corners. Be generous applying the dye, but wipe off the excess. Once the dye is dry, wipe on a coat of gel stain directly over it and wipe off the surplus after a couple of minutes. This helps make the grain and pore structure more pronounced, while leaving the ray-fleck pattern pale. I used General Finishes Brown Mahogany, a deep, warm brown. This dye-and-stain combination results in a deep, aged brown like you'll find on many antiques.

Allow the gel to dry completely (about 24 to 36 hours) before applying a topcoat. If you're not sure it's dry, do the smell test: If there is a strong, discernible smell of oil, wait. I applied three coats of an oil-based varnish to give the table decent protection. If you want to use a water-based finish, seal the gel stain first with a coat of dewaxed shellac. Zinsser's Seal-Coat works very well and can be used at its regular 2-lb. cut.

DYE COLORS THE WOOD

Filter first. Before using the dye, pour it through a fine paint filter to remove any lumps of powder.

Apply dye liberally. Use a folded piece of cloth or paper towel to dye the wood (above). After a minute or two, wipe off the surplus with a clean cloth.

GEL STAIN POPS THE GRAIN

Wipe on, wipe off. Applied straight to the dyed wood, the gel stain packs the pores and emphasizes the grain pattern of the white oak.

Antique Pine

Sealing the surface is the secret to an even color on this notoriously blotch-prone wood.

If white oak is predictable when finishing, pine is anything but. A soft wood, it can take dye stain in a very uneven way and leave dark blotches. If the dyed sample boards indicate blotching, apply one or two washcoats of a 1-lb. cut of SealCoat shellac (three parts shellac with two parts denatured alcohol). When the shellac is dry, sand it with P220-grit paper and clean off the dust.

For this shelf, I used Early American Maple medium-yellow dye. I mixed roughly 1/4 oz. of powder in 8 oz. of water so that it would have just enough color to give the pale pine a little boost. When dry, apply a coat of undiluted SealCoat, and when this is dry, sand it with P320-grit paper to flatten the surface.

Now that the surface is sealed, the gel becomes a glaze. Instead of quickly soaking into the wood, it sits on the surface and you can move it around. You can leave it denser in corners to simulate aging, or even remove it altogether if you don't like the appearance. When using any stain in this way, you need to dilute it by about 10% with mineral spirits to extend the working time. Don't overthin, or the gel will become watery and you'll lose the color strength. Instead of mineral spirits, you can add a little colorless glaze base such as Benjamin Moore's Studio Glaze to get even more working time and control over the color. The gel-stain glaze can be applied with a pad or brush, but if you choose a pad, use a dry China-bristle brush to feather out any application lines. Let the glaze dry prior to topcoating.

Because the shelf won't see as much wear and tear as the table, I used SealCoat shellac as a topcoat (three coats). When brushing on the first coat, use as few brush strokes as you can. If you work the shellac too much, it could pull the pigment and leave a patchy appearance. When the third coat of shellac is dry, lightly sand the surface with P320- or P400-grit paper. A coat of wax is an optional final finish, but it gives the piece a soft look and a nice feel.

THE RECIPE
- Lockwood #142 Early American Maple Medium Yellow water-soluble dye
- General Finishes Prairie Wheat gel stain
- Blond shellac

SEAL FIRST
Sealing is the solution. This pine needed only a thin, 1-lb. cut of shellac. Wipe it on, let it dry, and then apply the dye.

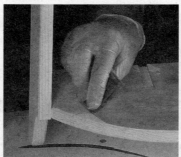

DYE, THEN SEAL AGAIN

Yellow adds depth. Wipe the sealed pine with the yellow dye (left). Apply a 2-lb. cut of dewaxed shellac (right) to seal the dye before using the gel stain as a glaze.

STAIN BECOMES A GLAZE
Reversible color. When applied to a sealed surface, the gel stain becomes a glaze and can be wiped on and off until the appearance is just the way you want it.

Glowing Mahogany

A vibrant dye brings the wood to life while a layer of dark gel stain adds depth to the appearance.

Instead of the normal mahogany brown, let's have a little fun with this mahogany jewelry box. Start with a Bismarck Brown, but don't be fooled by the name; this alcohol-soluble dye is a deep, fiery red.

With an open-pored wood like mahogany, sealing is optional. If you want to emphasize the pore structure, skip this step. Just be aware that the gel will be darker on raw wood. In this case, the grain pattern was nothing special so I sprayed on a single coat of SealCoat shellac. For the glaze (gel stain), I used Bartley Espresso. I added a second coat of glaze to the bracket feet to deepen them. After applying the glaze coats, let the piece sit for a few days to

dry completely and then seal it with shellac.

For a softer sheen, smooth the finish with 1,000-grit CAMI-grade wet-or-dry sandpaper or a 1,000-grit Abralon pad, and then rub it down with 0000 steel wool and wax.

THE RECIPE
- Lockwood #350 Bismark Brown alcohol-soluble dye
- Bartley Espresso gel stain
- Solvent-based lacquer

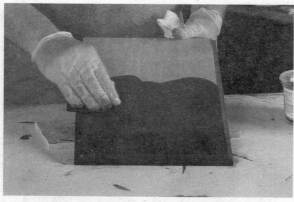

TRY AN ALCOHOL-BASED DYE
A brighter option. Powders dissolved with denatured alcohol are more vibrant.

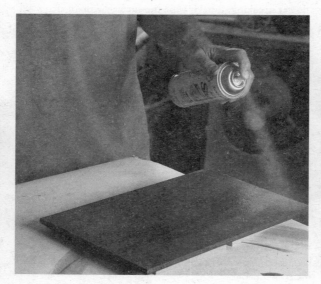

Seal by spraying. When sealing an alcohol-based dye with shellac, spray it on. Brushing or wiping could pull the dye and leave a blotchy appearance. SealCoat is available in an aerosol can.

GLAZE IS A COOLER BROWN

Another shot of color. Wiped on over the shellac, the Espresso gel stain becomes a glaze. Use a dry brush to remove pad marks.

Continued ➡

Tea as a Low-Tech Dye

by Sean Clark

You may have heard of food-safe finishes, but how many finishes are safe as food? My guess is not many.

There is one such product lurking in the kitchen. The humble teabag not only revives me after a long day in the shop, but it also serves as an inexpensive, easily available, and environmentally friendly dye.

Tea imparts an attractive warm, golden color that can be built up with additional coats with no loss of clarity. I've found that white oak, maple (both regular and tiger), and pine all benefit from this dye. It is particularly useful on pine, a wood prone to blotching, since the weak consistency and finer color particles of the tea stain tend not to collect in the blotch-prone areas.

Brew it, Brush it, Seal it in

The color and density produced by different brands of tea varies significantly, so do a little experimenting on sample boards first. I have tried different brands and blends (as dyes and drinks), including Lipton, Royal World Indian green tea, Tetley's British Blend, and PG Tips. While green tea produces too weak a dye, my favorite brew is to combine 12 oz. of hot water and six PG Tips tea bags in a plastic container and allow it to sit overnight.

Sand all the surfaces at P150-grit followed with P220-grit paper. To raise the grain before the application of the water-based dye, wet the surface with distilled water, allow two to four hours of drying time, and then resand with P220-grit paper to remove the whiskers.

Apply the tea using an artificial-bristle brush (the kind recommended for latex paint). Allow the stain to soak in for a few minutes, wipe off any excess with a cotton cloth, and then allow one to two hours of drying time. If a deeper color is required, repeat the application and when dry, lightly sand with P320-grit paper to dull any raised grain.

I like to seal in the dye before applying a topcoat, especially if it is water based, as this can reactivate the dye. Brush on two coats of a dewaxed blond shellac such as SealCoat. Allow the sealer to dry for at least four hours and then sand with P220-grit paper.

If you want the piece to have a subtly darker color, you can tint the clear coat. You can add dye concentrates such as TransTints to many finishes, but if you are using a water-based finish you can continue using tea. Add one part of the tea stain to five parts of finish and stir, but be sure to read the directions on the can, because some water-based finishes have limits as to how much they can be diluted. If you are happy with the color of the piece, simply apply two or three clear coats of your choice, such as more shellac, lacquer, or polyurethane in either solvent or water-based form. Then, if you want a low-luster look, rub the surface with 0000 steel wool and apply a thin coat of paste wax before buffing the surface with a soft cotton cloth.

After all that, you'll have earned that cup of tea.

Colorize Your Turnings

by Jimmy Clewes

On many turnings, adding a bright dye can transform a competent piece of work that might not get a second glance into a piece of art that stands out from across the room. Wood turning is a creative craft, and coloring is an even more creative process. Even if you've never applied dye to furniture, I hope you'll break the bonds of inhibition and try dyeing a turning.

When it comes to dyes, my first choices are alcohol-based, and in particular those by Chestnut Products. These are pre-mixed and can be used at full strength or diluted with denatured alcohol. These dyes have a 5% shellac content, so each application progressively seals the wood. Therefore, the later colors soak in less and become more like glazes, creating a layered look rather than mixing into the previous ones.

Two Ways to Confine the Color

Unless you plan to dye the entire piece, you have to create a clean break between the dyed and undyed parts. The safest way is to turn and sand the whole piece, then seal the section that will remain undyed. Wipe a 1-lb. cut of shellac onto the platter's recessed center, and once that was dry, apply a coat of Danish oil. If any dye seeps onto the sealed and oiled surface, it comes right off with steel wool. On the other hand, avoid leaving either finish on the section to be dyed or you'll end up with a blotchy appearance.

If you are a confident turner, a quicker method is to turn and sand the area to be dyed, but leave some waste wood on the adjacent section. After the dyes have been applied and dried, come back and turn the rest of the piece, removing the unwanted dye at the same time.

Prep the Surface and Apply the Dye

The surface must be flawless, because any blemishes will show up when you apply the dye. If you are using curly or burl wood (both give pleasing results), the grain may be running in different directions, so inspect the surface very closely.

After the last sanding, raise the grain. I do this by spraying the surface with denatured alcohol because it evaporates quickly. Water works as well but takes longer to dry. Don't resand the wood; you want the dye to penetrate deeply.

Coloring is best done on the lathe: You can turn the piece slowly without touching it by revolving the chuck, and then turn on the power for sanding. Apply the dye with a brush, cloth, sponge, or folded-up paper towel, but be sure to cover the whole surface evenly and quickly because alcohol-based dyes dry in under a minute. If you do get streaking, quickly wipe the surface with an alcohol-dampened cloth.

Once the surface is dry, lightly sand it with CAMI 600-grit wet-or-dry paper. If you are satisfied with the appearance, you can go ahead with the clear coat, or apply another coat of the same color.

Layers of Color Give a Dramatic Effect

After you've mastered using a single color, there are a couple of ways to use multiple hues. On curly wood, dyes penetrate the short grain more than the long grain. To exploit this effect, let the first color dry completely, then sand the surface with CAMI 400-grit wet-or-dry paper. This step removes some of the color and leaves a striped effect.

Next, apply a lighter complementary or contrasting color, which will show most where the first dye was removed. Now sand the surface again, this time with CAMI 600-grit paper.

You can either stop here or make the figure pop more with a third color. You can apply the third color to the whole area or just to certain sections. On curly wood, this

Alcohol Dyes are Brighter and Dry Faster

Compared with water-based dyes, alcohol-based ones are brighter and dry faster. You can buy them as liquids or as powders that dissolve in alcohol. Solar-lux liquids and alcohol-soluble dye powders are available at woodworker.com. You can view Chestnut Products dyes at toolpost.co.uk. To order, contact peter.hemsley@btinternet.com.

1. SEAL ADJACENT AREAS

Shellac barrier. If you aren't going to dye the whole piece, wipe a washcoat of shellac onto the areas to remain undyed. Follow with Danish oil.

2. APPLY THE DYE

Start at the inside edge. Use the chuck to turn the platter by hand as you dye the wood.

A light sanding. When it's dry, sand the dyed area. You can then move on to the topcoat or add more color.

3. POP THE FIGURE

Make the tiger roar. To enhance the stripes of the tiger maple, sand the first coat with 400-grit paper and then adds more color.

Bolder stripes. On the third round, instead of dyeing the whole rim, Focus on the darker sections of the curl.

ANOTHER WAY: DYE FIRST, TURN LATER

A more surefire way to get a crisp break between dyed and natural wood is to apply the dye and then complete the turning, cutting away unwanted dyed areas.

Finish the rim. Shape, sand, and dye the rim of the platter but don't hollow the center.

Finish the center. With the rim colored, use a parting tool to define the inner edge of the rim. Then finish turning the center.

4. BLEND THE COLORS AND FINISH

- **Soften the contrast.** If you want the colors to flow slightly together, spray the piece with denatured alcohol. Don't wipe it off.

- **Easy cleanup.** If any dye does get onto the sealed section, 0000 steel wool removes it.

- **Frame the rim.** Coloring the edge of the platter with a permanent marker conceals any dye that bled through and provides a nice break between the dyed and undyed parts of the rim.

- **Quick finish.** Gloss lacquer pops the colors, and using an aerosol gets the job done quickly.

---

can be just the lighter parts of the stripes, or on non-curly wood, you can use a dappled pattern. Continue coloring and sanding until you are pleased with the result.

A Gloss Finish Brings the Dye to Life

While I favor a low- or medium-luster finish for most of my undyed pieces, a thin, high-gloss finish really makes the dyes vibrant and the wood almost iridescent. Although you could wipe or brush on a finish (don't use shellac or you'll pull and blotch the alcohol-based dyes), the easiest and fastest finish is spray lacquer. Use a spray gun if you have one, but for small projects, an aerosol is economical and won't leave you with a gun to clean.

Spray several light coats of lacquer, letting each coat dry for 20 to 30 minutes. Smooth the surface with CAMI 800-grit wet-or-dry paper followed by 1,000-grit and finally 1,500-grit. For a glasslike finish, buff the piece using liquid car polish.

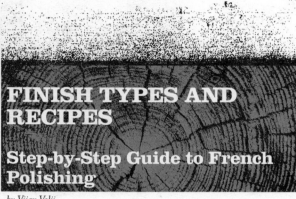

FINISH TYPES AND RECIPES

Step-by-Step Guide to French Polishing

by Vijay Velji

When I was growing up in Calcutta, India, my family's apartment had a clear view of a workshop that made high-end cabinets for radios. Standing there, I could watch the master craftsman make a carcase, veneer it, and finally finish it. For the latter, he used a curious circular motion with his hand that produced a most gleaming finish. Over time I talked to him about his technique, called French polishing, and after I had made a few pieces of furniture, I decided to try it myself.

In the years since, I've spent many hours reading articles about this mysterious finish, but practice was the key to getting the method correct. I will guide you through the process, from prepping the surface to filling the grain, from applying the shellac in very thin coats to giving the surface that final mirror shine. No other finish can match the clarity and depth of French polishing or the way it reveals a wood's beauty. There are no deep secrets to this finish, but there are some tips you need to know.

Careful Sanding Lays the Foundation

Whether you are refinishing a piece or finishing a new piece, the steps are the same. To start, the surface has to be dead flat with a uniform scratch pattern, because any irregularities will be magnified after the shellac is applied. Start sanding with P100-grit paper and work your way up to P320-grit. You can use a random-orbit sander until the last grit, which must be done by hand using a cork-faced block, sanding with the grain. There are no short cuts, so take your time.

You can French polish both flat and curved surfaces, but you can't get a polishing pad into inside corners. If a piece is already assembled, Brush shellac on the inside corners of the base. However, it is perfectly possible on a new piece to polish the components first, and then carefully assemble them. The only exceptions are small areas such as molding or trim.

Use Fresh Flakes

The best shellac for French polishing is dewaxed orange, garnet, beige, super blond, or platina flakes. Always use dewaxed shellac when finishing new or restoring old furniture. It is the wax in the shellac that gives rise to poor water

---

resistance. Decanting seedlac or machine-made shellac can never get rid of enough wax, so use dewaxed varieties that have a wax content of 0.2% to 0.5%. Even in flake form, shellac has a shelf life of only two to three years, so don't use flakes you picked up at a tag sale. Also don't use premixed shellac sold in cans for French polishing, as the additives that extend its shelf life make it hard to pad on very thin coats.

Open-Grained Wood Must Be Filled

To achieve a mirror-like finish, the polished surface must remain perfectly smooth. Because shellac shrinks over time, if you try to use it to fill wood pores, eventually the pore structure will reappear on the surface. On close-grained species such as cherry or maple, grain filling may not be necessary, but on open-grained woods like walnut and mahogany it certainly is. Use superfine 4F pumice, a white volcanic rock. Sprinkle the pumice with a simple cotton bag made from a roughly 8-in. square of T-shirt material held together with a rubber band.

MAKE TWO PADS

You will force the pumice into the pores with the first of two pads, so take a moment to create these tools. Take an 8-in.-square piece of linen and a ball of cotton batting that fits in your palm. Place the ball on the linen, grasp the four corners of the linen, bring them together, and twist them tightly over the ball to form a pad. The second pad, used later, is almost identical but has a cheesecloth core. All three materials can be found at fabric stores.

Open the first pad and dampen the core with alcohol and a 1-lb. cut of shellac in roughly a 10:1 ratio, working it into the batting. Close the pad and sprinkle some pumice on the wood. Now work the pad with firm pressure in a circular pattern mostly across the grain. The pumice soon takes on the color of the wood. Avoid working with the grain, because that will remove the pumice that has been packed into the pores.

The tiny amount of shellac is enough to create a kind of mastic that will glue the pumice in the pores. If you add too much shellac and the pad becomes sticky, simply add more alcohol. Grain filling is hard work, so take frequent breaks and try not to leave obvious swirls of the sawdust and pumice mixture on the surface. Recharge the pad with alcohol and shellac and sprinkle more pumice as required. Once you are satisfied, lightly run your fingernail across the grain. A smooth slide indicates that the pores are full. Add a 1-lb. cut of shellac on the outside of the pad and lightly coat the surface. Let it dry for at least four hours.

Slightly wet the surface with water and lightly sand in a circular pattern using 1,500-grit wet-or-dry sandpaper. Dry sanding would create heat, melt the shellac, and clog the sandpaper, causing uneven sanding. Run your palm on the surface to determine if it is smooth and flat. Remove the residue with a clean cloth.

Thin Coats Dry Almost Instantly

To get a mirror surface, the finish has to be perfectly smooth. Any waves or ridges will scatter the light rays. The easiest way to build a smooth finish is to apply very thin layers using a 1-lb. cut of shellac. With experience, you can move toward a 2-lb. cut.

The process of applying the shellac is known as bodying. Switch to the second pad. Dampen the cheesecloth core slightly with alcohol, then work in an equal mixture of alcohol and a 1-lb. cut of shellac. Twist the linen around the core and flatten the pad on a scrap of wood. Move the pad in a small circular pattern over the surface. Look for a faint glow of shellac seeping through the linen as it flows out of the core. As well as the circular pattern, you can employ a figure-eight pattern both along and across the grain, covering the entire surface of the wood. As the pad dries out, open it and add equal amounts of shellac and alcohol to the core. Never add shellac from the outside of the pad because the shellac must flow in a controlled manner from the core.

Continued ➜

As the shellac builds up in the pad, it may get sticky. This can cause the linen fibers to separate and end up in the finish. There are three ways to deal with a sticky pad: Recharge the core with alcohol. If you see any accumulation of shellac on the linen cover, move the inner core to a new part of the linen. As a last resort, add a drop of mineral oil on the outside of the pad. Any oil added now has to be removed at the later stage of burnishing, so use it sparingly. Luckily, fresh flakes usually don't need much oil.

Bodying is the most time-consuming part of French polishing. You can do it in one long stretch or spread it out over several days. I can't give you a rule on how much shellac to apply; a grain-filled, open-pored wood will usually require more than a close-pored wood. To determine if the bodying process is complete, look at the surface from an angle against the light. If you see any pores of wood grain, you have more work to do. The initial bodying process is complete once you've have laid a flat and even layer of shellac over the entire surface.

Let it dry overnight. The next morning, because shellac shrinks as it dries, you may see some areas that require more work. Continue with the bodying process but if you have been using one of the darker grades of shellac, switch to super blond or platina. These grades have the best resistance to moisture.

Once the pores are filled with shellac and the surface looks perfectly smooth again, start using alcohol alone to get rid of all the shellac from the core as well as the linen. Again let the piece sit overnight to double check that shellac shrinkage doesn't reveal any more pores.

Burnish the Surface for That Mirror Finish

Burnishing is where you evenly stretch the shellac and remove any oil used when bodying the finish. You can use the same pad, but if the linen cover looks thin and worn, replace the whole pad.

Burnishing is hard labor because pressure must be applied on a pad that is almost dry to the touch. If you are using an old pad, wet just the core with alcohol. Use a little more alcohol to wet the core of a new pad. Move the pad with the grain and sometimes in small circular patterns, always applying pressure, and always moving. If you stop, the pad will stick and mar the surface. If this happens, try burnishing away the blemish; if this doesn't work you will have to apply more shellac. If the pad gets too dry, add alcohol very sparingly.

Working this way will give you the mirror finish you have heard about. By the way, you do not have to apply a layer of wax, because the shellac is hard and durable enough to stand on its own merits for a long time.

How to Handle Small Surfaces

1. Brush tight spots. Use an artist's brush to apply shellac to inside corners that a pad can't reach.

2. Blend the surface. Immediately after brushing on shellac, use the pad to feather the wet edge into the rest of the surface.

3. Don't forget the edges. Only the top surface needs to be grain filled and fully French polished, but you can use the pad to apply shellac to the rest of the workpiece while bodying the top.

---

1. Fill the Grain

Before being polished, open-pored wood must be filled with a mixture of shellac and pumice. Applying the mixture with a pad is good practice for later steps.

Pounce the pumice. Pour some superfine 4F pumice into a cotton bag and then knock the bag at even intervals on the workpiece.

Prepare the pad. The pad consists of a cotton batting core inside a linen covering. Dampen the core with very dilute shellac.

Fill the grain. Force the pumice into the wood's pores using a circular motion. Sprinkle on more pumice until the pores are filled.

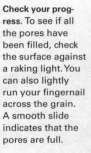

Check your progress. To see if all the pores have been filled, check the surface against a raking light. You can also lightly run your fingernail across the grain. A smooth slide indicates that the pores are full.

2. Build the finish

This is the heart of French polishing: padding on multiple layers of shellac. The thin layers dry so fast that you can build up a deep, smooth finish in one session, without stopping.

Start at the core. The second pad has a cheesecloth core and a linen cover. Dampen the core with alcohol and shellac.

Knock it flat. After charging the pad, press it onto a scrap of wood to form a flat, wrinkle-free surface that will contact the workpiece.

Apply the shellac and raise the shine. Move the pad across the surface in a circular motion. You can employ a figure-eight pattern both along and across the grain, covering the entire surface of the wood. The shellac builds surprisingly quickly. Never stop the pad on the surface, as this will leave a mark.

3. Now Burnish Everything

Pause for a pore check. After letting the surface dry overnight, check to see if the shellac has shrunk into the wood pores and more shellac needs to be applied. Then use a barely dampened pad to burnish the shellac to a mirror finish. At the same time, the pad removes any oil that was used when building the layers of finish.

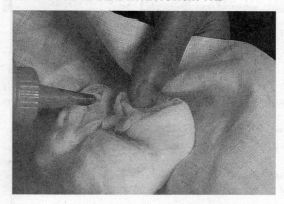

Recharge the pad with just alcohol. When the pad becomes sticky, try dampening the core with alcohol alone.

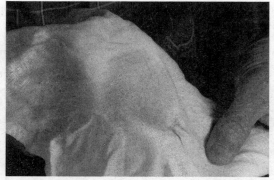

Move the core. If shellac starts to build up on the outside of the pad, it is more likely to stick. Move to a clean part of the linen.

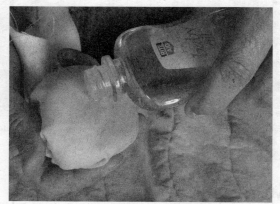

A little oil. Apply a drop of mineral oil to the pad. You will remove the oil from the workpiece later, so use as little as possible.

Stunning Results with Shellac

by Mario Rodriguez

My first experience with shellac, at age 14, was a disaster. I almost ruined a bookcase I'd built, and I swore off shellac altogether. But in time I learned how to use it correctly, and today shellac is one of my favorite finishes.

It's a cinch to apply, and because it dries so fast, you can apply multiple coats in a day and repair mistakes with ease.

It doesn't take an expert to get great results with shellac. Follow a few simple steps, and you can create a lustrous, satiny finish that makes grain and figure pop, no matter the species.

Fresh, Dewaxed Shellac Is Plenty Durable

Shellac gets a bad rap for durability, in part because of confusion between waxy and dewaxed versions. Stick with dewaxed shellac; it dries to a hard, impermeable film that protects against heat and moisture and is compatible with all finishes. True, shellac won't hold up against spilled alcohol. But since dewaxed shellac bonds beautifully with every other finish, you can always follow it up with a wipe-on varnish to protect vulnerable surfaces.

Shellac's freshness affects its performance and durability. That's where I went wrong with my bookshelf: I used old shellac and it never fully dried. To be sure it's fresh, buy and mix shellac only as needed. Store it in a cool, dry place, like a basement or refrigerator. If its freshness is in doubt, brush some onto a scrap. If it's still tacky in two hours, it's not fresh.

Thin Shellac to Suit the Project

Whether you're using flakes or premixed shellac, adjust the thickness to suit the job. The "cut" refers to the ratio of flakes to alcohol: Add 1 oz. of flakes to a cup (8 oz.) of alcohol to make a 1-lb. cut, 2 oz. of flakes to a cup for a 2-lb. cut, and so on. If you don't have a scale, you can measure flakes by volume with standard kitchen measuring cups. One oz. by weight is roughly equal to 1 oz. by volume, or 1/8 cup.

For a small project mix about a pint of shellac, half at a 1-lb. cut and half at a 1-1/2-lb. cut. Start with a 1-lb. cut as a sealer, to raise the grain and ensure that successive coats build uniformly. Follow with two coats at a 1-1/2-lb. cut to build the finish. I use a 1-lb. cut for the final coat because, with more alcohol, it flows and levels better, which minimizes brush marks.

Zinsser's SealCoat comes in a 2-lb. cut; for a 1-lb. cut, combine one part SealCoat to one part alcohol. For a 1-1/2-lb. cut, mix two parts SealCoat with one part alcohol.

Prep Surfaces and Seal

Sand all surfaces, working from P120 grit to P150, then P220. Between grits, flush the surface with alcohol to remove lingering abrasive particles and reveal any surface flaws that might need fixing.

I apply shellac with a brush because it builds the finish in fewer coats than a rag. I use a 2-in. Chinex brush, but natural China bristle or Taklon work well, too.

To help avoid drips and detect brush marks and other imperfections, lay parts flat if possible.

To start, apply one coat of 1-lb. cut shellac as a sealer. Hit the edges first. Then, for flat surfaces, load the brush and tap the tips of the bristles on the inside of the container so that it's full, but not dripping. To avoid reaching over drying finish, start at a far corner and work toward your body. Use long, continuous strokes, overlapping them by 1/4 in.

If you miss a spot or leave a drip, don't go back and touch it up—overworking it will leave deep brush marks that have to be sanded out. In two hours, sand with P320-grit to knock down the raised grain. Don't use alcohol to remove dust after sanding shellac, because it will reactivate the finish. Use a tack cloth or compressed air instead.

Heavier Coats Build Faster

The second and third coats—at a 1-1/2-lb. cut—can be applied generously, in the same fashion as the first. Heavier

---

Choosing the Right Version

Shellac is widely used as a sealer coat under other finishes, but it can prod[...] on its own. For maxi[...] durability, use dewax[...] shellac, whether pre-[...] or flakes. Shellac is m[...] durable when it's fres[...] so try to buy only wha[...] you'll use in the next [...] months.

FLAKES OFFER SAFE, SUBTLE TONES

Dewaxed flakes range in color from clear to amber (orange) to deep reddish browns, like garnet. Unlike dyes and stains, shellac flakes offer a foolproof way to impart warm, subtle tones without any blotching. Color differences are more apparent on lighter woods like maple and cherry than they are on darker woods like walnut. Dewaxed flakes are available from online retailers.

PRE-MIXED IS CONVENIENT

If you want a clear finish that adds just a hint of warmth, Zinsser's SealCoat, is the right choice. It's the only dewaxed shellac that's available premixed at home centers and hardware stores. Keep in mind when buying any shellac that if the packaging doesn't specify "dewaxed" or "wax-free," it probably isn't.

Skip the wax. Wax is an ingredient in some shellacs, including Zinsser's "clear" and "amber" products. When waxy shellac dries, the wax allows moisture to permeate the finish, making it less durable.

Use dewaxed instead. Without the wax, shellac dries to a hard film that's impervious to moisture. For premixed, you have one choice: Zinsser's SealCoat.

HOW TO MIX YOUR OWN

Grind for speed. Ground flakes dissolve completely in a few hours. If you don't grind them, it's best to give them a full day.

Mix with denatured alcohol. Give the mixture an occasional shake to keep the shellac from congealing at the bottom of the jar.

Strain solution before brushing. When the flakes are fully dissolved, pour the solution through a medium-mesh paint strainer to remove any impurities.

Denatured alcohol	1-lb. cut	1½-lb. cut	2-lb. cut
1 cup (8 fluid oz.)	1 oz. flakes (by volume)	1-½ oz. flakes (by volume)	2 oz. flakes (by volume)

Continued →

cuts get tacky almost as soon as they're applied, so work quickly to avoid brush marks.

You can apply your third coat two hours after the second coat, then let everything dry overnight. The finish will appear very glossy, but don't sweat—you're not done.

Finish the Finish

Before the final coat, it's time to address any drips or imperfections. Use a fresh razor like a card scraper to knock down drips, then rub out all surfaces with a maroon abrasive pad for an even matte sheen. Use the 1-lb. cut for the final coat, and let everything dry overnight.

For the final rubout, use super fine (0000) steel wool to knock down the sheen. If you want to add a coat of oil-based varnish for extra durability, now's the time. Apply paste wax with a soft cotton T-shirt rag, then buff it off for a deep, satiny finish.

Easy Finish, Step by Step

Preparation
Beautiful finishes start with careful prep. All surfaces should be sanded thoroughly, to remove machine and mill marks.

- **Prep surfaces with sandpaper.** To ensure uniformity, sand all surfaces, starting at P120 grit and finishing with P220.
- **Flush between grits.** Before moving to a finer grit, flush surfaces with alcohol and wipe them down with a rag to remove any loose abrasive particles, which can leave scratches.

The First Coat acts as a Sealer
Brush on a coat of 1-lb. cut shellac to raise the grain and seal the surface, creating a level foundation for subsequent coats.

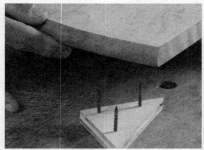

Tack strips elevate the workpiece. Use scraps of plywood with protruding drywall screws to hold the workpiece, allowing you to flip it as needed without marring the finish.

- Coat brush in alcohol first. Whether you're softening an old brush or using a new one, work alcohol into the bristles to help the brush flow smoothly and keep shellac from drying in the reservoir (the hollow area where the bristles meet the metal ferrule).
- Hit the edges first. When brushing narrow edges with a big brush, drips are likely to form on adjacent surfaces. If you brush the edges first, drips will form on the large, flat, dry surfaces, where they can be cleaned up quickly and easily.
- Brush on a sealer coat. A thin 1-lb. cut raises the grain and dries quickly. In two hours, it can be sanded with P320-grit paper.
- Don't look back. Apply shellac in long, continuous strokes with little overlap. If you miss a spot, don't go back. "Backbrushing" into drying finish will leave deep brush marks. Subsequent coats will cover small missed spots without any problem.

Wipe-on Alternative
Where brushing would cause excessive drips, like on a chair splat, shellac can be applied with a pad.

- **Charge the pad.** Fold up a piece of wool (or other absorbent cloth) and place it at the center of a lint-free cotton rag. Use a squeeze bottle to fill the wool until it's soaked but not dripping.
- **Slow, but safe.** Wrap the pad so its surface is wrinkle-free. The wool releases a thin coat of shellac through the cotton onto the surface, so it takes more coats to achieve the same look as parts that have been brushed. Seal the pad in a glass jar to keep it supple between coats.

Build the Finish
Sand the first coat smooth, then apply two coats of shellac at a 1-1/2-lb. cut to build a uniform protective film.

- Sand between coats. When the surface is completely dry, sand with P320 grit. Use a stearated paper, like Norton's 3X, which has a soapy coating that resists clumping and clogging.
- Dry finish won't clog sandpaper. Sanding dry shellac will produce a fine powder (right). If the finish isn't quite dry, the sandpaper will clog almost immediately.

A Final Thin Coat
Repair drips and brush marks, then brush on a coat of 1-lb. cut.

- Eliminate drips. Use a fresh razor like a miniature card scraper to level drips and other imperfections. Don't bear down; instead, take multiple light passes until the drip is flush with the rest of the surface.
- Follow up with a rubdown. After making repairs, rub everything down thoroughly with a maroon abrasive pad (equivalent to 000 "extrafine" steel wool).
- Finish with a 1-lb. cut. For the final coat, go back to the thinner, 1-lb. cut. It has longer open time, so it flows and "self-levels" a little better, minimizing brush marks.

Finish the Finish
Use steel wool to get a level, matte surface. Then, apply paste wax to create a lustrous, satiny finish that's soft to the touch.

- Knock off the gloss. For the final rubout, use 0000 "super fine" steel wool to transform shellac's naturally glossy sheen into a uniform matte surface.
- Wax on. Paste wax is the key to this satiny finish; use a soft T-shirt rag to distribute a very thin layer of wax across the surface.
- Wax off. When the wax has hazed over, use a fresh cotton rag to remove it, working in a brisk, circular motion.

▶ **TIP** **Brush Care Is Easy**

To store your brush, give it a few dips in alcohol and wrap it in a paper sleeve to keep the bristles straight and clean. The shellac that remains in the bristles will harden, further protecting the brush's shape during storage. When you're ready to use it again, just soak it in alcohol to soften it up.

Pigmented Lacquer
by Sean Clarke

Whether in modern or traditional interiors, bookcases, built-ins, and cabinets sparkle when finished in a crisp, classic white. For maximum impact, this finish requires a very even application and a smooth finish, so it is typically sprayed on. But don't despair if you aren't set up to spray: I will show you how to get an off-the-gun-looking finish just by brushing and wiping. It will take longer than spraying, but the quality of this finish is well worth the wait.

While I could reach for oil-based or latex paint, I find that pigmented lacquer provides a superior look in terms of evenness and lack of residual brush marks. I prefer acrylic lacquers over nitrocellulose ones because they are non-yellowing and retain brilliance better. I'm going to use a pre-catalyzed version here, which has better durability than a non-catalyzed lacquer and is easier to apply than a post-catalyzed lacquer. You can buy this type of lacquer from Sherwin Williams or M.L. Campbell paint stores and, if you like, they can tint it to match an existing color in your house.

Right at home. You should design a built-in or entertainment center to match the design of the room, and a paint company can tint your lacquer to match, too.

A Flawless Finish Needs Perfect Prep Work

The best woods for painting are close-pored, such as poplar, maple, pine, or birch plywood. The high-solids primer that I'll use can fill medium-pore woods, but if you find yourself having to paint an open-pored wood such as oak it would be best to apply an oil-based grain filler first.

I begin to prep the surfaces by filling any imperfections with water- or solvent-based, natural-colored wood filler. Using a utility blade or flat spatula, I lay the wood filler into any indentations, leaving the filler slightly proud of the surface. For minor indentations (less than 1/16 in. deep and 3/16 in. wide), let the filler dry for one or two hours. Larger fills will require more drying time. Next, I sand the whole surface up to P180- or P220-grit. Wrap the sandpaper around a sanding block for a smooth, even surface. The block also ensures that the filled areas end up even with their surroundings.

Since this project is made from pine, I next apply a 2-lb. cut of shellac as a sealer on any knots or sap pockets. Without it, these areas can emit resin that eventually leaches through the finish. I apply a generous coat of dewaxed shellac to any knots, spreading it away from the center of each knot to blend into the unsealed surfaces. Let the shellac dry for about four hours, or until it is not tacky to the touch, then lightly dull the shellac with a purple abrasive pad, being careful not to cut through it.

Primer Creates a Smooth Foundation

White lacquer primer is one of the big secrets. It builds a film that overcomes any imperfections too small to fill and it sands easily, leaving a flat, seamless surface devoid of grain texture, critical for a flawless finish. I work in a large, well-ventilated area; otherwise, I'd use a respirator.

I reduce the primer approximately 40% with the manufacturer's recommended solvent. This is slightly thinner than for spraying but it makes the primer more workable and forgiving for a hand application. I prefer a large lacquer mop brush because of the amount of finish that it can carry, but a quality 2-in. natural-bristle flat brush is also a good choice. If possible, work on a horizontal surface, as this greatly reduces the chance of runs. Tip cabinets onto their sides and let one side dry before turning it over.

Brushing tips for primer and lacquer—Both the primer and topcoat are applied in the same way. I apply the first coat with the grain, starting a few inches from an edge and applying the finish about half the length of a normal brush stroke. Then I go back and forth to spread it out on each side of the initial brush stroke. After recharging the brush, I land it about an inch or two away from the wet area, ensuring even coverage without a ridge of surplus finish.

On narrow moldings or details, I use a smaller #6 or #8 lacquer mop or a 1-in. natural-bristle flat brush. I let this whole first coat dry at least one to two hours, depending on temperature and humidity, and then evaluate the surface. Fill any imperfections that may have been missed in the initial filling; let the filler dry one to two hours (or longer for larger areas), and then block-sand the filled spots.

If the surface is fairly smooth (and didn't need more filling), you can skip sanding as long as you apply the next coat within 60 to 90 minutes. If you wait longer, or the surface is rough, sand it with P220-grit paper to smooth the surface and to create a mechanical bond with the next coat.

To apply the second primer coat, I work perpendicular to the grain, using the same technique. By applying coats alternately with and across the grain, you minimize a buildup of brush lines. If you are brushing a confined area, apply all the coats in the longer of the two directions. I allow this coat to dry for a minimum of two to four hours, depending on temperature and humidity, but overnight is fine too.

I repeat the horizontal application for the third primer coat, let that dry for two to four hours, and then block-sand all the primed surfaces with P220-grit sandpaper. I use a vacuum with a brush attachment to carefully remove all the sanding dust. Wipe your hand across the surface. If it comes up white, gently use a tack cloth to remove any remaining dust.

Remove Any Flaws

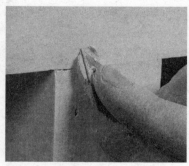

More flaws show up. The uniform appearance of the primer will probably reveal surface defects that were camouflaged by the natural wood. Fill and smooth them.

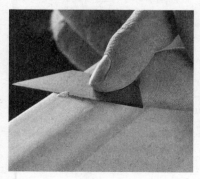

Deal with drips. If you can't catch a drip or run immediately, don't wipe the sticky surface. Let it dry, then shave it flush with a sharp knife or use a utility blade.

Apply Topcoats Until You Get the Desired Look

It's time to apply the tinted lacquer topcoats. Start by thinning the lacquer by approximately 30% with the manufacturer's recommended solvent and then add a further 10% in retarder. This gives the lacquer time to flow out before drying, minimizing brush marks. I apply the first coat across the grain, as described above, and let it dry for a minimum of two to four hours. Using P220-grit sandpaper and a block, I lightly sand this coat to remove any surface debris and brush marks, and then vacuum away the dust. I apply a second coat of lacquer with the grain, and then allow the workpiece to dry overnight.

Stop here? The next day I assess the workpiece. As long as there is no streaking, and if you like a little grain pattern showing, then you can stop here. If desired, you can rub the surface with 0000 steel wool wrapped around a cork block and then apply wax, to both level the surface and then even out the sheen.

Brush Two More Coats and Then Pad on a Topcoat for a Flawless Finish

Even if you aren't set up to spray, you can still achieve the formal look of a factory finish; it just takes a little longer.

Lightly block-sand all the surfaces with P220-grit sandpaper to remove dust nibs and brush marks. Then rub all the surfaces with a maroon abrasive pad, dulling down the finish to make really sure that a mechanical bond can be achieved with the next coat. Follow up by wiping all surfaces with a tack rag to remove any fine sanding debris.

> **BRUSHING RECIPE**
>
> 60% lacquer
> 30% thinner
> 10% retarder

I apply two more coats in the same manner as the first two, sanding after each and allowing for an overnight drying period.

To approach the smoothness achieved by spraying, pad on a final application of lacquer. To form the pad, I cut a cotton bed sheet roughly 8 in. square, removing any hems. I then cut a piece of cotton wadding (available at fabric stores) about 6 in. square and fold it into a wad roughly 2 in. wide and 3 in. long, with a point at one end.

I further thin the topcoat by 10%, and then add it directly to the core of the pad. After squeezing out the excess, I place it in the center of the sheet, bring each corner of the sheet in to the center, twist the corners into a grip for the pad, and make sure that the polishing side of the pad is tight and free of creases or wrinkles.

I start the process perpendicular to the grain, beginning at the far edge, working the pad left to right and slowly moving toward me. When you begin to feel some resistance, it's time to charge the pad with more lacquer. Open the pad and add lacquer to the inner face of the wadding, let it absorb, re-wrap the pad tightly, and gently squeeze the pad to remove any excess material.

When working in an area where the light source is fluorescent tubes, place the workpiece in a position so that your strokes are perpendicular to the light source for a better surface reading.

Working a small area such as the side of a cabinet, I cover the whole surface two or three times, let it dry for about 10 minutes, and then repeat the process with the grain. I pad in alternating directions up to four times, with a 10-minute drying break after each application, until I am satisfied with the build and evenness of the surface.

In tight corners, moldings, and narrow surface areas, you can try using a smaller pad. Or you can allow the larger surface areas to cure overnight, and then tape them off with low-tack blue tape before padding the adjoining smaller areas.

Let the finish cure for two or three days before moving it into the house. This will allow it to off-gas in the workshop and avoid the risk of heavy object imprinting into the finish while it is still soft.

Brush on the Top Coats

Like the primer, the lacquer topcoat is thinned and applied in multiple coats.

Doctor it for brushing. Thin the topcoat to make it easier to apply and add retarder to leave fewer brush marks.

Brush in sequence. When finishing complicated surfaces, do the large surfaces first with a big brush, then cover molding and trim with a smaller one.

Sand between coats. Sanding not only removes dust nibs and brush marks, but it also creates a mechanical bond between layers of finish.

Work horizontally. On large and small pieces, when possible, work on a horizontal surface to reduce the risk of runs.

Continued ➔

Choose Your Final Sheen

As with clear coats, you have a choice of final sheen. You can use steel wool and wax for a low-luster look, or pad on the last coat for a high gloss.

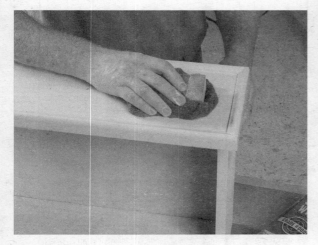

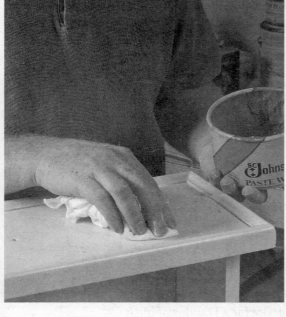

LOW LUSTER

Steel wool and wax. Unwrap a pad of 0000 steel wool and fold it around a sanding block. Rub the surface in one direction to smooth and dull the surface. Wipe on and buff off a coat of paste wax for an even sheen and a pleasing feel.

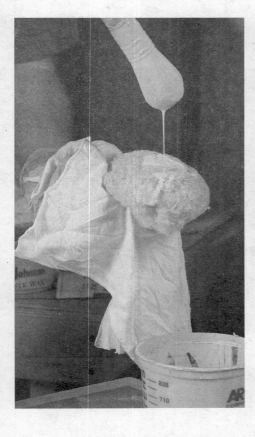

HIGH GLOSS

Pad on a final coat. Make a pad with cotton cloth and cotton wadding. To get an even flow of finish, always add the finish directly to the core and not to the outside of the pad. Pad on a last coat, wiping lightly to keep the coat very thin.

Isolate the trim. If you can't pad the whole surface at once cleanly, let the large areas dry overnight, then mask off areas adjacent to the trim, and work on it with a smaller pad.

PADDING RECIPE

50% lacquer
40% thinner
10% retarder

Wiping Varnish
by Michael Pekovich

For me, the ideal finish for handmade furniture is a silky smooth, low-luster finish that lets the beauty of the wood shine through. Over the years, I've tried countless products and techniques trying to achieve this look. Some required elbow grease and homemade concoctions. Some took weeks to apply. Some looked great at first only to fade over time.

Finally, I've found a finish that gives me the durability and flawless look I want along with easy application. The answer is wiping varnish. It's a versatile finish that is thin enough to wipe on, but dries hard even when applied in thicker coats. This allows me to build the finish quickly, then end with thin coats that give me just the look I want. My brand of choice is Waterlox, a tung-oil-based varnish. It builds quickly, levels well when brushed on, and adds a beautiful amber tone to the work.

In finishing, the technique is just as important as the product, and the directions on the back of the can just don't cut it. I'll share the simple steps I've discovered for fast, dependable results. I'll also show you how to apply wiping varnish for a high-luster look, suitable for high-style furniture.

Simple Steps to a Flawless Finish

As opposed to oil finishes, which must go on in thin coats, wiping varnish lets you build the finish fast, level it, then continue with thin coats that dry quickly. One secret to a durable finish is to build to a little higher gloss than you're aiming for, then rub it out to a lower luster. This way you have a thick enough film for adequate protection with the sheen you want.

STEP 1

FLOOD IT ON AND WIPE IT OFF

For this thin-film approach to work, careful surface prep is crucial to remove any mill marks, sanding scratches, or tearout. Be sure to sand to P320 grit, or higher for blotch-prone woods.

With that done, begin applying the finish by brushing on a liberal coat. The finish will penetrate the bare wood, so apply more finish to any areas that begin to look dry. After 10 minutes or so, wipe the entire surface dry.

On open-pored woods like oak, the soaked-in finish can sometimes seep back out of the pores for a few minutes. Wipe away these shiny damp spots; they're tough to remove later. Let this coat dry overnight.

A brush is fast. It allows you to apply a heavy coat evenly, and the bristles let you work into the corners. Any brush will do. Wipe away the excess finish, working in the direction of the grain.

STEP 2

WIPE ON A COAT AND LEAVE IT

The second coat also will go on heavy, but this time you'll leave more of it behind. So now you should switch to a clean cotton cloth, as wiping is easier to control than brushing.

After coating the surface with circular strokes, wipe the finish gently in the direction of the grain, working to level it without wiping it off. Let it dry overnight.

Apply the finish with circular strokes. This helps to ensure an even coat. Smooth the finish with straight strokes. Follow the grain along the length of the workpiece for the smoothest application.

STEP 3

LEVEL THE SURFACE

Once the first two coats have dried, there may be areas of raised grain or dust nibs, so it's important to smooth the surface. The easiest way is to apply a thin third coat of finish and wet-sand it with P400-grit paper. The result is a sealed, smooth starting point from which to begin applying the remaining coats. Wet-sanding lubricates the sandpaper and prevents clogging, allowing the paper to cut more aggressively while still leaving a fine scratch pattern. Let it dry overnight.

Wet-sand the third coat. Use a cloth to apply a third coat, then use folded sandpaper to work the wet finish with the grain. Afterward, use the cloth again to even out the still-damp finish, as you did in Step 2.

STEP 4

ADD A FEW THIN COATS

With the foundation coats applied and the surface smoothed, continue building the finish in a series of thin coats that level easily and dry quickly enough to avoid dust nibs.

Again, start with a circular motion to apply the varnish. Then follow the grain with light strokes to even out the finish without completely wiping it off, and allow it to dry. Four to six of these light coats should build up enough finish to protect the wood without encasing it in a heavy film.

Work in a thin coat. Apply the finish in a circular motion, working it into the wood in a thin layer. Then wipe lightly with the grain. The thin coats should dry quickly enough to allow a couple of coats a day.

STEP 5

RUB IT OUT WITH STEEL WOOL

For years, I applied wax with steel wool. Why not? It killed two birds with one stone, rubbing out and waxing the piece in one step. Trouble is, wax makes it hard to see the scratch pattern created by the steel wool, and it's easy to end up with an uneven sheen.

Rubbing out the surface first with steel wool alone lets you see what you're doing. Afterward, you can apply the wax with a cloth. For broad, flat surfaces, you can also wrap the 0000 steel wool around a cork-faced sanding block. Wipe the surface clean to check your progress. The finished result should be a dull, even sheen.

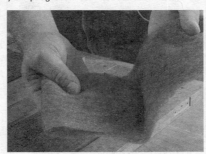

Create a wider pad. Start by unrolling the narrow pad and folding it into a square. Work every surface, being careful not to rub through the finish along the edges.

Cleanup is key. Use compressed air to clear the corners of steel-wool fragments and dust.

STEP 6

WAX IS THE FINAL TOUCH

A coat of wax will protect against scuffing and bring out the shine. The solvents in wax can soften a fresh finish, so let the finish cure for a week or so before applying the wax. When wiping on wax, I dampen the cloth with mineral spirits first. It thins the wax and allows me to apply an even coat that's easier to buff when dry.

Work the wax into the wood. The mineral spirits will help the wax spread evenly and thinly. Then buff with a soft cloth. The surface should have a pleasing satin luster.

Want More Protection, or a Higher Shine?

A higher luster requires a thicker layer of finish. Tabletops do, too. By the way, on open-pored woods like mahogany, you may also need to fill the grain first.

Seal and level the surface as in steps 1 to 3 of the low-luster finish. Then continue building the finish by brushing on heavier coats and letting them dry without wiping. Use an inexpensive foam brush for an even coat on flat surfaces and a rag for everything else. These slower-drying coats gather more dust nibs and need another round of leveling with fine sandpaper followed by steel wool to achieve an even scratch pattern.

For a satin finish, you could follow the steel wool with paste wax and buff. But for a higher polish, use a fine automotive polishing compound applied with a clean cotton cloth. It isn't strictly necessary to apply wax afterward; the luster is already nice. Still, it makes sense to apply wax to tabletops to add scuff resistance.

BUILD IT THICKER

A foam brush works fine. Apply the finish in slightly overlapping passes. Don't worry about small bubbles or brush strokes; the finish levels well as it dries.

Sand between coats. Use P600-grit paper wrapped around a cork-faced sanding block to remove any dust nibs and level the finish.

RUB IT OUT

Wet-sand to level the finish. The wood is sealed, so the water won't raise the grain. Use 600-grit paper. For curved parts, skip this step and go right to the steel wool.

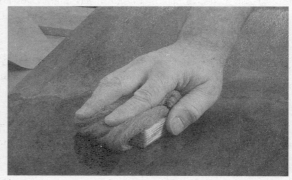

Steel wool. Follow the sandpaper with 0000 steel wool. Dip it in water mixed with a few drops of liquid soap for an even scratch pattern. You can stop here for more protection with the same satin finish.

Continued ➡

Bring out the shine. The fine abrasives in commercial auto polishes offer a higher luster than steel wool. Squirt some polishing compound onto the surface and buff with a clean rag. Remove the residue with a clean cloth and apply wax.

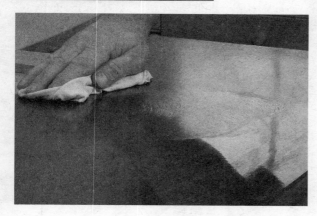

Wipe-On Finishes

by Hendrik Varju

Wipe-on finishes are a favorite of many woodworkers, both amateur and professional, because of their easy application. However, there is great confusion over what exactly constitutes a wipe-on finish: You'll hear one woodworker talk of wiping varnish, another of an oil/varnish blend; then somebody throws around the term "Danish oil," and pretty soon you have no idea which finish is which.

These finishes are not identical. To make the right choice, you need to know what each finish is made from, the pros and cons, where to use each one, and how to apply it. Only then will you discover how practical these finishes really are.

Different Ways to Create a Wipe-On Finish

It may help to think of varnishes, oils, and their various offspring as occupying a kind of grid (see drawing): In the top right-hand corner is varnish, which is hard to apply (brush marks, sags, runs, and a magnet for dust) but offers enormous protection. In the bottom left-hand corner is pure oil finish, which is easy to apply (wiped on with a cloth, surplus wiped away, no dust problem) but offers minimal protection.

Between these two extremes are wiping varnishes and oil/varnish mixes. In making these finishes, manufacturers wanted to combine the good points of varnish and oil and avoid the negatives.

Wiping varnish is made by thinning varnish with mineral spirits. It dries faster, attracting less dust, but because each coat is thinner, it offers less protection than a coat of undiluted varnish.

Wiping Varnish

Brushing varnish is thinned with mineral spirits to create a wiping varnish. This offers a thicker film than an oil/varnish blend, but it must be wiped on more carefully

Choosing a Wipe-On Finish

When choosing among pure varnish, pure oil, wiping varnish, or an oil/varnish blend, you make a trade-off between ease of application and the amount of protection you are giving the wood.

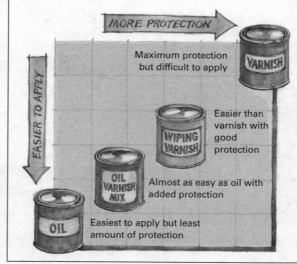

MORE PROTECTION

EASIER TO APPLY

Maximum protection but difficult to apply — VARNISH

Easier than varnish with good protection — WIPING VARNISH

Almost as easy as oil with added protection — OIL VARNISH MIX

Easiest to apply but least amount of protection — OIL

An oil/varnish blend is made by combining linseed or tung oil with varnish. This product gives more protection than oil alone, but less than a wiping varnish. Because it allows you more time to manipulate the finish, it is even easier to apply than wiping varnish.

How to Recognize Each Product

One of the main reasons for the confusion between wiping varnishes and oil/varnish blends is the way manufacturers name their finishes. What is Danish oil? What is salad-bowl finish? Why is Minwax Tung Oil Finish an oil/varnish blend and Formby's Tung Oil Finish a wiping varnish?

There are two ways to make certain of what you're using. The directions on the can may provide the first clue: If the can says to apply the finish with a cloth and let it dry, but doesn't mention wiping off the excess, then you have a wiping varnish. If it tells you to wipe off the excess a short time after applying it, then you have an oil/varnish blend. You also can compare how a puddle of the finish dries.

Blend Your Own

To make a wiping varnish, thin regular brushing varnish, either alkyd or polyurethane, with equal parts low-odor mineral spirits. For an oil/varnish blend, combine two parts boiled linseed oil or tung oil with one part brushing varnish. If you are using tung oil, add Japan drier to speed up drying time. Or, combine three parts Danish oil (a relatively thin oil/varnish blend) with one part varnish. You can reduce the amount of varnish if you find the finish too sticky, or increase it for a faster build.

Place half a teaspoon of finish on a dished, impermeable surface and wait 24 hours. If the dried finish has a smooth surface it's a wiping varnish. If the surface is wrinkled, it's an oil/varnish blend.

Picking the Best Option

So when is one finish better than the other? Here's some advice. For a piece of fine furniture that won't be heavily used, you can't beat an oil/varnish blend. This finish isn't technically a film finish or a penetrating finish; it's a hybrid that you might call "semi-film forming." It keeps the wood looking natural, but is only moderately resistant to water, heat, and chemicals, and it offers very limited protection from wear and scratches. If you need a protective finish, say, for a kitchen table, no off-the-shelf finish works as well as varnish. Thinning it to a wipe-on consistency makes it really easy to apply.

Varnish forms a cross-linking film: It interlocks on a molecular level, making it resistant to water, heat, scratches,

chemicals, and so on. By wiping it on, you can still obtain a protective film for high-wear areas; it will just take you longer than brushing on thicker coats. Use a polyurethane varnish for even more protection.

Feel free to combine both finishes on one project to put additional protection where you need it most. For example, you can finish the base of a table with an oil/varnish blend but the top with a wiping varnish.

Oil/Varnish Blend: Be Sure to Wipe Off Excess

Apply the blend generously and wipe it around with a cloth, a cheap brush, or a roller. Particularly with the first coat, you can apply more finish after 10 minutes or so if the wood has absorbed the first lot. Because an oil/varnish blend has a long open time, it is very forgiving. It's easy to remove sags and runs, and if you miss a spot, you can still apply more an hour later and it will never show a mark.

After the finish soaks in, but before it becomes tacky, you must wipe off the excess with a cloth, going with the grain. If you forget to remove the surplus finish, it will stay sticky for many days, and eventually it will dry with a wrinkled surface. Let each coat dry for 24 hours or until it no longer feels oily.

Oil/Varnish Blend: Widely Available

Oil/varnish mixes are popular because they are easy to apply, so almost every hardware store will stock one or two brands. Three or four coats build very little film, giving the wood a low-luster finish that is easy to repair but offers only a little protection.

ADD PROTECTION
If your commercial oil/varnish blend is too thin, mix in some brushing varnish in a 3:1 ratio to add protection.

APPLICATION: WIPE ON, WIPE OFF

Goes on easily. Apply an oil/varnish blend liberally and allow it to soak into the wood. You can use a small paintbrush to get finish into tight spots. Because of the long open time, you have plenty of time to remove any sags and runs. Once the finish soaks in, use a clean cloth to wipe off any surplus; otherwise, you will end up with a thick, sticky mess.

One of the real bonuses of an oil/varnish blend is that it isn't thick enough to catch much dust, so it's a great finish in the average workshop. Although there are no real dust nibs to deal with, a tiny bit of fine sanding with 600-grit paper helps make the surface smoother just before the final coat.

The modest final thickness, even after numerous coats, isn't suitable for rubbing out. The final coat already has an attractive hand-rubbed look and rarely needs to be rubbed to an even sheen. But a coat of paste wax gives the surface a smooth feel.

Wiping Varnish: Sand Lightly Between Thin Coats

You can use a lint-free cotton cloth or an untextured paper towel to apply wiping varnish, but you have only a few minutes to manipulate the finish. Apply a thin coat, then let it dry at least eight hours and possibly overnight, depending on the temperature and humidity. Any attempt to wipe off the excess after the finish has begun to tack up will result in a mess of disturbed, half-dried finish.

One of the downsides of varnish is that the long open time allows dust to settle into the finish. Even wiping

varnish can have this problem, particularly if you put on a good amount with an overwet cloth. Fine sanding between coats will remove dust nibs and give the next coat some mechanical bonding power (particularly if more than 24 hours has passed since the last coat was applied). I use 600-grit wet-or-dry paper, lubricated with mineral spirits.

For the final coat, I use a rubbing pad, similar to one used in French polishing, to apply a superthin coat that dries very quickly. Take two pieces of lint-free cotton cloth about 10 in. square. Fold up one piece, place it in the center of the other piece, and then gather the sides of the second piece around the first piece, making sure the round end is wrinkle-free. Secure the ends with an elastic band.

Unlike French polishing, you can only cover the surface once, with slightly overlapping, straight strokes. Dip the finishing pad into a small amount of wiping varnish every few strokes to maintain a wet edge while putting down a superthin film. In fact, this finish film is so thin that the surface dries within minutes, barely giving dust a chance to settle into it.

Remember that varnish can look like a plastic film if applied too thickly, particularly on open-pored woods like walnut and mahogany. You can leave the pores crisp and defined under a thin film of three or four coats, or use grain filler first and then build up a thicker, more durable finish. After at least six to eight coats, wiping varnish can be rubbed out to a satin, semigloss, or glossy sheen using materials such as steel wool, pumice and rottenstone, or automotive polishing compound.

Remember the spontaneous combustion risk with all oil finishes. Make sure to unwrap the finishing pad when you're done, leaving it flat or hanging it outside to dry.

Wiping Varnish: More Protection

You may need to visit a paint or woodworking store to find a commercial wiping varnish, but you can make your own. You have less working time than with an oil/varnish blend, but each coat adds more protection until eventually it reaches the same level as brushed varnish.

Application: Wipe and Let Dry

Use overlapping passes. Apply wiping varnish in a thin layer, but don't keep going back over the same area or you'll pull the finish as it starts to dry.

Make Your Own

You can thin oil-based brushing varnish with mineral spirits in a 1:1 ratio to create a finish thin enough to wipe on with a cloth.

Remove the dust nibs. Wiping varnish, especially if applied thickly, will dry slowly enough to allow dust and other debris to stick to it. Before the final coat, sand the surface with 600-grit paper lubricated with mineral spirits.

Pad on the final coat. To apply a final thin coat of varnish, create a rubbing pad by wrapping a folded piece of cotton cloth inside another piece and securing the ends with an elastic band. Pad on the very thin coat of wiping varnish in long strokes, landing on the middle of the surface and lifting off at either end.

Edge treatment. The pad also can be used to apply a thin final coat to the edge with one long stroke.

 TIP

Shortcut to a thicker coat. You can brush on full-strength varnish if you want to build a protective finish quicker. Sand between coats, and then finish off with thin coats of wiping varnish, applied with a cloth.

All about Wax

by Peter Gedrys

There is a quality to a wax topcoat that can't be matched by more durable, modern finishes. The soft sheen and tactile quality of a waxed surface just begs to be touched. Not only does a waxed surface look good and feel good, but it also helps protect the finish underneath.

Besides being a final coat on finished wood, wax has a number of other uses. It can serve as a minimal finish to maintain a wood's natural beauty, or it can give a just-made piece an antique look. Colored waxes can create special effects. Best of all, the tools are simple and the techniques are easy. Whatever your furniture-making ability, your projects will look and feel better after a proper waxing.

Wax Polish Finishes a Finish

The most common use for wax is to apply it as the final layer of finish. It can go on top of any type of finish, from an in-the-wood couple of coats of oil to high-gloss, rubbed-out shellac. The wax helps to even out the sheen and adds a measure of protection that can be renewed easily. However, don't be in a rush to apply it: Almost all waxes contain solvents, which can damage a film finish that isn't fully cured. For most finishes, this means waiting a week; but wait at least a month before applying a paste wax to solvent-based lacquer.

For best results, use an applicator—Using widely available but hard paste waxes, beginners tend to put on too much, then wonder why the surface smears when they try to buff it. The answer is to make a wax applicator.

Take some good, dense cheesecloth and fold it over. Place a small amount of wax on the middle of this pad. Gather up the edges and twist them to form a small knob that encloses the wax. As soon as you rub the surface, the wax will start coming through the cloth evenly and thinly. Although you can use softer semi-paste wax this way, you gain the most benefit when using harder paste waxes. For closed-pore, light-colored woods such as maple, I use a clear wax, but for open-pore woods such as oak or mahogany and darker closed-pore woods like cherry, I use a colored wax.

When you rub the surface, you will apply a very thin film of wax. The applicator prevents you from applying too much. I begin by applying the wax in circles, forcing it into any open pores, and then I give it a once-over with the grain to straighten everything out. If you run out of wax, don't apply more to the outside of the applicator; just unwrap it and replenish the inside. When finished, you can store the applicator inside the can of wax.

To get the best results, you must wait for the solvent to evaporate before you remove the excess wax and buff the surface. If you do this too soon, you'll either remove the wax or just move it around. If you wait too long, it becomes progressively harder to remove the surplus. Although the wax won't get hazy like car polish, it will change from glossy to dull. The time this takes varies by brand and atmospheric conditions, but 20 minutes is average.

Although using the applicator should prevent excess wax, I still rub the dried wax with a white nylon nonabrasive pad. The open weave picks up any thicker patches or small lumps of wax. The final step is to buff the surface with a soft cloth like terrycloth, an old T-shirt, or even a paper towel. Rub the surface vigorously and turn the cloth frequently so that you burnish the wax rather than just redistribute it.

At this stage, if you find you simply can't get the surface to shine, you probably put on too much wax or let it harden for too long. Rub the surface with a cloth dampened with mineral spirits to remove most of the wax. Wait an hour for the solvent to evaporate, and then reapply the wax more carefully.

Rub out the surface with wax—If you prefer a medium luster, an option when waxing a cured finish such as shellac, varnish, or lacquer is to apply the wax with 0000 steel wool or a gray abrasive pad. This will reduce the sheen and soften the look. To better lubricate the steel wool, I use a softer semi-paste wax. To avoid cross-grain scratches, apply the wax with the grain only. It is easy to apply too much wax with this method, so you'll probably need to go over the wax once it has dried with clean steel wool or a white abrasive pad. When the wax has cured, buff the surface in the same way as previously described.

Waxing intricate shapes and carvings—By highlighting areas that are proud and leaving recesses dull, wax can give carvings and moldings a more three-dimensional appearance. The softer the wax, the easier it is to work into the corners using either a cloth or a small stiff brush. When dry, a vigorous buffing with a dry and moderately stiff-bristle brush will yield good results.

Renewing a waxed surface—When a waxed surface begins to look dull, try buffing to renew the sheen. If this doesn't do the trick, simply apply and buff another layer of wax in the same way as described earlier. When done correctly, the layers of wax are so thin you need have no concern about wax buildup.

If the surface becomes worn or dirty, wax can be removed with mineral spirits or one of the proprietary wax washes. If it is very grimy, use either 0000 steel wool or a gray abrasive pad with solvent to loosen the wax. Wipe well with paper towels, and then rewax the surface.

Wax Bare Wood for a Natural Look

Wax also can be used on its own as a finish. It has the advantage of barely changing the natural color of the wood, just giving the surface a slightly higher sheen. The downside is that it gives minimal protection, but this is not a problem for objects such as picture frames that are subject to infrequent handling. As with waxing a finish, you need to match the wax color to the wood.

A variation on this is one of my favorite finishes. I seal the bare wood with a coat or two of a 1- to 2-lb. cut of shellac, lightly sand it when dry, and then apply the wax. I've used it with great success on lightly used furniture and on architectural components such as paneling. The thin barrier of shellac barely changes the wood's appearance yet makes it smoother and less porous, allowing a more even luster. It also allows me to easily remove the wax at a later date, if required.

Colored Wax Gives a Range of Looks

Wax comes in a range of colors, from wood tones to specialty colors such as black and white. These colored waxes can be used either for decorative finishing or for replicating antiques.

A limed finish on white oak is the most famous decorative wax finish. First, open up the pores with a brass brush or a slightly stiffer bronze brush, then vacuum and blow out the pores thoroughly. Seal the surface with a thin coat of shellac, and then rub white wax well into the pores. Wipe off the excess and apply either a couple of coats of paste wax or, for a higher sheen, a coat of shellac. Other applications include adding colored pigments or mica powders to clear wax to color the pores.

If your taste runs more toward period than contemporary, wax can give furniture an aged appearance. Using wax a shade or two darker than the wood will add accent lines around moldings and carvings. There are brown and black waxes sold as patinating waxes, but you can make your own or use dry pigment powders on top of a clear wax.

Don't use shoe polish. Many include silicone, which will play havoc with any film finish that you apply afterward.

Continued ➔

Choose One Made for Furniture

In general, if the first use mentioned on the can is polishing wood floors, don't use the wax on furniture. It is likely to contain a high percentage of carnauba wax and is designed to be buffed with a mechanical floor buffer. You'll have a hard time buffing it by hand. However, these hard paste waxes can be used as a clear base for custom-coloring. In general, waxes designed for furniture are easier to use. They usually are softer in consistency (what I call a semi-paste wax) due to their higher percentage of solvent, which makes them easier to apply.

Colored Wax

If you do one thing after reading this, I hope you'll try using a dark wax. A clear wax on a dark, open-pored wood can leave white residue in the pores. Even if the pores are filled, the clear wax can leave a slight haze on a dark surface. Conversely, wax the same color or darker than the wood can enhance the appearance. See the box below for more detail and to learn how dark wax can be used to give an aged look.

You can buy wax in a range of wood tones, or you can take clear paste wax and color it yourself. You must first melt the wax, but because wax is flammable, never heat it over an open flame. Instead, place it in a container over heated water, a device known as a double boiler. Add artist's oils or universal colorants and mix them in thoroughly. Let the wax solidify before use.

- **Buy the right color.** Find one that matches the wood and it won't show in pores and recesses.

- **Or color your own.** If you need only a small amount of colored wax or you want an unusual color, melt some clear paste wax in a container over hot water, and then mix in artist's oil colors.

Clear-Wax Basics

Although brands of wax vary greatly in price, they all draw from the same limited number of raw waxes and solvents.

The best-known wax is beeswax. After the honeycomb has been melted and refined, it can be left dark or placed in the sun and bleached. Medium-soft, beeswax produces a medium-gloss finish.

The cheapest component is paraffin wax, derived from refining crude oil. Relatively soft and colorless, it serves as the base for many wax blends. Also obtained from petroleum is microcrystalline wax, a highly refined and expensive wax that has excellent resistance to water. It is favored by museums because of its neutral pH.

To offset paraffin wax's softness, manufacturers add harder waxes: Carnauba, obtained from scraping the leaves of a Brazilian palm tree, produces a very high shine but is also very hard to buff out when used alone; candelilla, obtained from the leaves of a Mexican plant, is much like carnauba, but somewhat softer.

The speed at which a solvent evaporates will determine how long you have to wait before you can buff the wax. Traditionally, turpentine was used to dissolve beeswax, but its relative expense means this medium-paced solvent is rarely used in commercial waxes.

Mineral spirits is the most common solvent and can be formulated for slow or medium-paced evaporation. Faster-evaporating solvents include naphtha and toluene. I avoid toluene waxes such as Briwax for a number of reasons. First, I dislike their strong odor; second, toluene is most likely to damage a finish that is not fully cured; third, I find they harden very fast, making them somewhat difficult to work with.

Rediscovering Milk Paint

by Nancy Hiller

Milk paint has been around at least 20,000 years. The Egyptians used it, and it has been found decorating ancient cave dwellings. Woodworkers who specialize in Colonial and Shaker furniture are familiar with it, as milk paint was a common finish on both types of furniture. But milk paint offers interesting possibilities for all woodworkers, from makers of period reproductions to those who prefer contemporary furniture and cabinetry. And it contains no toxic ingredients. This durable and versatile finish comes in a variety of colors and can be used with different topcoat treatments to create unique effects. Opaque surfaces, color washes, layering, and decorative painting are just the beginning.

Many woodworkers are reluctant to try milk paint, concerned that it may be difficult to use. Nothing could be further from the truth. This finish is so easy to mix and apply that you can't mess it up, and slight imperfections will only enhance the finished look.

What Is Milk Paint?

Milk paint's durability comes from its ingredients. Casein, a protein found in milk, is extremely hard when dry and adheres to a variety of substrates, including solid woods, plywood, and medium-density fiberboard (MDF). Manufacturers mix casein with lime. When combined with water, the lime and casein react to form a natural coating that cures over time, somewhat like concrete. If you want to apply milk paint over some other type of finish, be sure to follow the manufacturer's instructions. You'll usually have to scuff up the existing finish with sandpaper, and then clean the surface with water or vinegar and water. Finally, use a bonding agent (supplied by milk-paint manufacturers) mixed in with the water and powder of the first coat when refinishing.

Supplied as a dry powder, milk paint has a limited shelf life once it is mixed with water, so you should make up only as much as you can use in a day. Unused powder, however, can be stored indefinitely in an airtight, sealed container. Moisture makes the powder unusable, so the trick is to keep out humidity. You can purchase many different colors. The paint dries lighter than it looks when it's wet, so test colors on scraps.

Close-grained species such as pine, poplar, and maple will give the smoothest finish under milk paint. While you can use it on open-pored species such as oak or ash, the grain structure will be pronounced and must be considered part of the design.

Applying Milk Paint Is Easy but Different from Other Paints

To prepare the surface, sand to P180-grit and remove dust using a vacuum or tack cloth. Milk paint is not like premixed latex and oil-based paints that form a layer on top of the wood's surface. It's thinner and, when used on clean, unfinished surfaces, is self-priming: The first coat is partially absorbed by the wood and, when cured, forms its own bond coat. This makes applying the first coat very different from applying the first coat of a premixed paint. The wood will absorb the milk paint as you apply it, so don't expect it to glide on. Compensate for this by reapplying paint to the brush more often and dabbing the paint into the wood.

The most common approach is an opaque finish, which obscures the figure of the wood and covers your piece with the intense, velvety color that is milk paint's hallmark. Mix equal parts warm water and powder in a nonmetallic container and stir briskly. Let the paint slake for about 10 minutes. An opaque application is between two and four coats. Although some people recommend raising the grain with a light spray of water before applying the paint, I don't. I find this step to be redundant. Since I am applying multiple coats of milk paint, I'm not worried about sanding through the first coat.

Wax Can Give an Aged Appearance

CREATE INSTANT DUST

Dirt in the crevices. Apply softened paste wax into the nooks and crannies of carvings. Then tap in some rottenstone with a stiff-bristled brush (top). When the wax has dried, rub the area with crumpled newspaper to remove the bulk of the rottenstone, and then burnish the high points with a cloth. This leaves a line of gray similar to that found on antiques.

ADD YEARS OF POLISH

Stimulate wax buildup. To replicate the dark recesses found on antiques, use dark wax in these areas (above), or apply dry pigments to freshly applied clear wax. When the wax is dry, burnish the high points with a cloth or a brush.

With an inexpensive natural-bristle brush, apply a generous first coat with the grain. Stray bristles or small chunks of undissolved paint can be picked off the surface as you go. Applying a second coat of base color before the first has fully dried seems to help even out the coverage. When the first two coats have dried, scuff-sand with P220-grit paper to a smooth surface and decide whether you need subsequent coats. You can tell a coat is dry by the characteristic papery appearance. Drying time is quick—you can usually recoat in one to two hours—depending on humidity.

Apply as many coats as needed to produce the opacity you want. There is no rule about how many coats to apply. If you want a very smooth finished surface, sand each time between coats. I don't always do this (sometimes I want to achieve a more imperfect-looking surface), but I always sand before applying the topcoat in order to create optimal conditions for adhesion. Let the milk paint dry completely—at least overnight—before protecting it with clear topcoats.

Topcoats: Different Looks and Levels of Protection

Topcoats add protection but alter the color of the paint. The bare finish has a distinctive shaded look with subtle imperfections that can be left natural or burnished to a soft sheen using 0000 steel wool. Milk paint is compatible with almost any topcoat, but topcoating is not required; the paint itself is hard and stands up to normal wear on furniture. However, if left unfinished it will quickly pick up and show oils from fingers. A high-traffic area such as a kitchen or a bathroom will need more protection than a keepsake box, picture frame, or wall shelf. Waxes, shellac, and oils provide less protection than polyurethanes.

Whether water-, alcohol-, or oil-based, topcoats will alter the final look, making it darker. Whichever topcoat you plan to use, prepare the painted surface by sanding with P220-grit paper along the grain, then remove the colored dust.

Wax, Alcohol, and Oil-Based Topcoats

These topcoats all tend to leave the paint color warmer and darker. Because visually the end result is almost the same, you should consider the level of protection when choosing between them.

Wax, like oil, will darken milk paint. While it is one of the traditional coatings used over milk paint, it won't afford substantial protection from common household substances. Shellac will create a clear, glossy look but give only limited protection against damage by water and oils. Boiled linseed oil and Danish oil are two traditional protective coatings. Apply as many coats as necessary to build up the luster you desire. These oils will darken the paint's tone and give colors a warmer look. It is important to take this ambering effect into account if you are working with blues, which will shift toward green under oil-based polyurethane. If you are concerned about yellowing, you can always use a water-based polyurethane instead.

The availability of matte and glossy finishes adds yet another dimension to consider.

Water-Based Topcoats

Unlike oil-based topcoats, water-based topcoats can make a finish look colder and give it an artificial appearance. This can be a problem over warm colors such as reds and browns. However, this effect can be a positive if the design of the piece calls for a starker look.

Once dry, milk paint forms a coating that is non-soluble, so it won't dissolve when water-based topcoats are applied. In days past, water-based finishes were not resistant to damage from oil, so you couldn't rely on them to protect a milk-painted surface from such common hazards as a pastry baker's buttery fingers opening cabinet latches in the kitchen. But these days, many water-based finishes are as good as, if not better than, their oil-based counterparts and offer full protection from oils, water, and alcohol. Some even mimic the warm yellow cast of the oils.

Topcoats Make a Big Difference

Steel Wool and Wax

Wax is simple and easy. After scuff-sanding with P220-grit, burnish the milk paint with 0000 steel wool and use the steel wool to work in a fairly heavy coat of paste wax for a natural look.

Danish Oil

Oils offer more protection. Apply a generous amount of an oil finish and allow it to penetrate for about 30 minutes. Wipe off the excess with a clean, lint-free cloth to give the surface more protection than wax as well as a subtle sheen.

For a tough topcoat, go with poly. Oil-based polyurethanes darken and warm the color of milk paint, but they also can change the color, as shown above. Water-based finishes give a colder, brighter appearance, a plus for bright colors and contemporary designs.

Breaking the Mold: Special Effects

In addition to the opaque finish, you can get a variety of looks with milk paint, depending on how the film is applied.

Layering—Layering different colors and then sanding through in spots so that the base hues appear is a good way to age a piece instantly. When you layer different colors, you should use two coats of the base to ensure that the buildup will be adequate. And whenever you switch colors in layering, be sure to let the paint dry well to prevent the wet colors from mixing together.

Washcoat—A wash made from a dilute solution of paint adds color while allowing the figure to show. Because the finish becomes more opaque with each coat, I use one washcoat only.

My wood of choice for washcoating is cypress because it's close-grained yet has pronounced figure that shows through under the color. Other woods that could work well with a washcoat are yellow pine, furniture-grade Douglas fir, and maple.

Decorative painting—To paint intricate pictures and graphics, mix milk paint as you would any other artist's paint. To cover a large surface, mix larger quantities of dry powder, adding more of particular colors to obtain the look you want. For small designs, you can blend small batches of color on a ceramic plate just as you would on a painter's palette, adjusting hues as you go.

Because the first coat of milk paint soaks into the wood, it's best to decorate on a background that has already been coated at least twice. The consistency should be thicker when you are decorating than when you are covering an entire surface with one color. Test it on a sample piece that matches the piece you'll be painting. Experiment and have fun.

Milk Paint 101

Work in the first coat. Milk paint soaks into the wood as it is applied. Reapply paint to the brush often, and push the paint into the wood. The second coat glides on more smoothly, like regular paint. After two coats, scuff-sand lightly with P220-grit paper and decide if you need more.

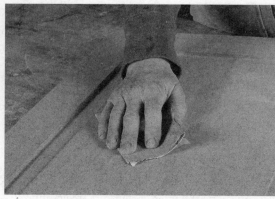

Powder first. To reduce clumping, add some water to the powder, and then stir to a paste before adding the rest. Alternatively, you can add all of the water, cover the mixing container tightly, and shake vigorously for several minutes.

Continued ➔

Water-Based Finishes

by Jeff Weiss

No finishing topic creates more controversy, head scratching, and general mayhem than water-based finishes. Much of the misunderstanding stems from the rather checkered history of these finishes. They've always promised fast drying time, low odor, easy cleanup, and nonflammability, but early versions were hard to apply and gave many woods a cold, dead look.

However, today's formulations match the clarity, hardness, and durability of most, if not all, of the solvent-based clear-coat cousins that they are increasingly replacing. As the founder of a company that makes water-based finishes, I'll shed some light on their history, describe the increasingly sophisticated science behind them, and give some tips on how to apply them. In this way, I hope to give you the confidence to make the switch.

Water-Based Finishes Started Life on the Floor

The history of many of today's water-based wood-finish resins can be traced back more than a century to the floor-care industry. Early developments included water emulsion paste-wax blends for protecting wood and tile floors. These blends had the advantage of being lower in odor and less flammable than solvent versions. After the Second World War, we began to see the development of polymer acrylates for tile floor finishes and waterborne urethanes that featured the early polyester, and later polycarbonate, resins used to waterproof fabric and leather. In the early 1980s, these technologies became the first generation of water-based finishes for wood floors.

Water-based latex and acrylic paints were developed before water-based clear finishes for two reasons: First, the market volume for paint is much greater; second, paint was easier to develop because early water-based resins demonstrated poor clarity and were better suited to blending with pigments.

In many ways, water-based clear finishes are following the same track as water-based paints, but are about 20 years behind in terms of market share. In the early 1980s, solvent-based wood finishes occupied almost 100% of the industrial and DIY market. Today, their share is estimated at 70% and is rapidly declining, with most of the decline within the last seven years.

The Link Between Solvent Finishes and Air Pollution

The event that transformed water-based finishes from various niche products into increasingly widespread use was the Clean Air Act of 1970. One of the terms popularized by the act was volatile organic compound (VOC). Aromatic solvents such as toluene, xylene, mineral spirits, and various ketones found in solvent-based finishes create low-level, or ground-standing, ozone—commonly known as smog. These VOCs also cause upper respiratory problems and can aggravate asthma.

Efforts to improve air quality placed limits on the amount of VOCs a finish can contain. These restrictions, in turn, gave a boost to water-based finishes. With a few exceptions, water-based coatings also contain VOCs. But because their components contain far fewer VOCs than those in solvent finishes, it is much easier to formulate a water-based finish to comply with clean-air regulations.

In recent years, state regulations on air quality have become more restrictive than federal ones. In particular, those of southern California and a coalition of northeastern states increasingly set the parameters used when formulating finishes. For example, the national limit for solvent lacquer is 680 grams of VOC per liter, whereas the northeast limit is 550 grams, and in southern California the limit is 275 grams. The benefit for woodworkers is that these restrictions are causing a migration to water-based finishes. As that market grows, companies are devoting more time and money into developing better finishes.

So What is a Water-Based Finish?

To better understand water-based finishes, it helps to know what goes into them. Water-based is a generic term for coatings in which the resin is suspended in a water medium. In basic terms, a primary glycol solvent dissolves the resin, allowing it to form a crude film, and water acts as the diluent (or secondary solvent) that evaporates with the glycol as the film dries.

Two families—Water-based coatings can be either waterborne or water-reducible. Waterborne coatings start with a resin, which can be a urethane, an acrylic, or a blend of the two in a solution of water and surfactants. This is known as the crude resin. Next, glycol ethers and performance additives based on the intended use of the finish are blended in. These include leveling agents to help it flow out during brush or spray applications, defoamers to minimize bubbles, anti-scuffing agents to stop marring, and ultraviolet additives to protect the wood from sunlight.

The second group of water-based finishes is known as water-reducible coatings. They consist of oil-based resins such as tung, linseed, and castor oils, blended with alcohols, glycol ethers, and neutralizers to allow the absorption of water and create a homogenous solution of oil and water. Like waterborne finishes, these coatings contain synthetic resins and performance additives. They are sometimes referred to as hybrids.

Application is Now Much Easier

One legacy of the early water-based finishes designed for floors is that they developed a reputation as being hard to apply. They performed well with tools used for finishing floors, but due to their low viscosity, most could not be sprayed successfully. They were also a challenge to brush, as many dried too fast or developed runs and sags. Generally speaking, water-based finish manufacturers suggest dilution rates ranging from 5% to 20% by liquid volume to help thin the viscosity of the coating or to slightly retard the drying time. However, some can be reduced more than 50% with basic tap or distilled water and will still maintain their film-formation qualities, although thinner and less protective. Refer to the specific product's technical data sheet or contact the manufacturer for the best dilution rate.

The right brush makes all the difference—Instead of large, high-volume paintbrushes designed for thick house paints, I recommend the use of fine arts and special-purpose brushes that feature shorter bristles and a thin nap. Consider such brands as daVinci's Cosmotop and Top-Acryl Series, Winsor & Newton's Athena and Monarch Series, as well as Purdy's Syntox brushes. Appropriate sizes range from 1 in. to 3 ½ in. wide.

Many finishes can be sanded within an hour. On most finishes, if re-coated within the first 24 hours, the next series of coats will chemically bond, or burn in, with the previous coat. But check the specific instructions on the can.

New advances in finishes for spraying—As large industrial users are restricted in the amount of VOCs they can release, water-based finish manufacturers are creating finishes for them that more closely match solvent finishes in both application and performance. With proper guidance from the manufacturer, you can switch to water-based finishes in an afternoon with minor tip size and air pressure adjustments. Like solvent finishes, water-based finishes have a shelf life, in most cases about a year. Signs of a finish past its prime include gelling in the can and either a pink or greenish/blue color.

Water-Based Finishes for All

Woodworkers have much to look forward to as they explore the range of water-based finishes now available. As research and development continues, more and more water-based finishes will successfully replace the solvent-based finishes of the past.

Explosion-Free Spraying

Solvent-based finishes should be sprayed in an explosion-proof spray booth. Water-based finishes can be used in a simple knockdown booth in a garage or basement.

RESIN TYPE	PHYSICAL CHARACTERISTICS (poor/good/excellent)		SPRAY/ BRUSH/ WIPE
Acrylic Blends — Commonly marketed as the water-based equivalent of solvent lacquer finishes, these finishes are designed only to be sprayed. They harden rapidly and give good gloss development. Those made with styrene acrylics have good corrosion resistance to household chemicals such as salt or vinegar, but yellow with age.	Hardness	G-E	S
	Chemical resistance	G	
	Clarity	G-E	S
	Burn-in	E	
	UV resistance	P-G	S
	Repairability	G-E	S,B
Copolymers — Due to rapidly changing technologies, these resins offer a unique range of performance values that are difficult to compare to old-world solvent-based finishes. They generally fall into the post-catalyzed lacquer and pre-catalyzed conversion varnish range of performance.	Hardness	G-E	B
	Chemical resistance	G-E	
	Clarity	G-E	B
	Burn-in	P-G	
	UV resistance	G	B
	Repairability	P-G	
Urethanes — These finishes develop a hard, chemical-resistant film, so they are used for wood floors, architectural trim, tabletops etc. This durability also means that successive coats tend to form layers rather than melting together like acrylic blends.	Hardness	E	B
	Chemical resistance	E	
	Clarity	G-E	S,B,W
	Burn-in	P	
	UV resistance	G	
	Repairability	P	S,B
Urethane/Acrylic Blends — These are the most common type of water-based finish because the blend can be fine-tuned for specific uses.	Hardness	G-E	S,B
	Chemical resistance	G-E	
	Clarity	G-E	S
	Burn-in	P-G	S,B
	UV resistance	G	
	Repairability	P-G	B
Hybrids — The newest type of water-based finishes, they combine the warm tones, clarity penetration, and in some cases exterior protection of solvent finishes with the low odor and quick-drying benefits of a water-based finish.	Hardness	E	S,B,W
	Chemical resistance	E	
	Clarity	G-E	S,B,W
	Burn-in	P-G	
	UV resistance	P-G	
	Repairability	E	S,B,W

Spraying Water-Based Finishes

by Teri Masaschi

The first time I used a water-based finish, I promised it would be my last. In the late 1980s and 1990s, companies launched a mass of water-based finishes and used the consumer as the testing lab. I wasn't alone in finding the new finishes too difficult, too finicky, and too unpredictable.

Today the air-quality laws are more stringent than ever and the end is approaching fast for many solvent-based finishes. The good news is that during this period, the formulators of water-based finishes have been busy. As a hardened "lacquer head," I never thought you'd hear me say this, but when it comes to water-based finishes, I like what I have used recently.

Switching to water-based finishes has been a relief: No more headache or solvent hangover at the end of a long day, and far less use of flammable solvents. However, the transition has not been easy, in part because solvent lacquer and water-based lacquer are as alike chemically as chalk and cheese. Therefore, fellow lacquer heads have to forget much of what they know and in some ways become novice sprayers again. However steep the learning curve, it is well worth the climb. And for newcomers to spraying, here is your chance to finally achieve professional-looking finishes without the need for an explosion-proof spray booth.

The Right Tools and Conditions are Critical

One thing that hasn't changed is that water-based finishes remain generally fussier than solvent-based ones. Your spray gun needs to have either stainless-steel or plastic fluid passages because water-based finishes corrode aluminum quickly.

Everything must be clean, clean, clean! Keep the surface contaminant-free, the gun dedicated to water-based finishes, the air source (if compressor driven) filtered to remove moisture and oil, and the spray gun's cup clean (a disposable lining is best).

I have sprayed solvent-based finish as low as 45°F and gotten away with it, but water-based finishes are more temperature sensitive. The safe range is about 60° to 80°F.

One thing you don't have to worry about is compatibility with no-load sandpaper, which has stearates to prevent the paper from gumming up. Stearates used to leave a waxy coating that fouled up water-based finishes, but modern stearates don't have this problem.

Anyone who has refinished old furniture is familiar with "fish eye," the shallow craters in the finish caused by contaminants, in particular silicone. You can add a fish-eye destroyer to solvent-based finishes but not to water-based ones, so if you are working on antique furniture, be prepared to use shellac as a sealer coat over the contaminants first. On most woods it isn't necessary to pre-raise the grain before spraying a water-based finish, but you should on gnarly or figured wood.

Not Your Dad's Lacquer

For more than 80 years, nitrocellulose lacquer has been the benchmark against which all other finishes are found wanting. Each coat melts into the previous one, creating a single film of finish no matter how many coats are applied. This creates the dimensional and reflective sheen that allows you to look down into the beauty of the wood.

Trying to associate their new finishes with the industry standard, manufacturers started calling many water-based formulations lacquer. However, the ingredients of the two have nothing in common. Water-based lacquers usually consist of a glycol solvent, an acrylic resin, a glycol ether, and various leveling agents, defoamers, and other performance enhancers. This is not your father's lacquer but it will, most likely, be yours.

How to Warm Up the Color

One of the main differences between solvent- and water-based finishes is the latter's cold appearance and inability to warm the wood. If you are finishing maple, birch, ash, or any white wood, water-based can be perfect. On cherry,

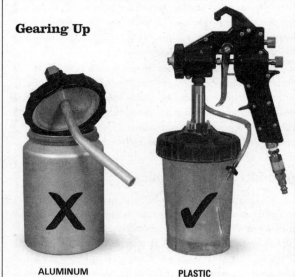

Gearing Up

ALUMINUM ✗ PLASTIC ✓

CHOOSE YOUR GUN CAREFULLY
Water-based finishes will corrode an aluminum cup. Instead, make sure the cup and the gun's fluid passages are either stainless steel or plastic. 3M's PPS system of plastic cups with disposable liners works well.

STAINLESS STEEL ✓

CLEAR THE AIR
Water-based finishes are very sensitive to contamination. Use a filter to remove moisture and oil coming from the compressor.

NO TACK CLOTH, PLEASE
Use a damp cotton or microfiber cloth to wipe away sanding dust. A sticky tack cloth can leave residue that will repel water-based finishes.

walnut, mahogany, or figured woods (including maple), it isn't. You can solve the problem by tinting the coating with an amber dye to mimic the tone of solvent lacquers and oil-based products. But water-based finishes have a milky appearance at first, making it hard to judge the tone.

A better approach is to coat the bare wood with dewaxed shellac. You can tint light-colored shellac such as beige or blond, or use darker grades such as orange or garnet. This eliminates any need to pre-raise the grain. Also, if you wipe on a coat of oil to enhance a wood's figure, apply a coat of dewaxed shellac before using a water-based finish.

Big Pluses: Faster Build, Fewer Fumes

If the preparations for spraying water-based finishes are more elaborate than for their solvent siblings, the actual spraying is easier. Unlike solvent-based lacquers, which tend to be sticky and syrupy, water-based coatings spray thin and wet but have excellent "cling," which means fewer sags and runs. They dry in about the same amount of time as solvent-based ones—30 to 45 minutes. With any type of finish, the number of coats is subjective. However, because the solids content of water-based finishes is generally higher than for solvent-based ones, you will be pleasantly surprised after only the second coat. This faster build offsets the fact that water-based finishes cost 20% to 30% more.

Use a small setup for the gun, such as Accuspray's 0.043-in. needle and a No. 5 aircap. You could use a No. 7 aircap for a large surface. After prolonged spraying, crusted coating may build up on your spray gun. I apply a thin film of Vaseline on the horns of the air cap first, so I can flick off the buildup later with my fingernail.

Water-based finishes are safer—The moment when solvent finishes are the most dangerous is not when spraying them—you're wearing a respirator and the fan is drawing off the fumes—but when they have just dried. You've removed your respirator and are scuff-sanding the surface. The fan has been shut off, but all the solvents are lifting off the surface and hanging heavy in the air. This is incredibly lethal exposure. Water-based products give off gas, too, but are far less toxic. The gas has a smell similar to mild ammonia.

Rubbing Out and Cleaning Up

Most water-based materials contain a blend of resins such as acrylics and urethanes that offers durability and clarity, and you can often get a perfect finish off the gun, particularly for a satin sheen.

However, if you want a polished-out surface, don't assume that these coatings are going to behave like solvent lacquer. Successive coats do not melt completely into the previous layer. In this way, water-based finishes are more like solvent-based varnishes or polyurethanes in that the finish builds in layers rather than melting into a single film. Consequently, there is a higher risk of "witness lines" when you polish through one coat into another.

The solution is to apply two or three coats and then completely flatten the surface. This will create numerous white witness lines, but they will disappear when the next couple of coats are applied. You can then polish the last coat with less risk of burning through the layers. Cure time for a successful rubout is the same as for solvent-based finishes: A minimum of 200 hours is preferable.

When you are done spraying, flush and clean the gun with water and ammonia, and then flush it with alcohol or lacquer thinner (you can't escape flammable solvents entirely).

Go ahead and use the new generation of water-based finishes. Just don't try them at the last moment! It is much less stressful to use test samples, and get a feel for these products first.

Continued →

Secrets of Success

FILTER FIRST
Before spraying, pour the finish through a fine-mesh paint filter to remove any contaminants that could block the gun.

NO FANCY BOOTH NEEDED
If you don't have a purpose-built spray booth like this one, build a simple knock-down one. An exhaust fan draws air through the filters, pulling away overspray.

SAND BETWEEN COATS
With a quick-drying, water-based finish in a clean environment, you shouldn't need to sand away dust nibs between coats. However, if you let the finish dry for longer than the time specified on the can, you must sand the surface to give the next coat a mechanical bond.

BROWN BAG: A PRO'S SECRET WEAPON
You can use brown shopping bag paper to smooth and polish the last coat of stain or semi-gloss water-based finish.

Simple High-Gloss Finish

Nothing matches a high-gloss, rubbed-out finish for enhancing the color, depth, and figure in wood. However, you won't get this flawless and glossy look from brushing or spraying alone: It is achieved by applying certain types of film finish and then polishing them either by hand or machine.

I recommend shellac or lacquer (not water-based) for this process. While I'll demonstrate by brushing on lacquer, I'll also give recipes for spraying lacquer and for brushing or spraying shellac.

Although certain styles of furniture such as Art Nouveau may have the whole surface polished (or "rubbed out"), with other styles it is quite acceptable to rub out just the most noticeable surface, such as a tabletop. Or, you can start the rubbing-out process but stop before a high gloss is reached, and instead achieve a flawless, semigloss sheen.

A Perfect Surface is Critical

For this highly reflective finish, the surface of the wood must be absolutely flat and smooth. This means that all milling marks, whether the telltale ripples of a power planer or the ridges from a handplane, must be removed. Start sanding at P150 grit and work up to P220 grit. If you are working with a harder wood such as maple, you may need to start with P120 grit. If you plan to use a water-based dye, wet the surface with water to raise the grain, let the wood dry for one to two hours, and sand lightly with P320-grit paper to remove the raised grain. Apply the stain, allow it to dry for at least four hours, and lightly sand with P220-grit paper.

Open-pored woods need to be filled—When applying a film finish to open-grained species such as oak, walnut, and mahogany, use grain filler. You'll need fewer coats of finish and less sanding between coats to achieve a flat surface, and you'll avoid the risk of the grain structure reappearing as the finish cures and shrinks down into the pores. Cherry and maple are sufficiently close-grained not to need filling. Before applying grain filler, apply a washcoat of dewaxed shellac to prevent staining.

You can use oil-based filler (I like Bartley's), or water-based (I use Behlen's). Both come in light, dark, and neutral, but you can tweak them with water- or oil-soluble dye powders to customize the color. The oil-based filler gives you a longer working time, which first-time users may appreciate, but the water-based is ready more quickly for topcoating.

Apply the filler with an old natural-bristle brush, working across the grain. Wait about five minutes, then use a plastic scraper or credit card to gently remove the excess from the surface. Wait about 15 minutes and then use a piece of burlap or a white abrasive pad to remove the remaining excess. The next day, lightly sand to leave the pores uniformly filled but with no filler on the surface.

Build a Finish Thick Enough to Sand Flat

Whether working with lacquer or shellac, I recommend two to three fully cured coats depending on how thickly you apply it. This gives you enough material to sand flat and then polish out. After applying a sealer, don't go beyond four coats, or you risk achieving a thick, plastic look. I'll focus on brushing lacquer; see the facing page for spraying lacquer and using shellac.

I use M.L. Campbell's Magnasand sealer and Magnamax clear gloss lacquer. Sold by the gallon, they are designed to be brushed or sprayed. Alternatively, Deft, Watco, and Behlen sell quarts of sealers and lacquers. Begin by applying two coats of lacquer sanding sealer,

1. Fill the Grain on Open-Pored Woods

Seal
Shellac prevents stains. When using grain filler, first apply a washcoat of shellac to prevent the filler from staining the wood.

Fill
Use a stiff brush. Apply the filler using an old, paint-stiffened brush, going across the grain. Commercial fillers come in neutral, light, and dark tones, but you can tint them with dye powder to match the finished wood.

Scrape
Remove the surplus. After the filler has started to dry but before it becomes hard, use a plastic spreader or an old credit card at 45° to the grain to scrape away surplus filler on the surface.

Wipe
Clean the surface. Use a piece of burlap (or a white abrasive pad) to remove remaining surface filler that the scraper missed. Work at right angles to the grain so you don't pull the filler out of the pores. Let the filler cure overnight and then sand the surface lightly with P220-grit paper.

2. Build Up a Topcoat

Seal
Two sealcoats. Working with the grain, apply a coat of lacquer sanding sealer using either a conventional flat brush or a mop brush, which can hold more finish. Wait an hour, then apply a second coat, but this time go across the grain. Let the sealer dry for at least four hours.

Sand
Block keeps surface even. After the sealer dries, sand it with P220-grit paper wrapped around a cork block. Sand across the grain, then with the grain.

Build
Layer on the topcoats. Thin the lacquer and then brush on two coats across the grain. After an hour, brush on two coats with the grain. Let the finish dry for four hours, wet-sand the surface with 600-grit paper, and apply four more coats.

3. Level the Topcoat

Start sanding across the grain. Wrap some 600-grit paper around a cork block and start sanding. Stop frequently to check your progress, and rinse the paper in warm water to resist clogging. Sand away almost all the low, shiny spots, but use caution near edges to avoid sanding through.

Uniformly dull. Work your way up through the grits until all the shiny spots are removed.

Alternate Directions When Leveling the Finish

Your first shop teacher told you never, ever to sand across the grain, but here is an exception to this rule. Level the surface with 600-grit paper, then progressively reduce the size of the scratches until they are small enough to be rubbed out with polishing compound. It is critical to remove all the scratches, and by alternating the sanding direction, it is much easier to see any scratches that remain from the previous paper.

4. Polish to a Mirror Finish by Hand

New material, traditional method. Automotive polishing compound is less messy than traditional pumice and rottenstone, but you can still work small surfaces and edges by hand using a damp cloth wrapped around a cork block.

By Machine

Labor-saving method. An electric polisher with a sponge pad brings up a high-gloss shine in a matter of minutes. Keep the machine moving to avoid overheating the finish.

Wet-look wood. Remove any remaining compound with a dry cloth or paper towel. This leaves a rubbed-out, high-gloss finish that gives the wood great clarity and depth.

brushing with the grain. Wait one hour, then brush on two more coats across the grain. No sanding is necessary between coats as long as you recoat within four hours.

Reduce the lacquer by 25% to 50% with lacquer thinner until it flows out evenly on a test board, and brush on two coats across the grain. Within two hours, brush on two more coats, this time with the grain. These four coats count as one fully cured coat. Allow four hours of drying time, then sand with P220-grit paper and dust off the residue. Repeat the four coats as described above. Depending on how thickly the lacquer was applied and how lightly you sanded, the build might be adequate at this point. To be safe, once this application has dried for four hours, sand with P320-grit paper, brush on two more coats with the grain, and let it dry overnight.

You are now ready to begin flattening the surface with increasingly finer grits of wet-and-dry sandpaper (all wet-and-dry grits specified are CAMI grade). To lubricate the paper, add one drop of hand soap per 8 oz. of warm water, and change the water each time you move to a higher grit. Start by wrapping a piece of 600-grit paper around a solid cork block (or stick some cork flooring tile to a block of wood), splash a little water on the surface, and sand across the grain in straight strokes. Wipe off the sanding residue frequently with a cotton cloth to monitor your progress and to prevent the paper from clogging too quickly.

Although you aren't aiming to eliminate 100% of the shiny brushed surface, you should come very close, with only a few slight depressions unsanded. Use caution near edges so that you don't sand through the finish. Switch to 1,000-grit paper and sand with the grain, removing the 600-grit lines. Repeat with 1,500 grit across the grain, then 2,000 grit with the grain until all the sanding lines have been removed and the surface is dull but flawless.

At this point, if you choose a hand-rubbed, semigloss sheen, wrap a cork block with Liberon 0000 steel wool and buff with the grain, applying firm, even pressure in long, straight strokes to dull the surface. Apply paste wax and then buff with a clean cotton cloth.

Rub Out to a High Sheen

In the past, woodworkers used pumice and rottenstone, lubricated with oil, to rub out a finish. Today's automotive polishing compounds are much easier to use. I use 3M's Imperial Microfinishing Compound-Liquid.

Elbow Grease for Small Surfaces

If the surface area is small, I polish it by hand. Wrap a cork block with a clean, damp cotton cloth. Apply a small amount of compound and a few drops of water directly to the surface. Begin to polish in a circular motion, working in an area about 8-in. square. As the compound starts to dry out, add a few more drops of water and continue to polish. Apply more compound and water until a high gloss appears and all of the 2,000-grit sanding lines are gone.

Change often to a fresh section of cloth and move across the surface, adding water and compound until all areas are covered. When the whole surface has a high gloss with no lines, wrap a clean cloth around the block. Sprinkle water on the surface, add a small amount of compound to the cloth, and do a final polish with the grain. Finally, use another clean, dry cloth or paper towel to polish off any residue.

An Electric Polisher Saves Time

On a larger surface, I use a polisher with a sponge pad attachment. A right-angle grinder also can be used, if it has variable speed. If you don't have a polisher, you can use a variable-speed electric drill or a random-orbit sander and polishing pads. Be very careful to keep water away from electrical parts.

Moisten the sponge pad to soften it, and then spin the disk a few times to remove surplus water. Apply a few drops of compound directly to the surface, start at one end, and slowly move the buffing wheel back and forth across the grain, polishing out the 2,000-grit sanding lines. Use a slow speed to reduce friction that could blister the finish.

Apply more compound and water as needed. Be cautious near the edges where the finish may be slightly thinner.

Once the sanding lines begin to disappear, reduce the amount of compound and increase the water to keep the surface lubricated and cool. Now work the buffer in a circular motion. The surface should take on a high gloss. Once all of the sanding lines are gone, finish polishing by hand, using a cloth-wrapped cork block.

Two Alternatives to Brushing Lacquer

Spray lacquer and normal shellac are both easy to apply and repair. While the former has greater resistance to impact, chemicals, and heat, thick coats can look synthetic. Shellac gives rich amber tones with a deep, organic feel.

For a Fast Build, Spray Lacquer

Apply two coats of lacquer sanding sealer in quick succession, allowing them to dry for four hours. Sand with P220-grit paper and spray on two coats of clear gloss lacquer reduced by 20%. Wait at least four hours and then block-sand with P320-grit paper. Wipe off the sanding residue and apply two more coats of the clear gloss lacquer, also reduced by 20%, and allow at least eight hours of drying time. Now follow the rubbing-out process described in the article.

Shellac Can Be Brushed or Sprayed

Brush on two coats of shellac sanding sealer such as SealCoat. Allow to dry for a minimum of four hours, then block-sand with P220-grit paper. Brush or spray on two coats of a 2-lb. cut of super-blond shellac, allowing 15 minutes between coats. You can use either SealCoat or dissolved flakes. After four hours, block-sand with P220-grit paper, first across the grain, then with the grain. Apply two more coats. Let dry for one or two days before starting the rubbing-out process.

Fast Finish with Oil, Shellac, and Wax

by Jeff Jewitt

I've had to learn to do quick finishing jobs and make fast fixes in my refinishing business. This method is both fast and attractive, whether you're working on a holiday gift on Christmas Eve or you just prefer no-fuss finishes. I came up with the technique based on necessity, but I'm sure it will save you when time is tight.

This finish is ideal for a low-build, "in-the-wood" type of look, where durability is not the key factor. However, you can build the shellac to increase the level of protection. The ingredients—boiled linseed oil, denatured alcohol, a can of amber shellac, and a few rags—can be found in most woodshops or at the nearest hardware store. The wipe-on technique avoids the hassle of most oil finishes, which can take days to complete. In fact, it works so well that it might become your favorite finish.

A Thin Coat of Oil Lays the Foundation

For surface preparation, scrape, plane, or sand the wood with the grain to P220-grit. Wipe with naphtha or denatured alcohol to remove dust, dirt, and sanding debris. The solvent will highlight potential problems like glue spots and scratches.

Applying boiled linseed oil is the first step in French polishing, a more tedious and time-consuming technique from which this finish is derived. In fact, you could call this a "down and dirty" French polish.

I'm a big fan of boiled linseed oil for this step, because it contains driers that cause it to cure faster than tung oil.

Pour a small amount onto a small cotton cloth. Apply just enough oil to make the wood appear "wetted," which is about a teaspoon per square foot depending on wood species. Don't use the "flood on, let sit, then wipe" method. If you do, the oil will seep from figured areas through the thin shellac that is applied in the next step.

Remove excess oil with a clean rag, then lightly buff the surface with a gray synthetic abrasive pad such as 3M Scotch-Brite or Mirka Mirlon. The pad will pick up residual oil and will smooth the wood surface further.

Begin with a Light Coat of Linseed Oil

Because this finish does not provide time for the oil to dry, compensate by using a whisper-thin coat. Use just enough to bring out the beauty of the wood. Immediately remove any residual oil with a clean, lint-free cloth. A good rubdown with a synthetic pad will smooth the surface and add a nice sheen.

Pad on Shellac Right Away

Normally, you would let the oil cure for 24 to 48 hours. You can wait, but if you go directly to the shellac application, it will speed things up and the oil will provide a bit of lubrication for the shellac. The thin coat of oil cures fine below the shellac.

Plain, orange, waxy shellac (sold in a can as amber shellac) works well and is easy to find. The brand I use comes in a 3-lb. cut that I dilute by mixing 2 parts denatured alcohol with 5 parts shellac. Put the mixture in a squeeze bottle with a dispensing spout.

I use a padding cloth to wipe on the shellac. It should be as absorbent, clean, and lint-free as possible. Old, clean T-shirts work fine. Cotton is preferred, because polyester does not hold or absorb liquids as well. Wad up the cloth so that the bottom part is as smooth and free of wrinkles as possible. Make the pad a manageable size. Large pads are great for big, flat surfaces but don't work for smaller and more intricate projects.

Dispense about 2 oz. of denatured alcohol into the pad and compress the pad with your hand several times to work the solvent through it. Then squeeze the pad to remove excess solvent. Pour about 1 oz. of shellac solution onto the pad bottom.

Padding shellac simply means wiping it on thinly with this cloth pad. It is best to practice on a flat surface to get a feel for applying it smoothly and evenly.

Wipe on Shellac

Thin the shellac you'll use by mixing 5 parts shellac with 2 parts denatured alcohol. This thinner shellac is easier to apply, especially on small or intricate surfaces. Wipe it on thinly with a cloth pad, starting with flat surfaces and then working the sides and edges. Use 600-grit sandpaper to smooth out application marks or remove debris.

Finishing Different Surfaces Requires an Assortment of Techniques

For flat surfaces, bring the pad down lightly near one edge and drag it across the top and off the opposite edge, like an airplane landing and then taking off again. Come in from the other side and repeat the stroke. Continue down the board in alternating stripes, with the grain. When you've reached the bottom, start again at the top. One of the great benefits of shellac is that it dries quickly enough for you to repeat the sequence rapidly. Work the sides and edges in a similar fashion. As the pad starts to dry out, reload it with shellac.

Continued →

For complex surfaces such as furniture interiors, tight corners, or other challenging areas, you'll need to modify things a bit. Start with the pad anywhere that's convenient and move it toward corners, right angles, and such. Always keep the pad moving. When you recharge, make sure you don't put too much shellac in the pad or you'll pool it. Bring the pad down on the surface and immediately begin to move it using just the pressure of your fingers or the weight of your arm.

To finish routed or other three-dimensional surfaces, wad up the cloth and compress it into the profile of the edge. Use a small, well-wetted portion of the pad to get the shellac into small or tight areas. But again, don't get the pad too wet or you'll create problems.

It probably took you longer to read about the shellac application than it will to actually do it. For a medium-size project like a small cabinet or table, I spend only about 30 minutes with the shellac. Smaller projects are a little harder, because you risk returning to an area before it dries, and dragging the gummy shellac. Move the pad more slowly, or try using a smaller pad.

You may encounter streaks or fibers in the sticky shellac. Any application marks or debris can be rubbed out with some 600-grit (CAMI grade) sandpaper followed by 0000 steel wool after the shellac has cured for about eight hours. Because there are no "coats" of finish in the conventional sense, just keep applying the finish to achieve the look you want.

Applying the Final Touch

Near the end of the process, if you use all the shellac in the pad and keep rubbing with the dry pad, it will burnish the surface and give it a nice soft glow. For a lower luster and extra protection, wait a day and then apply some paste wax with 0000 steel wool. Buff the wax with a soft cloth.

Finish with Steel Wool and Wax

Paste wax adds a more even sheen and a nice feel to your project. Apply it with 0000 steel wool. When the wax appears hazy, buff it with a soft, clean cloth.

Easy, Durable Finish with Varnish and Turpentine

I wasn't asking for much: I wanted a finish with a rich, hand-rubbed luster, neither too glossy nor too dull, that illuminates rather than hides the grain—one that would offer real protection from moisture and sunlight and yet still feel like wood, not plastic. I also wanted a finish I could apply quickly and easily, and something I could use right out of the can. And it would be awfully nice if it smelled good. That isn't too much to ask of a finish, is it?

The answer turned out to be rather simple: high-gloss spar varnish, turpentine, wet-or-dry sandpaper in various grits, a few rags and a bit of elbow grease. Simply rubbing plain gloss varnish into the raw wood provided the protection, sheen, feel and ease of application I was looking for.

Start with a Well-Prepared Surface

The key is to scrape, plane or sand each of the pieces of your project before you assemble it. Even if you have to touch up the sanding after final assembly, this step will save lots of time.

During the building process I sand by machine (belt sander, 120 grit), then sand by hand with a wood sanding block padded with felt. The sanding sequence will depend, in part, on the type of wood. On hard maple, for example, use 100 grit, then 120, 150 and finally 220 grit. With mahogany and its much more open grain, stop dry-sanding at 150 grit. Be sure to change sandpaper frequently.

Make sure the surface is clean by using a vacuum to pull out the sanding grit from the pores of the wood. Don't worry if the surface is less smooth than what you normally shoot for. The sanding doesn't stop when the finishing begins. I wet-sand with finer and finer grits during the application of the finish itself.

Materials Are Easy to Obtain

The heart of my finish is a high-gloss spar varnish, which has several advantages: Unlike plain oils, it hardens overnight; it's readily available; and it has much greater clarity than semigloss or satin finishes, whose additives not only dull the finish but also cloud the grain. Spar varnish also contains ultraviolet protection that will help keep the wood from fading or yellowing. I've used this varnish for years on boats, protecting the wood from salt water and abuse, so I know it provides the tough tabletop film I'm looking for. As an added bonus, this finish is quite easy to renew by scuff-sanding with 220-grit paper and simply wiping on an additional coat of varnish if the surface ever needs it. In addition, this finishing method will also work with other types of varnish, urethanes and even some finishing oils.

Though it's counterintuitive, gloss varnish does not produce a glossy surface when it's rubbed on. Because you're wiping off any excess varnish, not letting it stand on the surface, it doesn't get a chance to build up to its normal gloss.

To thin the varnish for the initial coat, I like to use natural turpentine instead of paint thinner, simply because it smells good. As a general rule, thin a finish with whatever the label suggests for cleanup.

You will need a few sheets of 220-, 320-, 400- and 600-grit wet-or-dry sandpaper for sanding in the varnish. For dry-sanding between coats, use open-coat, self-lubricating 320-grit paper. A box of soft cotton rags from the paint store ensures that you won't run out of clean rags just when you need one. Lastly, disposable gloves are essential. Not only will they protect your skin from solvents, but they also make the job a lot less messy.

Application Is Straightforward

Before starting, spread out a plastic sheet to contain drips and spills. This is also a good time to change into an old shirt and pants. (I might even follow my own advice about this one of these days.) Pour a small amount of varnish into a container using a piece of nylon panty hose as a strainer. Thin with one part turpentine to about three parts varnish. The first coat saturates the wood more effectively if it is thinned down a bit.

Wearing gloves, quickly flood the entire surface on all sides until it's completely coated, adding more varnish as needed. It's important to cover the piece completely, not in sections. Working on a small area at a time may leave a line where different areas of finish overlap.

Sand the wet varnish into the wood using 220-grit wet-or-dry paper. Sand with the grain until you produce a slurry. This helps fill the pores of open-grained woods, such as mahogany or oak, and the color match is perfect. While the varnish is still wet, wipe with a soft cotton rag to remove any varnish that has not soaked into the wood. When removing the excess varnish, there's a point at which the varnish gets quite sticky and difficult to wipe. Working on something like a large tabletop might require a helper. Rub across the grain to avoid pulling the slurry out of the wood pores. Be sure to spread out the oil-soaked rags to dry before disposing of them, to avoid the danger of the rags spontaneously igniting.

Buff with a fresh cloth until the surface is slick and smooth. Polish the piece every half hour or so to make sure no wet spots emerge on the surface. Joints, such as on the breadboard ends of a tabletop, will absorb excess varnish, which will gradually seep out after the rest of the surface has dried. To avoid this, I blast the joint with compressed air, forcing the surplus varnish out of the gap.

Let the piece sit at room temperature overnight. You can carry on working in the shop because it doesn't matter if dust lands on the piece, but it is a good idea to ensure adequate ventilation to avoid a concentration of fumes. The next morning the surface should feel smooth and dry. Lightly dry-sand it with 320-grit nonloading, or stearated, paper. Use a felt-padded block, and sand with the grain. Clean the surface with a vacuum or compressed air. Apply a flood coat of unthinned varnish and use 320-grit wet-or-dry paper to sand the varnish into the surface. Wipe and buff the excess varnish as before.

Repeat this process each day; wet-sanding with finer and finer grits until you have at least three coats. Additional coats will produce slightly more luster. Some folks like to wax the surface when it's dry, but I prefer to leave it unwaxed, because it's easier to recoat should the surface become damaged over time.

I haven't yet been tempted to throw away either my spray guns or my badger-hair brushes, but after using this finishing process on several projects, I can't remember the last time I used those tools. This simple technique meets all of my criteria for an ideal finish and produces very consistent results, all without a large investment in equipment.

First Coat: Thinned Varnish

THREE PARTS VARNISH

ONE PART THINNER

220-GRIT WET-OR-DRY PAPER

Additional Coats: Unthinned Varnish

Build the finish. Apply subsequent coats the same way as the first coat. Rub in each coat with a higher grit of wet-or-dry paper. The last coat is rubbed in with 600-grit paper to create a very smooth surface.

A final buffing. After the final coat has dried, the surface will be silky smooth with the pores filled. Rub the surface briskly with a clean cotton rag.

UNTHINNED VARNISH

FINER-GRIT PAPER

Fast-Drying, Wipe-On Varnish Blend

by Roland Johnson

We'd all like a finish that can be applied easily by hand, stands up to the rigors of everyday use, and is easy to repair or renew. Several years ago, in my search for this Holy Grail finish, I started sampling varnishes. I rejected polyurethane because it's hard to repair and worse to remove if a piece needs a total refinish. I narrowed my search to alkyd-based varnishes, eventually choosing Pratt & Lambert's No. 38 clear. However, I wanted it to have more water resistance and to dry faster, and I wanted to wipe it on.

So I started tweaking the stock No. 38 and, through trial and error, came up with a brew that fulfilled my needs. I mixed equal parts of No. 38 and pure tung oil, added some pure spirits of gum turpentine, and zapped the mix with a dose of Japan drier.

This custom oil-varnish mixture has a number of advantages. It is easily wiped on and off with a paper towel. It can be wet-sanded into the grain to act as a pore filler. The thin coats dry quickly, reducing the opportunity for dust to get trapped in the wet finish. Often I apply finish in an area that is less than white-room clean, so eliminating the worry about dust is a real bonus. This finish is water-resistant and tough enough to hold up to everyday use, it's easy to repair or replace, it resists yellowing, and it dries hard enough to be rubbed out to a high-gloss sheen if desired. There are a couple of drawbacks, though. It has a short shelf life (a few weeks before it starts to solidify), so mix only the amount you'll need for the project. More than with other oil-based finishes, cloths used with this mixture must be laid out to dry because the fast catalytic reaction caused by the Japan driers may create enough heat to spontaneously combust if they are left wadded up.

The Recipe

5 parts	Pratt & Lambert No. 38 alkyd varnish
5 parts	Pure tung oil for water resistance
2 parts	Japan drier to speed drying time
2–3 parts	Pure gum spirits turpentine to make wiping easier

Flood on the First Coat

A clear finish looks only as good as the wood beneath it, so good surface preparation is important. I typically sand to P240-grit, then use compressed air or a shop vacuum to clean off the dust, and wipe the surface with a tack rag before applying the first coat.

On horizontal surfaces, pour some finish onto the wood and use a disposable foam or bristle brush or a good-quality paper towel (Bounty works well) to cover the surface with varnish. On vertical areas, apply the finish with the brush. The key to success is an even coating. Keep applying finish until it is no longer absorbed quickly. Areas that absorb the finish will have a dull appearance. A raking light across the surface will help you see the dull spots.

You've applied an even film when the sheen across the entire piece is reasonably consistent. At that point, wipe off the excess with a dry paper towel or a lint-free cotton cloth and then allow the finish to dry thoroughly. If the temperature is at least 65°F, 24 hours should be enough time for this first coat.

A combination filler and finish—If you want a glossy film finish on open-pored wood, you will need to fill the pores. Spread on the first coat as above, and then sand the surface with P400-grit paper. The resulting slurry will form a paste that fills the pores. Lightly wipe the excess finish off the surface, going across the grain, and allow the finish to dry for 24 hours. To avoid pulling the filler out of the pores, don't sand the next one or two wiped-on coats.

Sand Between Coats and Build the Film, Then Rub Out

I sand between each coat of finish with P400-grit paper. The real importance of sanding between coats is to even the surface tension of the next coat of finish. If the surface is left shiny, or with an inconsistent gloss, the wet finish will not flow out evenly.

The varnish is dry enough to sand when the sanding dust is white and doesn't gum up the paper: "When the swarf is white, the drying is right." If the dust is brown and forms tiny clumps on the paper, the finish isn't ready for sanding. Vacuum the dust.

After the first coat, where the wood absorbs a lot of finish and needs longer to dry, successive coats may be applied as quickly as every three or four hours, depending on the temperature and humidity. However, I wouldn't apply more than three coats in one day as you might trap solvent under the topcoat, resulting in a prolonged curing time. For most surfaces, three or four coats give a nice, even build. For tabletops or other surfaces likely to receive occasional liquid spills, I would apply a minimum of six coats.

I prefer medium-luster finishes, and to get there I use steel wool and wax. Unfold a pad of 0000 steel wool and lightly rub the surface. Keep checking the surface under a raking light until it shows an even dullness. At that point, vacuum away the steel-wool dust and rub on a thin coat of clear paste wax. Let this dry for 30 minutes and then buff the surface with a clean cotton cloth.

If you prefer a higher gloss, wait several weeks for the varnish to harden, then sand the surface with 600-grit (CAMI) paper, rub it with car polish, and finish with a coat of paste wax. Your piece will now have a finish worthy of your craftsmanship.

Foolproof Finish with Shellac, Varnish, and Wax

by Mark Schofield

When I joined *Fine Woodworking* in the summer of 2000, I was made responsible for the finishing articles. The editor made it seem like an honor, but in truth I don't think any of my colleagues wanted the job. Like most woodworkers, they'd rather cut wood than finish it. But today, after hundreds of hours watching finishing experts such as Peter Gedrys, Jeff Jewitt, Teri Masaschi, and Chris Minick work their magic, I have a confession to make. I like finishing.

I haven't completely bought in, however. While I'll attempt a perfect French polish, I can still relate to my fellow woodworkers who above all want a finish they can't mess up.

To meet this need, I have developed what I call the "Fine Woodworking foolproof finish." You first seal the wood with shellac, then apply three or more coats of gel varnish, and complete the finish with a coat of paste wax. You get a medium-luster, in-the-wood finish that can be built up to give varying degrees of protection. All three steps are applied by hand, the only "tools" are pieces of cloth, and I promise you'll be proud of the results.

It All Begins with Careful Preparation

I've lost track of how many projects I've seen (including one or two of my own early efforts) that prominently display the telltale tracks of jointer or planer knives. Like most finishes, this one doesn't hide poor preparation; it magnifies it. So the first task is to prep the wood's surface.

If you have mastered the bench plane and/or the scraper, you can remove machine marks fairly quickly. Then use a random-orbit sander with P180-grit sandpaper followed by P220-grit paper, and finally hand-sand with the grain using P220-grit paper wrapped around a sanding block. Remove the dust with a vacuum or

compressed air. If you don't handplane, start power sanding with P100-grit, move to P150-grit, and then follow the steps above.

The second step is to create a sample board on scraps from the project. After making this cabinet, designed by Garrett Hack (FWW #175), I could tell after wiping the bare wood with denatured alcohol that the walnut crotch used for the panels would appear darker under a finish than the walnut used for the rest of the project. I did the full finishing sequence on samples of both woods and found that a dark wax would bring the plain walnut close enough in color to the crotchwood (which gets clear wax).

Seal with Shellac, Then Apply Gel Varnish

If your project includes a floating panel, it is always a good idea to finish it before inserting it into the frame. In this way you won't see a strip of unfinished wood when seasonal changes cause the panel to shrink. I also finish the inside edges of the frame components with shellac and gel varnish before assembling them. This is much easier than trying to finish the narrow strip of frame and not get finish on the panel.

I've found that giving bare wood a single coat of dewaxed shellac has a number of benefits. On blotch-prone woods like cherry or pine, shellac helps prevent the uneven shading you can get from applying gel varnish to bare wood. On dyed wood, the shellac prevents pulling away some color when you rub on the gel varnish. And finally, sealing the wood with shellac and then sanding it gives a smoother base than bare wood for the gel varnish. Use a dewaxed shellac, like Zinsser's SealCoat. It comes as a 2-lb. cut, and I apply it as is, by dipping a small piece of cloth in the can, gently squeezing out the surplus, and then wiping the wood with the cloth. A couple of strokes over each area are usually sufficient. Let the shellac dry for about 30 minutes, and then lightly hand-sand the surface with the grain using P320-grit sandpaper. Vacuum or blow the dust out of the pores.

A gel varnish (also known as gel polyurethane or gel topcoat) has much the same resin, oil, and mineral spirits as a liquid clear finish, plus a thickening agent. This makes it much easier and less messy to wipe on. And because the product is designed to be wiped, it needs no thinning. Best of all, each layer dries too quickly to attract dust, so there is no need to sand between coats.

To apply, you simply dip a cloth into the gel, work it into the wood, and remove the surplus with a clean cloth. There are a few tricks to getting the best results. First, don't apply too much gel or work on too large an area at once. The varnish gets tacky in minutes and becomes progressively harder to remove. If you find yourself trying to wipe away gel the consistency of lard, simply dampen a cloth with mineral spirits, wipe away the gel, let the surface dry, and then apply the finish again.

Start with an area of about 2 sq. ft. You can increase the area if you find you are having no trouble removing the surplus. I rub the gel well into the wood. After you first wipe off the surplus, small wood pores appear filled; but as the gel cures, it sinks down to line the inside of the pores, leaving an open-grain look.

When removing the surplus gel, keep re-folding the cloth so that you don't smear the finish. The final rub-down should be with the grain. You can let the finish cure overnight, but in reasonably warm and dry conditions you can apply two coats in a day. To avoid spontaneous combustion, always spread used finishing cloths outside to dry before throwing them away.

You should apply at least three coats to build an even luster. On a piece like a side table, where the top will get slightly heavier use, you can apply four or five coats. But don't try to build up a plastic-looking finish. In theory, you could wipe on enough coats to protect a kitchen table-top, but liquid polyurethane would be quicker. By the way, all gel varnishes leave a satin finish.

Continued ➡

Top It Off with Wax

After the last coat of gel has cured for at least three days, I give the workpiece a coat of paste wax. Though gel varnish, applied and wiped off correctly, leaves a very smooth surface, it still has a slight grab to it when you touch it. Nothing beats the silky feel of a surface that has been waxed and buffed. Wax also gives some scratch protection, since objects are more likely to slide across the surface than to dig in and scratch it. And wax conceals any differences in sheen, though these should be minimal if you removed all the surplus gel.

Finally, dark wax left in corners and crevices emphasizes the three-dimensional aspects of the piece, and it can cover up minor blemishes in craftsmanship. You may never build the perfect piece, but at least it'll have a perfect finish.

1. Shellac

Dip and squeeze. Fold up a small piece of clean cotton cloth and dip it into a can of dewaxed shellac. Squeeze out the surplus so that it doesn't drip.

Seal the surface. Wipe the cloth over the surface no more than a couple of times to leave a thin film of shellac on the wood. Use P320-grit sandpaper wrapped around a sanding block to smooth the surface. Remove the dust with a vacuum or compressed air.

2. Gel Varnish

One thick finish. The easiest way to control how much gel varnish goes onto the cloth is to place it on with a stirring stick.

Rub on the gel varnish, then wipe off the surplus. Work the finish into the wood using small, circular movements, then wipe with the grain to remove any thicker deposits. Don't try to cover too large an area or the finish will become tacky before you can buff it. Use a clean cotton cloth to wipe away the surplus gel varnish, turning the cloth frequently to keep exposing a clean surface.

3. Wax

Colored wax can be used to subtly change the tone of a whole piece or to harmonize sections. I used a really dark brown wax on most of the walnut but a clear wax on the panels. Allow the wax to dry for 20 to 30 minutes and then buff the surface with a clean cloth.

Apply Clear Wax Thinly

A thin film of wax. Fold over a piece of cheesecloth a couple of times and then place a lump of paste wax in the center. Gather the corners of the applicator and then press down until the wax begins to ease out through the rounded face of the applicator. To avoid having light wax show up in the pores of dark wood, use light pressure on the applicator.

Work Dark Wax into Pores

Apply dark wax directly. If you want dark wax to enter the pores to change the tone of a piece, wipe the cloth into the wax. Work it into the wood and then wipe with the grain to remove the surplus. Buff the wax, clear or dark, until the surface is silky to the touch.

---

by Mark Scholfield

After my article "One Editor's Foolproof Finish" appeared, several readers asked whether the wipe-on finish I described would be suitable for kitchen cabinets or dining tables. I replied that while you could build up the extra protection these surfaces need by wiping on many more coats of the gel polyurethane, it would be far quicker to brush on several coats of liquid polyurethane and then switch to the wipe-on gel for the final few coats. In this way, you get the rapid build of a brushed finish, without any brush marks or dust nibs in the final surface.

This approach to a durable yet smooth finish is so foolproof, we decided to share it with all of our readers in this step-by-step article. By the way, because it starts with a quick washcoat of shellac, it is also a great finish for pieces made from blotch-prone woods, such as cherry. The table also demonstrates how this finish can be used in tandem with my original wipe-on-only Foolproof finish: I used the durable finish on the tabletop, where food and liquids will be a hazard, and on the feet, which are likely to be rubbed by shoes. But I used the simpler finish on the rest of the piece.

Sand Carefully, Then Seal

Although this won't be a high-gloss finish that magnifies every ripple or void in the surface, we're still dealing with an eye-catching large, flat surface, so good preparation is essential.

If you are more comfortable with a random-orbit sander, start at P100 grit and work your way up to P220 grit, then hand-sand with the grain using the final grit. Remove the dust using a vacuum or compressed air to clean out the pores.

The next step is to apply a thin coat of shellac to the whole piece. As well as greatly reducing the likelihood of blotching, the shellac gives the wood a slightly warmer tone and lets you build a sheen faster with the gel finish. You may have heard that polyurethane will not adhere to shellac. This is true if you use shellac containing wax, such as Zinsser's clear or amber Bulls Eye Shellac. Polyurethane will adhere perfectly to dewaxed shellac such as Zinsser's SealCoat or your own mixture using dewaxed shellac flakes.

Mix a 1-lb. to 1 1/2-lb. cut (dilute the SealCoat by about a third with denatured alcohol). You can apply the shellac with a natural or synthetic filament brush, but I find it just as quick (and easier on vertical surfaces) to wipe on the shellac with a cotton cloth. It also requires less sanding afterward.

Let the shellac dry for two to four hours depending on the temperature and the humidity, and then lightly sand the surface with P320-grit paper wrapped around a cork or cork-faced block. All you are doing is removing any particles, dust nibs, etc. to leave a smooth surface. Wipe and vacuum away the dust.

Brush Polyurethane to Add Toughness

Because you won't be brushing on the final coats, you don't need a really expensive brush that leaves a perfect surface. A $10 to $20 natural-bristle brush, 2 in. or 2 1/2 in. wide, works fine for most surfaces. If you have no experience brushing finishes, or if your attempts have been below par, this is a painless way to build your brushing skills and confidence.

You can use any brand of oil-based gloss polyurethane, even those recommended for floors, but the viscosity between different brands varies greatly. The Minwax Fast-Drying Polyurethane I used is about the consistency of 1% or 2% milk and can be used straight from the can. If your finish is closer to heavy cream, then thin it with mineral spirits.

You need to apply a roughly equal thickness of finish to both sides of the top to prevent uneven moisture changes, which cause cupping and warping. Start with the underside of the table, a good place to practice your brushing technique where the appearance is less important. Brush on three coats. You don't need to sand between coats as long as you apply the next coat within 24 hours.

As soon as the underside is finished, start on the top. Let the first coat cure overnight, then sand the surface with P320-grit paper. Use stearated paper, which is designed to resist becoming clogged with finish. Most sandpaper is stearated (it has a slightly white, opaque look) but avoid garnet paper designed for bare wood. Even stearated paper clogs fairly quickly, so follow finishing expert Jeff Jewitt's advice and wipe the paper frequently on a carpet remnant.

Don't overuse the sandpaper. It is meant to be disposable, and you'll get much better results if you switch to a new piece as soon as the paper no longer feels rough or becomes clogged almost instantly.

When the whole surface feels smooth to the touch, including the edges, remove the dust with a vacuum. You should apply a minimum of three coats. Sand intermediate coats with P320-grit paper, but sand the last one with P400-grit.

Unlike a high-gloss, rubbed-out finish, you don't need to make the surface dead-flat before applying the satin gel poly, so don't try to sand away all the small, shiny depressions. However, the shininess will show through, so after sanding rub the surface with the grain using Liberon 0000 steel wool to dull these spots and to give the whole surface an even scratch pattern. Use raking light to check your progress. It is worth ordering the Liberon steel wool because it lasts longer, produces better results, and sheds less than the product found in hardware stores.

Brushed Poly Builds a Base

Three or four coats of liquid polyurethane, sanded smooth between coats, are enough to give the wood real protection without a thick, plastic look.

A light touch. Lay on a coat of polyurethane starting a few inches from one edge and brushing off the opposite edge. Use a light touch, holding the brush at about 45° to the surface. After the first pass, land the brush just inside the far end and return, smoothing the strip of wet finish until you cover the small dry area and go lightly off the end. By brushing off the ends and not onto them, you avoid having finish run down the edges.

Layers of protection. The subsequent coats of polyurethane are applied in the same way. Moving the brush slowly minimizes bubbles in the finish. You are not looking for a perfectly flat surface, but high points and depressions should be well covered with finish.

Gel Poly Removes Topcoat Terror

After you carefully vacuum away all the remnants of steel wool, the surface should look pretty good—smooth, with a fairly even sheen. Normally, you would brush on the final coat of polyurethane and leave it, risking dust nibs and brush marks. With my approach, you'll top off the surface by wiping on and buffing off several coats of gel finish. These super-thin coats dry so quickly, dust doesn't have time to settle on them. Again, the brand doesn't matter: I've had good results with Bartley's Gel Varnish, Petri's Gel Poly Finish, and General Finishes' Gel Topcoat. They are all satin polyurethane turned into a gel.

Take a piece of cotton cloth about 4 in. square and dab some gel varnish onto it with a small stick. Wipe the gel onto the surface in a circular motion. Don't try to cover more than 2 or 3 sq. ft. before immediately coming back with a larger piece of clean cotton cloth and buffing the surface in quick strokes with the grain. If you wait too long and the surface becomes sticky, wipe on a little more gel to reactivate the finish and then immediately buff the surface. What you are doing is obscuring the fine scratches left by the steel wool. However, you are applying an extremely thin coat of finish, so be prepared to apply at least three coats. The directions on the can will probably say to wait overnight between coats, but in warm, dry conditions, eight hours is plenty.

For the areas of the table that don't need the extra protection of the brushed-on polyurethane, just wipe on the gel finish as described above. Four or five coats should be sufficient to get a sheen that matches the brushed areas.

Adding a coat of wax is optional. On pieces likely to be handled regularly, I use it as much for the feel as any extra protection. But on a dining table likely to be wiped frequently with a damp cloth, wax is a waste of time.

Tips for Gel Poly

Use a stirring stick to place some of the thick finish on a small piece of cotton cloth. Dipping the cloth is too messy. Apply the gel in a circular motion until you've covered a few square feet in an even layer. Buff off the surplus finish right away using quick, firm strokes and turning frequently to a fresh section of cotton cloth. Repeat until the whole tabletop is done. You'll be very happy with your flawless finish.

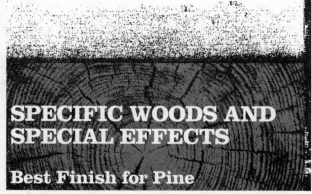

SPECIFIC WOODS AND SPECIAL EFFECTS

Best Finish for Pine

by Tom Wisshack

I have never understood why so many woodworkers consider pine an inferior wood. I think it's one of the most beautiful woods available, and it only gets better with time, taking on a marvelous color and patina. But poor staining and finishing techniques have given pine a bad rap.

Pine does present unique challenges. You want the wood to look as if it has aged naturally to its present color. You'll never achieve that look if you apply stain directly to pine, because the color penetrates deeply and unevenly. Softer portions of the wood become very dark, while the harder and more resinous areas resist the stain. Worse, this blotchiness is irreversible. That is, the drastic measures you'd have to take to correct the blotchiness could ruin the piece.

Fortunately, you can achieve superior results if you apply thin layers of shellac and stain with patience and a delicate touch. When you wipe away the excess stain, some will remain in the crevices of moldings and joints, giving the subtle feeling of age that I prefer on pine.

Let the Pine Age Naturally

I smooth my pieces with a handplane and polish them by hand with P600-grit wet-or-dry paper. If you use sandpaper alone, begin with P120- or P180-grit, then work up to P320- or P400-grit.

Whenever I build a piece from pine, I sand it and then allow it to stand in the shop for at least a month before finishing. Pine will take on a natural patina, which I call shop aging. When I apply the finish, the resulting color is always deeper and richer than it would be if I finished the piece right away, so a very light stain normally is adequate. Waiting for the wood color to change is a luxury, but the results are worth it. Applying a finish too soon after constructing a piece of furniture is, in my opinion, a mistake.

TIP

First, Do Nothing

Unfinished pine will take on a golden color naturally after a few weeks' exposure to the air. This patina will enhance any color you apply.

Seal the Grain

A washcoat of shellac comes first. This serves as a sealer; it's essential to close the pores of the pine and provide a foundation for the stain. Shellac dries very quickly and gives the wood absolute clarity. You can stain over it and—what's critical—remove most or all of the stain if you make a mistake or don't like the look.

I have had good luck with Zinsser shellac, which is widely available. I usually mix the clear and amber varieties, which gives the wood a warm, antique hue. Fill a quart glass jar about one-fourth full of clear shellac. Add small amounts of amber shellac until the mixture is about the color of honey. Note how much shellac you have, then add about half that amount of denatured alcohol. The result is close to a 2-lb. cut, but exact proportions aren't critical.

Brush the shellac onto one horizontal surface at a time, using long, even strokes. Rotate the piece as needed to coat all the surfaces with this thin washcoat. When covering a wide surface, work quickly, overlapping strokes only slightly. Seal a piece of scrap, too, so you can dial in the stain color before tackling the workpiece.

For best results, apply two washcoats. Wait about an hour between coats and two hours after the second coat. Then scuff-sand with worn P600-grit wet-or-dry paper.

TIP

Test the Stain on a Sample Board

Test the color on a sample board that's been given a washcoat of shellac. This lets you tweak the proportions of the stain recipe before finishing the real piece.

Mix and Apply the Stain

Oil-based stain is the best type for pine. It can be brushed or wiped on, and it dries relatively slowly. Regardless of the brand, thin it with mineral spirits. That not only gives you more working time, it also keeps the addition of color subtle. A small amount of boiled linseed oil makes the stain more translucent.

Off-the-shelf stains vary considerably in the amount of pigment they contain. The Olympic stains I usually use are very heavy-bodied and require considerable thinning. Stain/sealer products that contain some tung-oil varnish are watery and weaker.

Don't be afraid to experiment with color, intermixing stains and trying different dilutions to get just the shade you want. The box at left gives a good basic stain recipe to use as a starting point. The amount of thinner required depends on the opacity and thickness of the stain you choose. Start with a mixture that's roughly 30% mineral spirits to 70% stain. If that's too intense or opaque, add more spirits. Very

often, I end up with 60% thinner to 40% stain.

When the color is right, brush a liberal amount of stain onto the wood, let it stand about five minutes, then remove the excess very lightly. A soft cotton cloth works well; quilted bathroom tissue, even better.

The stain mixture normally will stay workable for 15 to 20 minutes. If it begins to set up, lay down another coat of stain before continuing to wipe. A single coat of stain may have a minimal effect on the wood's color. But if you layer three or more coats of stain, you will steadily achieve a rich and increasingly aged look. Let the individual coats of stain dry for at least a week.

Apply stain generously. Brush on a thick coat of stain, working in a defined area such as this door panel. Use the brush to work the stain into corners and the recesses of moldings.

Wait, then wipe lightly. Let the stain dry for 15 to 20 minutes (temperature and humidity will affect drying times). Then wipe away the excess. Work in a circular motion at first, then with straight strokes. Use a very light touch—no pressure on the wood at all.

Additional Coats Provide Depth

Subsequent coats of stain give the wood a warm, amber tone. The layers of finish also add uniformity, minimizing differences in color from one area or board to the next. A coat of thinned shellac seals in the color.

More stain if needed. Brush on a second coat of stain (above), then wipe carefully (right) to avoid hitting an area you've already wiped. If you slip, dab on more stain, then wipe again.

Brush on more shellac. Let the initial coats of stain dry thoroughly, which can take as long as a week. Then brush on another washcoat of shellac. Rotate the piece as needed so you're always working on a horizontal surface.

Add protection with a topcoat. Use a mixture of varnish and mineral spirits, brushing it on with long, smooth strokes.

Add Another Coat of Shellac, Then the Topcoats

Once you are happy with the color of your pine, protect the stain with another coat of shellac. If you don't, the stain may dissolve when you apply a topcoat. Use a somewhat thicker mixture this time, say 70% shellac to 30% denatured alcohol.

Don't overbrush or overwork the barrier coat because the alcohol can dissolve the stain beneath. Allow the barrier coat to dry several hours or overnight.

I've found that varnish makes the best topcoat because it adheres well to shellac and gives the wood an additional amber tint. Avoid polyurethane varnish, though; it won't adhere well to the waxy shellac.

Lightly scuff-sand the piece with P400- or P600-grit paper, dilute the varnish by 30% to 40% with mineral spirits, and brush on three thin coats. Smooth the final coat with P600-grit wet-or-dry paper and rub the surface with 0000 steel wool and mineral oil for a satin sheen.

Continued ➞

Stain Recipe for Pine

This recipe makes about 1 qt. of stain. It uses three Olympic oil stains, which I've found to be very heavily pigmented. If you use another brand, it may not contain as much pigment, so you may have to adjust the amounts.

1 pt. mineral spirits
⅓ cup boiled linseed oil
⅔ cup Olympic Dark Walnut oil stain
⅔ cup Olympic Colonial Maple oil stain
⅓ cup Olympic American Cherry oil stain

Mix the ingredients and stir well. The resulting mixture should have a medium golden-brown look and the consistency of 2% milk. Test the stain on a sample board. If the stain looks too dark, add more Colonial Maple; too light, more Dark Walnut; too brownish, more American Cherry.

Mix well. Fill a jar with the mineral spirits and linseed oil, then add the stains. You don't have to measure precisely. Let the color of the mixture tell you when you have the right amounts. Err on the side of making the stain too thin.

Blotch-Free Cherry

by Mark Schofield

Cherry's popularity for fine furniture is no surprise: It is hard but not heavy; it cuts easily with power tools or by hand; the grain is restrained but interesting; and over time it takes on a beautiful, deep, red-brown color.

However, like a scorpion, there is a sting in the tail for the unwary. Many woodworkers apply an oil-based clear finish only to see the wood break out in random, dark, ugly blotches. Those who stain the wood, intending to instantly turn pallid, freshly cut cherry into the rich look of a 200-year-old antique, can see even worse results.

Not all cherry behaves like this. I'll show you how to spot the problem areas in advance. I'll also give you tips on how to pretreat your project before you apply a stain or a clear coat. When you start with a wood as nice as cherry, it's worth learning how to finish it.

Everyone agrees blotching is caused by uneven absorption of a liquid, whether it is a dye or a clear finish. There is less agreement on the causes. Some say it is resin deposits from kiln drying, while others point to alternating grain, similar to that found in curly wood.

No matter the cause, to locate these blotch-prone areas and to anticipate the degree of blotching, wipe all of the wood with a cloth soaked in denatured alcohol. Most of the wood should stay a uniform shade, but certain parts may soak up the alcohol, turning the wood much darker. These areas, which also will take longer to dry, are the ones that will blotch when a dye or oil-based finish is applied.

Now that you know trouble lies ahead, forewarned is forearmed. You can use a variety of different products and techniques, depending on the severity of the blotching, to pretreat the wood before applying a dye, stain, or clear

finish. However, even if there are only one or two problem areas, the whole workpiece will need to be treated in order to achieve an even appearance when finished.

Many Methods of Blotch Control; Not All Work

The objective of all blotch prevention is to even out the absorption capacity of the wood, and there are at least a dozen products and techniques that claim to achieve this. The majority aim to restrict the wood's ability to absorb a dye or clear finish by burnishing or semi-sealing the surface. The second method is to saturate the wood with another liquid prior to applying the finish.

To discover which methods worked best and how much time and effort they took, I initially made three sample boards of blotchy cherry. I sanded half of each board to P150-grit, while the other half was treated with six methods of blotch control. One board was finished with Danish oil, another wiped with a water-based dye, and the last was wiped with an oil-based pigment stain. After discussing the results with the other editors, I did further testing using larger areas, to explore various grain situations and types of stains.

Some Clear Finishes Cause Blotching

We've all sighed with content as that first coat of Danish oil reveals the true color and shimmering depth of cherry. This is what woodworking's all about, we think, and happily press on. The next morning is when the shock hits: What is that dark area on that drawer front? Why doesn't it disappear when you look at it from a different angle? It's not poor sanding, because the surface feels uniformly smooth. Welcome to the world of blotchy cherry.

It's not just oil/varnish blends like Danish oil that cause blotching, but also wiping varnishes such as Waterlox Original, and oil-based alkyd varnishes or polyurethanes. Any blotching will be less noticeable than when dyeing or staining, but the darker patches still will be blemishes. The three most effective ways to control blotching are described on this page, while two techniques to avoid are on the next.

Add Color to Cherry, but Not Bare Wood

While many woodworkers recoil from the concept of coloring wood, with cherry in particular it's tempting to fast-forward the aging process and achieve an antique look in hours. Alternatively, you may be trying to blend cherry boards with different tones or to match an existing piece of furniture.

As well as the sample boards tested with water-based dye and oil-based pigment stain, I also tried a gel stain and colored Danish oil. Without exception, all of the coloring methods looked better when applied to cherry that had been pretreated with a washcoat of shellac. On bare wood, all of the dyes and pigment stains caused blotching to a greater or lesser extent.

On the next page, I give three ways to color cherry based on the amount of color you want to add, the ease of application, and the number of colors available. Also I give a couple of coloring options to avoid.

The bottom line? Never apply any pigment stain or dye to blotch-prone cherry that has not been treated with a washcoat. Whatever dye or clear finish you use, try it on a sample board from scraps of wood left over from your project. Discover the hidden surprises there and not on your cherry workpiece.

Shellac Prevents Blotching

A thin coat of shellac, known as a washcoat, is the most effective form of blotch control. However, it is important that you use dewaxed shellac, as waxy shellac can prevent some topcoats from adhering.

---

3 Ways to Reduce Blotching from Clear Finishes

Oil-based finishes are the most likely of the clear finishes to cause blotching on cherry. These include wiping varnish, oil/varnish mixes, Danish oil, and polyurethane, and the blotching can occur whether the finish is wiped, brushed, or sprayed on. The sample board shows how Watco Danish Oil is affected by various treatments.

1. FOR MINIMAL BLOTCHING, KEEP ON SANDING

If the alcohol test reveals that only minimal blotching is likely, the simplest method of blotch control is to sand to a higher final grit. Instead of stopping at P150- or P180-grit sandpaper, carry on through the grades until you reach P400 grit. This smooths and burnishes the wood, making it less able to absorb a liquid. It will still allow the deep, lustrous look associated with oil-based finishes, but it does involve more time sanding—a task that few of us find appealing.

2. A WATER-BASED CONDITIONER SEALS IN MODERATE BLOTCHING

Minwax's Water-Based Pre-Stain wood conditioner feels and looks like a greatly thinned water-based clear finish, and dries to a thin film on the surface. Brush on a single coat, let it dry thoroughly, and then sand it with P320-grit paper. Remove the dust and apply the oil-based clear coat of your choice. This method works well on wood with moderate blotching, yet the results still resemble a penetrating finish. Don't be tempted to thin a water-based finish by 50% and use that as a blotch controller; it won't work.

3. NOTHING BEATS SHELLAC ON SEVERELY BLOTCHY WOOD

If the alcohol test reveals severe blotching is likely, stop sanding at P180-grit and apply a single coat of a film finish that has been heavily thinned. Known as a washcoat, the most common choice is a 1-lb. cut of dewaxed shellac. The blotch-prone areas will soak up the washcoat more than the rest of the wood. After the washcoat dries, sand it lightly with P320-grit sandpaper. You'll remove much of the sealer but leave the blotch-prone areas lined with it, allowing the surface to absorb clear finish more evenly. This will almost eliminate blotching, but the reduced oil penetration will also leave more of a film-finish look.

Two Blotch-Control Methods to Avoid

GLUE SIZE: EFFECTIVE BUT TIME-CONSUMING

You've probably noticed how remnants of glue squeeze-out leave annoying pale areas after you've applied a dye or an oil-based clear finish. You can exploit this by diluting some yellow glue with about eight parts of water to create a glue size. Brush on a single coat, let it dry, and then sand the surface with P320-grit paper. Like a washcoat of shellac, this seals the blotch-prone areas so they will end up the same color as the rest of the board. However, the water-based glue size raises the grain more than shellac, takes longer to sand smooth, and can't be used under a water-based dye or water-based clear coat. So stick with shellac.

SOLVENT-BASED CONDITIONER LEFT SPLOTCHES

Just as an inoculation gives your body a small amount of the disease, in theory you can treat blotching by first applying a much-diluted coat of a penetrating finish. The directions call for flooding the surface and then wiping off the surplus. Then you apply the dye or clear coat. I found pre-saturation less effective than sealing the wood, especially on heavily blotchy cherry. I applied a coat of Minwax's Pre-Stain wood conditioner (not to be confused with the water-based product of the same name, which actually seals the surface), but it left orange splotches on the wood that showed through the clear finish.

Alcohol Reveals Trouble Spots

It is very difficult to spot blotch-prone areas on bare boards, especially after sanding. The best way to find them is to wipe the wood with denatured alcohol. This will leave blotch-prone areas that are darker than their surroundings and take longer to dry.

FIGURE IS ONE CAUSE OF BLOTCHING

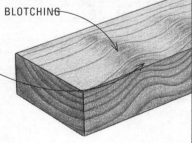

BLOTCHING

Where curly grain rises to the surface, it exposes end grain. This absorbs more liquid, whether stain or clear finish, than the surrounding wood and causes blotching.

3 Ways to Add Color to Cherry Without Blotching

To narrow down the options, I first tested a number of dyes and stains on separate sample boards, each treated with various stain controllers. Then I made the board at left to illustrate how the best stain controller—a washcoat of shellac—can help with three good methods of coloring cherry.

TINTED OIL ADDS MINIMAL COLOR WITHOUT FUSS

Penetrating pigment. Tinted oil was liberally applied and then wiped off. The washcoated side didn't blotch; the bare-wood side did.

Watco's cherry Danish oil is a pigmented stain, and as expected caused severe blotching on bare cherry. However, on blotch-prone cherry washcoated with shellac, the result was a light but even application of color. If you want only a slight change in your cherry's tone (remember, cherry will darken as it ages, even under a dye) and prefer the look of a penetrating finish, this is the way to go.

GEL STAINS ADD EXTRA COLOR WITH EACH COAT

While Bartley's Pennsylvania cherry left bare wood blotchy, it left wood washcoated with shellac evenly colored and blotch-free, but with the grain slightly highlighted. Each coat of gel stain adds incremental color with minimal fuss, so if you are looking for an easy way to harmonize different-colored boards, try a gel stain. However, because gel stains are mostly pigment-based, each extra coat after the second or third will gradually make the finish more opaque, hiding the wood's figure.

WATER-BASED DYES OFFER CLARITY AND COLOR CHOICE

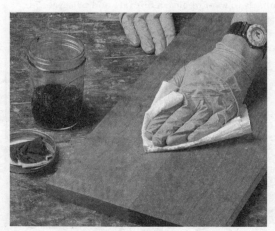

With dyes, the particles of color are far smaller than in pigment stains, so they remain suspended in the liquid (there's no need to stir the container) and they don't collect in the wood pores, highlighting them. However, they will still create darker areas on blotch-prone wood, so pretreating is advisable. A washcoat of shellac will reduce the overall impact of the dye when compared to bare wood, but you can get around this by mixing a more concentrated batch.

Avoid Oil-Based Pigment Stains for Cherry

Walk into any hardware store or home center and the first choice for coloring wood will be rows of wood stains. The choice of colors is extensive and the application method (apply, leave on for five minutes, and then wipe off with a clean cloth) seems simplicity itself. Just say no. On a sample board that was sanded to P150-grit, I applied a single coat of Minwax Wood Finish, an oil-based pigment stain. On the right-hand side of the board that was sanded to P150-grit, it brought out the worst in this blotchy cherry. Various methods of blotch control on the same sample board had mixed results. An oil-based conditioner and a water-based one reduced but didn't eliminate blotching; a coat of glue size or a washcoat of shellac eliminated blotching and most of the color but still left pigment in the grain; sanding to P400-grit and P220-grit made little difference.

Bring Out the Best in Mahagony

by Peter Gedrys

Before I start a finishing project, I always let the wood tell me what it needs. I wipe the surface with denatured alcohol to preview the appearance of a clear finish. There are times when dyes and stains are called for, perhaps to enhance otherwise plain boards. On a mahogany bookcase I finished, the top and sides had beautiful figure and color, and the piece had been left unfinished for a long time, allowing the wood to develop a rich, natural hue.

So I knew I could use my basic mahogany approach for most of this bookcase: Fill the open pores and then apply a thin coat of shellac for a warm, even glow. Leave out the grain filling, and you get a hungry, half-finished look. Put a thick film finish everywhere, and the topcoat is the star, not the wood.

However, like all pieces, this one had specific needs. A characteristic of mahogany is its wide range of colors. After wiping the surface with denatured alcohol, the face frame was much lighter than the rich, warm tone surrounding it. The solution was to dye it to match. Finally, some varnish on the top would give that most vulnerable surface some added water resistance. One of the big lessons here is that not all parts of a piece need the same finish.

Harmonize Color Inconsistencies

To give the face frame a subtle color change, I started by dampening the wood to raise the grain and sanding it lightly when dry. Then I used a water-based dye. A quick note on mixing dye: I mix new batches into a concentrated or "saturated" color: 1 oz. of dye to a pint of very hot water. Once cooled and filtered through a fine paint or coffee filter, just add it incrementally to clear water for the desired strength. For the face frame, I used the dye at approximately half strength. Be sure to test the dye on scraps from the same board.

An industrial-strength paper towel makes an effective application tool. Fold it over a couple of times to create a reservoir. Wet it well with dye and squeeze out the excess.

Fill the Grain with Paste Filler

Prior to filling the pores, you need to seal the wood with a thin washcoat of finish. This washcoat acts as a barrier so color in the filler doesn't stain the wood. The goal is to seal the wood yet still leave the pores open enough to accept the filler. I used Zinsser's SealCoat, a dewaxed clear shellac compatible with any topcoat.

Continued ➤

I prefer the speed and control given by a pad, but you also can apply the shellac with a brush. I use a fairly large pad that will cover the surface quickly. It consists of a high-quality cheesecloth core wrapped in a piece of smooth cotton such as a well-used bedsheet or a piece of linen. Whatever size pad, the one rule is to have no wrinkles on the bottom that will leave lines on the surface of the wood. To charge the pad, wet it with a little alcohol first and then add the shellac, which becomes slightly diluted. Go over the wood with the pad once or twice but no more. When dry, sand lightly with P320-grit sandpaper or a gray abrasive pad, and clean the surface and pores thoroughly with a vacuum.

Seal the Wood

Go over the surface a couple of times with a pad to apply a thin coat of shellac. Keep the pressure light to avoid filling the pores. It is easier to get into corners, carvings, and moldings by applying the shellac with an artist's brush.

In the past, most commercial paste fillers were made with quartz as the main filling component. Many fillers on the market today contain cheaper and, in my opinion, less-effective ingredients. Sherwin-Williams still uses 100% quartz, but it's sold only in gallons. Pore-O-Pac uses some quartz, but is cheaper and comes in quarts. Both these fillers are oil-based, which I find easier to apply and control than water-based filler.

In either case, buy the uncolored or "natural" filler; it enables you to customize the color to suit the wood. Stir the filler thoroughly to get the solids off the bottom. Pour some filler into a small container and add mineral spirits to get it to the consistency of heavy cream.

The filler's color is a matter of personal choice. I like the pores somewhat darker than the lightest part of the wood, but not dark enough to make them stand out. For this project, I added equal parts of burnt umber and Van Dyke brown artist's oils. I first mix the pigment with some mineral spirits and a portion of the filler. This way, when I mix the color concentrate into the filler, they will readily incorporate.

On large, flat surfaces, apply the filler with a pad, squeegee, or brush, working in small sections. For carved or curved surfaces, use an old brush and apply filler sparingly. For this bookcase, I filled all the outside surfaces (except the back) and the tops of the shelves.

As the solvent evaporates and the filler begins to dry, it will change from shiny to dull. Run a plastic scraper across the surface, slightly diagonal to the grain, to see if the surplus is ready to be scraped off. If it hasn't set enough, it will be slightly runny. If it's too dry, it will come off in flakes. When it rolls up in wrinkles onto the scraper, it's just right.

You need to get all the filler off the surface or the residue will show through the topcoat as unattractive gray spots. After removing the bulk of the surplus with the scraper, wait about 10 minutes (less on a hot, dry day), and then do the second removal. Wiping the surface with burlap is the traditional way, but I prefer a white woven pad. Again working slightly diagonal to the grain and using moderate pressure, remove the filler left on the surface. As the pad starts to load, switch to a clean section. I also use the pad to remove all the surplus filler from the moldings. The object is to remove only the surplus, not pull filler out of the pores.

When finished, wait about an hour and inspect the surface. If there are areas not completely filled, reapply the filler. If everything looks good, lightly wipe the surface with a dry cotton rag going with the grain. If there's any dried filler on the surface, lightly dampen the rag with mineral spirits to rub it off. When the rag comes up clean, all the filler is removed.

Two Topcoats for One Piece

I give filler at least two days to dry, longer if necessary, before applying a topcoat. If the piece smells of oil, wait.

For this bookcase, I again reached for the SealCoat to be the body of the finish and applied it with a pad. You only need to go over the surface a few times for an effective finish. This is where filling the pores fully pays off. You can keep the coating thin, maintain a close-to-the-grain look, and still have the wonderful glow that shellac produces on a smooth surface. I brushed the interior with a couple of unthinned coats of SealCoat.

To give the top added protection and water resistance, I used an alkyd varnish. I used a foam brush to apply two thin coats, lightly sanding between the coats. Once the varnish has cured for a few weeks, you can refine it by rubbing it out. For a soft sheen, rub the surface with 0000 steel wool going with the grain, and then apply some paste wax. For a higher sheen, lightly abrade the surface with some 600-grit (CAMI) wet-and-dry sandpaper lubricated with water. Then rub the surface with a fine-cut automotive rubbing compound, and finally, apply some paste wax.

Two Options for Topcoats

Shellac is fast and easy

End with shellac. A few thin coats give the filled mahogany a beautiful glow. This can be done with a pad or a brush.

Varnish Adds Protection

Two coats of varnish over the shellac will protect the top of the bookcase from spilled liquids.

Rub Out Varnish for a Low Luster or a High Gloss

Low-luster look. After the varnish has cured, you can rub the surface with 0000 steel wool. Then apply a coat of paste wax, wait 30 minutes, and buff the surface with a soft cloth.

For a glossy surface. First sand away any dust nibs using 600-grit (CAMI) paper lubricated with water. Then use an automotive compound to rub the surface to an even shine before applying wax.

Bleach Mahogany for a Unique Look

by Sean Clarke

Rich red tones are the colors most associated with mahogany, but you can also achieve a light golden-amber color by bleaching and then dying the wood. Honduras, Philippine, and African (khaya) mahogany all respond well to bleaching, but Cuban mahogany will darken if bleached and is therefore not a good choice (in any case, you are unlikely to want to bleach this rare and pricey wood).

Eye-Catching Contrast

You can make an entire project from bleached mahogany or use it for part of a piece of furniture. The bleached wood stands out beautifully against ebonized wood.

Faux Satinwood

This picture frame is made entirely from mahogany, but the strip of inlay is ribbon-stripe mahogany bleached and then dyed to imitate satinwood.

While bleaching flatsawn boards produces a unique-looking wood, bleaching quartersawn boards with ribbon-stripe figure is a great way to imitate satinwood. Cut into thin, narrow strips, it can be used as a border or inlay and is a great deal cheaper and more easily available than genuine satinwood.

1. Raise the grain

Bleach will raise the grain. Excessive sanding after bleaching may sand through to unbleached wood and result in uneven color. To avoid this, pre-raise the grain. After sanding the surface up to P220 grit, wipe the entire surface with lukewarm water and allow it to air dry. Re-sand the surface lightly with the P220-grit paper.

2. Use the right bleach

Use a two-part bleach designed for wood, such as Klean-Strip. Mix equal parts A and B in a plastic container. Wearing gloves, apply the bleach with a brush or a clean white cloth. The brush should have synthetic bristles, which will not react with the bleach. Apply it evenly, soaking the surface. Then remove any excess with a white cotton cloth and let it dry for eight hours.

3. Evaluate the color

With a white cotton cloth, wet the surface with lukewarm water to evaluate the color and neutralize any active bleach. If you like the color, let the surface dry, lightly sand with P220-grit paper, and move to finishing. However, one coat of bleach usually leaves areas with a pinkish tone. If so, re-bleach the whole piece, wait eight hours, and re-test the color.

4. Neutralize it

While water will neutralize a single coat of bleach, for two or more coats you need to apply diluted white vinegar (two parts water, one part vinegar). This prevents blistering in the topcoat. Apply the vinegar solution with the same brush used for the bleach and wipe off any excess. Let the piece dry for at least eight hours and then lightly sand again with P220-grit paper.

5. Warm Up the Wood

You could finish the mahogany in its bone-white state, but I prefer to warm it up slightly with a water-based golden amber dye (Lockwood #144). Mix 1 teaspoon of dye with 8 oz. hot water, and apply evenly with a cloth or brush. Let it cool, wipe off any excess with a clean cotton cloth, and allow the piece to dry overnight.

6. Seal the surface

Brush on a 1- to 2-lb. cut of super blond shellac, such as SealCoat, or if you'd prefer a deeper amber tone, use button or garnet shellac. Once the shellac has dried for two to four hours, lightly sand with P320-grit paper and apply a topcoat of your choice.

Dyes Bring Out the Best in Figured Maple

by James Condino

If you've ever attended an outdoor custom-car show, you've noticed how some paint schemes appear to change color. That '49 Mercury appears black from a distance, but closer inspection under the sun's rays reveals a dark-purple shimmer with a subtle iridescent red.

This multidimensional, layered color is what I try to accomplish on figured maple, a wood uniquely suited to being enhanced with dyes. First, the wood's light-blond color puts no limit on your imagination (stick with wood tones, but my process works just as well with other, brighter colors). Second, the striped and quilted figure

becomes almost three-dimensional with added color. This is because the ripples present alternating sections of long grain and end grain to the viewer.

Prep the Surface and Select Your Colors

Your goal is to reveal the depth and clarity of the wood, so use a finely burnished scraper to remove tearout or machine marks. Vacuum fine dust particles; don't blow them into the pores.

Once you have a color scheme in mind, test it on some scrap, ideally from the same boards as the workpiece. Take careful notes on dye concentrations, color combinations, and the number of coats. I use water-soluble dye powders. They penetrate the wood, giving me a margin of error if I accidentally sand through the shellac later.

The Wood is Alternately Dyed and Sanded

To prepare the dye, mix the powder in hot, but not boiling, water. The ratio is 1 oz. of dye to 1 qt. of water, but you'll need only a few fluid ounces of each dye. So just gradually add dye powder to the water until a maple stirring stick turns roughly the color you want. Allow the mixture to cool and then strain it through a piece of old T-shirt or a paper coffee filter.

To apply the dye, I use a pad similar to that used for French polishing. Cut out two 5-in. squares of lint-free cotton cloth (well-washed T-shirts work great). Fold one of them to form a 1-in.-wide strip, and then fold the strip into a 1-in. square. Wrap this in the other piece, and secure the ends with rubber bands to give you a handle. You'll need a pad for each dye, so make several. To prevent the wood from absorbing too much dye initially, I first rub the wood with a damp pad, using distilled water.

With the wood still damp, apply a very dark base coat—dark brown or, in this case, black. Dip the pad into the dye and then rub it lightly into the wood in overlapping small circles.

After the dye has dried, sand the entire surface back to natural wood with P220-grit sandpaper, leaving only the figure darkened. Repeat the wetting and dyeing, this time using a warm dark color—amber or even a dark red. Once it is dry, sand this coat back until the figured grain stands out against the natural wood. Although you won't see it until the clear finish is applied, the two dyes will come out subtly when your viewing angle changes, just like when you walked around that '49 Mercury.

You can test the finished look by wiping the surface with denatured alcohol. Be careful not to make the figure too dark and unnatural looking.

Now that you have brought out the curl and figure, apply an overall tone to the piece, perhaps yellow or light amber for an antique tiger-maple look.

A Coat of Oil Adds Depth

After letting the piece dry overnight, the brilliant image that you created will appear somewhat dull and washed out. But don't worry; the next two steps will more than restore the appearance.

To bring out the huge curl and deep figure in the maple, apply a thin coat of walnut or boiled linseed oil. Add a few drops of oil to a pad and very gently coat the entire surface you are working on. Then wipe it off with a clean cloth. This brings out the wood's depth and luminosity, making the grain appear to move as your perspective changes.

Seal the Surface with a High-Gloss Clear Coat

The final step is to apply a clear coat to enhance the three-dimensional look of the wood. The finish needs to be as thin as possible with a high gloss. French polishing is the best method for this effect, and I urge you to try it.

Alternatively, you can brush or spray on a few coats of super-blond shellac, or for a more durable finish, seal in the oil with a coat of dewaxed shellac, and then apply some lacquer.

The reaction from woodworkers and non-wood-workers alike when they see the finished piece will be, "Wow."

Finishing Oily Woods

by Jeff Jewitt

Many woodworkers use exotic tropical woods such as rosewood, cocobolo, jatoba, bubinga, wenge, teak, and others. If you've ever applied an oil-based finish to one of these woods, you have probably run into problems: Either the finish took a very long time to dry, dried only partially and stayed tacky, or wouldn't dry at all. And even if the finish dried, it might have peeled or flaked off later. Your first reaction probably was to blame the finish or yourself, without realizing that the wood was in fact the culprit.

Natural Oils Protect Tropical Wood

Tropical and rain-forest woods have developed a natural resistance to the accelerated decay caused by their hot and steamy environments. Extract-ives (commonly referred to as oils) produced by the trees are naturally water repellent and rich in chemicals known as antioxidants. These impede or slow down the oxidation of other molecules, which is the first step in the decay process.

To understand why these wood oils affect oil finishes, you have to understand how oil finishes cure. Drying oils like soya, tung, and linseed (and the varnishes and polyurethanes based on them) begin to dry by absorbing oxygen from the air into the liquid finish on the wood's surface. The oxygen combines with molecular components of the finish, forming other chemical molecules, one of which is a free radical. A free radical is like a molecule on steroids. It has too many electrons, making it highly reactive (chemists call this unstable). The free radical accelerates the final stage, which is polymerization (curing) of the finish.

On tropical woods, this process is impeded by the anti-oxidants in the oily wood. Antioxidants donate a portion of their electrons to stabilize the free radical, thus neutralizing it. As a result, the final curing or hardening of the oil-based finish is slowed down dramatically.

Shellac Is the Answer

When I was learning to finish, I was told to wipe down oily woods with lacquer thinner or acetone prior to applying oil-based stain or finish. This helps with the adhesion issue (finishes don't bond well to oily woods) as long as you apply a finish within minutes, but it may not help with the curing problem. This is because the evaporation of the solvent pulls more oil to the surface of the wood.

A better strategy is to seal the wood with a thin barrier of a finish that isn't affected by the oils. For solvent lacquer, you can spray on a barrier of vinyl sealer, but for most finishes, use a coat of dewaxed shellac. You should use either ready-made, wax-free Zinsser SealCoat or make the shellac from dewaxed flakes.

One coat of a 2-lb. cut of shellac (SealCoat comes in this concentration) does the trick. You can brush, spray, or wipe it on. However, on projects made with dark tropical wood as accents (like inlay), color from the dark wood can leach out and be smeared onto adjacent lighter woods if you brush or wipe on the shellac. Here, the best strategy is to spray the shellac, using an aerosol if you lack spray equipment.

Once the shellac is dry, lightly sand the surface with P600-grit (or 400-grit CAMI) sandpaper and then continue with the finish of your choice. You can safely use oils, oil-based finishes, water-based finishes, lacquers, or urethanes. Or, just continue with an all-shellac finish.

Mahogany and Veneer Are the Exceptions

Finishing wouldn't be fun (or exasperating, depending on your point of view) if there weren't exceptions to the rule. Mahogany poses no problems, because it doesn't have these types of oils. Commercial veneers also are benign, as the hot water used to prepare tropical logs for slicing chemically breaks down the oils.

Finally, on decorative objects not subject to much handling, you can simply apply wax (with or without the shellac sealer), or nothing at all. You can produce a great shine on some tropical woods just by buffing.

Seal with Shellac

Wipe on a single coat of dewaxed shellac such as SealCoat. This seals in the wood's natural oils.

TROPICAL WOODS CAN BLEED

Two-tone problem. When dark tropical wood is adjacent to light-colored wood, don't wipe or brush on a barrier coat of shellac. You might stain the lighter wood with the dark wood's pigment (left). Spraying is the solution. If you don't own a spray gun, you can buy a can of aerosol shellac and use it to seal the wood.

Safe to finish. With the shellac dry, it is safe to apply a clear topcoat of your choice.

Lacquer Finish

Two steps to a lacquer finish. First, spray on a coat of vinyl sealer to shut in the tropical wood's oils. With the sealer dry and sanded, spray on topcoats of solvent lacquer.

Continued ➜

No Finish at All

A natural fifinish. You can exploit the oil in many tropical woods and bring up a high shine by simply polishing the bare wood on a buffing wheel.

Finishes for Foodware

by Mike Mahoney

At college, my industrial arts professor cautioned me many times about the harmful finishes I was using for my wooden bowls. Specifically, he stressed that oil finishes with metallic dryers were dangerous for food contact. Now that lead has been banned as a drier, studies have shown that almost all finishes are benign to humans: Ingesting fully cured finish is similar to eating a piece of plastic—the body won't digest it.

If safety is no longer an issue, how do you decide which finish to use? From the many finishes available, you should base your choices on durability, ease of application and repair, and the intended use of the piece.

Penetrating Oils Are Easily Renewable

For wooden items that will get constant wear and tear in the kitchen (for example, salad bowls, plates, spatulas, and butcher blocks), penetrating oils are the preferred finish. They are the easiest to apply, and the ability to reapply them easily will keep your work looking great year after year.

With penetrating finishes in particular, you need to carefully sand away any tool marks. For a turned piece, sand it on the lathe, sanding in both directions if the lathe has a reversing switch. It also helps if you raise the grain with water and let the piece dry before giving it a final sanding.

The two most popular oils are boiled linseed oil and tung oil. They are both curing oils and will slowly harden in the wood, reducing the need for reapplications. Boiled linseed oil is cheaper and more widely available, but it has a tendency to yellow the wood more than other oils. Pure tung oil gives a little more water protection but is harder to rub to an even sheen.

Oil/varnish blends such as Danish oil, if heavily diluted and thinly applied, are easy to apply and repair. Just don't apply so many coats that you start to build a film, as this will break down and be hard to repair.

Nut oils, such as walnut, macadamia, and almond, are more expensive and will cure more slowly and only partially. Mineral oil is widely available in drugstores and forms no film or sheen no matter how many coats are applied, but it also requires more frequent renewal.

I don't recommend using olive or vegetable oils for finishing. These oils will not cure at all; they can go rancid under the wrong conditions; and if kept in a closed, oxygen-deprived area, or if too much finish is applied, the piece can become sticky.

Regarding the objection that oil finishes don't offer any resistance to abrasion, my contention is that if you're using a wooden item to serve food and are worried about staining or scratching the wood's surface, you may be better off using ceramic, plastic, or glass. The lack of a moisture barrier is not important for foodware, as wood naturally absorbs and evaporates moisture. I have been using wooden butcher blocks, bowls, and dinner plates in my house for nearly 20 years and they look better than the day they were made—stains, cut marks, scratches, and all.

Film Finishes: Instant Appeal but Problems Down the Road

There is no denying the eye-catching shine that a film finish can give to a piece. However some topcoats, such as lacquer, shellac, and waxes, while easy to apply, aren't durable enough for items that get regular use and need to be cleaned occasionally. These finishes may be relatively easy to repair if damaged, but eventually you'll get tired of doing so.

The case for or against using varnishes is more complicated. Many wooden foodware items such as spoons, rolling pins, butcher blocks, and mortars and pestles are rubbed, washed, knocked, cut on, and pounded in everyday use. A tough surface film would seem ideal to stand the rigors of time. But when a varnish or polyurethane breaks down and especially if water penetrates it, it is much harder to repair.

However, these tough film finishes may be quite appropriate for objects that contain dry goods, such as sugar bowls or lidded boxes for cookies. These items rarely receive any abrasion, and usually need dusting only. Therefore the membrane will take many years of wear.

Since oil/varnish finishes are very slow to dry, their odor can linger, sometimes for months. This is especially true on lidded containers. I would not let food be in contact with this finish until the odor has completely dissipated. Instead of waiting, you can either leave the inside unfinished or finish it with quick-curing shellac.

A Few Tips for Preserving Woodenware

A third choice is the finish left by sandpaper—in other words, no finish at all. The wooden plates I use in my kitchen have never had a finish. They are 20 years old and are barely broken in yet. A closed-pored wood such as maple, cherry, or birch is best.

However, there are some secrets to letting woodenware age gracefully. When washing these items, do not leave them in standing water; use mild dish soap, scrub gently, and rinse. Then either dry the piece with a towel or let it air-dry.

Never put wooden items in the dishwasher or the microwave. Some timbers, especially fruitwoods, are also sensitive to cold and may crack if refrigerated.

The Best Woods for Foodware

The best woods for the kitchen and dining room are what I call the soft hardwoods. These include maples, cherry, walnut, ash, birch, poplar, and sycamore. These timbers are flexible and shock resistant. In contrast, the hard hardwoods such as locust, rosewoods, hickory, and Osage orange will shatter if dropped or knocked and won't last very long in the kitchen. White oak is the exception: Tough yet flexible, it makes excellent foodware. Red oak, on the other hand, is too porous.

Expect Wear and Tear? Use Oil

BOILED LINSEED OIL

Pour on the oil. Boiled linseed oil is a good penetrating oil. Flood the surface and use a disposable brush to ensure uniform coverage.

Sand in the oil. Another way to apply oil is to place a few drops on a foam-backed sanding pad chucked into an electric drill (left), and then sand it into the wood with the workpiece slowly turning. This deepens the penetration and brings out any curl.

OIL/VARNISH MIX

Use oil/varnish mixes sparingly. You can use oil/varnish mixes and wiping varnishes as penetrating-oil finishes, but don't apply too many coats or you'll build up a film, which is hard to repair.

MINERAL OIL

Renewable mineral oil. Because it never forms a film, no matter how many coats you apply, mineral oil is easy to use. But it has to be renewed frequently.

Creating a Patina Finish

by Peter Gedrys

Building any reproduction involves a great deal of time, effort, and expense, so when the last drawer is fitted you might be tempted to apply the finish as quickly as possible. After all, you've put a lot of hours into the piece and you just want it done. You might also be afraid that anything more than the simplest of finishes could ruin all your hard work.

However, just as your cabinetmaking skills have progressed from butt joints and basic boxes to dovetails and desks, so you should expand your finishing horizons beyond wiping on oil. Finishing is no harder than woodworking, just a different skill set.

I'll show you how to imitate a century or three of use and age to form that unique surface known as a patina. It involves choosing and using dyes, filling open-pored woods, adding depth to the color with a glaze, applying a clear topcoat, and using surface tricks to age a piece. Unquestionably, it takes longer than applying a wipe-on varnish, but when you are already months into an heirloom project, what's a couple of weeks more? Give your reproduction the finish it deserves, one that creates a wow factor each time someone sets eyes on it.

Practice and Experiment—But Not on the Piece

Start by looking at finishes that you'd like to replicate. This is similar to getting ideas when you design a piece. Look at books, magazines, auction catalogs, and websites and see what colors and finishes please you.

Once you've settled on the look you want, see where you're starting from. Take the sample boards from each part of the piece and wet them with a solvent to see the base color of the wood. You can use alcohol for a quick preview or slower-drying mineral spirits for a longer study.

On this Federal desk, built by *FWW* Managing Editor Mark Schofield, I wanted to darken the main veneer, which had a strong, pinkish-red base to it. On the first sample board, I applied Chippendale Red Brown dye (all the dye powders I used are water-soluble) and when it dried, applied several coats of shellac. This left the wood darker but still with too much red, so then I used Georgian Brown Mahogany instead. This cool, greenish-brown dye neutralized the base red to a more pleasing brown.

I also experimented on samples of the tiger maple on the legs and the bird's-eye maple drawer fronts before settling on a combination of colors.

Sand the Whole Piece but Seal it Selectively

It's better to spend a little extra time fine-tuning the surface than to discover flaws after you start applying the dyes. After a final hand-sanding with P180-grit paper, I remove the dust and wipe the surface with alcohol. This reveals any areas with glue residue that require a little extra sanding.

Once I'm satisfied that all is well with the surface, I clean it well, blowing out the pores with compressed air, vacuuming it, and giving it a good wipe-down with clean, dry, lint-free cloths.

If you have the steady hand of a marksman, you can try to apply the dye up to but not onto the holly stringing and banding. For the rest of us, it's safer to isolate the areas you don't want to dye. I've found that masking tape, even when burnished, isn't effective because the thin dye seeps under the edge.

Instead, I dilute varnish to a water-like viscosity, and use it to seal the stringing and banding. Apply it with a small sable artist's brush. You should be able to go 8 in. to 10 in. before having to reload your brush. When you begin again, land the brush gently like a plane, overlapping the previous stroke about an inch or so. This ensures you don't miss a spot on the stringing.

It is a good idea to practice with denatured alcohol before trying it with varnish. One trick I have for areas close to an edge is to use my baby finger as a kind of guide fence. Don't be in a rush: With all the stringing on the base, drawers, and top of this desk, this step took me the

better part of a day. It is exacting work but no more so than laying in the stringing or the fans in the first place.

Let the Coloring Begin

Once the inlays and stringing are isolated, apply the dye. For confined spaces I use a #20 bright artist's brush, but for larger areas I use a non-embossed industrial paper towel folded over a couple of times. I like these because they hold a lot of dye, flatten out nicely to a sharp edge, and give me a great deal of control. Even though the inlays are coated, try to avoid running the dye over them. You know the old saying: An ounce of prevention is worth a pound of cure.

I used the same yellow dye on the rosewood that I used

on the maple because it creates color harmony to the eye. Later, I'll tweak the rosewood's appearance by glazing it. After I've dyed the whole piece, I let it dry overnight and then look for areas either missed or dyed by mistake. You can try sanding any dyed sections of holly, but if this doesn't work, apply a matching gouache (an opaque artist's watercolor) with a #2 artist's brush.

I next rub the surface very sparingly with boiled linseed oil. I used less than 3 oz. for the whole desk but this is enough to set the dye in the wood. After the oil has cured overnight, I apply a 1½-lb. cut of blond, dewaxed shellac. This can be done by brush, pad, or spray and serves to isolate the base colors you just applied from the color in the grain filler applied next.

Dyes Add Decades of Darkening

SEAL SELECTIVE AREAS BEFORE YOU DYE

Stain controller. Before applying any dye, washcoat end grain with a thin coat of shellac to prevent it from absorbing too much dye.

Protect light-colored woods. To prevent the holly stringing from being discolored, use a narrow brush to seal it with a thin coat of varnish.

TOUCH UP TROUBLE SPOTS

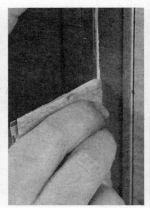

Sand away mistakes. If dye strays onto the wrong wood, wrap medium-grit sandpaper around a credit card and sand that section. A straight edge helps guide the sandpaper.

Pigment trumps dye. If you can't sand away errant dye, use opaque artist's watercolors to cover the affected area.

APPLY THE DYE

The whole surface of this desk was dyed, with the exception of the inlays, which were presealed to resist the dyes and retain their color. Dye numbers refer to W.D. Lockwood's catalog.

Apply the dye. A flat artist's brush works well in confined areas, while a folded paper towel covers large areas quickly. Try to even out the color while the dye is wet. (For more, see "Success with Dyes," on page 270)

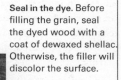

Seal in the dye. Before filling the grain, seal the dyed wood with a coat of dewaxed shellac. Otherwise, the filler will discolor the surface.

Stains replace dyes. If you discover a section that wasn't dyed after you've sealed the surface, use a pigment stain to apply color over the sealer. Two choices are gel stains or universal tints. If using the latter, mix it with a binder such as shellac.

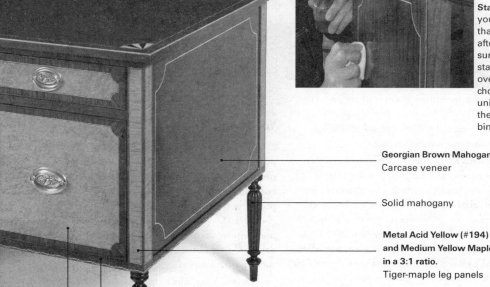

Georgian Brown Mahogany (#22)
Carcase veneer

Solid mahogany

Metal Acid Yellow (#194)
and Medium Yellow Maple (#142)
in a 3:1 ratio.
Tiger-maple leg panels

Rosewood banding

Bird's-eye maple drawer fronts

Finish Alone Can't Fill Open-Pored Wood

A formal finish needs to have a flat surface. If you apply a film finish to open-pored wood, it will leave the surface with a hungry look. Instead you need to apply a grain or paste filler. You can get paste filler already colored, but I prefer to tint my own to get a better match with the wood. I use an oil-based filler from Sherwin Williams, which in this case I tinted with raw umber and a dash of black artist's oils.

Paste filler requires thorough mixing to be effective. Once I have it colored, I'll pour it into a cup lined with cheesecloth folded over a couple of times. Then I gather the cheesecloth at the top and pull down on it, forcing the paste filler through it. This ensures my filler is lump free and the color is well incorporated.

You can apply the filler with a brush or a plastic blade. The pores on this wood are large and pronounced, so I used a short-bristle brush to force the filler in. Be sure to apply filler in manageable sections; otherwise, it will become very difficult to remove as it dries. Start with an area of a couple of square feet.

Although burlap is often recommended for removal, I've never liked it. I scrape off most of the excess with a plastic spreader going at 45° or perpendicular to the grain to avoid pulling filler out of the pores. Then I use a white abrasive pad to erase any filler that remains on the surface. These work great, and I can use a clogged pad to apply filler to carved areas such as the reeded legs. I simply rub the pad around the leg a few times, and then come back with a sharpened dowel to remove any filler from the groove between each reed. After letting the filler cure for five or six hours, I wipe all the surfaces with a clean cloth dampened with mineral spirits and let the piece sit overnight.

Don't be surprised if very open-pored wood requires a second round of filling. Don't skimp on this step or you'll find yourself trying to compensate later with the clear coat.

Once the pores are filled, let the piece dry for a few days and then seal the surface with a 2-lb. cut of dewaxed shellac in preparation for glazing.

Glazing Adds Depth to the Color

If you study antiques closely, one of their major differences with modern pieces is the subtle darkening found on some surfaces, particularly on carvings. The best way to imitate this combination of buildup in the recesses and greater wear on the high points is by a technique known as glazing.

Glaze is a translucent color applied over a sealed surface. It is a versatile tool in the finisher's arsenal because it is very forgiving. If you don't like what you see, simply wipe it off before it dries.

In this case I used asphaltum as my glaze. A black, naturally occurring, tar-like substance, it mixes well with mineral spirits to produce a rich golden brown. It's easy to adjust the color strength by adding more asphaltum to the thinner. During application, less is more. Light applications read better to the eye than thick ones. Remember, you can always add more glaze if required.

I apply the glaze with a pad, paper towel, or brush on flat areas such as the rosewood banding, but for carved areas I use an artist's fan brush to reach into the recesses. This brush has short, stiff bristles that allow me to quickly apply a thin coat of glaze to, in this case, the reeded legs. Next, use a paper towel to remove the glaze from the high points. To feather out or blend the resulting unnaturally sharp line between the glazed and unglazed areas, gently go over the surface with a dry artist's brush to give the glaze a harmonious appearance.

Use Filler on Open-Pored Woods

Tint the grain filler. I like to use uncolored, oil-based grain filler that he tints using artist's oils.

Filter the filler. After adding the colors, squeeze the filler through layers of cheesecloth to mix in the color and remove lumps.

Pack the pores. Use an old paintbrush to force the filler into the pores. Let the filler cure for a few minutes and then pull a plastic squeegee across the surface perpendicular to the grain to remove the excess.

Clean the surface. A white abrasive pad does a great job scrubbing any remaining filler from the surface while leaving the pores filled. Don't wait or the filler will harden on the surface.

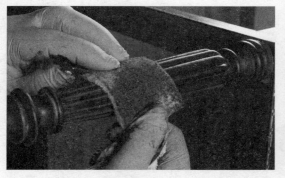

Fill grain on carvings, too. A clever way to fill the pores on carvings is to take a pad used to remove surplus filler from flat surfaces, and rub it over the carving, working it into the recesses, too.

Glazing Simulates Wear and Tear

Seal again, then glaze. Tint an oil-based glazing stain to the desired color or use diluted asphaltum. Apply it to the sealed surface.

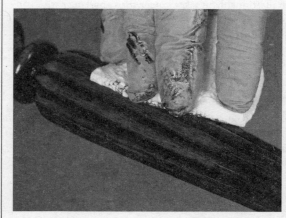

Wipe the high points. Use a paper towel to remove the glaze from the prominent surfaces, which are lighter on antiques.

Blend the transition. Use a dry brush to soften the line between the glazed and unglazed areas.

You Have a Choice of Clear Finishes

Set the piece aside for a few days to dry well before you apply the clear topcoat. You have a number of choices based on the application method you feel most comfortable with and the amount of use the finished piece will receive. It is perfectly fine to use two different types of finish on a single piece. On this desk, I padded shellac onto the base and used wiping varnish on the top for extra protection, but you could also brush on either of those finishes or spray the top with lacquer.

On the base, after I sand the sealer coat well on the non-glazed areas with P320-grit paper, I pad on shellac. I use an identical pad to one used for French polishing (see "Step-by-Step Guide to French Polishing, page 275), and basically the same technique. This includes the same circular and figure-8 patterns, but I lay down slightly thicker coats and finish by going with the grain. The advantage of the pad is that it doesn't leave any brush marks and the

surface is refined during application, eliminating the need to rub it out afterward. Take the time to practice this technique. You'll be happy you did.

On the top, I sealed the surface with a 2-lb. cut of dewaxed shellac and then wiped on four coats of Behlen's Rockhard Tabletop Varnish, thinning the varnish by about 40% with mineral spirits. This is enough protection for a desktop, but dining tables would be safer with three brushed-on coats, thinning the finish by 10% to 15% and sanding between each coat.

The Finishing Touches

When all the finish coats were done I set the desk aside for a week prior to any rubbing out. This also gave me the chance to look at the piece and to consider whether it needed any more aging.

There are some subtle surface techniques done with a little wax and rottenstone that imitate the buildup of dust, grime, and polish. Whether you wax the whole piece is entirely optional. In this case it doesn't affect the look of the piece but it does give a uniquely attractive quality to the touch.

The beauty of this finish is its visual depth. Once you've tried it, experiment with some of the steps and colorants to create your own patinas.

Topcoats Seal in the Beauty

It is fine to use one type of finish such as shellac on the base and add a more durable one such as varnish or lacquer to the top.

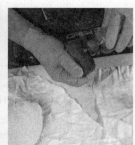

Color with shellac. If you choose shellac as your finish coat, tweak the final appearance by selecting a color ranging from super blond to garnet.

Make your pad. Use a cheesecloth core inside a linen wrapping. Add the shellac to the core for a consistent release onto the workpiece.

Build the finish. The advantage to padding on shellac over brushing is that you end up with a smooth finish (devoid of brush marks) that doesn't need rubbing out.

A durable top. To give the desktop extra protection, wipe on some thinned varnish over the shellac sealer.

Wax and Dirt Add the Final Touches

Wax the recesses. To imitate dust buildup, begin by using an old artist's brush to push clear paste wax into the recesses of carvings.

Add your dust. Brush rottenstone onto the freshly waxed areas. Rottenstone's pale blue/gray cast mimics dust well.

Complete the effect. After 20 minutes, use a piece of folded newspaper to remove most of the rottenstone but leave traces deep in the recesses.

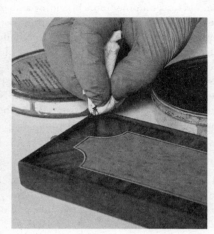

Patinating pulls. To add contrast to the antique-finish pulls, first use brass polish to give shine to the wear points, then rub some dark wax into the recesses. Finally, buff the whole surface with a clean cotton cloth.

Dark wax in the corners. Wipe on some dark wax, letting it build up in the corners to imitate antiques.

Period Finish for an Arts-and-Crafts Look

by Nancy Hiller

Whenever clients want cabinets to look original to a late-nineteenth- or early-twentieth-century-style home, I use this finish. I have borrowed techniques from two well-known finishers to create a period look. While the five steps to this Arts-and-Crafts-finish may seem daunting, the execution is actually quite painless.

Dye and Stain Increase Color and Contrast

Before applying any finish, sand all parts to P180-grit, then use water to raise the grain and gently sand again with P180-grit.

Jeff Jewitt introduced me to using dyes under oil-based stains to bring out the contrast between the basic grain and the ray-fleck patterns of quartersawn oak.

301

First, dye the oak with a water-based dye solution (I use TransTint's honey amber, dissolved in water at the ratio of 1 oz. to 1 qt.), applying it quickly and liberally with a foam brush and wiping off the excess with a lint-free cloth. During this step and the next (depending on the woods used), it may be necessary to block out and/or stain the inlay to maintain contrast. In this case, I carefully placed a sealer coat of clear shellac over the inlay after it had been glued in place and sanded, but before applying the amber dye. To knock back any raised grain, lightly sand with P320-grit paper.

Next, use an oil-based stain (in this case, Minwax's Early American) to bring out the wood's full figure. Apply the stain generously using a foam brush and leave it on for 5 to 10 minutes. Wipe off any excess stain using a clean, lint-free cloth and allow the piece to dry overnight. Make sure to check periodically for stain weeping out of the oak's open pores, removing any you find.

Seal in the Previous Steps with Shellac

A professional floor finisher once advised me that I could get an old look on pine floors by adding amber shellac. So once the stain has dried, I brush on a thin coat of Zinsser's premixed amber shellac to achieve a look similar to the shellac-based varnish that was used in many older houses. The shellac also seals the piece before the aging steps. When the shellac has dried, scuff-sand with P320-grit paper and wipe off the dust with a tack cloth. Now you can judge the final tone of the finish and fill any holes with matching wood putty. Scuff-sand again.

Simulate Signs of Aging

Teri Masaschi's suggestion to use gel stain for shading enables me to mimic signs of age without heavy-handed distressing, and make built-ins look like part of the original fabric of the home.

Apply gel stain in a compatible color to areas where dirt would typically have built up, such as joints, crevices, and around hardware. Let the gel stain set for 10 minutes or so, then with a lint-free cloth, gently rub and feather out the shading to create a natural-looking patina. Allow the gel stain to dry overnight.

Two coats of oil-based polyurethane finish the piece. You can follow it with a generous application of paste wax, applied with 0000 steel wool and buffed out with a soft, lint-free cloth.

Easy Finish Ages a Classic Cherry Piece

by Dan Faia

Like many furniture projects I worked on, a porringer-top tea table in cherry wouldn't be the first piece of furniture in its new home. There is a spot all picked out for it in the living room, between pieces of age-darkened cherry and stained pine.

So my first goal was to tone down the table's bright natural cherry a little to help the new piece blend in.

Cherry's tendency to blotch can make dyeing tricky, but this staining method helps to minimize the problem. For a topcoat afterward, I chose Waterlox Original Satin Finish because it allowed me to build a durable finish quickly, with a minimum of fuss.

Surface preparation is important to all finishes, but especially when dyeing and staining. Coloring wood highlights and magnifies minor imperfections like overlooked glue squeeze-out or small areas of tearout. Glue will absorb less dye and appear lighter than the surrounding wood. Sanding scratches and tearout will do just the opposite.

Begin the process by handplaning to level the surfaces and to remove mill marks. A thorough scraping will refine the surfaces, helping to clean up any tearout. How the wood is scraped will determine the sanding grit to begin with—P180-grit is most likely. To preserve the feeling of hand-worked surfaces on this period reproduction, I sanded only by hand, without using a sanding block.

Even though I seal the surface before applying the water-based dye, I still start by raising the grain. After sanding, slightly dampen the surface with distilled water. If you use tap water, be sure to test it on a piece of scrap first. Some tap water has a high iron content that can stain the wood, leaving black or yellow spots. Allow the wood to dry thoroughly and resand the wood lightly with P220-grit paper.

1. The First Coat Is Shellac

Sealing the piece with a washcoat of shellac will even out the wood's absorption properties, resulting in a more uniform color throughout the piece.

Whether you're using premixed shellac or flakes, adjust the heavy cut with denatured alcohol until you have roughly a 1-lb. cut.

Apply the shellac with a brush. It will dry quickly, so don't do much reworking as you go. Sand lightly with some used P220-grit paper or 0000 steel wool to level any fuzzy fibers.

2. The Key to Applying Dye: Keep Moving

Water-based aniline dye is easy to mix. I used Homestead Finishing's TransFast dye powder in antique cherry red. Start with a capful (about 1/2 oz.) of dye powder in a pint of warm water and add small amounts of dye or water to adjust the color. Always test the color on a scrap piece of project lumber that also has been sanded and sealed.

To achieve a uniform color when applying the dye, it's best to be methodical. Brush dye on one element of the project at a time, then mop away the excess with a rag. If the dye puddles or sits too long, it could darken the piece unevenly. You can make the overall color darker by applying further coats. The dye shouldn't raise the grain enough to require any additional sanding, but you can smooth the surface with 0000 steel wool.

3. Full-Strength Varnish Builds Quickly

I apply Waterlox Original without thinning. It is heavy and flows slowly, but the advantage is that it is self-leveling and leaves very few brush marks. Be sure to use a high-quality brush for fewer stray bristles. Brush on three or four coats (maybe more for porous woods), rubbing out between coats with 0000 steel wool.

If you are nervous about brushing, you can apply the finish with a rag. Ragging requires the product to be thinned. The downside is that this means more coats—and more rubbing out—to achieve the same build of finish.

After the final rubout, apply a coat of paste wax for a uniform sheen and an extra layer of protection. Use a lint-free rag and work on a few sections at a time. If the wax hardens for a long period of time, it will become very labor-intensive to rub out.

Finally, use a clean rag to buff the piece to its final luster.

Texture Wood to Highlight the Grain

by Geoff Guzynski

I've always liked the textured look of weathered cypress. It reminds me of old playground equipment where the wood's texture has been polished by thousands of small hands. It turns out that traditional Japanese craftsmen loved this look too. They called it jin-di-sugi and created it by burying the wood in the ground and allowing it to decay for several years. I wasn't about to invest that much time, but I was determined to incorporate the look in my furniture. After some experimenting, I came up with a fast and simple technique using an angle grinder fitted with a wire brush.

The process works best on boards with a dramatic difference in density between the early and latewood growth rings. You should be able to run your thumbnail across the grain and leave marks in the earlywood but not in the latewood. I've seen pine, cedar, and fir boards that pass this test, but I've had the best results with cypress. Be sure to test each board individually, however.

Texture the Wood in Three Steps

Dimension the wood in the normal way. It's not necessary to start with a board that's thicker than the intended final thickness, because only the softer early wood is removed. The dense latewood remains unchanged.

Begin removing softwood, keeping the brush's rotation in line with the grain and moving the grinder parallel with the grain. For a less aggressive cut, and to avoid snagging the panel edges, let the brush pull the grinder along the surface.

If you're going to color the wood, the stain mostly penetrates the soft early wood, so you need to adapt your grinding technique to the grain pattern. In areas where the grain is more flatsawn, use a very light touch with the brush or you will get rid of all or almost all of the early wood, and the surface won't absorb stain later. A panel with a flatsawn area adjacent to a more quartersawn section would then end up with uneven color. After the grinder, hand-brush the surface with a sparse, stiff-bristled wire brush. The final step is to smooth the panel with a nylon flap brush chucked in a drill.

You can stop here and apply the clear finish of your choice. Be careful to keep any film finish thin because a thick finish that fills the grooves looks really bad.

Dye and Stain Highlight the Texture

Using separate dye and pigment stains allows me to manipulate the color balance between the latewood and early wood. I start with a very light dye stain in an acetone and water base. The acetone gives the dye a bit more bite on the densest parts of the latewood. I combine brown, red, and yellow dye concentrates from Sherwin-Williams until the mix is a little brighter than if it was the only color being used. If you are using TransTints, Homestead No. 6006 dark mission brown, No. 6010 red mahogany, and sometimes No. 6020 lemon yellow give good results, too.

Once the dye has dried, flood the panel with a black pigment stain, like Minwax ebony diluted with five parts of mineral spirits. Wipe off the excess stain almost immediately. The deep grooves really hold onto the pigment.

Since I spray-finish my work, I don't topcoat the panel before assembling it into the frame. If you are applying finish with a brush, I would definitely recommend a seal coat of shellac before brushing on a topcoat, because there is a lot of color you could pick up and drag to the frame.

Reveal the Grain

You need a 4-in.-dia. crimped wire wheel and a nylon flap brush

Go lightly. Hold the angle grinder so that the wire wheel is parallel to the grain and just touching the surface. The goal is to remove the soft, early wood while leaving the harder, later wood intact.

Brush hard. Pull a stiff wire brush across the surface to define the grooves in the early wood. Use heavy pressure.

Remove the fuzz. A nylon brush attached to a drill removes loose wood fibers and leaves the surface ready for finishing.

Light or Dark? This texturing method looks great with a clear finish, but if you really want the patter to pop, try an ebonized treatment.

Kick Up the Contrast with Color

First dye the surface. Apply a dye with a slightly brighter color than the intended final look.

Then add a pigment stain. A diluted black pigment stain mutes the dye and also darkens the denser late wood.

A thin coat, please. The textured surface looks best under a minimal clear finish.

FIXES AND TROUBLE-SHOOTING

10 Best Finishing Fixes

by Teri Masaschi

Hobbyists and professionals alike make mistakes in the shop. When you're building a piece, fixing an error is fairly straightforward: Back up and start again by milling a new piece, recutting a joint, or fitting in a patch. But finishing mistakes can be harder to overcome—hence the dread many woodworkers feel.

Problems can pop up at any one of three points in the finishing process—surface preparation (and assembly), staining and coloring, and applying the topcoat. I'll show you some of the methods I use as a professional to back out of a mistake and to try to keep it from happening in the first place.

The best way to avoid mistakes altogether is to practice on a sample board. Testing the colors and materials you want to use will alert you to problems before you risk ruining an expensive project. Also, resist the urge to rush through the finishing process. You can nearly always tell when someone has taken a shortcut.

And finally, even if you make mistakes you can't fix, after suffering through them you probably won't repeat the same ones again.

Continued ➜

Surface Flaws

The most common pitfalls are sanding swirls and tearout, sanding through the veneer of hardwood plywood, and glue squeeze-out. Many of these maladies can occur even if you're trying to be meticulous. And you might not see the problem until it glares at you through a freshly applied coat of oil or stain.

1. Scratches and Tearout

Problem: A random-orbit sander left its signature pigtail marks, or you didn't use the right paper to eliminate scratches left by coarser grits. Or, cutting or planing tore out some wood fibers, leaving a divot in the surface. If the first swipe of stain shows vivid swirls or scratches all over the work, stop.

Solution: Sand the piece again, this time changing paper frequently and working your way systematically through the grits. If you've oiled or stained the piece and find that swirls show up in only one or two spots, sand those areas by hand with P220-grit wet-or-dry paper, wetting it with some of the same finish you used. This method works well with most oil finishes or oil-based pigment stains. If you used stain, reapply it carefully to match the surrounding stained areas.

If you used a dye, resand a stand-alone area, such as an entire stile. If it is a large surface, sand the damaged area, feathering the edge between sanded and unsanded parts. Then apply more dye.

To eliminate tearout, sand, plane, or scrape the surface. Wipe the surface with mineral spirits to check the smoothness. If the imperfections are small enough (generally no larger than a pinhead), you can fill them after you've stained and sealed the piece, using fill sticks, the wax crayons sold for touching up scratches.

If you aren't coloring the wood, small amounts of tearout can be OK in some places (legs, frames, etc.). But stain makes them pop.

- **Smoothing slurry.** Wet-sanding with the oil or stain you used helps eliminate swirls more rapidly without ruining the color.

2. Glue Residue

Problem: You used too much glue, leaving squeeze-out around the joint. Or you got sloppy and left a gluey fingerprint on the workpiece. Oil or stain won't penetrate the glue residue, leaving an unsightly light spot.

Solution: You can get rid of some fingerprints by wet-sanding with the stain you used, or by lightly sanding and reapplying the stain.

Use a sharp chisel to eliminate dried glue from around a joint. Use sandpaper to clear up areas where you didn't completely wipe away squeeze-out. Wrap P220-grit paper around a hard block and sand with the grain, using firm pressure. To avoid scratching adjacent surfaces, use a 6-in. flexible drywall knife as a shield.

- **Touch-up.** When removing glue squeeze-out, sand with the grain using P220-grit sandpaper. Keep the block flat against the work to avoid rounding over an edge. Shield adjacent surfaces with a wide drywall knife.

3. Sand-through

Problem: You sanded away some face veneer on a large, expensive piece of plywood after you had glued up everything.

Solution: Use a scrap of the same plywood to duplicate the mistake and serve as a sample board for the remedy. Apply the same finish you plan to use on the piece, then sand through a portion of the face veneer to give yourself a place to experiment with a repair.

Mix thin shellac with a touch-up powder such as Behlen Master Furniture Powder or Mohawk Blendal Powder Stain. Put a piece of glass next to the sand-

through on the practice board and begin developing your color. Quickly dip the brush into the shellac, then into one of the touch-up powders. Swirl the brush around on the glass to incorporate the powder and shellac. Dab on more shellac and a different powder to blend the color you need. Work in thin layers, sneaking up on the color rather than painting it in. If you aren't happy with the results, wipe away the color and start over.

When you've done a reasonable job of covering the sand-through on the scrap, take a deep breath and do the same thing on the real project. A glaze—a type of stain used on a semisealed surface—brushed on and then lightly wiped off will help blend in the patch.

- **Practice patch.** Make a similar burn-through on a scrap of the same plywood. Mix touch-up powders with thinned shellac to match the color of the face veneer and hide the sanded-through spot.

- **Faux finish.** Carefully paint the tinted shellac over the sand-through. Apply a glaze to help blend the patch into the surrounding wood.

Color Mistakes

By far the biggest finishing problems can occur when you apply dye or stain. A color you thought would look great comes up garish. Or the first coat of color takes unevenly, leaving blotches or streaks. Here's how to get around drawbacks like these.

4. Uneven Dye Stain

Problem: A dye-based stain looks stronger or more intense in some areas than in others. Consequently, you have an unevenly colored surface or lap marks where you wanted uniformity.

Solution: Pull a damp rag over the surface. That will lift the dye, so you can "move" or remove it to make the color even. Work the rag around to blend the color evenly. Then apply a washcoat of shellac and the stain you want to use.

5. Wrong Stain Color

Problem: The stain you applied threw the wood color way off. Generally, a stain will appear either too red or not red enough. Either way, it spoils the appearance of the piece.

Solution: Correct the color with a glaze. Apply a washcoat of shellac over the stain, then gently scuff-sand with P320-grit paper when it's dry. Use a glaze that contrasts with the stain to bring the color back into line.

For example, if the stain looks too red, tone it down with a raw umber glaze, which is greenish in tone. Alternatively, you can use a black glaze to change the color's tone.

If the stain doesn't have enough red, warm up the color with burnt umber or burnt sienna, which is predominantly reddish.

Brush on the glaze liberally, let it sit for a minute or so, then lightly remove most of it with a clean rag, leaving a thin film of color. Once you've corrected the color to your liking, protect the glaze with another washcoat of shellac before you apply the topcoat.

6. Blotchy Stain

Problem: You chose a pigmented stain that didn't take evenly on the wood. Pine, cherry, maple, birch, and alder are the most likely to blotch.

Solution: If the surface is very blotchy, you'll have to remove the stain by stripping, sanding, or both, and start over. This time, apply a washcoat of shellac and then the stain.

If the blotching isn't too severe, try using a glaze to soften the contrast between the deeply colored and lighter areas. Once the initial stain is dry, apply a washcoat of shellac. Let it dry, then gently scuff with P320-grit paper. Brush on a burnt umber or other brownish glaze; wipe gently to remove most of the excess.

Topcoat Trouble

Problems can occur in laying down the final coats, whether you brush, wipe, or spray. Apply multiple light layers of the topcoat rather than one or two thick ones. Sand carefully, wiping away the sanding dust to check surfaces frequently. Rubbing out, the last step, is incredibly important because it "finishes" the finish. However, the idea of abrading a carefully applied topcoat scares many people, and rightly so. You don't want to have problems so close to the finale. Use a light touch.

7. Drips and Sags

Problem: You used too heavy a hand in applying the topcoat, so the coating drools down the side of your beautiful project.

Solution: Wait until the sag is totally dried. It should feel hard, not resilient, when you push on it. Wrap a cork or hardwood sanding block with P320-grit paper and lightly sand to level the mess. If you start sanding while the sag is still gummy, you'll just make the mess worse. Check your work frequently and change the paper often. You want to flatten the lumps without going through the stain color or down to the bare wood.

Or, if you only have one or two drips, you can use a fresh single-edge razor blade to scrape them off. Be sure to scrape carefully to avoid cutting through the finish.

8. Contaminated Finish

Problem: Flat surfaces are pockmarked with small craters. Often from the first brushful, the coating literally "crawls" into an odd formation that resembles a crater or fisheye. You can't do anything ahead of time to prevent this contamination. It may come from lubricants used on a tablesaw or jointer bed. It can also occur if you put a water-based finish over an oil-based stain.

Solution: Stop. Don't even begin to think you can keep brushing to eliminate the problem. Wipe off all the coating, then brush or spray on a light coat of shellac. If spraying, use a very fine, almost dry spray. The shellac forms a barrier to keep the contaminant from coming up through subsequent layers of finish. When the shellac dries, continue applying the topcoat you want.

9. Burnthrough

Problem: You have either sanded through the finish (a frequent occurrence on edges, moldings, and carvings) or burned through the color (removing both the topcoats and the stain).

Solution: If you've burned through the color, carefully apply more stain, protect it with a light coat of shellac, and then replace the topcoats. If you've only burned through the finish, delicately reapply it. When the repairs are thoroughly dry, rub out those areas to blend them in with the rest of the surface.

10. Witness Lines

Problem: When rubbing out a film finish like varnish, you cut through the layers of finish. Witness lines are shadowy craters of this cut-through. Witness lines seldom occur with shellac or lacquer because new coats of those finishes dissolve into the old ones.

Solution: Keep leveling the finish, then apply at least two more fresh coats of finish.

- **Witnesses.** Sanding too much can produce witness lines, whitish areas exposing earlier coats of finish.

- **Keep sanding.** Using fine sandpaper and a light touch, sand the surface to level it as much as possible before applying more topcoat.

- **Add another topcoat.** Apply more of the topcoat to the entire surface, not just where the witness lines had been.

How to Prevent Surface Flaws

Sand with progressively finer grits, ending with P220. Finish by hand-sanding with the grain with P180- or P220-grit paper. Vacuum or blow off the dust. Wet the surface with mineral spirits or shine a bright light across it to reveal flaws. If you're working with hardwood-veneer plywood, sand with a very light touch and check your progress often. Use glue sparingly and remove squeeze-out carefully.

How to Prevent Color Mistakes

To avoid problems with stain or water-based dye in the first place, use a sample board to test the finish you want to use. You'll greatly increase the odds of having the color go on evenly if you apply a wash-coat of thinned shellac beforehand. That will help ensure that subsequent coats of color take uniformly. A good washcoat is a 1-lb. cut: Combine premixed shellac (which is a 3-lb. cut) and denatured alcohol in a 3:2 ratio.

Revive a Finish

by Jeff Jewitt

Stripping a piece of furniture must be the nastiest finishing task. Not only are the fumes unpleasant, but it's messy and requires cumbersome safety equipment. Yet for many, stripping is the first thing that comes to mind when they see a piece of furniture whose finish is worn or damaged. However, stripping is the nuclear option of refinishing.

In many cases, if the finish is just worn but still in good shape, you should consider cleaning and reviving it. This approach is used extensively in the antiques and museum trades and uses simple materials and surprisingly few tools.

I'll show you several no-strip methods for refreshing different kinds of finish. I'll discuss which finishes respond well and which don't. Go ahead and experiment on an old piece. You'll most likely be amazed at the results,

but if you aren't, you can always strip it afterward without having invested a great deal of time.

Evaluate the Damage and Determine the Finish

Woodworkers usually get to finish new furniture, but there are a couple of reasons why it is good to know how to refinish a piece. The finish on your early creations may have deteriorated; or perhaps you own an heirloom or two, or couldn't resist a flea-market bargain. The first step is to see if the finish has damage that puts it beyond reviving (see photos at right).

If it looks like a good candidate for reviving, the second step is to see what type of finish you're dealing with, because this determines the method. The best finishes to clean and revive are old oil, oil/varnish, shellac, and lacquer finishes. The first two types are generally wipe-on, penetrating finishes with little to no surface build and will have a flat, dull look when old. You may even have applied them yourself when you built the piece.

With a film finish, test to see if it is lacquer or shellac. If the finish responds to neither solvent it is probably oil-based polyurethane, a waterborne finish, or a high-tech catalyzed finish, none of which revive very well. However, you can still put these finishes through the two-step cleaning process explained below.

A Good Cleaning Reveals the Finish

First, remove any loose dust from the surface. Next, take a rag, ideally with a little texture such as terrycloth, and wet it with mineral spirits or paint thinner. Rub the surface in small circles, paying attention to crevices and corners that might contain old wax as well as areas that get contact with hands and fingers, such as around knobs and pulls. I often wear a respirator when using either solvent indoors, but if you work in a well-ventilated area (as I am above) you can probably get by without one. Or you can substitute odorless mineral spirits (Klean-Strip is one brand) or naphtha, which evaporates faster and doesn't have a lingering solvent odor.

If you don't see a lot of grime on your rag when you do this step, all that means is that the finish probably wasn't waxed often or exposed to oil-based products such as lemon oil. However, if there's some grime on the surface that doesn't seem to be coming off with the cloth, you can use a piece of 0000 steel wool.

Evaluate the Finish

Is It Beyond Repair?

To see if any finish is worth reviving, wipe it down with some paint thinner or mineral spirits. Wetting the surface not only helps you preview what the piece will look like under a revived finish, but more importantly, it reveals any major flaws in either the finish or the wood that can be fixed only by stripping the piece.

MISSING FINISH
You can't revive a finish if it's missing. The mineral spirits will darken areas with no finish.

DAMAGE TO THE WOOD
Cracks and blisters in veneer make reviving a finish pointless. On solid wood, if long, deep scratches and gouges have gone through the finish into the wood, cleaning and reviving may make them look worse.

BLACK/GRAY AREAS
Cleaning and reviving will not remove gray or black areas. These problems usually indicate water damage to the wood and not the finish.

STICKY FINISHES
Finishes around pulls that are routinely in contact with skin will become sticky over time. If you press a cotton swab on the finish and parts of the cotton remain, go right to stripping. Cleaning and even putting new finish over a sticky finish will never harden it.

ALLIGATOR SKIN
Some finishes that have been applied thickly become brittle and crack as they get older. The resulting finish is rough and bumpy. Don't bother trying to clean or revive these finishes.

READY FOR REVIVAL
After 30 years, the original penetrating oil finish on this table is still intact but has become dull and is obscured by a layer of dirt and grime. The fix isn't refinishing, but cleaning and renewing the finish.

Continued →

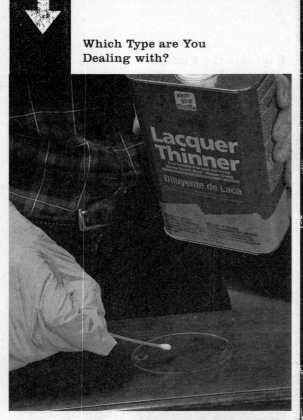

Oil finishes are easy to spot, but a film finish could be a number of things. Rub a cotton swab soaked in lacquer thinner on an unobtrusive area. If the finish comes away, it is lacquer. If it doesn't, try denatured alcohol to see if it is shellac.

For the second cleaning, put about ½ oz. of dish detergent in a pint of lukewarm water. I like to use Dawn because it contains grease-cutting chemicals known as surfactants. Dampen a cloth (don't get it dripping wet) and wipe the surface in the same manner as before. Most of the grime and dirt is removed with this second step because the soapy water pulls off the oily residue from the first step and also removes water-soluble grime like sugary food spills. Change the cloth frequently to a clean part. When you're done, lightly wipe the surface using distilled water to remove any soap residue.

How to Revive a Wipe-On, Oil-Based Finish

One of the most popular finishes used by non-professional woodworkers is some type of an oil finish. This includes pure tung oil or boiled linseed oil, one of the Danish oils, a wiping varnish, or an oil/varnish mix. All these finishes are popular because they penetrate deep into the wood, accentuate figure and detail, and provide a very natural, low-luster finish that woodworkers like.

A downside of these in-the-wood finishes is that over time they get dull and the wood loses its luster. The steps below are a good way to really liven these finishes back up. This was probably the first finish you used, and luckily for you, it is among the easiest to revive.

Wet-sand to remove minor scratches—You're bound to find minor surface scratches on pieces that have seen normal household use, but this next step should repair them. You'll need some type of wiping varnish such as Seal-A-Cell, Waterlox Original, or Minwax Antique Oil. If you know the original finish was a pure tung or linseed oil and you want to avoid adding any kind of film finish, you can substitute Danish oil.

Pour a small puddle of the finish onto the surface and then use a small piece of wet-or-dry sandpaper (600-grit CAMI or P1000-grit FEPA) to wet-sand in circles or with the grain. Sand until any slight scratches are gone and the surface looks uniform. Remove the excess with a dry cloth and let it dry at least six hours.

These penetrating finishes aren't usually used with dyes or glazes so you probably won't need to touch up any missing color, but if you do, let any color repairs dry for about an hour and then apply a coat of the same finish you used for wet-sanding. Using a small piece of paper towel or old cotton T-shirt, I apply just enough to make the surface look wet and then allow it to dry. Apply another coat or two if you want a deeper luster to the wood or more protection. As a final step, you can apply and buff out a coat of paste wax.

Sand and Wax Shellac or Lacquer

Reviving a shellac or lacquer finish is even quicker, because you don't have to add finish. You could, of course, as new shellac or lacquer will melt right into old, but it's easier to level what is already there than try to brush on a new, level coat. Do the two-step cleaning process, then instead of wet-sanding, dry-sand the finish lightly with P600-grit stearated sandpaper like Norton 3X or 3M Fre-Cut. If the finish is slightly crazed (rough and cracked), sand it back as much as you can without sanding through to the stain or bare wood.

Touch up any missing color—If the piece was originally dyed or stained, or if you sanded through to lighter wood underneath, you may need to repair some colors. I mix dry furniture powders with SealCoat dewaxed shellac.

You can blend a custom color and it dries very fast, so you can proceed to the next step without waiting. Use a No. 4 artist's brush (from Art-and-Crafts stores) and play with the colors on a piece of white paper until you get a reasonable match to the wood. Apply it sparingly, just enough to disguise the problem. Avoid the temptation to make it perfect, because you are more likely to make the touch-up obvious.

Instead of more finish, I find that a coat or two of paste wax works better and is a lot easier. It adds a bit of luster and lends that silky feel that old furniture gets over time when it has been cared for. If you deliberately leave a little dark wax in corners and crevices, it adds an antiqued look. Always use tinted paste waxes on dark finishes. Clear wax can dry whitish and look bad on open-grained woods like oak.

Thick Film Finishes Can Only Be Cleaned

Film finishes like oil-based polyurethane, waterborne finishes, or high-tech, two-part finishes often found on kitchen cabinets don't revive very well. If you try to sand them, you are likely to go through a layer of finish and leave a witness line that can only be covered up by applying a new topcoat to the whole surface. However, these tough finishes are harder to damage, so there is a good chance that after the two-step cleaning they will be ready for many more years of useful service.

Restore an Oil Finish

Thin, wipe-on finishes don't offer much protection, so over the years the surface becomes scratched. Fortunately they are easy to revive.

STEP 1. WET-SAND AND WIPE

Pour on a liberal amount of a wiping varnish and then sand the surface with fine sandpaper. This removes most of the scratches and leaves an even sheen. Once you've sanded the whole surface, wipe off the extra finish and let the piece dry.

STEP 2. WAX AND BUFF

Dark wax can enhance a dark wood by concealing minor scratches and not leaving a cloudy residue. If left a little heavy in corners, it can add an aged look. Buff the wax to leave the restored piece looking beautiful again.

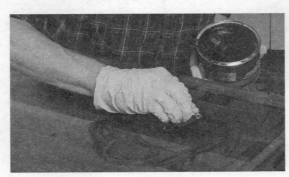

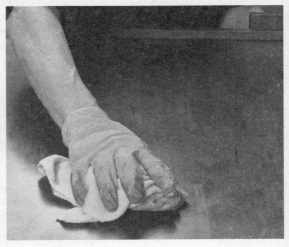

Revive Lacquer or Shellac

These thicker film finishes can be sanded smooth and then just waxed. Although unsightly, most surface scratches and dull areas are only skin deep.

STEP 1. SAND IT SMOOTH
Use 600-grit sandpaper to remove the damaged surface of the finish, leaving a more even appearance.

STEP 2. RETOUCH MISSING COLOR

Any old piece that was originally dyed or stained is likely to need the color touched up. The edges of pieces are often worn down, revealing bare wood. A single brush stroke of color instantly restores their look. Combine different shades of furniture powders and some dewaxed shellac on a piece of white paper until you get a good match.

STEP 3. FINISH WITH WAX
After sanding away the damaged finish, apply a coat of paste wax and then polish it to an even sheen.

How to Troubleshoot a Spray Gun

by Jeff Jewitt

As the technical troubleshooter for my business, I've been asked to solve just about every spray-gun problem imaginable, from a new gun that just hisses air to an old gun that used to spray perfectly and now leaves a horrible finish. The good news is that in most cases, you can diagnose the cause of the problem by analyzing the spray pattern. In a few other situations, a slight change in your spraying technique can help. Even if you're just considering taking the leap into spray finishing, knowing how to achieve and maintain a good spray pattern will give you the confidence you need.

Since all spray guns operate on the same basic principle, it doesn't matter whether you have a high-volume, low-pressure (HVLP) gun or a non-HVLP gun, a turbine-driven system or a compressor-driven system. When differences exist, I'll call them out.

Most of the time some finish comes out of the gun, just not in a manner to give that thin, even coating that makes spraying so worthwhile. One of the most common problems is uneven coverage, which leaves a repeating light/dark effect when the finish dries. You can study the spray pattern with a light shining through it. If you find this difficult, spray some dark finish or stain onto cardboard. If you substitute a dark finish for a clear one just to test the pattern, be sure that it has a comparable viscosity.

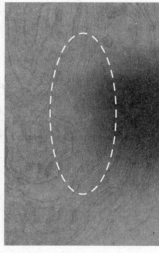

TEST YOUR GUN
You want the gun to spray an elliptical pattern consisting of fine, even-sized droplets (far right). Most of the time, spraying clear finish onto cardboard will give you a legible spray pattern while the finish is wet. For an even clearer pattern, spray black stain or paint onto the cardboard as shown in the following test panels.

PATTERN HEAVY ON ONE SIDE
The typical culprit for this is a plugged or partially clogged air-cap port. It's easy to diagnose: Just rotate the air cap 180° and if the problem side reverses, then it's the air cap. Remove the air cap and soak it in lacquer thinner. Use micro-brushes to clean the air-cap ports as best you can. The ports meet inside the air cap at a 90° angle, so come in from both sides. A blow gun that has a protective rubber tip can be used to blow out the ports, but wear eye protection in case some thinner splashes out (I speak from painfuexperience).

If the pattern does not reverse when you rotate the air cap, then it is the fluid nozzle that is clogged, causing the spray to veer to one side as it exits the gun. If you have a gravity gun, you can easily diagnose a partially obstructed nozzle by unhooking the air line and pulling the trigger completely back with solvent or finish in the gun. The liquid should come out in a steady stream if the nozzle is clear. If you have a compressor-driven pressure cup and the gun has a cheater valve (an internal air shutoff), simply close the cheater valve and pull the trigger. Again, the finish/solvent should come straight out the front. On suction and turbine-driven pressure cups you can't do this, so you'll just have to see if cleaning the nozzle helps.

Which Type of Gun Do You Have?

Spray guns come in two basic designs. Siphon cups (also called suction cups) have the storage cup under the spray gun, while gravity guns put it on top. To troubleshoot correctly, you need to know which type you have.

SIPHON CUPS
In a standard siphon cup, air exiting the front of the gun creates suction, pulling the finish up into the gun through a metal tube. With a pressurized siphon cup (usually called a pressure cup), the cup is pressurized by an external or internal tube that diverts a small amount of air from the gun. This pushes the finish up into the gun. All turbine systems use pressurized siphon cups.

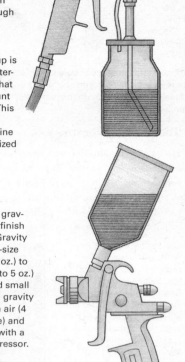

GRAVITY CUPS
With the cup on top, gravity alone pushes the finish down into the gun. Gravity guns range from full-size cups (about 20 to 25 oz.) to detail guns (about 4 to 5 oz.) used for touchup and small projects. These small gravity guns don't use much air (4 cubic feet per minute) and typically can be run with a small portable compressor.

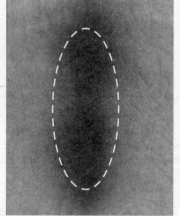

PATTERN SPLIT IN THE CENTER
If there is no finish in the center of the spray pattern, more than likely the air pressure is too high. Lower it and see if the problem gets better. On the few turbine models that lack air regulation, switch to a smaller fluid nozzle.

PATTERN HEAVY IN THE CENTER
If most of the finish is in the center, the air pressure is too low. If you can adjust the pressure, turn it up. On a compressor-driven system, turn down the atomizing air using either the compressor output regulator or a secondary supply regulator. This regulator can be wall-mounted if you have a metal air pipe, or a mini-regulator attached to the base of the gun. With turbines, all you can do is to turn down the atomizing air with an air-control valve mounted on or near the base of the gun. If your turbine has a speed control, you can adjust it for a slower speed, which reduces the air. If you can't adjust the pressure, try thinning the product or switching to a larger fluid nozzle.

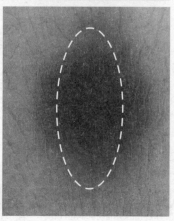

Continued ➜

COARSE SPRAY PATTERN

If your dried finish has little dimples all over it resembling the skin of an orange, you have "orange peel." Poor atomization (large droplets) is the main culprit, and this is often easiest to see if the spray pattern is backlit.

On all compressor-driven guns, try increasing the air pressure and see if the coarse pattern improves. If it doesn't, you can try thinning the product in 10% increments until it improves. If neither works, try a smaller nozzle.

With a turbine gun, make sure the air control (if you have one) or the speed control for the turbine is opened all the way. If this doesn't work, try thinning the material and then switching to a smaller nozzle.

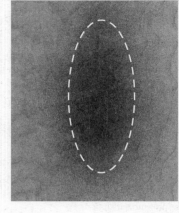

Too Much Overspray

HVLP systems should limit overspray to 20% to 30% of the finish. If you think you're getting more, you can reduce it by turning down the air pressure. Just keep in mind that when you do this, the finish quality will start to suffer, at some point resulting in the orange-peel effect described above.

Throttle back the air. To reduce overspray, simply reduce the air pressure. If you build a dedicated spray booth, consider installing a combination regulator and air cleaner attached to the wall. The cleaner ensures that no contaminants reach the finish.

Bounce back. Old-fashioned spray guns created large amounts of overspray. Modern HVLP guns are designed to avoid this.

Dry or Rough Spray, or No Spray at All

If the finish feels rough when it dries, there are some possible causes common to all guns. You may not be depositing enough finish: Try slowing down your motion as you spray to leave more finish on the surface. Likewise, the gun may be too far from the surface. The correct distance is 4 in. to 6 in. for HVLP and 6 in. to 8 in. for non-HVLP. It could be that the overspray is landing on your work after you spray. Use a fan to remove the overspray. Last, the finish may be drying too fast because it's hot and dry. Use a retarder specified by the manufacturer to give the finish a longer time to flow out into a smooth film.

In extreme circumstances, you may get no finish coming out of the gun. You pull the trigger and hear air coming through the front but no finish comes out, or it sprays a little and then stops. All standard siphon and gravity cups have a small vent hole that allows air to enter the cup to displace the finish volume as it's pulled out through the fluid nozzle. Use a toothpick or micro-brush to clear the vent hole. If there's a fair amount of hardened finish in the hole, soak the top in lacquer thinner, but be sure to remove any gaskets first.

If that doesn't work, remove the fluid nozzle and see if it's clogged. Soak it in lacquer thinner to soften any dried finish and ream it clean with a micro-brush. Finally check the fluid pickup tube and see if it is clogged.

Remove dried-on finish. Soaking gun parts in lacquer thinner is the best way to remove hardened finish, but first remove non-metal parts.

Trouble in the tube. If the tube that pressurizes a pot is clogged, finish will not fully flow to the gun. Remove the tube from the base of the gun and the top of the pot (above), and then blow through the tube to see if the check valve or tube is blocked (below).

Clean the splash guard. The small pressure vent can get plugged with dried finish, interrupting the flow. Use micro-brushes in a spray-gun cleaning kit to clean the hole.

REGULAR CLEANING PREVENTS MOST PROBLEMS

If you are spraying a fast-drying finish such as shellac, solvent-based lacquer, or a water-based finish, each coat is likely to be 1 to 2 hours apart, so leaving finish in the gun between coats doesn't cause problems. However, if the finish needs to dry overnight, or if you change to a different finish, you should clean the gun.

When you use solvent-based lacquer and shellac, any new finish in the gun will re-melt any dried finish, so you typically don't have to clean the gun thoroughly. Just run some lacquer thinner or denatured alcohol through it, depending on the finish.

Finishes that require more diligence in cleaning are water-based and oil-based products (including latex and oil paint) because the cleanup solvent won't remove the dried finish. Therefore you should clean the gun soon after use. When cleaning guns that sprayed paints, remove the air cap, fluid nozzle, and needle so you can clean more thoroughly. The chart below tells you which solvent works best to clean the different finish types, or you can check the finish container for the proper solvent. Note that some products require a different cleaner once they have dried.

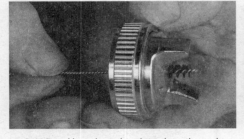

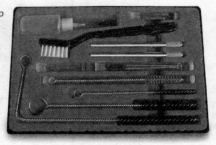

Let fluid flow. Use a large brush to clean the main nozzle in the center of the air cap where finish exits the gun.

Air supply. The small holes on either side of the fluid nozzle supply air that atomizes the finish. Clean them; using thin needles.

Don't forget the needle and nozzle. After removing the air cap, unscrew the nozzle, and then use a micro-brush to clean inside it.

Buy a full cleaning kit. To keep spray guns working properly, a cleaning kit should contain special brushes and needles to access the different parts of the gun.

FOR CLEANUP, MATCH SOLVENT TO FINISH

Finish	To Rinse/Clean	To Remove Dried Finish
Shellac	Denatured alcohol	Denatured alcohol
Solvent lacquer	Lacquer thinner	Lacquer thinner
Waterborne finishes and latex paint	Water followed by denatured alcohol	Acetone/lacquer thinner
Oil-based finishes and oil paint	Mineral spirits/paint thinner/naphtha	Lacquer thinner

Projects

THE LANGUAGE OF FURNITURE CONSTRUCTION

Tables, Case Pieces, and Chairs

by Steve Scott

An old Czech proverb says that to learn a new language is to gain a new soul. That transformative power also exists in woodworking, where the craft's dialect can seem as bewildering to the newcomer as a foreign tongue. Grasp it, though, and you'll begin to see and think in new ways.

Like any craft, woodworking has specialized terms for its tools and techniques. It is full of everyday words that live different lives in the woodshop—from frogs and fences to stretchers and aprons. A comprehensive glossary could fill a book, and has, but this short one will get you started.

Because the furniture itself is the heart of furniture making, we decided to begin with a visual glossary of furniture parts. When you start researching projects you'd like to tackle, or you find yourself describing what you want to build, this guide will help.

Knowing the language of woodworking won't make you a woodworker, but it can help you learn the craft, share your ideas, and express yourself. It also connects you to the history and tradition of the craft. And there's a lot of soul in that.

Tables

People commonly talk about tables in terms of their function—dining table, sofa table, end table, etc. But furniture makers must go deeper, knowing the name of every part.

Continued →

Trestle Table

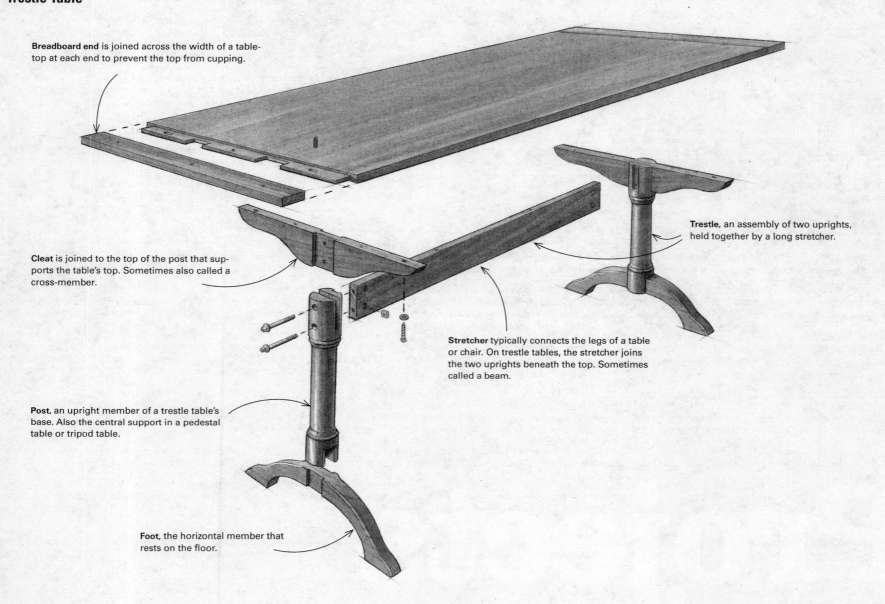

Breadboard end is joined across the width of a table-top at each end to prevent the top from cupping.

Trestle, an assembly of two uprights, held together by a long stretcher.

Cleat is joined to the top of the post that supports the table's top. Sometimes also called a cross-member.

Stretcher typically connects the legs of a table or chair. On trestle tables, the stretcher joins the two uprights beneath the top. Sometimes called a beam.

Post, an upright member of a trestle table's base. Also the central support in a pedestal table or tripod table.

Foot, the horizontal member that rests on the floor.

ExpandingTable

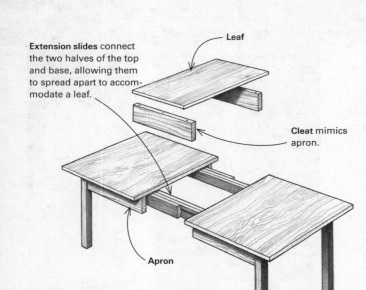

Extension slides connect the two halves of the top and base, allowing them to spread apart to accommodate a leaf.

Leaf

Cleat mimics apron.

Apron

Demilune Table

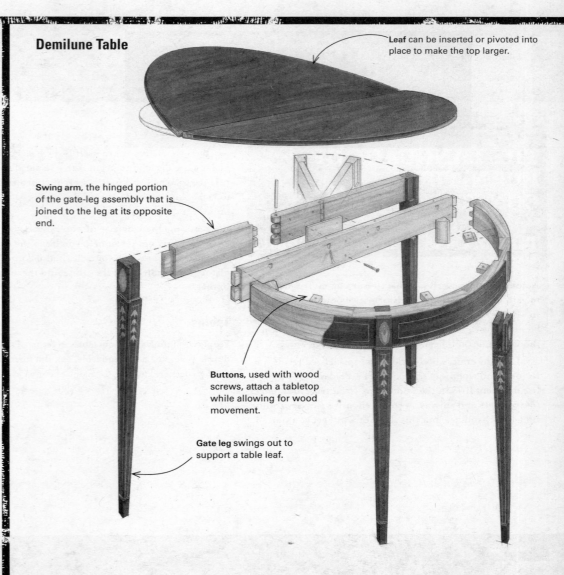

Leaf can be inserted or pivoted into place to make the top larger.

Swing arm, the hinged portion of the gate-leg assembly that is joined to the leg at its opposite end.

Buttons, used with wood screws, attach a tabletop while allowing for wood movement.

Gate leg swings out to support a table leaf.

Table with Drawer

Kicker vs. Runner

How is a dresser or table drawer like an open sleigh? It slides on its runners. Remember that and you won't confuse runners and kickers, a common mistake. Together, they control a drawer's movement inside the case.

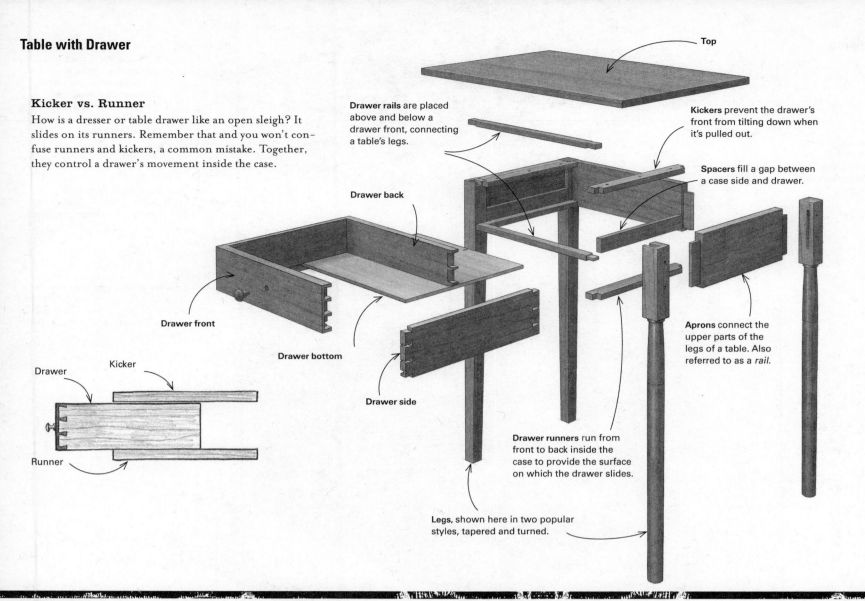

Drawer rails are placed above and below a drawer front, connecting a table's legs.

Top

Kickers prevent the drawer's front from tilting down when it's pulled out.

Drawer back

Spacers fill a gap between a case side and drawer.

Drawer front

Aprons connect the upper parts of the legs of a table. Also referred to as a *rail*.

Drawer bottom

Drawer side

Drawer runners run from front to back inside the case to provide the surface on which the drawer slides.

Legs, shown here in two popular styles, tapered and turned.

Drawer

Kicker

Runner

Wall Cabinet

A conversation about a case piece can start out simply enough. After all, it's just a carcase—or box—with the standard top, bottom, back, and sides. But once you get inside the box, things get more complicated.

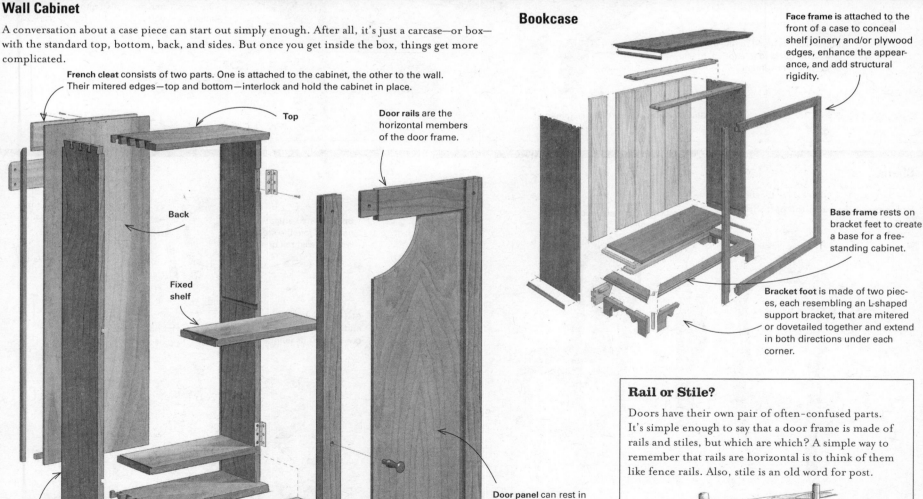

French cleat consists of two parts. One is attached to the cabinet, the other to the wall. Their mitered edges—top and bottom—interlock and hold the cabinet in place.

Top

Door rails are the horizontal members of the door frame.

Back

Fixed shelf

Sides

Bottom

Door stiles are the vertical members of the door frame. Sometimes referred to as *hinge-side stile* and *strike-side stile.*

Door panel can rest in grooves or be held by different combinations of rabbets and moldings on the front and rear of the frame.

Bookcase

Face frame is attached to the front of a case to conceal shelf joinery and/or plywood edges, enhance the appearance, and add structural rigidity.

Base frame rests on bracket feet to create a base for a free-standing cabinet.

Bracket foot is made of two pieces, each resembling an L-shaped support bracket, that are mitered or dovetailed together and extend in both directions under each corner.

Rail or Stile?

Doors have their own pair of often-confused parts. It's simple enough to say that a door frame is made of rails and stiles, but which are which? A simple way to remember that rails are horizontal is to think of them like fence rails. Also, stile is an old word for post.

311

Chest of Drawers

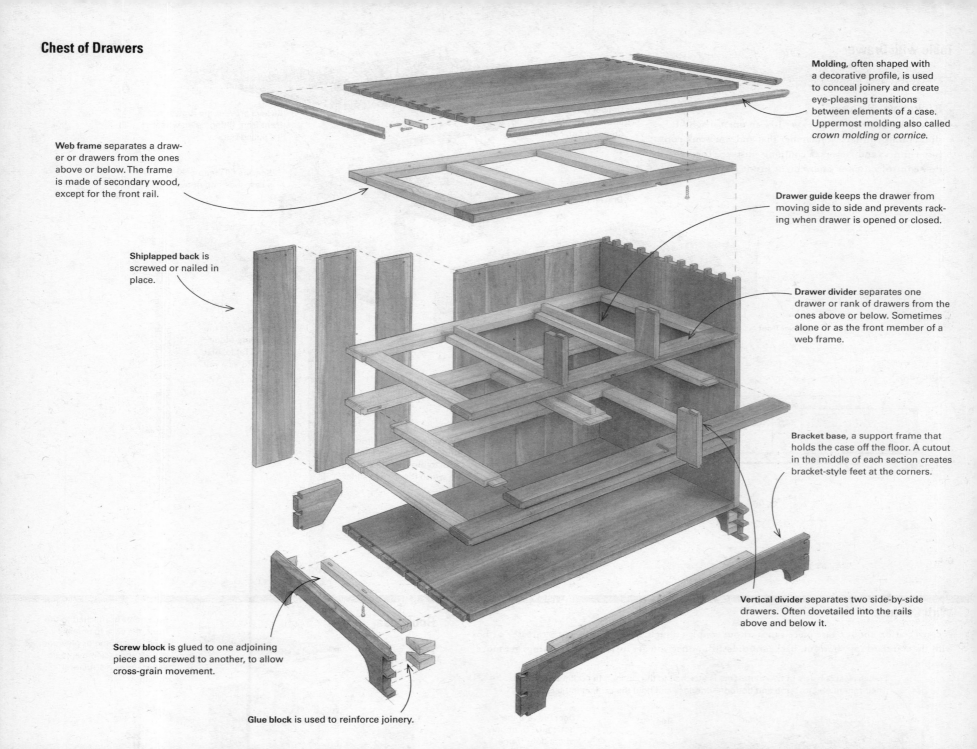

Molding, often shaped with a decorative profile, is used to conceal joinery and create eye-pleasing transitions between elements of a case. Uppermost molding also called *crown molding* or *cornice*.

Web frame separates a drawer or drawers from the ones above or below. The frame is made of secondary wood, except for the front rail.

Drawer guide keeps the drawer from moving side to side and prevents racking when drawer is opened or closed.

Shiplapped back is screwed or nailed in place.

Drawer divider separates one drawer or rank of drawers from the ones above or below. Sometimes alone or as the front member of a web frame.

Bracket base, a support frame that holds the case off the floor. A cutout in the middle of each section creates bracket-style feet at the corners.

Vertical divider separates two side-by-side drawers. Often dovetailed into the rails above and below it.

Screw block is glued to one adjoining piece and screwed to another, to allow cross-grain movement.

Glue block is used to reinforce joinery.

Chairs

The language of chairs pays special attention to the back, the part with the most variety.

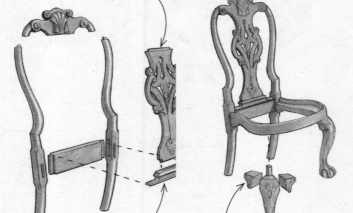

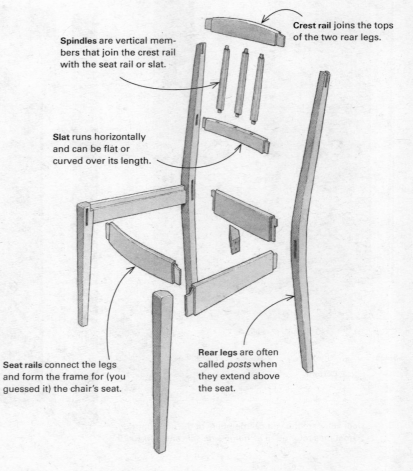

Splat runs vertically. Sometimes decoratively shaped or carved, it can be flat or bent along its profile.

Spindles are vertical members that join the crest rail with the seat rail or slat.

Crest rail joins the tops of the two rear legs.

Slat runs horizontally and can be flat or curved over its length.

Shoe is a block attached to the top of the chair's seat rail, into which the back splat is mortised.

Transition block is attached between a cabriole leg and the chair rail, to blend the curves of the leg into the structure of the seat.

Seat rails connect the legs and form the frame for (you guessed it) the chair's seat.

Rear legs are often called *posts* when they extend above the seat.

BOXES AND SMALL ITEMS

Box Design Tips

by Doug Stowe

I've been making boxes for over 30 years. Indeed, I've made thousands of them and I hope to make a few thousand more in the years to come.

I can't cover decades of box-making knowledge in a single article, but I can share some of the things I consider when designing a box—wood, corner joints, lid, bottom, feet, pulls, and dividers. Armed with a few good options for each element, you'll have no trouble designing all sorts of beautiful boxes on your own.

Box making appeals to me for many reasons. I enjoy the process of design. And because boxes come together more quickly than many other woodworking projects, I have more opportunities to try new designs and learn new woodworking techniques. Consider, too, that you can make a box from bits of lumber left over from larger projects, so wood costs are minimal.

Not only can they be beautiful to look at—masterpieces in miniature—but boxes are perfect for storing everything from jewelry to stamps, and keepsakes to odd change.

Contrast Adds Interest

Unlimited design possibilities open up when you vary the texture and color of the wood or introduce contrasting materials such as stone, metal, or fiber.

Mix the woods. Stowe often makes the sides and top from two different woods, playing with the contrast in color and grain.

Vary the texture. Don't be afraid to explore different textures. Knots, knotholes, and live edges accentuate the natural look of the wood. Rough-carved surfaces encourage both looking and touching. Roughsawn sides married to finished tops and bottoms create interesting visual conflicts.

Resaw for Continuous Grain

I like small boxes to have thin sides, in proportion with the overall scale. Rather than running stock through a thickness planer and wasting a lot of beautiful wood, I get thinner stock by resawing. Resawing also means I can get all of the parts for a box from a single board, with matching grain at all four corners.

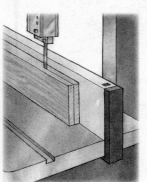

1. On the bandsaw, resaw stock to produce a pair of book-matched halves.

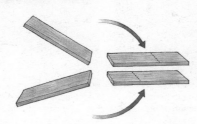

2. Open the halves to put the resawn surfaces on the outside of the box. Cut at the dotted lines to create four sides.

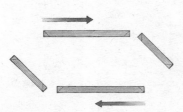

3. Then miter the ends and assemble the box as shown for continuous grain around all four sides.

Choose Corner Joints Early On

Most corner-joint options are more than strong enough to hold together a relatively light box. And joints with minimal strength, like butt joints and miter joints, are easily reinforced. So, most times, I base my choice of corner joint on appearance rather than strength.

Splined miters add interest to the corners, especially when the splines are made from a wood that contrasts with the box sides (left). A hidden, vertical spline works well if you don't want to disturb the appearance of the grain as it wraps around the corners. If the stock is thick enough, you can make the job a little easier by substituting biscuits for splines (center). A more rustic appearance can be had by adding dowel pins to a rabbet joint (right).

SPLINED MITER

Slot for spline

Spline

BISCUITED MITER

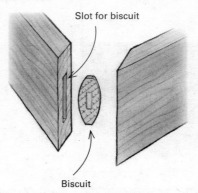

Slot for biscuit

Biscuit

PINNED RABBET

Rabbet joint

Dowel pins

Traditional Favorites

The classic dovetail joint (left) never goes out of style. Feel free to vary the dovetail angle and spacing to get the look you want. Finger joints (right) are also eye-catching and easy to make on the tablesaw using a shopmade crosscut jig.

Don't Overlook the Feet

Add feet to a box and you immediately create a different look. Feet can be as unassuming as small, rounded disks. You also can make feet simply by cutting away some of the bottom edge of each side, or mounting the box to a mitered base frame with the bottom edge cut away.

Sometimes, to give a box a more balanced look, I make an oversize bottom that gives the look of a continuous molding around the perimeter. Generally, I simply round over the edges of this base, and attach it with screws to the bottom edge of the sides. Oversize holes for the screw shanks allow the base to expand and contract in width due to seasonal changes in humidity. Countersink the screw holes so they sit just below the surface.

Rounded disk. A single countersunk screw driven through the bottom of the disk secures it to the corner of the box.

Cutaway sides. By cutting away the bottom edge of the sides, the box effectively ends up with four feet.

Cutaway base frame. Cutting away the bottom edge of a base frame also produces feet.

Oversize flat bottom. An oversize flat base creates the look of a molding around the bottom of the box.

Dividers and Trays Add Versatility

Some boxes become more useful when you add dividers or trays. A box I make for holding stationery has a sliding tray with three routed recesses for stamps and paper clips, plus a groove to hold a favorite writing pen. My jewelry box has a fully divided bottom with additional dividers in a sliding tray. A keepsake box has a mix of six small and three large compartments.

It pays to plan. If you're building a box for a specific use, plan any dividers and trays early in the process. Their size, number, and location will have a lot to do with the ultimate size and shape of the box.

Lid Choices Abound

Design possibilities soar when you start thinking about the lid. Choices include two-part lids (top), sliding lids (center) and rabbeted lift-off lids (bottom).

Lids can be made from a single piece of solid wood or some variation of a frame and panel. I commonly use an overlapping raised panel that locks into the sides of the lid (below).

Space inside the grooves allows room for wood movement caused by seasonal changes in humidity. To allow that movement, it's important not to glue the panel in place.

Two-part lid. Stowe used shopmade wooden hinges here. The hinge pins are brass.

Sliding. You open and close the top on this pencil box by sliding it.

Rabbeted lift-off. Gravity holds this lid in place. A rabbet around the underside of the lid keeps it centered.

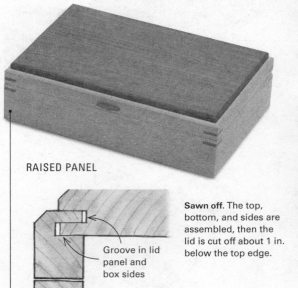

RAISED PANEL

Sawn off. The top, bottom, and sides are assembled, then the lid is cut off about 1 in. below the top edge.

Groove in lid panel and box sides

A Pull Can Push the Envelope

A well-designed pull looks good while making it easier to open a box. Shown here are some of my favorites. There are as many possibilities as there are types of boxes, so don't restrict yourself to only these designs. Add a little imagination and soon you'll be inventing your own.

Turned. Small lathe turnings make wonderful pulls. A single brass screw holds each one in place.

T-shaped. This profile quietly invites the thumb and forefingers, and is good for heavier lids.

Fan-shaped. Rounded and softened edges give this pull a delicate look that works nicely with lightweight lids.

Hinges, from Hidden to Handmade

Sliding and rabbeted lift-off lids can become awkward to use when boxes get around 12 in. square or bigger. At that size, I generally find that hinged lids work better.

Depending on the box design, there are several hinge types that I commonly use. Each type adds a distinctive look.

Wood. Shopmade hinges add to the handmade appeal. The flat version is screwed from the bottom. Wood pins secure an L-shaped hinge.

Leather. Three pieces of leather—two end pieces and a center piece—are secured with brass tacks to create a unique hinge.

Bent-wire. A single bent wire gives a unique look. This one is from Horton Brasses (www.horton-brasses.com).

Flat. Flat stock doweled to a pair of posts adds an Asian flavor. Scale the size up or down depending on the box dimensions.

Front-mounted. Mounted to the front of a hinged lid, the pull serves as a lifting point.

Live-edge. The natural curve of a live edge works perfectly as a lift for some boxes.

Two Fast Ways to Build a Box

by Bill Nyberg

One of the challenges of building a small, decorative box is deciding how to align and attach the top to the base. The most common way is hinges, but they can be time-consuming and fiddly to install. The simple rabbet joint works fine and leaves an attractive, clean look, but it can be troublesome, too.

The traditional method is to create a solid box, cut off the lid on the tablesaw, and then use a bearing-guided rabbeting bit to rout a rabbet on the inside of one piece and the outside of the other. You finish the joint by either squaring or rounding one set of corners and finessing the joint for a good fit. Simple to explain, harder to accomplish. Cleaning up and fine-tuning the inside rabbet is tedium defined, and is done mostly by hand-sanding. I'm sure that's what kept my father—Helge Nyberg—an extremely accomplished woodworker from using a rabbet joint on anything but the fanciest box. The joint is seductive, however.

My cousin Carl taught me a way to streamline the traditional method for a rabbeted lid, and then I came up with a radical new way that I call "the inside-out box." Either technique is much simpler than cutting the rabbets after the box has been glued up. The inside-out method works so well that I use it for functional boxes as well as for fancy work. I'd bet even old Dad would consider it.

The Traditional Method, Streamlined

The traditional method is to cut the box apart on the tablesaw and then rabbet the two parts, which is tedious and fussy. This method combines those steps into one. Also, because the section you need to take out is only the width of a single sawkerf, you can use wood with figure or swirly grain, and you'll end up with almost no jump in the pattern.

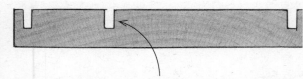

1. Before mitering the sides, cut grooves for the top and bottom in the normal way. But cut an additional groove on the tablesaw to serve as the inside part of what will become the rabbet joint.

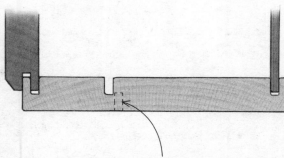

2. After the box is glued up, cut the outside rabbet on the tablesaw. This cut also separates the lid from the base.

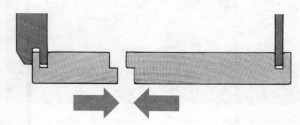

3. The rabbet joint slides together.

The Revolutionary Inside-Out Box

Even the streamlined version of the traditional method leaves an inside rabbet in the lid that is difficult to clean up. But here is a way to build the box inside out, letting you sand the rabbets before assembly. The downside of reversing the box and lid (see drawing) is poor figure and grain continuity. So choose fairly straight-grained boards. Vertical patterns such as tiger maple or small, random figure such as bird's-eye also work well.

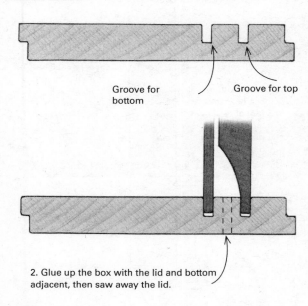

1. Cut and smooth both rabbets on either side of the board when the box sides are one long piece. Also, cut the grooves for the top and the bottom.

Groove for bottom   Groove for top

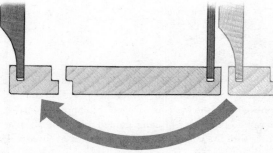

2. Glue up the box with the lid and bottom adjacent, then saw away the lid.

3. Swing the lid around to the top and bring the rabbet joint together.

Option 1: Cut One Rabbet Before Assembly, One After

Take all four sides from one board. Mill it to the right thickness and width (taking into account the width of the rabbet), but leave it a little long to allow for planer and jointer snipe and possible re-dos when mitering.

While you're at the tablesaw, instead of just cutting grooves for the top and bottom of the box, cut the inside rabbet along the entire length of the workpiece. Now miter the corners and assemble the box, inserting the top and the bottom. You can use the masking-tape clamping method or 45° clamping cauls, as shown. Once the glue has dried, use an offcut from the box sides to set the tablesaw fence so that the kerf creating the outside rabbet will be alongside the inside one. Also use the offcut to set the blade height so that it just meets the inside rabbet. Make the cut on all four sides, separating the lid and creating the rabbet joint at the same time.

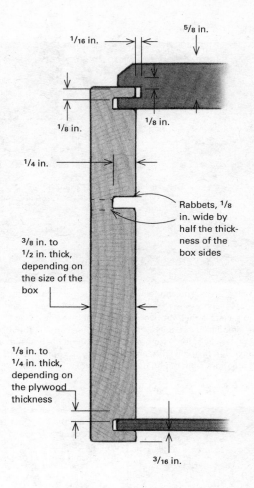

1/16 in.   5/8 in.

1/8 in.   1/8 in.

1/4 in.

Rabbets, 1/8 in. wide by half the thickness of the box sides

3/8 in. to 1/2 in. thick, depending on the size of the box

1/8 in. to 1/4 in. thick, depending on the plywood thickness

3/16 in.

CUT THE FIRST RABBET

One piece, three grooves. While the sides of the box are one continuous piece, cut grooves for the top and bottom panels, and then cut a third groove that becomes the inside rabbet. Use a rip blade for these cuts; it leaves a square kerf.

Continued →

GLUE UP THE BOX

Assemble the box. You can reinforce the miters with biscuits. In any case, apply glue to the mitered ends, place the top and bottom panels in their grooves, and assemble the box. Use 45° blocks, glued to 1/4-in.-thick MDF, to align the clamping force with the joint. Use light force from clamps resting on the bench to align the cauls with the box sides, and then apply the upper clamps, which are more centered on the joint (above).

CUT THE SECOND RABBET

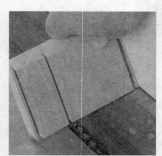

Align the rabbet joint. Use an offcut from the box sides to set the tablesaw fence so that the outside rabbet will just touch the inside one.

Cut the outside rabbet. Run all four sides across the blade, maintaining steady pressure against the fence. A tall auxiliary fence provides greater stability.

The rabbet revealed. Once the fourth side has been cut, the lid will come away, revealing the two halves of the rabbet joint. Sand or plane the rabbets to clean up the saw marks and fine-tune the fit.

Option 2: Make the Rabbets Before Making the Box

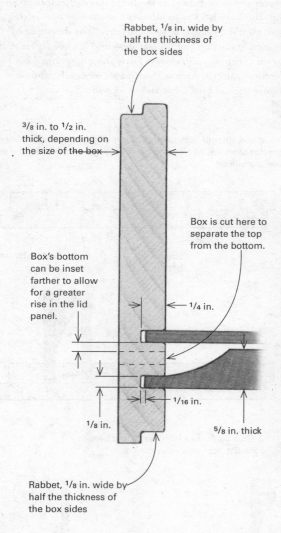

Rabbet, 1/8 in. wide by half the thickness of the box sides

3/8 in. to 1/2 in. thick, depending on the size of the box

Box's bottom can be inset farther to allow for a greater rise in the lid panel.

Box is cut here to separate the top from the bottom.

1/4 in.

1/16 in.

1/8 in.

5/8 in. thick

Rabbet, 1/8 in. wide by half the thickness of the box sides

Mill the board to the same specifications as the first method. Cut a rabbet along both long edges, but on opposite faces, the way you do when shiplapping boards. You can do this with a bearing-guided rabbeting bit in a router, with the same bit or a straight bit in a router table, or with either a regular or dado blade on the tablesaw. Set the depth of the rabbets to just under half the thickness of the wood.

Next, cut grooves for the top and bottom panels. Their precise location is determined by the design of the box and the thickness of the lid panel. A full-size drawing is sometimes helpful to decide exactly where to cut the grooves and where you'll eventually cut apart the box. Before mitering the sides, use a shoulder plane and/or a sanding block to trim and clean up the two fully exposed continuous rabbets. Now assemble the box.

After the glue dries, cut apart the box between the top and bottom panels, switch the positions of the two pieces, and fit them together. If the fit is not perfect, it can be adjusted easily by trimming the half with the exposed rabbet. The interior rabbet is already finished and can be left alone.

Among the benefits of this method is that when the bottom and top are separated on the tablesaw, minor inaccuracies are easier to deal with than if the cut had formed the joint. Joints leave little room for error, but nobody knows if you sand away another fraction of an inch of the top or bottom.

CUT ALL THE JOINERY

Cut rabbets and grooves. Cut the two parts of the rabbet joint on opposite edges of the board. Then cut the grooves for the top and bottom panels.

Easy cleanup. Trim and clean both continuous rabbets with a shoulder plane and a sanding block. Use a short section cut from one end to tell when the rabbet joint comes together flush.

ASSEMBLE THE BOX INSIDE OUT

Use the cauls again. Because the box is open, you can use a spring clamp to hold the cauls to the box sides. Place the top and bottom panels in their grooves with the outsides facing each other, and assemble the box. Align these miter joints carefully, as any inaccuracy will affect the fit of the rabbets.

Cut the box in two. Set the blade height just greater than the thickness of the sides, and cut between the hidden top and bottom panels in a carefully marked location.

The inside-out box. With the cuts complete, the top and bottom of the box are revealed. Sand away the saw marks on the top and bottom edges. The rabbets should need very little trimming.

Four Ways to Top a Box

by Matthew Kenney

Boxes are fun to make and can be a pleasant diversion between larger projects. With a bit of nice wood and a clever design, you can turn out a beautiful box in just a few hours. But there is one part of making a box that is never fun: installing high-quality hinges and getting them just right. And don't forget that you also have to buy them, for a box that might otherwise cost you nothing more than some leftover cutoffs.

You can avoid that hassle by making a box without hinges. Of course, you'll need another way to keep the top on, but the challenge of figuring out how to do that can lead to elegant and unique designs. Here are four great ways to do it. One is mine, one is from a *FWW* author, and two are from *FWW*'s art director and most prolific wood-worker, Michael Pekovich.

1. Inserts Hold the Top in Place

One of my favorite ways to make a box is to glue up the sides, top, and bottom as a single unit. Once the box is assembled, I simply slice it in two. One half becomes the box, the other, the lid. To avoid hinges, you need some way to align the lid with the box. The answer is a handsome liner that extends above the edge of the box and keeps the lid snugly in place.

Cut off the top on the bandsaw. All four edges end up level—something that never seems to happen at the tablesaw, where you cut into one side at a time. To smooth the bandsaw cuts, just rub the parts on a sheet of sandpaper stuck to a flat surface, like your tablesaw's table.

Fit the inserts. Do the two ends first and then the front and back. For each side, miter one end at the tablesaw, mark the length directly from the box, and then miter the second end. The goal is a snug fit, so no glue is needed.

ONE BOX BECOMES TWO PIECES

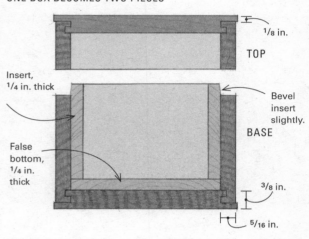

- 1/8 in.
- TOP
- Insert, 1/4 in. thick
- Bevel insert slightly.
- BASE
- False bottom, 1/4 in. thick
- 3/8 in.
- 5/16 in.

Bevel their top edges. Otherwise, the top won't fit easily over them. Mark the inserts so that you know how wide to make the bevels. The only practical way to do the job is with a block plane, because the inserts are small and the bevels are shallow.

Continued →

ROUT THE RABBETS

Align the router table's fence with the bit's bearing. Keep the side pressed down firmly; small deviations in the rabbet's depth are noticeable on a little box. (The groove is for the box's bottom.)

2. One Box Tops Another

I see this box as a stripped-down version of box No. 1. Here, the bottom of the box acts like its own box liner. The lid nests over it almost completely, so lifting it off is like revealing a hidden box. Make the two out of contrasting woods for a more surprising revelation.

TWO BOXES FIT TOGETHER

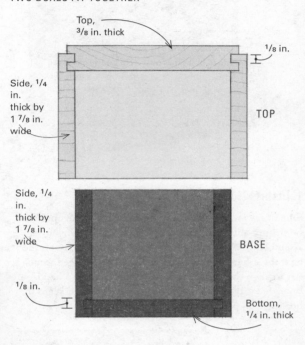

Top, 3/8 in. thick

1/8 in.

Side, 1/4 in. thick by 1 7/8 in. wide

TOP

Side, 1/4 in. thick by 1 7/8 in. wide

BASE

1/8 in.

Bottom, 1/4 in. thick

V-GROOVE BIT DIVIDES BOX

It should be as wide as the divider is thick and set up to cut its full width. Use a large backer board to keep the side square to the bit, and stop the cuts when they reach the bottom groove.

The same bit shapes the divider's ends. Attach a zero-clearance face to your fence and align it with the middle of the bit. You shouldn't need to adjust the bit's height.

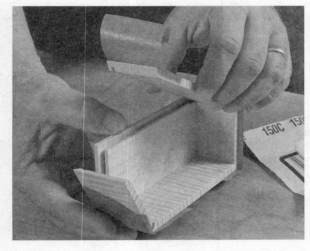

Glue up the top first. Treat it like a box without a bottom, using blue tape at the corners to create clamping pressure on the miter joints.

3. Drop the Top into a Rabbet

I wanted a box with a modern look and a thin top. So I gave a contemporary turn to the old trick of holding the top in a rabbet, putting in a full-height divider that splits the top in two (something that would have required four hinges in a traditional box). By the way, the lifts are attached with cyanoacrylate glue.

Fit the divider. Do it after gluing up the box (use blue tape in place of clamps). If the divider is long, plane a shaving or two from one tip and re-rout it.

How to make the bottom box. Attach an L-shaped fence to a miter gauge to prevent tearout. Start with pieces that are longer than the side's final dimension and make the first miter cut on each one. Then mark each side for final length by putting the mitered end inside the larger box and marking directly from it at the opposite end. To cut it to length accurately, line up the mark with the miter cut in the L-shaped fence on the miter gauge.

Cut the two-panel top. Square one end of your lid stock, mark and cut the longer side to length, and then mark, cut, and fit the shorter one from the adjacent section.

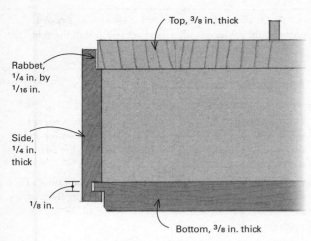

Top, 3/8 in. thick

Rabbet, 1/4 in. by 1/16 in.

Side, 1/4 in. thick

1/8 in.

Bottom, 3/8 in. thick

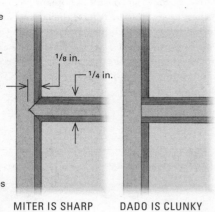

You could leave the divider inside the box, but it looks better full-height, separating the top into two parts. To join the divider to the sides, the best choice is a bird's-mouth joint, because it has a cleaner look that echoes the mitered corner joints.

1/8 in.

1/4 in.

MITER IS SHARP   **DADO IS CLUNKY**

4. Tip the Lid and Stand It Up

The lid of this box is a more sophisticated version of a lid in a rabbet, with the rabbets functioning like a hinge. The side rabbets are sloped at the back and the back rabbet is deeper than the other three. To open the box, you press on the back of the lid, bringing up the front edge so you can grab it. It rocks gently into the back rabbet, which holds it upright.

1. Press down. Because the side rabbets are tapered toward the back, the lid's front edge raises up.

2. Lift. The back edge turns smoothly down the rounded corner of the side rabbets, as if it were hinged.

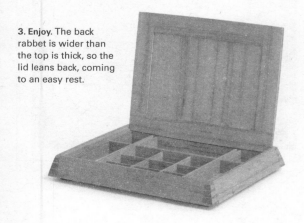

3. Enjoy. The back rabbet is wider than the top is thick, so the lid leans back, coming to an easy rest.

MODIFIED RABBETS ACT LIKE HINGES

The back rabbet functions like a built-in stop, holding the lid slightly past vertical so that it won't fall forward.

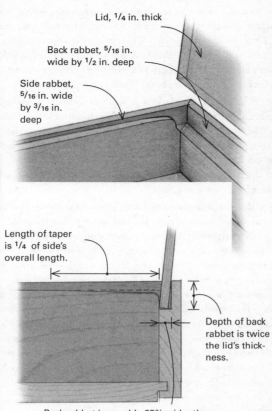

Lid, 1/4 in. thick

Back rabbet, 5/16 in. wide by 1/2 in. deep

Side rabbet, 5/16 in. wide by 3/16 in. deep

Length of taper is 1/4 of side's overall length.

Depth of back rabbet is twice the lid's thickness.

Back rabbet is roughly 25% wider than thickness of top.

Start with straight rabbets. The back one is deeper to hold the standing lid. Next, square off the end of the side so that the miter doesn't stick into the back rabbet. Then taper the side rabbet. Start at the back corner and take a slightly longer stroke each time. The final stroke should be the taper's full length.

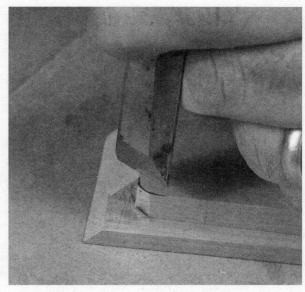

Round the ends. Pencil in the layout. Then use a flat chise, making a big chamfer first and then nibbling away ever smaller facets. Smooth the arc with sandpaper.

Handsome Tool Chest

by Steve Brown, head of Woodworking at the North Bennet Street School

Originally conceived simply as a place to put your tools, the tool chest project has become a familiar step in the two-year Cabinet and Furniture Making curriculum at the North Bennet Street School. Though simple in design and appearance, it challenges our students in genuine and surprising ways. They learn the value of planning the order of tasks; fitting the actual pieces, not just working from the drawing; and choosing between various methods and techniques.

This tool chest is the students' first major project, so we've narrowed the parameters to make sure that the focus stays on the craftsmanship and not the overall design and dimensions. Primary woods can be maple, cherry, walnut, or mahogany. Choices for secondary woods are soft maple, poplar, and pine (for drawer parts only). We allow students to use highly figured woods only for the panels. This tool chest (16 in. deep by 24 in. wide by 14 in. tall) is at the small end of our size range, but students can build them up to 18 in. deep by 30 in. wide by 17 in. tall. Drawer size and configuration is another place where individual designs vary, and so is the frame-and-panel lid.

The typical chest starts with a drawing, scaled or full-size, and consists of a through-dovetailed carcase with dovetailed drawers running on mortise-and-tenoned divider frames. The lid provides a means of locking the box as well as an introduction to setting a full-mortise lock. Above the top divider is a space to put the lid when the box is unlocked.

Continued ➡

Although every aspect of building this tool chest—from the dovetails to the shiplapped back—creates a valuable learning experience, I can't go into all of it in one article. Here, I'm going to focus on machining the dadoes and rabbets, fitting and installing the horizontal dividers, cutting and fitting the vertical dovetailed partition, and installing the lid and its hardware. Not designed to be portable, the chest looks great on a countertop, or fits neatly under a typical workbench.

Plenty of Learning Opportunities

There is nothing stronger than a dovetailed carcase, and dovetails are one of the fundamentals of woodworking. So the choice for the carcase joinery is a natural. With the panels cut to length and width, the dovetails can be laid out, cut, and fitted all by hand. At NBSS, we start with pins and then scribe and fit the dovetails. Once all four corners are dry-fit, we check the case for square before laying out the dadoes and rabbets. A very important component of the layout is that the front and back edges of the case must be flush to serve as consistent reference surfaces.

How to cut stopped dadoes safely on the tablesaw— The dadoes hold the divider frames securely. But they also provide the opportunity to learn layout principles and techniques, as well as safe and effective ways to make plunge and stopped cuts.

The key is to reference from the inside surfaces of the case while it is dry-fitted, with joints closed and the case square. From the inside face of the case bottom, use a marked story stick to transfer the dado locations to the inside faces of the case ends.

Use a marking gauge off the front edges of the case to lay out the front end of the stopped dado. Because the front is already flush, the front edges of the divider and the drawer fronts will lie in the same plane, in front of the stopped dadoes. The dado will run out the back edge, so it will show in the rabbet until it is covered by the shiplapped back.

Once the dadoes are laid out, I cut them on the tablesaw with a 1/2-in.-wide dado set because it's faster and easier than cutting them with a router. One of the most important safety rules in the NBSS shop is that we never do stop-cuts on the tablesaw without a clamped block backing up the workpiece. The process requires careful layout, labels to help with orientation, and mental focus. Because you are working on the two opposite sides and it's safest to keep the end of the panel closest to the dado against the rip fence, each pair of dadoes involves one plunge and one stopped cut. So for every dado you are either plunging in at the front and running out the back, or starting through the back and stopping at the front. Mark the fence to show the extent of where the blade will cut to know where to stop and start.

We finish the dadoes with a router plane for consistent depth, and square up the ends to the layout lines with a chisel.

Rabbets are the next step—After the dadoes, cut the rabbets for the case back. The rabbets in the top and bottom run all the way through. I lay out my pins so they are at least as wide as the rabbet, and that allows me to run the rabbet through them. The sides get stopped rabbets on each side. I cut them on the tablesaw as I would the dadoes. The only difference is that each piece has a plunge cut and a stopped cut instead of one or the other.

Drawers Run on Mortise-and-Tenoned Frames

The drawer dividers live in the dadoes in the sides and provide a place for the drawers to ride, and the top one creates a spot for the lid when it's tucked away. Simple mortise-and-tenon joints keep them together. We use a router table with a 3/16-in. bit for the mortises and cut the tenons on the tablesaw. When milling the parts, leave them slightly thick so their fit in the dadoes can be fine-tuned with a handplane.

After gluing up the frames, clean up the glue, flush the joints, and skim any mill marks with a handplane. Check

the length of the frame to the space from dado to dado. Trim the frame if needed. Test-fit the thickness of each frame to its dado. If the frame has been skimmed, plane only the bottom of the frame to fit. Once each frame fits in its dado, skim the front edge of each frame with a handplane, and then lay out the notch and trim with a handsaw. Check the front edges for alignment relative to the case front. If both the stopped dadoes and the frame notches were laid out and executed carefully, the frames' front edges should lie in a plane. If not, adjust them.

The top drawer divider is laid out so there is enough space above it to store the lid. It also has brackets attached to the front, which act as a stop for the lid. They lie in the same plane as the stepped stop at the bottom of the case, which I make by gluing a slightly oversize block to each side of the front of the divider, shaping it at the bandsaw, and cleaning it up at the bench.

Bottom drawer runs on a different system—You've created the spaces for the lid and most of the drawers, but the bottom drawer space isn't complete. The bottom drawer rides on a stepped stop (which is also a transition from the plane of the drawer fronts and door stop) and blocks glued in behind it. The dimension between the front edge and the top fillet or step has to be accurate, as does the position of the piece in the case. An effective way to guarantee this is to make the distance between the steps a hair larger than needed. Dry-clamp the stop in place, according to the back step. Then glue in the first block behind the stop, making sure not to glue the stop yet. Now you can check and adjust the front step as needed and accurately position it when gluing it in.

Dovetailed partition—A requirement of the project is that one level of drawers be divided by a vertical dovetailed partition. Before gluing the divider frames in, lay out and fit the dovetailed partition. Again, use a story stick to establish its location. Often a student's first inclination is to align one divider with the other and mark the top and bottom of the partition. Our method is to use a story stick and reference off one of the inside faces of the case. The results are more consistent this way.

Locate the first side of the dado for the partition. The shoulders of the dovetail are sunk into a 1/8-in. dado in the dividers. This registers the partition and gives it rigidity that the dovetail alone doesn't.

After notching the partition so that the shoulders bottom out in the dado, the front 1/2 in. of the partition becomes the dovetail. Make the dovetail and, using a sharp pencil, scribe the socket lines onto the dividers. These lines are transferred to complete the socket layout. Once sawn and pared to the lines, the dovetail is test-fitted to the socket. If adjustments are needed, do them to the socket.

With dividers and partition fitted, dry-clamp everything so you'll know your procedure and what clamps are needed. Glue is only applied to the front 3 in. to 4 in. of the dado. The rest of the frame needs to be free enough for the case to expand and contract. The clamps should be ready to pull the frame tight to the front given the real possibility of the joint grabbing before it closes fully.

A Handsome Lid and Well-Fitted Drawers

Size the lid frame to fit the lid space created in the front of the case. After making the frame, dry-fit it and mark the groove depths on the face of the frame to outline the panel sizes. This provides the exact size for the panels.

Raise the panel on the tablesaw and then fit it by hand with a rabbet plane. Prefinish the panels before gluing them into the frames.

A well-fitted drawer is a hallmark of our program. We want a drawer that slides in and out easily and quietly, with only enough clearances for its function and wood movement.

First, fit the drawer parts to their corresponding spaces. You want no gaps at this point. I cut the drawer back 1/32 in. shorter than the front to aid in the fitting process. Once the drawer is dovetailed and glued up, check it for wind by setting it on a flat surface. If needed, correct it with a smoothing plane before fitting.

As for the back of the chest, I make the shiplapped parts on the tablesaw with a dado set and install them by counterboring and using round-head screws.

Add the Hardware and Finish

The lid is held in place by pins and sockets on the bottom edge and the full-mortise lock in the top edge. I put the lid in place to lay out the location of the pins and sockets and drill the small holes, and then the hardware simply presses into place.

The lock set is a matter of a deeper mortise with a shallow hand-cut mortise so the whole piece sits flush in the lid, and a shallow strike plate mortised in the top to catch the bolt.

Before applying finish I handplane, scrape, and sand the chest up to P220 grit. I use shellac and wax on the interior and areas of sliding contact. On the exterior, I wipe on Minwax Fast-Drying Polyurethane. After the first coat, I sand with P400 grit. After the second coat, I smooth the surface with steel wool and wax with Boston Polish butcher's wax.

Lid Stows Away

A secure lid. A lock mortised into the top edge and two pins on the bottom hold the lid in place.

Dedicated storage space. When not locked in place, the lid tucks neatly away in the space between the top drawer and the top of the chest.

Dovetailed Tool Chest

Through-dovetails are an attractive, traditional joinery option for this tool chest, but the lesson doesn't end there. Mortise-and-tenoned dividers, a dovetailed partition, and a frame-and-panel lid round out the list of furniture fundamentals you'll learn as you make the chest.

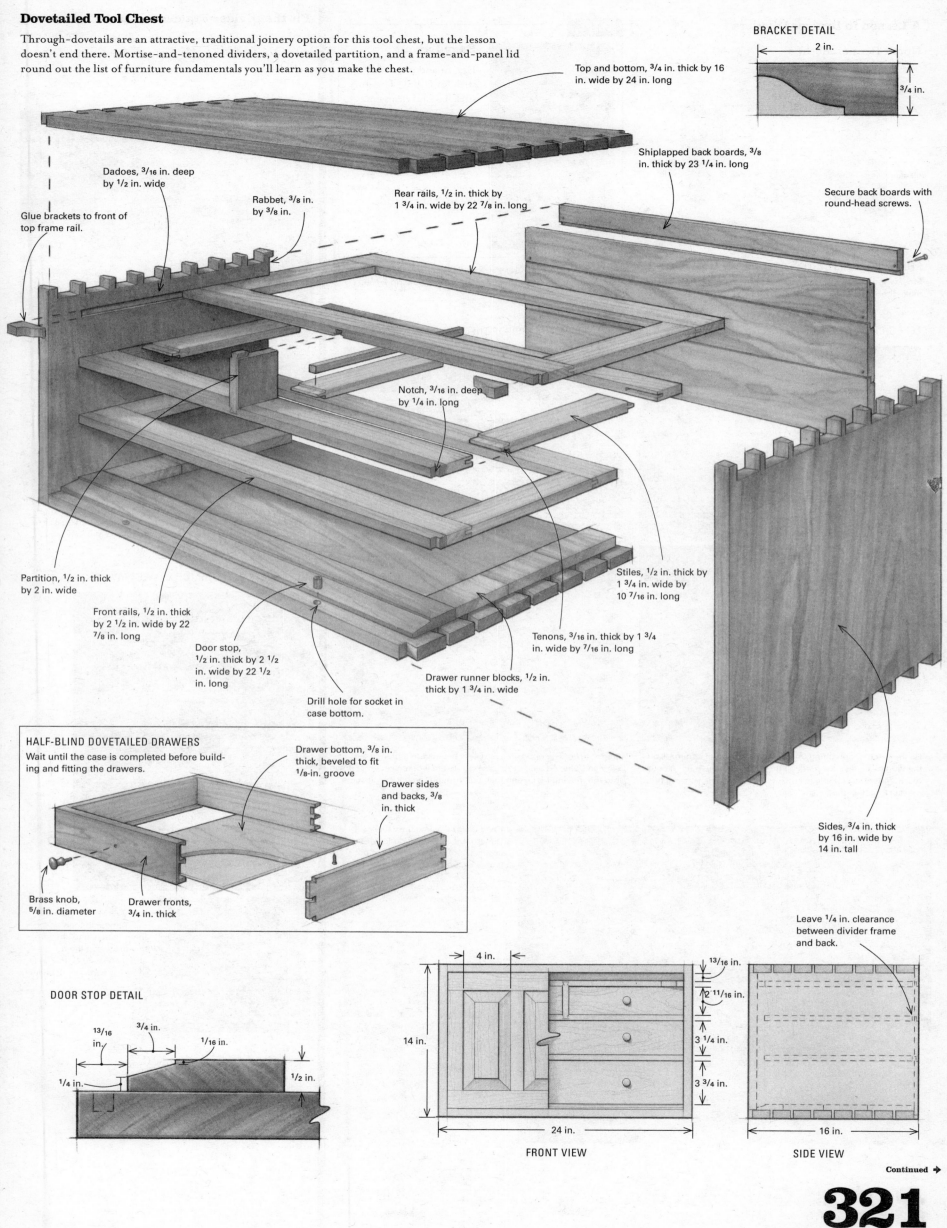

BRACKET DETAIL

2 in.

³/₄ in.

Top and bottom, ³/₄ in. thick by 16 in. wide by 24 in. long

Shiplapped back boards, ³/₈ in. thick by 23 ¹/₄ in. long

Secure back boards with round-head screws.

Dadoes, ³/₁₆ in. deep by ¹/₂ in. wide

Rabbet, ³/₈ in. by ³/₈ in.

Rear rails, ¹/₂ in. thick by 1 ³/₄ in. wide by 22 ⁷/₈ in. long

Glue brackets to front of top frame rail.

Notch, ³/₁₆ in. deep by ¹/₄ in. long

Partition, ¹/₂ in. thick by 2 in. wide

Front rails, ¹/₂ in. thick by 2 ¹/₂ in. wide by 22 ⁷/₈ in. long

Door stop, ¹/₂ in. thick by 2 ¹/₂ in. wide by 22 ¹/₂ in. long

Drill hole for socket in case bottom.

Drawer runner blocks, ¹/₂ in. thick by 1 ³/₄ in. wide

Tenons, ³/₁₆ in. thick by 1 ³/₄ in. wide by ⁷/₁₆ in. long

Stiles, ¹/₂ in. thick by 1 ³/₄ in. wide by 10 ⁷/₁₆ in. long

Sides, ³/₄ in. thick by 16 in. wide by 14 in. tall

HALF-BLIND DOVETAILED DRAWERS

Wait until the case is completed before building and fitting the drawers.

Drawer bottom, ³/₈ in. thick, beveled to fit ¹/₈-in. groove

Drawer sides and backs, ³/₈ in. thick

Brass knob, ⁵/₈ in. diameter

Drawer fronts, ³/₄ in. thick

Leave ¹/₄ in. clearance between divider frame and back.

DOOR STOP DETAIL

13/16 in.

3/4 in.

1/16 in.

1/4 in.

1/2 in.

4 in.

14 in.

24 in.

13/16 in.

2 11/16 in.

3 1/4 in.

3 3/4 in.

16 in.

FRONT VIEW

SIDE VIEW

Continued ➡

A Lesson in Drawer Dividers

North Bennet Method

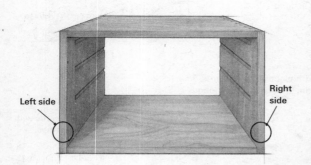

Left side — Right side

TIP

Easy Layout

Dry-fit and use a story stick for layout. The story stick has one clean end and knife nicks along the edge to indicate the dadoes. Reference from the inside faces of the sides and the bottom. Then carry the marks to the back of each side.

STOPPED DADOES ON THE TABLESAW

Most woodworkers do these with a plunge router, but a dado set is faster. To keep the same reference end against the rip fence, make these stopped cuts in both directions.

LEFT-SIDE DADOES: CUT THEN LIFT

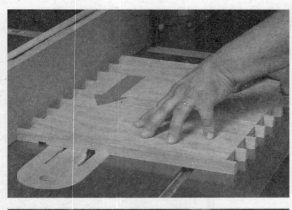

Go then stop. Start cutting into the side. When the end mark on the workpiece meets a mark on the fence, use the miter slot to reach under the workpiece and lift it off the blade, keeping the pressure against the fence.

RIGHT-SIDE DADOES:DROP THEN CUT

Stop then go. The opposite dado cuts begin with a plunge cut. With an L-shaped stop block backing up the workpiece, pivot down into the moving blade and then cut through the back of the side.

Hand tools complete the dadoes. Square the end of the dado with a chisel, and clean out the bottom with a router plane.

Fit the Divider Frames

Simple mortise-and-tenon frames are carefully fit into the dadoes and notched at the front, but not glued in until later.

Test-fit the dividers. If the fit needs adjustment, plane the bottom face of the frame to fit. That way, if there is tearout or any other issue, it won't be noticeable. With the dividers pushed up against the end of the dado lay out the notch and use a handsaw and chisel to cut it.

ADD BRACKETS TO THE TOP DRAWER DIVIDER

Glue, then shape. It's easier to glue oversize blocks to the frame and then shape them than it is to shape tiny pieces on the bandsaw and then try to clamp these irregular parts to the divider.

Dovetailed Partitions by Hand

When there are only one or two vertical partitions, Brown cuts their small dovetails by hand.

North Bennet Method

Dry-fit and use a story stick. Use the story stick to mark the near side of the partition and then the actual partition to mark the far side. Now remove the two dividers and cut the shallow dadoes in them. Before fitting the partition into its dadoes, clamp in a spacer block. Base it on the space at the ends of the drawer pocket.

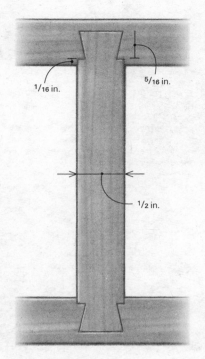

1/16 in.

5/16 in.

1/2 in.

DOVETAILED PARTITION

Angled guide block makes the dovetail easy. Chop the dovetail, transfer the location to the divider, and cut the socket.

Lid Is a Good Place to Show Off Grain

The panels are the only place where students are allowed to use highly figured wood, and these molded panels are an ideal place to showcase beautiful grain.

Prefinish the panels. Brown applies the polyurethane finish to the panels before gluing them into the frames so seasonal movement doesn't expose unfinished wood.

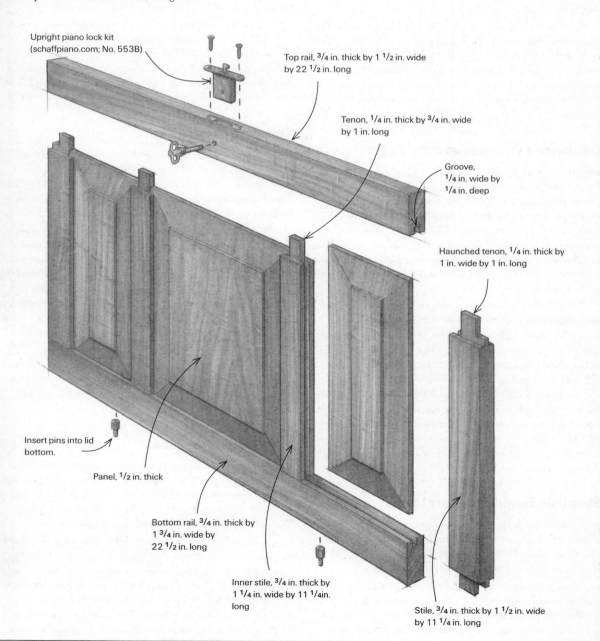

Upright piano lock kit (schaffpiano.com; No. 553B)

Top rail, 3/4 in. thick by 1 1/2 in. wide by 22 1/2 in. long

Tenon, 1/4 in. thick by 3/4 in. wide by 1 in. long

Groove, 1/4 in. wide by 1/4 in. deep

Haunched tenon, 1/4 in. thick by 1 in. wide by 1 in. long

Insert pins into lid bottom.

Panel, 1/2 in. thick

Bottom rail, 3/4 in. thick by 1 3/4 in. wide by 22 1/2 in. long

Inner stile, 3/4 in. thick by 1 1/4 in. wide by 11 1/4 in. long

Stile, 3/4 in. thick by 1 1/2 in. wide by 11 1/4 in. long

Pins and sockets keep the lid in place. Basic brass hardware (rockler.com; No. 32334) is pressed into holes drilled into the case and lid bottom.

Continued ➜

Blanket Chest by Hand

by Andrew Hunter

Trends in furniture come and go, but Early American country furniture endures. Country pieces, with their simplicity and practicality, can find a home in any setting, from an 18th-century farmhouse to a New York City loft. The clean, unpretentious designs, born of necessity, have an honesty that gives them lasting beauty. But for a woodworker, the real beauty of country furniture is in the making. Everything from fine dovetails to clinched nails is appropriate as joinery, and eastern white pine—the wood of choice for so much Colonial furniture, and my choice for this chest—is a dream to work.

Country designs are ideal for building solely with hand tools, and the classic six-board chest is a great project for developing your skills. It is small enough not to overwhelm yet chock-full of enjoyable joinery. One can work without the pressure to be perfect. Imperfections and stray tool marks in a country piece only add to the feeling of authenticity. Although I'll demonstrate using only hand tools, you can choose your battles depending on the skills you have or wish to develop.

Preparing the Boards

My father and I sawed up a large white pine tree 10 years ago, and I've made a number of country pieces with those beautiful planks. But even though pine is my preference, any locally abundant, easily worked wood fits the bill for this project. And while I had the luxury of using full-width boards for my chest, you can always glue up narrower boards if wide boards are not available, matching two boards to look like one or simply using random boards for an uncalculated country look.

I milled all the stock for my chest with hand tools. Of course, you could mill your wood with a jointer and planer instead, and begin the hand-tool work after that. Once you have straight, flat boards, rip and crosscut the four main boards and the lid to their final dimensions. But leave the bottom boards and the lid cleats wide and long for now.

Construction Work Begins at the Bottom

Start the joinery by laying out and cutting the grooves for the bottom boards and the cutouts that form the feet. Locate the grooves in the mitered section of the corner joints, so they can be through-grooves, which are much easier to cut. Plow these grooves before you make the cutouts so you still have the bottom edge of the sides to use as a reference surface. I used a grooving plane with a fence for this job. Alternately, you could use a panel saw with a guide block and a chisel.

Next come the arched openings. To lay them out, I made templates cut from cereal-box cardboard. I first drew a number of curves freehand, and when I had one I liked, I made a template from it. To be sure the two ends of the cutout were mirror images, I made the template for just half the opening and used it to lay out both sides. I cut out the curves with a bowsaw and followed it up with spokeshaves and chisels to smooth the cut and fair the curves. You could use a coping saw, or even make multiple relief cuts with a handsaw and chisel away the waste. The best tool is the one you have—making do goes along with the country theme.

Story Pole Simplifies Joinery Layout

Accurate layout is the most important part of the project, and I try to focus all my attention while I'm doing it. After that I can relax a little and just enjoy working wood—all I have to worry about is not going over the lines.

Start by laying out the baselines for the dovetails on all four boards in pencil with a sliding square. Because the dovetails will be proud, set the square to the thickness of the stock plus 1/16 in. Leaving the dovetails proud is not

just an aesthetic choice. Over time, as the wood moves, joints that are cut flush don't stay exactly that way, and protruding joinery will accommodate any such changes. With the baselines marked, locate the pins and the mitered foot with a story pole. Using a story pole will ensure that all four corners of the chest are laid out identically.

I drew the pin cheeks using a bevel gauge set to about 14°. Then I used a marking gauge to score the baseline of the pins. The tail layout waits, since you'll trace the tails from the pins. Take care when laying out the mitered foot—because the dovetails are proud, they'll extend 1/16 in. past the point of the miter.

Create the Dovetail Pins

I used a Japanese ripsaw to cut the cheeks of the dovetail pins, but of course a Western saw will get the job done, too. I cut the dovetails while sitting on a stool with the board lying on my bench. This puts the workpiece at eye level for great control of the cut.

With the cheeks sawn, begin chopping away the waste between the pins, chiseling about 1/16 in. from the scored baseline. Be sure the workpiece is well supported beneath, since any give will steal force from the chisel blow. Working in soft wood, such as pine, there's a greater tendency for end-grain tearout. To minimize it, use low blade angles on sharp chisels and give firm blows, working from both sides toward the middle. To protect my bench, I support the board at both ends on scraps of 1/4-in. plywood.

After chopping close to the baseline, pare away the rest of the waste, inserting the chisel point into the scored line. Then pare the cheeks, working up to the pencil line but leaving it as a reference.

Pins Generate the Tails

To trace the pins, lay the tail board on the bench with its outside face down. Then stand the pin board along the tail board's shoulder line. If the pin board has any cup, use a caul and clamps to keep it straight while you are tracing. The joinery will keep the boards flat after assembly.

With the pin board in place, make a short pencil mark to register the location of each pin. Then remove the pin board and use the bevel gauge to complete the lines. Use a square and the bevel gauge again to transfer the layout to the second face. When you've finished the layout on all four joints, saw the tail cheeks. Then use a narrow chisel to chop close to the baselines. Because the space between

the tails is so narrow, I used a narrow chisel, tapped into the end grain, to split the waste so I could remove it as I chopped. After paring to the baselines, pare the cheeks as well.

The last part of the joint to be cut is the mitered section at the foot. First, with the workpiece clamped so the feet are pointing up, make the angled crosscut. Then clear the waste with an angled ripcut. Clean up the sawcuts by paring with a chisel.

Getting Ready for Glue-Up

Before test-fitting the corner joints, put a slight chamfer on the ends of the pins. Go slow with the test-fitting, using light blows and a scrap block to protect the project. If the going is tough, separate the parts by hammering down on the tail board, check for excessive denting, and pare where necessary. When you've made the bottom boards, dry-fit the case to see that they are a good fit.

Once all the parts are fitted, disassemble the chest and use a smoothing plane set very fine to put a finished surface on all the parts. Then plane a small chamfer on the exposed edges. Handplaning the surfaces was my final finish—I didn't apply any coating. The sheen of the wood is from the keenness of the plane blade, and the lustrous surface will attain a rich patina over time. Dents, scratches, and stains will attest to its years of usefulness.

Bringing the Box Together

Assemble the chest with a bit of glue on the pins only, and try to keep any squeeze-out to the inside where it can be cleaned with a chisel after it dries. I used hide glue, which gives me more time for assembly and also means that in the future parts can be reglued, since new hide glue will bond with old.

I did the glue-up with the back of the chest lying facedown on the bench. I fit the two ends to it, and then fit the bottom boards. I didn't use any glue on the bottom boards, although you could put a dab at the center of each one, as long as you ensure there's a gap between them to allow for seasonal movement.

Put a Lid on it and Add Appropriate Hinges

Two quartersawn hardwood cleats in dovetailed sockets keep the chest's lid flat yet allow for seasonal movement. To excavate the sockets, I started with a saw and finished with chisels. I used a Japanese panel saw, which has a convex head, enabling me to start a cut in the middle of the board.

After sawing, clean out the waste with a long chisel or a router plane. Then plane the cleat to its layout lines and test the fit in the socket. The cleat should stop 1/4 in. before the closed end of the socket to allow the lid to move with the seasons. Hammer the cleat home and mark it to length. Also mark where the back edge of the cleat will need to be relieved to allow the lid to sit flat. Remove the cleat one last time and make the two cuts. The cleat, which gets no glue, is fixed at the back end by the snipe hinge.

Cotter-pin or "snipe" hinges, common in Colonial furniture, are a simple way to attach the lid, and they function quite nicely, with the added benefit of securing the cleats. You can make them from 1/8-in. steel rod or simply use cotter pins from the hardware store. To install the hinges, drill holes where the back and top meet, centered on the cleats. Loop the cotter pins together and slide them through their holes. With pliers, fold the tips outward 90°. Then hammer each leg over, supporting the blows from below.

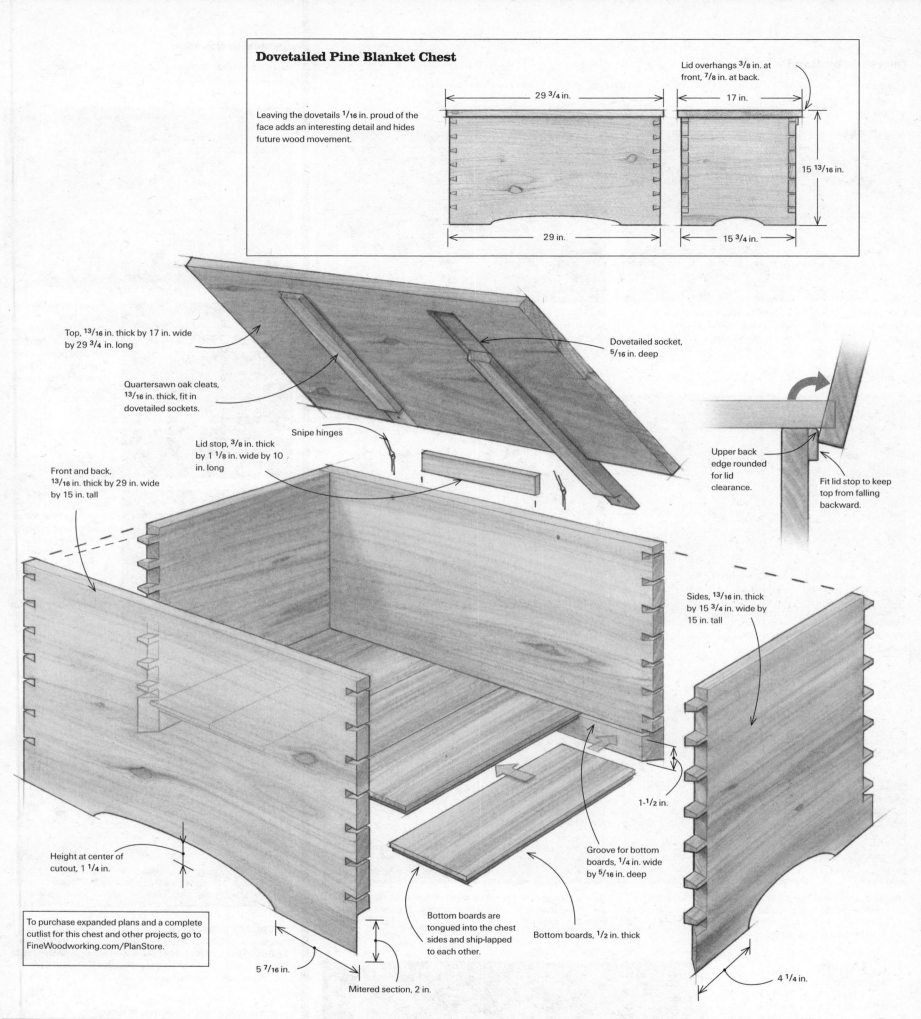

Dovetailed Pine Blanket Chest

Leaving the dovetails 1/16 in. proud of the face adds an interesting detail and hides future wood movement.

Lid overhangs 3/8 in. at front, 7/8 in. at back.

29 3/4 in.

17 in.

15 13/16 in.

29 in.

15 3/4 in.

Top, 13/16 in. thick by 17 in. wide by 29 3/4 in. long

Dovetailed socket, 5/16 in. deep

Quartersawn oak cleats, 13/16 in. thick, fit in dovetailed sockets.

Lid stop, 3/8 in. thick by 1 1/8 in. wide by 10 in. long

Snipe hinges

Upper back edge rounded for lid clearance.

Fit lid stop to keep top from falling backward.

Front and back, 13/16 in. thick by 29 in. wide by 15 in. tall

Sides, 13/16 in. thick by 15 3/4 in. wide by 15 in. tall

1-1/2 in.

Height at center of cutout, 1 1/4 in.

Groove for bottom boards, 1/4 in. wide by 5/16 in. deep

Bottom boards are tongued into the chest sides and ship-lapped to each other.

Bottom boards, 1/2 in. thick

To purchase expanded plans and a complete cutlist for this chest and other projects, go to FineWoodworking.com/PlanStore.

5 7/16 in.

Mitered section, 2 in.

4 1/4 in.

START WITH THE GROOVE

After milling and cutting the boards to size, begin the chest by cutting the groove for the bottom boards. A grooving plane makes short work of the task. Then create the cutouts at the bottom of the chest, sawing close to your layout lines with a bowsaw or coping saw and smoothing the surfaces with spokeshaves and chisels or files.

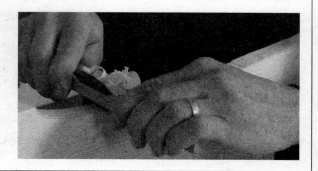

Dovetails by Hand

These protruding dovetails also have a short miter at the bottom, giving the chest a clean base section.

1. LAYOUT

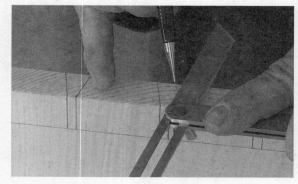

Mark and score. Hunter lays out the dovetail pins with a mechanical pencil and a sliding bevel, then scores along the baseline, in the waste areas only, with a marking gauge.

Mark the miters. When you lay out the 45° miters on all four boards, begin at the baseline. The miter's tip should end 1/16 in. shy of the end of the board. The dovetails need the extra length, since they're proud.

2. PINS COME FIRST

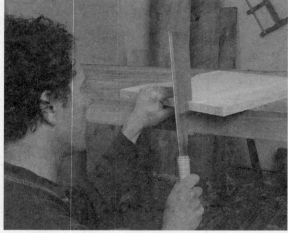

Rip the pins. Hunter saws just shy of his layout line, then pares right to it, leaving the line for reference.

Chop and pare. Chop away the waste between the pins with heavy blows, leaving 1/16 in. or so along the baseline. Follow with paring cuts, starting with the tip of the chisel in the score line. Work from each face of the workpiece toward the middle to avoid blowout.

3. TAILS FOLLOW

Two-step layout. With the pin board simply standing along the baseline on the tail board, Hunter makes a short pencil mark inside each pin cheek. Then he removes the pin board and extends the marks with a sliding bevel.

Saw, chop, and pare. Saw close to your lines, and then chop out the waste, staying away from the baseline. Last, pare to all of your layout lines.

4. MITER THE FEET

Cut all of the miters now. Cut the mitered faces first with a ripsaw. Then saw in from the side to cut the waste free. Use paring cuts with a chisel to clean up the miters, and fit one to the next.

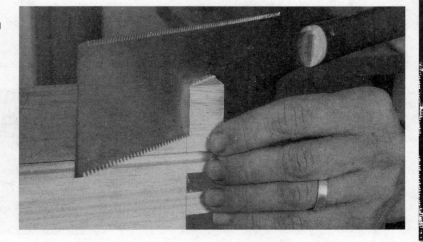

Assemble the case

After a few final steps and a dry-fit, you can glue up the whole case in one shot.

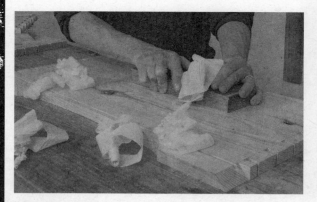

Final touches before assembly. With all the joinery cut, Hunter creates a glassy finished surface with light passes of a Japanese smoothing plane and chamfers all exposed edges.

Tiny chamfers are a big help. Chamfered edges give the proud dovetails a distinctive look and also make assembly go more smoothly.

RABBET THE BOTTOM BOARDS

SHOPMADE RABBET FENCE

Quick rabbets. To cut the tongues and shiplaps on the bottom boards, Hunter fits his rabbet plane with a simple shopmade fence. To prevent tearout on cross-grain cuts, he scores the workpiece with a marking gauge.

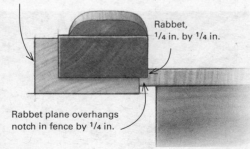

Scrap of solid wood notched to fit rabbet plane is held in place during cut.

Rabbet, 1/4 in. by 1/4 in.

Rabbet plane overhangs notch in fence by 1/4 in.

GLUE UP THE CASE

Knock home the ends. After applying hide glue to the cheeks of the pins, Hunter hammers home the joint. Then he installs the bottom boards. Scraps of 1/4-in. plywood under the case accommodate the through-dovetails.

Proud and square. Seat the joints with a scrap block placed just inside the pins. Then measure the diagonals to check for square. If necessary, pull the chest into square by lightly clamping from corner to corner.

Top it Off

Tapered dovetailed cleats are the backbone of the lid. Simple snipe hinges are its elbow joints.

CLEATS KEEP THE LID FLAT

Cleat socket layout

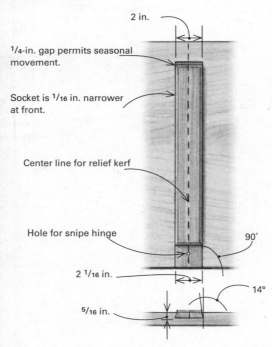

2 in.

1/4-in. gap permits seasonal movement.

Socket is 1/16 in. narrower at front.

Center line for relief kerf

Hole for snipe hinge

90°

2 1/16 in.

14°

5/16 in.

Cleats fit in a dovetailed socket. The socket, tapered slightly along its length, is 1/16 in. wider at the back of the lid than the front.

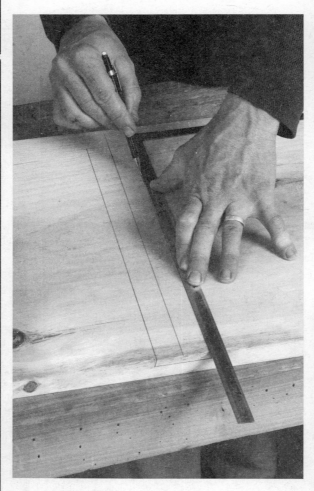

Automatic angle. A block of scrap cut to a 14° angle guides the saw to cut the dovetail socket. Hunter draws a line on the sawblade with an erasable marker to gauge the depth of cut.

Rough removal. Working toward himself with the bevel down, Hunter chisels out all the waste, first on one side of the central relief cut, then on the other.

Out comes the long chisel. Hunter flattens the bottom of the cleat socket with a long, wide paring chisel. He checks his progress with a straightedge.

Continued ➔

Two-Sided Standing Picture Frame

by Christian Becksvoort

I have a black-and-white woodcut print and a piece of needlepoint that are dear to me. Since wall space is limited in my house, I decided to make a free-standing frame to display them. Both pieces of art fit in the same frame, one on each side facing out, and the frame can be placed on a tabletop, shelf, desk, dresser, anywhere you have free, flat space—at home or in the office. The frame also makes a great gift.

Because both sides are visible, I knew this frame would be a bit trickier to design than a typical, wall-hung picture frame. I also needed a way to take apart the frame, should the artwork ever need to be replaced.

The frame required a relatively wide base to stand on. Playing around with several designs, I settled on a wide base, a narrower top, and through-tenons on the uprights to allow for disassembly. Although the frame dimensions will vary depending on what it is to hold, the building process can be adapted to any size.

Cut the Joints

Once you've measured both pieces of art, added a proportional border/mat, and come up with an overall dimension, you can rough out the frame parts for the base, the top, and the two sides. Use a drill press to rough out the mortises in the top and the base.

Cut the through-grooves in the two sides, and then move on to the stopped grooves in the top and bottom pieces. The grooves line up with the mortise holes and run between them.

Square up all four mortise holes in the bottom and top. Both the top and bottom now have a groove centered on the wide faces, ending at the square mortises.

Cutting tenons on the sides of the frame is the last structural operation. With only one height setting, I cut the tenons on the tablesaw using a wide dado blade. Small bevels on the tops of the tenons make the frame easier to assemble.

Simple Anatomy

The sleek design and basic mortise-and-tenon joinery in this standing frame make it a quick project and a great gift.

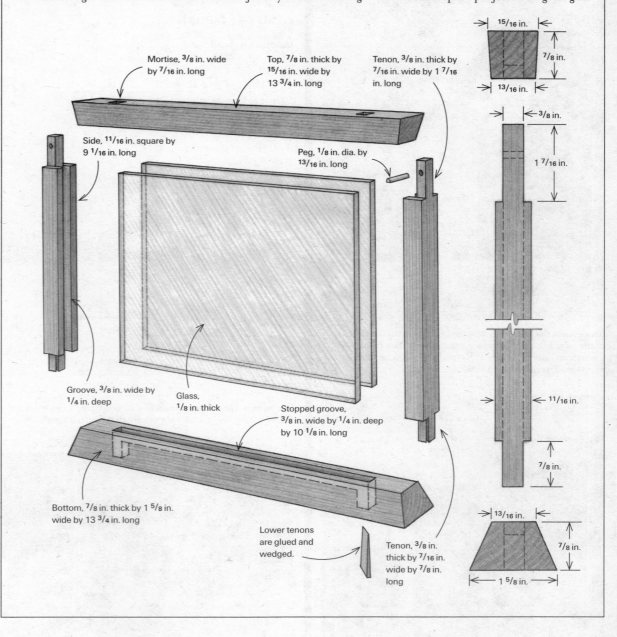

Mortise, 3/8 in. wide by 7/16 in. long

Top, 7/8 in. thick by 15/16 in. wide by 13 3/4 in. long

Tenon, 3/8 in. thick by 7/16 in. wide by 1 7/16 in. long

Side, 11/16 in. square by 9 1/16 in. long

Peg, 1/8 in. dia. by 13/16 in. long

Groove, 3/8 in. wide by 1/4 in. deep

Glass, 1/8 in. thick

Stopped groove, 3/8 in. wide by 1/4 in. deep by 10 1/8 in. long

Bottom, 7/8 in. thick by 1 5/8 in. wide by 13 3/4 in. long

Lower tenons are glued and wedged.

Tenon, 3/8 in. thick by 7/16 in. wide by 7/8 in. long

15/16 in.

7/8 in.

13/16 in.

3/8 in.

1 7/16 in.

11/16 in.

7/8 in.

13/16 in.

7/8 in.

1 5/8 in.

Grooves, Bevels, and Mortises are Simple to Make

Start on the drill press. Drill through the top and bottom, centering the mortise holes in the stock.

Through-grooves on the sides. With a straight bit on the router table, run through-grooves on the two side pieces.

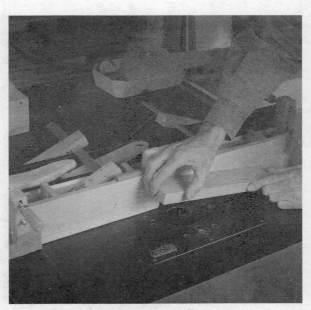

Stopped grooves in the top and bottom. With two stop blocks clamped to the fence so that the bit lines up in the mortise holes at each end, pivot down into the first hole with the router running, run the groove, and lift the workpiece out of the second hole.

Assemble the Frame

When I was working out the original design and the artwork and glass panes were in place, everything fit well but looked too clunky. So, to give it a lighter appearance, I ripped a bevel down the sides of the top and bottom and crosscut an angle on each end.

Once you've completed the joinery and beveling, sand all the parts to P220-grit and glue the sides to the bottom, wedging the tenons diagonally on the underside. Plane and sand the bottom flush. With the frame fully assembled, but without the artwork or glass, take a knife and mark the spot where each tenon protrudes through the top. Then remove the top and drill holes through the tenons, using shims so the tenons lie flat and are supported on the drill-press table. I make sure the hole overlaps the knife marks by about $1/2$ in. By offsetting the holes like this, the dowels with a flat sanded on one side are then forced into the space, pulling everything tight.

Using a dowel plate, make two dowels out of any very hard, tight-grained wood such as apple, rock maple, dogwood, or hornbeam. Begin with square stock and use a knife to cut a series of bevels around the end. Rounding the ends helps start the stock in the dowel plate. Then simply hammer the stock through the dowel plate. Fit the dowels (see photos, below) and cut them to length. The dowels are removable with hand pressure, although if you insert them in January and then want to open the frame in August, it helps to have a small block to push the dowels out.

Finally, I applied two coats of Tried & True Danish Oil, polishing the first coat with 0000 steel wool after it dried.

Tenons, Wedges, and Pegs Keep the Frame Together

Quick and easy tenons. Using a dado set, miter gauge, and the rip fence as a stop, form the tenons on the side pieces.

Lower tenons are wedged. Saw a diagonal kerf in the bottom tenons. When the wedges are tapped in, the tenons will spread in all directions.

Tap in wedges. Glue the sides into the bottom, set the top in place for clamping, glue the wedges, and tap them into place. Saw the tenons and wedges flush, and then smooth the bottom with a block plane.

Chisel the mortises square. Now square up the mortise holes all the way through the top and bottom pieces.

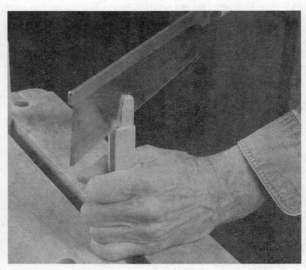

Bevels lighten the look. Becksvoort rips a bevel down the length of the top and bottom, refining the look.

Angle the ends, too. With the tablesaw blade still tilted from the bevel, use a miter sled and cut angles on the ends of the top and bottom.

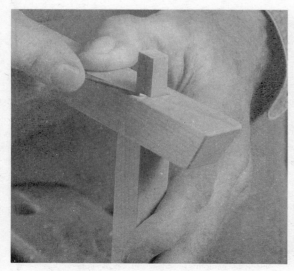

Dowels secure the top. Dry-fit the frame to mark for the dowels. Mark the point where the tenon protrudes. Drill a hole at that point, overlapping the knife mark by about $1/32$ in.

Flatten the dowels to create a perfect fit. Sand a flat into each dowel and then insert it, flat side against the top of the frame, until hand tight.

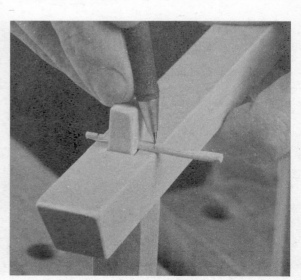

The final cut. Mark the dowels and cut them to length, flush with the sides of the frame.

Show off Two Pieces of Art in One Frame

Installing artwork is a breeze. Just sandwich the art between two glass pieces and slide the package into grooves in the bottom and sides. The mortised and grooved top fits onto the sides, and dowels lock it all in place.

Style Cutting Board with Inlay

by Scott Lewis

When I was asked to make a cutting board as a special gift, I wanted to do something new and eye-catching. Tired of squares and straight lines, I envisioned curving accents—not shallow inlay, but strips extending through the full thickness of the board so they would be visible on the top, bottom, and both ends. I drew some flowing S-curved lines, and one soon overlapped another. I liked the way they looked, but I thought, how am I going to make all the curved pieces nest together perfectly?

When I broke the process down, it was actually quite simple. I make the through-inlays as bent-laminations: Each accent line is made of thin, flexible strips sandwiched together to look like a solid piece of wood. The critical step is getting the solid parts of the cutting board to fit together. After routing a shallow groove in the blank using a curved template, I bandsaw most of the waste from the groove and use a flush-trimming bit to remove the rest from each half. When I add the inlay strips, the curves match exactly.

Although the three lines of through-inlay in my cutting board differ in thickness and appear to have different shapes, I use a single template to do all the routing required to establish their paths. I trim the inlays flush once they are glued in. So far, I've only used the technique on cutting boards, but I can also imagine using it on chair backs, box lids, or cabinet doors.

One Template Guides the Routing

I create the through-inlays one at a time—gluing in the first one, then trimming it to length and flushing it off before beginning work on the second. I use different diameter router bits for each inlay, but just the one router template. By flipping the template and moving it laterally, I get different results for each line of inlay.

To design the curves, I sketch freehand right on the cutting-board blank, keeping in mind that I will have to bend the strips to that shape, so the curves can't get too crazy. And to avoid problems with wood movement, I keep the inlay curve roughly parallel with the grain of the cutting board.

When I have a curve I like, I transfer it to a piece of tracing paper cut to the size of the cutting-board blank. Then I tape the paper to a piece of ³⁄₄-in. MDF and bandsaw along the line. So that the router will be supported at the beginning and end of the cut, I make this template several inches longer than the cutting board.

For tight gluelines, the curves of the template must be free of bumps and dips, so I bandsaw carefully and sand with a flexible sanding block. If you mess up a template, you can try again with the offcut.

To prevent the router from tipping while using the template, I hot-glue a ³⁄₄-in.-thick piece of scrap to the router base. I rout the paths for the through-inlays in a number of shallow passes. When the groove is about ¹⁄₄ in. deep, I bandsaw first along one wall of the groove and then the other, leaving just a bit of waste to clean up on the router table.

If you push the halves of the cutting board together now, the curves won't match. Add the through-inlay—which is exactly as thick as the routed groove—for a perfect match. I make the individual inlay strips ¹⁄₈ in. thick, and they flex easily around the curves. I cut them about ¹⁄₄ in. wider than the thickness of the cutting board so that during glue-up they extend slightly above and below the board. I also cut the strips over length by about 6 in. This allows me to cut off any planer snipe. Even minimal snipe is noticeable when a number of strips are stacked together.

Interesting Assembly

Having sliced your cutting board apart, you may look at the two halves and think, "What have I done?" Not to worry; with the right clamps and clamping cauls, the whole thing will come back together. The glue-up is a bit of challenge, though, since you have to clamp in three directions.

I glue up the cutting board on a flat bench and use shopmade cauls that have notches to accommodate the inlay. I use a quick-grip-style clamp to bring the halves most of the way together, squeezing the stack of inlay strips to the curved shape. I then add pipe clamps with light pressure to close the joint. Next, I tighten clamps on the notched cauls that hold everything flat and push the inlay strips into place. As I tighten the pipe clamps, I check that the ends of the halves line up.

After glue-up, I use a handsaw to cut the inlay to length, then rout it and scrape it flush. Then I start the process over to add the subsequent inlay strips.

When I've finished the inlays, I bandsaw the sides of the cutting board to gentle curves and sand them smooth. Then I give the edge a radiused profile and cut finger grips into the ends.

I sand all surfaces with P150 grit, and sand the end grain to P220. Before wrapping this gift and mailing it off, I coat it with my favorite food-safe finish—mineral oil, which never goes rancid and is easy for the owner to maintain.

One Template Handles All the Curves

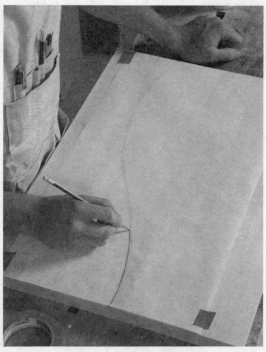

Sketch a pleasing curve. Lewis begins by sketching an S-curve freehand on the cutting-board blank, keeping it roughly parallel with the grain. He transfers the curve to tracing paper, which he tapes to ³⁄₄-in. MDF and bandsaws out to make a template.

Make it smooth. Fairing the template's curves is vital, since any bumps could be visible in the inlay gluelines. Lewis used the tablesaw to cut slots in a piece of MDF, creating a pliable sanding block that conforms to convex and concave curves.

Cut the Board Apart

MAKE ROOM FOR THE INLAY

By routing away the same amount of material he is adding, Lewis ensures perfectly mating curves and tight gluelines. It's vital to start with a blank that's dead flat so that everything goes back together properly.

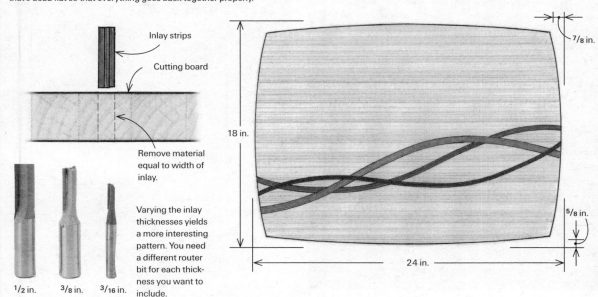

Inlay strips

Cutting board

Remove material equal to width of inlay.

Varying the inlay thicknesses yields a more interesting pattern. You need a different router bit for each thickness you want to include.

1/2 in.   3/8 in.   3/16 in.

18 in.

24 in.

7/8 in.

5/8 in.

1. ROUT A GROOVE

Template-routing a 1/4-in.-deep groove creates smooth, accurate reference edges for the next steps. Get to final depth in multiple passes.

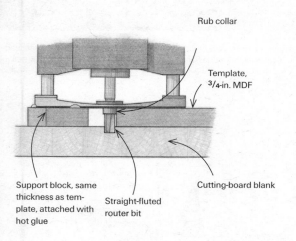

Rub collar

Template, 3/4-in. MDF

Support block, same thickness as template, attached with hot glue

Straight-fluted router bit

Cutting-board blank

2. SAW OUT THE CENTER

Before sawing, Lewis darkens the corners of the groove with a pencil for visibility. Then he carefully bandsaws the waste, staying 1/16 in. away from each wall of the routed groove.

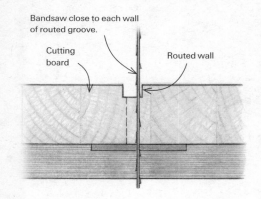

Bandsaw close to each wall of routed groove.

Cutting board

Routed wall

3. FINISH WITH A FLUSH CUT

Placing the workpiece groove-side down on his router table, Lewis flush-trims the bandsawn surface with a 1-in.-dia. straight bit, guided by a bottom bearing.

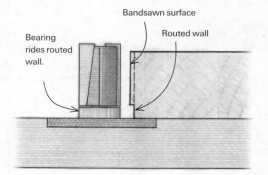

Bandsawn surface

Routed wall

Bearing rides routed wall.

Glue It Back Together

FIT THE STRIPS

Dial in the thickness. Lewis uses melamine-coated MDF as an auxiliary bed to keep the thin strips from getting chewed up in the planer, bending the strips to create downward pressure at the point of the cut. A straight groove cut in a piece of scrap tests the pack of strips for a perfect fit.

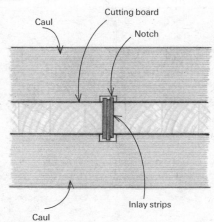

This glue-up takes some guile. A quick-grip clamp, with its pump action and long travel, is ideal for making the flat strips conform to the S-curve.

Caul

Cutting board

Notch

Inlay strips

Caul

Hold it flat. Cauls with shallow notches center the inlay strips. Lewis uses a deep-reach clamp (left) to adjust end-to-end alignment of the cutting board's halves.

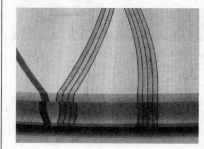

Verify the alignment. Before putting on the final pipe clamps, Lewis uses a notched piece of MDF (left) to make sure the halves are lined up perfectly.

ADD VARIETY WITH PIN STRIPES

For a jazzy alternative, try adding thin commercial veneers between each of the thicker strips.

331

Smooth and Repeat

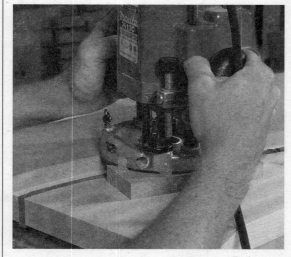

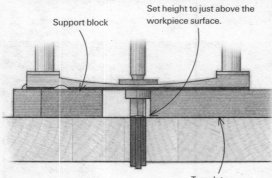

Support block

Set height to just above the workpiece surface.

Template

A few steps to smooth strips. After cutting the end of the inlay flush with a handsaw, Lewis uses a router to get it close to flush with the surface. Then he uses a card scraper for final smoothing.

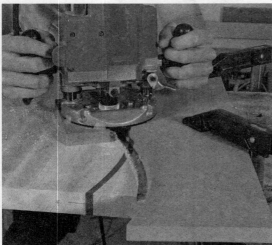

Repeat for additional strips. With the first strip glued in and flushed off, Lewis starts the process for the second strip. After repositioning the template on the cutting board, he routs a new groove, bandsaws away the waste, and flush-trims it on the router table. He clamps the new curve, and when that is all glued up and scraped flush, he repeats the process for the third strip.

Shape the Profile

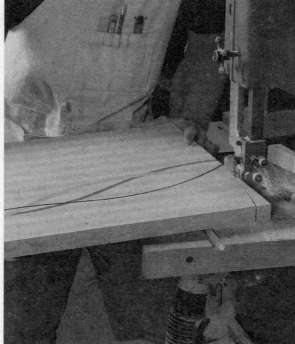

1-in. radius roundover bit

Cutting board

Use just a portion of the bit.

Soft edges. After bandsawing and smoothing the cutting board's curved perimeter, Lewis gives the edges a shallow radiused profile. He uses the top section of a 1-in. roundover bit, taking light passes.

Finger grips in a curved surface. To rout the finger grips on the curved ends of a cutting board, Lewis makes a curved fence for the router table. He uses a fluting bit and takes multiple shallow passes. He controls the length of the finger grip by adding end stops to the fence.

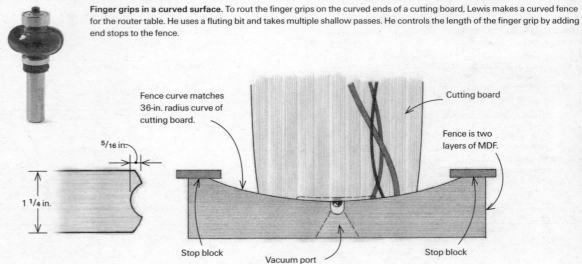

Fence curve matches 36-in. radius curve of cutting board.

Cutting board

Fence is two layers of MDF.

5/16 in.

1 1/4 in.

Stop block

Vacuum port

Stop block

Veneer Chessboard

by Craig Thibodeau

At some point in your woodworking life, you'll probably make a chessboard. The classic parquet pattern adds fun and function to an ordinary table. And a stand-alone chessboard makes a great gift.

If you haven't worked with veneer, you may be tempted to make your game board from thick squares of solid wood. Don't. You'll have to contend both with wood movement and weak end-grain joints. Veneer is much easier to cut accurately and is easy to apply to a stable MDF substrate. Also, veneer is available in hundreds of beautiful species and grain patterns. By the way, the following technique works for other parquetry patterns, too, such as diamonds.

Standard chessboard squares range from 2 in. to 2½ in. square, but you can size the squares to fit the chess pieces you have on hand.

Chessboard or chess table? Add solid-wood edging for a simple chessboard that can be stowed away, or incorporate the veneered panel into a table design of your choosing, like Thibodeau's Art-Deco-style game table.

Veneer Taping 101

Because of the V-groove that a knife or veneer saw leaves behind, it's important to keep track of your "glue face" and "show face," as they are called. When cutting the veneer, keep the glue face on top, which guarantees that the lower edges of all of your cuts meet cleanly on the opposite show face. And generally, as you assemble any veneer pattern, you bring the pieces together by using blue masking tape on the glue face, and then thin moisture-activated veneer tape goes on the show face. When the veneer tape is dry, you peel off the masking tape and you are ready to apply the veneer to a substrate.

Simple Jig Ensures Accuracy

Start by making a straight block of hardwood or plywood roughly ¾ in. thick by 20 in. long. Rip it precisely 2 in. wide, and stick coarse sandpaper to the bottom to help keep it in place. This will be the guide you use to cut the strips of veneer into equal squares, so make sure the sides of the jig are truly straight and parallel.

When cutting with the veneer saw (a single-bevel marking knife or razor also works), make sure the blade stays 90° to the cutting guide so you will have square edges on the strips. If you decide to use a more delicate veneer for your squares, such as burl or heavily figured woods, it may be necessary to cover the face of the veneer with a layer of veneer tape to prevent chips and breakage along the cut line. Cut a sample strip or two to check.

Using your guide, cut one straight edge on each piece of veneer. Start with a light pass just to create a path for the blade, and then bear down a bit more on the next few strokes until the waste veneer falls away cleanly. Next, align one edge of the guide with the cut edge of the veneer and cut the first 2-in. strip. Repeat this process, using the straightedge as the sizing guide, until you have four dark strips and five light strips or five dark and four light—it doesn't really matter. Ensure that all of the strips have clean edges free of tearout and chips, and replace any damaged strips.

Strips Become Squares

Now use blue masking tape to create an array of alternating strips, applying the tape on the glue face, where you did your cutting. Start by just taping across the joints every 2 in. or so, and then run long pieces of tape along the joints.

The next step is to square off one end of the veneer sheet. This is critical, so use an accurate square to line up your guide. Now use the guide to crosscut 2-in.-wide strips from the veneer sheet until you have eight equal strips of alternating squares.

All of the strips now need to be flipped over to the show face so you can see the veneer and align the squares when taping. Just flip one strip at a time end for end so they stay in order and the grain remains aligned. Now slide every other strip down one square to create the chessboard pattern. Use more blue tape to join the strips one at a time, being careful to align the intersections of the squares. Use enough tape to hold the joints together but don't run tape along the entire joint at this time. Peel away the overhanging squares that remain outside the playing surface and you have your chessboard pattern. These blue tape strips on your show face are for alignment only, so your taping is far from over. It goes quickly, though.

Whole Lotta Taping

To get the veneer tape where it belongs, you need to flip the pattern over again and cover the other side with blue tape, pulling it across the joints first and then putting long strips along the joints.

Now flip it over once more and remove the small amount of blue tape from the show face. Then apply moist veneer tape to this face one long strip at a time, making sure the strips overlap slightly and cover the entire chessboard. When all the wet strips are in place and burnished, place the entire veneer assembly under a piece of MDF or plywood for a few hours. Otherwise the wet tape will distort the veneer and pull the squares apart as it dries.

After the tape has dried, trim off any overhanging pieces with a razor knife, and remove all of the remaining blue tape from the glue face.

Tips for a Handsome Border

A nice way to create a transition between solid-wood edging and chessboard squares is to add a decorative veneer banding, in a color that contrasts with both chessboard colors and the edging. Black is an easy choice, but any contrasting veneer will create a transition.

Before you add any decorative banding, it is likely that the outside edges of the chessboard pattern will need to be straightened slightly. Line up the straightedge with each side of the pattern and trim just enough veneer to clean up any misalignment of the squares.

Now, using your guide, slice four ¼-in.-wide strips of banding veneer. Flip the pattern over so the veneer tape is facing up and lay a strip of blue tape around the perimeter

leaving about half overhanging. Flip the sheet again and begin sticking the banding strips onto the tape, pressing the banding strips up against the chessboard to create tight joints. Allow the banding strips to overlap each other at the corners.

Now you miter the corners simply by aligning the cutting guide at 45° on each corner and cutting through both pieces of banding with a razor knife. Remove the excess pieces, and then press the mitered corner together, pulling it tight with a piece of blue tape across the joint if necessary. Once the corners are finished, do the whole tape dance again. Apply blue tape to the joints between the banding and the chessboard pattern. Flip it over and remove the blue tape from the veneer-tape side. Check for tight miter joints, and veneer tape all along the banding line, and then stick the whole thing under that piece of MDF again.

Now Turn It Into a Real Chessboard

Cut your MDF substrate as close as possible to the size of the veneer pattern but not smaller, and join and cut a backer veneer too. Normal yellow glue works fine, and the panel is small enough that you can use clamps to do the pressing, as opposed to a vacuum bag. Scuff-sand the MDF on both sides to help with adhesion.

Use MDF or particleboard cauls for the glue-up, a layer of thin cardboard to spread the pressure, and thin plastic sheeting to resist the glue. You'll need plenty of clamps, and either some deep-reach versions or bowed cauls to get pressure in the center of the panel.

Apply an even layer of glue, and then carefully place your veneer (tape side up) on the substrate and press it all over to help secure it. Then quickly tape it in place with several pieces of blue tape wrapped from the backer veneer over the top of the chessboard veneer.

After the panel is dry, remove the veneer tape. Wet the surface with a sponge, allow the tape to soften, then peel and scrape it off. You'll also need to clean up the edges of the panel before gluing on solid-wood edging. I find it easiest to sand one edge flat with a hard block and some 60-grit paper, before placing that flat reference edge against the fence of a crosscut sled on the tablesaw. Trim 1/16 in. off each of the four edges, or whatever it takes to get the miters of the veneer edging to line up perfectly at the corners.

Then fit and glue mitered pieces of solid wood to the edges, just as you would with any veneered or plywood tabletop.

Chessboards are beautiful and functional, and look great in a variety of tables.

A Short List of Supplies

VENEER

Standard commercial veneers work great for this project. For a 2-in. grid you'll need two pieces of contrasting veneer, each about 10 1/2 in. wide by 18 1/2 in. long. If need be, you can cut the strips from a narrower stack of matching veneer. For a more decorative pattern, try alternating the grain direction of one color. Use an even darker wood for the banding at the edges, and don't forget to veneer the back to prevent the panel from warping. Any species will do there.

SQUARES

BACK

EDGING

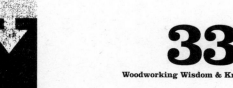

TAPE

For initial assembly, you'll need blue masking tape. It has some stretch to it, so when you pull on it as you apply it, it draws the pieces together tightly. It also peels off easily. Moisture-activated veneer tape goes on next and stays on until the veneer is applied. I prefer the wide, thin variety (34-gram, 50 mm veneer tape; from veneersystems.com), which covers more ground and is easier to remove after your panel is done and dry.

VENEER SAW

You can use a razor knife or a sharp veneer saw to do the cutting, but I greatly prefer the veneer saw because it cuts quickly, and doesn't tend to follow the grain of the veneer and wander off the cut line. Veneer saws are inexpensive, but they require a quick tuneup with a fine file. It only takes a few minutes, and then you are ready to make perfect cuts.

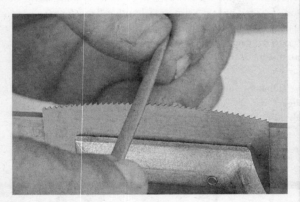

Quick tuneup. First, sharpen the teeth with a fine file, following the angles already established. Then bevel the outside edge to bring each tooth to a sharp point. Last, knock the burr off the back.

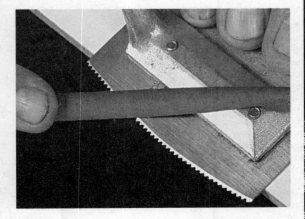

From Strips to Stripes to Squares

PRECISE STRIPS

Straightedge doubles as a template. Make a plywood guide exactly as wide as your desired squares, and use it to guide a sharp veneer saw. Glue sandpaper on the bottom to keep the guide from slipping. For each new strip, line up the guide with the edge you just cut, and simply saw along the opposite side.

Tape the strips together. Use blue tape to pull the strips together tightly and then tape each seam. Alternate four of one color with five of the other; it doesn't matter which.

Burnish for a better bond. Here's a tip for both blue tape and veneer tape: Burnish them with a brass-bristle brush after applying, and they will hold much better.

THE CHESSBOARD EMERGES

Crosscut the strips. Use the guide again, setting up the first cut with a framing square.

Blue tape for assembly. Keep the strips in order as you create the chessboard pattern. Work on the show face, which allows you to see the alignment clearly. Just a few pieces of tape are fine here, and then flip to the glue face and put blue tape both across the seams and along them.

Veneer tape locks in the pattern. Peel off the small pieces of blue tape from the show face. Then veneer-tape the entire surface, overlapping the pieces slightly and trimming away the excess. Draw the tape across a wet sponge to dampen it. After the veneer tape has dried, remove the blue tape from the opposite face.

Finishing Touches

ADD MITERED BANDING

Blue tape again. Put a strip around each edge of the show face, leaving about half of the tape overhanging. Then flip the pattern over.

Place the banding. Pull it tight to the edges of the pattern as you press it down, and simply overlap the ends.

Cutting guide strikes again. Line up your cutting guide with the corners of the overlap, and use a sharp knife to cut through both layers. Remove the waste pieces, and you should have a perfect miter. Do the blue-tape dance again to get veneer tape on the show face and you are ready to lay up the panel.

MOUNT THE PATTERN ON A PANEL

Veneer both sides. Get your clamps, cauls, glue, and other materials together, and start with the backside veneer when making the sandwich. Put glue on the substrate only, using a roller or a finely notched spreader to control the amount.

Lock it down quickly. Wrap a few pieces of tape around the bottom and top veneers to keep them from curling or sliding around.

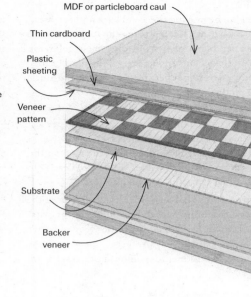

MDF or particleboard caul
Thin cardboard
Plastic sheeting
Veneer pattern
Substrate
Backer veneer

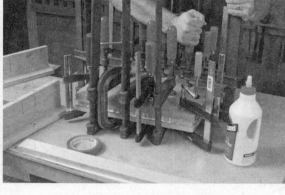

You don't need a vacuum bag. A vacuum bag is easier, but clamps and cauls will work, too. If you come up short on clamps, add extra cauls to distribute the pressure.

CLEAN UP THE EDGES

Use a crosscut sled. Start by scraping and sanding the squeeze-out off one edge, and put that edge against the fence on your crosscut sled. You might need to add a shim to align this first cut.

Turning a Pen From Scraps

by Barry Gross

More furniture makers should try turning a pen. You already have most of the tools you need, you probably have the wood, and if you've done any wood turning at all, you have the skills. Not only is pen turning fun, but pens also make great gifts both for the recipient and for the maker. In the time you'd spend making a box—never mind a small piece of furniture—you can make half a dozen pens and get six heartfelt thank-yous instead of one.

Pen turning can be done on any lathe with a few specialized tools. I'll tell you which of these tools are essential and which ones can be duplicated by tools you probably already own. I'll tell you what pen hardware to buy, what woods work well, how to turn and finish the blanks, and last, how to assemble the pen.

Preparing the Pen Blank

Woodworkers often ask me what wood makes the best pen and I half-jokingly reply any wood they rejected for furniture making. Examples include gnarly or crotch sections of boards, isolated patches of figure or curl, or even pieces of firewood with spalting in it. Remember, you want a blank that is less than 1 in. square by 5 in. long. For this reason, burls are a good choice because their tight, swirly grain pattern is the right scale. If the scrap bin or the firewood pile is exhausted, one of the benefits of wood turning is the opportunity to try new and exotic species such as amboyna burl, lignum vitae, or red palm for $2 to $8 a blank. You can also buy eye-catching composite woods and acrylic blanks.

Once you've selected the pen kit and the material for the body, you can get started. Depending on whether your kit has a one-part or two-part body (or barrel), place the pen tube(s) on the pen blank and mark it for length, adding $1/16$ in. to each end. Label the sections and then cut the parts to length.

What makes pens different from a typical spindle turning is the long hole through the center, and the metal tube(s) you glue into it. You can drill the pen blank on the drill press or on the lathe. For the former you'll need to clamp the blank and ensure it is in line with the drill bit. On the lathe, a dedicated pen-drilling chuck is the easiest way to center the blank to the drill bit, but you also can hold the workpiece in a four-jaw chuck.

Once the pen blanks have been drilled, glue the tubes into them. Roughen the outside of the pen tubes with 80-grit sandpaper. I also size natural or unstabilized wood by dripping some thin cyanoacrylate (CA) glue down the holes. Both actions give the glue for the tubes a better surface to bond to. When it is dry, place some medium-thick CA glue or 5-minute epoxy on a piece of glossy paper or plastic, roll a tube in it, and then use a specialized insertion tool or a nail punch to hold the pen tubes so you do not get glue all over your fingers. Push the tubes into the blanks until they are about $1/16$ in. inside each end. You'll bring the ends flush to the tubes later when trimming them clean and square. You can do this before or after rough-turning the blank using either a barrel trimmer in a handheld drill or a squaring jig and a disk sander equipped with a miter gauge. Take off the excess slowly until you just reach the brass tube.

Turning and Finishing the Blanks

To secure the pen blank while you turn and finish it, you use a mandrel, which goes into those tubes you inserted earlier. Hold the mandrel in the head stock of the lathe via a Morse taper or an attachment to a chuck, and place the step bushings and prepared pen blanks on the mandrel following the instructions in the pen kit. Do not overtighten the nut on the mandrel because this will cause the mandrel to bow slightly, and you'll turn the blanks out of round. I prefer to turn one pen blank at a time to reduce the chances of vibration.

With the lathe speed set at approximately 2,000 rpm, start with a roughing gouge to get the blank round. Next, use a skew and turn the blank down to the step bushings, adding a little shape to the blank if desired. If you are skew "challenged," use a Spindlemaster. This tool is a beginner's best friend because it does not have the sharp points of a skew to catch and dig in, and it leaves almost as good a finish.

For the last pass, use the skew or the Spindlemaster as a scraper to lightly pass over the blank and bring the ends almost flush with the bushings. Start sanding with P180- or P220-grit sandpaper and work your way up to 800 grit. To remove the microscopic scratches that sandpaper will leave, I give the blanks a very brief touchup with 500, 1,000, 2,000, and 4,000-grit Abralon sanding pads.

Super glue is the pen-turner's secret finish—A high-gloss finish best displays the wood's beauty, but because of the frequent handling that pens get, it needs to be durable. You can use solvent-based lacquer, but the most durable shine comes from CA glue, which is in fact a type of acrylic. With the lathe turning at around 150 rpm, and wearing disposable gloves, dribble some medium thick CA glue onto the blank while holding a paper towel against the underside. Thin glue wicks into the towel too fast and will not apply evenly.

Apply the glue by moving the towel back and forth as the pen blank is turning. Keep moving the towel so it does not stick to the pen blank, then spray on some accelerator to dry the glue quickly, and apply three more coats in the same way. Don't worry about getting glue on the bushings; you'll remove it later.

Once you've applied four coats, turn off the lathe and sand parallel to the lathe with 320-grit sandpaper to remove any ridges. Turn the lathe back on at 2,000 rpm and with a small parting tool, remove the glue on the bushings close to the pen blank. This will make it easier to remove the bushings from the pen blank later.

Wet-sanding and polishing—With the finish smooth, you can use acrylic sanding pads to polish it. The six grits range from 600 up to 12,000 and are color-coded by grit. Place a towel on the lathe bed to protect it and wet a 600-grit pad with water. Use a medium amount of pressure and wet-sand for about 10 seconds per pen blank. Wipe off the resulting white slurry, move on to the next grit, and repeat the process.

Remove the pen blanks from the mandrel. If a blank is stuck to the bushings, lightly tap it on the lathe to break the bond. Your blanks will almost certainly have a higher sheen than anything else you've made, but if tiny scratches are still visible, you can buff them off. Hold the pen blanks perpendicular to a buffing wheel treated with a compound (in this case a blue acrylic polish), and apply a bit of pressure. Then polish the blanks on a cotton flannel wheel to bring up the ultimate shine.

Line up the pen parts according to the instructions in the kit. Use a pen press, drill press, or bench vise to apply light pressure to press (not glue) the pieces into the pen blanks. Use scraps of wood to avoid any metal-to-metal contact that might damage the pen components. Congratulations, you've just finished what I'm sure will be the first of many pens.

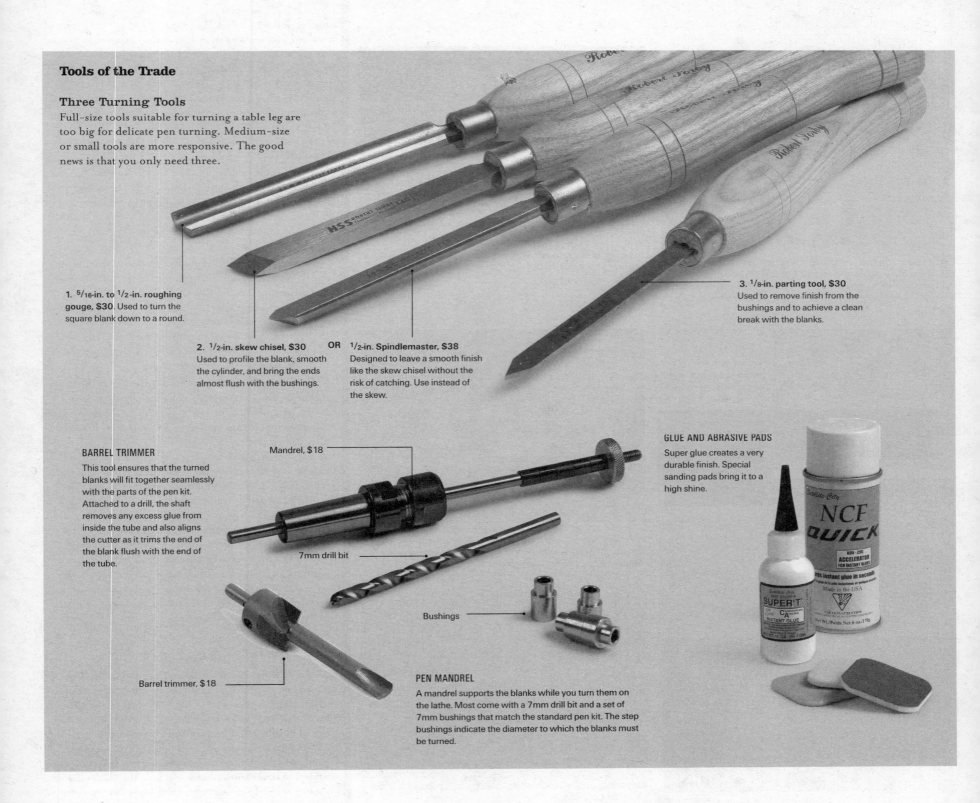

Tools of the Trade

Three Turning Tools
Full-size tools suitable for turning a table leg are too big for delicate pen turning. Medium-size or small tools are more responsive. The good news is that you only need three.

1. ⁵/₁₆-in. to ¹/₂-in. **roughing gouge, $30.** Used to turn the square blank down to a round.

2. ¹/₂-in. **skew chisel, $30** OR ¹/₂-in. **Spindlemaster, $38** Used to profile the blank, smooth the cylinder, and bring the ends almost flush with the bushings. Designed to leave a smooth finish like the skew chisel without the risk of catching. Use instead of the skew.

3. ¹/₈-in. **parting tool, $30** Used to remove finish from the bushings and to achieve a clean break with the blanks.

BARREL TRIMMER
This tool ensures that the turned blanks will fit together seamlessly with the parts of the pen kit. Attached to a drill, the shaft removes any excess glue from inside the tube and also aligns the cutter as it trims the end of the blank flush with the end of the tube.

Mandrel, $18

7mm drill bit

Bushings

Barrel trimmer, $18

PEN MANDREL
A mandrel supports the blanks while you turn them on the lathe. Most come with a 7mm drill bit and a set of 7mm bushings that match the standard pen kit. The step bushings indicate the diameter to which the blanks must be turned.

GLUE AND ABRASIVE PADS
Super glue creates a very durable finish. Special sanding pads bring it to a high shine.

Prepare the Pen Blanks

Before you turn the blanks, you need to drill them and insert the brass tubes that come with the pen kit.

1. Lay out the blank. Each section should be a little over ¹/₈ in. longer than its respective tube. Label the parts and mark their relationship for grain continuity.

2. Drilling on the lathe is easiest. Cut the parts to length, then secure each blank in a pen-drilling chuck or a conventional four-jaw chuck (shown).

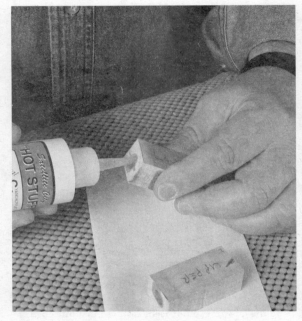

3. Stabilize the blanks. In any natural wood (as opposed to impregnated or stabilized woods sold for pen turning), you should "size" the holes with thin CA glue.

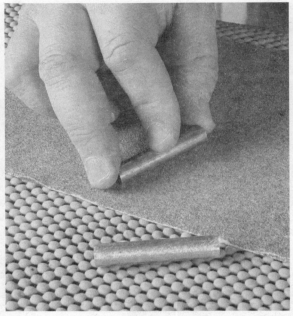

4. Rough up the tubes. Rub the pen tubes on 80-grit sandpaper to give them better adhesion when you glue them into the blanks.

5. Work fast. Spread medium-viscosity CA glue on some glossy paper. Roll a tube in the glue and then use either a dedicated insertion tool or a nail punch to push it into the blank.

6. Square up the ends. To bring the ends of the blank flush with the ends of the tubes, you can use a barrel trimmer mounted in a handheld drill as shown, or a miter gauge on a disk sander.

Turn and Sand

Round it. Insert the correct size bushing. Use a roughing gouge to turn the square blank round.

Refine it. Use a Spindlemaster, or if you are comfortable with it, a skew chisel to bring the blank to its final size and shape. To bring the ends of the blank flush with the bushings, use the skew or Spindlemaster like a scraper.

Sand it. Smooth the wood with sandpaper to 800 grit, then switch to Abralon cushioned abrasive pads and go up to 4,000 grit. Each grit needs to be applied for a few seconds only.

Finish and Polish the Blanks

A super finish. Apply medium-thick CA glue to the turning blank as you spread it with a paper towel. Wear a disposable glove or wrap your finger in a plastic bag. Use an aerosol accelerator to instantly cure the CA finish.

Smooth the finish. After four coats of finish are applied, use 320-grit paper to remove any ridges.

Unstick the blank. Use a parting tool to scrape off any glue from the bushings.

Polish the finish. Use a series of increasingly fine abrasive pads designed for acrylic to polish the finish.

ASSEMBLE THE PEN

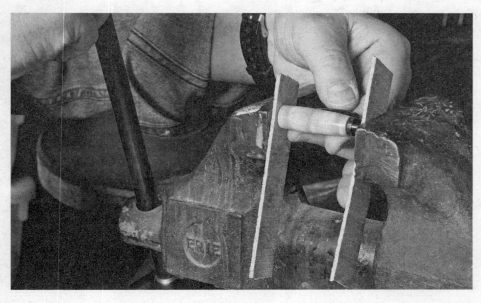

Any vise works. You can buy a pen press to assemble the pen, but as long as you protect the components, a metalworking (or woodworking) vise works almost as well.

by Ernie Conyer

Of all the things I make on the lathe, one of the most eye-grabbing is the barley-twist candlestick, which owes its name to a type of English candy traditionally made with a twist. Whether on a dining-room or a kitchen table, the candlesticks, usually made in right- and left-twist pairs, never fail to be the center of conversation, with woodworkers and non-woodworkers alike wondering how they are made. Although one would think that such work must require a router and complicated jigs, the design predates the router by at least 300 years. A lathe and a few simple tools are all you need.

This is a good project for novice turners, as the only turning is where you bring the blank to shape. The spirals are cut entirely by hand, with the lathe used as a vise to hold the work.

Besides a lathe you need some sharp gouges: I use a #9-7mm (#9 sweep, 7mm wide), a #9-15mm, a #7-20mm, and a #8-18mm. Gouges close to these in sweep and size would work as well.

Choose wood that is easy to carve. Mahogany is a good choice for your first try; walnut is durable and looks good on a dining table; basswood is easiest to carve and looks fine in a less-formal setting; and oak was a common choice in seventeenth-century England.

Prepare the Blank and Lay Out the Twists

Before you turn the blank to the cylindrical pattern and drill out the center, be sure to imprint drive-center marks on both ends so that you can chuck the work in the same exact position at either end for carving. When creating the turning, put a gentle cove just inside the bead at each end to allow an easy start and finish with the gouges when carving the threads.

The next task is the layout lines. If your lathe has indexing, then use it to draw the four horizontal lines, but you can also use dividers or the lines drawn earlier on the end grain to find the center. Now divide the shaft into 3/4-in.-long segments, holding a pencil against the work to create a series of circles.

Although our forefathers would have used a piece of string to lay out the spiral, masking tape does a better job. Wind the tape in a left or right spiral so that one edge crosses each intersection of the 90° lines and circles. Repeat for the other spiral.

The next step is to center-drill the blank. For the 11/12-in.-dia. column on this design, drill a 3/8-in. hole. Drill from both ends to ensure better centering of the bore.

Saw, Carve, and Sand the Spirals

Use a backsaw to cut a 1/4-in.-deep kerf following the curve of the cylinder on the spiral lines you just laid out. Place the #9-7mm gouge on the tool rest, just as if you were going to make a sheer cut with a turning tool, but skewed to follow the line of the kerf. You want to cut to the right side of the sawkerf to be cutting downhill with the grain. Now turn the work with the lathe's handwheel or an auxiliary wheel (see the drawing on the next page). If you have the tool at the correct angle, you'll automatically follow the spiral, but if not, simply correct on the fly.

Now reverse the piece end-over-end on the lathe and carve the other side of the kerf, blending in the middle as much as possible. Come back and repeat both cuts using a #9-15mm gouge to widen the channel.

When you have cut to the bottom of the kerf, deepen the sawkerf and repeat the process. Before you break through to the drill hole and weaken the workpiece, use a #7-20mm or #8-18mm gouge inverted to round over the top edges of the grooves.

The breakthrough to the drill hole presents the greatest danger of cracking one of the twists. It is easy for the gouge to become a wedge along the grain line. Reduce this risk in three ways: Clear enough wood from both sides of the groove to keep clearance for your gouge; make only light cuts; and use a rasp when breaking through. If all else fails, a bottle of medium-viscosity super glue is a good standby.

Once you have a good gap between the spirals, use a gouge on its side or upside down on the tool rest and carve the inside of the spiral by halves to avoid carving against the grain. If you'll be making a lot of these barley twists, use an in-cannel gouge; having the bevel on the inside of the flute gives greater control. You can find them at old tool sales, or regrind an old gouge. You'll need one whose sweep is slightly greater than the diameter of the spiral you're carving.

With the spirals roughly cut to shape, it's time to sand. Because you will not turn the lathe on, it's safe to use cloth-backed abrasive cut into strips. Start with P80-grit and work up to P180-grit paper.

Turn the Other Parts and Apply a Finish

Once everything is sanded to final smoothness, face-plate-turn the base, and spindle-turn the candle holder/wax cup. I turn a 3/8-in. tenon on the bottom of the wax cup to glue into the main shaft. I attach the base with a spindle-turned 3/8-in. dowel of the same wood I used for everything else.

Apply a coat of Minwax Antique Oil Finish and sand it in with P220-grit sandpaper. Sanding the wet oil ensures good bonding between coats and forms a slurry of wood dust and oil that fills the pores. When the finish is slightly tacky, wipe it with a clean cloth until almost dry. Repeat the steps with P320-grit, and finish with P400-grit. Aim for a very smooth, glossy surface but not a shiny, plastic look.

Turn a Cylinder and Lay Out the Spirals

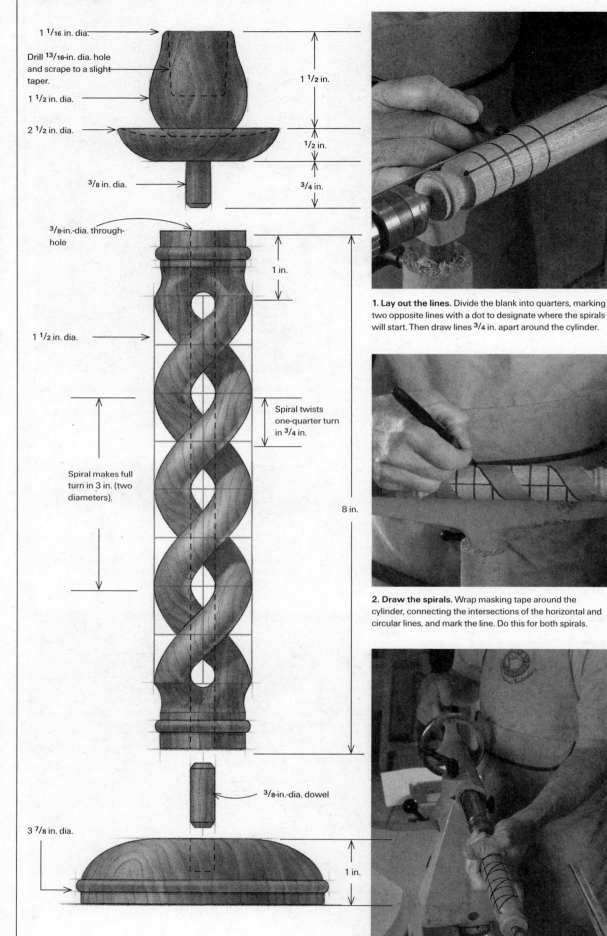

1 1/16 in. dia.

Drill 13/16-in. dia. hole and scrape to a slight taper.

1 1/2 in. dia.

2 1/2 in. dia.

1 1/2 in.

1/2 in.

3/8 in. dia.

3/4 in.

3/8-in.-dia. through-hole

1 in.

1 1/2 in. dia.

Spiral makes full turn in 3 in. (two diameters).

Spiral twists one-quarter turn in 3/4 in.

8 in.

3/8-in.-dia. dowel

3 7/8 in. dia.

1 in.

1. Lay out the lines. Divide the blank into quarters, marking two opposite lines with a dot to designate where the spirals will start. Then draw lines 3/4 in. apart around the cylinder.

2. Draw the spirals. Wrap masking tape around the cylinder, connecting the intersections of the horizontal and circular lines, and mark the line. Do this for both spirals.

3. Center-drill the cylinder. Drill the blank from each end to keep the hole centered.

Saw and Carve the Spirals

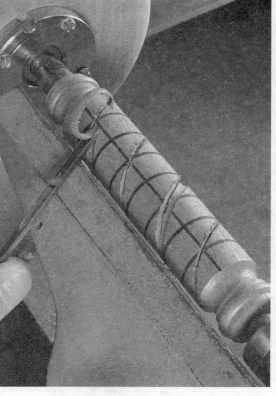

Saw the layout line. Use a backsaw to cut a kerf roughly 1/4 in. deep along the spiral lines. Gradually spin the piece by hand as you cut.

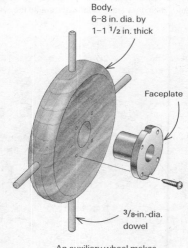

Body,
6–8 in. dia. by
1–1 1/2 in. thick

Faceplate

3/8-in.-dia.
dowel

An auxiliary wheel makes
hand-turning easier.

Carve the channel. Use a narrow gouge to carve a channel along each spiral. Stay to the right of the sawkerf so that you are cutting downhill and not against the grain. Flip the workpiece to carve the second half.

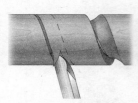 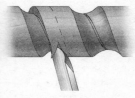

1. Stay to the right of
the sawkerf.

2. Flip the blank to carve
the other side.

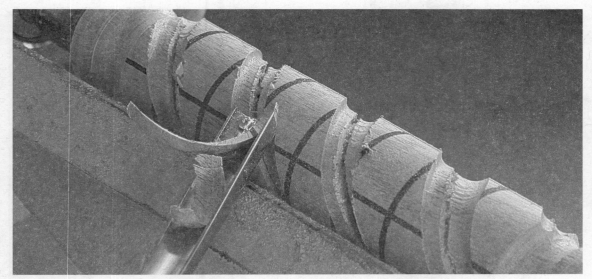

Widen the channel. Come back with a wider gouge to enlarge the channel. Again, always cut on the right side of the kerf. When complete, saw down another 1/4 in. and repeat the carving with the narrow and wide gouges.

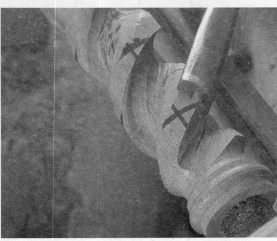

Round over the spiral. Use an inverted gouge to shape the outside of the spirals.

Shape the Inside of the Spirals

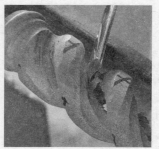

Reveal the center hole and refine the spirals. The workpiece becomes much weaker once you break into the drill hole. To reduce the risks of cracking a spiral, use a rasp when breaking through. Taking light cuts, delicately shape the insides of the spirals.

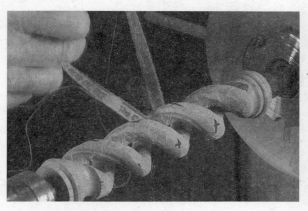

Sand and finish on the lathe. With the lathe off, begin sanding the spirals with cloth-backed P80-grit sandpaper. The best method is to tear the abrasive into strips known as shoelaces. Wipe on an oil/varnish mix and sand it into the wood to create a smooth, medium-luster finish.

TIP

Work on Both Sides of the Lathe

When cutting a left-hand spiral or certain sections of a right-hand spiral, it is easiest to move the tool rest and work from the back of the lathe.

A Simpler Way to Make a Comfortable Chair

by Michael C. Fortune

I have designed dozens of chairs during my career and made several hundred. Whenever I design one, I strive to make it beautiful, comfortable, and strong. Meeting those goals often means the chairs are difficult to build, with parts meeting at compound angles. And then all those parts must be hand-shaped so they join seamlessly.

So, I began looking for a less complex way to make chairs, while remaining true to my design goals of beauty, comfort, and strength. In traditional chairmaking the legs, rails, seat, and back are part of a single unit, which complicates construction quickly. With this design, I borrowed from techniques developed in Scandinavia during the mid-twentieth century. By separating the seat and back from the legs and rails, you build the chair's base first and then add the seat and back to it. As a result, the legs and rails can be square to one another, which simplifies the joinery. But the seat and back can be highly contoured for comfort, and then attached to the base with screws (I have a great technique for the shaping).

A chair like this is for a dining table, so you'll be planning to make at least four, but more likely six or eight. Since you're basically taking your woodworking into production mode, I'll show you some nifty jigs that will make the process go more smoothly and quickly.

I've now made a lot chairs this way, and I couldn't be happier with the results. The basic structure and technique is flexible enough to accommodate a variety of designs. Best of all, even a novice chairmaker can use the technique and make great chairs right away.

One Jig Handles Many Mortises

The curved legs give the chair an air of complexity. But that's an illusion. The rails and legs meet at right angles and slip tenons hold them together, except for an integral tenon where the side rail joins the back leg. Making the joinery comes down to routing a bunch of straight mortises. The slip tenons are basically straight sticks planed to fit. As for

the curves in the legs, don't sweat them. Use the drawings on the following pages to get you close and trust your eyes when making templates.

While the legs and rails are still straight and square, but before routing the mortises, drill holes in the back legs and side rails for attaching the back and seat.

I rout all the mortises with the help of one shopmade jig, starting with the double mortises that join the side rails to the front rail. These are oriented horizontally, because vertical mortises cut across too much grain and weaken the rails. The double mortises are laid out so that the ones in the face grain and the ones in the end grain can be routed with a single setup on the jig (and a 5/16-in.-dia., two-flute aluminum-cutting end mill). The secret is a spacer.

Rout the bottom mortises on the front rail. Then put the spacer between the rail and vertical clamping surface on the jig. This moves the rail out so you can rout the top mortises. I rout the entire through-mortise from one side of the rail, taking shallow cuts (about 1/8 in.). I don't use a backer block, because I've never experienced tearout with this type of end mill (it is an upcutting bit). Just don't take too big of a cut.

Now rout the mortises in the side rail's end grain, adjust the jig's stop block, and rout the double mortises that join the back rail to the side rails. Then set up to rout the vertical mortises in the front legs. Put a 3/8-in.-dia., two-flute aluminum-cutting end mill in the router and adjust the jig to center the mortises on 1 1/4-in.-thick material. Once that's done, adjust the jig to center the bit on 7/8-in.-thick material and rout the matching mortises in the end grain of the front rail.

Finally, rout the mortise in the back leg for the integral tenon on the side rail. The tenon is stepped, with a large base section that carries the weight, and a pair of smaller wedged through-tenons that lock the joint. Rout the mortise for the tenon's base first and then the two through-mortises.

Time for Tenons

To make the slip tenons, start with two blanks milled to the final thickness and width. Rip a groove down both faces of one blank. The grooves give the glue a place to go. Next, round over the edges of both blanks to match the ends of the mortises. Finally, cut individual slip tenons from

the blanks. For the tenons that fit a stopped mortise on one end only, use a handsaw to cut a small kerf (with the grain) on that end. Now cut the integral tenon into the side rail. Start at the tablesaw, cutting the cheeks with a dado set. Then head to the bandsaw and cut the two small through-tenons. Finally, cut slots in the tenons for the wedges and make the wedges.

Shape the Parts and Assemble the Base

Now shape the legs and rails. Start with the side rails, which have a beveled taper on their top edges to accommodate the curved seat. (The beveled edge sits higher than the front legs and rail so that the seat clears them.) Then cut the compound taper at the top of the back legs to fit the curved back. Clean it up with a block plane.

Next, cut the curves on the legs. Trace the profile from a full-size template, rough out the shape at the bandsaw, and then clean up the curves. Convex curves are easily smoothed with a handplane, but concave curves are trickier. For those, I use a template and rout the parts flush to it at the router table—making sure to always rout down the curve and with the grain.

The front legs are also tapered along their length and across their width. Both tapers can be done at once at the bandsaw. I use an L-shaped jig that has a tapered shim added to its vertical side.

The rails are much easier to shape. Just trace the curve onto the bottom edge, cut it out at the bandsaw, and rout it flush to a template at the router table.

After shaping the legs and rails, assemble the base. Glue the front rail to the front legs. Next, glue the side rails to the back legs. Wedge the tenons. Then glue the back rail between the two side rails and wedge those tenons. This creates an assembly made up of the back legs, back rail, and side rails. Let the glue dry. Finally, glue and wedge the side rails into the front rail. After the glue has dried, trim all of the wedges and tenons, cutting them close with a handsaw and handplaning them flush.

The Secret to a Comfortable Seat

A chair is either made or broken by how comfortable it is. With traditional methods, shaping the seat and back for comfort is difficult, but the technique I use on this chair makes it easy.

Both the back and seat are made by cutting curved ribs from large blanks and then stacking them on edge and gluing them together to create a curved blank. The concave side becomes the scoop that your back and backside rest against.

Because both the back and seat are made in the same way, I'll show you how to make only the back. Start with a flatsawn board. The grain exposed by the bandsaw cuts will complement the curve. Also, the board should be wide enough to make all of the ribs (use a second board for the seat).

To cut the curves, I use my bandsaw and a modified circle-cutting jig. It has a large base that pivots on a center point. The blank sits on top of the base as I feed it through the blade. I then advance the blank 1 in. closer to the blade and make a second cut to free another rib. Repeat until you've cut out all of the ribs. The outside curve is cut from the other end of the base, so rotate it, adjust the center-point, and cut the curve on all of the ribs.

Next, edge-glue the ribs together to make the curved back blank. I do this in steps, first gluing up the ribs in pairs. Then glue all the pairs together. After the glue is dry, I smooth the inside and outside curves using shopmade sanding blocks. I start with P120-grit sandpaper and work up to P220-grit.

Now shape the perimeter of the back. Because it's curved, you need a cradle to hold it: a piece of MDF for the base and two supports, both curved on the top edge to match the curve of the seat back. Draw the perimeter shape on the back and cut it at the bandsaw, with the table square to the blade. Sand the cuts smooth.

Finish the base, the seat, and the back. For a chair like this, I use Watco Danish Oil. Then screw the seat and back in place.

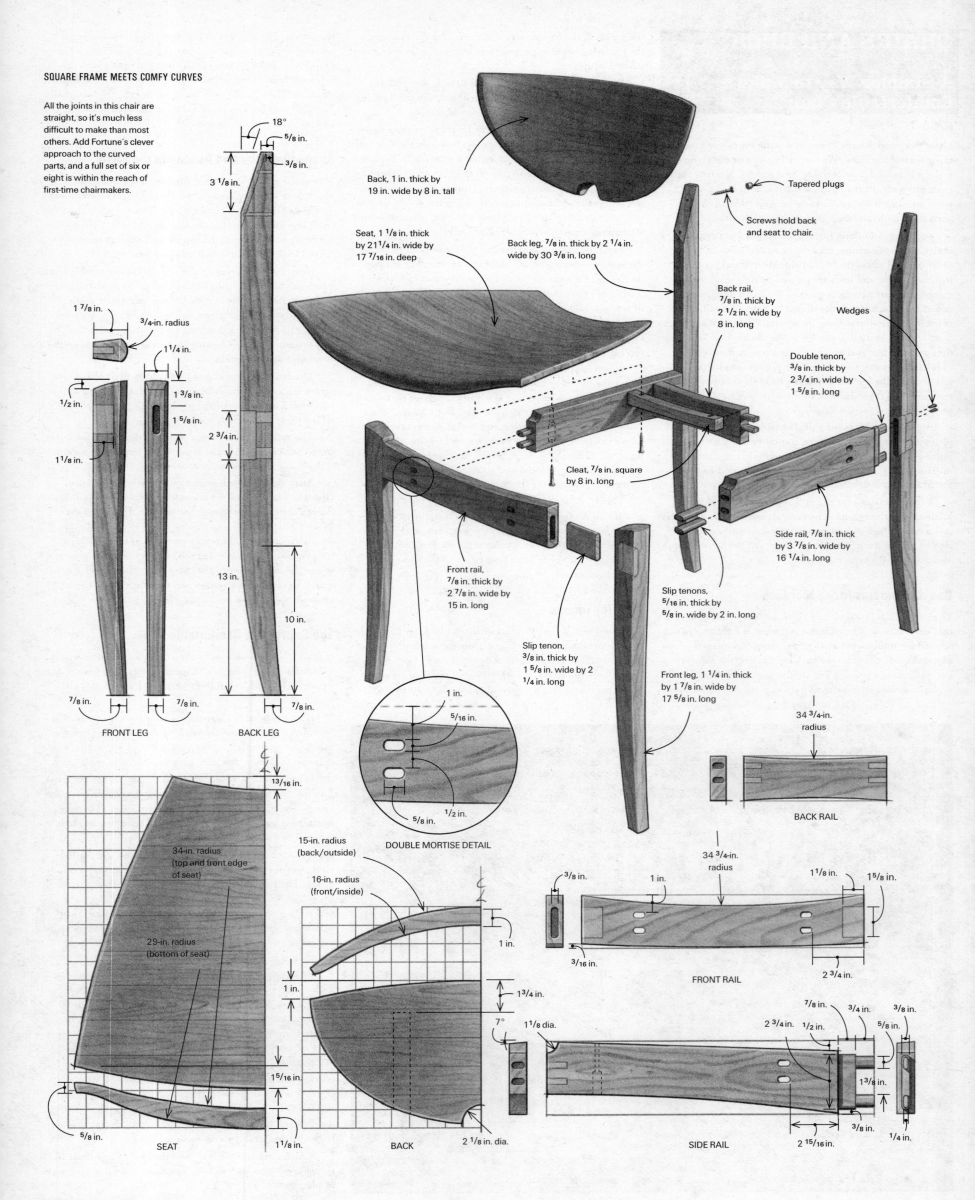

SQUARE FRAME MEETS COMFY CURVES

All the joints in this chair are straight, so it's much less difficult to make than most others. Add Fortune's clever approach to the curved parts, and a full set of six or eight is within the reach of first-time chairmakers.

Back, 1 in. thick by 19 in. wide by 8 in. tall

Tapered plugs

Screws hold back and seat to chair.

18°
5/8 in.
3/8 in.
3 1/8 in.

Seat, 1 1/8 in. thick by 21 1/4 in. wide by 17 7/16 in. deep

Back leg, 7/8 in. thick by 2 1/4 in. wide by 30 3/8 in. long

Back rail, 7/8 in. thick by 2 1/2 in. wide by 8 in. long

Wedges

Double tenon, 3/8 in. thick by 2 3/4 in. wide by 1 5/8 in. long

1 7/8 in.
3/4-in. radius
1 1/4 in.
1/2 in.
1 3/8 in.
1 5/8 in.
1 1/8 in.
2 3/4 in.

Cleat, 7/8 in. square by 8 in. long

13 in.
10 in.

Side rail, 7/8 in. thick by 3 7/8 in. wide by 16 1/4 in. long

Front rail, 7/8 in. thick by 2 7/8 in. wide by 15 in. long

Slip tenons, 5/16 in. thick by 5/8 in. wide by 2 in. long

7/8 in.
7/8 in.
7/8 in.

FRONT LEG   **BACK LEG**

Slip tenon, 3/8 in. thick by 1 5/8 in. wide by 2 1/4 in. long

Front leg, 1 1/4 in. thick by 1 7/8 in. wide by 17 5/8 in. long

1 in.
5/16 in.
13/16 in.
1/2 in.
5/8 in.

DOUBLE MORTISE DETAIL

34 3/4-in. radius

BACK RAIL

34-in. radius (top and front edge of seat)

29-in. radius (bottom of seat)

15-in. radius (back/outside)

16-in. radius (front/inside)

34 3/4-in. radius

3/8 in.
1 in.
1 1/8 in.
1 5/8 in.

1 in.
1 3/4 in.
7°

3/16 in.
2 3/4 in.

FRONT RAIL

1 5/16 in.
1 in.

5/8 in.
SEAT

1 1/8 in.
BACK

1 1/8 dia.
2 1/8 in. dia.

7/8 in.
3/4 in.
3/8 in.
2 3/4 in.
1/2 in.
5/8 in.
1 3/8 in.
3/8 in.
1/4 in.
2 15/16 in.

SIDE RAIL

ULTIMATE JIG FOR SLIP TENONS

This jig's usefulness goes far beyond this article. We first presented it in FWW #197, but we've included it here for those of you without access to that issue.

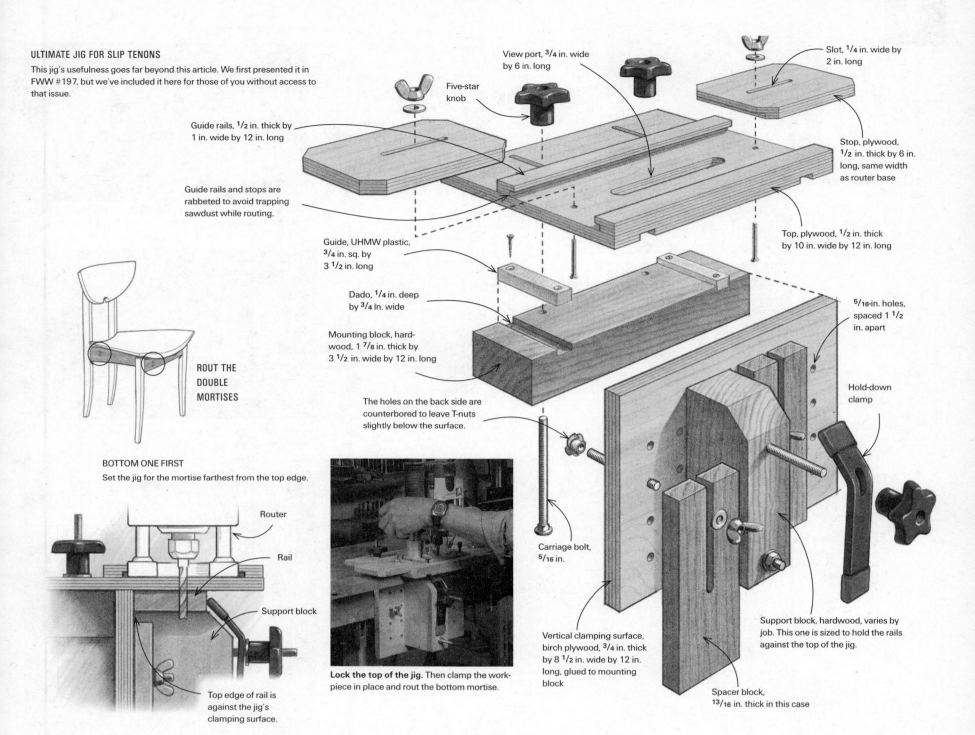

View port, ³/₄ in. wide by 6 in. long

Five-star knob

Slot, ¹/₄ in. wide by 2 in. long

Guide rails, ¹/₂ in. thick by 1 in. wide by 12 in. long

Guide rails and stops are rabbeted to avoid trapping sawdust while routing.

Stop, plywood, ¹/₂ in. thick by 6 in. long, same width as router base

Guide, UHMW plastic, ³/₄ in. sq. by 3 ¹/₂ in. long

Top, plywood, ¹/₂ in. thick by 10 in. wide by 12 in. long

Dado, ¹/₄ in. deep by ³/₄ in. wide

Mounting block, hardwood, 1 ⁷/₈ in. thick by 3 ¹/₂ in. wide by 12 in. long

⁵/₁₆-in. holes, spaced 1 ¹/₂ in. apart

The holes on the back side are counterbored to leave T-nuts slightly below the surface.

Hold-down clamp

Carriage bolt, ⁵/₁₆ in.

Support block, hardwood, varies by job. This one is sized to hold the rails against the top of the jig.

Vertical clamping surface, birch plywood, ³/₄ in. thick by 8 ¹/₂ in. wide by 12 in. long, glued to mounting block

Spacer block, ¹³/₁₆ in. thick in this case

ROUT THE DOUBLE MORTISES

BOTTOM ONE FIRST

Set the jig for the mortise farthest from the top edge.

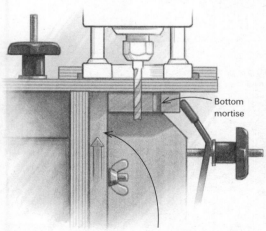

Router

Rail

Support block

Top edge of rail is against the jig's clamping surface.

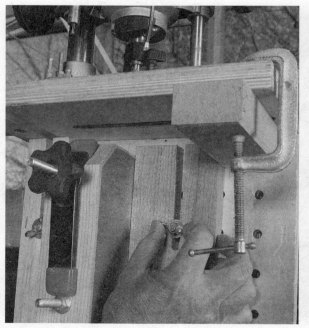

Lock the top of the jig. Then clamp the workpiece in place and rout the bottom mortise.

NOW ADD A SPACER

This lets you cut the top mortise without changing your setup.

Bottom mortise

Add a ¹³/₁₆-in.-thick spacer between the jig and top edge of the rail.

Space out for the second mortise.
The spacer lets you keep the overall setup locked in and ready for the next workpiece.

END GRAIN MORTISES MOUNT VERTICALLY

Rout the ends of the rails with the workpiece clamped against the support block, which stays exactly where it was when you were routing the face-grain mortises.

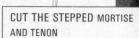

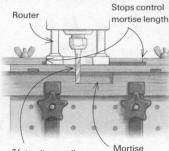

Mortise the back legs. Fortune adds a long piece of plywood behind the vertical clamping surface and notched to fit around the jig's mounting block, so he can use a stop block to quickly locate all of the legs (and that's a lot when you're making six or eight chairs).

CUT THE STEPPED MORTISE AND TENON

Had Fortune used a slip tenon here, the mortise in the end grain of the rail would be too close to the double mortises for the back rail, weakening the side rail.

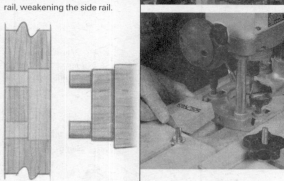

Another spacer to the rescue. When routing the two through-mortises in the back leg, Fortune puts a small block in the jig to lock in their length. Switch it to the other end of the jig for the second mortise.

STEP 1: ROUT THE LONG MORTISE

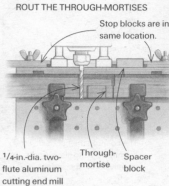

Router — Stops control mortise length.

$3/8$-in.-dia. two-flute aluminum cutting end mill — Mortise

STEP 2: ROUT THE THROUGH-MORTISES

Stop blocks are in same location.

$1/4$-in.-dia. two-flute aluminum cutting end mill — Through-mortise — Spacer block

CUT THE STEPPED TENON

Two-part cheeks. After cutting thinner cheeks at the end of the board, lower the dado set, adjust the rip fence, and cut the thicker base section of the tenon.

Form the double tenon. Fortune makes all of the cuts at the bandsaw, using diagonal cuts to clean out the waste between the tenons.

JIGS DIAL IN THE LEG SHAPES, TOO

When you're making a set of chairs, it pays to make jigs for the repetitive tasks, especially shaping. Your parts are guaranteed to be exactly the same and you'll get them done much quicker.

Angle the Tops of the Back Legs

The curved back is screwed onto beveled tapers at the tops of the legs, so these cuts are critical. This jig handles the taper, and the bandsaw table creates the bevel.

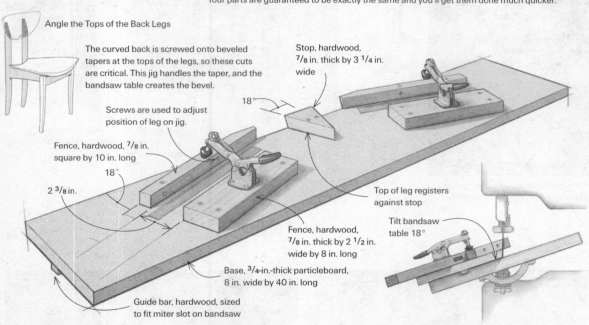

Stop, hardwood, $7/8$ in. thick by $3 1/4$ in. wide

18°

Screws are used to adjust position of leg on jig.

Fence, hardwood, $7/8$ in. square by 10 in. long

18°

$2 3/8$ in.

Top of leg registers against stop

Fence, hardwood, $7/8$ in. thick by $2 1/2$ in. long

Base, $3/4$-in.-thick particleboard, 8 in. wide by 40 in. long

Guide bar, hardwood, sized to fit miter slot on bandsaw

Tilt bandsaw table 18°

One jig, two legs, two angles. The angled table (18°) and jig combine to cut a compound angle on both legs in one shot. A wooden guide bar on the bottom rides in the table's miter slot.

CURVE THE FRONT LEGS

Clean up with a router. A flush-trimming bit leaves a clean, fair surface.

Fortune bandsaws all the curves on these chairs, cleaning up with hand tools where possible. For concave surfaces, he uses router templates.

Roundovers on the router table, too. Fortune uses part of a $3/4$-in. radius roundover bit to put a softer edge on these front legs. The pin at rear helps him enter the cut safely.

NOW TAPER THEM

With their curves cut, Fortune bevels and tapers the legs with sleds. He holds them in place by hand, reaching past the blade when necessary.

FIRST CUT

Leg is tilted 5° and fed foot-first through blade.

Hardwood wedge, 5°

Fence, $5/8$-in.-thick particleboard, $3 7/8$ in. wide by $18 1/4$ in. long

$2 1/4$ in.

Support block holds up foot.

Base, $5/8$-in.-thick particleboard, 2 in. wide by $18 3/4$ in. long

Small cutout in base acts as stop.

SECOND CUT

Leg is tilted 10° and fed top-first through blade

Hardwood wedge, 10°

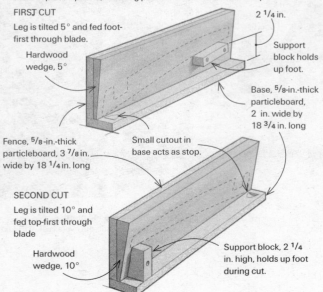

Support block, $2 1/4$ in. high, holds up foot during cut.

Wedge-shaped fence is the key. Tilting the leg into the blade creates an angle on the side and raising the foot (pushing it farther out than the leg's top) cuts a taper along the leg's length.

Second jig for the second side. The wedge's angle is double that on the first jig, and the leg is fed through the blade top-first, so it's raised on the trailing end.

SEAT AND BACK: STACK AND CONQUER

Rather than cooper the curved seat and back or sculpt them from solid slabs, both tedious techniques, Fortune cuts curved sections on the bandsaw and then simply stacks them. Little cleanup is required.

CUT THE SECTIONS

ANOTHER INGENIOUS JIG
You'll need two of these, one to form the curved sections for the seat, and the other to handle the slightly different curve of the back. Both jigs work the same. The seat jig is 24 in. wide by 36 in. deep with reference lines 1 1/8 in. apart. The one for the back is 21 in. wide by 19 in. deep, with reference lines 1 in. apart. *See plan (p. xx) for radii.

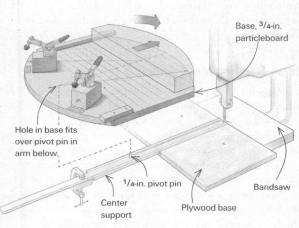

Base, 3/4-in. particleboard

Hole in base fits over pivot pin in arm below.

1/4-in. pivot pin

Center support

Plywood base

Bandsaw

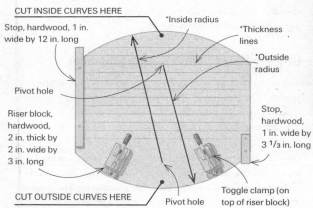

CUT INSIDE CURVES HERE

Stop, hardwood, 1 in. wide by 12 in. long

*Inside radius

*Thickness lines

*Outside radius

Pivot hole

Riser block, hardwood, 2 in. thick by 2 in. wide by 3 in. long

Stop, hardwood, 1 in. wide by 3 1/3 in. long

CUT OUTSIDE CURVES HERE

Pivot hole

Toggle clamp (on top of riser block)

Cut the inside curve first. No clamps are needed, because the force of the cut pushes the blank against the stop. But as the blank gets narrower, use a bit of hot-melt glue on the leading end.

Other side now. The other side of the jig has a smaller radius, so the blank ends up thinner at the edges than in the center, eliminating the need to taper it by hand.

GLUE AND SHAPE THE BLANKS

Clamp it up in sections. Fortune starts by gluing up pairs of ribs and then glues those together into a single blank. Cauls across the blank's width keep the ribs aligned, which makes it much easier to smooth it.

Cut it out at the bandsaw. Use hot-melt glue to hold the blank in place. Fortune puts the blank in the cradle first and then adds a few drops of glue along the seams.

USE A CRADLE FOR CONTROLLED CUTS
Again, you need one for the seat and one for the back.

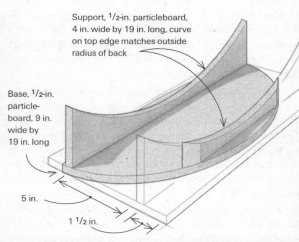

Support, 1/2-in. particleboard, 4 in. wide by 19 in. long, curve on top edge matches outside radius of back

Base, 1/2-in. particleboard, 9 in. wide by 19 in. long

5 in.

1 1/2 in.

Soften the edges. Fortune hogs off most of the waste with a Shinto saw rasp and then follows up with files and sandpaper. To smooth the curves, use a sanding block that's been shaped to match the radius. Wrap the sandpaper around the ends of the block and staple it in place.

ASSEMBLE IN STAGES

To avoid making an unintentional rocking chair, glue up a single joint or subassembly at a time. Then add subassemblies together for a square, solid chair.

Slope the walls. Use a rat-tail file with a diameter that matches the bit used to rout the mortise—5/16 in. for all but those mortises on the back legs (use a 1/4-in.-dia. file there). An angled guide block ensures that the shape is correct.

Put glue in the mortises. Spread some on the area around the joint, too, but not on the tenons. They'll swell and the joint will be much harder to get together. Assemble the front legs first. Fortune elevates the parts and uses shaped cauls to create a flat surface for clamping and protect the legs from the clamp heads.

Then glue the side rails to the back legs. Don't use a caul over the through-tenons. They need to stick out a bit for the joint to be pulled tight. Hammer in the wedges right away. After the glue is dry, the tenon won't spread for them. Also, sink them all the same amount so that after being flushed to the leg they are same thickness (looks better than wedges that vary in thickness).

Finish the base and attach the back. When gluing the back rail between the side rails, Fortune dry-fits the front leg assembly to keep things square. Then, when gluing on the front legs, he clamps a board to the back rail, providing a large, flat clamping surface so that he can get a clamp on both sides of the two joints. Finally, the back gets pilot holes for the screws, making it easier to get the screw in and preventing splits along the grain.

Smart comfort. Reminiscent of the classic chairs found at cafés, Fortune's design combines a welcoming seat and back with straightforward joinery. It's a chair you can build and that everyone will want to sit in.

← 17 in. →

10 in.

Original back profile

EASY TO CHANGE THE LOOK
A café-style chair isn't right for every dining table, but by adding 1⅛ in. to the height of the back legs and adjusting the back's dimensions, you get a more traditional dining chair.

Windsor Rocker Without Special Tools

by Peter Galbert

I've been a professional woodworker for 20 years, but for the last 10, I've produced Windsor chairs exclusively, because they are comfortable, durable, beautiful, and fun to make. Rocking chairs are the most popular because they fit a unique niche in modern lives. The human body just isn't meant to sit in one position for long periods. The easy motion of a rocking chair helps keep blood moving and allows the sitter to shift positions easily while relaxing different muscle groups. I think of it as a subtle exercise machine.

Designing this version of a Windsor rocker, I was inspired by Sam Maloof's chairs to extend the sculptural quality of the seat to the arms, crest, and spindles. For me, this strengthens the visual unity of the chair, and the fluid lines invite the sitter to relax. I've also updated some traditional techniques to make this project more accessible to new chairmakers. You'll get plenty of opportunity to use hand tools, but don't worry about having to buy lots of Windsor-chairmaking tools: While specialized tools may speed the process, you can use general shop tools for most tasks. The turnings are all elementary and only require a lathe with at least 18 in. between centers.

Windsor chairs traditionally had pine seats, as pine is easily carved, while the rest of the chair was made from a wood such as oak or ash that was strong or steam-bent well. The mismatch in appearance disappeared when the chair was painted. Because this chair will be clear-coated, I chose to make it from white oak with a butternut seat because these two woods take on a similar shade when fumed with ammonia.

For most chairs, I prefer green wood for the bent parts, but this chair can be made successfully using air-dried or even kiln-dried oak and butternut. The bends are gentle enough that the risk of breaking during bending is low.

Select boards that are as straight-grained as possible whether the parts are to be bent or not. Not only is the fiber alignment important for strength, but it also makes shaving the surface of the wood more predictable. To obtain parts with dead-straight grain, rip the board along its grain lines on the bandsaw.

All the white-oak parts, except for the rockers, can be cut from an 8/4 board that is approximately 10 in. wide by 120 in. long or the equivalent square feet. The rockers are cut from 4/4 stock, preferably quartersawn to display the ray fleck.

Wet-Dry Joints Are Tried and True

On the mortise-and-tenon joints (excluding the spindles and the crest rail), I use a variation of the wet-dry joint: The tenon is super-dried in a simple kiln (heated to 100°F–140°F with light bulbs) and then inserted in a mortise with a higher moisture content. As the moisture equalizes, the tenon swells and the mortise shrinks, creating a locked joint.

Start by cutting out the blanks for all the parts except the rockers and the seat. Rough-turn the legs, stretchers, and arm posts slightly oversize, and place them in the kiln until fully dry, which takes about five days for air-dried wood. Then finish-turn them, making sure the tenons taper at exactly 6° and match the length in the plans. Keep them in the kiln until ready to be assembled or, if your work on the chair is intermittent, place them back in the kiln a couple of days before you will use them. Cut the back posts to octagons on the tablesaw before rough-turning the tenon. If your lathe can't handle the length, you can shape the tenon using a drawknife and a spokeshave.

Steam-Bending Made Simple

I steam-bend the back posts, spindles, and crest rail in a simple plywood box hooked up to a wallpaper steamer. Green-wood parts only need about 40 minutes, but kiln-dried wood takes about an hour. Leave the back posts and crest rail in their overbend forms overnight (the spindles only need 10 minutes), and then clamp them in their final forms to open up the curve a bit.

Leave the crest rail in the final form for a few days before placing it in the kiln for a couple of days. For the spindles, I use a jig that acts like a press, capturing the spindles front and back to ensure even pressure. Don't dent the moist, softened wood.

Drill the Holes Before Shaping the Seat

The seat is the chair's anchor both visually and structurally. The arm posts, back posts, and legs have tapered tenons that lock into the seat at various angles. Accurately drilling and reaming the tapered, angled holes is essential.

Drill all the holes from the top of the seat, but transfer the sightlines to the underside and use them to ream in the tapers for the leg tenons. On rocking chairs, proper leg alignment simplifies mounting and balancing the rockers. Put the leg in position and place the bevel gauge next to it and parallel to the sight line. Use the reamer to adjust the angle of the hole if necessary.

The position of the back posts greatly affects the final look and feel of the chair. Draw a line perpendicular to the sight line on the seat, place the post in the hole, and align the flat on the front of the top with this line. By lining up a square on the sight line with a mark on the center of the top of the post, you can tell if the post needs to move left or right (splay) as you ream.

To get the proper tilt back (rake) on the post, connect a string to a spot on the front of the post at the height of the arm mortise and to the top center of the post. The rake is correct when this string is at 100° tilted back along the sight line and parallel to the string on the other back post.

Given the potential for slight variations in the bends, it is wise to practice by drawing the rear portion of the pattern on a 2x8, drilling and reaming in the back posts to check their alignment. Once you've done this, measure the exact rake and splay of the mortise using a straight dummy post. Now use the new numbers and the dummy post to start the actual mortises in the right direction.

Many tools aid shaping the seat—Carving a seat reminds me of why I became a woodworker. Watching the shapes emerge while the shavings fly is pure joy. Transfer the pattern onto the blank, drill two holes to locate the deepest part of the seat, and then start excavating down to this level. Create a rough bowl shape at the back of the seat, then carve a ramp from the bowl to the front of the seat, forming a shovel shape. Come back to refine and smooth the area that you carved away, making sure that you stay just inside the line that demarcates the flat area around the back of the seat.

Next, round over the front of the seat, removing enough material so the seat doesn't cut off circulation behind the knees. Shape the underside of the front and create a curved bevel on the underside of the sides. A drawknife is the fastest tool for this, and with practice you can take fine shavings and get into tight corners. Or, use flat and curved-sole spokeshaves, rasps, files, and scrapers. I find that power carvers and sanders soften the sculptural qualities of the seat. Last, bandsaw the back of the seat and carve a convex profile.

Stretchers and Rockers Brace the Legs

Now that the seat is carved, turn to the undercarriage. Dry-fit the legs, mark each one where it enters the seat, and measure its length from this point. Now cut them to length on the lathe to get perfectly square ends. Place the legs in their mortises and turn them so that the growth rings seen on the ends of the legs are parallel to the front and back of the seat, as this reduces the effect of seasonal movement on the joint.

This design uses only cross-stretchers because the rockers act as front-to-back stretchers. Mark the height of the stretcher mortises on the adjacent faces of each pair of legs. The exact radial location isn't important, because you can twist the legs in their mortises. Attach some white masking tape to the front face of the front legs and the back face of the back ones. Using a board with one end cut at 85°, draw a line on each piece of tape. Now clamp a leg in a V-shaped holder that mounts in a bench vise. Using a straightedge and a mirror, align the leg until the line on the tape is parallel to the top of the bench. On its angled end, stand the same board you used to draw the line on the tape and use it as an angled drilling guide. In this way, the stretchers will be perfectly parallel to the floor. Drill the mortises 1 1/16 in. deep with a 5/8-in.-dia. brad-point bit.

Place the legs back in the chair, measure for the stretcher lengths, and finish-turn the oversize stretchers that have been super-drying in the kiln. Turn the stretcher tenons until they just fit the mortises. These joints should be so tight that they can only be dry-fit to about one third of the depth. Glue the front and rear assemblies together, being careful to ensure that the legs are in the same plane when you drive in the second leg with a dead-blow mallet.

I use liquid hide glue (oldbrownglue.com) for all the joints on this chair. Not only is it repairable without having to disassemble the whole chair, but it also remains slippery when assembling a joint instead of grabbing like yellow glue. With the latter, you run the risk of not being able to drive a tight joint all the way home. Don't glue these pairs of legs into the seat until after you rout the rocker slots.

Align the Rocker Slots Precisely

Tap the leg assemblies in the seat and make a mark 1 1/4 in. down on the part of the leg that faces its corresponding leg (left front to left rear, and right front to right rear). This marks the approximate depth of the rocker slot. You want the rockers to continue in the same plane as the legs. Place a rubber band around a pair of legs covering the point you just marked, thread some thin string under each rubber band, draw the ends of the string tight, and allow the rubber bands to snap back. In this way the string will locate the closest points between the two legs. Lay a straightedge over the ends of the legs parallel to the string and make a mark on the ends of the legs. This gives an end point so you can

connect the two points to get your vertical axis. Use the straightedge to connect the points on the ends of the legs and extend the line across the end of the legs to give you a horizontal axis.

To cut the rocker slots, make a couple of simple jigs: First, use a router with a fence and a 1/2-in.-dia. spiral upcut bit to rout a slot about 4 in. long and about 5 in. from the edge of a piece of plywood or MDF. Drill a hole slightly larger than the diameter of the leg in the center of the slot. Clamp the plywood to a workbench so that the slot is parallel to and in the middle of an opened vise.

For the second jig, take a 15-in.-long piece of 3-in. square softwood (a 4x4 works well) and turn it into a cylinder with a slightly smaller diameter at both ends. It will look rather like a rolling pin. Rip the cylinder down the middle on the bandsaw, and then cut a V-shaped notch in the middle of each half. Attach cork floor tile to the two faces of each notch and place a rubber band around each "handle" of the jig.

Remove the pairs of legs from the seat and place one of the legs in the notch of the jig. With the rubber bands holding the jig around the leg, place the jig in the vise and adjust it until the vertical axis of the leg is parallel to the

front of the bench and the end of the leg is just below the surface of the first jig. Shift the plywood jig so that the slot is parallel to and centered over the axis drawn on the end of the leg. Finally, use the router to cut the slot for the rocker.

You'll add the rockers last. The rest of the chair needs to be assembled in order to get the right balance. You can, however, now glue the two leg assemblies into the seat. Many of the mortise-and-tenon joints on this chair are reinforced with wedges. These are about 1 1/4 in. long and taper at a 3° or 4° angle down from 1/8 in. thick. Use a thin-kerf saw to cut a slot parallel to the stretcher for the wedge in the tenon of each leg. I pre-fume the wedges and pegs with ammonia in a small plastic container until they are almost black to give contrast. Glue in the legs, followed immediately by the wedges. After the glue has dried, cut away the bulk of the protruding tenons, and then bring them flush to the seat with a gouge. You'll now have what resembles a wide and rather low stool. Before assembling the top half of the chair, use a scraper and sandpaper to finish smoothing the seat.

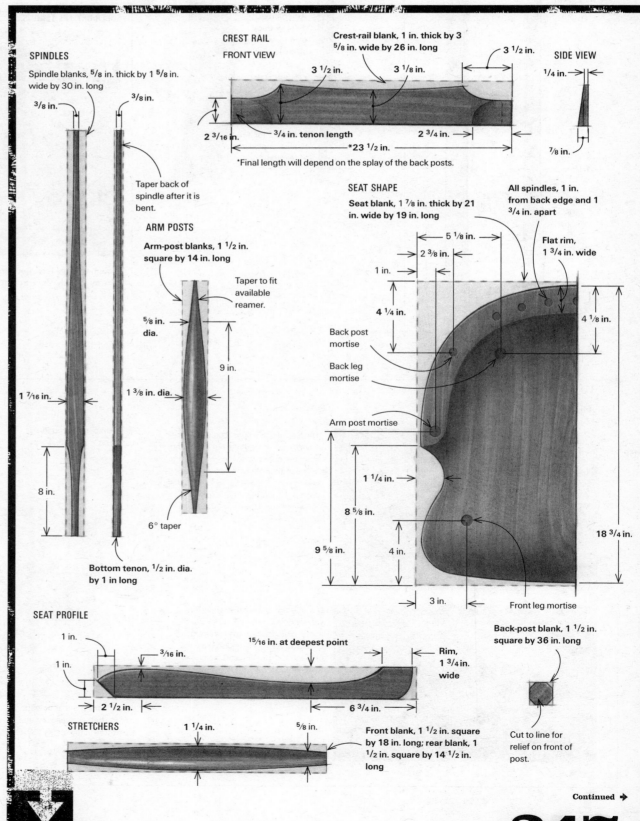

ROCKERS

Rocker blanks, 1/2 in. thick by 5 in. wide by 35 1/2 in. long.

LEGS

6° taper

2 in.

Leg blanks, 2 in. square by 15 in. long

15/16 in. dia.

1 3/4 in. dia.

11 in.

9 1/2 in.

5 1/2 in.

1 1/2 in.

FRONT

Trim after leg is glued into seat.

12 in.

Rocker slot, 1/2 in. wide by 1 1/4 in. deep

5 3/4 in.

REAR

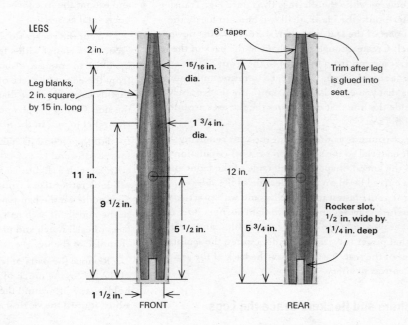

BACK POSTS

1 1/8 in.   1 1/8 in.

6 1/4 in.

Mortise for crest rail, 3/8 in. wide by 7/8 in. deep by 2 1/4 in. long

36 in.

1 1/8 in.   1 1/2 in.

9 3/4 in.   8 3/4 in.

7/8 in.

2 1/4 in.   2 1/4 in.

5/8 in.

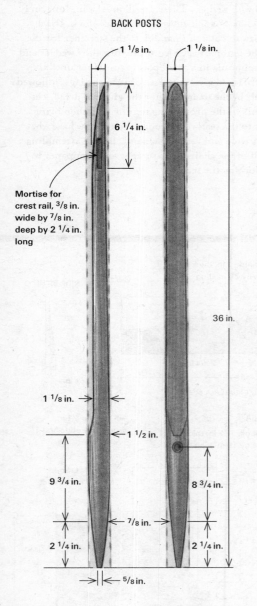

ARMS

SIDE VIEW   TOP VIEW

Stepped tenon, turned to match arm-post to back-post distance

Arm blanks, 1 3/4 in. thick by 4 in. wide by 17 in. long

Arm post location

Mortise for arm post, angled and reamed

SUPER-DRY THE TENONS

Rough-turn the legs. Because the tenon needs to be super-dried, turn the whole leg over-size by roughly 1/8 in. at first.

SHOPMADE DRYING KILN

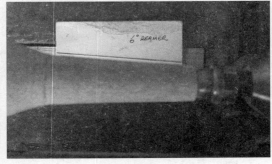

The legs and back posts only need to have their tenons dried, but the drying chamber needs to be long enough and tall enough to hold the spindles and crest rail later. Place the tenon end of each leg in the kiln. After a few days, the tenon's moisture content will be between 4% and 5%.

Dry and tight. Once the tenons are super-dry, you can turn the legs to their final profile. To taper the tenons at exactly 6°, draw the angle on a piece of magnetic sheeting and attach this to the lathe's bed under the tenon.

3/4-in.-thick plywood lined with 1/2-in.-thick, foil-faced foam insulation

Thermometer

Light bulbs

-in. plywood with 1-in.-dia. holes for back post and leg tenons

Rack

9 in.

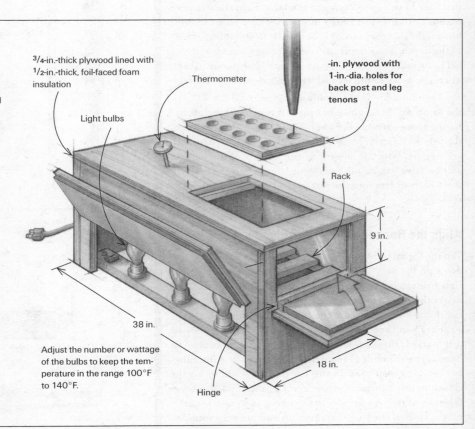

38 in.

18 in.

Adjust the number or wattage of the bulbs to keep the temperature in the range 100°F to 140°F.

Hinge

BENDING

Two forms for each steam-bent part

Steam the back posts. After roughly shaping the back posts, place them in the steam box. Leave the super-dried tenons sticking out, but stuff an old T-shirt around them to prevent the steam from escaping.

Overbend them. After removing the posts from the steamer, clamp them overnight in a form that deliberately overbends them.

The final form. Transfer the posts to a setting form that opens up the curve slightly and reduces the chances of spring-back.

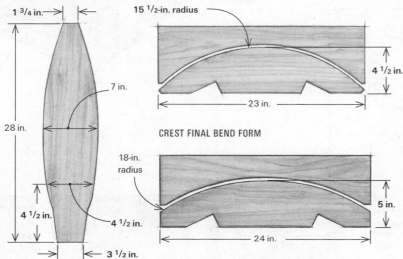

BACK-POST OVERBEND FORM

1 3/4 in.
28 in.
7 in.
4 1/2 in.
4 1/2 in.
3 1/2 in.

CREST OVERBEND FORM

15 1/2-in. radius
4 1/2 in.
23 in.

CREST FINAL BEND FORM

18-in. radius
5 in.
24 in.

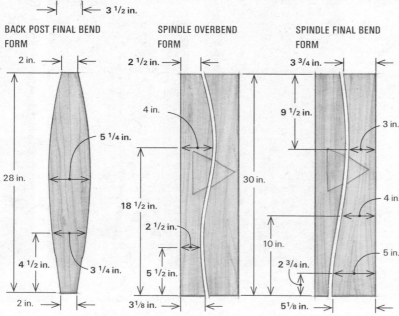

BACK POST FINAL BEND FORM

2 in.
28 in.
5 1/4 in.
4 1/2 in.
3 1/4 in.
2 in.

SPINDLE OVERBEND FORM

2 1/2 in.
4 in.
30 in.
18 1/2 in.
2 1/2 in.
5 1/2 in.
3 1/8 in.

SPINDLE FINAL BEND FORM

3 3/4 in.
9 1/2 in.
3 in.
4 in.
10 in.
5 in.
2 3/4 in.
5 1/8 in.

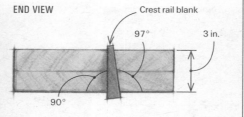

END VIEW

Crest rail blank
97°
3 in.
90°

Curving the crest rail. Both the overbend and the setting form for the crest rail have one face cut at 97° to accommodate the rail's tapered profile.

Simple form for the spindles. Like all the other forms, the ones for the spindles are made from 2x6 or 2x8 lumber.

Continued ➡

DRILL THE SEAT

The mirror trick. By correctly positioning two mirrors, Galbert can dart his eyes from one to the other to check that he is drilling at the correct angle.

ANGLES AND SIGHT LINES

For each angle, the drill is tilted along the sight lines. The drill is angled toward the center of the seat for the leg mortises and away for the back posts, arm posts, and spindles. All holes are drilled from the top of the seat.

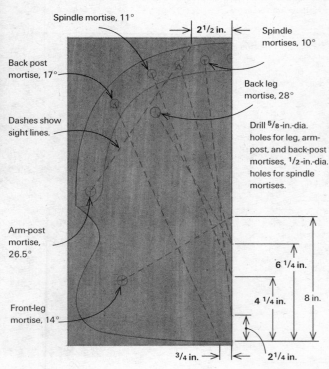

Spindle mortise, 11°

2 1/2 in.

Spindle mortises, 10°

Back post mortise, 17°

Back leg mortise, 28°

Dashes show sight lines.

Drill 5/8-in.-dia. holes for leg, arm-post, and back-post mortises, 1/2-in.-dia. holes for spindle mortises.

Arm-post mortise, 26.5°

6 1/4 in.

4 1/4 in.

8 in.

Front-leg mortise, 14°

3/4 in.

2 1/4 in.

Use two mirrors, one with a bevel gauge placed parallel to the sight line, and one with a square placed perpendicular to the sight line.

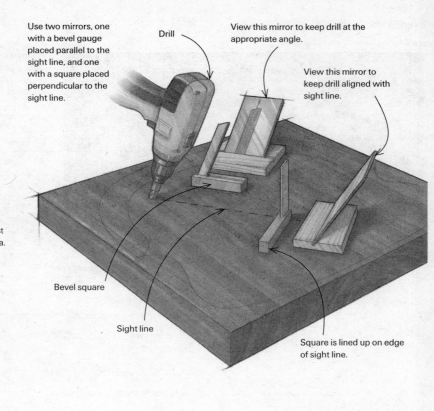

Drill

View this mirror to keep drill at the appropriate angle.

View this mirror to keep drill aligned with sight line.

Bevel square

Sight line

Square is lined up on edge of sight line.

TAPER THE MORTISES FOR THE LEGS, ARM POSTS, AND BACK POSTS

REAMER REFINES THE HOLE

The reamer is one chairmaking tool you do need. It creates a 6° taper to match the turned tenons, and also allows you to fine-tune the hole's angle.

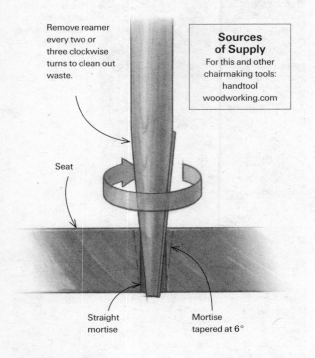

Remove reamer every two or three clockwise turns to clean out waste.

Sources of Supply
For this and other chairmaking tools: handtoolwoodworking.com

Seat

Straight mortise

Mortise tapered at 6°

Highlighted lines. Blue tape along the edge of the sight lines and at the top of the bevel gauge helps you align the top of the reamer in both planes simultaneously while you turn it.

Check your progress. After every few turns of the reamer, insert the leg to see that it is angled correctly. Stop reaming once the leg has reached the correct depth.

String trick. It is hard to align the curved back posts with the bevel gauge when setting their rake angle. Tie a piece of string from the top of each post to the location of the mortise for the arm and then compare the angle of the string to the gauge.

SHAPING THE SEAT IS FUN

You can use dedicated chairmaking tools or regular woodworking tools—or a combination of the two—to sculpt the seat.

Hollowing is a process. An adze is the traditional tool for creating the seat's recess, but a wide carving gouge and a mallet also get the job done. An inshave is the tool of choice for refining the surface. A curved cabinet scraper works too, but takes longer.

Profile the front edge. The top side is gently rounded, and the bottom is beveled. With a slight change in the cutting angle, a drawknife can either hog off wood quickly or make fine finishing cuts. The beveled S-shaped curves on the sides of the seat can be shaped with a drawknife, a spoke-shave, rasps, files, and scrapers.

Bandsaw the back. Once you've finished shaping the top and front of the seat, there is less need for a flat clamping surface, so band-saw the back curve and then round that edge under.

Mark the splay. Set the legs at their final depth and then cut each one to length on the lathe. To help align the bit when drilling the mortise, use an angled board to draw a line 5° from vertical on each leg.

Mortise the leg. Clamp the leg into a V-notched jig held in a bench vise. Pivot the jig until the line on the leg is parallel with the benchtop. Now use mirrors to align the drill bit with the same angled board and drill the mortise in the locations marked earlier.

A tight fit. Once the stretchers are glued in, you'll have to pry the legs apart to fit them into the seat.

CUT THE ROCKER SLOTS AND GLUE UP THE BASE

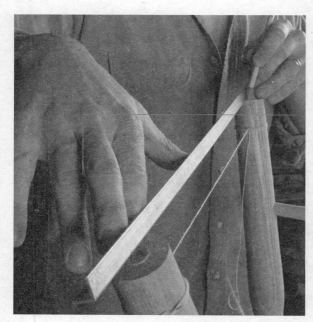

Another string trick. Place rubber bands around each leg 1¼ in. from the ends. Snap a thread between the bands to find the closest points between legs. Then use a straightedge to eyeball and mark the router slots.

Align the slot. Place each leg in a V-notch jig so the layout line is parallel to the front of the bench.

Rout the slots. Put a support panel over the leg and run a fence-guided router against it. Enter from both ends to avoid tearout.

Glue in the legs. Unlike yellow glue which can bind prematurely, liquid hide glue remains slippery while the joints are brought together. Be sure to cut a sawkerf in each leg tenon (for wedging) before assembling the base.

Finish the job. With the legs glued and wedged into the seat, cut away most of the protruding tenons and then bring them flush with the seat using a gouge.

Join the Arms to the Seat and Back Posts

The two frames formed by the seat, arms, arm posts, and back posts form a very strong connection between the chair's seat and back. Finish shaping the lower half of the back posts with a spokeshave, but leave the top portion until after you have chopped the mortises for the crest rail. Mark the location of the arm's mortise on each back post.

Select dry stock with matching grain for the arms. Transfer the pattern to the top and inside of each rectangular arm blank. Extend the center line down both ends of the arm and scribe a horizontal line ⅝ in. from the top face all the way around the blank to create centers for turning. This is offset turning, so make sure that the piece doesn't strike the tool rest. Turn the tenon until the line on the inside of the curve nearly vanishes.

Dry-fit the arm and back post—Cut a test block roughly matching the length and thickness of the arm and drill a ½-in.-dia. hole at 62° for the arm post. Ream the test block until the underside of the block is aligned with the baseline of the arm tenon on the arm post. The reamer used for the seat mortises may not fit this smaller hole, but a plumber's 6° reamer used to de-burr pipes (available at hardware stores) works fine. Now see if the other end of the test block centers on the location of the mortise in the back post. If you're close, you can tweak the angle when you drill the arm. If not, make another test block and try again.

Drill the mortise at 62° (or whatever angle worked on the test block), using the centerline as a sightline. Cut away a section of the underside of the arm down to the layout line on either side of the arm-post hole. This will enable you to ream the hole until the bottom of the arm just touches the arm post's baseline. Ream both arms at the same time to ensure matching angles. Once both arms are seated, note the actual height of the mortises on the back posts.

The mortises in the back posts directly face the arm posts. To find this point, place a large rubber band around the back post at the height of the mortise and stretch it

Continued →

across to the point you reamed down on the arm post. Measure halfway across the gap at the back post end of the rubber band to find the center, and check the alignment by visually centering the arm post on the back post. To find the correct angle of the mortise in the back post, use the same block with an 85° angle cut on one end. Set the block on the arm and mark the angle on the outside of each back post. Place the roughed-out arm tenons into the top of the shopmade kiln and let them dry for at least 24 hours.

Drill the mortise in the same way you drilled the mortises in the legs, using the V block holder and keeping the line marked on the posts parallel to the benchtop with the mortise location pointing straight up. Drill the mortise with a 7/8-in. to 3/8-in. stepped bit (morriswoodtool.com/Counterbores) until the shoulder is about 1/8 in. below the surface of the post. It's important to note that the obtuse, or larger of the two angles, is toward the top of the chair. This mortise also can be drilled with the combination of a 7/8-in.-dia. Forstner bit for the shoulder and a 3/8-in.-dia. brad-point bit for the mortise, as long as the tip on the brad-point is long enough to correctly center in the dimple left by the Forstner.

Place the back post in the seat and measure the distance between where the arm-post tenon exits the arm and the shoulder of the rear-post mortise. Use this distance to mark the shoulder on the arm's super-dry tenon. Finish-turn the shoulder and tenon.

Shaping the arms and the back posts—Bandsaw the side profile on each arm, then tape the waste back on and cut the top profile. Draw a midpoint line around the sides of the arm to give a reference point for shaping. I shape the arms with drawknives and spokeshaves while holding them in a shave horse, but you also can secure the arm in a vise or with clamps. While the tops of the arms will be sanded smooth, I leave clean spokeshave facets on the underside for the sitter to discover.

While the tops of the back posts still have flat sides, cut the mortises near the top for the crest rail. Now you can round the rear of each back post and start to taper the tops. Leave a 1/4-in.-wide flat section on each top, as it helps to rest the chair on these points when assembling the rockers.

To dry-fit the arm/posts assembly, place the arm post in the seat and slide the back post onto the arm while dropping the arm and back post into position. To disassemble the joint, twist the arm post in the seat, and lift up the back post and arm. If all the joints look good, go ahead and glue both assemblies, adding wedges to each joint. I use a clamp to draw the arm all the way into the joint.

Shape and Fit the Crest Rail and the Spindles

Once the crest rail has been set in the final form and has spent a couple of days in the kiln, you can begin shaping it and making the tenons. Clamp the crest rail across the front of the back posts in line with the mortises. If there is any twist or misalignment, shave the crest until it sits flat against the back posts. Mark the back of the rail where it meets the outside of the posts to get the location and angle of the tenons. Even though the crest mortises don't go all the way through, the extra length is easily taken up by the flexibility of the posts, and the extra splay looks good in the final piece.

Lay out the cove and recessed area on each end. Bandsaw the cove and then use a drawknife and spokeshave to remove the bulk of the recessed area. Leave the tenon parts a little thick and scrape them to final thickness when smoothing the crest. Cut the tenons about 1/16 in. shorter than the mortises to ease installation.

It is now time to work on the spindles. Lay out and

then bandsaw the recesses on the bottom ends, then shave the tenons round. Once all of the spindles are dry-fitted into the seat, number the sequence and then draw an oval on them that roughly encloses where the sitter's back will make the most contact. Shave from these marks to the ends and facet the edges. Then shave, scrape, and sand the fronts and backs. Dry-fit the crest rail and mark the spindles where they intercept it. Cut the spindles to length including 7/8 in. for the top tenons, and then finish shaping them.

The spindles splay out from the center, so they require angled mortises in the crest rail. Evenly space the spindles and then mark their angle in the back of the crest rail. To keep the crest rail vertical and stable, clamp it to the final bending form and use the mirror technique to drill each hole at the required angle.

To orient the spindles in their holes, hold a thin strip of wood along the curve at the mid-back region to make sure that they align smoothly where the greatest body contact and weight will be. Mark this alignment on masking tape attached to the bottom of the spindles and the chair seat.

Glue the spindles into the seat and let them dry. Then, in quick succession, glue them into the crest rail, glue one end of the crest rail into a back post, and finally spread the back posts to seat the other end of the crest rail. Glue a wedge into the gap above each crest-rail tenon and peg the crest-rail-to-back-post joints.

It Don't Mean a Thing if It Ain't Got That Swing

Balancing the rockers for the smoothest motion is vital to the success of the chair. Being pulled too far back or pitched forward will leave the sitter struggling to stay in the chair.

The bottom of each rocker is beveled to match the splay of the legs. Measure the rocker slots with a bevel gauge and then tilt the bandsaw table to this angle. Lay out one rocker using the design provided and then cut it on the bandsaw, beveling just the bottom curve. Fair the curve using coarse sandpaper on a curved block of wood and plane or scrape the sides until it slides into the slots. Trace this rocker onto the other blank and repeat the process.

Turn the chair upside down and line up the front of each rocker with the front legs. Use winding sticks to see if the rockers are in the same plane. They almost never are, so tap a rocker out of the slot until they are in plane. Tap a wedge in from both ends of the gap, tape the rockers to the chair legs, then turn the chair over and see how it feels to sit in. If the rocker needs to rock back more, simply tap the rockers out of the front slots. Once you're happy, mark where the rockers enter the legs. Remove the wedges, measure the largest gap between the rocker and the bottom of the mortise, scribe the distance on all sides of the other legs, and pare to the line. Once the joints are set, shape the rest of the rocker tops, bevel the ends of the legs, and then glue and peg the rockers.

A Fumed Finish

Before applying a finish, fine-tune the shape. I fume the chair with janitorial-strength ammonia followed by four coats of an oil/varnish mix.

MAKE AND FIT THE ARMS

1. ROUGH THEM OUT FIRST

Rough-turn the tenon. Bandsaw the top profile for each arm, mount it on the lathe using the center points at each end, then mark the centerline of the tenon. Turn the tenon until the line drawn on the inside almost disappears.

2. DRILL THE ARM-POST MORTISE

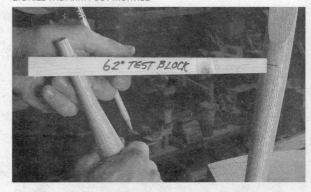

62° TEST BLOCK

Check the angle. The mortise in the arm needs to be angled so that the arm tenon is at the correct height on the back post. Start with a test block drilled at 62°. Adjust the angle from there.

Drill the arm-post mortise. In the same way that you drilled the leg mortises, drill into the arm for the arm post with the bevel gauge set to the test-block angle.

Ream to fit. Bandsaw down to the layout line on the underside of the arm so you can see when the arm post is home. That way, when you ream the mortise, you can be sure that the arm will enter the post at the right spot.

3. DRILL THE POST AND SHAPE THE ARM

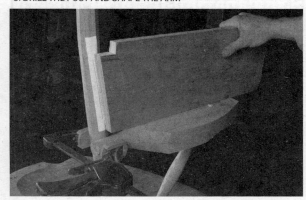

Lay out the back-post mortise. Place the same board used to lay out the leg stretchers onto the arm and trace a line on a piece of tape on the back post.

Drill the mortise. Angle the post until the line you just drew is parallel to the benchtop. Using the angled board and a mirror, drill a stepped mortise through the post with two brad-point bits.

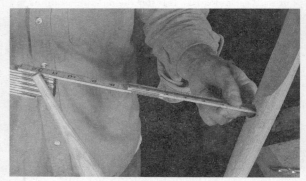

At arm's length. With the stepped mortise drilled, measure from the bottom of the wide part of the mortise to the midpoint of the arm post.

Two-step tenon. Mark the location where the tenon steps down and then turn it on the lathe. A shopmade gauge aids accuracy.

Shave your arms. Mark the centerline of the arm. With the joinery complete, sculpt the arms using a drawknife, spokeshave, files, and sandpaper.

THE TWO-STEP MORTISE

A two-step mortise is much stronger than a single-diameter joint. If the whole joint were $7/8$ in. dia., this would weaken the back post. If the whole joint were $3/8$ in. dia., the arm post would be weak where it enters the post, the most likely point of failure.

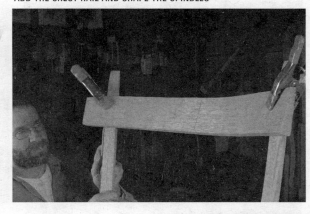

Back post

Arm

Mortise, $7/8$ in. dia. by $1/8$ in. deep

Wedge

$3/8$-in.-dia. tenon extends through the back post.

Four-way glue up. The back post, arm post, and arm need to be glued and wedged all at one time. Use a clamp to ensure the stepped arm-to-back-post joint fully closes.

ADD THE CREST RAIL AND SHAPE THE SPINDLES

Fit the crest rail to the chair. With the back posts glued in, clamp the crest rail to them in line with the mortises. Slide the rail back and forth to find the best fit and then mark out the tenons. The scalloped ends of the crest rail transition into tenons that enter the back posts. Because the posts need to be splayed later when inserting the crest rail, having a tenon that fits tight on four sides is awkward. So leave a slight gap above the tenon.

Start on the spindles. Use a template to lay out and then bandsaw the profiles on the bottom of each spindle. Then use a spokeshave to create round tenons.

Point of contact. Number and dry-fit the spindles into the seat. Draw an oval across all the spindles where the sitter's back will make contact (have someone sit on it to lay out the oval). Narrow the spindles above and below the oval and smooth the fronts and backs using a drawknife, a spokeshave, and a scraper.

Space the spindles. Because the spindles splay outward from the center, mark the location and angle where they enter the crest rail.

Drill the crest rail. For stability, clamp the crest rail to the angled bending form. Drill each angled hole for the spindles, starting nearer to the back of the rail to avoid breaking through the tapered front.

Back support. Dry-fit the spindles, then bend a thin strip of wood against their widest part. Alter the angle of individual spindles until you get a smooth, flowing curve.

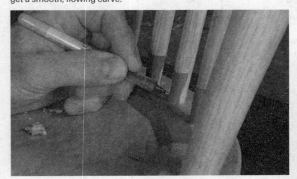

Mark the location. Place masking tape on the top and base of the spindles to show the correct depth of each tenon. Then mark the orientation of each spindle so that you keep the flowing curve after glue-up.

All together now. Glue the spindles into the seat, glue in one end of the crest rail, then glue the spindles into the rail. Then splay the back posts and glue in the other end of the crest rail. Install a small wedge to close the gap above each tenon, and trim it flush later.

How splayed are the legs? Use a bevel gauge to discover the angle of the rocker slots versus the ground. If the front and back legs on the same side have different angles, average the readings.

ROCKERS

Bandsaw along dotted line. Rocker is trimmed later to match the front and rear leg locations.

Rocker blanks, 1/2 in. thick by 5 in. wide by 35 1/2 in. long

2 1/4 in.

2 1/2 in. wide at front

3 in. wide

1 1/2 in.

3 1/4 in.

4 in.

2 in.

14 in.

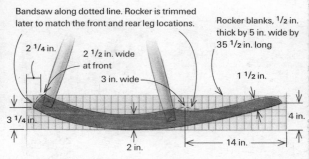

Bevel the rockers. Set the bandsaw table at the angle of the rocker slots and bevel the bottom edge of each rocker. Bandsaw the top edge square.

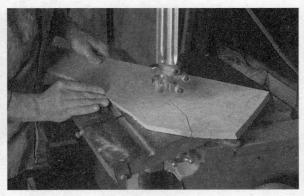

A rocker that rolls. Use a pair of straightedges to align the rockers and set them at the correct depth in each slot.

Measure the gap and deepen the slots. Discover which rocker is farthest from the bottom of the slot and measure the distance. Mark this distance on either side of the other three legs, remove the rockers, and then chop down to the line to bring all four slots level.

Scandanavian-Inspired Modern Bench

by Mark Edmundson

This bench has been part of my entire woodworking career. I designed it as a student in the College of the Redwoods fine woodworking program. A chair by famed Swedish furniture designer Carl Malmsten inspired the shape of the armrests and legs; the Danish-cord seat adds texture. Over the years I've made a half-dozen benches like this one and used the Danish-cord weave on many pieces.

The bench is a good project for mastering mortise-and-tenon joinery, for working with gently curved components, and, of course, for making a woven seat. You can get all the parts from one 8/4 plank that's 7 in. to 8 in. wide and 8 ft. to 10 ft. long. In a pinch you can use a secondary wood or sapwood for the seat rails because the Danish cord hides the wood completely.

Cut the legs, armrests, and lower side rails from the outside edges, where you'll have straight quartersawn grain. It's a good idea to have enough stock for an extra leg blank. Take the long seat-support rails from the middle of the plank.

Legs Are Square Where It Matters

Using the drawing on p. xx as a guide, make templates for the leg, the curved rails, and the armrests. It's imperative that you know which legs go left, right, front, and back, because of the way they're curved. Label them clearly.

Mark the leg template with the locations of the top and bottom of each mortise. Transfer the mortise locations to the leg blanks, beginning with the side-to-side mortises. Remember not to mark mortises for a lower support rail on the front two legs. Similarly, transfer the locations of the front-to-back mortises from the template to the leg blanks, then trace the curve on the outside of each leg.

Refer again to the drawing for the widths of each mortise, the distances from the edge of the leg to the mortises, and the spacing between double mortises. Tenon lengths tell you the depth of each mortise. Transfer these measurements to each leg, then cut all the mortises, using a router or a hollow-chisel mortiser. If you use a router, chop the ends of each mortise square with a chisel.

Saw Tenons on the Stretchers

Dimension the rails and cut them to length, then mill the tenons. Use the tablesaw and miter gauge to cut the tenon shoulders first, and then use a tablesaw tenoning jig to cut the cheeks.

To mill the double tenons, cut the tenon shoulders, then load the piece in the tenoning jig and saw away the 3/16-in.-wide space between the double tenons. I make one pass over the blade, then rotate the piece 180° and make another pass, checking it with the leg to see if the gap is tight.

When the fit seems good, cut all the spaces between double tenons, then change the setup to cut the outside cheeks. Lower the blade to 1/8 in. above the table and make a cut, checking the results against the mortise in the leg. When it's to your liking, raise the blade so that it is just below the shoulder crosscut and make a pass. Rotate the work and cut the other side. You'll have to clean up a bit of wood between the tenons with a narrow chisel or file.

Finally, cut the two small mortises on the inside of the long support rails. These will house two short auxiliary stretchers. Wait to cut those stretchers until you have dry-fit the rest of the bench.

Dry-Fit and Cut the Curves

Assemble one pair of legs and short rails, fit the long rails in place, then press the remaining legs and short rails in place. Pull the joints together with clamps to be sure the mortises and tenons seat properly.

Lay out the legs. A cabinetmaker's triangle marked on the ends of the leg blanks helps keep them oriented properly. A template not only gives you a pattern for the two curved faces on the legs, but it can also hold all the information you need to mark mortise locations on the leg blanks.

Be sure there's at least a 1/8-in.- to 3/16-in.-wide gap between the long weave rails and the support rails below them. A smaller gap will make it hard to weave the Danish cord. Plane the support rail if you have to widen the gap between the rails. Also, be sure that the tenon shoulders on the long weave rails don't interfere with the tenon shoulders on the adjacent support rail.

If everything looks good, make the auxiliary stretchers to fit between the long support rails. After the initial dry-fit, cut the curves on the legs, lower side rails, and front rail on the bandsaw.

There are several tools you can use to clean up the bandsaw marks. I use a thin piece of wood wrapped in P100-grit sandpaper, a shopmade plane with a gently curved sole, a spokeshave, a scraper, and a block plane. Check your progress against the leg template. No two faces will be exactly the same, but that's all right. Just be sure the legs don't seem too bottom-heavy and that they flare out a bit at the top.

Finish shaping the legs by chamfering the corners. I also like to plane a gentle taper on the inside straight faces. Scribe a line 1/16 in. from the top inside edges. Plane from the top of the mortises to those scribe lines.

The top and bottom faces of the lower side rails have the same inside curve as the armrest. Align the armrest template 1/16 in. below the top and bottom faces of the rail, then trace the curve. You may want to plane the outside edge of the rail so it aligns with the edges of the legs. Chamfer the corners as you did the legs.

You also can use the inside curve of the armrest template to plot the gentle curve at each end of the long support rails.

Shape and Join the Armrests

When the legs and rails are to your liking, rough out the armrest on the bandsaw, and clean up the curves with sandpaper and a scraper. Use a router table and a core-box bit to cut a 1/4-in.-radius cove on the underside. Finally, round over the ends of each armrest.

Join the armrests to the legs with dowels. Use dowel centers to mark the locations of corresponding holes in the armrests.

Prepare the Seat Rails

Round over the four weave rails at the router table. The short ones have a 3/8-in. radius on all four edges. The long ones have a 3/8-in. radius on the top outside and lower inside edges and a 1/4-in. radius on the other edges. That's partly for comfort, partly to make it easier to cinch the cord.

Finally, drill rows of 1/16-in.-dia. pilot holes in the weave rails and drive in the L-shaped nails to hold the Danish cord.

Also, drill a pair of holes on top of the front support rail for #8 2 1/2-in. screws. They secure the weave rail to the support rail and keep it from bowing.

Prewrap the long weave rails with Danish cord. While the cord will cover the short weave rails, the front-to-back warp strands won't cover the long rails by themselves. The wrapping fills in the spaces (see photos and drawing, above).

Glue Up the Bench, Then Weave

I finish all the pieces before glue-up.

Glue the legs and short rails together first, using the leg offcuts as pads. Then attach the armrests.

Spread the cord on the long weave rails so it's evenly spaced over the screw holes in the support rails. Drive the screws until they begin to seat; stop before they pull the two rails together.

Weaving the Danish-cord seat is the final step. It takes me about three hours. But if this is your first experience with a woven seat, allow more time until you get the hang of things.

Cut the mortises. If you use a plunge router with an adjustable edge guide, you can easily dial in the depth of the different mortises and their distances from the edge of the blank. Stop blocks clamped to the blank control the length of the mortises. After routing, use a chisel to square up the ends of the mortises.

Bandsaw the curves. Once you've cut the curve in one face, tape the offcut onto the blank. It will help keep the leg square on the bandsaw table as you cut the second curve. Use coarse sandpaper, a scraper, or a spokeshave to smooth the curves. Don't worry if the curves aren't identical; the eye won't pick up minor variations.

Continued →

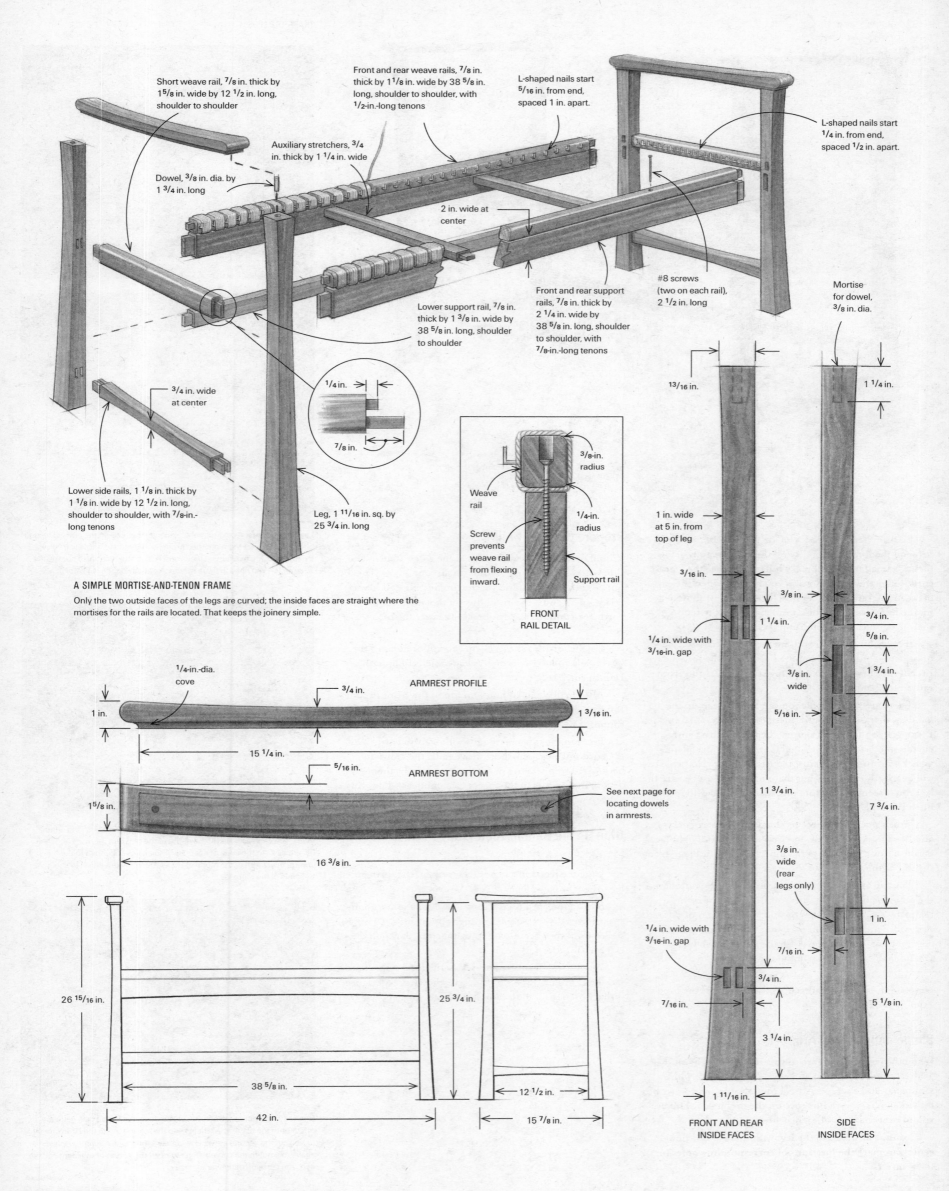

Short weave rail, 7/8 in. thick by 1 5/8 in. wide by 12 1/2 in. long, shoulder to shoulder

Front and rear weave rails, 7/8 in. thick by 1 1/8 in. wide by 38 5/8 in. long, shoulder to shoulder, with 1/2-in.-long tenons

L-shaped nails start 5/16 in. from end, spaced 1 in. apart.

L-shaped nails start 1/4 in. from end, spaced 1/2 in. apart.

Auxiliary stretchers, 3/4 in. thick by 1 1/4 in. wide

Dowel, 3/8 in. dia. by 1 3/4 in. long

2 in. wide at center

Lower support rail, 7/8 in. thick by 1 3/8 in. wide by 38 5/8 in. long, shoulder to shoulder

Front and rear support rails, 7/8 in. thick by 2 1/4 in. wide by 38 5/8 in. long, shoulder to shoulder, with 7/8-in.-long tenons

#8 screws (two on each rail), 2 1/2 in. long

Mortise for dowel, 3/8 in. dia.

3/4 in. wide at center

Lower side rails, 1 1/8 in. thick by 1 1/8 in. wide by 12 1/2 in. long, shoulder to shoulder, with 7/8-in.-long tenons

Leg, 1 11/16 in. sq. by 25 3/4 in. long

1/4 in.

7/8 in.

A SIMPLE MORTISE-AND-TENON FRAME

Only the two outside faces of the legs are curved; the inside faces are straight where the mortises for the rails are located. That keeps the joinery simple.

Weave rail

Screw prevents weave rail from flexing inward.

3/8-in. radius

1/4-in. radius

Support rail

FRONT RAIL DETAIL

13/16 in.

1 1/4 in.

1 in. wide at 5 in. from top of leg

3/16 in.

1/4 in. wide with 3/16-in. gap

3/8 in.

3/4 in.

5/8 in.

1 1/4 in.

3/8 in. wide

3/8 in. wide (rear legs only)

1 3/4 in.

5/16 in.

11 3/4 in.

7 3/4 in.

1/4 in. wide with 3/16-in. gap

1 in.

7/16 in.

3/4 in.

7/16 in.

3 1/4 in.

5 1/8 in.

1 11/16 in.

FRONT AND REAR INSIDE FACES

SIDE INSIDE FACES

1/4-in.-dia. cove

ARMREST PROFILE

3/4 in.

1 in.

1 3/16 in.

15 1/4 in.

5/16 in.

ARMREST BOTTOM

1 5/8 in.

See next page for locating dowels in armrests.

16 3/8 in.

26 15/16 in.

25 3/4 in.

38 5/8 in.

12 1/2 in.

42 in.

15 7/8 in.

CUT THE TENONS ON THE RAILS

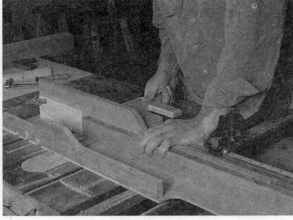

Cut tenon shoulders first. Edmundson uses a narrow, shopmade sled to cut the tenon shoulders, with a stop block clamped to it.

Add a tall fence to cut tenon cheeks. An auxiliary fence clamped to the sled supports the work when cutting the cheeks.

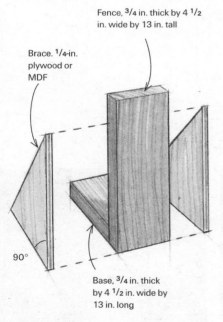

Fence, ³/₄ in. thick by 4 ¹/₂ in. wide by 13 in. tall

Brace. ¹/₄-in. plywood or MDF

90°

Base, ³/₄ in. thick by 4 ¹/₂ in. wide by 13 in. long

CUTTING THE DOUBLE TENONS

Begin in the middle on the double tenons. Once you've cut the shoulders, cut away the waste between the tenons in the middle of the stock. Cut the inside face of one tenon, then rotate the stock 180° for the second cut. Creep up on the right distance, using the leg to check the fit. Finally, cut the outside cheeks and ends.

SHAPE THE ARMRESTS

Bandsaw curves. Begin with the curve for the top of the armrests, then bandsaw the curves for the sides.

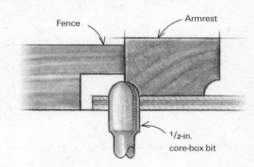

Fence

Armrest

¹/₂-in. core-box bit

Rout a cove on the underside. The cove gives the thick armrest a lighter look. Edmundson uses a narrow shopmade guide that clamps to the router table and sits above the blade. It follows both the convex and concave sides of the armrests. Reset the stop for the end-grain cuts.

Drill for dowels. Use ³/₈-in.-dia. dowels to connect the legs to the armrests. Drill the legs first, then use dowel centers to locate the holes in the armrests. Position the armrest and press down. Now you can drill the mating hole in the armrest.

ADD NAILS AND WRAP THE LONG RAILS BEFORE ASSEMBLY

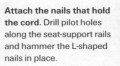

Attach the nails that hold the cord. Drill pilot holes along the seat-support rails and hammer the L-shaped nails in place.

Wrap the long rails.

ASSEMBLE THE BENCH

Five wraps between nails

⁵/₁₆ in.

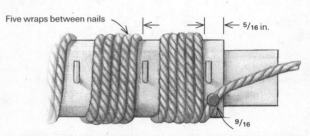

9/16

Glue up the end frames. Curved offcuts again make ideal clamping pads. Because Edmundson oils the components before glue-up, he puts leather scraps between the leg and offcut to protect the finish.

Add the long rails. Once the glued-up end frames are dry, connect them with the long rails. Then screw the weave rails to the support rails.

Clamp armrests last.

Continued →

HOW TO WEAVE WITH DANISH CORD

Danish cord resembles thick hemp twine, but it's made from strands of tightly rolled paper. You weave the seat by looping the cord over L-shaped nails driven into the inside of the weave rails. The cord comes in 2-lb. bundles, about enough for a single chair seat, or in 10- to 11-lb. rolls, ample for two benches. You can order the nails and cord from several retailers, including www.caning .com, www.caneandreed.com, and http://catalog.countryseat.com. Before you begin, wrap the long weave rails with cord, as shown on the previous page. Then do the weaving in two stages: First, run warp strands from front to back; then, weave cord from side to side. No need to measure; you're always taking a loop of cord from the bundle, hooking it on a nail, passing a looped end to the other side of the bench, and hooking it onto a nail.

STEP ONE: WEAVE FRONT TO BACK

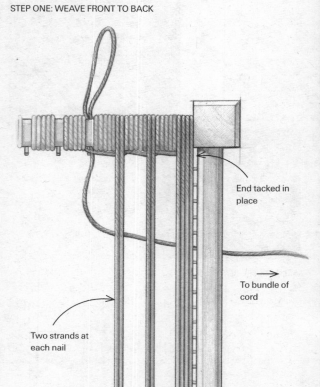

End tacked in place

To bundle of cord

Two strands at each nail

Four strands at each end

Front and rear rails are wrapped prior to assembly

1. Start the warp. Loop a length of cord, keeping the strand from the bundle toward the center of the bench. Push the loop under the front weave rail next to the leg.

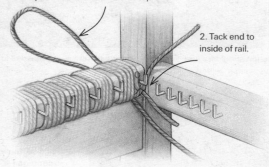

1. Pull loop under front rail and over top.

2. Tack end to inside of rail.

2. Bring the loop to the rear rail and hook it on a nail. This makes the first two warp strands. Repeat for a total of four strands on the first nail.

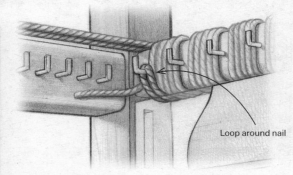

Loop around nail

3. Hook the cord and drag it to the next nail. Pull the cord taut and hook it over the first nail. Bring it across the top of the next nail. Make a loop with the strand from the bundle to the outside, and push it under the front rail.

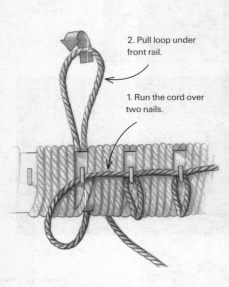

2. Pull loop under front rail.

1. Run the cord over two nails.

4. Continue running the cord from front to back, with a pair of warp strands hooked over each nail. Finish with four strands at the end, twisting the loop so that the strand from the bundle is closest to the leg.

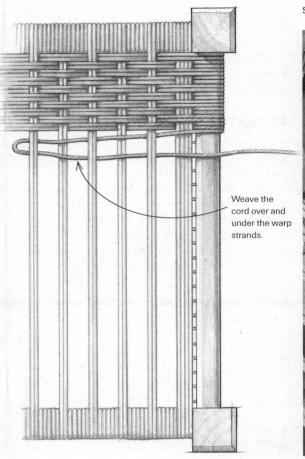

Weave the cord over and under the warp strands.

1. Begin the weaving. Start at the rear of the bench, tacking the cord in place at the corner of a leg. Make a loop, and bring the cord over the short weave rail. Push the loop over the group of four warp strands, under the next pair, over the next, and so on until you reach the opposite side. Keep the weave strands snug, but not so tight that they make the warp strands flex up and down.

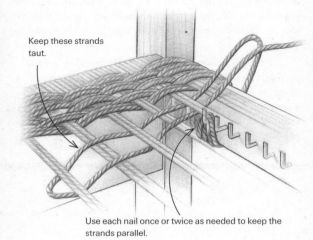

Keep these strands taut.

Use each nail once or twice as needed to keep the strands parallel.

2. Hook the cord and weave it again. As you weave toward the front of the bench, hook the cord twice over each nail in the short rails. In order to keep the weave strands parallel to the long rails, you may need to hook the cord only once over some nails.

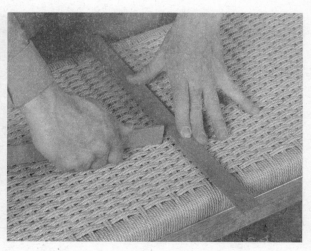

3. Push each weave strand in line. Each time you weave the cord through the warp strands, use your fingers to push the cord snug against the weave. When you're about halfway through the weave, sight down the length of the bench to be sure the weave strands are straight.

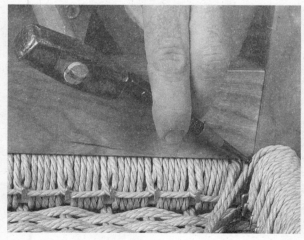

4. Tack down the weave cord. Turn the bench upside down and tack the end of the weave cord to the leg. Work the pigtails of cord at the corners out of sight, tucking them under the L-shaped nails.

5. Clinch the nails. Carefully tap the short leg of the L on each nail down over the cord. If you break a nail, use pliers to pull out the stub and tap in a replacement, making sure you catch all the loops of cord.

6. Straighten the weave. Use a thin stick to push any wayward strands into alignment. Don't try to make everything perfect; it's better if the seat has some small variations to signal that it's been woven by hand.

Contemporary, Comfortable Bench

by Daniel Chaffin

This bench's clean, contemporary style and comfortable seat let it sit well in the foyer, bedroom, mudroom, or on the front porch. It even works under a tree in the backyard, if made with exterior woods and finishes.

The slight taper on the tops of the seat slats complements their beveled edges. The legs, which are glued up from two boards, have a routed groove that both hides the glueline and ties the legs to the spaced seat slats. The legs also are arched along the bottom, a detail repeated on the stretchers.

These design details seem difficult, but they are surprisingly straightforward. Tapering the seat slats would be tough by hand, but I'll show you how a simple stick turns a planer into a tapering machine. Templates simplify the shaping of the legs and stretchers and make it easier to produce multiple benches.

Make a Template for the Legs

You could make the legs from a single 15-in.-wide board, but few people have a jointer and planer wide enough to handle it. I recommend using two narrower boards for each leg.

Leave some extra width on the boards. That will help keep the glueline centered so it will be hidden by the routed groove. Keep the boards a bit long as well, so there's room to adjust them for the best grain match. After gluing the boards together, joint one edge and rip the leg to width, keeping the glueline centered.

Making a template for the legs is time well spent. A Forstner bit large enough to cut the hole in the leg will leave tearout on the walls of the hole. The template allows you to drill the hole undersize and rout it to finished diameter with a spiral bit, leaving a smooth surface.

I guide the spiral bit with a bushing, so the hole in the template needs to be 3½ in. dia. to account for the offset and create a 3⅜-in.-dia. hole. The arc, on the other

hand, is made with a bearing-guided, flush-trimming bit, so it should be actual size on the template. To draw the arc, use a ⅛-in.-thick batten made from quartersawn lumber. Register the ends of the batten against two small clamps, push it to its apex, and trace the arc.

Remove the waste at the bandsaw. Smooth the cut by sanding to the line. Bore the hole at the drill press and attach the fences.

Put That Template to Work

Use the template to mark the arc and hole on your leg stock. Then bandsaw and drill out the waste. Put the leg back in the template and secure it to the bench—I use holdfasts. There's no need for double-faced tape, because the three fences and clamping pressure hold the leg in place. Rout the arc and hole to final size.

I clean up the routed surfaces with a card scraper—using a narrow one for the hole—and sandpaper. While you have the router out, rout the cove detail on the show

BUILD IT IN A WEEKEND
Aside from the mortise-and-tenon joints, everything else—from tapers, grooves, and bevels to pocket screws—is simple to execute.

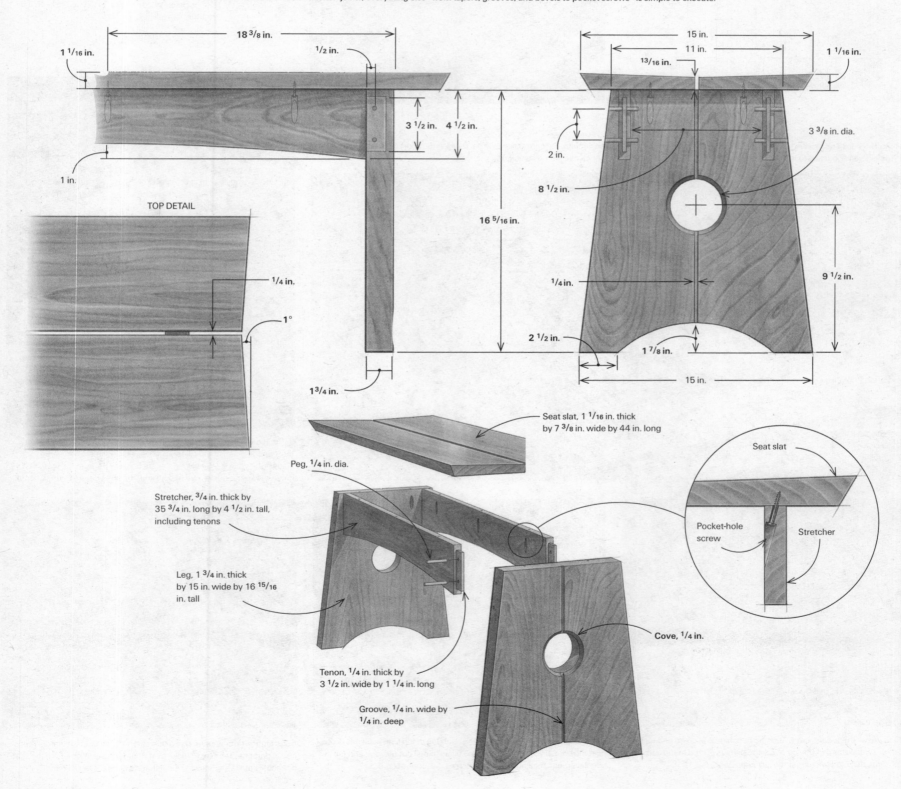

TOP DETAIL

Seat slat, 1 1/16 in. thick by 7 3/8 in. wide by 44 in. long

Peg, 1/4 in. dia.

Stretcher, 3/4 in. thick by 35 3/4 in. long by 4 1/2 in. tall, including tenons

Leg, 1 3/4 in. thick by 15 in. wide by 16 15/16 in. tall

Tenon, 1/4 in. thick by 3 1/2 in. wide by 1 1/4 in. long

Groove, 1/4 in. wide by 1/4 in. deep

Seat slat

Pocket-hole screw

Stretcher

Cove, 1/4 in.

sides of the holes and then groove the center of the legs. Now mortise the legs. I do this before tapering them because I use a hollow-chisel mortiser to cut them, and I want square edges to register against its fence. A router and edge guide would also work.

After all the mortises are cut, lay out the leg tapers with a straightedge and cut close to the lines at the bandsaw. Clean up the cuts with a smoothing plane. Mark the arc on the stretchers. I make a plywood template, using a batten to lay out the arc, so that they're the same. Cut the tenons and trim them to fit. Then cut the arc at the bandsaw and clean it up with a spokeshave.

Simple Stick Tapers Seat

Nearly every surface on the seat slats is beveled or tapered, and it's important to cut them in the right order. First, taper the slats' thickness. Then cut the compound angles on the ends. Finally, bevel the outside edges.

I've tapered the seat slats across their width with a handplane, but it took forever. I've also used an elaborate sled for my planer. Every taper I cut with it had to be fixed with a handplane, so I rethought my approach and came up with a simple solution—so simple, I wonder how I could have missed it earlier.

All you need so that your planer will make this cut time after time is a stick that lifts the inside edge of the slat higher than the outside edge. Ironically, the stick I use is an offcut from the elaborate sled. Attach the stick to the bottom of the slat on the inside edge with double-faced tape, and use a pencil to mark lines over its entire face. When the last bit of pencil has been removed, you're done. It's that simple.

With the ends still square, clamp the slat between benchdogs and plane all the surfaces smooth.

Tilt the tablesaw blade to 60°, adjust the miter-gauge fence to 89°, and crosscut the slats. Move the gauge to the

continues on pg. xx

A TEMPLATE MAKES QUICK WORK OF THE LEGS

This template not only helps lay out the arc and hole before roughing them out, but it also works as a guide for your router, ensuring that both legs are the same and that the hole and arc are accurate and clean.

1. MAKE THE TEMPLATE

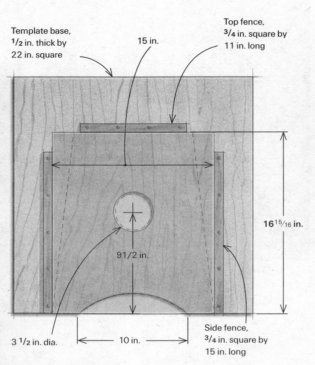

Template base, 1/2 in. thick by 22 in. square

15 in.

Top fence, 3/4 in. square by 11 in. long

16 15/16 in.

9 1/2 in.

3 1/2 in. dia.

10 in.

Side fence, 3/4 in. square by 15 in. long

Attach three fences—one for the top and two for the sides—to align the legs in the template so that they're marked and routed consistently. After attaching the first two, place the leg blank against them, and use it to align the third.

2. REMOVE THE WASTE BEFORE ROUTING

Place the leg blank in the template, and trace the arc and circle onto its inside face. Cut the waste from the arc, leaving about 1/16 in. to be routed away. For the hole, Chaffin uses a 3 1/4-in. Forstner bit, which leaves about 1/8 in. of waste. Any tearout on the outside is removed by the router.

---

3. ROUT THE ARC AND CIRCLE

Rout the arc. Because the legs are 1 3/4 in. thick, it takes two passes with a pattern bit to rout the arc flush. On the first pass, the bearing rides against the template. For the second pass, remove the template and register the bearing against the routed surface.

FIRST PASS

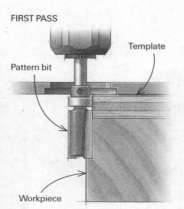

Template

Pattern bit

Workpiece

SECOND PASS

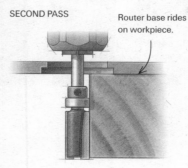

Router base rides on workpiece.

ROUT THE HOLE WITH A SINGLE PASS

Rout the hole. A 2-in.-long spiral bit cuts end grain and long grain cleanly, and is long enough to trim the walls in one pass.

Guide bushing, 5/8 in. O.D.

Template

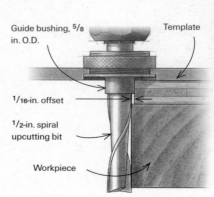

1/16-in. offset

1/2-in. spiral upcutting bit

Workpiece

FINISHING TOUCHES

Cove the edge. A 1/4-in. bearing-guided cove bit routs a nice detail on the outside edge of the hole.

Groove the glueline. Use a 1/4-in. straight bit to rout a 1/4-in.-deep groove over the glueline.

Continued →

TAPER AND BEVEL THE SEAT

A flat seat isn't comfortable. Taper the slats across their widths so that they are thinner on the inside edge than the outside.

TAPER FIRST

TIP

A SIMPLE TRICK FOR BIG TAPERS

All you need to taper the seat slats is a 1/4-in.-square stick. Attach it to the inside edge of the slat with double-faced tape. Chaffin puts cross-hatching on the board to gauge his progress.

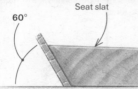

BEVEL SECOND

60°   Seat slat

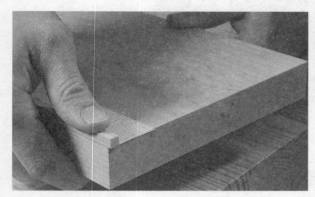

Ends get a compound angle. With the blade tilted to 60° and the miter gauge set at 89°, crosscut the slat to length. The outside edge should be against the fence. For the second cut, move the miter gauge to the other side of the table and turn the board over.

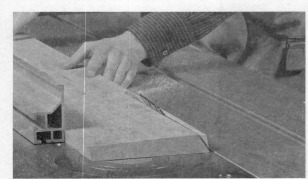

Edges last. Leave the blade at 60° and bevel the outside edge of the seat slat.

ASSEMBLY IS STRAIGHTFORWARD

With only four joints, assembly isn't tough. Glue the base together, then peg the joints.

Glue the stretchers to the legs. Spread glue on the tenons and tap them home. Scrape away the squeeze-out when the glue starts to gel, but leave the clamps on for a few hours.

Peg the joints. Saw off the waste, and use a sharp block plane to bring them flush.

Add the seat. Secure the top with pocket-hole screws. Note the 1/4-in.-thick spacer on the bench keeping the tapered slats flat against the legs.

Oil finish for warmth. Three coats of a linseed oil/varnish finish brings out the natural color of cherry, and protects the seat.

other side of the table and flip the board onto its other face to cut the second end. With the blade still at 60°, bevel the outside of each slat.

Prep all the surfaces for finishing now. If you wait until after assembly, you'll find places that you can't get at well enough to do a good job, like between the stretchers. I use a smoothing plane and break the edges with a block plane. Because cherry is prone to blotching, I lightly sand all the parts with P320- or P400-grit sandpaper so that it absorbs the oil finish more evenly.

Assemble and Finish the Bench

I use pocket screws—located on the inside of the stretchers and legs—to attach the seat slats. Cut the pocket holes before assembling the bench.

Begin the assembly by gluing and clamping the stretchers and legs together, making sure that their top edges stay aligned. Let the glue set for a few hours and then drill holes for the pegs that pin the tenons. I make cherry pegs with a dowel plate, but you also can buy them. Don't use much glue on the pegs. They're a tight fit in the holes, and the pressure created when you drive them in could force glue out through the faces of the legs. Cut the pegs close and plane them flush. Now place the slats on top of the legs, aligning their inside edges with the groove cut into the legs. Drive in the pocket screws and you're ready to finish the bench.

You can build this bench in a weekend, but the finishing might take longer. I applied three thin coats of Tried and True varnish oil, wiping away excess oil after an hour. Allow plenty of time for each coat to dry before applying the next. In Kentucky, that can mean four days between coats in the summer, less in the winter. Buff the first coat with 0000 steel wool, and the last two with a soft cloth. Top it off with a coat of paste wax.

Adirondack Chair

by Tom Begnal

This quintessentially American outdoor chair was born in the early 1900s in the Adirondack mountain region of New York state. The generous slant of the seat and back make it an inviting place to relax outdoors. And for those who like to graze while relaxing, armrests the size of small tables offer plenty of room for a plate of snacks and a favorite beverage.

Unlike the original, our chair has a curved seat and back, making it a place where you won't mind spending a lot of downtime. It is made from western red cedar, a weather-resistant, lightweight wood available at most lumberyards. Cypress, mahogany, and redwood also are lightweight and enjoy the outdoors. Ipé and teak are at home outdoors, too, but expect a chair made from either to be a muscle-strainer.

Most of the parts are made from presurfaced "1-by" stock, but for the parts that carry extra load—sides, legs, risers, and cradles—I used 5/4 presurfaced stock. Much like a 2x4, the actual dimensions end up slightly less. That said, if you use teak, ipé, or any other hardwood, you can build the entire chair from 1-by boards.

Begin with the Sides

The sides are the foundation of the framework. Cut a full-size pattern, then transfer it to the stock, and cut out the shape on the bandsaw. Smooth the sawblade marks on the edges of the sides with a plane, scraper, or sanding block.

Cut Seat Slats, Stretcher, and Lower Back-Slat Cradle

Cut the seat slats to size before moving on to the front stretcher. To lay out the curve along the bottom edge of the stretcher, make a jumbo compass (see tip on the next page) Measure 33 in. from the compass pivot point and drill a 1/8-in.-dia. hole to accept a pencil point.

Before scribing the curve, add reference points to the stretcher. At a point 3/4 in. from the front edge, draw a line across the length of the piece. On that line, mark the center point. Now, place the stretcher on a workbench. Align the pivot point of the compass with the center mark on the stretcher, positioning the pencil on the center point. Use the compass to scribe the arc across the stretcher, use a bandsaw to cut it out, then smooth the sawn edges.

Again, turn to the jumbo compass to scribe the curved front edge of the lower cradle. Relocate the pencil hole to create a 10¾-in. radius. At a point 2⅛ in. from the front edge of the cradle, draw a reference line across the length of the piece. Then, mark the end-to-end center point on the line and cut the curve on the bandsaw. After that, smooth, sand, and round over the edges.

Move on to the Leg Assemblies, Then the Back

Each of the two leg assemblies is made up of a leg, a leg bracket, and an arm-support block. With the parts disassembled, drill all the shank holes in the legs and support block. Use a bandsaw to cut the taper on the bracket, and then smooth with a smoothing plane. Now, sand all the leg parts and round over the edges. But do not round edges where parts meet. Screw one block to the top of each leg. For each leg assembly, screw a bracket to the underside of a block and outside of a leg.

The back assembly is made up of two parts: a pair of vertical risers and a pair of riser brackets. Once the parts are cut, rounded, and smoothed, screw them together. To locate the proper position for the riser brackets, place a leg assembly on the riser with both bottom ends flush, then use the arm-support block as a straightedge to scribe a line across the riser. Position the bracket so that its face is flush with the front edge of the riser and its top edge is at the marked line. Secure each bracket in place by driving three screws through the inside face of the riser and into the bracket.

Make the Upper Cradle

To create the curved front edge, use the jumbo compass again. This time, though, locate the pencil hole 12¾ in. from the nail hole. Again, add a reference point to the cradle. Draw a line 2¼ in. from the front edge of the cradle, and then mark the end-to-end center point on the line. Use the compass to scribe the arc.

The end curves are next. I experimented with several shapes on the end of a 4½-in.-wide piece of cardboard. When I hit on one that looked good, I cut out the curve and used the cardboard to trace the shape on each end of the cradle. Use a bandsaw to cut them out, and then smooth the sawn edges.

Cut Out the Arms

The arms are the focal point of the chair. Enlarge the drawing to trace a full-size pattern on stiff paper or cardboard. Cut out the pattern and use it as a template to trace the shape on each length of stock. Then use a bandsaw to cut out both arms at the same time. Smooth the edges, round them over, and sand through P150-grit.

Taper the Back Slats

To taper the seven back slats, I use an old jointer trick that makes the process quick and easy. First, apply a piece of tape to the jointer fence to establish a point about 1 in. from the front edge of the outfeed table. Lower the infeed table 1/8 in. (the amount of taper you want on each edge). Then wedge the guard open so that you can lower a slat onto the cutterhead.

Next, with the machine turned on, rest the bottom end of the slat on the infeed table (or, if the infeed table is short, overhanging the end), and align the top end of the slat with the tape. Holding the slat against the fence with your hands well behind the cutterhead, lower the end onto the outfeed table. Use a push block to feed the slat through the cutterhead. Repeat on the opposite edge.

Now you're ready to trace the top curve on the back slats. Start by placing all the back slats edge to edge with a pair of spacers between each. Redrill the pencil hole on the jumbo compass 10 in. from the nail. Position the pivot point 10 in. from the top end of the slats and centered on the middle slat. Scribe the arc across all the slats.

Cut out the curved ends with a bandsaw. Sand or scrape each sawn edge and sand the faces through P150-grit before rounding the edges.

Continued →

Assemble all the Parts

You are ready to start putting the chair together. Stainless-steel screws (countersunk) and carriage bolts eliminate the need for glue. Start the assembly by screwing the stretcher to the front end of each side piece. With the stretcher mounted, add the lower back-slat cradle to give some rigidity to the subassembly.

Now, on each side piece, mark a line 5¼ in. from the front face of the stretcher. Elevate the stretcher until the back ends are flat on the worksurface. Then place a leg against the side piece, and use a square to make sure it is square to the worksurface and on your mark. Add a clamp to make sure it won't inadvertently shift out of position as you drill a pair of ⅜-in.-dia. holes through the legs and sides. Bolt the leg in place, then attach the other leg.

With the legs safely at first base, the back assembly is now at bat. At a point 4 in. from the back end of the side, clamp a riser to a side piece. Check for square with the worksurface, then drill the holes and add the bolts. Follow the same procedure for the second riser.

The upper cradle is next. Position the cradle so that its back edge is set back ¼ in. from the back edges of the risers. Measure and drill for a pair of shank holes at each end of the upper cradle.

After you attach the upper cradle, add the arms, as it becomes a chore to attach them once the back slats are in place. Position each arm so that the notch fits around the riser, and screw through the riser and arm-support block.

The back slats are attached to the lower and upper cradles. I attach the center slat first, then move to the two outside slats and work inward. Before drilling the shank holes, it is important to align them from left to right, up and down, and keep the spacing even to maintain a nice curve on the bottom and the top.

Give the entire project a quick once-over with P150-grit sandpaper, and break any sharp edges. You can leave the chair unfinished and let it weather naturally. Or, three coats of spar varnish provide a finish that will hold up well in an outdoor environment. A fresh coat every couple of years should keep the chair happy and fit for decades to come.

> **▶ TIP**
>
>
>
> **Make a jumbo compass.** The compass is a thin strip of wood about 36 in. long. Measure 1 in. from the end, and drill a hole to accept a nail. Create a pivot point by driving the nail through the strip and into a square block of ¾-in.-thick stock. The location of the pencil hole will vary depending on the radius of the arc.

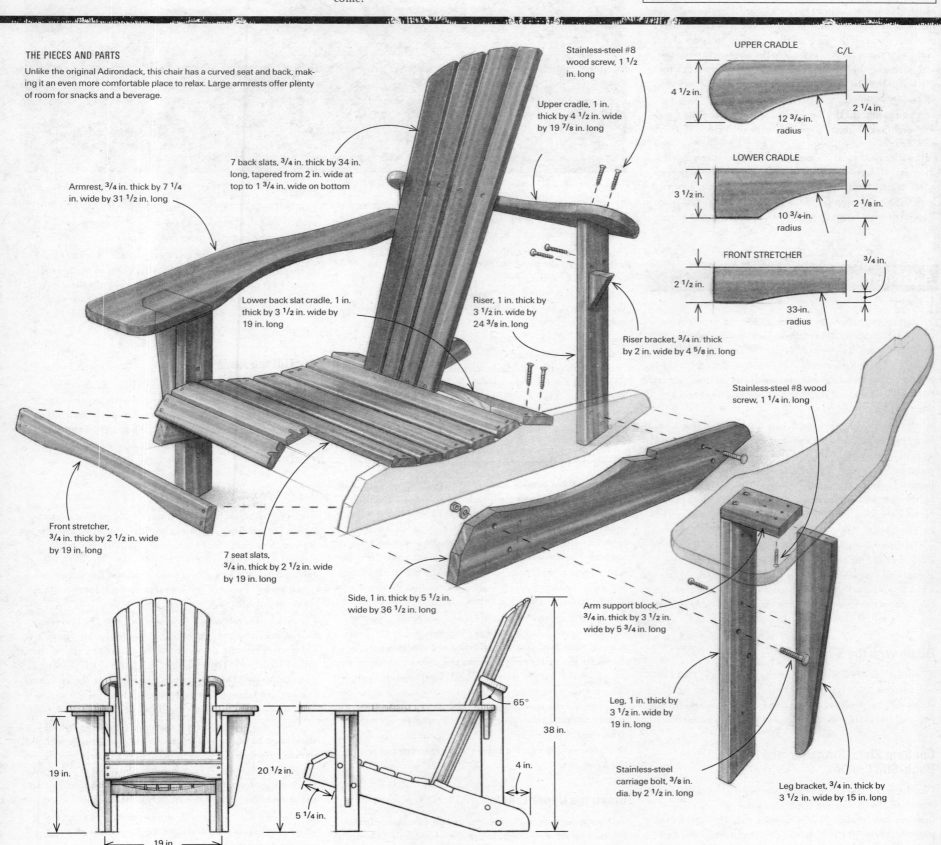

THE PIECES AND PARTS

Unlike the original Adirondack, this chair has a curved seat and back, making it an even more comfortable place to relax. Large armrests offer plenty of room for snacks and a beverage.

Stainless-steel #8 wood screw, 1½ in. long

Upper cradle, 1 in. thick by 4½ in. wide by 19⅞ in. long

7 back slats, ¾ in. thick by 34 in. long, tapered from 2 in. wide at top to 1¾ in. wide on bottom

Armrest, ¾ in. thick by 7¼ in. wide by 31½ in. long

Lower back slat cradle, 1 in. thick by 3½ in. wide by 19 in. long

Riser, 1 in. thick by 3½ in. wide by 24⅜ in. long

Riser bracket, ¾ in. thick by 2 in. wide by 4⅝ in. long

Stainless-steel #8 wood screw, 1¼ in. long

Front stretcher, ¾ in. thick by 2½ in. wide by 19 in. long

7 seat slats, ¾ in. thick by 2½ in. wide by 19 in. long

Side, 1 in. thick by 5½ in. wide by 36½ in. long

Arm support block, ¾ in. thick by 3½ in. wide by 5¾ in. long

Leg, 1 in. thick by 3½ in. wide by 19 in. long

Stainless-steel carriage bolt, ⅜ in. dia. by 2½ in. long

Leg bracket, ¾ in. thick by 3½ in. wide by 15 in. long

UPPER CRADLE C/L
4½ in.
12¾-in. radius
2¼ in.

LOWER CRADLE
3½ in.
10¾-in. radius
2⅛ in.

FRONT STRETCHER
¾ in.
2½ in.
33-in. radius

19 in.

19 in.

20½ in.

5¼ in.

65°

38 in.

4 in.

BEGIN WITH THE SIDE PIECES

FULL-SIZE TEMPLATES MAKE CURVES EASY

Copy these patterns to the measurements indicated and use them to draw templates. Cut out the templates and transfer the shapes to the workpieces.

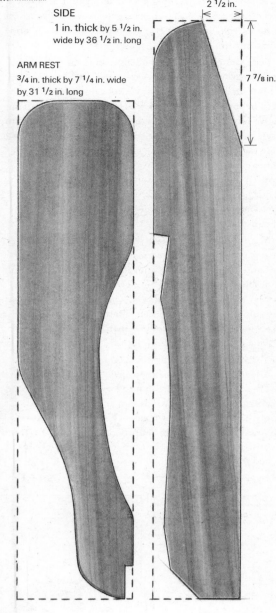

SIDE
1 in. thick by 5 1/2 in. wide by 36 1/2 in. long

ARM REST
3/4 in. thick by 7 1/4 in. wide by 31 1/2 in. long

2 1/2 in.

7 7/8 in.

Trace the shape. Use a thick-paper template to outline the side shape on stock.

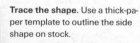

Tape sides together. Begnal uses double-sided tape to hold the boards together as he cuts them.

Keep the parts taped together. A file, followed with sandpaper, is a good way to smooth the edges of inside or outside curves. Start sanding with coarse paper, say P80-grit, working up to P150-grit.

TAPER AND SHAPE THE BACK SLATS

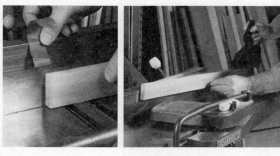

Easy tapering on the jointer. With the infeed table set to make a 1/8-in.-deep cut, add a piece of tape to the fence 1 in. from the front edge of the outfeed table. Also, wedge the guard open 1 in. or so. Now, with the machine running, lower the top end of a slat onto the outfeed table, using the tape as a guide and keeping your hands a safe distance from the cutterhead.

One pass per side. Use a push block to feed the back slat through the cutterhead. Flip the slat over and repeat. The short untapered portion at the top end won't be visible after sanding.

SCRIBE AN ARC ON THE BACK SLATS

Use the tip on the previous page to create a jumbo compass. After that, measure 10 in. from the nail hole and drill a 1/8-in.-dia. hole—a size just big enough to accept a pencil point.

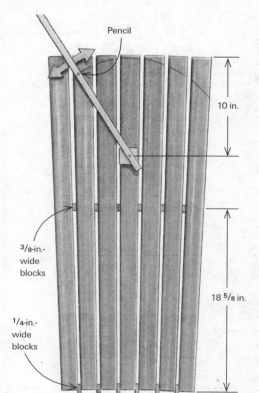

Pencil

10 in.

3/8-in.-wide blocks

1/4-in.-wide blocks

18 5/8 in.

Mark the arc. A clamp and some light pressure keep the back slats and spacers from shifting while Begnal uses the jumbo compass.

ASSEMBLE THE BASE

#8 wood screw

Countersink and 1/8-in.-dia. shank hole

No pilot hole needed for soft woods.

SCREW DETAIL

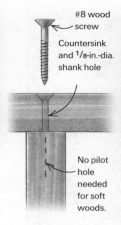

Make a subassembly. Screw the stretcher to the front and follow with the lower cradle.

Add one leg assembly at a time. Use a spring clamp to temporarily clamp each one to a side piece, then square it to the worksurface.

Secure the leg assemblies. Once the leg assemblies are in place, drill 3/8-in.-dia. holes through the sides and legs and add bolts, nuts, and washers.

Attach the upper cradle. Use a temporary spacer board to ensure that the risers stay parallel when the upper cradle is attached.

Continued →

ADD THE ARMS AND SLATS

Position the back slats. Start with the center slat, then the two end slats, and work your way in. The slats must be aligned at the bottom of the lower cradle, with even spacing between them.

Layout trick. Place the chair on its back and use spring clamps to level it. This will allow you to rest the slats on the cradles and adjust positioning without slippage.

Add the arms. Drive the riser screws (at the back-first to be sure the arm notch fits snugly around the riser. Begnal conceals the screws by driving them in from the inside of the riser and the underside of the support block.

Seat slats are the final step. The seven slats are attached at each end. The $3/8$-in. spacers between each slat make placement a snap.

Five Ways to Build a Bed

by Matthew Teague

Beds may be the most important pieces of furniture in the house. Not only do you spend a third of your life in them, but their sheer size makes them the focal point of whatever room they inhabit, and a grand canvas for fine wood and craftsmanship.

Beds also pose unique challenges to the woodworker. Headboards (and footboards) are usually held upright by only two joints, which must also knock down to allow the bed to be moved. Beds are also large and bulky, requiring creative methods to deal with the big workpieces. Furniture makers past and present have addressed these challenges in a wide variety of ways; in fact, supporting a mattress may be the only thing beds have in common. For this article, I scoured the woodworking world to find six of the best approaches to bed design, taking a close look at how their makers managed the dance between looks and construction.

All of these skilled pros started with the same realities: mattress size and the desired mattress height. Then they confronted the knock-down joinery, making the side rails removable. While there are numerous ways to support a mattress, most custom makers go with some version of ledger strips and simple wood slats. Mattress manufacturers make a lot of money selling box springs, but slats achieve the same end while saving you hundreds of dollars. Either way, the choice affects mattress height.

After you deal with the inescapable realities, though, a bed leaves you plenty of room to express yourself. Some makers rely on tradition for design and construction, while others make their own rules. Whether your tastes lean toward the eighteenth century or the twenty-first, the six construction methods shown here should cover almost any bed you can imagine.

Traditional Pencil-Post

"This pattern was probably taken from an eighteenth-century bed that came into the shop for my father to repair," says Lou Irion, former owner of Irion Company Furniture Makers in Christiana, Pennsylvania Jonathan Sanbuichi, who now runs the company, builds this bed the same way it was done for generations.

When assembled, the headboard and footboard on this bed are too tall to fit through standard doorways, so tall-post designs are engineered to break down completely.

To this end, posts attach to the headboard, footboard, and side rails using shallow tenons and traditional bed bolts hidden by bolt covers of varying designs.

The upper portions of the posts are tapered and hexagonal at the top, with hand-carved lamb's tongues where the taper begins. The upward sweep of the posts draws the eyes upward toward the tester, or canopy. Joining the tester to the posts is straightforward: The maker drives nails into the tops of the posts, removes their heads, and the four corners of the tester are then drilled so that they simply slide in place over the headless nails.

To replicate the look of period rope beds, this design is often built using thick, heavy rails that could have resisted the lateral pull of the rope. To accommodate modern box springs, bed irons must be mortised low on the side rails, a look that almost requires the bed to be dressed with a dust ruffle. A cleaner look, which is also historically accurate, skips the box spring altogether and uses slats to support the mattress.

TRADITIONAL BED BOLTS, OFFSET FOR CLEARANCE

The tall posts mean this bed must knock down completely for transport. To prevent the criss-crossing bed bolts from colliding mid-post, the side rail's bolt hole is centered, but the end rail's bolt enters $\frac{1}{2}$ in. below. As with all beds, the exact height of the rails is determined by mattress height and placement.

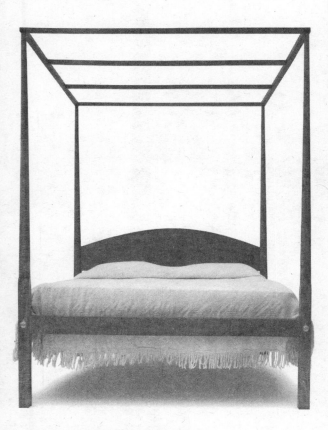

Shaker simplicity, canopy optional. Irion's clean design is a tribute to 1800s-style pencil-post beds, and features brass covers over the hardware.

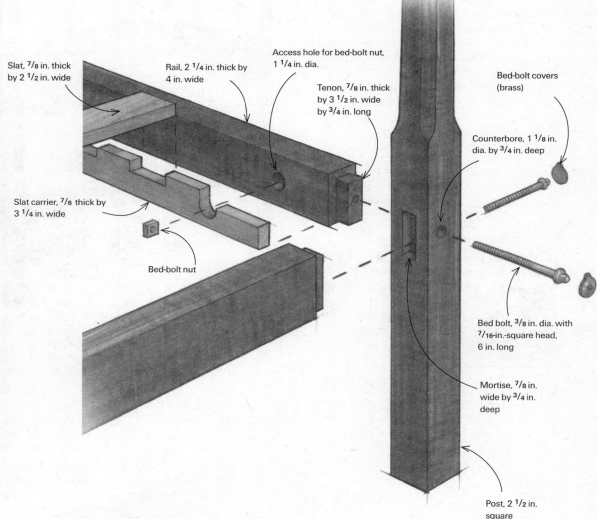

Slat, $\frac{7}{8}$ in. thick by 2 $\frac{1}{2}$ in. wide

Rail, 2 $\frac{1}{4}$ in. thick by 4 in. wide

Access hole for bed-bolt nut, 1 $\frac{1}{4}$ in. dia.

Tenon, $\frac{7}{8}$ in. thick by 3 $\frac{1}{2}$ in. wide by $\frac{3}{4}$ in. long

Bed-bolt covers (brass)

Counterbore, 1 $\frac{1}{8}$ in. dia. by $\frac{3}{4}$ in. deep

Slat carrier, $\frac{7}{8}$ thick by 3 $\frac{1}{4}$ in. wide

Bed-bolt nut

Bed bolt, $\frac{3}{8}$ in. dia. with $\frac{7}{16}$-in.-square head, 6 in. long

Mortise, $\frac{7}{8}$ in. wide by $\frac{3}{4}$ in. deep

Post, 2 $\frac{1}{2}$ in. square

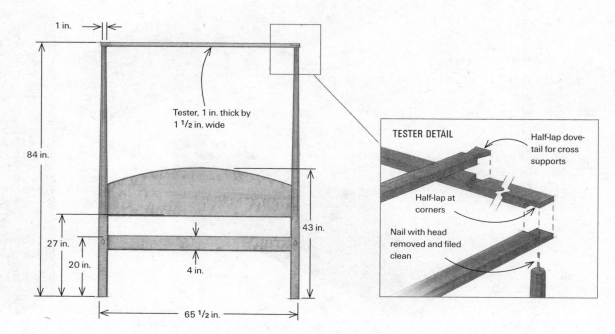

1 in.

Tester, 1 in. thick by 1 $\frac{1}{2}$ in. wide

84 in.

27 in.

20 in.

43 in.

4 in.

65 $\frac{1}{2}$ in.

TESTER DETAIL

Half-lap dovetail for cross supports

Half-lap at corners

Nail with head removed and filed clean

Continued →

Contemporary Pencil-Post

Designer and maker Bill Huston of Kennebunkport, Maine, is drawn to simple forms like this variation on a traditional pencil-post bed. While eight-sided posts are more common, tapered four-sided posts offer a similar visual presence yet appear more streamlined and contemporary, a look Huston prefers. He also chose a simple pattern for the headboard, then centered three wenge inlays near the top, a modern touch that has become a signature on his work.

Like the traditional pencil-post design, the posts, rails, and headboard of this bed break down completely to fit through doorways. Where tradition calls for through-bed bolts, however, Huston uses shopmade bed bolts that are invisible from the outside of the bed. Instead of buying specialty bolts, Huston opts for inexpensive 6-in. hanger bolts that have machine threads on one end and wood threads on the other. The wood threads are permanently screwed into the posts. The other end of the hanger bolt is let into a hole drilled into the end of the bed rail. To secure that end of the bolt, a nut and washer are set into a mortise drilled on the inside of the rail. Shallow ¼-in. tenons on the ends of the rails make quick work of assembly and alignment. "As with any spare design," says Huston, "the more straightforward the design, the more important the choice of woods and graining."

HIDDEN VARIATION ON TRADITIONAL BED BOLTS

Hanger bolts are the key, with one side simply screwed into the wood. An easy way to drive them is to lock two nuts halfway down the machine-threaded end, and then turn the outer nut with a wrench. Ultimately the machine-threaded end goes into the end of the rail and emerges in an oval slot where a nut and washer can draw the rail and post tight.

Tall posts with hidden hardware. Huston's modern take on the pencil post does away with the tester and visible bed bolts for a sleeker look.

HEADBOARD DETAIL

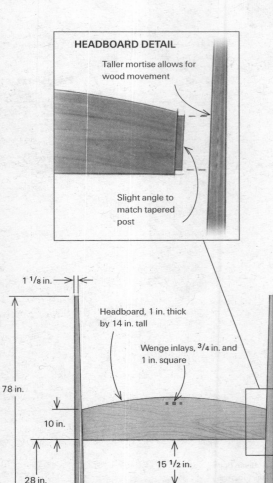

Taller mortise allows for wood movement

Slight angle to match tapered post

1 ⅛ in.

Headboard, 1 in. thick by 14 in. tall

Wenge inlays, ¾ in. and 1 in. square

78 in.

10 in.

15 ½ in.

28 in.

7 in.

65 ¼ in.

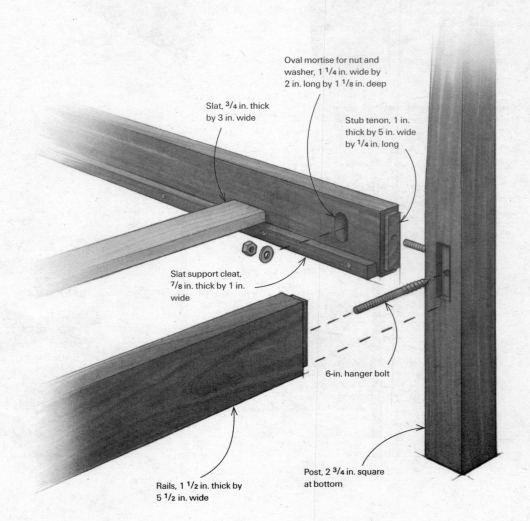

Oval mortise for nut and washer, 1 ¼ in. wide by 2 in. long by 1 ⅛ in. deep

Slat, ¾ in. thick by 3 in. wide

Stub tenon, 1 in. thick by 5 in. wide by ¼ in. long

Slat support cleat, ⅞ in. thick by 1 in. wide

Rails, 1 ½ in. thick by 5 ½ in. wide

6-in. hanger bolt

Post, 2 ¾ in. square at bottom

Frame-and-Slats

Kevin Rodel's clients requested a four-post, slat-type, Stickley-style Arts and Crafts bed in quartersawn white oak, but left the other details to his own tastes. In the end, Rodel guided them toward the Glasgow style, in keeping with his other work. He began by working out the shape of the posts as well as the slat size and orientation. Once the basic shape was determined, he turned to the joinery. Because the bed is a low-post design, the headboard and footboard can be solid assemblies glued up using traditional mortise-and-tenon joinery. For knockdown joints where the side rails meet the head and footboard, he opted for through-bed bolts (horton-brasses.com; part No. H-73) located using shallow tenons on the rails, much like those used on Irion's pencil-post bed. Instead of using traditional bolt covers, however, Rodel squared up the mortises used to recess the bolt heads and then plugged them with ebony caps. The edges of the caps are lined with tape or leather, which compresses just enough to create a friction fit, making them removable.

Because his clients already owned a mattress and box springs, he attached simple bed irons (also available from Horton Brasses) as low as possible on the side rails.

Hide the hardware, show off the artistry. The slats on Rodel's Arts and Crafts bed showcase the maker's detailed inlay and relief carving, while a clever cap conceals the hardware.

A PRETTY WAY TO HIDE BED BOLTS

Rodel opted for traditional bed bolts but covered up the bolt heads with a sleek alternative that harmonizes with the bed's Arts and Crafts style.

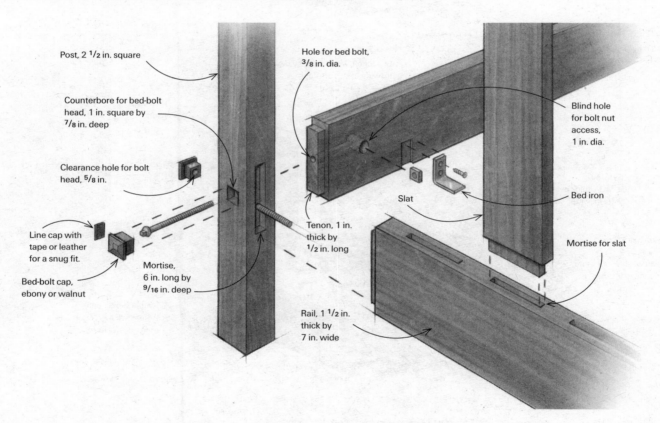

Post, 2 1/2 in. square

Counterbore for bed-bolt head, 1 in. square by 7/8 in. deep

Clearance hole for bolt head, 5/8 in.

Line cap with tape or leather for a snug fit.

Bed-bolt cap, ebony or walnut

Mortise, 6 in. long by 9/16 in. deep

Hole for bed bolt, 3/8 in. dia.

Blind hole for bolt nut access, 1 in. dia.

Slat

Bed iron

Mortise for slat

Tenon, 1 in. thick by 1/2 in. long

Rail, 1 1/2 in. thick by 7 in. wide

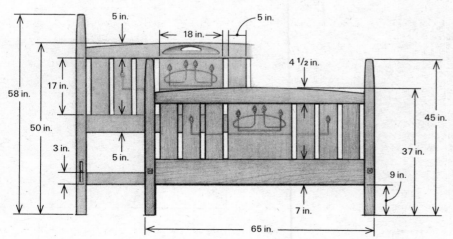

58 in.
50 in.
17 in.
3 in.
5 in.
5 in.
18 in.
5 in.
4 1/2 in.
45 in.
37 in.
9 in.
7 in.
65 in.

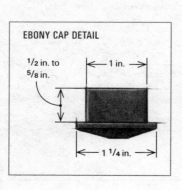

EBONY CAP DETAIL

1/2 in. to 5/8 in.

1 in.

1 1/4 in.

Continued ➡

Frame-and-Panel

Design ideas often come from unexpected places. The inspiration for Seattle woodworker Ross Day's bed came while he was watching a commercial promoting travel to Japan and featuring someone playing a koto, a Japanese instrument with strings stretched over a long, convex wooden soundboard. "The shape of the instrument attracted me," he said, "I just really liked the curves."

Day began with the curves in the top rail of the headboard, and later mimicked that curve throughout the bed in both the shapes of the panels and in the compound angles of the legs.

A few years earlier, Day had purchased a few planks at the lumberyard, convinced that their curved graining would one day come in handy. He bandsawed the planks into veneer, jointed the seams with a plane, and attached them to plywood cores. The veneered panels are grooved on edge and glued into the tenoned frames using solid cherry splines. Small gaps around the panels create interesting shadowlines.

Day's ingenious version of a hidden knockdown joint uses cap-head screws, accessed at one end by a hidden mortise in the rails and secured at the other end in threaded inserts that are set into the back side of a slip tenon in the headboard and footboard.

Harmonious lines, veneer construction. Matching curves inspired by musical instruments are paired with the beautiful grain of custom-sawn veneer.

SLIP TENONS MAKE FOR A STRONG AND ACCURATE JOINT

Day's bed features panels and rails joined to the posts by slip tenons. They're strong, forgiving, and the matching mortises are easy to make with a router or a slot mortiser.

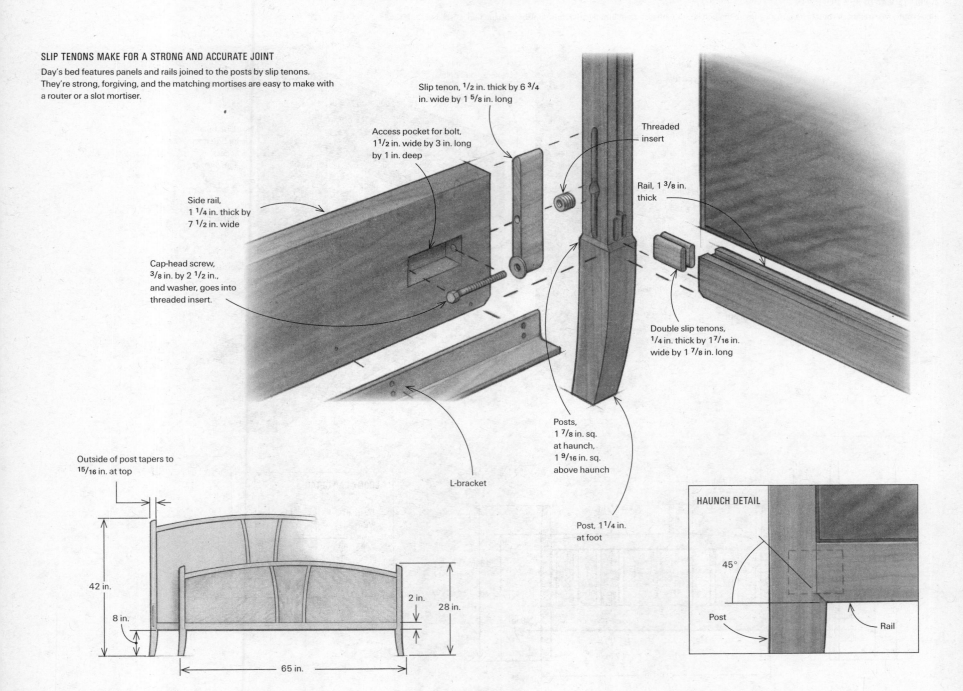

Slip tenon, 1/2 in. thick by 6 3/4 in. wide by 1 5/8 in. long

Access pocket for bolt, 1 1/2 in. wide by 3 in. long by 1 in. deep

Side rail, 1 1/4 in. thick by 7 1/2 in. wide

Cap-head screw, 3/8 in. by 2 1/2 in., and washer, goes into threaded insert.

Threaded insert

Rail, 1 3/8 in. thick

Double slip tenons, 1/4 in. thick by 1 7/16 in. wide by 1 7/8 in. long

L-bracket

Posts, 1 7/8 in. sq. at haunch, 1 9/16 in. sq. above haunch

Post, 1 1/4 in. at foot

Outside of post tapers to 15/16 in. at top

42 in.

8 in.

2 in.

28 in.

65 in.

HAUNCH DETAIL

45°

Post

Rail

Platform with Thick Timbers

Robert Spangler's inclination toward Asian design ties in well with a renewed interest in platform beds. This low-slung platform bed is an evolution of earlier designs. "I've always really liked the wide rails around the side," says Spangler, "because it accentuates the horizontal lines in the furniture."

Spangler's design is easily the least traditional of the lot. Not only is it a platform design, it also features a headboard that doesn't run all the way to the floor but instead appears to float. The headboard is tenoned into an angled riser block on the bed frame, which tilts it backward about 11° to make it comfortable when sitting up in bed.

While many platform beds are built so that the mattress slides around on top, Spangler set his inside the frame, with 1x4 slats resting on angle brackets. This not only allows the mattress to sit lower, but it also locks it into place.

Another interesting joinery detail is in the feet, which are simply blocks of wood that are joined in pairs by a simple rail, and notched to hug the frame above. The frame is joined with shopmade bed bolts let into the horizontal members, and a pair of alignment dowels. The bed bolts are nothing more than a 5-in. length of threaded rod outfitted with a nut and washer on each end.

Graceful curves crown strong, solid-wood construction. Asian elements in the headboard work well with thick timbers that cradle a low-slung, futon-like mattress.

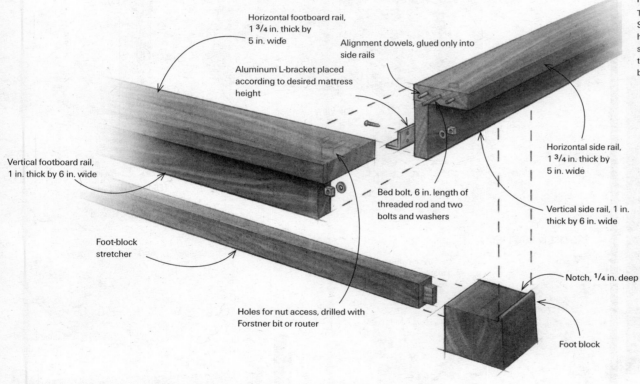

Horizontal footboard rail, 1 3/4 in. thick by 5 in. wide

Alignment dowels, glued only into side rails

Aluminum L-bracket placed according to desired mattress height

Vertical footboard rail, 1 in. thick by 6 in. wide

Foot-block stretcher

Bed bolt, 6 in. length of threaded rod and two bolts and washers

Horizontal side rail, 1 3/4 in. thick by 5 in. wide

Vertical side rail, 1 in. thick by 6 in. wide

Notch, 1/4 in. deep

Holes for nut access, drilled with Forstner bit or router

Foot block

PHYSICS KEEP HEAVY PLATFORM IN PLACE

There's little mystery to the L-shaped frame geometry that defines Spangler's Port Blakely bed. What might seem more mysterious is how the bed attaches to its pylon-like feet, but the answer is strikingly simple. Gravity and the sheer weight of the bed help keep it in place; the only additional locator is a 1/4-in.-deep notch at the top of the foot blocks that keeps the frame from sliding sideways.

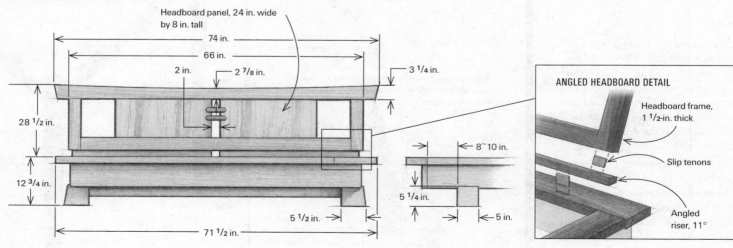

Headboard panel, 24 in. wide by 8 in. tall

74 in.
66 in.
2 in.
2 7/8 in.
3 1/4 in.
28 1/2 in.
12 3/4 in.
5 1/2 in.
71 1/2 in.
8~10 in.
5 1/4 in.
5 in.

ANGLED HEADBOARD DETAIL

Headboard frame, 1 1/2-in. thick

Slip tenons

Angled riser, 11°

Continued ➜

TABLES AND DESKS

Triangle Side Table

by Ray Finan

After 25 years of hopscotching from state to state working for a large company that makes paper for magazines like *Fine Woodworking*, I recently settled in Vermont and turned my woodworking hobby into a second career. To help launch my business, I decided to produce some pieces of furniture inspired by the Art Deco and mid-century modern styles. This little table was one of those pieces. I was eager to make a successful start, so of course I wanted my table to be distinctive in its design, but I also wanted it to be straightforward to make.

A few key decisions helped streamline the building process. When I hit on the idea of a curved-sided triangular shape for the tabletop, I found a simple way to generate the shape full size, first on paper and then on the workpiece. When it came to the legs, I thought turning and tapering them would nicely complement the shape of the top. But wouldn't that make for challenging leg-to-apron joinery? I greatly simplified the matter by dispensing with shouldered tenons and mortising the aprons full-size right into the legs. On a small, light table like this, that would give me plenty of joint strength. To cut the mortises, I built a router jig that took the guesswork out of what might have been a tricky process.

It takes very little wood to make the table, so this could be an opportunity to use some favorite scraps kicking around your shop. I made the top of mine from a beautiful small board of curly ash I'd been saving.

Lay It Out Full Scale

Although this is a fairly simple table, I found it beneficial to build it from full-size drawings. They made it a snap to lay out precise mortise locations, helped ensure that the legs didn't splay during assembly, and provided a controlled method for tapering the legs, even for a novice turner like me. Two drawings are needed: a plan view and a leg profile. The good news is that the drawings are very quick to make and you'll soon be building furniture.

I drew the plan view on drafting paper. I used a beam compass to draw the curved outlines of the top and a straightedge to draw the equilateral triangle that represents the centerlines of the aprons. Next, with a regular compass, I drew three concentric circles at each point of the triangle. The small circle is the circumference of the leg where it meets the floor; the middle circle is the circumference of the leg at the top; and the large circle represents

the edge of the table where it is cut away to allow the leg to penetrate the top.

I drew the full-scale leg profile on a scrap of ¼-in. hardboard so that I could use it as a frequent reference when turning the legs to a taper. After drawing the tapered elevation, I added a series of lateral lines across the leg. While turning, I took caliper measurements at these points and transferred them to the leg.

Three Legs, Three Stages

Cutting mortises in the legs after they had been tapered would have been a challenge. I simplified matters by making the legs in three steps. First, I turned the square blanks to 1¾-in. cylinders. Then I mortised the cylinders in the router jig. And last, I remounted the cylinders and turned them to a taper.

Since I had the full-scale plan-view drawing, marking the mortise locations was easy. I simply stood the cylinders in place on the drawing and transferred the apron centerlines to the leg. I carried those marks around to the top of the leg and used them to register the leg in the router jig. One important thing to note is that the mortises will be cut on the face opposite these marks—so be sure to make the registration marks on what you want to be the outside face of the leg.

Full-Scale Layout is Key to Success

Finan draws a top view of the table full-scale on paper and uses the drawing at several critical points as he builds. A full-scale front view of the leg, drawn on a thin piece of MDF, guides him on the lathe.

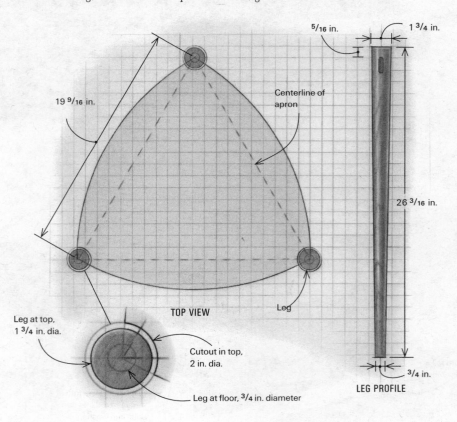

19 9/16 in.

5/16 in.   1 3/4 in.

Centerline of apron

26 3/16 in.

3/4 in.

TOP VIEW

Leg

LEG PROFILE

Leg at top, 1 3/4 in. dia.

Cutout in top, 2 in. dia.

Leg at floor, 3/4 in. diameter

EXERCISE IN GEOMETRY

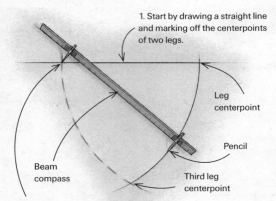

1. Start by drawing a straight line and marking off the centerpoints of two legs.

Leg centerpoint

Beam compass

Pencil

Third leg centerpoint

2. Place the pin of a beam compass on the first two leg centerpoints and draw crossing arcs to find the third leg centerpoint (above).

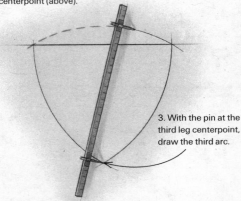

3. With the pin at the third leg centerpoint, draw the third arc.

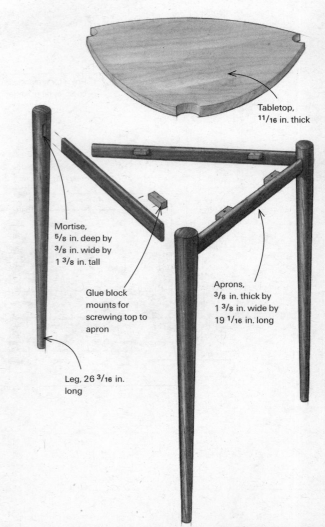

Tabletop, 11/16 in. thick

Mortise, 5/8 in. deep by 3/8 in. wide by 1 3/8 in. tall

Glue block mounts for screwing top to apron

Aprons, 3/8 in. thick by 1 3/8 in. wide by 19 1/16 in. long

Leg, 26 3/16 in. long

After cutting all the mortises, I put the leg cylinders back between centers on the lathe and shaped the tapered profile. I don't do much turning, so I tried to make things as foolproof as possible. I started by using a parting tool to cut a series of evenly spaced, progressively deeper grooves along the leg. I used calipers to transfer measurements from the leg profile drawing to the appropriate grooves. Then, using a 3/4-in. roughing gouge, I removed the waste wood between the grooves. I faired the leg with a long block of wood with 100-grit self-stick sandpaper adhered to it. Then I finish-sanded the legs to 400-grit while they were still on the lathe. With the sanding finished, I used the parting tool to form a slight crown at the top of the leg, paring back at a slight angle until the leg separated from the drive center.

The Base Comes Together

After thicknessing and ripping the apron stock to size, I rounded over all four long edges with a quarter-round bit on the router table. I used a test piece of apron stock and a test mortise to sneak up on a snug fit. After applying glue and getting the pieces knocked together, I stood the base up on the drawing and tweaked the stance until the tips of the legs stood precisely in the small circles. Then I cinched the band clamp, rechecked the stance, and let the glue cure.

Top It Off

The full-scale drawing came in handy again when it was time to lay out the tabletop. I taped the drawing to the tabletop blank and used an awl to mark the centerpoints of the three legs. Then I removed the drawing and used the beam compass—with its pin in the holes made by the awl—to draw the curved sides of the top. I used the regular compass, its pin in the same awl holes, to draw a 2-in.-dia. circle at each point.

I bandsawed out the long arcs of the top, but before I did so I used a Forstner bit at the drill press to create the tightly curved cutouts for the legs. To get a clean cut, it's a good idea, especially in wood with difficult grain, to make the blank large enough to allow full contact of the Forstner bit. I cleaned up the bandsawn arcs with rasps and files.

Different Finishes for Top and Base

To showcase the spectacular grain pattern of the curly ash, I applied multiple coats of Waterlox Original, wet-sanding it in with 600-grit wet-or-dry paper. I wanted a sharp contrast between the light-colored top and the white-oak base, so I darkened the base with a recipe from Teri Masaschi that produces a look reminiscent of lightly fumed white oak—without the ammonia fumes. I let the finish cure for a week, then lightly wet-sanded the top and base with a 2,000-grit Abralon pad and a 50/50 blend of mineral spirits and paraffin oil, and gave it a light coat of paste wax.

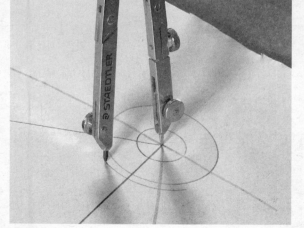

Two compasses create the plan. Finan uses a beam compass—in this case simply a yardstick fitted with a movable pin and pencil—to lay out the curve-sided triangle of the top. He uses a regular compass to establish the circumferences of the legs and the corner cutout of the tabletop.

Do the Leg Work

1. TURN A CYLINDER

And mark the mortises. After turning the leg blank to a 1 3/4-in.-dia. cylinder (not tapered yet), Finan puts it in place on the drawing and transfers the apron centerlines. These will register the leg in the mortising jig.

2. ROUT THE MORTISES

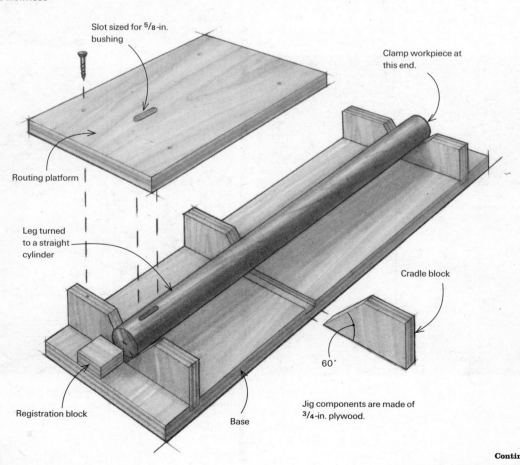

Slot sized for 5/8-in. bushing

Clamp workpiece at this end.

Routing platform

Leg turned to a straight cylinder

Cradle block

Registration block

Base

60°

Jig components are made of 3/4-in. plywood.

Continued →

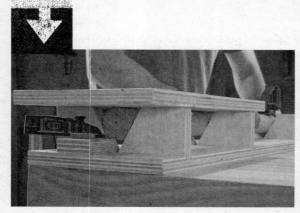

Snug in the jig. A clamp at the far end is critical, but the mortise jig is sized so the leg is also held firmly between the routing platform and the cradle blocks. If necessary, Finan unscrews the platform to insert the leg.

ALIGNMENT IS EASY

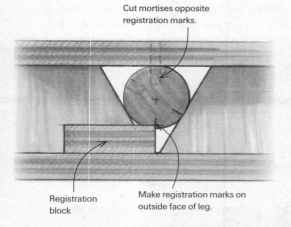

Cut mortises opposite registration marks.

Registration block

Make registration marks on outside face of leg.

Plunge with a bushing. Using a $^5/_8$-in. guide bushing and a $^3/_8$-in. spiral upcut bit in his plunge router, Finan cuts the mortises in a series of progressively deeper passes.

3. NOW TURN THE TAPER

Tapering tricks. To achieve a consistent taper, Finan starts by cutting a series of grooves with a parting tool, using his full-scale leg drawing to set his calipers. He uses a roughing gouge to remove the waste between the grooves, then smooths the taper with a long, straight sanding block.

Round the top. After shaping the top of the leg with the parting tool, he sands it smooth.

ADD THE APRONS

The apron is a tenon. Finan shapes the aprons with a roundover bit on the router table, preparing them to be inserted fully into the leg mortises. This means he won't have any shoulders to fit to the round, tapered leg.

Perfect placement. Because there are no shoulders on the aprons, the legs can be adjusted vertically. With the joints just glued, Finan tweaks the legs until they stand within the $^3/_4$-in. circles on the drawing.

A little belt tightening. After adjusting the stance of the table, Finan cinches up a band clamp. He checks the stance once more and then leaves the table on a flat surface to cure. He will remove the blue tape (which makes glue cleanup easy) before the glue dries.

Screw blocks. Preparing to attach the top, Finan rubs on screw blocks, holding them in place with finger pressure for a minute or two until the glue stiffens.

Good point. Finan tapes the full-scale drawing to the tabletop blank and uses an awl to transfer the centerpoints of the legs. The awl holes allow him to quickly lay out the outlines of the tabletop.

Drill first, saw later. Using a Forstner bit, Finan drills the cutouts for the legs at the corners of the top. Then it's on to the bandsaw to cut the curved sides of the tabletop.

English-Inspired Dropleaf Side Table

by Chris Gochnour

Cricket tables were common in England during the eighteenth century. Typically distinguished by round tops and three-legged bases, many cricket tables, like the one featured here, also included drop leaves, adding an extra measure of charm and utility. Although this piece is based on an early English table, I made a few changes to give it a look that's distinctly American Arts and Crafts.

Make the Diamond-Shaped Legs

Rip blanks for the legs out of two boards, each 1¾ in. thick by 3¼ in. wide by 28 in. long. Go to p. 377 to see the right sequence of tablesaw cuts. I found that using two boards simplifies the leg-making process even though it produces one more blank than needed. The extra blank comes in handy as a test piece. My sawblade tilts to the right, but the procedure is the same for a left-tilt saw as long as the fence is oriented correctly.

Now cut the legs to length—Because the legs splay out under the table, the crosscuts must be made at an angle. Begin by labeling, on a side surface, the top and bottom ends.

On both ends of each leg, draw a reference line from the 120° corner to the 60° corner. This line must always be horizontal when you trim the ends.

Now, set your miter-saw blade 7° to the left. Clamp a support cradle (see p. 377) slightly to the left of the blade, and place the leg in cradle A with the top end at the blade and the reference line horizontal. Now, while holding the leg in place on the jig, trim the top end at 7°. Do the same for the top ends of the other two legs.

Next, shift the cradle to the right side of the blade. Mark the leg's total length at 25⅜ in. and cut the bottom end of each leg parallel to the top end.

Cut the angled mortises—Each leg has four mortises—two for the aprons and two for the stretchers—all cut on the narrow sides of the legs and inset ¼ in. from the wide side of the leg. With a dozen to cut, I put my hollow-chisel mortiser to work, along with the leg jig. After the machine

work, I used a chisel to shave the ends of the mortises to 6°. Taper the legs as shown (bottom photo, facing page).

Tenon the Aprons and Stretchers

You are ready to make the three aprons and three stretchers. Rip the parts to width, then use the tablesaw miter gauge set at 6° to crosscut them to length.

Cut the outside cheeks—The tenons are next, starting with the aprons. Decide which side of the parts you want on the outside of the table.

Set up the tablesaw with a ⅝-in.-wide dado blade raised slightly less than ¼ in. above the table. Position the rip fence ¾ in. from the outside of the blade. Use a miter gauge, angled away from the blade at 6°, to reference the end of the apron so it's parallel to the fence.

Then, with the outside face of the apron against the saw table and the end butting against the rip fence, cut one of the outside tenon cheeks. You'll need two overlapping passes to remove all the waste. Because the outside faces of the aprons, stretchers, and legs are flush to each other, the tenon location is important. Repeat on all the parts, making the cuts only on the same outside cheeks.

Now, readjust the miter gauge to angle toward the blade at 6°. Make the outside cheek cut on the other end of each part. After the last cut, you'll have all the outside tenon cheeks cut to align flush with the outsides of the legs.

Cut the inside cheeks—At this point, it's just a matter of cutting the inside cheeks to fit snugly in the mortises. That's done by making several cuts to "sneak up" on a perfect fit. Start by placing the inside face of an apron against the saw table and butting the end against the rip fence. Also, butt the edge of the apron against the miter gauge, which is still facing toward the blade at 6°. Then, make a shallow (about 3/16 in.) cut. As before, you'll need to make two passes.

Check the tenon fit; you can expect the tenon to be too big because the dado-blade cut was shallow. Raise the dado blade slightly, then recut and recheck the fit. Continue increasing the depth of cut until the tenon fits just right. Now, make inside cheek cuts on all the aprons and stretchers with the miter gauge angled toward the blade.

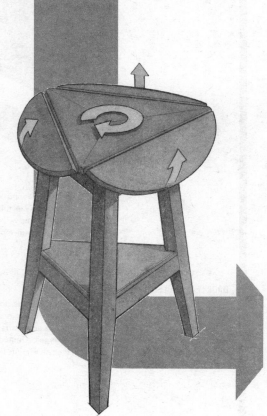

GIVE IT A SPIN
With the leaves lowered, the table has an eye-catching triangular top. To expand top until the leaves are over the legs.

Continued →

Readjust the miter gauge to angle away from the blade at 6°. Then make the inside cheek cut on the other end of each part. After the last cut, you'll have all the cheek cuts done.

Last, lay out and mark the location of the top and bottom cheeks and shoulders. Cut to the lines with a backsaw.

Bevel the aprons and stretchers—The upper edges on all the aprons and stretchers must be beveled so they end up parallel with the tabletop and bottom shelf. Cut the bevels on the tablesaw with the blade tilted to 4°.

Now you can go ahead and smooth all of the surfaces with a handplane to remove any mill marks.

Band Clamps Ease Assembly

Assemble the legs, aprons, and stretchers. The joints are angled and the base is triangular, but band clamps work wonderfully. You'll need just one for the aprons and one for the stretchers.

The glue-up is a five-minute operation. Use a small brush to apply glue to all the mortises and tenons. Assemble each one, and then add the band clamps.

Install the axis board—The axis board runs parallel with one apron and is notched into the other two. A slightly oversize hole through the center of the axis board accepts a machine screw that secures the top to the base and serves as a pivot point.

Notch the base for the hinge barrels—When the top of the table is rotated 60° to open or close the leaves, the hinges pass over the top end of the legs and aprons. So, at each of the three corners of the base, you'll need to cut a 1/8-in.-deep notch to allow clearance for the hinge barrels.

Mark the notch locations with a trammel, then use a router to remove the waste between scribe marks. Finish with a chisel.

The Top is Fun

The top is an interesting geometric array made up of six boards. Three are isosceles triangles joined with splines to create a central equilateral triangle. The other three are circular segments, and attach (with hinges) to the central triangle to form the drop leaves and create a full circle. From the drawing on p. 50, make a full-size template of the triangle and the drop leaf.

Use the two templates to lay out the isosceles triangles and leaves in a row on a single board. Cut all six parts on the bandsaw, making sure all are slightly oversize. Then, use the tablesaw with a cutoff table and protractor fence to trim the two inside edges on each triangular piece so they're straight and meet at exactly 120°. Later, after the sections are glued, handplane the three outer edges to exact size.

The splines keep the triangles aligned during assembly and add glue area, which means a stronger joint, important because wood movement will stress these areas. You can cut the stopped grooves on a router table with a 1/4-in. slot-cutter buried in the router fence. Elevate the slot-cutter so the cut will be centered on the 3/4-in.-thick stock. Then, set the fence to make a 3/8-in.-deep cut.

Note that each triangular piece has one long edge, and two shorter edges of identical length. Each of the two shorter edges gets the stopped groove for the splines. On one of the edges, you begin the groove at the stopped end by plunging the slot-cutter into the stock and then feeding the entire edge of the triangle through the cutter. When making the plunge cut, it's important to make sure the triangle corner nearest the plunge is kept firmly against the router fence to serve as a pivot point. Don't use the opposite corner as you'll likely run into some kickback as the stock is plunged.

To cut the remaining edge, place it against the fence, then feed the stock into the slot-cutter. Stop the cut just short of the triangle corner before using the opposite corner as a pivot point to swing the edge away from the cutter.

To clamp the three triangles, I make a clamping table out of melamine and hardwood braces (see p. 50). It uses a system of wedges to apply even clamp pressure to the tri-

angles. When the glue has set, remove the excess glue with a scraper and handplane. If handplaning isn't your forte, you can simply sand the top and bottom surfaces smooth. Complete the triangular top by planing the outer edges to their final dimensions.

With the triangular portion completed, use a trammel set to a 10 1/2-in. radius to make reference marks where the circular leaves will be attached. The points of the triangle will be trimmed later to align with the leaves.

The shelf is like the top—The triangular shelf is a thinner version of the one on top, but the construction is essentially the same. Make a full-size template of the isosceles triangle from the drawing on p. 50.

Mount the Leaves and Attach the Top

Now you can attach the drop leaves. First, use a spokeshave to smooth the curved edge of each leaf to the line traced earlier.

The hinges are 7/8-in. by 1 1/2-in. butt hinges from White Chapel Ltd. (www.whitechapel-ltd.com). To mount them, mortise the hinges into the leaves at a point 3 in. from each end. With the hinges installed on the leaves, align them with the triangular top and transfer the hinge locations. Then mortise the top and screw the hinges in place. Now use a bandsaw, file, and sander to shape the points of the tabletop to align with the drop-leaf curves.

The top is fastened to the base with a machine screw that slips through a slightly oversize hole in the axis board and into a threaded brass plate mortised into the underside of the top. Drill and tap for a 1/4-20 thread in the center of the plate. Then, bore and countersink for four 1/8-in.-dia. holes near the corners of the plate. Cut a mortise to accept the plate, and secure it with #6 by 1/2-in.-long brass wood screws. Now, attach the top and enjoy this unique side table.

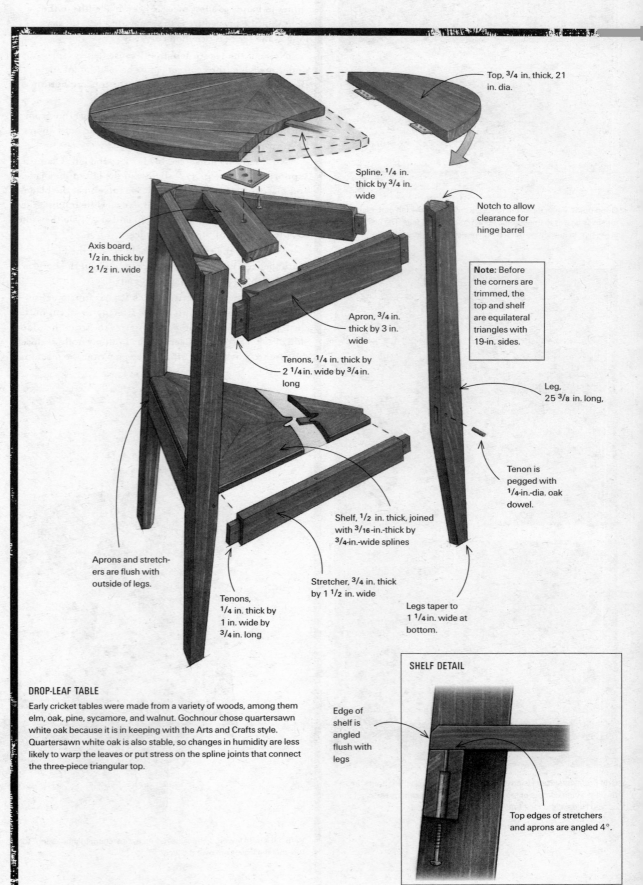

Top, 3/4 in. thick, 21 in. dia.

Spline, 1/4 in. thick by 3/4 in. wide

Notch to allow clearance for hinge barrel

Axis board, 1/2 in. thick by 2 1/2 in. wide

Apron, 3/4 in. thick by 3 in. wide

Tenons, 1/4 in. thick by 2 1/4 in. wide by 3/4 in. long

Note: Before the corners are trimmed, the top and shelf are equilateral triangles with 19-in. sides.

Leg, 25 3/8 in. long,

Tenon is pegged with 1/4-in.-dia. oak dowel.

Shelf, 1/2 in. thick, joined with 3/16-in.-thick by 3/4-in.-wide splines

Stretcher, 3/4 in. thick by 1 1/2 in. wide

Legs taper to 1 1/4 in. wide at bottom.

Aprons and stretchers are flush with outside of legs.

Tenons, 1/4 in. thick by 1 in. wide by 3/4 in. long

DROP-LEAF TABLE

Early cricket tables were made from a variety of woods, among them elm, oak, pine, sycamore, and walnut. Gochnour chose quartersawn white oak because it is in keeping with the Arts and Crafts style. Quartersawn white oak is also stable, so changes in humidity are less likely to warp the leaves or put stress on the spline joints that connect the three-piece triangular top.

SHELF DETAIL

Edge of shelf is angled flush with legs

Top edges of stretchers and aprons are angled 4°.

Cut the Leg Blanks

Leg geometry simplifies construction
Splayed legs usually require fussy-to-cut compound-angle joinery, but not on this table. Viewed from above with the table assembled, the aprons and stretchers meet the diamond-shaped legs at right angles. So, to splay the legs, the aprons and stretchers need only be angled in one direction.

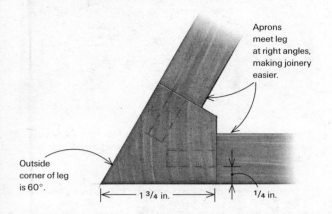

Aprons meet leg at right angles, making joinery easier.

Outside corner of leg is 60°.

1 3/4 in.

1/4 in.

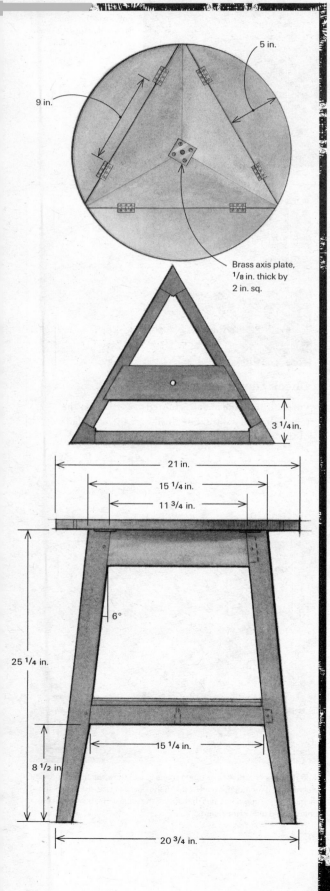

5 in.

9 in.

Brass axis plate, 1/8 in. thick by 2 in. sq.

3 1/4 in.

21 in.

15 1/4 in.

11 3/4 in.

6°

25 1/4 in.

8 1/2 in.

15 1/4 in.

20 3/4 in.

Rip the stick into two blanks.
Angle the blade and set the rip fence as shown. Cut the first blank, rotate the offcut piece, and cut the second blank. Rip the other stick to get four blanks total. For all cuts, use a push stick near the blade.

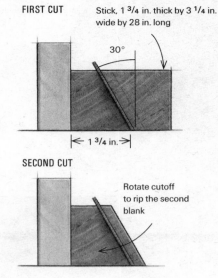

FIRST CUT

Stick, 1 3/4 in. thick by 3 1/4 in. wide by 28 in. long

30°

1 3/4 in.

SECOND CUT

Rotate cutoff to rip the second blank

A final cut completes the shape. Move the rip fence to the other side of the blade. Use the spare blank to make test cuts until the top face is 1 3/4 in. Rip the remaining three blanks at the same setting.

THIRD CUT

Move rip fence to opposite side of blade

1 3/4 in.

30°

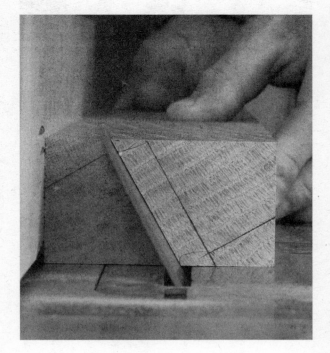

A Cradle Makes Joinery Easier

A JIG HOLDS THE LEG IN TWO POSITIONS

The odd shape of the legs makes them difficult to clamp in place for cutting to length, cutting mortises, or planing the tapered bottoms. This support jig simplifies all three operations.

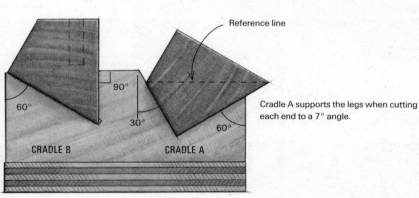

Reference line

Cradle B is used to support the legs when cutting the apron and stretcher mortises, and when handplaning the leg tapers.

90°

60°

30°

CRADLE B

CRADLE A

60°

Cradle A supports the legs when cutting each end to a 7° angle.

MAKING THE JIG

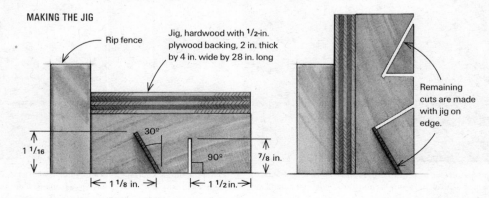

Rip fence

Jig, hardwood with 1/2-in. plywood backing, 2 in. thick by 4 in. wide by 28 in. long

30°

90°

Remaining cuts are made with jig on edge.

1 1/16

7/8 in.

1 1/8 in.

1 1/2 in.

The blade is at 90° for the first cut, 30° for the remaining three. You end up with two channels, each cut at different angles and used for different purposes as the legs are made.

Continued ➔

Cut mortises. Gochnour uses a mortiser to remove most of the waste. Then he angles the ends of the mortises to 6° with a bench chisel.

Trim to length. With the jig clamped to the left side of a miter saw set to 7°, trim one end of each leg. Then slide the leg to the right side of the saw and cut to length at the same 7°.

Taper the legs. After using a bandsaw to remove most of the waste, use the cradle jig to hold the legs in place so a handplane can clean up the surfaces.

Aprons Have Angled Tenons

Cut to length. Cut the aprons (shown) and stretchers to length with the tablesaw miter gauge at a 6° angle.

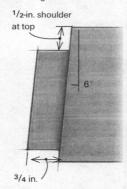

1/2-in. shoulder at top

6°

3/4 in.

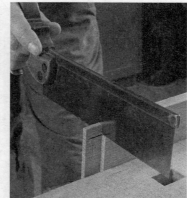

Cut the top and bottom. With a tenon saw, make a pair of parallel cuts to establish the top and bottom of the tenon. Then cut across the grain to form the shoulders.

Outside cheeks are first. With a dado blade in the tablesaw, the miter gauge facing 6° away from the fence, and the rip fence positioned to establish the tenon length, cut all the outside cheeks on the left end of each apron and stretcher. Then, reset the miter gauge to face 6° toward the fence and cut all the outside cheeks on the right end of each apron and stretcher. Then flip the workpieces and cut the inside faces.

> ▶ **TIP**
>
>
>
> ## Check the Shoulder Depth.
>
> When the outside cheek is butted against a leg, the tenon shoulder should be flush with the outside face of the mortise.

Band Clamps Aid Glue-Up

Glue and clamp. Add glue to all the mortises and tenons, then assemble the parts. A pair of band clamps—one around the aprons, one around the stretchers—provides all the pressure needed.

Plane the outside surfaces perfectly flush. With a piece of plywood clamped to the workbench to serve as a planing platform, Gochnour uses a smoothing plane to make sure the outside faces of the legs, aprons, and stretchers are perfectly flush.

Add the axis board. An axis board spans two of the stretchers to provide a centerpoint for mounting the top. Cut the board to size, then mark the location of the apron notches that accept the ends of the board. Cut the notches and glue in the board.

Make the Top and Leaves

For consistent color and grain, cut the top pieces from a single 7-ft. board. Make a template of both shapes, and then arrange and trace them on the board.

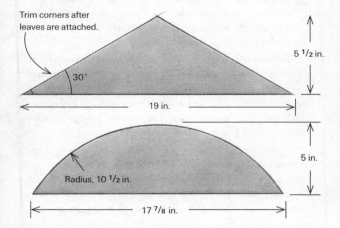

Trim corners after leaves are attached.

30°

5 1/2 in.

19 in.

Radius, 10 1/2 in.

5 in.

17 7/8 in.

Rough-cut the parts. Cut the circular parts and triangular parts with a bandsaw. Stay just outside the marked lines so the parts end up slightly oversize.

Trim the triangles to exact size. Gochnour uses a shopmade cutoff table with a protractor fence to trim the two inside edges of each triangular part. He handplanes the outside edges after assembly.

SPLINES STRENGTHEN THE TOP AND SHELF

Cut the spline grooves. Cut a stopped groove on the inside edges of the triangles. The grooves accept splines that restrain wood movement.

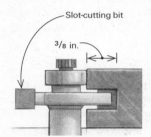

Slot-cutting bit

3/8 in.

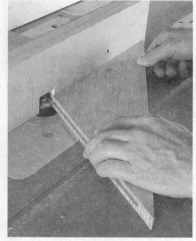

Assemble the triangles. A clamping table, made from melamine so glue won't stick, has three wood cleats screwed to it, two of them angled to accept wedges. Assemble the three triangular parts using glue and splines, then add the assembly to the clamping table and drive wedges between the cleats and the triangle.

Add the Leaves and Attach the Top

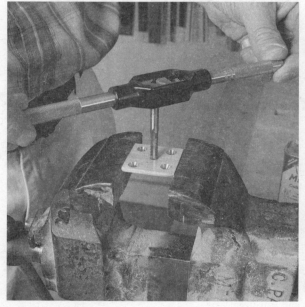

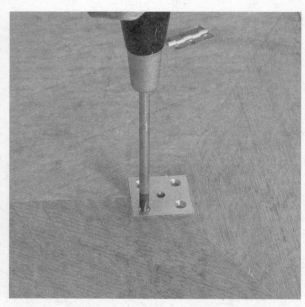

Set the hinges. Lay out and scribe the location of the hinges on the leaves, then mortise them in. Then use a clamp to hold each leaf to the triangular top, and transfer the hinge locations.

Make the axis plate. Use a hacksaw to cut a brass plate to size, then drill four mounting holes and a center hole. Tap the center hole for a 1/4-20 thread.

Mount the plate. After mortising in the axis plate, attach it with four brass wood screws.

Mount the top. To attach the top to the base, add a washer to a single round-head machine screw, then slip the screw through a slightly oversize hole in the axis board. Tighten the screw until it's slightly snug.

Hall Table with Floral-Inspired Curves

by Jennifer Anderson

I designed this entryway table when I was a student in the Fine Woodworking program at College of the Redwoods. Many of my classmates were designing furniture with legs that tapered from thick at the bottom to thin at the top, a style we called "Gumby" legs. Inspired by the calla lilies that grow wild near the school on California's north coast, I took a different approach.

To echo the flower's shape, I gave each leg a pronounced taper, topped with a gentle curve, on both outside faces. I cut away the table's top at each corner to put these graceful shapes on full display, and I shaped the apron faces to harmonize with the profile of the legs. I built the table from shedua, with maple for the drawer sides and bottom.

The piece is a treat to build. The design is not as complex as a carcase piece but goes beyond a simple table with drawer, adding a few wrinkles that will help you grow as a woodworker.

There's a variety of joinery, from traditional mortise-and-tenon joints to dovetails to dowels, and real pleasure in shaping the legs and aprons. For this, I blend machine work and hand tools.

Start with the Joinery

Cut all of the joinery while the stock is still square, but first take a few moments to make a template for your leg shape, and use it and a bevel gauge to mark the legs and aprons for the curves and tapers you'll cut later. To join the narrow legs and aprons, I interlocked the mortise-and-tenon joints. I routed the mortises and cut the tenons at the tablesaw.

When cutting the tenons, test each setup on sample material until the machines and jigs are dialed in. Use a marking gauge to lay out the shoulders and cheeks on each piece. Clamp a stop to a crosscut sled for cutting the shoulders. Cut all the wide surfaces first, then adjust the blade to the proper height for cutting the shoulders on the apron edges. Before making this cut, put a piece of blue tape on the stop to offset the shoulder slightly. This leaves a small strip of extra material on the shoulder that can easily be pared flush.

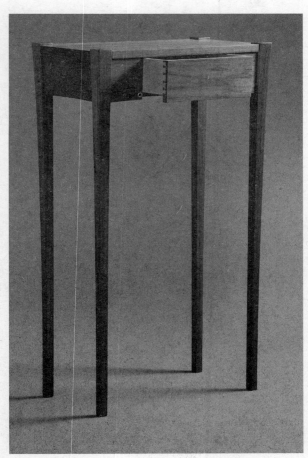

I used a tenoning jig to cut the cheeks, then a bandsaw to remove the remaining waste at the ends and between the tenons. Clean up and fit the joints with chisels and files. I round my tenons instead of chopping the mortises square. When all the joinery is cut, saw the drawer front from the front apron. Next, dry-fit the end assemblies and measure the inside distance between the front and rear aprons to determine the length of the interior rails. For greatest accuracy, take this measurement as close to the legs as possible.

Create the Drawer Pocket

The drawer enclosure is formed by a pair of interior rails—each slightly narrower than the aprons—that run front to back and guide the drawer sides. Each rail is joined by dowels to the front and rear aprons and rabbeted along the bottom to accommodate a framed panel. This panel closes the compartment, adds rigidity, and supports the drawer from underneath.

For smooth drawer movement, the interior rails must be parallel to one another, with dowel joints that are precisely aligned, front to back. To accurately lay out the joints on the face of the rear apron, I used the front aprons as a reference.

A jig aids doweling—I drilled my dowel holes using a shopmade jig created especially for this project.

To drill a front apron, set the jig in place so its reference face is flush with the apron's interior edge. Clamp the jig temporarily while you fasten it with a couple of brads. At the drill press, take a moment to set the bit depth, using the layout for your shaping as a guide. Drill through your layout marks, simultaneously completing the jig and drilling your first set of dowel holes.

After drilling the apron, carefully align the jig on the end of the corresponding rail and drill the mating holes.

Repeat the process on all the aprons and corresponding rail ends. Once all the holes are bored, test the fit. One way to simplify the test-fitting of dowel joints is to use dowels in only half the holes. It also helps to compress them by rolling them between a file and your bench. This keeps the dowel holes from loosening during multiple dry-fits.

Build and Fit the Frame-and-Panel Bottom

The drawer pocket's bottom is a panel set in a frame held together with bridle joints. These joints are easy to cut with a tablesaw tenoning jig, and their ample glue surface makes them very strong. Because the drawer runs directly on the frame, I oriented the frame's joinery so the grain is uninterrupted from front to back. I made the frame slightly wide, so I could handplane a perfect fit later. I added 1/8-in.-thick edge-banding to hide the end grain on the frame's front edge.

Although it is hidden most of the time, the panel inside the frame is more for beauty than strength. Use your primary project wood, and take care in assembling and finishing.

I cut the tongue on the panel, and the stopped grooves that hold it, on the router table with a fence and straight bit. Sand the panel before this step. Heavy sanding afterward may loosen the fit. Prefinish the panel and the inside edges of the frame. After glue-up, saw 1/8 in. from the front edge and add the edge-banding. Flush the edge-banding and then plane the edges for the final fit.

Shaping Is the Fun Part

Once all joinery has been cut and fit, the shaping begins. I shaped both outside faces of each leg in a pronounced taper that ends in a graceful curve at the top of the leg. I also shaped the face of each apron to follow the taper of the legs for a consistent reveal where the two meet. Lastly, I planed a slight bevel into the edge of the top to match the rest of the piece.

To start shaping the legs, bandsaw close to one of your template layout lines. After the first cut, lay the template on the bandsawn surface and strike a new line for cutting the adjacent face. At the bench, use a combination of block and smoothing planes, scraper, and sandpaper to fair the curves and smooth the surfaces.

The taper in the apron's face is slight and easily planed in by hand. To lay out for the taper, dry-fit each leg-and-apron connection, measure the reveal at the top of the joint, and mark the bottom edge of the rail with this measurement. Strike a line at this mark along the bottom edge, and connect the mark with the top edge of the apron front. This pair of lines guides the planing.

I used a block plane to chamfer the top and bottom edges of each leg to prevent chipout. I also used a spoke-shave and block plane to shape a subtle curve on the bottom edge of each apron.

Dry-fit the table to make sure all the tapers and reveals are consistent. The cut-out gap around the legs should be consistent and wide enough to let the top expand and contract.

Pre-Finish and Glue Up

I almost always prefinish a piece before glue-up. When the parts are separate, there's no struggling to get a brush or pad into tight corners. The result is a very even finish, even one applied in multiple coats as with the shellac and wax on this piece. Prep by breaking edges and sanding parts to P400 grit, paying special attention to end grain. Tape off any surfaces that will get glue.

Gluing up a piece with a lot of components can become a desperate race to apply glue to all of the many surfaces and then get the joints together and clamped before parts start seizing. For greater control, I broke the process into four manageable stages.

Start by gluing and clamping the two side assemblies. With those in clamps, you have time to glue the dowels into the ends of the drawer rails.

After the glue has dried, glue the drawer rails into the front and rear aprons. Once this assembly is together, dry-fit it into the legs, check for square, and clamp.

When the glue is dry, unclamp and remove the leg assemblies. Apply glue to the tenons on the front and rear aprons, seat them in their mortises, and clamp.

When this assembly comes out of clamps, the last step is to glue the frame-and-panel bottom into its rabbets.

With the base complete, finish cutting and fitting the drawer joinery. Assemble the drawer after shaping its bottom edge to match the curve on the underside of the front aprons.

Once the drawer is glued up, shape its front and its bottom edge to match the aprons. Put the drawer all the way into the drawer pocket. Use a sharp pencil to scribe the shape from the front rail to the end grain on the drawer face. Be sure to scribe both sides of the drawer face. Plane close to the lines. Sneak up on the final shape by checking it in the drawer pocket frequently as you work.

There are many ways to fasten the tabletop to the base. I used handmade brass brackets, but commercially made figure-eights would work well, too. Cut the recess for the fasteners into the aprons. Pre-drill and attach the brackets to the aprons and then pre-drill and attach the top.

Natural Grace

Anderson's entryway table combines gentle, organic curves with rock-solid joinery for a sturdy piece with delicate looks.

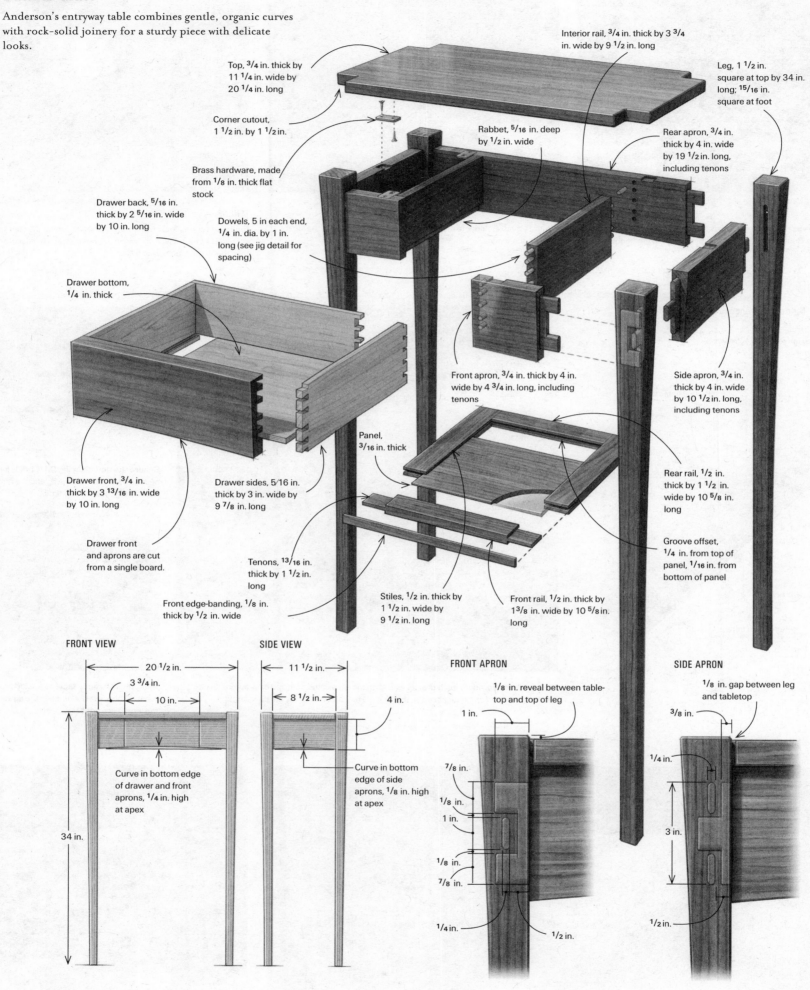

Top, 3/4 in. thick by 11 1/4 in. wide by 20 1/4 in. long

Interior rail, 3/4 in. thick by 3 3/4 in. wide by 9 1/2 in. long

Leg, 1 1/2 in. square at top by 34 in. long; 15/16 in. square at foot

Corner cutout, 1 1/2 in. by 1 1/2 in.

Rabbet, 5/16 in. deep by 1/2 in. wide

Rear apron, 3/4 in. thick by 4 in. wide by 19 1/2 in. long, including tenons

Brass hardware, made from 1/8 in. thick flat stock

Drawer back, 5/16 in. thick by 2 5/16 in. wide by 10 in. long

Dowels, 5 in each end, 1/4 in. dia. by 1 in. long (see jig detail for spacing)

Drawer bottom, 1/4 in. thick

Front apron, 3/4 in. thick by 4 in. wide by 4 3/4 in. long, including tenons

Side apron, 3/4 in. thick by 4 in. wide by 10 1/2 in. long, including tenons

Drawer front, 3/4 in. thick by 3 13/16 in. wide by 10 in. long

Drawer sides, 5/16 in. thick by 3 in. wide by 9 7/8 in. long

Rear rail, 1/2 in. thick by 1 1/2 in. wide by 10 5/8 in. long

Panel, 3/16 in. thick

Drawer front and aprons are cut from a single board.

Groove offset, 1/4 in. from top of panel, 1/16 in. from bottom of panel

Tenons, 13/16 in. thick by 1 1/2 in. long

Stiles, 1/2 in. thick by 1 1/2 in. wide by 9 1/2 in. long

Front rail, 1/2 in. thick by 1 3/8 in. wide by 10 5/8 in. long

Front edge-banding, 1/8 in. thick by 1/2 in. wide

FRONT VIEW

20 1/2 in.
3 3/4 in.
10 in.
34 in.

Curve in bottom edge of drawer and front aprons, 1/4 in. high at apex

SIDE VIEW

11 1/2 in.
8 1/2 in.
4 in.

Curve in bottom edge of side aprons, 1/8 in. high at apex

FRONT APRON

1/8 in. reveal between tabletop and top of leg

1 in.
7/8 in.
1/8 in.
1 in.
1/8 in.
7/8 in.
1/4 in.
1/2 in.

SIDE APRON

1/8 in. gap between leg and tabletop

3/8 in.
1/4 in.
3 in.
1/2 in.

Join the Base

Anderson uses two types of joinery to bring together the table's base. Interlocking mortise-and-tenon joints provide a sturdy connection between the aprons and the slender legs. Dowels fortify and align the butt joints between the aprons and interior rails.

MORTISES

Lay out the curves first. Anderson uses a template to trace layout lines that serve as a visual reminder to avoid mortising into the portion of the leg that will be cut away. Rout in progressively deeper passes to create the stepped mortises for the tenons.

TENONS

Rounded tenons for routed mortises. After cutting the cheeks and shoulders at the tablesaw, remove the waste with a bandsaw and chisel, then round the tenons with a file.

Dowels

A shopmade jig ensures accurate dowel holes.

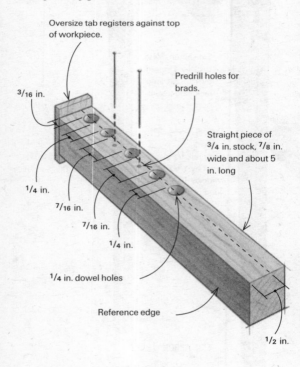

Oversize tab registers against top of workpiece.

Predrill holes for brads.

3/16 in.

Straight piece of 3/4 in. stock, 7/8 in. wide and about 5 in. long

1/4 in.

7/16 in.

7/16 in.

1/4 in.

1/4 in. dowel holes

Reference edge

1/2 in.

Mark the back apron for each drawer rail. Align the ends of the front and back aprons. Scribe a line along the front apron's inner edge, marking the rear apron to locate the doweling jig.

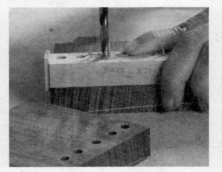

Secure the doweling jig. Drive brads just far enough to hold it. Drill the jig and the first set of dowel holes at the same time.

Mind the reference face. To ensure proper alignment of the dowel holes, keep the jig aligned with the workpiece edge.

Drilling goes quickly. For the holes in the rear apron, keep the jig's reference face oriented toward the interior of the piece. Align the edge with the layout line you scribed on the apron's inner face. A large hand screw secures the rail for drilling into the end grain.

Shape the Parts

Anderson's table is distinctive because of the organic curves that require shaping on every major component. Aside from a few bandsaw cuts, much of the work is done by hand with spokeshaves, planes, scrapers, and sandpaper.

LEGS

Start at the bandsaw. Cut close to the lines to create the long, gentle curves on the outside faces.

Smooth the shape with hand tools. The curve is gentle enough to accommodate the sole of a skewed smoother or a block plane. Anderson follows up with a scraper.

Flexible sanding pad. Anderson attaches adhesive-backed sand paper to strips of plastic laminate for a flat backer that is rigid but gives enough to easily follow the curve.

Aprons and Top

To give the table a graceful, cohesive appearance, Anderson shapes the aprons and tabletop to match the legs.

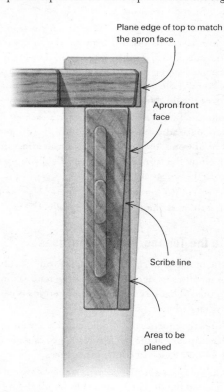

Plane edge of top to match the apron face.

Apron front face

Scribe line

Area to be planed

Mark the profile on the apron. Measure the reveal between leg and apron at the top of the assembly, then mark the apron's bottom and end grain to match.

Make shavings. The taper on the apron faces is gentle, so the waste can be removed with a handplane. Start with the iron set for an aggressive cut, then adjust for a finer cut as you approach the layout line to minimize tearout.

More curves. Anderson bandsaws a very gentle curve into the bottom edge of each apron. Afterward, she smooths the bandsawn edges. She shapes the curve in the underside of the drawer front after it is assembled and installed.

Assembly

Anderson pre-finishes the entire table (other than the joints) before the glue-up, which takes place in several stages for simplicity's sake and to ensure the assembly remains square throughout. Afterward, she assembles, fits, and shapes the drawer.

Stage one: Side aprons go into the legs. Because the parts are prefinished, Anderson makes her cabinetmaker's marks on blue tape to help orient the parts for proper assembly.

Stage two: Inner rails are next. Glue the dowels into both ends of each rail. Tap the dowels home with a hammer to prevent them from seizing. Anderson uses a measured reference block to set the depth of each dowel. Let this glue dry before adding the front and back aprons.

Continued ➜

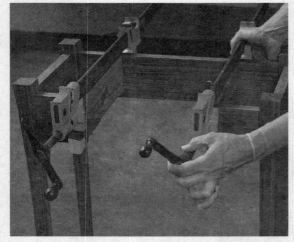

Dry-fit the legs to aid clamping. The legs hold the aprons in proper position, making it easier to clamp the rails in place squarely.

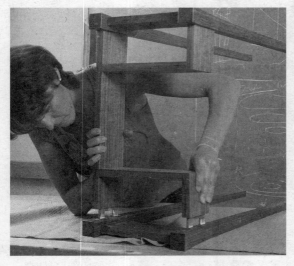

Stage three: Add the leg assemblies and drawer support. After adding the legs, the frame-and-panel bottom of the drawer compartment goes into a pair of rabbets milled into the bottom edge of the drawer rails.

Harmony in the details. The organic curve of the leg is echoed in the shaped apron faces and the beveled edge profile on the tabletop.

Bow-Front Hall Table

by Charles Durfee

A simple, rectangular table can be functional and quite lovely. But give it a gentle curve along the front and you'll have a table with elegance. A subtle curve grabs attention without being loud and distracting.

The large drawer in the front apron of this table is functional without detracting from its clean look. I cut its face from the front apron, so with the drawer closed, the sweep of the apron runs uninterrupted from side to side. I also beveled the front legs, so the curve of the apron extends seamlessly across them.

Making a curved-front table isn't as hard as you might think. A single pattern can be used to make both a form for laminating the front apron and a full-size top-view drawing that helps you lay out and assemble the drawer, its guides, and the rest of the table base. I'll also show you a few very simple jigs that make it easy to crosscut the curved apron and cut tenons on its ends.

Everything Follows the Curve

With most curved furniture, it's best to start with the curve, in this case the front apron. It's far easier to make the other parts fit the curve than to make the curve fit the other parts. I laminated the front apron rather than cutting it from solid stock, which can result in unattractive grain patterns.

To begin, make a full-size pattern of the curve. You'll use it to make the bending form for laminating the front apron and for laying out the apron and top when you do the full-size drawing. Mark, cut, and smooth the curve carefully, because the pattern affects the accuracy and beauty of everything that follows. To mark the curve, spring a flexible strip of wood, known as a batten, between two nails, but make sure the curve is symmetrical before marking it. Do this by measuring from the baseline to the curve in 5-in. increments. If the curve is symmetrical, the two measurements farthest from the center on either side will be the same, the next two farthest will be the same, and so on. If it's not symmetrical, adjust the batten and secure it with brads as needed.

Smooth the curve with a cabinetmaker's rasp, then a file, and finally a sanding block (120 grit). Hold the rasp and file diagonally across the MDF to get as much body on the surface as possible. That helps to keep the curve smooth.

Full-scale Drawing Simplifies Construction

With your pattern in hand, use it to make a full-size, top-view drawing of the table. Include the top, aprons, legs, drawer, drawer rails, and joinery details.

The front apron is cut into three parts, and the drawer rails double as stretchers to reinforce the right and left sides of the apron. Their position and length must be exact, or the table won't be square or the curve continuous. The drawing makes it a snap to get them right. It also makes assembling the table much easier.

Use a thin piece of plywood for the drawing rather than a sheet of paper. It is more durable and will make a good base for marking joinery and assembling parts.

Lamination without Perspiration

The form isn't difficult to make. A router and flush-trimming bit ensure that when you're done, you'll have a uniform curve and a smooth surface.

A plywood base attached to the form allows you to clamp it to the bench and acts a fence to keep the plies aligned. Cover the curved surface with packing tape to keep glue from sticking to it.

I used six plies to laminate the front apron. Leave them a few inches long so the drawer front can be cut out. I resawed them from 8/4 stock, first cutting them a bit fat and then planing them down to 1/8 in. thick. To keep the plies from being torn up by the planer, I put a long, 3/4-in.-thick MDF auxiliary bed in it.

It's important to keep the plies in sequence so that the top edge of the drawer front will look clean and unified when the drawer is open. Before resawing, draw a carpenter's triangle on the edge of the board to help keep the plies in order.

To laminate the plies, I used yellow glue and applied it with a small paint roller. I know that others recommend urea-formaldehyde glue because it creeps less after drying, which prevents springback, but I've never had any problem with yellow glue. Work quickly, and stack the plies on the form as you go.

Once you have all the plies on the form, start clamping down the lamination, beginning in the middle. Use as many clamps as you can fit onto the assembly.

Leave the clamps on for 24 hours. After removing the apron from the form, scrape any glue squeeze-out from one edge and joint it. Then rip the apron to width on the tablesaw. If you don't immediately crosscut it to make the drawer front, clamp it lightly from end to end to help it keep its shape.

Make the Base before the Top

While you're waiting for the glue to dry, you can mill the rest of the parts, except for the top. There's no guarantee that the table base will come out precisely as planned. That could be disastrous if the top is already made, because there isn't much overhang.

Mill your parts a bit oversize and let them sit for a day or two. This allows them to release internal stresses, which can cause warping, cupping, and twisting. Then mill the parts to final dimensions.

To cut the drawer front from the apron, you'll need a support block. Bandsaw it from solid wood, and attach it to the apron with double-faced tape. The bandsawn surface needs to be smooth for the tape to stick, so smooth it like you did the pattern. I wrapped tape around both to reinforce the double-faced tape.

Cut the drawer front 1/8 in. long on each end so you can make adjustments when you fit the drawer. The amount of wood lost during fitting won't affect the grain match along the front apron, especially if you use quartersawn or riftsawn stock.

Next, cut the apron pieces to length. Use the full-size drawing to mark their lengths accurately.

Angle the Tenons, Not the Mortises

Cut the mortises using the method of your choice. I cut all of the mortises straight and angled the tenons on the front apron pieces, because cutting angled tenons is easier than cutting angled mortises.

After the mortises are done, cut the tenons on the side and back aprons at the tablesaw with a stack dado cutter, using a miter gauge to control the pieces.

On the front aprons, the tenon cheeks are cut at the tablesaw and the shoulders are cut by hand. Before you do any cutting, scribe the shoulders on the edges with a marking gauge and then use a knife to scribe across the faces. Cut the first cheek on both apron pieces. Then adjust the fence and cut the second cheek. Cut the tenons a bit thick. After the cheeks have been cut, use a backsaw to cut the shoulders, and trim the tenons to fit with a shoulder plane.

When all of the joints are cut and fit, glue the side aprons into their legs. Having the side assemblies together will make it easier to lay out the joinery for the drawer rails. Before you glue them up, however, taper the two inside faces of the legs. I did this on the tablesaw with a tapering jig, but you could do it on a bandsaw.

After the glue is dry, take the side assemblies to the jointer and bevel the front faces of the front legs.

Use the Drawing to Dial in the Drawer Pocket

Before you can attach the front and back aprons to the side assemblies, you need to cut dadoes in the back apron and rabbets on the front apron pieces to hold the drawer rails.

Those dadoes and rabbets, however, must be located precisely to get a square hole for the drawer to slide into. The best way to lay them out is by dry-fitting the front and back aprons into the side assemblies. Do this upside down

on top of the full-scale drawing. The drawing will help you align all the parts square before you clamp them. You can then transfer the joint locations directly from the drawing to the aprons.

To cut the rabbets on the front apron pieces, I ran them vertically past the dado cutter. Use the support block used for cutting the tenons between the apron and the tall fence of the tenoning jig. The dadoes in the back apron are cut by guiding the apron over the dado cutter with a miter gauge. At this point you also can mark the length of the drawer rails directly from the assembly and crosscut them to length.

Now is the best time to cut pocket holes in the front apron for attaching the top. These fix the front edge of the tabletop, locking in its short overhang. The seasonal movement is then transferred to the back, where the tabletop is attached to the rear apron with wooden buttons. Rout the slots to house the buttons now.

Reassemble the side assemblies and legs upside down on the drawing. Dry-fit the drawer rails to the assembly and check your results.

The next step is to cut the joinery for the stretcher that runs between the drawer rails. The stretcher is located so that there's about a 1/16-in. gap between it and the back of the drawer front. I glued a strip of cork to the stretcher to fill the gap. That way, the drawer closes with a solid, but muted, thump.

Cut the tails on the stretcher, and then transfer them to the drawer rails. I roughed out the sockets with a router and then cleaned them up with a chisel.

The Drawing Guides the Glue-Up, Too

After the stretcher is fitted, finish gluing up the base. Do this on top of the drawing to ensure that everything is square and aligned properly. Before brushing on any glue, dry-fit everything and check to make sure that the table is square. If it's not, correct the problem now.

Put waxed paper between the plywood drawing and any glue joints so that you don't accidentally glue them together.

After the assembly is dry, reinforce the rabbet joint connecting the drawer rails to the front aprons with screws and plug the holes. The drawer runners can just be glued in. The two long-grain glue surfaces are strong enough without reinforcement.

Tips for a Curved Drawer

I used traditional dovetail joinery to make the drawer, with a solid bottom that's slid in from the back.

I think a pull or knob would detract from the front's beauty, so I routed a finger recess into the stretcher that runs between the drawer rails. Use a 1/2-in. cove bit and a handheld router, and center the recess.

Crosscut the drawer front to fit its opening, using the same support block used to separate the drawer front from the apron.

To rout the groove for the drawer bottom in the curved drawer front, I attached the curved support block I used earlier when cutting out the drawer front. This gives a wider surface for the router base. Clamp the drawer front in a vise, and use a bearing-guided slot-cutting bit to rout the groove.

Make and Attach the Top

Glue up the boards and check the bottom assembly to get the correct width and length. Rip the top to width, crosscut it to length, and plane it to final thickness.

It's important that the curve of the top matches the curve of the front apron. The curve is shallow enough that you can use the original pattern as a template and flush-trim the top to create an even overhang.

I prepped the surfaces for finishing using a smoothing plane and then a card scraper with a fine hook. I used three coats of Minwax Antique Oil Finish. Let each coat dry for at least 24 hours. Wet-sand the second and third coats with P320-grit paper before wiping off the excess.

Attach the top to the bottom, and stand back and admire your work. Then move it into your house, where its beauty and elegance will surely be welcomed.

Table with a Curve

A bow front gives the table elegance, but it complicates the construction. Draw a full-size top view to guide you.

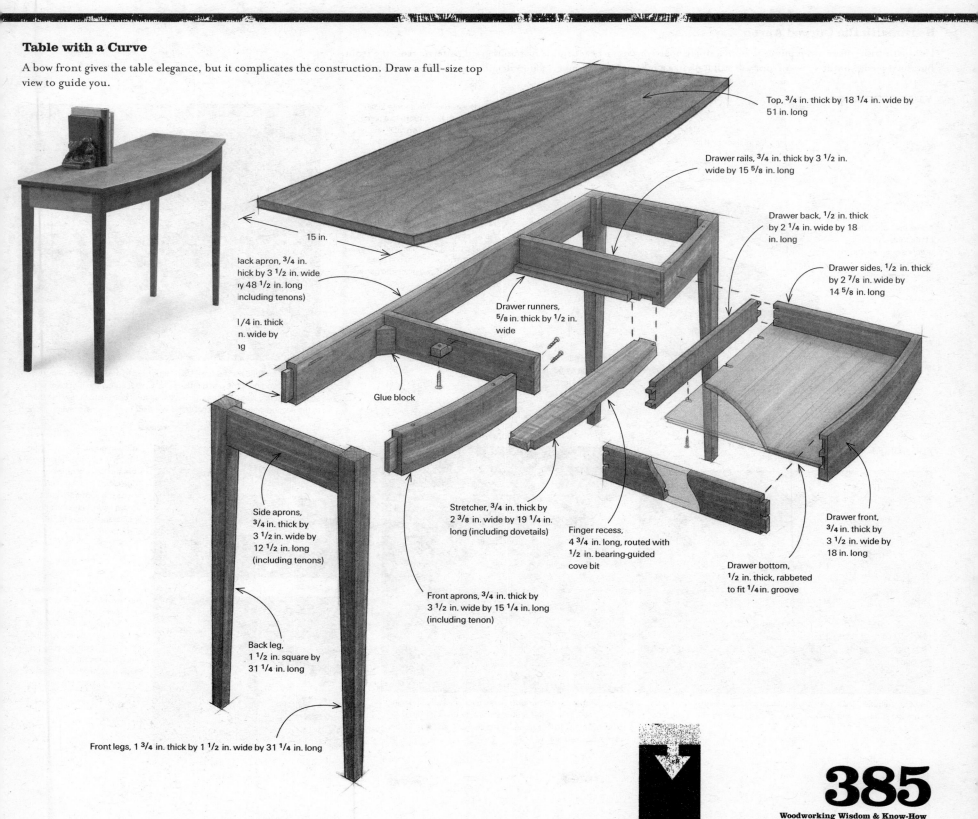

Top, 3/4 in. thick by 18 1/4 in. wide by 51 in. long

Drawer rails, 3/4 in. thick by 3 1/2 in. wide by 15 5/8 in. long

Drawer back, 1/2 in. thick by 2 1/4 in. wide by 18 in. long

Drawer sides, 1/2 in. thick by 2 7/8 in. wide by 14 5/8 in. long

15 in.

Back apron, 3/4 in. thick by 3 1/2 in. wide by 48 1/2 in. long (including tenons)

1/4 in. thick in. wide by g

Drawer runners, 5/8 in. thick by 1/2 in. wide

Glue block

Side aprons, 3/4 in. thick by 3 1/2 in. wide by 12 1/2 in. long (including tenons)

Stretcher, 3/4 in. thick by 2 3/8 in. wide by 19 1/4 in. long (including dovetails)

Finger recess, 4 3/4 in. long, routed with 1/2 in. bearing-guided cove bit

Drawer front, 3/4 in. thick by 3 1/2 in. long by 18 in. long

Drawer bottom, 1/2 in. thick, rabbeted to fit 1/4 in. groove

Front aprons, 3/4 in. thick by 3 1/2 in. wide by 15 1/4 in. long (including tenon)

Back leg, 1 1/2 in. square by 31 1/4 in. long

Front legs, 1 3/4 in. thick by 1 1/2 in. wide by 31 1/4 in. long

CORNER DETAIL

Bevel front leg after side is assembled.

The front legs are 1/4 in. deeper so they appear square after beveling.

Apron tenon is inset 3/8 in. to accommodate bevel.

1/4 in.

1 1/2 in.

1 3/4 in.

1 1/2 in.

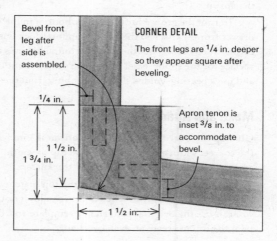

TOP VIEW

Overhang, 1/2 in. on all sides

Dado, 3/4 in. wide by 3/16 in. deep

Top is attached to sides, back, and drawer rails with shopmade buttons.

Top is attached to front apron with pocket screws.

Rabbet, 3/4 in. wide by 1/2 in. deep

14 in.

17 1/4 in.

16 in.

25 in.

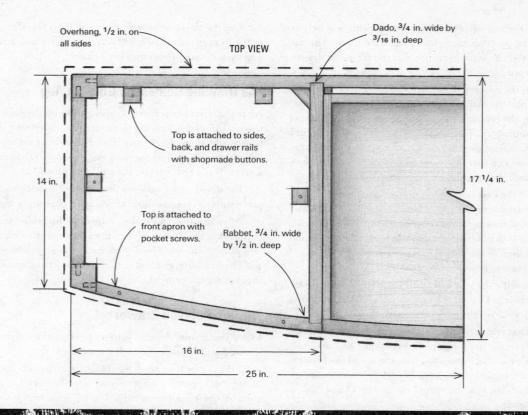

Begin with the Curved Apron

Laminating the apron from plies cut from a single board ensures a beautiful, continuous grain pattern across the front. But the top edge of the drawer front will still look like a piece of solid lumber, a nice detail when the drawer is open.

MAKE THE BENDING FORM

Layer, 3/4 in. thick by 6 in. wide by 53 in. long

Curve the back side of the form and cut notches at either end so that clamps are always perpendicular to the form's bending surface.

Base, 1/2 in. thick by 7 3/4 in. wide by 53 in. long, attached last

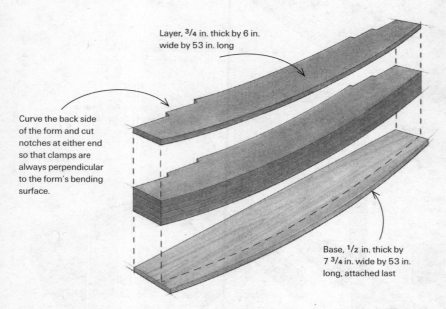

Mark the curve. Use double-faced tape to attach the pattern to a piece of 3/4-in.-thick MDF. The MDF should be the same length as the pattern, but about 1/4 in. wider.

Rout flush to the pattern. After cutting away most of the waste at the bandsaw, use a router and a flush-trimming bit to clean up the curve and shape it to the pattern. Leave about 1/16 in. of waste to be routed. Durfee uses a bottom-bearing bit and places the pattern below it. You can use a top-bearing bit if you place the pattern above.

Second layer follows the first. Use the pattern to mark the remaining layers of the bending form, and bandsaw the waste. Screw the first layer to the second and use it as a pattern to rout the second one flush. Screw the third to the second, and rout it flush. Do the same for the remaining layers.

GLUE AND TRIM THE APRON

Roll out the glue. Use a foam paint roller to spread an even coat of glue on mating surfaces, and stack the plies in front of the form, outside face down on the bench.

Clamp from the center out. To get even pressure and minimize creep, start in the center and work outward from side to side. Small MDF cauls under the clamp heads spread the clamping pressure.

Joint an edge. After the glue has dried, remove the apron from the form, scrape one edge clean, and then run it across the jointer. To get a square edge, keep the apron against the fence near the cutterhead.

Rip to width. The second edge can be cleaned and squared, and the apron cut to width, all at once at the tablesaw. Rip it concave side up, keeping the piece against the table at the leading edge of the blade. Use a splitter to keep the piece on track.

Cut Apart the Drawer and Aprons

To give the illusion of a continuous apron, the drawer front is cut from the middle of the lamination. A support block makes it easier to cut it out accurately and to get square ends. A second block simplifies trimming and tenoning.

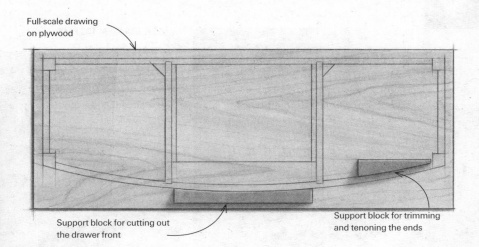

Full-scale drawing on plywood

Support block for cutting out the drawer front

Support block for trimming and tenoning the ends

SUPPORT BLOCKS ARE THE KEY

Cut out the drawer front. To get cuts parallel to the drawer's eventual sliding motion, use a support block shaped to cradle it parallel to the table. Guide it through the blade with a miter gauge, and hold the offcut securely so that it doesn't fall into the blade.

Trim the apron to length. A second block, shaped to match the inside of the apron, makes it possible to crosscut the front apron pieces to length and get them square.

THE APRONS HAVE ANGLED TENONS

Use the second block for tenons, too. Attach it to the apron with double-faced tape to cut the cheeks of the angled tenons. A shopmade tenoning jig straddles the fence and guides the workpiece through the cut.

Saw the shoulders by hand. There's no need to jig up and cut the shoulders at the tablesaw. A backsaw or pullsaw will take care of them quickly and accurately, and a bench hook is all you need to hold the pieces steady.

Clean up with a shoulder plane. Durfee flips over his bench hook and uses it to hold the curved apron pieces for trimming the shoulders and cheeks. You'll need a chisel to get into the most acute corner.

Assemble the Base in Stages

Because the front apron is curved and there are so many parts, sizing the parts and gluing up the table could be a challenge, but not if you do it in stages.

MAKE THE SIDES

Clamp and let glue dry. Apply glue to the tenons and then fit the legs to the apron.

Now bevel the front legs. Use a bevel gauge and the full-size drawing to set the jointer fence to the correct angle. Take light cuts, and use push sticks near the cutterhead.

Continued ➜

Size the rails. After cutting the dadoes in the back apron, dry-fit the table again and clamp it down to the full-size drawing. Crosscut one end of the rail, and align that end with the dado. Then mark and cut the rail to length.

MAKE PARTS FROM THE PLAN

Mark the stretcher joinery. Cut the tails on the stretcher. Then, with the rails in place, lay out the dovetail sockets.

COMPLETE THE ASSEMBLY

Full-size drawing keeps things square. Clamp one side to the drawing (left), glue up the back apron, and attach the other side. Use the drawing to align the parts and then clamp everything together and down to the bench. To keep the parts square, check their alignment with the drawing as you tighten the clamps.

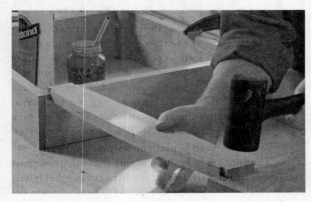

Stretcher is the keystone. The last piece to glue in place is the stretcher. By bridging the drawer pocket, it keeps the table square, adds stability, and helps prevent racking.

TIP

SIMPLIFY DOVETAILS ON A CURVED DRAWER

The smartest way to cut dovetails in a curved drawer front is to flatten the curve so that the sides can have straight shoulders.

Plane here

Tails on drawer side

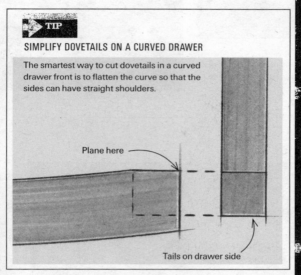

Plane it flat. Mark the area to be flattened and plane away the waste. The small flats simplify the next step.

Transfer the tails. Clamp the drawer front in a vise and shim the drawer side until the tails sit flat.

Versatile Trestle Table

by Gary Rogowski

With a simple form that allows many variations, the trestle table can look contemporary or classic. The trestles, the stretcher that joins them, and even the top can be shaped in myriad ways. The design offers easy access for diners, with no table apron to knock a knee against and more chair room on each side. And it is expandable, scaling up easily from this kitchen-sized table to a large dining table.

A key feature on many trestle tables, including this one, is the wedged joinery for the stretcher, which is rock-solid even though it's called "knockdown." With a through-mortise-and-tenon joint, the stretcher locates and holds the trestles upright. In a marvel of engineering, the wedges lock everything together, preventing the table from racking along its length. I know of no stronger joint. It's also good looking: The projecting tenons and the wedges add another design element.

In this section, I'll focus on the stretcher joinery—the most challenging aspect of the project. Executing the joinery successfully relies on careful fitting of the through-tenons and the wedges to their respective mortises.

How to Cut Large, Clean Mortises

Furniture construction is like painting a floor. Careful planning keeps you out of the corners. In this case, it's important to lay out and cut the large through-mortises in the posts before shaping the posts to preserve a parallel reference edge for guiding the router.

I use a template guide bushing and a simple shopmade mortising jig to rout mortises. The jig consists of a 1/4-in. MDF routing template attached to a fence that registers against the stock. The jig centers the mortises on the width of the posts, but you'll still need to do a little layout. First, measure from the top of each post to mark the tops and bottoms of the mortises. Use a square to carry the lines around to the board's opposite face, then check the edges of both boards side by side to ensure that the marks line up. Then, because the jig's slot is slightly larger than the mortise itself, make a separate registration mark to locate the jig accurately.

Clamp the mortising template securely in place on the outside face of the post. To cut the mortises, I use a plunge router and a 3/8-in. spiral-fluted bit. It's possible to rout all the way through the post or stop short of full depth and clear the remaining waste with a chisel. But for a technique that will work for posts of greater thickness, start by routing away—in shallow passes—about half of the mortise depth. Then remove the template, flip the workpiece, reattach the template on the opposite face, and finish the cut.

After routing the mortises, chop them out square, working in from both faces. Now you can shape those posts.

Cutting Tenons on a Long Board

The size of the stretcher makes it generally difficult to handle. For example, it's too long to support safely in a tablesaw tenoning jig. Whatever tenoning method you use, it needs to be clean and accurate—all the more so because the tenon's fit will be visible where it exits the big through-mortise.

As with the big posts, joinery comes before shaping. After laying out the stretcher shape and tenon location, I cut the shoulders on the tablesaw, using a miter gauge with a long fence or a crosscut sled with a long stop-block attachment to hold the work and locate the cut. To cut the tenon cheeks, I use the bandsaw with a roller stand for infeed support and a 6-tpi blade for a smooth surface.

Before cutting the tenon to width (height), I clean up the cheek cuts, trimming the tenon to the proper thickness. To keep the cheeks flat near the shoulder, I use a shoulder plane, but I'll switch to a block plane for quicker stock removal near the tenon ends. Remember that the last 2 in. or so of the tenon won't be housed in the assembled joint, so that section can have a slightly looser fit.

I also cut the tenon to width on the bandsaw, again leaving it just oversize and cleaning up with hand tools until it slides through the mortise with no gaps showing on the outside face.

The Wedge Mortises

The last step in making the tenon is to create the mortise for the wedge. In addition to cutting the mortise straight through the entire width of the tenon, the trick here lies in cutting the outer end of the mortise at an 8° angle. The secret is that the inside wall of the mortise is buried in the post and doesn't need to be chopped out square, so you can cut the entire mortise at 8° on the drill press. If your drill press doesn't have a tilting table, use a jig like the one on the page 391.

Mark out the wedge mortise with a center line in the tenon thickness. Mark the mortise end at ¾ in. past the post, but have it start ⅜ in. inside the post. In this way, the wedge won't bottom out against the back side of the mortise. Using a brad-point bit, drill the holes at each end of the mortise first. Work slowly and clear out the waste often. Then drill out the middle section. To chop out the remaining waste, clamp the stretcher on the bench and use layout lines on the tenon at the 8° angle or a sliding bevel placed on the bench to sight against for chopping. Chop in toward the center of the mortise from both the top and bottom, flipping the workpiece as needed. Chamfer the wedge mortise on both top and bottom so the wedge slides through more easily.

I cut the wedges on the bandsaw using a simple holding jig. Set a sliding bevel to the angle of the mortise and mark out the shape of the wedge on a piece of ¼-in. MDF. Carefully cut out that shape and file the edges straight. Glue another piece of MDF to the bottom of this template to hold the workpiece in place. Make up wedge stock at the proper thickness and length and at roughly the correct width. Then set the bandsaw fence to cut out the wedge. Clean up the wedges with a bench plane, holding them in a vise or in the jig on a shooting board.

Modern Trestle Table

The trestle design is centuries old, yet its rock-solid construction and easy access for sitting remain unequalled. It can be made in any size—from breakfast to banquet table—and its wedged through-tenons let you break down the base for easy transport. What's more, it is a designer's playground, with the feet, posts, stretcher, through-tenons, wedges, and tabletop each offering room for interpretation. I like this smallish version, sized to be a desk or a kitchen table for four.

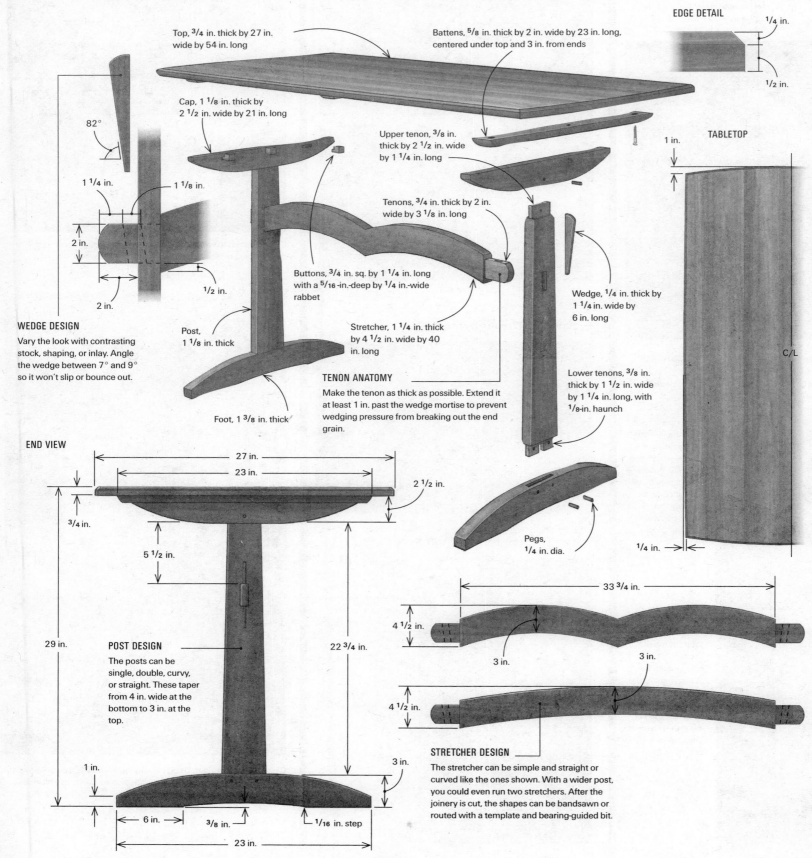

Top, ¾ in. thick by 27 in. wide by 54 in. long

Battens, ⅝ in. thick by 2 in. wide by 23 in. long, centered under top and 3 in. from ends

EDGE DETAIL
¼ in.
½ in.

82°

Cap, 1⅛ in. thick by 2½ in. wide by 21 in. long

Upper tenon, ⅜ in. thick by 2½ in. wide by 1¼ in. long

TABLETOP

1 in.

1¼ in.

1⅛ in.

2 in.

2 in.

½ in.

Tenons, ¾ in. thick by 2 in. wide by 3⅛ in. long

Buttons, ¾ in. sq. by 1¼ in. long with a ⁵⁄₁₆-in.-deep by ¼ in.-wide rabbet

Wedge, ¼ in. thick by 1¼ in. wide by 6 in. long

C/L

WEDGE DESIGN
Vary the look with contrasting stock, shaping, or inlay. Angle the wedge between 7° and 9° so it won't slip or bounce out.

Post, 1⅛ in. thick

Stretcher, 1¼ in. thick by 4½ in. wide by 40 in. long

TENON ANATOMY
Make the tenon as thick as possible. Extend it at least 1 in. past the wedge mortise to prevent wedging pressure from breaking out the end grain.

Lower tenons, ⅜ in. thick by 1½ in. wide by 1¼ in. long, with ⅛-in. haunch

Foot, 1⅜ in. thick

END VIEW

27 in.
23 in.
2½ in.
¾ in.
5½ in.

Pegs, ¼ in. dia.

¼ in.

33¾ in.
4½ in.
3 in.
3 in.

29 in.

POST DESIGN
The posts can be single, double, curvy, or straight. These taper from 4 in. wide at the bottom to 3 in. at the top.

22¾ in.

4½ in.

1 in.
6 in.
⅜ in.
1⁄16 in. step
3 in.
23 in.

STRETCHER DESIGN
The stretcher can be simple and straight or curved like the ones shown. With a wider post, you could even run two stretchers. After the joinery is cut, the shapes can be bandsawn or routed with a template and bearing-guided bit.

Continued →

Cut a Flawless Wedged-Tenon Joint

1. Rout the Through-Mortises

A TEMPLATE TAMES THE TASK

A simple template, used with a guide bushing, makes it easy to cut through-mortises to the right size, in the right place.

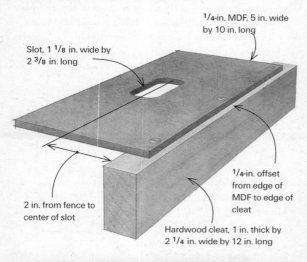

Slot, 1 1/8 in. wide by 2 3/8 in. long

1/4-in. MDF, 5 in. wide by 10 in. long

2 in. from fence to center of slot

1/4-in. offset from edge of MDF to edge of cleat

Hardwood cleat, 1 in. thick by 2 1/4 in. wide by 12 in. long

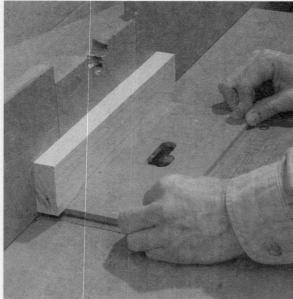

How to make the template. Drill a hole in the MDF, then move to the router table. The jig's cleat rides the table's fence, so the slot is cut parallel to the cleat. Start the router bit in the drilled hole and go from there. Reposition the fence for a second pass and a bigger mortise.

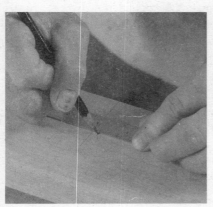

Offset the layout. The template slot is bigger than the mortise, so make a separate registration mark to locate the template accurately and carry that mark around to the other side.

Rout the mortise. With the template in place, cut halfway through the stock. Then flip the board end for end to ensure that the jig is clamped to the same reference edge for the second cut.

TEMPLATE GUIDE

A guide bushing rides the template's rim and shields it from the spinning bit. Be sure to factor in the bushing diameter when sizing the slot in the template.

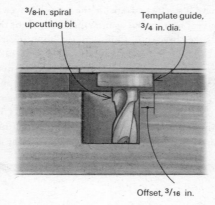

3/8-in. spiral upcutting bit

Template guide, 3/4 in. dia.

Offset, 3/16 in.

2. Saw the Through-Tenons

Cut the shoulders on the tablesaw. Use a miter gauge with a long fence or a crosscut sled to manage the long stock.

Move to the bandsaw. Use a test cut to adjust the fence for drift. Leave the cheeks slightly fat for trimming and cleanup.

Cut the tenon to width. Again, leave the tenon slightly oversize. Make the adjoining cut with a handsaw to remove the waste.

Clean up the shoulder. Using the tablesawn shoulders as a reference, walk the chisel's edge across the hand-sawn section to establish your line, then chop away the waste.

3. Drill the Wedge Mortises

DRILLING JIG
Rogowski built this simple jig to secure the stretcher at an 8° angle for drilling out the wedge mortises. The jig clamps to the drill-press table and the work is clamped to the jig.

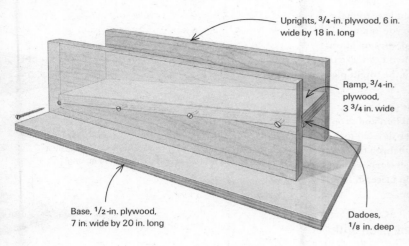

Uprights, 3/4-in. plywood, 6 in. wide by 18 in. long

Ramp, 3/4-in. plywood, 3 3/4 in. wide

Base, 1/2-in. plywood, 7 in. wide by 20 in. long

Dadoes, 1/8 in. deep

Position the jig. The jig stays put on the drill-press table. Slide the workpiece in the jig to reposition it, and clamp it in place for each new hole.

Support the cut. Place a block underneath the tenon to prevent blowout where the drill bit exits the cut.

Start at the ends. Where holes overlap, make sure the bit's centering point hits wood so it locates properly.

Layout line is a visual reference. Mark the angle on the tenon's cheek and sight down the line while chopping away the waste.

4. Cut the Wedges and Assemble

Bandsaw is safer than tablesaw. Rogowski uses a simple jig made of 3/8-in. MDF with an 8° notch cut into it.

Tap the wedges home. When the wedges are tightly driven, they pull the tenon shoulders firmly against the post for an assembly that won't budge.

Dining Table with Two-Way Drawers

by Stephen Hammer

Many of my favorite designs began with a challenging request from a client, and that was definitely the case with this table. The client wanted a dining table that would double as a worktable with a lot of storage, so I added double-fronted drawers accessible from either side. That required a drawer with half-blind dovetails at both ends, and a support system that could handle the extra stress of deep drawers when fully loaded. So I designed a table with upper and lower drawer stretchers that have the vertical dividers mortised in solidly. In addition, I wanted a clean design that would emphasize the beauty of the wood, and in this case tie into the eclectic setting that would be its home. I chose walnut because the table would be paired with a set of walnut Nakashima benches.

The table has the usual parts: legs, stretchers, dividers, runners and kickers, aprons, and drawers. But because it is built like a torsion box and the drawers have double fronts, the how-to is more like a cross between a chest of drawers and a basic table. Keep track of the joinery and work in the right order and you'll have no trouble reproducing this versatile dining table.

Mortises, and Lots of Them, Are the Key to This Construction

To begin, I go to my hollow-chisel mortiser and mortise the legs and stretchers, about 52 mortises in all. The upper and lower stretchers are mortised through their faces for the vertical dividers that separate the drawers. Take extra care that all these mortises line up top to bottom, because their alignment is critical or the vertical dividers will be crooked. To do this, I clamp all four pieces together and, using my square as a guide, score a line across the inside edge of the stretchers. Then I transfer those lines across the faces of the stretchers to lay out the exact mortise locations.

Keep in mind that the legs are designed with a very simple double-sided taper that begins at the base of the apron. I cut the joinery before tapering the leg, so I can work on it while it is still flat and square. I cut the mortises for the lower stretcher and the haunched mortises for the side aprons. The upper stretchers connect to the legs with lap dovetails. The socket for the dovetail is cut later.

Now that the mortises are cut, it's time to move on to the tenons on the aprons, the drawer runners and kickers, the lower stretchers, and the vertical dividers.

The side aprons have haunched tenons. These tenons are cut with several passes on the tablesaw with a 1/2-in. dado set. I lay the boards flat on the table and crosscut them, using the fence to set the tenon length. The tenons on the runners and kickers are cut using the same method. To keep from interfering with the vertical drawer divider joinery, the center runners and kickers have two tenons. I remove the waste between the tenons on the tablesaw with the same sled and method I use for the vertical dividers, below. This isn't necessary on the end runners and kickers.

The tenons on the lower stretchers aren't as straightforward. They are joined with a double stub tenon into the leg and a single tenon into the lower apron spacer. I cut the stub tenons on the bandsaw and use the router table and a straight bit to create the tenon that lands in the spacer. I measure for the mortise in the lower apron spacer and cut it. Later, when the legs are glued to the apron, I dry-fit the lower stretcher system to the legs and apron, setting the apron spacer in place. It automatically registers itself, which allows me to mark its location and glue it in place.

Continued →

Upper Stretchers Get Dovetails

While the lower stretchers have mortises and tenons, the upper stretchers are connected to the leg and apron spacer with dovetails. This makes assembly much easier. I use a simple jig to establish the sides of the tails on the bandsaw, and then I cope out the waste and clean up with a chisel. These structural dovetails are never seen, so appearance is not critical.

With all the leg joinery completed, I now feel comfortable cutting the tapers in the legs. With only four legs to do, I mark the taper on the legs, cut it freehand on the bandsaw, and then clean it up on the jointer, making sure to register one side against the fence to keep the taper square. Later, after the legs are glued to the aprons, I'll mark and cut the dovetail socket in the top of the leg post, using a plunge router freehand. Then I clean it up with chisels.

How to Simplify a Complex Glue-Up

Because there are so many parts in the drawer system, this glue-up is more complicated than the average table glue-up. But you can break it into manageable stages: the leg/apron assembly, and then the stretcher assembly. Before glue-up, do a final sanding and finishing of the table parts. I use a finely set smoothing plane to remove mill marks, followed by a random-orbit sander up to P320-grit sandpaper. Then I apply Tried & True Original Wood Finish to all the parts. I can always sand more after assembly, but this step saves time, gives a nicer finish, and helps a lot with glue cleanup.

Attach the aprons to the legs—Gluing the apron to the front and back legs is straightforward, and the mortises dictate the alignment of the parts. The side aprons have upper and lower spacers glued to them that allow the drawers to clear the legs, which are thicker than the aprons. However, I do not attach and cut the joinery in these spacers until the legs are glued to the aprons. It is easier to cut the joinery when they are separated from the apron, but I need the leg/apron assembly together to mark the exact location of the joinery on the spacers. With the joinery done, the spacers can be glued in place.

Two sets of stretcher frames, upper and lower—This is where things get a little complicated (but just a little). I glue up the front and back lower stretchers with the drawer runners as one frame, then the front and back upper stretchers with the drawer kickers as a second frame.

Put it all together—Next, glue the vertical drawer dividers into the lower stretcher frame. You have to make sure they stay straight as they are drying, so you can use a slow-dry glue such as Titebond Extend and work on gluing the upper stretcher assembly right away, or you can take the pressure off the glue-up and simply dry-fit the top in place until the dividers are dry.

The final steps happen all at once. Glue the lower stretcher assembly into the leg/apron assemblies, and drop the top stretcher assembly into place over the dovetail sockets and drawer divider tenons. It is critical that you check all the parts for square. Measuring the diagonals works well for this. Here you also can just dry-fit the top in place while the bottom stretcher dries, and then add the top.

Quick and Easy Drawer Construction, Even with Two Fronts

With the base assembled, it is time to focus on the drawers. I combine power tools and handwork to create consistent dovetails efficiently while keeping a hand-cut appearance. I use quartersawn white oak for the drawer sides. Its hardness lets the drawer slide easily and with little wear. It also contrasts with the walnut to show off the dovetails. Custom walnut handles are the finishing touch.

Top It Off

With the base complete, you can make the top. I made mine from a series of boards picked for grain appearance and glued up side by side using biscuits for alignment. After cutting the top to final size, I shaped the edge with a 12° bevel that matches the bevel on the stretchers. Wooden buttons secure the top to the frame.

To finish the top, I use a finely set smoothing plane to take out all the milling marks, and then sand it up to P320 grit. I then apply several coats of Tried & True Original Wood Finish wiped on and rubbed off by hand. Even though all parts were pre-finished, I go over the entire piece again with a final few coats.

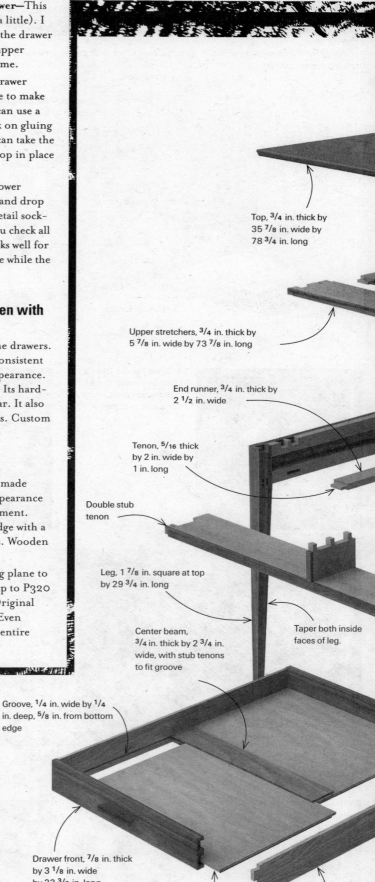

Top, 3/4 in. thick by 35 7/8 in. wide by 78 3/4 in. long

Upper stretchers, 3/4 in. thick by 5 7/8 in. wide by 73 7/8 in. long

End runner, 3/4 in. thick by 2 1/2 in. wide

Tenon, 5/16 thick by 2 in. wide by 1 in. long

Double stub tenon

Leg, 1 7/8 in. square at top by 29 3/4 in. long

Taper both inside faces of leg.

Center beam, 3/4 in. thick by 2 3/4 in. wide, with stub tenons to fit groove

Groove, 1/4 in. wide by 1/4 in. deep, 5/8 in. from bottom edge

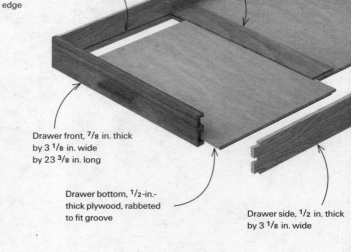

Drawer front, 7/8 in. thick by 3 1/8 in. wide by 23 3/8 in. long

Drawer bottom, 1/2-in.-thick plywood, rabbeted to fit groove

Drawer side, 1/2 in. thick by 3 1/8 in. wide

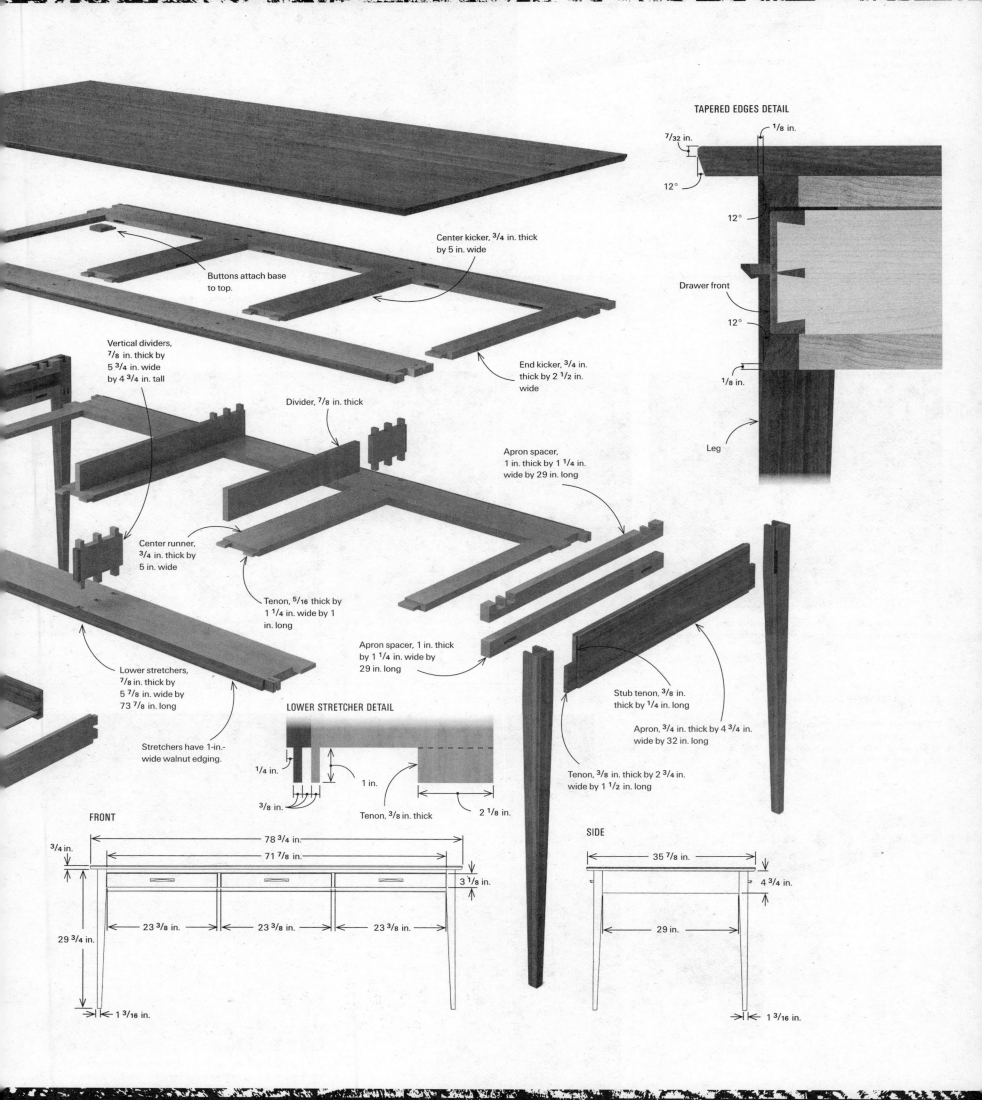

TAPERED EDGES DETAIL

7/32 in.

1/8 in.

12°

12°

Drawer front

12°

1/8 in.

Leg

Center kicker, 3/4 in. thick by 5 in. wide

Buttons attach base to top.

End kicker, 3/4 in. thick by 2 1/2 in. wide

Vertical dividers, 7/8 in. thick by 5 3/4 in. wide by 4 3/4 in. tall

Divider, 7/8 in. thick

Apron spacer, 1 in. thick by 1 1/4 in. wide by 29 in. long

Center runner, 3/4 in. thick by 5 in. wide

Tenon, 5/16 thick by 1 1/4 in. wide by 1 in. long

Apron spacer, 1 in. thick by 1 1/4 in. wide by 29 in. long

Stub tenon, 3/8 in. thick by 1/4 in. long

Lower stretchers, 7/8 in. thick by 5 7/8 in. wide by 73 7/8 in. long

Apron, 3/4 in. thick by 4 3/4 in. wide by 32 in. long

Stretchers have 1-in.-wide walnut edging.

Tenon, 3/8 in. thick by 2 3/4 in. wide by 1 1/2 in. long

LOWER STRETCHER DETAIL

1/4 in.

1 in.

3/8 in.

Tenon, 3/8 in. thick

2 1/8 in.

FRONT

3/4 in.

78 3/4 in.

71 7/8 in.

3 1/8 in.

29 3/4 in.

23 3/8 in.

23 3/8 in.

23 3/8 in.

1 3/16 in.

SIDE

35 7/8 in.

4 3/4 in.

29 in.

1 3/16 in.

MAKE SHORT WORK OF MULTI-TENON JOINTS

The bulk of the joinery is mortise-and-tenon joints. The most challenging ones are the multiple tenons on each vertical drawer divider. Here's how to tackle them successfully.

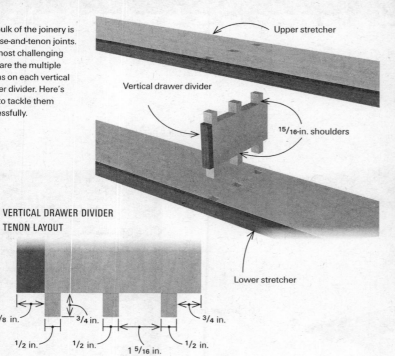

Upper stretcher

Vertical drawer divider

15/16-in. shoulders

Lower stretcher

VERTICAL DRAWER DIVIDER TENON LAYOUT

7/8 in.   3/4 in.   3/4 in.

1/2 in.   1/2 in.   1 5/16 in.   1/2 in.

Mortises first. Mark the upper and lower stretchers for the location of the vertical drawer dividers, and then cut these through-mortises with a hollow-chisel mortiser, using a backer board to prevent blowout.

Graze the tenon cheeks. Before cutting the tenons, skim 1/16 in. of material from the tenon cheeks with a dado set. This gives a clean edge where the tenons end.

Mortises locate tenons. Use the mortises on the stretchers to locate and mark the tenons on the vertical dividers.

A simple sled. Hammer uses a very basic sled to hold the vertical dividers as he removes the waste between tenons. He works carefully to his layout lines without using a stop, test-fitting as he goes.

WAIT TO DO THE UPPER STRETCHERS

Unlike the lower stretchers, the upper stretchers get dovetailed into the legs and apron spacers. The quirk in the process is this: Because the dovetail sockets go partially into the apron spacers, they can't be laid out and cut until after the legs are glued to the aprons.

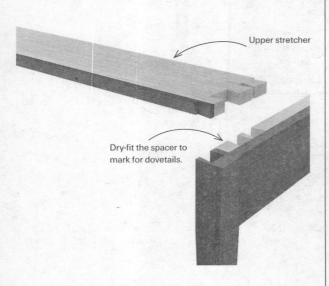

Upper stretcher

Dry-fit the spacer to mark for dovetails.

UPPER STRETCHER DOVETAIL LAYOUT

1/4 in.   1 in.   1/2 in.

1 in.   1:6 slope   1/2 in.   1 in.

Dovetail the stretcher and lay out the sockets. Saw and chop the dovetails and clean to the line with a chisel. Dry-fit the apron spacers into the apron/leg assembly and mark the dovetail locations in the leg and spacer.

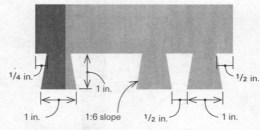

Remove the spacers to notch them. Using the tablesaw sled again, this time with an angled fence, Hammer makes the cuts to form the sides of the dovetail sockets. Then he runs the spacers through the same dado setup but on a 90° sled to remove any waste in the center.

MANAGE THE GLUE-UP IN STAGES

This is a little trickier than your average table glue-up, so it's best to take it in steps. The legs are already glued to the aprons, so you'll need to glue in the apron spacers, make two frames of the stretchers, runners and kickers, and then piece it all together.

Glue in the spacers. Clamp the apron spacers into the leg-to-apron assembly.

Create two frames. The two lower stretchers are connected by the drawer runners. The two upper stretchers are connected by the kickers.

Add the lower frame to the legs. One long clamp on each side is enough to pull it all together.

MAKE HANDSOME HANDLES

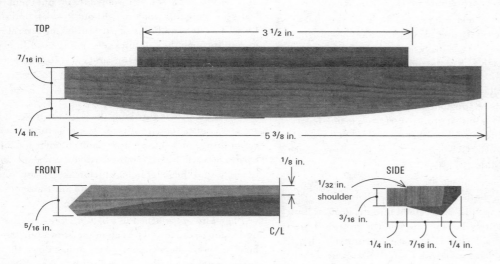

TOP

3 1/2 in.

7/16 in.

1/4 in.

5 3/8 in.

FRONT

5/16 in.

C/L

1/8 in.

1/32 in. shoulder

SIDE

3/16 in.

1/4 in.   7/16 in.   1/4 in.

Drop the vertical dividers in place and top it off. With the vertical dividers glued into the lower stretchers, you can dry-fit the top stretcher assembly until the vertical dividers are set, and then glue the top assembly in place. Or use glue with a longer open time and do it all at once.

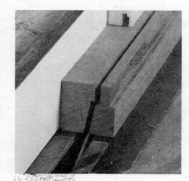

Rip tricks. The first two rip cuts form the tenon. Leaving the angled cheek cut for last lets the handle stock fall away from the blade.

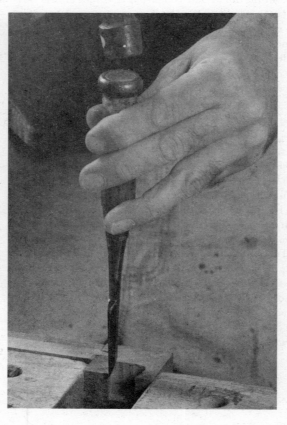

Create the sockets in the legs. Hammer clamps the leg-and-apron assembly into his end vise with the top of the leg flush with the top of the bench. With the router base sitting on the bench, he routs close to the layout line, then cleans to the line with a chisel.

Continued →

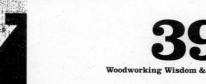

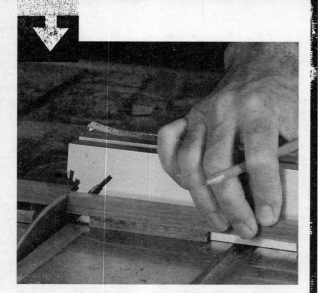

Final shape. Using the tenons to secure the handles in a vise, do the shaping with a block plane.

Pivot-Leaf Table

by Michael C. Fortune

When it comes to expanding tables, nothing beats a butterfly table for grace, beauty, and just overall coolness. Its leaf lies under the tabletop and then, like a mechanical wonder, swings up and open, coming to rest fully expanded on the aprons. As the name suggests, it's like a butterfly emerging from its cocoon—sure to draw a gasp of admiration from your dinner guests and fellow woodworkers, too.

The mechanism is both simple and ingenious. The leaf is two pieces joined by barrel hinges. It is connected to the table by a pair of pivot pins, and stores neatly under the tabletop. Then, as your guests arrive, you slide the top apart, take hold of the top half of the leaf, and pull up. As you do, it rotates on the pins and opens, rising up from beneath the top and unfolding until it rests on the aprons. At that point, you simply push the sides of the top against it and, voila, you have a bigger table. To stow the leaf, you just reverse the process. No struggle, and no loose leaves to store in a closet.

The genius of the mechanism, paired with your craftsmanship, is the perfect way to show how far you've come as a furniture maker. It's not as hard as you might think. Locating the pivot pins properly is the trick, but I'll show you a trouble-free way to do it. And the mechanism is

simple enough to work with just about any type of table. The one I've made here is fairly conventional—four legs joined to aprons—but you can make one with a pedestal or trestle base. The top can be rectangular, round, oval, or just about any shape. I even have made tops with a serpentine leaf. It works on big tables, too, as long as you beef up the slides (ball-bearing slides are best for big tables) and use more hinges on the leaf.

Straight-Grained Slides Won't Bind

The basic structure of this table is simple. I joined the legs and aprons with slip tenons. The aprons are curved and the legs tapered, but I keep them square until after I've made the butterfly mechanism and routed the mortises. However, the butterfly mechanism does need some explanation. The two halves of the top are attached to slides that ride in notches cut into both the end aprons and a pair of cross-stretchers that run between the side aprons. The slides and notches are T-shaped and work much better than dovetail-shaped slides, which tend to bind when the top is extended.

Make the notches and then fit the slides to them. Cut the vertical part of the notch at the tablesaw, using a standard blade and crosscut sled. After the vertical part is cut, rout the horizontal part of the notch. I use a handheld router and a spiral upcut bit. A pair of edge guides ensures a straight slot and a pair of stops controls the length. After the notches are done, cut the end aprons to length, cutting both ends of the apron to locate the notches properly.

Now make the matching slides. They are assembled from two pieces of hardwood, which should be straight-grained because it is less likely to warp, twist, cup, and bind in the notches. Rip the pieces to width and then cut them to length. Use a dado set to cut a shallow groove down the middle of the piece that becomes the horizontal part of the slide. A tongue routed in the vertical part of the slide registers in that groove during glue-up. Then round over all four edges so that the slide moves smoothly through the notch. Glue the two pieces together to make the T-shaped slide.

The slide mechanism also has a pair of L-shaped runners attached to both sides of the top. They ride in grooves cut in the side aprons. Stops glued into the grooves limit the in-and-out travel of the top. Cut the grooves (I use a dado set at the tablesaw), then make the runners. They're just a length of hardwood with a rabbet that I cut at the tablesaw with a standard blade—one pass for each wall of the rabbet.

For the top to close completely after the runners are installed, the cross-stretchers need to be notched to allow the runners to pass through. To make the notch, first stand the cross-stretchers on edge and guide them past the tablesaw blade with a crosscut sled. Then make a ripcut at the bandsaw to free the waste. I notch the runners in the same way.

Finally, make the stops, but don't install them until after the base is assembled and the runners have been attached to the top.

Now, before moving on to the top and leaf, assemble the base. Rout mortises in the aprons, cross-stretchers, and legs. Make slip tenons to fit. I start with a long board, round the edges, and then crosscut tenons from it. Gluing the base together is difficult if you do it all at once, so I don't. Instead, I glue up one pair of legs and an end apron, then the second pair to their apron. The side aprons and cross-stretchers are then glued together as a unit. To help keep it square, I cut a piece of particleboard to fit in the space between the cross-stretchers, assemble the side aprons and cross-stretchers around it, and then put on clamps. I leave it there while the glue dries. After the glue has dried on all three components, I glue them together to form the base.

How to Hinge the Leaf

To make the leaf, glue up an oversize panel and, after the glue has dried, rip it to width. Leave it long for now; it will be cut to length after a dry-assembly of the top and leaf, so you can mark it directly from the two halves of the top.

After ripping the leaf, cut it in half and install the hinges. The perfect hinge for this application is a concealed barrel hinge. On a top like this, which is 7/8 in. thick, a 16mm hinge is the right size (leevalley.com; No. 00H36.16). The two hinges on the outside are 2 in. from the edge. Space the rest equally between them.

To drill the holes for the hinges, I make a jig at the drill press. One half of the leaf is drilled from first side of the jig and the other half from the opposite side. This ensures that the holes in both halves are mirrors of one another and align perfectly. After the holes are drilled, install the hinges.

Pins Align Tabletop Sections

Now it's time to install alignment pins in the leaf and tabletop halves. To do that, I use a jig similar to the one I used for the hinges. The holes in the two halves of the top must mirror one another, and the holes in both sides of the leaf must mirror those in the top that they align with.

There are two parts to the alignment pins (leevalley.com; part No. 00S10.06): the pin and sleeve. One half of the top gets only pins, and the other half gets only sleeves. After you've installed them, put them in the leaf, too. Now close the top (without the leaf) and shape it. I used a router and full-size pattern, taking several passes to rout through the full thickness. Put the leaf in place, mark both ends from the top, and cut it to final length.

Install the Pivot Pins Last

Now that the base is glued together and the top and leaf are made, install the pivot pins. The pins for this table are nothing fancy. I use window bolts bought at a local hardware store. I like them because you can slide the bolt in and out of the pivot hole, which makes it easy to test-fit the leaf, take it out for finishing (and any time you need to move the table), and then put it back in.

The pins are attached to a batten screwed to the underside of the leaf. The batten serves two purposes. First, it lowers the pivot point far enough down the cross-stretchers to allow the leaf to clear the underside of the slides when it is stored in the table. Second, it helps to keep the leaf flat. Because it is screwed across the width of the leaf, use elongated screw holes in the batten to accommodate the seasonal movement of the leaf.

With the pins installed, drill the pivot holes in the cross-stretchers. I use a drilling guide made at the drill press to ensure the hole is straight and square to the face of the cross-stretcher. It is long enough to register against the side apron, ensuring that both holes are the same distance from the apron. If the holes aren't aligned properly, the leaf sits askew under the table and won't open properly.

Now install the leaf. Make sure that it opens and closes without problem. (If you've drilled the holes in the wrong place, plug and re-drill them.) Close the leaf and screw a narrow hardwood shelf to the underside of the cross-stretchers. When closed, the leaf rests on it, taking the weight off of the pivot pins and holes. Remove the leaf. Place the top upside down on the bench and then put the base on the top. Put the slides in their notches and then screw them to the top. Now glue the stops into the grooves in the side aprons, and screw the runners to the top.

Butterfly Leaf Rises and Spreads Its Wings

The secret to this expanding table is a hinged leaf that swings on pivot pins. It stays hidden under the table when not in use, but quickly spreads open when you need extra space.

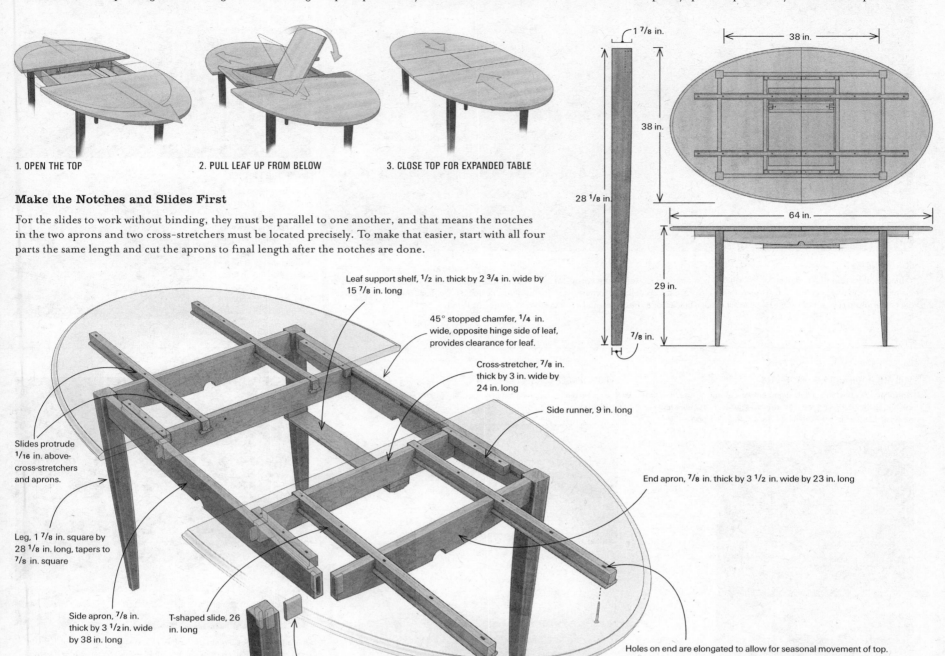

1. OPEN THE TOP

2. PULL LEAF UP FROM BELOW

3. CLOSE TOP FOR EXPANDED TABLE

Make the Notches and Slides First

For the slides to work without binding, they must be parallel to one another, and that means the notches in the two aprons and two cross-stretchers must be located precisely. To make that easier, start with all four parts the same length and cut the aprons to final length after the notches are done.

Leaf support shelf, 1/2 in. thick by 2 3/4 in. wide by 15 7/8 in. long

45° stopped chamfer, 1/4 in. wide, opposite hinge side of leaf, provides clearance for leaf.

Cross-stretcher, 7/8 in. thick by 3 in. wide by 24 in. long

Side runner, 9 in. long

End apron, 7/8 in. thick by 3 1/2 in. wide by 23 in. long

Slides protrude 1/16 in. above cross-stretchers and aprons.

Leg, 1 7/8 in. square by 28 1/8 in. long, tapers to 7/8 in. square

Side apron, 7/8 in. thick by 3 1/2 in. wide by 38 in. long

T-shaped slide, 26 in. long

Slip tenon, 3/8 in. thick by 2 in. wide by 1 1/4 in. long

Holes on end are elongated to allow for seasonal movement of top.

38 in.

38 in.

28 1/8 in.

1 7/8 in.

7/8 in.

64 in.

29 in.

T-SLIDES MAKE THE TOP A SMOOTH OPERATOR

When fully open, the top naturally wants to tip down. That would bind dovetail-shaped slides, but T-shaped ones continue to glide easily.

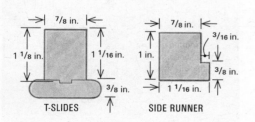

7/8 in.
1 1/8 in.
1 1/16 in.
3/16 in.
3/8 in.
T-SLIDES

7/8 in.
1 in.
3/16 in.
3/8 in.
1 1/16 in.
SIDE RUNNER

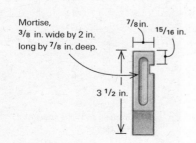

Mortise, 3/8 in. wide by 2 in. long by 7/8 in. deep.
7/8 in.
15/16 in.
3 1/2 in.

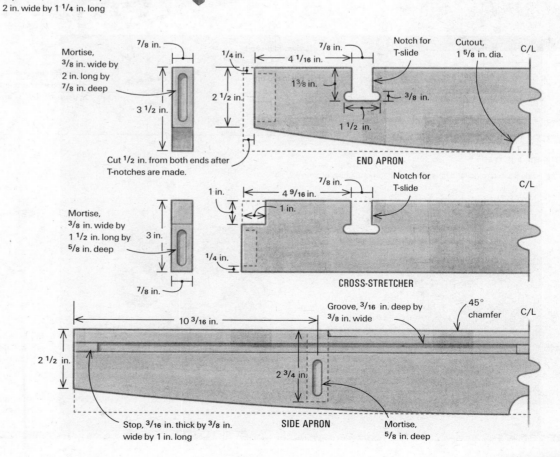

Mortise, 3/8 in. wide by 2 in. long by 7/8 in. deep
7/8 in.
1/4 in.
4 1/16 in.
7/8 in.
Notch for T-slide
Cutout, 1 5/8 in. dia.
C/L
3 1/2 in.
2 1/2 in.
1 3/8 in.
3/8 in.
1 1/2 in.
Cut 1/2 in. from both ends after T-notches are made.
END APRON

Mortise, 3/8 in. wide by 1 1/2 in. long by 5/8 in. deep.
7/8 in.
3 in.
1 in.
4 9/16 in.
7/8 in.
1 in.
1/4 in.
Notch for T-slide
C/L
CROSS-STRETCHER

10 3/16 in.
Groove, 3/16 in. deep by 3/8 in. wide
45° chamfer
C/L
2 1/2 in.
2 3/4 in.
Stop, 3/16 in. thick by 3/8 in. wide by 1 in. long
SIDE APRON
Mortise, 5/8 in. deep

MAKE THE T-SLIDES

Two-part T-slide. First cut a groove down the center of the horizontal part. Fortune uses a dado set for that. Then round its edges to match the notch (above). Rout a tongue on the upright to fit the groove. Two passes along a straight bit (right) is all it takes.

CUT THE NOTCHES

Tablesaw, then router. A pair of stops on a sled's fence controls the width of the notch. Cut the sides and then nibble away the waste in between. Flip the part end for end to cut the second notch. Repeat for the other six notches. Fortune uses a $^3/_8$-in.-dia. spiral upcut bit to make the horizontal part of the notch, taking several light passes. Use a pair of edge guides for a straight cut and a pair of stops to control the length.

JIGS ALIGN TOP AND LEAF PERFECTLY

The location of the hinges and alignment pins is critical, ensuring that the halves of the top and the leaf are perfectly level when the table is expanded, but simple drilling guides lock in their location.

BARREL HINGES CONNECT THE LEAF

The round hinges are installed in holes drilled in the adjoining edges of the leaf parts.

Drill holes for the hinges. The drilling guide keeps the bit straight and can be used from both sides, so the holes are guaranteed to line up.

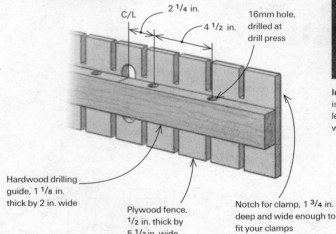

Install the hinges. Pound the hinges into one leaf with a mallet. If the fit is too tight, sand the barrels lightly with P320-grit paper. Add the second leaf, tapping back and forth across the end. The clamp keeps one side on while you tap the other.

C/L
2 $^1/_4$ in.
4 $^1/_2$ in.
16mm hole, drilled at drill press

Hardwood drilling guide, 1 $^1/_8$ in. thick by 2 in. wide

Plywood fence, $^1/_2$ in. thick by 5 $^1/_2$ in. wide

Notch for clamp, 1 $^3/_4$ in. deep and wide enough to fit your clamps

PINS ALIGN THE TOP AND LEAF

A similar drilling guide is used to drill the holes for the alignment pins and sleeves.

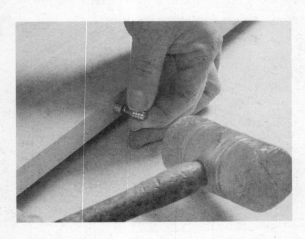

Tip for the sleeves. To sink the sleeve without marring the surface, put in a pin and tap it.

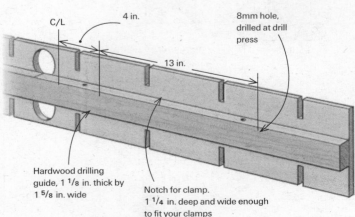

C/L
4 in.
8mm hole, drilled at drill press

13 in.

Hardwood drilling guide, 1 $^1/_8$ in. thick by 1 $^5/_8$ in. wide

Notch for clamp. 1 $^1/_4$ in. deep and wide enough to fit your clamps

ATTACH THE TOP TO ITS SLIDES

The top doesn't attach to the base with buttons or screws as on a conventional table that doesn't expand. Instead, it's attached to T-shaped slides that allow the two halves to move freely in and out, and prevent the open halves from tipping.

Install the slides. Center the halves of the top first, and leave a bit of space between the ends of the slides.

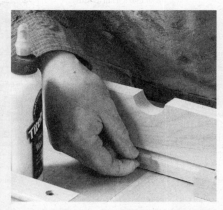

Put the stops in next. A bit of glue is strong enough to hold them in place. There are three stops per groove: one in the center and one at each end.

Add the side runners last. Fortune drills a clearance hole in the runner, transfers its location to the top with a punch, and then drills a pilot hole in the top.

Small shelf supports the folded leaf. Turn the table over and open the top so that you can clamp the shelf in place. Add blocks as shown below to lower the shelf. Drill clearance and pilot holes and screw the shelf in place.

INSTALL THE LEAF

This is where the rubber meets the road. The holes for the pivot pins have to be located precisely. The dimensions shown are for this specific table. For others, see the next page.

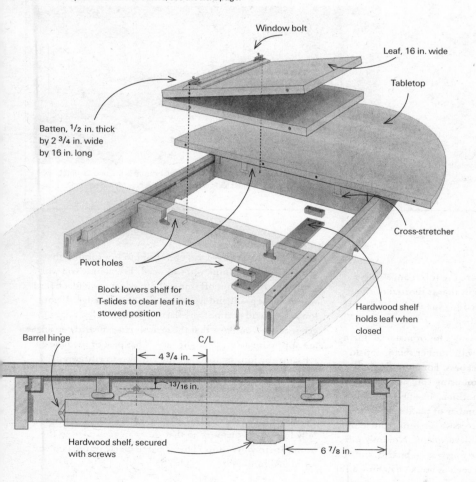

Window bolt

Leaf, 16 in. wide

Tabletop

Batten, 1/2 in. thick by 2 3/4 in. wide by 16 in. long

Cross-stretcher

Pivot holes

Block lowers shelf for T-slides to clear leaf in its stowed position

Hardwood shelf holds leaf when closed

Barrel hinge

C/L

4 3/4 in.

13/16 in.

Hardwood shelf, secured with screws

6 7/8 in.

Drill the pivot hole. Use a drilling guide that references off the side apron. That keeps the two holes aligned and the leaf swinging freely.

Attach the pivot pins. Fortune uses a window bolt because they make it easy to take the leaf in and out for fitting, finishing, and moving the table.

Put the leaf in place. Fold the leaf and let one end rest on the shelf while you lock the bolts into their holes.

Continued

Different Table Dimensions?

Here's how to locate the pivot.

To calculate this dimension, add $1/4$ in. to distance from top of stretcher to bottom of slide. Divide in half.

Horizontal pin location is $1/8$ of leaf's total length from center line

C/L

The thickness of the batten is equal to the distance from the underside of the tabletop/leaf to the base of the window-bolt bracket.

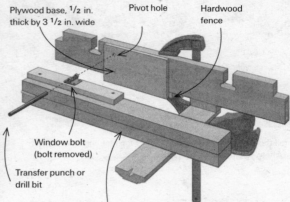

Top

Proper location of pivot hole creates $1/4$ in. of clearance.

Batten

Window bolt

T-slide

Side apron

Cross-stretcher

Measure from the table base's centerline one-eighth of the leaf's final length. Draw a vertical line down the cross-stretcher there. Next, add $1/4$ in. to the distance from the top of the cross-stretcher to the bottom of the T-slide and divide in two. Use the result to find the center point of the pivot hole on the vertical line.

In theory, that should be perfect, but I found out on my first butterfly table that there is more to it than theory. The leaf must be able to clear the slides and the apron. So, I now use a narrow mock-up of the leaf to test the pivot hole location. It is 2 in. wide and as long as the leaf, cut in half and hinged with tape. Add a spacer as thick as the batten and screw on a window-bolt bracket that has had its bolt removed. Use a drill bit or transfer punch the same diameter as the bolt in its place.

I then drill a hole in a piece of plywood and attach a fence to it. Clamp it in place so that its hole lines up with the location you marked on the cross-stretcher. Put the narrow leaf in place and insert the drill bit. Swing the leaf open and closed. If it swings without hitting the T-slide and side apron, use that location for the hole. But before you drill, locate the support shelf so that as you open the leaf, it rides on the support and just clears the side apron. That's best done by trial and error. I clamp the support to the cross-stretchers about 1 in. from the side apron and test the leaf's swing. If it hits the apron on its way up, move the support closer to the table's centerline and try again. Repeat this process until the leaf opens with no problems. Then screw it in place and drill the pivot holes.

Put a temporary leaf in place. Fortune clamps a piece of plywood with a pivot hole to the cross-stretcher. He then puts a transfer punch (or drill bit) in place of the window bolt.

VERIFY YOUR MATH WITH TWO JIGS

One jig lets you place the pivot hole where you think it belongs. And a simple leaf mockup lets you dial in the location of the window bolt.

Plywood base, $1/2$ in. thick by $3 1/2$ in. wide

Pivot hole

Hardwood fence

Window bolt (bolt removed)

Transfer punch or drill bit

Narrow leaf mockup, 2 in. wide and same thickness and length as full-size leaf. Use tape for the hinge.

LOCATE THE HARDWOOD SHELF

Place the shelf so that the leaf just clears the apron when opened. If the leaf shelf is positioned too close to the apron, the leaf will hit the apron and not ride over it.

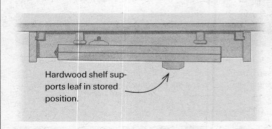

Hardwood shelf supports leaf in stored position.

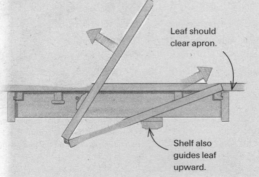

Leaf should clear apron.

Shelf also guides leaf upward.

Swing it open to check for problems. The side on the bottom is the one to watch. As it rides up the leaf support, it should just slide over the apron's chamfered edge.

Creating an Attractive Tabletop

by Bob Van Dyke

Part 1: Lumber Selection and Rough Milling

The top is the most visible part of the table, so you need to get it right. This sounds easy on the surface, but the process is loaded with pitfalls. In this three-part series, I'll describe my method for producing a tabletop you can be proud of. In this issue, you'll learn how to choose the best boards, mill them, and arrange them for the best-looking sequence. In part two, I'll show you how three glue-ups are less traumatic than one. In part three, I'll show you how to achieve a perfectly flat and smooth tabletop.

Remember, someone (probably you) is going to be living with this table for many years. And as a furniture maker, one of the advantages you have over the factory is that you can hand-pick beautiful boards. Those early decisions make or break a tabletop.

PICK THE RIGHT BOARDS

The best design option is to make the top from a single wide board. Realistically, though, that is limited to small tabletops. Most often you'll need to glue up boards, and the lumber selection will be critical.

Start thick—You'll be removing a lot of material during flattening and planing, so start with lumber that is considerably thicker than the final thickness. For a top that will be $3/4$ in. to $7/8$ in. thick, plan on using roughsawn 4/4 lumber, typically 1 in. to $^{11}/_{16}$ in. thick. The best-looking tops are usually made from a number of planks cut from the same board. You can cut successive sections from a long board, or resaw boards from a thicker plank. Not only will the color match perfectly when using resawn boards, but you can create symmetrical patterns such as book-matching and slip-matching. However, when resawing you will need stock at least 10/4 ($2 1/2$ in.) or even 12/4 (3 in.) thick because the resaw parts will move a lot after they are cut and may become severely cupped, twisted, or bowed.

Select as many boards as you will need and try to match the color as best you can. You may have to spend a considerable amount of time sorting through the lumber stack.

Watch the grain—Don't be afraid to buy lumber that is wider than you think you will need. Frequently you will bandsaw a few inches off one or both edges to yield a board with straight grain and no sapwood along the edge. If you look at the end grain of any flatsawn board with straight-grain edges, you'll see that the growth rings near those edges are approximately 45° to the face. That part of the board is riftsawn. By joining together the riftsawn to riftsawn parts of the boards, you are ensuring that the top will stay flat. And because the face grain of any riftsawn section is mostly straight, you have the advantage of hiding the glueline.

After bringing the boards home, stack them horizontally for a week or more so that they can acclimate to the humidity in your shop. This is particularly important for air-dried lumber.

Rough-Cut the Boards to Length and Width

Begin rough milling by deciding where you will chop each individual board that will make up the top. Are there knots, sapwood, or other obvious defects you need to cut out or hide?

All planers and jointers leave some snipe—the tendency of the tools to take a deeper bite at the end of a cut. Make the sections at least 5 in. longer than final length, so you can cut away areas of snipe. Now lay out the width of the board you will need on the roughsawn plank (typically about 3/4 in. wider than the final width). Note which edges have straight grain that you can use for the glue joint. If the boards are wide enough, you can angle the sections so that the edges are parallel to the grain (see drawing). Crosscut the boards on the chopsaw and rip them on the bandsaw (or with a circular saw) and not the tablesaw.

Anatomy of a Perfect Panel

A well-made tabletop begins with the lumber: Look for boards with consistent color, straight grain along the edges to disguise the gluelines, and boards that can be milled flat and straight so that you don't build stresses into the finished top. It is worth spending extra time and even extra money to find the right sequence of boards. Just milling the first boards that come to hand will create a top where the boards clash and the gluelines are obvious.

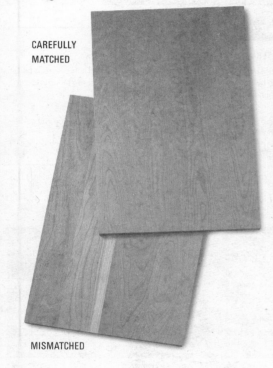

CAREFULLY MATCHED

MISMATCHED

Surface the Boards and Lay Them Out

Once your boards are sawn to rough width and length, you're ready to joint and plane them. At this point, you only want the boards roughly flat and planed so that the faces are just parallel. If you take too many passes on the jointer and planer, you may not have enough material left to plane after the glue-up. Joint one edge straight and rip the opposite edge parallel, leaving it about 1/4 in. to 3/8 in. over final width. Each pair of boards combined should be narrow enough to fit through your planer. Pass the ripped edge over the jointer to remove the sawmarks.

With the boards planed enough to reveal the grain and the color, you're ready to make the final decision on how they will go together. Shuffle them to find the most pleasing combination. Don't try to arrange boards so that the grain lines run from one board into the next. More often than not, the match will get thrown off as soon as you plane the boards to final thickness.

As you try different combinations, step back and look at them from a few angles. The color and figure of many boards will change dramatically depending on the direction from which you view them because light is being reflected differently from the wood cells within the board. This effect is known as chatoyance.

Try to align boards so the grain is going the same way. Doing so will make it easier to plane the top smooth later. But don't sacrifice aesthetics for practicality. Appearance is the number one priority.

Many woodworkers make a big deal over alternating the direction of the end grain because they think it will help to keep the top flat over time. However, I give priority to a board's best appearance on the top face and pay little attention to the end-grain orientation because I am milling the boards carefully before glue-up.

As you shuffle the boards, keep track of the different combinations by drawing small triangles with a number inside them across the gluelines. Most of the time, the best combination will hit you as soon as you see it. When you've made the final decision, put a large triangle across all the boards to show clearly how they go together.

In part two, I'll show you how to prep the boards for glue-up.

What to Look for at the Yard

Sneak preview. At the lumberyard, if the boards are roughsawn, ask permission to block-plane a small section to get a better view of the wood's color and grain.

Riftsawn edges add stability. Try to find boards where the growth rings run at about 45° to the face where the finished edges will be. This ensures that the sections of the top will stay flat.

STRAIGHT GRAIN HIDES JOINTS

It is much easier to conceal the joint between two boards if the grain on both runs parallel to the edge. Another advantage to selecting boards with riftsawn edges is greater stability across the tabletop.

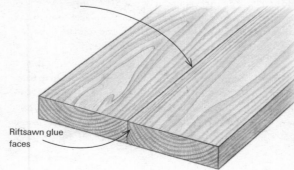

Straight grain along the board edges conceals the joint best.

Riftsawn glue faces

ROUGH-MILLING REVEALS TRUE CHARACTER

Start extra long. After laying out the parts of the tabletop on the rough boards, cut them 4 in. or 5 in. overlong to allow for snipe from the jointer and planer.

Bandsawing is safer. Ripping the un-jointed boards on the tablesaw might cause kickback. So cut them 3/4 in. over final width on the bandsaw.

FOLLOW THE GRAIN

One advantage of using rough boards a few inches wider than finished width is that if the grain runs at a slight angle, you can saw the finished board so that its edges are parallel to the grain.

Location of desired board

Joint a face. With the boards cut slightly wide and long, joint a face of each board. If the board is warped, joint the concave side. At this stage there is no need to completely smooth the board. Just remove enough to stop it from rocking.

Plane the other face parallel. Run the boards through the planer until the face opposite the jointed one is just smooth. Don't aim for final thickness yet.

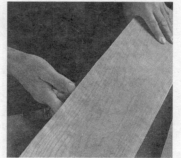

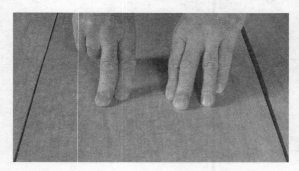

Joint one edge, then rip to width. Run one edge over the jointer until it is flat and at 90° to the face that is against the fence. With the jointed edge against the fence of the tablesaw, rip each board slightly over final width.

The right combination. With the faces and edges flat and square, you can place the boards next to each other and look for the best sequence.

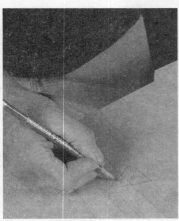

Record good matches and make the final choice. When you find two boards that go well together, draw a small triangle across the joint and number both sides. This will make it easier to come back to this pairing after you've tried other combinations. After you have found the best sequence of boards, draw a large triangle across the whole top.

Part 2: Edge-Jointing and Glue-Up

PUT A SPRING IN YOUR JOINTS

The first step is to run the adjoining edges of each board over the jointer to form the glue joint. Check that the jointer fence is at 90°, but alternate the faces of boards against the jointer fence to cancel any error in the jointer setup. If one edge measures 91°, the angle on the adjacent edge will measure 89° and the boards will lay up flat. Sometimes this means jointing against the grain and risking tearout, so make light cuts with a slow feed rate.

To ensure that the joint closes along the edges of the boards, take a bit more wood from the middle than from the ends, creating a slight gap in the middle of the joint. This is called "springing" the joint. As the clamp pressure closes the gap in the middle, the joint will only get tighter toward the ends of the boards.

To spring the joint, set the jointer to take a light cut and use a slow feed rate. Begin the cut by exerting a small amount of downward pressure on the board as it goes across the cutterhead. When about 6 in. of the board is on the outfeed table, push down hard on the board with your left hand just past the cutterhead. Continue with this slow feed and heavy pressure until about 6 in. remains. At that point, lighten up on the board until you're exerting almost no downward pressure, and finish the cut. Do the same to the adjacent board.

The gap in the center will be too small to see, but you can test the joint by standing the boards up with their sprung edges together. Now try to swivel the top board. The points of contact at either end should provide enough friction to prevent this. If the top board swivels on the bottom one, you have a small lump somewhere. Rip 1/16 in. off the sprung edge of one board, spring it again, then re-test the joint. If you still feel the swivel, re-joint the other board.

LEVEL THE JOINTS AS YOU GLUE THEM UP

A properly made butt joint will be stronger than the wood itself, eliminating the need to add biscuits or dowels for strength. As a matter of fact, biscuits and dowels can sometimes hinder you from aligning the boards during glue-up. A common problem is that the glued-up top will be wider than your planer. The simplest way to handle this is to divide the top into two or more subassemblies, each one sized to fit through the planer. Then glue the two subassemblies together, leaving very little flattening to do on the completed tabletop.

A level surface to clamp on is very important because you do not want any distortion. I use a flat sheet of melamine cut to the size of my benchtop, which also protects it from glue drips. I typically will use an odd number of clamps, in this case three on the bottom and two on top. Placing clamps on the top and bottom helps equalize pressure and produces a flatter glue-up.

Space the bottom clamps evenly and lay out the boards on top of them, using the triangle you drew earlier as a guide.

After applying the glue, make sure the triangle lines are aligned, then tighten the middle clamp slightly, pushing down on the joints to align them. Work your way out to the ends, maintaining moderate clamp pressure and aligning the joints as you go. Remove any glue squeeze-out before putting on the top clamps.

Once all the clamps are in place, apply an even amount of pressure to each one. Turn over the assembly and remove the excess glue between the clamps. Place a straightedge across the boards in several places to make sure uneven clamping pressure hasn't bowed the workpiece. Adjust the clamp pressure if necessary.

After the subassemblies dry, run them through the planer to remove any misalignment between the boards. Then flip them end for end and plane the other side parallel. Plane them down to less than 1/32 in. over final thickness, taking light cuts near the end to minimize tearout. Now repeat the glue-up procedure, this time gluing the

two subassemblies together. Take extra care to get a flush glue joint as you have very little surplus thickness to work with. Once the glue dries, you're ready to flatten, dimension, and smooth the tabletop. I'll describe how to do that in the third and final part of this series

Spring-Joint the Edges

Is it square? Adjust the jointer's fence so that it is 90° to the outfeed table just past the cutterhead.

 TIP

ALTERNATE FACES AGAINST THE FENCE

If the jointer fence is not exactly 90°, you can still achieve a flat tabletop by putting one board facing inward (I) against the fence and the adjacent board facing out (O).

Alternating faces when jointing will make up for any fence inaccuracy. (Angle is exaggerated for clarity.)

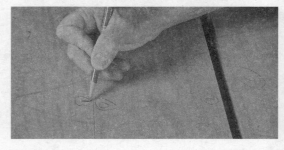

Vary the force. While jointing each edge, bear down in the middle to create a very shallow hollow.

No swinging allowed. If the sprung joint has been cut correctly, the two boards will not move when placed edge to edge. If they pivot, then one or both boards need to be ripped and re-jointed.

GLUE UP IN SECTIONS

Don't spare the glue. Van Dyke applies a generous bead of glue on one edge, spreading it out with his finger.

Press and rub. Place the glued edge against its mating edge and slide the two surfaces back and forth to distribute the glue evenly.

Align and clamp. Apply light force, aligning the surfaces with your fingers. Use a caul on the face that will be glued to the other half.

Easy cleanup. Before putting on the top clamps, scrape off most of the surplus glue with a putty knife.

More force applied. Place clamps on top of the glue-up. Then tighten down all of them, applying firm, even pressure.

FLATTENING FOR THE FINAL GLUE-UP

Don't get lost. You are about to plane away the large triangle that marked the sequence of all four boards. To keep the correct order, mark the adjacent ends of the boards.

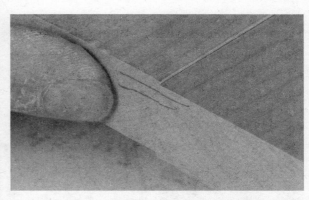

Final assembly. Pay close attention to board alignment when clamping the two subassemblies to form the tabletop. Doing so will minimize the work needed to flatten the top later.

Part 3: Flattening, Dimensioning, and Smoothing

TOP NOT PERFECT? DON'T PANIC

If you started with straight, flat boards and your glue-up went well, your top may be flat enough to proceed to final smoothing. It's more likely, however, that the top will be slightly cupped, or the glue joint between subassemblies won't be perfect.

Don't sweat it. Flattening a top is not difficult. I prefer handplanes for flattening and smoothing. They work faster than sandpaper and guarantee a flat surface. But careful sanding, by power or hand, will work, too. To plane the top, secure it between benchdogs, cupped side up. It should not move when you press on it. If it rocks or deflects, tap in wedges underneath to stabilize it.

With a long handplane (preferably at least a No. 5, but you can use a No. 4 if the top is narrow), begin planing diagonally across the surface. Start at one end and work down the length, overlapping strokes. Check your progress with a straightedge. The plane should be cutting the high spots only. Once it takes a shaving the whole way across, the face is flat. Stop planing.

Begin planing along the length, starting at the far end and working your way back, overlapping the strokes. Here you are just trying to remove most of the tearout from the diagonal planing. Final surfacing comes later. When you are done, flip over the top end for end and flatten the other side.

DIMENSIONING: HOW TO HANDLE A LARGE PANEL

At this point, the top is still a little bigger than its finished size. To get to the final width, first re-joint one edge using a handplane or the jointer. Rip the top to width on the tablesaw and then joint or handplane the ripped edges to smooth them.

Now that the sides are parallel, crosscut the top to length. This can be tricky, as almost all tabletops are too big for a miter gauge. A crosscut sled is the easiest, safest,

Continued ➜

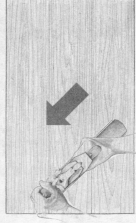

Flatten with a handplane. Even if the glue-up went well, there usually will be small steps between boards and a bit of cupping. To remove these defects, first plane diagonally to the grain.

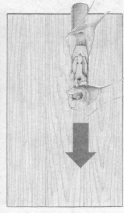

Now go with the grain. Clean up marks from the diagonal passes by planing with the grain.

and most accurate way to do the job. Cut one end square, then flip the top and cut the other end to finished length. If you used a jointer to prep the edges before glue-up, cut off at least 1 in. from each end of the top. Doing so removes any snipe from the jointer that can weaken the very end of the glue joint. If the top is too large for a crosscut sled, use a square to draw a layout line across the ends and use a circular saw or jigsaw to cut about 1/16 in. outside the lines. Clamp a straight piece of plywood on the line, then flip over the top and use a router with a flush-trimming bit, running against the plywood edge, to clean up the end. A spiral flush-trimming bit works well.

SMOOTH THE EDGES

With the top cut to size, it is time for final surfacing. There are many ways to do this, and you should use tools you are comfortable with. I usually use a smoothing plane, a block plane, a card scraper, and some P320- or P400-grit sandpaper, but many people use cabinet scrapers, random-orbit sanders, or belt sanders. To begin, use a very sharp block plane on the ends to smooth out any marks left from the tablesaw or the router. End grain is tough to plane, so take very light cuts and skew the plane. A little furniture wax on the sole of the plane also will help it cut smoothly. To avoid tearing out the long grain of the far edge, stop planing an inch or two before the end and then come at it from the opposite side. Now wrap a piece of P320- or P400-grit sandpaper around a cork sanding block and, with a few strokes, you will have ends that feel like glass.

Remove the jointer marks on the long edges with a handplane or a card scraper. These machine marks and light tearout can be hard to see. To help highlight any tearout, lightly sand the edges with stearated P320- or P400-grit paper wrapped around a cork sanding block. Any tearout will show up because the fine sanding dust will fill in the voids from the tearout.

NOW SMOOTH THE BOTTOM AND THE TOP FACE

Once the edges are smooth, it's time to smooth the top and bottom. I generally use a No. 4½ smoothing plane, but you also can use a No. 4. Make sure the handplane is as sharp as possible, the mouth is closed up fairly tight, and it is set for a light cut. Secure the tabletop, bottom face up, between benchdogs, using scrapwood to protect the ends. I plane or scrape only the portion that will overhang the base, but some people surface the entire bottom. I see no point in doing this. The only people who will ever see it are just way too nosey!

Now you are ready to make the top surface perfect. Work slowly and methodically, starting at the far side and working across using overlapping passes. Plane with the grain to avoid tearout in the final surface. If you are getting tearout where two boards meet, try taking light cuts diagonally across the joint. Now sand the surface with P320-grit paper. This step will highlight any areas of tearout. Go over the surface with a card scraper. Because the surface left from the scraper feels a little rough, sand the top again with P320- or P400-grit paper. If you are planning to use a pigment stain on the piece, then sand the whole surface with a coarser paper—usually P180 or P150 grit.

I lightly chamfer all the edges and corners with the block plane. Congratulations: Your top is done, so don't drop it.

Two Ways to Cut to Length

1. USE A CROSSCUT SLED ON THE TABLESAW

Does it fit your sled? If your tabletop is narrow enough, use a crosscut sled to cut it to length quickly and safely.

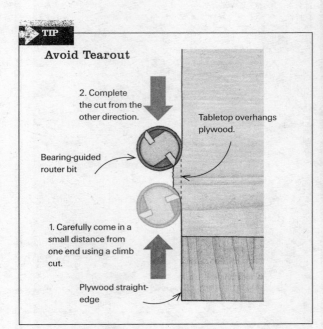

TIP

Avoid Tearout

2. Complete the cut from the other direction.

Tabletop overhangs plywood.

Bearing-guided router bit

1. Carefully come in a small distance from one end using a climb cut.

Plywood straight-edge

2. ROUGH-CUT, THEN ROUT

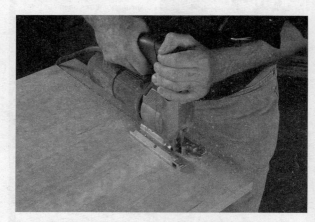

Use a router for wide tabletops. If the top is too big to be crosscut safely on the tablesaw, lay out the cut, and use a jigsaw or a circular saw to cut just outside the line. Then use a bearing-guided router bit riding against a straightedge to trim the waste up to the line. Whichever way you cut the top to length, use a sanding block, a low-angle block plane, or better still a low-angle smoother to clean up the ends of the tabletop (below).

3. A PERFECT TOP

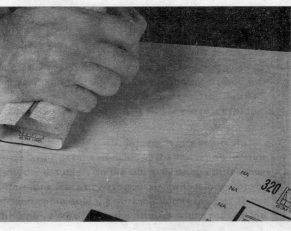

Tearout revealed. It can be hard to see minor tearout left by handplanes. Lightly sand the surface with P320- or P400-grit paper to highlight the torn-out areas.

A sharp card scraper quickly removes any tearout you find, but be careful not to create hollows.

Break the edges. Use a block plane to create small chamfers on all the edges. This lessens the chances of the top being damaged, makes applying a finish much easier, and feels better to the touch.

Customize Tabletop Edges

by Garrett Hack

I expect a lot from a tabletop edge. On one hand, I need it to be tough, able to endure a life full of bumps and bruises, even spills. Yet I want the edge to be attractive, with lines that are in keeping with the overall piece and with a profile that is pleasant to touch. It's not an easy dance to master, but it's a fun challenge.

I treat table edges with respect, spending a great deal of time on them. My goal is to design edges that are as alluring as the rest of the piece. I use the edges as a canvas to add detail or create interest by incorporating facets that catch light or add shadows. But make the edges too delicate, and they won't hold up to the ruthless wear and tear of use. I look to soften sharp, square surfaces so that they're friendly to hand and body. Subtle shapes can be very appealing, and less is usually more.

Consider the Overall Piece

When designing a tabletop edge, make the profile an important part of a cohesive design. Generally, simple furniture calls for simple edges while more intricate designs call for more elegant profiles. I consider the shape or aesthetic of the table and its function, the size of the overhang, the wood the top is made of, and how thick it is or how thick I would like the top to appear. You can make the top look thinner by shaping the underside of the edge with, say, an underbevel. You can accentuate thickness by using a simple bullnose or roundover, or using a beveled top edge.

The overhang of a tabletop is a critical part of a table's design. Dining tables may have wider overhangs to accommodate seating, while an overhang on a sideboard may be shorter to allow access to a door or drawer. The size of the overhang will have a direct impact on the width of the edge profile and the way it's seen. Wide overhangs can be nice, but they partially conceal the aprons or any drawers from

standing view. In such a case, you may choose an underbevel profile, which exposes details below the top. Shorter overhangs limit the size of the edge profile to the thickness of the top, such as a bullnose or beaded edge.

Hardwood vs. Softwood Tops

If you are really on your toes, you'll choose a profile that works with your wood selection, whether softwood or hardwood, figured or plain.

Softwoods and hardwoods each have working characteristics that make them suitable for particular profiles. Softwoods age to a beautiful patina, but they dent easily and don't take or hold detail as well as harder woods. So for softwood tops, you may incorporate pronounced chamfers or bold profiles with less complex shaping and no sharp edges. The harder the wood, the better it holds detail, so harder tops are better for multifaceted edges.

Finally, think about the figure; a tabletop with abundant figure or prominent grain may beg for a less-detailed edge that doesn't compete for attention.

Custom Edges that Sing

Some woodworkers choose an edge profile based on the router bits they have. I avoid that approach because I don't want my furniture to look factory made. Production furniture has a certain look, with predictable edges—perfect 45° chamfers, blunt bullnoses, and other recognizable profiles cut with routers or shapers. The edges are good and durable, but they don't seem very creative or interesting.

However, when I create one-of-a-kind edges that fit my style, common router bits can be a starting point. They certainly make things easier. So I sometimes use a router to rough out the profile, then refine the machined edge with hand tools. Sometimes all it takes is delicate passes with a block plane or a spokeshave, or even scrapers and sandpaper.

From simple to complex, the edge profiles illustrated here can be used individually or combined to create dazzling designs.

Chamfers—I often incorporate chamfers in my work to create light-catching facets along edges. A light chamfer is created by kissing the corner with a block plane. More passes with the plane create wider chamfers. The detail can be incorporated into any number of edge profiles. Cham-

fers can be cut at any angle, even a different angle on the top than the bottom. You also can cut multiple chamfers into an edge, creating a multifaceted surface.

Bevels—A bevel is simply a wide chamfer. Cut on the top edge or the bottom, they are often used to disguise or play up the thickness of the top. Steep angles generally accentuate thickness, while wider, sweeping bevels tend to play it down, especially when used on the bottom edge.

Roundovers—Though I think of bullnose-style roundovers as a rather unimaginative staple of the modern furniture industry, these edges work well at deflecting dings in a high-traffic area. One way to make an otherwise bland roundover more attractive is to reshape it so that it's not just a radius or section of a circle; sometimes an asymmetrical roundover is best. Another way is to use just part of the full radius, so the roundover has hard edges. To add even more interest, I often lick the top and bottom of the profile with a block plane to create fine, light-catching chamfers. I also combine a roundover with other profiles, creating any number of elegant custom variations.

Complex profiles—High-style tabletops often feature complex edge profiles with multiple shapes. Here's where I use a router to rough out the profile, and then planes or custom-made scrapers to refine it. When working this way, I often create a small wooden mock-up to dial in the profile and then use it to gauge my progress on the real edge.

Beads—I use beaded profiles in many ways: along table aprons, on drawer fronts, and on legs. But they also work well as part of a table profile. I prefer to cut beads with hand tools in order to create a fine quirk (the narrow indentation on the inside edge of the bead). Bead-cutting router bits leave a wide quirk. You can combine a bead with a chamfer to create an elegant edge with lots of light-reflecting and shadow-catching surfaces. You also can incorporate multiple beads for a traditional look.

Last, Make It Personal

Unless you are making a strict period reproduction, it's difficult to say that one profile is better than another; it all depends on your design and taste. By adding subtle details to the basic profiles presented here, you can come up with a unique shape that fits your furniture. Explore the possibilities. For me, playing with the edges has become one more fun part of building special pieces.

Chamfers and Bevels

A chamfer cut along the top or bottom of a tabletop is a simple and very effective profile that catches light, draws the eye, and softens hard edges. A bevel is simply a wide chamfer. Both can be cut with handplanes, but bevels often are cut with a router or a tablesaw and refined with a block plane.

Chamfers are quick to make with a block plane. You can kiss an edge for a light facet or make repeated passes to create a wider flat. Use your fingertips to register the tool at a consistent angle for each pass.

Continued ➡

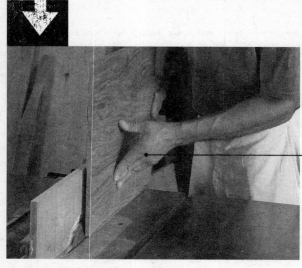

Two steps to a bevel. Rough out the bevel on the tablesaw. Be sure to support the top with a tall fence as you make the cut. Clean up the sawn surfaces with a handplane.

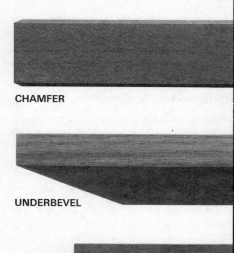

CHAMFER

UNDERBEVEL

BEVELED TOP WITH FILLET

2. Mark the boundaries. Extend a line across the top, indicating where the profile will end. The lines will provide a consistent stopping point for all the shaping cuts to follow.

3. Round the edge with a block plane. After making a few chamfers on the tablesaw, take light cuts with the plane, removing corners of the facets with each pass.

BEYOND THE BASIC BEVEL

COVE

You can shape a concave profile, or cove, on a beveled edge using hand tools. First, make thick marks along the top and bottom edges of the bevel. Next, use a convex spokeshave (or curved scraper) to remove material between the marks. Finally, use a bullnose sanding block to fine-tune the shape and remove the reference marks.

ROUNDOVERS

Expecting dings and bumps? Rounded edges are especially effective at deflecting them. This classic quarter-round is roughed out on a tablesaw, then refined with hand tools.

BULLNOSE

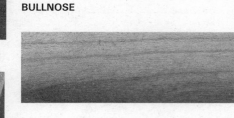

BULLNOSE WITH BEVEL

QUARTER-ROUND

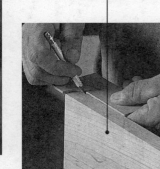

1. Make a template of the profile. Then use the template to trace the profile on the corners.

4. Check your progress. The template will show where you need to remove more material.

FILLETS

Adding a fillet to a simple roundover creates a shadowline and catches light. Rough out the profile with a router, then use hand tools to customize the shape.

ROUNDOVER WITH FLAT AND FILLET

Router and planes work hand in hand. Use a quarter-round bit to remove most of the material. The bit will carve a fillet at the top and base of the profile. Next, scribe lines to indicate the stopping point of the handwork on top. Finally, refine the edge with a block plane. Remove corners of the facets in steps until you have a round surface. You can leave fine facets to stimulate the tactile senses or smooth the surface with sandpaper.

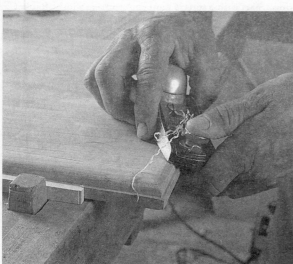

COMPLEX PROFILES

It's easy to use a router bit to get an edge on a tabletop. But you wind up with a cookie-cutter look that adds no dazzle to the design. To personalize your furniture, design your own profiles, then combine power tools and handwork to get the shape you want.

OVOLOS

This classic edge is simply a modified ovolo profile, created with a tablesaw, router, and handplanes. Start by making a template of the profile and tracing it on the table edge.

OVOLO

OVOLO WITH FILLET

1. Round the tip. Use a quarter-round bit to rout the lower edge of the profile.

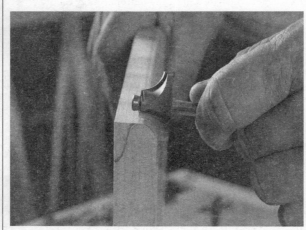

2. Hollow a channel. Use a core-box bit to rout the concave area of the profile.

3. Refine with hand tools. Following the layout lines on the edge, smooth the curves with handplanes and sandpaper.

BEADS

A beaded edge works well to introduce a round surface and shadowlines in an otherwise rectilinear edge. To create beads with fine quirks, use a scratch stock or a beading tool.

BEAD WITH CHAMFER

TRIPLE BEAD

Two ways to scratch a bead. Hack avoids router-cut beads, preferring to incise them with finer hand tools. A homemade scratch stock cuts custom beads and quirks. You also can use a beading tool for a fine detail.

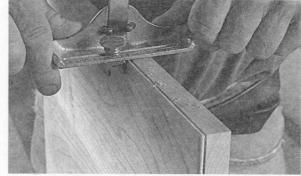

Quirky sanding block. To refine the bead, use a thin sanding block that reaches into the narrow quirk.

Continued ➡

Curved-Front Desk

by Chris Gochnour

Of all the furniture that I've designed, this desk is one of my favorites. I love its graceful lines and the inward curve of the front. The stepped drawer fronts echo that arc, but are also practical, creating space for your legs. The shape of the legs—a simplified turn on the cabriole—is curvaceous, too. And the top, which has a curved edge to match the front of the base, completes the picture.

Because it's a study in curves, I know this desk might seem too difficult for many woodworkers. Joinery on curved parts can be demanding. But actually it isn't. All of the joints are cut when the parts are still straight. The shaping is done after they're complete. That's even true of the drawers, which have curved fronts. And you'll be surprised at how easy it is to cut the dovetails, after I show you a trick that lets you treat them as if the front were square to the sides.

Another key is to make templates of all of the curves. You can use a batten or flexible ruler to make the leg template. But because the template for the front rails and top is also used for shaping those parts, I recommend Paul Schürch's jig for large-radius arcs because it produces a smooth, perfectly shaped arc.

Start with the Legs and Aprons

The side and back aprons are standard fare, straight with tenons on both ends. However, the legs have curves on all four sides—the shape is a version of a cabriole leg. They aren't difficult to make: Just trace and bandsaw a pattern onto the two outside faces. But before you shape them, you'll need to mortise them and cut a bevel on the front face of the front legs, so that they flow seamlessly into the curve of the front rails and drawers. Also tenon the side and back aprons to fit their mortises.

Now you can shape the front legs. Cut the sides of the legs first by cutting the shape marked on the front. Next, cut the front and back profiles of the leg by cutting out the pattern marked on the outside face. Last, break off the waste from the first two cuts and clean up the leg with a spokeshave and block plane.

Make the Top Rail and Connect It to the Back

There are three drawers in the desk. To make fitting them easier, it's important to build the rail and divider assembly so that the drawer pockets are square. I do that by dry-fitting the back apron between the two side assemblies, clamping a precise spacer near the front, and then fitting the top rail and drawer dividers.

The top rail is dovetailed into the legs and side aprons, while the divider assemblies are tenoned into the rail and joined to the back apron with a sliding dovetail. After the rail and dividers have been dry-fitted to the rest of the base, the base is square and the drawer pockets are defined. Then the bottom center rail is fitted to the dry-assembled base. Only then are the parts shaped.

After gluing up the side assemblies, dry-clamp the back apron between them. Clamp a spacer between the side aprons on the front of the base to help locate the top rail.

Put the back edge of the top rail blank against the front edge of the spacer. It should stick out 1/8 in. beyond the corner of the leg where the front and inside faces meet and be centered on the base's length. Scribe a baseline where the leg and side apron intersect the rail. Repeat the process at the other end, take the rail off, and extend the lines around to the top of the rail. Lay out two dovetails at each end of the rail: One goes into the leg and the other into the side apron.

Cut the tails and transfer their locations to the leg and the side apron. Make the sockets. Fit the joints and put the rail in place. Lay the template on the top rail, aligning it with the inside corner of the front legs, and trace the curve. Knowing the curve's location helps with the next step.

The top rail has mortises to hold the drawer dividers in place. After laying out and cutting the mortises, set the rail aside. It won't be shaped until after the dividers and bottom center rail have been made.

Next up are the drawer dividers. Rout the sliding dovetail sockets in the back apron and then rout the mating keys. Cut the dividers to length and make the end caps. Finally, cut the tongue-and-groove joint that joins each end cap to its divider. Glue together the two parts. Reassemble the base and fit the bottom center rail.

Shape the Parts in Steps

Now start shaping the front, beginning with the top rail. Rough out the curve at the bandsaw and then rout it flush to the template. Dry-assemble the top rail to the dividers and transfer the arc onto the top edge of the end caps. Disassemble the parts and cut that bevel. Reassemble the parts dry, this time adding the bottom center rail. Mark that rail where the dividers run into it. Pull the assembly apart and use the template to draw the arc. Rough it out and then rout it flush. That's all the shaping for now.

Add the Bottom Outside Rails

You could cut the bottom outside rails from a wide blank. However, if you did this, the grain would run out toward the edges, creating short-grain weakness. Instead use a narrower blank, angling its ends so that it fits between the leg and the divider.

First, make a template with ends that run on a slant from the leg to the divider, giving you the distance between the shoulders and the tenon locations. Use it to lay out the shoulders and tenons of the rails. Lay out the lap dovetail, too. Cut and fit the joints. These rails are the last parts glued up during assembly. To make that work, round over the top of the tenon ends (a 3/4-in. radius works), so that you can pivot them into the mortise as you put the dovetail into its socket. Now rough out the curve on the rails and clean it up with a spokeshave.

There is one last thing to do before you can finish gluing up the base: rout grooves in the drawer dividers for the runners.

The Drawers Ride on Side Runners

The wooden drawer runners are glued into grooves in the drawer dividers and, on the ends, filler blocks that bring the runners out past the legs. I rout all of the grooves at the router table.

After they're routed, finish gluing up the base. First glue the back apron between the two side assemblies. Then glue the bottom center rail to the dividers, and add the top rail. After that assembly is dry, glue it into the base. Finally, glue the bottom outside rails into place. Don't

glue the filler blocks in yet. Do that after you've made the runners, because they are used to locate the filler blocks level with the runners in the dividers.

The runners aren't complicated. After rounding over one end of a wide board, I rip the runners from it and crosscut them to length. The two that go in the filler blocks need to be notched at the front and back to fit over the legs. The others just need one notch at the front to fit over the dividers. Make the notches long enough that the runners can move back and forth in the grooves (that extra space comes into play when the runners are glued in).

Now dry-fit the runners in the grooves. Place the head of a combination square on the top edge of the divider and extend the rule down to the top edge of the runner. Lock it at that distance. Use the combination square, referenced on the top edge of the side aprons, to locate the filler blocks (the runners are dry-fitted into them). This guarantees that the two runners are level with one another. Glue on the filler blocks, but don't glue in the runners. That will be done after the drawers are made, because the runners also function as stops.

Now turn to the drawers. The curved fronts are cut from blanks after the dovetails have been cut, and their final shaping is done after the glue-up, with the drawers in their pockets so that the fronts can be blended seamlessly into the curve of the rails. Start by routing grooves in the sides for the drawer runners.

To set the router table's fence for these cuts, I make a long spacer block that fits between the top of the drawer pocket and the top of the runner. Use the block to set the distance between the fence and the bit—it should fit snugly between them. Rout the grooves, referencing the top of the drawer side off the fence.

After the grooves are routed, dovetail the drawer sides to the front and back. There is nothing tricky about the through-dovetails at the back of the drawers, because both the sides and back are straight. But the half-blind dovetails at the front can be a challenge, so I'll give you a few tips.

First, don't cut the fronts from thick blanks. Rather, make them the same way the bottom outside rails were made. Then rabbet the ends. This creates a square recess for the sides and allows you to cut the dovetails as if the parts meet at 90°.

After the joinery is done, dry-assemble the drawers and slide them onto the runners and into their pockets. Set the drawer in so that you can trace the top rail's curve on the drawer front. Do this for both the front and back curve. Take the drawers apart, rough out the curve at the bandsaw, and smooth the cuts with a spokeshave.

Now it's time to cut the grooves for the drawer bottom. I do it at the tablesaw with a dado set. The challenge here is the groove in the back of the drawer front, because it's curved. The groove is narrow and shallow, and the curve on the drawer's back is gentle, so it can be done safely. To ensure that the groove is the same depth along its length, rock the front as it enters the dado blades, so that the back is always on the table as it passes them.

Now glue up the drawers. After the glue dries, clean up the drawer sides with a handplane. Then make the bottoms. Start with a square panel cut to final width. Rabbet the sides and slide the panel into the grooves as far as it will go. Then use a small spacer block and pencil to scribe the curve of the drawer front onto the bottom. Cut the curve on the bandsaw and rout a rabbet on the front end.

Now glue in the runners. Put some glue in the grooves and then insert the runners and push them toward the front. Now put the drawers on the runners and push them in so that the drawer front is flush with the rails. This sets the runners at the right location to also function as stops.

Pull out the drawer and clamp the runners in place. Let the glue dry. Make the drawer pulls and screw them on.

Then make the top. It starts as a large panel glued up from several boards. I use a template to draw the curve on the front edge, rough it out at the bandsaw, and rout it flush to the template. The top is held to the base with shopmade buttons.

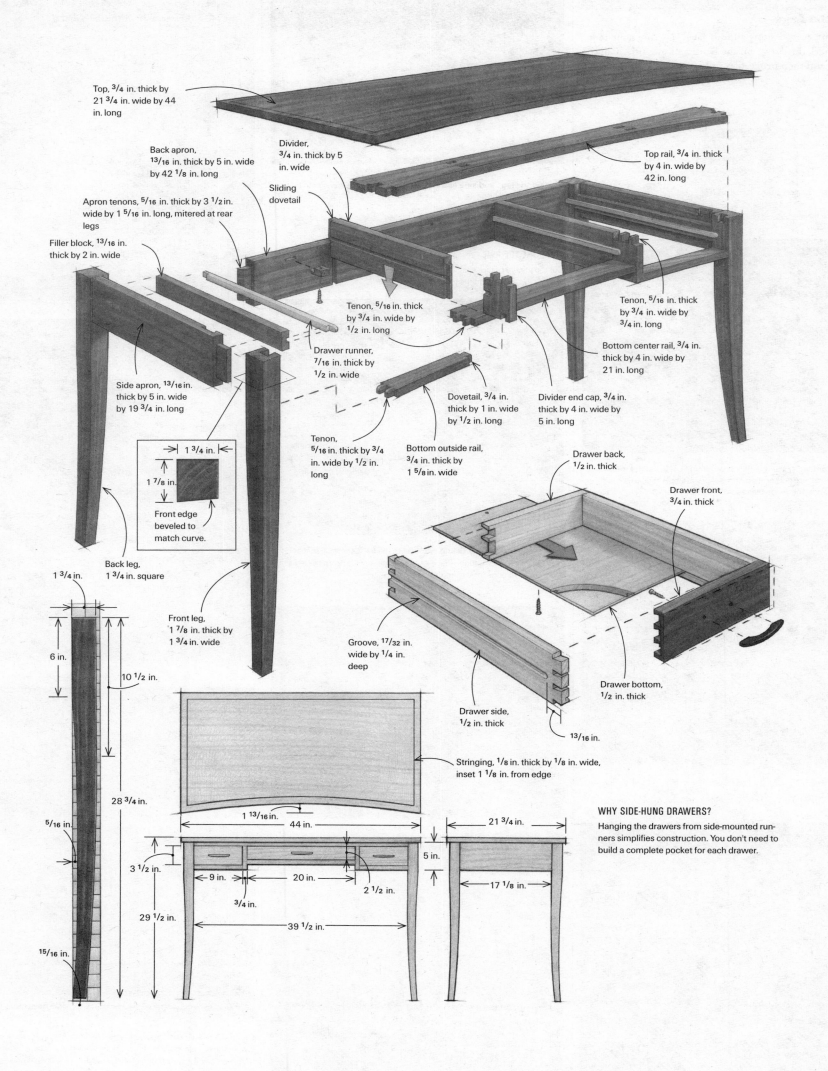

Top, 3/4 in. thick by 21 3/4 in. wide by 44 in. long

Back apron, 13/16 in. thick by 5 in. wide by 42 1/8 in. long

Divider, 3/4 in. thick by 5 in. wide

Top rail, 3/4 in. thick by 4 in. wide by 42 in. long

Apron tenons, 5/16 in. thick by 3 1/2 in. wide by 1 5/16 in. long, mitered at rear legs

Sliding dovetail

Filler block, 13/16 in. thick by 2 in. wide

Tenon, 5/16 in. thick by 3/4 in. wide by 1/2 in. long

Tenon, 5/16 in. thick by 3/4 in. wide by 3/4 in. long

Bottom center rail, 3/4 in. thick by 4 in. wide by 21 in. long

Side apron, 13/16 in. thick by 5 in. wide by 19 3/4 in. long

Drawer runner, 7/16 in. thick by 1/2 in. wide

Dovetail, 3/4 in. thick by 1 in. wide by 1/2 in. long

Divider end cap, 3/4 in. thick by 4 in. wide by 5 in. long

1 3/4 in.

1 7/8 in.

Front edge beveled to match curve.

Tenon, 5/16 in. thick by 3/4 in. wide by 1/2 in. long

Bottom outside rail, 3/4 in. thick by 1 5/8 in. wide

Back leg, 1 3/4 in. square

Front leg, 1 7/8 in. thick by 1 3/4 in. wide

Drawer back, 1/2 in. thick

Drawer front, 3/4 in. thick

1 3/4 in.

6 in.

10 1/2 in.

5/16 in.

28 3/4 in.

15/16 in.

Groove, 17/32 in. wide by 1/4 in. deep

Drawer bottom, 1/2 in. thick

Drawer side, 1/2 in. thick

13/16 in.

Stringing, 1/8 in. thick by 1/8 in. wide, inset 1 1/8 in. from edge

1 13/16 in.

44 in.

21 3/4 in.

3 1/2 in.

5 in.

9 in.

20 in.

2 1/2 in.

17 1/8 in.

3/4 in.

29 1/2 in.

39 1/2 in.

WHY SIDE-HUNG DRAWERS?

Hanging the drawers from side-mounted runners simplifies construction. You don't need to build a complete pocket for each drawer.

Shape the Legs

The legs are curved along all four faces. Use the same template to mark the curves on the front and one side. Cut the mortises, and then proceed as follows.

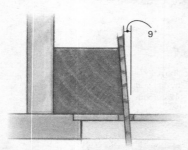

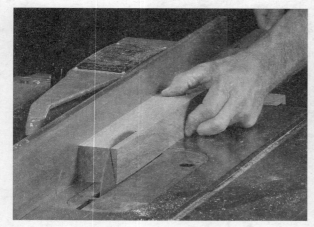

Bevel the front leg. It's part of the curved front, too. Do it after the mortises are cut, but before shaping, because after it's shaped the leg can't be guided through the blade safely.

Shape the sides. Stop the bandsaw cuts about 1/8 in. before freeing the waste, so you don't lose the layout you drew on the side.

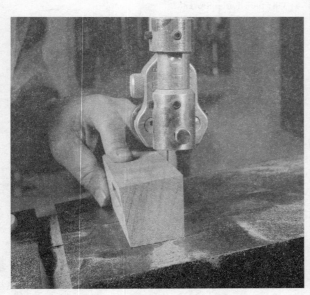

Tilt the table and shape the front. Match the bevel you cut earlier, so the curved section is just a smooth continuation of the top of the leg.

Glue up the legs and side aprons. Doing it now makes it easier to build the rest of the table base.

MAKE THE TOP RAIL

Cut the joinery before shaping the rail. That saves you the hassle of trying to align the curves and the joints at the same time.

Dry-assemble the base. Clamp the sides to the back apron. A spacer up front keeps the base square. Place its front edge 3 7/8 in. from the leg's front, as a reference for locating the top rail.

Mark the joint. Center the top rail, clamp it to the spacer, and mark a shoulder line by scribing around the leg and apron.

Double dovetail. After cutting two tails on the end of the rail, transfer their locations to the leg and apron. Make the sockets and fit the joint.

Finish the rail. Dry-fit it and scribe the arc, lining it up with the legs. Now lay out the double mortises for the drawer divider end caps. Simplify the mortising using a spacer between the rail and fence when making the second mortise. Rough out the curve on the bandsaw, then rout the rail flush to the template.

COMPLETE THE FRONT RAIL ASSEMBLY

JOINERY IS A STEP-BY-STEP PROCESS

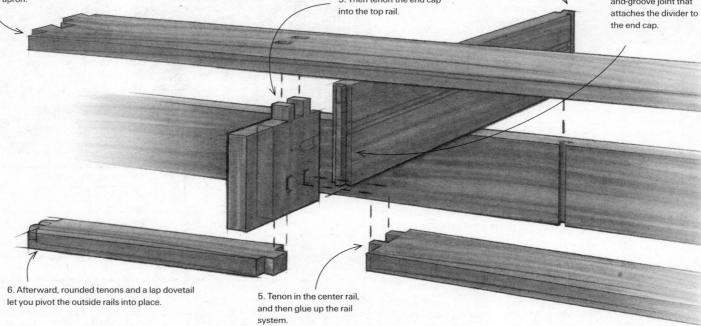

1. You've already made the lap dovetails that attach the top rail to the leg and apron.

2. Now cut the sliding dovetail that allows you to drop the whole rail assembly into the base during glue-up.

3. Then tenon the end cap into the top rail.

4. And cut the tongue-and-groove joint that attaches the divider to the end cap.

6. Afterward, rounded tenons and a lap dovetail let you pivot the outside rails into place.

5. Tenon in the center rail, and then glue up the rail system.

DOVETAIL THE DIVIDER

Router

MDF router jig

Dovetail bit

3/8 in.

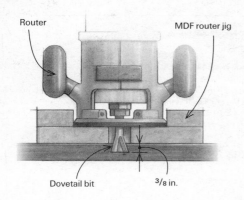

Sliding dovetails at the back. Using a router jig and a dovetail bit, Gochnour routs the socket in the rear apron in a single pass. After the socket is done, he routs the dovetail key, making it slightly shallower than the socket so that it's easier to get the two parts together during glue-up.

Glue the end cap to the divider. They're joined with a simple tongue-and-groove joint, similar to the mortise and tenon used to join legs to aprons. The caps are extra-wide at this point.

SHAPE THE FRONT FROM THE TOP DOWN

Using one part to guide the shaping of its neighbor guarantees that all of the pieces end up perfectly aligned.

Bevel the end cap to match the curve. The curve intersects the end cap as a straight line. Mark the angle directly from the top rail and then cut it at the tablesaw after tilting the blade to match the layout line.

Mark the center rail from the end caps. The marks show exactly where the curve hits it. Next, use the template to lay out the rest of the curve. Rough out the shape at the bandsaw and rout the rail flush to the template.

ANGLE THE BOTTOM RAILS FOR STRENGTH

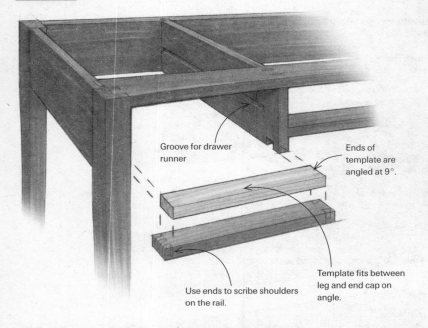

Groove for drawer runner

Ends of template are angled at 9°.

Use ends to scribe shoulders on the rail.

Template fits between leg and end cap on angle.

Make a template first. Use a piece of scrap, and trim the ends at 9° so it fits between the leg and end cap.

Put the tenon locations on it. Mark directly from the mortises on the leg.

GROOVE THE DIVIDERS

The groove for the center drawer is offset. That's because its centered on the drawer's height, which is less than the divider's.

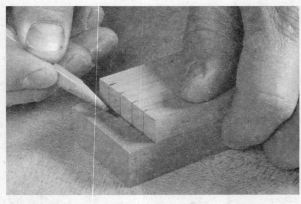

Lay out the joints on the rail. Use the template to lay out the shoulders and tenons.

Round over the top of the tenons. This will let you pivot the piece into place later.

NOTE: You need to rout all the grooves for the drawer runners before assembly, but don't glue in the outside grooved filler blocks until afterward.

THE RIGHT ORDER OF ASSEMBLY

Glue the side assemblies to the back apron. Then drop in the rail assembly and locate the outer drawer runners.

The rail assembly goes in all at once. For the sliding dovetails at the back, use glue only at the bottom end of the socket and top end of the tail. Otherwise, the joint swells and you can't get it together.

POSITION THE FILLER BLOCK TO POSITION ITS RUNNER

Notch the runners. This allows them to extend over the end caps without creating any cross-grain problems.

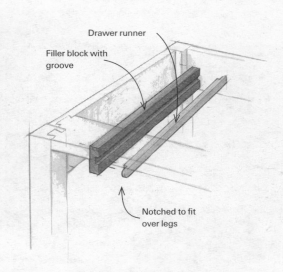

Drawer runner

Filler block with groove

Notched to fit over legs

Position the filler block. Use the square to locate it. Glue the filler block in place, but not the runner.

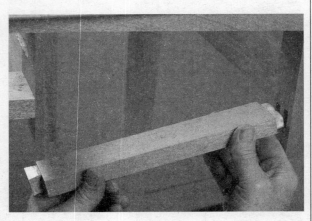

Add the bottom outside rails last. Put in the tenons and then pivot the rail upward, seating the lap dovetail into its socket.

Measure to the side runners. Set a combination square to the top edge of the side drawer's runner that's dry-fitted into the groove on the divider.

Drawers

The big lesson from making the base is that it's best to do joinery before shaping the parts, and it applies here, too. Not only that, but the drawer front blanks are angled like the bottom rails are.

GROOVE THE DRAWER SIDES

Make a spacer block. Like the actual drawer, it should slide smoothly between the top of the runner and the bottom of the rail. Use it to set up the router-table fence for the next step.

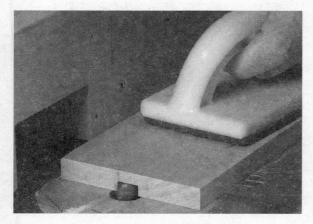

Then rout the groove. To make the groove ¹/₃₂ in. wider than the ¹/₂-in. runners, just reset the fence to remove extra material from the bottom edge of the groove.

DOVETAIL DRAWERS BEFORE SHAPING THE FRONTS

The fronts start thick to accommodate the curve. The side-drawer fronts are angled to make them stronger. Rabbets create a square recess for the joinery.

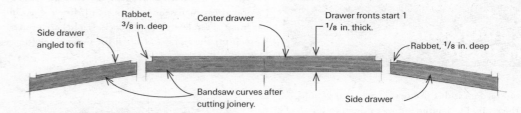

Side drawer angled to fit

Rabbet, ³/₈ in. deep

Center drawer

Drawer fronts start 1 ¹/₈ in. thick.

Rabbet, ¹/₈ in. deep

Side drawer

Bandsaw curves after cutting joinery.

Bevel the ends of the side-drawer fronts. Use the same angle as on the bottom rails (9°). Make the two ends parallel to one another.

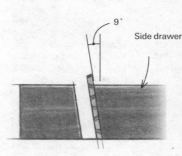

9°

Side drawer

Rabbet the back edge. For the rabbet on the other end, you need to reverse the setup, moving it to the other side of the fence.

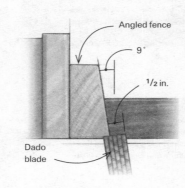

Angled fence

9°

¹/₂ in.

Dado blade

DRY-FIT TO MARK THE CURVE

Assemble the drawer dry. You'll need to pull it apart after the next step to shape the front.

Mark the curve. On the back, the curve lines up with the dovetail shoulder. Then push the drawer in and mark the front curve.

Shape it at the bandsaw. Cut both the back and front proud of the lines. Smooth both with a spokeshave.

THE RUNNERS ARE THE STOPS, TOO

It's a simple matter to set them so that the drawer stops flush with the front when the ends of the grooves hit the ends of the runners.

Use the drawer to adjust them. Immediately after putting in the runners, slide in the drawer, stopping when the front is flush with the rails. Now remove the drawer and clamp the runners in place.

Glue in the runners. After spreading the glue and putting it in the groove, push the runner as far forward as it will go.

Continued ➤

Like many avid readers and collectors, I have a lot of bookcases. Over the years, I've jammed some of them so full that paperbacks are wedged into any usable opening. The shelves are so crowded, in fact, that it's almost impossible to see the back of the case. For strictly functional cabinets like these, a sturdy back can be as simple as a plain sheet of plywood.

But there are other types of cases that need a good-looking back, and some instances in which an attractive back also must be rock solid.

I have display cases, for example, that house ceramics, antique tools, and other prized possessions. For cases like these, the back needs to look good. The case that holds my collection of first-edition books needs a different kind of back. It has a pair of inset glass doors, so the back must look good and also be quite rigid. That helps hold the case square and keep the doors from racking and binding, regardless of the substantial weight of the books.

Fortunately, there are several ways to make an attractive back; some combine great looks with construction rigid enough for the most demanding applications.

Apart from that bare sheet of plywood, most cabinet backs fall into two basic designs: slats or frame-and-panel. Slats offer a wide variety of looks—from rustic to refined—and their joinery allows for wood movement. They work well with open-front cases but aren't rigid enough for cabinets with inset doors. A frame-and-panel back, whether it's made with floating panels or glued-in plywood, is sturdier.

Slat-Back Options

The basic aesthetic goal for any slatted back is a pleasing, consistent pattern that doesn't involve very narrow or wide slats on the edges. I stagger the width of the slats, using pieces around 4 in. and 5 in. wide. Wider boards look better on larger backs.

For slatted backs, three basic forms of joinery come into play. In order of simplicity, these are shiplapping, splining, and tongue-and-groove.

Shiplapping—Shiplapping involves rabbetting opposite sides of the same board so that the edges of adjoining slats overlap. Use a router table, a tablesaw with dado head, or a shaper; make the rabbets about 1/4 in. wide and half as thick as the stock.

For small cases like the one shown here, (the back is 28 1/2 in. wide and 42 3/4 in. tall), slats as thin as 5/16 in. would work. But because shiplapped joints are not truly interlocking, large cases require thicker slats to avoid having edges twist out and pull away from the case. Another strategy for this is to use a splined or tongue-and-groove back, both of which join the slats more securely.

Splining—For boards of this size and length, cut a groove 1/8 in. to 3/16 in. wide. Keep the groove no deeper than 3/16 in. to 1/4 in. or you risk breaking off one of the sides. It's simplest to center the groove on the slat's edge unless you plan to add a bead or chamfer on the front of the board. In that case, cut the groove closer to the back of the board, but not so close that it compromises the strength of the groove's back lip.

On the tablesaw, use a featherboard and a tall auxiliary fence for safety and consistency of cut. A zero-clearance insert adds safety and prevents tearout.

You also can cut the grooves with a slot cutter mounted on a shaper or router table. Most slot-cutter sets are designed to cut a groove about 1/2 in. deep, so I bury the cutter in the fence to get a shallower cut and to reduce tearout. A fence-mounted featherboard adds both safety and accuracy.

Two Stylish Options

A bookcase stuffed to the gills with paperbacks doesn't need a fancy-looking back. On the other hand, a case for displaying collectibles probably needs something dressier than a plain sheet of plywood. Slat backs (left) made of solid wood are attractive enough to set off fine collectibles or rare books, and provide sufficient strength for an open-front cabinet. Frame-and-panel backs (right) are even more handsome. With glued-in plywood panels, this back is also exceptionally rigid, making it the best choice for a cabinet with inset doors.

CASE CONSTRUCTION

Regardless of solid-wood or plywood construction, the case should be built to accommodate sturdy attachment of the back. The key is to rabbet the sides and inset the subtop and case bottom flush with the rabbets.

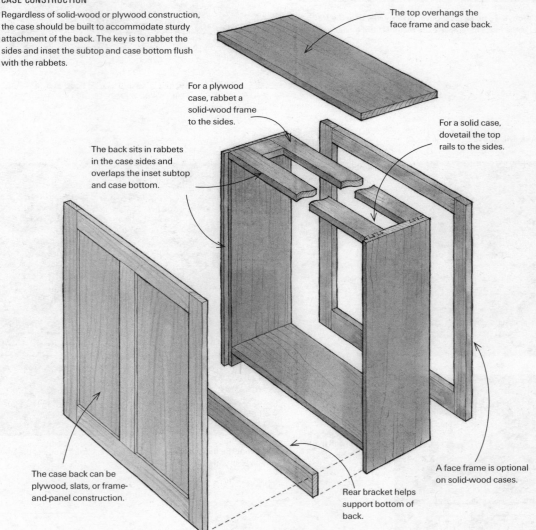

The top overhangs the face frame and case back.

For a plywood case, rabbet a solid-wood frame to the sides.

For a solid case, dovetail the top rails to the sides.

The back sits in rabbets in the case sides and overlaps the inset subtop and case bottom.

The case back can be plywood, slats, or frame-and-panel construction.

Rear bracket helps support bottom of back.

A face frame is optional on solid-wood cases.

After cutting the grooves, I create splines by thickness-planing a board of slat stock to a little less than the combined depth of the two grooves and using the tablesaw to rip off strips that fit snugly in the grooves. When mounting the slats in the case, leave a slight gap, no more than 1/16 in., between the pieces to allow for movement.

Tongue and groove—Positioning and cutting the grooves for tongue-and-groove slats is the same as for splining. Because these boards aren't very wide, there will be minimal movement, so the groove does not need to be very deep.

Amana sells a two-wing, slot-cutting assembly marketed under the name of Quadraset that can be adjusted to cut both halves of the joint with a slot width as narrow as 1/8 in. and expandable in 1/32-in. increments. There is a distinct advantage in cutting both the top and bottom rabbets at the same time, because the tongue is guaranteed to be consistent and fit the groove. In my experience, cutting one side at a time, regardless of setup efforts, leads to variations in the tongue thickness that may require touch-up with a rabbet plane.

Embellishments—Chamfers and beads are the two most common forms of edge detail on slat backs. For chamfers on splined or shiplapped slats, bury the bit into an auxiliary fence to ensure that the chamfer doesn't take up the entire edge. For tongue-and-groove slats, I make a special fence that allows me to chamfer both the tongued and the grooved slats with one router-table setup. I cut one of the lips off an extra piece of grooved stock, then bury the V-groove bit into the lower lip. (Don't use a chamfering bit here. The tongue on your slats will ride the bit's bearing and push the work away from the cutter.) The small flat that was left below the chamfer rides the edge of the rabbet.

I typically bead only tongue-and-groove slats, using a high fence and a beading bit in a table-mounted router. I cut the bead on the tongued section. When using thin stock, I don't bead the grooved edge because it will weaken the lip. This isn't an issue for larger cases with thicker back boards. If possible, set the top of the bead a little below the surface of the board so that it is not flattened during subsequent planing, scraping, and sanding stages.

Easy Frame and Panel

Frame-and-panel backs are much more rigid than slat backs and, as a result, are more effective at keeping a case from racking. Frame-and-panel backs are also quite attractive, and the use of contrasting panels adds a contemporary feel.

A very traditional back can be made with full tenons and a solid, raised panel, but I prefer another method, using plywood panels. This is just as attractive yet easier and more rigid. Plywood frame-and-panel backs can be made with a simple, quick method. For a case of this size, use 5/8-in. to 3/4-in. frame stock with panels made from 3/8-in. or 1/2-in. plywood. Plywood is available rotary cut in common species such as walnut, mahogany, cherry, and red or white oak. Since the panels aren't large, it is not difficult to cut a sheet for optimum appearance. Plain-sliced plywood has a more uniform look, but may not be as readily available in most species.

Size the back about 1/8 in. taller and wider than the rabbeted case opening. Design the back so that interior stiles and rails are proportional to each other. In my bookcase (see photo), the back is divided into two panels for a balanced look. The center stile is about 1/2 in. narrower to compensate for the edges of the side, which rest in a rabbet in the case.

Making the frame—I use stub-tenon joinery, which is a wonderful way to make frames quickly for a variety of applications such as cabinet backs and dust panels. By itself, this frame isn't as strong as one made with traditional mortise-and-tenon joinery. But with plywood panels glued in place, you wind up with a lightweight back that is more rigid than its traditional cousin.

Options for Slat Backs

A slat back is relatively simple solid-wood construction. Each of these joinery choices is designed to allow for its own wood movement, so don't glue the slats to each other. Each slat should expand and contract as an individual unit.

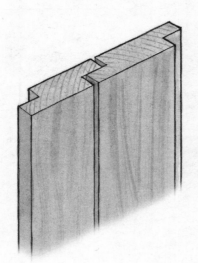

SHIPLAP
This is a practical choice for thinner slat stock because rabbetting divides the narrow edge of each slat into just two elements. In contrast, a groove plowed in the edge of a too-narrow slat will have skinny, fragile walls that could snap off.

SPLINES
Cutting a simple groove along the edges of each slat allows the boards to be held together with splines. Stronger than shiplap, but not as strong as tongue and groove, a splined back is much quicker to make than the latter.

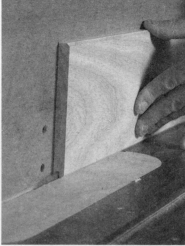

Cut a groove. A tablesaw kerf is wide enough to house a spline. The spline should be slightly narrower than the combined depth of the grooves to allow for movement.

Matched rabbets form a joint. With the bit height set at half the thickness of the stock, all of the cuts can be made with one router-table setup.

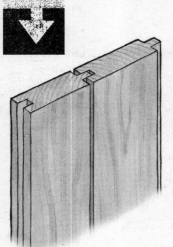

TONGUE AND GROOVE
Tongue-and-groove joinery makes a sturdier back. The joints interlock more securely than splined slats, reducing the likelihood of a piece cupping or twisting.

A slot cutter plows a groove. Tongue-and-groove joinery requires a wider groove. Make one pass in each direction to ensure that the groove is perfectly centered.

A straight bit cuts the tongue. Set the bit height to match the bottom of the groove.

Edge Details

CHAMFERS
Chamfers work well on all three styles of slat backs, and they're easily cut using a block plane or a chamfering or V-groove bit chucked into a router table.

A shiplap fence simplifies the work. Allowing the stock to overlap the fence means both edges can be chamfered with one router-table setup.

Cut a chamfer on each edge. Make sure that the profile doesn't compromise the integrity of the rabbet at either edge.

BEADS
Beading works best on a shiplapped or tongue-and-groove back. On a splined slat, however, the bead can weaken one of the groove walls.

Cut the decorative element after cutting the joinery. Cutting the tongue first yields a cleaner cut because the beading bit isn't forced to hog away large amounts of waste material.

The joinery is easy to cut. Start by plowing a full-length groove, 1/2 in. deep and 1/4 in. wide, along the inner edges of the frame members. You can do this with a slot cutter or dado head. Lay out the tenons so they are centered on the stock. You can cut them quickly using any tenoning jig.

With all the joints cut, fit the frame together and size the panels. Measure the panel openings and add 7/8 in. to the length and width to account for the panel's rabbeted edges. Cut the rabbets about 1/2 in. to 9/16 in. wide. There is no need to make the reveal precisely even, as the rabbets are not visible from the front of the case.

Glue up in stages—It's best to approach the glue-up very systematically, starting with the top and bottom rails and the center stile. Next, apply a bead of glue along the back edges of the grooves only. In this way, any squeeze-out will be on the back of the plywood panel. Slide the panels in, mount the side stiles dry, and clamp the whole assembly, making sure everything is flat and square. After about half an hour, unclamp the assembly, glue on the side stiles, and reclamp.

Fit the panel to the case—Taking special care to keep the panel square, size it for a snug fit in the case back. Racking is devastating if you plan to use inset doors. Rather than nails, use screws to hold paneled backs in place. This facilitates easy removal for finishing or any other reason that might arise.

INSTALLING SLATS

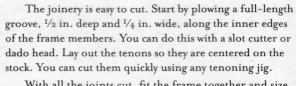

Start in the middle. Space the slats about 1/16 in. apart. Rip the outer boards to fit. Nail or screw the outer slats along the edge. Use two nails in each middle slat, about 3/4 in. from each edge.

Frame-and-Panel Backs

Frame-and-panel backs are much more rigid than slat backs and as a result they're much more effective at keeping a case from racking. They are also quite attractive, and the use of contrasting panels adds a contemporary feel.

TRADITIONAL JOINERY WITH A SOLID PANEL

A traditional frame-and-panel back uses a solid-wood panel floating in a mortise-and-tenon frame.

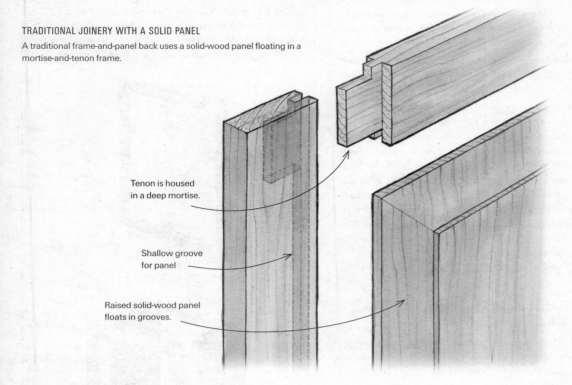

Tenon is housed in a deep mortise.

Shallow groove for panel

Raised solid-wood panel floats in grooves.

STUB TENONS WITH A PLYWOOD PANEL

With plywood panels chosen for good-looking face veneer and glued in place, this approach is just as attractive as a traditional frame-and-panel back, but is both more rigid and easier to make.

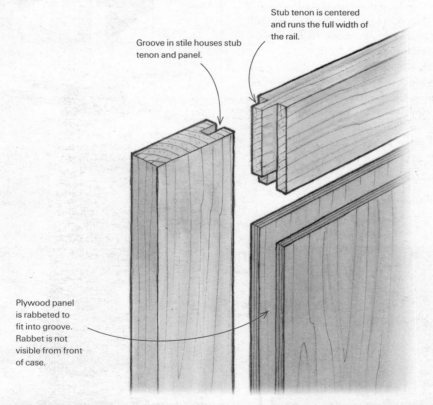

Groove in stile houses stub tenon and panel.

Stub tenon is centered and runs the full width of the rail.

Plywood panel is rabbeted to fit into groove. Rabbet is not visible from front of case.

Cut a continuous groove in the frame members. On the stiles, the groove that houses the panel also serves as a mortise for the stub tenons on the rails. Because the cutter is buried into the fence, tearout is radically reduced. Make one pass in each direction to center the groove.

Cut the stub tenons. Raise the tablesaw blade enough to barely nick the bottom corner of the groove. This ensures a clean, snug-fitting corner at the base of the tenon. Raise the blade to trim the tenon cheeks.

Assemble the back. The 1/2-in.-thick plywood is rabbeted on the back side, ensuring a good fit in the grooves. Check carefully once the clamps are on to make sure the assembly is flat, tapping the components into place with a deadblow hammer, if needed, as you tighten the clamps.

Building Bookshelves to Last

by Steve Latta

This small but classic bookcase is one of my favorite projects. The finished piece is practical and attractive, and for the fledgling woodworker it presents a great introduction to face-frame case construction.

A face frame on a case piece serves a couple of different roles. It improves how the piece looks, letting you hide through-dadoes and change proportions to make the front of the piece appear more substantial and formal. And, if you're adding doors, it can keep the opening square and allows a good mounting surface for the hinges.

Like anything else in woodworking, though, there's more than one way to get the job done. Many furniture makers build the case first and then assemble and attach the face frame. I take a different approach. My early woodshop training was in commercial cabinetry, where the practice was to build the frame first. I do it that way for fine furniture, too, because it offers several advantages.

First, building the frame at the outset gives me the freedom to alter its dimensions slightly to fix any tearout or minor mistakes in its construction. For instance, this

Continued ➔

frame is decorated with a bead around its inner edge with miters in the corners that can be easy to miscut. I'd lose the flexibility to make an easy fix if I were building the frame to fit an already glued-up case.

Second, I like joining the face frame to the case with strong and positive tongue-and-groove joinery as opposed to just gluing the frame in place. Assembling the face frame before building the case makes it easier to locate that joinery. I like that positive connection because the assembled frame helps align the whole assembly during glue-up of the case, simplifying the process and helping to ensure that it goes together squarely.

If you've never tried the face-frame-first method, read on. This handsome bookcase project will illustrate all of the advantages.

Put Your Best Face Forward

The face frame on this cabinet is decorated with a 1/4-in. bead that runs around the inside edge and is mitered at the corners. I cut this bead at the router table while the stock is still wide and long, so that any bead marred by tearout, snipe, or other mistakes can be cut away and redone.

Afterward, rip the frame members extrawide and run them through the planer on edge to a finished width that is 1/32 in. greater than called for in the drawing. Later, after the case and frame are glued up, you'll plane away this extra material to bring the frame flush with the case sides.

As I mentioned, mitering the beaded corners on the frame can be challenging because it's possible to miscut by a fraction and wind up with a gappy miter. If that happens, simply cut the miter again and recut the corresponding parts to match. You'll end up with a slightly shorter or narrower frame, but that won't be an issue since my process ensures that the case will fit the frame.

If, instead, I messed up a miter while trying to fit the frame to an already assembled case, I wouldn't have room for that sort of adjustment. My only choice would be to waste time and stock milling up new frame parts.

Once the miters are cut, you can cut the joinery for the face frame and then glue up the frame. When gluing up, be sure to clamp carefully to avoid twist, and check diagonal measurements to ensure that the frame stays square.

It's Impossible to Go Wrong on the Case

Here's a great feature of this approach. Notice how the process ensures a perfectly sized case. Because the case isn't built yet, and the parts are still oversize, I can now rabbet the front edge of the case sides, cut grooves in the rear of the frame stiles, and then dry-fit the two to find the exact length of all the case's crosspieces.

Also, this case-to-frame joinery is easier to execute than locating biscuits on a face frame, and it's much stronger and more manageable to glue up than a simple butt joint between the case and frame.

Still, it's important to locate the grooves in the back of the frame carefully so the frame ends up 1/32-in. proud of each side, for planing flush later. To ensure a snug fit and accurate placement of the groove, I cut test joints in scrap stock.

With the case-to-frame joinery cut, you can use the frame to find the exact sizes of all the case parts, and locate the dadoes in them. After squaring the bottom of each side, dry-fit them to the face frame, mark their height and width, and then cut them to size on the tablesaw.

The face frame also serves as a reference for sizing and locating the bottom shelf and the rails across the top. With the sides cut to size and once again dry-fit into the face frame, I locate the dadoes that will hold the bottom shelf, to ensure that it ends up perfectly level with the frame's lower rail. Once these dadoes are cut, I go ahead and rabbet the back edges of the case sides to accept the back. Then, I dry-fit the frame and sides again to measure for the bottom shelf's length. When the shelf is cut to length

and dry-fitted, you can mark and then rip it so it ends at the rabbet.

The screw rails that support the case's top are joined to the sides with a pair of shouldered through-dovetails at each end. Working with the frame, sides, and bottom all dry-fit allows me to quickly fit the shoulders very accurately with no measuring or even marking.

I start with the rails about 1/16 in. longer than the outside width of the case. This will leave about a 1/32-in. overhang on each side that will be easily pared with a chisel.

Using a miter gauge and the saw's fence, make a shoulder cut on each end that you know is too short. At the bandsaw, remove just enough of both cheeks to let you butt against the shoulder for test-fitting. Now you can sneak up on the fit by moving the fence farther away from the blade in small increments and recutting the shoulders until the rail drops in place. For accuracy's sake, make sure you are fitting right behind the face frame. Once the shoulder cuts are established, cut the cheeks using a tenoning jig or a high fence. Now you can cut the tails and easily lay out the mortises in the tops of the sides.

As a last step before glue-up, drill the shelf-pin holes.

Let's Get This Straight: The Frame Simplifies Glue-Up, Too

The case glue-up is another stage where having an assembled frame is a distinct advantage. Keeping the case parts together during glue-up can be a challenging exercise in positioning cauls and shifting clamps. But the tongue-and-groove connection to the frame helps to keep everything aligned and eliminates a lot of fussing. I start by dry-fitting the top screw rails in place and then gluing the bottom into the case sides. Then I immediately dry-fit the frame to the sides to help keep them parallel before putting the assembly in clamps. Then I glue in the screw rails at the top. When the glue is dry, I remove the face frame, apply glue, and reattach it to the case.

When the assembly comes out of clamps, I use a plane, scraper, and sanding block to bring the face-frame stiles flush with the case sides. Check often to make sure the corners stay square, especially at the bottom where the cove molding will be attached. When this work is done, you are ready to add the base and top.

Frame is the Foundation

Latta builds the case by first assembling the face frame (1). Next, he rabbets the sides into grooves in the back of the frame (2). With the frame dry-fitted to the sides, Latta marks out and fits the bottom shelf and top rails (3). After gluing up the case and attaching the frame, he can size and attach the top and base (4).

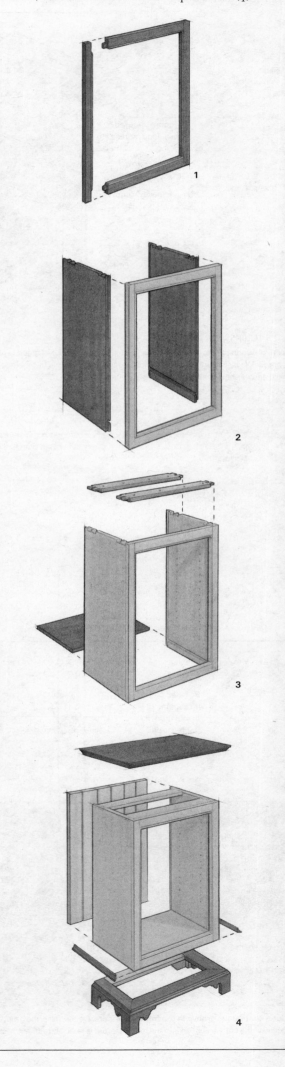

A Case Study

Building a case frame-first lends itself well to the practice of fitting parts to a piece as you build it, a process known as "verify in field." The face frame becomes a template for sizing and locating other major components, so do not pre-cut parts to final size for this bookcase, or any project for that matter.

Top molding, 5/8 in. by 5/8 in.

Top, 3/4 in. thick by 12 5/16 in. wide by 32 5/8 in. long

Back boards, 1/2 in. thick, with 1/4-in.-wide by 1/4-in.-deep rabbets

Groove, 5/16 in. wide by 3/8 in. deep

TOP DETAIL
1 sq. = 1 in.

Sides, 3/4 in. thick by 10 1/4 in. wide by 43 1/2 in. long

Top rails, 3/4 in. thick by 2 3/8 in. wide by 30 in. long

Face-frame bead, 1/4 in. wide

Tongue, 5/16 in. thick by 5/16 in. wide

Stiles, 3/4 in. thick by 1 1/4 in. wide by 43 1/2 in. long

Bottom shelf, 3/4 in. thick by 9 3/4 in. wide by 29 1/4 in. long

Dado, 3/8 in. deep by 3/4 in. wide, 1 1/4 in. from bottom edge

Cleat

Base molding, 5/8 in. by 5/8 in.

Rails, 3/4 in. thick by 2 in. wide by 29 in. long

Tenons, 1/4 in. thick by 1 3/8 in. wide by 3/4 in. long

BASE DETAIL
1 sq. = 1/2 in.

4 in.

2 3/8 in.

6 1/4 in.

Base frame front, 3/4 in. thick by 3 in. wide by 32 3/8 in. long

Base frame sides, 3/4 in. thick by 3 in. wide by 12 3/16 in. long

FOCUS ON THE FRAME
By building the frame first, you can ensure there are no flaws in the most prominent part of the bookcase.

Cut clean joinery. Because the case is not yet constructed, any problems with the corner joints can be corrected by recutting them and making the frame slightly smaller.

Glue up the frame. Check that the frame is square and flat. The joints should come together cleanly with no gaps.

TIP

Milling Trick

After cutting the bead on the rails and stiles, run the pieces on edge through the planer to guarantee consistent widths.

Continued ➔

CONNECT THE SIDES

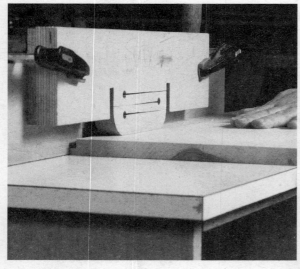

1. RABBET THE CASE SIDE

Rabbet the front of the case sides to create a tongue for the face frame, but leave the sides wide so you can trim away any mistakes. Putting the cutter above the work ensures consistent thickness for the tongue, as long as there is a hold-down pushing down on the workpiece.

2. GROOVE THE FACE FRAME

Cut test grooves in a piece of scrap to locate the groove accurately. When this is done, the frame should overlap the rabbeted side by $1/32$ in. Now cut the grooves in the frame. Clamp a piece of long stock to a sawhorse or table to help support the workpiece.

DRY-FIT PARTS AS YOU BUILD

A PERFECT BOTTOM SHELF

Locate the dadoes in the case sides. To ensure that the bottom shelf ends up level with the bottom rail of the face frame, use a combination square to pick up the width of the rail.

Transfer the dimension. Put the square against the outside of the dado set to position the rip fence. You can trust that it's right.

Dado with no doubts. Verify the cut's location in a test piece, then cut the dado. Use a wide push paddle with a cleat in the rear to guide the workpiece.

Dry-fit and measure. Use a tape measure or, better yet, two overlapping rulers to measure between the dado bottoms for the precise length of the shelf.

Cut with confidence. Because you used the face frame to position the sides, you know this shelf will fit perfectly.

UPPER RAILS ARE STRAIGHTFORWARD, TOO

Leave them oversize. With the rails $1/16$ in. longer than the width of the case, Latta begins cutting the shoulders.

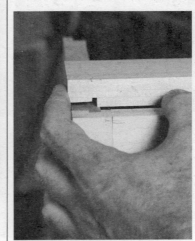

Shoulders first. Working again with the rest of the case dry-fitted, Latta can cut the shoulders accurately. He removes material in small increments from both ends until the shoulders drop snugly between the case sides.

One part determines the next. With the shouldered dovetails cut, Latta marks their mating sockets in the top of the case sides.

ASSEMBLE THE CASE IN STAGES

Dry-fit the top to glue up the bottom. With the top rails holding the sides in place, Latta brushes glue into the dadoes that will hold the bottom shelf. Cleats that allow for cross-grain movement will be added later to reinforce this joint.

Add the frame, too. Dry-fitting the frame helps square the assembly and hold it rigid. With the frame in place, you can clamp the sides tight to the bottom.

Now glue in the top rails. Leave the dry-fitted frame in place.

Now glue on the frame and trim to fit. When the bottom shelf and top rails are dry, remove the frame, apply glue, and clamp it in place. Later, use a block plane or scraper to remove the excess frame stock that overhangs the sides of the case. Everything will be square and perfect now, and ready for the crown moldings and base.

Stickley-Inspired Portable Book Rack

by Gregory Paolini

Years ago, while researching American Arts and Crafts designs, I took an immediate liking to Gustav Stickley's No. 74 book rack. It's shorter than most bookcases, with slats that form a V-shaped trough to hold books spine up. Its D-shaped handholds make it easy to move.

I've made a dozen racks based on that design, from small desktop versions to extra-tall ones that hold DVDs. I've also modified Stickley's design. Simple through-tenons replace the wedged tenons. I added a second V-shaped trough in the middle to make the rack more functional, and I tapered the end panels, reflecting the look of the Roycroft designs that I favor. Despite the changes, the book rack retains its Arts and Crafts character. This version, made from quartersawn white oak, is sized to sit between a couple of Morris chairs.

Make the End Panels and Router Template

Since the end panels are the focal point, you want boards with maximum figure. Use single wide boards if you have them, or edge-glue narrower boards.

While the panels are drying, make a router template from 1/4-in. medium-density fiberboard (MDF) or plywood, which you'll use to cut slots for the shelf mortises.

The template (see next page) simplifies construction in several ways. It locates the shelf mortises, of course. And because I clamp the template to the inside face of one end piece and the outside face of the other, it ensures that the mortises will line up. When laying out the slots in the template, all you have to do is draw the dimensions for the 3/4-in.-thick shelves and cut a slot that wide. When using those slots to cut the through-mortises, use a bit and guide bushing. The offset between bit and bushing equals the width of the tenon shoulders. I get a mortise the right width, in the right location.

To avoid tearout when routing through-mortises, I work from one face toward the middle, without popping out the other side. So I rout the bulk of the mortises with the guide bushing, then use a flush-trimming bit from the other side to finish them cleanly.

Continued ➨

Make the template 11½ in. wide by 29 in. long. Draw the panel side tapers, handle, and lower arch. Then draw rectangles representing the full size of the ends of the narrow V-shelves and the wide bottom shelf. With the template drawn, draw layout lines ¼ in. from each end of the V-shelf rectangles. For the bottom shelf, draw layout lines 1 in. from the ends. These define the starting and stopping points for the shelf mortises. To cut the mortise slots, clamp a shopmade fence jig flush with the long side of each shelf outline and plunge cut from one line to the next with a router and a ¾-in. bit. Cut out the handle and bottom arch with a jigsaw, then smooth the curves and clean up the sawmarks with sandpaper.

Mill the Oak and Cut the Mortises

Next, I mill all the oak shelves to size and cut the glued-up end panels to length. However, I won't taper the panels until I've finished making all the cutouts with the router.

I make the mortises and cutouts on one panel at a time. Rather than clamping them together and cutting everything at once, I set up the template so that the panels are oriented as copies, not mirror images. In other words, the template goes on the outside face of the left-hand panel but on the inside face of the right-hand panel.

Register the template to the side and bottom of the end panel. You can use a long scrap of wood as a fence to help align the template with the side. Clamp the assembly

to the bench and mark a small dot on the bottom of the right foot. You'll use that mark to reference how you laid out the panel.

Set up the router and bushing. The ¾-in.-wide slots in the template will produce a ½-in.-wide mortise in the oak, using a ¼-in. spiral bit and a ½-in. bushing. You could also use a ⅜-in. bit and a ⅝-in. bushing. However, the smaller bit leaves a tiny ridge dead-center in the groove, which comes in handy later on.

Rout the outlines for the D-shaped handle, the lower arch, and the shelf mortises in several passes. Don't cut all the way through. When the cuts are about ⅝ in. deep, stop and remove the template. Use a jigsaw to remove most of the waste from the handle and the lower arch.

Drill a hole through each shelf mortise. This is where you can use that ridge left by the ¼-in. bit. I like to use it to center a 1/16-in.-dia. pilot hole. Then I flip the panel over and enlarge the pilot hole with a 13/32-in. bit. This gives me a starting place for the router bit I use next.

Flip the panel over, and finish all the cuts with a ⅜-in. flush-trimming bit. I chuck the bit in a laminate trimmer. It's easy to control and lets me easily see what I'm doing.

These extra steps guarantee that you won't have any tearout. Square up the mortises with a chisel, working from each face toward the middle to avoid tearout. Finish the panels by tapering the sides on the bandsaw, cutting

just to the waste side of the line. I clean up the cuts with a router, using my shopmade edge guide and a straight bit.

Cut the Tenons on the Tablesaw

The through-tenons on the shelves project ¼ in. from the side panels. They have narrow shoulders on their wide faces, and deep shoulders on the sides. The shoulders hide some imperfections and make glue-up much easier. I cut the tenons on the tablesaw, defining the shoulders with a combination blade to minimize tearout, then switching to a stacked dado set to finish.

You should purposely make the shoulder cuts a hair too deep, which prevents a ridge at the inside corner that you'd have to clean out later.

Trade the combination blade for a stacked dado set to finish the tenons. Cut the wide cheeks first. Set the blade low and raise it gradually through a series of cuts to sneak up on the proper tenon thickness. Test the fit after each cut. Once that first tenon fits the mortise just right, cut the rest. Follow the same procedure to cut all the short cheeks.

Next, chamfer the ends of the tenons. Mark a line 7/32 in. from the ends, then plane to that line at roughly a 45° angle. Plane the long edges first, then plane the short edges.

Finally, soften the remaining sharp edges of the shelves and side panels with a ¼-in. roundover bit in the router.

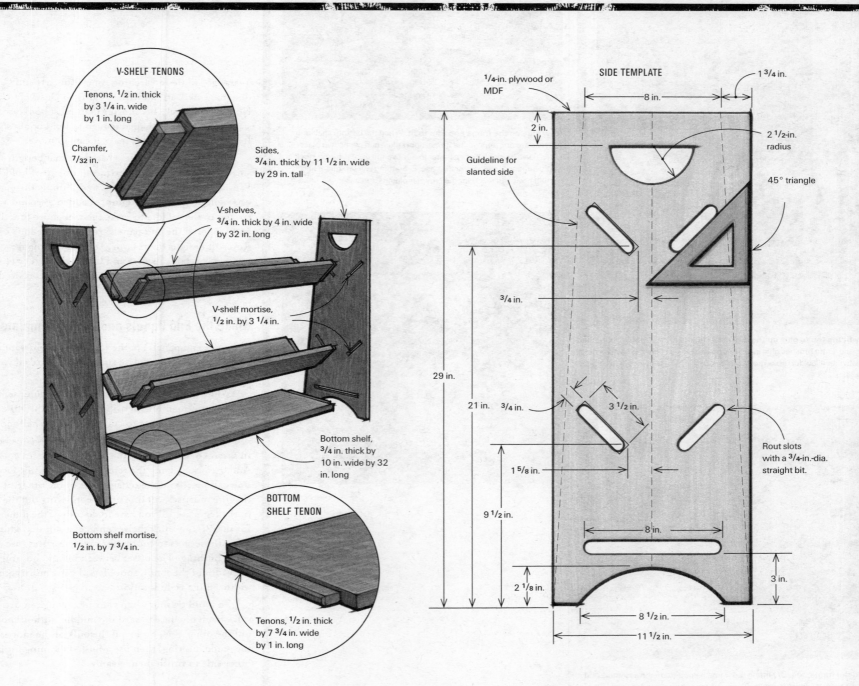

Fit and Finish

Dry-fit the piece. The tenons should slip into their mortises with hand pressure. If you need a mallet, the joints are too tight and you'll need to pare down the tenons with a shoulder plane or a coarse file.

Smooth the pieces with a random-orbit sander, finishing with P180-grit. Then hand-sand all the pieces with P180-grit paper, working with the grain, to minimize any sanding swirls.

I like to do some of the finishing before assembly, when the pieces are easy to handle. To keep finish off the tenons, I wrap them with 1/2-in. masking tape.

For a simple finish, I like Minwax Early American 230 stain followed by clear shellac or varnish, which looks remarkably like one of Stickley's original finishes.

After the stain has dried, glue up the piece. If you get any squeeze-out, let it dry, then peel it off.

In keeping with the Arts and Crafts tradition, I use shellac as a topcoat. I typically brush on six or seven coats of Zinsser SealCoat thinned to a 1-lb. cut. After the shellac has cured, I rub out the piece with mineral oil and 0000 steel wool, giving the piece the satin sheen typical of this style of furniture. The finish should provide plenty of protection for a few generations of readers.

MAKING THE TEMPLATE

The 3/4-in.-wide slots in the template will guide a router bushing for making the 1/2-in.-wide mortises in the workpieces.

Lay out the slots. Align the template and the triangle against a straight-edge clamped to the bench to draw the shelf outlines.

Make the cutouts. Use a straight bit and a fence jig to cut the 3/4-in. slots for the shelf mortises. Use a jigsaw for the other cutouts.

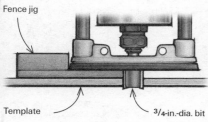

First trim edge of jig with router, then align jig with layout lines.

Fence jig

Template   3/4-in.-dia. bit

Secret to Clean Through-Mortises

1. ROUT TO PARTIAL DEPTH

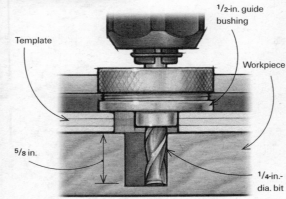

Use a guide bushing for initial cuts. Clamp the template to the workpiece. Begin cutting the shelf mortises with a plunge router equipped with a 1/4-in.-dia. spiral upcut bit and a 1/2-in. guide bushing. Use the same setup to make the curved cutouts. Make these cuts only about 5/8 in. deep; don't cut through the work at this stage.

Template

1/2-in. guide bushing

Workpiece

5/8 in.

1/4-in.-dia. bit

2. DRILL, FLIP, AND CLEAN UP

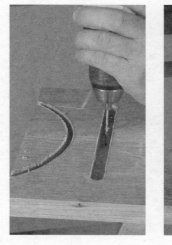

Starter holes for the next step. Drill a hole to allow the flush-trimming bit to enter the mortise. Start with a small pilot hole to locate the center. To prevent blowout, follow with a larger bit from the other side.

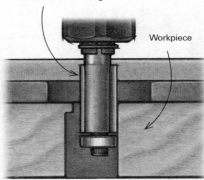

3/8-in.-dia. flush-trimming bit

Workpiece

Flip the work and finish with a flush-trimming bit. Finish the mortises and other cutouts with a 3/8-in. flush-trimming bit, working from the opposite face. To clean up the D-shaped handle and the cutout at the foot, cut away most of the waste with a jigsaw, then use the same bit to smooth the edge.

Square up the corners. Cut away the waste in the corners with a chisel. Chop about halfway down, then flip the work and finish by paring from the opposite face toward the center.

Continued →

CUT TENONS ON THE TABLESAW

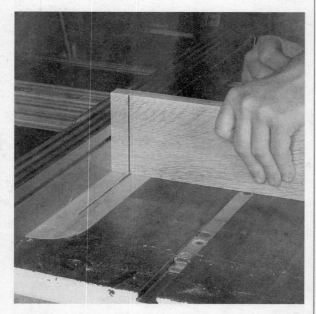

Define the shoulders. Use a combination blade to make the initial cuts for the tenon shoulders. Make these cuts about $^1/_{32}$ in. deeper than the tenon, to define the shoulders cleanly.

Finish with a dado set. Use a stacked dado set to cut away the waste on each tenon. Check the first tenon often against its mortise to creep up on the right blade height.

The result. You should have tenons with even shoulders, smooth cheeks, and a nice fit.

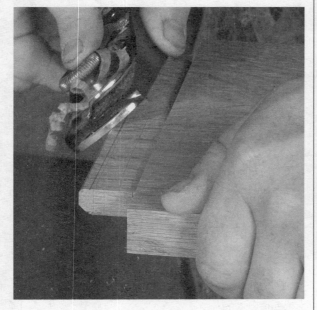

Chamfer the tenon ends. Use a block plane to chamfer the portion of each tenon that will be proud of the side pieces, working to a layout line. To minimize tearout, plane the wide cheeks first, then the narrow ends.

Fine-tune the fit. The tenons should fit into the mortises with hand pressure. At the end, you may need to remove a small amount of excess with a coarse file or a shoulder plane.

Dye, then stain. A brownish dye, followed by a darker oil stain, produces a finish that's very close to fumed oak. Mask the tenons to keep finish off glue surfaces. When applying the finish, work carefully to keep the stain out of the mortises.

Glue, then shellac. To reduce squeezeout, put most of the glue on the tenons and only a dab in the mortises. When the glue has cured, apply several coats of thinned shellac. As a final step, rub out the finish.

Decorative Wall Cabinet

by Garrett Hack

I made this nice little wall-hung cabinet to hold tools, but it could easily find a spot inside a home and hold small knickknacks. What's interesting about this project is the uncommon way I build the case. The process is efficient, and it yields a strong and very attractive piece with a lot of room for design variations.

The main joints are sliding dovetails, which are rock-solid and easily made with a tablesaw and router. Using sliding dovetails forces me to inset the top and bottom of the cabinet, but that works to my advantage, as you'll see.

Also, I use an unusual face-frame variation, which blends more seamlessly with the case. Basically, I cut a deep rabbet in the front edges of the case and glue the stiles into that rabbet. That leaves the glueline very close to the corner, where I can disguise it easily with a chamfer, a bead, or a bit of banding, for a variety of looks. Note that the rails are added later, simply glued to the top and bottom of the case. These also act as blocking for any moldings you want to add.

You might ask, why have a face frame at all? The first reason is that the sides are thin and a face frame allows you to create whatever thickness looks best at the front edges. Also, it lets you run through-dadoes for the shelves. Without a face frame, you would have to cut stopped dadoes to create a clean look at the front. Finally, it is easier to cut hinge mortises in the face-frame stiles while they are loose than it is to cut them in the sides themselves.

The design is best for hanging cabinets, but it works for floor-standing cabinets as well. The "ears" (the part of the sides that extends above the sliding dovetails) can be as short as 3/4 in. and hid behind a molding. Or an overhanging top can be added.

Banding Determines the Cabinet Width

I often add a banding under the crown molding to serve as a transition between the molding and the case. It might seem like an unusual place to start, but to get the cabinet width and the length of the top and bottom pieces, I need to know this banding length. The idea is to end up with a uniform black square on each end of the banding.

So after I ripped up the black and white pieces (ebony and holly) on the tablesaw, I laid out the sandwich and

then used it to tick off the full banding length on a story stick. Then, to get the width of the cabinet, I had to subtract the slight overhang of the banding. Last, I marked the length of the crosspieces on the story stick. Because the dadoes and dovetails are the same depth, you can cut the shelves, top, and bottom to the same length with the same setup—another bonus.

Cut the Joinery

Start with the sides of the case. Leave them a bit long and tape them together as shown (facing page). Mark the finished length of the sides and lay out the dadoes for all the crosspieces (even the sliding dovetails start out as dadoes). After cutting those dadoes, move to the router table to turn the dadoes for the top and bottom of the case into

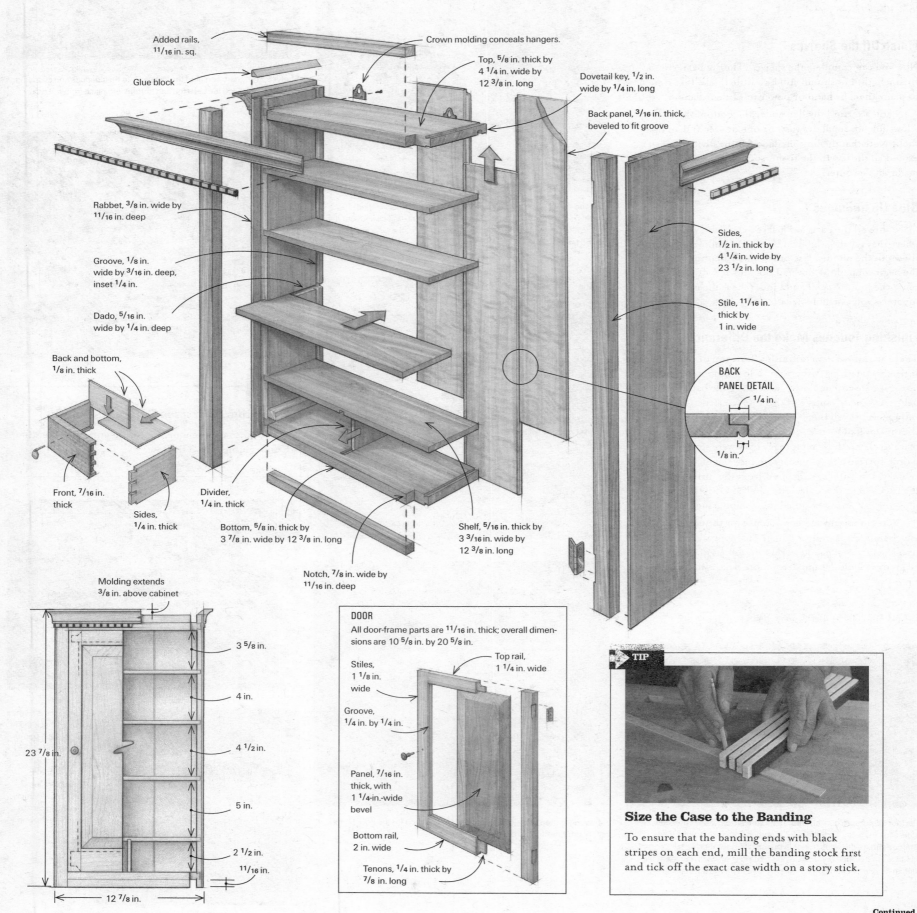

Added rails, 11/16 in. sq.

Glue block

Crown molding conceals hangers.

Top, 5/8 in. thick by 4 1/4 in. wide by 12 3/8 in. long

Dovetail key, 1/2 in. wide by 1/4 in. long

Back panel, 3/16 in. thick, beveled to fit groove

Rabbet, 3/8 in. wide by 11/16 in. deep

Groove, 1/8 in. wide by 3/16 in. deep, inset 1/4 in.

Dado, 5/16 in. wide by 1/4 in. deep

Sides, 1/2 in. thick by 4 1/4 in. wide by 23 1/2 in. long

Stile, 11/16 in. thick by 1 in. wide

Back and bottom, 1/8 in. thick

Front, 7/16 in. thick

Sides, 1/4 in. thick

Divider, 1/4 in. thick

Bottom, 5/8 in. thick by 3 7/8 in. wide by 12 3/8 in. long

Notch, 7/8 in. wide by 11/16 in. deep

Shelf, 5/16 in. thick by 3 3/16 in. wide by 12 3/8 in. long

BACK PANEL DETAIL

1/4 in.

1/8 in.

Molding extends 3/8 in. above cabinet

23 7/8 in.

3 5/8 in.

4 in.

4 1/2 in.

5 in.

2 1/2 in.

11/16 in.

12 7/8 in.

DOOR

All door-frame parts are 11/16 in. thick; overall dimensions are 10 5/8 in. by 20 5/8 in.

Top rail, 1 1/4 in. wide

Stiles, 1 1/8 in. wide

Groove, 1/4 in. by 1/4 in.

Panel, 7/16 in. thick, with 1 1/4-in.-wide bevel

Bottom rail, 2 in. wide

Tenons, 1/4 in. thick by 7/8 in. long

TIP

Size the Case to the Banding

To ensure that the banding ends with black stripes on each end, mill the banding stock first and tick off the exact case width on a story stick.

sliding dovetails. The next step is to cut the dovetail keys on the top and bottom of the case. Run both sides of the dovetail past the bit, and creep up on a nice fit. The dovetail key should slide partway in with only a small amount of pressure.

Now you can rabbet the sides and notch the top and bottom of the case for the face-frame stiles. Plane the stiles to fit perfectly later.

A Raised Back in Three Pieces

You can put any type of back into a cabinet like this, but I use a three-piece solid-wood back, shiplapped together. This lets me distribute the wood movement over four gaps instead of two. It also allows me to add a bead to the joints that looks great inside the cabinet. I beveled the edges to fit into a small groove in the sides and top, making the back look like a raised panel.

Finish Off the Shelves

Now you can complete the shelves. They've been cut to final length, but should still be a little thick. Take time now to plane them by hand or power to fit their dadoes.

I add a vertical divider under the bottom shelf. That allows for two small drawers, or one drawer and an open shelf. Note that the bottom dado for the divider doesn't extend all the way to the front, so it must be a stopped cut, made with a router.

Glue Up in Stages

Make sure all the parts are marked clearly so you know where they go and which end is which. Follow the stages shown in the photos. Use only a small amount of glue on the beginning of the dovetail slot and key. Too much will cause the joint to swell and bind. Check the case with a square as you assemble it.

Finishing Touches Make the Difference

There are lots of ways to finish off the top of a wall cabinet. It needs something; otherwise, it looks too much like a box. I used a cove molding, with that little banding just below it. One advantage of this case construction is the extra pieces (I call them "ears") that stick up beyond the sliding dovetail to give it strength. They are the perfect place to clamp those moldings. They were so short that I wasn't worried about cross-grain movement. With a deeper cabinet, I might screw them on from the inside, running the back screws through slotted holes. Of course, the front molding can always be glued on with no issues.

You can use any method you like for the door, drawer, and even the back of the cabinet. This approach to construction is very versatile, and works for cabinets of all sizes with all kinds of molding and decoration. That's why I love it.

CUT ALL THE JOINERY AT THE SAME TIME

Perfect alignment, guaranteed. To be sure all the dadoes and dovetail slots align perfectly, tape the sides together when you cut the joints. Start by cutting the sides to length on the tablesaw, then install a dado blade to cut the shelf dadoes. Cut the same 5/16-in.-wide dadoes at the sliding-dovetail locations. This will clear a path for the dovetail bit.

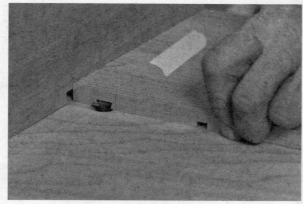

Rout the dovetail slots and keys. With the case sides still taped together, set a dovetail bit at the same height as the dadoes and rout the slots. Without moving the bit, adjust the fence to cut the keys in the case top and bottom.

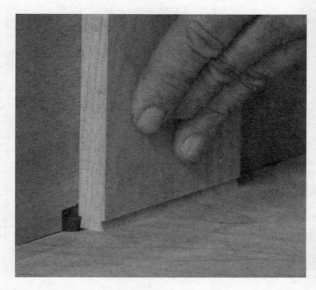

A few more steps. After grooving the sides and top for the back panel, rabbet the sides for the face frame.

ASSEMBLE IN AN ORDERLY FASHION

Shelves first. Start by gluing the shelves into their dadoes and clamping them in place. Slide the case top and bottom into place from the rear.

> **TIP**
>
> ### Cut Hinge Mortises Before Assembly
>
> It's easier to cut the mortises for the hinges in the stile before gluing it into the case.

Face frame comes next. Check the fit of the face-frame stiles, and then glue them into their rabbets. Complete the face frame simply by gluing rails to the case top and bottom.

Install the divider and back. Press the divider into place and plane it flush after the glue has dried. The back consists of three ship-lapped boards that are beveled to fit the grooves in the case sides and top. Slide them in from the bottom and nail them to the shelves.

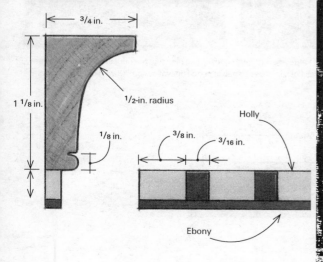

Add the molding. The "ears" that extend beyond the dovetailed case top provide a convenient clamping surface for the molding. A bead, cut with a scratch stock, is a nice transition for the banding.

Handcrafted Vanity Cabinet

by Mario Rodriguez

Browsing at a country flea market one weekend, I came across a vendor selling interesting architectural pieces. There were fireplace mantels, stained-glass panels, doors, and some odd lengths of ornate moldings. What really caught my eye, though, was a bathroom wall cabinet of Victorian vintage. It was simple and graceful, with a soaring cornice and nearly perfect proportions. Miraculously, it still wore its original finish. Over the years the cabinet had developed a deep, rusty color and a wonderful patina, punctuated by a brass Victorian cupboard latch. This was a piece worth copying.

I took some measurements, snapped a few photos, and then returned to my shop to draw up plans for a similar piece. This cabinet is the result. I made it out of quarter-sawn white oak. The ray-fleck grain patterns give a nice flair to the simple lines of the cabinet. What's really nifty is how the mirrored door is made. I assembled the parts with slip tenons—nothing revolutionary—but before cutting the joinery, I rabbeted the pieces for the mirror. This method creates half-lap joints and a perfectly square recess for the mirror without any need for chisel work in the corners.

This piece is a popular class at my school, and I understand why. It doesn't take long to build, and it adds a handmade touch to any bathroom.

Case Joinery Comes First

The joinery is really straightforward, and it's all done at the tablesaw using a dado set. However, all the joints are visible, so make sure they're clean and tight. Once the case joinery is done, use a bandsaw to cut out the arc on the bottom of each side. This arc gives the cabinet a slimmer look and provides more clearance to reach items stored on the bottom shelf.

Plane and sand all the parts, then you're ready to glue up the case. After assembly, drill for the shelf pins that will support the adjustable shelves. To ensure the shelf-pin holes were aligned side to side, I made a drilling template out of $1/4$-in.-thick plywood. I clamped it to one side of the cabinet, drilled the holes, then slid it to the other side to drill the others.

Cut the Cove for the Cornice

Making your own molding is a great way to add a custom touch. Most can be done with a router, but the cove molding for this piece is too large for standard bits, so I used a slick technique on the tablesaw. I passed the stock over the spinning blade at an angle, guiding it between two fences clamped to the saw top.

You don't need a complicated formula to determine the angle of the fences. Simply raise the blade to the full height of the cut and angle the stock until the ends of the arc align with the leading and trailing teeth of the blade. Now clamp the two fences on either side of the stock, raise the blade to about $1/16$ in., and run the stock over it. Raise the blade in $1/16$-in. increments with each pass. As you approach the finished profile, take smaller, $1/32$-in. bites, which will leave a slightly smoother surface that will be easier to clean up.

After finishing the cove profile, make a series of 45° edge cuts on the tablesaw. These cuts project the cove molding at a 45° angle from the cabinet, which looks attractive and presents a solid and stable surface for installation.

Pre-Built Miters Stay Tight

Most people fit and miter cornice moldings right on the case, but it can be difficult to get gap-free miters. I have a better way. I preassemble the moldings, ensuring that the corners are tight, then attach the entire assembly to the case. Attaching an assembled cornice lets me build it square with tight miters, and then coax it into position.

The cornice requires a compound-angle miter. It's common to make this cut with a tablesaw or compound-miter saw. With the tablesaw you need to angle both the workpiece and the blade; with the compound-miter saw you need to angle the blade in two directions and find a way to support the molding. Once again, I have an easier way. I cut the miters on a simple chopsaw, with the workpiece nestled in a cradle that holds it at the correct angle.

After mitering and attaching the crown, install the back panel and French cleat.

Mirrored Door Is Easy

I could have made a traditional door frame, with mortise-and-tenon joints, and then routed out a rabbet for the mirror. But routing the rabbet after assembling the door often results in tearout when you change direction. It also can be difficult to support the router on the frame without tipping, which leads to a bumpy or wavy cut. And you have to square up the corners with chisels afterward. Instead, I cut the rabbets for the mirror in the rails and stiles first, and I joined the parts using slip tenons. This gives me a strong door with a perfectly square rabbet for the mirror.

Continued →

3/4 in.

1 1/8 in.

1/2-in. radius

1/8 in.

Holly

3/8 in.

3/16 in.

Ebony

For an easy door installation, I chose Horton's non-mortised hinges (NM-7, $9 a pair; horton-brasses.com). When installed, these hinges allow a generous 1/16-in. reveal. After cutting the door to size, allowing 1/16 in. spacing all around, you have to cut a 3° back bevel on the hinge side/edge of the door to give clearance for the door to open and close without binding. Once the door is hung, install the pantry latch and strike (SL-4, $17), and then the door stop.

Now cut the mirror and cardboard backing to fit the door rabbet. Then cut and screw the plywood backing over those pieces.

For the finish, you need to choose something that will hold up in a steamy environment. I warmed the oak with amber shellac, then sprayed the cabinet with lacquer. If you don't have a sprayer, any wipe-on varnish or oil/poly mixture will work.

Mirrored Vanity Shines

This white-oak vanity cabinet is a warm departure from manufactured cabinets, giving your bath a handmade touch. The case joinery is simple, and the door assembly makes installing a mirror a breeze. The custom cove molding on top is all done at the tablesaw.

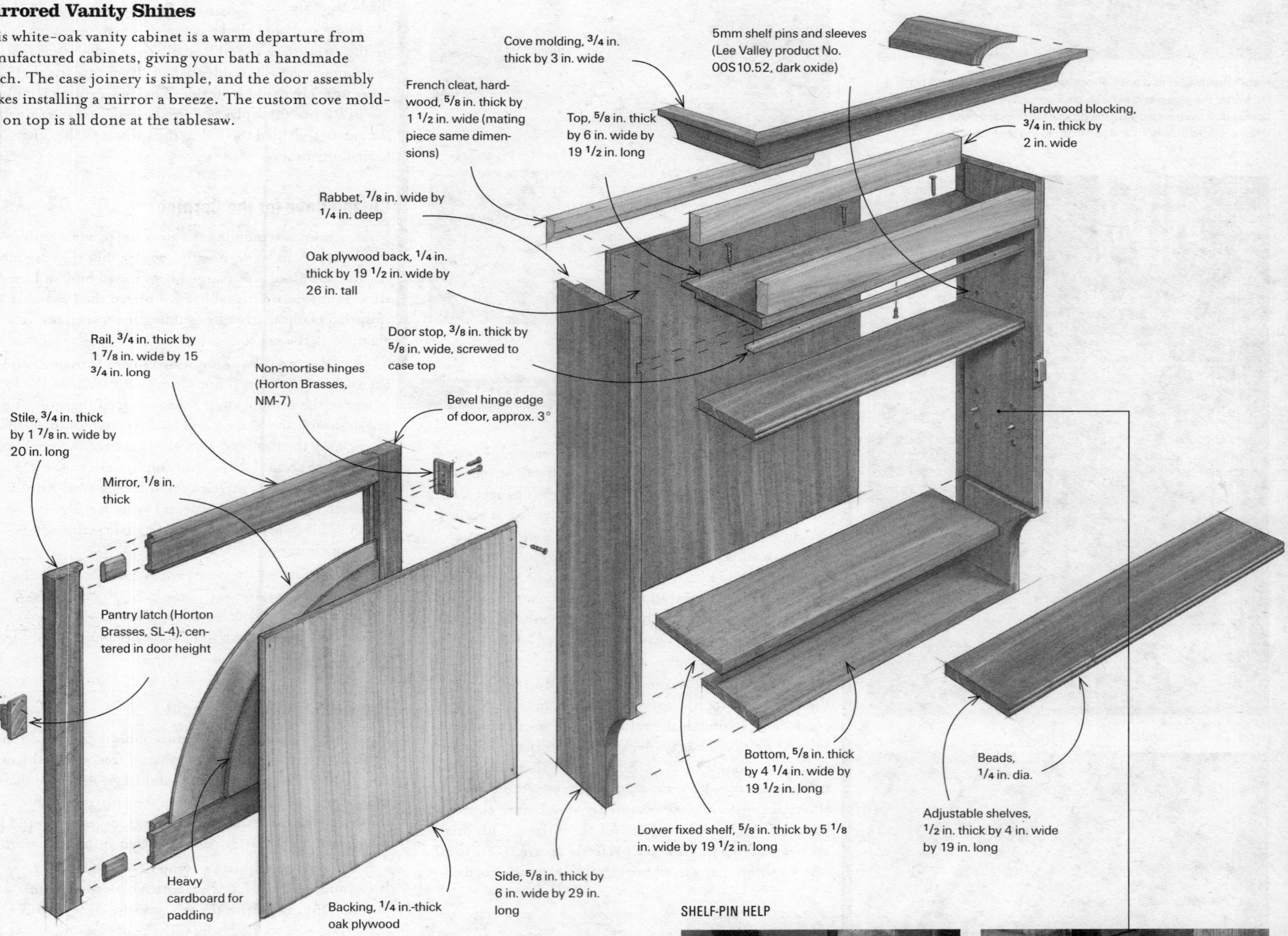

Cove molding, 3/4 in. thick by 3 in. wide

5mm shelf pins and sleeves (Lee Valley product No. 00S10.52, dark oxide)

French cleat, hardwood, 5/8 in. thick by 1 1/2 in. wide (mating piece same dimensions)

Top, 5/8 in. thick by 6 in. wide by 19 1/2 in. long

Hardwood blocking, 3/4 in. thick by 2 in. wide

Rabbet, 7/8 in. wide by 1/4 in. deep

Oak plywood back, 1/4 in. thick by 19 1/2 in. wide by 26 in. tall

Door stop, 3/8 in. thick by 5/8 in. wide, screwed to case top

Rail, 3/4 in. thick by 1 7/8 in. wide by 15 3/4 in. long

Non-mortise hinges (Horton Brasses, NM-7)

Bevel hinge edge of door, approx. 3°

Stile, 3/4 in. thick by 1 7/8 in. wide by 20 in. long

Mirror, 1/8 in. thick

Pantry latch (Horton Brasses, SL-4), centered in door height

Heavy cardboard for padding

Backing, 1/4 in.-thick oak plywood

Side, 5/8 in. thick by 6 in. wide by 29 in. long

Lower fixed shelf, 5/8 in. thick by 5 1/8 in. wide by 19 1/2 in. long

Bottom, 5/8 in. thick by 4 1/4 in. wide by 19 1/2 in. long

Beads, 1/4 in. dia.

Adjustable shelves, 1/2 in. thick by 4 in. wide by 19 in. long

FRONT

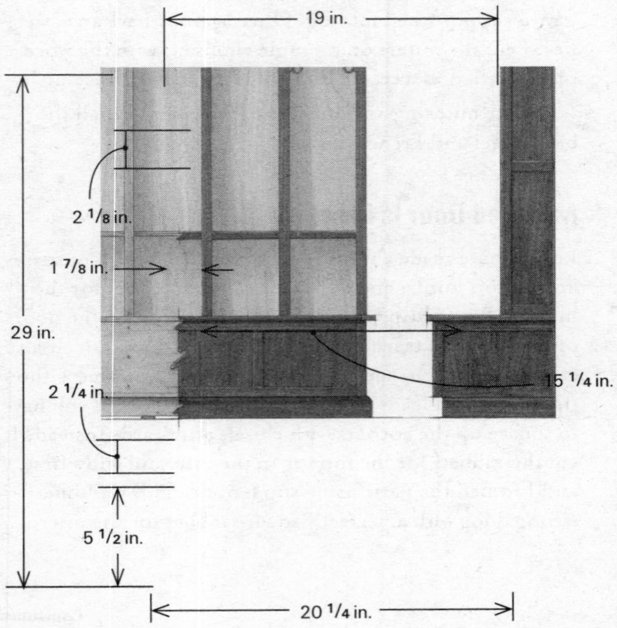

19 in.
2 1/8 in.
1 7/8 in.
29 in.
2 1/4 in.
5 1/2 in.
15 1/4 in.
20 1/4 in.

SIDE

2 1/4 in.
6 in.
2 1/2-in. radius

SHELF-PIN HELP

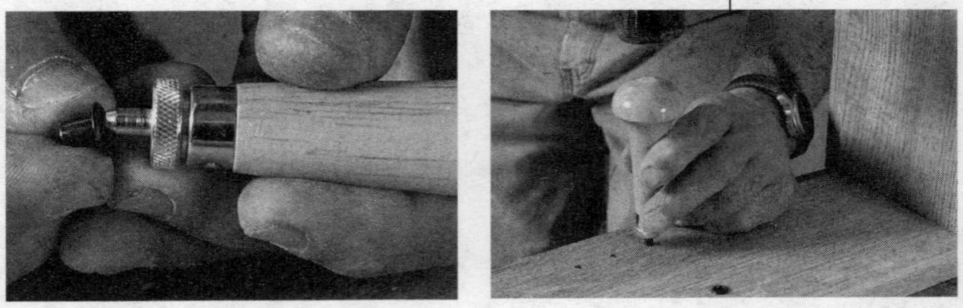

No-fuss shelf supports. To add longevity, Rodriguez chose shelf pins that are housed in hollow sleeves. The easiest way to set the sleeves flush is to use a special punch (leevalley.com, 00K61.02) as shown.

COVE DETAIL

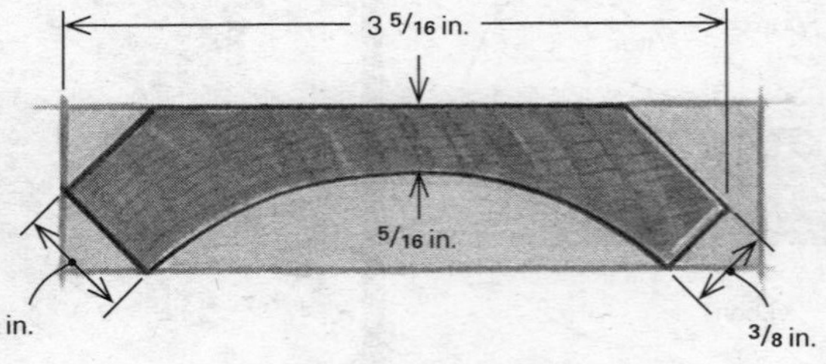

3 5/16 in.
5/16 in.
1/2 in.
3/8 in.

Dado Set Handles All the Joinery

The joinery is really straightforward—nothing more than a few dadoes and rabbets cut at the tablesaw using a dado set.

Dadoes and bottom rabbet. After cutting the rabbet for the bottom, cut the dadoes for the top and fixed middle shelf. Any tearout on the back will be removed when you cut the rabbets for the back panel and French cleat. Bury the blade in a sacrificial fence when rabbeting.

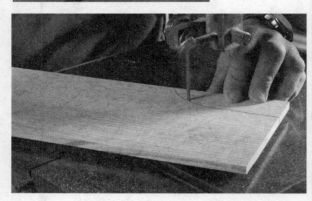

Bandsaw the bottom curve. The cutout at the bottom of the cabinet gives the case a slimmer look. Smooth the bandsaw marks with a spindle sander, a spokeshave, or curved sanding blocks.

Clamp it up. After planing and sanding the case parts, glue them up. Do a dry run first to make sure that everything comes together cleanly and squarely.

Cove-Cutting on the Tablesaw

You can't cut a cove this big with a router bit, but a time-tested tablesaw technique handles it easily. Take time to set up the cut accurately, and take light passes to creep up on the profile.

SETUP

Height, then angle. Raise the blade to meet the apex, or high point, of the arc. Now angle the fences so that the ends of the arc align with the leading and trailing teeth of the blade. Mark that angle on the tablesaw top and then clamp the fences in place.

SET UP THE FENCES

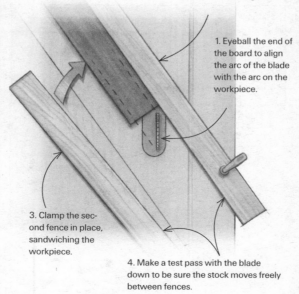

2. Mark the approach angle on the tablesaw top, and clamp the first fence along that mark.

1. Eyeball the end of the board to align the arc of the blade with the arc on the workpiece.

3. Clamp the second fence in place, sandwiching the workpiece.

4. Make a test pass with the blade down to be sure the stock moves freely between fences.

First pass. After clamping both fences securely, make a test pass with the blade below the table, just to be sure that the stock slides without binding. Then raise the blade to 1/16 in. high and make the first pass. Use a push stick or pad in your back hand and stop your front hand short of passing over the blade

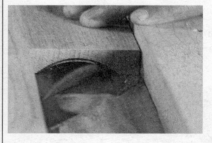

The final cuts. Raise the blade in 1/16 in. increments until you get within about 1/16 in. of the profile mark. Then make lighter passes, in 1/32-in. increments, until you hit the mark.

Trim the moulding. Now make the 45° trim cuts on both edges to finish off the moulding.

Clean up before mitering. Use a gooseneck scraper and a curved sanding block to remove the tablesaw marks.

Continued ➡

Better Way to Miter Molding

Rodriguez assembles the molding before attaching it to the cabinet. This way he can ensure tight miters with no gaps.

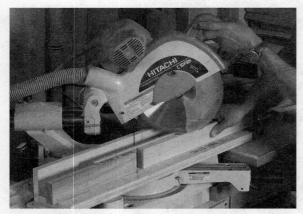

No rocking in this cradle. To turn the compound-angle miters into simple 45° cuts, Rodriguez supports the work in a cradle. He makes both left and right cuts in the front fence first, and then uses those kerfs to line up the molding cuts.

CRADLE MAKES COMPOUND-ANGLE CUTS EASY

With this cradle you can make a compound-angle cut with a simple 45° miter cut on the chopsaw. The key is that the molding is held at its installed angle. All parts are plywood, except for the front fence, which is poplar.

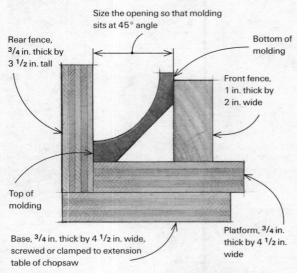

Size the opening so that molding sits at 45° angle

Rear fence, 3/4 in. thick by 3 1/2 in. tall

Bottom of molding

Front fence, 1 in. thick by 2 in. wide

Top of molding

Base, 3/4 in. thick by 4 1/2 in. wide, screwed or clamped to extension table of chopsaw

Platform, 3/4 in. thick by 4 1/2 in. wide

From cradle to case. After carefully cutting the miters, using the case as a guide for the length of the front piece, cut the side moldings to final length. Assemble the sections on the bench using glue and a pin nailer. Let the assembly dry, slide it onto the top of the case, and nail it in place.

Simple but Sturdy Door Joints

The door is assembled with slip tenons. But before cutting the mortises, Rodriguez cuts the rabbets for the mirror. The process creates a perfectly square recess plus half-laps at the joints.

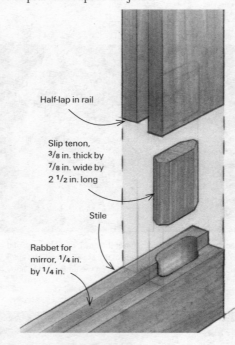

Half-lap in rail

Slip tenon, 3/8 in. thick by 7/8 in. wide by 2 1/2 in. long

Stile

Rabbet for mirror, 1/4 in. by 1/4 in.

CLEVER JIG FOR MORTISING

This simple shopmade jig makes it easy to center a 3/8-in.-wide by 7/8-in.-long mortise on both the rails and stiles, using a 3/4-in. O.D. bushing and 3/8-in. spiral bit.

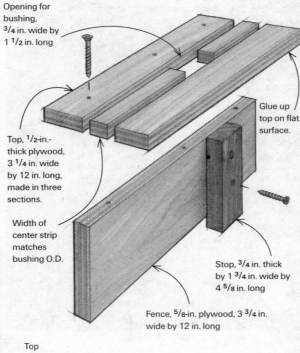

Opening for bushing, 3/4 in. wide by 1 1/2 in. long

Top, 1/2-in.-thick plywood, 3 1/4 in. wide by 12 in. long, made in three sections.

Width of center strip matches bushing O.D.

Glue up top on flat surface.

Stop, 3/4 in. thick by 1 3/4 in. wide by 4 5/8 in. long

Fence, 5/8-in. plywood, 3 3/4 in. wide by 12 in. long

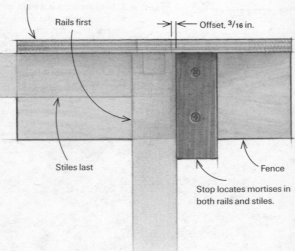

Top

Rails first

Offset, 3/16 in.

Stiles last

Fence

Stop locates mortises in both rails and stiles.

Make way for the mirror. Use the same dado set to rabbet the stiles and rails and to cut half-laps in the rails.

ROUT FOR LOOSE TENONS

Rout the rail first. Clamp the jig in a vise, with the bottom of the rail tight against the stop and with the end tight to the top, then rout using a 3/8-in. spiral bit and guide bushing.

Bushing, 3/4 in. O.D.

3/8-in. spiral bit

Fence

Stock, same thickness as opening width, ensures mortise is centered

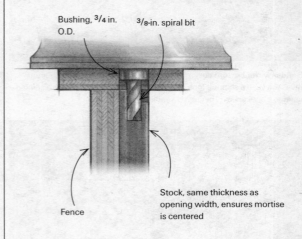

Stiles next. Butt the end of the stile tightly against the stop and tight to the top.

FINAL TOUCHES

HINGES

Non-mortise hinges are easy to install. And they can be adjusted slightly to dial in the gap. But you have to bevel the hinge side of the door to create clearance for the hinge barrel.

MIRROR

The plywood backer over the mirror is cut from the same 1/4-in. oak plywood as the case back.

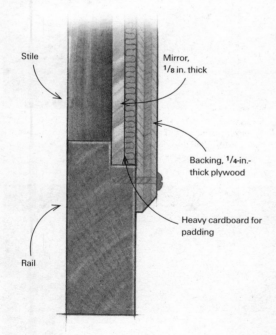

Stile

Mirror, 1/8 in. thick

Backing, 1/4-in.-thick plywood

Heavy cardboard for padding

Rail

Stunning Bombé Chest

by Thomas McKenna

On the surface, a bombé chest is a beautiful piece, with friendly curves on every side. But woodworkers know it's really a wolf in sheep's clothing. Those drastic swells confound traditional construction, creating a conundrum of surfaces that stymie every step of the way, from shaping the sides and drawer fronts to fitting the drawers. Even the hardware has to be shaped to fit.

As you might guess, not many craftsmen are willing to embark on this quest. But it's not just the technical aspects of the project; it's also the cost of the lumber. To achieve the carefully matched grain patterns on the sides and front, you need to sculpt the parts from monstrous slabs of solid mahogany.

So I was thrilled when longtime *FWW* contributor Dan Faia told me he was commissioned to build a bombé for a local client. It is hard to imagine anyone better suited for the job. Faia has strong Boston roots, as does the American bombé, and possesses terrific technical skills with an attentive eye for detail. He also happens to run the Cabinet and Furniture Making program at Boston's North Bennet Street School.

It was a perfect storm for *Fine Woodworking*. We had a once-in-a-lifetime piece being built by one of the best period furniture makers in the country. So we decided to go along for the ride. This is a brief account, in pictures, of Faia's long journey—so long you can see his beard come and go in the photos.

American Bombés Have Boston Roots

"Many furniture makers are fixated on making their piece mimic the original," said Faia. "But I did not want to simply re-create a piece that had already been done." Fortunately, his client gave him broad freedom to explore different options. But, he said, "it was important that I keep the details—and the construction—authentic to the period."

He pored over historical examples—in books and in museums—searching for elements that he could incorporate, and trying to piece together the steps. It was like "CSI Boston."

Bombé furniture didn't originate in America, but the form was refined and perfected in Boston in the late 1700s. Many scholars believe it first appeared in the states in the Brattle Square Church. The church had a number of wealthy and politically influential members, such as John Adams and John Hancock. When the church was rebuilt in the late 1700s, its most prominent architectural element was the pulpit, which exhibited the iconic serpentine shapes of the bombé form.

Wealthy church members, eager to showcase their cultural status, commissioned local cabinetmakers to build pieces based on the pulpit's design. One of the most notable of these makers was John Cogswell, whose signature adorns many of the original bombé chests and desks still in existence.

Cogswell and other makers stepped away from the European take on bombé pieces, where the swelled case sides were shaped from narrow boards that were coopered together and then covered with veneer. American makers,

in a nod to the wealth and prosperity of their clients, built their chests out of solid, thick slabs of plentiful mahogany. They adorned the pieces with opulent hardware and occasionally incorporated fine carvings, such as ball-and-claw feet and leafage motifs.

Building drawers to fit these curvy cases was perhaps the greatest challenge, and makers came up with a number of solutions. Some made vertical sides, with the pocket blocked out, or angled the sides inside the pocket. In both cases, the front was shaped to fit the curves. More complex designs featured drawers whose sides and fronts were shaped individually to fit the case. That approach was a hallmark of later Cogswell pieces.

No Repeats

Faia began with a number of sketches. He wanted to incorporate period-perfect details, but the mix had to be right. "My intention was to replicate the very best elements of the very best period examples," he said.

His piece has roots in the original Cogswell chests. He sculpted the sides and the front parts (drawers, dividers) from solid mahogany. He shaped the drawer sides and front to fit the inside curves of the case. And he added ball-and-claw feet and leafage patterns carved on the knees and transitions.

But that wasn't enough. "To make my bombé different," he said, "I also incorporated a number of unique carving details, such as the fretwork at the top of the case and the egg-and-dart base molding."

Having settled on his savory stew of traditional details, Faia's next challenge was figuring out the steps. "The project required the greatest amount of planning of any piece I have ever made," he said. "Work sequences had to be well-timed for everything to come together right. I knew a mistake at any stage would be devastating."

Faia figured it all out, and when he was finished, he was as understated as always. He didn't jump for joy. He wasn't interested in a high-five or a flying chest bump. He said, "I'm happy with it. It came out pretty good."

Staggering Amount of Stock Removal

Cutting and milling the rough stock was the most physically demanding part of the entire project. The 12/4 board, from which Faia took all the case parts, weighed close to 350 lb. and was too big for a jointer or planer, so he did all of the flattening by hand. Luckily, he said, "I enjoy handwork, so it didn't feel too much like hard labor."

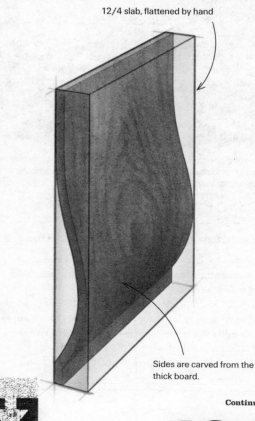

12/4 slab, flattened by hand

Sides are carved from the thick board.

Continued ➡

Kerfs guide the work. Faia laid out the side profiles on the thick blank, then cut a series of tablesaw kerfs that would guide the sculpting to come.

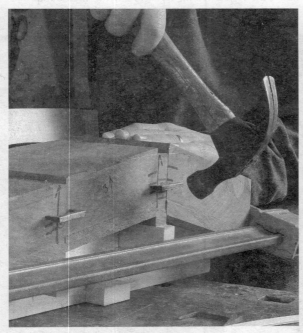

Chop to the lines. Faia chipped away the bulk of the waste using a wide chisel and mallet. He followed with a travisher (inset) to rough in the curves.

Smoothing the rough spots. As the work became more refined, Faia faired the curves using a smoothing plane and a card scraper. At this point, the bull's-eye grain pattern really started to pop.

These dogs pinch. Faia spot-glued and clamped the parts, in sequence, on top of the supports and used pinch dogs to hold the components tightly together for shaping.

Drawers and Dividers Done As One

To ensure fair curves on the front of the chest, Faia shaped all the parts at the same time: drawer fronts, dividers, even the fretwork molding at the top. He sandwiched the pieces on a pair of curved supports—shaped to match the curve of the sides—which later-served as the rear supports for the drawer runners. He learned this clever technique from Lance Patter-son, a colleague at North Bennet Street School.

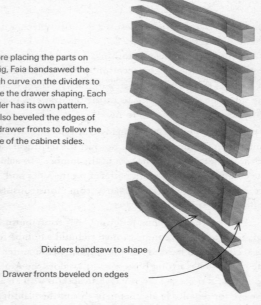

Before placing the parts on the jig, Faia bandsawed the rough curve on the dividers to guide the drawer shaping. Each divider has its own pattern. He also beveled the edges of the drawer fronts to follow the curve of the cabinet sides.

Dividers bandsaw to shape

Drawer fronts beveled on edges

Heavy handwork. As with the case sides, waste material was hogged away with hand tools. The arsenal included a drawknife, chisels, a travisher, spokeshaves, and other handplanes. He started with the flatter sections at the outside of the drawer fronts.

3-D pattern has multiple uses. Once the end sections of the drawers were flush with the dividers, Faia used a 3-D pattern to mark where the serpentine shape begins. The same pattern was used to mark the shape on the ends of the drawers and to lay out the front of each case side. Faia followed those lines as he sculpted the front of the case.

Bull's-eye. As the shaping neared the end, the telltale bull's-eye grain pattern on the case front was revealed. A scraper handled the final fairing.

CRAZY CURVES COMPLICATE ASSEMBLY

Once the shaping was done, Faia cut all of the carcase joinery. The bottom is joined to the sides with half-blind dovetails. The top and dividers connect to the sides with sliding dovetails. The fretwork molding is mitered into the case, while the lower egg-and-dart molding in front of the pine bottom is dovetailed. Before glue-up, he carved the fretwork pattern into the sides.

Does it fit? Before shaping the top, Faia dry-assembled the case to make sure all the joinery was perfect. Then he bandsawed the top to shape and used the router table to cut the edge profile. He used custom scrapers to give the routed shapes a hand-cut look and feel.

Time for glue. The top and bottom were glued to the sides first. Then Faia installed the drawer dividers. Last to go on was the fretwork molding.

DEVILISH DRAWERS ARE TRICKY TO FIT

With compound-angle dovetails and rounded sides, the drawers were one of the most challenging parts of the piece. To top it off, each one has a different shape, requiring a different set of compound angles. After cutting the joinery, Faia shaped each drawer to fit its opening, one at a time.

Never-ending array of curves. Each of the dovetailed drawers has a different shape on the ends, requiring compound-angle joinery and meticulous hand-shaping and fitting on the sides.

Shaping needs a heavy hand. Faia used a smoothing plane to shape the drawer sides to fit the curved pocket. He started with heavy cuts and finished with light, smoothing cuts to refine the curve. He checked the fit often.

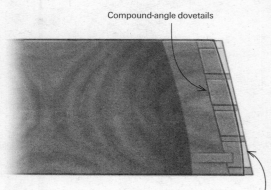

Compound-angle dovetails

Sides and front are planed to fit the case curves.

FRETWORK ADDS PIZZAZZ

During his research, Faia had seen a few bombé secretaries and chest-on-chests with fretwork molding around their midsection and sometimes at the cornice. He liked the idea of fretwork at the top of the low bombé, but for this smaller piece he had to scale it down.

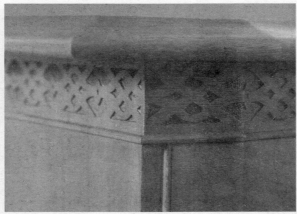

Worth fretting over. The fretwork molding at the top was a period-correct twist to Faia's bombé. The front is a separate molding, mitered into the case. The side patterns were hand-carved into the carcase.

In the zone. While carving, Faia followed a pattern marked from a full-size template. "It looks like a daunting job," he said, "but I find carving to be very meditative."

Knockout punches. To create the texture in the recesses of the fretwork, Faia used a series of custom punches he made using flat and triangular files.

FLOOR-LEVEL DETAILS ARE FANTASTIC

Many original bombé chests had spare bases, with simple moldings and feet. Perhaps the makers believed the voluptuous shape and fancy hardware were enough decoration. But Faia loaded up on hand-carved details at the base to take his bombé to another level.

Boston ball and claw. With the side toes raking back, Boston feet are unique to the region. Faia borrowed the leafage pattern on the knees and transition blocks from an original piece at the Museum of Fine Arts Boston.

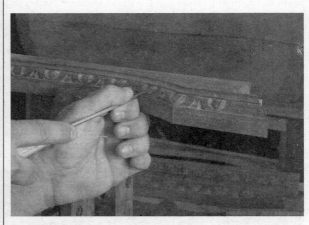

How do you like your eggs? Faia carved the egg-and-dart molding so that the corners would meet perfectly in the center of an egg. "It was time consuming," he said, "but in a piece of this magnitude, the details are everything."

EVEN THE HARDWARE HAS CURVES

Pulls must be shaped to the case. Faia had to shape the brass hardware to fit the front. He placed each piece on a curved pine block and tapped it into shape using a deadblow mallet. And the pilot holes had to be perpendicular to the curve at each location, or the screw heads wouldn't sit flush.

Continued ➜

Low Home-Theater Console

by Steve Casey

Just a few years ago, building an entertainment center for a large-screen TV meant designing a case piece big enough to hide an elephant. Today's slimmer sets can hang on a wall or sit attractively in the open, offering furniture makers new options. Among the most practical is a low console that can house media and electronics. It's a great way to bring that glorious high-definition picture out of the armoire.

I designed this console for a self-contained small home-theater system built around a 52-in. projection-style TV, but it would work just as well with a slimmer flat-panel model. Visually, it's tasteful and tame enough to harmonize with quite a few furniture styles, and you can feel free to adapt its style to fit your room. Look below the surface, though, and it becomes clear this piece is media furniture through and through.

At 24 in. tall, the console is still low enough to place the center of most TVs at eye level for a seated viewer. And it's strong enough to support any set, so you won't need a tricky wall-mount.

At 22 in. deep, the cabinet will comfortably hold most electronic components. I designed the drawers specifically to house DVDs, VCR tapes, and CDs without making the case too tall. The back and shelves are engineered to promote ventilation for the equipment and to simplify cable management. And I put the whole piece on casters so it would be easy to pull away from the wall for system setup, maintenance, or cleaning. Small casters will work on a hardwood floor, but carpet calls for larger ones.

None of those features call attention to themselves. What you see and live with is a nice piece of furniture. The project is a good example of building a sturdy carcase in an efficient way, using sheet goods and techniques I developed and use for building large-scale entertainment center furniture and cabinetry.

Sheet Goods Make a Stable Case

One of the greatest challenges in building furniture to house electronic equipment is that the gear generates heat that causes wood movement. So, I always use stable composite material (in this case, two sheets of cherry plywood) for media furniture carcases.

The first step is to lay out and cut the carcase parts. When cutting sheet goods, never assume that the original edges are straight or square. If you want a 20-in.-wide finished piece, cut it at least 1/8 in. larger, then turn it around and cut off the factory edge. If things are not square, it is usually best to square the ends of smaller ripped parts rather than the whole sheet. After all the parts are cut, I drill holes for adjustable shelves in the equipment rack space. Then I join the carcase together.

The carcase is joined entirely with biscuits and screws—no dadoes, no rabbets, no glue. I don't want to chip out the veneer on a $100 sheet of plywood while cutting dado and rabbet joinery, or fret over squeeze-out marring my finish in the corners. A glueless carcase also lets me disassemble the piece as needed during construction to check fit and measurements, making it much easier to fix mistakes.

There's no harm, of course, in using glue if you want to. But, after years of gluing everything to last an eternity, I've discovered that biscuits and screws are more than strong enough to hold a piece like this together…forever.

I predrill for the screws using a tapered bit with an integral countersink. I use #7, 15/8-in. bugle-head construction screws with sharp, coarse threads and put them in carefully so they don't strip. It's easy to get splitting near the outside joint edges, so I put a clamp on the thread side of the joint so the wedge action of the screw doesn't split the panel.

Attach the Solid Trim

Solid-wood edging and other details elevate the console's appearance from cabinetry to furniture. The most prominent of these features are the frame-and-panel caps on the ends. The front stiles are cut from the same stock as the side panels and are mitered to wrap the grain continuously from the sides to the face. The frames are assembled with biscuits, and the inside of each frame is rabbeted to accept a floating panel of 1/2-in. solid cherry or cherry plywood. This creates a 1/4-in. reveal for the panel while maintaining consistent thickness for the exterior trim. The assembly is attached with screws driven into the frame from inside the case.

A solid-cherry stretcher across the top of the case combines with solid edging to dress out the rest of the case front. Before attaching the edging, I hand-sand a small 1/16-in. roundover radius on the inside corners of each adjoining piece of plywood and solid stock, including the pieces on the top. This creates a very fine parting line where the plywood and edging meet, accentuating what many folks would try to hide and, in the process, making an eye-pleasing detail. After the edging is attached, I rout a 3/16-in. roundover onto all the outside and inside corners.

The Drawers Have Simple Joinery and False Fronts

I build the drawers from 1/2-in.-thick prefinished Apple-Ply or Europly. The bottoms are two-sided, 1/4-in. black melamine, in keeping with the high-tech contents. The joints are rabbeted, glued, and pinned with brads to hold them together while the glue dries.

I hang the drawers on black, side-mounted, full-extension slides. Undermount slides might yield a cleaner look, but they steal depth from the drawer at the bottom. In a console with limited overall height, this can make the difference between a drawer that can be used for media storage and one that isn't deep enough. I size the drawer boxes to accommodate a 3/4-in.-thick separate front, with the faces recessed very slightly behind the front radius detail. Separate drawer fronts allow for perfect alignment after the piece is finally placed and loaded with equipment.

Edge the Top and Attach It

The top is plywood with a 1-in. by 2½-in. solid border, which is biscuited and mitered. This three-sided border creates a nice effect, making the piece appear to belong up against a wall. The raw edge on the back of the top is dressed with ¼-in. solid stock.

To make room for the cables that connect the TV to the other equipment, make a small cutout in the back of the top. This also lets some heat escape when the case is tight against the wall. The top is held in place with screws driven from the underside through the solid cross-members of the case. Because the solid border is thicker than the top, you'll need to shim and fill the space between the plywood and the cabinet.

The back is two-sided, ¼-in. black melamine. Although thin, this material creates a rigid back that lends the piece much of its structural strength, so be sure to size the back to fit snugly between the rear stiles of the end caps. I fasten the back with screws countersunk and driven every 8 in. into the rear edges of the plywood carcase.

Get the Popcorn Ready

Before finishing, break down all removable components, then sand everything that wasn't sanded prior to assembly. I used clear oil to bring up the color before spraying on a standard lacquer finish: one coat of sanding sealer and two coats of 40-sheen lacquer, sanding with 320-grit paper between coats. For an alternative hand-applied topcoat, try dewaxed shellac or a traditional oil finish.

Install the equipment, roll the finished unit into place, and you're all done. Time to pop in a DVD or watch some drivel on TV!

Media-Friendly Features

OPEN SHELVING

The components are accessible to hands and remote controls and become part of the design. The center shelving adjusts to fit a wide variety of components.

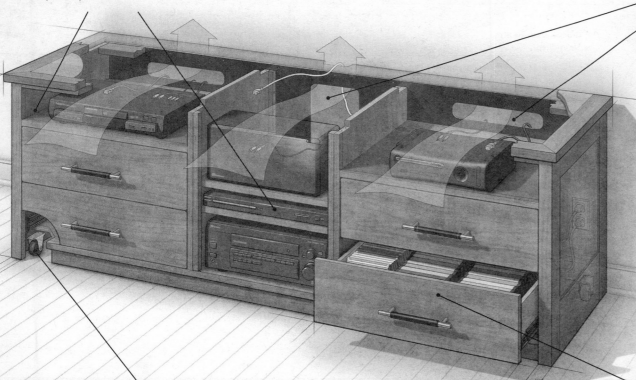

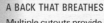

A BACK THAT BREATHES

Multiple cutouts provide ample airflow for electronic components. The recessed back also creates space behind the piece for cords to drop freely.

TALL DRAWERS

Side-mounted slides allow deep storage for DVDs, CDs, and VCR tapes. Dividers keep everything organized.

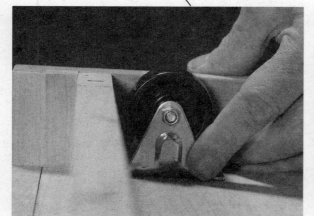

WHEELS

Six casters make it easy to reach the back for setup, maintenance, or cleaning. The wheels are inset to avoid a distracting gap between the floor and the bottom of the piece.

Continued →

Efficient Construction

The plywood carcase is held together with biscuits and screws. Solid-wood drawer faces, end caps, and edging give the piece a furniture feel.

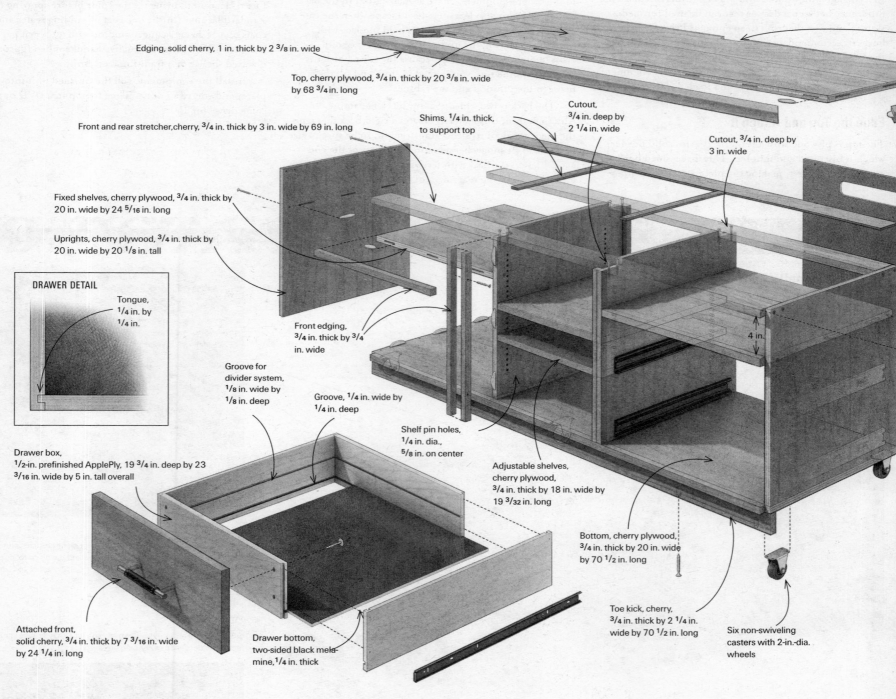

Edging, solid cherry, 1 in. thick by 2 3/8 in. wide

Top, cherry plywood, 3/4 in. thick by 20 3/8 in. wide by 68 3/4 in. long

Front and rear stretcher, cherry, 3/4 in. thick by 3 in. wide by 69 in. long

Cutout, 3/4 in. deep by 2 1/4 in. wide

Cutout, 3/4 in. deep by 3 in. wide

Shims, 1/4 in. thick, to support top

Fixed shelves, cherry plywood, 3/4 in. thick by 20 in. wide by 24 5/16 in. long

Uprights, cherry plywood, 3/4 in. thick by 20 in. wide by 20 1/8 in. tall

DRAWER DETAIL

Tongue, 1/4 in. by 1/4 in.

Front edging, 3/4 in. thick by 3/4 in. wide

Groove for divider system, 1/8 in. wide by 1/8 in. deep

Groove, 1/4 in. wide by 1/4 in. deep

Shelf pin holes, 1/4 in. dia., 5/8 in. on center

Adjustable shelves, cherry plywood, 3/4 in. thick by 18 in. wide by 19 3/32 in. long

Drawer box, 1/2-in. prefinished ApplePly, 19 3/4 in. deep by 23 3/16 in. wide by 5 in. tall overall

Attached front, solid cherry, 3/4 in. thick by 7 3/16 in. wide by 24 1/4 in. long

Drawer bottom, two-sided black melamine, 1/4 in. thick

Bottom, cherry plywood, 3/4 in. thick by 20 in. wide by 70 1/2 in. long

Toe kick, cherry, 3/4 in. thick by 2 1/4 in. wide by 70 1/2 in. long

Six non-swiveling casters with 2-in.-dia. wheels

4 in.

MAKE THE SIDE PANELS

The panel sits in a rabbet. Rout the rabbet with a bearing-guided bit and square up the corners with a chisel.

A NO-CLAMP GLUE-UP

Blue tape tames this miter. Bevel the front stile after glue-up. Cutting it beforehand would deprive you of a square clamping surface. The mating piece is cut from the same stock. Strips of painter's tape align the edges and create a hinge for the glue-up. Casey wraps the assembly with several bands of painter's tape to secure the pieces. No biscuits or clamps are needed.

ASSEMBLED BACK DETAIL

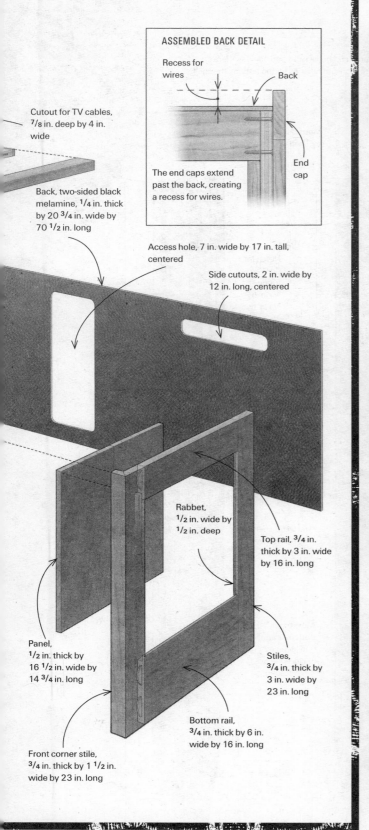

Recess for wires

Back

End cap

The end caps extend past the back, creating a recess for wires.

Cutout for TV cables, 7/8 in. deep by 4 in. wide

Back, two-sided black melamine, 1/4 in. thick by 20 3/4 in. wide by 70 1/2 in. long

Access hole, 7 in. wide by 17 in. tall, centered

Side cutouts, 2 in. wide by 12 in. long, centered

Rabbet, 1/2 in. wide by 1/2 in. deep

Top rail, 3/4 in. thick by 3 in. wide by 16 in. long

Panel, 1/2 in. thick by 16 1/2 in. wide by 14 3/4 in. long

Stiles, 3/4 in. thick by 3 in. wide by 23 in. long

Bottom rail, 3/4 in. thick by 6 in. wide by 16 in. long

Front corner stile, 3/4 in. thick by 1 1/2 in. wide by 23 in. long

The mitered return hides the plywood. The face grain wraps around to the front of the case and gives the look of thick, solid stock. The assembly is attached to the case with screws driven from inside. The panel is prefinished to prevent wood movement from exposing any unfinished areas at the edges.

The fixed shelves are first. Construction begins with two H-shaped subassemblies. These assemblies are then connected by a plywood bottom. The space between them creates the central shelving area.

Solid-wood stretchers connect the piece at the top. These also create a place to attach the back and top of the cabinet. The front stretcher protrudes 3/4 in. from the case, to meet the other edging, so Casey uses a piece of 3/4-in. scrap to set the reveal.

FIT THE DRAWERS

No measuring, no marking. The lower slides sit right on the case bottom. To ensure proper spacing between the slides, Casey rips a piece of 1/2-in. MDF to match the drawer-face height.

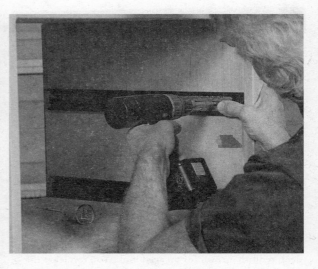

Use the spacer to locate the upper slides. With the spacer positioned on top of the lower slide, its top edge supports the upper slide at the correct height for installation.

Attach the matching hardware. Casey uses a combination square referenced off the bottom of the drawer side to pencil a layout line for the runner. Mounting screws are centered on this line and driven through factory-drilled holes in the hardware.

False fronts and media storage. Casey drills oversize holes and uses a 1-in. washerhead screw with a 1/2-in.-dia head (some manufacturers call them "drawer-front adjusting screws"). This creates wiggle room for slight adjustments in the position of the drawer front to get it square and even in the opening. The central horizontal groove houses the divider hardware.

Traditional Country Hutch

by Martin Milkovits

Being self-employed as a furniture maker, it's always tough to find time to build a piece for my own use. But my wife and I had always wanted a cupboard to store our collection of dinnerware, so I relented and spent what little spare time I had building a cupboard that fits not only the space available in our dining room but also the overall décor.

The design of this piece germinated while I was building a large cupboard for a client. That piece was twice as wide as this version, and was made of maple with a rather plain frame-and-panel façade. I wanted something a little smaller, with more flair. So I scaled down the size and revised a few details to enliven the piece.

This version is made mostly of cherry, stained to a deep reddish-brown for an aged look. You can leave the cherry natural, and it will darken over time. The glass doors showcase our prized plates and glassware, and are easy to make on the router table. The beaded, painted back slats add texture and contrast, while the custom hand-forged door hinges contribute to the classic feel.

Lower Case Is a Complex Assembly

The lower case of the cupboard consists of a frame-and-panel bottom, back, and sides. The legs do double duty as the stiles of the frame-and-panel assemblies. As such, there are a number of mortises and grooves to be cut into each leg, as well as mortises for the front stretchers. The legs also are notched for the bottom and the drawer guides. For strength, the shelf sits in grooves in support members that also are mortised into the legs.

Taken individually, the lower case assemblies are relatively simple to construct. After dry-fitting everything together, begin assembling the back of the lower case. Don't forget to add the rear shelf support before gluing on the last leg. Set it aside to dry, then glue up the bottom frame-and panel assembly. Put together the front top and bottom stretchers and the drawer divider, and attach them and the lower front apron to the front legs. Check frequently for square.

After the glue in the front, back, and bottom assemblies is dry, make up the drawer-guide assembly and glue it to the bottom stretcher. Glue the case bottom to the

LAYOUT BEGINS WITH THE LEGS

The legs of the lower case also work as the stiles of the frame-and-panel sides and back, so there are a number of joints that need to be laid out. You'll also have to mark out notches for the bottom, the shelf, and the drawer guides.

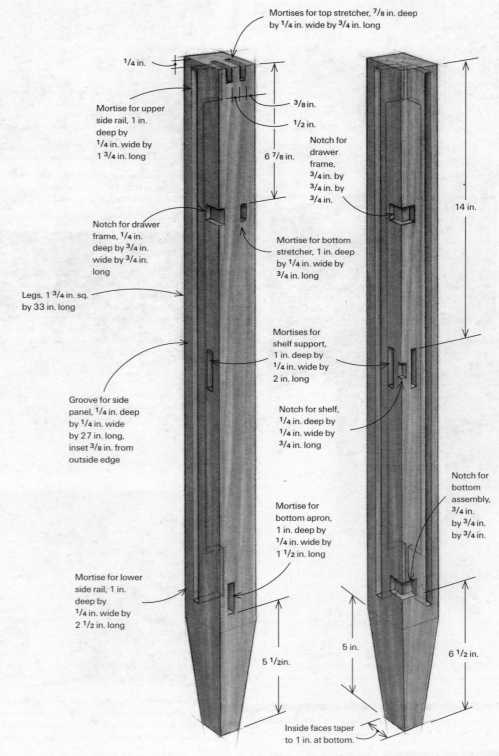

Mortises for top stretcher, 7/8 in. deep by 1/4 in. wide by 3/4 in. long

1/4 in.

Mortise for upper side rail, 1 in. deep by 1/4 in. wide by 1 3/4 in. long

3/8 in.

1/2 in.

6 7/8 in.

Notch for drawer frame, 3/4 in. by 3/4 in. by 3/4 in.

Notch for drawer frame, 1/4 in. deep by 3/4 in. wide by 3/4 in. long

Legs, 1 3/4 in. sq. by 33 in. long

Mortise for bottom stretcher, 1 in. deep by 1/4 in. wide by 3/4 in. long

14 in.

Mortises for shelf support, 1 in. deep by 1/4 in. wide by 2 in. long

Groove for side panel, 1/4 in. deep by 1/4 in. wide by 27 in. long, inset 3/8 in. from outside edge

Notch for shelf, 1/4 in. deep by 1/4 in. wide by 3/4 in. long

Notch for bottom assembly, 3/4 in. by 3/4 in. by 3/4 in.

Mortise for bottom apron, 1 in. deep by 1/4 in. wide by 1 1/2 in. long

Mortise for lower side rail, 1 in. deep by 1/4 in. wide by 2 1/2 in. long

5 1/2 in.

5 in.

6 1/2 in.

Inside faces taper to 1 in. at bottom.

FRONT RIGHT LEG

REAR RIGHT LEG

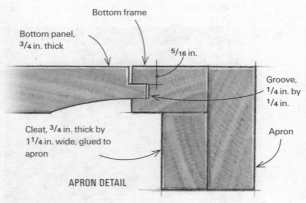

Bottom frame

Bottom panel, 3/4 in. thick

5/16 in.

Groove, 1/4 in. by 1/4 in.

Cleat, 3/4 in. thick by 1 1/4 in. wide, glued to apron

Apron

APRON DETAIL

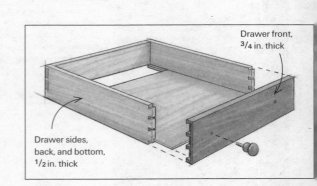

Drawer front, 3/4 in. thick

Drawer sides, back, and bottom, 1/2 in. thick

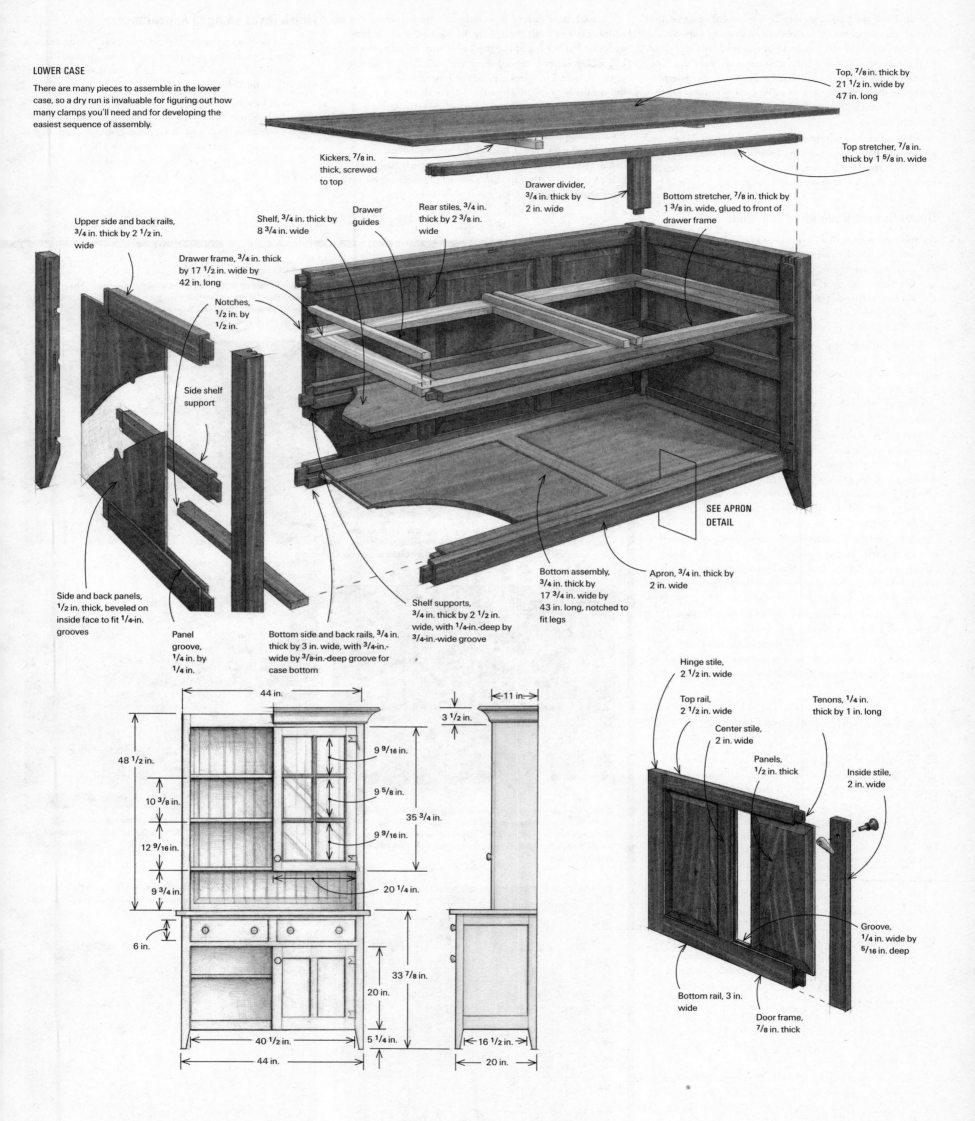

LOWER CASE

There are many pieces to assemble in the lower case, so a dry run is invaluable for figuring out how many clamps you'll need and for developing the easiest sequence of assembly.

Top, $^7/_8$ in. thick by 21 $^1/_2$ in. wide by 47 in. long

Kickers, $^7/_8$ in. thick, screwed to top

Top stretcher, $^7/_8$ in. thick by 1 $^5/_8$ in. wide

Drawer divider, $^3/_4$ in. thick by 2 in. wide

Bottom stretcher, $^7/_8$ in. thick by 1 $^3/_8$ in. wide, glued to front of drawer frame

Upper side and back rails, $^3/_4$ in. thick by 2 $^1/_2$ in. wide

Shelf, $^3/_4$ in. thick by 8 $^3/_4$ in. wide

Drawer guides

Rear stiles, $^3/_4$ in. thick by 2 $^3/_8$ in. wide

Drawer frame, $^3/_4$ in. thick by 17 $^1/_2$ in. wide by 42 in. long

Notches, $^1/_2$ in. by $^1/_2$ in.

Side shelf support

Side and back panels, $^1/_2$ in. thick, beveled on inside face to fit $^1/_4$-in. grooves

Panel groove, $^1/_4$ in. by $^1/_4$ in.

Bottom side and back rails, $^3/_4$ in. thick by 3 in. wide, with $^3/_4$-in.-wide by $^3/_8$-in.-deep groove for case bottom

Shelf supports, $^3/_4$ in. thick by 2 $^1/_2$ in. wide, with $^1/_4$-in.-deep by $^3/_4$-in.-wide groove

Bottom assembly, $^3/_4$ in. thick by 17 $^3/_4$ in. wide by 43 in. long, notched to fit legs

Apron, $^3/_4$ in. thick by 2 in. wide

SEE APRON DETAIL

44 in.

48 $^1/_2$ in.

10 $^3/_8$ in.

12 $^9/_{16}$ in.

9 $^3/_4$ in.

6 in.

9 $^9/_{16}$ in.

9 $^5/_8$ in.

9 $^9/_{16}$ in.

20 $^1/_4$ in.

35 $^3/_4$ in.

11 in.

3 $^1/_2$ in.

33 $^7/_8$ in.

20 in.

40 $^1/_2$ in.

44 in.

5 $^1/_4$ in.

16 $^1/_2$ in.

20 in.

Hinge stile, 2 $^1/_2$ in. wide

Top rail, 2 $^1/_2$ in. wide

Center stile, 2 in. wide

Panels, $^1/_2$ in. thick

Tenons, $^1/_4$ in. thick by 1 in. long

Inside stile, 2 in. wide

Groove, $^1/_4$ in. wide by $^5/_{16}$ in. deep

Bottom rail, 3 in. wide

Door frame, $^7/_8$ in. thick

Continued ➡

apron. Place the back assembly on the bench, add the shelf and its side supports (glue the shelf to the rear support only), then glue in the top and bottom side rails and slide in the side panels. When these two assemblies are dry, drop the case front and bottom assembly onto the rear assembly using the dadoes in the bottom side rails as guides. Drive the parts home with a mallet, then lift the case onto its legs and add clamps.

When the glue has dried, finish building the drawer system and cut the slots for the buttons that will secure the top to the lower case. Once that's done, you can make and install the doors and drawers and cut and fit the top.

Upper Case Is Dovetailed Together

A cupboard is designed to hold stacks of plates and other dinnerware, which can put great demands on the structure. For maximum strength, the top and sides of the upper case are dovetailed together, and the shelves mate with the sides via tapered sliding dovetails. The tapered pins and slots add strength through the wedging action and make it easy to slide the shelves home without binding during glue-up.

After cutting the dovetail joint that connects the top to the sides, rout rabbets in the top and sides for the back panel frame and the front face frame. Stop the cuts short of the ends on the top piece to prevent an unsightly gap in the corners when the pieces are put together. Square up the corners after the case has been glued up.

Now lay out the shelf locations so that they will line up with the horizontal muntins in the glass doors. Set up a fence for the router to cut the dovetail slots and adjust the fence so that the slot tapers toward the front of the case. Cut the tapered pins on the shelves using a router table, working one shelf at a time to allow for any differences in the slot widths.

After cutting the pins on the shelves, rout a stopped groove in each one for a plate rail, which is handy if you simply want to display fancy plateware. Now glue up the top and sides of the upper case and slide in the shelves (see the sequence in the photos).

Once that is complete, build the front face frame, which will hold the glass doors, and the back assembly, which is basically a series of shiplapped boards that float in a frame to allow for expansion and contraction. The case is topped off with a simple crown molding cut on the tablesaw.

Glass Doors Add Interest and Elegance

To simplify construction, the frame of the glass doors in the upper case is assembled with loose mortise-and-tenon joints. Mill the rails and stiles to size, cut the mortises and tenons, then rout the profile on the inside edges.

To shape the profile on the frame and the muntins, I used a divided-light door router-bit set from CMT (item No. 800.525.11). The set has a sticking bit to cut the profile, a cope bit to shape the mating profile on the muntin and rail ends, and a rabbeting bit to cut the recesses for the glass panes.

To make routing the narrow muntin stock safer, I did a few things. First, I routed the ovolo profile on wider stock, then ripped the pieces to width. To rout the rabbets on the back of the thin muntins, I mounted the pieces in a cradle, simply a 3½-in.-wide piece the same thickness as the muntin stock, with one edge shaped in the negative image of the ovolo profile. The cradle holds the piece securely and keeps my fingers clear of the rabbeting bit.

To hold the thin stock for coping, I used a sled that rides in the miter slot of the router table. The muntin is clamped between a fence and a backer board to prevent tearout as the bit exits the cut.

Once you have completed all the profiling, chop the mortises in the stiles and rails and the vertical muntin using a hollow-chisel mortiser or chisels. When the frame is glued together and the door is fitted to the opening, add the glass panes, securing them with brads and glazing putty.

I used hand-forged iron butterfly hinges, which can be a bit tricky to install. I align the bottom edge of the hinge with the inside edge of the top or bottom rail. Lay the hinge backward on the stile with the back flap on the edge of the stile and the back side of the butterfly flap facing out on the face side of the stile. Locate the center hole and install a screw, making sure that the butterfly flap is still flat on the stile. Remove the screw, and place the hinge in the normal position, reinstall the screw, and then scribe around the back flap. Chop in the hinge mortise and install the rest of the screws. If done correctly, the back side of the butterfly flap should be in the same plane as the door and stile face.

Finish Gives an Aged Appearance

For final sanding, first wet the piece to raise minor dents that happened during construction. Power-sand to P180-grit, wet the piece again to raise the grain, then hand-sand with P150 and P180 grits.

To add an antique patina, I used 100 drops of TransTint dark walnut #6005 dye per 1 pint of denatured alcohol as a washcoat, followed by General Finishes candlelight stain and several coats of Minwax Antique Oil and wax. The back panel and upper case interior are painted an ivory color.

ASSEMBLE THE CASE IN STAGES

1. After gluing up the bottom assembly, attach it to the front legs. Put together the stretchers and the vertical drawer divider, and then attach them and the lower front rail to the front legs. Check frequently for square.

2. Glue the rear panels and stiles into the rails. Attach one leg (remember, the panels are not glued to the legs), slide in the rear shelf support, then attach the other leg. Glue in one side shelf support, slide the shelf into place (glue it to the rear support only), then install the other side support.

3. Glue the front to the back. Place the back assembly on the bench. Install the side panels, then hoist the case front and drop it down on the rear assembly.

UPPER CASE

The top case is a bit simpler to glue up than the lower case. The top and sides are dovetailed together first, then the front face frame is added. The shelves mate with the sides via tapered sliding dovetails, and the back assembly sits in a rabbet.

1. Connect the top to the sides. To ensure that the assembly remains square, the author clamps square sections of plywood into each corner.

2. Add the front face frame. For a good fit, rip the rail and stiles so that they're a hair proud of the case, then plane the frame flush to the sides after the glue dries.

3. Slide in the shelves. Flip the case onto its front to install the shelves. You should be able to drive each shelf home with only a few light blows of a mallet.

4. Drop the back panel in place. Remember to rout the rabbet on the bottom of the frame to mate with the groove in the top of the lower case.

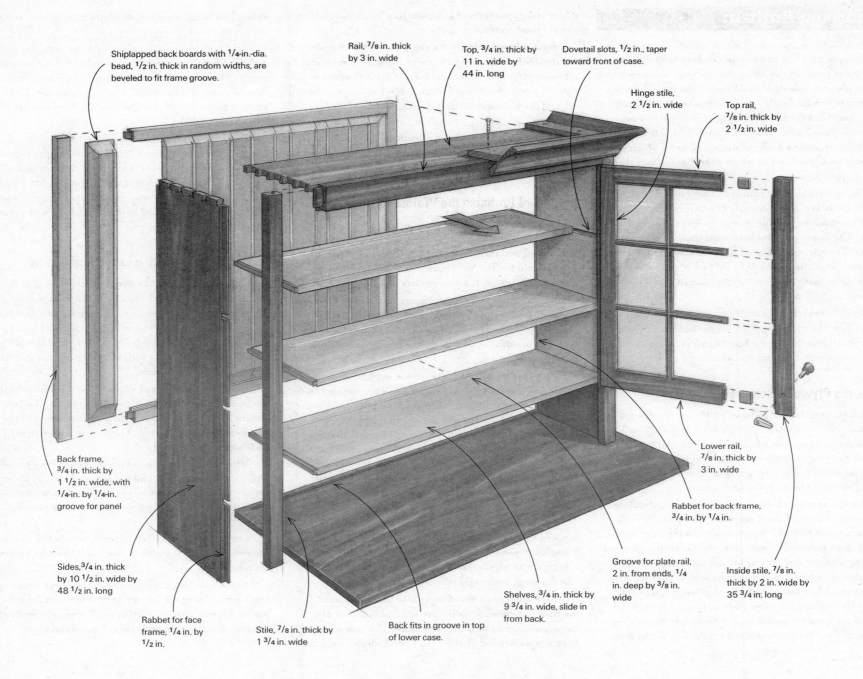

Shiplapped back boards with 1/4-in.-dia. bead, 1/2 in. thick in random widths, are beveled to fit frame groove.

Rail, 7/8 in. thick by 3 in. wide

Top, 3/4 in. thick by 11 in. wide by 44 in. long

Dovetail slots, 1/2 in., taper toward front of case.

Hinge stile, 2 1/2 in. wide

Top rail, 7/8 in. thick by 2 1/2 in. wide

Back frame, 3/4 in. thick by 1 1/2 in. wide, with 1/4-in. by 1/4-in. groove for panel

Sides, 3/4 in. thick by 10 1/2 in. wide by 48 1/2 in. long

Rabbet for face frame, 1/4 in. by 1/2 in.

Stile, 7/8 in. thick by 1 3/4 in. wide

Back fits in groove in top of lower case.

Shelves, 3/4 in. thick by 9 3/4 in. wide, slide in from back.

Groove for plate rail, 2 in. from ends, 1/4 in. deep by 3/8 in. wide

Rabbet for back frame, 3/4 in. by 1/4 in.

Lower rail, 7/8 in. thick by 3 in. wide

Inside stile, 7/8 in. thick by 2 in. wide by 35 3/4 in. long

A SIMPLE WAY TO ATTACH THE CROWN

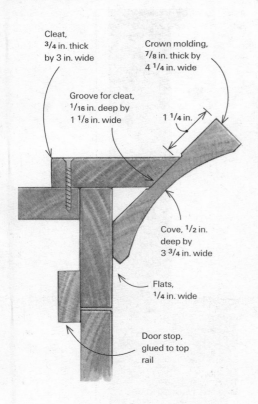

Cleat, 3/4 in. thick by 3 in. wide

Crown molding, 7/8 in. thick by 4 1/4 in. wide

Groove for cleat, 1/16 in. deep by 1 1/8 in. wide

1 1/4 in.

Cove, 1/2 in. deep by 3 3/4 in. wide

Flats, 1/4 in. wide

Door stop, glued to top rail

Continued ➡

Mudroom Built-In

by Tony O'Malley

An enclosed porch or mudroom can help keep dirt and snow from reaching the living areas of your house. It's also a great place to stow stuff you'd rather not have cluttering the kitchen or family room: boots, shoes, book bags, sports gear, and the like. But without designated storage areas, a mudroom becomes a minefield. An elegant solution is to make a built-in storage cabinet, which will not only look good and organize your life, but can also add value to your home.

This mudroom unit features a base cabinet topped with open locker-type cabinets. The base cabinet has a lift-lid section for stowing out-of-season stuff like winter boots. The upper cabinets have fixed shelves and hooks for jackets. This piece is designed for a family of four—with each person getting his or her own locker space—but it can easily be made larger or smaller to suit a different-size family.

The construction is simple: maple plywood cases with walnut face frames and applied frame-and-panel assemblies, which give the piece a furniture feel. Most of the parts are made in the shop and assembled on site.

Build the Plywood Boxes First

For this project, I used prefinished 3/4-in.-thick maple plywood for all the cases. Though not commonly available at major home centers, the plywood often can be special-ordered at lumberyards. It saves you considerable finishing time, and creates a bright, durable interior that looks great with the dark walnut exterior.

For the upper lockers, I made four identical skinny cabinets and screwed them together. These smaller cabinets are easier to build, move around in the shop, and install. And this method can make the difference between needing a helper and getting the job done on your own. The plywood edges on the upper lockers are hidden with solid-walnut face frames, which are glued and nailed in place. To help align the face frames, I used 1/8-in.-thick splines cut from tempered Masonite. Before assembling the cases, I cut the grooves for the splines in all the front edges using a router and a slot-cutting bit. To assemble the cases, I used screws and biscuits.

Base cabinet is built the same way—The base cabinet for this built-in goes together with the same biscuit and screw joinery as the locker cabinets. One difference is that I used an adhesive-backed maple edge-banding on the top edge of the two exposed partitions.

Put on the edge-banding before you cut the partitions to size. That way, the banded partitions don't vary in size from the unbanded ends of the case. Trim the edge-banding with a chisel.

Make and Prefinish the Walnut Parts

Once the plywood cases are glued up, you can begin working on the walnut face frames, the frame-and-panel assemblies, and the lift-lid assembly. All of the walnut parts should be finished (I used Minwax Wipe-On Poly) before installation. It's much easier that way.

Because most walls aren't square or flat, you'll need to fit the end pieces of the built-in to that irregular surface. So leave any piece that butts against the wall about 3/8 in. oversize in width (or length for the moldings) to allow for scribing and fitting.

Face frame—Mill the face-frame stock to thickness and width, but leave the pieces long. They'll be trimmed to fit the case during installation. That will leave the end grain unfinished, but no one will see it. I chamfer the edges and ends of every face-frame part to create a small V-groove at each intersection; this detail not only looks good but also masks any minor unevenness at the joints. You can't chamfer the ends now, because the pieces aren't cut to final length, but you should chamfer the edges and prefinish the pieces.

Frame-and-panel assemblies—The front and exposed side of this built-in are covered with applied frame-and-panel assemblies made from solid walnut and 1/4-in.-thick plywood and assembled with simple joinery (see drawing, next page).

Base and crown moldings—Like the face frames, both the base and crown molding are solid walnut. For efficiency, mill up both at the same time. The base molding has a simple beveled profile. It's a good idea to leave it a bit wider than its finished size and trim it to fit after installation. The crown molding also is simple.

All four bevel cuts are made with the tablesaw blade at 42°. Clean up any saw marks with a handplane or sandpaper. The miters and scribing are done during installation. To support the crown, I use a beveled plywood strip screwed to the top of the case. Cut the strip and bevel its edge.

Last, the lift lid—The top of the lower cabinet features a lift lid, a fixed back (on which the upper cabinets will sit), and two pieces of side trim. I decided to use 3/4-in.-thick walnut plywood for the lid and fixed back to eliminate any wood movement worries. To ensure a good grain match, cut the fixed back and lid from one piece of plywood.

Assembly: Start with a Level Foundation

Built-in cabinetry must be installed level and plumb, no matter how out of whack the floors and walls may be. One of my favorite tricks is to install a separate base that can be leveled without moving the entire cabinet back and forth in the process (see photos). Once the base is complete, install the cases, starting with the lower cabinet and finishing with the upper lockers.

Cover up the plywood edges—Now it's time to install the front frame-and-panel assembly, the lid, the face frames, and the moldings. The front is screwed to the lower case from the inside. The lid is attached to the fixed back with a piano hinge.

When gluing and nailing on the face-frame pieces, attach the verticals first and the horizontals last. Because they're for alignment only, you need only one spline per vertical piece, even though the three middle pieces cover two cabinet sides.

On the horizontal frame pieces, remember to chamfer the ends, and apply finish to that small chamfer before installation.

Now all you have to do is install the crown molding and base molding. Once you're finished, you'll have a handy place to store all sorts of stuff, and a convenient seat where you can put on and take off shoes and boots. •

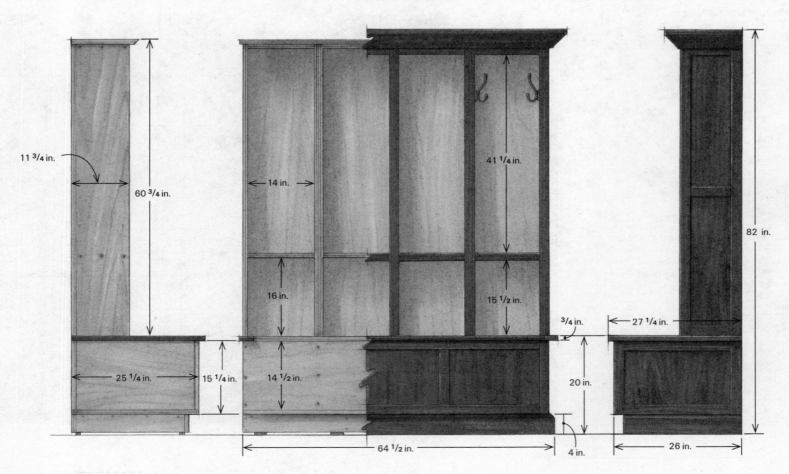

Base Cabinet Offers Seating and Storage

The lower cabinet is a plywood box faced with walnut frames and panels. The height is perfect for sitting to change shoes, and the lidded box has plenty of room for items you don't want to see, like boots and outdoor gear.

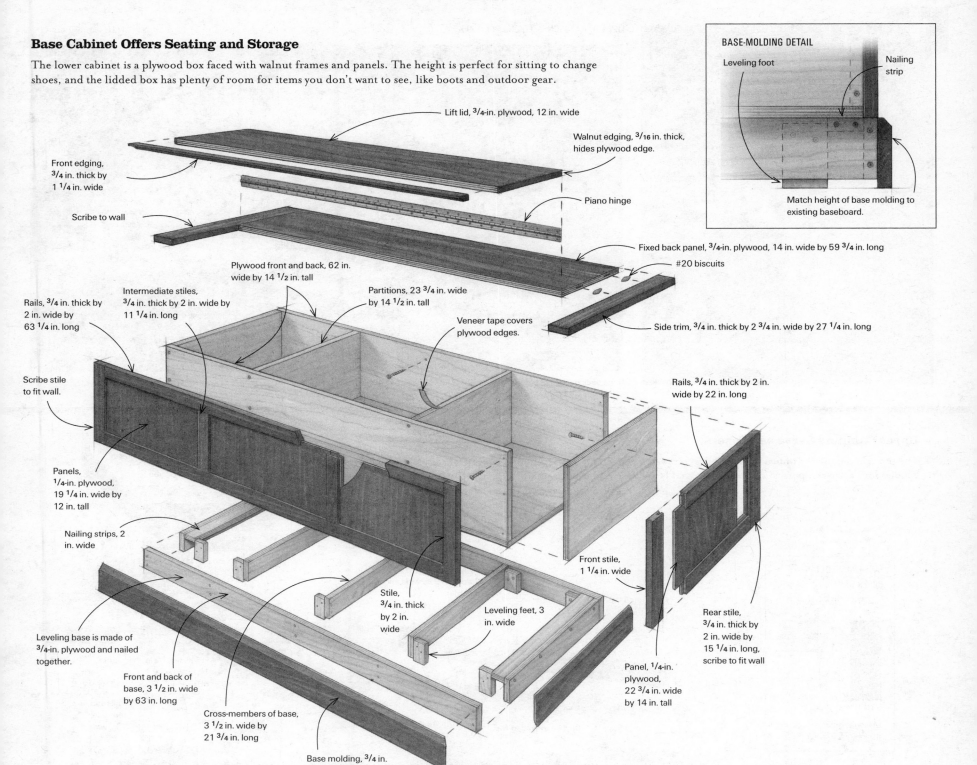

BASE-MOLDING DETAIL

Leveling foot

Nailing strip

Match height of base molding to existing baseboard.

Lift lid, 3/4-in. plywood, 12 in. wide

Walnut edging, 3/16 in. thick, hides plywood edge.

Front edging, 3/4 in. thick by 1 1/4 in. wide

Scribe to wall

Piano hinge

Fixed back panel, 3/4-in. plywood, 14 in. wide by 59 3/4 in. long

#20 biscuits

Plywood front and back, 62 in. wide by 14 1/2 in. tall

Intermediate stiles, 3/4 in. thick by 2 in. wide by 11 1/4 in. long

Partitions, 23 3/4 in. wide by 14 1/2 in. tall

Veneer tape covers plywood edges.

Rails, 3/4 in. thick by 2 in. wide by 63 1/4 in. long

Side trim, 3/4 in. thick by 2 3/4 in. wide by 27 1/4 in. long

Scribe stile to fit wall.

Rails, 3/4 in. thick by 2 in. wide by 22 in. long

Panels, 1/4-in. plywood, 19 1/4 in. wide by 12 in. tall

Nailing strips, 2 in. wide

Front stile, 1 1/4 in. wide

Stile, 3/4 in. thick by 2 in. wide

Leveling feet, 3 in. wide

Rear stile, 3/4 in. thick by 2 in. wide by 15 1/4 in. long, scribe to fit wall

Leveling base is made of 3/4-in. plywood and nailed together.

Front and back of base, 3 1/2 in. wide by 63 in. long

Cross-members of base, 3 1/2 in. wide by 21 3/4 in. long

Panel, 1/4-in. plywood, 22 3/4 in. wide by 14 in. tall

Base molding, 3/4 in. thick by 4 in. wide

CLEAN CUTS IN PLYWOOD

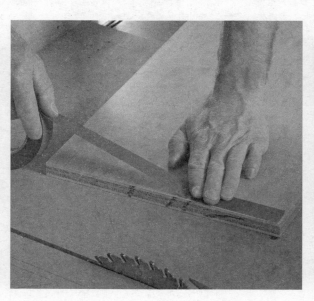

Rip, then crosscut. When breaking down a full sheet of plywood on a tablesaw, rip the pieces to size, then crosscut them using a sled.

The final cuts. To reduce tearout, keep the show face on top, and use a good combination blade and a zero-clearance insert or crosscut sled. To further reduce the chances of tearout during a crosscut, apply masking tape over the bottom side of the cut line.

BISCUITS AND SCREWS SPEED ASSEMBLY

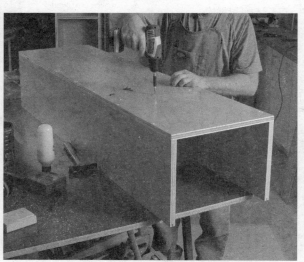

No clamps required. Assemble the shelves, top, and sides with biscuits and screws. The screws not only reinforce the biscuits, but they also eliminate the need for clamps. Drill clearance holes and countersinks in the top pieces, and pilot holes in the edges below to prevent splitting.

Continued →

443

Woodworking Wisdom & Know-How

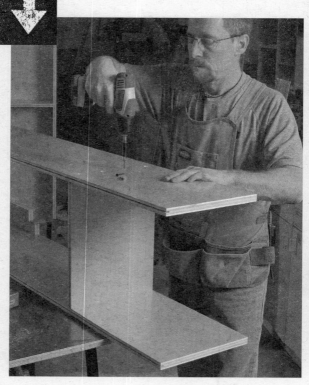

LIFT LID: A LESSON IN EDGING PLYWOOD

Fixed back gets solid edges. Attach the side trim pieces to the fixed back with biscuits.

Upper Cabinets Serve as Lockers

The top cabinets are individual plywood boxes screwed together and faced with solid walnut. These lockers have small cubbies for backpacks, purses, and briefcases, and larger spaces to hang coats and jackets.

CROWN-MOLDING DETAIL

Plywood support frame

3/8 in.

7/8 in.

2 3/4 in.

3/8 in.

1 1/4 in. exposed

FACE-FRAME DETAIL: UPPER RAIL

1/4-in.-deep groove

Masonite spline, 1/8 in. thick by 1/2 in. wide

FACE-FRAME DETAIL: STILE

Only one alignment spline needed.

Face-frame stile

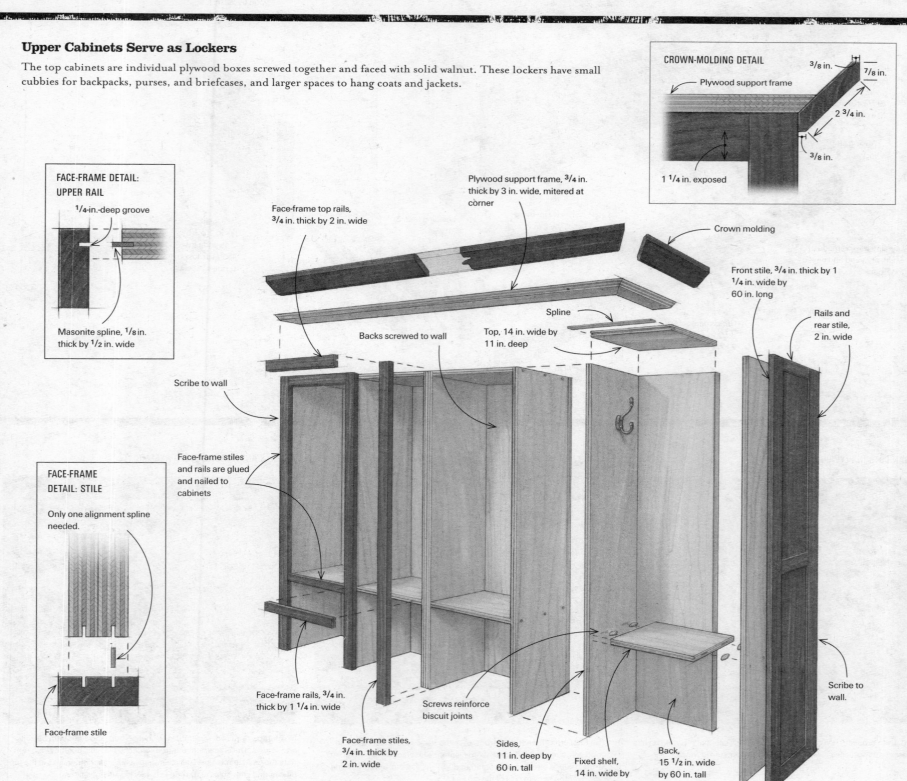

Plywood support frame, 3/4 in. thick by 3 in. wide, mitered at corner

Face-frame top rails, 3/4 in. thick by 2 in. wide

Crown molding

Front stile, 3/4 in. thick by 1 1/4 in. wide by 60 in. long

Spline

Rails and rear stile, 2 in. wide

Backs screwed to wall

Top, 14 in. wide by 11 in. deep

Scribe to wall

Face-frame stiles and rails are glued and nailed to cabinets

Face-frame rails, 3/4 in. thick by 1 1/4 in. wide

Face-frame stiles, 3/4 in. thick by 2 in. wide

Screws reinforce biscuit joints

Sides, 11 in. deep by 60 in. tall

Fixed shelf, 14 in. wide by 11 in. deep

Back, 15 1/2 in. wide by 60 in. tall

Scribe to wall.

Hide exposed edges on lid. The side edge-bandings are glued on with masking tape as the clamps, and the front edging is attached with biscuits. All the edging is trimmed flush with a block plane and cleaned up with sandpaper.

Soft landing for fingers. After gluing on the front edging and trimming it flush with the plywood, rout a cove along the bottom edge to serve as a finger pull.

INSTALL FROM THE GROUND UP

BASE: SET IT AND FORGET IT

Installing the cabinets over a separate base makes leveling easy. Assemble the base from scrap plywood, using nails or screws; set it in place and level it. Once that's done, you know that all the cabinets above will be level.

Add feet. Use shims to get the base perfectly level and up to the target height. Once the base is at the target height, screw on the plywood feet.

SCREW IN THE LOWER CABINET

First, screw the cabinet to the base and to the wall. Then add the side panel and the fixed back of the lid assembly.

Put the cabinet on the base. Screw it to the base and to the wall with finish-head screws. Shim behind the cabinet if the wall isn't plumb.

Top it off. Place the fixed back panel on top and screw it to the lower cabinet from above. The screws will be hidden by the upper lockers.

Side panel is next. Scribe the rear stile to the wall and trim the panel flush with the front of the cabinet. Screw it to the cabinet from inside.

DETAILS, DOORS, DRAWERS, LEGS, AND HARDWARE

Illustrated Guide to Cabinet Doors

by Andy Rae

Doors are what we see when we look at a cabinet. Thanks to their relatively large surface area, they're the most visible component in many projects, and they will make a lasting impression if you design them carefully and thoughtfully.

In addition to looking good, doors must function properly. A well-made door opens with little resistance, closes without clatter or fuss, and has a comfortable pull that fits the hand.

Begin by choosing the style of door you want: overlay, rabbeted, or flush. After that, it's a design exercise in proportioning components carefully, choosing the appropriate joinery, and understanding wood movement.

The illustrations on the following pages will help you work out the best door design for whatever project you're planning. This guide covers frame-and-panel doors, the most popular type, used in many furniture styles and periods. Some of the design considerations, however, also apply to slab-style plank doors and veneered doors.

Begin with Good Proportions

Because doors are the focal point of many pieces, it's important to proportion them so they will work in harmony with each other and with other case components. People frequently make doors and their case openings too wide or, less commonly, too tall. Whenever possible, divide the case opening into reasonable sections and build the doors to suit.

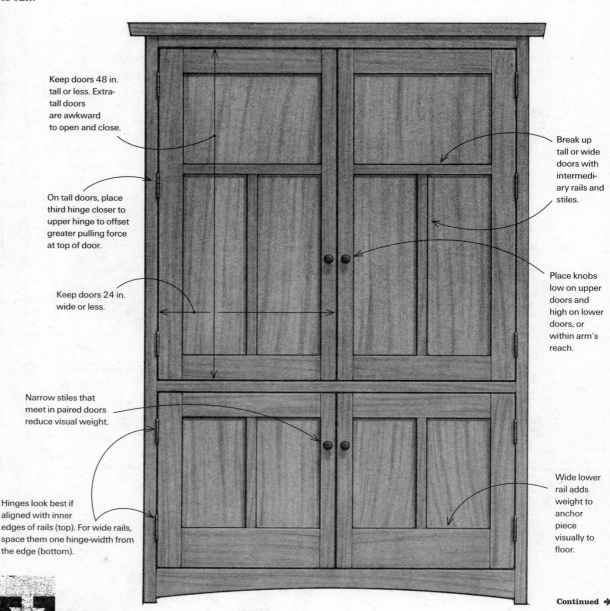

Keep doors 48 in. tall or less. Extra-tall doors are awkward to open and close.

On tall doors, place third hinge closer to upper hinge to offset greater pulling force at top of door.

Keep doors 24 in. wide or less.

Narrow stiles that meet in paired doors reduce visual weight.

Hinges look best if aligned with inner edges of rails (top). For wide rails, space them one hinge-width from the edge (bottom).

Break up tall or wide doors with intermediary rails and stiles.

Place knobs low on upper doors and high on lower doors, or within arm's reach.

Wide lower rail adds weight to anchor piece visually to floor.

Continued ➡

Mounting Options

For fine furniture and cabinets, there are three main options. Flush and rabbeted doors are seen in contemporary as well as period furniture. Overlay doors are used most often in kitchen and bathroom cabinets. Each style has some pluses and minuses when it comes to fitting and mounting.

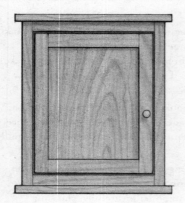

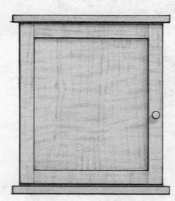

FLUSH DOORS

These require the most attention during fitting because the doors hang inside the face of the case. They call for reveals of 1/16 in. or less between the door and case opening.

RABBETED DOORS

These sit partially proud of the case, and a rabbet on the back allows them to rest slightly inside the case opening. Because the door gap is concealed, this type is generally the easiest to fit.

FULL OVERLAY DOORS

These cover the entire face of the cabinets. Avoid unattractive partial-overlay doors, which are used in factory-made cabinets because they require no fitting.

Basic Door Anatomy

In frame-and-panel door construction, a narrow outer framework surrounds and captures a wide panel. The vertical frame pieces are called stiles; the horizontal pieces, rails. The panel can be made of solid wood, plywood, or medium-density fiberboard (MDF). Typically, stiles run full-length and are mortised for tenons on the rails. But you can reverse that for aesthetic reasons: On paired doors, for example, full-width rails add a visually unifying element. Full-width rails also provide better screw purchase for knife hinges.

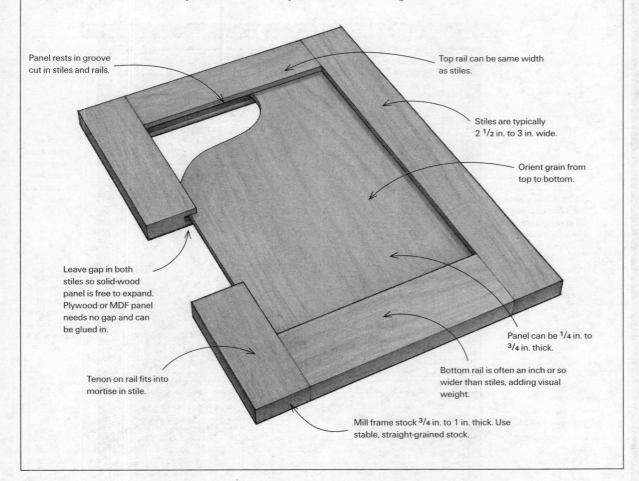

Panel rests in groove cut in stiles and rails.

Top rail can be same width as stiles.

Stiles are typically 2 1/2 in. to 3 in. wide.

Orient grain from top to bottom.

Leave gap in both stiles so solid-wood panel is free to expand. Plywood or MDF panel needs no gap and can be glued in.

Tenon on rail fits into mortise in stile.

Panel can be 1/4 in. to 3/4 in. thick.

Bottom rail is often an inch or so wider than stiles, adding visual weight.

Mill frame stock 3/4 in. to 1 in. thick. Use stable, straight-grained stock.

Flat panels offer simplicity and are a hallmark of Shaker work. Raised panels are more traditional. Rabbets or bevels can be positioned on the back to keep the front plain. As a rule, keep the panel flush with or below the surface of the frame.

THIN, FLAT PANEL

Essentially the same thickness as the groove in the frame. Made from plywood or MDF, or glued up from narrower solid stock.

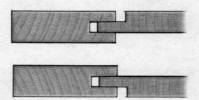

RABBETED PANEL

Profiled on front or back and designed to be flush with the frame. Or, it can be the same thickness as the frame and rabbeted equally front and back.

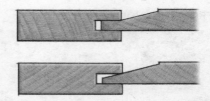

RAISED PANEL

Panel has a flat tongue made on a router table or shaper (top). Alternatively, you can cut the profile on the tablesaw, or form it with a handplane (bottom).

Frame Edge Profiles

Edges offer a chance for you to be creative by cutting different profiles or applying a molding. This is usually done to the inside edge of the frame, though rabbeted doors typically have a thumbnail or roundover profile on their outside edge.

SQUARE EDGE

Simple in design, simple to make. Smooth the surface with a plane before assembling the frame.

BEAD WITH QUIRK

Make bead 1/8 in. to 1/4 in. wide with a 1/16-in. quirk. Cut it on the router table or shaper. Requires a mitered frame so the bead is continuous.

THUMBNAIL

Quarter-round, quarter-round with fillet (shown), ogee, or other profiles. Shape on a router table or shaper, or by hand.

APPLIED BEAD

Shape a 1/8-in. to 1/4-in. bead. For all applied beads and moldings, miter the ends, then attach with glue and/or brads.

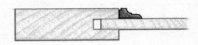

APPLIED MOLDING

Use stock 1/4 in. to 1/2 in. thick, profiled on a router table or shaper. Glue to frame and panel if panel is sheet goods; otherwise, glue only to frame.

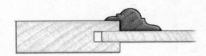

BOLECTION MOLDING

Complex profile with a rabbet that rests over the frame. Glue to frame only, unless panel is made from plywood or MDF.

Options for Corner Joints

Doors with solid-wood panels get their strength mainly from the corner joints in the frame; a glued-in plywood or MDF panel adds considerable rigidity. The time-honored mortise-and-tenon joint is quite common, but the type of joint you use will depend on the look you want and the strength you need, as well as the ease of construction. Here are nine good options.

MORTISE AND TENON

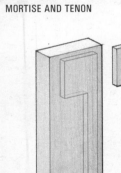

The basic joint: Rails are grooved their full length for the panel; stiles require a stopped groove. Mortises should be as deep as possible for maximum strength; Rae tries to make his at least 1 1/4 in. deep.

HAUNCHED TENON

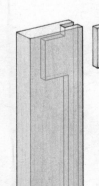

A variation on the basic mortise-and-tenon joint that's easier to make. Both stiles and rails are grooved their full length for the panel. The tenon is cut with a step, or haunch, on one side that fills the groove in the stiles.

MITERED MORTISE AND TENON

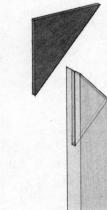

Another variation on the basic joint. The inside edges of the stiles and rails are mitered after the mortise and tenon are cut. The miter makes it easy to mold a continuous profile along the inside edge.

BRIDLE JOINT

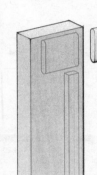
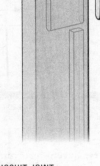

A strong and easily made joint. You can cut the open mortise and the tenon on the tablesaw, using a tenoning jig.

FLOATING TENON

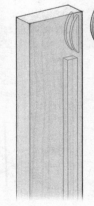

Mortise both stiles and rails, then join the parts with a separate tenon sized to fit. Making this joint means you can size the rails without having to take into account the extra length of the tenons.

BISCUIT JOINT

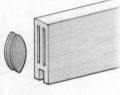

Biscuits don't yield an especially strong joint. Make the rails at least 3 in. wide to accept #20 biscuits, and use two biscuits for maximum strength. Best with a glued-in plywood panel for added strength.

COPE AND STICK

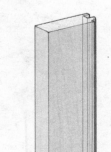

Matched router bits cut mating profiles in the inside edges of the stiles and rails. Easy to make but not especially strong, it may need reinforcement with a floating tenon or a plywood panel glued into the grooves.

STUB TENON

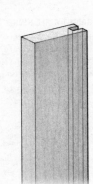

A variation on the basic mortise-and-tenon joint that's very easy to make. Stiles and rails are grooved their full length, and the tenons are cut to a length equal to the depth of the grooves. A plywood panel glued into the grooves gives the door additional strength.

REINFORCED MITER

A miter reinforced with a wood key makes a very strong joint. It's also fairly easy to make, since you can use the tablesaw for all the cuts. You'll need a cradle-type jig to hold the frame at 45° when cutting the key slots.

Hinge Options

Well-made hinges installed with care will yield a door that swings smoothly and closes easily. Be sure to select the correct type of hinge for the style of door you're hanging. Buy quality hardware: Look for solid castings or extrusions, thick leaves, and knuckles that pivot smoothly without play.

BUTT HINGE

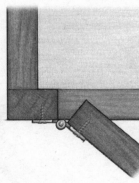

Used for overlay and flush doors. Requires mortising one or both leaves into the case and door.

SURFACE HINGE

The easiest type to install. Used for flush and rabbeted (right) doors.

SURFACE HINGE FOR RABBETED DOORS

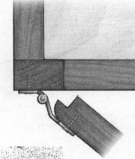

One leaf is bent to accommodate the offset. Installation is a snap.

Continued ➡

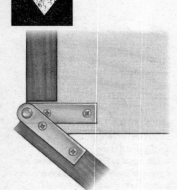

STRAIGHT KNIFE HINGE
Used for overlay doors where the case top and bottom extend over the sides. Requires careful mortising of case and door.

OFFSET KNIFE HINGE
Used for flush doors. Requires careful mortising of both case and door.

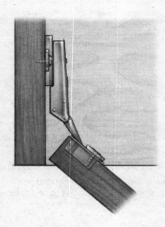

CUP HINGE
Available for all types of doors. Easy to mount in hole drilled in back of door. Lots of adjustability after door is mounted.

When Doors Meet

Paired doors are common, offering easier access inside a case. For the tidiest look and one that seals out dust, design the doors with some sort of overlapping element. It's customary to have the right-hand door open first. Also, cut a slight bevel in the side of one door, to keep it from binding.

OPPOSING RABBETS
Close the gap by cutting matching rabbets in the edges of the stiles. Make each rabbet half the thickness of the doors, so they sit flush with each other when closed. When planning the cabinet, you may need to widen the stile of the door rabbeted on its front (top drawing), so that the stiles appear the same width when closed.

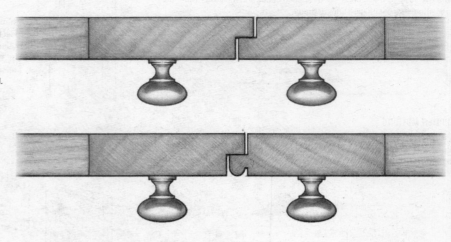

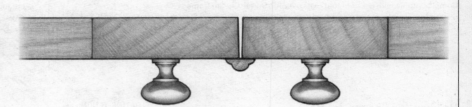

ADD AN ASTRAGAL
This is a strip of wood glued either to the face of one door or attached to the back of the captured door. Be sure to cut the astragal a hair short so it won't interfere with the case top or bottom.

Good Options for Glass Doors

Glass doors dress up a cabinet and add a practical touch, because you can see what's inside. Use translucent or textured glass if you want to light up the inside without revealing precisely what's there. There are several options when it comes to rabbeting the door to accept the glass.

RABBET THE FRAME AFTER ASSEMBLY
Glue up the door, then use a bearing-guided router bit to cut the rabbet for the glass in the back of the frame.

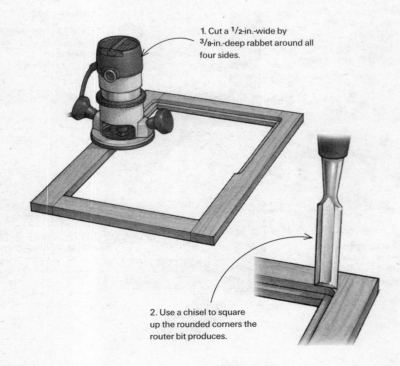

1. Cut a 1/2-in.-wide by 3/8-in.-deep rabbet around all four sides.

2. Use a chisel to square up the rounded corners the router bit produces.

INSTALL THE GLASS

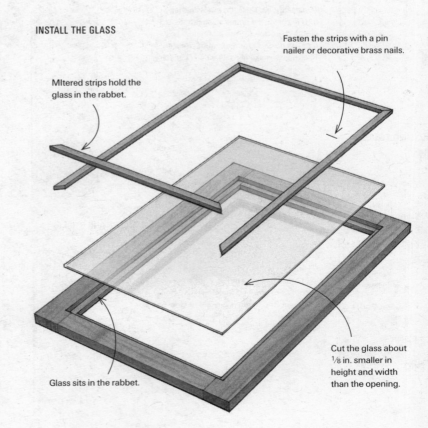

Fasten the strips with a pin nailer or decorative brass nails.

MItered strips hold the glass in the rabbet.

Cut the glass about 1/8 in. smaller in height and width than the opening.

Glass sits in the rabbet.

TWO FRAMES THAT CAN BE RABBETED BEFORE ASSEMBLY

It's easier to cut the rabbet before assembly by grooving or rabbeting parts on the tablesaw, but not all frames allow this.

KEYED MITER

Cut the rabbet in the frame stock, then cut the miters, assemble the frame, and add the keys.

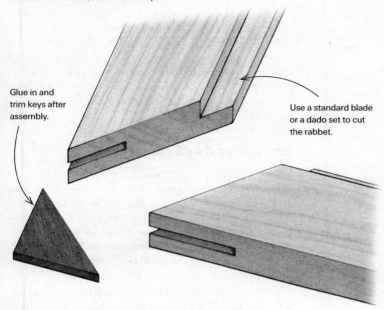

Glue in and trim keys after assembly.

Use a standard blade or a dado set to cut the rabbet.

MITERED MORTISE AND TENON

When making a batch of doors this way, you can use the same machine setups to create a rabbet for a glass door.

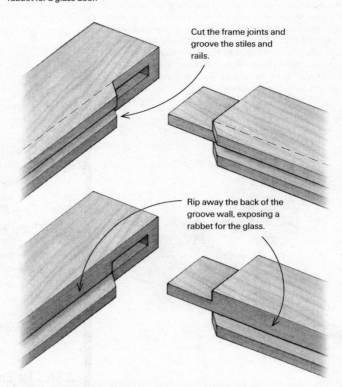

Cut the frame joints and groove the stiles and rails.

Rip away the back of the groove wall, exposing a rabbet for the glass.

Frame-and-Panel Doors Made Easy

by Michael Pekovich

This past summer, during the remodeling of my kitchen, I was faced with the task of making 31 cabinet doors. I needed speed and simplicity, so I broke out my router table and a set of cope-and-stick router bits. These bit combinations allow you to rout door frames quickly, in two steps. The first bit routs a profile and panel groove on the inside edge of all the frame parts. The second bit is a mirror image of the first, routing a coped profile and a stub tenon on the ends of the frame rails.

What you create is not a traditional mortise-and-tenon joint. But done right, it gives you a cabinet door that's just as strong. The key is to use a flat panel of plywood or medium-density fiberboard (MDF) that's glued in place—not a raised panel, which is designed to float. All in all, I was able to build all 31 doors in the course of a weekend, from milling lumber to finish sanding.

Different types of cope-and-stick bits are available, with an array of profiles from simple thumbnails to more ornate ogees. In general, these bits are designed for 3/4-in.-thick doors, but there are cope-and-stick bits available for stock 1/2 in. or thinner.

Start with Straight, Square Stock

I began by milling the door-frame stock. I prefer quartersawn or rift-sawn boards because the tight, straight grain is both good-looking and stable. It's important that the stock be straight and square. Any slight bow or twist will make fitting the door a nightmare.

Don't be tempted to flatten an entire wide board and then rip the frame parts from it; that will lead to bowed or twisted stock. Instead, start with rough-sawn 4/4 stock and rip the parts oversize on the bandsaw. Crosscut the stock to remove any serious twist, bowing, or knots, but keep it as long as possible to reduce the number of pieces you'll have to rout. Then joint and plane the boards to final thickness (mine finished at 3/4 in.), and rip to the exact width on the tablesaw.

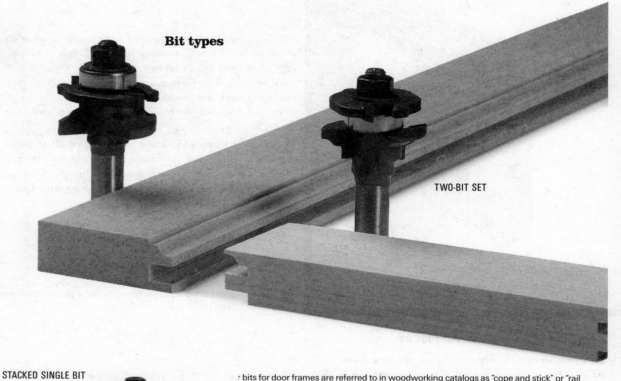

Bit types

TWO-BIT SET

STACKED SINGLE BIT

...r bits for door frames are referred to in woodworking catalogs as "cope and stick" or "rail
...ile" bits. Their function is to rout a profile and a panel groove on the inside edge of the
...parts and to cope the ends of the rails to fit that profiled edge. The bit style I use consists
...ir of matched bits (above). Another style of bit that is available is a stacked bit (left), in
...the cutters necessary for each profile are included on a single bit. The stacked style does
...with bit changing and may be more convenient for occasional use, but the two-bit style
... used with two dedicated routers for a better production setup. Both styles range from
... $150. A less-expensive alternative is a reversible bit, with cutters that are reconfigured
...aft for each cut. These sell for $80 to $100, but I don't think the savings is worth the
...renience.

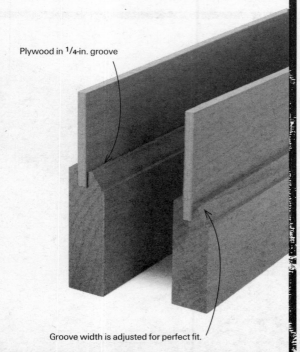

Plywood in 1/4-in. groove

Groove width is adjusted for perfect fit.

Rout the Edge Profile on All Pieces

Now you can rout the edge profile on all of the door-frame pieces while they are still long. Start with the "stick" bit in your router. Adjust the height until you produce a profile with a 1/16-in. fillet at the top. A shallower fillet would create a weak upper portion of the joint and a deeper fillet would locate the panel groove too far toward the back, creating a thin rear wall. Align the router-table fence precisely with the guide bearing on the bit. Attach featherboards to hold the stock against the table and fence when routing. If you're using a smaller router or a very hard wood such as oak or maple, you may need to take two passes to reach final depth. In that case, set up for a three-quarter-depth cut and rout all the stock before adjusting the fence for the final pass. Removing the bulk of the waste on the first pass will yield a cleaner surface on the second.

Use a Story Stick for Crosscutting

Once the edges have been profiled, it's time to cut all the parts to final length. Instead of a tape measure, I made a "story stick" to record the width and height of the case openings, along with the number of doors that fit in the

opening. For cases with two doors, I measured the width and marked the halfway point.

I then used the story stick to set up the tablesaw for crosscutting. I started with the stiles, which run top to bottom in the case opening. First I clamped a stop block to the rip fence in front of the blade, to prevent the stile from binding between the blade and the fence during cutting. Then it was simply a matter of aligning the mark on the story stick with the blade and setting the fence so that the stop block was flush with the end of the stick. Cut the stiles, making sure to mark the door number on each piece.

Cutting the rails to length is a bit trickier. Because they fit between the stiles, you must account not only for the width of the stiles but also the depth of the stub tenons. This can lead to some head-scratching, but I found a simple method that let me dispense with the math. First, make a setup block that is equal to the width of the two stiles minus the depth of the panel grooves. Use this setup block in conjunction with the story stick to quickly dial in the right dimensions for the rails. Because rails are usually short, use a stop block clamped to the crosscut-sled fence to set the length. Again, align the mark on the story stick with the blade; then rest the setup block on the story stick flush with the end, and pencil a line on the sled to mark the end of the rail. Clamp the stop block at the line and cut the rails.

A Sled for End-Routing

With the parts cut to length, it's time to install the coping bit and profile the ends of the rails. Do not try to run these rails against the router-table fence without additional support; the pieces are too narrow to stay square against the fence. Instead, use a simple plywood sled fitted with hold-down clamps to run the stock squarely and safely across the bit. But before setting up the sled, cope the long edge of an extra piece of frame stock to make a special backing block. This piece will marry with the profiled edge of the rail stock and prevent tearout. When the other end of the rail is routed, the trailing edge will be flat, and a flat backer block will suffice.

After the backing block is made, clamp an offcut in the sled and take a test cut. Adjust the bit's height until the two pieces are flush and you're ready to cope the rails. Start with the flat edge against the sled fence and cope the first

end. Then rotate the rail, insert the backing block into the panel groove, and cope the second end.

Make the Panels Undersize in Width

With the frames complete, all that's left to do is to size the panels. I made them 1/16 in. narrower than the length of the rails. This is to accommodate the slight amount of seasonal movement (yes, even MDF moves), and to make sure the panel allows the frame parts to seat fully during glue-up. The panels' length equals the stile length minus the setup-block length. The MDF I used fit very snugly into the panel groove, so I knocked the panels' corners off quickly with a block plane. (Unlike plywood, which is thinner than its nominal thickness, MDF measures out on the mark.)

How to Keep It All Square

Gluing up cope-and-stick doors is a challenge. One concern is that the stub tenons could slide along the panel groove, making it difficult to glue up the parts square. Or, the panel could fit so tight that it seizes up on contact with the glue, making it very difficult to square up the parts. Fortunately, this procedure eliminates both potential problems. I installed the panel in a stile groove first, then slid the rails on, and finally, added the second stile.

To position the panel correctly, mark its location on the stile by holding a rail in place and marking the width of its tenon. Apply glue along the panel grooves of the stiles only. Then apply glue to the coped ends of the rails. If there is glue in the rail grooves, they won't slide along the panel. Install the panel, making sure it's fully seated. Then push a rail onto the panel, fully seating it, and slide it down onto the stile. Install the second rail in the same manner, using the panel to align the rails parallel to each other and square to the stiles. All that's left is to install the last stile.

Once that's done, clamp along the entire joint. Be careful not to apply too much pressure across the panel, because it's slightly narrower than the rails, and the stiles could bow inward. Use a straightedge to make sure the stiles are flat with the rails. The short tenons provide little resistance against flexing upward.

1. Rout the profile

Make the edge profiles first. Even before the frame pieces are cut to size, rout their edge profiles to accept the panel. Do this in one or two passes, using the sticking bit.

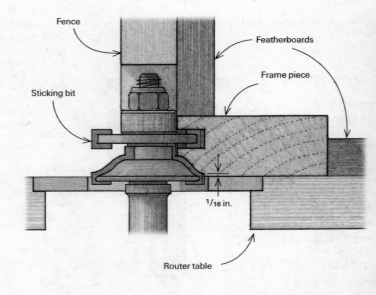

Fence

Featherboards

Frame piece

Sticking bit

1/16 in.

Router table

2. Cut the Stiles

Put away your tape measure. Mark the door-frame length and width measurements on a thin "story" stick. You'll transfer the marks directly to the tablesaw.

Clamp a stop block to the rip fence. Use the story stick to set the rip fence for crosscutting the stiles.

Cut all the stiles. Lead with the profiled edges to keep them free of chipout. A well-made crosscut sled keeps the cuts square.

3. Cut the Rails

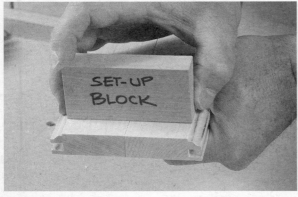

Cutting the rails requires an extra step. Start by cutting a block to the width of two rails minus the combined depth of their grooves. When you subtract this distance from the door width, you'll get the correct length of the rails.

Use the block to set up the cut. With the story stick's door-width mark aligned with the sawblade, use the block to draw a line on the sled fence.

Cut the rails. With a stop block clamped at the line, you can cut all the rails to a precise and uniform length for a specific door size.

4. Cope the Rails

A SHOPMADE SLED FOR PRECISE COPING

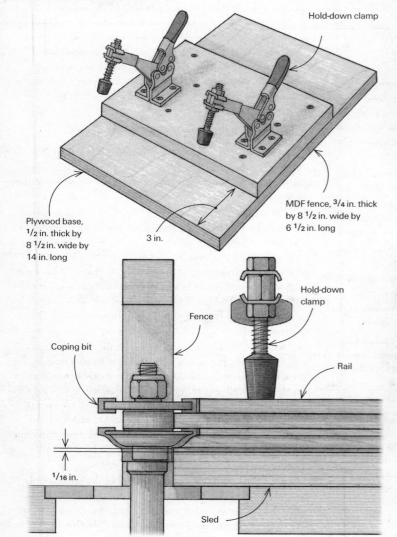

Hold-down clamp

MDF fence, 3/4 in. thick by 8 1/2 in. wide by 6 1/2 in. long

Plywood base, 1/2 in. thick by 8 1/2 in. wide by 14 in. long

3 in.

Fence

Hold-down clamp

Coping bit

Rail

1/16 in.

Sled

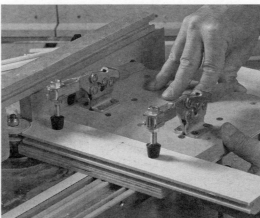

Profile the rail ends. Switch to the coping bit and use the sled to keep the rails square and secure for their end cuts. After making test cuts to ensure the faces will be flush, begin by coping the rail with the flat edge against the fence.

Back the profile with its mate. Before coping the opposite end, run a short length of scrap past the coping bit to make a backer block for the rail's profiled edge. With the backer block mated behind the piece, cope the second rail end.

Continued ➡

5. Assemble the panels

Placing the panel is key. Line up the panel precisely between the layout marks, and push it down to the groove bottom. This will keep the rest of the assembly square.

Attach the rails. After applying glue to the leading end of one rail, slide it down the panel edge and fit its stub tenon into place in the stile groove. Do the same with the second rail. Complete the assembly by gluing on the last stile.

Check and clamp. Before tightening the clamps, use a straightedge to make sure the panel is flat in all directions. Adjust the clamps if necessary, and tighten.

Mark and glue one stile. After marking the location of the panel on one of the stiles, apply glue inside the entire length of the stile's groove. The panel will be glued to the stiles only.

Glass Doors Made Easy

by Doug Stowe

I live in Eureka Springs, a small town in northwest Arkansas that's home to many artisans and art collectors. And so I've made several cabinets with glass doors to house art collections. Glass doors are also great for kitchen cabinets, allowing you to display decorative dishes while protecting them, and for enclosed bookshelves. But many people build them in a tedious way, by making a normal mortise-and-tenoned door and then rabbeting the pieces for the glass in a separate series of steps. I've learned that the best way to make those doors is with a bridle joint. Not only is the joint easy to make—I do it with a tenoning jig at the tablesaw—but by shortening the length of the tenon cheek on the back face of the rails, I can cut through-rabbets for the glass at the same time. That saves you the hassle of routing stopped rabbets and squaring their corners after the door is glued up.

As simple as this joint is to make, it is one of those assemblies—like the dovetail—that can be hard to wrap your mind around, at least at first. That's because it can be difficult to imagine how the offset tenon shoulder on the back of the rail fills the rabbet on the stile. But don't worry, it does. And the steps are easy.

Make the Bridle Joint First

There are two parts to the joint. A slot is cut into the end of the stile, and a tenon onto the end of the rail. On a door with a wood panel, both of the tenon's shoulders are the same distance in from the end of the rail. However, in order to cut through-rabbets on the back of the parts, the cheek is shorter on the back than it is on the front so that the shoulder on the back fills the rabbet on the stile after the door is glued up. That means there are no unsightly gaps in the door frame from the through-rabbets.

Before you make the joint, lay the parts on the bench

and mark their faces and inside edges to help keep them properly oriented as you cut the joints and rabbets. Also, I start with rails and stiles that are about 1/8 in. longer than final size. I cut the joints so that the ends of the tenons and slots are 1/16 in. proud after assembly and then trim them.

Start with the slots on the stiles. I use a tenoning jig to hold the stile on end as I run it through the tablesaw blade. Use a blade with a flat-top grind, like a ripping blade. Some combination and crosscut blades leave a V-shaped notch in the bottom of the kerf that would be visible after assembly.

Put the back face of the stile against the jig and clamp the stile in place. Cut the first side of the slot. Make the same cut for the remaining three slots. Adjust the fence to align the blade with the other side of the slot and make that cut for all four slots. I use a blade that's 1/8 in. thick, so those two cuts form the entire slot. A thinner blade requires a third cut to clean out the middle.

Now it's time to cut the tenons on the ends of the rails. This joint will seem strange at first, because the tenon's cheeks are different lengths. But after you put the joint together, it makes perfect sense.

I cut the shoulders at the tablesaw with a crosscut sled and a jig that has two different stops built into it. One stop lets me cut the shoulder for the shorter cheeks on the rail's back, and the other is set to cut a shoulder for a cheek that is 1/4 in. longer. Cut the back shoulders of the rails first. Then switch the stop to its second position and cut the front shoulders.

Now cut the cheeks using the tenoning jig. Because the cheeks on the front are longer than those on the back, cut them first. Put the rail in the jig with its back against the main fence and cut all of the front cheeks. Then lower the blade and cut the cheeks on the backs.

Finally, trim the tenons to their final width. This is more critical than usual for a tenon, since the fit will show

on the outside of the frame. After setting the blade height so that it is just lower than the length of the tenon, I clamp the rail into the tenoning jig with its inside edge against the main fence. I then define the final width of the tenon with a single cut of the blade. Then I use a crosscut sled with a stop to make the shoulder cut that frees the waste piece. The stop ensures that the shoulder aligns with the shoulder on the front of the rail.

Cut the Rabbets and Assemble the Door

Now that the bridle joints are finished, you can cut the rabbets that hold the glass. Because of the way the bridle joint is cut, these are through-rabbets, made quickly at the tablesaw.

Set the blade height to 3/8 in. Set the rip fence so that the outside edges of the blade's teeth are 1/4 in. from it. Lay the rail back down on the saw's table and cut the first side of the rabbet. Next, lower the blade to 1/4 in. and adjust the rip fence so that the outside teeth are 3/8 in. from it. Stand the rail on its inside edge and cut the second side of the rabbet. The blade can push the waste back toward you after it's cut free, so don't stand directly behind the blade.

After the rabbets are cut, the joint fits together and you can see why the tenon's cheeks are different lengths. Now I dry-assemble the door and rout a slight chamfer on the inside edges of the rails and stiles, using a chisel to square the rounded corners left by the bit. The joint fits tightly enough that you don't need clamps, which would get in the way at the router. Disassemble the door and sand the inside edges of the parts, which would be more difficult to do after the door is glued together.

Now glue up the door. Apply glue to the tenons only and push them into the slots. If you put glue in the slot as well, the tenon will push most of it out, creating a mess on the outside edge of the joint. You should be able to bring the joint completely together with hand pressure. Then

use a C-clamp and cauls (to protect the door from the clamp heads) to hold the joints together. No other clamps are needed.

After the glue has dried, trim the rails and stiles to length and sand the frame, but don't re-sand the inside edges.

I use glass that is $1/8$ in. thick, so the stops (wood strips) that hold the glass in place are made from $1/4$-in.-square hardwood. After milling them, I sand them and then fit them to the frame, using butt joints at the corners. Fit the sides first, and then the top and bottom. That way, if you make a mistake cutting the sides, you can cut them shorter and use them for the top and bottom.

I hold the stops in place with $1/2$-in.-long #20 gauge brad nails. To prevent the stops from splitting, pre-drill for the nails at the drill press. Now apply a finish to the frame and stops. Clean the glass and put it in place. Use a tack hammer and nail set to drive the nails into the stops, placing a piece of cardboard between the hammer and glass so that it doesn't get scratched or broken. The nail set helps you direct the hammer's force and keep the nail moving straight in. Once a small brad nail begins to bend, there is no correcting it, so just cut your losses by pulling it out and starting a new one. Finally, I install hinges. I generally use knife hinges because they are less visible, but butt hinges will work fine, too.

START WITH A SIMPLE SLOT IN THE STILES
Offset it toward the front to allow room for the stops that hold the glass in place.

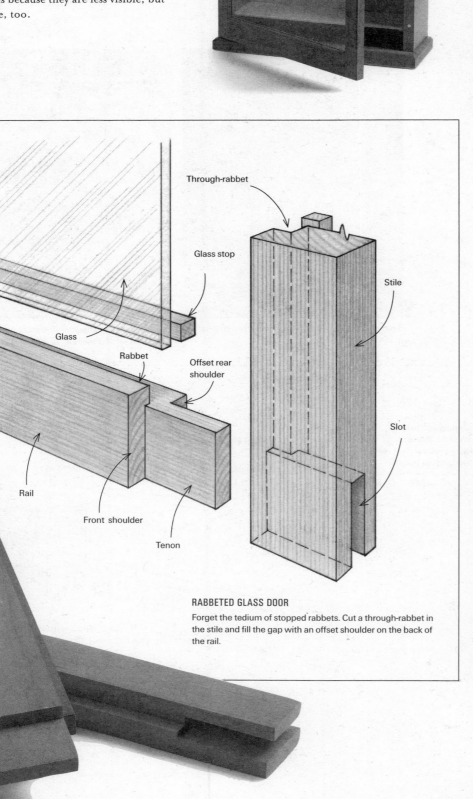

RABBETED GLASS DOOR
Forget the tedium of stopped rabbets. Cut a through-rabbet in the stile and fill the gap with an offset shoulder on the back of the rail.

Labels: Through-rabbet, Glass stop, Glass, Rabbet, Offset rear shoulder, Stile, Slot, Rail, Front shoulder, Tenon

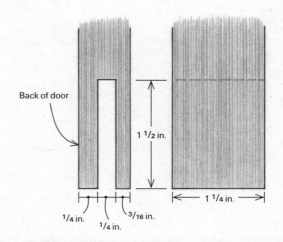

Labels: Back of door, $1\ 1/2$ in., $1\ 1/4$ in., $1/4$ in., $1/4$ in., $3/16$ in.

Use a tablesaw tenoning jig. Set up the jig so that the blade cuts the side of the slot closest to the jig first. The slot is $1/4$ in. wide, so with a standard blade, the second cut will complete the slot.

Continued ➔

CUT SHOULDERS ON THE RAILS

Use your tablesaw sled to cut the offset shoulders.

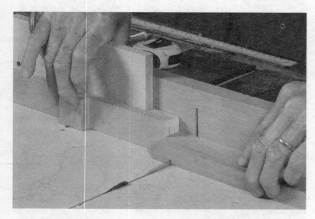

Cut the short shoulder first. Use the end with the longer stop to make the shorter side.

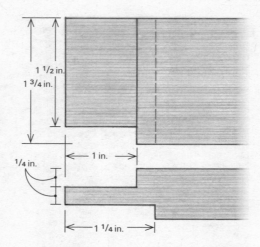

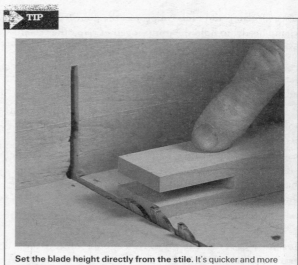

Set the blade height directly from the stile. It's quicker and more reliable than transferring a measurement from the slot.

TWO-SIDED STOP BLOCK MAKES PRECISE CUTS

For this joint to work, the shoulders' offset must be precise. That's no trouble with this jig. Flip it end for end to create the 1/4-in. offset between them.

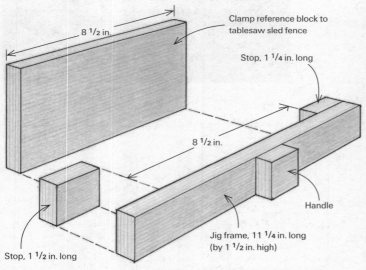

8 1/2 in.

Clamp reference block to tablesaw sled fence

Stop, 1 1/4 in. long

8 1/2 in.

Stop, 1 1/2 in. long

Handle

Jig frame, 11 1/4 in. long (by 1 1/2 in. high)

All parts made from 1/2-in.-thick plywood

Flip the stop. The reference block ensures that it ends up in the right place.

Then cut the long shoulder. The second stop is 1/4 in. shorter than the first, so the second cheek is 1/4 in. longer.

NOW THE CHEEKS

Using the right jigs, you can cut these quickly, accurately, and safely at the tablesaw.

Pull out the tenoning jig again. Set the blade to cut the shorter cheeks first. Then adjust the jig, raise the blade, and cut the longer cheeks.

ALTER YOUR STOP SETUP FOR THE FINAL CUT

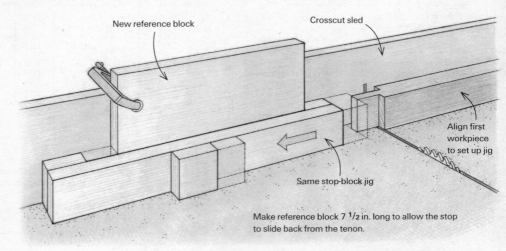

New reference block

Crosscut sled

Align first workpiece to set up jig

Same stop-block jig

Make reference block 7 1/2 in. long to allow the stop to slide back from the tenon.

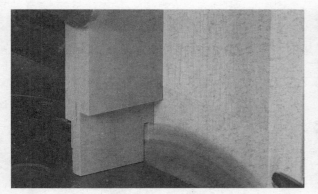

Use the jig to cut the tenon's width, too. Set the blade height to the lower (rear) shoulder.

Position the workpiece. Push the stop block toward the blade, and the workpiece toward the block.

Move the stop and make the cut. This allows the waste piece to move away freely.

CUT THE RABBETS AND ASSEMBLE

None of the rabbets (for the glass) are stopped, so you can cut them all quickly on the tablesaw.

TWO CUTS FOR THE RABBET

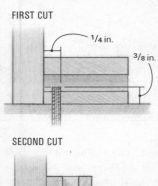

FIRST CUT

1/4 in.

3/8 in.

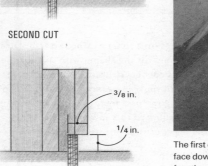

SECOND CUT

3/8 in.

1/4 in.

The first one is made with the rails and stiles face down, the second is with them on edge to free the waste.

One clamp for each joint. If the frame is square and the joints tight, you don't need clamps across the width and length.

THEN INSTALL THE GLASS

Hold it in place with stops. Stowe predrills clearance holes in these thin wood strips and nails them in using a hammer and nail set. He uses a piece of manila folder to protect the glass. Use butt joints between the stops, not miters, so they are easy to remove for repair.

Modern Twists on Cabriole Legs

by Jonathan Binzen

The cabriole leg was like a flourished signature on furniture of the eighteennth century. From Queen Anne through Chippendale, the S-curved cabriole, with its outcurved knee and incurved ankle, was produced by European and American furniture makers in thousands of variations, on pieces from dining tables and side chairs to highboys and footstools. But use of the cabriole—which takes its name from the Italian word for a leaping goat—neither started nor stopped in the eighteenth century. Versions of it have been around since ancient Egypt, Greece, and China. And now many furniture makers are giving it a contemporary twist of their own.

The reversing curves of the cabriole can provide a powerful visual impact whether the legs are long or short and whether the curves are sharp or shallow. The challenge for the furniture maker is to create a handsome cabriole that also suits the overall design of the piece. Here is a handful of examples that show how the ancient cabriole is being deftly put to use by some of today's top makers.

Smoothed Out and Stretched

"I think subtle can be powerful," says Ted Blachly, and the slightly sinuous legs of his table prove the point. The legs are notable not only for their restraint but also for combining a fairly hard line down the outside corner with softly rounded inside faces.

Blachly's design started with a small freehand sketch and proceeded to a full-scale drawing. To generate the lines of the legs' curves full size, he used a spline and spline weights. This simple technique, an essential in a boat-designer's kit, involves placing a thin, flexible strip of solid wood (the spline) right on the drawing paper and bending it to the desired curves. A few weights placed strategically along the spline hold it still while you trace the curve with a pencil. The longer the curve, the thicker the spline should be, Blachly says. For these legs, he used a cherry spline about 3/16 in. thick and 7/8 in. wide. To ensure that the spline takes an even curve when bent, it should be made from straight-grained stock. Specially made spline weights can be purchased (woodenboatstore.com; no. 835-073S), but Blachly improvises with blocks of soapstone.

To make the legs, Blachly started with squared-up blanks milled from a 12/4 mahogany plank. He transferred the curves from his drawing to the leg blanks with a flexible template he made from 1/4-in.-thick lauan plywood.

After tracing the template on one face of each leg, he bandsawed those curves. Then, to provide a flat bearing surface for cutting the second face, Blachly taped the bottom offcut back in place. He positioned the template on the now-curved upper face, traced it, and cut the second set of curves. He smoothed the curves with spokeshaves and bench planes, including a flexible-soled compass plane.

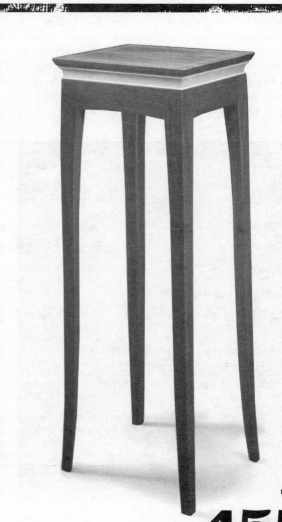

tinued ➜

1. USE A SPLINE TO CREATE THE DRAWING

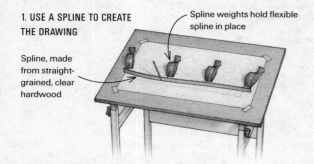

Spline weights hold flexible spline in place

Spline, made from straight-grained, clear hardwood

2. TRACE THE TEMPLATE ON ONE FACE OF THE BLANK

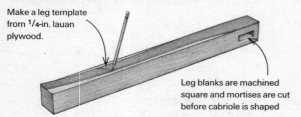

Make a leg template from 1/4-in. lauan plywood.

Leg blanks are machined square and mortises are cut before cabriole is shaped

3. BANDSAW THE CURVES ON THE FIRST FACE

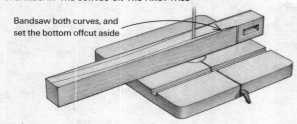

Bandsaw both curves, and set the bottom offcut aside

4. BANDSAW THE CURVES ON THE SECOND FACE

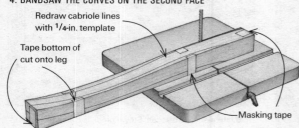

Redraw cabriole lines with 1/4-in. template

Tape bottom of cut onto leg

Masking tape

Shaped Top and Bottom

Peter Shepard tapped a longstanding furniture tradition when he carried the legs of his bureau through to the top of the case and had them serve as corner posts for the frame-and-panel carcase. But where in many such case pieces the upper portion of the post is left square, Shepard shaped it with a pair of incurving bevels accented with an ebony bead. This makes the whole leg read as one piece, rather than as a post with a leg below it, and helps deliver the sprightly feeling he was seeking.

After cutting the joinery, Shepard roughed out the legs on the bandsaw and used an MDF template to refine them on the router table. With the curves cut, he used a handheld router with a bearing wheel and a chamfer bit to create the bevels on the upper half of the leg. After the bead was glued in, Shepard worked with rasps and files to extend the bottom of the bevels and create a crisp transition to the lower half of the leg.

How to Make the Leg

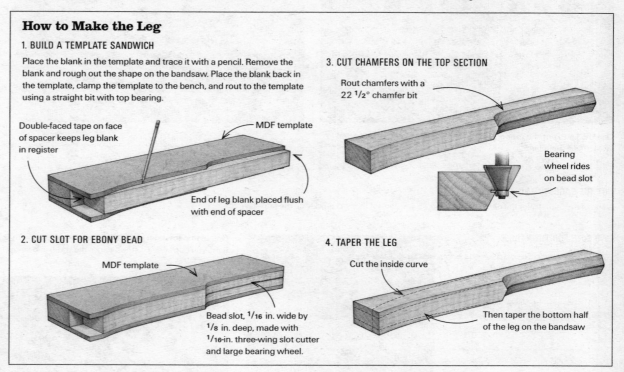

1. BUILD A TEMPLATE SANDWICH

Place the blank in the template and trace it with a pencil. Remove the blank and rough out the shape on the bandsaw. Place the blank back in the template, clamp the template to the bench, and rout to the template using a straight bit with top bearing.

Double-faced tape on face of spacer keeps leg blank in register

MDF template

End of leg blank placed flush with end of spacer

2. CUT SLOT FOR EBONY BEAD

MDF template

Bead slot, 1/16 in. wide by 1/8 in. deep, made with 1/16-in. three-wing slot cutter and large bearing wheel.

3. CUT CHAMFERS ON THE TOP SECTION

Rout chamfers with a 22 1/2° chamfer bit

Bearing wheel rides on bead slot

4. TAPER THE LEG

Cut the inside curve

Then taper the bottom half of the leg on the bandsaw

Upside Down and Twinned

For 50 years, Jere Osgood has been making furniture that exhibits a sculptor's flair for invented forms and an engineer's eye for the creative technical solution.

The legs of this square dining table are an inverted cabriole. Osgood originally designed the shape not for this table but for the back legs of his wishbone chair. When he decided to use a similar leg for the table, he knew it would have to be beefier than on the chair both for visual and structural reasons. Rather than scaling up the leg, however, he paired it up.

This unconventional decision instantly added strength and visual panache, but it also posed a daunting technical challenge—how to attach the legs firmly to the aprons, especially without joining the legs to each other, which he did not want to do. Osgood's equally unconventional solution was to create a V-shaped extension at the junction of the aprons. The forked extension offers a true tenon to each leg and is fixed to the rails with a series of slip tenons oriented to maximize long-grain glue surface.

Osgood made the legs on a shaper using two templates for each leg. The leg comes off the shaper with its cabriole curves established but its corners still square. From there it's all hand-shaping with spokeshaves, rasps, and files. To guide the handwork, Osgood uses templates made from illustration board or cardboard that help him check the cross-section of the leg at critical points.

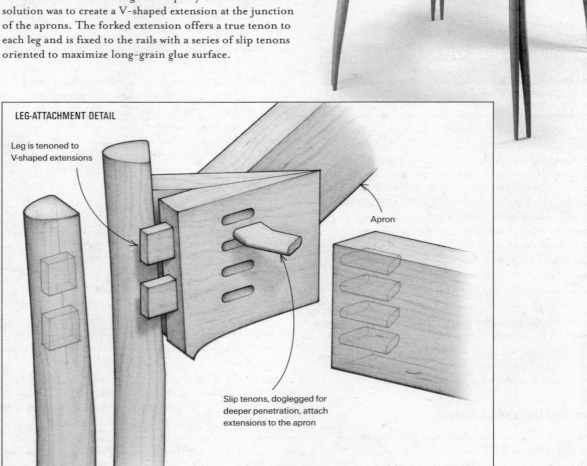

LEG-ATTACHMENT DETAIL

Leg is tenoned to V-shaped extensions

Apron

Slip tenons, doglegged for deeper penetration, attach extensions to the apron

With a Sense of Fun

James Schriber set out to design a little table that could also serve as a magazine or book rack and include a drawer. He decided to make the case and box out of sheet aluminum and the legs out of solid wood. This let him balance the flat, cool, hard-edged aluminum with lively, S-curved legs, softly pillowed, rounded at the edges, and coated with a milk-paint finish. "I liked the purposefulness of the box," Schriber says, "against the playfulness of the legs."

The legs may have a lighthearted air, but they required some serious shaping. Schriber roughed out the curves on a bandsaw and then pattern-shaped them with a router. Then he took them back to the bandsaw to taper them in thickness. Seen from the edge, the legs are thickest at the middle and thinner at the top and bottom. He turned the leg on its edge to make the cuts.

To begin shaping the pillowed sides, he tilted the bandsaw table to 45°, laid the legs on their face planes, and cut bevels along the cabriole curves. From there, the majority of the shaping was done with the legs hand-held against the spindle end of his edge sander. This technique left a series of facets that required smoothing with a balloon sander. He finished with a random-orbit sander fitted with a soft pad. Much of the shaping, Schriber

is by eye, "and calipers wouldn't find these legs identical. That's fine, though—and it's true of most all cabrioles."

Schriber had the aluminum case fabricated by a metal shop. To provide joinery for the legs, he had the shop fix metal pins to the case. The pins, three for each leg, were 1/4 in. dia. and protruded 1 in. from the case. Schriber drilled mating holes in the legs and fastened them to the case with epoxy.

HOW TO MAKE THE LEG

1. BANDSAW AND ROUT

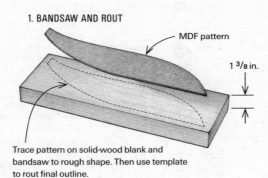

MDF pattern

1 3/8 in.

Trace pattern on solid-wood blank and bandsaw to rough shape. Then use template to rout final outline.

2. TAPER THE LEG PROFILE

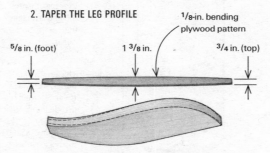

1/8-in. bending plywood pattern

5/8 in. (foot)   1 3/8 in.   3/4 in. (top)

Cut taper on bandsaw, rocking workpiece as needed, but leave pencil lines.

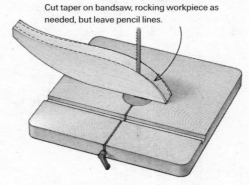

3. SHAPE THE FRONT EDGE
VIEW FROM BOTTOM

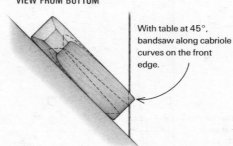

With table at 45°, bandsaw along cabriole curves on the front edge.

Smooth the edge first against a spindle sander, move to a balloon sander inflated soft, and then a random-orbit sander. Final sanding is done by hand.

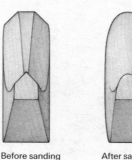

Before sanding   After sanding

Turn a Pad-Foot Leg

by Jon Siegel

There are many names for the furniture leg that's less elaborate than a cabriole but more complex than a simple taper. I've heard it called pad foot, spoon foot, and Dutch foot. By any name, it was most popular on Queen Anne tables and lowboys. It also can complement Federal or Shaker-inspired furniture.

Unlike cabriole legs, pad-foot legs are produced entirely on the lathe, with no bandsaw work beforehand or hand-finishing afterward.

Making a pad-foot leg involves multi-axis turning—that is, using two pairs of center points. The leg is partially turned while mounted in one pair of centers, then moved to the second pair to finish.

One pair falls at the true center of each end of the leg blank. The second pair is offset in from the true centers in two directions by a fraction of an inch at the bottom of the leg, and a smaller fraction at the top. The two axes—that is, the imaginary lines connecting the centers—cross at a transition point. That's usually at the base of the pommel, the square section that receives the mortises for a table apron or the carcase of a chest.

Accurate Layout Is Critical

To produce these legs, you must precisely locate the two sets of center points and the transition point. That involves careful marking and a little arithmetic.

For the leg shown here, begin with 8/4 stock, milled to about 1 7/8 in. square. (I prefer maple, but any hardwood will do.) A blank that size will give you a well-proportioned leg for many tables. The leg will measure 1 3/4 in. dia. at the widest part of the foot (that's the line defining the toe), and 3/4 in. dia. at the ankle, where the leg is narrowest. The square pommel can be whatever length suits your design.

To find the true center at each end of the blank, I normally use a marking gauge, but for these legs I use a center square because it gives me diagonal lines for the next stage of layout. Don't just connect opposite corners, because that method is not accurate enough. If you use the center square at each corner, the lines will create a tiny square in the center. Punch a hole in the center of this square.

Next, evaluate the appearance of each of the faces, and choose the outside corner where the best faces meet. Make a distinct mark for reference on the inside corner; that will help you orient the offset centers.

To locate the offset centers, you need to know two radii (for the ankle and the foot) and two lengths (for the square pommel and the turned section).

To calculate the offset at the bottom of the leg, subtract the radius of the ankle from the radius of the foot. Measure that distance from the true center along the diagonal pointing to the inside corner, and punch a hole.

The offset at the top of the leg will be a fraction of the offset at the bottom. The fraction is the ratio of the pommel length to the turned length. That is, if the pommel is 6 in. and the turned section 18 in., the ratio is 1 to 3. That means the top offset will be one-third the length of the bottom offset. Measure from the true center along the diagonal pointing to the outside corner and punch another hole.

Finally, draw a dark pencil line to mark the length of the pommel and locate the transition point for the turning. If you mark all four faces of the leg blank, it will be easier to see the transition point when the blank is turning on the lathe.

Begin Turning On the Offset Centers

Mount the blank on the offset center points, with the top of the leg at the headstock. Start the lathe and look carefully at the shadow lines—the multiple images you see as the blank spins eccentrically. Be sure there's only one shadow line at the transition point—the mark you made for the length of the pommel. To tweak the alignment, shut off

Continued ➡

the lathe and tap the blank near one end to shift it slightly on its centers. Be sure to tighten the blank again so it won't wobble.

Use a 5/8-in. skew with its long point down to make the transition cut. Cut about 1/8 in. to 1/4 in. deeper than the flats on the square pommel.

Move to the foot, where you'll see two shadow lines. Use a 3/4-in. roughing gouge to cut down to within 1/8 in.

of the second shadow line (see photo). Because the blank is turning off-center, you'll round off only one corner. Mark a line to locate the height of the foot.

Next, use a 5/8-in. or 1/2-in. spindle gouge to shape the curve that forms the ankle and the flare at the toe. Begin these cuts well to the left of where you want the toe and widen the curve as you make it deeper. Use calipers to check the diameter at the ankle.

Finally, use the roughing gouge to taper the leg from transition to ankle. Steady the blank with your free hand as you cut, a technique that also allows you to feel any irregularities in the taper. Use a straightedge to check that the taper is even when you make the final smoothing cuts. When this part of the turning is completed, sand it before going on to the next step. I like to use broken P100- and P120-grit sanding belts for the first pass, then finish to at least P220 grit.

Start with Careful Layout

The most important step in turning a pad-foot leg is locating the offset centers on the blank. It's easiest to begin with the offset at the foot, then mark the offset at the top.

1. Mark the pommel. This defines the transition line where the two axes intersect. Marking all four faces will help you see the line when the leg is turning.

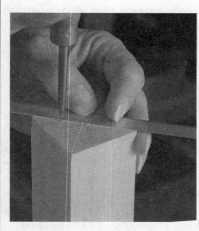

2. Mark the bottom offset. Measure from the true center toward the inside corner of the leg.

3. Mark the top offset. Measure from the true center along the diagonal pointing to the outside corner of the leg for this offset point.

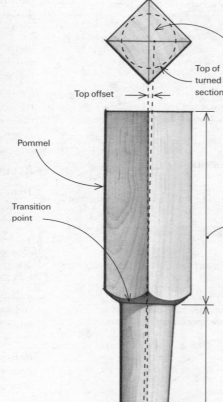

Top of turned section

Top offset

Pommel

Transition point

The offset at the top is a fraction of the bottom offset. To determine the fraction, calculate the ratio of the pommel length to the length of the turned section. It's 1:3 for a 6-in. pommel and an 18-in. turned section. So, in that example, the top offset will be one-third of the bottom offset.

The length of the pommel is one factor in determining the location of the offset centers. The pommel also affects the leg's overall proportions.

Turned section

Offset axis

True axis

The foot is centered on the leg's true center and should be as close as possible to the blank's rough dimensions. To locate the bottom offset, subtract the radius of the ankle from the radius of the foot, and measure that distance on the appropriate diagonal.

Ankle — Toe

Bottom offset — Foot

Ankle

Finish on the True Centers

Mount the blank on the true centers. Use the 1/2-in. spindle gouge to shape the bottom of the foot, beginning at the toe. It's the same kind of cut you'd use to shape a bead. Round that part of the leg down so that it's between 3/4 in. and 1 in. dia. at the very bottom.

Lightly sand the foot, being careful not to blunt the sharp line that defines the toe.

If you've done everything correctly, that sharp line should blend smoothly into the taper at the back of the leg. If you see a bulge instead of a smooth taper, you can turn or sand it away, although that will reduce the diameter of the toe slightly.

SHAPE THE LEG

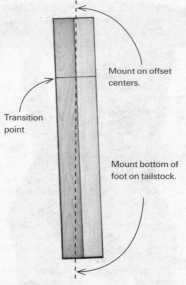

Mount on offset centers.

Transition point

Mount bottom of foot on tailstock.

1. Begin on offset centers. Most of the leg will be turned with the blank mounted askew. The bottom of the leg, with the greatest offset, goes on the tailstock.

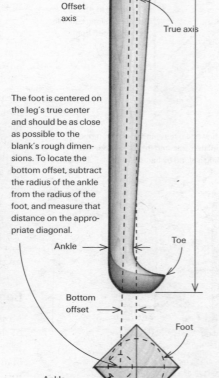

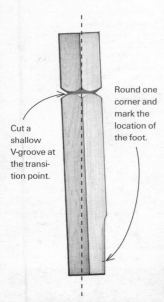

Cut a shallow V-groove at the transition point.

Round one corner and mark the location of the foot.

2. Cut the transition and mark the foot. Using a skew, cut a V-groove and slightly round the corners of the pommel. Next, you'll need to rough the foot area a bit to round one corner. Stop just short of the inner shadow line; the author's pointing to the spot you want, about 1/8 in. above the second shadow line. Now you can mark a line for the height of the toe.

Turn a large cove to form the top of the foot.

3. Watch the lines. A large cove cut forms the ankle and the top of the foot. Enlarge the cove until you reach the line marking the height of the toe.

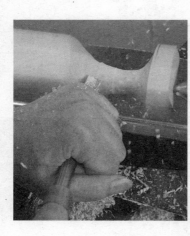

Turn the straight taper.

4. Cut the taper. When cutting, use your free hand to steady the blank. Check the line with a straightedge.

FINISH THE FOOT

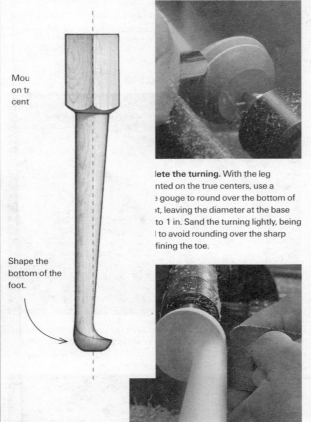

Mou[n]...
on t[r]...
cent...

...[ete] the turning. With the leg ...[mou]nted on the true centers, use a ...[round] gouge to round over the bottom of ...[the foo]t, leaving the diameter at the base ...to 1 in. Sand the turning lightly, being ...[carefu]l to avoid rounding over the sharp ...[re]fining the toe.

Shape the bottom of the foot.

VARIATIONS

Sample legs from Siegel's shop show the range of design options. Siegel's porringer table adapts one of those styles to a Queen Anne design. The legs are splayed slightly to compensate for the angle of the offset.

by Dan Faia

Ogee bracket feet, often linked to the Chippendale style, have been around since the late seventeenth century, and they remain one of the most recognized forms in furniture.

The distinctive S-curve on the faces (the ogee) and the ornate profiles on the ends of the feet traditionally were made with hand tools—a time-consuming, labor-intensive process. My method blends the best of the new and old. I've replaced the molding planes with the tablesaw to rough out the ogee profile, and the bandsaw has replaced the coping saw for cutting the end profile. However, machines can't replace the scrapers and other hand tools that are necessary to refine those machine-cut shapes.

Tablesaw Takes the Big Bites

The front pairs of feet typically are mitered. To get the best possible grain match and flow, and for efficiency, start with a long blank, milled to the right size. You'll need a board long enough to make six pieces. You'll also need enough stock to make the unshaped portions of the rear pairs of feet, which are dovetailed together. Often these unshaped pieces were made of a secondary wood, because they were not seen.

The key to success is making a couple of full-size patterns out of 1/8-in.-thick plywood, which will guide both machine and handwork. I use one pattern to draw the ogee profile on each end of the blank. After the ogee shaping is complete, I use another pattern to lay out the miters and to draw the profile on the inside of the foot.

For speed and consistency, I shape the face of the long blank on the tablesaw, using a cove-cutting technique. This is done by passing the piece diagonally across the blade, guided by an auxiliary fence, and raising the blade a bit more for each pass. You can use any straight material for the fence, as long as it's thick enough to support the workpiece. The fence I made is simply two 3/4-in.-thick strips of MDF. After screwing the pieces together, I ripped both long edges straight. I don't use a special blade for the cove cut; it's just a combination blade.

Because this cove cut is symmetrical, the blade will be perpendicular to the table (an asymmetrical cove would require the blade to be tilted). Start by raising the blade to the apex of the cove, using the pattern as the guide.

Now dial in the width of the cove by pivoting the auxiliary fence. Place the end of the pattern against the fence. To ensure accuracy, use the head of a combination square to keep the pattern 90° to the table and fence. With your eyes level with the table, pivot the fence until the blade aligns with the cutout on the pattern. Clamp the fence in place and make a test cut.

To do that, lower the blade so it projects about 1/16 in. above the table. Make the first pass or two and then compare the cut to the pattern you traced on the end of the blank. Because you're taking such light cuts, any errors in the setup are easily corrected by adjusting the fence as you go. Continue making passes over the blade, raising it about 1/16 in. at a time, until you're cutting the full depth of the cove.

Once the cove has been cut, it's time to create the convex (top) portion of the foot on the blank. This job is started at the tablesaw, with the blank on edge. Tilt the blade to remove the bulk of the waste in one pass. Then readjust the blade angle to creep up on the layout line with smaller passes. You'll end up with a faceted surface.

Hand Tools Heal the Tablesaw Scars

Following the layout lines on the end of the blank, I clean up the machine marks on the blank and refine the curves.

To shape the convex portion, I use No. 5 (jack) and No. 4 (smoother) planes, gradually removing the table-sawn facets to create a smooth curve. To smooth the concave area, I use a gooseneck scraper and sandpaper.

Continued ➡

Finally, I sand all the curves smooth. Once the face is complete, you can start cutting the individual feet from the blank and mitering them.

Accurate Miters Are a Must

True to the period forms, I typically miter the front pairs of feet, but I use half-blind dovetails in the rear pairs. The dovetail is a strong way to join the thin, flat back piece to the shaped piece.

To ensure a continuous grain match around the feet on the front, it's important to lay out the parts in pairs. When laying out the parts, leave extra material on the straight-cut ends. This will give you room to make test cuts until you have perfect-fitting miters.

Once the miters are cut, trim all the feet to their final length using the inside profile pattern as a guide. Now cut the dovetails in the rear pairs of feet: tails in the flat feet and sockets in the molded feet. Don't glue any of the feet together yet.

Profile the Feet Before Assembly

Once the joinery is done, lay out and cut the inside profiles on the feet. Use the full-size pattern to draw the design, and bandsaw close to the lines. Now glue the feet together—both the miters and the dovetails. For the miters, I use clamping cauls that direct the clamping pressure to the corners. I also seal, or size, the porous end grain with glue before assembly. Don't rush here. The glue must dry completely to adequately seal the end grain; otherwise, the joint will be compromised.

It may seem counterintuitive to glue the feet before fairing the end profiles, but doing so makes it easier to clamp the feet in a vise for the final shaping.

After the glue dries, fair the inside profile. First, I remove most of the bandsaw marks with rasps and files. Then I use gouges and chisels to back-cut the shapes at a slight angle. The back-cut makes it easier to finesse only the visible portion of the profile in front with rasps and files. I also break the inside edges by chamfering them with a chisel.

The final step is to add reinforcing corner blocks to the inside of the feet. The blocks strengthen the miter and add to the overall glue surface for attaching the feet to a base frame. Here's a trick to avoid a potential problem with cross-grain glue surfaces on the vertical section. I cut a series of small glue blocks and stack them, alternating the grain direction of the blocks. This creates a super-strong block assembly that will remain stable over time. No need to clamp any of the glue blocks in place; a simple rub joint will do the trick.

After the glue dries on the blocks, I trim the vertical pieces flush, then chisel a slight chamfer on the outside corner to make sure the pieces can't be seen by any probing eyes. Now the feet are ready to mount to the case.

1. CARVE OUT THE COVE ON THE TABLESAW

Reference lines. Use a full-size pattern to lay out the face profile on each end of the blank. You'll reference those lines as you rough out and refine the profile.

Eyeball it. Raise the blade to the apex of the cove. Then pivot the fence to set the cove's width, using the head of a combination square to keep the pattern 90° to the fence and table. Once you're there, clamp down the fence.

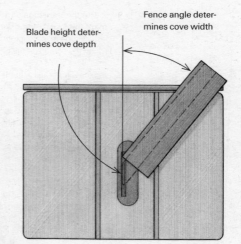

Blade height determines cove depth

Fence angle determines cove width

Nibble away. Start with the blade about 1/16 in. above the table. Then make multiple passes over the blade, raising it in 1/16-in. increments, until you've removed as much waste as possible.

2. FINISH THE CURVES

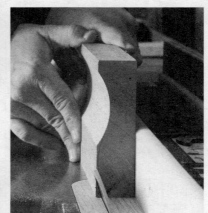

Stay at the tablesaw. A few bevel cuts rough out the rest of the profile. Using the layout lines on the end of the blank as a reference, take multiple passes to remove the waste, adjusting the angle as you work. You'll end up with a faceted surface.

Hand tools take over. Use handplanes to fair the faceted surfaces made by the tablesaw. A gooseneck scraper works quickly in the cove area. Finish with sandpaper.

3. CUT THE JOINTS AND PROFILE THE ENDS

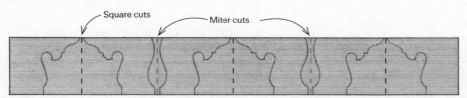

Square cuts — Miter cuts

How to get a great grain match. You want the grain at the miters to flow seamlessly around the corner, so lay out the blank as shown. Note that the parts on the ends are the back feet, which are left square.

Perfect miters. Leave the mitered sections extra long, so you can creep up on a perfect fit. Then cut the feet to length.

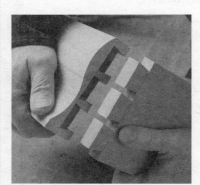

Dovetails in back. Because the rear of the case was not seen, period makers didn't bother to shape the back pieces. Those flat parts join to the shaped side pieces with dovetails.

Cut the inside profile. First trim the feet to length. Then trace the pattern onto the back of each foot, aligning the inside edge of the pattern with the square-cut end. Cut the profile at the bandsaw. Work carefully—clean cuts here mean less work later.

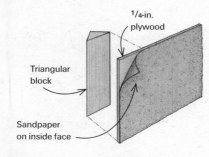

4. GLUE AND FINE-TUNE THE FEET

1/4-in. plywood

Triangular block

Sandpaper on inside face

Pinpoint clamping. Faia uses a pair of simple clamping cauls to apply pressure directly on the miter. Start by clamping the cauls to the mitered parts. Then clamp across the triangular blocks to bring the joint together firmly and evenly.

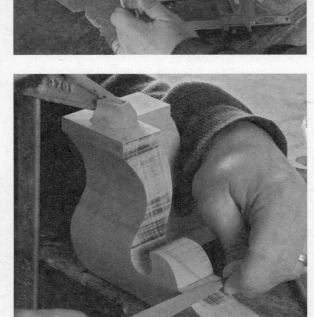

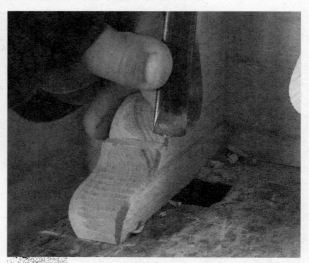

Cleanup work. First remove sawmarks using rasps and files . Use gouges to back-cut the edges slightly, then go back and refine only the outside profile using rasps and files. Finally, chamfer the inside edges with a chisel. It's OK to leave unseen, inside surfaces rough.

Continued ➜

Quench Thirsty Miters

End grain soaks up glue quickly, drawing it from the surfaces and weakening the joint. The solution is to seal the end grain with an initial coat of glue, a process called "sizing." Let the glue absorb for a minute or two, then wipe it off with a rag moistened with water. Let the pieces dry completely before applying more glue and clamping them.

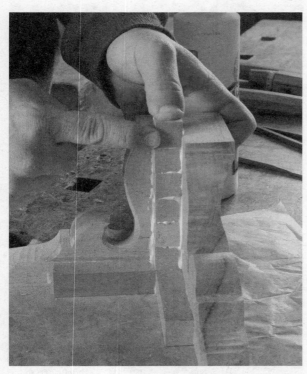

Reinforce the corners. To strengthen the miters, add glue blocks to the back of the feet. No need for clamps here; a rub joint works fine. Rub each block until the glue grabs and holds it.

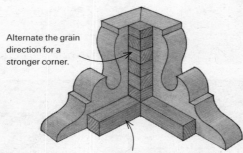

Alternate the grain direction for a stronger corner.

Include long blocks for gluing or screwing the feet to the case.

Chamfer when dry. A wide chamfer helps hide the glue blocks.

462

Projects

Illustrated Guide to Drawers

by Matthew Teague

Whether it's a tiny drawer in a jewelry box or the wide, deep drawer of a dresser, all drawers are little more than a box that slides into an opening. But there are nearly endless combinations of construction methods that can be used to build that box. By understanding the various ways in which drawers are made, you'll be able to choose the best construction method for your project, with the ideal blend of beauty, strength, and efficiency.

Drawers can be made of solid wood, plywood, or both. Drawer fronts often become the focal points of a piece, showing off spectacular figure, molded edges, or a handsome pull. The actual drawer front can be integral to the drawer, meaning that it is joined directly to the drawer sides, or it can be attached to a fully constructed drawer box. Joinery options at both the back and front can range from simple butt joints to classic hand-cut dovetails. Drawer bottoms can be made from solid wood or plywood.

To size a drawer correctly, you need to know not only the size of the opening, but also the depth of the inset. Drawers can be designed flush to, recessed into, or overlapping the front of the case.

Different styles of furniture call for different types of drawers. While a plywood drawer with a false front makes sense in a shop cabinet, it would be quite out of place in a high-style eighteenth-century reproduction. The joinery and materials you choose should fit the type of furniture you want to build. So should the way the drawer will slide in and out of its pocket. So let's start there.

Drawer Slides Influence Design and Construction

Like all drawer decisions, drawer-slide options range from simple and efficient to finely handcrafted. Traditionally, the sides of a wooden drawer slide directly on a wooden frame within the case. Most drawers with integral fronts work well with this design because the drawer is sized and constructed to fit the opening.

Manufactured drawer slides have long been common on kitchen cabinets, but they're being used more and more on high-end furniture today. Although frowned upon by some purists, contemporary slide designs install quickly and painlessly, and it's difficult to find fault with their smooth action, soft-close mechanisms, and full-extension capability. These slides can be side- or bottom-mounted, and are perfect for use with false-front drawers or drawers with sliding dovetails.

Each type of commercial slide has its own drawer requirements, so you'll have to build the drawer to accommodate the slides. For instance, side-mounted slides typically require $1/2$ in. of space on both sides of the drawer box. If you're using commercial slides, it's a good idea to have them on hand before you build either the case or the drawers.

Front Joints Are the Critical Ones

Regardless of whether a drawer has an integral front or a false front, most pulling and racking stresses on a drawer box occur at the front corners; after all, a drawer is opened and closed by pulling and pushing on the front. Any action that isn't straight in or out of the drawer pocket also causes racking stress, which hits the front-corner joints hardest.

For these reasons, front-corner joints should be as strong as possible and have some mechanical reinforcement. This mechanical connection can be as simple as pegs or pins in a rabbet joint, or it can be the interlocking strength of the classic half-blind dovetail.

While it's also important to have a sound mechanical joint at the back of the drawer, aesthetics are less of a concern because these corners are rarely seen. For these reasons, rear-corner joints often are different from the front-corner joints. If you are using a machine setup to cut the front joinery, however, it makes sense to use those same setups to cut the back joinery.

Drawer Bottoms: Fancy or Functional

The choice of material and the design of the drawer bottom depend on the style of drawer you are building, whether it's a quick-and-dirty shop drawer or a drawer for an 18th-century secretary.

Both solid wood and plywood are commonly used for drawer bottoms. Solid wood is the traditional choice, and aesthetically, it's hard to beat. But you must allow solid wood to expand and contract with changes in humidity so that it doesn't cause the drawer to bind in its opening.

Plywood is a much more stable choice for a drawer bottom because it does not expand and contract with humidity changes as much as solid wood. Although reproduction builders and a few purists resist plywood bottoms, it's easy to argue their superiority. A plywood bottom can be housed completely in grooves in the sides, back, and front, and glued in place to strengthen the drawer box. Or it can be slid in from the rear and screwed to the drawer back, or even glued and nailed to the bottom of a drawer box with a false front.

Integral-Front Drawers

A traditional drawer is built with the front joined directly to the sides. This is the most lightweight and attractive design overall. Aim for drawer sides that are half to one-third the thickness of the front. Once the drawer has been assembled, the sides often must be planed or sanded carefully so the drawer fits in the opening. In most of these examples, the joinery is hidden from the front for a clean look.

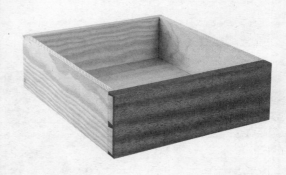

Rabbet should be half to two-thirds as thick as the drawer front.

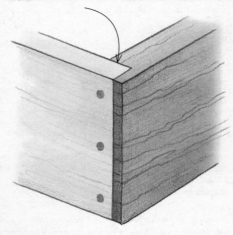

PINNED RABBET

The rabbet is easy to make, but it's not very strong. It should be reinforced with some kind of fastener, such as recessed screws, cut copper nails, or wooden dowels or pegs, which offer a clean, handmade look. With this style of construction, the back of the drawer usually is set into simple dadoes in the drawer sides.

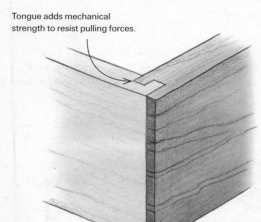

Tongue adds mechanical strength to resist pulling forces.

TONGUE AND RABBET

Although it takes a few more tool setups, a half-blind tongue and rabbet adds built-in mechanical strength (beyond glue alone) to the joint. Dado or dadoed rabbet joints are suitable options for the back of the drawer.

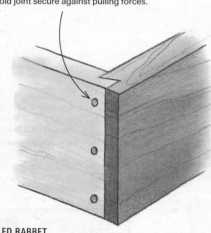

Pins hold joint secure against pulling forces.

DOVETAILED RABBET

A dovetailed rabbet is stronger and more attractive than a simple rabbet joint. This type of corner joint also should be reinforced with pegs, brads, or some kind of mechanical fastener. The rear joints can be rabbeted dadoes or sliding dovetail joints.

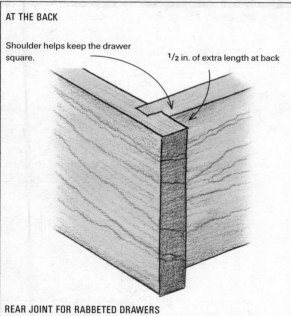

AT THE BACK

Shoulder helps keep the drawer square.

½ in. of extra length at back

REAR JOINT FOR RABBETED DRAWERS

A rabbeted dado is an easy and effective means of attaching the back to the sides, plus it helps keep the drawer square. Leaving the sides long at the back allows the drawer to be pulled out farther, providing better access.

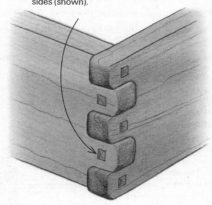

Joint can be reinforced with pegs at the top and bottom, or through the front or sides (shown).

BOX JOINT

The box joint is the beefier, more handsome cousin of the finger joint, and it's quite comfortable at the front of a piece of furniture. The design seen here, reminiscent of Greene-and-Greene construction, features wide fingers with rounded corners. Square, pillowed pegs reinforce the joint and add visual interest. If you're using box joints at the front of a drawer, it's efficient to use them at the back, too, though the fingers should not protrude.

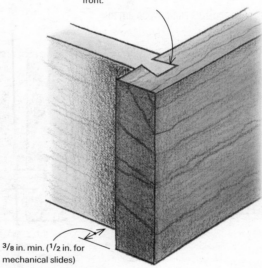

Tail portion, or key, should extend at least halfway into the drawer front.

³⁄₈ in. min. (¹⁄₂ in. for mechanical slides)

SLIDING DOVETAIL

The sliding dovetail has built-in mechanical strength to keep it together. It offers a quick, strong joinery option, but requires the drawer front to overhang the sides a bit. So it usually is used either on drawers designed with overlay fronts or on flush drawers that ride on mechanical slides or are fitted between wood guides in the case.

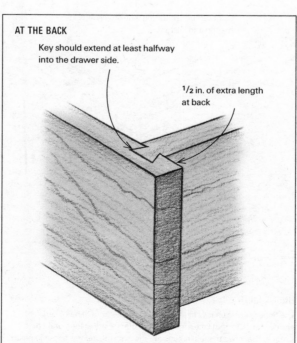

AT THE BACK

Key should extend at least halfway into the drawer side.

½ in. of extra length at back

REAR JOINT FOR SLIDING-DOVETAIL DRAWERS

If you're using sliding dovetails to join the front of the drawer, it's efficient to use the same joints to attach the back. Leaving the sides long at the back will give you access to the full depth of the drawer when it's open.

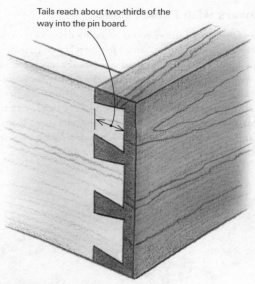

Tails reach about two-thirds of the way into the pin board.

HALF-BLIND DOVETAIL

Many regard the half-blind version as the king of dovetail joints because of its attractiveness and superior strength. To highlight the craftsmanship, many furniture makers use contrasting woods on the front and sides. Through-dovetails are easier to cut than half-blinds, so the former are the usual choice for the rear corners.

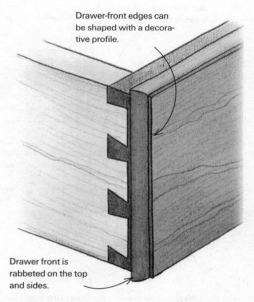

Drawer-front edges can be shaped with a decorative profile.

Drawer front is rabbeted on the top and sides.

LIPPED HALF-BLIND DOVETAIL

For overlay drawers with excellent strength, use lipped half-blind dovetails. With this joint, the front is rabbeted and joined to the sides with dovetails. Again, through-dovetails are a good option for the rear-corner joints.

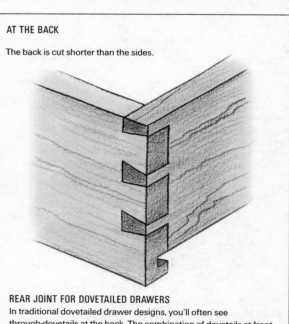

AT THE BACK

The back is cut shorter than the sides.

REAR JOINT FOR DOVETAILED DRAWERS

In traditional dovetailed drawer designs, you'll often see through-dovetails at the back. The combination of dovetails at front and back creates a sturdy drawer that will last a lifetime. The pin board typically is cut shorter than the sides to allow the drawer bottom to be slid in after the rest of the box is assembled.

Continued ➡

Drawers with False Fronts

Using false fronts allows you to separate drawer construction from drawer fitting, which ultimately makes both processes easier. With this method, the drawer box is glued up and installed in its opening. Then the false front is cut to size, applied to the box temporarily, adjusted for a perfect reveal (the gap between the drawer and the case), and then permanently attached to the box. These drawers are ideal for use with manufactured slides, which typically require 1/2 in. of space on each side of the drawer box.

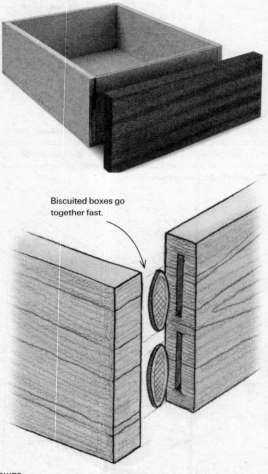

Biscuited boxes go together fast.

BISCUITS

Biscuits offer a quick, strong option to join the sides to the front of a drawer. Once a false front is applied, the end-grain (or plywood) ends of the drawer sides are completely concealed. This joinery system is a good option for kitchen cabinets, built-in units, and utility drawers. Biscuits also can be used to join the back of the drawer to the sides.

Drawer Bottom Options

Solid wood and plywood are the most common materials used for drawer bottoms. A solid-wood panel will expand and contract with humidity changes, so it must be sized and installed to allow for that movement. A plywood bottom offers a more stable (and simple) option, but traditionalists see it as thin and bland. Plywood's stability, however, gives a furniture maker more options when it comes to drawer design.

SOLID WOOD IS ELEGANT, BUT IT MOVES

Traditionally, solid-wood panels slide into place after the sides, front, and back of the drawer have been assembled. The back is cut shorter, allowing you to slide the bottom in place, and the bottom is screwed to the back through an elongated hole to allow for wood movement. Building a drawer in this way allows you to take it apart for repairs.

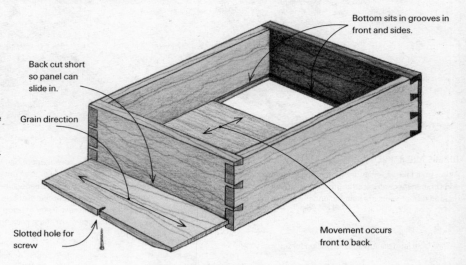

Bottom sits in grooves in front and sides.

Back cut short so panel can slide in.

Grain direction

Slotted hole for screw

Movement occurs front to back.

THREE EDGE PROFILES FOR A WOOD BOTTOM

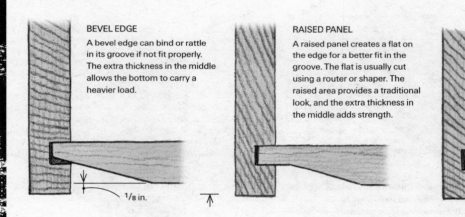

BEVEL EDGE
A bevel edge can bind or rattle in its groove if not fit properly. The extra thickness in the middle allows the bottom to carry a heavier load.

1/8 in.

RAISED PANEL
A raised panel creates a flat on the edge for a better fit in the groove. The flat is usually cut using a router or shaper. The raised area provides a traditional look, and the extra thickness in the middle adds strength.

RABBETED
A rabbeted bottom is easier to make, yet offers the same strength as a beveled or raised panel. Watching the gap around the rabbeted edge makes it easy to keep the drawer square during assembly.

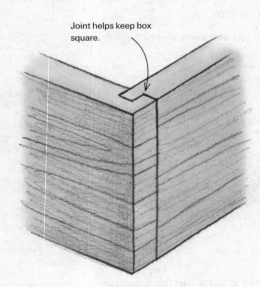

Joint helps keep box square.

DADOED RABBET

The dadoed rabbet offers a strong mechanical connection at the front of the drawer box, but it's not very attractive. Attaching a false front to the drawer in this case gives the option more appeal. Simple dadoes or tongue-and-rabbet joints are suitable options for the rear joints in this style of drawer construction.

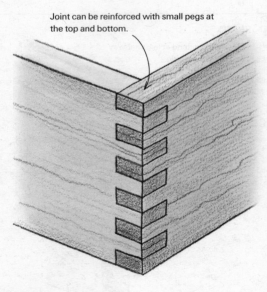

Joint can be reinforced with small pegs at the top and bottom.

FINGER JOINT

The finger joint is usually hidden behind a false front. It has a series of narrow knuckles that lace together and offer plenty of long-grain glue surfaces. Because the tool setups are the same, if you use finger joints at the front of a drawer, use them at the back, too.

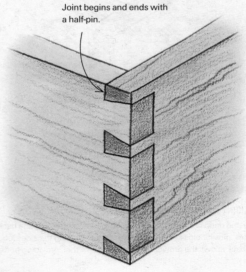

Joint begins and ends with a half-pin.

THROUGH-DOVETAIL

The angled tails and pins of a through-dovetail create a secure joint that resists pulling and racking forces. If you're cutting through-dovetails by machine (with or without a router jig), it's usually efficient to employ the same joint at the back of the drawer.

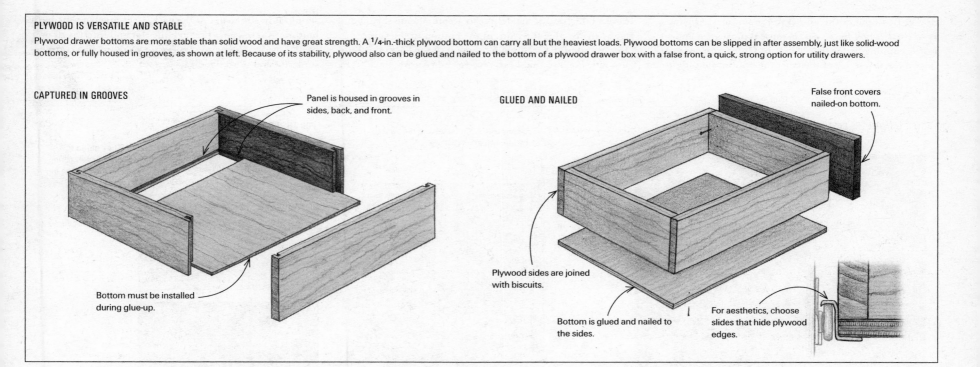

PLYWOOD IS VERSATILE AND STABLE

Plywood drawer bottoms are more stable than solid wood and have great strength. A ¼-in.-thick plywood bottom can carry all but the heaviest loads. Plywood bottoms can be slipped in after assembly, just like solid-wood bottoms, or fully housed in grooves, as shown at left. Because of its stability, plywood also can be glued and nailed to the bottom of a plywood drawer box with a false front, a quick, strong option for utility drawers.

CAPTURED IN GROOVES

Panel is housed in grooves in sides, back, and front.

Bottom must be installed during glue-up.

GLUED AND NAILED

False front covers nailed-on bottom.

Plywood sides are joined with biscuits.

Bottom is glued and nailed to the sides.

For aesthetics, choose slides that hide plywood edges.

Build Drawers That Fit

by Rob Porcaro

You don't need to know any mysterious art passed down from a master to fit a drawer successfully. All you need is a logical process. And that's what I'd like to share with you. I've distilled what I've learned through the years into a clear path that guarantees success. The key is that it eliminates—rather than compounds—errors as you move through the steps.

I start with an old cabinetmaker's trick: I taper the width of the drawer pocket slightly. Then I fit the drawer front to its opening. It's easy to take that one board and plane its ends and edges so that it fits perfectly into the opening, even if the opening itself is slightly out of square. I then make the sides and back to match the front. There's nothing new about these steps. But after them, I do one thing that will be new to some of you. Instead of marking and cutting my dovetails so that the pins are proud, I leave the drawer sides slightly proud. That makes gluing the drawer together much easier and takes all the hassle out of fitting it. All you need to do is plane the sides down to the pins and the drawer slides right in.

Taper the Pocket

A drawer fits into a pocket. And you won't get a truly good fit for the drawer unless you take care when making the pocket. They can be made in variety of ways and from a variety of materials. No matter how you do it, I've got a tip that makes the pocket a perfect partner for the drawer.

The pocket should be slightly wider at the back than at the front—about ¹⁄₆₄ in. How that's accomplished depends upon how the case is made. For a cabinet with solid-wood sides dovetailed into a top and bottom, I assemble the piece dry, use a shopmade bar gauge to measure the front of the pocket, and then slide it to the back to see how wide it is in relation to the front. I then disassemble the case and use a handplane to remove a few shavings, typically from the back. For a plywood cabinet, you would simply make the back panel of the cabinet a hair longer/wider than the face frame. The exact process might vary, but the result will be the same: a slightly wider pocket at the back.

Fit the Drawer Front to Its Opening

After you have the cabinet assembled, mill the drawer front to near final thickness and rip it to width. It should be just narrow enough to fit the height of the opening. Then crosscut it about ¹⁄₃₂ in. larger than the opening's width. Now turn off the machines and get out your shooting board and handplane. They offer a level of precision and control that let you easily sneak up on the perfect fit.

That's important because this is incremental work. The way to get a perfect fit is to remove a shaving at a time. And a shooting board lets you angle the drawer front a bit so that you can plane the end to match a pocket that's slightly out of square.

Plane the bottom edge of the drawer front to remove milling marks and to ensure that it is straight and square. Next, register it against your shooting board's fence and plane the left end of the drawer front. It should be parallel to the left side of the drawer pocket. If the opening is out of square, place a shim between the shooting board's fence and the drawer front. Check your progress frequently.

After the left end has been fitted, it's time to get really careful. Fitting the right end is a critical step. If you take too much off or the end isn't parallel to the side of the opening, the fit will be sloppy and you'll need to start over. As you did with the left end, shoot the right end until it's parallel to the right side of the pocket and the front barely makes it into the opening. The fit should be very snug at this point.

Now it's time to plane the top edge, keeping it parallel to the top of the opening. Don't worry if it's no longer parallel to the bottom edge. It doesn't need to be. As for the size of the gap at the top, it needs to be large enough to accommodate seasonal movement, but don't guess at how much movement to expect. Rather, consult something like the Lee Valley Wood Movement Reference Guide (leevalley.com, No. 50K24.01) or an online wood-movement calculator to determine it precisely.

Prep the Other Parts and Cut the Dovetails

The drawer sides and back are next. I prefer straight-grained, quartersawn stock for the sides and back, because it is more stable than flatsawn. I typically make the sides slightly greater than half the thickness of the front, but I make the back just a bit thinner than the front for stronger joints and to help balance the drawer as you pull it out. It also is a good idea to orient the grain on the sides so that they can be planed cleanly from front to back after assembly. If you plane the sides from back to front, you might blow out the end grain on the drawer front.

Rip both sides so that they are as tall as their mating ends on the drawer front. Now crosscut them a bit longer than final length. Head back to the shooting board and square up both ends (bring them to their final length in the process), registering the bottom edge against the fence. Rip the back slightly wider than its final dimension, and then crosscut it a bit long. Shoot its ends to match those of the front, making it the same length or a hair longer, but never shorter.

I use dovetails to join the parts: half-blinds up front,

and through in the back. This article isn't about cutting dovetails, so I'll spare you a detailed explanation. However, there is one step that is critical to my fitting process. When laying out the pins, set your marking gauge just a hair shallower than the thickness of the tails. The sides will be proud after assembly, but you'll plane them flush to ends of the drawer front.

Now, glue together the drawer. That couldn't be easier. Because the sides are proud of the front and back, no clamping cauls are needed if you're using parallel jaw clamps. If you're not using them, use a straight caul—no need to shape it to fit around the pins—to spread pressure across the entire joint.

A Few Quick Shavings and the Drawer Slides in Like a Piston

After the glue has dried, take off the clamps and get your handplane ready for action. Planing drawer sides can be tricky, because vises don't hold assembled drawers very well. So, I use a simple jig made from a piece of ¾-in.-thick MDF. It has notches cut deep enough to hold the widest drawer and spaced so that you can plane the sides and front. I clamp the jig between benchdogs and then slide the drawer into the notches. (If you don't have benchdogs, just use a piece of MDF wide enough to be clamped down at the back of the bench.) The side is supported by the MDF, so you have a good flat surface for planing. But the drawer isn't clamped in, so you can quickly move from one drawer side to the other, and from one drawer to the next.

Plane down the sides until they are level with the ends of the front. At this point, the drawer will barely fit inside the pocket, because the front was already fit snugly to it (and the back was made to match). You'll probably need to take another shaving or two to fine-tune the fit. Before doing that, put the drawer on a flat surface, such as your tablesaw, and check that it sits flat, without any twist. Plane any high spots until it does. Now you are ready to fine-tune the drawer's fit. Slide it into the pocket to get a sense of how tight it is. Pull it out and take a few conservative shavings from both sides. That should be enough for the drawer to gently swish back into its opening, but keep in mind the season in which you're working. If it's winter, which can be quite dry, you should take a few extra shavings from the sides. Experience has taught me that the sides can get slightly thicker in more humid weather, which is enough to bind the drawer.

Now it's on to the bottom. You might not think that making the bottom is part of fitting the drawer, but if you get it wrong it could fall out in the winter or push the

Continued ➜

drawer front out of the pocket in the summer. Quater-sawn stock is best here, too, because it moves less and resists cupping better than flatsawn. Unless you are working on the driest day of the year, the bottom should extend beyond the back of the drawer to accommodate shrinkage. I lightly glue the front of the bottom into its groove, forcing all of the seasonal movement to the back. But I do use hide glue, so that I can reverse and remove the bottom should it need repair. At the back, I cut opened slots in the bottom. A screw goes through the slot and into the drawer back. I use washer-head screws, but you can cut a counter-sunk slot and use a flat-head screw, too.

STEP 1. TAPER THE CASE...

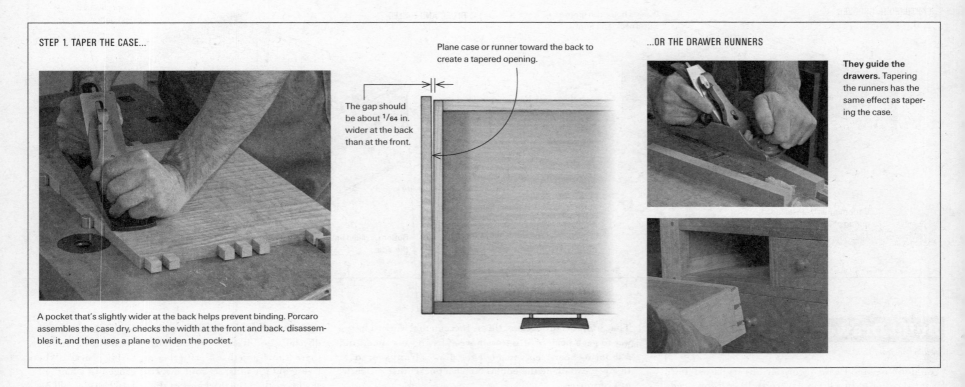

Plane case or runner toward the back to create a tapered opening.

The gap should be about 1/64 in. wider at the back than at the front.

...OR THE DRAWER RUNNERS

They guide the drawers. Tapering the runners has the same effect as tapering the case.

A pocket that's slightly wider at the back helps prevent binding. Porcaro assembles the case dry, checks the width at the front and back, disassembles it, and then uses a plane to widen the pocket.

STEP 2. FIT THE DRAWER FRONT

Get this part right and the rest of the drawer is no problem, because it is built to match. As a result, the drawer fits nicely with very little planing after the glue is dry. You'll need a shooting board..

1. The bottom edge is a reference for fitting the ends. Plane away any machine marks, keeping it straight and square as you do.

2. Plane the left end of the front parallel to the left side of the pocket.

3. Then do the same for the right end.

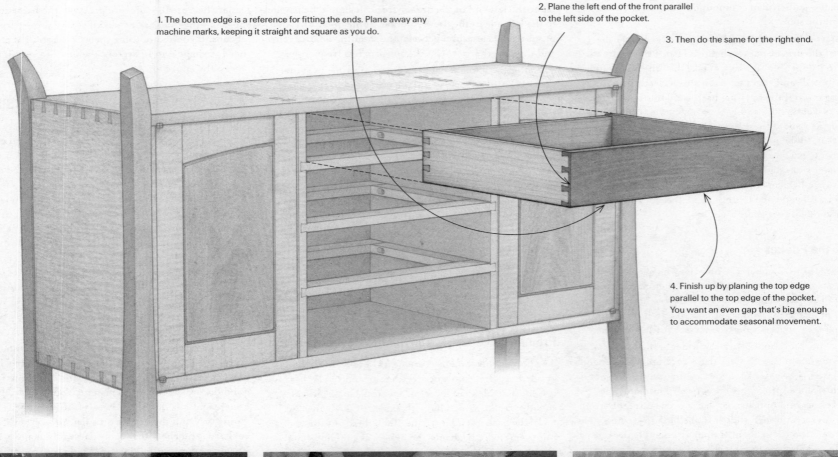

4. Finish up by planing the top edge parallel to the top edge of the pocket. You want an even gap that's big enough to accommodate seasonal movement.

1. Clean up the bottom edge. This is your reference edge, so you don't want to touch it again.

2. Shoot the left end. Put the bottom edge of the drawer front against the shooting board's fence. Porcaro has shimmed it with a piece of tape because the opening isn't square. That brings the end of the drawer front parallel to the side of the pocket.

3. Now fit for length. Trim the right end just like the left, parallel to the opening. At this point, the fit should be tight.

4. Plane the top edge, too. Porcaro uses his shooting board to ensure that the edge stays square.

STEP 3. LEAVE THE SIDES PROUD WHEN DOVETAILING

The front already fits the opening snugly. To avoid removing too much from the pins when cleaning up the joint after assembly, leave the sides proud and plane them flush.

Leave the pins a little short. Set your gauge about 1/64 in. shy of the side's thickness, and use it to mark the tails' depth on the drawer front.

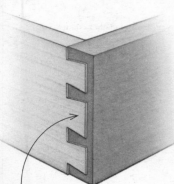

Another benefit of proud sides. Because the sides are proud of the pins, you don't need any special cauls, and that makes the glue-up less stressful.

Put clamp directly onto tails.

▶ TIP

How to Beat Squeeze-Out

To catch the squeeze-out in the inside corner, put a piece of blue tape on both parts of the joint. As soon as the glue sets, pull up the tape, leaving a clean corner.

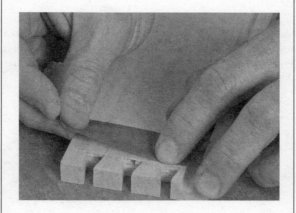

STEP 4. PLANE FOR A PERFECT FIT

Here's when you see the big payoff for fitting the drawer front first. After planing the sides down to the pins, it takes just a few more shavings for the drawer to fit nicely into the pocket.

Do the sides first. This simple jig holds the drawer box much better than a vise can for this job. It's a piece of 3/4-in.-thick MDF clamped between the benchdogs. The slots are spaced so the sides and the front and back can be planed. And you don't need to clamp the drawer in place.

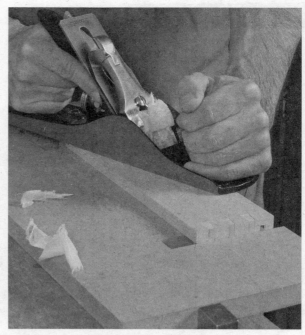

Plane front to back. Porcaro uses a jack plane (a smoother works, too), which is long enough to maintain a flat side. Because there is so little material to remove, he sets it for a light shaving.

Clean up the top edge. After planing the sides, take a few shavings from the top edge of the drawer front. Then plane the sides to match.

▶ TIP

Bottom Grain Goes Side to Side

This is a must on a solid-wood drawer bottom, so when it expands, it doesn't push out the sides, locking the drawer into the pocket or worse, breaking the joints.

467

A Guide to Drawer Pulls

by Matt Kenney

Drawers are made to be opened and closed, and that means every drawer needs a pull. And although attaching pulls is one of the last things you do when making a drawer, you can't wait until then to think about the style of pull you'll use and where on the drawer it will go. Because they are attached to the drawer fronts, pulls are highly visible and can have a dramatic effect on the beauty of a piece of furniture.

There's plenty to say about which types of pulls go with which pieces, but this article will focus on where to put them. Placing a pull on a drawer front is not as simple as "put it in the center." After all, it's not exactly clear how you center something like a pendant pull. And of course some drawers need two pulls, which should be spaced so that they are comfortable to use. Then there is the visual pattern created by the overall array of pulls, and that is determined mostly by how you size and orient the drawers themselves.

When I started to think about everything it takes to place pulls just right, I was overwhelmed. That's why I asked several successful furniture designers and makers for help. I not only learned some great basic guidelines, but also that there are situations you'll have to take one at a time.

Don't Always Center the Screws

Typically, pulls are centered vertically. How that is done depends on the pull's style. Because their height is balanced above and below the point of attachment, place knobs and handles by centering their screw holes or tenons. However, a pendant or bail pull would appear low on the drawer if centered this way. Instead, balance its overall outline above and below the drawer's centerline. It's the same for every other pull type: Think about the overall height, not just where the screw or tenon goes in.

One Pull Or Two?

SIMPLE ANSWER: DRAWER WIDTH DECIDES

Drawers less than 14 in. wide need only one pull because they are small enough to open and close by pulling or pushing on the center.

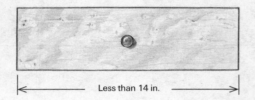

Less than 14 in.

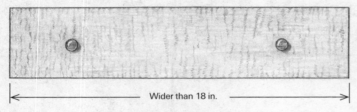

Wider than 18 in.

Drawers wider than 18 in. definitely need two pulls. A single, centered pull would be stressed by the weight of the drawer, eventually causing it to break or break free of the drawer front.

MAKE TWO PULLS COMFORTABLE TO USE

Space pulls between 18 in. and 22 in. apart, roughly the distance between a pair of outstretched hands. If the drawer is too narrow to space the pulls 18 in. apart, they should be separated by at least one-half of the drawer's width.

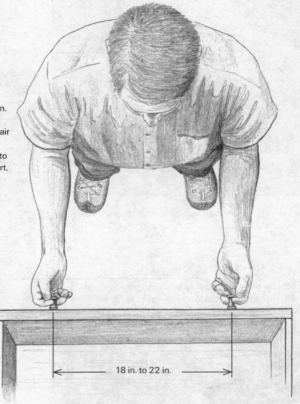

18 in. to 22 in.

ON MEDIUM-SIZE DRAWERS, CONSIDER THE WHOLE ARRAY

Between 14 in. and 18 in. is a gray area. The choice between one pull or two comes down to aesthetics.

BLAH   14 in.   BETTER

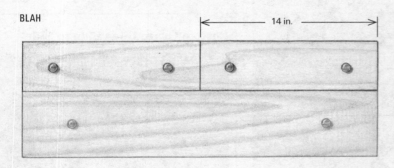

1. With two knobs on each of the small top drawers, this array looks top-heavy. Centering a single knob on each small drawer balances the pattern. It also brings the knobs on the top drawers closer together, creating two inward slanting diagonals, which suggests a solid base and upward movement.

2. A single, centered knob on the bottom drawer creates an inverted triangle and a top-heavy pattern. However, placing two knobs on the bottom drawer—and aligning them under the knobs on the top drawers—gives the array a more solid feel.

BLAH   BETTER

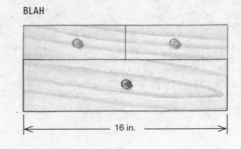

16 in.

NOW CONSIDER THE WHOLE PIECE

On a piece with multiple drawers, the number, size, and arrangement of the drawers affects how the pulls are arrayed. You'll have a better chance of integrating the array into the overall design if you begin to think about drawers and pulls as soon as you start to sketch out a piece.

STEPPED DRAWERS CREATE CONVERGING LINES

The stepped drawers on Hank Gilpin's sideboard (left)—narrower at the bottom than at the top—mirror the arc of the middle legs. By centering a single pull on the drawers in the two lower rows and placing two pulls on the center drawer in the top row, Gilpin uses the pulls to echo the arc as well. Garrett Hack used centered knobs to emphasize the stepped rise of the two outer columns of drawers on his sideboard (right).

LEARN FROM THE CLASSICS

Gerald Curry's reproduction of a Chippendale block-front chest of drawers (above) is a perfect example of how the arrangement of drawers affects the array formed by their pulls. The brasses on each drawer form an arc. Because the drawers are graduated, the most dramatic arc is at the bottom and the most gentle at the top. The tighter arc on the bottom drawer complements the arc suggested by the bracket base, and the more relaxed arc on the top drawer transitions nicely to the straight line of the top. Moreover, the series of arcs reinforces the strong, stable stance while drawing the eye upward at the same time.

RULES ARE MADE TO BE BROKEN

Michael Fortune knew the usual rules wouldn't work on this seven-drawer cabinet. If he had centered the pulls vertically (see drawing below), the lowest one would be too close to the floor and awkward to use. Also, while the pulls are nicely proportioned, on the large drawers they would appear lonely if centered vertically. So he positioned all of the pulls the same distance from the top of the drawer.

BLAH 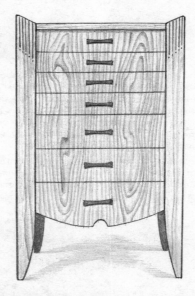 BETTER

Centered, but off-target. When centered vertically on the lower three drawer fronts, the delicate pulls get lost. Also, the column of pulls no longer enhances the graduation of the drawer fronts.

WHAT WORKS ON ONE HIGHBOY DOESN'T ON ANOTHER

On Jeffrey Greene's bonnet-top highboy (above), the pulls on the lower drawers are farther apart than the pulls on the two drawers in the top row. The pattern they create mirrors the lines of the piece created by the sides and the bonnet top. The same drawer arrangement doesn't work on a flat-top highboy (right). Adding a third drawer to the top row makes for a more successful pull array. The outer pulls on the top row are moved out, pulling the eye up and out toward the cornice, and the top two rows create an angle that mirrors the angled corner joint of the cornice. The top row also emphasizes the thinness of the piece's waist, making the pulls on the lower drawers appear closer together and balancing the three pulls on the bottom row of drawers. Note that the pulls on the lower half are directly in line with the knees, giving the base a wonderful grounded stance while drawing the eye up and into the waist. From there the eye is pulled up to the cornice.

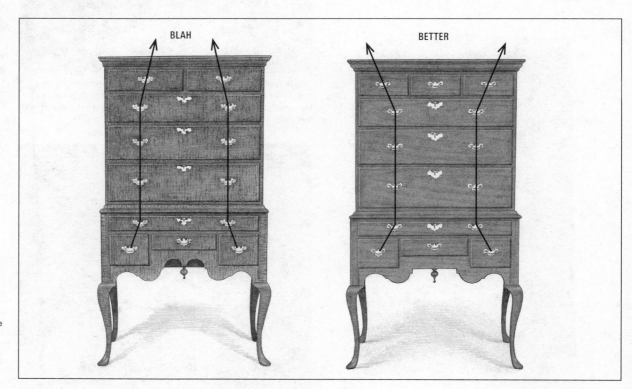

BLAH

BETTER

Continued ➜

TWO WAYS TO SPICE UP SHAKER

Christian Becksvoort and Gerald Curry used drawer design and pull arrangement to put a spin on Shaker design. By alternating rows of one and two drawers (top), Becksvoort created a pattern of diamonds. Curry's take (bottom) is more aggressive. The small second drawers on the third and fifth rows create an asymmetric diamond pattern.

Two Classic Pulls

by Michael Pekovich

I've made a lot of traditional furniture and I've learned the importance of getting the drawer and door pulls just right. Fortunately, you don't need to own a lathe to make the elegant turned pulls that are the hallmark of Shaker furniture, and you don't need to commission hand-hammered hardware every time you tackle an Arts and Crafts project. Instead, there's a really easy way to customize store-bought pulls, and I'll share a simple jig that will help you make your own classic pyramid pulls quickly and safely.

SHAKER PULLS MADE BY MACHINE, PERFECTED BY HAND

Before and after. The mass-produced piece (below) is rough and rounded over. A little sanding at the drill press reshapes it into a period-perfect Shaker pull (below).

You can get turned pulls in a variety of woods from most woodworking retailers. They are a convenient option, but the machine-duplicated profiles leave a lot to be desired. Typically, they lack the crisp detail and graceful curves of a hand-turned pull. They also tend to have heavy scratch marks and a nib at the center of the cap. Finally, the limited size selection often forces you to choose between a knob that's slightly too large and one that's too small.

The good news is that it doesn't take special tools or a lot of time to remedy any of these shortcomings. All you need is a drill press (even a hand-held drill will do) and five minutes of sanding to change the profile or the diameter and to transform a generic pull into one suited for fine furniture.

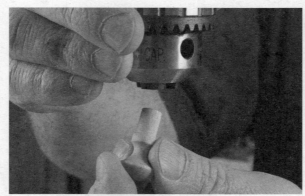

Two ways to mount the pull in the drill press. A tenoned end-grain pull can be mounted directly in the drill-press chuck (top). To mount a face-grain pull with a hole, cut the end off a bolt, chuck it onto the drill, and thread the knob in place (bottom).

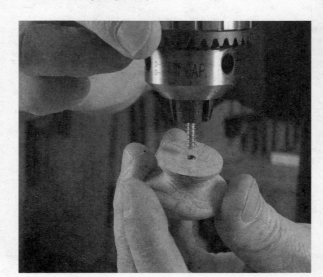

FROM ROUGH TO REFINED IN MINUTES: THREE STEPS TO A FINISHED PULL

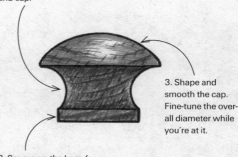

1. Hollow out the waist to create crisper transitions at the base and cap.

3. Shape and smooth the cap. Fine-tune the overall diameter while you're at it.

2. Square up the base for a hand-turned look.

Trim the waistline. Wrap coarse sandpaper around a dowel to establish the waist, then sand up to 600 grit before moving on to the base. To shape and smooth the base, wrap the sandpaper around a small block to establish a flat face.

▶ TIP

The Secret to a Scratch-Free Cap

Sanding while the pull is spinning will result in rings or a nib at the center. The trick to removing them is to stop the drill after every grit and sand across the cap by hand. Just a couple of strokes will do.

High-speed finish. With the pull spinning, wipe on a thin coat of shellac; it will dry almost instantly. Burnish with wax and fine steel wool for a satin luster that's pleasing to the touch.

PYRAMID PULLS ARE BEST MADE FROM SCRATCH

You can buy square pulls, but the profiles are usually rounded over, lacking the crisp facets that catch the light. Also, the wood selection offers few choices of species or grain orientation. You can do better on your own. The trick, when working with any small part on power tools, is to do it safely. A simple jig solves the problem. Not only is it easy to make, it's also a true multi-tasker. Use it on the drill press to drill the screw hole and shape the waist. Then move it to the tablesaw to bevel the top.

MAKE THE BLANK

HOLLOW THE WAIST

BEVEL THE CAP

TRIM THE BASE

START WITH PERFECT SQUARES

Mill the stock to ⅞ in. thick and 1 ¼ in. wide. Make the strip longer than you need and save the excess to make the jig at right.

1. A sliding stop is safe and accurate. Use the width of the blank to set the stop's distance from the blade.

2. Position the workpiece. Hold the stop firmly in place while sliding the stock against it.

3. Slide the stop out of the way before making the cut. This prevents the block from being trapped against the blade.

MAKE THIS SMART JIG

This jig takes you through the rest of the steps. But it's nothing more than two pieces of the leftover blank glued to a fence.

Fence, 1 ¼ in. thick by 2 in. wide by 18 in. long

Pull blank, ⅞ in. thick by 1 ¼ in. square

Alignment blocks, ⅞ in. thick by 1 ¼ in. wide by 4 in. long

Use a blank to position the blocks for gluing.

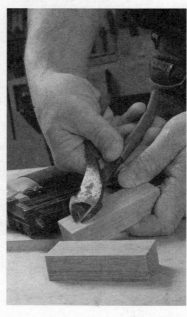

Set the spacing during glue-up. When assembling the jig, sandwich a blank snugly between the two pieces to set the proper distance between them.

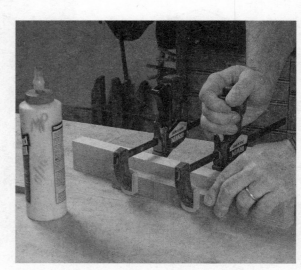

Secure the blocks with pins. To prevent the blocks from sliding around during glue-up, Pekovich drives 23-gauge pins into the inside face and clips them off just above the surface.

Continued ➜

DRILL THE SCREW HOLE AND WAIST ON THE DRILL PRESS

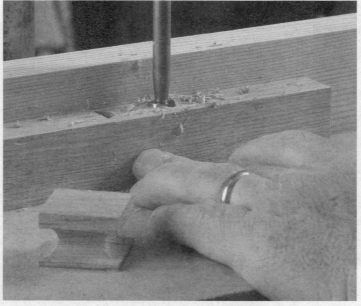

Center point, ⁵⁄₁₆ in. from fence, aligned with edge of blank.

¹⁄₂ in. dia.

A Forstner bit shapes the waist. Install a blank with its bottom toward the jig's fence and position the jig so that the bit is centered on the edge of the blank. Drill the blank and rotate until all four sides are complete.

Drill the mounting holes. Insert a blank facedown on the table with the center point marked. Align the blank with the drill bit and clamp the jig in place. Now all the mounting holes can be drilled after marking just a single blank.

BEVEL THE CAP ON THE TABLESAW

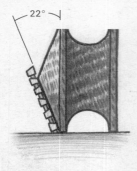

22°

Set up the bevel cut. Draw a center line on the jig, tilt the blade 22°, and adjust the rip fence until the blade cuts just to the line. When the setup looks right, insert the first pull.

Cut the facets. Use a normal push stick on the jig and a simpler stick (a piece of scrap will work) to keep the pull in place throughout the cut. Rotate the blank after each pass until all four sides are beveled.

USE A CROSSCUT SLED TO TRIM THE BASE

Final cuts. Clamp a stop block to the crosscut sled and cut each edge of the base.

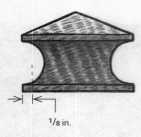

¹⁄₈ in.

> ▶ **TIP**
>
> ### How to Sand the Facets Cleanly
>
>
>
> Place sandpaper on a flat surface and rock the piece up onto one of its facets. Keep it flat as you sand to maintain a crisp profile.

Projects for Traditional Styles

18TH CENTURY DESIGNS

Classic Corner Chair

by W. Mickey Calahan

The corner chair, sometimes called a roundabout chair, became fashionable in England and America in the late 17th and early 18th centuries. Supposedly created for a gentleman to sit on while wearing his broad coat and sword, it may owe its name simply to the fact that it sits nicely in the corner of a room. Regardless, it provides today's sitter with an optimal amount of back and arm support, especially when writing at a table or a desk.

Though the chair has lots of curves, the construction is simple mortise-and-tenon joinery without the compound angles found on many chairs. If you aren't a confident carver, eliminate the shell, replace the ball-and-claw foot with a pad foot, and you'll still have a very handsome chair.

Shapely Legs for a Shapely Chair

The two side legs and the back leg transition into the arm supports, while the front leg terminates at the seat. Pay close attention to the end-grain orientation when you lay out the stock: The front leg should be oriented for a bull's-eye grain pattern on the exposed knee. The other legs should have straight, vertical grain.

Transfer your patterns onto 16/4 stock machined to 3 in. square, but leave enough length for two knee blocks per leg. The knee blocks serve primarily as a transition between the legs and the seat rails.

While the leg blanks are square, lay out and cut all the mortises, then create the tenons that enter the arm rail. All the tenon shoulders must be at the same elevation for the arm to fit flush. Cut around the perimeter of the blank using a dado blade. The tenon is not centered, so set the elevation of the blade carefully for each cut. Drill a 7/8-in.-dia. hole in a piece of scrap to use as a gauge when rounding the tenons.

Cut away the knee-block stock and then rough out the cabriole legs on the bandsaw. Cut the square sections housing the mortises proud of the pattern, as you will flush them to the fronts of the glued-in seat rails later. This is particularly important for the front leg because you will remove a large amount of stock, and leaving it square also aids clamping the leg to the rails.

Shape the legs and carve ball-and-claw feet, but hold off on the knee shell until the post of the front leg is rounded into the adjoining seat rails.

Continued →

Anatomy of an Heirloom

This chair is loosely based on one that was made in New York around 1765. The cabriole legs, relief-shell carving, and curved front rails reflect the earlier Queen Anne period, while the ball-and-claw feet and intricate splats reflect the later Chippendale style.

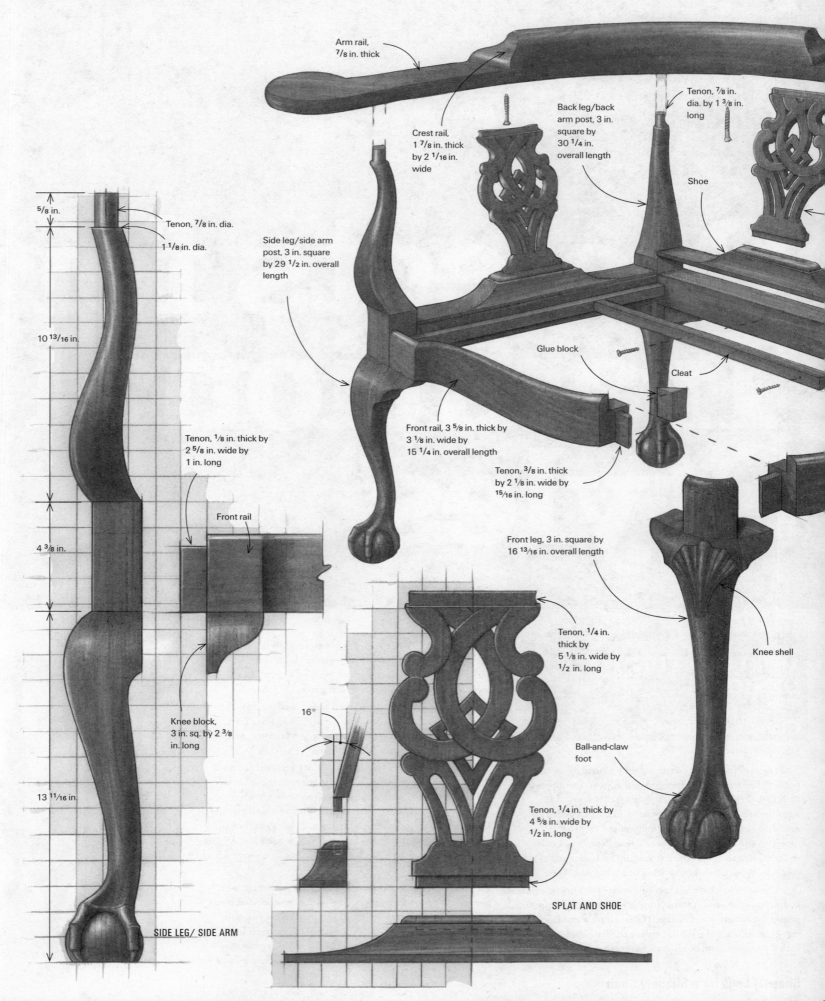

Arm rail, $^7/_8$ in. thick

Crest rail, 1 $^7/_8$ in. thick by 2 $^1/_{16}$ in. wide

Tenon, $^7/_8$ in. dia. by 1 $^3/_8$ in. long

Back leg/back arm post, 3 in. square by 30 $^1/_4$ in. overall length

Shoe

Side leg/side arm post, 3 in. square by 29 $^1/_2$ in. overall length

$^5/_8$ in.

Tenon, $^7/_8$ in. dia.

1 $^1/_8$ in. dia.

10 $^{13}/_{16}$ in.

Tenon, $^1/_8$ in. thick by 2 $^5/_8$ in. wide by 1 in. long

Front rail

Glue block

Cleat

Front rail, 3 $^5/_8$ in. thick by 3 $^1/_8$ in. wide by 15 $^1/_4$ in. overall length

Tenon, $^3/_8$ in. thick by 2 $^1/_8$ in. wide by $^{15}/_{16}$ in. long

Front leg, 3 in. square by 16 $^{13}/_{16}$ in. overall length

4 $^3/_8$ in.

Knee block, 3 in. sq. by 2 $^3/_8$ in. long

16°

Tenon, $^1/_4$ in. thick by 5 $^1/_8$ in. wide by $^1/_2$ in. long

Knee shell

Ball-and-claw foot

13 $^{11}/_{16}$ in.

Tenon, $^1/_4$ in. thick by 4 $^5/_8$ in. wide by $^1/_2$ in. long

SIDE LEG/ SIDE ARM

SPLAT AND SHOE

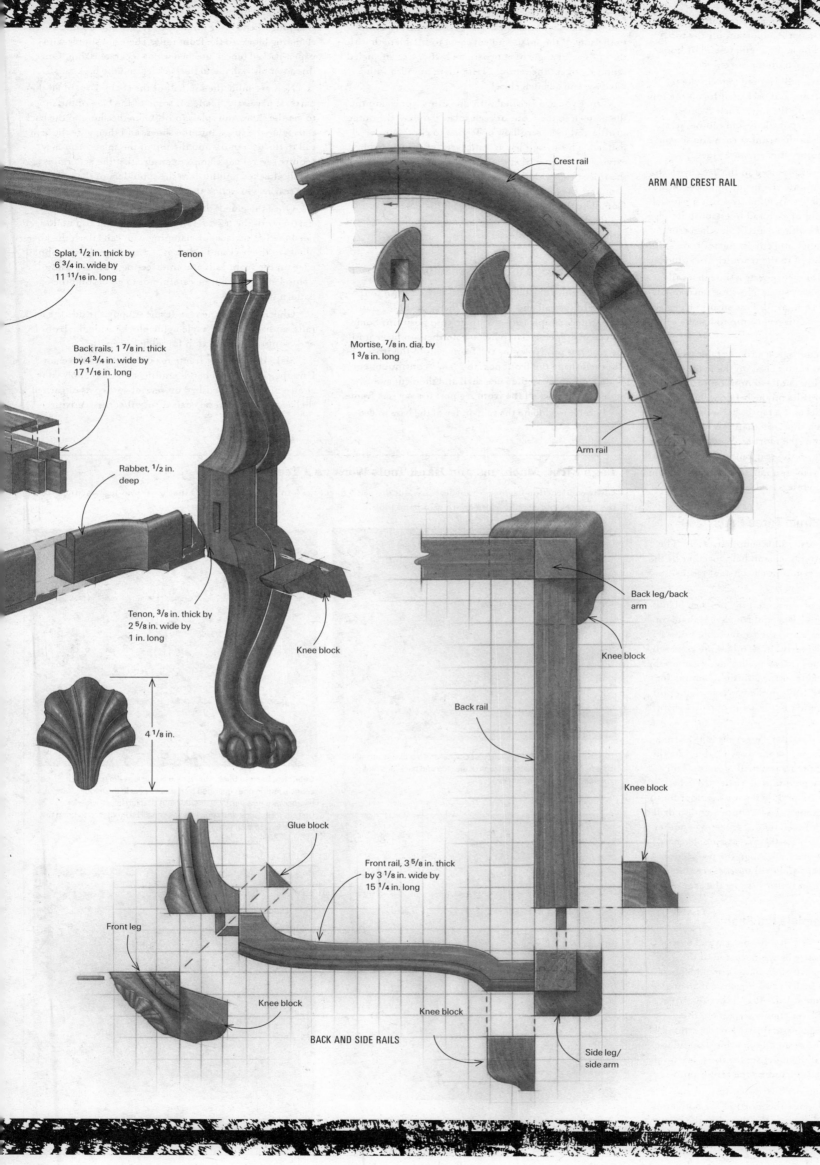

ARM AND CREST RAIL

Crest rail

Splat, 1/2 in. thick by
6 3/4 in. wide by
11 11/16 in. long

Tenon

Mortise, 7/8 in. dia. by
1 3/8 in. long

Back rails, 1 7/8 in. thick
by 4 3/4 in. wide by
17 1/16 in. long

Arm rail

Rabbet, 1/2 in.
deep

Back leg/back
arm

Knee block

Tenon, 3/8 in. thick by
2 5/8 in. wide by
1 in. long

Knee block

Back rail

Knee block

Knee block

4 1/8 in.

Glue block

Front rail, 3 5/8 in. thick
by 3 1/8 in. wide by
15 1/4 in. long

Front leg

Knee block

Knee block

Side leg/
side arm

BACK AND SIDE RAILS

Curved Rails, Square Joinery

Try to get all the rails from one board for grain and color consistency. This is particularly important for the two front rails, which should be laid out end to end or book-matched for a pleasing pattern on the curved faces.

Starting with the front rails, lay out and cut the tenons, and then trace the front and back profiles on the top of each rail. Bandsaw close to the lines, then clean up the surfaces with a curved-sole spokeshave and cabinet scrapers. Leave extra material on the front at each end so you can fair the rail-to-leg joints after they are glued.

The slip-seat frame is supported in the back by cleats, but it rests on a rabbet cut into the inside top faces of the front rails. To cut the rabbet, first lightly scribe a parallel line 1/2 in. from the front of each rail to establish its edge. Remove most of the waste with a dado blade, then trim to the scribe line using a gouge and chisel. Again, leave a little extra to be removed adjacent to the front leg after glue-up.

The two rear rails also incorporate a shoe that will house the bottom of the back splat. The shoe starts out as part of the back rail but is cut away. This ensures a perfect grain match and provides a bigger section to handle when shaping the shoe.

Before cutting the tenons, use a router table to shape the cove and the quarter-round bead on the front face and top edge of each shoe. Now cut the tenons on each end and cut the shoes' side profiles on the bandsaw. Finish shaping them with a chisel and scraper. Excavate the mortise in the top of each shoe and then carefully carve the bead returns at each end of the mortise. When both shoes are profiled, saw them from the rear rails.

Dry-fit the four legs to the seat rails to ensure that all joinery is correct and that all four legs land firmly on the floor.

One Long Arm Made from Three Parts

The construction of the arm rail is simplicity itself: The bottom two parts are butt-joined and held together by the crest rail. The arc of the arm is not a constant radius, so use care when laying out the parts.

To ensure matching profiles, nest the two arm blanks together using double-stick tape and rough-cut them on the bandsaw. Clean them up on the router table using a template and a bearing-guided bit. Bandsaw the crest rail to rough shape. Using the arms as a template, clean up the crest rail on the router table, using a flush-trimming bit. Now cut the ogee-shaped ends on the bandsaw. Glue and screw the three parts together but leave any further shaping until later.

Once the glue dries, locate the mortises in the arm rail for the leg tenons. First, use the drawing to locate the mortise for the back-leg tenon and drill it on the drill press. Place the tenon gauge you used earlier over the end of each side-leg tenon, and then use a Forstner bit to mark the center of each tenon. Use a clipped nail to drill a small hole in the center of each tenon. Inserting another clipped nail in each hole, place the dry-assembled chair base upside down on the arm rail. Align the two sections, push the nails into the rail, and drill mortises centered on the nail holes. You can now finish shaping the arm rail.

The Back Splats Complete the Chair

To make the back splats, first dry-fit the arm rail to the base to establish the distance between the top of the shoe and the arm rail. On a piece of scrap the same thickness as the back splats but an inch or two longer, cut an angled tenon that fits into the shoe. Rip off a 1/4-in.-thick piece and crosscut it in two. Clamp these two parts so they overlap and use them as a measuring stick to determine the distance. Crosscut the scrap piece to this size and use it to mark the location of the mortises for the splats on the underside of the crest rail, including the center points.

Resaw the splats from one board, but leave them about 1 in. extralong. Because the mortises for both ends of the splats are perpendicular to the floor but the splats lean outward from the seat, you must angle the tenons accordingly.

With the same measuring stick used earlier, determine the total length of each splat, locate the tenon shoulders, and tweak the tenon angles. Transfer this information to the side of the splats and cut them to final length with the ends at an angle of approximately 16°. Use an angled tenon jig to cut the tenons. Trim them to width with a handsaw and a bench chisel.

Once you are satisfied with the joints, spray-mount the pattern to the front of each splat. Bandsaw the outer profile and use a scrollsaw or fretsaw to cut the inner pattern. This design has an interlaced effect created by carving away material at the points of intersection. Make the initial cuts with the pattern attached, but remove it to complete the carving to get a better feel for the final look. Complete the splats by smoothing all the saw cuts and lightly chamfering all the exposed edges on the rear faces with curved and flat files.

Carve and Shape as You Assemble

Add the front knee blocks, which should fit flush to the bottom of the rail and the face of the adjacent leg post. Once fitted, simply rub-glue them into position. Sometimes a bed-spring clamp helps hold them in place until the glue sets up. Now glue the front rails to the front post, and then shape the front post to form a continuous curve. Then you can carve the knee shell and then cut away the rabbet in the back of the front leg post for the seat frame.

I prefer to glue up the remainder of the base in two stages, as it is less frantic and there is enough flex in the base to allow this. Because you can't use the front leg post for clamping when gluing on the side legs, you'll need to attach clamping blocks to the front rails. These are simply sandpaper-backed blocks attached with a separate clamp. Once this assembly is dry, add the back leg and the back rails.

Now assemble the top half of the chair. Dry-fit all the parts. If necessary, plane off some of the base of the shoes to get the shoes and splats to fit. Glue the shoes to the back rails, glue the splats into the shoes, and then glue the arm rail to the leg tenons and the top of the splats. You may require several bar clamps to ensure that the arm rail is firmly attached and flush to the shoulders of the two side and rear legs as well as the top shoulder of each splat.

Once the glue is dry, you can finish shaping the base starting with the leg-to-rail joints. Now that you no longer need the flat surface for clamping, you can attach the knee blocks to the back and side legs. Last, create the thumbnail edge on the front rails and intersecting front leg using a chisel and rasp, but be careful not to go beyond the pattern lines.

Glue and screw the seat-frame supports inside the back rails, and add a small angled glue block inside the front leg and front rail intersection for added strength.

Make the slip-seat frame for upholstering the chair. Give the chair a final hand-sanding and then apply your choice of finish. I brushed on several washcoats of garnet shellac and then several coats of an oil/varnish mixture.

Legs First: Machines and Hand Tools Work as a Team

Chair construction begins with the legs. Lay out the pattern, cut the joinery, and then shape the curvaceous legs starting at the bandsaw and moving on to a variety of hand tools.

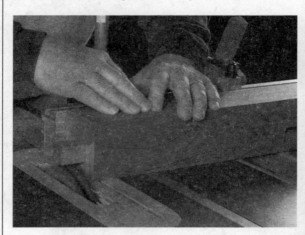

Cut the leg tenons using a dado set. While the leg blanks are still square, cut the tenons on the tops of the side and back legs that connect them to the arm rails.

Cabrioles, back to back. The back and side legs are really two cabriole legs in one separated by a square post in the middle. Careful bandsawing now (left) will reduce hand shaping later (below). Chisels, rasps, files, and spokeshaves can all be employed to bring the cabriole legs to their final shape.

Round the tenons. Guided by a drilled template, round the square tenons using chisels and carving gouges.

Shapely Rails, But Straightforward Joinery

The chair's front rails are S-shaped and include a rabbet to support the upholstered seat. Each back rail begins life attached to a shoe that receives the carved back splats.

FRONT RAILS

Rough-cut the rabbet. Remove the bulk of the waste using a dado blade. Cut to the lowest point of the rabbet with one pass, then clamp a stop block to the tablesaw and raise the blade into the stationary front rail as shown to make the deeper cuts.

BACK RAILS

Shape the shoes. Use a bullnose bit in a router table to cut the shoe's cove. Cut the bead with a corner round bit.

Bandsaw the ends. With the front profile cut, draw the side profiles on the back of the shoe and cut them on the bandsaw.

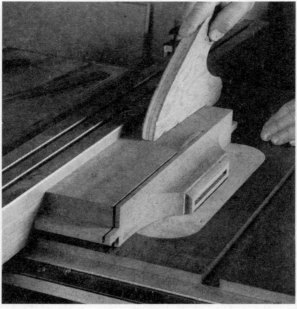

Take off your shoes. When you've finished shaping the shoes, cut them away from the back rails. Remove the small tab at each end.

Arm Rail Curve It and Carve It

The armrest flows around the back and sides of the chair. You need to locate the mortises accurately for the arm posts and the splats.

Two parts shape the third. After shaping the two sections of the arm, screw them to the crest rail to act as a template for shaping it to match. Use a flush-trimming bit in the router table.

A tricky cut made easy. A hand screw provides a stable platform for bandsawing the ogee-shaped ends of the crest rail.

Trick for marking mortises. Use a clipped brad nail to drill a hole in the center of the side-leg tenons. Then place another clipped nail in the hole (above). Place the back leg tenon into its mortise in the arm rail. Set the side leg tenons an equal distance from the inside edge of the arm rail (below). Push down on the legs so that the nails mark the arm rail.

Finish shaping the crest rail. Use a flat chisel to rough out the front curve and then refine it using a spokeshave and scrapers (above). On the back side at both ends of the crest rail, use carving gouges to create the small, tapering recesses that are purely for ornamentation (below).

Continued →

Back Splats: How to Get a Perfect Fit

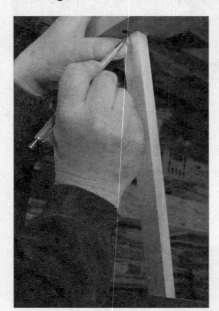

Scraps help. Use a scrap of wood to find the height of the splat and the angle and location of the joinery.

Carving tips. To give a three-dimensional look to the back splat, carve away material where the pattern intersects. After making the initial chop cuts at each intersection (left), remove the paper pattern and complete the carving (right).

Chop the mortise. Carefully clamp the arm rail so that you can chop the splat mortises.

Assembly: Clamp, Then Shape

Keep the front leg post square to provide a flat surface for clamping the front rails to it. After glue-up, you can also extend the seat-frame rabbet onto the back of the front post.

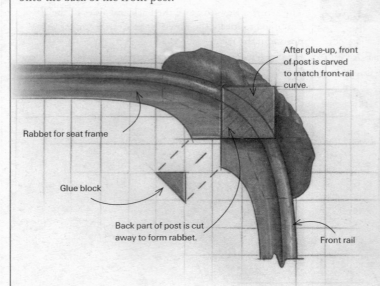

After glue-up, front of post is carved to match front-rail curve.

Rabbet for seat frame

Glue block

Back part of post is cut away to form rabbet.

Front rail

Finish shaping the front post. After you have clamped on the front rails, you can extend their curve and rabbet onto the post.

Angle the tenons with accuracy. Use a tenon jig and narrow dado set to form the tenons at each end of the back splats.

Final assembly. Clamping the arm/crest rail to the rest of the chair can be tricky given the chair's numerous curves. Do a dry-fit first. The easiest way to fine-tune the fit is to plane a bit off the shoes at the base of each back splat.

Porringer-Top Tea Table

by Dan Faia

When a client asked for a tea table recently, I built this one in the Queen Anne porringer style, named for the top's rounded, soup-bowl-shaped corners. I found the design in an antiques catalog. The original was built in Wethersfield, Conn., sometime between 1740 and 1760.

Tea tables were most popular from the William and Mary period in the early 1700s through the Empire period in the mid-1800s. Today, even though earlier dinnertimes have put an end to daily afternoon "teas," these tables still are useful as end tables or occasional tables.

This piece is also a great way to get started in building period reproductions. The design is simple, but there are challenging details in matching the grain, shaping the cabriole legs and transition blocks, and creating the uniquely shaped top. The project requires careful machine work and a delicate touch with hand tools. When you're done, you'll have a handsome, highly functional piece of furniture.

Seek Consistent Grain for a Coherent Look

Lumber selection and grain orientation are critical details for any furniture project. Using the right grain for individual parts can make the difference between a good piece and a great one. For grain consistency, I made the aprons and the slip-matched top from a single board. It might seem shameful to rip wide lumber into narrow pieces, but it pays off in the finished appearance.

Grain selection for the cabriole legs is even more important. Look for a 12/4 board with a rift-sawn end section, but be prepared to spend some time picking through the lumber to find it. Most pieces that will fit the bill will be rift for only half or three-quarters of the width. You'll rarely find a board that will yield any more than two legs side by side in the rift.

Turn the Feet Before Shaping the Legs

Start by rough-cutting the leg blanks longer than the finished leg. This leaves matching stock for two transition blocks, which you should trim off after the leg is turned and before it is shaped.

Begin by turning the pad foot on the center of the blank. Layout is done using plywood patterns derived from full-scale drawings. On the lathe, use a parting tool and a pair of calipers to set the pad's maximum diameter and to cut the fillet on which the foot will rest. Then make a rolling cut with a spindle gouge to establish the curve between

the foot's widest point and the fillet. The last step on the lathe is to use the corner of the skew to make a shallow scribing cut that just begins the top of the foot. This will help you locate the toe later in the leg-shaping process.

While the blanks are square, cut or chop the mortises for the aprons, making sure to choose the proper inside corner for the grain selection. Label and trim off the transition blocks, and cut the legs to length.

Time-Honored Cabriole Layout Method

Lay out the leg pattern on the two inside faces and bandsaw the profile. Do not bandsaw the top of the post, and stay proud of the pattern line by 1/16 in. or more above the knee. It is important to leave plenty of wood here for shaping later. Clean up the cuts with a spokeshave and a rasp, making each surface a fair curve.

I shaped the legs primarily with wide, flat chisels, removing wood in a series of chamfers until I arrived at a rounded profile. For consistency, I laid out the chamfers using a technique called the 5/7 rule.

At this small scale, the 5/7 rule isn't a precise measuring technique. It's a way of eyeballing the layout with consistent results (consistent enough, anyway, to please the eye). Start at the ankle by marking the center point of each side of the leg. From these marks, draw centerlines up

Bandsaw the Legs

and down the blank, maintaining the same dimension and following the curves created by the saw.

Your next marks should be a little less than halfway from these centerlines to each adjacent corner. To estimate this distance consistently, imagine that the space between each center point and each adjacent corner is divided into 12 equal parts. From each center, count five units toward the corners and make your marks at those locations. Draw additional layout lines from these marks up and down the blank.

Use a chisel and rasp to remove the material between these second layout lines, creating a broad chamfer. Now mark the centerlines of the chamfers. Refine the profile by paring about halfway in from these centerlines and the original ones to remove the newly created corners. This will create a set of narrower, secondary chamfers. Last, remove the ridges along these faces with a spokeshave. The corners should now be so close to round that no other division is needed. Use a rasp, file, and scraper to achieve the final shape.

Blocks Transition from Apron to Knee

Cut the apron stock to the appropriate lengths and rip the aprons slightly wider than the finished width. I used a dado head on the tablesaw to cut the tenons. Remove milling marks from the aprons with a handplane. Locate the center of each apron, measuring from the shoulders. Trace the apron patterns and bandsaw to shape. Clean up the bandsaw marks with a spokeshave, chisels, and files.

With the base dry-fitted together, trace the outside face of the aprons onto the leg posts, which were left fat earlier. Bandsaw the posts just proud of these lines, leaving wood that can be planed flush to the aprons after assembly. Glue up the base, checking for square and using moderate clamp pressure. Finish the assembly by trimming the posts flush to the apron fronts with a shoulder plane.

To begin fitting the transition blocks, first handplane their mating surfaces so that they fit tightly to the legs and aprons. Now clamp the transition block temporarily into place, aligning it roughly with the flat bottom of the apron, and use it as a reference surface for the shoulder plane. You want to plane the top of the leg where it meets the post, bringing its height flush with the top of the transition block.

Rough-cut the profile on the bandsaw. After turning the pad foot, trace the layout onto two faces of the blank and cut one face (above). Leave the waste area above the knee intact for now. Then tape the cutoffs back in place and cut the second face (left). The cutoffs support the work for safe and accurate cutting of the adjacent sides.

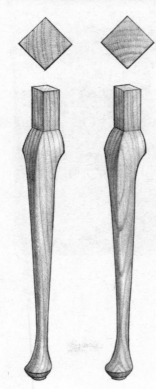

TWO WAYS TO ORIENT THE GRAIN

There are two options for the look of the legs: flow lines and bull's-eyes. Flow lines, used on this piece, keep a parallel vertical pattern that follows the leg's contours. Bull's-eyes are the sunburst patterns seen at the peak of the knee. You can get either pattern from the same blank, depending on how you orient the leg. End grain that runs from inside corner to outside corner will create flow lines (left). Side-to-side grain will produce bull's-eyes (right).

Do not remove the waste until after dry-fitting the legs to the aprons.

Continued ➡

Remove the blocks and use a bandsaw to cut the curved side profiles on each one. Use chisels and sandpaper to smooth the outer profiles to a fair shape, and then glue the blocks onto the legs and aprons. Chisel the leg profile to shape with the transition blocks. Curve the transitions across their width from the leg to the apron. Continue shaping diagonally over the blocks to a final rounding.

Shape and Attach the Top

I like to spring-joint the top boards. To "spring" the joint, plane away a minimal amount of wood from the middle section of each edge, so clamping pressure is moderate. Then the joint requires only one center clamp for glue-up. After planing and/or sanding the top flat, lay out and bandsaw the top pattern slightly proud of the lines. A jigsaw is a good alternative for cutting these shapes, especially the large-radius corners. Fairing these shapes by hand will require the use of many tools—spokeshave, chisel, file, and scraper.

The edge profile is not a half-round shape. It's a section of a larger radius, which is a common profile used in 18th-century furniture. Layout is simple. Draw a single centerline on the edge, and a pair of lines (one on each face) marking the top and bottom of the curve.

The makers of many original pieces used glue blocks to attach their tabletops; however, I don't recommend this because it restricts seasonal movement. Six wood screws, driven through pocket holes in the aprons, hold this top down. Mount the two end screws tightly and widen the slots for the four side screws to allow wood movement.

Shape the legs

LAY OUT THE PRIMARY CHAMFERS

Mark the edges of the curves. Begin the layout for shaping the leg by drawing a pair of reference lines on each side, at equal distances from the corners (left). These are called centerlines because the two meet at the center of the leg's narrowest point.

Mark the edge of the first chamfer. Faia visualizes a "5/7" ratio to draw a new set of lines a little less than halfway from the reference lines to the corner on each side. He chisels to these lines in creating the first chamfers.

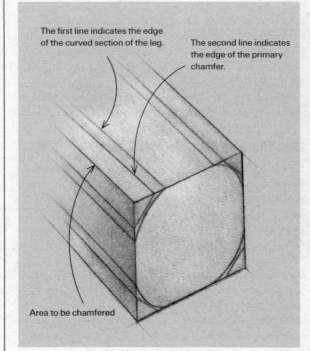

The first line indicates the edge of the curved section of the leg.

The second line indicates the edge of the primary chamfer.

Area to be chamfered

Cut the first chamfer. Use a chisel to remove the wood between the second layout lines (above). Stop the cut at the narrowest part of the leg, where the grain direction changes, and then work from the opposite direction. The sharply curved area just above the foot is hard to negotiate with the chisel. Follow up with a rasp to smooth the transition (below).

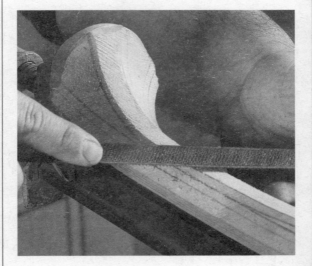

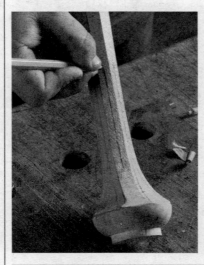

Lay out the next chamfers. Mark centerlines on the newly created faces. These lines will be used in cutting a second set of chamfers.

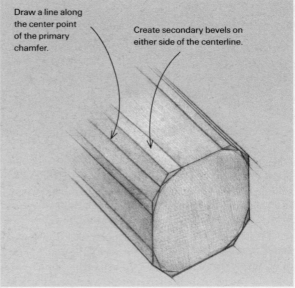

Draw a line along the center point of the primary chamfer.

Create secondary bevels on either side of the centerline.

Cut the new facets. Chisel away a triangular section of waste between the two centerlines. This cut is only about halfway to the line on either side of the corner (above). The remaining ridges are small enough to remove with a spokeshave (left). Use rasps, files, and sandpaper to shape the leg to its finished contour (below).

Assemble the Base

Profile the aprons. Use chisels, rasps, and files to create a smooth surface after bandsawing the apron shape.

Mark and trim the posts. Dry-fit the aprons into the mortised leg posts and trace cut lines on the front of each post (right). The finished posts will be flush with the aprons. Cut on the waste side of the line (below) and plane the posts flush with the apron after glue-up.

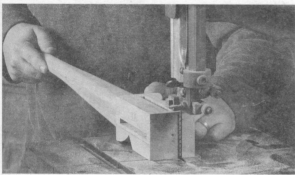

Glue up the base. Use moderate clamping pressure and be sure to check the assembly for square.

Prep the Leg for Corner Blocks

Plane the post flush. Use a shoulder plane, referencing off the surface of the apron.

Locate the transition block. Clamp the rough stock in place, aligned roughly with the bottom of the apron. Plane the top of the leg to match the block's height.

Add Transition Blocks

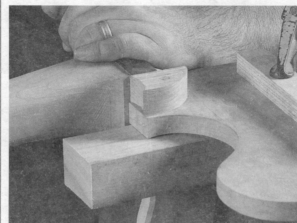

Mark and cut the corner block. Mark the block at the knee's apex to determine its thickness (top). Cut the block to shape and glue it in place before shaping it with a chisel (above).

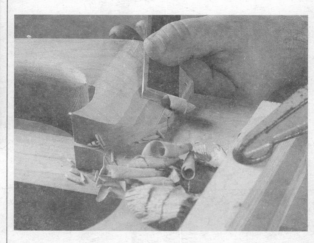

Shape the transition block. Pare across the top of the block, using the leg as a reference surface. As you near the apron, round over the ledge made by the shoulder plane.

Change directions. Next, work toward the top of the leg, rounding the transition block until it meets the apron.

Fair the curves underneath. Use a rasp to smooth the underside of the transition block where it meets the bottom of the apron.

Shaping the Tabletop's Edge

Using chisels, rasps, and files, work between a centerline drawn on the edge and layout lines on the faces.

Continued →

Basic Joinery Supports a Graceful Design

Simple mortise-and-tenon joinery brings the leg posts and aprons together, while the details lend distinction to the piece. The aprons are flush with the leg posts, and the curves in the cabriole legs are echoed by the rounded corners and edge details of the tabletop.

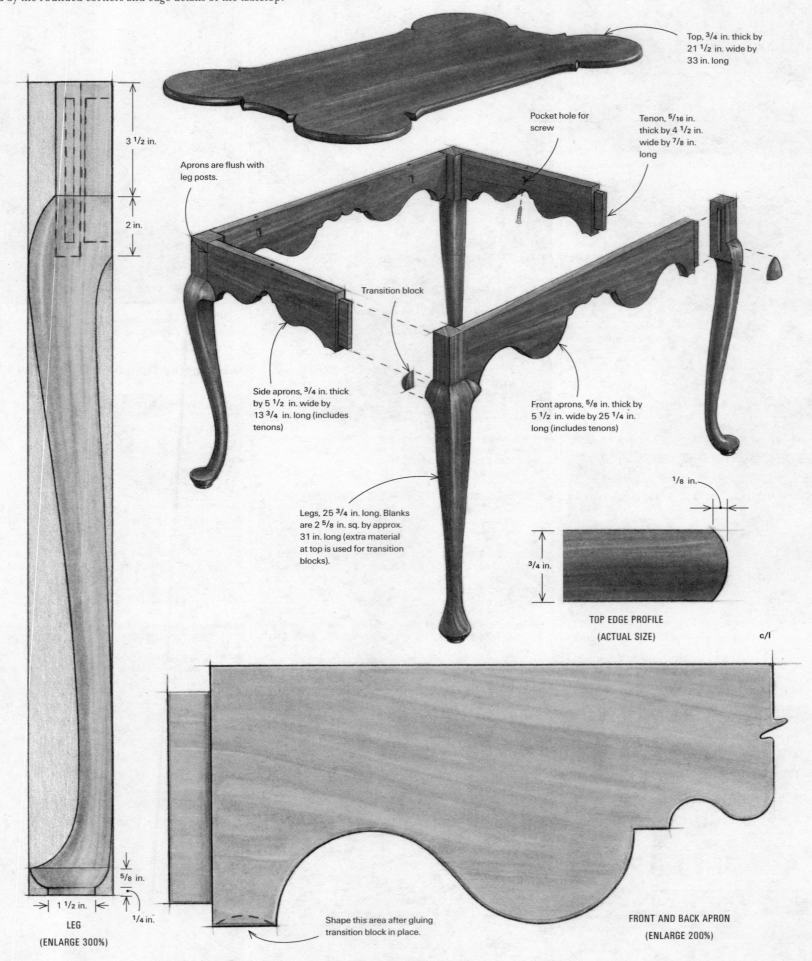

Top, 3/4 in. thick by 21 1/2 in. wide by 33 in. long

Pocket hole for screw

Tenon, 5/16 in. thick by 4 1/2 in. wide by 7/8 in. long

Aprons are flush with leg posts.

3 1/2 in.

2 in.

Transition block

Side aprons, 3/4 in. thick by 5 1/2 in. wide by 13 3/4 in. long (includes tenons)

Front aprons, 5/8 in. thick by 5 1/2 in. wide by 25 1/4 in. long (includes tenons)

Legs, 25 3/4 in. long. Blanks are 2 5/8 in. sq. by approx. 31 in. long (extra material at top is used for transition blocks).

1/8 in.

3/4 in.

TOP EDGE PROFILE
(ACTUAL SIZE)

c/l

5/8 in.

1 1/2 in.

1/4 in.

LEG
(ENLARGE 300%)

Shape this area after gluing transition block in place.

FRONT AND BACK APRON
(ENLARGE 200%)

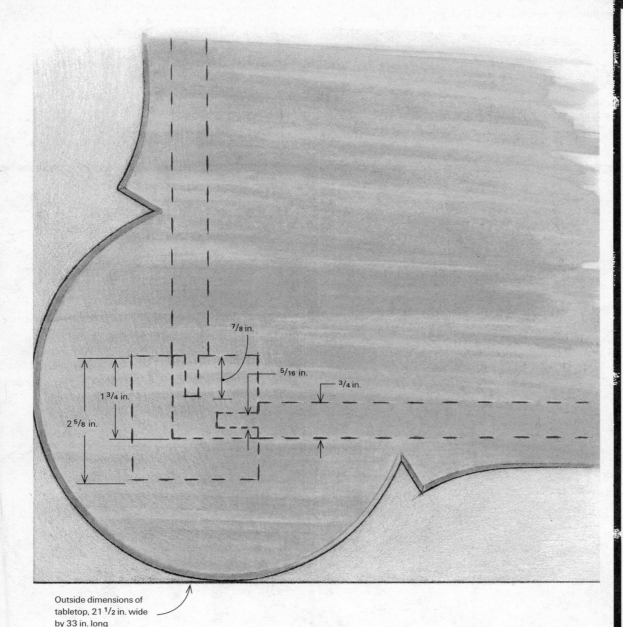

7/8 in.

5/16 in.

3/4 in.

1 3/4 in.

2 5/8 in.

Outside dimensions of
tabletop, 21 1/2 in. wide
by 33 in. long

TABLETOP CORNER
(ENLARGE 200%)

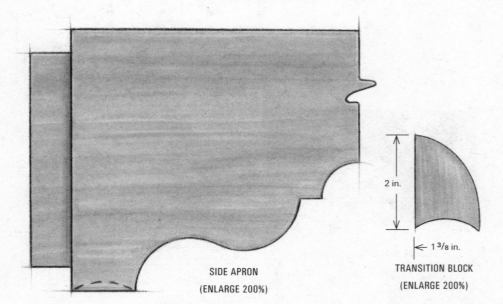

SIDE APRON
(ENLARGE 200%)

2 in.

1 3/8 in.

TRANSITION BLOCK
(ENLARGE 200%)

Regal Queen Anne Lowboy

by Dan Faia

The Queen Anne lowboy is about as traditional as American furniture gets, but from a modern perspective this 18th-century piece is still highly practical. The lowboy can be used as a dressing table or hall table, and the design has lost none of its elegance in the last 300 years.

For an intermediate woodworker looking to grow as a craftsman, the lowboy is an ideal project. It's not overly big or complex, but it is a satisfying, high-level test of many skills; so many, in fact, that you're almost guaranteed to learn one or two new ones before you're done. The piece combines a mortise-and-tenoned case with cabriole legs, dovetailed drawers, and a tabletop with a hand-shaped edge profile. A fan carving decorates the center drawer.

I've modified some of the period construction details to build a case that will accommodate seasonal wood movement. It's not an exact reproduction, but it captures the spirit of the early pieces.

The Cabriole Leg: Grace Under Pressure

These cabriole legs are slender, but balanced and strong enough to support a heavy case piece without stretchers. They also do more than just hold the case off the floor; their long top posts are an integral part of the case itself. The case can't go together until the legs are done, so let's begin with the four legs.

It's most practical to turn the foot and cut the mortises before sawing and shaping the curved cabriole profile. The first step is to orient the leg blanks for the best figure. Mark the inside corners of each leg, then trace the cabriole pattern on these two adjacent surfaces. On each leg, use a cutting gauge to score a line defining the post block. Set the gauge to the dimension of the waste to be cut away. Score these lines on the tops of the legs, too; this helps keep the position of the leg clear.

To lay out the turned foot, scribe a line around the bottom of the blank to mark the top of the foot. Draw center marks on the two ends of the blank to locate the points of the lathe centers for the offset turning.

Turning and mortising—At the lathe, use a parting tool to turn a cylinder for the foot from the layout line to the end of the blank. Then turn a narrower cylinder at the very end of the blank to establish the pad at the bottom of the foot. Next, use the point of a turning skew to score a line where the square corners of the blank meet the cylinder, defining the top of the foot. Use the skew to soften the hard corners of the square and then shape the foot by rounding off the cylinder to a quarter-round. Sand the foot while it is on the lathe.

Each leg is mortised on the two inside faces to accommodate one case side and either the solid back or the front apron and rails. Referencing from the top of each blank and factoring in the extra inch, use a combination square to mark the tops and bottoms of the mortises. Use a cutting gauge and reference from the inside corner of each blank to mark the fronts and backs of the mortises. Cut the mortises at the drill press or mortiser.

Continued →

Saw and refine the shape—At the bandsaw, cut the leg's curved profile into one of the laid-out faces. Tape on the waste piece at the back of the leg and cut the other face. Be sure to save the long waste piece sawn from the post. You can use this material for transition blocks. Next, with the leg held in a bar clamp and vise, use a spokeshave to remove the bandsaw marks and smooth all four surfaces.

After cleaning up the sawcuts, finish shaping the leg by cutting a series of chamfers at the corners to round the profile. File the leg smooth and scrape with a card scraper. Then trim the post blocks and cut the posts to length.

Precise Joinery Ensures a Square Case

Building the case is a challenge in precision. There are no steps or reveals to mask inaccuracies where the sides, back, or rails meet the corner posts. Everything is flush.

With the mortises already cut in the posts, the next step is to lay out and cut the tenons on all of the mating pieces. I begin with the back and the front rails. These pieces must match exactly in overall length from tenon shoulder to shoulder. This helps ensure that the case comes together squarely and cleanly, with no gaps.

It's also crucial to locate all of the tenons correctly on the thickness of the stock so that the outside case surfaces are flush with the posts when the joint is assembled. To do this consistently, scribe the end grain for both cheeks using the outside face as a reference for your marking gauge. Set the gauge for 1/4 in. to scribe the outside cheeks and 1/2 in. to scribe the inside cheeks.

To cut the cheeks, set the stock face-side down on the tablesaw and raise a dado cutter to just under the lower scribe line on the end of the first workpiece. Adjust the rip fence for 1/32 in. less than the tenon's length and use

Mahogany lowboy

This small piece lets you develop your turning, joinery, and carving skills, and learn how to apply an antique-looking finish.

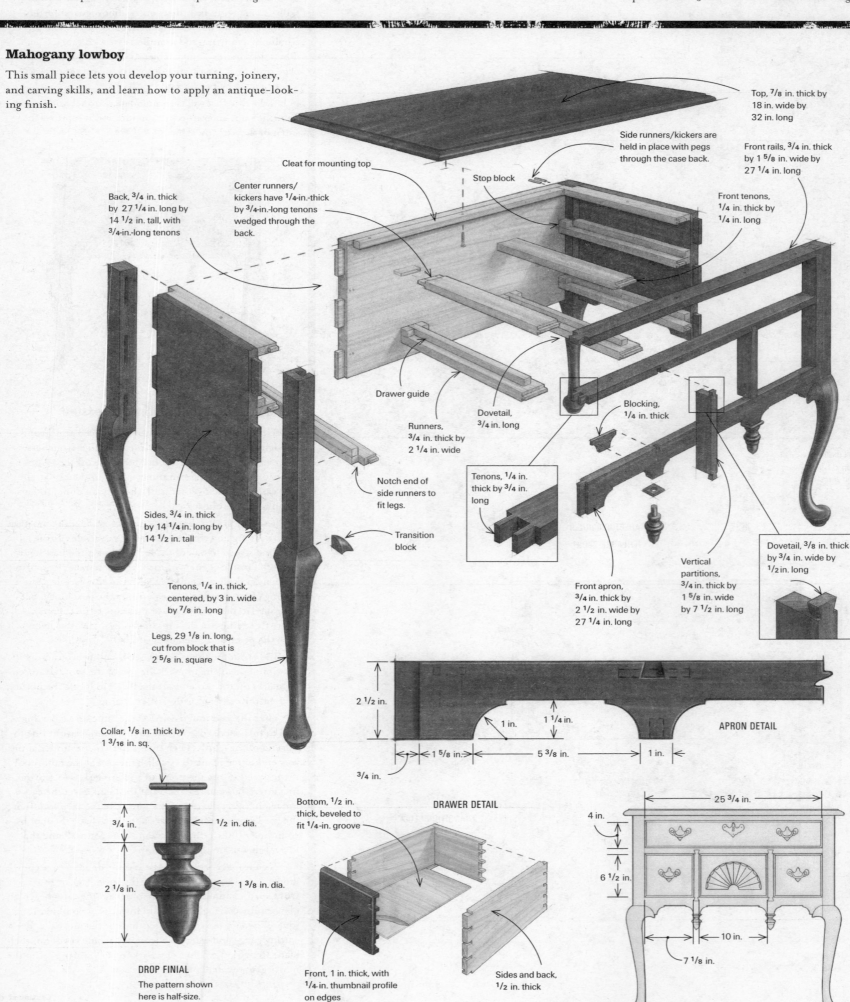

Top, 7/8 in. thick by 18 in. wide by 32 in. long

Side runners/kickers are held in place with pegs through the case back.

Front rails, 3/4 in. thick by 1 5/8 in. wide by 27 1/4 in. long

Cleat for mounting top

Stop block

Front tenons, 1/4 in. thick by 1/4 in. long

Back, 3/4 in. thick by 27 1/4 in. long by 14 1/2 in. tall, with 3/4-in.-long tenons

Center runners/kickers have 1/4-in.-thick by 3/4-in.-long tenons wedged through the back.

Drawer guide

Runners, 3/4 in. thick by 2 1/4 in. wide

Dovetail, 3/4 in. long

Blocking, 1/4 in. thick

Tenons, 1/4 in. thick by 3/4 in. long

Sides, 3/4 in. thick by 14 1/4 in. long by 14 1/2 in. tall

Notch end of side runners to fit legs.

Transition block

Tenons, 1/4 in. thick, centered, by 3 in. wide by 7/8 in. long

Front apron, 3/4 in. thick by 2 1/2 in. wide by 27 1/4 in. long

Vertical partitions, 3/4 in. thick by 1 5/8 in. wide by 7 1/2 in. long

Dovetail, 3/8 in. thick by 3/4 in. wide by 1/2 in. long

Legs, 29 1/8 in. long, cut from block that is 2 5/8 in. square

Collar, 1/8 in. thick by 1 3/16 in. sq.

2 1/2 in.

1 in.

1 1/4 in.

1 5/8 in.

5 3/8 in.

1 in.

3/4 in.

APRON DETAIL

3/4 in.

1/2 in. dia.

Bottom, 1/2 in. thick, beveled to fit 1/4-in. groove

DRAWER DETAIL

25 3/4 in.

4 in.

6 1/2 in.

2 1/8 in.

1 3/8 in. dia.

DROP FINIAL
The pattern shown here is half-size.

Front, 1 in. thick, with 1/4-in. thumbnail profile on edges

Sides and back, 1/2 in. thick

10 in.

7 1/8 in.

the miter gauge to help control the workpieces. For the intermediate front rail, use a 1/2-in. dado stack to remove the waste from between the twin tenons. Hold the piece vertically against a miter gauge. Use a sacrificial backer block and use the miter fence as a stop. Raise the blade to just below the scribe line before making the cut.

At the workbench, use a shoulder plane to fit the tenons to their mortises. To help keep the outer surfaces flush, avoid paring too much stock from either tenon cheek. After paring to the shoulder lines with a chisel, cut the multiple tenons from the full-length tongues on the back and side panels.

Before you can start gluing up, you'll need to dovetail the top rail, then mortise the front rails and the case back for the kickers and runners that will support the drawers. Then, with the case dry-fit, locate and fit the dovetailed vertical partitions. Finally, bandsaw out the shape of the front apron and clean up the profile.

Transition Blocks Marry Legs to Case

Start building the case by gluing up the back and front assemblies separately. The legs transition into the case with blocks that are glued on and shaped to match the curved profile. It's much easier to apply and shape the two blocks on the front apron now than when the case is fully glued up.

Begin by holding each block in position to see whether it is flat against the apron and the back of the knee. If needed, plane the block to fit. When this is done, draw the pattern on the front and saw the front profile, saving the offcut. Now return to the bench, hold the block in position again, and trace the shape of the leg onto the surface of the block that mates to the leg. To bandsaw this profile, set the transition block back onto the offcut and saw, staying 1/16 in. from the line.

Glue the two front transition blocks in place using a rub joint and hold them with a spring clamp if needed. Use a chisel, rasp, and scraper to shape the blocks. The side transition blocks are attached and shaped in the same way, but are installed after the case has been glued up.

Dry-Fit the Case for Layout

The next step is to add the sides without glue and clamp the case snug so you can accurately fit the crossmembers that span the interior. These are the runners that support the drawers from underneath and the kickers that sit above the drawers and prevent them from tipping downward when pulled out. In the space separating the upper and lower drawers, the crossmembers serve both of these functions. Rip all of the runners and kickers and crosscut them to a little over final length.

Measure from the back side of the apron and middle rail to the inside of the back. Use a knife to mark these distances on the parts. Cut the tenons with a dado blade and fit them. On the center runners and kickers, make handsaw cuts 1/4 in. from the edge and 1/4 in. from the shoulder to accept wedges for the through-tenons in the back panel. The left and right runners and kickers are notched to fit around the post blocks.

20 Mortises, 20 Tenons, One Glue-Up

The case is ready to come together. With clamps ready, apply glue to the mortises in the back legs and to the corresponding tenons on the sides. Seat the sides. Next, glue the center runners and kickers into their mortises in front, then apply glue to the front leg mortises and matching side tenons. Gently lower the front into place, taking care to seat the unglued tenons of the runners and kickers in the rear-panel mortises. Stand the assembly upright and use bar clamps to seat the joints. Before the glue sets, check the diagonals for square. When all is square, drive the wedges into the through-tenons at the back of the case. Clamp the side runners in place, drill into them through the back, and drive wooden pegs to secure them.

Drop Finials Adorn the Front Apron

In order to create a 1-in.-square platform for each drop finial and collar, glue 1/4-in.-thick backer blocks to the rear of the 3/4-in.-thick front apron, matching the latter's profile. Drill a 1/2-in.-dia hole into the center of each platform and into two blanks for the collars. Turn and sand the finials, including the 1/2-in.-dia. tenon.

To mark the size of the collar, slip it over the finial's tenon and insert the tenon into the apron. Using a 3/32-in.-thick spacer held against each edge of the platform, scribe a line around all four sides of the collar. Handsaw to these lines and then clean up the edges with a block plane. To create the bead, bevel all eight edges, moving the piece across the bottom of a plane, then refine the curve with sandpaper. Lastly, glue the collar to the platform and the finial into the apron.

Crowning Touch: A Hand-Shaped Top

The two-board top has a thumb-molding profile that is characteristic for this period, and I enjoy creating it with hand tools. The top is fastened with screws through the front rail, the two top kickers, and the cleat on the top inside surface of the back panel. Elongate the screw holes in the back to accommodate movement.

Stain and Shellac for a Flattering Finish

I finished the piece with a water-based stain (Cuban mahogany from www.wdlockwood.com) and shellac. This approach evens out variations in the color, shows the figure well, and yields a richer tone than the brassy color that natural mahogany sometimes has. Next, I applied dark grain filler to help show the pore structure and followed with a few more coats of shellac. The last step is to rub out the finish with 0000 steel wool and apply a coat of paste wax.

Turn and Shape the Legs

The legs take shape in two distinct stages. Start by laying out and turning the pad foot. Then rough out the leg's overall shape at the bandsaw and refine it with chisel, rasp, file, and scraper.

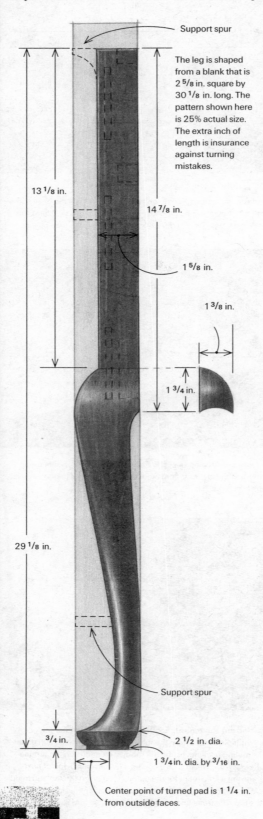

Support spur

The leg is shaped from a blank that is 2 5/8 in. square by 30 1/8 in. long. The pattern shown here is 25% actual size. The extra inch of length is insurance against turning mistakes.

13 1/8 in.

14 7/8 in.

1 5/8 in.

1 3/8 in.

1 3/4 in.

29 1/8 in.

Support spur

3/4 in.

2 1/2 in. dia.

1 3/4 in. dia. by 3/16 in.

Center point of turned pad is 1 1/4 in. from outside faces.

The foot is turned. Use a parting tool to turn cylinders for the foot and pad, then use a skew chisel to create the quarter-round profile.

BANDSAW THE BLANK

Cut the curved profile. Start cutting the profile by first defining the edge of the spurs. Then make cuts to complete the basic profile.

Rotate the blank and cut again. Save the cutoff with the pattern drawn on it and tape it back in place to guide this second cut. The spurs will steady the leg for these subsequent cuts.

Continued →

Layout lines guide the shaping. Start with a centerline on each face, then split the distance from the centerline to the edge of the leg with a line that runs from the knee to the ankle.

Trim the post. Dimension the post block with a pair of stopped cuts on the tablesaw. These cuts are made to the right and left of the fence so that the inside corner of the post block is against the fence. The untrimmed waste just above the knee is removed after glue-up.

SHAPE WITH HAND TOOLS

Chamfer the corners to form an octagon. Use a flat chisel. To stay with the grain, always work from the convex surfaces to the concave ones.

Case Construction

MULTIPLE TENONS MADE EASY

Lay out matching tenons. Clamp one of the front rails to the back panel and scribe the shoulder lines for both pieces simultaneously. Clamp the scribed rail to its mates and scribe shoulders on the remaining pieces.

MORTISE FOR THE RUNNERS AND KICKERS

Dovetail the top rail to the legs. The top rail is dovetailed into the tops of the leg posts. Lowe rabbets the tail to enhance accuracy when transferring the layout.

Shave away the remaining corners. Use a flat-soled spokeshave to cut a second, narrower set of chamfers, effectively rounding the leg.

Cut the joinery with a dado set. For consistency, cut face-side tenon cheeks on all of the pieces before adjusting the setup— if needed—to cut the opposite cheeks.

Smooth the surface. Finish rounding the profile with a rasp and a smooth file.

Mark out and cut the tenons. For the sides and back panel, you need to fashion multiple tenons from the full-width tongues. Hold each panel against its mating post and scribe the mortise locations on the tongue (above). Remove the waste with a coping saw and chisel (top of next column), leaving a little room for the tenons to move in the top and middle mortises. This allows room for seasonal expansion of the sides and back toward the top. The transition blocks prevent downward expansion.

Locate the kickers and runners. They are tenoned into the front rails and apron, and those mortises can be cut by machine, but the back panel's width means its mortises must be cut by hand. The mortise locations are picked up from the dry-fit front assembly (above) and marked on both faces of the back panel. Use a 1/4-in. chisel to chop the through-mortises, working in from each surface (left).

LOCATE THE DIVIDERS

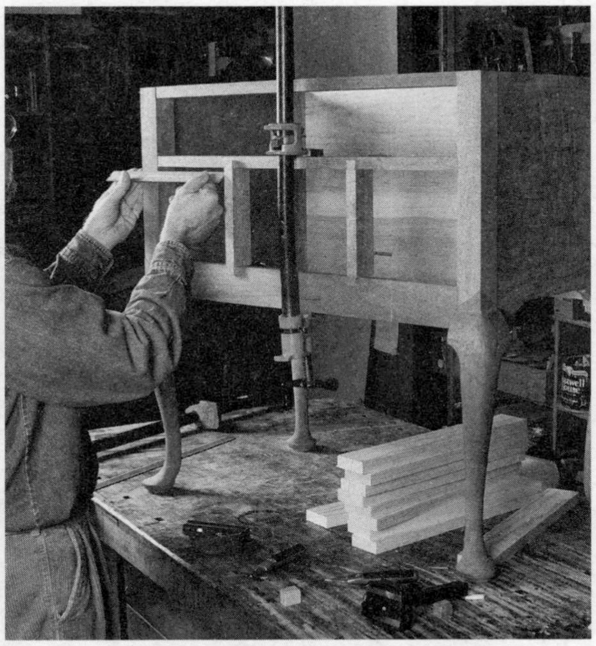

Measure to locate the drawer partitions. The whole case is dry-fit at this point (above). The vertical drawer partitions are dovetailed into the top of the apron and the bottom of the intermediate rail. The clamp helps hold the partitions in place while you knife the profile on the front surfaces of the apron and rail (below). Now disassemble the case, saw the mortise, and chop and pare to fit.

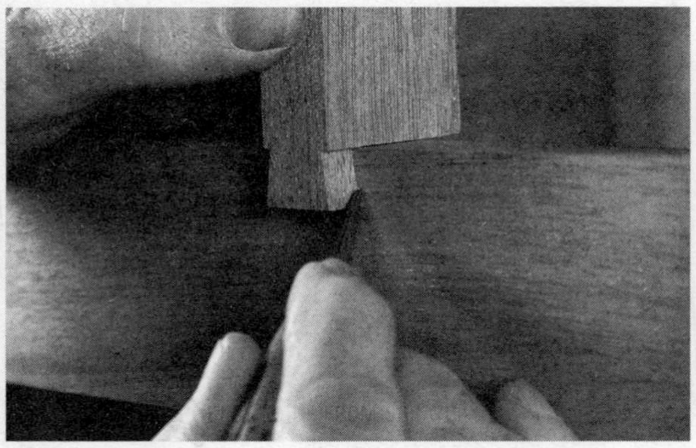

The Case Comes Together

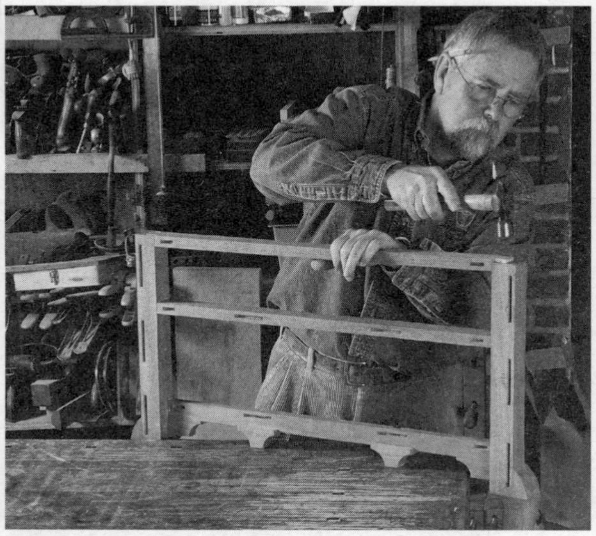

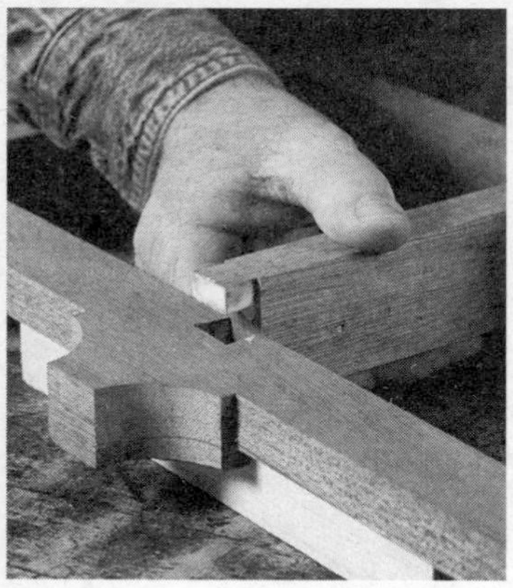

GLUE UP THE FRONT AND BACK

Apply yellow glue to both mortises and tenons. Once each assembly is in clamps, lay a straightedge across both post blocks to make sure they don't twist out of square. On the front assembly, check the diagonal dimensions and adjust the clamps to bring it into square. Glue the partitions in place after the front assembly has dried (left).

ADD THE TRANSITION BLOCKS

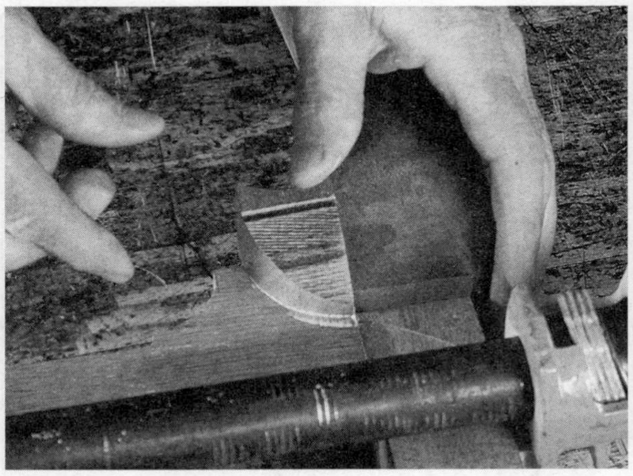

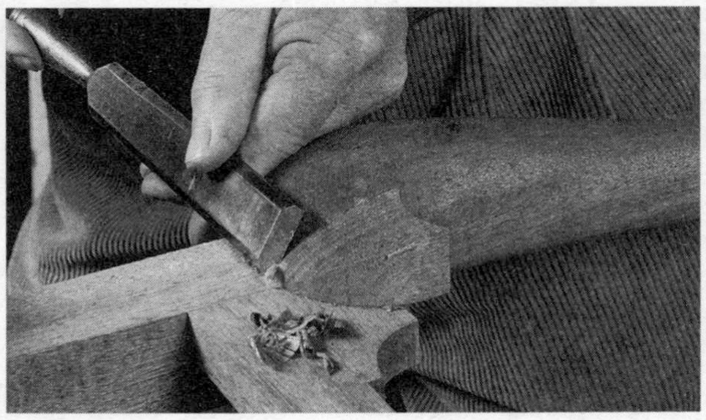

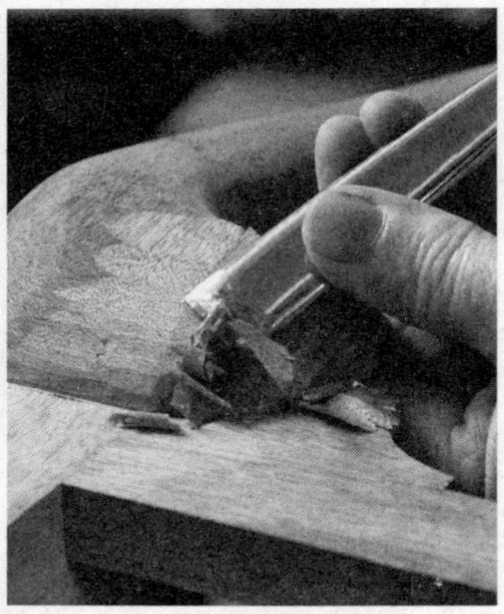

The blocks are shaped in place. After cutting the basic curves in the bottom and front of the block, glue it in place with a rub joint (top). With the block in place, pare away excess material to reach the final, rounded shape. Start with a chisel, making a series of side-to-side passes (above right). Then use a carving gouge with a shallow profile in a series of bottom-to-top passes to blend the curve further (left).

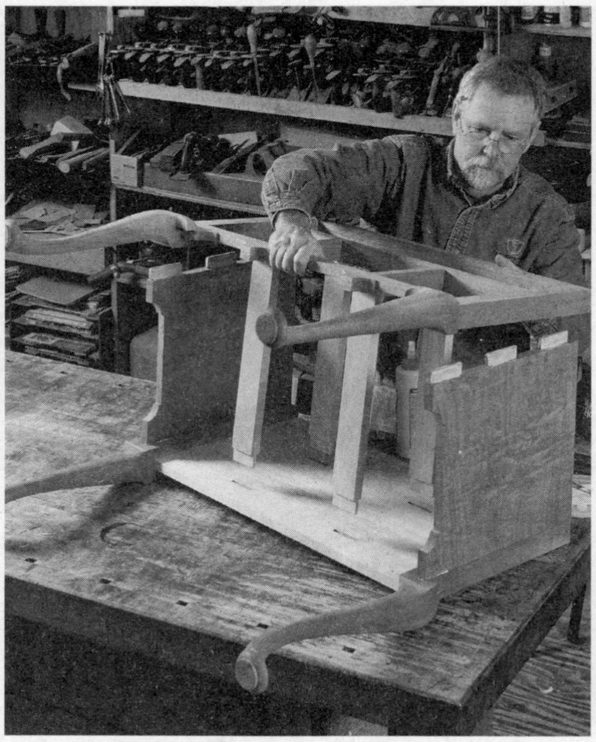

The final glue-up. Back and front assemblies are joined by gluing the side panels into the rear posts, gluing the interior kickers and runners into their mortises in the front, and then settling the front assembly into position.

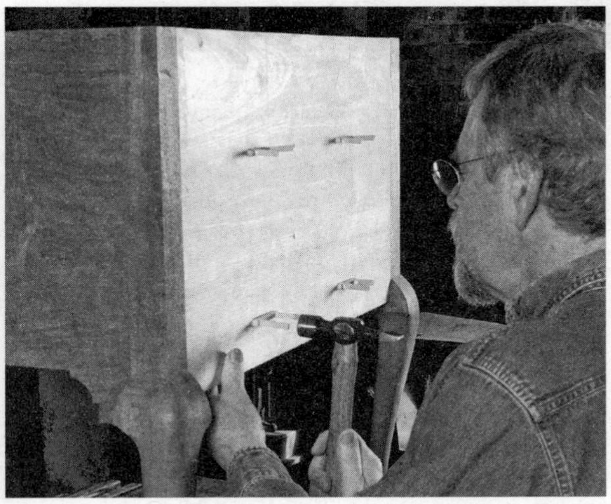

Wedge the tenons. The center runners are secured in back with wedged through-tenons. Glue the wedges and tap them home. When dry, saw them off and plane them flush.

HAND-SHAPED EDGE PROFILE

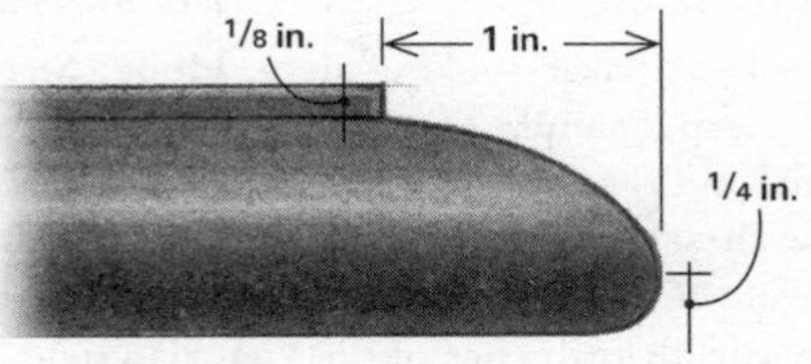

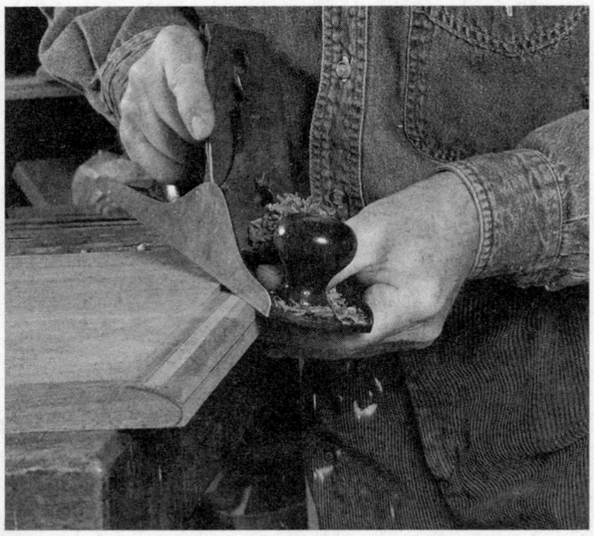

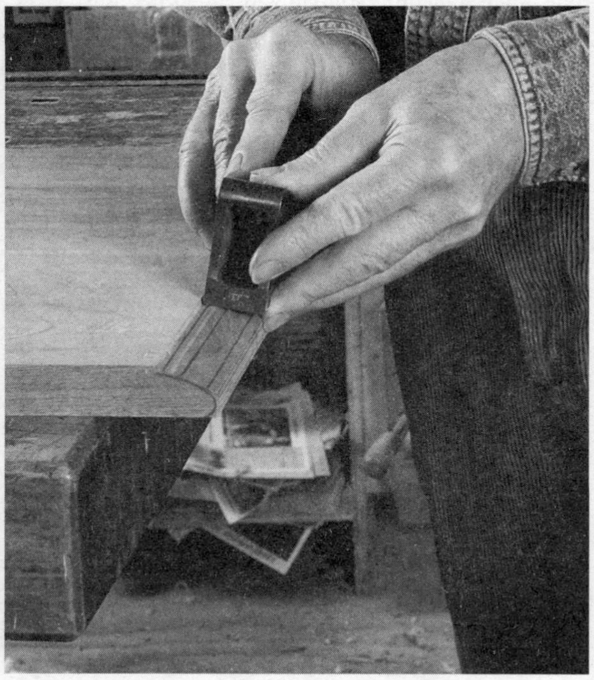

No router in sight. Start by using a dado blade to cut a 1/8-in.-deep rabbet. Then use a handplane to shape the profile (top). A shoulder plane allows you to work all the way into the corner (above).

Continued ➔

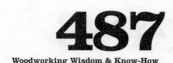

Elements of Shaker Style

by Chris Becksvoort

Woodworking masters Jere Osgood, Sam Maloof and George Nakashima each evolved a style and explored it to its ultimate conclusion, and to hell with what was in vogue. The Shakers did the same thing, continually refining their idiom until they approached perfection, without regard to the latest trend. They developed a style of furniture that blends well and fits comfortably in any type of house. The Shakers went out of their way to eschew fashion: The result is timelessness.

I grew up in a house full of Danish modern furniture, which was, it turns out, heavily influenced by Shaker designs. Like the Danish furniture makers, I fell under the sway of Shaker furniture the moment I discovered it—in my case, during a slide lecture in an architecture appreciation course I took in college. The simplicity and utility of the furniture I saw in the slides stunned me. In the late 1970s, I began restoring Shaker furniture, and much of my own work has been in the Shaker vein ever since. I very seldom reproduce slavishly, but you can look at my work and without batting an eye see its derivation is Shaker.

To make a Shaker-looking piece, adopt a Shaker attitude: Keep it simple in design and materials, make it functional and incorporate authentic details. The details shown on these pages were commonly used by the Shakers until about 1860, after which their furniture began to show the worldly influence of the Victorian style.

The Shakers believed "that which has in itself the highest use possesses the greatest beauty." It took the rest of the world nearly a century to come to the same conclusion, when, in the early 20th century, Louis Sullivan declared "form follows function." But these dictums alone do not lead inevitably to a particular style, much less to a specific set of elements and details. In addition to being inspired by their beliefs, the Shakers and the furniture they made were influenced by their historical context.

In short, the Shakers took the furniture they were familiar with, the local styles from New England to Kentucky, and stripped it of superfluous ornamentation. The Shaker craftsman Orren Haskins (1815-1892) perhaps said it best: "Why patronize the outside world? ... We want a good plain substantial Shaker article, yea, one that bears credit to our profession & tells who and what we are, true and honest before the world, without hypocrisy or any false covering. The world at large can scarcely keep pace with it self in its stiles and fassions which last but a short time, when something still more worthless or absurd takes its place. Let good enough alone, and take good common sense for our guide in all our pursuits, and we are safe within and without."

Shaker furniture, especially from the classic period of 1820 to 1850, contains little in the way of excessive moldings and virtually no carving or veneer. The Shakers favored native materials and were dead set against materials they felt were decadent, such as brass. The Western communities tended to follow the local vernacular style to a much greater degree than their Eastern counterparts. So the Shaker furniture from Ohio and Kentucky appears more ornate.

Some forms of furniture were never built by the Shakers. You will never see Shaker coffee tables, for example, nor tea tables, highboys, pencil-post beds or upholstered pieces. Some furniture companies market these items "in the Shaker style," including improbable pieces such as entertainment centers.

Certain elements appear over and over in Shaker furniture and make sense within the idiom. In striving for a design that remains faithful to the Shaker style, be mindful of their approach—just as you wouldn't build Queen Anne out of poplar, you wouldn't build Shaker out of rosewood. And pay close attention to the details.

Crown Moldings

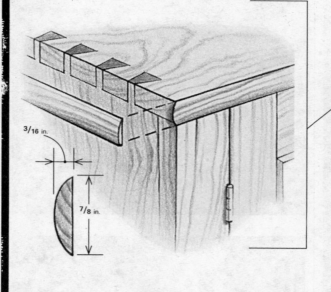

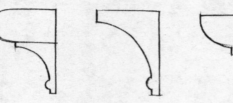

Moldings along the tops of Shaker case pieces are hard to justify as anything but decorative. Most styles of furniture (and architecture) incorporate moldings or some type of overhang at the top. To the eye, a crown molding or overhang denotes an ending; it is much like a period at the end of a sentence. The Shakers, presumably, were not immune to this near-universal need for closure.

Base Moldings

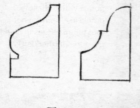

Shaker craftsmen used base moldings and profiled bracket bases for protection, not decoration. A rounded or shaped edge is far less prone to splintering or chipping than is a sharp, square corner. This is especially true near the floor, where base molds and brackets are likely to encounter brooms and mops or shoes and boots.

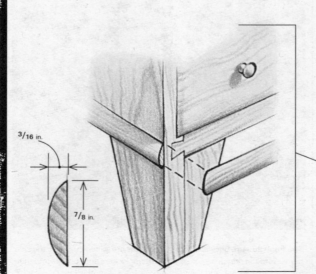

CHERRY CUPBOARD
80 in. by 44 in. by 19 in. Canterbury, New Hampshire, Circa 1850-1900

Door Frames and Panels

The doors on early Shaker pieces usually had raised, fielded panels. Over time, however, the raised panel fell out of favor, perhaps because it appeared too decorative or possibly because the shoulder was seen as just another dust collector. In any event, the flat panel ultimately replaced the more traditional raised panel as the first choice of Shaker cabinetmakers. In the transition, the pillow panel, as I call it, was sometimes used. Instead of having a well-defined, shouldered field, the panel was planed on all four edges to fit the groove in the frame. The result was a field that was barely noticeable.

Although square-shouldered door frames were used on occasion, more often than not, the frames featured a quarter-round thumbnail profile along their inside edges. To me, this represents a perfect example of a utilitarian, as opposed to a strictly decorative, molding. Rounded edges along the inside of the door frame are much easier to keep clean than straight, square shoulders.

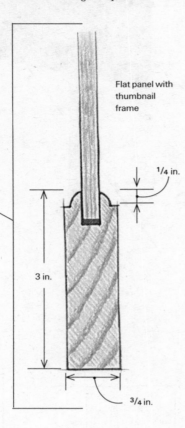
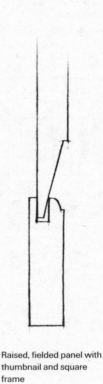

Flat panel with thumbnail frame

1/4 in.

3 in.

3/4 in.

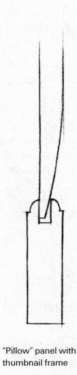

Raised, fielded panel with thumbnail and square frame

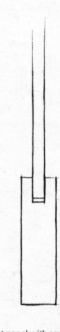

"Pillow" panel with thumbnail frame

Flat panel with square frame

Drawers

Shaker craftsmen built both flush and lipped drawers. Flush drawers had square edges and fit fully into their openings. Lipped drawers, although more difficult to make, covered the gap around the drawer front to keep out dust. The lips, however, were usually on the top and two sides only. A lip on the bottom was considered too fragile, should the drawer have to be set on the ground. The quarter-round and thumbnail profiles were commonly used on all four edges of lipped drawers. Neither the Shakers nor their worldly contemporaries used the bevel-edged, raised door panel as a drawer front. That design fiasco was perpetrated on consumers by the kitchen-cabinet industry.

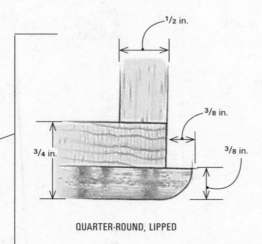

1/2 in.

3/4 in.

3/8 in.

3/8 in.

QUARTER-ROUND, LIPPED

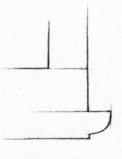

THUMBNAIL, LIPPED

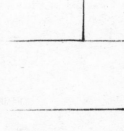

FLUSH

Continued ➜

Knobs

Shaker craftsmen continued the theme of simplicity right down to the knobs. Prior to the 1850s, most Shaker knobs were shopmade, although some early pieces had commercially manufactured porcelain knobs in either white or agate, a marbled brown color. After 1860, manufactured knobs became more and more common.

The typical Shaker knob was a variation of the mushroom form. Sizes ranged from 3/8 in. dia. on tiny desk drawers to 2 1/4 in. dia. on large built-ins. Knobs up to 1 1/2 in. dia. were typically spindle turned, with either a plain tenon (glued and wedged through the door or drawer front) or a threaded tenon. Larger knobs were usually face turned and attached with steel screws from the inside. Shop-built Shaker knobs were always made of hardwoods, often of a contrasting species to the rest of the piece.

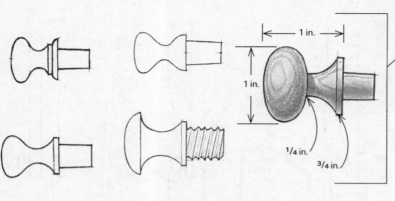

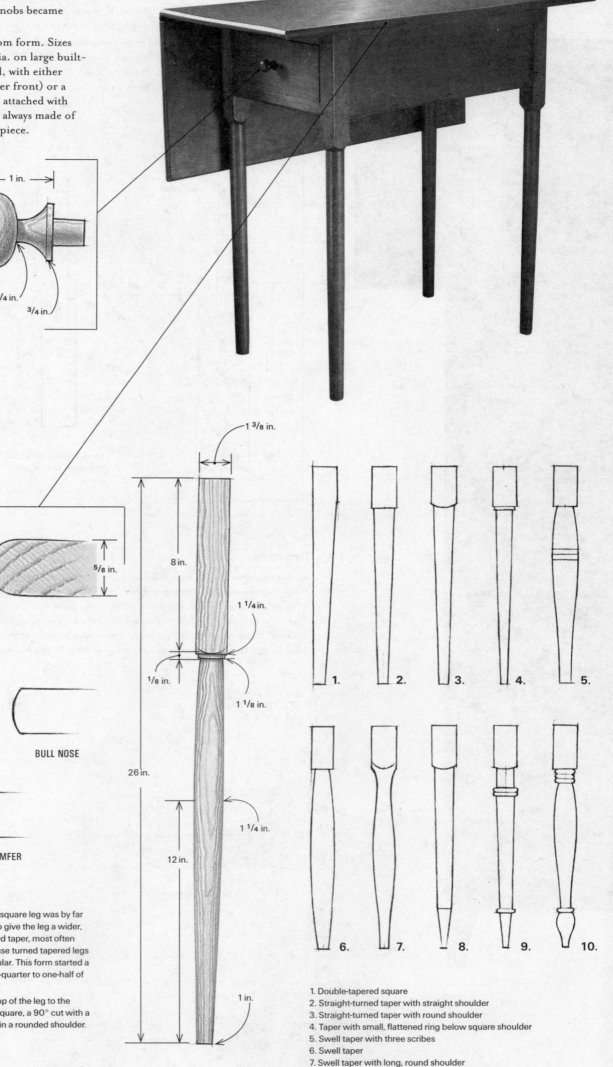

Tabletop Edges

A fair number of Shaker tabletop edges were square or only slightly eased. A square edge, however, was by no means the only profile used. Shaker craftsmen realized that a simple, shaped profile was not only less prone to damage than a square edge but also less painful when bumped.

Rule joints were used on drop-leaf tables. The joint looked crisp and was less likely to lodge crumbs or pinch items hanging over the edges.

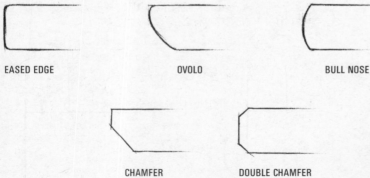

EASED EDGE OVOLO BULL NOSE

CHAMFER DOUBLE CHAMFER

Legs and Turnings

Shaker table legs were, for the most part, quite simple. The double-tapered square leg was by far the most common form. The tapers were cut only on the two inside faces to give the leg a wider, sturdier stance and appearance. Another favorite leg was the straight-turned taper, most often seen on drop-leaf tables. These legs are often splayed a few degrees, because turned tapered legs attached at 90° to the top appear pigeon-toed. Swell tapers were also popular. This form started a bit narrow under the shoulder, then swelled to a maximum diameter at one-quarter to one-half of the way down.

Shaker craftsmen handled the transition from the square area at the top of the leg to the turned portion in several ways. Frequently, they cut the shoulder perfectly square, a 90° cut with a parting tool. An easier, more common transition was the 45° cut, resulting in a rounded shoulder.

1. Double-tapered square
2. Straight-turned taper with straight shoulder
3. Straight-turned taper with round shoulder
4. Taper with small, flattened ring below square shoulder
5. Swell taper with three scribes
6. Swell taper
7. Swell taper with long, round shoulder
8. Telescope or double taper
9. Straight taper with rings
10. Swell taper with rings and pear foot

Shaker Dining Table

by Christian Becksvoort

This table is based on a piece built at the Shaker community in Hancock, Mass. (It's now in the collection of the Fruitlands Museum in Harvard, Mass.) The original, made from cherry, is almost 11 ft. long, with a third trestle to support the center. Such a length made good sense for communal dining, but it's not practical for most homes today. My version has only two trestles, and I typically make the top either 8 ft. or 9 ft. long.

A trestle table has appeal for a few reasons. For one, it can be "knocked down" without fuss. Remove the top from the base parts and the stretcher from the trestles, and you can move the table through doors and up or down stairs. Unlike most tables, which have aprons around the perimeter to stiffen the structure, trestle tables have a single center stretcher. This gives more vertical legroom. On the other hand, most trestle tables have flat feet, which tend to get in the way of the feet of diners sitting at either end. This Shaker design solves that inconvenience by replacing the flat feet with arched feet. This simple change not only makes the piece more ergonomic, but also gives it an especially graceful look.

Most Lathes will Handle These Posts

I make the posts first, using 16/4 stock. If this size isn't readily available, consider face-gluing two pieces of 8/4 stock from the same board. Using the same board means the grain and color of the pieces will be close and the glue joint less visible.

Mill the stock to about 3⅝ in. sq. and crosscut it to 24½ in. long. Then mount it in a lathe and turn it to 3½ in. dia. At a point 6 in. from the top and 4 in. from the bottom, use a parting tool and calipers to establish the 2⅜-in. diameter of the center section.

Continue using the parting tool to make a series of 2⅜-in.-dia. cuts between the end cuts. With these cuts serving as a depth guide, use a gouge to reduce the entire center section to 2⅜ in. dia. At each end of the center section, turn a small cove and a bead with a small flat at each end of it. If your turning skills are rusty, practice first on a shorter blank.

Jig Simplifies Post Joinery

Once both posts are turned and sanded, they need to be notched for the braces, feet, and stretchers. To hold them for layout and machining, I clamp the posts to a shop-made cradle that consists of a couple of U-shaped saddles screwed to a rectangular piece of plywood. A narrow piece of paper towel in each saddle, held in place with masking tape, helps prevent scratches on the posts.

Place the cradle on a bench (with the clamp between the opened jaws of the vise so the cradle can rest flat). Use a square to lay out the width and length of the notch on each end of the post. To lay out a notch, first use a square to mark a vertical line through the center of the turning. Using that centerline as a reference, mark the width of the notch. Finally, mark the depth of the notch. The notches can be cut by hand with a deep backsaw; but a bandsaw does as good a job in less time. With the post clamped in the cradle, carefully saw between the lines to the bottom of the notch. Then, nibble out the bottom of the notch with the blade. As you switch from one end to another, you'll need to reposition the clamp so that it doesn't bump into the saw table as you cut.

Rout a shallow groove for the stretcher—There's one more machine cut to make on each post—a groove, ¼ in. deep by 1 in. wide by 5 in. long, that will accept the end of the stretcher. You can cut the groove with a chisel, but it's easier on a router table.

Again, I use the cradle to support the post. A clamp gets in the way on the router table, so I made a wooden yoke that serves as a clamp. With the yoke screwed to the base of the cradle, the post stays securely in place. Before tightening the yoke, make sure the cheeks of the slot are parallel with the router-table surface.

Install a 1-in.-dia. straight bit in the router, and raise the bit to make a ¼-in.-deep cut in the post. Adjust the router-table fence so that when the cradle slides against it, the bit is centered on the post. Also, clamp a stop block to the fence to stop the cradle when the groove is 5 in. long. Hold the cradle firmly against the fence as you slide it forward to feed the post in the bit.

The router bit leaves rounded corners at the end of each groove. Use a chisel to cut them square.

Fit the Other Parts to the Posts

Templates for the brace and feet can be found on p. 20, but you'll need to enlarge them to full size. I'm not fussy about pattern stock; light cardboard or poster paper works just fine.

Use the patterns and a pencil to transfer the profiles to the stock. Cut the parts on the bandsaw, staying just outside the lines. Next, lay out and mark the location of the dadoes in the braces and feet. These mate with the deep notches in the posts. They can be cut by hand, with a router, or with a dado blade on the tablesaw. To save time, I use the dado blade set for the widest possible cut.

To support the braces and feet during the dado cuts, clamp a long fence to the miter gauge. The fence should extend at least 15 in. on either side of the dado blade. Add a pair of stop blocks to ensure that the shoulders of the dadoes align perfectly on both sides of the joint. When setting the depth of cut, I leave the areas between the dadoes a bit thick. That way, I can trim them with a rabbet plane for a perfect final fit.

With the dadoes cut, I smooth concave edges of the braces and feet using a spindle sander, and convex edges using a stationary disk sander. Smooth the curved edges further by hand-sanding.

Now use the router table and a chamfer bit to rout a ¼-in. chamfer along the top edges of the feet. Stop each chamfer at a point ½ in. from the dadoes.

To fit a joint, first make a knife cut at the shoulders of the dado to sever the wood fibers before trimming the dadoes with a rabbet plane. When the joint begins to engage, I mark the leading edges of the slots with a pencil, which shows me exactly where the joint is still tight. A few more strokes with the rabbet plane and the joint should fit snugly.

Once all braces and feet are fitted to their respective posts, the parts can be glued and clamped to create a trestle. A pair of clamps, each spanning from brace to foot, is all that's needed. After that, at one end of the trestle, measure the distance from the top edge of the brace to the bottom edge of the foot. Do the same at the other end. The measurement should be the same. If they differ, adjust the

pressure on the two clamps until the measurements agree. Once dry, sand the bottom of the post and the underside of the arched foot until flush.

When making the stretcher, I start with slightly thicker stock. Then I make light passes with a thickness planer until the stretcher fits snugly in the groove routed in the top of the post.

How to Install Bed Bolts

Each trestle attaches to an end of the stretcher with a pair of ⅜-in. by 6-in. bed bolts and nuts (available from Horton Brasses; www.horton-brasses.com). Each bolt extends through a post and brace and into the end of the stretcher. The end of the bolt threads through a nut mortised into the stretcher. When the bolt and nut are tightened, the stretcher and trestle are pulled together to produce a rock-solid joint.

The bed-bolt work starts at the drill press. Once again, the cradle comes in handy. Use the yoke to secure the trestle to the cradle, with the stretcher groove facing down. Make sure the sides of the brace and trestle are parallel to the worksurface. If the parts tilt, the holes won't be square.

Measuring from the top end of the post, mark the hole centers at 1 in. and 4 ¼ in. Position the cradle so that a 1-in. Forstner bit is centered on the upper hole. Clamp the cradle to the drill press, and then bore a ⅝-in.-deep hole to accept the head of the bed bolt. Replace the Forstner bit with a ⅜-in.-dia. brad-point bit and bore a hole completely through the post and brace. Repeat the process for the remaining holes.

Next, clamp the stretcher in a vise and temporarily mount one of the trestles. Transfer the ⅜-in.-dia. bit from the drill press to a portable drill. Using the holes in the trestle as guides, drill matching holes in the end of the stretcher. Remove the trestle and continue drilling until the hole is at least 3 ½ in. deep, measured from the end of the stretcher.

Portable drills rarely produce a hole perfectly square to the stretcher ends. So, to make sure the mortise for the nut is properly located, I use a bed bolt as a guide. Allow a good portion of the bolt to extend from the hole. Then place a long ruler so it's centered along the length of the exposed bolt. Use a pencil to extend the centerline along the face of the stretcher. With the centerline showing the location of the bolt hole, measure 2 ½ in. from the end of the stretcher, and lay out the location of the mortise for the nut. A few minutes' work with a chisel yields a mortise just big enough to accept the nut. You'll know the alignment is OK if you can slip the bolt into the hole and thread it into the nut. I use a special bed-bolt wrench (available from Horton Brasses; a 12-point socket also works) to turn and tighten the bolts.

With the holes drilled and all the mortises cut, you can mount the trestles to the stretcher.

Build the Top and Breadboard Ends

I make the tabletop by edge-gluing 1-in.-thick stock, using three or four well-matched boards across the 36-in. width.

Breadboards are applied to either end. The original table, made from ⅞-in.-thick stock, had a ¼-in.-thick by ½-in.-long tongue cut fully across each end of the top and pinned to allow for wood movement. The tongue fit into a corresponding groove cut across the entire length of the breadboard end. I make my tenons longer for added strength.

The top is attached with screws driven through counterbored holes in the braces and stretcher. To allow the top to expand and contract in width due to seasonal changes in humidity, be sure to elongate the shank holes in the braces.

For a finish, I use an oil-and-varnish mix (equal parts of each), applying three coats to all the table surfaces, including the top and bottom of the top and breadboard ends. For added durability, the top then gets two more coats.

Continued ➔

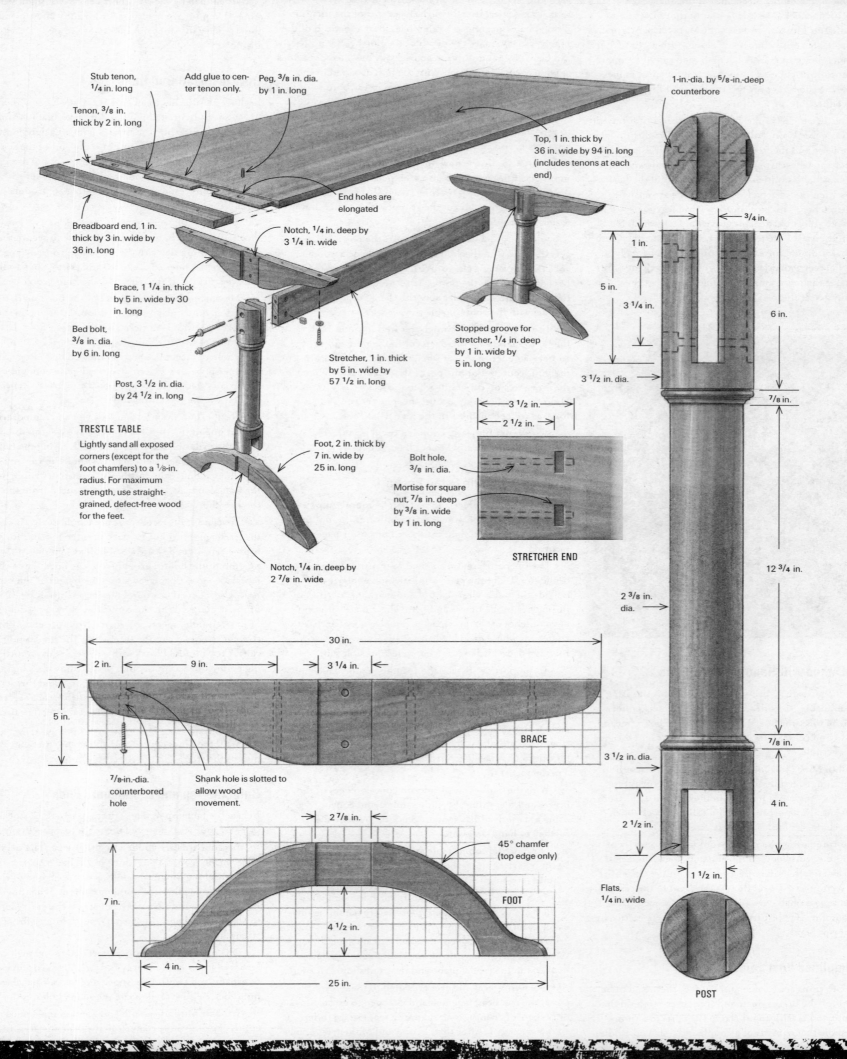

Stub tenon,
1/4 in. long

Add glue to cen-
ter tenon only.

Peg, 3/8 in. dia.
by 1 in. long

Tenon, 3/8 in.
thick by 2 in. long

1-in.-dia. by 5/8-in.-deep
counterbore

Top, 1 in. thick by
36 in. wide by 94 in. long
(includes tenons at each
end)

End holes are
elongated

Breadboard end, 1 in.
thick by 3 in. wide by
36 in. long

Notch, 1/4 in. deep by
3 1/4 in. wide

Brace, 1 1/4 in. thick
by 5 in. wide by 30
in. long

Bed bolt,
3/8 in. dia.
by 6 in. long

Stretcher, 1 in. thick
by 5 in. wide by
57 1/2 in. long

Stopped groove for
stretcher, 1/4 in. deep
by 1 in. wide by
5 in. long

3/4 in.

1 in.

5 in.

3 1/4 in.

6 in.

3 1/2 in. dia.

7/8 in.

Post, 3 1/2 in. dia.
by 24 1/2 in. long

TRESTLE TABLE

Lightly sand all exposed
corners (except for the
foot chamfers) to a 1/8-in.
radius. For maximum
strength, use straight-
grained, defect-free wood
for the feet.

Foot, 2 in. thick by
7 in. wide by 25 in. long

3 1/2 in.

2 1/2 in.

Bolt hole,
3/8 in. dia.

Mortise for square
nut, 7/8 in. deep
by 3/8 in. wide
by 1 in. long

STRETCHER END

2 3/8 in.
dia.

12 3/4 in.

Notch, 1/4 in. deep by
2 7/8 in. wide

3 1/2 in. dia.

7/8 in.

2 1/2 in.

30 in.

2 in.

9 in.

3 1/4 in.

5 in.

BRACE

7/8-in.-dia.
counterbored
hole

Shank hole is slotted to
allow wood movement.

4 in.

1 1/2 in.

Flats,
1/4 in. wide

2 7/8 in.

45° chamfer
(top edge only)

7 in.

FOOT

4 1/2 in.

4 in.

25 in.

POST

The Posts are Simple Turnings

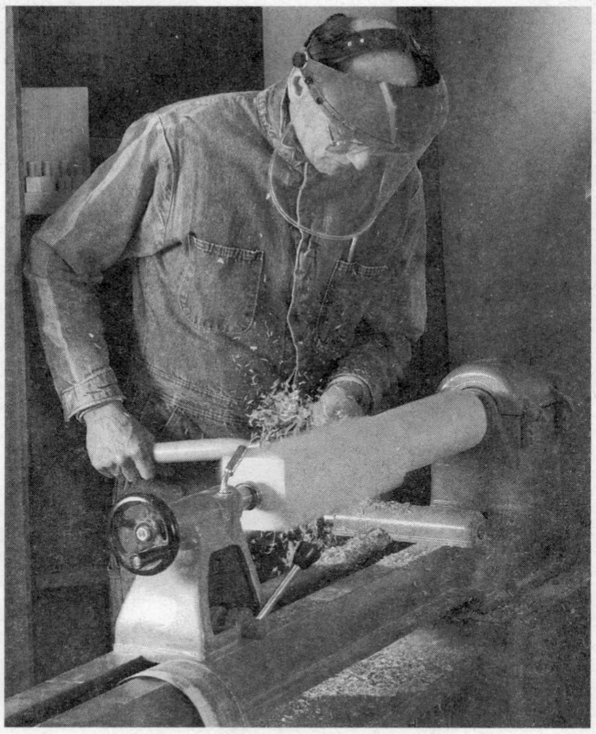

Turn the blank. Becksvoort turns a 3 5/8-in.-sq. blank to 3 1/2 in. dia. (above), then makes a series of 2 3/8-in.-dia. parting cuts along the midsection, checking the diameter with calipers (below). After that, with the parting cuts serving as guides, he reduces the entire midsection to 2 3/8 in. dia.

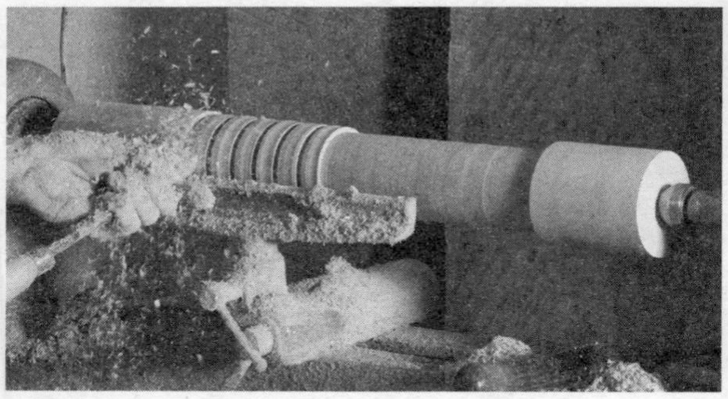

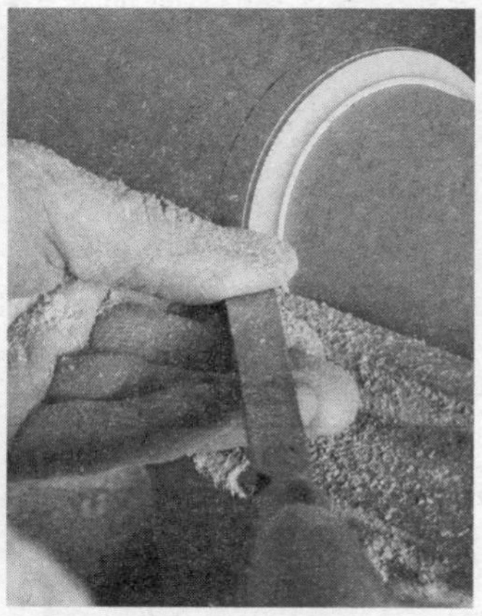

Coves and beads. Each end of the midsection terminates in a cove and bead. Mark the 7/8-in. width of the detail by lightly touching a pencil point against the spinning post. Cut the cove with a roundnose chisel or small gouge, then the bead with a diamond-point or skew chisel.

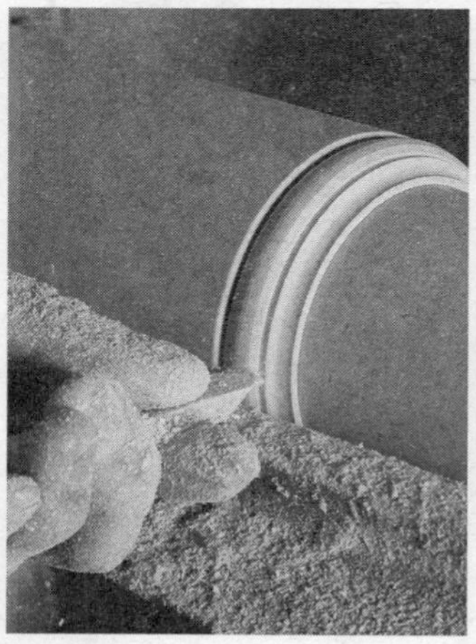

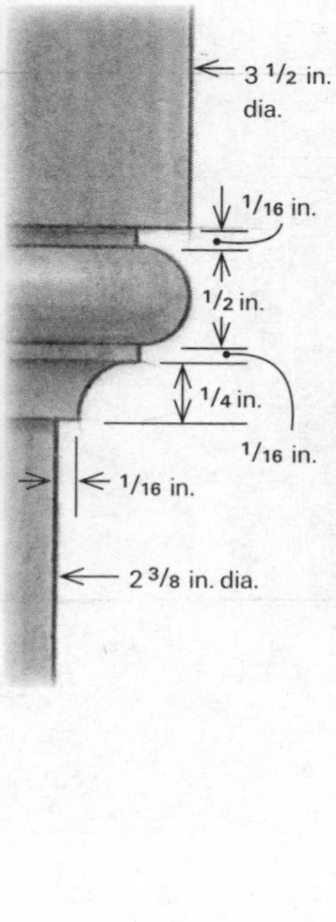
3 1/2 in. dia.
1/16 in.
1/2 in.
1/4 in.
1/16 in.
1/16 in.
2 3/8 in. dia.

Notch the Posts

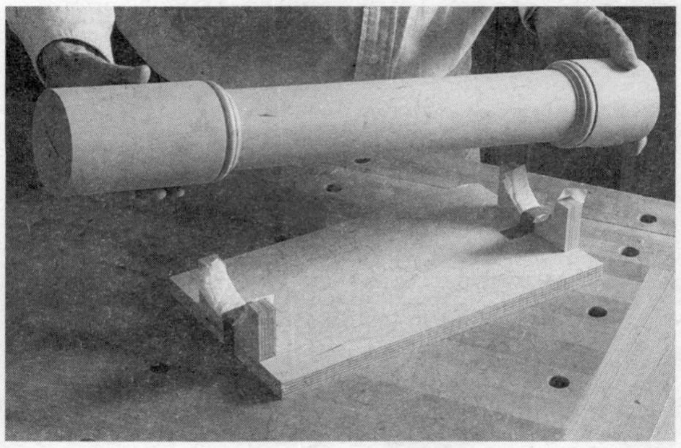

Build a cradle. Two saddles screwed to a base, 3/4 in. thick by 8 in. wide by 12 1/2 in. long, create a cradle for the post that simplifies a number of construction steps.

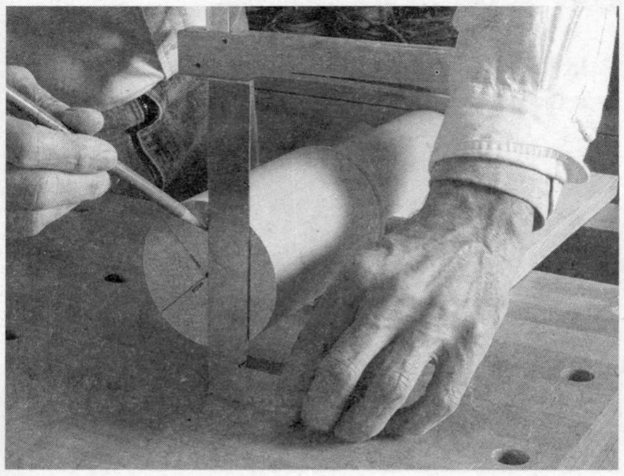

Lay out the location of the notches. With the cradle on a flat surface, use a square to mark a vertical centerline on each end of the post (above). Measure and mark the width of the notch, then use a square to scribe the notch depth (below).

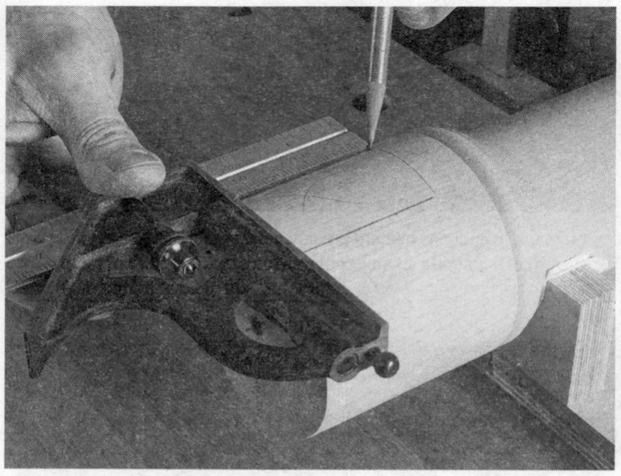

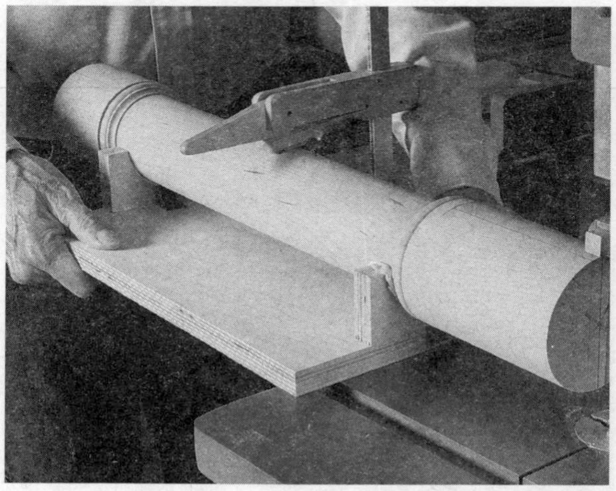

Cut the two notches. With the post securely clamped in the cradle, use a bandsaw to cut the notch on each end, following your layout lines by eye.

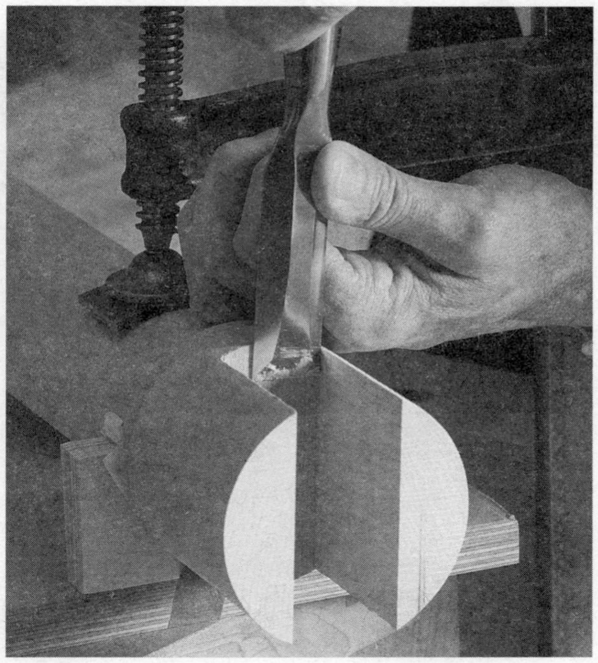

Hand work. Smooth the ends of the notches and the cheeks with a sharp chisel.

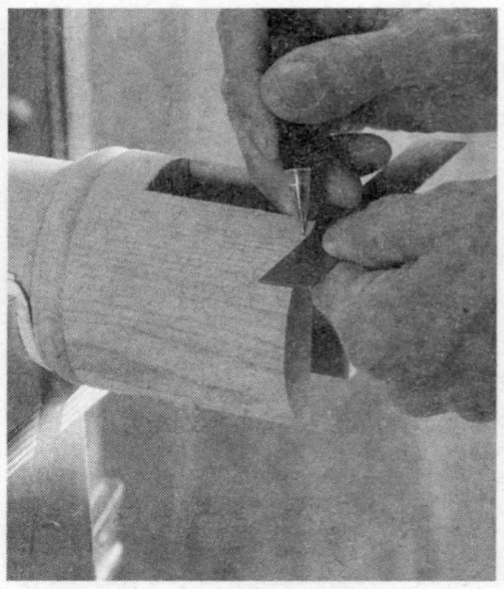

Cut small shoulders. Cut a flat on each side of the notches to ensure gap-free contact between the post and the brace and foot. First, lay out each flat with a pencil and ruler (left), then make a vertical cut with a chisel to establish the end point. Finally, make horizontal cuts with the chisel to pare the stock to the layout line (below).

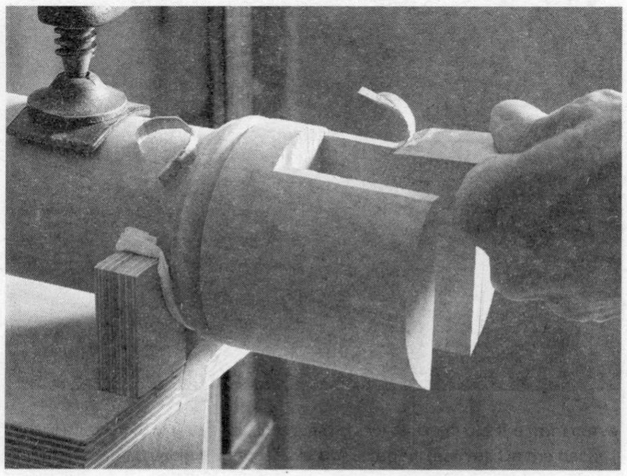

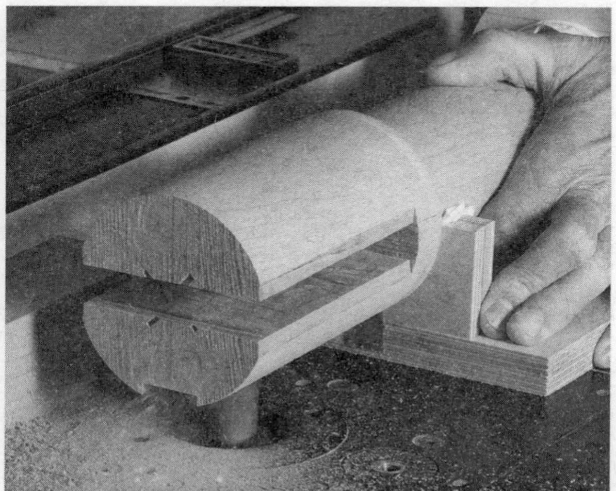

Continued →

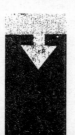

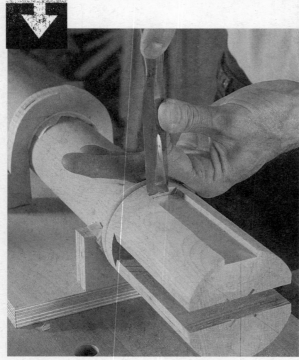

Rout chamfers. A chamfer bit in a router table is used to chamfer the top edges of the feet. Stop the cut 1/2 in. short of the dado.

Assembly is Easy

Put it together. After all the parts have been sanded and finished, it's finally time to put the table together. With the table parts upside down, slide the ends of the stretcher into the post grooves and slip the bed-bolt nuts into the mortises in the stretcher. Then, insert the bolts (below).

Cut the groove for the stretcher. With a U-shaped yoke screwed to the cradle serving as a clamp, use a router table to cut a stopped groove in the top end of the post (above). Square the rounded end left by the router bit with a chisel.

Complete the Trestles

Dado the legs and braces. Cut a wide dado on each side of the brace and foot (above). Use the tablesaw miter gauge with a long auxiliary fence to support the parts during the cuts. A pair of stop blocks helps ensure that the ends of the dadoes end up perfectly aligned on both sides of the parts.

Dry-fit the parts. Check the fit of the posts to each dado (above). If too tight, use a rabbet plane to trim the sides or bottom of the dado.

Add the Bed Bolts

Start by drilling. With a trestle clamped in the cradle, and the cradle clamped to the drill-press table, use a 1-in.-dia. Forstner bit to drill a 5/8-in.-deep hole (left). Then, remove the Forstner bit and use a 3/8-in.-dia. brad-point bit to drill a hole completely through the post.

Drill holes in the ends of the stretcher. Add a trestle to the stretcher temporarily, then use a 3/8-in.-dia. brad-point bit to extend the bed-bolt hole slightly into the end of the stretcher. After that, remove the trestle and drill deeper to complete the hole.

Lay out the location of the bed-bolt nuts. With a bed bolt in a stretcher hole serving as a guide (in case the hole isn't drilled perfectly square), mark the location of the bed-bolt nut (above). Cut the mortises for the nuts (left) just deep enough to allow the bolt to thread into the nut.

Attach the top. A screw and washer go into each counterbored hole in the braces. The slotted shank hole allows wood movement.

494

Shaker Chest of Drawers

by Christian Becksvoort

Years ago, clients wanted me to make a blanket chest to store shirts and sweaters. Blanket chests are great for quilts and blankets, but they tend to allow small items to drift toward the bottom and get lost. For clothes, I mused, drawers would make the contents more accessible. And if I used the same outside dimensions as a blanket box, they could still place the chest at the foot of the bed and sit on it, or push it against the wall to use as a dresser. The different drawer depths would add to the versatility of what the chest could hold. They took my advice and they still love the finished chest.

As with much of my work, this design is heavily influenced by the Shaker design ethic, with its simple lines, functional design, solid construction, and cherry wood. There are a number of parts, but the construction is straightforward. I use half-blind dovetails to secure the sides to a subtop, and a sliding dovetail to secure the bottom to the sides. A vertical divider gets centered in the top and bottom and dadoed in place. Front and back rails are notched around the vertical divider and dovetailed into place. I use a sturdy frame-and-panel back, glued into a rabbet, so the piece looks beautiful from all directions. And the main top gets screwed in place from the underside of the subtop. This is the same construction I use on all my case pieces, so the anatomy could work for a taller chest, too.

Tackle the Sides First

Most of the business happens on the side pieces. But before I hand-chop any half-blind dovetails, the side pieces get a rabbet, leg arches, a sliding dovetail, and a dado with a dovetail at the front.

First, rabbet the side pieces with two ripcuts on the tablesaw. This rabbet will accept the back. Then, draw the leg arches on the side pieces and use a bandsaw to cut them out and a block plane to smooth the straight edges. I clean up the arches using a balloon sander on my lathe and finish up with hand sanding.

Now it's time to pick up the router and tackle the dado/dovetail that holds the front and back rails and the drawer runners, as well as the sliding dovetail that holds the bottom. For all three I use a shopmade jig with two parallel bars, spaced the width of the router base, clamping it square to the carcase side. The same jig works for the dadoes on the sides of the vertical divider and the dadoes in the subtop and bottom that hold the vertical divider. While the router and jig are out, cut the dadoes in each side of the vertical divider. Along with the dadoes in the sides, these will hold the drawer runners. Line them up with the dadoes on the sides, but leave the piece a bit long until you glue up the carcase and get an exact measurement.

Dovetailing a Large Case Piece

Cutting dovetails on a large piece is very similar to cutting dovetails on a smaller box or drawer, but there are a few more things to consider. Holding the pieces is more challenging, keeping them flat is important, and of course there is more material to remove. The good news, at least with this piece, is that even if your dovetails don't look perfect they'll be hidden by the subtop. I always lay out and cut the tails first, then transfer them and finish up with the pins (see photos, p. 496).

Once you have the dovetails cut, it's time to glue the subtop to the sides. But first rout the dadoes for the vertical divider in the subtop and bottom (using the same jig as before). To find the center of both, it isn't necessary to do a dry-fit. The subtop, the bottom piece, and the rails are all the same length, so just stack the top and bottom together with the ends flush and measure for the center. After routing the dadoes, glue the dovetailed subtop to the sides. The bottom doesn't go in yet, so use spacers at the bottom of the legs to keep everything straight and square.

While that assembly is drying, move to the router table to cut the sliding dovetails in the ends of the bottom and front and back rails. Then slide the bottom into place. I glued only the last 3 in. to 4 in. at the front of the sliding dovetail. Because the dovetail slot is deep, it weakens the sides of the case, so I added five glue blocks underneath each side. This strengthens and anchors the lower sections of the case sides to the bottom, yet still allows for wood movement.

Divider Helps Drawers Run Smoothly

The four drawers are separated by a vertical divider that is cut to fit after the case is assembled. With a handsaw, notch the vertical divider to accept the notched front and back rails, and then slide it in place. These notches line up with the dadoes that are already in the vertical divider. Don't glue the vertical divider in place because it is an end-grain to long-grain joint, and glue won't hold. Instead, screw it in place, plugging the holes in the bottom. The holes in the subtop will be covered by the top.

The bottom drawers run on the bottom of the case, but the top drawers run on a frame: two rails and four drawer runners. The runners are tenoned into the front and back rails. The tenons get glued into the front rail but are left loose in the back rail to allow for wood movement.

Finish Panels Before Gluing in Frames

A frame-and-panel back, although more work, gives as much diagonal racking resistance as plywood (unlike nailed shiplapped, tongue-and-groove boards) and looks much better. Once the case and all the dividers are in place, make the frame-and-panel back, leaving it a little too wide so you can sneak up on the perfect fit with a block plane. I profile the four panels with a 22 ½° panel-raising bit. I pin the rails and stiles for extra support and a nice design detail. Then I sand the inside face and fit the back to the case. I glue the back in place, secure it with small brads, countersink them, and plug the holes.

Complete the Base and Profile the Top

To finish the front of the case, miter and spline the three-piece base assembly, bandsaw the arches to the same radius as the sides, and glue it into place. A one-piece base would introduce cross-grain gluing and could self-destruct. This way, the base expands and contracts (up and down), while the case side it is glued to does not change in length.

Next, sand the entire case, and then cut the top of the case to size, allowing a ½-in. overhang on the front and on each side. Rout the profile into the front and sides, sand the top, and screw it into place from underneath through the subtop.

Drawers Are the Final Step

Before starting the dovetails on the drawers, groove the sides and front. Now lay out the tails, saw and chop them, and move on to the pins. I cut the pins and tails slightly proud and flush everything up with a belt sander after the drawers are glued. Knob holes also can be drilled at this point. I use a pencil to mark the tight spots and a belt sander to remove material as I carefully fit the drawers to their openings.

Insert the drawer bottoms, and hold them in place with two saw slots and round-head screws in the underside of the drawer backs. The knobs are turned on the lathe, tenons cut to length, and then glued into place.

Before applying a finish, I go over the entire piece to break and sand all edges including around the drawer openings, and the gaps between the frames and panels on the back. Then I sign the piece and give it three coats of an oil finish. The first coat is straight Danish oil, and the final two coats are a mixture of Tried & True varnish oil and spar varnish.

Pro Method

DUAL PURPOSE JIG FOR DADOES AND DOVETAILS

Like many chests of drawers, the sides of this one need a dovetail/dado combo for the rails and drawer runners, and a long sliding dovetail for the bottom. One simple jig handles them all.

Setup is easy. Registering off the front edge of the side, it's easy to clamp the jig square and cut dadoes and dovetails precisely.

Dovetail meets dado. Use a ³/₄-in. dovetail bit to cut the dovetail notch for the front and back rails (left). Without moving the jig (Becksvoort has two identical routers so he doesn't have to change bits), use a ³/₄-in. straight bit to cut the dado that will hold the drawer runners (below).

Two cuts for a long sliding dovetail. Before the final pass with a ³/₄-in. dovetail bit, Becksvoort uses a smaller straight bit to waste away the material, making the dovetail cleaner and easier to cut.

Continued ➡

Pro Method

HALF-BLIND DOVETAILS IN LARGE PANELS

Half-blind dovetails make a strong but clean-looking case. They can be a challenge on big pieces, but Becksvoort has tricks for keeping the pieces flat and aligned.

Tails first. On the subtop, Becksvoort marks the centers of the pins and uses a dovetail guide to lay out the tails (above). To saw the long, wide board, he rests it on the floor and secures it in a vise. A thick, straight hardwood board clamped near the action keeps the wide board flat (below).

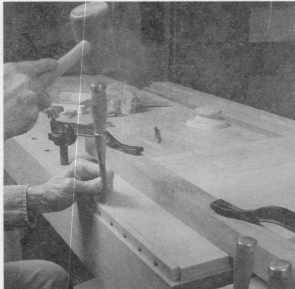

Chop and pare, chop and pare. Keeping the wide workpiece flat, make a vertical cut in the scribed line, tipping the chisel slightly forward (above). Make the first cut light. Then, paring horizontally in from the end grain, remove a chip (top of next column). Alternate between cutting down and cutting in until about halfway through, then turn the board over and repeat the process until you've met in the middle. Follow the same procedure after sawing the pins.

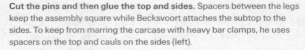

Cut the pins and then glue the top and sides. Spacers between the legs keep the assembly square while Becksvoort attaches the subtop to the sides. To keep from marring the carcase with heavy bar clamps, he uses spacers on the top and cauls on the sides (left).

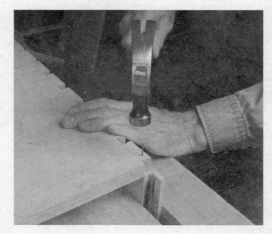

TIP

Nail Down the Tail Board to Mark Pins

Mark the location of the tails on the pin board. On long, wide workpieces, Becksvoort uses a small nail to help in the transfer. Align the boards and predrill. Tap in the nail partway so it can be easily removed (above). Using a marking knife and working from the nailed corner, scribe the tails onto the pin board (left). Pivot the tail board into alignment whenever necessary.

Pro Method

HOW TO TAME LONG SLIDING DOVETAILS

Long sliding dovetails can bind and freeze during assembly, but not if you follow Becksvoort's steps closely.

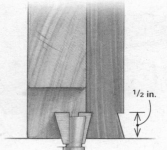

Big workpiece is an added challenge. A featherboard applies even pressure, keeping the long board on track and the cut precise. Go for a snug fit.

1/2 in.

Please don't freeze. To prevent binding, don't use glue yet, and keep the bottom as straight as possible as you slide it in most of the way. Glue only the front 3 to 4 in. of the bottom; otherwise, the joint will seize while you are trying to bring the piece home. Use clamps to pull the bottom evenly and steadily. Clamping blocks that extend over the side keep the workpieces from getting damaged, but, more importantly, stop the bottom when it is exactly flush with the sides.

RAILS AND DIVIDERS GUIDE THE DRAWERS

This simple system keeps drawers from racking back and forth, tipping up, or dropping down.

1. Fit the vertical divider, and tap it into position without glue. Screw it in from the top and bottom.

2. Fit the front rail and glue it into the sides and onto the vertical divider panel.

3. Install the four drawer runners. Apply glue only to the front tenons.

4. The back rail is glued into the dovetail slots and onto the vertical divider. The back mortise-and-tenon joints are not glued. This allows the web frame to telescope in and out as the case expands and contracts. .

5. Fit the back. The end stiles extend beyond the bottom rail and become an integral part of the back legs. Use a block plane to sneak up on the fit before clamping and gluing.

6. Apply the mitered front base assembly. Add glue blocks afterward to strengthen the corner joints.

Continued ➜

Built to Last

Half-blind dovetails, sliding dovetails, and dadoes ensure decades of flawless function. A frame-and-panel back makes the chest look good from all directions.

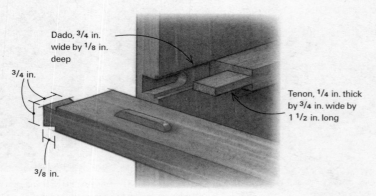

Dado, ³/₄ in. wide by ¹/₈ in. deep

³/₄ in.

³/₈ in.

Tenon, ¹/₄ in. thick by ³/₄ in. wide by 1 ¹/₂ in. long

A. STRETCHER END DETAIL

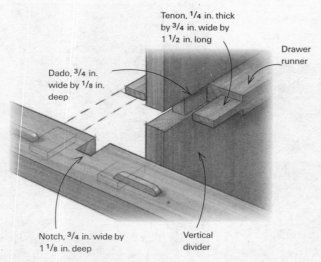

Tenon, ¹/₄ in. thick by ³/₄ in. wide by 1 ¹/₂ in. long

Drawer runner

Dado, ³/₄ in. wide by ¹/₈ in. deep

Notch, ³/₄ in. wide by 1 ¹/₈ in. deep

Vertical divider

B. STRETCHER/VERTICAL DIVIDER DETAIL

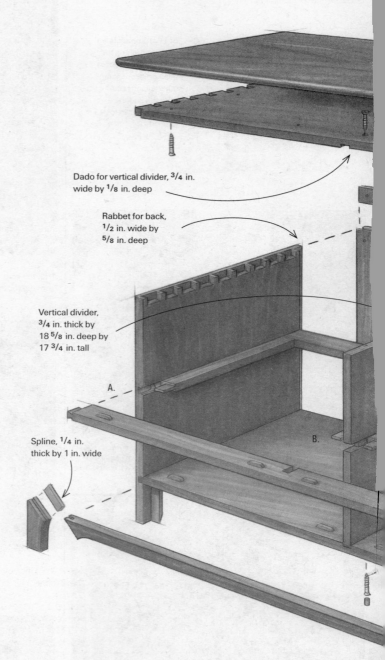

Dado for vertical divider, ³/₄ in. wide by ¹/₈ in. deep

Rabbet for back, ¹/₂ in. wide by ⁵/₈ in. deep

Vertical divider, ³/₄ in. thick by 18 ⁵/₈ in. deep by 17 ³/₄ in. tall

A.

B.

Spline, ¹/₄ in. thick by 1 in. wide

Rail, ³/₄ in. thick by 2 ¹/₈ in. wide by 46 ¹/₂ in. long

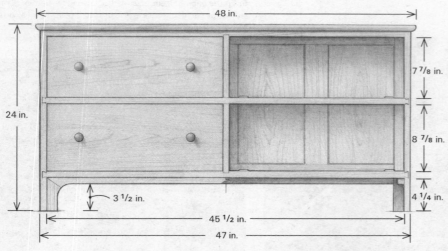

48 in.

24 in.

7 ⁷/₈ in.

8 ⁷/₈ in.

4 ¹/₄ in.

3 ¹/₂ in.

45 ¹/₂ in.

47 in.

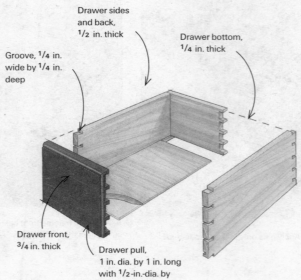

Drawer sides and back, ¹/₂ in. thick

Drawer bottom, ¹/₄ in. thick

Groove, ¹/₄ in. wide by ¹/₄ in. deep

Drawer front, ³/₄ in. thick

Drawer pull, 1 in. dia. by 1 in. long with ¹/₂-in.-dia. by ⁵/₈-in.-long tenons

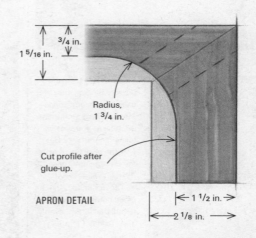

³/₄ in.

1 ⁵/₁₆ in.

Radius, 1 ³/₄ in.

Cut profile after glue-up.

APRON DETAIL

1 ¹/₂ in.

2 ¹/₈ in.

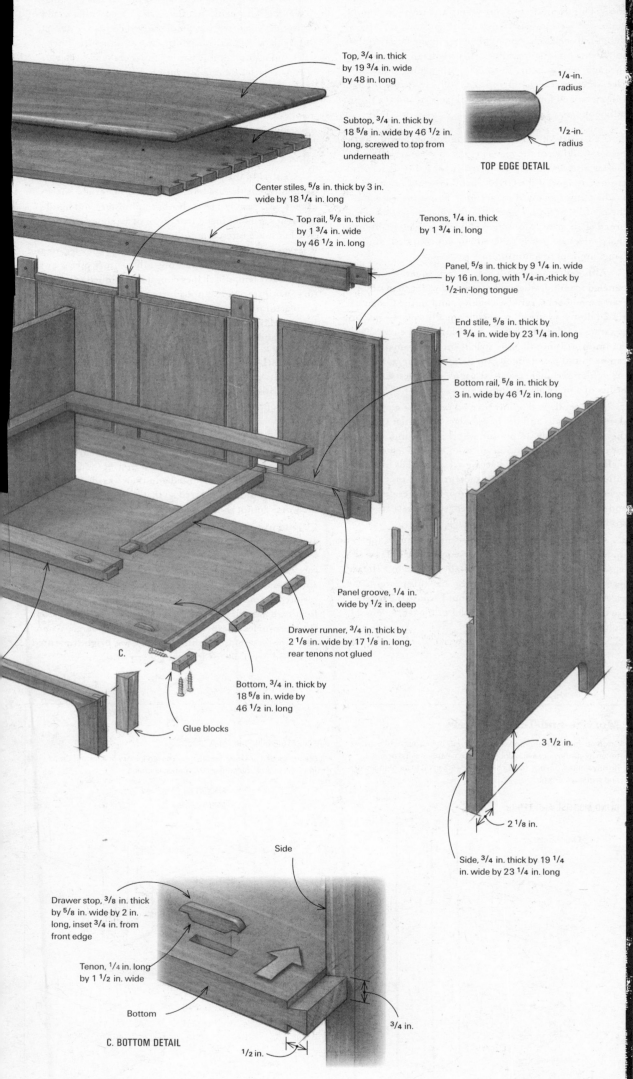

Top, 3/4 in. thick by 19 3/4 in. wide by 48 in. long

Subtop, 3/4 in. thick by 18 5/8 in. wide by 46 1/2 in. long, screwed to top from underneath

1/4-in. radius

1/2-in. radius

TOP EDGE DETAIL

Center stiles, 5/8 in. thick by 3 in. wide by 18 1/4 in. long

Top rail, 5/8 in. thick by 1 3/4 in. wide by 46 1/2 in. long

Tenons, 1/4 in. thick by 1 3/4 in. long

Panel, 5/8 in. thick by 9 1/4 in. wide by 16 in. long, with 1/4-in.-thick by 1/2-in.-long tongue

End stile, 5/8 in. thick by 1 3/4 in. wide by 23 1/4 in. long

Bottom rail, 5/8 in. thick by 3 in. wide by 46 1/2 in. long

Panel groove, 1/4 in. wide by 1/2 in. deep

Drawer runner, 3/4 in. thick by 2 1/8 in. wide by 17 1/8 in. long, rear tenons not glued

C.

Bottom, 3/4 in. thick by 18 5/8 in. wide by 46 1/2 in. long

Glue blocks

3 1/2 in.

2 1/8 in.

Side, 3/4 in. thick by 19 1/4 in. wide by 23 1/4 in. long

Side

Drawer stop, 3/8 in. thick by 5/8 in. wide by 2 in. long, inset 3/4 in. from front edge

Tenon, 1/4 in. long by 1 1/2 in. wide

Bottom

3/4 in.

1/2 in.

C. BOTTOM DETAIL

ARTS & CRAFTS DESIGN

Elements of Arts and Crafts Style

Text and Illustrations by Graham Blackburn

The Arts and Crafts style has been popular for a hundred years; there are examples in every antique and secondhand furniture store; reproductions abound; and it's a perennial favorite with woodworkers—but what exactly defines Arts and Crafts? Ask anyone familiar with the style—also known as Mission, Craftsman, Crafts, Cloister or even Quaint—how they identify it, and you'll get answers that typically contain words such as "foursquare," "straightforward construction,""exposed joinery" and "quartersawn oak." Such elements make the Arts and Crafts style inviting to many woodworkers who are new to the craft and who are less intimidated by Arts and Crafts furniture than they are by other, more sophisticated styles. Despite its apparent simplicity, however, it's just as easy to get a piece of Arts and Crafts furniture wrong as it is to fail at your first attempt at constructing a Chippendale piece that features cabriole legs—unless you have a full understanding of what the essential design details are and how they work together.

It's true that the Arts and Crafts style originated partly in response to overdecorated and directionless 19th-century furniture, but equally important were concerns about the shoddy quality of mass-produced factory furniture and its effect not only on the consumer but also on the people who made it. Arts and Crafts was conceived as an essentially utilitarian style affordable by all; the idea that its manufacture should be something in which the maker could take pride was central to the philosophy underlying what became known as the Arts and Crafts movement.

A piece of furniture built in the genuine Arts and Crafts style is therefore first and foremost completely functional. The furniture is solidly constructed with a minimum of superfluous ornament, unashamed yet not boastful of its joinery and, more often than not, made of oak—which is a supremely appropriate wood for hard-wearing furniture and a species that harks back to the period in furniture-making history when craftsmanship was valued more than commercial success.

The movement embodied the writings of a variety of influential 19th-century art critics, philosophers, architects and designers such as John Ruskin and William Morris, as well as the work of 20th-century furniture makers Gustav Stickley (and his brothers), Elbert Hubbard and the Roycrofters. Other seminal figures included the noted California architects Charles and Henry Greene; Frank Lloyd Wright; and internationally known and influential designers and furniture makers Charles Voysey, Ernest Gimson and the Barnsley brothers.

Because the movement that resulted in this style of furniture began as far back as the middle of the 19th century, the range of design elements that belong to this style is, in fact, much broader than many people realize.

Six Quintessential Elements

1. MATERIAL—Quartersawn oak does have much to recommend it: strength, durability, relative stability and an attractive figure characterized by the medullary rays not visible in flatsawn stock. Although a hardwood, oak is not excessively difficult to work—it is easier, in fact, to produce a crisp surface with a less than perfectly sharp tool on a piece of oak than on a piece of softwood. Oak is not toxic and may have a wide range of color—red, white or brown—depending on the species. The wood also takes stain well and can be fumed, a technique that can produce a wonderful aged look. Although most factory-built Arts and Crafts furniture was made of oak, many well-known designers have used other species, such as walnut, mahogany and cherry.

Continued ➔

Quartersawn Lumber Suits the Style

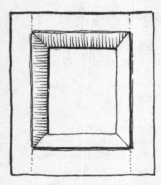

FLATSAWN OAK
Most boards from a tree sawn in this pattern show no medullary rays and are less stable.

Medullary rays

QUARTERSAWN OAK
When a tree is first quartered, the boards cut by any of the patterns shown are less likely to warp and will show medullary rays.

2. CONSTRUCTION TECHNIQUES—Although cabinet construction with veneered surfaces is occasionally used for the body of an Arts and Crafts piece, the majority of authentic pieces are made using solid wood and frame-and-panel construction.

Consistent with the directness and honesty that are the hallmarks of this style is the use of slats where a solid piece or a frame-and-panel section would be overkill. Unlike the furniture of the Gothic Period, turned elements are rare in Arts and Crafts designs. All of this is in keeping with the principle of using the simplest possible methods of work for the most honest and unpretentious result.

Simple does not, however, mean sloppy, especially in terms of the construction of a piece. In fact, because the aim of the Arts and Crafts movement was to design furniture that the maker could be proud of, a nice execution, particularly of exposed joinery, is essential when building a genuine Arts and Crafts piece.

3. JOINERY—Without a doubt, the mortise and tenon is the king of Arts and Crafts joints (see the drawings below right). Dovetailing, doweling, lapped and housed joinery also are used where appropriate, but in keeping with the demands of strength and honesty, the mortise-and-tenon joint plays a major role in the majority of Arts and Crafts pieces.

Paneling

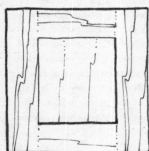

18th- and 19th-century paneling typically has a frame consisting of stiles and rails of different widths, invariably molded on the inner edges surrounding a fielded or raised panel.

Arts and Crafts paneling is typically square, with equal-width rails and stiles. Panels are sometimes carved, but more often than not they are plain and flat in unmolded frames.

Several varieties of tenons are used, including stub, blind, through- and tusk, but each is used only when and where necessary for maximum strength without compromise. This means that if, for example, a through-tenon is the strongest possible form in a given situation, the design will make a virtue of the necessity by not attempting to hide or disguise the joint. This results in the ends of through-tenons being finished a little proud of the surface, often nicely chamfered and with any wedges thoughtfully arranged for a pleasing visual pattern and the most efficient use.

4. DESIGN PARADIGMS—In American Arts and Crafts pieces, whether of the mass-produced variety typified by Gustav Stickley's Craftsman furniture or the higher-end custom designs of the Greene brothers, there is an immediate impression of squareness. This is most evident in the profiles of tops, edges and other flat surfaces, such as broad chair arms. Molding is almost completely absent, sharp edges are gently relieved but not rounded, and overhangs are kept to a minimum.

Although many details are, in fact, square—such as in paneled framing, where a bottom rail wider than other frame members is rare (see below), and in the design of glazed doors, where all panes are equally square—absolute squareness is largely illusory, and slopes and curves are common. It is not that the style is inelegant—many pieces can be found based on elegant design paradigms such as the golden rectangle (see next page)—but the strength and utility of a piece always dominate.

Both gently and boldly formed curves are common in skirts, chair rails and the lower edges of cabinet sides, but they are invariably simple and rarely compound, except for occasional tight cutouts on stool bases. Such shapes, including ogees and intersecting arcs, are nods to the influence of medieval Gothic oak furniture, much valued by leaders of the Arts and Crafts style for its craftsmanship and honesty. Curved yet square-edged brackets are another common feature of many pieces.

One other detail that would seem to belie an apparent squareness and angularity is the frequent use of tapered legs. The tapers, however, are usually limited to a short section near the base. Tapering legs like this prevents the piece from appearing too heavy, but because the tapers are equally formed on all four sides of the leg, a general feeling of squareness persists.

5. DECORATION—Despite a superficial plainness characterized by square edges, the lack of molding, the use of a relatively homogenous material and the flatness of panels, Arts and Crafts furniture often is decorated with a variety of techniques ranging from simple curved cutouts to delicate floral inlays. Reflecting a continuing sensitivity to other styles and fashion on the part of designers such as Harvey Ellis or Charles Rennie Macintosh, who are perhaps better known for their Art Nouveau styles, the influence of the more flowing, nature-based Art Nouveau style is felt in many Arts and Crafts pieces—for example, in the products of various "utopian" workshops such as the Byrdcliffe Arts Colony in Woodstock, N.Y.—in the form of pastel-colored painted sections, tulip inlays and lily patterns.

Central to the principle of craftsmanship in this style of furniture is the use of other natural materials, such as reed and rush for seats, leather upholstery and hand-wrought hardware made from iron or hammered brass. The hardware often is as square and sturdy as the furniture it serves and stands in complete contrast to the elegant and finely wrought shapes found on 18th-century pieces or the overworked fantastic shapes common on much 19th-century furniture. A gratuitous form of decoration in terms of structural function, but one that is consistent with the incorporation of natural materials, is the frequent use of a row of hand-wrought nails as an edge decoration.

6. FINISH—It would be inappropriate to finish an Arts and Crafts piece with a glossy lacquer. But while natural finishes like simple oiling and waxing may predominate, other processes, such as filling, staining and fuming, are common.

Careful surface preparation is most important. In the case of an open-grained wood like oak, a matching wood filler should be used. If oak is filled first, it then may be waxed or perhaps lightly oiled and then waxed. If wax alone is used, it should be colored so that the wax-filled pores in the wood do not show white.

Fuming, the process of exposing oak to the fumes of ammonia, is a common method of turning oak darker without producing the irregular color that can result from careless staining. The popularity of fuming, especially among early proponents of Arts and Crafts furniture, resulted from the misconception that genuine Gothic furniture was extremely dark. That darkness, in fact, came from centuries of exposure to smoky atmospheres. When new, however, most Gothic furniture was brightly painted or valued precisely for its light golden color.

Mortise-and-Tenon Joinery

Stronger and more appropriate than dowels or biscuits, mortise-and-tenon joints may be unshouldered (as for seatback slats) or shouldered on anywhere from one to four sides, depending on their intended use and particular design.

BLIND MORTISE AND TENON

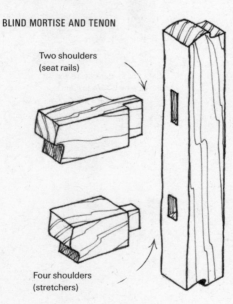

Two shoulders (seat rails)

Four shoulders (stretchers)

DECORATIVE REINFORCEMENTS
Lacking applied ornamentation, the exposed joinery of Arts and Crafts furniture became the primary decorative element.

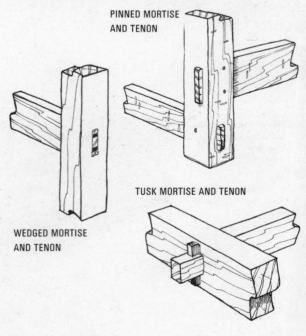

PINNED MORTISE AND TENON

TUSK MORTISE AND TENON

WEDGED MORTISE AND TENON

Designing Using the Golden Rectangle

The perfect squareness of the upper glazing and the general rectilinearity of this cabinet are based on a sophisticated design paradigm in which the height (H) equals the base (B) multiplied by 1.618, a proportion called the golden rectangle. The upper portion of the cabinet also is a golden rectangle.

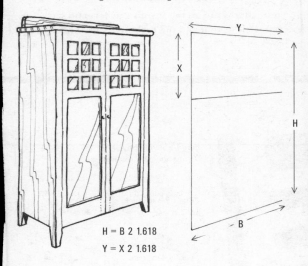

H = B 2 1.618

Y = X 2 1.618

Brackets and Cutouts

Not all details are perfectly rectilinear. Small accents, many in the form of brackets or cutouts, enliven otherwise straightforward designs.

Brackets, though square-edged, unmolded and flat, often are given a gently curved profile.

The angularity of wedges and curved cutouts lends a refined look to Arts and Crafts pieces.

Craftsman-Style Morris Chair

by Gregory Paolini

Craftsman furniture is known for its straight lines, quartersawn oak, and sense of earthen mass and solidity. No piece displays those features better than a Morris chair, with its large, square legs and wide arms decked out in beautiful ray-fleck figure. The gracefully bowed arms of this version, designed by Brian Murphy of American Furniture Design and related to a design by Gustav Stickley, lighten the mass just enough to give it the feel of irresistible comfort. Throw in a reclining back and firm, but giving, cushions, and you have a chair that you'll never want to leave.

For the most part, the construction is straightforward. But the most distinctive part of the chair—its arms—presents two big challenges: making bowed arms with attractive grain, and cutting a mortise-and-tenon joint on the curved arms and side frame. I'll show you how laminating the arms gets you around those challenges. And I'll show you how to get striking quartersawn grain everywhere it counts, including a simple and authentic method for making a leg with four quartersawn faces.

Legs that Look Good from Every Angle

The legs of a traditional Morris chair have four quartersawn faces. Lumber like that doesn't grow on trees, but it can be made in the shop. There are several different methods to achieve the look, but the one Stickley used, which is the easiest by far, is to glue up a core of quartersawn lumber and then laminate two quartersawn veneers over the flatsawn edges of the core.

After the glue is dry, trim the veneers flush to the core with a router and flush-trimming bit. Then crosscut the bottom of each leg to square it up. Don't worry about the tops right now.

Mortises, then Tenons

When making a mortise-and-tenon joint, I usually start with the mortises. It's much easier to fit a tenon to a mortise than the other way around. You can cut all of the mortises now, except the four in the arms. They're laid out and cut after you make the tenons on the tops of the legs.

Remain consistent with your reference edges. When cutting the mortises on the legs, for example, reference the same fence against the outside face of each one. Otherwise, the position of the mortises will vary, resulting in sloppy joints and possibly a chair that's out of square.

Now cut all of the tenons, except those on top of the legs, at the tablesaw. Cut a full tenon on the back of the upper rail; you'll just saw away part of it later.

Router-cut mortises have round ends, so I round the tenons with the rasp portion of a Nicholson 4-in-hand file. Its smooth edges won't mar the tenon shoulders, and its aggressive teeth make quick work of the rounding.

The tenons on the lower side rails will interfere with those of the front and back stretchers where they meet inside the legs. The best way around this is to insert the side rails into their mortises and trace the front and back mortises onto them. You'll need to trim the tenons' thickness about 1/8 in. in those areas.

Drawing Brings Arms and Legs Together

The upper rail and the tops of the legs must be curved to match the bow of the arms. The easiest way to do this is to make a full-size drawing of the arm's profile. You'll use this drawing to make a pattern for marking the curve on the upper rails and legs and to make the bending form used to laminate the arms. Here's an easy way to make the full-size drawing of the profile. Spring a batten between two nails located at both ends of the arc. Push the center of the batten up to the high point of the arc and trace the line.

To make the pattern for marking the curve on the legs and upper rail, use graphite paper to transfer the arm's profile to a piece of MDF. Cut the curve on the bandsaw and use files and sandpaper to smooth it.

Laminated Arms are a Cut Above

Because the bowed arms are so prominent in this design, the figure and grain that shows on the top of each arm must be just right. Arms sawn from solid lumber would have a wild, distracting grain pattern. But laminating the arms allows you to control their look, choosing your best stock for the top and orienting it for the best effect. A laminated arm is also more stable than one cut from solid lumber, and concerns about short grain weakness disappear.

Laminating form keeps plies in line—Bent laminations can be tricky, but they don't need to be. A fence and a stop on the form keep the plies aligned, and a simple caul applies even pressure over them. Using the right kind of glue will prevent the plies from creeping after you remove them from the form. Start by making a laminating form. First, transfer the arm's profile to a piece of 3/4-in.-thick MDF. The pattern for marking the curve won't work here, because the arms are longer than it.

Cut close to the line of the curve on a bandsaw and sand or file down to the line. You need eight 3/4-in. layers to get a form 6 in. wide. Use the first layer to make the remaining seven.

Screw a fence to the side of the form and a stop to its front end. They will keep the plies aligned as you glue up the arms. Cover all of the working surfaces with packing tape to prevent glue from sticking to them.

Low-stress resawing—It takes a finely tuned bandsaw to resaw wide lumber. To make things easier, I begin resawing at the tablesaw and finish up at the bandsaw. The tablesaw removes most of the material and its kerfs help me guide the bandsaw blade through the arm. After resawing all of my laminates to 5/16 in. thick, I plane them to 1/4 in.

The right glue for laminations—The best glue for laminating curved parts is urea formaldehyde. It has a long open time and doesn't creep once dry. Those benefits outweigh its longer drying time. It is, however, a known carcinogen, so wear gloves and use a respirator or work in a well-ventilated area.

I use a piece of whiteboard for a caul, because it bends well and is glue-resistant. Available at home centers, whiteboard is 1/8-in.-thick Masonite covered on one side with white thermofoil.

Once both arms are laminated, scrape the glue from one edge, joint it, and rip the arm to width on the tablesaw, concave side up. Then cut the arm to length using a crosscut sled and a shim to get a square cut on the end.

Curved Arms Mean Curved Sides

To mark the curve of the arm on the upper rails and legs, dry-fit the side assemblies together. Align the bottom of the pattern with the bottoms of the rails. The ends of the pattern will align with the outside edges of the front and rear legs. Mark the curve on the inside and outside faces of the legs. And mark the inside of the legs on the pattern so you can realign it to mark the rail. Disassemble the side, and mark the curve there, too.

Cut the curve on the upper rail on the bandsaw. When you do this, the back tenon will be cut down to its final width. To cut the tenons on the legs, first use a combination blade to cut all four shoulders square to the leg, in line with the highest shoulder (the one of the front of each leg). Then use a dado set to cut the cheeks. To cut down to the curved shoulder lines on the sides and back of the leg, use a chisel and mallet. I back-bevel the shoulders to ensure a tight fit with the bottom of the armrests.

Through-tenons require careful layout—Dry-fit and clamp the side assemblies in preparation for cutting and fitting the arm mortises. Then clamp an assembly on the bench, inside face down with the tenons overhanging

Continued ➔

the edge. Set the arms on the tenons and press them snug against the shoulders. Mark the fronts and backs of the mortises directly from the tenons. Remove the arms and mark the mortise sides. Use a Forstner bit to remove most of the waste from the mortises, then pare down to the lines with a chisel. Next, chamfer the tenons that come through the arms. Cut them 3/8 in. proud of the arms and bevel them at 15°.

After the arms are fit and the tenons chamfered, lay out and drill the holes for the back support pins. A drill press will ensure that they're perpendicular. Be sure to bore the holes before cutting the outside back corner of the arm.

While you're at the drill press, drill the holes for the pivot pins in the legs.

Shape Corbels to Fit the Arms

With the arms temporarily in place, you can fit and attach the corbels. I make a pattern for the corbels, mark out four, and cut them out at the bandsaw.

The front and back corbels are the same length, but they hang down lower on the rear legs because of the arm's curve. The corbels are centered on the legs, and their tops need some shaping for a snug fit against the bottom of the arm. After they're shaped, predrill them and the legs for screws, and use a Forstner bit to create a countersink for the screw head. Put a bit of glue on the corbels and screw them in place. Plug the countersinks with shopmade tapered plugs to get a good grain match.

Next, cut the arc on the front stretcher, and screw the seat-frame cleats to it and the back stretcher. Then glue up the base.

Arts & Crafts Recliner

Bowed arms and beautiful quartersawn oak stand out on this Craftsman classic. All the joints are mortise and tenon, which makes this a chair that will last.

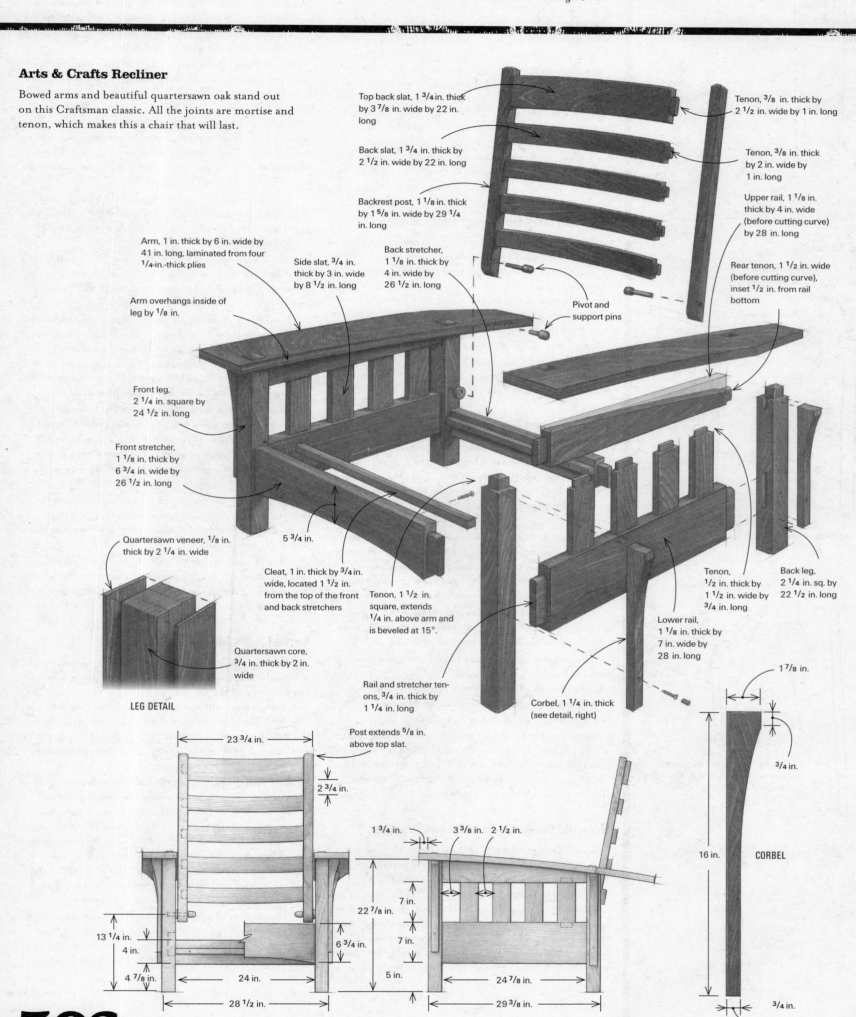

Top back slat, 1 3/4 in. thick by 3 7/8 in. wide by 22 in. long

Back slat, 1 3/4 in. thick by 2 1/2 in. wide by 22 in. long

Backrest post, 1 1/8 in. thick by 1 5/8 in. wide by 29 1/4 in. long

Arm, 1 in. thick by 6 in. wide by 41 in. long, laminated from four 1/4-in.-thick plies

Side slat, 3/4 in. thick by 3 in. wide by 8 1/2 in. long

Arm overhangs inside of leg by 1/8 in.

Back stretcher, 1 1/8 in. thick by 4 in. wide by 26 1/2 in. long

Front leg, 2 1/4 in. square by 24 1/2 in. long

Front stretcher, 1 1/8 in. thick by 6 3/4 in. wide by 26 1/2 in. long

Quartersawn veneer, 1/8 in. thick by 2 1/4 in. wide

Quartersawn core, 3/4 in. thick by 2 in. wide

LEG DETAIL

5 3/4 in.

Cleat, 1 in. thick by 3/4 in. wide, located 1 1/2 in. from the top of the front and back stretchers

Tenon, 1 1/2 in. square, extends 1/4 in. above arm and is beveled at 15°.

Rail and stretcher tenons, 3/4 in. thick by 1 1/4 in. long

Pivot and support pins

Tenon, 3/8 in. thick by 2 1/2 in. wide by 1 in. long

Tenon, 3/8 in. thick by 2 in. wide by 1 in. long

Upper rail, 1 1/8 in. thick by 4 in. wide (before cutting curve) by 28 in. long

Rear tenon, 1 1/2 in. wide (before cutting curve), inset 1/2 in. from rail bottom

Tenon, 1/2 in. thick by 1 1/2 in. wide by 3/4 in. long

Back leg, 2 1/4 in. sq. by 22 1/2 in. long

Lower rail, 1 1/8 in. thick by 7 in. wide by 28 in. long

Corbel, 1 1/4 in. thick (see detail, right)

Post extends 5/8 in. above top slat.

23 3/4 in.

2 3/4 in.

1 3/4 in.

3 3/8 in. 2 1/2 in.

7 in.

22 7/8 in.

7 in.

13 1/4 in.

4 in.

6 3/4 in.

4 7/8 in.

24 in.

5 in.

24 7/8 in.

28 1/2 in.

29 3/8 in.

1 7/8 in.

3/4 in.

16 in.

CORBEL

3/4 in.

After the glue dried, I made a hardwood frame with webbing for the seat cushion because I sent this chair to an upholsterer, and a hardwood frame is better than the plywood frame some upholsterers use. I used ash to make the frame, joining the parts with mortise-and-tenon joints. The length and depth of the frame should be 1/4 in. undersize to allow room for upholstery to be wrapped around the sides and stapled to the bottom.

Back slats: Tenon the Curve

I cut the tenons on the back slats at the same time as the other tenons because it is much easier to cut tenons on a square piece than on a thin, curved piece. Use a pattern to lay out the curve and then cut it at the bandsaw. I cleaned up the sawmarks with a stationary belt sander, but a spoke-shave or sanding blocks also works.

Authentic Look Without the Fumes

Stickley's furniture is well-known for its rich brown finish, which can be had by fuming with industrial ammonia. But you can forgo the ammonia and still get a great finish. After sanding this chair, I applied an antique cherry aniline dye. I let it dry overnight and then applied a dark walnut oil-based pigment stain. I finished it off with Min-wax Polycrylic water-based polyurethane.

When the finish is dry and the upholstery done, bring your chair into the house, put it in a welcoming spot, and take a moment to enjoy its grace and beauty. Then take a seat—and maybe a nap—to enjoy its comfort.

Build the form layer by layer. Make the first layer at the bandsaw, cleaning it up with sandpaper. Glue and screw on each successive layer and rout it flush.

Finish the form. Screw a melamine fence to the rear of the form and a stop to its front edge. Packing tape keeps the glue from sticking to the form and stop.

Tips for Accurate Joints

Every joint in this chair is a mortise and tenon, the traditional Craftsman joint. They must fit well to get a square and strong chair. Here's how to cut the joints accurately with two common tools: a router and a tablesaw.

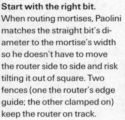

Start with the right bit. When routing mortises, Paolini matches the straight bit's diameter to the mortise's width so he doesn't have to move the router side to side and risk tilting it out of square. Two fences (one the router's edge guide; the other clamped on) keep the router on track.

Tenons at the tablesaw. First, cut the shoulders a hair deeper than the cheeks using a combination blade. Then, use a dado set to cut the cheeks. Support the piece with the miter gauge.

Resaw the plies. Start the cuts on the tablesaw and use the kerfs to guide the bandsaw blade as you finish the cut freehand.

Clamps, clamps, clamps. After coating the plies with glue, press them against the stop and fence. Add a flexible caul on top and start clamping next to the stop. Work progressively down along the form. Place a clamp every 2 in. You'll need two dozen.

Double the parts for stable routing. Thin pieces, like the side posts, don't provide a stable surface for a router. Clamp two or three of them together to get a wider bearing surface.

How to Laminate the Arms

The bow of the arms needs to match the curve cut onto the upper rails and legs. Use a full-scale drawing of the arm's profile to make the bending form and you'll get a great fit.

2 1/4 in.   1 in.

Pivot pin holes, 5/8 in. dia. by 2 1/4 in. deep

13/16 in.

Leg mortise, 1 1/2 in. sq.

24 1/4 in.   4 in.

4 in.

6 in.

10 in.

40 3/8 in.

Continued →

Same Pattern For the Sides

The hardest part of building this chair is fitting the arms to the sides. The tops of the upper rails are curved, and so are the tenon shoulders. Make a pattern of the upper rails and use it to mark the curve. It's easier to align and hold in place than one of the arms.

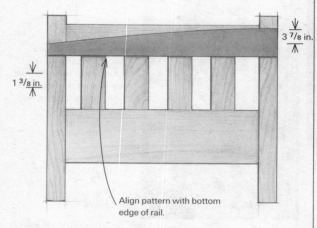

3 7/8 in.

1 3/8 in.

Align pattern with bottom edge of rail.

Mark the curve. With the sides dry-fitted, align the bottom of the rail pattern with the bottom of the rail and mark the curve on the legs. This locates the tenon's shoulders on the legs. Then disassemble the sides, realign the pattern on the rail, and mark its curve.

Cut the tenons. Start by cutting the shoulders square. Cut the cheeks with a dado set. Then chop and pare away the waste with a chisel as shown to define the curved shoulders.

Mortise the Arms

The most accurate way to locate the arm mortises is to mark directly from the leg tenons. That way, you're not guessing where they should be.

First, cut arms to size. After scraping the glue from one edge and jointing it, rip the arm to width with the concave side up. Crosscut the arms to length, using a sled and small shim to get a square cut.

LOCATE AND CUT THE MORTISES

1. Lay the side assembly on your bench and stand an arm on the tenons, flush against their shoulders. The front mortise is 2 in. from the front edge. Use that measurement to align the arm before transferring the tenon locations to the arm. Lay out the underside, too.

2. Now clamp the arm in a vise so the mortise area is level and use a Forstner bit to remove the waste. To avoid tearout, go halfway from one side, flip the arm, and complete the cut from the other side.

3. Use a chisel to chop away the remaining waste and square the corners. As you did when drilling, go halfway from one side and finish up from the other.

Assemble the Base

Glue up the base before making the back, so you can take measurements for the back directly from it.

Work in stages. Assemble the sides first (right). The slats don't need glue if they fit snugly. Glue the rails to the legs and leave the clamps on overnight. Next, glue up and clamp the stretchers. Attach the arms (below), brushing glue on them and on the leg tenons. Leave the clamps on for 24 hours.

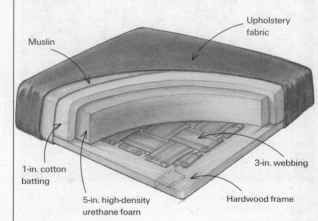

Over and under. After stapling four courses of webbing across the frame's opening, weave webbing through them to create a strong but comfortable base for a cushion.

CUSHION ANATOMY

Ask your upholsterer to make a layered cushion like this one. It's firm and durable yet comfortable.

Upholstery fabric

Muslin

1-in. cotton batting

5-in. high-density urethane foam

3-in. webbing

Hardwood frame

Then Make the Back

Cut the tenons before shaping the slats. Using a half-pattern to mark the curve of the slats will ensure that they're symmetrical.

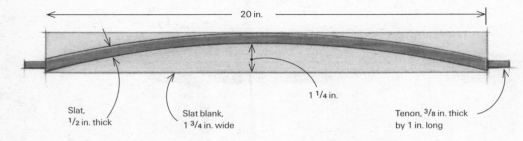

20 in.

Slat, 1/2 in. thick

Slat blank, 1 3/4 in. wide

1 1/4 in.

Tenon, 3/8 in. thick by 1 in. long

Cut the slats. Bandsaw and smooth the curves after cutting the tenons. Because the slats are curved, they tend to flex a little under clamping pressure. Hardwood spacers limit the force of the clamps.

PIVOT AND SUPPORT PINS

Even a novice can turn these pins. Check the diameter of the shaft with a 5/8-in. open-end wrench. Use a gouge until you're close, and finish up with sandpaper.

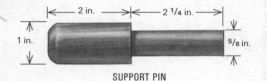

1 in.

2 in.

2 1/4 in.

5/8 in.

SUPPORT PIN

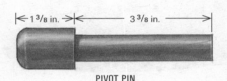

1 3/8 in.

3 3/8 in.

PIVOT PIN

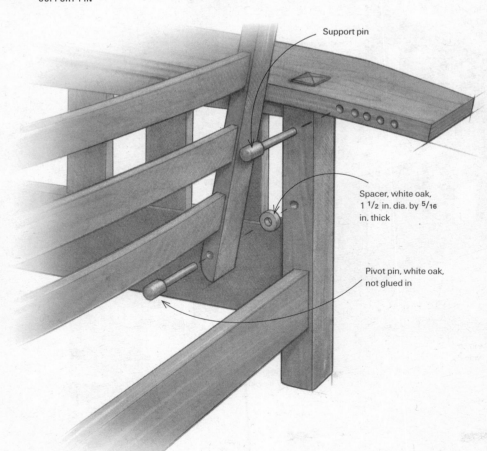

Support pin

Spacer, white oak, 1 1/2 in. dia. by 5/16 in. thick

Pivot pin, white oak, not glued in

Limbert-Style Coffee Table

by Gregory Paolini

There are many well-known designers of Arts and Crafts furniture, like the Stickleys and the Greenes. But a lesser-known designer, Charles Limbert, has always held a special appeal for me. I'm especially fond of his oval library table. That's why I jumped at the chance to design and make a scaled-down version, to be used as a coffee table.

I've preserved the elliptical top and shelf, the gently curved legs, the decorative piercings in the stretchers, and Limbert's choice of wood—quartersawn white oak. I kept the overall proportions as well, so the parts come together just as harmoniously as they do in the original table.

A variety of joints are used. Bridle joints hold the legs and aprons together, and a half-lap joint is used where the stretchers and aprons intersect. The legs and shelf are notched where they meet, and slip tenons join the stretchers to the legs. Some of those joints can be tricky, but I'll show you some techniques to help you get flawless results. I'll also show you how to draw an accurate ellipse to take the mystery out of the top and shelf.

Pattern-Rout the Top and Shelf

Begin by gluing up panels for the top and shelf and milling all of the parts. Then make full-size patterns for them. You'll need to draw two ellipses, which is easy to do with string, a pencil, and two small nails. To begin, draw the ellipse's axes on a piece of plywood 1 in. longer and wider than the ellipse and mark its length and width. Next, locate the foci, drive a nail into both foci, and tie a loop of string around them. When you stretch out the loop, it should just reach the side of the ellipse (see drawing, above left). Put a pencil inside the loop and draw, keeping the string taut.

With both ellipses drawn, cut them out at the bandsaw. Use 100-grit (CAMI) sandpaper, glued to a thin strip of wood, to remove the saw marks and fair the curves. Then trace the patterns on the panels for the top and shelf. Before cutting out the top and shelf, cut the notches in the shelf that join it to the legs. This is far easier to do now, when the sides and ends are square, than after cutting the shelf into an ellipse. Lay out the notches by placing the legs on the shelf and transferring their thickness onto it. Then cut them at the tablesaw, using a crosscut sled. The width of the notches is critical, so cut the notch sides first and then nibble away the inside. Cut the notches a bit tight and fit them with a chisel later.

After all four notches have been cut, head to the bandsaw and cut out the elliptical top and shelf. The top is heavy and unwieldy, so cut away the bulk of each corner first. Then make a second pass close to the line. I use a flush-trimming bit to rout the top and shelf flush to their patterns (see page 508).

Continued →

Strength and Beauty

An elliptical top, arched legs, and decorative piercings add grace and beauty. Slip tenons and bridle joints ensure decades of service.

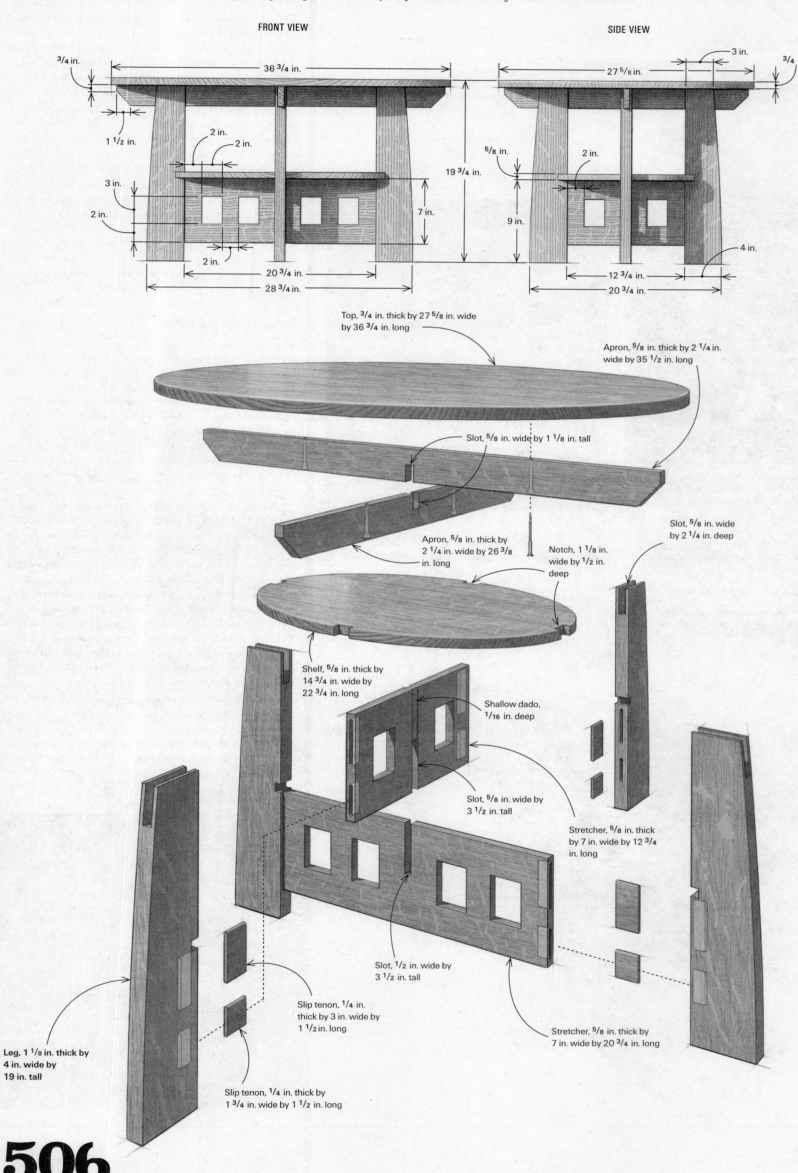

FRONT VIEW

36 3/4 in.
3/4 in.
1 1/2 in.
2 in.
2 in.
3 in.
2 in.
2 in.
19 3/4 in.
7 in.
20 3/4 in.
28 3/4 in.

SIDE VIEW

3 in.
3/4 in.
27 5/8 in.
5/8 in.
2 in.
9 in.
4 in.
12 3/4 in.
20 3/4 in.

Top, 3/4 in. thick by 27 5/8 in. wide by 36 3/4 in. long

Apron, 5/8 in. thick by 2 1/4 in. wide by 35 1/2 in. long

Slot, 5/8 in. wide by 1 1/8 in. tall

Apron, 5/8 in. thick by 2 1/4 in. wide by 26 3/8 in. long

Notch, 1 1/8 in. wide by 1/2 in. deep

Slot, 5/8 in. wide by 2 1/4 in. deep

Shelf, 5/8 in. thick by 14 3/4 in. wide by 22 3/4 in. long

Shallow dado, 1/16 in. deep

Slot, 5/8 in. wide by 3 1/2 in. tall

Stretcher, 5/8 in. thick by 7 in. wide by 12 3/4 in. long

Slot, 1/2 in. wide by 3 1/2 in. tall

Slip tenon, 1/4 in. thick by 3 in. wide by 1 1/2 in. long

Stretcher, 5/8 in. thick by 7 in. wide by 20 3/4 in. long

Leg, 1 1/8 in. thick by 4 in. wide by 19 in. tall

Slip tenon, 1/4 in. thick by 1 3/4 in. wide by 1 1/2 in. long

Join Legs and Aprons

With the top and shelf done, you can get started on the joinery. The stretchers are joined to the legs with slip tenons. Because the stretchers are 7 in. wide and could expand as much as 1/16 in., break the mortise into two. The tenon will fit tight in the upper mortise but loose in the lower one, forcing the stretcher's movement downward and away from the shelf. I make the slip tenons by milling some white oak to the correct thickness and width, rounding over the edges at the router table, and then crosscutting the tenons to length. Now cut a notch in each leg. Paired with the notches in the shelf, they form a strong joint that holds the shelf in place and prevents the base from twisting or racking. Cut them just as you did the notches in the shelf. While you're at the tablesaw, go ahead and cut the slot for the bridle joint into the top of each leg. I use a tenoning jig, starting at the center of the slot and working outward. As you get close to the sides of the slot, use the apron to test the fit.

A half-lap joint is used to connect the aprons where they intersect. For this joint, I cut a slot halfway through each apron. Unlike the notches in the legs and shelf, which were cut from the sides in, cut this joint from the center out. That will keep the joint centered on the aprons.

To complete the legs, cut the curve on the outside edge. I made a pattern out of 1/4-in.-thick plywood and traced it on the legs. Save the offcuts to use as cauls during glue-up.

Slot and Rout the Stretchers

As with the aprons, a half-lap joint is used where the stretchers intersect. However, cut a shallow dado on both sides of the shorter stretcher to conceal the joint and reinforce it against racking.

After cutting the dadoes, raise the blade and cut a slot on the bottom edge of the stretcher. You won't be able to get the full depth with a 10-in. sawblade, so cut as deep as you can and finish up the slot with a handsaw and chisel. With the short stretcher done, cut the slot in the longer stretcher.

Now it's time to rout mortises in the ends of the stretchers to accept the slip tenons that join them to the legs. Do this the same way you routed the mortises in the legs, with a router and spiral bit.

After routing the mortises, use a template, plunge router, guide bushing, and spiral bit to rout the decorative piercings in the stretchers. Make the template from a piece of plywood and lay out the piercing on it, taking the bushing's offset into account. Head to the router table and cut out the opening. Attach a fence to the bottom side, lay out the location of the piercings on the stretchers, and you're ready to rout the openings.

Hog out most of the waste with a Forstner bit at the drill press. With most of the waste removed, clamp the template to the stretcher and the stretcher to the bench. Make a clockwise pass around the opening, increase the bit's depth, and make a second pass. Make a third pass to complete the piercing.

Dry-Fit, Stain, and Glue Up

This little table is kind of like a puzzle, in that there are pieces that interlock and must be assembled in a particular order for the table to come together. Dry-fitting the table will help you not only learn and get comfortable with that puzzle, but also find any joints that need to be tweaked.

Begin by putting the stretchers together and adding one leg. Fit the shelf into that leg and add the opposite leg. Then add the last two legs. Now add the aprons and put the top in place. Before you take the table apart, use a pencil to mark the joint where the aprons intersect and where they pass through the legs. The marks will remind you not to sand those areas, which would cause the joints to become loose. Also, as you take off the legs, number

Top and Shelf

HOW TO MAKE A PERFECT ELLIPSE

Both the top and shelf are elliptical. You can use a simple nail-and-string technique to make patterns for these. Each pattern does double duty. First, it lays out a line to follow at the bandsaw. And after the shape has been roughed out, the pattern serves as a template for a bushing-guided router.

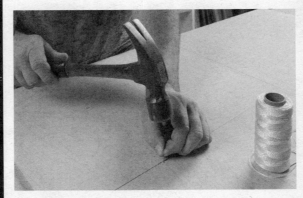

Nails and string. Driven into the focal points, nails guide the string loop, which in turn guides the pencil along the perimeter of an ellipse.

KEY DIMENSIONS

Here's how to lay out the nails and size the string for each ellipse:

Top: x = 13 13/16, y = 24 1/4   Shelf: x = 7 3/8, y = 17 5/16

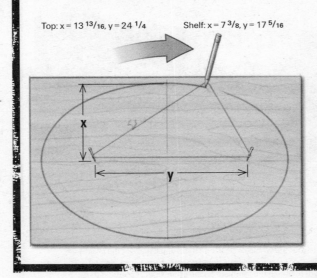

the inside of the notches—I use a felt-tipped marker—and number the corresponding legs to match. Numbering the aprons on the top edge also is a good idea.

After disassembling the table, break the edges with a block plane and then use a random-orbit sander to sand all of the parts up to P180 grit. Do not sand the areas you marked earlier: the half-lap joint where the aprons intersect and the area where the aprons pass through the bridle joint in the legs. Next, wipe all of the parts with a damp rag to raise the grain, then use a sanding block and P220-grit paper to remove the raised grain.

I finish the table before the glue-up. The advantage of finishing first is that any glue squeeze-out will not soak into the grain and become a problem when you try to finish over it. And squeeze-out doesn't stick to the finish, so it just peels away without fuss. To stain the table, I used the same finishing recipe that I used on my bow-arm Morris chair. Tape off any area where glue will be applied, like the bridle and half-lap joints on the aprons, and use caution when staining around them and the slots.

Now you're ready for the glue. You can do it in stages or, if you're feeling lucky, all at once. Repeat the assembly order from the dry-fitting and use the leg cutoffs as cauls for the clamps. After the glue is dry, peel away any squeeze-out. Then rub out the finish with 0000 steel wool and paste wax, and buff the wax with a shoe-shine cloth or brush. Finally, attach the top with four screws, driving through the aprons and into the top. Slot the holes on the short apron to allow for wood movement.

Simple, accurate ellipses. Size the string so the pencil reaches the x dimension (see diagram). Then keep the string taut as you trace an ellipse.

Cut the pattern at the bandsaw. Cut just outside the line, so there is less waste to remove when smoothing the curves.

Notch the shelf before cutting the ellipse. Because its width is critical, cut each side of the notch first and then remove the middle. Use stop blocks on your crosscut sled to ensure that notches on opposite sides will line up.

Continued ➡

Cut the top and shelf at the bandsaw. Use the patterns to trace the shapes. When bandsawing, leave about ¹⁄₈ in. of waste for the next step: routing the edges flush to your template.

Always rout downhill. If you try to rout the whole circle in one pass, you'll tear out the grain in some areas. So you'll need to flip the workpiece. Use a double-bearing, flush-trimming bit so there's no need to change bits or re-attach the template on the other side. Just adjust the bit height to use the other bearing.

1. ROUT TWO QUARTERS WITH TEMPLATE UP

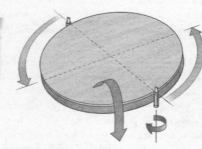

Template

Top bearing
guides router.

Workpiece

Rout downhill to eliminate tearout. To avoid climb cuts, which can be dangerous, you'll only be able to trim two of the ellipse's quarters.

2. THEN FLIP THE WORKPIECE

Workpiece

Bottom bearing
guides router.

Template

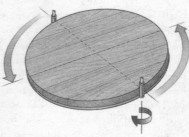

With template and workpiece flipped, the two remaining quarters can now be trimmed cleanly.

Base

A LESSON IN BRIDLE JOINTS AND SLIP TENONS

Other than the mortises and slip tenons holding the stretchers to the legs, every joint in this table is some type of bridle joint or half-lap joint. A router makes quick work of the mortises, and a tablesaw, equipped with a standard combination blade, is the right tool for the bridle joints and half-laps.

Rout mortises in the legs. Use a spiral bit that matches the mortise's width, and use a fence on both sides of the router: Set up the router's edge guide and then clamp on a simple shopmade fence. The mating mortises in the stretchers are done the same way.

LEGS

Bridle joints must be centered. Using a tenoning jig for the slot, cut in the middle of the leg first. Then flip the leg side to side to make the subsequent cuts. As you work out to the sides of the joint, it remains centered on the leg.

Cut the curve last. After tracing the shape onto the leg, cut away the waste on the bandsaw, and then clean up the saw marks with a handplane or sander.

TIP

Fence and Guide Block Keep the Mortise on Line

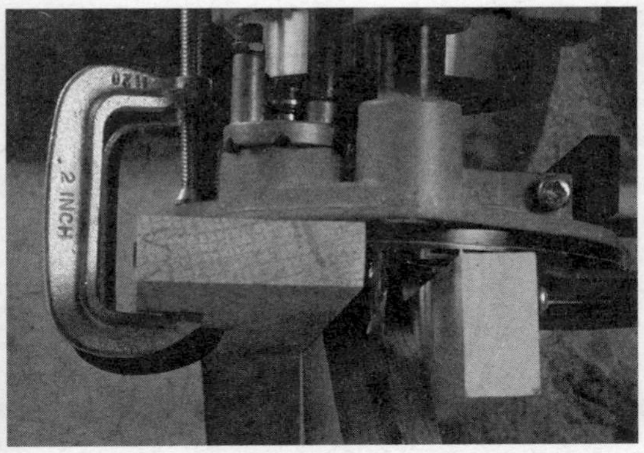

No wiggle room. It will be straight and parallel to the sides because the fence and guide block prevent the router from wandering.

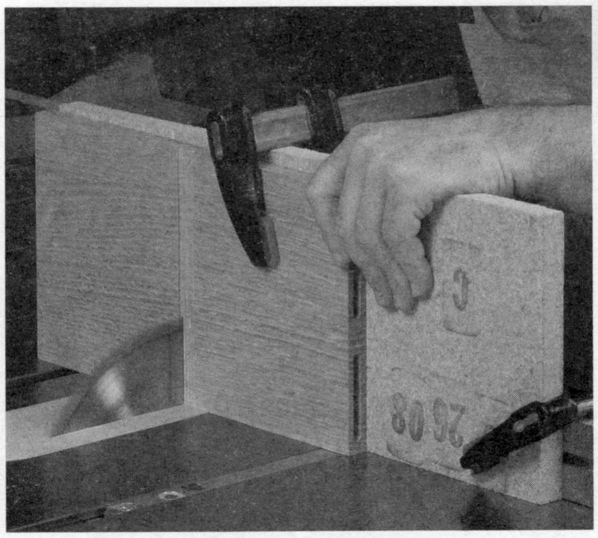

Start the slot at the tablesaw. With the blade as high as possible, cut the sides to line up with the dado, and nibble away the waste in between.

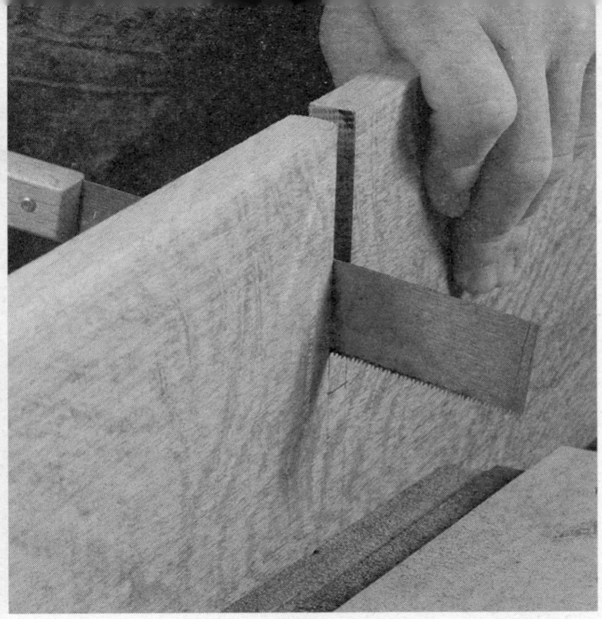

Go deeper with a handsaw. Follow the sides of the slot with the saw and then remove the rest of the waste with a chisel.

RONS

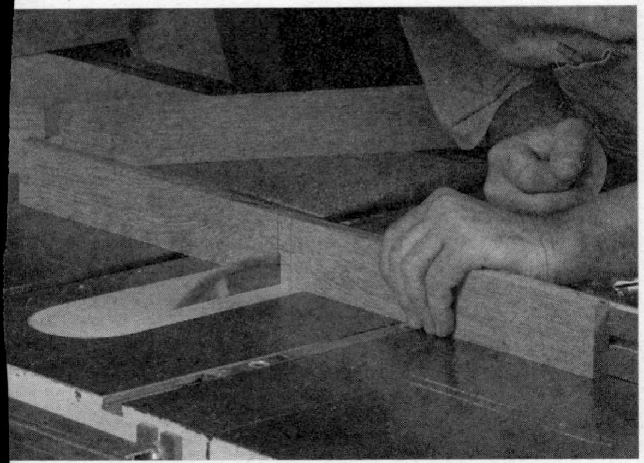

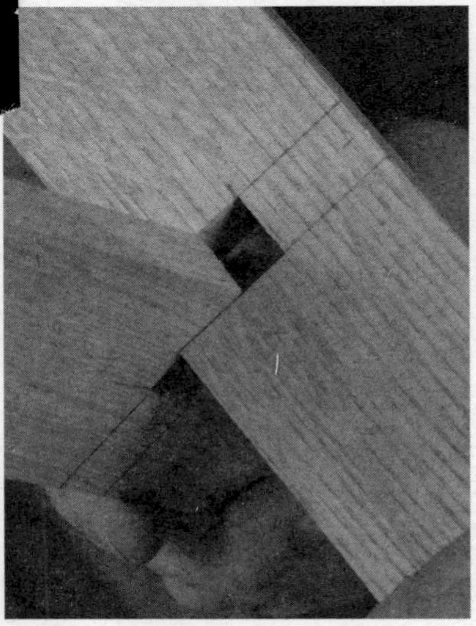

Slot the aprons and test the fit. After marking the joint, cut each side first and then nibble away the waste one pass at a time (above). Cut the slots a bit tight at first, and then sneak up on a tight joint, checking the fit (left) after each trimming cut.

STRETCHERS

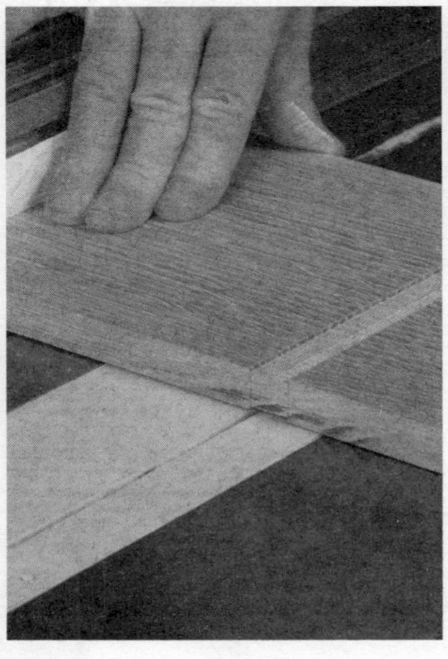

Cut the dado with a standard-kerf blade. That way you can sneak up on the final width, testing how well the long stretcher fits into it as you go.

Aprons

USE A ROUTER TEMPLATE FOR CLEAN CUTOUTS

There are six rectangular piercings. Use a router and template to make them all the same. A spiral bit is best because its shearing action will cut the end grain areas smoothly.

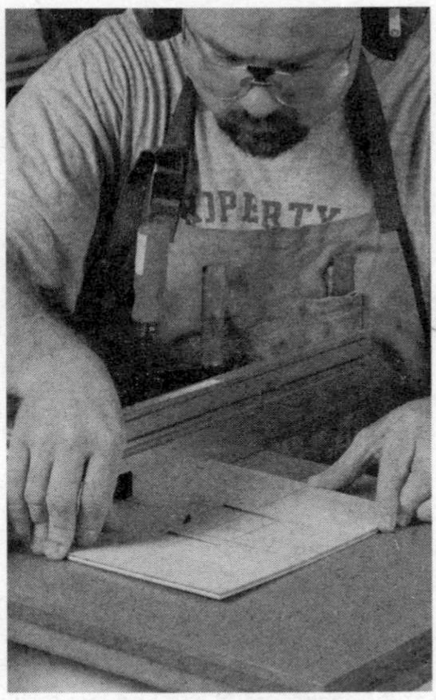

Make the template at the router table. Paolini routs one side of the opening at a time, lowering the template onto a 1/4-in.-dia. spiral bit. He stops the last cut about 1/2 in. before the end and finishes it with a handsaw and sandpaper.

TEMPLATE FOR CUTOUTS

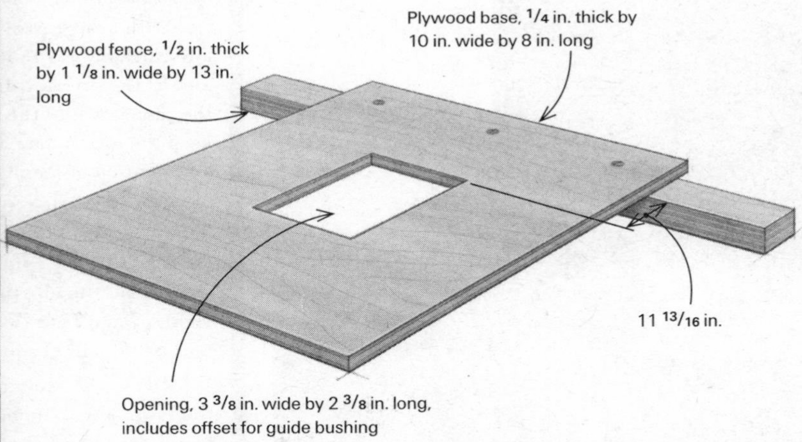

Plywood fence, 1/2 in. thick by 1 1/8 in. wide by 13 in. long
Plywood base, 1/4 in. thick by 10 in. wide by 8 in. long
11 13/16 in.
Opening, 3 3/8 in. wide by 2 3/8 in. long, includes offset for guide bushing

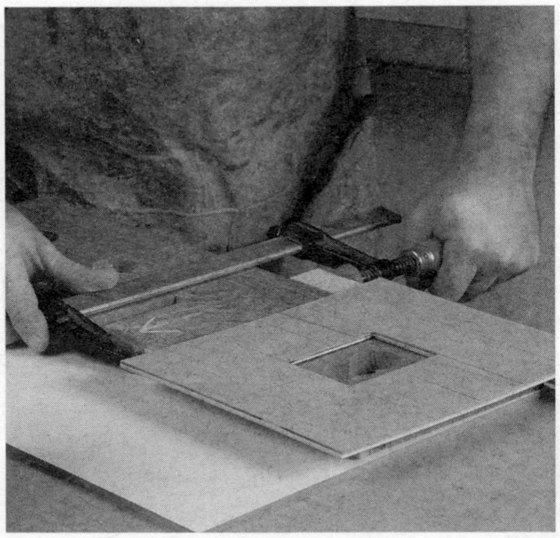

Clamp the template in place. Remove most of the waste in the cutout using a Forstner bit. Then clamp the template to the stretcher. Place scrap beneath the stretcher to protect your bench.

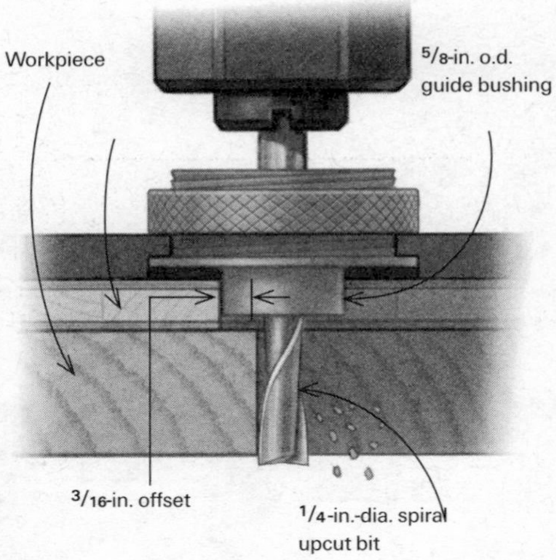

Workpiece
5/8-in. o.d. guide bushing
3/16-in. offset
1/4-in.-dia. spiral upcut bit

Trim flush in three passes. Set the bit depth to 1/4 in. for the first pass, 1/2 in. for the second (right), and 5/8 in. on the last one.

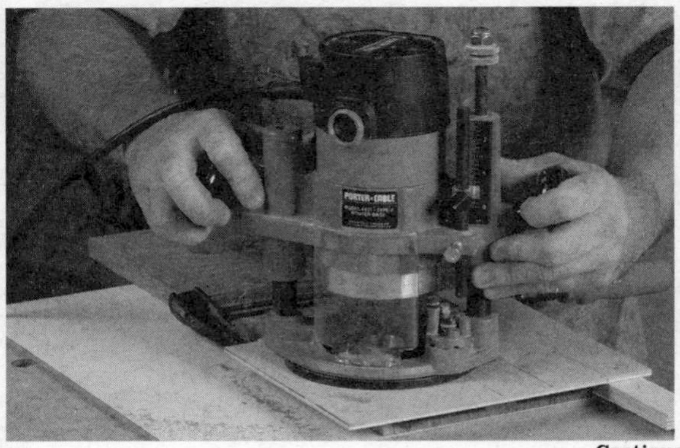

Continued

Assembly

A DRY RUN SORTS OUT SURPRISES

The table's base is a three-dimensional puzzle, and you don't want to be figuring it out with glue on the joints. So do a dry run to get comfortable with the steps.

Start with the stretchers. As the core of the table, these should fit snugly and squarely.

Fit the slip tenons. The top should be a close fit, but leave the bottom tenon a bit narrow to allow for wood movement.

The shelf is next. Lock it in place with opposing legs, then add the last two. If you assemble the legs first, you won't be able to get the shelf in place.

Aprons are the last piece to the puzzle. They hold the legs in place and make the base rigid.

Stickley-Style Cabinet

by Michael Pekovich

Simple is not always easy. Take Arts and Crafts furniture. Woodworkers fond of the style—with its beefy parts, rectilinear lines, and exposed mortise-and-tenon joinery—may think the furniture is easy to make. But this simple form is unforgiving of mistakes. Make one slip-up in proportions, hardware choice, or finish, and the design falls down. I've been building Arts and Crafts furniture for a long time, and I've worked through the challenges in making a piece that's true to the style.

This case piece is an original design, yet it would not be out of place in an antique Stickley catalog. With its quartersawn white oak, exposed joinery, fumed finish, and hand-hammered hardware, it breathes Arts and Crafts. The leaded-glass doors are typical, too, and add to the handcrafted look. You can have panels made by a local artist or you can make them yourself. If you are interested in building in this style, I hope you'll find a few valuable lessons here. Also, this piece is a versatile one: I designed it to hold books and cherished items, but it could work as a sideboard, too.

When building an Arts and Crafts piece, the most important step is to choose good wood. The tight grain and magnificent ray fleck of quartersawn oak is the primary ornamentation, so don't skimp on the lumber. I found some great boards online that I supplemented with lumber from a local yard.

With a large project like this, I start from the outside and work my way in because it's easier to build the case first and fit the interior dividers after. The top and bottom of the case attach to the sides with through-tenons. To help keep the case square and the wide boards flat, I added a stub tenon between the through-tenons.

The through-tenons are prominent features of the design, so you must get them right. For clean cuts and no gaps, I fitted the router with a guide bushing and straight bit and cut the mortises using a full-size template (see right). Then I cut the dadoes between mortises for the stub tenons. Finally, I squared up the mortises with a chisel.

To cut the remaining mortises for the backsplash and the lower apron, attach a fence to the router and use a spiral upcut bit. Then square them with a chisel.

Once the mortises have been cut, cut out the foot recess and profile the tops of the sides. Clean up the cuts with a block plane, a spokeshave, and files. The last task is to drill holes for the tenon pins. For this, I used a doweling jig to help keep the bit aligned.

Crosspieces Must Line Up Shoulder to Shoulder

Now it's time to cut the tenons on the top, the bottom, the horizontal divider, the back splash, and the apron. These parts have three different tenon lengths among them, but they all have the same shoulder-to-shoulder length. To ensure the case remains square, it is critical to get this dimension exactly right.

To help, I use a trick I learned from contributing editor Steve Latta. Cut the parts all the same length, and then cut the tenon shoulders using the same setting on the tablesaw. Test the fit, and then trim the through-tenons to width. Next, cut the stub tenons to length using a bandsaw. Once you're sure everything is fitting well, trim the through-tenons to their final length and chamfer their ends.

Now rout the slots for the stopped sliding dovetails that connect the vertical dividers to the top, the bottom, and the horizontal divider. Then cut the rabbets in the sides and top for the back panel.

Assembly: Keep it Square

It's critical that the case remains square as you assemble it. Otherwise, you'll be fighting to fit the doors and drawers. To simplify the glue-up and to help keep the case square, I first glued the backsplash and apron to the case top and bottom, respectively. Then I glued up the sides, top, and bottom.

After the glue is dry, drill holes though the tenons and dry-fit the pins. Cut the pins to length and chamfer the exposed end of the pins before gluing them in.

Once the case is assembled, cut the vertical dividers to length and rout the dovetail keys on the ends, using the same dovetail bit used to rout the slots. After installing the dividers, cut and fit the shiplapped back panels.

Build the Drawers and Doors

With the case glued up, it's time to build and fit the drawers and doors. All three drawer fronts are cut from one board for continuous grain and color. Original Stickley pieces typically use white oak for the drawer sides as well, but I chose beech because of its dense, fine grain.

Full-Size Template Simplifies the Sides

To cut matching mortises that align perfectly, make a full-size template from 1/4-in.-thick MDF. The template is quick to make using a 3/8-in. straight bit on the router table.

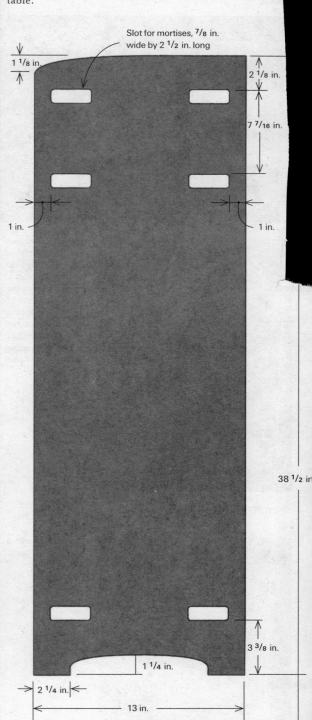

The outside dimensions of the template are the same as the case sides. The template mortises are larger than the case mortises to accommodate the guide bushing used to rout them.

The doors are rabbeted for simple leaded-glass panels (see p. 516). I wanted them to be inset 5/16 in. from the front of the case, which means I couldn't hinge them directly to the case sides. So I added 1/4-in.-thick hinge strips to the inside of the case, inset 1/4 in. from the front edge. The strips provide clearance for the doors to open, and it's easy to cut the hinge mortises prior to installing them.

Details that Would Make Stickley Proud

No matter how true you are to the Arts and Crafts ideals when you build a piece, you can kill the design if you choose the wrong hardware or mess up the finish. For this piece, I chose traditional hand-hammered hardware and fumed the wood before applying a topcoat. Fuming may intimidate people, but I've developed a low-tech method (for details, see p. 515).

After fuming, I warm up the wood with a coat of garnet shellac. Then I switch to Waterlox, a wipe-on tung oil varnish. The last step is to rub out the finish with steel wool and apply a dark wax. This fills the open pores of the oak and pops the rays.

Now screw on the back slats, add the glass panels to the doors, install the traditional hardware, and the piece is ready for your living room.

Second cuts. After the first passes, remove the spacer between the fence and template and finish routing the mortise slots (above and below). Adjust the fence and repeat the process for each set of mortise slots.

STOP BLOCKS AND A SPACER ENSURE AN ACCURATE TEMPLATE

First cuts. Clamp stop blocks on both sides of the bit for the stopped cuts. With the spacer in place (see drawing below), plunge through the template and make one pass in the first mortise slot. Just flip the template to do the opposite slot.

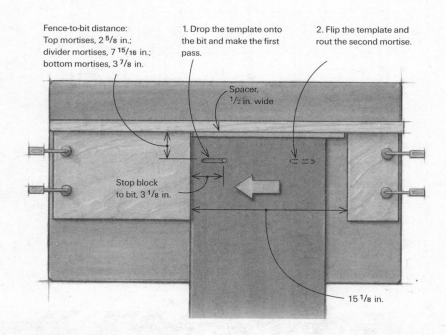

Fence-to-bit distance:
Top mortises, 2 5/8 in.;
divider mortises, 7 15/16 in.;
bottom mortises, 3 7/8 in.

1. Drop the template onto the bit and make the first pass.

2. Flip the template and rout the second mortise.

Spacer, 1/2 in. wide

Stop block to bit, 3 1/8 in.

15 1/8 in.

Continued ➡

Original Piece, Traditional Design

In Arts and Crafts furniture, it's all about the wood and small details. The tight grain and magnificent ray fleck of quartersawn oak is the primary ornamentation. To give the piece a solid feel without being clunky, Pekovich varied the thickness of the parts. The sides are a full inch thick, the top and bottom are 7/8 in. thick, and the remaining interior dividers are 3/4 in. thick. Also, each piece is slightly inset from the other, creating subtle shadow lines.

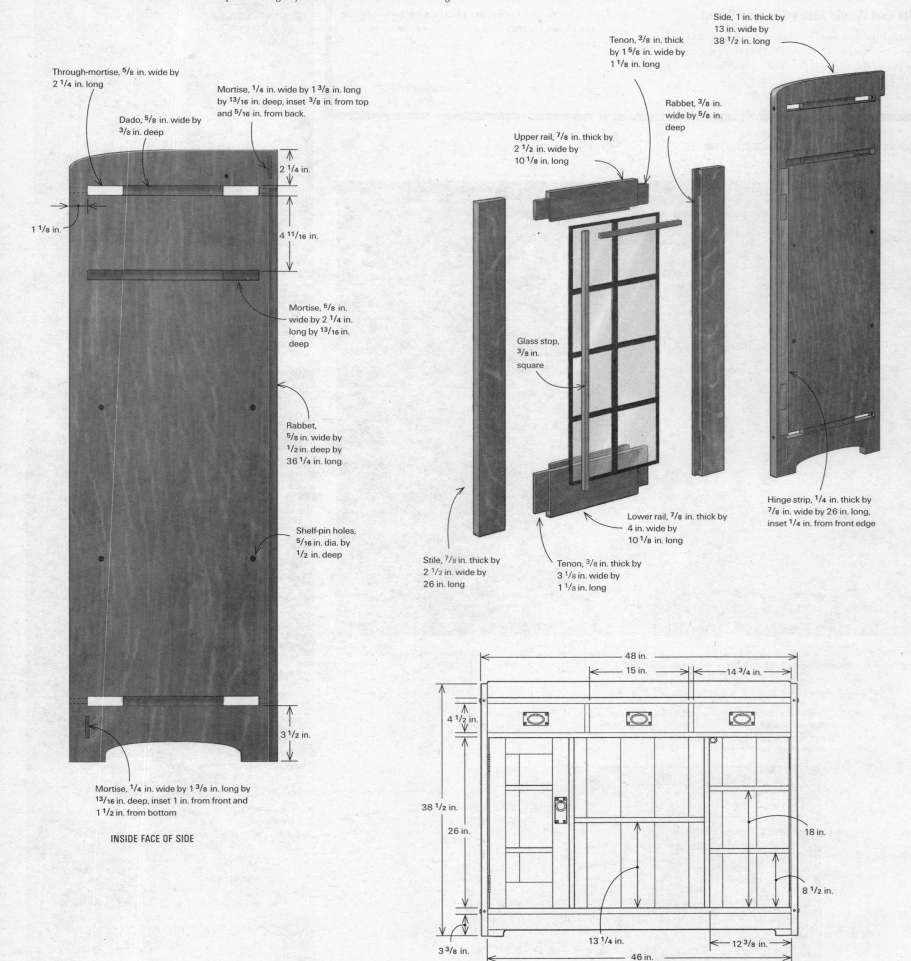

Through-mortise, 5/8 in. wide by 2 1/4 in. long

Dado, 5/8 in. wide by 3/8 in. deep

Mortise, 1/4 in. wide by 1 3/8 in. long by 13/16 in. deep, inset 3/8 in. from top and 5/16 in. from back.

1 1/8 in.

2 1/4 in.

4 11/16 in.

Mortise, 5/8 in. wide by 2 1/4 in. long by 13/16 in. deep

Rabbet, 5/8 in. wide by 1/2 in. deep by 36 1/4 in. long

Shelf-pin holes, 5/16 in. dia. by 1/2 in. deep

3 1/2 in.

Mortise, 1/4 in. wide by 1 3/8 in. long by 13/16 in. deep, inset 1 in. from front and 1 1/2 in. from bottom

INSIDE FACE OF SIDE

Side, 1 in. thick by 13 in. wide by 38 1/2 in. long

Tenon, 3/8 in. thick by 1 5/8 in. wide by 1 1/8 in. long

Rabbet, 3/8 in. wide by 5/8 in. deep

Upper rail, 7/8 in. thick by 2 1/2 in. wide by 10 1/8 in. long

Glass stop, 3/8 in. square

Hinge strip, 1/4 in. thick by 7/8 in. wide by 26 in. long, inset 1/4 in. from front edge

Lower rail, 7/8 in. thick by 4 in. wide by 10 1/8 in. long

Stile, 7/8 in. thick by 2 1/2 in. wide by 26 in. long

Tenon, 3/8 in. thick by 3 1/8 in. wide by 1 1/8 in. long

48 in.

15 in.

14 3/4 in.

4 1/2 in.

38 1/2 in.

26 in.

18 in.

8 1/2 in.

3 3/8 in.

13 1/4 in.

12 3/8 in.

46 in.

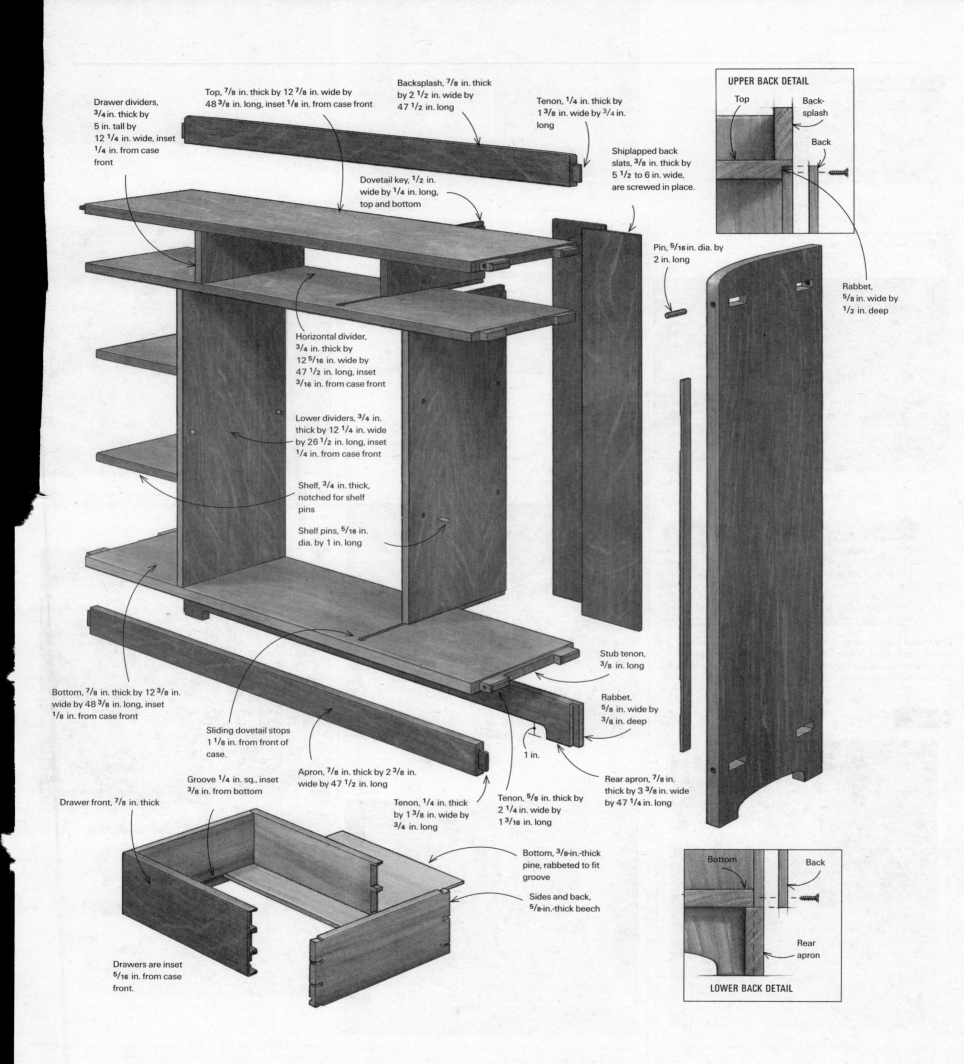

Drawer dividers, 3/4 in. thick by 5 in. tall by 12 1/4 in. wide, inset 1/4 in. from case front

Top, 7/8 in. thick by 12 7/8 in. wide by 48 3/8 in. long, inset 1/8 in. from case front

Backsplash, 7/8 in. thick by 2 1/2 in. wide by 47 1/2 in. long

Tenon, 1/4 in. thick by 1 3/8 in. wide by 3/4 in. long

Shiplapped back slats, 3/8 in. thick by 5 1/2 to 6 in. wide, are screwed in place.

Dovetail key, 1/2 in. wide by 1/4 in. long, top and bottom

Pin, 5/16 in. dia. by 2 in. long

Horizontal divider, 3/4 in. thick by 12 5/16 in. wide by 47 1/2 in. long, inset 3/16 in. from case front

Lower dividers, 3/4 in. thick by 12 1/4 in. wide by 26 1/2 in. long, inset 1/4 in. from case front

Shelf, 3/4 in. thick, notched for shelf pins

Shelf pins, 5/16 in. dia. by 1 in. long

Rabbet, 5/8 in. wide by 1/2 in. deep

Stub tenon, 3/8 in. long

Bottom, 7/8 in. thick by 12 3/8 in. wide by 48 3/8 in. long, inset 1/8 in. from case front

Sliding dovetail stops 1 1/8 in. from front of case.

Rabbet, 5/8 in. wide by 3/8 in. deep

1 in.

Groove 1/4 in. sq., inset 3/8 in. from bottom

Apron, 7/8 in. thick by 2 3/8 in. wide by 47 1/2 in. long

Tenon, 1/4 in. thick by 1 3/8 in. wide by 3/4 in. long

Tenon, 5/8 in. thick by 2 1/4 in. wide by 1 3/16 in. long

Rear apron, 7/8 in. thick by 3 3/8 in. wide by 47 1/4 in. long

Drawer front, 7/8 in. thick

Bottom, 3/8-in.-thick pine, rabbeted to fit groove

Sides and back, 5/8-in.-thick beech

Drawers are inset 5/16 in. from case front.

UPPER BACK DETAIL

Top

Back-splash

Back

LOWER BACK DETAIL

Bottom

Back

Rear apron

Case joinery

THROUGH-MORTISES WITHOUT MESS-UPS

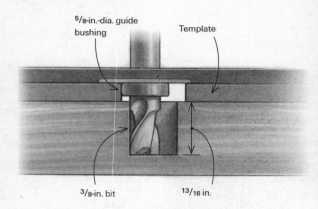

5/8-in.-dia. guide bushing
Template
3/8-in. bit
13/16 in.

Start on the inside face. To make it easier to hold the workpiece and template, Pekovich uses an elevated clamping table. A bushing guides a spiral upcut bit.

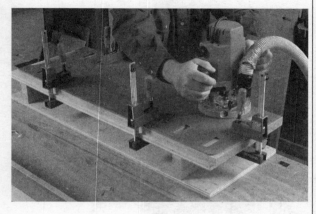

1/2-in. bearing-guided bit

The Paolini trick. To complete the through-mortises with no tearout, Pekovich uses a trick he learned from Greg Paolini. Drill a hole through each mortise (below, tip), flip over the piece, insert a bearing-guided bit in the hole, and rout out the remaining waste (top of next column).

> **TIP**
>
> Place tape over the divider mortises so you don't drill through them accidentally.

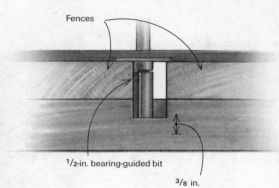

Fences
1/2-in. bearing-guided bit
3/8 in.

Connect the slots. To rout the shallow dadoes that connect the through-mortises, clamp fences on both sides of the mortises, and use a top-bearing-guided bit.

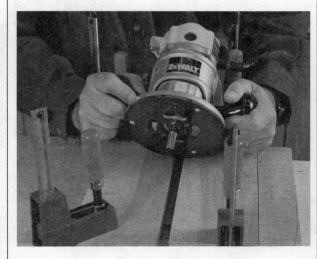

TWO-PART TENONS

Dado blade does most of the work. After cutting the tenon cheeks and shoulders with a dado set, cut the through-tenons to width, using a tall fence to support the board. The scrapwood behind the tenons backs up the cut and reduces tearout.

Saw off the stub tenon. Use the bandsaw to cut the stub tenons to length. The fence ensures a parallel cut.

SLIDING DOVETAILS MADE EASY

Use a fence to guide the slot cuts. To ensure that the dovetail slots are parallel, clamp an MDF fence to the workpiece to steer the router's guide bushing.

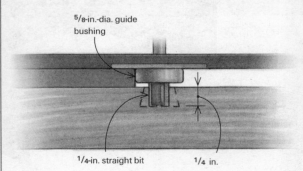

5/8-in.-dia. guide bushing
1/4-in. straight bit
1/4 in.

Remove the waste. Drill a 1/2-in.-dia. hole at the stopped end, then rough out the slot using a 1/4-in. straight bit. The 1/4-in. piece of MDF opposite the fence prevents the router from tipping.

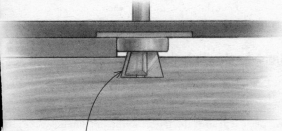

¹/₂-in. dia. 14° dovetail bit

Final cut. Use a ¹/₂-in. dovetail bit to finish the slot. The hole at the end of the slot lets you drop the bit into the cut before turning on the router. The hole will be hidden by the divider.

Glue-Up Without Screw-Ups

The case glue-up involves eight pieces. That many solid parts can be a pain to assemble and align during a single glue-up. So assemble the piece in stages.

Backsplash and apron first. Dry-fit the case to ensure proper alignment when gluing the backsplash and apron to the case top and bottom. These parts will help keep the case square in the later stages.

Top, bottom, and sides. Use grooved clamping cauls over the through-tenons to get pressure where it's needed (left). Place the case on T-supports to make clamping easier (below). Be sure to keep glue off the ends of the through-tenons.

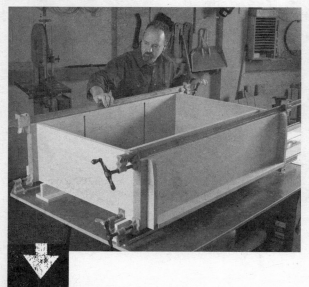

Fumed Finish Made Easy

Fuming wood involves exposing it to ammonia fumes, which react with tannins in the oak to darken its color. The longer the wood is exposed, the darker it becomes.

Most people build a complicated tent to house the workpiece and contain the ammonia fumes. But I just drape plastic sheeting over the piece. It works as well as the tent and makes it easier to take the cover off the ammonia once it's safely inside. The sheeting also makes it easy to remove sample blocks to check the finish.

Though my method is low-tech, I still treat the ammonia carefully because it's a toxic chemical that can damage your lungs, skin, and eyes. Be sure to set up the fuming area in a low-traffic, well-ventilated area. Wear goggles and gloves when you're pouring it, and be sure to wear gloves when you take the lid off the container once it's under the plastic. Also, when you remove the sheeting, it's a good idea to run a fan in the space to help ventilate the area. The good news is that the fumes dissipate quickly.

Respirator not required. Drape plastic sheeting over the piece as a tent. Then put the ammonia in a covered container and slide it under the tent. Wear gloves when you reach under the cover to remove the lid.

How to dial in the color. The effect won't be apparent until finish is applied, so it's a good idea to throw in a few sample blocks, remove them at hour intervals, and wipe on some finish to preview the final effect (right).

Warm it up. Fuming imparts a greenish-gray cast to the wood. Pekovich warmed up the look with a coat of garnet shellac prior to applying Waterlox. He rubbed out the finish with steel wool and brown wax made from melting Kiwi brown shoe polish into paste wax using a double-boiler setup (below).

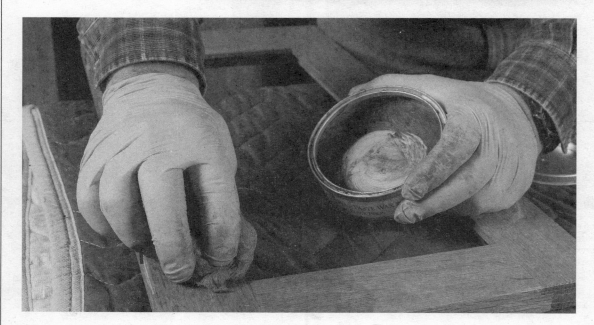

Continued ➜

Rout the dovetail keys. After cutting the dividers to length, use the dovetail bit to cut the keys. A tall fence supports the long boards and a featherboard keeps the piece snug against the fence.

Long sliding dovetails with no binding. The trick is to slide in the dividers from the back almost all the way without glue, leaving about 2 in. exposed, and then apply glue to that exposed end and into the slot at the front. Now you can drive the divider home with a mallet.

Leaded Glass Cabinet Doors

by Michael Pekovich

Not only is leaded glass attractive and true to Stickley furniture, but it's also simple to make and an alternative to glass panels divided by wood mullions. The simple pattern on these doors is a great introduction to the craft, but the techniques apply easily to more intricate designs.

Choose Your Glass First

You will need a few special tools and materials to make leaded-glass panels (see box, below). For the panes, I chose a slightly distorted glass (5/16 in. thick) that my local glass shop referred to as restoration glass. There are a lot of glass options available online and from stained-glass supply stores, but for this display case, stay away from anything too textured or bubbly. Clear plate glass would be better than something that draws too much attention to itself.

The process of making a leaded-glass panel involves cutting the glass into small pieces and reassembling them between strips of lead called came. Lead came is available in a few profiles, but for this panel I used a simple H-profile. Surrounding the assembly is a U-shaped zinc channel that adds some rigidity to the panel. After assembly, the joints are soldered, and cement is forced between the came and the glass pieces. Finally, the came is buffed, which has the added benefit of darkening the lead.

Use a Template to Cut the Glass

It's always best to start with a full-size pattern of the glass panel. In this case, it's easy enough to lay the glass on the pattern and use it as a guide to cut the rectangles. For ornate designs, I'd transfer the pattern onto heavy paper and cut the pieces apart to use as individual templates for the glass. When cutting the rectangles, offset the cuts 1/16 in. inside the pattern lines to allow for the 1/16-in.-thick rib inside the lead came; otherwise, the panel will end up too large.

As you cut the glass, number each rectangle to correspond with the numbers on the pattern.

Right-Angle Jig Is the Key

To keep the panel square during assembly, use a jig with a 3/4-in.-thick plywood base and two fences that meet at a right angle. Trim the pattern along two adjoining edges and place it against the fences of the jig. Then cut the zinc border to length and place two pieces against the fences. Put the first piece of glass in the corner, securing it with a horseshoe nail and a short piece of came.

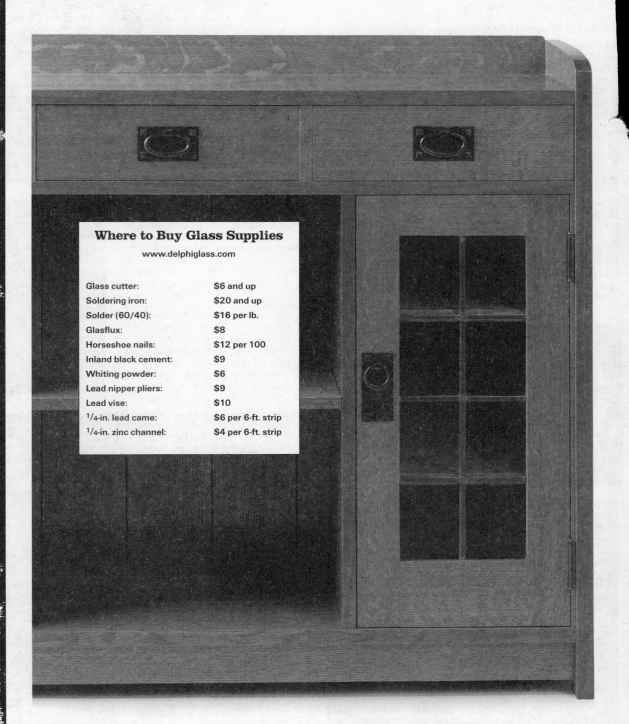

Where to Buy Glass Supplies

www.delphiglass.com

Glass cutter:	$6 and up
Soldering iron:	$20 and up
Solder (60/40):	$16 per lb.
Glasflux:	$8
Horseshoe nails:	$12 per 100
Inland black cement:	$9
Whiting powder:	$6
Lead nipper pliers:	$9
Lead vise:	$10
1/4-in. lead came:	$6 per 6-ft. strip
1/4-in. zinc channel:	$4 per 6-ft. strip

Cut a piece of came to length, place it along the side of the glass, and install the second rectangle. Continue until the first row of panels is completed. Cut the center strip of came to length and install it and the second row of panels. Once the last two pieces of zinc border are secured, solder the joints on both sides of the panel.

To cement the glass in place, you can use glazing compound, but I prefer the dark look of black cement. Apply the cement liberally, brushing it into all crevices, then use whiting and sawdust to solidify the mix and to clean the glass. Do both sides of the panel.

When the glazing is complete, the panel is ready to be installed in the door.

Assembly: Follow the Pattern

The glass panes are installed between sections of lead came. The entire assembly is framed with zinc channel.

¹/₄-in. zinc u-channel

¹/₄-in. lead came

Clamp and pull. The lead-came strips are flexible when shipped. To straighten them and make them rigid, you need to stretch them. Put one end in a lead vise (above) or other clamp and pull hard on the other end.

Cutting Glass Cleanly

Although a steel-wheel glass cutter from a hardware store will work, you'll get better results with a diamond-wheel cutter.

Steel-wheel cutter

Diamond-wheel cutter

Use a full-size pattern as a guide. A drywall square ensures a straight, square cut. Make one pass only, pressing hard enough with the cutter to hear a slight crackling sound. Offset the cuts ¹/₁₆ in. inside the lines to account for the lead came.

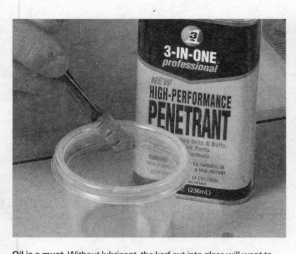

Oil is a must. Without lubricant, the kerf cut into glass will want to close up, leading to a coarse edge. A simple steel-wheel cutter gets dipped (above), while a self-lubricating cutter gets filled (below).

Breaking up isn't hard to do. With a properly lubed cutter, the glass should snap apart cleanly after scoring.

Square from the start. To keep the glass panel square, assemble it on a right-angle jig, placing the full-size pattern underneath.

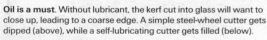

Corner first. Slide the first piece of glass into the zinc channel. Snug a short section of came against the glass and use it as a guide to cut the horizontal section of came to length.

Continued ➡

One row at a time. Tack the glass rectangles in place with horseshoe nails, using short pieces of came as a cushion. Horseshoe nails can be removed and reused.

Secure the frame. Once all the panes are in place, install the last two sections of the zinc frame. Use horseshoe nails to prevent the assembly from shifting.

Solder the Joints

To achieve a smooth solder joint, let the soldering iron heat until the solder melts easily and doesn't stick to the iron.

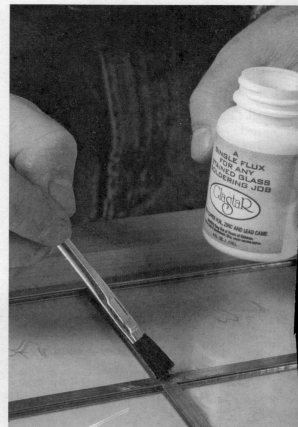

1. Flux first. Flux cleans the joint before soldering. It also helps the solder to flow more easily when it's melted, making a better-looking joint.

2. Solder on. Melt some solder onto the iron (left), and apply it to the joint (right). Do not leave the iron in contact with the came too long or it will melt the came and create a gap.

3. Do the second side. Once the joints on one side have been soldered, remove all the nails along the border and carefully flip the panel to solder the other side.

Glaze the Panel

Use black cement to fill any gaps and make the panel more rigid. Whiting firms up the cement and helps clean the panel.

Apply the cement liberally, then sprinkle on whiting. Use a stiff-bristle brush to work the cement into the gaps between the came and glass. Sprinkle on the whiting and rub it in (top, above). You can use plaster of paris in place of the whiting.

Burnish with sawdust. The final step is to pour sawdust on the panel and brush (top). This step not only helps clean the glass, but it also darkens the lead and the solder joints. The more you brush, the darker the look. Use a thin stick to remove excess material in the corners (above).

518

Projects for Traditional Styles